AF361479

A Biographical Dictionary
of the Maryland Legislature,
1635-1789

A BIOGRAPHICAL DICTIONARY OF THE MARYLAND LEGISLATURE, 1635-1789

Volume 1: A-H

Edward C. Papenfuse, Alan F. Day, David W. Jordan,
and Gregory A. Stiverson

THE JOHNS HOPKINS UNIVERSITY PRESS, BALTIMORE

The reprint of this volume in 2010 has been made possible by the generous support of an anonymous donor in honor of the editors and research staff of the Legislative History Project.

Publication in 1979 was assisted by a generous grant from the Maryland Bicentennial Commission, the Honorable Louise Gore, Chairman.

This work was made possible through the assistance of a research grant from the National Endowment for the Humanities. The findings and conclusions presented here do not necessarily represent the views of the Endowment.

The Johns Hopkins University Press
2715 North Charles Street
Baltimore, Maryland 21218-4363
www.press.jhu.edu

The 1979 publication was cataloged by the Library of Congress as follows:
Library of Congress Catalog Card Number 78-18042

ISBN 13: 978-0-8018-9096-3
ISBN 10: 0-8018-9096-9

The seal on the title page first appeared in 1765 on the title page of the Reverend Thomas Bacon's compilation of the Laws of Maryland, and until 1793 it ornamented printed editions of the session laws of the Assembly. Carved on a wood block by Thomas Sparrow, ward and employee of the Annapolis printer Jonas Green, the Sparrow seal bears the Latin motto *Crescite et Multiplicamini,* which means "increase and multiply."

The Johns Hopkins University Press uses environmentally friendly book materials, including recycled text paper that is composed of at least 30 percent post-consumer waste, whenever possible. All of our book papers are acid-free, and our jackets and covers are printed on paper with recycled content.

Dedicated to the memory of

MISTRESS MARGARET BRENT, SPINSTER
(ca. 1600–1670/71)

landowner, businesswoman, agent and executrix of Governor Leonard Calvert,
whose claim to a vote in the Maryland Assembly was denied

Contents

FIGURES

Acknowledgments

It is always a happy occasion to compose this segment of a book because the text is complete and we can now acknowledge those individuals and institutions that helped to make it possible. First and foremost, George R. Lewis, former secretary of the Department of General Services, J. Max Millstone, the present secretary, and Robin J. Zee, director of the Office of Central Services, unfailingly gave us their support. The same is true of the Hall of Records Commission, under the chairmanship of Robert C. Murphy, chief judge of the Court of Appeals, which not only endorsed our proceeding with the two volumes that follow but also strongly recommended that we seek funding to continue the biographical study of Maryland legislators whose service began after 1789.

The major portion of funds for the biographical research came from the National Endowment for the Humanities, although the Maryland Bicentennial Commission did provide a grant to compile a *Directory of Maryland Legislators, 1635–1789* and supplied a most generous subsidy for this publication.

Money is critical for an undertaking of this magnitude, but the expertise of scholars and friends is also essential. Several individuals gave freely of their time and knowledge to advise us as the project developed. Russell R. Menard, an authority on the early history of the Chesapeake Bay region, contributed significantly by researching many of the biographies of the legislators who served before 1715. Lois Green Carr, historian for the St. Mary's City Commission, granted us access to extensive biographical files on legislators who served from that county, and members of her staff helped us sift through the wealth of information the commission has collected. Both Morris L. Radoff, archivist emeritus of the Hall of Records, and Jack P. Greene, Andrew Mellon Professor of History at The Johns Hopkins University, gave advice and encouragement. J. Randall Miller assembled a preliminary draft of many of the session lists. David A. Bohmer and Allan Kulikoff shared the results of their research on different aspects of Maryland history, and Jackson Turner Main loaned his notes on late-eighteenth-century legislators. We also benefited from the insight of Marian Schallcross, Margaret Cook, and the late Louise Hienton, all extraordinarily knowledgeable on the history of Prince George's County, and Evelyn Parran Mackall, an authority on Calvert County. Carol Van Voorst assisted us with those clergy who either served in or were related to men who sat in the General Assembly. We are indebted to Michael J. Milton, assistant attorney general, for legal advice rendered to the project. A note of special appreciation and commendation must also be extended to William Jabine II and his staff artist, Helen Stone, from the Maryland Department of Natural Resources, for preparing the maps depicting legislative districts.

Except for the front matter, this book was keyboarded on an in-house text-editing system. This minicomputer was to prove indispensable. It furnished a reviseable data base for future editions, reduced the cost of composition, and enabled last-minute changes to be made easily. Use of such a device requires an expert "Tessy" (the acronym for "Text Editing System Operator"), and we were fortunate to have several who are adept at inputting and correcting. Donna McDonald, Fran Reilly, and their supervisor, Stephanie Tooles, deserve special recognition because they assumed the major responsibility for this task, drawing on reserves of tolerance as well as skill.

Sally Mason toiled profitably for long hours in the Maryland Historical Society, checking private papers relating to legislators. Kay Smith Jordan worked on the biographies of those men who served in the pre-1715 period. Louise Townsend, Lynn Bohmer, Marianne Braun, Diana Tyson, Maxine Keller, Dawn Donaldson, Winona Wright, Sarah Davis, Lillian Bayly Marks, Mr. and Mrs. C. R. Hutchins, William S. Hemsley, and Thomas Hunter McLean all deserve our thanks for their contributions. Finally, the staff of the Hall of Records supported the project with their unstinting cooperation and their accustomed professional acumen. In particular, we would like to thank Phebe Jacobsen, whose extensive work with Maryland records and singular interest in the project made her an invaluable asset; Frank White, an expert in the history of Maryland law, officeholding, and politics; Patricia Vanorny, an authority on local records and director of the archives' county records project; and Susan Nettles, who understands the machinations through which an entail could be cleared from the title to a tract of land in the colonial period.

The bulk of the records required to write the biographies of the men who governed Maryland from 1635 through 1789 are located at the Hall of Records, although other repositories were searched for relevant materials. Since our travel funds were limited we occasionally intruded upon vacation itineraries, suggesting stops at archives or historical societies. When a senior staff archivist accompanied her husband to Philadelphia, where he was to participate in a championship tennis tournament, we persuaded her that visiting the City Bureau of Archives and History and the Historical Society of Pennsylvania would be more absorbing than watching her husband attempt to vanquish his cross-court foe. On another occasion, a staff member's sister made a trip from her upstate New York home to Kentucky, and we prevailed upon her to spend a diverting day or so at the Kentucky Division of Archives and Records, locating probate materials on Maryland legislators.

The holdings of the Maryland State Library and the Maryland Historical Society were frequently consulted. The collections at the Virginia State Library, Archives Division, the Virginia Historical Society, and the Research Department of the Colonial Williamsburg Foundation were rich in reference materials on men who served in the Maryland General Assembly prior to 1715. Other information was secured from the Library of Congress, the Milton S. Eisenhower Library of The Johns Hopkins University, the North Carolina State Division of Archives and History, the Kentucky Historical Society, the Filson Club, the University of Pennsylvania Archives and Records Center, Princeton University Library, the William R. Perkins Library at Duke University, the Nicholas Murray Butler Memorial Library at Columbia University, and Yale University Library. We found relevant documents in London at the Public Record Office, the British Museum, the Institute of Historical Research, the Friends' House Library, and the Lambeth Palace Library; in Edinburgh, at the Scottish Record Office and the National Library of Scotland; and in Paris, at the French National Archives, where Jean Baker ably acted as translator and guide. At all of these institutions we received the most courteous attention, for which we are grateful.

Undoubtedly in such a cooperative enterprise a few names will remain obscured through oversight. A project of this nature, involving the collaboration of so many people, inevitably results in omissions when writing acknowledgments. To those we have inadvertently forgotten we extend our apologies and our sincere appreciation.

A Biographical Dictionary
of the Maryland Legislature,
1635-1789

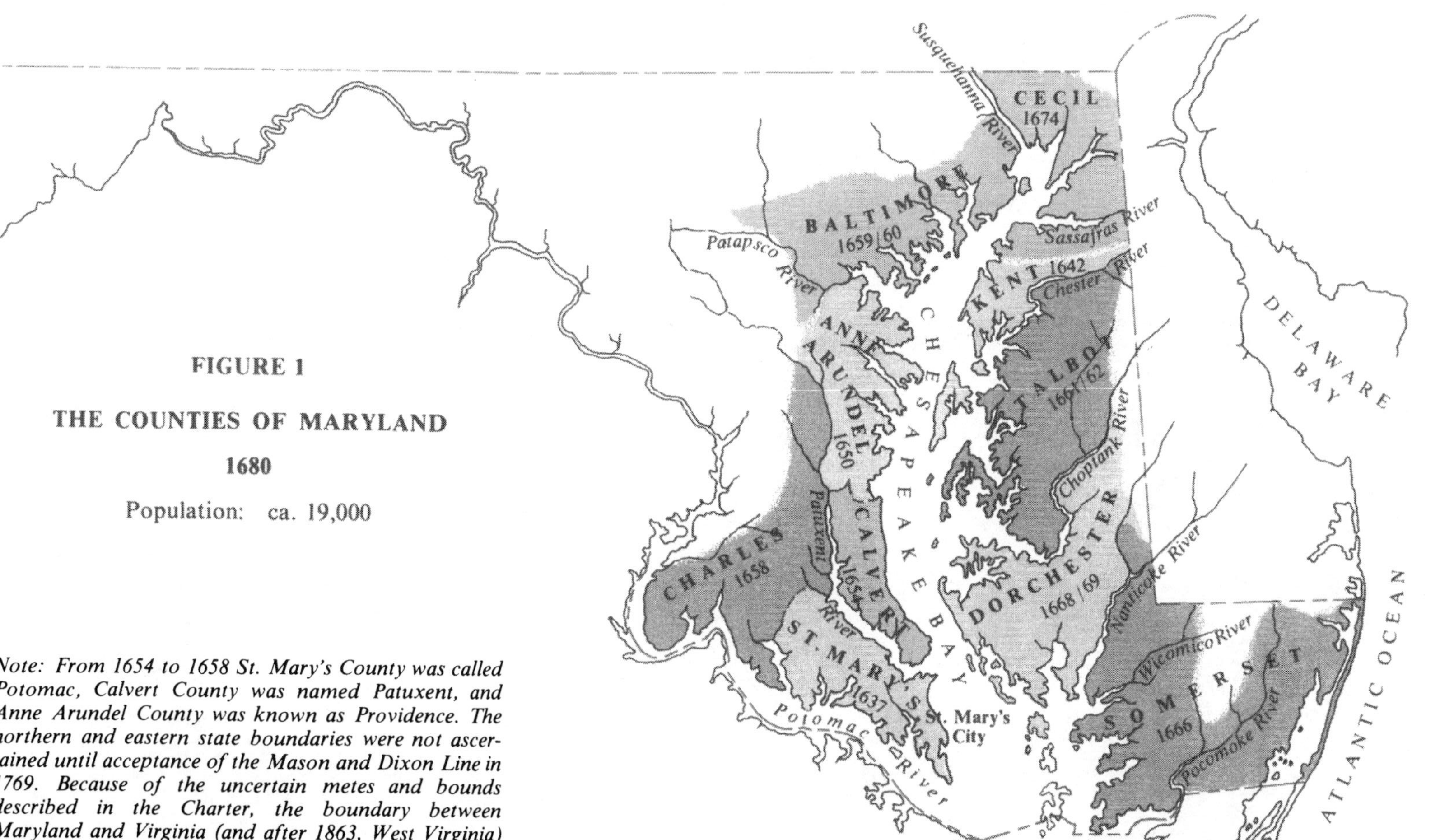

FIGURE 1

THE COUNTIES OF MARYLAND

1680

Population: ca. 19,000

Note: From 1654 to 1658 St. Mary's County was called Potomac, Calvert County was named Patuxent, and Anne Arundel County was known as Providence. The northern and eastern state boundaries were not ascertained until acceptance of the Mason and Dixon Line in 1769. Because of the uncertain metes and bounds described in the Charter, the boundary between Maryland and Virginia (and after 1863, West Virginia) was not officially determined until the 20th century.

Shading indicates county boundaries and extent of settlement as determined by Edward B. Mathews.

FIGURE 2

THE COUNTIES OF MARYLAND

1730

Population: ca. 82,875

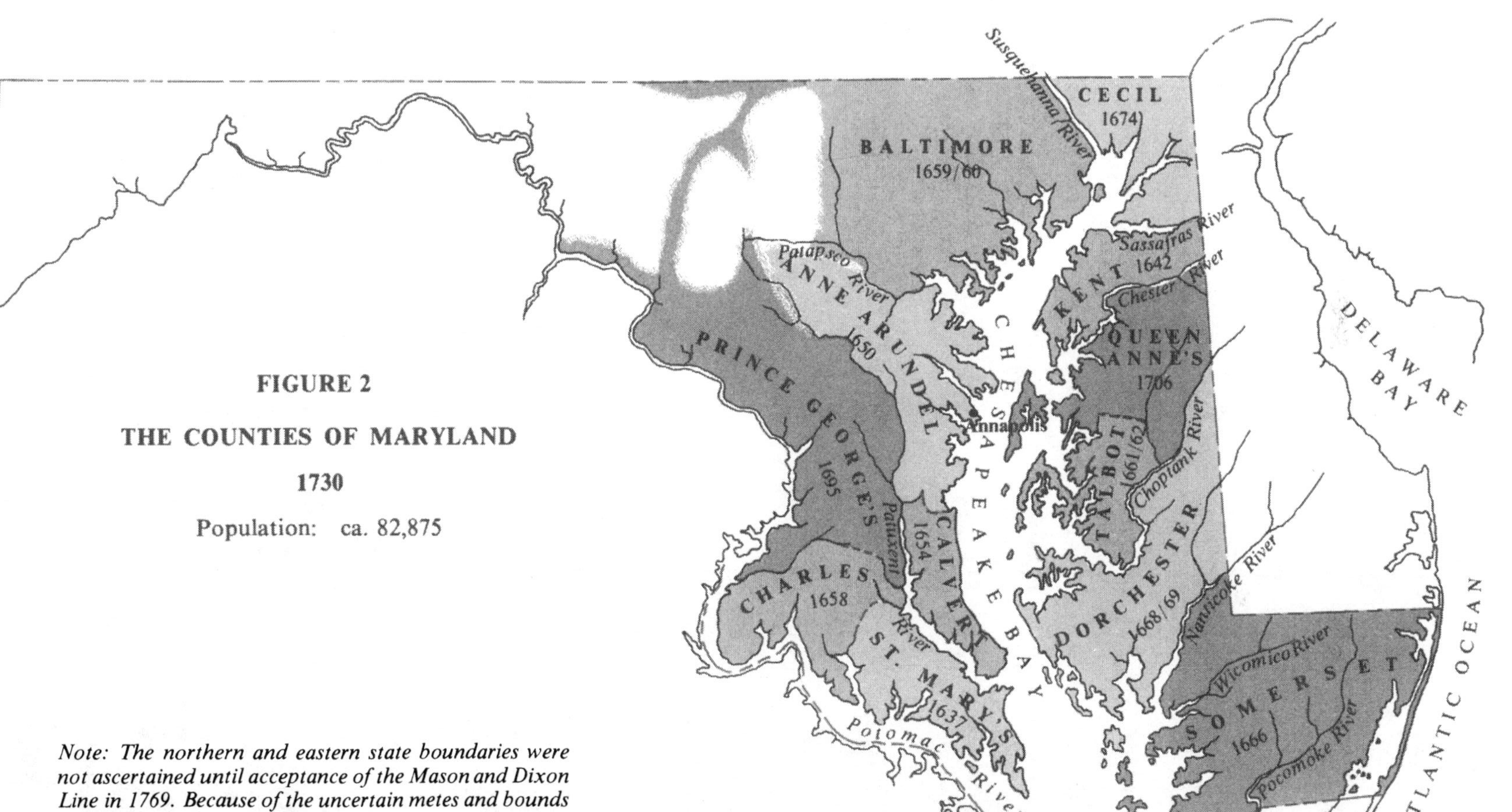

Note: The northern and eastern state boundaries were not ascertained until acceptance of the Mason and Dixon Line in 1769. Because of the uncertain metes and bounds described in the Charter, the boundary between Maryland and Virginia (and after 1863, West Virginia) was not officially determined until the 20th century.

Shading indicates county boundaries and extent of settlement as determined by Edward B. Mathews.

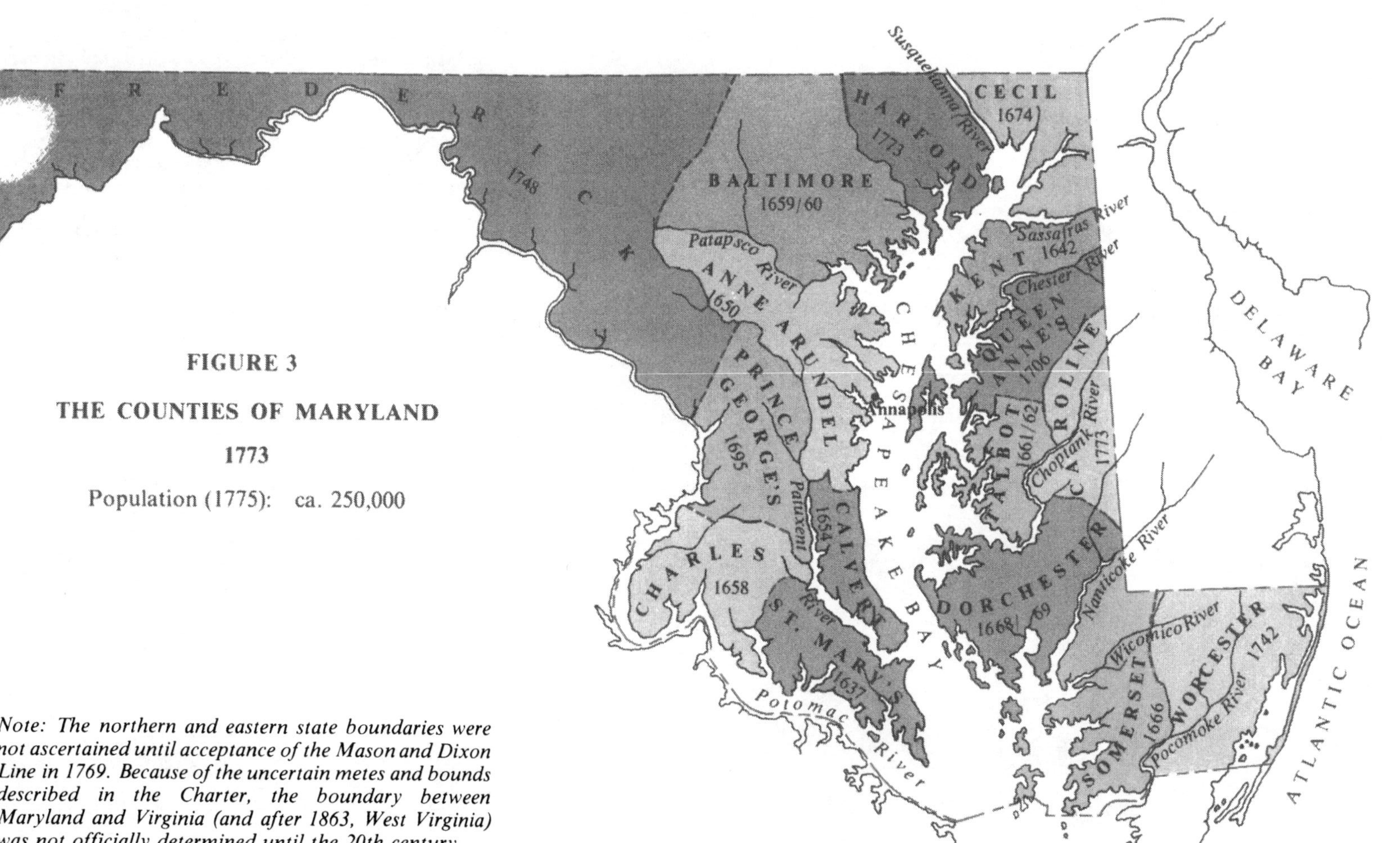

FIGURE 3

THE COUNTIES OF MARYLAND

1773

Population (1775):   ca. 250,000

Note: The northern and eastern state boundaries were not ascertained until acceptance of the Mason and Dixon Line in 1769. Because of the uncertain metes and bounds described in the Charter, the boundary between Maryland and Virginia (and after 1863, West Virginia) was not officially determined until the 20th century.

Shading indicates county boundaries and extent of settlement as determined by Edward B. Mathews.

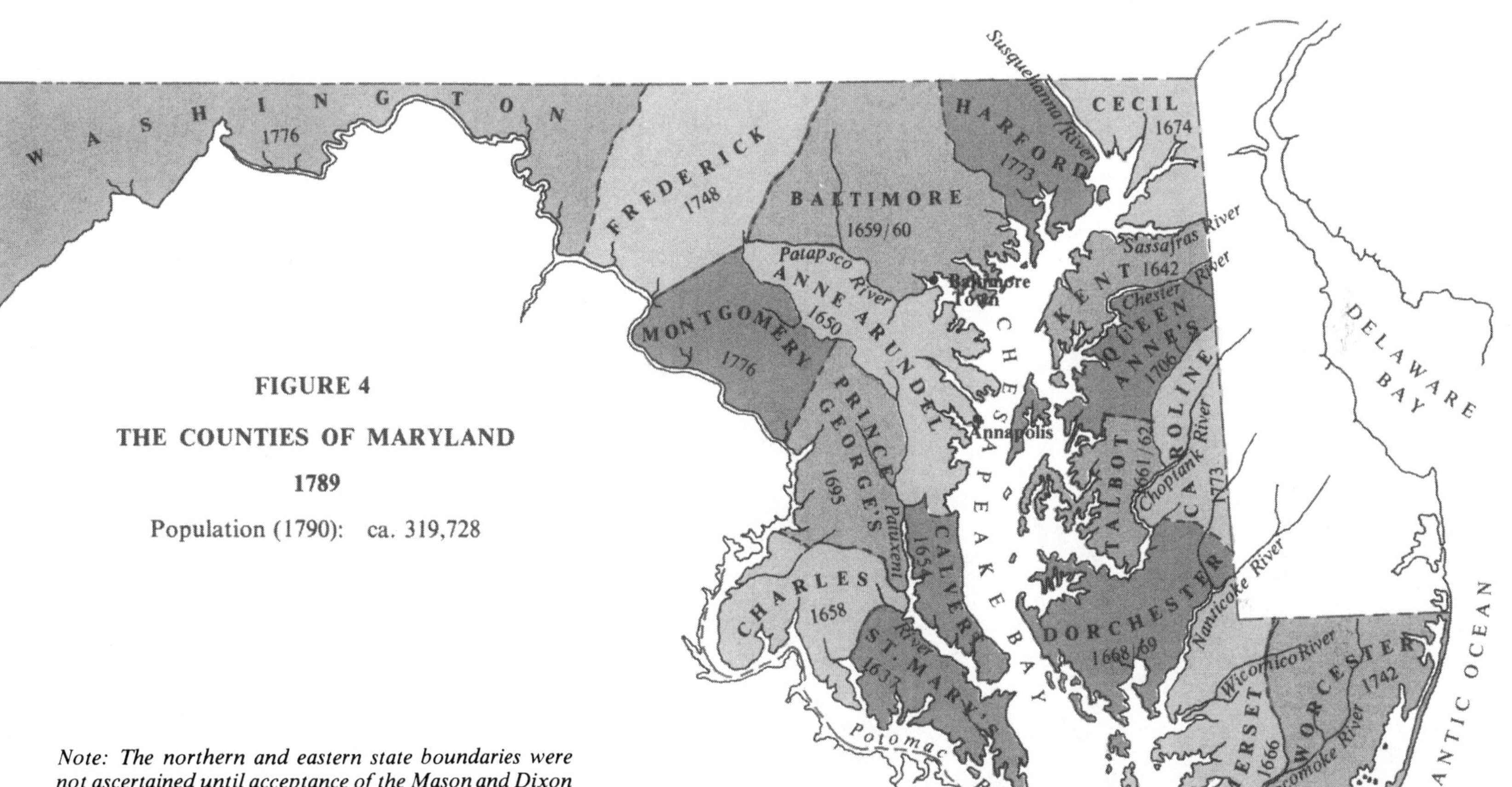

FIGURE 4

THE COUNTIES OF MARYLAND

1789

Population (1790):   ca. 319,728

Note: The northern and eastern state boundaries were not ascertained until acceptance of the Mason and Dixon Line in 1769. Because of the uncertain metes and bounds described in the Charter, the boundary between Maryland and Virginia (and after 1863, West Virginia) was not officially determined until the 20th century.

Shading indicates county boundaries and extent of settlement as determined by Edward B. Mathews.

Introduction

No facet of American history is more thoroughly scrutinized than the political. Studies of institutions, celebrated individuals, and conspicuous events abound. Paradoxically, with the exception of preeminent legislators the thousands of participants who contributed to the evolution of representative government remain faceless. To understand the dynamics of our political system it is imperative to know more about each of these men—their education, social background, economic position, values, and public and private lives. Perhaps it is not surprising that scholars have made scant effort to compile a substantial biographical profile of any American legislature.[1] The sheer magnitude of such an undertaking, abetted by often incomplete records, can be a formidable deterrent.

Despite the obstacles, Maryland presented an irresistible challenge. The number of legislators formed a manageable population that, because of the state's geographical location, economic development, and remarkably full records, seemed likely to permit generalizations applicable to other areas. Neither wholly northern nor southern, Lord Baltimore's colony contained aspects of both regions. Though it was initially an English-settled, tobacco-growing area, by the late eighteenth century Maryland possessed a culturally varied population, a predominantly rural but diversified economy, and the beginnings of urban, commercial, and administrative centers such as Baltimore and Annapolis.

The nature, scope, and extent of the records, coupled with their excellent preservation, rendered Maryland an ideal choice for a legislative dictionary and analytical history. Unlike some states, Maryland has long had a strong local records program to complement its distinguished collection of state records. Directed by Morris L. Radoff, state archivist from 1939 until 1975, the Hall of Records staff generated tens of thousands of index references to the records that, in ever increasing numbers, were systematically brought under archival control. A similar but computer-assisted endeavor is the newly issued *An Inventory of Maryland State Papers, Volume 1: The Era of the American Revolution, 1775–1789*, a massive finding aid to more than 31,000 previously inaccessible loose papers vital to any legislative history of that period.[2] These and other finding aids enabled the project team to extract biographical data more efficiently than perhaps could be accomplished elsewhere.

The first prerequisite of research was to create a master list of all men who held legislative office between 1635 and 1789, including proprietors, governors or acting governors, parliamentary commissioners, members of the Upper House (or the Senate, as it was reconstituted in 1776 by the ninth Maryland Convention), members of the Council, Executive Council, and Council of Safety, members of the Lower House (renamed the House of Delegates after 1776), and members of the nine provincial conventions held between 1774 and 1776.[3] The second

---

1. Two notable exceptions to this generalization are the *Biographical Directory of the American Congress, 1774–1961* (Washington, D.C.: Government Printing Office, 1961), and Walter B. Edgar, ed., *Biographical Directory of the South Carolina House of Representatives*, 2 vols. (Columbia: University of South Carolina Press, 1974, 1977).

2. Annapolis, Md.: Maryland Department of General Services, Hall of Records Commission, 1977.

3. For an early version of this list, see Edward C. Papenfuse et al., comps., *Directory of Maryland Legislators, 1635–1789* (Annapolis, Md.: Maryland Department of Economic and Community Development, 1974). David Jordan and

preliminary task was to group legislators on the master list into regional categories: (1) St. Mary's, Calvert, and Charles counties; (2) Anne Arundel, Baltimore, and Harford counties; (3) Prince George's, Frederick, Montgomery, and Washington counties; (4) Kent and Cecil counties; (5) Caroline, Talbot, Queen Anne's, and Dorchester counties; and (6) Somerset and Worcester counties. Investigating the careers of legislators who lived in contiguous counties, rather than proceeding alphabetically, chronologically, or in some other sequence, simplified collection of data and made it easier to perceive the ample synchronic and diachronic connections between legislators living in the same or adjoining counties.

After these preparatory steps, the arduous labor of constructing profiles of the political, public, social, and economic careers of legislators began. Information collected by David Jordan and Russell Menard on those men who served before 1715 was restructured to conform with the final element and category arrangement devised for all biographies. Researchers entered their findings for the 903 post-1715 legislators on worksheets following a carefully devised methodology explained more fully in the section on biographies below. Their first goal was to identify positively the legislators whose names appear in the journals of the General Assembly from 1635 through 1789. Highly visible leaders like William Paca, Charles Carroll of Carrollton, and Samuel Chase are readily recognizable, as is the legislator who had no other contemporary with the same name. On occasion, too, a newspaper obituary would mention a man's legislative service, thereby distinguishing him from other candidates. Prominence, uniqueness of name, or indisputable linkage, however, were atypical. The incidence of two or more men of the same name living in the same county and serving in the legislature occurred with depressing regularity. The predilection of eighteenth-century Maryland families for perpetuating a particular Christian name, generation after generation, or for indiscriminately using differentiating appellations compounded the frustration.

The cases of the two Henry Ennalls and the seven Samuel Hansons exemplify the dilemmas posed by the intricacies of identification. A Henry Ennalls sat in the House of Delegates in 1785. Two men emerged from the records as distinct possibilities of being that legislator. The first was born about 1741 and had died by 1788. Known as "Sr." after 1777, this Henry was a substantial Dorchester County landowner and justice of the peace. His mother was the daughter of a legislator, his brother was a member of the provincial conventions from Dorchester County, and his nephew, Henry Waggaman (1753–1809), also sat in the 1785 session. The other candidate was born about 1757 and died in debt in 1803. This latter Henry Ennalls, known as "Jr.," owned more land than the first, and was the scion of a wealthy, but not politically prominent, branch of the Ennalls family. In 1785, however, the year of the legislative service in question, Henry Ennalls, Jr., married Sarah, daughter of Robert Goldsborough (1733–1788), a prominent lawyer and member of the Maryland Senate. The House *Journal* of 1785 uses no distinguishing titles for Henry Ennalls, and no probate records survive for Dorchester County from 1777 until 1851. Given the more or less equal claim of both candidates to be designated as the Lower House member, it was reluctantly decided that the legislator, Henry Ennalls, could not be positively identified. Therefore, biographies of both men are included.

Perhaps even more enigmatic was the allocation of legislative service among the multitude of Samuel Hansons. A Samuel Hanson represented Charles County in the second, fourth, and fifth

Russell Menard were responsible for the basic work in assembling the list of pre-1715 legislators. For the qualifications for voting and holding office before 1776, see Newton D. Mereness, *Maryland as a Proprietary Province* (New York: Macmillan, 1901), pp. 195–202, and Charles Albro Barker, *The Background of the Revolution in Maryland* (Hamden, Conn.: Archon, 1967), pp. 171–83. For the period 1776 through 1789, see Edward C. Papenfuse and Gregory A. Stiverson, *The Decisive Blow is Struck: A facsimile edition of The Proceedings of the Constitutional Convention of 1776 and the First Maryland Constitution* (Annapolis: Hall of Records Commission, 1977).

provincial conventions held between 1774 and 1776 and in the House of Delegates from 1777 to 1784. The proceedings of the conventions and the journals of the house cause immediate confusion because the distinguishing titles appended to Samuel's name ("Jr.," "of Samuel," "Major") follow no pattern. Preliminary research into Charles County probate, land, court, and assessment records produced six recognizable Samuel Hansons, with the hint of a seventh. Of the six definite possibilities, three customarily added their father's name as a distinguishing characteristic (i.e., "of Walter," "of William," and "of John"). This evidence, along with their military service in the War for Independence, which indicated that they were either too young for legislative service or had enlisted in the Maryland Continental Line, eliminated them from consideration. After further study it became clear that all three of the other Samuel Hansons— Samuel (1716–1794), Samuel of Samuel (1752–1830), and Samuel (ca. 1738–1817)—were members of the Lower House, and legislative service was assigned as it appears in their respective profiles.

Such a systematic exploitation of sources, even in the most difficult cases, was extraordinarily successful. It led to the isolation, with a reasonable degree of certainty, of all but one-half of one percent of the 1,445 legislators studied. Moreoever, profiles constructed of men who ultimately proved not to be legislators contributed clues about men who were, and made it possible later to assign correctly further biographical details. The process of identification also clarified one of the salient characteristics of Maryland's political life, namely, the labyrinthine interconnections among legislative families.

With basic linkage solved, the next step was to create more complete profiles, adding data not already ascertained through the identification process, including birthplace, residence during adulthood, family, marriages, education, church membership, occupation, officeholding, landholding, and wealth. Lawrence Stone has called such an endeavor "prosopography," defining it as "the investigation of the common background characteristics of a group of actors in history by means of a collective study of their lives."[4] It might be argued that a new word, "profilography," understood as the writing of biographical sketches or profiles, more appropriately encompasses what we attempted here. But "profilographical" is as difficult to pronounce as "prosopographical," and possibly both words should be abandoned for the more comprehensible phrase "collective biography." Whatever term is adopted, we cannot claim to have written full biographies of the men included in this *Dictionary*. For example, we omitted embellishments that would color, but not add substantively to, a profile. The sketch of Charles Carroll of Carrollton does not reveal that before the bombardment of Fort McHenry by the British in 1814, he invested heavily in the fund that built the British navy; nor does the entry for the last proprietary governor of Maryland, Sir Robert Eden, show his greater concern with a "bedfellow" and duck hunting than with the fast-approaching revolution. Such miscellany are in the working files of the project, which are organized in such a way as to encourage corrections and additions as well as further study.

By its very nature prosopography, profilography, or collective biography demands sensitive evaluation of sources and clear guidelines on how far to carry the investigation of a given man. The lack of personal papers for legislators in Maryland is compensated by an abundance of public records that must be sifted with discretion to prevent unproductive and expensive forays in pursuit of elusive details. We adhered to strict criteria governing the parameters of research and severely limited the average time spent on files. The biographies are thus not definitive, but they are as rounded as available material and self-imposed constraints allowed.

---

4. Lawrence Stone, "Prosopography," *Daedalus* (Winter 1971): 46.

The profiles stand as independent entities, but they also form the basis for three companion monographs: the first will analyze the political history of the colony from its inception through 1715; the second, from the return of the colony to the Calverts through the effective end of proprietary government in 1774; and the third, from the provincial conventions that began in 1774 through the ratification of the federal Constitution. These monographs will not adhere to the traditional but overly narrow conception of early American politics as institutional history. They will not be mere descriptions of the powers of the proprietor and governor or recitations of the role of the Council or accounts of the rise of a representative assembly. They will correlate legislators' professional and economic interests, social status, family background, political experience, education, national origin, religious affiliation, geographical distribution, and other variables, in the hope that a broader vision and interpretation of the Maryland political process will be made manifest.[5]

The underlying purpose of the research project thus is not solely to produce a biographical dictionary, but to fashion, coordinate, and interpret a corpus of evidence that will, as Lawrence Stone has written, "make sense of political action, identify social reality, and describe and analyze with precision the structure of society and the degree and the nature of the movements within it."[6] In the truest sense, then, this book represents only a beginning.

SESSION LISTS

The session lists, basically drawn from the official journals of the Assembly, represent as nearly as possible a record of election or attendance. Where dates or knowledge of membership come from other than the Assembly journals, sources are footnoted. To avoid confusion because of frequent variations in the spelling of names in colonial and state records, first, middle, and last names have been standardized, but distinguishing characteristics, such as "Jr.," "John of John," and "III," are retained. It should be noted that the biographical profiles exclude freemen invited to attend, but not elected to, the first few sessions of the Assembly but include all proprietors, governors, and men elected or ordered to attend by special writ.

Governor. Prior to 1777 the actual title of the governor changed from lieutenant general during the first proprietary period to governor during the time of royal rule and to lieutenant governor after 1715, when the Calvert family regained control of the colony. For purposes of clarity and because the duties of the office, irrespective of title, remained essentially the same, the term governor is used throughout the session lists, complying with the constitutional designation adopted in 1776.

Acting Governor. When the governor expected to be absent from the colony, he usually selected the senior councillor as the acting governor. Upon the death of a governor, the senior councillor (normally referred to as president of the Council) served as chief executive until the arrival of a duly commissioned governor. Footnotes to individual assemblies explain the occasional variations in this nominating process. The constitution of 1776 imposed consistency on the appointment of acting governors. It stipulated that upon the death or resignation of a governor, the ranking executive councillor would assume the position of acting governor and would immediately

---

5. Already in progress at the Hall of Records and an outgrowth of the biographical research is a quantitative analysis of legislative behavior in the eighteenth century. Funded by the National Endowment for the Humanities. this project will seek to analyze every piece of legislative action between 1715 and 1789, involving more than 2,600 roll-call votes, and all motions, committee assignments, reports, bills, resolutions, and petitions.

6. Stone, "Prosopography," 47.

call a meeting of the General Assembly to elect a new chief executive for the remainder of the unexpired term.

Council/Upper House. The Council, officially promulgated as an executive body in 1637, consisted of those confidants upon whom the governor depended heavily for guidance on a wide variety of subjects. The proprietor technically commissioned councillors, but he usually accepted gubernatorial recommendations. The governor ensured the presence of these advisers by extending special writs commanding their attendance. After the mid-seventeenth century the governor issued such writs less frequently. Appointees to the Council, except those on special writ, served indefinitely, usually for life unless they were removed for disloyalty or they resigned for personal reasons. From 1650, when the Assembly officially became bicameral, until the American Revolution, the members of the Council performed separate and distinct legislative functions as the Upper House, whose membership also included others summoned on special writ for particular sessions, and, before 1675, the governor. The membership lists for the Upper House are in descending order according to seniority. They incorporate not only the individuals physically present as they appear in the journals but also the eligible, but nonattending, councillors, who are given the parenthetical designation DNS ("did not serve"). After 1776, the new constitution separated executive and legislative responsibilities and the Upper House was called the *Senate*. The reader should refer to the footnotes to the session of the General Assembly of 1777 for a discussion of the composition of the legislative and executive branches of government for the post-1776 period.

Lower House. The order in which county and city delegations appeared in the Lower House journals varied only slightly during the seventeenth and eighteenth centuries. In the colonial period, the clerk recorded the delegations in chronological order of county formation. Figures 1–4 depict the changes in legislative districts (counties and towns) through 1789. After the revolution, the same rule of listing delegates applied, apart from the reversal in position on the membership roster of the Annapolis and Prince George's County delegations. Only during the conventions of 1774 to 1776 was there a significant alteration made in the method of membership presentation. The proceedings of these extralegal conventions list delegations geographically rather than chronologically, beginning with St. Mary's County at the southern end of the Western Shore and progressing clockwise to Worcester County at the southern end of the Eastern Shore. To be consistent and to facilitate comparison, the order of all session lists for the Lower House parallels the chronology of county erection. With the constitution of 1776 the Lower House became the House of Delegates.

Committee Service. Before 1692, the Assembly journals report occasional committee appointments, as noted. It was not until the royal period, however, that standing committees became a feature of legislative activity. A standing committee, as defined here, was a committee that was named in the series of appointments generally made at the beginning of a session and that existed for more than one assembly. The session lists include standing committees but exclude ad hoc committees and committees assigned only to investigate specific pieces of legislation, petitions, or issues.

A legislator's committee service for a particular session of the Assembly stems either from the original appointment list or from an additional appointment resolution approved during a session. There are, however, two exceptions to these rules. First, the Lower House often voted to continue standing committees from the previous session by a blanket resolution, with no repetition of individual names. The second, much less common, occurrence is where the journal contains no indication of any appointments or reappointments to obviously functioning standing committees. In these cases legislators named in the last complete committee listing are credited with continuing service.

All committees on the session lists are Lower House committees, unless otherwise noted as a joint committee. Joint committee membership lists are presented with Upper House (or Senate) members first, followed by Lower House members.

Figure 5
BIOGRAPHICAL ELEMENTS AND CATEGORIES

Elements	*Major Categories*	*Elements*	*Major Categories*
[NAME]*		PUBLIC CAREER	LEGISLATIVE SERVICE
[PERSONAL BACKGROUND]*	BORN IMMIGRATED NATIVE RESIDED		OTHER PROVINCIAL/ STATE OFFICES LOCAL OFFICE(S) JURY SERVICE MILITARY SERVICE OUT OF COLONY/ STATE SERVICE
FAMILY BACKGROUND	FATHER STEPFATHER GUARDIAN MOTHER STEPMOTHER UNCLE AUNT BROTHERS SISTERS FIRST COUSIN NEPHEWS NIECES OTHER KINSHIP	[VALUES AND OPINIONS]*	STANDS ON PUBLIC/ PRIVATE ISSUES
		WEALTH DURING LIFETIME	PERSONAL PROPERTY ANNUAL INCOME LAND AT FIRST ELECTION SIGNIFICANT CHANGES IN LAND BETWEEN FIRST ELECTION AND DEATH
MARRIED			
CHILDREN	SONS DAUGHTERS		
PRIVATE CAREER	EDUCATION RELIGIOUS AFFILIATION SOCIAL STATUS AND ACTIVITIES OCCUPATIONAL PROFILE	WEALTH AT DEATH	DIED PERSONAL PROPERTY LAND
		IDENTIFICATION PROBLEMS	

* A square bracket denotes element titles that do not appear in print.

BIOGRAPHIES

The format of the biographies is designed so that the major public and private aspects of a legislator's career are quickly discernible. In formulating research procedures, we adopted eleven elements as an organizational framework for the collation of evidence as it accumulated (see figure 5). After an individual's name and dates of birth and death come concise statements of his personal and family background, marriages, children, private and public career, values and opinions, and wealth. Elements are set in boldface type in small capital letters, with categories of data within each element set in regular type in small caps. The section dealing with a legislator's familial connections, for example, begins with the element FAMILY BACKGROUND (boldface type), followed by categories such as FATHER, MOTHER, UNCLE, and AUNTS (regular small caps). Elements and categories do not appear where research elicited no information. If we could not ascertain the name of a legislator's wife but did know the name of his offspring, only CHILDREN will appear and not the element MARRIED. The names of all legislators in a man's biography are in boldface italic type in order to highlight legislative connections. If a legislator's father, two uncles, and four sons sat in the legislature, their names will be in boldface italics and reference should be made to their biographies. The voluminous number of sources consulted precluded using footnotes, but the documented files on each legislator are at the Hall of Records. Upon completion of the three monographs, these files will be open to the public and the contents placed on microform.

The first element of a biography consists of the legislator's name, with variant spellings indicated parenthetically, followed by birth and death dates. For an explanation of date qualifiers "by," "ca.," and slash dates (e.g., 1744/45), see Abbreviations and Notes.

If we know the precise date of a legislator's birth, it appears after the category BORN in the element [PERSONAL BACKGROUND]. Where the term "of age by" precedes a year after BORN, it means that the man was of legal age—twenty-one—by that date. Also included in this category, where available, is the legislator's birthplace and rank within his family (that is, first son, younger son, etc.). The category IMMIGRATED explains when a legislator came to Maryland. For the purpose of numbering generations, an immigrant was considered first generation if he was of age upon arrival in the colony. When a legislator immigrated to the colony as a minor with his parents, he was counted as second generation. The final category under personal background is the legislator's residence. If a man lived in several locations, they are listed in chronological order. Only one location and the absence of a date denotes a legislator who maintained a single residence throughout his adult life.

One of the main concerns of the project was to document legislative connections within and between family groupings. Thus, primary stress in the element FAMILY BACKGROUND was the delineation of a legislator's relationships, through blood or marriage, to other legislators. Marriages of brothers are not shown if the father sat in the Assembly, but those of sisters are given if they married legislators. This rule applies to all male and female relatives. If a man's father did not sit in the Assembly, however, available information on the legislator's immediate family is included.

The research files contain much additional information on familial ties. For the sake of brevity in publication, however, the relationships are limited to the immediately preceding and the two succeeding generations. Specific relatives sought were: father, stepfather/guardians, mother, stepmothers, uncles, aunts, brothers and sisters, first cousins, nephews, and nieces. We did not usually list half brothers, unless they were legislators, or half sisters, unless they married legislators.

Under MARRIED, the name or names of a legislator's wife or wives are in chronological sequence. Because marriage into a politically influential family began or greatly enhanced many legislative careers, the same criteria that applied to FAMILY BACKGROUND determined which of the wife's relations merited inclusion.

The element CHILDREN encompasses a chronological ordering by sex of the legislator's progeny. Last names are given only for male offspring who became legislators, and for illegitimate sons and daughters.

Most of the categories in the element PRIVATE CAREER are self-explanatory. Caution should be exercised in interpreting titles in SOCIAL STATUS AND ACTIVITIES because they no longer bore the same social connotation after the mid-eighteenth century as in the first hundred years of settlement. Both this category and OCCUPATIONAL PROFILE are chronological, with dates noted where possible. No date appears, however, if a man held one occupation throughout his adult career. The occupational entry "officeholder" signifies that at least a portion of the legislator's income derived from a public office in which he performed the duties of the post. The term "placeman" means that a man secured one or more lucrative positions in the colonial bureaucracy through the intercession of the governor, the proprietor, or, during the period of crown rule, the monarch. Before 1692, Catholics as well as Protestants could hold office in Maryland. From that year until 1774, when the first extralegal convention met, only Protestants who took an oath of office could serve in the legislature. Therefore, under RELIGIOUS AFFILIATION, legislators who served between 1692 and 1774 for whom we cannot find definite proof of church membership carry the designation "probably Protestant." Under the constitution of 1776 discrimination abated, with Catholics, Quakers, and other religious groups again permitted to participate in public life.

Within the element PUBLIC CAREER the category LEGISLATIVE SERVICE is chronological according to each assembly or convention a legislator attended. Committee service, along with any necessary explanatory information, is in parentheses after the relevant assembly or convention. MILITARY SERVICE is by no means comprehensive for many legislators, because the information came incidentally during the process of identification, rather than through a concerted attempt to search all military-related records. OUT OF COLONY/STATE SERVICE is also not complete, because we did not always have the resources to trace a man's public career outside of Maryland.

The crucial category STANDS ON PUBLIC/PRIVATE ISSUES is used sparingly in most biographies of eighteenth-century legislators, and then chiefly for matters of a private nature. The quantitative analysis of legislative behavior in progress will determine more sharply than presently possible what constituted public issues for these men and will be a focus of the subsequent monographs.

The appraisal of total personal property for the element WEALTH DURING LIFETIME was possible only for a fraction of the legislators. Nonetheless, for specific points in time considerable information did accrue for many men from the few assessment and census lists that survive as well as from extant records of mortgages, inheritances, insolvencies, and bankruptcies.

Because of the abundance of documentation, a much greater degree of precision proved feasible in computing a legislator's interest in land, the prerequisite of social, economic, and political status in early America. In many cases research not only determined the amount, geographical distribution, and method of acquisition of real property at first election but also charted any significant changes between the beginning of a legislative career and death.

The time, place, and manner of death comes as the first entry in the penultimate element, **WEALTH AT DEATH**. When the date of a legislator's demise is not known from family papers, an obituary notice, or the public record, we relied upon probate. The year of death often remains ambiguous with wills registered in January or February, because of the time permitted for filing or because of dilatory executors. In those cases "ca." (circa) precedes the ascribed death date. If a man died intestate, or if no will survives, the sole evidence of death was usually an estate inventory or account, and "ca." again appears before the death date because many months—even years— could elapse before the recording of these documents.

The category PERSONAL PROPERTY summarizes the legislator's assets at death, exclusive of land. That there are so many estimates of personal property here is due to extensive probate materials preserved at the Hall of Records. Parenthetically included after the total estate value are more important items in the inventory, such as the number of servants and slaves, ounces of silver plate, books, and ships.

The final element, **IDENTIFICATION PROBLEMS**, occurs only when there was insufficient evidence for positive identification of a legislator. A short explanation sets forth the problems encountered.

Abbreviations and Notes

1, 2, etc.	Arabic numbers in session lists after a legislator's name and in the biographical category LEGISLATIVE SERVICE after the Assembly date refer to sessions of the given General Assembly.
A	Appointed before or during the designated session or convention of the Assembly
by	The word "by" preceding a birth or death date means that the birth or death of the legislator happened within ten years prior to the given date. Elsewhere in the profile, "by" preceding a date connotes the earliest documented reference to a marriage, elevation to a military post, or any other event.
C	Council
ca.	Circa. With birth and death dates, the year given after circa generally represents the middle year of a span of three.
Chm.	Chairman of a committee
Cv	Convention. A meeting of an assembly that passed no legislation and that ended prematurely because of some extraordinary event or an impasse in the proceedings. The Assembly itself first used the term to describe the meetings held between 19 March 1735/36 and 10 April 1736. These meetings are distinct from, and should not be confused with, the de facto governing bodies of the colony, also called conventions, that existed during the Glorious Revolution and again between 1774 and 1776.
D	Died before or during the indicated session or convention of an assembly
Dating	*See* "by," "ca.," and Slash Dates
Dcl	Declined to serve
DNS	Did not serve
Ds	Discharged during the designated session or convention of an assembly because of failure to meet the requirements of office
E	Elected before or during the indicated session or convention of an assembly
Estate Overpaid	*See* FB
EV	Election declared void because of irregular election procedures
FB	Final Balance. The figure given is the known value of personal property remaining after payment of debts. Totals are rounded to the nearest penny. "Estate overpaid" immediately following "FB" denotes insufficient personalty to meet outstanding charges against the estate. The phrase "as calculated" indicates that the research staff corrected clerical errors.
R	Resigned before or during the designated session or convention of an assembly
S	Sheriff. The designation connotes a legislator's disqualification from sitting before or during the numbered session or convention of the Assembly because he chose to accept the office of sheriff.

Slash
  Dates   Before 1752, when the Gregorian replaced the Julian calendar, dates from 1 January through 24 March are given in Old Style (e.g., 14 February 1722/23).

SW   Special Writ. A personal summons issued by the governor for attendance at an assembly.

TEV   Total Estate Value. The figure given represents the amount of an inventory or inventories of personal property plus collectable debts due to the estate. It does not include the value of real property except for leaseholds. Totals are rounded to the nearest penny. The phrase "as calculated" indicates that the research staff corrected clerical errors. Where known, the type of currency or commodity (such as sterling, paper money, or tobacco) is given. If the type of currency or commodity is unknown, no qualifying remarks follow.

Session Lists

PROPRIETARY ASSEMBLY OF 1634/35 [1]

Cecilius Calvert, 2nd Lord Baltimore, proprietor

Leonard Calvert, governor

February 26, 1634/35

(No record of membership)

[1] The only record of this Assembly is a reference to an act passed on February 26, 1634/35, by a "General Assemblie" at St. Mary's.

PROPRIETARY ASSEMBLY OF 1637/38

Cecilius Calvert, 2nd Lord Baltimore, proprietor

Leonard Calvert, governor

A GENERAL ASSEMBLY OF ALL FREEMEN

January 25–29; February 8, 26; March 5, 12–24, 1637/38 [1]

IN ATTENDANCE [2]

Leonard Calvert, lieutenant general and president of the Assembly

Thomas Cornwaleys, of the Council
Robert Wintour, of the Council

John Lewger, of the Council
Jerome Hawley, of the Council

George Evelyn, commander of Kent Isle (SW) [3]

Thomas Greene	James Cauther	John Hill	John Medley
William Bretton	William Lewis	John Richardson	Isaac Edwards
Henry Fleet	Thomas Franklin	Thomas Hebden	John Courtis
Robert Philpott [4]	Thomas Nabbs	John Halfehead	Cuthbert Fenwick
William Brainthwaite	Thomas Baldridge	John Hillierd	Christopher Thomas
John Wyatt	Edward Fleet	Edward Bateman	Richard Lowe
Robert Clarke	Robert Percy	Richard Lusthead	John Nevill
Richard Garnett (Gardiner), Sr.	John Price	John Fleet	Richard Thompson
Justinian Snow	Thomas Morris (Maurice, Morrison)	Anthony Cotton	Reinold Fleet
Marmaduke Snow	Thomas Stent	Andrew Chappell	William Broughe
Francis Rabnett	John Robinson [5]	Cyprian Thoroughgood	Henry Crawly
Robert Vaughan	Zachary Mottershead	Christopher Martin	Thomas Bradnox [4]
James Baldridge	John Langford	Nathaniel Pope	Edward Beckler [4]
Francis Gray	Edward Parrie (Perry)	John Smithson	
		Robert Smith	

Committee Service

LAWS [6]	Evelyn	L. Calvert
Cornwaleys	Wintour	J. Snow

[1] The Assembly met only during the dates listed and was otherwise in adjournment.

[2] Membership is listed generally in order of appearance. Many of the men attended for only a brief period, while others attended regularly. Twenty-four men, who did not attend personally, were represented by proxies.

[3] The clerk erred several times the first day of the first session in referring to "Captain Robert Evelyn" as commander of Kent Isle. The commander was actually George Evelyn, commissioned in December 1637. By the second day of the session, the error was noted and Robert Evelyn was no longer referred to as commander of Kent Isle, although a man of that name did attend subsequent assemblies.

[4] Robert Philpott, Thomas Bradnox, and Edward Beckler were elected to this Assembly to represent the freemen of Kent Isle. The freemen were also eligible to attend, however, and several did.

[5] A carpenter named John Robinson attended this Assembly, but a second man with the same name may also have been present.

[6] This was an elected committee charged with drafting legislation. Each person voted for five members and these were the five men with the most votes, in order of strength. Later in the session, a smaller committee of three men—Thomas Cornwaleys, Leonard Calvert, and George Evelyn—was elected to prepare laws.

PROPRIETARY ASSEMBLY OF 1638/39

Cecilius Calvert, 2nd Lord Baltimore, proprietor

Leonard Calvert, governor

February 25–March 19, 1638/39

SPECIAL WRITS

Thomas Cornwaleys, of the
Council

Giles Brent, of the Council
John Lewger, of the Council

Fulke Brent
Thomas Greene

John Boteler [1]

ELECTED MEMBERS

MATTAPANIENT HUNDRED
Henry Bishop

ST. MICHAEL'S HUNDRED
James Cauther

John Price

ST. MARY'S HUNDRED
Thomas Gerard
Francis Gray

ST. GEORGE'S HUNDRED
David Wickliff
Randall Revell

KENT ISLE
Nicholas Brown
Christopher Thomas

NONELECTED FREEMEN [2]

Cuthbert Fenwick

Robert Clarke

[1] There is no evidence that John Boteler attended.

[2] Both men claimed a voice in the Assembly, because they did not assent to the election of burgesses from St. Mary's Hundred.

PROPRIETARY ASSEMBLY OF 1640–1641

Cecilius Calvert, 2nd Lord Baltimore, proprietor

Leonard Calvert, governor

FIRST SESSION: October 12–24, 1640
SECOND SESSION: August 2–12, 1641

SPECIAL WRITS

Giles Brent, of the Council [1]
Thomas Greene [2]

Fulke Brent [3]
Thomas Gerard, lord of St.
  Clement's Manor [3]

Cuthbert Fenwick [4]
John Lewger, of the
  Council [5]

ELECTED MEMBERS

MATTAPANIENT HUNDRED
Richard Lusthead [6]
Cuthbert Fenwick (E–2)

ST. MICHAEL'S HUNDRED
Thomas Baldridge

Thomas Morris

ST. MARY'S HUNDRED
John Lewger
Thomas Greene

ST. GEORGE'S HUNDRED [7]
Francis Gray
George Pye

ST. CLEMENT'S HUNDRED
Robert Vaughan [6]

KENT ISLE [8]
Giles Brent
Thomas Adams
Thomas Allen
John Abbott

[1] Elected a burgess from Kent Isle, as well as being summoned on a special writ.

[2] Elected a burgess from St. Mary's Hundred, as well as being summoned on a special writ.

[3] Attended only the second session.

[4] Served at the first session on a special writ as attorney for Councilor and Manor Lord Thomas Cornwaleys, who was out of the country; at the second session he was elected a delegate from Mattapanient Hundred.

[5] Elected a burgess from St. Mary's Hundred, as well as being summoned as a councilor on a special writ.

[6] Attended only the first session.

[7] St. George's Hundred sent only George Pye to the second session in an effort to reduce expenses.

[8] Kent Isle sent only Giles Brent and Thomas Adams to the second session in an effort to reduce expenses.

PROPRIETARY ASSEMBLY OF 1641/42

Cecilius Calvert, 2nd Lord Baltimore, proprietor

Leonard Calvert, governor

A GENERAL ASSEMBLY OF ALL FREEMEN [1]

March 21–23, 1641/42

SPECIAL WRITS

Thomas Cornwaleys, of the Council	John Lewger, of the Council	Thomas Greene	John Langford
	Giles Brent, of the Council	Fulke Brent	Thomas Gerard

FREEMEN IN ATTENDANCE [2]

William Lodington [3]	Robert Wiseman	John Medley	David Wickliff
Richard Thompson [3]	John Prettiman	Nathaniel Pope	John Hampton
Henry Lee	John Robinson, barber	Richard Garnett	John Nevill
Thomas Davison	Angat Baker	(Gardiner), Sr.	Henry Wiseman
Richard Duke	John Cockshott	Henry Bishop	Mathias de Sousa
Thomas Baldridge	Nicholas Keptin	Randall Revell	Francesco van Rynden
Marmaduke Snow	Cyprian Thoroughgood	William Assiter	Edward Coming
John Halfehead	Thomas Charington	John Hallows	Nicholas Herby (Hervey)
Thomas Hebden	Joseph Edlo	John Thatcher	Richard Purlivant
John Weyvill	Isaac Edwards	Robert Clarke	John Gresham
James Johnson	Walter Bayne (Beane)	Philip Conner	Ralph Bayne (Beane)
Francis Posey	George Pye	William Bretton	Christopher Carnall
Robert Kedger	Thomas Morris	Nicholas Causine	
John Harwood	Richard Cole	John Worthy	

Committee Service

AGGRIEVANCES	Lewger	Lodington	Greene
Cornwaleys	Langford	Thompson	Pope
G. Brent			

[1] Writs were initially issued for this to be an elected Assembly, but it in fact became a General Assembly for all freemen or their proxies.
[2] At least twenty-nine other men, who never attended personally, were represented by proxies.
[3] These men were elected burgesses from Kent Isle with proxies for all of the inhabitants.

PROPRIETARY ASSEMBLY OF 1642A

Cecilius Calvert, 2nd Lord Baltimore, proprietor

Leonard Calvert, governor

July 18–August 2, 1642

SPECIAL WRITS

Thomas Cornwaleys, of the Council	Giles Brent, of the Council	William Blount	Cuthbert Fenwick
	John Langford, of the	Thomas Gerard	Robert Clarke
John Lewger, of the Council	Council [1]	Robert Evelyn	William Bretton, clerk

ELECTED MEMBERS

MATTAPANIENT HUNDRED	John Langford [1]	ST. GEORGE'S HUNDRED	KENT ISLE
Henry Bishop [2]		David Wickliff	Richard Thomas
	ST. MARY'S HUNDRED	George Pye	Robert Vaughan
ST. MICHAEL'S HUNDRED	Thomas Greene		
Thomas Sturman	Nathaniel Pope	ST. CLEMENT'S HUNDRED	
		William Broughe	

Committee Service

ACCOUNTS	Vaughan	LAWS [3]	Greene or Pope
Lewger	Pope	Cornwaleys (chm.)	Thompson
Greene	Pye	Lewger	Vaughan
Thompson		Evelyn	Wickliff or Pye

[1] Two men of this name attended the Assembly; the burgess for St. Michael's Hundred was identified as a carpenter.

[2] His initial election to represent a St. Leonard's Hundred was ruled invalid because the hundred was not yet legally established and no writ had been issued for an election there. Bishop's election to represent Mattapanient Hundred was then reported.

[3] Representation on this committee, appointed "to consider all bills," was clearly based on a rudimentary sense of geographical balance and probably on literacy.

PROPRIETARY ASSEMBLY OF 1642B

Cecilius Calvert, 2nd Lord Baltimore, proprietor

Leonard Calvert, governor

A GENERAL ASSEMBLY OF ALL FREEMEN

September 5–13, 1642

SPECIAL WRITS

Thomas Cornwaleys, of the Council	Giles Brent, of the Council [1]	William Blount, of the Council (DNS) [2]	Francis Trafford, of the Council (DNS) [2]
John Lewger, of the Council	John Langford, of the Council		

FREEMEN IN ATTENDANCE

Thomas Weston [3]	George Pye	Thomas Franklin	Thomas Sturman
Thomas Greene	Robert Clarke	Thomas Hebden	William Durford
George Binks	Cyprian Thoroughgood	John Medley	William Broughe
Nicholas Herby (Hervey)	John Hollis	Francis Posey	Nicholas Causine
David Wickliff	John Weyvill	Randall Revell	

Committee Service

LAWS	Brent	Langford	Binks
L. Calvert	Lewger	Greene	Herby
Cornwaleys			

[1] Although he was removed from the Council on September 5, this did not affect his sitting on a special writ. He also represented by proxy seventy-three inhabitants of Kent Isle.

[2] Blount and Trafford, as members of the Council, were entitled to sit by special writ in this Assembly, but neither man actually attended.

[3] Thomas Weston "pleaded he was no freeman because he had no land nor certain dwelling here &ca.," but by vote the Assembly decided he was a freeman.

PROPRIETARY ASSEMBLY OF 1644/45 [1]

Cecilius Calvert, 2nd Lord Baltimore, proprietor

Leonard Calvert, governor

February 1644/45

(No record of membership)

[1] No journal survives from this Assembly, which met during the month when Capt. Richard Ingle successfully challenged the proprietary government and caused Leonard Calvert to flee to Virginia. One act is known to have been passed on February 11, which was published under seal on February 13.

18

PROPRIETARY ASSEMBLY OF 1646–1646/47[1]

Cecilius Calvert, 2nd Lord Baltimore, proprietor

Leonard Calvert, governor

Edward Hill, deputy governor 1 (Ds–2)[1]

FIRST SESSION: Fall 1646[1]

SECOND SESSION: December 29, 1646–January 2, 1646/47

UPPER HOUSE[2]

John Lewger   Thomas Greene   Thomas Gerard

LOWER HOUSE[3]

(No definite record of membership)

[1] The first session of this Assembly, called by Deputy Governor Edward Hill, apparently met in the fall of 1646 following Hill's commission in July of that year. The Assembly's legality was later questioned because Hill's appointment was invalid due to his not being a councilor. The second session, also challenged later because it met under the same summons from Hill, was chaired by Leonard Calvert, who had returned to Maryland by the late fall of 1646.

[2] This was the first Assembly to meet in two houses; the division had occurred at least by the second session.

[3] The Assembly of 1649 would charge that "the whole house of Commons (two or three only excepted) consisted of that Rebelled Party and his [Calvert's] Professed Enemies." It is very likely that the membership included the nine men who swore to the oath of fealty to the proprietary government on January 2, 1646/47 along with Lewger, Gerard, and Greene, the three known members of the Upper House at the second session. Those men and their probable constituencies were: Francis Gray (St. George's Hundred), John Hampton (probably Kent Isle), John Hatch (St. Mary's Hundred), Francis Pope (probably Newtown Hundred), William Thompson (Newtown Hundred), William Bretton (Newtown Hundred, probably clerk of the Assembly), Nathaniel Pope (St. Mary's Hundred), Thomas Sturman (St. Michael's Hundred), John Hollis (St. Mary's Hundred). Of these men, at least Sturman, Gray, and Hampton were "rebels."

PROPRIETARY ASSEMBLY OF 1647/48

Cecilius Calvert, 2nd Lord Baltimore, proprietor

Thomas Greene, governor

A GENERAL ASSEMBLY OF ALL FREEMEN

January 7; January 17–March 4, 1647/48

SPECIAL WRIT

Giles Brent, of the Council

FREEMEN IN ATTENDANCE

John Price	Richard Banks	Robert Clarke	George Manners
Robert Vaughan	Barnaby Jackson	Francis Posey	Robert Percy
Cuthbert Fenwick	George Saphyr	John Hatch	Margaret Brent[1]
Thomas Bradnox	George Akerick	William Thompson	Nicholas Gwither[2]
Philip Conner	John Medley	John Wyatt	"& divers other
Thomas Thornborough	Walter Waterlin	Edward Cotten	inhabitants"
Francis Brookes	Walter Pakes (Peake)	John Halfehead	
Thomas Allen	Edward Packer	William Bretton	

Committee Service

ACCOUNTS		DEFENSE	
G. Brent	Price	Bretton	Banks
Vaughan	Saphyr	Hatch	Saphyr
	Jackson		Jackson
	Packer		

[1] Denied the right to vote by Governor Greene.

[2] Denied the right to vote when Cuthbert Fenwick claimed that Gwither still owed him service on an indenture.

PROPRIETARY ASSEMBLY OF 1649 [1]

Cecilius Calvert, 2nd Lord Baltimore, proprietor

William Stone, governor

April 2–21, 1649

SPECIAL WRITS

John Pile	Thomas Greene	Robert Vaughan
Thomas Hatton	John Price	

ELECTED MEMBERS

ST. MARY'S [2]	Richard Brown	Thomas Thornborough	George Manners
Richard Banks	John Mansell	Robert Clarke	KENT ISLE
Walter Peake	Cuthbert Fenwick	William Bretton [3]	Philip Conner

Committee Service

ACCOUNTS	Banks	Brown
Fenwick	Conner	Peake

[1] Only the journal of the last day's proceedings and the acts of this Assembly survive. It is not known if the Assembly met as one house or two.

[2] The specific hundred that each man represented is unknown, therefore they are listed collectively under St. Mary's County.

[3] William Bretton may have attended as clerk, rather than as an elected member.

PROPRIETARY ASSEMBLY OF 1650–1650/51

Cecilius Calvert, 2nd Lord Baltimore, proprietor

William Stone, governor

FIRST SESSION: April 6–29, 1650
SECOND SESSION: March 11, 1650/51

UPPER HOUSE

John Pile (DNS)	Robert Vaughan (A–1) [2]	Robert Brooke (DNS)	William Mitchell (A–2, DNS)
Thomas Greene (Ds–2) [1]	Robert Clarke (Ds–1) [3]	William Eltonhead (DNS)	
John Price	Thomas Hatton		

LOWER HOUSE

ST. MARY'S HUNDRED	ST. MICHAEL'S HUNDRED	NEWTOWN HUNDRED	KENT ISLE
Philip Land	Thomas Sturman	William Broughe	Robert Vaughan (C–1) [2]
Francis Brookes	George Manners	John Medley	PROVIDENCE
ST. INIGOE'S HUNDRED	ST. GEORGE'S HUNDRED	Robert Robins	(ANNE ARUNDEL)
Thomas Mathews (Ds–1) [4]	John Hatch	ST. CLEMENT'S HUNDRED	James Coxe, speaker
Cuthbert Fenwick (E–1)	Walter Bayne	Francis Posey	George Puddington

Committee Service

ACCOUNTS (JOINT)	Hatch (1)	Clarke (1a)	Land (1a, 1b)
Price (1)	Broughe (1)	Greene (1b)	Robins (1a)
Vaughan (1)	Robins (1)	Price (1b)	Bayne (1a)
Coxe (1)	Puddington (1)	Vaughan (1a, 1b)	Fenwick (1b, chm.)
Land (1)	LAWS (JOINT) [5]	Puddington (1a, 1b)	
	Hatton (1a)	Hatch (1a, 1b)	

[1] Dismissed as a councilor and member of the Upper House at the second session.

[2] Began the first session as an elected member from Kent Isle, but was sitting in the Upper House by April 25.

[3] Discharged from the first session upon his own request.

[4] Dismissed from the first session for failure to take the oath of secrecy.

[5] Two separate committees worked on the laws in the first session.

COMMONWEALTH ASSEMBLY OF 1652 [1]

Richard Bennett, commissioner of Parliament
William Claiborne, commissioner of Parliament

June 24–28, 1652(?) [1]

[1] The Bennett-Claiborne commission issued a call on March 29, 1652, for elections to be held for an Assembly to meet on June 24, 1652. At least one election, that of Thomas Gerard to represent St. Mary's County, was held on June 12. It is unclear if the Assembly ever convened, although Gerard did later sue to recover his expenses. On June 28 the reinstated proprietary officials declared "there is no Absolute necessity of a General Assembly at present."

PROVINCIAL PARLIAMENTARY COMMISSIONERS OF 1654–1657/58 [1]

Richard Bennett, commissioner of Parliament
William Claiborne, commissioner of Parliament

July 22, 1654–March 24, 1657/58

William Fuller	John Hatch	Sampson Waring	Thomas Thomas
Richard Preston	Richard Wells	Michael Brooke	Philip Thomas
William Durand	Richard Ewen	John Pott	Samuel Withers
Edward Lloyd	William Parker	Woodman Stockely	Richard Woolman
John Smith	Robert Slye	William Parrott	
Leonard Strong	Thomas Meeres	Philip Morgan	
John Lawson	Thomas Marsh	William Ewen	

[1] Richard Bennett and William Claiborne, with authorization from the Puritan government in England, issued an ordinance July 22, 1654, to ten Marylanders as commissioners "for the well Ordering, directing and Governing the affaires of Maryland" with powers that included the right to summon assemblies. Later additions to the body of commissioners were Parker (October 20, 1654), Slye (April 24, 1655), Meeres and Marsh (June 26, 1655), Waring, Brooke, Pott, and Stockley (August 13, 1655), Parrott (March 23, 1656/57), and Morgan, Ewen, the two Thomases, Withers, and Woolman (by spring, 1657). Thomas Marsh died in 1656/57 and Leonard Strong was serving as agent in England ca. 1655, but the other commissioners presumably remained active. The records, however, are incomplete and therefore the full service of all the commissioners cannot be established. The commissioners surrendered their powers to the restored proprietary government March 24, 1657/58.

COMMONWEALTH ASSEMBLY OF 1654 [1]

Richard Bennett, commissioner of Parliament
William Claiborne, commissioner of Parliament

October (?)–20, 1654

POTOMAC (ST. MARY'S) [2]	KENT	Leonard Strong	Richard Ewen
John Hatch	Thomas Hynson	Richard Wells	William Parker
Thomas Hatton (Dc1)	Joseph Wickes	William Durand	Sampson Waring
Job Chandler (Dc1)	PROVIDENCE	Edward Lloyd	James Berry
Arthur Turner (E)	(ANNE ARUNDEL)		William Ewen
John Wade (E)	William Fuller	PATUXENT (CALVERT)	
		Richard Preston, speaker	

[1] The Assembly, under the Puritan government of the parliamentary commissioners, was unicameral.
[2] Thomas Hatton and Job Chandler declined to serve because of their previous oaths to Lord Baltimore. They were replaced by Arthur Turner and John Wade.

COMMONWEALTH ASSEMBLY OF 1657[1]

Richard Bennett, commissioner of Parliament
William Claiborne, commissioner of Parliament

September 24, 1657

POTOMAC (ST. MARY'S)
Robert Siye
James Johnson

KENT
Robert Vaughan

Joseph Wickes

PROVIDENCE
(ANNE ARUNDEL)
Thomas Besson

PATUXENT (CALVERT)
Richard Ewen, speaker
Robert Taylor

Peter Sharpe
Philip Morgan
Michael Brooke

[1] This Assembly, like its predecessor, was unicameral and was summoned by the provincial parliamentary commissioners.

PROPRIETARY ASSEMBLY OF 1658

Cecilius Calvert, 2nd Lord Baltimore, proprietor
Josias Fendall, governor

April 27–by May 6, 1658

UPPER HOUSE

Philip Calvert
William Stone (DNS)

Thomas Gerard
Robert Clarke
John Price

Job Chandler (DNS)
Baker Brooke (SW) [1]

Nathaniel Utie (SW) [1]

LOWER HOUSE

ST. MARY'S [2]
Richard Willan (St. Mary's)
Thomas Cornwaleys (St.
  Inigoe's)
William Lucas (St.
  Michael's)
George Mee (St. Michael's)

William Evans (Newtown)
Zachary Wade (Newtown)
James Langworth (St.
  Clement's)

KENT
Philip Conner

ANNE ARUNDEL
William Fuller
Edward Lloyd
William Ewen

CALVERT
Richard Preston

Michael Brooke
Richard Smith
Woodman Stockley

CHARLES
John Hatch

[1] Baker Brooke and Nathaniel Utie sat in the Upper House for this Assembly by special writ. Both men were lords of manors and would soon be officially appointed to the Council.
[2] Elections in St. Mary's County were by hundreds.

22

PROPRIETARY ASSEMBLY OF 1659/60 [1]

Cecilius Calvert, 2nd Lord Baltimore, proprietor

Josias Fendall, governor

February 28–March 14, 1659/60

UPPER HOUSE

Philip Calvert	John Price	Robert Clarke	Nathaniel Utie
Thomas Gerard	Luke Barber	Baker Brooke	Edward Lloyd

LOWER HOUSE

ST. MARY'S [2]	Henry Morgan	Robert Clarkson	Zachary Wade
Robert Slye	John Russell		John Jenkins
William Barton (EV)		CALVERT	
William Evans (EV, E)	ANNE ARUNDEL	William Parker	BALTIMORE
James Langworth (EV, E)	Richard Ewen, speaker	Sampson Waring	Samuel Goldsmith
Luke Gardiner (E)	Thomas Howell	Richard Preston (DNS) [3]	George Goldsmith
	Richard Woolman	Michael Brooke	Godfrey Bayley
KENT	William Burgess		Francis Stockett
Joseph Wickes	William Fuller	CHARLES	
Thomas Hynson	Thomas Taillor	John Hatch	
		Robert Henley	

[1] Before this Assembly ended, Gov. Josias Fendall, Nathaniel Utie, and Thomas Gerard joined with members of the Lower House in a rebellion against Lord Baltimore's government in an effort to reestablish a commonwealth.

[2] For unexplained reasons Barton, Evans, and Langworth were ruled unduly elected. The subsequent election returned Evans and Langworth, but replaced Barton with Gardiner.

[3] On a trip to England, he did not attend this Assembly.

PROPRIETARY ASSEMBLY OF 1661

Cecilius Calvert, 2nd Lord Baltimore, proprietor

Philip Calvert, governor

April 17–May 2, 1661

UPPER HOUSE

Henry Coursey, secretary	Baker Brooke	John Bateman
Robert Clarke	Edward Lloyd	

LOWER HOUSE

ST. MARY'S	KENT	CALVERT	CHARLES
William Evans	Thomas Stagwell	Richard Preston, speaker	Henry Adams
Luke Gardiner	William Leeds	Thomas Manning	Joseph Harrison
Thomas Mathews		Richard Smith	
William Barton	ANNE ARUNDEL	Thomas Trueman	BALTIMORE
	John Brewer		Thomas Stockett (DNS)
	Samuel Chew		George Utie

PROPRIETARY ASSEMBLY OF 1662

Cecilius Calvert, 2nd Lord Baltimore, proprietor

Charles Calvert, governor

April 1–12, 1662

UPPER HOUSE

Philip Calvert, deputy governor
Henry Sewall, secretary

Robert Clarke
Baker Brooke
Edward Lloyd

John Bateman
James Neale
Henry Coursey [1]

LOWER HOUSE

ST. MARY'S
William Evans
Luke Gardiner
Thomas Turner
Richard Willan

KENT
Robert Vaughan
Richard Blunt

ANNE ARUNDEL
Robert Burle
Richard Beard
Ralph Hawkins

CALVERT
Richard Preston, speaker
Thomas Manning
Thomas Trueman
Richard Smith

CHARLES
Zachary Wade

BALTIMORE
Nathaniel Utie
Thomas Stockett

TALBOT
Richard Woolman

[1] Excused from attendance.

PROPRIETARY ASSEMBLY OF 1663–1664

Cecilius Calvert, 2nd Lord Baltimore, proprietor

Charles Calvert, governor

FIRST SESSION: September 15–October 3, 1663
SECOND SESSION: September 13–21, 1664

UPPER HOUSE

Philip Calvert, deputy governor
Henry Sewall, secretary [1]

Robert Clarke (D–2)
Baker Brooke
Edward Lloyd

John Bateman (D–2)
Henry Coursey
Jerome White

William Evans (A–2)
Nathaniel Utie (SW–2)

LOWER HOUSE [2]

ST. MARY'S
William Calvert
Robert Slye, speaker
Thomas Notley
Nicholas Gwither

KENT
Henry Carline

Robert Dunn

ANNE ARUNDEL
Thomas Meeres
George Puddington
Richard Beard
John Homewood

CALVERT
Richard Preston
Thomas Brooke
Thomas Letchworth

CHARLES
Henry Adams
Joseph Harrison

BALTIMORE
Samuel Goldsmith
Thomas Stockett
Francis Wright [1]
Richard Bennett

TALBOT
Richard Woolman

[1] Sewall, who was in England, did not attend the second session, nor did Wright, who was away on official business at the Susquehannah Fort.
[2] Lower House journals do not survive for either session. Membership of the Lower House for the first session is recorded in the Upper House journal, but no complete list is available to determine attendance or possible new members at the second session.

PROPRIETARY ASSEMBLY OF 1666

Cecilius Calvert, 2nd Lord Baltimore, proprietor

Charles Calvert, governor

April 10–May 3, 1666

UPPER HOUSE

Philip Calvert, deputy governor

Richard Boughton, secretary (DNS) [1]

Henry Coursey

Jerome White (DNS) [1]

Baker Brooke

Edward Lloyd

William Evans

Thomas Trueman

LOWER HOUSE

ST. MARY'S
William Calvert
Robert Slye
Thomas Notley, speaker
Nicholas Young

KENT
Nicholas Pickard

Richard Blunt

ANNE ARUNDEL
Robert Burle
Richard Beard
Thomas Besson

CALVERT
Richard Preston

Richard Smith
Thomas Brooke
Richard Hall

CHARLES
James Neale
Zachary Wade
Gerard Fowke
Thomas Thorowgood

BALTIMORE
Thomas Howell
Nathaniel Utie

TALBOT
William Coursey
William Hambleton

Committee Service

LAWS [2]
Neale (a)
Thorowgood (a, b)

Young (a)
Beard (a)
Slye (a)

Utie (b)
Smith (b)
Coursey (b)

[1] There is no record that either Boughton or White received a summons to, or attended, this Assembly, although both men were members of the Council and thus members of the Upper House.

[2] There was not yet a permanent Committee of Laws which served an entire session, but these two committees were each delegated responsibility for more than one bill and represent more than ad hoc bodies; each brought back approximately four draft bills.

PROPRIETARY ASSEMBLY OF 1669

Cecilius Calvert, 2nd Lord Baltimore, proprietor

Charles Calvert, governor

April 13–May 8, 1669

UPPER HOUSE

Philip Calvert, chancellor
Jerome White

Baker Brooke
Henry Coursey

Thomas Trueman
William Calvert (SW) [1]

LOWER HOUSE

ST. MARY'S
Thomas Notley
John Morecroft [2]
Robert Slye
Thomas Dent

KENT
Robert Dunn
Richard Blunt

ANNE ARUNDEL
William Burgess
Samuel Withers
Thomas Taillor
Edward Selby

CALVERT
Hugh Stanley
Thomas Manning, speaker
Edward Keene
Richard Hall [3]

CHARLES
Thomas Thorowgood
John Bowles
Richard Boughton
Stephen Mountague

BALTIMORE
John Vanhack
Nathaniel Utie

TALBOT
Richard Woolman

Joseph Wickes
William Hambleton
Daniel Clarke

SOMERSET
William Stevens
Stephen Horsey (DNS) [4]

DORCHESTER
Richard Preston

AGGRIEVANCES (JOINT)	W. Calvert	Preston	Taillor
P. Calvert	Utie	Withers	Wickes
Coursey	Burgess	Slye	Boughton
Trueman			

[1] Calvert apparently attended this Assembly on a special writ, because he was not yet officially appointed to the Council when the Assembly convened; perhaps he was replacing William Evans, who died in March 1668/69.

[2] Impeached by the Lower House during the session for irregular actions as a lawyer; the Upper House ruled the impeachment procedure improper and cleared him of all charges.

[3] The surviving Upper House journal does not record Hall's attendance, but he was an elected delegate from Calvert County.

[4] Horsey never attended the session. Somerset, like Dorchester, a newer and less populated county, may have desired a smaller delegation.

PROPRIETARY ASSEMBLY OF 1671–1674/75

Cecilius Calvert, 2nd Lord Baltimore, proprietor

Charles Calvert, governor

FIRST SESSION: March 27–April 19, 1671
SECOND SESSION: October 10–19, 1671
THIRD SESSION: May 19–June 6, 1674
FOURTH SESSION: February 12–24, 1674/75

UPPER HOUSE

Philip Calvert, chancellor	Baker Brooke	Samuel Chew	Thomas Taillor (A–3)
William Talbot, secretary 1 (R–1) [1]	William Calvert, secretary 3, 4 [1]	Edward Fitzherbert (R–2) [2]	Nathaniel Utie (A–3)
	Thomas Trueman	Jesse Wharton (A–3)	

LOWER HOUSE

ST. MARY'S	CALVERT	John Vanhack (R–4) [4]	DORCHESTER [6]
Luke Gardiner (S–3)	Thomas Brooke	John Waterton	Daniel Clarke
William Boarman	Charles Brooke (D–3)	Thomas Howell	Henry Trippe [4]
William Hatton	Richard Perry (R–3) [4]	Thomas Todd (E–4)	William Ford (E–4) [4]
Thomas Dent (E–3)	Daniel Jenifer (R–3) [4]	George Wells (E–4)	
John Jarbo (E–3)	Richard Hall (E–3)		ST. MARY'S CITY [7]
	William Berry (E–3)	TALBOT	John Morecroft (E–2, D–3)
KENT	Henry Darnall (E–3, S–4)	Richard Woolman	Thomas Notley (E–2),
Arthur Wright		Philemon Lloyd	speaker 2–4
William Bishop	CHARLES	Joseph Wickes	Robert Carvile (E–3)
	Humphrey Warren (DNS, D–1) [5]	William Hambleton	
ANNE ARUNDEL			CECIL [8]
Thomas Taillor, speaker 1 (C–3) [3]	Henry Adams	SOMERSET [6]	Henry Ward (E–4)
	Ignatius Causine	Paul Marsh	Abraham Wilde (E–4)
William Burgess	John Bowles	Roger Woolford	John Vanhack (E–4) [4]
Cornelius Howard		Ambrose Dixon (DNS) [5]	Thomas Salmon (E–4)
Robert Franklin	BALTIMORE	Ambrose London (DNS) [5]	
	James Browne (DNS) [5]		

Committee Service

ACCOUNTS (JOINT) [9]	Adams (2)	Carvile (3a, 3b)	Clarke (3b)
B. Brooke (1, 2)	Burgess (3)	Lloyd (3a, 3b)	Berry (3b)
Trueman (1, 3)	Hambleton (3)	Adams (3a)	Howell (3b)
Chew (1, 2)	Howell (3)	Vanhack (3a)	Boarman (4)
Taillor (3)		Hatton (3a)	Wells (4)
Jenifer (2)	LAWS (JOINT) [10]	Waterton (3a)	Ward (4)
T. Brooke (2)	B. Brooke (2)	Dent (3b)	Hall (4)
Lloyd (2, 3)	Trueman (2, 3)	Burgess (3b)	Wright (4)
Franklin (2)	Chew (3)	Woolman (3b, 4)	
	Wharton (3)		

[1] Talbot returned to England and Ireland after the first session; Calvert had succeeded Talbot as secretary by the third session.

[2] Fitzherbert apparently left the colony permanently after the second session.

[3] In England during the second session; promoted to the Upper House before the Assembly reconvened in 1674.

[4] Questions arose in this Assembly of replacing delegates who were temporarily or permanently out of the colony. When Henry Trippe was absent from the second session, Dorchester County's justices or freemen elected a replacement, identity unknown, who apparently was never seated by the Lower House. By the third session Calvert County voters had replaced Richard Perry and Daniel Jenifer, who had moved to England and Virginia respectively. It is uncertain whether William Ford of Dorchester County was a third delegate, or was replacing Daniel Clarke, who did not attend the fourth session but was still alive. John Vanhack ceased serving from Baltimore County when he was elected as a burgess from newly erected Cecil County in 1674/75. Thomas Todd and George Wells probably replaced both him and James Browne at the fourth session.

[5] Warren died before the first session convened; Browne went to New England; Dixon and London never attended, perhaps because of Somerset County's expressed desire to send only two delegates for financial reasons.

[6] Somerset and Dorchester both requested that they be allowed to send only two delegates due to the heavy financial burden their expenses placed on newer counties.

[7] Representation for St. Mary's City was first granted at the second session as an act of Governor Calvert to ensure the presence in the Assembly of John Morecroft and Thomas Notley, two devoted proprietary supporters.

[8] Cecil County, created in 1674, sent its first delegates to the fourth session.

[9] Lower House membership on the Committee of Accounts at the first session is unknown.

[10] Lower House membership on the Committee of Laws, which first appeared at the second session, is unknown for that session. Two committees sat in the third session, with men marked (3a) serving early in the session and those marked (3b) working on legislation late in the session. The entire Upper House met in conference with the Lower House members at the fourth session.

PROPRIETARY ASSEMBLY OF 1676–1682

Charles Calvert, 3rd Lord Baltimore, proprietor [1]

Cecilius Calvert, governor [2]

FIRST SESSION: May 15–June 15, 1676
SECOND SESSION: October 20–November 14, 1678
THIRD SESSION: August 16–September 17, 1681
FOURTH SESSION: November 1–12, 1681 [3]
FIFTH SESSION: April 25–May 13, 1682

UPPER HOUSE

Philip Calvert, chancellor	Jesse Wharton (D–2)	Henry Coursey (A–2)	William Stevens (A–3)
William Calvert, secretary	Thomas Taillor	Benjamin Rozer (A–2, D–3)	George Talbot (A–3) [4]
Baker Brooke (D–3)	Thomas Notley (A–2, D–3),	Vincent Lowe (A–3)	William Digges (A–3)
Samuel Chew (D–2)	deputy governor 2 [2]	Henry Darnall (A–3)	

LOWER HOUSE [5]

ST. MARY'S
Thomas Notley, speaker 1 (C–2) [2]
John Coode [6]
William Hatton
Walter Hall (D–2)
Clement Hill (E–2) [7]
Richard Gardiner (E–3)

KENT
Joseph Wickes
Thomas Marsh (D–3)
Henry Hosier
Samuel Tovey [8]
John Hynson (E–3)
Thomas Smith (E–3?) [8]

ANNE ARUNDEL
William Burgess
James Rigby (D–3)

John Homewood
William Richardson
Richard Hill (E–3)

CALVERT
Thomas Brooke (D–2)
Richard Hall
Richard Ladd
Christopher Rousby [9]
Francis Billingsley (E–2)

CHARLES
John Allen (D–2)
John Douglass (D–3)
Robert Henley
Henry Adams
Josias Fendall [10]
John Stone (E–2)
Randolph Brandt (E–3)

BALTIMORE
George Wells
John Stansby (S–3)
John Waterton
John Scott
James Mills (E–4 or E–5) [11]

TALBOT
Philemon Lloyd, speaker 2–5
John Edmundson
Richard Woolman (D–3)
Wenlock Christison (D–3)
George Robotham (E–3)
John Rousby (E–3)

SOMERSET
William Stevens (C–3)
Roger Woolford
James Dashiell
John White (S–3)

John Goddin (E–3)
Henry Smith (E–3)

DORCHESTER
John Stevens
William Ford (D–3)
Bartholomew Ennalls
John Hudson (D–2)
Anthony Tall (E–2, D–3)
John Brooke (E–3)
Henry Trippe (E–3)

ST. MARY'S CITY
Kenelm Cheseldyne
Robert Carvile

CECIL
James Frisby
Jonathan Sybray
William Pearce
Nathaniel Garrett

ACCOUNTS (JOINT) [12]
Taillor (2–5)
W. Stevens (3)
Coursey (3)
Lowe (4)
Burgess (1, 3)
T. Brooke (1)
R. Hall (1, 3)
W. Stevens (1)
Douglass (1)
Henley (1)

C. Rousby (2)
Coode (2)
Cheseldyne (2)
Christison (2)
Carvile (2, 4)
Edmundson (3)
Ennalls (3)
J. Rousby (4)

ELECTIONS AND PRIVILEGES
Homewood (2)
Ladd (2)

Woolman (2)
White (2)
Ford (2)

LAWS
C. Rousby (2)
Coode (2)
Cheseldyne (2)
Christison (2)
Carvile (2)

SECURITY AND DEFENSE
C. Rousby (2)
Cheseldyne (2)
Coode (2)
Christison (2)
Douglass (2)
Richardson (2)

TRADE
Robotham (5)
Edmundson (5)

[1] Present for the first session as both proprietor and resident governor, he returned to England soon after that session for his investiture as third Lord Baltimore. He was back in Maryland by the third session and personally presided over the third, fourth, and fifth sessions of this Assembly.

[2] Before leaving the colony in June 1676, Calvert commissioned his infant son Cecilius as nominal governor, and Councilor Jesse Wharton, his stepson-in-law, as deputy governor. Wharton died within a month, and as predetermined by Calvert, Notley became Wharton's successor. Speaker of the first session, Notley was now elevated to the Council. Notley presided over the second session, but died in April 1679.

[3] The November 1681 session was actually a continuation of the third session, which had been adjourned, rather than prorogued, on September 17, 1681. For convenience it is counted here as a separate session.

[4] There is no evidence that he attended any of the three sessions of this Assembly at which he was eligible to sit.

[5] Although four delegates were elected from each county for this Assembly, Charles Calvert actually summoned only two delegates per county for the first session, an action that caused much discontent. All elected members received the proper summonses for subsequent sessions. Those individuals known to have been present at the first session were Thomas Notley, John Coode, Joseph Wickes, William Burgess, Thomas Brooke, Richard Hall, John Douglass, Robert Henley, Henry Adams, Philemon Lloyd, John Edmundson, William Stevens, Kenelm Cheseldyne, and Robert Carvile, the latter being summoned after the Assembly convened at the special request of the Lower House.

[6] Calvert sought the dismissal of Coode from membership in the Assembly at its third session for Coode's alleged conspiracy with Josias Fendall earlier in 1681. The Lower House strenuously and successfully resisted the effort to unseat one of its members on as yet unproven charges.

[7] Hill, who was serving as sheriff in 1676 and 1677, was apparently elected to replace Thomas Notley.

[8] The journal of the fifth session mentions a Capt. Thomas Smith as a member, and the records of the third session refer to both a Mr. Smith and Capt. Henry Smith of Somerset County. The reference may represent a clerical error, or Thomas Smith may have replaced Samuel Tovey of Kent County, who was excused from the second session for illness and may have subsequently resigned.

[9] Returned to England in 1681 on business arising from his controversies with Lord Baltimore over the collection of customs duties; he missed the third through the fifth sessions.

[10] Voters of Charles County attempted to elect Fendall to the vacancy created by John Allen's death, but the Council issued a clear warning that he was ineligible to sit because of the prohibition placed on his holding office after his overthrow of the proprietary government in 1659/60.

[11] Definitely present at the fifth session, when he signed a declaration with other delegates; he may have been elected to the fourth session, but the records are incomplete.

[12] Lower House membership for the joint Committee of Accounts is unknown for the fourth and fifth sessions.

PROPRIETARY ASSEMBLY OF 1682–1684

Charles Calvert, 3rd Lord Baltimore, proprietor and governor

FIRST SESSION: October 26–November 17, 1682
SECOND SESSION: October 2–November 6, 1683
THIRD SESSION: April 1–26, 1684 [1]

UPPER HOUSE

Philip Calvert, chancellor (D–2)
Thomas Taillor
Henry Coursey

Vincent Lowe
Henry Darnall
William Stevens
William Digges

William Burgess
Nicholas Sewall
George Talbot [2]
John Darnall (A–2)

Thomas Trueman (A–2)
Edward Pye (A–3)

LOWER HOUSE [3]

ST. MARY'S
William Hatton
Clement Hill

KENT
Joseph Wickes
Henry Hosier

ANNE ARUNDEL
Richard Hill
William Richardson

CALVERT
Francis Hutchins
Richard Hall
[Richard Ladd] [4]

CHARLES
Henry Adams
Thomas Burford

BALTIMORE
Miles Gibson (S–2)

Henry Johnson
Thomas Long (E–2) [5]

TALBOT
Philemon Lloyd, speaker 1–3
John Rousby

SOMERSET
Henry Smith
John Osborne

DORCHESTER
Bartholomew Ennalls
John Brooke

ST. MARY'S CITY
Robert Carvile
Leonard Greene

CECIL
James Frisby
William Pearce (S–3)

Committee Service

ACCOUNTS (JOINT)
Taillor (1)
Stevens (1, 2)
Digges (1–3)
Burgess (3)
Hatton (1)
H. Smith (1–3) [6]
C. Hill (1–3)
Frisby (2, 3)
R. Hall (2)

R. Hill (2) [6]

ELECTIONS AND PRIVILEGES
Carvile (2)
H. Smith (2) [7]
Osborne (2) [7]

LAWS (JOINT) [8]
Lowe (3a, chm.)
H. Darnall (3a)
Stevens (3b, chm.)
J. Darnall (3b)

Carvile (2)
R. Hall (2)
Richardson (2)
Osborne (2, 3b)
C. Hill (3a)
H. Smith (3a)
Frisby (3a)
Rousby (3b)
Burford (3b)
R. Hill (3b)

TRADE (JOINT)
Lowe (1)
Burgess (1)
Carvile (1, chm.)
Rousby (1, 2)
Hosier (1)
Osborne (1)
Burford (2)
Ennalls (2)

[1] The session of April 1684 was actually a continuation of the previous session, which had been adjourned, rather than prorogued, in order to save temporary laws. For convenience it is listed here as a separate session.

[2] There is no evidence that he sat at either the first or third session.

[3] Following the ordinance he had proclaimed in 1681, Lord Baltimore issued writs to elect only two delegates per county instead of four.

[4] The mention of "Captain Richard Ladd" as a member of the first session was probably a clerk's error. Francis Hutchins and Richard Hall were present at all three sessions, and the county was allowed only two delegates. The clerk probably meant to write Capt. Richard Hill, a delegate from Anne Arundel County.

[5] Elected on October 11, 1683, to replace Miles Gibson.

[6] Henry Smith and Richard Hill were appointed later in the session to replace Clement Hill and Richard Hall.

[7] Osborne was appointed late in the session to replace Henry Smith.

[8] Early in the third session a joint Committee of Laws (3a) was appointed to examine the temporary laws and to prepare a report; another Committee of Laws (3b) was appointed later to perfect bills and amendments.

PROPRIETARY ASSEMBLY OF 1686–1688

Charles Calvert, 3rd Lord Baltimore, proprietor
Benedict Leonard Calvert, governor [1]

FIRST SESSION: October 27–November 19, 1686
SECOND SESSION: November 14–17; November 19–December 8, 1688

UPPER HOUSE

Thomas Taillor [1]	William Stevens (D–2)	Nicholas Sewall	Henry Coursey (SW–1),
Vincent Lowe	William Digges	Edward Pye	speaker 1 [2]
Henry Darnall	William Burgess (D–2)	Clement Hill	William Joseph (A–2) [1]

LOWER HOUSE

ST. MARY'S
Clement Hill (DNS, C–1) [1]
Joseph Pile
Richard Gardiner (D–2)
John Coode (E–2)

KENT
Henry Hosier (DNS, D–1) [4]
Michael Miller
William Harris (E–1)

ANNE ARUNDEL [5]
Richard Hill

CALVERT
Henry Jowles
George Lingan

CHARLES
John Stone
Thomas Burford (D–2)
Henry Hawkins (E–2)

BALTIMORE
Thomas Thurston
George Wells

TALBOT
George Robotham
John Edmundson

SOMERSET
James Round
Stephen Luffe

DORCHESTER
Edward Pindar (DNS, S–1) [6]

John Brooke
Daniel Clarke [7]

ST. MARY'S CITY
Kenelm Cheseldyne, speaker 1(?), 2
Anthony Underwood

CECIL
William Dare
Edward Jones

Committee Service

ACCOUNTS (JOINT)	Hill (2)	Underwood (2)	Round (2)
Digges (2, chm.)	Robotham (2)	Pile (2)	

[1] Benedict Leonard Calvert, Lord Baltimore's infant son and heir, was nominal lieutenant general and governor, but actual executive power devolved upon a Board of Deputy Governors consisting of the councilors. In 1688 William Joseph was appointed to the Council and elevated to the presidency, replacing Thomas Taillor in that leadership role.

[2] Attended the first session and presided in the Upper House at the request of the other members; Lord Baltimore later reprimanded these men for that request.

[3] Appointed to the Council and Upper House before the Assembly convened in its first session. It is not known whether Joseph Pile or Richard Gardiner was elected to replace him.

[4] Died before the first session convened; William Harris was elected to replace him.

[5] The second delegate from Anne Arundel County has not been identified. No journal survives for the first session of this Assembly, and only Hill's name appears in the records of the second session.

[6] Appointed sheriff prior to the convening of the first session; it is not known whether John Brooke or Daniel Clarke replaced him.

[7] The Dorchester County commissioners detained Daniel Clarke from attending the second session, which resulted in a complaint from the Lower House.

30

PROTESTANT ASSOCIATORS' CONVENTION OF 1689–1692 [1]

FIRST SESSION: August 22–September 4, 1689
SECOND SESSION: April 1–4(?), 1690
THIRD SESSION: September 29–October 6, 1690
FOURTH SESSION: April 12(?)–25, 1691
FIFTH SESSION: August (?)–September 10, 1691
SIXTH SESSION: April 9, 1692

ST. MARY'S
John Coode [2]
Nehemiah Blakiston, speaker 4–6
Kenelm Cheseldyne, speaker 1–2 [2]
John Campbell

KENT
William Harris
Michael Miller
Hans Hanson
Thomas Davis

ANNE ARUNDEL [3]
Thomas Tench
William Hopkins

Nicholas Gassaway (D–6)
Nicholas Greenberry

CALVERT
Henry Jowles
Ninian Beale
Henry Mitchell
James Keech

CHARLES
John Addison
John Courts
Henry Hawkins
John Stone

BALTIMORE
John Thomas

Thomas Staley
Thomas Thurston
Christopher Gist (D–4)

TALBOT
John Edmundson
William Sharpe
George Robotham, speaker 3
Robert Smith

SOMERSET
Francis Jenkins
David Browne
Robert King [2]
Samuel Hopkins

DORCHESTER
John Brooke
Henry Trippe
Charles Hutchins
Thomas Cooke (S–6)

ST. MARY'S CITY
William Blanckenstein
Gilbert Clarke (S–2)
Robert Mason (E–3) [4]

CECIL
Charles James
Edward Jones
William Dare [5]
James Frisby [5]

Committee Service

ACCOUNTS
Cheseldyne (1)
Coode (1)

Blakiston (1)
Jowles (1)
Clarke (1)
Addison (1)

Courts (1)

SECRECY
Blakiston (1)

Jowles (1)
Clarke (1)
"& one or two more"

Grand Committee of Twenty [6]

Coode, president
Cheseldyne
Blakiston
Miller
Harris
Gassaway

Greenberry
Jowles
Beale
Addison
Courts

Thomas
Staley
Robotham
Edmundson
Browne

King
Brooke
Trippe
Jones
James

[1] Except for a portion of the first session, no journal for this revolutionary convention survives. Unless otherwise noted, membership is derived from the signatures of delegates on "The Address of the Representatives of their Majestys Subjects in the Province of Maryland Assembled," dated September 4, 1689, Colonial Office Papers 5/719, part 1, no. 1 (Public Record Office, London). For the dates of individual sessions and identification of speakers, see William Hand Browne et al. eds., *Archives of Maryland,* 72 vols. to date (Baltimore, 1883–), 8:117, 172, 207, 242–50, 260; ibid., 13:247; Thomas Bacon, *Laws of Maryland with Proper Indexes* (Annapolis, 1765), note after laws of 1688; Charles County Court and Land Record, R no. 1, ff. 3, 129, 189, 275; Talbot County Land Record, NN no. 6, f. 317; Edmund B. O'Callaghan, ed., *The Documentary History of the State of New York,* 4 vols. (Albany, 1849–51), 2:117–18, 126–27; Edmund B. O'Callaghan, ed., *Documents Relative to the Colonial History of the State of New York,* 15 vols. (Albany, 1853–87), 3:788–89.

[2] Coode and Cheseldyne, who went to England in the late summer of 1690 to defend the revolution they had led, did not serve in subsequent sessions, and their replacements, if elected, are unknown. Robert King of Somerset County may also have accompanied them.

[3] Anne Arundel County did not send delegates to the first session. These four men were probably elected to the second session, when Gassaway and Greenberry were named to the Grand Committee of Twenty. Tench and Hopkins were definitely sitting by the fourth session.

[4] Elected to replace Gilbert Clarke, who resigned upon becoming sheriff prior to the second session. Mason was definitely sitting by the fourth session and was probably a member by the third meeting.

[5] A contemporary account of the first session reported that only two delegates participated from Cecil County, but the signatures of four delegates were affixed to the September 4, 1689, address from the Assembly. There is no other record of service for William Dare and James Frisby, who are known later to have opposed the government of the Protestant Associators, and probably declined to serve further.

[6] The second session appointed this group as an interim executive agency. Nehemiah Blakiston succeeded Coode as president by September 1690.

ROYAL ASSEMBLY OF 1692–1693

Lionel Copley, governor (D–2)

Thomas Lawrence, acting governor, as president of the Council 2 [1]

Edmund Andros, acting governor 2 [1]

FIRST SESSION: May 10–June 9, 1692
SECOND SESSION: September 20–26, 1693

UPPER HOUSE

Thomas Lawrence [1]	Nicholas Greenberry	David Browne	John Courts
Henry Jowles (Ds–2) [2]	Charles Hutchins	Thomas Tench	Thomas Brooke
Nehemiah Blakiston	George Robotham	John Addison	James Frisby (DNS, Ds–2) [3]

LOWER HOUSE

ST. MARY'S
Kenelm Cheseldyne, speaker
John Campbell
Philip Clarke
John Watson

KENT
William Harris
Hans Hanson
Elias King
Samuel Wheeler

ANNE ARUNDEL
John Hammond
Henry Ridgeley
James Saunders
John Dorsey

CALVERT
Thomas Greenfield
Thomas Tasker
Henry Mitchell
John Bigger

CHARLES
William Dent
Henry Hawkins
James Smallwood
Philip Hoskins

BALTIMORE
George Ashman
Edward Boothby
Francis Watkins
Thomas Staley

TALBOT
Robert Smith
William Finney
Hugh Sherwood
John Edmundson (Ds–1) [4]
Thomas Robins (E–1)

SOMERSET
William Whittington
John Huett (Ds–1) [4]
Thomas Everden (Ds–1) [4]
John Goddin (Ds–1) [4]
Roger Woolford (E–1)
John Bozman (E–1)
Lazarus Maddox (E–1)

DORCHESTER
Henry Trippe

John Brooke (D–2)
Thomas Ennalls
Edward Pindar (D–2)

ST. MARY'S CITY
Edward Wynn (D–2)
Robert Mason (S–2)

CECIL
William Dare (Ds–1) [4]
St. Leger Codd (Ds–1) [4]
Edward Jones [4]
George Warner (Ds–1) [4]
James Wroth (E–1)
Thomas Theakston (E–1)
Robert Crooke (E–1)

Committee Service

ACCOUNTS (JOINT)
Addison (1)
Tench (1)
Mason (1)
Hammond (1)
Harris (1)
Pindar (1)
Trippe (1)
Whittington (1)

AGGRIEVANCES
Watson (1)
Smith (1)
Hoskins (1, 2)
Dent (2, chm.)
Hammond (2)
Greenfield (2)
Boothby (2)
Whittington (2)

ELECTIONS AND PRIVILEGES
Hammond (1)
Pindar (1)
Harris (1)
Clarke (1)
Brooke (1)

LAWS (JOINT)
Jowles (1)
Greenberry (1)
Addison (1)

Hutchins (2)
Tench (2)
Browne (2)
Dent (1)
Clarke (1)
Smith (1)
Trippe (1)
Greenfield (1)
Whittington (1)
Boothby (1)

---

[1] Sir Thomas Lawrence, the provincial secretary, had not arrived in Maryland at the time of the first session. In March of 1693, approximately six months after Lawrence's arrival, Governor Copley suspended him from the Council and imprisoned him for alleged opposition to the royal government in a power struggle between the two men. The Lower House ordered Lawrence's release from prison on September 22, 1693. It is uncertain who had been serving as acting governor in the power struggle since Copley's death on September 12, 1693, but Lawrence now resumed his position as senior councillor and presided in the Upper House until the arrival of Gov. Edmund Andros from Virginia on September 26. Andros claimed succession by virtue of his commission and served as acting governor through the remainder of this session. Andros's right to that post was later successfully challenged by Lawrence.

[2] Suspended from the Council by Governor Copley in November 1692 for alleged improper behavior in accepting a clerkship, and did not sit in the second session.

[3] Suspended from the Council by Governor Copley on July 9, 1692, for his alleged opposition to the government of the Protestant Associators and to the new royal government. Frisby had not attended the first session.

[4] Edmundson, Everden, Goddin, and Warner were discharged because as Quakers they were unable to subscribe to the oaths required of delegates. Huett, as a minister and "man in sacred orders," was ruled ineligible by English law to sit in the Assembly. The Lower House voted to discharge Codd for his opposition to the revolution and Protestant Associators' government. Dare, under suspicion for similar opposition, refused to provide security for his good behavior and was not seated. Jones, also suspected of opposition to the Protestant Associators' government, gave security and held his seat.

ROYAL ASSEMBLY OF 1694–1697

Francis Nicholson, governor

FIRST SESSION: September 20–October 18, 1694
SECOND SESSION: February 28–March 1, 1694/95
THIRD SESSION: May 8–22, 1695
FOURTH SESSION: October 2–19, 1695
FIFTH SESSION: April 30–May 14, 1696
SIXTH SESSION: July 1–10, 1696
SEVENTH SESSION: September 16–October 2, 1696
EIGHTH SESSION: May 26–June 11, 1697

UPPER HOUSE

Thomas Lawrence [1]
Henry Jowles
Nicholas Greenberry

Charles Hutchins
George Robotham
David Browne

Thomas Tench
John Addison
John Courts

Thomas Brooke
James Frisby
Edward Randolph [2]

LOWER HOUSE

ST. MARY'S
Kenelm Cheseldyne,
    speaker 4–8 [3]
Robert Mason (S–6)
Philip Clarke
John Bayne (S–6)
John Coode (E–7, Ds–7) [4]
John Lowe (E–8)
Henry Smith (E–8)

KENT
Hans Hanson
John Hynson
Thomas Smith
William Frisby

ANNE ARUNDEL
John Hammond
Edward Dorsey
Richard Hill
James Saunders

CALVERT
Thomas Greenfield (S–5)
Francis Hutchins
George Lingan (S–6)
Richard Johns (Ds–1) [4]
Thomas Tasker (E–2)
James Crawford (E–5)
Walter Smith (E–7)

CHARLES
Henry Hawkins
James Smallwood
William Dent
William Hutchinson (R–5) [6]
Philip Hoskins (E–7)

BALTIMORE
Edward Boothby
John Fery
James Maxwell (S–6)
Francis Watkins (D–5)
George Ashman (E–6)

John Hall (E–7)

TALBOT
Robert Smith, speaker 1–4 [3]
Henry Coursey (D–4)
Thomas Smithson
John Edmundson (Ds–1) [4]
Nicholas Lowe (E–2, S–6)
William Hemsley (E–5)
William Coursey (E–7)

SOMERSET
William Whittington (S–4)
Matthew Scarborough
John Bozman
Thomas Dixon
Francis Jenkins (E–5)

DORCHESTER
John Pollard
Henry Hooper
Thomas Ennalls
Thomas Hicks

ST. MARY'S CITY
John Watson
Thomas Waughop
Samuel Watkins (EV–7) [5]

CECIL
St. Leger Codd
John Thompson
William Pearce (S–6)
Casparus Augustus Herman
    (D–8)
Edward Blay (E–7)

PRINCE GEORGE'S [6]
Ninian Beale (E–5)
William Hatton (E–5)
William Barton (E–5)
William Hutchinson (E–5)
Thomas Hollyday
    (E–7, EV)

Committee Service

ACCOUNTS (JOINT)
Addison (1)
Frisby (1)
Randolph (1)
Whittington (3, chm.)
Mason (3–6, chm. 5–6)
T. Smith (3–8, chm. 8)
Lingan (3–5)
Watkins (3, 4)
Greenfield (3, 4)
Pollard (5–8)
Tasker (7, 8)
Thompson (7)

W. Smith (7, 8)

AGGRIEVANCES
Smithson (3–5, 8, chm.)
Watson (3, 4)
Hanson (3, 4, 8)
Hutchins (3)
Ennalls (3, 4, 8)
Pearce (4, 5)
W. Frisby (5)
Saunders (5, 8)

ELECTIONS AND PRIVILEGES
Hammond (7, chm.)
Dent (7)

T. Smith (7)
Clarke (7)
Saunders (7)
Boothby (7)

LAWS (JOINT)
Jowles (1)
Robotham (1, 7)
Randolph (1)
Addison (7)
Dent (3–5, 7, 8, probably
    chm. 3–5)
Boothby (3–5, 7, 8)
N. Lowe (3, 5)

Thompson (3–6)
Hill (3, 5, 8)
Scarborough (3, 4)
Clarke (5–8, chm. 8 and
    probably 6)
Hemsley (5)
Codd (4, 6)
Hammond (7)
Smithson (7)
Barton (7)
Crawford (8)
Hutchinson (8)
R. Smith (8)

[1] In England from 1694 to 1696 on official business and did not sit in the second through sixth sessions of this Assembly.

[2] Randolph, surveyor general of customs, was not a resident colonist. He was in Maryland for only the first three sessions of the Assembly.

[3] Robert Smith became ill during the fourth session, resigned the speakership, and returned home. Cheseldyne was immediately elected to replace him.

[4] Johns and Edmundson were dismissed from the first session, because as Quakers they were unable to subscribe to the oaths required of delegates. Coode was dismissed from the seventh session after a prolonged debate, because as a former minister he was ruled ineligible by English law to sit in the Assembly.

[5] His election was ruled invalid because there was no official vacancy; the voters were apparently seeking to replace John Watson, who was in England in 1696.

[6] Prince George's, recently established as a county, had its first representation at the fifth session. One of its delegates, William Hutchinson, previously sat from Charles County. Confusion over his status led to the election of Thomas Hollyday to the seventh session, but that election was declared invalid because no vacancy existed.

ROYAL ASSEMBLY OF 1697/98–1700

Francis Nicholson, governor 1, 2

Nathaniel Blakiston, governor 3, 4

FIRST SESSION: March 10, 1697/98–April 4, 1698
SECOND SESSION: October 20–November 12, 1698
THIRD SESSION: June 29–July 22, 1699
FOURTH SESSION: April 26–May 9, 1700

UPPER HOUSE

Thomas Lawrence (R–2) [1]
Henry Jowles
Charles Hutchins
George Robotham (D–2)

Thomas Tench
John Addison
John Courts
Thomas Brooke

James Frisby
Robert Smith (SW–2, A–3) [2]
John Hammond (A–3)

Thomas Tasker (A–3)
Francis Jenkins (A–3)
William Dent (SW–2) [2]

LOWER HOUSE

ST. MARY'S
Philip Clarke (D–3)
John Lowe
Jacob Moreland
Thomas Beale
John Nutwell (Nuthall)
 (E–3, EV–4) [3]

KENT
Michael Miller (D–4)
Thomas Smith
John Whittington
Simon Wilmer (D–4)
Solomon Wright (E–4)
Charles Hynson (E–4)

ANNE ARUNDEL
John Hammond (C–3)
Richard Hill
James Saunders

Samuel Young
John Worthington (E–3)

CALVERT
James Crawford (D–3)
Walter Smith
Elisha Hall
John Leech
William Parker (E–4)

CHARLES
James Smallwood
Philip Hoskins
Henry Hawkins (D–3)
Benjamin Hall
Philip Briscoe (E–3)

BALTIMORE
John Hall
George Ashman (D–4)
Thomas Staley (S–4)
John Fery (D–3)

James Phillips (E–3)

TALBOT
Thomas Smithson,
 speaker 1–4
Edward Lloyd
William Hemsley (D–3)
Richard Tilghman
Nicholas Lowe (E–3, EV) [4]
Philemon Lloyd (E–4)

SOMERSET
Francis Jenkins (C–3)
John Bozman
Walter Lane
Samuel Collins
William Whittington (E–3)

DORCHESTER
Thomas Hicks
Walter Campbell

Jacob Lookerman
Thomas Ennalls

ST. MARY'S CITY
Thomas Waughop
William Taylard (R–4) [5]

CECIL
William Harris
Hans Hanson
John Thompson
John Carvile (S–4)
William Pearce (E–4)

PRINCE GEORGE'S
William Hutchinson
Ninian Beale
John Wight
William Barton (S–3)
Thomas Greenfield (E–3)

Committee Service

ACCOUNTS
T. Smith (1–4, chm.)
J. Hall (1, 2)
Thompson (1–4)
Hoskins (1–4)

AGGRIEVANCES
Saunders (1, 2, 4)
Harris (1–3)
Ashman (1)
Wilmer (1, 2)
Hutchinson (1, 2)
Taylard (1)
E. Hall (2, 3)

Lane (2, 4)
E. Lloyd (2)
W. Smith (2, 3)
J. Hall (4)
J. Lowe (4)
Campbell (4)

ELECTIONS AND PRIVILEGES
Hammond (1, chm.)
Hawkins (1)
Hoskins (1)
Harris (1, 3, chm. 3)
Miller (1)
Leech (3)
Taylard (3)

J. Whittington (3)
E. Hall (3, 4)
W. Smith (3)
Saunders (3)
J. Lowe (4)
Greenfield (4)
Worthington (4)
Young (4)
Briscoe (4)

LAWS
Clarke (1)
Hill (1, 3, 4)
Crawford (1–3)
Hemsley (1)

Taylard (1, 3)
E. Lloyd (1, 3, 4)
Jenkins (2)
Miller (2, 3)
Carvile (2, 3)
Beale (2)
Wilmer (2, 3)
Tilghman (2–4)
Hutchinson (3, 4)
Young (3)
W. Whittington (4)
Ennalls (4)

[1] Returned to England in 1698, where he resigned his offices as provincial secretary and as a member of the Council and Upper House prior to the second session.

[2] Smith, chief justice of the Provincial Court, and Dent, attorney general of the colony, were invited on special writs to sit with the Upper House for part of the second session. Both men also sat on special writs during 1698 in the Council to ensure a quorum and to provide special advice. Smith later received royal appointment to the Council and was sitting as an official member by May 1699.

[3] His election to the third session was challenged and referred to the fourth session for final action, when it was ruled invalid because the election was not conducted according to law.

[4] His election to the third session was ruled invalid because proper notice had not been given to all freeholders.

[5] Resigned early in the fourth session to accept the position of clerk of the Lower House.

ROYAL ASSEMBLY OF 1701–1704

Nathaniel Blakiston, governor 1–3 (R–4)

Thomas Tench, acting governor, as president of the Council 4

John Seymour, governor 5

FIRST SESSION: May 8–17, 1701
SECOND SESSION: March 16–25, 1701/02
THIRD SESSION: June 25–26, 1702
FOURTH SESSION: October 26–29, 1703
FIFTH SESSION: April 26–May 3, 1704

UPPER HOUSE

Thomas Tench
John Addison
John Courts (D–4)
Thomas Brooke
James Frisby [1]

Robert Smith
John Hammond
Francis Jenkins
Edward Lloyd (A–2)

William Holland (A–2)
James Saunders (A–2)
Kenelm Cheseldyne (A–4, DNS) [2]

Thomas Ennalls (A–4, DNS) [2]
William Coursey (A–4) [2]
Robert Quarry (A–4, DNS) [2]

LOWER HOUSE

ST. MARY'S
Kenelm Cheseldyne (C–4)
John Lowe (D–2)
Thomas Beale
William Watts
John Baker (E–2)

KENT
Thomas Smith
John Whittington
John Hynson
John Salter

ANNE ARUNDEL
William Holland (C–2)
James Saunders (C–2)
Samuel Young
John Dorsey
Charles Greenberry (E–2)

Lawrence Draper (E–2)

CALVERT
Walter Smith
Elisha Hall (Ds–5) [3]
William Parker
John Smith

CHARLES
William Dent, speaker 5
James Smallwood
Philip Lynes
Benjamin Hall

BALTIMORE
John Hall
Edward Dorsey
Samuel Sicklemore
Thomas Hammond

TALBOT
Thomas Smithson, speaker 1–4 [4]
Edward Lloyd (C–2)
Philemon Lloyd
Richard Tilghman
William Coursey (E–3, EV) [5]

SOMERSET
William Whittington
James Round (DNS, D–1)
John Bozman
John Franklyn
Peter Dent (E–2)

DORCHESTER
Thomas Ennalls (C–4)
Jacob Lookerman

Hugh Eccleston
John Lecompte

ST. MARY'S CITY
Henry Lowe (Ds–5) [6]
George Muschamp

CECIL
William Harris
St. Leger Codd
John Thompson (D–2)
Matthias Vanderheyden
Thomas Frisby (E–3, EV, E–5) [7]

PRINCE GEORGE'S
Thomas Greenfield
William Hutchinson
John Wight
Robert Bradley

35

ACCOUNTS
T. Smith (1–3, 5, chm.)
Thompson (1)
J. Hall (1–3)
J. Smith (1–3, 5)
Bradley (1–3, 5)

AGGRIEVANCES
Harris (1, 5, probably chm.)
Salter (1)
Lynes (1, 5)

Wight (1)
Greenberry (5)

ELECTIONS AND PRIVILEGES
Greenfield (1, probably
    chm.)
E. Hall (1, 3)
P. Lloyd (1, 2)
Sicklemore (1)
Eccleston (1)
Harris (2, 3, probably chm.)

Muschamp (2)
Salter (2)

LAWS
Dent (1–3, probably
    chm. 1, 3)
Cheseldyne (1, 2, probably
    chm. 2)
E. Lloyd (1)
Tilghman (1, 2, 5)
Holland (1)

P. Lloyd (1, 5, probably
    chm. 5)
Vanderheyden (1)
Muschamp (1)
Ennalls (1)
Harris (1)
Hutchinson (2, 3)
Salter (2, 3, 5)
E. Dorsey (2)
H. Lowe (2)

[1] Attended only the first session and never attended a meeting of the Council during this period. He may have been in poor health, because he was dead by June 19, 1704.

[2] Cheseldyne, Ennalls, and Coursey were appointed to the Council and Upper House in the instructions of Gov. John Seymour on March 11, 1702/03, but news of their appointments probably did not reach the colony until after the fourth session. Neither Cheseldyne nor Ennalls served in the Upper House during this Assembly, but Coursey attended the fifth session. There is no evidence that Cheseldyne or Ennalls sat in the Lower House during the fifth session. Quarry, appointed in 1703/04, was successor to Edward Randolph as surveyor general of customs. Quarry was rarely in the colony and did not serve in this Assembly or in most sessions of subsequent assemblies in which he was eligible to sit.

[3] Dismissed from the fifth session for failure to subscribe to the required oaths.

[4] Thomas Smithson was absent from the fifth session due to illness and thus replaced as speaker.

[5] Election to the third session was apparently voided, for reasons unknown.

[6] Dismissed from the fifth session for failure to subscribe to the required oaths.

[7] Election to the third session was voided because he had been underage at the time of the election. Cecil County freeholders returned him in the next election to fill the vacancy, by which time he qualified. He may have been elected to the fourth session, for which no Lower House records survive.

[8] Membership lists are incomplete, since no journals of the Lower House survive for the fourth session.

ROYAL ASSEMBLY OF 1704–1707

John Seymour, governor

FIRST SESSION: September 5–October 3, 1704
SECOND SESSION: December 5–9, 1704
THIRD SESSION: May 15–25, 1705
FOURTH SESSION: April 2–19, 1706
FIFTH SESSION: March 26–April 15, 1707

UPPER HOUSE

Thomas Tench
John Addison (D–4)
Thomas Brooke [1]
Robert Smith (D–5)

John Hammond
Francis Jenkins
Edward Lloyd

William Holland
James Saunders
Kenelm Cheseldyne

Thomas Ennalls
William Coursey
Robert Quarry (DNS)

LOWER HOUSE

ST. MARY'S
Thomas Beale
William Watts
William Aisquith
Peter Watts

KENT
Thomas Smith, speaker 2–5
William Frisby
Elias King (D–5)
John Wells

ANNE ARUNDEL
Samuel Young
Charles Greenberry
John Hammond (Ds–1) [2]
Joseph Hill
Richard Jones (E–1)

CALVERT
Robert Skinner
John Mackall
Thomas Howe
John Leech

CHARLES
William Dent, speaker 1
(D–2)
James Smallwood
William Stone
John Contee (E–3)
Gerard Fowke

BALTIMORE
Edward Dorsey (D–4)
James Maxwell
James Phillips
Francis Dollahyde (S–5)

John Hall (E–5)
Richard Colegate (E–5)

TALBOT
Thomas Smithson
Robert Goldsborough
Henry Coursey (D–5)
Nicholas Lowe

SOMERSET
John Waters
Joseph Gray
John Jones
John McClester

DORCHESTER
Hugh Eccleston
John Taylor (D–4)
John Hudson
Joseph Ennalls

Roger Woolford (E–5)

ST. MARY'S CITY
George Muschamp
James Hay

CECIL
William Pearce
Edward Blay
Thomas Frisby
William Dare

PRINCE GEORGE'S
Thomas Greenfield
William Barton (D–4)
Robert Tyler
Samuel Magruder
Robert Bradley (E–4)

Committee Service

ACCOUNTS
Smith (1, chm.)
Hill (1–5, chm. 5)
Phillips (1–5)
King (1–4, chm. 2–4)
Leech (5)

AGGRIEVANCES
Greenfield (1, 4, 5, chm. 1, 4)
Maxwell (1, 2, 4, 5, chm. 5)

Wells (1, 2, 4, 5)
Dorsey (2, chm.)
Tyler (4, 5)

ELECTIONS AND PRIVILEGES
Dorsey (1, chm.)
W. Frisby (1)
Goldsborough (1)
Mackall (1)
Dollahyde (1)
Greenfield (3, chm.)

Maxwell (3)
T. Frisby (3)
Hill (4, 5, chm.)
Hay (4)
Aisquith (4)
Skinner (5)
Tyler (5)

LAWS
Smithson (1, 2, 5, chm.)
Goldsborough (1)

Greenberry (1–5, probably chm. 4)
Stone (1, 3, 5)
King (1)
H. Coursey (2)
N. Lowe (3, 4, probably chm. 3)
Eccleston (3, 4)
Contee (4, 5)
T. Frisby (4)

[1] Brooke did not attend the fifth session, nor did he sit with the Council after the spring of 1706; Governor Seymour dismissed Brooke as a councilor on August 16, 1708.
[2] Dismissed from the first session for his unwillingness to subscribe to the required oaths.

ROYAL ASSEMBLY OF 1708A

John Seymour, governor

September 27–October 5, 1708

UPPER HOUSE

Francis Jenkins	Kenelm Cheseldyne	Robert Quarry (DNS)	Thomas Greenfield
Edward Lloyd	Thomas Ennalls	Samuel Young	Philip Lynes
William Holland	William Coursey		

LOWER HOUSE [1]

ST. MARY'S [2]
John Coode (EV)
Thomas Trueman
  Greenfield (EV)
Henry Peregrine Jowles
  (EV)
Joshua Guibert (EV)

KENT
William Frisby
Samuel Wallis (EV) [3]
John Carvile
Thomas Covington
Daniel Pearce

ANNE ARUNDEL
Joseph Hill
Richard Jones
Charles Greenberry

Daniel Mariartee

CALVERT
Walter Smith
John Mackall
Robert Skinner
Nathaniel Dare

CHARLES
James Smallwood
William Stone
John Beale
William Harbert

BALTIMORE
Richard Colegate
James Maxwell
James Phillips
William Pickett

TALBOT
Thomas Smithson, speaker
Nicholas Lowe
Thomas Robins
Robert Ungle

SOMERSET
John West
George Gale
Samuel Worthington
John Franklyn

DORCHESTER
Hugh Eccleston
Roger Woolford
Joseph Ennalls
John Hudson

CECIL
Thomas Frisby

Matthias Vanderheyden
John Ward
John Hynson (DNS, D)

PRINCE GEORGE'S
Robert Bradley
Thomas Brooke (DNS) [4]
John Bradford
Robert Tyler

ANNAPOLIS [5]
William Bladen (EV)
Wornell Hunt (EV)

QUEEN ANNE'S
John Salter
John Whittington
Solomon Wright
Philemon Hemsley

Committee Service

ACCOUNTS	ELECTIONS AND PRIVILEGES	West	LAWS
Hill (chm.)	Smith (chm.)	Ungle	Greenberry (chm.)
Eccleston	Bladen	Mackall	Lowe
Phillips	Colegate	Jones	Worthington

[1] St. Mary's City ceased having representation in the Lower House with this Assembly. The writ of election was returned with the statement that no one was present in the town to hold an election.
[2] All four delegates from St. Mary's County were denied seats and their elections voided because the sheriff had not properly proclaimed the time and place of the election.
[3] Originally elected over John Carvile, Wallis's status as a freeholder in the county was successfully challenged, and he declined to swear that he possessed personal property worth £40 sterling. Carvile was then elected in Wallis's place by general consent.
[4] The former councilor was in Virginia and did not attend this Assembly.
[5] The Lower House, following receipt of objections from residents of Annapolis about the city's charter issued by Governor Seymour, ruled that the charter was invalid and thus rendered void the election of representatives from the city.

ROYAL ASSEMBLY OF 1708B–1711

John Seymour, governor 1 (D–2)

Edward Lloyd, acting governor, as president of the Council, 2–4 [1]

FIRST SESSION: November 29–December 17, 1708
SECOND SESSION: October 26–November 11, 1709
THIRD SESSION: October 24–November 4, 1710
FOURTH SESSION: October 23–November 3, 1711

UPPER HOUSE

Francis Jenkins (D–3) [1]
Edward Lloyd [1]
William Holland
Thomas Ennalls

William Coursey
Robert Quarry [2]
Samuel Young
Thomas Greenfield
Philip Lynes (D–2)

Charles Greenberry (A–2)
John Hall (A–2)
William Whittington (A–2)
Thomas Addison (A–3)

Richard Tilghman (A–4)
John Dorsey (A–4)
Philemon Lloyd (A–4)

LOWER HOUSE

ST. MARY'S
John Coode (Ds–1) [3]
Thomas Trueman
   Greenfield
Henry Peregrine Jowles
Joshua Guibert
James Bowles (E–3)

KENT
Daniel Pearce
Thomas Covington (D–2)
Edward Bathurst (DNS,
   D–2) [4]
John Carvile (DNS, D–2) [4]
Thomas Ringgold (E–3,
   D–4)
James Harris (E–3, S–4)
Edward Scott (E–3)

ANNE ARUNDEL
Richard Jones

Charles Greenberry (C–2)
Daniel Mariartee
Joseph Hill
John Brice (E–2, EV) [5]
Charles Hammond (E–3)

CALVERT
Walter Smith (D–4)
John Mackall
Robert Skinner
Nathaniel Dare

CHARLES
James Smallwood
William Wilkinson
Thomas Crabb
Walter Storey

BALTIMORE
James Maxwell
James Phillips

Aquilla Paca
Richard Colegate

TALBOT
Thomas Smithson
Nicholas Lowe
Robert Ungle
Thomas Robins

SOMERSET
John West
George Gale
Samuel Worthington
John Franklyn

DORCHESTER [6]
Hugh Eccleston (D–4)
Roger Woolford (S–3)
Joseph Ennalls (D–2)
Walter Campbell
John Hudson (E–3)
Thomas Hicks (E–3)

CECIL [6]
Matthias Vanderheyden
John Ward (S–3)
Edward Larremore (D–4)
Thomas Frisby
Henry Ward (E–4)

PRINCE GEORGE'S
Robert Bradley, speaker 1–4
Robert Tyler
John Bradford
Philip Lee

ANNAPOLIS [7]
Wornell Hunt (Ds–2, E–2) [8]
Thomas Bordley

QUEEN ANNE'S
John Salter
John Whittington
Solomon Wright
Philemon Hemsley (S–4)

Committee Service

ACCOUNTS
Phillips (1–4, chm.)
Hill (1–4)
Bradford (1, 3, 4)
Ungle (2)
Bordley (2–4)

AGGRIEVANCES
Smith (1–3, chm.)

Tyler (1–4, chm. 4)
Whittington (1–4)
Mackall (4)

ELECTIONS AND PRIVILEGES
Smith (1–3, chm.)
Jones (1, 2, 4, chm. 4)
Mackall (1–3)

West (1–3)
Ungle (1, 2, 4)
Eccleston (3)
Campbell (3)
Mariartee (4)

LAWS
Greenberry (1, chm.)
Lowe (1–4)

West (1–4)
Gale (1–4)
Skinner (1)
Worthington (1 –3)
Smithson (2–4, chm.)
Hunt (2)
Whittington (4)

[1] Although Jenkins was the senior councilor at the time of Governor Seymour's death in 1709, his colleagues argued that he had relinquished his right to the presidency of the Council by "not taking any notice of the Government after the Governour's death." The other councilors made Edward Lloyd, next in seniority, the president and thus the chief executive officer of the colony for the next five years.

[2] Quarry served only briefly in the second and third sessions of this Assembly.

[3] Dismissed from the first session, because as a man once in holy orders he was ineligible to sit in the Assembly.

[4] Both Bathurst and Carvile were absent from the first session and died before the second session convened.

[5] Election to the second session was voided because the sheriff denied a legally demanded poll by voters supporting Charles Hammond, who was subsequently elected to fill this seat at the third session.

[6] Neither the Cecil County nor the Dorchester County delegation attended the first session.

[7] The delegates from Annapolis were not seated at the first session until the bill on the Annapolis charter had passed the Assembly.

[8] Dismissed from the second session because he had not met the three-year residency requirement when he was first elected in November 1708; that requirement had been satisfied by October 1709, and he was immediately reelected to the same seat.

ROYAL ASSEMBLY OF 1712–1714

Edward Lloyd, acting governor, as president of the Council [1]

FIRST SESSION: October 28–November 15, 1712
SECOND SESSION: October 27–November 14, 1713
THIRD SESSION: June 22–July 3, 1714
FOURTH SESSION: October 5–9, 1714

UPPER HOUSE

Edward Lloyd [1]	Robert Quarry (DNS)	John Hall	Richard Tilghman
William Holland	Samuel Young	William Whittington	John Dorsey
Thomas Ennalls	Thomas Greenfield	Thomas Addison	Philemon Lloyd
William Coursey	Charles Greenberry (D–3)		

LOWER HOUSE

ST. MARY'S
Thomas Trueman
  Greenfield
Henry Peregrine Jowles
William Watts
Kenelm Cheseldyne

KENT
Daniel Pearce
Edward Scott
St. Leger Codd
Edward Blay (D–3)
William Blay (E–4)

ANNE ARUNDEL
Richard Jones (D–3)
Daniel Mariartee
Joseph Hill
Charles Hammond (D–3)
John Hammond (E–4)
Alexander Warfield (E–4)

CALVERT
John Mackall
John Leech (D–3)
John Broome (S–3)
James Mackall
John Rousby (E–4)
Alexander Parran (E–4)

CHARLES
James Smallwood
Philip Hoskins
Walter Storey
John Fendall

BALTIMORE [2]
Richard Colegate (EV–1,
  E–2)
William Talbott (EV–1,
  E–2, D–3)
Edward Stevenson (EV–1,
  E–2)

Thomas Hammond (EV–1,
  E–2)
James Maxwell (E–4)

TALBOT
Robert Ungle, speaker 1–4
Thomas Robins
Matthew Tilghman Ward
James Lloyd

SOMERSET
Samuel Worthington
William Whittington
John Purnell
Thomas Purnell

DORCHESTER
Roger Woolford
Henry Ennalls
Govert Lookerman
Henry Trippe

CECIL
James Frisby
Matthias Vanderheyden
William Dare
Peregrine Frisby

PRINCE GEORGE'S
Robert Tyler [3]
Thomas Sprigg
Thomas Claggett (S–2)
Thomas Brooke
James Stoddart (E–3)

ANNAPOLIS
Amos Garrett
Thomas Dockwra

QUEEN ANNE'S
Solomon Wright
John Whittington
Charles Wright
John Wells (D–3)
John Hawkins (E–4)

Committee Service

ACCOUNTS
Leech (1, 2, chm.)
Hill (1–4, chm. 3, 4)
Scott (1–4)
Greenfield (1, 3, 4)
Brooke (2–4)

AGGRIEVANCES
Tyler (1–4, chm.)

Mariartee (1–4)
J. Whittington (1–4)
Lookerman (1)
Garrett (1)
Trippe (2–4)

ELECTIONS AND PRIVILEGES
John Mackall (1–4, chm.)

Jones (1, 2)
Ennalls (1–4)
Jowles (1–4)
Codd (1–4)

LAWS
Ward (1–4, probably chm.)
Worthington (1–4)
Wells (1, 2)

Colegate (1–4)
Robins (1, 3, 4)
Garrett (2–4)
Lookerman (2–4)
John Mackall (2–4)
Stoddart (3, 4)

[1] See footnote 1 of the preceeding Assembly.

[2] The election of all four delegates from Baltimore County was voided at the first session because of the sheriff's "partiality and Neglect of his Duty in the Election of Members for that County." All four were reelected to the next session.

[3] After being elected speaker of the first session, Tyler declined to serve and recommended the election of Robert Ungle in his stead.

40

ROYAL ASSEMBLY OF 1715

John Hart, governor

April 26–June 3, 1715

UPPER HOUSE

Edward Lloyd
William Holland
Thomas Ennalls

William Coursey
Samuel Young
Thomas Greenfield

John Hall
William Whittington
Thomas Addison

Richard Tilghman
Philemon Lloyd

LOWER HOUSE

ST. MARY'S
Thomas Trueman
  Greenfield
John Baker
Samuel Williamson
Matthew Mason

KENT
James Harris
William Blay
St. Leger Codd
Andrew Hamilton

ANNE ARUNDEL
Daniel Mariartee
Joseph Hill
Alexander Warfield
Thomas Bordley

CALVERT
John Mackall
John Rousby
Alexander Parran
Thomas Holdsworth

CHARLES
John Fendall
Thomas Dent
Thomas Stone
Joseph Harrison

BALTIMORE
James Maxwell
James Phillips
Richard Colegate
Francis Dollahyde

TALBOT
Robert Ungle, speaker

Matthew Tilghman Ward
Thomas Robins
Foster Turbutt

SOMERSET
John Purnell
Thomas Dashiell
Charles Ballard
Samuel Hopkins

DORCHESTER
Roger Woolford
Henry Trippe
Peter Taylor
John Hudson

CECIL
John Ward
Matthias Vanderheyden

Ephraim Augustus Herman
Francis Mauldin

PRINCE GEORGE'S
Robert Tyler
Thomas Sprigg
Josiah Wilson
John Bradford

ANNAPOLIS
Amos Garrett
Benjamin Tasker

QUEEN ANNE'S
John Whittington
Charles Wright
Solomon Clayton
Edward Brown

Committee Service

ACCOUNTS
Hill (chm.)
Greenfield
Phillips
Bradford
Woolford
Dent

AGGRIEVANCES
Tyler (chm.)
Whittington
Mariartee
Trippe
Parran

ELECTIONS AND PRIVILEGES
Mackall (chm.)

Codd
Wilson
Harris
Baker

LAWS
Ward (chm.)
Mackall
Robins

Turbutt
Bordley
Colegate
Woolford
Dent
Harris
Hamilton

PROPRIETARY ASSEMBLY OF 1716–1718

Charles Calvert, 5th Lord Baltimore, proprietor

John Hart, governor

CONVENTION: April 24, 1716 [1]
FIRST SESSION: July 17–August 10, 1716
SECOND SESSION: May 28–June 8, 1717 [2]
THIRD SESSION: April 22–May 10, 1718

UPPER HOUSE [3]

Thomas Brooke	Thomas Ennalls	William Whittington (R–2)	Richard Tilghman
Edward Lloyd	Samuel Young	Thomas Addison	Thomas Smith
William Holland	John Hall	Philemon Lloyd	Henry Lowe (A–2)
William Coursey (D–3)			

LOWER HOUSE

ST. MARY'S
Thomas Trueman
  Greenfield [4]
Henry Peregrine Jowles
John Baker
Thomas Waughop

KENT
St. Ledger Codd
James Harris
Edward Scott
Nathaniel Hynson

ANNE ARUNDEL
Daniel Mariartee
Joseph Hill
Alexander Warfield
Richard Warfield

CALVERT
John Mackall

John Rousby
Nathaniel Dare
William Young

CHARLES
Philip Hoskins (D–3)
Thomas Dent
John Fendall
Samuel Hanson (S–3)

BALTIMORE
James Maxwell
Richard Colegate
Francis Dollahyde
Peter Bond (D–3)

TALBOT
Matthew Tilghman Ward,
  speaker

Thomas Robins
James Lloyd
Thomas Emerson

SOMERSET
Thomas Dashiell (S–3)
William Whittington
John Purnell
Samuel Hopkins

DORCHESTER
John Brannock
Peter Taylor
Tobias Pollard
John Meekins

CECIL
Matthias Vanderheyden
Ephraim Augustus Herman
John Ward

James Frisby

ANNAPOLIS
Thomas Bordley
Benjamin Tasker (S–3)
John Beale (E–3)

PRINCE GEORGE'S
Robert Tyler
Josiah Wilson (D–3)
James Stoddart
John Bradford

QUEEN ANNE'S
Charles Wright
William Turbutt
John Hawkins (D–3)
Edward Wright [4]

Committee Service [5]

ELECTIONS AND PRIVILEGES
Mackall (1–3)
Wilson (1, 2)
Baker (1–3)
Rousby (1–3)
J. Lloyd (1–3)
R. Warfield (3)

LAWS
Mackall (1–3)
Robins (1–3)
Bordley (1–3)
Colegate (1–3)
Stoddart (1–3)
Harris (1–3)
Dent (1)

Hanson (1)

AGGRIEVANCES
Tyler (1–3)
Mariartee (1–3)
Dent (1–3)
C. Wright (1–3)
Hynson (1–3)

ACCOUNTS
Hill (1–3)
Greenfield (1–3)
Scott (1–3)
Bradford (1–3)
Codd (1–3)
Beale (3)

[1] The one-day convention, held on April 24, 1716, is reported in the Lower House journal. Although no journal for the Upper House has survived, it was in session.

[2] The recorded Lower House proceedings for the second session begin on May 28, 1717. The recorded proceedings for the Upper House begin on May 29, 1717.

[3] The ranking of the Upper House members varies slightly throughout the proceedings.

[4] Greenfield, of St. Mary's County, and Wright, of Queen Anne's County, had one-half their allowance deducted for departing in "a contemptuous manner" without permission from the Lower House.

[5] There is no specific mention of committee appointments or reappointments in the Lower House proceedings of the second session, but the committees were definitely operating. It is presumed that the original committee members named in the first session were reappointed in the second session, and that Thomas Dent and Samuel Hanson, who were added to the Committee of Laws late in the first session, were not reappointed. The members of the second session committees were then reappointed to continue in the third session, but their names were not relisted.

PROPRIETARY ASSEMBLY OF 1719–1721/22

Charles Calvert, 5th Lord Baltimore, proprietor

John Hart, governor 1, 2

Charles Calvert, governor 3–5

FIRST SESSION: May 14–June 6, 1719
SECOND SESSION: April 5–22, 1720
THIRD SESSION: October 11–27, 1720
FOURTH SESSION: July 18–August 5, 1721
FIFTH SESSION: February 20–28, 1721/22

UPPER HOUSE

Thomas Brooke
William Holland
Samuel Young
John Hall

Thomas Addison
Philemon Lloyd
Richard Tilghman
Henry Lowe (D–5)

Matthew Tilghman Ward
Thomas Bordley (A–2, Ds–5) [1]

James Bowles (A–3)
John Rousby (A–5) [2]

LOWER HOUSE

ST. MARY'S
Henry Peregrine Jowles (D–2)
Thomas Trueman Greenfield (S–3, E–4)
George Clarke
Thomas Waughop
John Baker (E–4)

KENT
Nathaniel Hynson (D–4)
James Smith
St. Ledger Codd
Lambert Wilmer

ANNE ARUNDEL
Joseph Hill
Daniel Mariartee
Edmond Benson
Richard Warfield

CALVERT
John Mackall

John Rousby (C–5) [2]
Walter Smith
Benjamin Mackall

CHARLES
John Parry (D–2)
John Fendall
George Dent
Robert Hanson
Alexander Contee (E–3)

BALTIMORE
James Maxwell
Francis Dollahyde (D–4)
James Phillips (D–2)
Richard Colegate (D–5)
Roger Matthews (E–3)
John Dorsey (E–5)

TALBOT
Robert Ungle, speaker

James Lloyd
Thomas Emerson (D–2)
Thomas Edmondson
William Clayton (E–3)

SOMERSET
Benjamin Wailes
John Jones
John Caldwell
George Dashiell

DORCHESTER
Roger Woolford
John Brannock
John Rider
Peter Taylor (EV–1, E–2) [3]

CECIL
William Dare (S–4)
Ephraim Augustus Herman
James Frisby (D–2)
Roger Larramore [4]

Stephen Knight (E–3, Ds–3) [5]
John Ward (E–5)

ANNAPOLIS
Thomas Bordley (C–2) [1]
John Beale (Ds–2) [6]
Benjamin Tasker (E–2)
Amos Garrett (E–2)

PRINCE GEORGE'S
James Stoddart
Robert Tyler
Philip Lee
Ralph Crabb

QUEEN ANNE'S
Charles Wright (D–3)
Thomas Fisher
James Earle, Sr.
William Turbutt
James Earle, Jr. (E–4)

Committee Service

ELECTIONS AND PRIVILEGES
J. Mackall (1–5)
Rousby (1–4)
J. Lloyd (1–5)
Crabb (1–5)
Colegate (1–4)
Dashiell (5)

LAWS
Bordley (1)
Stoddart (1–5)
Lee (1–5)

Parry (1)
Benson (1, 3, 4)
Smith (1–4)
Woolford (1–5)
Brannock (1)
Dashiell (1)
J. Mackall (2–5)
Colegate (2, 3)
Contee (3–5)
Earle, Jr. (4, 5)

AGGRIEVANCES
Tyler (1–5)
Mariartee (1–5)
Wright (1, 2)
Hynson (1–4)
Fisher (1–4)
Turbutt (1)
Hanson (1)
Codd (1)
Maxwell (1)
Smith (1)

Emerson (1)
Colegate (1)
Warfield (3–5)

ACCOUNTS
Hill (1–4)
Phillips (1)
Codd (1–5)
Beale (1)
Turbutt (1, 3–5)
Rider (2–4)
Earle, Sr. (2–5)

[1] Originally elected a delegate to the Lower House, Bordley was appointed to the Council by April 6, 1720. However, in a letter dated September 1721, he was discharged from further service as a councilor after angering Governor Calvert with what the governor termed "Council of pernicious Consequence." In February 1721/22, the governor declared that since membership on the Council was the only qualification for membership in the Upper House, Bordley's discharge from the Council also removed him from service in the Upper House.

[2] Originally elected a delegate to the Lower House, Rousby was appointed to the Council prior to the fifth session.

[3] The election of Taylor was declared void on May 19, 1719, after the Lower House determined that the sheriff had been "very partiall and remiss in his Duty." He was declared duly reelected on April 7, 1720.

[4] Although his first name was usually given as Roger in the Lower House journal, it was occasionally listed as Robert.

[5] Knight was asked to withdraw from the Lower House on October 14, 1720, after the Committee of Elections and Privileges reported that no indenture was returned from the sheriff for his election. The sheriff was fined for not fulfilling his duties.

[6] The election of a new delegate from Annapolis was called for on April 6, 1720, to replace Beale, who had become clerk of the Council prior to the second session.

PROPRIETARY ASSEMBLY OF 1722–1724

Charles Calvert, 5th Lord Baltimore, proprietor
Charles Calvert, governor

FIRST SESSION: October 9–November 3, 1722
SECOND SESSION: September 23–October 26, 1723
THIRD SESSION: October 6–November 4, 1724

UPPER HOUSE [1]

Thomas Brooke (Ds–2) [2]	John Hall	Richard Tilghman	John Rousby
William Holland	Thomas Addison	Matthew Tilghman Ward	James Lloyd (A–1, D–3) [3]
Samuel Young	Philemon Lloyd	James Bowles	Benjamin Tasker (A–1)

LOWER HOUSE

ST. MARY'S
William Watts (D–3)
Justinian Jordan
Thomas Waughop
John Read

KENT
Samuel Wallis (D–3)
Robert Dunn
Philip Kennard
William Blackiston
Ebenezer Blackiston (E–3)

ANNE ARUNDEL
Thomas Bordley
Joseph Hill (D–3)
John Beale
Richard Warfield
Daniel Mariartee (E–3)

CALVERT
John Mackall
Benjamin Mackall
Walter Smith
William Young

CHARLES
George Dent
Henry Holland Hawkins
John Courts
Joseph Harrison

BALTIMORE
Thomas Tolley
William Hamilton
John Taylor
Thomas Hammond

TALBOT
Robert Ungle, speaker

James Lloyd (C–1) [3]
Daniel Sherwood
John Oldham
Thomas Bozman (E–2)

SOMERSET
Nathaniel Hopkins
Robert King
Thomas Purnell (D–2)
William Whittington
George Dashiell (E–3)

DORCHESTER
Henry Hooper
Matthew Travers
John Hudson, Secundus
Edward Pritchett

CECIL
John Ward

Josiah Sutton
Francis Mauldin
William Freeman

ANNAPOLIS
Thomas Humphrys
Daniel Dulany

PRINCE GEORGE'S
Robert Tyler
James Stoddart
Ralph Crabb
Thomas Gantt

QUEEN ANNE'S
Edward Wright
John Chaires
William Elliot
Solomon Wright

Committee Service [4]

ELECTIONS AND PRIVILEGES
J. Mackall (1–3)
J. Lloyd (1)
Crabb (1–3)
Humphrys (1–3)
Hooper (1–3)
Sherwood (1)
E. Wright (1)

Bozman (2)
S. Wright (2)

LAWS
Stoddart (1–3)
Dulany (1–3)
J. Mackall (1–3)
Dent (1–3)
King (1–3)

Sherwood (1–3)
Bordley (1)

AGGRIEVANCES AND COURTS
OF JUSTICE
Tyler (1–3)
Warfield (1–3)
Harrison (1–3)
Bordley (3)

ACCOUNTS
Hill (1, 2)
Beale (1–3)
J. Ward (1–3)
Gantt (1–3)

[1] The ranking of Upper House members as given in the proceedings varies. Members are listed here in the usual order of seniority.

[2] The precise reason for Brooke's dismissal is unknown.

[3] Originally elected a delegate to the Lower House from Talbot County, James Lloyd was appointed to the Council on the last day of the first session.

[4] The first few pages of the Lower House proceedings for the second session are missing. It is presumed that the original committee members appointed in the first session were reappointed in the second session, and that Sherwood, E. Wright, and Bordley, who were added late in the first session, were not reappointed. The proceedings of the third session state that the second session committee members were to be reappointed, but these members are not specifically named. It is assumed that Bozman and S. Wright, who were added in the middle of the second session, were not included in this reappointment.

PROPRIETARY ASSEMBLY OF 1725–1727

Charles Calvert, 5th Lord Baltimore, proprietor

Charles Calvert, governor 1–3

Benedict Leonard Calvert, governor 4

FIRST SESSION: October 6–November 6, 1725
SECOND SESSION: March 15–23, 1725/26
THIRD SESSION: July 12–25, 1726
FOURTH SESSION: October 10–30, 1727

UPPER HOUSE

William Holland
Samuel Young[1]
John Hall
Thomas Addison (D–4)

Philemon Lloyd
Richard Tilghman
Matthew Tilghman Ward

James Bowles
John Rousby
Benjamin Tasker

Philip Lee
Nicholas Lowe (A–3)
Charles Calvert (A–4)

LOWER HOUSE

ST. MARY'S
Samuel Williamson
Thomas Trueman
  Greenfield
Justinian Jordan
Thomas Waughop

KENT
James Harris
Philip Kennard
Simon Wilmer
Marmaduke Tilden (D–3)
Ebenezer Blackiston (E–4)

ANNE ARUNDEL
Thomas Bordley (D–4)
John Beale
Richard Warfield
Thomas Worthington
Daniel Dulany (E–4)

CALVERT
John Mackall, speaker 4
Benjamin Mackall
Walter Smith
Adderton Skinner

CHARLES
George Dent
John Courts
Joseph Harrison (D–4)
Henry Holland Hawkins

BALTIMORE
William Hamilton
Daniel Scott
James Maxwell
Thomas Sheredine (Ds–1)[2]
Roger Matthews (E–2)

TALBOT
Robert Ungle, speaker 1–3
  (D–4)

James Hollyday
Nicholas Goldsborough
Benjamin Pemberton

SOMERSET
Robert King
George Dashiell
Levin Gale
William Stoughton

DORCHESTER
Henry Hooper
John Rider
John Kirke
Edward Pritchett

CECIL
John Ward
Ephraim Augustus Herman

Francis Mauldin
Thomas Johnson

ANNAPOLIS
Robert Gordon
Vachel Denton

PRINCE GEORGE'S
James Stoddart (D–3)
Ralph Crabb
Thomas Gantt
Joseph Belt
John Magruder (E–4)

QUEEN ANNE'S
Edward Wright
Solomon Wright
John Chaires
William Elliott

Committee Service[3]

ELECTIONS AND PRIVILEGES
Greenfield (1–3)
B. Mackall (1–4)
Hooper (1–3)
Crabb (1–3)
Smith (1–4)
Stoughton (4)
Herman (4)
Matthews (4)

LAWS
Stoddart (1, 2)
Bordley (1–3)
Greenfield (1–4*)
Harris (1–4*)
Dent (1–4*)
Gale (1–4*)
King (1–4*)
Denton (1–4*)
Hollyday (3, 4)

Hooper (3)
J. Mackall (3)
Dulany (4)

AGGRIEVANCES AND COURTS
OF JUSTICE
Bordley (1–3)
Warfield (1–4)
Harrison (1–3)
Belt (1–4*)
Beale (1–4)

Dashiell (1)
Crabb (4)
Maxwell (4)

ACCOUNTS
Beale (1–4*)
J. Ward (1–4)
Hollyday (1–3)
Worthington (1–4)
Rider (1–4*)
Gordon (4)

[1] Last attended November 6, 1725. It is unknown if he remained in office, but no further evidence of attendance has been found.

[2] Declared not qualified to stand for election, because he was undersheriff at the time the election was held. He was dismissed on October 12, 1725.

[3] In the second session of the Assembly there is no mention of either committee appointment or reappointment, and in the third session the several committees were "appointed and sent out," but not relisted. It is presumed that the original committee members appointed in the first session were reappointed in both the second and third sessions. All committee members were named in the fourth session, but the worm-eaten condition of the original manuscript makes the composition of the committees of Laws, Aggrievances, and Accounts questionable. Members whose names are asterisked are assumed to have continued service in the fourth session. Those whose names are legible in the surviving portions of the manuscript are listed without an asterisk.

PROPRIETARY ASSEMBLY OF 1728–1731

Charles Calvert, 5th Lord Baltimore, proprietor
Benedict Leonard Calvert, governor

FIRST SESSION: October 3–November 2, 1728
SECOND SESSION: July 10–August 8, 1729
THIRD SESSION: May 21–June 16, 1730
FOURTH SESSION: July 13–July 29, 1731
FIFTH SESSION: August 19–September 6, 1731

UPPER HOUSE

Edward Henry Calvert (D–3)[1]
William Holland
John Hall

Philemon Lloyd
Richard Tilghman
Matthew Tilghman Ward

John Rousby
Benjamin Tasker
Philip Lee

Nicholas Lowe (D–2)
Charles Calvert[2]
John Rider (A–2)

LOWER HOUSE

ST. MARY'S
Thomas Trueman Greenfield
Thomas Waughop
Philip Key
John Young

KENT
James Harris
Philip Kennard
George Willson
Ebenezer Blackiston

ANNE ARUNDEL
John Beale
Daniel Dulany
Richard Warfield
Thomas Worthington

CALVERT
John Mackall, speaker

Benjamin Mackall
Walter Smith, of Leonard's Creek
Adderton Skinner

CHARLES
Robert Hanson
John Fendall
John Courts
Samuel Hanson

BALTIMORE
William Hamilton
Daniel Scott
Thomas Tolley
Roger Matthews

TALBOT
James Hollyday
George Robins

Samuel Chamberlaine
John Edmondson

SOMERSET
Robert King
Levin Gale
George Dashiell
William Stoughton

DORCHESTER
John Brannock
Peter Taylor
John Kirke
William Ennalls (Ds–1, E–2)[3]

CECIL
Thomas Johnson, Jr.
Ephraim Augustus Herman

Stephen Knight
Joshua George

ANNAPOLIS
Robert Gordon
Edmund Jennings

PRINCE GEORGE'S
John Magruder
Samuel Perrie (D–2)
Ralph Crabb
Joseph Belt
Edward Sprigg (E–2)

QUEEN ANNE'S
Augustine Thompson
William Elliott
William Hemsley
William Turbutt

Committee Service[4]

ELECTIONS AND PRIVILEGES
Smith (1–5)
Crabb (1–5)
Herman (1–5)
R. Hanson (1–5)
Hollyday (1–5)
B. Mackall (1–5)

LAWS
Harris (1–5)

Dulany (1–5)
George (1–5)
S. Hanson (1–5)
Jennings (1–5)
Key (1–5)
Perrie (1)
Magruder (1–5)
Greenfield (3)
Gale (3)

AGGRIEVANCES AND COURTS OF JUSTICE
Warfield (1–5)
Belt (1–5)
Beale (1–5)
Fendall (1–5)
Matthews (1–5)
Magruder (1–5)
Hamilton (1–5)

ACCOUNTS
Beale (1–5)
Worthington (1–5)
Hollyday (1–5)
Chamberlaine (1–5)
Turbutt (1–5)

[1] Edward Henry Calvert, brother of the proprietor, was apppointed "the first person" of the Council on June 19, 1728, and was sworn in on February 6, 1728/29.

[2] Charles Calvert was promoted to the first position on the Council after the death of Edward Henry Calvert in April 1730.

[3] Dismissed on October 12, 1728, after it was decided that he had not been duly elected. He was reelected and subsequently qualified on July 11, 1729.

[4] The original committee members named in the first session were reappointed but not relisted in the second, third, and fifth sessions. The members on the committees of laws, aggrievances, and accounts were renamed in the fourth session, but no mention was made of the Committee of Elections and Privileges. Since this committee was functioning during the fourth session, it is presumed that all former members continued to serve.

PROPRIETARY ASSEMBLY OF 1732–1734

Charles Calvert, 5th Lord Baltimore, proprietor

Samuel Ogle, governor 1, Cv [1]

Charles Calvert, 5th Lord Baltimore, governor 2 [1]

FIRST SESSION: July 11–August 8, 1732
SECOND SESSION: March 13, 1732/33–April 12, 1733
CONVENTION: March 19, 1733/34–March 25, 1734

UPPER HOUSE

Charles Calvert (D–Cv) [1]
William Holland (DNS, D–2)
John Hall [1]

Philemon Lloyd (D–Cv)
Richard Tilghman
Matthew Tilghman Ward
John Rousby
Benjamin Tasker

Philip Lee
John Rider
Michael Howard
George Plater

Edmund Jennings (A–2)
Samuel Ogle (A–2, R–Cv), president 2 [1]

LOWER HOUSE

ST. MARY'S
Thomas Waughop
Justinian Jordan
John Read
Richard Hopewell

KENT
Ebenezer Blackiston
George Willson
Matthew Howard
Christopher Hall

ANNE ARUNDEL
Daniel Dulany (Ds–Cv) [2]
John Beale (Ds–Cv) [2]
Philip Hammond
Richard Warfield

CALVERT
John Mackall, speaker
Benjamin Mackall
Walter Smith
Adderton Skinner

CHARLES
John Courts
William Middleton
Robert Hanson
Henry Hawkins

BALTIMORE
Daniel Scott
Thomas Sheredine
William Hamilton
Roger Matthews

TALBOT
John Edmondson

Perry Benson
Edward Needles
Nicholas Goldsborough

SOMERSET
Levin Gale (Ds–Cv) [2]
Francis Allen
John Caldwell
George Dashiell

DORCHESTER
Peter Taylor
Henry Hooper
Thomas Woolford
John Brannock

CECIL
Joshua George
Ephraim Augustus Herman
John Ward

Joseph Wood

ANNAPOLIS
William Cummings
Robert Gordon (EV, E–1, [3] Ds–Cv) [2]

PRINCE GEORGE'S
John Magruder
Edward Sprigg
Ralph Crabb (D–Cv)
Joseph Belt

QUEEN ANNE'S
Solomon Clayton
William Hemsley
William Elliott
Edward Wright

Committee Service [4]

ELECTIONS AND PRIVILEGES
Smith (1–Cv)
Crabb (1, 2)
Herman (1–Cv)
Hanson (1–Cv)
B. Mackall (1–Cv)
Hemsley (1–Cv)

LAWS
Dulany (1–Cv)
George (1–Cv)
Gale (1–Cv)
Hooper (1–Cv)
Allen (1–Cv)
Magruder (1–Cv)
Cumming (1–Cv)
Hammond (1–Cv)
Goldsborough (2)

AGGRIEVANCES AND COURTS OF JUSTICE
Warfield (1–Cv)
Belt (1–Cv)
Beale (1–Cv)
Matthews (1–Cv)
Magruder (1–Cv)
Hamilton (1–Cv)
Wright (1–Cv)

ACCOUNTS
Beale (1–Cv)
Gordon (1–Cv)
J. Ward (1–Cv)
Sprigg (1–Cv)
Smith (1)
Hemsley (Cv)
Hooper (Cv)
Cumming (Cv)

[1] The proprietor arrived during the winter of 1732 and assumed the office of governor. Ogle was appointed and sworn to the Council on March 21, 1732/33. He was listed in the first position of the Council and Upper House before Charles Calvert (the councilor), who had previously held that position. Ogle used the title of president in correspondence during his term on the Council and in the Upper House. He reassumed the office of governor on June 20, 1733. After the death of Charles Calvert (the councilor) in February 1733/34, John Hall assumed the first position on the Council and in the Upper House.

[2] Dulany, Beale, Gale, and Gordon were discharged by the Lower House on March 25, 1734, for receiving places of trust and profit from the government after their elections. Governor Ogle then dissolved the entire Assembly in objection to this action.

[3] Robert Gordon and Vachel Denton received an equal number of votes in the original election. Although Gordon was declared the winner and appeared in the Lower House as one of the Annapolis delegates, the election was disputed. On July 19, 1732, it was determined that Gordon had not been duly elected because of improper procedures. Gordon, however, won the subsequent election and was requalified one week later on July 26, 1732.

[4] The original committee members named in the first session were reappointed in the second session and again in the convention, but they were not specifically named. It is presumed that Smith, who was added to the Committee of Accounts in the middle of the first session, was not included in the reappointments. Likewise, it is assumed that Goldsborough, who was added to the Committee of Laws in the middle of the second session, was not included in the reappointments made in the convention.

PROPRIETARY ASSEMBLY OF 1734/35–1737

Charles Calvert, 5th Lord Baltimore, proprietor
Samuel Ogle, governor

FIRST SESSION: March 20, 1734/35–April 24, 1735
CONVENTION: March 19, 1735/36–April 10, 1736
SECOND SESSION: April 20–May 6, 1736
THIRD SESSION: April 26–May 28, 1737
FOURTH SESSION: August 11–16, 1737

UPPER HOUSE

John Hall, president 1, Cv, 2 (D–4) [1]
Richard Tilghman, president 3, 4 [1]

Matthew Tilghman Ward
John Rousby
Benjamin Tasker, president 3 [1]

Philip Lee
John Rider
Michael Howard
George Plater

Edmund Jennings
James Hollyday (A–Cv) [2]
Charles Hammond (A–Cv)

LOWER HOUSE

ST. MARY'S
Thomas Waughop (D–1)
Justinian Jordan
Philip Key
John Read
James Waughop (E–Cv)

KENT
James Harris, speaker 1, Cv, 2–4 [3]
Christopher Hall
George Willson
Philip Kennard

ANNE ARUNDEL
Philip Hammond
Vachel Denton
Daniel Dulany, speaker 1, Dcl [3]
Richard Warfield

CALVERT
John Mackall
Benjamin Mackall
Walter Smith
Adderton Skinner

CHARLES
Robert Hanson
John Courts
William Middleton
Henry Holland Hawkins

BALTIMORE
Thomas Sheredine
John Moale
William Hamilton
Roger Matthews

TALBOT
Edward Needles
Nicholas Goldsborough

John Edmondson
Tench Francis

SOMERSET
Levin Gale
Robert King
George Dashiell
William Stoughton

DORCHESTER
Thomas Woolford
Henry Hooper
James Brown
Henry Trippe

CECIL
Ephraim Augustus Herman (DNS, D–1)
Joshua George
Joseph Wood
Thomas Johnson, Jr.

John Ward (E–1)

ANNAPOLIS
Robert Gordon
Richard Francis (Ds–1, E–1) [4]

PRINCE GEORGE'S
John Magruder
Edward Sprigg
Joseph Belt
John Stoddert

QUEEN ANNE'S
William Hemsley (D–3)
William Elliott
Edward Wright
William Tilghman
Grundy Pemberton (E–4)

Committee Service [5]

ELECTIONS AND PRIVILEGES
Smith (1, Cv, 2–4)
Hanson (1, Cv, 2–4)
Hemsley (1, Cv, 2–4)
King (1, Cv, 2–4)
P. Hammond (1, Cv, 2–4)
George (1, Cv, 2–4)

LAWS
Dulany (1, Cv, 2–4)
Gale (1, Cv, 2–4)
Hooper (1, Cv, 2–4)
Key (1, Cv, 2–4)

T. Francis (1, Cv, 2–4)
George (1, Cv, 2–4)
P. Hammond (1, Cv, 2–4)
R. Francis (1, Cv, 2–4)

AGGRIEVANCES AND COURTS OF JUSTICE
Warfield (1, Cv, 2–4)
Stoughton (1, Cv, 2–4)
Goldsborough (1, Cv, 2–4)
Matthews (1, Cv, 2–4)
Magruder (1, Cv, 2–4)
Wright (1, Cv, 2–4)

Kennard (1, Cv, 2–4)
Hamilton (1, Cv, 2–4)
Belt (1, Cv, 2–4)
Key (3)

ACCOUNTS
King (1, Cv, 2–4)
Denton (1, Cv, 2–4)
Gordon (1, Cv, 2–4)
Sprigg (1, Cv, 2–4)
Dashiell (1, Cv, 2–4)

BILLS OF CREDIT–PAPER CURRENCY (JOINT) [6]
Tasker (1, Cv, 3)
Rider (1)
Plater (Cv, 2)
Gale (1, Cv, 2–4)
Trippe (1, Cv, 2–4)
Moale (1, Cv, 2–4)
Sprigg (1, Cv)
Hemsley (1, Cv, 2)
W. Tilghman (1, Cv, 2–4)
Key (Cv, 2–4)
Stoddert (3, 4)

[1] Hall signed himself as president of the Upper House in correspondence during the first session and the convention. Although he is not referred to as president during the second session, he still occupied that position. During Hall's absence in the third session, and after his subsequent death in 1737, Richard Tilghman assumed the position as senior councilor and used the title of president of the Upper House during the fourth session. Tasker acted in Tilghman's stead during Tilghman's brief absence in the third session, and accordingly signed letters as president of the Upper House.

[2] Hollyday was appointed to the Council on July 15, 1735, but did not attend until February 17, 1736/37, because he had been in Europe.

[3] Dulany declined to serve as speaker of the Lower House because of poor health. Harris was then chosen speaker. Dulany, however, did attend the Assembly as a delegate.

[4] The election of Francis was declared illegal on April 3, 1735. He was, however, reelected and qualified on April 12, 1735.

[5] The members of all first session Lower House standing committees were reappointed to continue in the convention, and the second, third, and fourth sessions. The only names actually relisted, however, were the members on the Committee of Bills of Credit in the convention, and the second and third sessions.

[6] This joint committee is referred to in the Lower House as the "Committee to inspect the accounts and proceedings of the Commissioners for emitting Bills of Credit," and in the Upper House as "the Committee to inspect the proceedings of the Commissioners of the paper currency." It originated on March 21, 1734/35. No Upper House member was named to this committee during the fourth session.

PROPRIETARY ASSEMBLY OF 1738

Charles Calvert, 5th Lord Baltimore, proprietor
Samuel Ogle, governor

CONVENTION: May 3–23, 1738

UPPER HOUSE

Richard Tilghman, president
Matthew Tilghman Ward

John Rousby (DNS)
Benjamin Tasker
Philip Lee
John Rider (DNS)

George Plater
Edmund Jennings
James Hollyday

Charles Hammond
Levin Gale (A) [1]

LOWER HOUSE

ST. MARY'S
John Read
James Waughop
James Swan
Thomas Aisquith

KENT
George Willson
Philip Kennard
Thomas Smith
Charles Hynson

ANNE ARUNDEL
Daniel Dulany [2]
Vachel Denton
Philip Hammond
Samuel Smith

CALVERT
John Mackall, speaker
Benjamin Mackall
Walter Smith
James Weems

CHARLES
John Courts
William Middleton
Bayne Smallwood
Robert Hanson

BALTIMORE
Thomas Sheredine
Roger Matthews
John Moale
Richard Caswell

TALBOT
Nicholas Goldsborough

William Thomas
Edward Lloyd
Robert Lloyd

SOMERSET
Levin Gale [1]
Robert King
William Stoughton
Robert Jenkins Henry

DORCHESTER
Henry Hooper
Henry Trippe
Bartholomew Ennalls
John Brannock

CECIL
Joshua George
Thomas Colvill
William Rumsey

Alphonso Cosden (DNS, D)

ANNAPOLIS
Daniel Dulany (DNS, R) [2]
Charles Carroll
Robert Gordon (E)

PRINCE GEORGE'S
John Stoddert
Edward Sprigg
John Magruder
Turner Wooton

QUEEN ANNE'S
Grundy Pemberton
Solomon Clayton
Thomas Wilkinson
Edward Wright

Committee Service

ELECTIONS AND PRIVILEGES
W. Smith
Hanson
King
P. Hammond
George

LAWS
Dulany
Gale
Hooper
George
P. Hammond

Denton
Carroll

ACCOUNTS
King
Denton
Sprigg
S. Smith
Sheredine

AGGRIEVANCES AND COURTS OF JUSTICE
Matthews

Stoughton
Goldsborough
Magruder
Wright
Kennard
Carroll
Moale
Pemberton

BILLS OF CREDIT
Gale
Moale

Stoddert
Trippe
Colvill

ARMS AND AMMUNITION [3]
W. Smith
Hanson
Hooper
Read
Wooton

[1] Although elected to the Lower House, he was appointed to the Council during this Assembly.

[2] Dulany was elected to represent both Annapolis and Anne Arundel County. He selected the latter seat, and Robert Gordon filled the vacancy left in Annapolis.

[3] The functions of this committee had been previously handled by the Committee of Accounts. The "Committee to Inspect into the Conditions of the Arms and Ammunition and Accounts Relating Thereto" was first appointed as a separate committee during the second session of the 1734/35–1737 Assembly. It had become a standing committee by the 1738 Assembly.

PROPRIETARY ASSEMBLY OF 1739–1741

Charles Calvert, 5th Lord Baltimore, proprietor
Samuel Ogle, governor

CONVENTION: May 1–June 12, 1739
FIRST SESSION: April 23–June 5, 1740
SECOND SESSION: July 7–29, 1740
THIRD SESSION: May 26–June 22, 1741

UPPER HOUSE

Matthew Tilghman Ward,
   president Cv, 1, 2 (D–3)
John Rousby (DNS)
Benjamin Tasker,
   president 3

Philip Lee
John Rider (DNS, D–1)
George Plater
Edmund Jennings

James Hollyday
Charles Hammond
Levin Gale

James Harris (A–Cv)
Samuel Chamberlaine
   (A–Cv)

LOWER HOUSE

ST. MARY'S
John Read
James Waughop
James Swan
Thomas Aisquith

KENT
Charles Hynson
George Willson
William Harris
James Calder

ANNE ARUNDEL
Charles Carroll
Vachel Denton
Philip Hammond, speaker
   1–3R [1]
Thomas Gassaway (D–1)
Henry Hall (E–1)

CALVERT
John Mackall, speaker Cv
   (D–1) [1]
Walter Smith
James Weems
Joseph Hall
John Brome (E–1)

CHARLES
Robert Hanson
Bayne Smallwood
William Middleton
John Courts

BALTIMORE
Thomas Sheredine
Roger Matthews (D–3)
John Moale (D–1)
Richard Caswell
Richard Gist (E–1)
Aquila Paca (E–3)

TALBOT
Nicholas Goldsborough
William Thomas
Edward Lloyd
Robert Lloyd

SOMERSET
Robert King, speaker 3 [1]
William Stoughton
Robert Jenkins Henry
John Gale

DORCHESTER
Henry Hooper
Henry Trippe (Ds–2, E–3) [2]
Bartholomew Ennalls
John Brannock (D–3)
Jacob Hindman (E–3)

CECIL
Joshua George
Thomas Colvill
William Rumsey

Thomas Johnson (DNS,
   D–Cv)
Benjamin Pearce (E–Cv)

ANNAPOLIS
Daniel Dulany
Robert Gordon

PRINCE GEORGE'S
Turner Wooton
Edward Sprigg
John Magruder
Osborn Sprigg

QUEEN ANNE'S
Grundy Pemberton
Solomon Clayton (D–1)
Thomas Wilkinson
Edward Wright (D–3)
Robert Norrest Wright
   (E–1)
Thomas Hammond (E–3)

Committee Service [3]

ELECTIONS AND PRIVILEGES
Smith (Cv–3)
Hanson (Cv–3)
Gassaway (Cv)
Magruder (Cv–3)
Hynson (Cv–3)
Willson (1–3)
Smallwood (1–3)

LAWS
Dulany (Cv–3)
Carroll (Cv–3)
P. Hammond (Cv)
Denton (Cv–3)
Hooper (Cv–3)
Calder (Cv–3)
George (Cv–3)

Henry (Cv–3)
Colvill (1–3)
Stoughton (1–3)

AGGRIEVANCES AND COURTS
OF JUSTICE
Matthews (Cv–2)
Stoughton (Cv–3)
Goldsborough (Cv–3)
Magruder (Cv–3)
E. Wright (Cv–2)
Carroll (Cv–3)
Moale (Cv, 1)
Willson (Cv–3)
Gassaway (Cv)
O. Sprigg (1–3)
J. Hall (3)

Pemberton (3)
Calder (3)

ACCOUNTS
King (Cv–3)
Denton (Cv–3)
E. Sprigg (Cv–3)
Sheredine (Cv–3)
Wooton (Cv–3)
Trippe (3)
R. Lloyd (3)

BILLS OF CREDIT–PAPER
CURRENCY (JOINT)
L. Gale (Cv, 1, 3)
Moale (Cv, 1)
Trippe (Cv–2)
Colvill (Cv–3)

E. Lloyd (Cv–2)
Caswell (Cv–3)
Rumsey (1–3)
Sheredine (1–3)
Hynson (1–3)
Pemberton (1–3)
Weems (3)
J. Gale (3)

ARMS AND AMMUNITION
Smith (Cv–3)
Hanson (Cv–3)
Wooton (Cv, 3)
Hooper (Cv–3)
Read (Cv)
H. Hall (3)

[1] Hammond was chosen speaker of the Lower House at the beginning of the first session after the death of John Mackall. He resigned as speaker on June 11, 1741, because of the increasing indisposition of his son, and was replaced by King.

[2] Trippe was discharged from the Lower House on July 21, 1740, for accepting the position of deputy commissary of Dorchester County after his election. The governor, objecting strongly to this action, decided to prorogue the Assembly. Trippe was reelected and qualified on June 4, 1741.

[3] The Lower House committee members appointed in the first session were reappointed to continue in the second session, but their names were not relisted. The Upper House member on the Committee of Bills of Credit–Paper Currency was not named during the second session.

PROPRIETARY ASSEMBLY OF 1742–1744

Charles Calvert, 5th Lord Baltimore, proprietor

Thomas Bladen, governor

FIRST SESSION: September 21–October 29, 1742
SECOND SESSION: May 1–June 4, 1744

UPPER HOUSE

John Rousby (DNS)
Benjamin Tasker, president
Philip Lee (D–2)
George Plater

Edmund Jennings
James Hollyday
Charles Hammond

Levin Gale (D–2)
James Harris (D–2)
Samuel Chamberlaine

Philip Thomas
Daniel Dulany (A–1) [1]
Edward Lloyd (A–2)

LOWER HOUSE

ST. MARY'S
James Waughop
James Swan
John Griffith
Robert Chesley

KENT
Richard Gresham
George Willson
James Calder
John Gresham

ANNE ARUNDEL
Charles Carroll
Philip Hammond
Henry Hall
Thomas Worthington

CALVERT
Walter Smith
James Weems

Joseph Hall
John Brome

CHARLES
Bayne Smallwood
Richard Harrison
William Wilkinson
Robert Yates (D–2)
John Courts (E–2)

BALTIMORE
Thomas Sheredine
Richard Caswell
Aquila Paca (D–2)
Daniel Scott
John Paca (E–2)

TALBOT
Nicholas Goldsborough
Robert Lloyd
William Thomas
John Goldsborough

SOMERSET
Robert King
William Stoughton
George Gale
James Martin (S–2)
David Wilson (E–2)

DORCHESTER
Henry Trippe
Bartholomew Ennalls
Jacob Hindman
Philemon Lecompte

CECIL
Joshua George
Thomas Colvill
Benjamin Pearce
Nicholas Hyland

ANNAPOLIS
Daniel Dulany (C–1) [1]

Robert Gordon
Benjamin Tasker, Jr. (E–1)

PRINCE GEORGE'S
John Magruder
Edward Sprigg, speaker
Turner Wooton
Osborn Sprigg

QUEEN ANNE'S
Grundy Pemberton
Robert Norrest Wright
Thomas Wilkinson
Thomas Hammond

WORCESTER [2]
John Purnell (E–2)
Thomas Robins (E–2)
Parker Selby (E–2)
John Henry (E–2)

Committee Service

ELECTIONS AND PRIVILEGES
Smith (1, 2)
Magruder (1, 2)
G. Willson (1)
Smallwood (1)
W. Wilkinson (1)
Worthington (1, 2)
Pemberton (2)
H. Hall (2)
J. Gresham (2)

LAWS
Dulany (1)
Carroll (1, 2)
George (1, 2)

Colvill (1, 2)
Stoughton (1, 2)
Calder (1, 2)
P. Hammond (1, 2)
R. Lloyd (1, 2)
King (1)
N. Goldsborough (1, 2)
G. Gale (1)
H. Hall (2)

AGGRIEVANCES AND COURTS
OF JUSTICE
Magruder (1, 2)
Stoughton (1, 2)
G. Willson (1, 2)
Carroll (1, 2)

J. Hall (1, 2)
N. Goldsborough (1, 2)
Pemberton (1, 2)
O. Sprigg (1, 2)

ACCOUNTS
King (1, 2)
Wooton (1, 2)
Sheredine (1, 2)
Worthington (1, 2)
A. Paca (1)
G. Gale (2)

BILLS OF CREDIT–PAPER
CURRENCY (JOINT)
L. Gale (1)

Plater (2)
Colvill (1, 2)
Caswell (1)
Sheredine (1, 2)
Pemberton (1, 2)
Weems (1, 2)
P. Hammond (2)

ARMS AND AMMUNITION
Smith (1, 2)
Wooton (1, 2)
H. Hall (1, 3)
Thomas (1, 2)
J. Gresham (1, 2)

[1] Although elected to the Lower House, he was appointed to the Council at the beginning of the first session.
[2] The law erecting Worcester County was passed at the first session. The delegates were seated at the second session.

PROPRIETARY ASSEMBLY OF 1745

Charles Calvert, 5th Lord Baltimore, proprietor
Thomas Bladen, governor

August 5–September 28, 1745

UPPER HOUSE

Benjamin Tasker, president
George Plater
Edmund Jennings

James Hollyday
Charles Hammond
Samuel Chamberlaine

Philip Thomas
Daniel Dulany
Edward Lloyd

Benjamin Young
Benjamin Tasker, Jr.
Richard Lee

LOWER HOUSE

ST. MARY'S
Zachariah Bond
Samuel Abell
Abraham Barnes
James Mills (EV) [1]

KENT
Richard Gresham
George Willson
John Gresham
Matthias Harris

ANNE ARUNDEL
Henry Hall
Charles Carroll
Philip Hammond
Thomas Worthington

CALVERT
Walter Smith

Joseph Hall
John Brome
James John Mackall

CHARLES
Bayne Smallwood
Richard Harrison
William Wilkinson
John Courts

BALTIMORE
Thomas Sheredine
John Hall
George Buchanan
John Paca

TALBOT
John Goldsborough
Robert Lloyd
William Thomas
Nicholas Goldsborough

SOMERSET
William Stoughton
David Wilson
John Dennis
Robert King

DORCHESTER
Henry Hooper
Bartholomew Ennalls
Philemon Lecompte
Daniel Sulivane (Ds) [2]

CECIL
Benjamin Pearce
Nicholas Hyland
Thomas Colvill
Joshua George

ANNAPOLIS
Robert Gordon

George Steuart (EV) [3]
Stephen Bordley

PRINCE GEORGE'S
Edward Sprigg, speaker
John Addison
Osborn Sprigg
Turner Wooton

QUEEN ANNE'S
Thomas Wilkinson
Grundy Pemberton
William Hopper
Thomas Hammond

WORCESTER
John Henry
John Purnell
Abraham Outten
Parker Selby

Committee Service

ELECTIONS AND PRIVILEGES
G. Willson
Smallwood
Worthington
J. Gresham
J. Goldsborough
Ennalls
Courts
Smith

LAWS
Carroll
George
Colvill
Stoughton

P. Hammond
R. Lloyd
N. Goldsborough
Hooper
H. Hall
Harris
Bordley

AGGRIEVANCES AND COURTS
OF JUSTICE
Stoughton
G. Willson
Carroll
N. Goldsborough
Pemberton

R. Gresham
Paca
O. Sprigg
Hooper

ACCOUNTS
King
Wooton
Sheredine
Worthington
Buchanan

BILLS OF CREDIT–PAPER
CURRENCY (JOINT)
E. Lloyd
Colvill

Sheredine
Pemberton
Henry
Barnes

ARMS AND AMMUNITION
Wooton
H. Hall
Thomas
J. Gresham
Hooper
D. Wilson
Addison
Smith

[1] The sheriff of St. Mary's County cast the deciding vote after James Mills and James Swan tied in the election. Mills attended as a delegate, but was dismissed on August 29, after the Lower House decided that the action of the sheriff was illegal.

[2] Sulivane continued to act as undersheriff of Dorchester County after the date of the election was posted. He was therefore not qualified to stand for election, and was discharged on August 29, 1745.

[3] Steuart was dismissed on August 10, after the petition of Stephen Bordley complaining of an irregular election was upheld. Bordley was determined duly elected, and took his seat.

PROPRIETARY ASSEMBLY OF 1745/46–1748

Charles Calvert, 5th Lord Baltimore, proprietor
Thomas Bladen, governor Cv1, 1, 2
Samuel Ogle, governor 3, Cv2, 4

FIRST CONVENTION: March 12, 1745/46–March 29, 1746
FIRST SESSION: June 17–July 8, 1746
SECOND SESSION: November 6–12, 1746
THIRD SESSION: May 16–July 11, 1747
SECOND CONVENTION: December 22–23, 1747
FOURTH SESSION: May 10–June 11, 1748

UPPER HOUSE

Benjamin Tasker, president
George Plater
Edmund Jennings
James Hollyday (D–Cv2)

Charles Hammond
Samuel Chamberlaine
Philip Thomas

Daniel Dulany
Edward Lloyd
Benjamin Young

Benjamin Tasker, Jr.
Richard Lee
Benedict Calvert (A–4)

LOWER HOUSE

ST. MARY'S
Philip Key
Zachariah Bond
Abraham Barnes
James Mills

KENT
John Gresham
George Willson
Richard Gresham
Matthias Harris

ANNE ARUNDEL
Henry Hall
Philip Hammond
Charles Carroll
Thomas Worthington

CALVERT
Walter Smith
Joseph Hall

John Brome
James John Mackall

CHARLES
Bayne Smallwood
Richard Harrison
William Wilkinson
John Courts (D–4)
William Middleton (E–4)

BALTIMORE
Thomas Sheredine
John Hall
George Buchanan
John Paca

TALBOT
Nicholas Goldsborough
William Thomas
Robert Lloyd
John Goldsborough

SOMERSET
William Stoughton (Ds–3) [1]
Robert King
George Dashiell
John Dennis (S–3)
Isaac Handy (E–3)
Robert Jenkins Henry (E–3)

DORCHESTER
Henry Hooper
Philemon Lecompte
Bartholomew Ennalls
Francis Lee (Ds–1) [2]
Daniel Sulivane (E–2)

CECIL
Nicholas Hyland
Joshua George
Benjamin Pearce
Peter Bayard

ANNAPOLIS
Robert Gordon
Walter Dulany

PRINCE GEORGE'S
Edward Sprigg, speaker
Turner Wooton
John Addison
John Stoddert

QUEEN ANNE'S
William Hopper
Thomas Hammond
Grundy Pemberton
Edward Tilghman

WORCESTER
John Henry
John Purnell
Thomas Robins
John Scarborough

Committee Service [3]

ELECTIONS AND PRIVILEGES
Worthington (Cv1, 1–3, 4)
Smallwood (Cv1, 1–3, 4)
J. Goldsborough (Cv1, 1–3, 4)
Ennalls (Cv1, 1–3, 4)
Dashiell (Cv1, 1–3, 4)
Smith (Cv1, 1–3, 4)
J. Gresham (Cv1, 1–3, 4)

LAWS
Stoughton (Cv1, 1–3)
Carroll (Cv1, 1–3, 4)
P. Hammond (Cv1, 1–3, 4)
R. Lloyd (Cv1, 1–3, 4)
Hooper (Cv1, 1–3, 4)

H. Hall (Cv1, 1–3, 4)
Harris (Cv1, 1–3, 4)
Key (Cv1, 1–3, 4)
N. Goldsborough (1–3, 4)
George (1–3, 4)
J. Gresham (3)
Tilghman (3, 4)
Addison (3)
R. J. Henry (4)

AGGRIEVANCES AND COURTS
OF JUSTICE
Carroll (Cv1, 1–3, 4)
R. Gresham (Cv1, 1–3, 4)
Paca (Cv1, 1–3, 4)
Hooper (Cv1, 1–3, 4)
Stoddert (Cv1, 1–3, 4)

J. Goldsborough (Cv1, 1–3, 4)
Willson (1) [3]
N. Goldsborough (1) [3]

ACCOUNTS
Wooton (Cv1, 1–3, 4)
Sheredine (Cv1, 1–3, 4)
Worthington (Cv1, 1–3, 4)
Dashiell (Cv1, 1–3, 4)
Buchanan (Cv1, 1–3, 4)
King (Cv1, 1–3, 4)

BILLS OF CREDIT–PAPER
CURRENCY (JOINT)
R. Lee (Cv1, 1, 4)
Chamberlaine (3)

Sheredine (Cv1, 3, 4)
J. Henry (Cv1, 1–3, 4)
Stoddert (Cv1, 1–3, 4)
Tilghman (Cv1, 1–3, 4)
Wooton (Cv1)
Barnes (1–3, 4)
H. Hall (1, 2)

ARMS AND AMMUNITION
Wooton (Cv1, 1–3, 4)
H. Hall (Cv1, 1–3, 4)
W. Thomas (Cv1, 1–3, 4)
Hooper (Cv1, 1–3, 4)
Addison (Cv1, 1–3, 4)
Smith (Cv1, 1–3, 4)

[1] Stoughton was discharged on May 18, 1747, after accepting the position of deputy naval officer of Pocomoke.
[2] Lee was discharged on June 20, 1746, after accepting the office of county clerk.
[3] The members of all first convention Lower House standing committees were reappointed to continue in the first, second, and third sessions. The only names relisted in those sessions were the members on the Committee of Bills of Credit–Paper Currency. It is presumed that George Willson and Nicholas Goldsborough, who were added to the Committee of Aggrievances and Courts of Justice during the first session, were not included in the reappointments made in the second and third session. No Upper or Lower House standing committees were mentioned, nor did any function during the two-day second convention. The Upper House member on the Committee of Bills of Credit–Paper Currency was named in all other sessions except the second.

PROPRIETARY ASSEMBLY OF 1749–1751

Charles Calvert, 5th Lord Baltimore proprietor
Samuel Ogle, governor

CONVENTION: May 9–11, 1749
FIRST SESSION: May 24–June 24, 1749
SECOND SESSION: May 8–June 2, 1750
THIRD SESSION: May 15–June 8, 1751

UPPER HOUSE

Benjamin Tasker, president
George Plater
Edmund Jennings

Charles Hammond
Samuel Chamberlaine
Philip Thomas

Daniel Dulany
Edward Lloyd
Benjamin Young

Benjamin Tasker, Jr. (DNS)
Richard Lee
Benedict Calvert

LOWER HOUSE

ST. MARY'S [1]
Zachariah Bond (EV–1, E–2)
Abraham Barnes (EV–1, E–2)
Philip Key (EV–1, E–2)
James Mills (EV–1, E–2)

KENT
Matthias Harris
Richard Lloyd
Simon Wilmer
Nicholas Smith

ANNE ARUNDEL
Philip Hammond, speaker
Thomas Worthington
Charles Carroll
Stephen Bordley

CALVERT
James John Mackall
James Heighe
Benjamin Mackall, Jr.
Benson Bond (D–3)
Thomas Reynolds (E–3)

CHARLES
John Stoddert
Bayne Smallwood
Jonathan Willson
Arthur Lee

BALTIMORE
George Buchanan (D–2)
John Paca
Thomas Sheredine (S–3)
Darby Lux (D–3)
William Smith (E–2)
John Matthews (E–3)
Walter Tolley (E–3, Ds–3) [2]
Thomas Franklin (E–3)

TALBOT
John Goldsborough
Nicholas Goldsborough
Robert Lloyd
Edward Oldham

SOMERSET
Robert King
Robert Jenkins Henry
Isaac Handy

Henry Waggaman

DORCHESTER
Henry Hooper
Philemon Lecompte
Daniel Sulivane
Henry Travers

CECIL [1]
Benjamin Pearce (EV–1)
Peter Bayard (EV–1)
John Baldwin (EV–1)
Richard Thompson (EV–1)
Thomas Colvill (E–2)
Nicholas Hyland (E–2)
Henry Baker (E–2)
James Baxter (E–2)

ANNAPOLIS
Robert Gordon
Walter Dulany (Ds–2, E–2) [4]

PRINCE GEORGE'S
Turner Wooton
Edward Sprigg

John Addison
William Murdock

QUEEN ANNE'S
Edward Tilghman (Ds–2) [4]
William Hopper
John Davis
Thomas Wilkinson
Nathaniel Wright (E–2, DNS, Ds–2) [5]
John Tillotson (E–3)

WORCESTER
Thomas Robins
John Selby
John Scarborough
John Henry

FREDERICK
Henry Wright Crabb
Thomas Owen
Joseph Chapline
Daniel Dulany, Jr. (EV–1) [6]
John Smith Prather [6]

Committee Service [7]

ELECTIONS AND PRIVILEGES
Sprigg (Cv–3)
Worthington (Cv–3)
Wooton (Cv–3)
Stoddert (Cv–3)
Tilghman (Cv, 1)
Smallwood (Cv–3)
J. Goldsborough (Cv–3)

LAWS
Carroll (Cv–3)
Robert Lloyd (Cv–3)
N. Goldsborough (Cv–3)
Hooper (Cv–3)
Harris (Cv–3)
R. J. Henry (Cv–3)
Key (Cv–3)
Bordley (Cv–3)
W. Dulany (Cv–3)

Sprigg (2)
Murdock (2)
Wooton (3)

AGGRIEVANCES AND COURTS OF JUSTICE
Carroll (Cv–3)
N. Goldsborough (Cv–3)
Hooper (Cv–3)
Addison (Cv–3)
Paca (Cv–3)
Stoddert (Cv–3)
J. Goldsborough (Cv–3)
Murdock (3)

ACCOUNTS
Worthington (Cv–3)
King (Cv–3)
Wooton (Cv–3)
Sprigg (Cv–3)

Sheredine (Cv–2)
Buchanan (Cv, 1)
Murdock (3)

BILLS OF CREDIT–PAPER CURRENCY (JOINT)
Chamberlaine (1)
R. Lee (2, 3)
Sheredine (Cv–2)
Tilghman (Cv, 1)
Barnes (Cv–3)
J. Henry (Cv–3)
Z. Bond (Cv–3)
J. Goldsborough (1)
Murdock (1)
Lux (1)
Richard Lloyd (1)
Waggaman (1)
Paca (1)

Hopper (1)
Willson (1)
A. Lee (1)
Wilmer (1)
Owen (1)
B. Mackall (1)
Colvill (2, 3)
Baxter (3)

ARMS AND AMMUNITION
Addison (Cv–3)
Lux (Cv–2)
Richard Lloyd (Cv–3)
J. J. Mackall (Cv–3)
Hooper (Cv–3)
B. Mackall (1)
Crabb (1)
Mills (2)
Hyland (2)

[1] The election of the St. Mary's County delegation was declared null and void on June 10, 1749, because of the illegal conduct of the sheriff, Robert Chesley. All delegates were subsequently reelected and returned on May 8, 1750.

[2] Tolley was discharged from the Lower House on June 1, 1751, for serving as an inspector of tobacco. Thomas Franklin, who had received the second highest number of votes cast, was declared the duly elected delegate and took his seat on June 4, 1751.

[3] Upon petition of various freeholders of Cecil County, the Lower House decided on June 6, 1749, that the election for delegates from Cecil County was not a free election, and was therefore null and void. A new election was called for, at which four different delegates were returned.
[4] Dulany and Tilghman were discharged from the Lower House on May 9, 1750—Dulany for accepting the office of deputy commissary of Anne Arundel County, and Tilghman for accepting the office of keeper of the rent rolls for the Eastern Shore. Dulany was subsequently reelected to the Lower House, and took his seat on May 16, 1750.
[5] Wright, who was elected to replace Edward Tilghman, was disqualified from serving on June 1, 1750, because he continued to act as inspector of tobacco after his election.
[6] Upon the petition of Prather, complaining of an illegal election and return by the sheriff of Frederick County, the Lower House determined on June 8, 1749, that Dulany had not been properly elected. Prather was declared the winner, and took his seat on June 9, 1749.
[7] The members of all Lower House standing committees appointed in the convention were reappointed to continue in the first, second, and third sessions, but the only names relisted in those sessions were the members on the Bills of Credit–Paper Currency Committee. It is presumed that Benjamin Mackall and Henry Wright Crabb, who were added to the Committee of Arms and Ammunition in the middle of the first session, were not included in the reappointment of members made in the second session, and that James Mills and Nicholas Hyland, who were added to this same committee in the middle of the second session, were not included in the reappointment made in the third. It is also assumed that Edward Sprigg and William Murdock, who were added to the Committee of Laws in the middle of the second session, were not included in the third session reappointment. The Upper House member on the Committee of Bills of Credit–Paper Currency was not named during the convention.

PROPRIETARY ASSEMBLY OF 1751–1754

Frederick Calvert, 6th Lord Baltimore, proprietor

Samuel Ogle, governor 1 (D–2) [1]

Benjamin Tasker, acting governor 2 [1]

Horatio Sharpe, governor 3–6 [1]

FIRST SESSION: December 7–14, 1751
SECOND SESSION: June 3–23, 1752
THIRD SESSION: October 2–November 17, 1753
FOURTH SESSION: February 26–March 9, 1754
FIFTH SESSION: May 8–30, 1754
SIXTH SESSION: July 17–25, 1754

UPPER HOUSE

Benjamin Tasker, president
George Plater
Edmund Jennings (R–3)
Charles Hammond
Samuel Chamberlaine
Philip Thomas
Daniel Dulany (D–4)
Edward Lloyd
Benjamin Young (D–4)
Benjamin Tasker, Jr.
Richard Lee
Benedict Calvert

LOWER HOUSE

ST. MARY'S
Zachariah Bond
Abraham Barnes
James Mills
Philip Key

KENT [2]
Alexander Williamson
William Rasin (Ds–1, E–2, S–4)
John Gresham (DNS, D–2)
Abraham Falconar (Ds–1, E–2, D–6)
Richard Gresham (E–2)
Hugh Wallis (E–5)

ANNE ARUNDEL
Thomas Worthington (D–3)
Philip Hammond, speaker
Charles Carroll
Henry Hall
John Gassaway (E–3)

CALVERT
James John Mackall
Benjamin Mackall, Jr.

Thomas Reynolds
Edward Gantt

CHARLES
Arthur Lee
John Stoddert
Bayne Smallwood
Richard Harrison

BALTIMORE [3]
William Govane (EV–1, E–2)
Lloyd Buchanan (EV–1, E–2)
Thomas Franklin (EV–1, E–2, S–3)
Charles Ridgely (EV–1, E–2)
John Paca (E–3)

TALBOT
John Goldsborough
Pollard Edmondson
Matthew Tilghman
Edward Oldham

SOMERSET
Henry Waggaman
Joseph Gillis
Robert Jenkins Henry
John Handy

DORCHESTER
Daniel Sulivane (S–3)
Ennalls Hooper (R–3)
Charles Goldsborough
Henry Hooper
Henry Travers (E–3)
Joseph Cox Gray (E–3)

CECIL
Michael Earle
Benjamin Pearce
Sidney George
Nicholas Hyland

ANNAPOLIS
Robert Gordon (D–3)
Walter Dulany
George Steuart (E–3, EV–3) [4]
Alexander Hamilton (E–3)

PRINCE GEORGE'S
Edward Sprigg (DNS, D–1)
Turner Wooton (S–3)
John Addison
William Murdock
George Fraser (E–2)
John Hawkins, Jr. (E–3)

QUEEN ANNE'S
Thomas Wilkinson
John Tillotson
William Hopper
James Hollyday

WORCESTER
John Scarborough
John Evans
John Selby (D–5)
John Purnell
John Henry (E–6)

FREDERICK
Daniel Dulany, Jr.
Nathan Magruder
Henry Wright Crabb
Joseph Chapline

Committee Service[5]

ELECTIONS AND PRIVILEGES
Worthington (1, 2)
Wooton (1, 2)
Stoddert (1–6)
Smallwood (1–6)
J. Goldsborough (1–6)
Hyland (1–6)
Tilghman (1–6)
Williamson (3–6)

LAWS
Carroll (1–6)
H. Hooper (1–6)
R. J. Henry (1–6)

Key (1–6)
D. Dulany, Jr. (1–6)
Tilghman (1–6)
Hall (1–6)
C. Goldsborough (1–6)
Hollyday (1–6)

GRIEVANCES AND COURTS OF JUSTICE
Carroll (1–6)
H. Hooper (1–6)
Addison (1–6)
Murdock (1–6)
J. Goldsborough (1–6)

Stoddert (1–6)
Smallwood (1–6)

ACCOUNTS
Worthington (1, 2)
Wooton (1, 2)
Murdock (1–6)
Waggaman (1–6)
Magruder (1–6)
Stoddert (3–6)
J. Goldsborough (3–6)

BILLS OF CREDIT–PAPER CURRENCY (JOINT)
R. Lee (2, 3, 5)

Barnes (1–6)
Bond (1–6)
Harrison (1–6)
W. Dulany (1–6)
A. Lee (1–6)

ARMS AND AMMUNITION
Addison (1–6)
J. J. Mackall (1–6)
Hopper (1–6)
Crabb (1–6)
Oldham (1–6)
Gantt (3)

[1] After the death of Ogle on May 3, 1752, Tasker, the president of the Upper House, assumed the duties of acting governor until the arrival of Horatio Sharpe on August 10, 1753.

[2] William Rasin and Abraham Falconar were discharged from the Lower House on December 11, 1751, Rasin for being an inspector within two years of his election, and Falconar for being an ordinary keeper at the time of his election. A new election was called, at which time Rasin was returned and Falconar was replaced by Richard Gresham. Falconar, however, was reelected later in the second session to replace the deceased John Gresham.

[3] The election for the Baltimore County delegation was declared void on December, 12, 1751, because of illegal actions of the sheriff in conducting it. The four men originally chosen were returned and took their seats at the beginning of the second session.

[4] The election of Steuart, the delegate chosen to replace the deceased Robert Gordon, was declared invalid on October 19, 1753. The petitioner, Alexander Hamilton, was declared the duly elected delegate for Annapolis and took his seat the same day.

[5] The members on all Lower House standing committees appointed in the first session were reappointed to continue in the second through sixth sessions, but their names were not relisted. It is presumed that Edward Gantt, who was added to the Committee of Arms and Ammunition in the middle of the third session, was not included in the reappointment of members made during the fourth session. The Upper House member on the Committee of Bills of Credit–Paper Currency was not named in the first, fourth, and sixth sessions.

PROPRIETARY ASSEMBLY OF 1754–1757

Frederick Calvert, 6th Lord Baltimore, proprietor

Horatio Sharpe, governor

FIRST SESSION: December 12–24, 1754
SECOND SESSION: February 22–March 26, 1755
THIRD SESSION: June 23–July 8, 1755
FOURTH SESSION: February 23–May 22, 1756
FIFTH SESSION: September 14–October 9, 1756
SIXTH SESSION: April 8–May 9, 1757

UPPER HOUSE

Benjamin Tasker, president
George Plater (D–3)
Charles Hammond
Samuel Chamberlaine

Philip Thomas
Edward Lloyd
Benjamin Tasker, Jr.
Richard Lee

Benedict Calvert
William Goldsborough
(A–2)

Robert Jenkins Henry
(A–5)[1]

LOWER HOUSE

ST. MARY'S
James Mills
Jeremiah Chase (D–3)
Thomas Reeder
William Hicks
John Reeder, Jr. (E–4)

KENT
Richard Gresham
Alexander Williamson,
   speaker 5, 6R [2]
Hugh Wallis
William Hynson

ANNE ARUNDEL
Henry Hall (D–4)
Charles Carroll (D–4)
John Gassaway
Philip Hammond
Charles Carroll, Barrister
   (E–4)
Brice T. B. Worthington
   (E–5)

CALVERT
William Fitzhugh
Benjamin Mackall, Jr.
James John Mackall
Thomas Reynolds

CHARLES
Bayne Smallwood
John Stoddert
John Jordan
Henry Moore (R–4)
Daniel of St. Thomas Jenifer
   (E–4)

BALTIMORE
William Govane
Walter Tolley
Lloyd Buchanan (Ds–3) [3]
John Paca
William Smith (E–4)

TALBOT
Matthew Tilghman
John Goldsborough
Pollard Edmondson
James Edge (D–6)

SOMERSET
Robert Jenkins Henry
   (C–5) [1]
John Handy (D–6)
John Dennis, Sr.
Henry Waggaman
Levin Gale (E–5)

DORCHESTER
Charles Goldsborough
Henry Travers
Joseph Cox Gray
Henry Hooper, speaker
   1–5R, 6 [2]

CECIL
Nicholas Hyland
Michael Earle
Henry Ward
Henry Baker

ANNAPOLIS
Walter Dulany
Stephen Bordley (Ds–5) [4]
Daniel Dulany, Jr. (E–5)

PRINCE GEORGE'S
John Addison
William Murdock
George Fraser
John Hawkins, Jr. (D–6)
Thomas Gantt (E–6)

QUEEN ANNE'S
Edward Tilghman
Henry Casson
John Bracco
Robert Lloyd

WORCESTER
John Scarborough, Sr.
John Henry
John Dennis, Jr. (S–4)
John Evans
Benjamin Handy (E–4)

FREDERICK
Henry Wright Crabb
Josiah Beall
Edward Sprigg
Joseph Chapline

Committee Service [5]

ELECTIONS AND PRIVILEGES
Stoddert (1–6)
Smallwood (1–6)
J. Goldsborough (1–6)
Hyland (1–6)
M. Tilghman (1–6)
Williamson (1–6)

LAWS
Carroll (1–3)
R. J. Henry (1–4)
M. Tilghman (1–4)
C. Goldsborough (1–4)
Hall (1–4)
Bordley (1–4)
E. Tilghman (1–4)
Chase (1, 2)
R. Lloyd (1–4)
P. Hammond (1–4)
Murdock (4)
Carroll, Barrister (4)

**GRIEVANCES AND COURTS OF
JUSTICE**
Carroll (1–3)
Addison (1–6)
Murdock (1–6)
J. Goldsborough (1–6)
Stoddert (1–6)
Smallwood (1–6)
Fitzhugh (1–6)
E. Tilghman (3)
P. Hammond (3)
C. Goldsborough (3)
M. Tilghman (4–6)
Carroll, Barrister (4)

**BILLS OF CREDIT–PAPER
CURRENCY (JOINT)**
Lee (1, 2, 5)
Chamberlaine (3, 4)
B. Calvert (6)
W. Dulany (1–6)
Earle (1–6)

J. Henry (1–6)
Edge (1–5)
Beall (1–6)
J. Handy (1–3, 5)
Bracco (2, 4–6)
Williamson (4–6)
Hynson (5)
Jenifer (5)
Gassaway (5)
Hawkins (5)
Casson (5)
Smallwood (5)
Reynolds (5)
J. J. Mackall (5)
Govane (5)
Travers (5)
Crabb (5)
Fraser (5)
Paca (6)
R. Lloyd (6)

ACCOUNTS
Murdock (1–6)

J. Goldsborough (1–6)
Stoddert (1–6)
Edge (1–5)
Hawkins (1–5)
Waggaman (5, 6)
J. Henry (6)
Govane (6)

ARMS AND AMMUNITION
Addison (1–4)
J. J. Mackall (1–4)
Crabb (1–4)
Fraser (1–6)
Jordan (1–4)
B. Mackall (4–6)
Paca (5, 6)
Govane (5, 6)
Casson (5, 6)
Fitzhugh (5, 6)
Hyland (5, 6)

[1] Originally elected a delegate to the Lower House, he was appointed to the Council on May 22, 1756.

[2] Williamson was chosen speaker of the Lower House on September 30, 1756, to replace the ailing Henry Hooper. On April 13, 1757, Williamson was reported ill, and Hooper was returned to the speaker's chair.

[3] Buchanan was discharged on June 28, 1755, for acting as prosecutor in the Baltimore County Court.

[4] A new election for a delegate from Annapolis was called for on September 14, 1756, to replace Bordley, who had accepted the offices of attorney general of the province and naval officer of Annapolis.

[5] The Lower House members on all first session standing committee were reappointed to continue in the second through fifth sessions, except the Committee of Laws which ceased to function after the fourth session. The only names relisted in those sessons were the members on the Committee of Bills of Credit-Paper Currency. In the sixth session the members on the committees of Bills of Credit and Accounts were relisted; the members on the committees of Elections and Arms and Ammunition were reappointed, but not relisted; and the members on the Committee of Grievances were neither relisted nor reappointed, but functioned as usual. Therefore, the members on the Committee of Grievances in the first through fifth sessions were credited with continued service in the sixth. It is presumed that Edward Tilghman, Philip Hammond, and Charles Goldsborough, who were added to the Committee of Grievances at the end of the third session, were not included in the reappointment made during the fourth session, and that Charles Carroll, Barrister, who was added to this committee in the middle of the fourth session, was not reappointed in the fifth.

PROPRIETARY ASSEMBLY OF 1757–1758

Frederick Calvert, 6th Lord Baltimore, proprietor
Horatio Sharpe, governor

FIRST SESSION: September 28–December 16, 1757
CONVENTION: February 13–March 9, 1758
SECOND SESSION: March 28–May 13, 1758

UPPER HOUSE

Benjamin Tasker, president
Charles Hammond
Samuel Chamberlaine

Philip Thomas (DNS)
Edward Lloyd
Benjamin Tasker, Jr.

Richard Lee
Benedict Calvert
William Goldsborough

Robert Jenkins Henry
Daniel Dulany, Jr.

LOWER HOUSE

ST. MARY'S
George Plater
John Reeder, Jr.
Henry Greenfield Sothoron
Edmund Key (Ds–1, E–1) [1]

KENT
John Tilden
William Rasin
William Hynson
Alexander Williamson

ANNE ARUNDEL
Brice T. B. Worthington
John Gassaway
Charles Carroll, Barrister
Philip Hammond

CALVERT
Benjamin Mackall
James John Mackall
Thomas Reynolds

Edward Gantt

CHARLES
John Hanson, Jr.
Arthur Lee
George Dent
John Truman Stoddert

BALTIMORE
William Govane
John Hammond Dorsey
Thomas Cockey Deye
Samuel Owings

TALBOT
Pollard Edmondson
Edward Oldham
John Goldsborough
Matthew Tilghman

SOMERSET
Samuel Wilson
Henry Waggaman

Henry Lowes
Levin Gale

DORCHESTER
Henry Hooper, speaker
Joseph Cox Gray
Daniel Sulivane
Philemon Lecompte

CECIL
Nicholas Hyland
Michael Earle
Henry Baker
Henry Ward

ANNAPOLIS
Walter Dulany
George Steuart (EV–1) [2]
Henry Woodward [2]

PRINCE GEORGE'S
Thomas Gantt

George Fraser
Francis King
William Murdock

QUEEN ANNE'S
Robert Lloyd
Emory Sudler
Edward Tilghman
John Bracco

WORCESTER
John Scarborough
John Henry
Benjamin Handy
Benton Harris

FREDERICK
Joseph Chapline
Edward Dorsey
Thomas Beatty
Thomas Cresap

Committee Service [3]

ELECTIONS AND PRIVILEGES
J. Goldsborough (1, Cv, 2)
Hyland (1, Cv, 2)
M. Tilghman (1, Cv, 2)
Williamson (1, Cv, 2)
Carroll (1, Cv, 2)
J. J. Mackall (1, Cv, 2)

GRIEVANCES AND COURTS OF
JUSTICE
Murdock (1, Cv, 2)
J. Goldsborough (1, Cv, 2)
M. Tilghman (1, Cv, 2)
Carroll (1, Cv, 2)
E. Dorsey (1, Cv, 2)
Bracco (1, Cv, 2)
P. Hammond (1, Cv, 2)

E. Tilghman (1, Cv, 2)

ACCOUNTS
Murdock (1, Cv, 2)
J. Goldsborough (1, Cv, 2)
R. Lloyd (1, Cv, 2)
Govane (1, Cv, 2)
Cresap (1, Cv, 2)
Waggaman (1, Cv, 2)
Lowes (1)
Tilden (1)
Hynson (1, Cv, 2)
Gassaway (1, Cv, 2)
Edmondson (1)
Plater (1)
Harris (1)
Sudler (1)

BILLS OF CREDIT–PAPER
CURRENCY (JOINT)
Chamberlaine (1, Cv, 2)
W. Dulany (1, Cv, 2)
Earle (1, Cv, 2)
J. Henry (1, Cv, 2)
R. Lloyd (1, Cv, 2)
Bracco (1, Cv, 2)
Williamson (1, Cv, 2)
M. Tilghman (1, Cv, 2)
Worthington (1, Cv, 2)
Gale (1)
Hanson (1, Cv, 2)

ARMS AND AMMUNITION
J. J. Mackall (1, Cv, 2)
Hyland (1, Cv, 2)

B. Mackall (1, Cv, 2)
Fraser (1, Cv, 2)
A. Lee (1, Cv, 2)
Cresap (1, Cv, 2)
Sudler (Cv)
Dent (Cv, 2)
Handy (2)
Rasin (2)

PUBLIC OFFICES [4]
E. Tilghman (1, Cv, 2)
M. Tilghman (1, Cv, 2)
R. Lloyd (1, Cv, 2)
Carroll (1, Cv, 2)
Murdock (1, Cv, 2)
P. Hammond (1, Cv, 2)
E. Dorsey (1, Cv, 2)

[1] Upon petition of the freeholders of St. Mary's County, Key's election was declared invalid and he was dismissed on October 12, 1757. A new election was called, and Key was returned, requalifying on November 19, 1757.

[2] The petition of Henry Woodward, complaining of the illegal election of Steuart as a delegate from Annapolis, was upheld. On October 1, 1757, the Lower House ordered Steuart's name erased from the election return and Woodward's name inserted in its place.

[3] During the convention the members on the committees of Accounts, Arms and Ammunition, Bills of Credit–Paper Currency, and Public Offices were relisted. During this same session the members on the committees of Elections and Grievances appointed in the first session were appointed to continue, but were not relisted. The members of all standing committees appointed in the convention were reappointed to continue in the second session, but the only names relisted were those of the members on the Committee of Bills of Credit–Paper Currency.

[4] This committee was established as a "Committee to inspect into the several Public Offices, and Report to the House the State and Condition thereof."

PROPRIETARY ASSEMBLY OF 1758–1761

Frederick Calvert, 6th Lord Baltimore, proprietor

Horatio Sharpe, governor

FIRST CONVENTION: October 23–November 4, 1758
FIRST SESSION: November 22–December 23, 1758
SECOND CONVENTION: April 4–17, 1759
SECOND SESSION: March 22–April 11, 1760
THIRD SESSION: September 26–October 15, 1760
THIRD CONVENTION: April 13–May 6, 1761

UPPER HOUSE

Benjamin Tasker, president
Charles Hammond
Samuel Chamberlaine
Philip Thomas

Edward Lloyd
Benjamin Tasker, Jr.
(D–Cv3)
Richard Lee

Benedict Calvert
William Goldsborough
(D–3)
Robert Jenkins Henry

Daniel Dulany, Jr.
Stephen Bordley (A–Cv2)
John Ridout (A–Cv3)

LOWER HOUSE

ST. MARY'S
Edmund Key (R–2)
Henry Greenfield Sothoron
George Plater
Thomas Greenfield
William Thomas (E–3)

KENT
Alexander Williamson
(D–3)
Richard Gresham
John Tilden
William Hynson
Thomas Ringgold (E–Cv3)

ANNE ARUNDEL
Brice T. B. Worthington
Philip Hammond (D–3)
Charles Carroll, Barrister
John Gassaway
John Hammond (E–3)

CALVERT
Benjamin Mackall, Jr.
James John Mackall

William Fitzhugh
Edward Gantt

CHARLES
Arthur Lee (D–3)
John Hanson, Jr.
John Truman Stoddert
George Dent
William Smallwood
(E–Cv3)

BALTIMORE
Thomas Cockey Deye
William Govane
John Hammond Dorsey
Samuel Owings

TALBOT
John Goldsborough
Pollard Edmondson
Samuel Bowman
Woolman Gibson

SOMERSET
Henry Waggaman (D–Cv3)

Levin Gale
Samuel Wilson
William Waters, Sr.

DORCHESTER
Henry Hooper, speaker
Charles Goldsborough
Daniel Sulivane
Henry Travers

CECIL
Michael Earle
Henry Baker
Henry Ward (D–3)
Francis Mauldin
John Veazey (E–Cv3)

ANNAPOLIS
Walter Dulany
George Steuart (EV–1,
E–Cv2) [1]

PRINCE GEORGE'S
William Murdock

George Fraser
Francis King
Josias Beall, Jr.

QUEEN ANNE'S
William Hopper
Edward Tilghman
Robert Lloyd
Thomas Harris (D–2)
Matthew Tilghman (E–3)

WORCESTER
Benton Harris
John Scarborough
Benjamin Handy (S–1)
Zadock Purnell
Parker Selby (E–Cv2)

FREDERICK
Henry Wright Crabb
Joseph Chapline
Edward Dorsey (D–3)
Thomas Cresap
Nathan Magruder (E–Cv3)

Committee Service [2]

ELECTIONS AND PRIVILEGES
J. Goldsborough (Cv1, 1,
Cv2, 3, Cv3)
Williamson (Cv1, 1, Cv2, 2)
Carroll (Cv1, 1, Cv2, 2, 3,
Cv3)
E. Dorsey (Cv1, 1, Cv2, 2)
Key (Cv1, 1, Cv2)
Murdock (Cv1, 1, Cv2, 2, 3,
Cv3)
Fitzhugh (2)
R. Lloyd (2, 3, Cv3)
M. Tilghman (3, Cv3)

GRIEVANCES AND COURTS OF
JUSTICE
Murdock (Cv1, 1, Cv2, 2, 3,
Cv3)
J. Goldsborough (Cv1, 1,
Cv2)
Carroll (Cv1, 1, Cv2, 2, 3,
Cv3)

E. Dorsey (Cv1, 1, Cv2, 2)
E. Tilghman (Cv1, 1, Cv2,
2, 3, Cv3)
R. Lloyd (Cv1, 1, Cv2, 2, 3,
Cv3)
Gassaway (Cv1, 1, Cv2, 2,
3, Cv3)
C. Goldsborough (3, Cv3)
M. Tilghman (3, Cv3)
J. Hammond (3, Cv3)

ACCOUNTS
Murdock (Cv1, 1, Cv2, 2, 3,
Cv3)
J. Goldsborough (Cv1, 1,
Cv2, 3, Cv3)
Gassaway (Cv1, 1, Cv2, 2,
3, Cv3)
Waggaman (Cv1, 1, Cv2)
Govane (Cv1, 1, Cv2, 2, 3,
Cv3)

Cresap (Cv1, 1, Cv2, 3,
Cv3)
Hynson (Cv1, 1, Cv2, 2, 3,
Cv3)
Travers (2, 3, Cv3)
Sulivane (2, 3, Cv3)

BILLS OF CREDIT–PAPER
CURRENCY (JOINT)
R. Lee (Cv1, Cv2)
B. Calvert (1, Cv3)
Chamberlaine (2, 3)
W. Dulany (Cv1, 1, Cv2, 2,
3, Cv3)
Earle (Cv1, 1, Cv2, 2, 3)
R. Lloyd (Cv1, 1, Cv2, 2, 3)
Williamson (Cv1, 1, Cv2, 2)
Worthington (Cv1, 1, Cv2,
2, 3, Cv3)
Hanson (Cv1, 1, Cv2, 2, 3,
Cv3)
Plater (Cv1, 1, Cv2)

Beall (1, Cv2, 2, Cv3)
Gale (1)
Stoddert (2, 3, Cv3)
Ringgold (Cv3)

ARMS AND AMMUNITION
Cresap (Cv1, 1, Cv2, 3,
Cv3)
Scarborough (Cv1, 1, Cv2)
J. H. Dorsey (Cv1, 1, Cv2,
2)
Deye (Cv1, 1, Cv2, 2)
Baker (Cv1, 1, Cv2)
Fitzhugh (2)
Dent (2)
Fraser (2, 3, Cv3)
Ward (2)
Chapline (3, Cv3)
King (3, Cv3)
Stoddert (3, Cv3)

PUBLIC OFFICES
E. Tilghman (Cv1, 1, Cv2, 2, 3, Cv3)
R. Lloyd (Cv1, 1, Cv2, 2, 3, Cv3)

Carroll (Cv1, 1, Cv2, 2, 3, Cv3)
Murdock (Cv1, 1, Cv2, 2, 3, Cv3)
E. Dorsey (Cv1, 1, Cv2, 2)

Wilson (Cv1, 1)
Govane (Cv1, 1, Cv2, 2, 3, Cv3)
King (2, 3, Cv3)
J. H. Dorsey (Cv3)

B. Harris (Cv3)
Smallwood (Cv3)

[1] The validity of Steuart's election as a delegate from Annapolis was again questioned through petition from Henry Woodward, who sought to disqualify some of the votes cast for his opponent. After some discussion, both parties agreed to avoid "giving the House any further Trouble in this Controversy," and requested that the election "so far as it concerns them should be declared Void." The Lower House called for a new election, at which time Steuart was again returned. He requalified on April 4, 1759.

[2] The members on all Lower House standing committees appointed during the first convention were reapointed to continue in the first session and second convention, but the only names relisted were the members on the Committee of Bills of Credit–Paper Currency. All committees were individually relisted in the second and third sessions. During the third convention the Lower House members of all third session standing comittees were reappointed to continue, but again the only names relisted were the members on the Committee of Bills of Credit–Paper Currency. An Upper House member of this committee was named each session.

PROPRIETARY ASSEMBLY OF 1762–1763

Frederick Calvert, 6th Lord Baltimore, proprietor

Horatio Sharpe, governor

FIRST SESSION: March 17–April 24, 1762
SECOND SESSION: October 4–November 26, 1763

UPPER HOUSE

Benjamin Tasker, president
Charles Hammond
Samuel Chamberlaine
Philip Thomas (DNS, D–2)

Edward Lloyd
Richard Lee
Benedict Calvert
Robert Jenkins Henry

Daniel Dulany
Stephen Bordley
John Ridout

Charles Goldsborough (A–2) [1]
Philip Key (A–2)

LOWER HOUSE

ST. MARY'S
Henry Greenfield Sothoron
Edmund Key
George Plater
John Hall

KENT
William Hynson
Richard Lloyd
Simon Wilmer
Thomas Ringgold

ANNE ARUNDEL
Thomas Johnson, Jr.
John Hammond
Brice T. B. Worthington
Henry Hall

CALVERT
Charles Grahame
James John Mackall
Benjamin Mackall
Edward Gantt

CHARLES
William Smallwood
John Truman Stoddert
George Dent
John Hanson, Jr.

BALTIMORE
John Paca
Thomas Cockey Deye
John Hammond Dorsey
Corbin Lee

TALBOT
Pollard Edmondson
James Tilghman
John Goldsborough
William Thomas

SOMERSET
William Hayward
William Waters
John Adams
William Adams

DORCHESTER
Henry Hooper, speaker
Joseph Cox Gray
Daniel Sulivane
Charles Goldsborough (C–2) [1]
Henry Steele (E–2)

CECIL
Michael Earle
Henry Baker
Francis Mauldin (DNS, D–1)
William Ward
Nathan Baker (E–2)

ANNAPOLIS
George Steuart
Walter Dulany

PRINCE GEORGE'S
William Murdock
Mordecai Jacob

Josias Beall, Jr.
Francis Waring

QUEEN ANNE'S
Robert Lloyd
Edward Tilghman
James Hollyday
Thomas Wright

WORCESTER
Benton Harris
Parker Selby
William Allen
Peter Chaille

FREDERICK
Joseph Chapline
Nathan Magruder
Thomas Beatty
Thomas Cresap

ELECTIONS AND PRIVILEGES		ARMS AND AMMUNITION	
J. Goldsborough (1, 2)	W. Thomas (2)	B. Mackall (1, 2)	Beall (1, 2)
Allen (1, 2)	Allen (2)	Selby (1)	Stoddert (1, 2)
J. Hall (1, 2)	E. Key (2)	J. J. Mackall (1, 2)	Earle (1, 2)
Edmondson (1, 2)	Harris (2)	Smallwood (1, 2)	Grahame (1, 2)
Ringgold (1, 2)		W. Thomas (1, 2)	H. Hall (1, 2)
Harris (1, 2)	GRIEVANCES AND COURTS OF	Cresap (2)	
Jacob (2)	JUSTICE	W. Adams (2)	PUBLIC OFFICES
	J. Tilghman (1, 2)		J. Hammond (1, 2)
ACCOUNTS	Steuart (1, 2)	BILLS OF CREDIT-PAPER	Allen (1, 2)
J. Goldsborough (1, 2)	H. Hall (1, 2)	CURRENCY (JOINT)	J. Hall (1)
Hayward (1, 2)	W. Dulany (1, 2)	Chamberlaine (1)	E. Tilghman (1)
Waring (1, 2)	E. Tilghman (1, 2)	B. Calvert (2)	Ringgold (1, 2)
Sulivane (1, 2)	Robert Lloyd (1, 2)	W. Dulany (1, 2)	Harris (1, 2)
Hynson (1, 2)	J. Hall (1, 2)	Worthington (1, 2)	Chaille (1, 2)
Dent (1, 2)	J. Adams (2)	Hanson (1, 2)	Johnson (2)
Richard Lloyd (1)	J. Hammond (2)	Ringgold (1, 2)	E. Key (2)
	Beall (2)	Robert Lloyd (1, 2)	

[1] Originally elected a delegate to the Lower House, he was appointed to the Council in July 1762.

PROPRIETARY ASSEMBLY OF 1765–1766

Frederick Calvert, 6th Lord Baltimore, proprietor

Horatio Sharpe, governor

FIRST SESSION: September 23–28, 1765
SECOND SESSION: November 1–December 20, 1765
THIRD SESSION: May 9–27, 1766
FOURTH SESSION: November 1–December 6, 1766

UPPER HOUSE

Benjamin Tasker, president	Edward Lloyd	Robert Jenkins Henry	John Ridout
Charles Hammond	Richard Lee	(D–4)	Charles Goldsborough
Samuel Chamberlaine	Benedict Calvert	Daniel Dulany	Henry Hooper (A–1)

LOWER HOUSE

ST. MARY'S
Henry Greenfield Sothoron
Daniel Wolstenholme
George Plater
Edmund Key (D–3)
Thomas Key (E–4)

KENT
Thomas Ringgold
Robert Buchanan
Richard Lloyd
William Hynson

ANNE ARUNDEL
Thomas Johnson, Jr.
Henry Hall
John Hammond
Brice T. B. Worthington

CALVERT
Edward Gantt
Benjamin Mackall
Charles Grahame

Young Parran

CHARLES
John Truman Stoddert
  (DNS, D–1)
William Smallwood
George Dent
John Hanson, Jr.
Francis Ware (E–1)

BALTIMORE
Thomas Cockey Deye
Corbin Lee
James Heath (D–4)
John Hall, Jr.

TALBOT
Pollard Edmondson
John Goldsborough
Woolman Gibson
Henry Hollyday

SOMERSET
William Winder

William Adams
John Adams
Samuel Wilson

DORCHESTER
Daniel Sulivane
Robert Goldsborough III
Philemon Lecompte
Henry Travers (D–2)
John Henry (E–3)

CECIL
Michael Earle
Henry Baker
Nicholas Hyland
William Ward

ANNAPOLIS
Samuel Chase
Walter Dulany (Ds–1, E–2,
  EV–2) [1]
John Hall (E–2)

PRINCE GEORGE'S
Josias Beall
William Murdock
Mordecai Jacob
Robert Tyler

QUEEN ANNE'S
Edward Tilghman
James Hollyday
Robert Lloyd, speaker
Thomas Wright

WORCESTER
Peter Chaille
William Allen
Parker Selby
Benton Harris

FREDERICK
Thomas Cresap
Joseph Chapline
James Smith
Fielder Gantt

ELECTIONS AND PRIVILEGES
Edmondson (2, 4)
Jacob (2, 4)
Travers (2)
H. Hollyday (2, 4)
Ward (2)
H. Hall (4)
Wright (4)

ACCOUNTS
J. Goldsborough (2, 3)
Hynson (2)
Sulivane (2–4)
Dent (2, 4)
Wright (2–4)
R. Goldsborough (2, 3)
Hanson (3, 4)
Earle (4)

GRIEVANCES AND COURTS OF
JUSTICE
W. Dulany (2)
J. Hammond (2–4)
Tilghman (2–4)
Murdock (2–4)

Hyland (2)
E. Gantt (2–4)
Chase (2, 3)
J. Adams (2, 3)
J. Hall, Jr. (2)
Cresap (2, 3)
Wolstenholme (2)
Smallwood (2)
Hynson (2)
J. Goldsborough (2)
Travers (2)
Selby (2, 3)
Jacob (3, 4)
Johnson (3)
Harris (3)
Allen (3, 4)
J. Hall (Annapolis) (4)

BILLS OF CREDIT–PAPER
CURRENCY (JOINT)
Chamberlaine (2)
B. Calvert (2, 4)
W. Dulany (2)
Worthington (2, 4)
Beall (2, 4)

Hanson (2, 4)
Grahame (2, 4)
Richard Lloyd (2, 4)
Wilson (2)
Ringgold (2, 4)
H. Hall (2, 4)
Earle (2, 4)
Buchanan (2)

ARMS AND AMMUNITION
Cresap (2)
W. Adams (2, 4)
Smallwood (2, 4)
Ware (2, 4)
Edmondson (2)

PUBLIC OFFICES [3]
Tyler (2–4)
Parran (2–4)
H. Hollyday (2)
Chase (2, 3)
Harris (2)
J. Hammond (2–4)
Johnson (2, 3)
J. Hall (Annapolis) (2–4)

R. Goldsborough (2)
Plater (2, 3)
H. Hall (3, 4)
J. Hall, Jr. (3)
Worthington (3, 4)
Wilson (3, 4)
Ringgold (3, 4)
Wolstenholme (3)
Beall (3)
Grahame (3)

LAWS TO EXPIRE [4]
J. Goldsborough (2, 3)
Johnson (2, 3)
Tilghman (2)
J. Hammond (2, 4)
Chase (2, 3)
J. Henry (3)
Grahame (4)
Hanson (4)
Wilson (4)
J. Hall (Annapolis) (4)
Worthington (4)

[1] Dulany was discharged on September 24, 1765, for accepting the office of naval officer of the Patuxent after his election. He was reelected, and returned November 1, 1765. The Annapolis voters, however, protested his election. They claimed that in addition to other improper procedures during the election, Dulany, who was mayor of Annapolis, "continued. . . on the Bench during the Time of the Election and. . . did Object to the Qualifications of some of the Voters who offered to vote against him." On November 12 the House declared that Dulany had been unduly elected.

[2] There were no committee assignments in the first session of this Assembly, and there is no evidence that the committees of Elections, Bills of Credit–Paper Currency, and Arms and Ammunition functioned during the third session.

[3] The function of the Public Offices Committee was slightly redefined to include inspection "into the several papers and records in the Public Offices." Formerly the committee had been primarily interested in the structures that housed the public records rather than with the records themselves.

[4] The Committee on Laws to Expire was first appointed during the fifth session of the 1754–1757 Assembly and was charged to "revise the laws, and make report to the House what laws will expire with the close of this session, unless they have a revival." It became a standing committee in 1765.

PROPRIETARY ASSEMBLY OF 1768–1770

Frederick Calvert, 6th Lord Baltimore, proprietor

Horatio Sharpe, governor 1

Robert Eden, governor 2–4

FIRST SESSION: May 24–June 22, 1768
SECOND SESSION: November 17–December 20, 1769
THIRD SESSION: September 25–November 2, 1770
FOURTH SESSION: November 5–21, 1770

UPPER HOUSE

Benjamin Tasker, president 1 (D–1)
Charles Hammond [1]
Samuel Chamberlaine (R–2)
Edward Lloyd (DNS, R–2)
Richard Lee
Benedict Calvert
Daniel Dulany
John Ridout
Walter Dulany
John Beale Bordley
George Steuart (A–2)
William Fitzhugh (A–2)
William Hayward (A–3) [2]

LOWER HOUSE

ST. MARY'S
William Thomas
Thomas Key
John Eden
Daniel Wolstenholme

KENT
Robert Buchanan
Thomas Ringgold
Stephen Bordley
Richard Gresham

ANNE ARUNDEL
Samuel Chase
Brice T. B. Worthington, speaker 4R [3]
Thomas Johnson, Jr.
Henry Griffith

CALVERT
Benjamin Mackall, of James John
Young Parran
Edward Gantt
Charles Grahame

CHARLES
Francis Ware

William Smallwood
John Hanson, Jr. (Ds–2) [4]
Joseph Hanson Harrison
Robert Hendly Courts (E–3)

BALTIMORE [5]
John Ridgely (EV–1, E–2, EV–2)
Thomas Cockey Deye (EV–1, E–3)
John Moale (EV–1, E–2, EV–2)
Robert Adair (EV–1, E–2, EV–2)
George Risteau (E–2, EV–2)
John Paca (E–3)
Aquila Hall (E–3)
John Matthews (E–3)

TALBOT
John Goldsborough
Matthew Tilghman
James Dickinson
Nicholas Thomas

SOMERSET
Levin Gale
Samuel Wilson
William Hayward (C–3) [2]
Thomas Dashiell
William Adams (E–3)

DORCHESTER
Henry Hooper, Jr.
Daniel Sulivane
Philemon Lecompte (DNS, D–2)
Henry Steele
Edward Noel (E–2)

CECIL
John Veazey
William Ward
William Baxter
Henry Baker (D–2)
Joseph Gilpin (E–3)

ANNAPOLIS
John Hall
William Paca

PRINCE GEORGE'S
Josias Beall
Robert Tyler

William Murdock (D–2)
Francis Waring (DNS, D–2)
Thomas Contee (E–2)
Mordecai Jacob (E–2)

QUEEN ANNE'S
Robert Lloyd, speaker 1, 2 (D–3) [3]
Edward Tilghman, speaker 3, 4R, 4 [3]
James Hollyday
Thomas Wright
William Hopper (E–3)

WORCESTER
William Allen
Parker Selby (S–3)
Joseph Dashiell
Zadock Purnell

FREDERICK
William Luckett
Thomas Cresap
Joseph Chapline (D–2)
Thomas Jennings (Ds–2) [6]
Andrew Heugh (E–2)
Thomas Sprigg Wooton (E–2)

ELECTIONS AND PRIVILEGES
Ward (1–3)
Hayward (1, 2)
Steele (1)
Goldsborough (1–3)
M. Tilghman (1–3)
J. Hall (3)
S. Bordley (3)

ACCOUNTS
Goldsborough (1–3)
Sulivane (1, 2)
Wright (1–3)
Steele (1)
Dickinson (1–3)
Hooper (3)
Gilpin (3)
A. Hall (3)

PUBLIC OFFICES
Tyler (1–3)
Parran (1)
Chase (1)
Johnson (1)
Hayward (1)
Goldsborough (1)
Mackall (1–3)
Worthington (1)

N. Thomas (1)
S. Bordley (1)
Hooper (2, 3)
Beall (2)
Harrison (2, 3)
J. Hall (2, 3)
Purnell (2, 3)
Buchanan (2)
Moale (2)
Griffith (2, 3)
Gantt (2, 3)
Selby (2, 3)
W. Thomas (2, 3)

GRIEVANCES AND COURTS OF JUSTICE
Murdock (1)
Hayward (1, 2)
Allen (1, 2, 4)
N. Thomas (1–3)
Cresap (1)
Hooper (1–3)
S. Bordley (1–3)
Parran (1)
Worthington (1–4)
Ridgely (1)
Veazey (1, 2)
Ware (1–3)

Hollyday (1–3)
Wolstenholme (1)
Jennings (1)
Johnson (1–4)
E. Tilghman (2)
Chase (2, 3)
Harrison (2, 4)
Gale (3)
Selby (3)
Ward (3)
Luckett (3)
J. Paca (3)
Gantt (3)
W. Thomas (3)
Tyler (3, 4)
W. Paca (3)
Wright (3)
Buchanan (3)
Beall (4)
Mackall (4)

LAWS TO EXPIRE
Johnson (1)
Goldsborough (1–3)
N. Thomas (1–4)
Wilson (2)
Chase (3, 4)
Ringgold (4)

W. Paca (4)

CLAIMS–BILLS OF CREDIT (JOINT)[8]
B. Calvert (1–4)
W. Dulany (1–4)
Ringgold (1–4)
Dickinson (1, 2, 4)
Steele (1–3)
Worthington (1–4)
Beall (1, 2, 4)
Grahame (1–4)
Hanson (1)
Eden (1, 3)
Tyler (1)
Buchanan (1)
Wilson (2)
Contee (3, 4)
Parran (3)

ARMS AND AMMUNITION
Cresap (1–3)
Smallwood (1–3)
Ware (1–3)
Purnell (1–3)
Griffith (1–3)

[1] After the death of Benjamin Tasker, Hammond assumed the senior position, but is not referred to as president in the proceedings.

[2] Originally elected a delegate to the Lower House, he was appointed to the Council on September 24, 1770.

[3] Tilghman was chosen speaker at the beginning of the third session to fill the vacancy caused by Lloyd's death. He continued as speaker through the fourth session except for a period of three days (November 9–11) when illness forced him to withdraw. Worthington served as speaker during Tilghman's absence.

[4] Hanson was discharged on November 25, 1769, after accepting the office of deputy surveyor of Frederick County.

[5] The original election of delegates from Baltimore County was declared void on June 14, 1768, after complaints of "treating" and other irregularities were brought by John Hammond Dorsey, Charles Ridgely, Jr., and others. A second election was held on July 5, 1768. Three members of the original delegation were returned, with only Thomas Cockey Deye being unseated and George Risteau selected in his place. However, on November 18, 1769, a petition from sundry Baltimore inhabitants complaining of misconduct by the sheriff was presented to the Lower House at Deye's request. Consequently, on November 30, this election was also voided. Although Robert Adair had died one month before the beginning of the second session, no notice of his death had been given by the Lower House, and his election was voided with the others by this action. The third election returned Deye to his seat, along with John Paca, Aquila Hall, and John Matthews.

[6] Thomas Jennings was discharged on November 17, 1769, after accepting the office of attorney general.

[7] In the third session the members of the Committee on Arms and Ammunition were reappointed to continue as in the second session. However, as there was no appointment made in the second session, it is presumed that the original members named in the first continued to serve in the second and third sessions. There is no evidence that the committees of Elections, Accounts, Public Offices, and Arms and Ammunition functioned during the fourth session.

[8] The Committee of Claims was named to "inspect the accounts and proceedings of the commissioners appointed by virtue of the Act of 1765 (Chapter 38) for the payment of the public claims, for emitting bills of credit and for other purposes therein mentioned." Although this committee served essentially the same function, it technically superseded the Committee to Inspect the Accounts and Proceedings of the Commissioners for Emitting Bills of Credit (also known as the Committee to Inspect the Loan Office) which was abolished by the same Act of 1765.

PROPRIETARY ASSEMBLY OF 1771

Frederick Calvert, 6th Lord Baltimore, proprietor

Robert Eden, governor

October 2–November 30, 1771

UPPER HOUSE

Charles Hammond
Richard Lee (DNS)
Benedict Calvert

Daniel Dulany
John Ridout
Walter Dulany
John Beale Bordley

George Steuart
William Fitzhugh
William Hayward

Daniel of St. Thomas Jenifer
George Plater

LOWER HOUSE

ST. MARY'S
John Reeder, Jr.
Thomas Key (DNS)
William Thomas
Jeremiah Jordan

KENT
Thomas Ringgold (DNS)
Richard Gresham
Stephan Bordley (DNS, D)
Robert Buchanan
William Ringgold (E)

ANNE ARUNDEL
Brice T. B. Worthington
Thomas Johnson, Jr.
Samuel Chase
John Hammond

CALVERT
John Weems
Charles Grahame

Young Parran
Benjamin Mackall IV

CHARLES
Josias Hawkins (Ds, E) [1]
Francis Ware (Ds, E) [1]
William Smallwood
Joseph Hanson Harrison

BALTIMORE
Samuel Owings, Jr.
John Moale
George Risteau
Thomas Cockey Deye

TALBOT
Edward Lloyd
James Lloyd Chamberlaine
Nicholas Thomas
Matthew Tilghman

SOMERSET
Levin Gale

Littleton Dennis
Isaac Handy
John Adams

DORCHESTER
Henry Steele
William Ennalls
Joseph Richardson
William Richardson

CECIL
John Veazey
Benjamin Rumsey
William Baxter
William Ward

ANNAPOLIS
John Hall
William Paca

PRINCE GEORGE'S
Joseph Sim
Robert Tyler

Josias Beall
Thomas Contee

QUEEN ANNE'S
Edward Tilghman, speaker
Richard Tilghman Earle
Thomas Wright
Solomon Wright

WORCESTER
Nehemiah Holland
John Purnell Robins
William Allen
Peter Chaille

FREDERICK
Jonathan Hagar (Ds, E) [2]
William Luckett
Charles Beatty
Thomas Sprigg Wooton

Committee Service

ELECTIONS AND PRIVILEGES
M. Tilghman
Chase
Hall
S. Wright
J. Hammond

ACCOUNTS
T. Wright
W. Richardson
Earle
Deye
Chamberlaine

GRIEVANCES AND COURTS OF JUSTICE
Beall
Tyler
Harrison
Mackall
Worthington
Chamberlaine
Johnson
Chase
Paca
Dennis

CLAIMS–BILLS OF CREDIT (JOINT)
B. Calvert
W. Dulany
Contee
Parran
Jordan
Rumsey
Ennalls
Worthington
Beall
Grahame

PUBLIC OFFICES
Tyler
Mackall
Harrison
W. Thomas
Handy
S. Wright
Ennalls
Steele

LAWS TO EXPIRE
Chase
Handy
N. Thomas

[1] A petition was presented by Robert Hendly Courts of Charles County complaining about the improper election of Ware and Hawkins, charging them with "treating" at the polls. A new election was ordered on October 14, 1771. Both men were reelected and qualified on November 18, 1771.

[2] The Committee of Elections and Privileges reported on October 5, 1771, that Hagar, although a naturalized Marylander, was "not a natural born Subject nor descended from a natural born Subject." He was determined to be ineligible for election and discharged on October 8. Three days later the Lower House introduced a bill that allowed naturalized subjects "all the Rights and Privileges of natural born Subjects." This bill became law on October 16. Hagar was reelected and qualified on November 16, but the dispute over his election continued.

PROPRIETARY ASSEMBLY OF 1773–1774

Henry Harford, proprietor
Robert Eden, governor

FIRST SESSION: June 15–July 3, 1773
CONVENTION: October 13–29, 1773 [1]
SECOND SESSION: November 16–December 23, 1773
THIRD SESSION: March 23–April 19, 1774

UPPER HOUSE

Richard Lee
Benedict Calvert
Daniel Dulany
John Ridout

Walter Dulany (D–Cv)
John Beale Bordley
George Steuart

William Fitzhugh
William Hayward
Daniel of St. Thomas Jenifer

George Plater
Benjamin Ogle (A–Cv)
Philip Thomas Lee (A–Cv)

LOWER HOUSE

ST. MARY'S
John Reeder, Jr.
Philip Key
Richard Barnes
Thomas Bond

KENT
Robert Buchanan
William Ringgold
John Maxwell
Emory Sudler

ANNE ARUNDEL
Samuel Chase
Thomas Johnson, Jr.
Brice T. B. Worthington
John Hall

CALVERT
Alexander Somerville
John Weems, Jr.
William Lyles
Richard Parran

CHARLES
Francis Ware

Robert Hendly Courts
 (D–3)
Josias Hawkins
William Smallwood

BALTIMORE
Charles Ridgely
Thomas Cockey Deye
Aquila Hall (R–2) [2]
Walter Tolley, Jr.
Charles Ridgely, of John
 (E–3)

TALBOT
Matthew Tilghman, speaker
James Lloyd Chamberlaine
Nicholas Thomas
Edward Lloyd

SOMERSET
Littleton Dennis (DNS)
Levin Gale (DNS)
Samuel Wilson
Peter Waters

DORCHESTER

William Ennalls
John Ennalls
Thomas White (R–2) [3]
William Richardson
Henry Steele (E–3)

CECIL
John Veazey
William Ward
Joseph Gilpin
Stephen Hyland

ANNAPOLIS
William Paca
Matthias Hammond

PRINCE GEORGE'S
Josias Beall
Robert Tyler
Joseph Sim
Thomas Contee

QUEEN ANNE'S
Solomon Wright
Richard Tilghman Earle
John Brown

Turbutt Wright

WORCESTER
Peter Chaille
William Purnell
John Purnell Robins
Nehemiah Holland

FREDERICK
Thomas Sprigg Wooton
Charles Beatty
Jonathan Hagar (Ds–Cv) [4]
Henry Griffith
Jacob Funk (E–2)

HARFORD [5]
Thomas Bond, of Thomas
 (E–3)
John Love (E–3)
Richard Dallam (E–3)
Aquila Hall (E–3) [2]

CAROLINE [5]
Thomas White (E–3) [3]

ELECTIONS AND PRIVILEGES
T. Wright (1, Cv, 2, 3)
Hammond (1, Cv, 2, 3)
Chase (1, Cv)
J. Hall (1, Cv, 2, 3)
Johnson (1, Cv)
Wooton (2, 3)
Lyles (2, 3)
Paca (2, 3)

GRIEVANCES AND COURTS OF
JUSTICE
Beall (1, Cv, 2, 3)
Tyler (1, Cv)
Worthington (1, Cv)
Johnson (1, Cv)
Chamberlaine (1, Cv, 2, 3)
Paca (1, Cv, 2, 3)
Thomas (1, Cv, 2, 3)
Lloyd (Cv, 2, 3)
Reeder (2, 3)

Deye (2, 3)

ACCOUNTS
Chamberlaine (1, Cv, 2, 3)
Richardson (1, Cv, 2, 3)
Deye (1, Cv, 2, 3)
Contee (1)
Sim (1, Cv, 2, 3)
Barnes (1, Cv)
Earle (1, Cv, 2, 3)
Wooton (Cv, 2, 3)
Veazey (Cv, 2, 3)
Griffith (Cv, 2, 3)
Tolley (Cv)
Weems (2, 3)

LAWS TO EXPIRE
S. Wright (1, 2)
Beall (1, Cv, 2)
Chase (1, Cv, 3)
Richardson (2)
T. Wright (2)

Johnson (3)
Paca (3)

CLAIMS–BILLS OF CREDIT
(JOINT)
Calvert (1, Cv, 2, 3)
Jenifer (1, Cv, 2, 3)
Worthington (1, Cv)
Beall (1, Cv, 2)
T. Wright (1, Cv, 2)
Key (1, Cv)
Bond (St. Mary's) (1, Cv, 2,
3)
Sudler (1, Cv, 2)
Wilson (1)
Contee (Cv, 2, 3)
Parran (2, 3)
Hawkins (2, 3)
Gilpin (2, 3)

PUBLIC OFFICES
Tyler (1, Cv)

Thomas (1, Cv, 2, 3)
Hawkins (1, 2, 3)
Griffith (1, Cv, 2, 3)
Ridgely (1)
J. Hall (1, Cv, 2, 3)
Ringgold (1, 2, 3)
Wooton (1, Cv, 2, 3)
Buchanan (1)
Smallwood (2, 3)
S. Wright (2, 3)

ARMS AND AMMUNITION
Lloyd (2, 3)
Ware (2, 3)
Sim (2, 3)
Deye (2, 3)
Weems (2, 3)
Griffith (2, 3)
Veazey (2, 3)

[1] On October 28, 1773, unexpectedly and without notice to the governor or Upper House, the Lower House adjourned itself to "consult their Constituents on the present distressed Circumstances of the Province." The following day, the governor, acting with the advice of the Council, prorogued the Assembly until November 16, 1773.

[2] Hall, originally a delegate from Baltimore County, was elected to represent the newly formed Harford County by the third session.

[3] White, originally a delegate from Dorchester County, was elected to represent the newly formed Caroline County by the third session.

[4] The dispute over Hagar's right to a seat in the Assembly continued from the preceding Assembly. Arguing that the Assembly should have been immediately dissolved after the death of the proprietor in September 1771, the Lower House determined that the act investing naturalized subjects with the same rights as natural born subjects "was not enacted by legal and Constitutional authority, and is therefore void." Hagar was then ruled ineligible to hold a seat in the Assembly, and was discharged on October 15, 1773.

[5] Harford and Caroline counties were formed by acts of the Assembly passed during the second session.

[6] No members were appointed to the Committee of Arms and Ammunition in either the first session or the convention. The members on all Lower House committees appointed in the second session were reappointed to continue in the third, but the only names relisted were the members on the committees of Laws to Expire and Claims–Bills of Credit.

PROVISIONAL GOVERNMENT OF 1774–1776 [1]

FIRST CONVENTION [2]

June 22–25, 1774

ST. MARY'S
Abraham Barnes
Henry Greenfield Sothoron
Jeremiah Jordan

KENT*
Thomas Smyth
William Ringgold
Joseph Nicholson, Jr.
Thomas Ringgold
Joseph Earle
William Hall (DNS)

ANNE ARUNDEL*
Brice T. B. Worthington
Charles Carroll, Barrister
John Hall
William Paca
Samuel Chase
Thomas Johnson
Matthias Hammond
Thomas Sprigg (DNS)
Samuel Chew
John Weems
Thomas Dorsey
Rezin Hammond
John Hood, Jr. (DNS)

CALVERT*
Alexander Somerville
  (DNS)
John Weems, Jr.
William Lyles (DNS)
Edward Reynolds
Benjamin Mackall IV
Richard Parran (DNS)

CHARLES*
William Smallwood
Francis Ware
Josias Hawkins
Joseph Hanson Harrison
Daniel Jenifer
John Dent
Thomas Stone
Walter Hanson (DNS)
Robert Townshend Hooe
  (DNS)

BALTIMORE*
Charles Ridgely
Thomas Cockey Deye
Walter Tolley, Jr.
Robert Alexander
William Lux
Samuel Purviance, Jr.
George Risteau
Charles Ridgely, of John
  (DNS)
John Moale (DNS)
Andrew Buchanan (DNS)

TALBOT
Matthew Tilghman,
  chairman
Edward Lloyd
Nicholas Thomas
Robert Goldsborough IV

SOMERSET
Peter Waters
John Waters
George Dashiell

DORCHESTER
Robert Goldsborough
William Ennalls
Henry Steele
John Ennalls
Robert Harrison
Henry Hooper
Matthew Brown

CECIL
John Veazey, Jr.
William Ward
Stephen Hyland

PRINCE GEORGE'S
Robert Tyler
Joseph Sim
Joshua Beall
John Rogers
Addison Murdock
William Bowie
Benjamin Hall, of Francis
Osborn Sprigg

QUEEN ANNE'S
Turbutt Wright
Richard Tilghman Earle
Solomon Wright
John Brown
Thomas Wright

WORCESTER
Peter Chaille
John Done
William Morris

FREDERICK*
Lower District:

Henry Griffith
Thomas Sprigg Wooton
Nathan Magruder (DNS)
Evan Thomas
Richard Brooke
Richard Thomas
Zadock Magruder (DNS)
William Baker (DNS)
Thomas Cramphin, Jr.
Allen Bowie

Middle District:

John Hanson, Jr. (DNS)
Thomas Price
George Scott (DNS)
Benjamin Dulany (DNS)
George Murdock (DNS)
Philip Thomas
Alexander Contee Hanson
Baker Johnson
Andrew Scott

HARFORD*
William West (DNS)
Aquila Hall (DNS)
Richard Dallam
Thomas Bond, of Thomas
John Love
John Paca
Benedict Edward Hall
Benjamin Rumsey (DNS)
Nathaniel Giles (DNS)
Jacob Bond

CAROLINE*
Thomas White
William Richardson
Isaac Bradley
Nathaniel Potter
Thomas Goldsborough
Benson Stainton (DNS)

---

[1] The Proprietary Assembly that adjourned on April 19, 1774, was the last legislative session of the proprietary government. After that, Governor Eden prorogued the Assembly regularly until he ordered it dissolved on June 12, 1776, and called for a new election.

During the years 1774–1776, the powers of government increasingly came to be exercised by the extra-legal assemblies. In all there were nine meetings of six appointed or duly elected provincial conventions. Apparently neither contemporaries nor subsequent publishers of the extant proceedings were certain how to differentiate separately elected and self-contained conventions from those sessions that were merely a continuation of an adjourned meeting. This confusion partly results from the ambiguity of the surviving journals. On July 3, 1776, the penultimate Convention decreed that its own dissolution date would be August 1, 1776. The last entry on July 6, however, recorded that "the convention adjourns till Thursday the first day of August next. . .." For convenience each session is designated numerically as a distinct convention, although there were elections only to what are here called the second, fourth, fifth, sixth, and ninth conventions.

The First Convention was an informal meeting of ninety-two delegates from the counties charged with formulating Maryland's response to the Boston Port Act. As the revolutionary movement grew, the conventions evolved into formal assemblies of representatives elected in much the same manner as the proprietary Lower House. These conventions were concerned with financial, legal, and military matters and gradually became the de facto, if not de jure, government.

Governor Eden's authority was acknowledged until June 23, 1776, when he boarded a British ship to return to England. Two days later the Eighth Convention resolved that his call for the election of a new proprietary assembly would not be obeyed and the proprietor's control of Maryland was officially denied.

[2] Formal appointments survive for only those counties marked with an asterisk; the lists of delegates for the other counties are based on attendance at the Convention.

PROVISIONAL GOVERNMENT OF 1774–1776

SECOND CONVENTION [1]

November 21–25, 1774

THIRD CONVENTION

December 8–12, 1774

ST. MARY'S
John Allen Thomas
Jeremiah Jordan
Richard Barnes
John DeButts

KENT
Thomas Ringgold
Joseph Earle

ANNE ARUNDEL*
John Hall, chairman 3
Thomas Johnson
Samuel Chase
William Paca
Matthias Hammond
Charles Carroll, Barrister
Charles Carroll of
   Carrollton
Brice T. B. Worthington
Thomas Dorsey
John Weems
Thomas Sprigg [2]
Samuel Chew [2]
Rezin Hammond [2]
John Hood, Jr. [2]

CALVERT*
John Weems
Alexander Somerville
Richard Parran
Edward Reynolds
Benjamin Mackall IV
William Lyles [2]

CHARLES*
Samuel Hanson [2]
William Smallwood [2]
Josias Hawkins [2]
Francis Ware [2]
Joseph Hanson Harrison [2]
Thomas Stone
Daniel Jenifer
John Dent
George Dent [2]
Robert Townshend Hooe [2]
Samuel Love [2]
Thomas Hanson Marshall [2]

BALTIMORE*
Thomas Cockey Deye
Charles Ridgely
Walter Tolley, Jr.
Benjamin Nicholson
Samuel Worthington
John Moale
John Boyd
William Buchanan

TALBOT
Matthew Tilghman,
   chairman 2 [2]
Edward Lloyd

SOMERSET
Peter Waters
George Dashiell
Samuel Wilson
Josiah Polk
Henry Waggaman

John Winder
Luther Martin

DORCHESTER
John Dickinson
Thomas Ennalls
Matthew Brown
Josiah Richardson
Zachariah Campbell

CECIL
John Veazey, Jr.
Joseph Gilpin

PRINCE GEORGE'S*
Richard Brooke [2]
Josias Beall [2]
Robert Tyler
John Rogers
Joshua Beall
William Bowie
Addison Murdock [2]
Walter Bowie
Thomas Gantt, Jr. [2]
George Lee [2]
Osborn Sprigg
Edward Sprigg
David Craufurd

QUEEN ANNE'S
James Hollyday
John Brown
Thomas Wright
Turbutt Wright

WORCESTER
Peter Chaille

William Purnell
Samuel Handy
Smith Bishop
Nehemiah Holland

FREDERICK*
Charles Beatty
Henry Griffith
Thomas Sprigg Wooton
Jacob Funk
Evan Thomas [2]
Richard Brooke
Upton Sheredine
Baker Johnson [2]
Thomas Price
Joseph Chapline
James Smith [2]

HARFORD
Thomas Bond
John Love
Josias Carvil Hall
John Paca
Aquila Paca
Francis Holland
Aquila Hall
Amos Garrett
Richard Dallam

CAROLINE
Henry Dickinson
Benedict Brice
William Molleston
Joshua Clarke

[1] There is very little extant source material from which to obtain a roster for the Second and Third Conventions. Elections were held in the various counties in late October and early November, 1774, to choose delegates to the Second Convention. The *Maryland Gazette* reports the results of these elections for Anne Arundel, Baltimore, Calvert, Charles, Frederick, and Prince George's counties, but there is no record of the results from the other counties.

Fifty-seven delegates assembled in Annapolis on November 21, 1774, but the only name noted in the proceedings of the Convention is that of Matthew Tilghman, chairman. Because a number of counties were not fully represented, the Second Convention adjourned on November 25, 1774.

On December 8, 1774, eighty-five delegates met in Annapolis, but again the proceedings do not include the names of any men present except John Hall, "in the Chair." The Convention adjourned on December 12, 1774. On December 19, the Baltimore *Maryland Journal* printed the names of the delegates appearing for the Third Convention. It is unclear from the wording whether the list includes only those men present on December 8, or is a complete roster of all those who appeared at any time during the Convention.

The session list for the Second and Third Conventions has been compiled from these meager sources. An asterisk has been placed after those counties for which election results are known, and all elected delegates were named. It is probable that those men who are listed as attending the Third Convention also represented their county in the Second Convention.

[2] These members were not reported in the December 19 issue of the *Maryland Journal*. They may not have attended any meetings of the Third Convention, or they may simply have been overlooked by the *Maryland Journal*.

PROVISIONAL GOVERNMENT OF 1774–1776

FOURTH CONVENTION [1]

April 24–May 3, 1775

ST. MARY'S*
John Barnes (DNS)
John DeButts (DNS)
John Reeder, Jr.
Richard Barnes
Henry Greenfield Sothoron (DNS)
John Allen Thomas
Jeremiah Jordan (DNS)

KENT
Richard Lloyd
Thomas Smyth
William Ringgold
Joseph Nicholson, Jr.
Joseph Earle
Thomas Bedingfield Hands
Thomas Ringgold

ANNE ARUNDEL
Brice T. B. Worthington
John Hall
Thomas Johnson
Samuel Chase
Matthias Hammond
Charles Carroll, Barrister
Charles Carroll of Carrollton
Rezin Hammond

CALVERT
Benjamin Mackall IV
John Weems
Edward Reynolds
William Lyles

CHARLES*
George Dent (DNS)
Samuel Hanson (DNS)
William Smallwood (DNS)
Josias Hawkins

Francis Ware
Joseph Hanson Harrison (DNS)
Thomas Stone
Daniel Jenifer
Robert Townshend Hooe
John Dent
Samuel Love (DNS)
Thomas Hanson Marshall (DNS)
Philip Richard Fendall (DNS)

BALTIMORE*
Charles Ridgely
Thomas Cockey Deye
Walter Tolley, Jr.
Charles Ridgely, of John
Robert Alexander
Samuel Purviance, Jr.
Benjamin Nicholson
Darby Lux
Jeremiah Townly Chase
George Risteau (DNS)
Thomas Harrison
John Moale (DNS)
Andrew Buchanan (DNS)
William Lux
Samuel Worthington (DNS)

TALBOT
Matthew Tilghman, chairman
James Lloyd Chamberlaine
Nicholas Thomas
Edward Lloyd
Francis Baker
Peregrine Tilghman
William Hindman

SOMERSET
Peter Waters

Henry Jackson
George Dashiell
Gustavus Scott

DORCHESTER
Robert Goldsborough
Henry Hooper
William Ennalls
James Murray
Joseph Richardson
Matthew Brown
John Ennalls
Thomas Ennalls
John Dickinson

CECIL
Nathaniel Ramsey
William Ward
John D. Thompson
John Veazey III

PRINCE GEORGE'S*
Richard Brooke (DNS)
Josias Beall (DNS)
Robert Tyler
John Rogers
William Bowie (DNS)
Walter Bowie
George Lee (DNS)
Thomas Gantt, Jr.
Joshua Beall
Osborn Sprigg
David Craufurd
Joseph Sim (DNS)
Thomas Contee
Benjamin Hall, of Francis
Luke Marbury (DNS)
Stephen West
John Contee (DNS)
Thomas Sim Lee

QUEEN ANNE'S
James Hollyday
Thomas Wright
Richard Tilghman Earle
Turbutt Wright
Solomon Wright
James Tilghman

WORCESTER
(none present)

FREDERICK*
Charles Beatty
John Hanson, Jr. (DNS)
Upton Sheredine (DNS)
Baker Johnson
Philip Thomas
Jacob Funk
Samuel Beall (DNS)
Joseph Chapline (DNS)
John Stull (DNS)
James Smith (DNS)
Henry Griffith
Thomas Sprigg Wooton (DNS)
Richard Brooke
William Deakins, Jr.
Thomas Cramphin, Jr.

HARFORD
Benjamin Rumsey
Francis Holland
Robert Lemmon
Benedict Edward Hall

CAROLINE
Thomas Goldsborough
Joshua Clarke
Henry Dickinson
Nathaniel Potter

[1] Election results survive for only those counties marked with an asterisk; the lists of delegates for the other counties are based on attendance at the Convention. According to the published proceedings, 100 delegates were present.

PROVISIONAL GOVERNMENT OF 1774–1776

FIFTH CONVENTION [1]

July 26–August 14, 1775

ST. MARY'S*
John Reeder, Jr.
Richard Barnes
John Allen Thomas
Jeremiah Jordan

KENT
William Ringgold
Richard Lloyd
Thomas Smyth
Joseph Earle
Thomas Beddingfield Hands
Thomas Ringgold
Joseph Nicholson, Jr.

ANNE ARUNDEL
Samuel Chase
Thomas Johnson
John Hall
Ephraim Howard
Charles Carroll, Barrister
Charles Carroll of
  Carrollton
Thomas Dorsey
Thomas Tillard
John Dorsey
William Paca
Rezin Hammond
Brice T. B. Worthington
Matthias Hammond

CALVERT
Edward Gantt
Samuel Chew
Edward Reynolds
Benjamin Mackall IV
Alexander Somerville

CHARLES*
George Dent (DNS)
Samuel Hanson (DNS)
William Smallwood
Josias Hawkins (DNS)
Francis Ware (DNS)
Joseph Hanson Harrison
  (DNS)
Thomas Stone
Daniel Jenifer

Robert Townshend Hooe
John Dent
Samuel Love (DNS)
Thomas Hanson Marshall
  (DNS)
Philip Richard Fendall
Samuel Hanson, of Samuel
William Harrison
John Hoskins Stone

BALTIMORE*
Thomas Cockey Deye
  (DNS)
Charles Ridgely (DNS)
Walter Tolley, Jr.
Charles Ridgely, of John
Charles Ridgely, of William
John Moale
William Buchanan
Benjamin Nicholson
John Cradock
Jeremiah Townly Chase
Thomas Harrison
Darby Lux
Walter Tolley (DNS)
Robert Alexander
James Gittings

TALBOT
Matthew Tilghman,
  chairman
James Lloyd Chamberlaine
Nicholas Thomas
Edward Lloyd
William Hindman
Richard Tilghman
James Benson
Francis Baker
Peregrine Tilghman

SOMERSET
William Waters
Josiah Polk
George Dashiell
John Steward
John Waters
Gustavus Scott

DORCHESTER
Robert Goldsborough
James Murray
Henry Hooper
Thomas Ennalls
Robert Harrison

CECIL*
John Veazey, Jr.
Joseph Gilpin
William Ward (DNS)
Stephen Hyland (DNS)
William Rumsey
Nathaniel Ramsay
John D. Thompson
Charles Rumsey
John Cox
Patrick Ewing (DNS)
Peter Lawson
William Currer

PRINCE GEORGE'S*
Richard Brooke
Josias Beall
Robert Tyler
John Rogers
William Bowie
Walter Bowie
George Lee
Thomas Gantt, Jr.
Joshua Beall
Osborn Sprigg
David Craufurd
Joseph Sim
Thomas Contee
Benjamin Hall, of Francis
Luke Marbury (DNS)
Stephen West
John Contee
Thomas Sim Lee

QUEEN ANNE'S
Turbutt Wright
James Tilghman
Thomas Wright
John Wallace
James Hollyday
John Brown

Richard Tilghman Earle
Solomon Wright

WORCESTER
Samuel Handy
Peter Chaille
Zadock Purnell
William Morris

FREDERICK
Henry Griffith
Charles Beatty
Baker Johnson
Richard Brooke
Jacob Funk
John Hanson, Jr.
Samuel Beall
William Deakins, Jr.
Thomas Sprigg Wooton
Thomas Cramphin, Jr.
Upton Sheredine
Joseph Chapline

HARFORD
Richard Dallam
Samuel Durham
Thomas Bond
Samuel Ashmead
Benedict Edward Hall
John Beale Howard
Francis Holland
Benjamin Rumsey
Ignatius Wheeler, Jr.
James MacComas
William Webb

CAROLINE
Nathaniel Potter
Joshua Clarke
Peter Adams
Richard Mason
William Molleston
Benson Stainton
John Stevens
William Hopper
William Richardson
Henry Dickinson

FIRST COUNCIL OF SAFETY [2]

August 29–October 21, 1775

WESTERN SHORE
Daniel of St. Thomas
  Jenifer, president
Thomas Johnson
William Paca

Charles Carroll, Barrister
Thomas Stone (DNS)
Samuel Chase
Robert Alexander
Charles Carroll of
  Carrollton

EASTERN SHORE
Matthew Tilghman
John Beale Bordley (Dcl)
Robert Goldsborough
  (DNS)

James Hollyday
Richard Lloyd
Edward Lloyd
Thomas Smyth
Henry Hooper

[1] Election results survive for only those counties marked with an asterisk; the lists of delegates for the other counties are based on attendance at the Convention. According to the published proceedings, 141 delegates attended.

[2] By the time of the Fifth Convention it was apparent that the extra-legal government needed an executive branch that would implement the resolves of the conventions on a continuing basis. This executive branch, termed the Council of Safety, was selected by the conventions. Its members were named to represent either the Western or Eastern Shore in all but the fourth Council.

PROVISIONAL GOVERNMENT OF 1774–1776

SIXTH CONVENTION [1]

December 7, 1775–January 18, 1776

SEVENTH CONVENTION

May 8–May 25, 1776

EIGHTH CONVENTION

June 21–July 6, 1776

ST. MARY'S•
Jeremiah Jordan
John Allen Thomas [2]
Richard Barnes
George Plater [6]
John Reeder, Jr.
Athanasius Ford (E–7)

KENT•
Robert Buchanan
Peregine Lethrbury
Thomas Smyth (Dcl)
Emory Sudler
William Sluby
Thomas Ringgold

ANNE ARUNDEL•
Charles Carroll, Barrister
Thomas Johnson
Samuel Chase [4]
William Paca [5]
Charles Carroll of
  Carrollton [4]

CALVERT•
Edward Gantt
Alexander Somerville
Patrick Sim Smith
Benjamin Mackall IV
William Allein

CHARLES•
William Smallwood [2]

Francis Ware [2]
Josias Hawkins
Thomas Stone [4]
Robert Townshend Hooe
William Harrison (E–7)
Joseph Hanson Harrison
  (E–7)

BALTIMORE•
Robert Alexander [2]
Benjamin Nicholson [3]
John Moale [4]
Walter Tolley, Jr.
Jeremiah Townly Chase

TALBOT
Matthew Tilghman,
  chairman 6, 8 [4]
Nicholas Thomas
Pollard Edmondson
James Lloyd Chamberlaine
Francis Baker (DNS,
  Ds–6) [7]
Edward Lloyd

SOMERSET
George Dashiell
Gustavus Scott
Peter Waters
William Adams [4]
John Adams [4]

DORCHESTER
John Ennalls [3]
James Murray
Henry Hooper
William Ennalls [4]
Robert Goldsborough [6]

CECIL•
Joseph Gilpin
John Veazey, Jr.
John D. Thompson
Nathaniel Ramsay [2]
Patrick Ewing
William Currer (E–7)

PRINCE GEORGE'S•
Joseph Sim [4]
Josias Beall
Thomas Contee
John Rogers [2]
Robert Tyler [3]

QUEEN ANNE'S
Turbutt Wright
James Tilghman
Richard Tilghman Earle
James Hollyday
Thomas Wright

WORCESTER•
Peter Chaille
Samuel Handy

Smith Bishop [4]
John Done
Joseph Dashiell

FREDERICK•

Lower District:

Henry Griffith

Middle District:

Charles Beatty
Baker Johnson

Upper District:

William Baird
John Stull
George Brent (E–7) [5]

HARFORD
John Love
Richard Dallam
Aquila Hall
Benjamin Rumsey
Thomas Bond, of Thomas

CAROLINE•
William Richardson [6]
Joshua Clarke [2]
Nathaniel Potter
Henry Dickinson
Richard Mason

Committee Service

CLAIMS [8]
Contee (6–8)
Sim (6)
Earle (6–8)

Hooe (6–8)
Moale (6)
Tolley (6–8)
Chamberlaine (7, 8)

MANUFACTORIES [9]
Gilpin (8)
Earle (8)
Ewing (8)

Beall (8)
Lethrbury (8)

SECOND COUNCIL OF SAFETY

January 18, 1776–May 25, 1776

WESTERN SHORE
Daniel of St. Thomas
Jenifer, president

Charles Carroll, Barrister
John Hall
Benjamin Rumsey

EASTERN SHORE
James Tilghman
Thomas Smyth
Thomas Bedingfield Hands

THIRD COUNCIL OF SAFETY

May 27–July 6, 1776

WESTERN SHORE
Daniel of St. Thomas
Jenifer, president

Charles Carroll, Barrister
John Hall
Benjamin Rumsey (DNS)

George Plater
EASTERN SHORE
James Tilghman

Thomas Smyth
Thomas Bedingfield Hands
William Hayward

FOURTH COUNCIL OF SAFETY [10]

July 6–November 11, 1776

John Hall
George Plater
Charles Carroll, Barrister

Daniel of St. Thomas
Jenifer, president
Thomas Bedingfield
Hands (Dcl)

Benjamin Rumsey
Thomas Smyth
James Tilghman

Joseph Nicholson, Jr.
Nicholas Thomas (A) [11]

[1] The members of the Sixth, Seventh, and Eighth Conventions were elected in September 1775 to serve for a period of one year. Election results survive for only those counties marked with an asterisk; the lists of delegates for the other counties are based on attendance at the conventions.

[2] These delegates attended only the Sixth Convention.

[3] These delegates attended only the Sixth and Seventh Conventions.

[4] These delegates attended only the Sixth and Eighth Conventions.

[5] These delegates attended only the Seventh Convention.

[6] These delegates attended only the Seventh and Eighth Conventions.

[7] Baker was dismissed on December 11, 1775, for a "breach of the continental association" prior to his election.

[8] The Committee of Claims (upon the Treasury) served essentially the same function as the committees of Accounts and Claims–Bills of Credit had in the proprietary assemblies.

[9] The Committee on Manufactories was first appointed during the Sixth Convention "to receive all proposals relative to the establishment of manufactories." By the Eighth Convention it had become a standing committee.

[10] The proceedings for the Eighth Convention do not designate Western or Eastern Shore representation in its recording of the election of members to the Fourth Council of Safety.

[11] Nicholas Thomas was appointed by the Council of Safety on September 18, 1776.

73

NINTH CONVENTION

August 14–November 11, 1776

ST. MARY'S
Richard Barnes
Ignatius Fenwick
George Plater
Jeremiah Jordan

KENT
Thomas Ringgold (D)
William Ringgold
Joseph Earle
Thomas Smyth

ANNE ARUNDEL
Rezin Hammond
Brice T. B. Worthington
  (R, E)
Charles Carroll,
  Barrister (R)
Samuel Chase (R, E)
John Hall (E)

CALVERT
Benjamin Mackall
Charles Grahame
William Fitzhugh
John Mackall

CHARLES
John Dent
Thomas Semmes
John Parnham

Robert Townshend Hooe

BALTIMORE
Charles Ridgely
Thomas Cockey Deye
John Stevenson
Peter Shepherd

TALBOT
Matthew Tilghman,
  chairman
Pollard Edmondson
John Gibson
James Lloyd Chamberlaine

SOMERSET
Gustavus Scott
George Scott
William Horsey
Henry Lowes

DORCHESTER
Robert Goldsborough
James Murray
John Ennalls
Joseph Ennalls

CECIL
Joseph Gilpin
Patrick Ewing
David Smith
Benjamin Brevard

ANNAPOLIS
William Paca
Charles Carroll of
  Carrollton

PRINCE GEORGE'S [1]
Walter Bowie (EV, E)
Luke Marbury (EV, E)
Osborn Sprigg (EV, E)
Thomas Sim Lee (EV)
Benjamin Hall (E)

QUEEN ANNE'S [1]
Turbutt Wright (EV, E)
James Kent (EV, E)
Solomon Wright (EV, E)
William Bruff (EV, E)

WORCESTER [2]
Peter Chaille (EV, E)
Smith Bishop (EV, E)
Samuel Handy (EV, E)
John Purnell Robins (EV)
Josiah E. Mitchell (E)

FREDERICK

Lower District: [1]

Thomas Sprigg Wooton
(EV, E)
Jonathan Wilson (EV, E)
William Bayly, Jr. (EV, E)

Elisha Williams (EV, E)

Middle District:

Adam Fischer
Upton Sheredine
Christopher Edelin
David Shriver

Upper District:

Samuel Beall
John Stull
Henry Schnebeley
Samuel Hughes

HARFORD
Jacob Bond
Henry Wilson, Jr.
John Love
John Archer

CAROLINE
Nathaniel Potter
William Richardson (Ds) [3]
Richard Mason
Henry Dickinson
Thomas Johnson (E)

BALTIMORE TOWN
John Smith
Jeremiah Townly Chase

Committee Service

ELECTIONS
Gilpin
S. Chase
Worthington
Wooton
Carroll, Barrister
Grahame
Fitzhugh
Paca

CLAIMS
J. Smith
Hooe
Grahame
Worthington
Sheredine

MANUFACTORIES
Gilpin
Lowes
Ridgely
Ewing
Beall

LOAN OFFICE [4]
Grahame
Barnes
Carroll of Carrollton
T. Ringgold
J. Smith
Worthington

FIFTH COUNCIL OF SAFETY

November 12, 1776–March 20, 1777

WESTERN SHORE	Brice T. B. Worthington	EASTERN SHORE [6]	Samuel Wilson (A)
John Hall	Charles Grahame (Dcl)	Joseph Nicholson, Jr.	William Hemsley (A, Dcl)
George Plater	Thomas Contee (A) [5]	Nicholas Thomas	James Lloyd Chamberlaine
Daniel of St. Thomas		William Rumsey (Dcl)	(A, Dcl)
Jenifer, president		James Tilghman (Dcl)	Turbutt Wright (A)

[1] According to reports made by the Committee on Elections, the judges appointed by the Eighth Convention to conduct the elections of delegates in the counties of Prince George's, Queen Anne's, and Frederick (Lower District) failed to act. The citizens of these counties appointed new judges, who held the elections and signed the returns. The Ninth Convention declared these elections void since they had not been held by the judges specifically appointed for that purpose, and ordered new elections.

[2] A remonstrance from the election judges appointed by the Eighth Convention to hold the election of delegates in Worcester County indicated that the election was held "contrary to the resolves of the last Convention, ascertaining and declaring the qualifications of voters." The Convention declared this election void and ordered a new one.

[3] Richardson's seat was declared vacated on August 17, 1776, upon his acceptance of a colonel's commission in the Flying Camp.

[4] The committee to "inspect the accounts and proceedings of the commissioners of the loan office" was similar in function to the Committee on Bills of Credit prior to the Revolution.

[5] Contee was appointed to the Council of Safety on November 11, 1776, to replace Charles Grahame.

[6] Wilson and Hemsley were appointed on December 13, 1776, to replace Rumsey and Tilghman. On January 3, 1777, Chamberlaine was appointed to replace William Hemsley who declined to serve. After Chamberlaine also declined to serve, Wright was appointed on February 3, 1777.

GENERAL ASSEMBLY OF 1777[1]

Thomas Johnson, governor

FIRST SESSION: February 5–April 20, 1777
SECOND SESSION: June 16–29, 1777

SENATE

WESTERN SHORE
George Plater
William Paca
Daniel of St. Thomas
  Jenifer, president
Charles Carroll, Barrister
Thomas Johnson (Dcl)

Charles Carroll of
  Carrollton
Thomas Stone
Brice T. B. Worthington
Thomas Contee
Charles Grahame (E–1)

EASTERN SHORE
Matthew Tilghman
Joseph Nicholson, Jr.
Robert Goldsborough
Turbutt Wright
James Tilghman (Dcl)
Samuel Wilson

Edward Tilghman (E–1,
  Dcl)
Thomas B. Hands (E–1,
  Dcl)[2]
Henry Hooper (E–1, Dcl)[2]
William Hindman (E–1)

HOUSE OF DELEGATES

ST. MARY'S
John Hatton Read
James Jordan
William Thomas
Athanasius Ford

KENT
Peregrine Lethrbury
Isaac Perkins
John Maxwell
Donaldson Yeates

ANNE ARUNDEL
Thomas Tillard
Rezin Hammond
John Hall
Benjamin Galloway

CALVERT
William Fitzhugh
John Mackall, Jr. (Ds–1)[3]
William Allein
Richard Parran
Alexander Somerville (E–1)

CHARLES
Joseph Hanson Harrison
Thomas Semmes
Zephaniah Turner
Alexander McPherson

BALTIMORE
Thomas Cockey Deye

Charles Ridgely
John Stevenson
Peter Shepherd

TALBOT
John Gibson
James Benson
Henry Banning (Ds–1,
  E–1)[4]
Edward Lloyd (DNS, R–1)
Nicholas Thomas (E–1),
  speaker 1, 2[5]
John Bracco (E–1, DNS,
  R–1)

SOMERSET[6]
Henry Lowes (DNS, EV)
William Horsey (EV)
William Stone (EV)
John Waters (DNS, EV)
Henry Jackson (E–1)
John Stewart (E–1, DNS,
  Ds–1)
Thomas Maddux (E–1)
William Polk (E–1)
William Winder, Jr. (E–2)

DORCHESTER
William Ennalls
John Henry, Jr.
James Murray (DNS, R–1)
Henry Steele (DNS, R–2)

John Smoot (E–1)

CECIL
Richard Bond
John Veazey, Jr.
Joseph Gilpin
Patrick Ewing

ANNAPOLIS
Samuel Chase
John Brice

PRINCE GEORGE'S
Walter Bowie
David Craufurd
Osborn Sprigg
Jeremiah Magruder

QUEEN ANNE'S
James Kent
William Bruff
Robert Wright
James Bordley

WORCESTER
Peter Chaille
John Selby
Smith Bishop
Josiah Mitchell

FREDERICK
Christopher Edelin
Upton Sheredine

John Hanson, Jr.
  (DNS, R–1)
Philip Thomas
David Shriver (E–2)

HARFORD
Jacob Bond
Thomas Bond
John Archer
William Smithson

CAROLINE
Henry Downes
William Douglass
Richard Mason
Henry Dickinson

BALTIMORE TOWN
John Smith
Jeremiah Townly Chase

WASHINGTON
Samuel Beall
Joseph Sprigg
Samuel Hughes
Henry Schnebeley

MONTGOMERY
Elisha Williams
Thomas Sprigg Wooton,
  speaker 1R[5]
Richard Crabb
Edward Burgess

Committee Service

ELECTIONS AND PRIVILEGES
Hall (1)
J. T. Chase (1, 2)
Lethrbury (1, 2)
Henry (1)
Beall (1)
Sheredine (2)
Bruff (2)
Maxwell (2)

CLAIMS (ACCOUNTS)[7]
Smith (1, 2)
Sheredine (1, 2)
Bruff (1, 2)

Yeates (1)
Turner (1, 2)
John Brice (2)

MANUFACTORIES[8]
Gilpin (1, 2)
Smith (1)
Ewing (1)
Banning (1)
Maxwell (1)
J. T. Chase (1)
Beall (2)
Wooton (2)
Hughes (2)
Veazey (2)

GRIEVANCES AND COURTS OF
JUSTICE
Henry (1, 2)
Veazey (1)
Sheredine (1)
Hall (1, 2)
J. T. Chase (1)
Chaille (1)
Bruff (1)
Beall (2)
J. Bond (2)
Gilpin (2)
Wooton (2)
P. Thomas (2)

LOAN OFFICE (JOINT)[9]
Worthington (1)
T. Wright (1)
Grahame (1)
Kent (1)
Beall (1)
Jordan (1)
Dickinson (1)

LAWS TO EXPIRE[9]
J. T. Chase (1)
Hall (1)
Maddux (1)

EXECUTIVE COUNCIL [10]

February 14–November 10, 1777 [11]

Charles Carroll, Sr. (Dcl)   John Rogers   John Contee (Dcl)
Josiah Polk   Edward Lloyd   Thomas Sim Lee (E)
Jame Brice (E, Dcl)   Joseph Sim (E)

[1] The Constitution of Maryland, as framed by the Ninth Convention, provided for two distinct legislative branches, a Senate and a House of Delegates. The House of Delegates consisted of four representatives from each of the eighteen counties and two delegates from both Annapolis and Baltimore Town. House members, elected *viva voce*, served one year terms. A popularly chosen electoral college, comprised of two men from each county and one from both Annapolis and Baltimore Town, elected members of the Senate, who served five-year terms. The method of selection was by ballot, with the electoral college choosing fifteen senators—nine from the Western Shore and six fom the Eastern Shore—either from their own number or from the population at large. The Senate, unlike the House, had constitutional authority to fill its own vacancies. The Senate and House, collectively termed the General Assembly, was directed to meet annually on the first Monday of November and more frequently if necessary.

The Constitution mandated that the governor and a five member Executive Council be selected by joint ballots of both houses of the legislature. The governor and Council served one-year terms, but they could be reelected. The governor, however, could serve no more than three successive terms, and he was ineligible to occupy that office again until four years after his last gubernatorial term.

The Ninth Convention directed that special elections be held in November and December of 1776, and that the first General Assembly convene in Annapolis in February 1777. The Council of Safety adjourned for the last time on March 20, 1777, the day on which the first governor and Council qualified; the Assembly dissolved the Council of Safety by resolution two days later.

[2] It is presumed that Hands declined to serve, and that Hooper (first name not given in the proceedings, but probably Henry) was chosen in his place. There is no record in the proceedings of either Hand's refusal or Hooper's election, but the Eastern Shore's delegation of six senators would be accurately accounted for by this presumption. After Hooper declined on April 12, 1777, William Hindman was elected to complete the Eastern Shore roster.

[3] Mackall was discharged on February 19, 1777, because he was not a resident of Calvert County at the time of his election.

[4] Banning was declared ineligible because he was a field officer at the time of the election. He was discharged on February 12, 1777, and Thomas was chosen to replace him. Banning was later reelected and qualified on April 10, 1777.

[5] Speaker Wooton was granted a leave of absence because of the indisposition of his brother. Thomas was chosen to replace him as speaker on March 13, 1777.

[6] After hearing depositions regarding the election of delegates from Somerset County in which it was reported that "a number of men armed with fire arms, to the amount of thirty, and a number with sticks and spears fixed in the end of them, came from several parts of said county, to the place of election," the Lower House declared the election void on March 5, 1777. Four new delegates were elected on March 19, 1777, three of whom were qualified on March 27. The fourth delegate, John Stewart, a field officer at the time of election, was ruled ineligible and discharged.

[7] The assignment of the Committee of Claims was to "examine and adjust all claims against the state, inspect and examine the books of account of the board of accounts, . . . accounts of the disposition and loan of all public monies, . . . accounts against the Continental Congress," and the journal of accounts.

[8] The assignment of the Committee on Manufactories was to "receive all petitions and proposals for the establishment of manufactories and to consider and devise the best ways and means of promoting trade and commerce" within the state.

[9] There is no evidence that the Loan Office joint committee or the Committee on Laws to Expire functioned during the second session.

[10] Charles Carroll and John Contee declined to serve on the Executive Council in February 1777 soon after their election. Contee cited the smallpox epidemic in Annapolis and his fear of contracting the disease in his letter dated February 24. Lee was elected to replace Carroll on March 26, and Brice to replace Contee on April 16. Brice, however, declined to accept the seat, and Sim was elected on April 19 in his place.

[11] Term in office for the Executive Council is stated from the day of election to the day before the election of the succeeding group. Although this first Council was elected on February 14, it did not begin to function until March 20, the day that the governor and three of its members qualified.

GENERAL ASSEMBLY OF 1777–1778

Thomas Johnson, governor

FIRST SESSION: October 21–December 23, 1777 [1]
SECOND SESSION: March 13–April 22, 1778 [2]
THIRD SESSION: June 1–23, 1778 [3]

SENATE

WESTERN SHORE
George Plater
William Paca (R–1)
Daniel of St. Thomas
 Jenifer, president

Charles Carroll, Barrister
Charles Carroll of
 Carrollton
Thomas Stone
Brice T. B. Worthington
Thomas Contee

Charles Grahame
Thomas Jennings (E–2)

EASTERN SHORE
Matthew Tilghman
Joseph Nicholson, Jr.

Robert Goldsborough
Turbutt Wright
Samuel Wilson
William Hindman

HOUSE OF DELEGATES

ST. MARY'S
Athanasius Ford
John Hatton Read
Richard Barnes
Edmund Plowden

KENT
Peregrine Lethrbury
John Maxwell
Ezekiel Forman (Ds–1) [4]
John Cadwalader (DNS,
 R–2)
Richard Gresham (E–1)
James Lloyd (E–2)

ANNE ARUNDEL
Thomas Tillard
Rezin Hammond (R–3)
John Hall (R–3)
Nicholas Worthington
Nicholas Maccubbin, Jr.
 (E–3)

CALVERT
William Fitzhugh, speaker
 2, 3
Samuel Hance (DNS)
Alexander Somerville (R–3)
John Mackall (Ds–1) [5]
Samuel Chew (E–1)

CHARLES
Zephaniah Turner (R–2)
Thomas Semmes

Alexander McPherson
James Forbes
Samuel Hanson, Jr. (E–3,
 Ds–3) [6]

BALTIMORE
Thomas Cockey Deye
Charles Ridgely (R–1, E–2)
John Stevenson
Peter Shepherd

TALBOT
Nicholas Thomas, speaker
 1, 2 (R–2)
James Benson (R–2)
John Gibson
Howes Goldsborough
Robert Goldsborough, Jr.
 (E–2)
Samuel Chamberlaine (E–2,
 DNS, R–2)
William Goldsborough
 (E–3)

SOMERSET
Thomas Maddux
William Strawbridge
William Winder
Levin Wilson

DORCHESTER
John Smoot
John Henry, Jr.
James Murray
Joseph Daffin

CECIL
John Veazey
John Ward
Amos Alexander
Stephen Hyland

ANNAPOLIS
John Brice
Samuel Chase (R–1)
Allen Quynn (E–1)

PRINCE GEORGE'S
Walter Bowie
Stephen West
Jeremiah Magurder
John Contee

QUEEN ANNE'S
James Kent
William Bruff (R–1, E–2)
Robert Wright (R–2)
Richard Tilghman Earle
William Hemsley (E–2,
 DNS)

WORCESTER
Peter Chaille (DNS, R–1)
Nehemiah Holland (R–2)
Thomas Purnell
Josiah Mitchell
William Holland (E–2,
 DNS, EV, E–3, DNS) [7]
Thomas Purnell, of Thomas
 (E–3, DNS)

FREDERICK
Christopher Edelin
Philip Thomas
Jacob Young
Upton Sheredine

HARFORD
Henry Wilson, Jr.
Jacob Bond
Aquila Hall
William Smithson

CAROLINE
William Douglass
Henry Dickinson
Henry Downes (DNS, R–2)
Richard Mason
Benson Stainton (E–3)

BALTIMORE TOWN
John Smith
Jeremiah Townly Chase

WASHINGTON
Joseph Sprigg
John Barnes
Samuel Hughes
Henry Schnebeley

MONTGOMERY
Edward Burgess
Elisha Williams
William Bayly
Richard Crabb

ELECTIONS AND PRIVILEGES
Sheredine (1–3)
J. Hall (1, 2)
J. T. Chase (1, 2)
Veazey (1, 3)
Edelin (1)
Bruff (2)
Lethrbury (2, 3)
West (3)
Deye (3)

GRIEVANCES AND COURTS OF JUSTICE
J. Hall (1)
S. Chase (1)
Maddux (1)
John Brice (1, 2)
Turner (1)

R. Barnes (1–3)
Forbes (1, 3)
Murray (2, 3)
Earle (2)
N. Worthington (2)
Bruff (2, 3)
Kent (2)
Henry (3)

LOAN OFFICE [8]
John Brice (1)
Kent (1)
Sheredine (1)
J. Contee (1)
Ford (1)
Earle (1)

CLAIMS
Sheredine (1–3)

Forbes (1, 3)
Forman (1)
Turner (1, 2)
J. Contee (1, 2)
West (1–3)
Smith (1–3)
Tillard (1, 2)
Earle (2)
Bruff (2, 3)
J. Barnes (2)
McPherson (2)
Murray (3)

MANUFACTORIES
T. Purnell (1)
J. Hall (1)
Turner (1)
Maddux (1)

Fitzhugh (1)
West (1–3)
Smith (1)
Maxwell (2, 3)
A. Hall (2)
Gibson (2)
Sprigg (2)
Edelin (3)
Hughes (3)
Douglass (3)

LAWS TO EXPIRE
J. T. Chase (1)
Maddux (1)
John Brice (1–3)
N. Worthington (2, 3)
Quynn (2, 3)

EXECUTIVE COUNCIL [9]

November 11, 1777–November 9, 1778

Thomas Sim Lee   Joseph Sim (Dcl)   Edward Lloyd   John Rogers (Dcl)
Josiah Polk (Dcl)   James Brice (E)   William Hemsley (E, Dcl)
Daniel Carroll (E)   James Hindman (E)

[1] The governor convened the General Assembly on October 21, 1777. Recorded proceedings begin for the Senate on October 22, and for the House on October 31.

[2] Recorded proceedings for the Senate begin on March 13, 1778, and for the House on March 17.

[3] The governor convened the General Assembly on June 1, 1778. Recorded proceedings begin for the Senate on June 4 and for the House on June 8.

[4] On November 4, 1777, Forman was determined ineligible to hold a seat in the House because of holding the office of Kent County clerk.

[5] Mackall was discharged on November 4, 1777, because he was not a resident of Calvert County at the time of his election.

[6] On June 11, 1778, an objection to the recent election of Samuel Hanson, Jr., from Daniel Jenifer, who was second on the poll, was read. Hanson was discharged on June 17, because he had been a field officer at the time of his election.

[7] The election of Holland to replace Peter Chaille was declared void on April 6, 1778, because the sheriff of Worcester County, prior to holding the election, had resigned his commission. Holland was reelected to the third session, but did not serve.

[8] The Loan Office Committee ceased to function as a standing committee following the first session.

[9] On November 25, 1777, the Council journal notes that Polk, Sim, and Rogers declined to qualify, and that the General Assembly had chosen Brice, Hemsley, and Carroll in their places. Hemsley declined on December 2 and Hindman was elected on December 23 in his place.

GENERAL ASSEMBLY OF 1778–1779

Thomas Johnson, governor

FIRST SESSION: October 19–December 15, 1778 [1]
SECOND SESSION: March 2–25, 1779 [2]
THIRD SESSION: July 15–August 15, 1779 [3]

SENATE

WESTERN SHORE
George Plater
Daniel of St. Thomas Jenifer, president
Charles Carroll, Barrister
Charles Carroll of Carrollton
Thomas Stone
Brice T. B. Worthington
Thomas Contee (DNS, R–1)
Charles Grahame (DNS, D–3)
Thomas Jennings (R–3)
Richard Barnes (E–1)

Andrew Buchanan (E–3, Dcl)
Joseph Sim (E–3)
Upton Sheredine (E–3, DNS)

EASTERN SHORE
Matthew Tilghman

Joseph Nicholson, Jr.
Robert Goldsborough
Turbutt Wright (DNS, R–1)
Samuel Wilson
William Hindman
William Paca (E–1)

HOUSE OF DELEGATES

ST. MARY'S
Athanasius Ford
Nicholas Lewis Sewell
John Allen Thomas
John Mackall

KENT
Peregrine Lethrbury
Richard Gresham
James Lloyd
John Lambert Wilmer

ANNE ARUNDEL
Nicholas Worthington
John Hall
Nicholas Maccubbin, Jr.
Henry Ridgely

CALVERT
William Fitzhugh, speaker
Edward Reynolds
Samuel Chew
John Mackall IV (Ds–1) [4]
Thomas Mackall (E–2)

CHARLES
Warren Dent
Joseph Hanson Harrison
Samuel Hanson, Jr.
John Digges

BALTIMORE
Thomas Cockey Deye
John Stevenson
Charles Ridgely, Sr.
Rezin Hammond

TALBOT
Robert Goldsborough IV
Howes Goldsborough
Thomas Sherwood (R–1)
John Stevens (EV–1) [5]
John Gibson (E–1) [5]
William Goldsborough (E–2)

SOMERSET
Thomas Maddux
Josiah Polk
Henry Jackson
William Strawbridge

DORCHESTER
John Smoot
John Henry, Jr. (DNS)
Thomas Firmin Eccleston
James Woolford

CECIL
John Veazey
John Ward

Archibald Job
James Evans

ANNAPOLIS
Allen Quynn
John Brice (R–3)
Samuel Chase (E–3)

PRINCE GEORGE'S
Josias Beall
Thomas Gantt, Jr.
Walter Bowie
Jeremiah Magruder

QUEEN ANNE'S
William Bruff
John Brown
Richard Bennett Carmichael
James Bordley

WORCESTER
Peter Chaille
Thomas Purnell, of John
Oughten Sturgis
Josiah Mitchell

FREDERICK
John Hanson
Adam Fischer
William Murdock Beall
John Ross Key

HARFORD
Henry Wilson, Jr.
James McComas (Ds–1, E–1) [6]
William Bond, of Joshua
Benjamin Bradford Norris

CAROLINE
Richard Mason
William Keene
Benson Stainton
Matthew Driver (DNS, Ds–1) [7]
Nathaniel Potter (E–1)

BALTIMORE TOWN
John Smith
Jeremiah Townly Chase

WASHINGTON
Joseph Sprigg
John Barnes
Samuel Hughes
Henry Schnebeley

MONTGOMERY
William Bayly
Thomas Cramphin, Jr.
Richard Crabb
Edward Burgess

ELECTIONS AND PRIVILEGES
Maddux (1)
Hall (1)
Thomas (1)
Deye (1)
Polk (1)
Lethrbury (2, 3)
Sprigg (2)
Ford (2)
Bowie (2)
Gresham (2)
S. Hanson (2)
J. T. Chase (2)
Stevenson (2)
Bayly (3)
Crabb (3)
Quynn (3)
Ward (3)
J. Mackall (3)
S. Chase (3)
Sewell (3)

GRIEVANCES AND COURTS OF
JUSTICE
Hall (1, 3)
Brown (1)
Polk (1)
J. Lloyd (1)
W. M. Beall (1)
Maccubbin (1)
Bordley (1)
Veazey (3)
N. Worthington (3)
Bowie (3)
Norris (3)
Sturgis (3)
Woolford (3)
Gresham (3)
J. Barnes (3)
Schnebeley (3)

CLAIMS
John Brice (1, 2)
Eccleston (1, 3)
Burgess (1)
Jackson (1)
Veazey (1)
Smith (1, 3)
Bruff (1)
J. Hanson (1, 2)
Maccubbin (2)
W. M. Beall (2, 3)
W. Goldsborough (2)
Bayly (2)

R. Goldsborough IV (2)
J. Mackall (2)
H. Goldsborough (3)
Brown (3)
Hughes (3)
H. Wilson (3)
Smoot (3)
Keene (3)
Fischer (3)

LAWS TO EXPIRE
N. Worthington (1)
Quynn (1)
Sprigg (1)
J. Beall (2)
J. Barnes (2)
H. Ridgely (2)
Fischer (2)
Burgess (2)
Magruder (2)
Bond (2, 3)
Thomas (3)
Evans (3)
Gantt (3)
Reynolds (3)
Harrison (3)
S. Hanson (3)

MANUFACTORIES
H. Ridgely (1)
Sewell (1)
Bruff (1)
Bordley (1)
H. Wilson (1)
Sprigg (1)
J. T. Chase (1)

TAX COMMISSIONERS[8]
Smith (1)
Hughes (1)
Brown (1)
W. M. Beall (1)
Bordley (1)
J. T. Chase (3)
W. Goldsborough (3)
Maccubbin (3)
Chew (3)
Burgess (3)
McComas (3)
Sprigg (3)
J. Beall (3)
Chaille (3)
C. Ridgely (3)

EXECUTIVE COUNCIL

November 10, 1778–November 8, 1779

Thomas Sim Lee   James Brice   Daniel Carroll
Edward Lloyd   James Hindman (R)

[1] The governor convened the General Assembly on October 19, 1778. Recorded proceedings for the Senate begin on October 29, and for the House on October 26.

[2] The governor convened the General Assembly on March 2, 1779. Recorded proceedings for both the Senate and the House begin on March 9.

[3] The governor convened the General Assembly on July 15, 1779. Recorded proceedings for the Senate begin on July 20, and for the House on July 22.

[4] Mackall was discharged on October 28, 1778, because he was not a resident of Calvert County at the time of his election.

[5] John Stevens was declared illegally elected on November 7, 1778, because of improper procedures by the sheriff. According to information given by John Gibson, the sheriff had "struck out the names of several voters who voted for the said Gibson," and "permitted a number of persons to vote . . . who had not taken the (prescribed) oath." The House ordered the sheriff to erase the name of John Stevens from his election return and insert the name of John Gibson.

[6] The House determined that James McComas was ineligible for a seat because he had not resigned his colonel's commission until the third day of the election. He was discharged on October 30, 1778, but was reelected and returned on November 25.

[7] According to information supplied by the sitting members from Caroline County, Matthew Driver "desired the people not to elect him, for that he was a field officer and would not resign his commission, and consequently could not serve them." Driver was discharged on October 28, 1778.

[8] During this Assembly a committee was established "to examine the returns of the commissioners of the tax from the several counties of this state." There is no evidence that the Committee of Grievances and Courts of Justice and the Committee to Examine the Tax Commissioners' Returns functioned during the second session, nor that the Committee on Manufactories functioned during the second or third sessions.

GENERAL ASSEMBLY OF 1779–1780

Thomas Sim Lee, governor

FIRST SESSION: November 1–December 30, 1779 [1]
SECOND SESSION: March 2–May 16, 1780
THIRD SESSION: June 7–July 5, 1780

SENATE

WESTERN SHORE
George Plater (DNS)
Daniel of St. Thomas
  Jenifer, president 1, 2, 3 [2]
Charles Carroll, Barrister
Charles Carroll of
  Carrollton
Thomas Stone
Brice T. B. Worthington
Richard Barnes
Joseph Sim
Upton Sheredine

EASTERN SHORE
Matthew Tilghman,
  president 3 [2]
Joseph Nicholson, Jr.
  (DNS)
Robert Goldsborough
Samuel Wilson (DNS, R–1)
William Hindman
William Paca (R–2)
William Hemsley (E–1)
John Henry (E–2, DNS)

HOUSE OF DELEGATES

ST. MARY'S
John Hatton Read
Philip Key
James Jordan
John Mackall

KENT
Richard Gresham (D–2)
John Lambert Wilmer
Peregrine Lethrbury
William Stevenson
John Cadwalader (E–2)

ANNE ARUNDEL
Nicholas Worthington
John Hall
Henry Ridgely
Nicholas Maccubbin, Jr.

CALVERT
William Fitzhugh
Charles Williamson
Alexander Hamilton Smith
Frisby Freeland

CHARLES
Joseph Hanson Harrison
John Digges
Warren Dent
Samuel Hanson, Jr.

BALTIMORE
Thomas Cockey Deye
John Stevenson
Rezin Hammond
Charles Ridgely, Sr.

TALBOT
Henry Banning
John Gibson
Richard Johns (R–3)
Christopher Birckhead

SOMERSET
John Williams (R–2)
John Winder
Josiah Dashiell
Isaac Henry

DORCHESTER
John Henry, Jr.
Samuel McGee (R–2)
John Smoot
Thomas Firmin Eccleston
Henry Hooper (E–3, DNS,
  R–3)

CECIL
John Ward
Archibald Job
John Veazey (DNS, D–2)

Elihu Hall (R–2)
Peter Lawson (E–3)
Timothy Kirk (E–3)

ANNAPOLIS
Allen Quynn
Samuel Chase

PRINCE GEORGE'S
Josiah Beall, speaker
David Craufurd
Benjamin Hall, of Francis
Jeremiah Magruder

QUEEN ANNE'S
William Bruff
John Brown
Richard Tilghman Earle
Jacob Ringgold

WORCESTER
Peter Chaille
Nehemiah Holland (R–3)
Henry Dennis
William Selby, of John

FREDERICK
George Stricker
John Hanson
John Beatty
Fielder Gantt

HARFORD
John Taylor (Ds–1, E–2,
  Ds–2, E–2) [3]
James McComas
John Archer
Benjamin Bradford Norris

CAROLINE
Matthew Driver
William Keene
Hugh McBryde (R–2, E–3)
Charles Daffin

BALTIMORE TOWN
David McMechen
Mark Alexander

WASHINGTON
John Stull (Ds–1, E–1) [4]
John Barnes
Joseph Sprigg
James Chapline

MONTGOMERY
William Bayly
Thomas Cramphin, Jr.
Thomas Sprigg Wooton
  (R–3)
Edward Burgess

ELECTIONS AND PRIVILEGES
S. Chase (1–3)
Lethrbury (1)
Deye (1, 3)
J. Hall (1)
J. Hanson (1)
C. Ridgely (2)
Earle (2)
J. Henry (2)
N. Worthington (2, 3)
Ringgold (3)
Fitzhugh (3)

GRIEVANCES AND COURTS OF JUSTICE
J. Hall (1)
Wooton (1)
J. Henry, Jr. (1, 2)
Bruff (1–3)
W. Stevenson (1–3)

Gantt (1, 2)
Jordan (1)
Fitzhugh (1)
Quynn (2, 3)
Winder (2, 3)
Brown (2, 3)
Chaille (3)
McMechen (3)

MANUFACTORIES [5]
Jordan (1)
Gresham (1)
McMechen (1, 2)
Wilmer (1, 2)
Alexander (1, 2)
J. Hanson (1)
Key (1)
Reed (1, 2)
S. Hanson (1)
I. Henry (2)

Gantt (2)
Gibson (2)

CLAIMS [6]
Craufurd (1, 3)
W. Stevenson (1–3)
Winder (1–3)
Eccleston (1–3)
J. Hanson (1)
Burgess (1–3)
Cramphin (1–3)
McBryde (1–3)
Smoot (1, 2)
Jordan (2)
C. Ridgely (2)
Sprigg (2)
Wilmer (2)
Harrison (2)
B. Hall (2)

LAWS TO EXPIRE
Quynn (1–3)
Lethrbury (1)
N. Worthington (1–3)
Maccubbin (2, 3)

TAX COMMISSIONERS [5]
Bruff (1, 2)
Wooton (1)
Key (1)
Gantt (1)
Gresham (1)
J. Henry, Jr. (1, 2)
Jordan (1, 2)
Eccleston (2)
H. Ridgely (2)
Earle (2)
W. Stevenson (2)
C. Ridgely (2)

EXECUTIVE COUNCIL

November 9, 1779–November 13, 1780

John Hoskins Stone   Jeremiah Townly Chase   James Brice
Daniel Carroll   John Brice

[1] The governor convened the General Assembly on November 1, 1779. The House adjourned daily until November 8, when a quorum was gathered. Recorded proceedings for the Senate begin on November 8.

[2] Tilghman was elected president at the beginning of the third session to replace Jenifer who was attending Congress. Jenifer returned from Congress on June 14 and was reelected to the presidency on June 15, 1780.

[3] John Taylor was discharged and fined on November 10, 1779, because, even though he was sheriff of Harford County, he had conducted his own election, received votes for himself, and signed the return which named him a delegate. A new election was held, and on March 25, 1780, Taylor was reported reelected. He was again ruled ineligible, however, because at the time of the second election he was collector of the tax for Harford County. A third election was held on April 12, by which time Taylor no longer held any government office. He was again reelected, and qualified on April 25, 1780.

[4] John Stull was discharged on November 9, 1779, for being a field officer at the time of his election.

[5] There is no evidence that the Committee on Manufactories and the Committee to Examine the Returns of the Tax Commissioners functioned during the third session.

[6] The Committee of Claims also assumed the responsibility for examining the state of the Treasury and the Loan Office.

GENERAL ASSEMBLY OF 1780–1781

Thomas Sim Lee, governor

FIRST SESSION: October 17, 1780–February 2, 1781
SECOND SESSION: May 10–June 27, 1781

SENATE

WESTERN SHORE
George Plater,
    president 1, 2 [1]
Daniel of St. Thomas
    Jenifer, president 1 [1]
Charles Carroll, Barrister

Charles Carroll of
    Carrollton
Thomas Stone (R–1, E–1)
Brice T. B. Worthington
Richard Barnes
Joseph Sim (DNS, R–2)
Upton Sheredine (R–1)

Richard Ridgely (E–1, Dcl)
Samuel Hughes (E–1)
Benedict Edward Hall (E–2)

EASTERN SHORE
Matthew Tilghman
Joseph Nicholson, Jr.

Robert Goldsborough
    (DNS)
William Hindman
William Hemsley
John Henry

HOUSE OF DELEGATES

ST. MARY'S
James Mills
Edmund Plowden
Philip Key
John Mackall

KENT
William Stevenson
Peregrine Lethrbury
John Lambert Wilmer
John Cadwalader

ANNE ARUNDEL
John Hall
Nicholas Worthington
Nicholas Maccubbin
William Brogden (Ds–1,
    E–1) [2]

CALVERT
Levin Mackall (R–1)
Frisby Freeland
Charles Williamson (R–1)
Thomas Gantt
William Fitzhugh (E–1)
Edward Johnson (E–1)

CHARLES
Warren Dent
Daniel Jenifer (DNS, R–1)
Gerard Blackstone Causin
Henry Boarman (DNS,
    R–1)
Samuel Hanson, Sr. (E–1,
    R–2)

Thomas Stone (E–1, R–1)
John Dent (E–2)
Michael Jenifer Stone (E–2)

BALTIMORE
Thomas Cockey Deye
John Stevenson
Charles Ridgely (R–1)
Rezin Hammond (R–2)
Robert Lemmon (E–2)
Charles Ridgely, of William
    (E–2)

TALBOT
James Hindman
James Lloyd Chamberlaine
    (R–2)
Nicholas Martin
Edward Lloyd

SOMERSET
John Winder
Thomas Maddux
Henry Jackson
John Done (DNS)

DORCHESTER
John Henry, Jr. (DNS, R–1)
Thomas Firmin Eccleston
    (DNS, R–1)
Gustavus Scott
Daniel Sulivane
James Shaw (E–1)
Arthur Whitely (E–1)

CECIL
John Ward
Peter Lawson
Archibald Job
Timothy Kirk

ANNAPOLIS
Allen Quynn
Samuel Chase

PRINCE GEORGE'S
David Craufurd
Thomas Duckett
Alexander H. Magruder
Thomas Clagett

QUEEN ANNE'S
William Bruff, speaker 1,
    2R, 2 [3]
James Kent (R–1, E–2)
Robert Wright (R–1)
Samuel Earle
Turbutt Wright (E–2),
    speaker 2R [3]

WORCESTER
Henry Dennis
William Morris
Joseph Dashiell
Isaac Houston

FREDERICK
Fielder Gantt
Richard Potts (R–1)
Normand Bruce (DNS,
    R–1)

John Hanson (DNS)
Thomas Johnson (E–1)
Thomas Beatty (E–2)

HARFORD
John Taylor
James McComas
Benjamin Bradford Norris
John Rumsey (DNS, R–1)
James Giles (E–1)

CAROLINE
Matthew Driver
Benson Stainton
William Whitely
William Hopper (DNS,
    R–1)
James Seth (E–1)

BALTIMORE TOWN
David McMechen
Mark Alexander

WASHINGTON
Thomas Sprigg
John Stull (DNS, R–1)
Joseph Chapline
James Chapline
John Barnes (E–1)

MONTGOMERY
Thomas Cramphin, Jr.
William Bayly
Laurence O'Neale
Charles Hungerford

ELECTIONS AND PRIVILEGES
N. Worthington (1, 2)
Wilmer (1)
Quynn (1, 2)
Deye (1)
Craufurd (1, 2)
J. Dent (2)
T. Wright (2)

GRIEVANCES AND COURTS OF
JUSTICE
Lloyd (1)
F. Gantt (1, 2)
Dashiell (1, 2)

Bayly (1, 2)
Potts (1)
S. Hanson (1)
Wilmer (1)
Chamberlaine (1)
Brogden (1)
Scott (2)
Morris (2)

CLAIMS
J. Hindman (1, 2)
W. Stevenson (1, 2)
Craufurd (1, 2)
Clagett (1, 2)
Cramphin (1, 2)

W. Dent (1)
Ward (1, 2)
Duckett (2)
Brogden (2)

LAWS TO EXPIRE
Quynn (1, 2)
Potts (1)
N. Worthington (1, 2)
Maddux (2)

MANUFACTORIES
McMechen (1, 2)
Wilmer (1)
Alexander (1, 2)

Key (1)
Duckett (1, 2)
Ridgely, of William (2)
Magruder (2)

PUBLIC TAXES [4]
T. Johnson (2)
Kent (2)
T. Wright (2)
Sprigg (2)
Ridgely, of William (2)
Morris (2)
Winder (2)

EXECUTIVE COUNCIL

November 14, 1780–November 20, 1781

Daniel Carroll   James Brice   Jeremiah Townly Chase
John Hoskins Stone   Samuel Turbutt Wright

[1] Plater was elected president on January 29, 1781, to replace Jenifer who was "indisposed and unable to attend."

[2] Brogden was a field officer in the militia at the time of his election. He was discharged on November 1, 1780, but was reelected and qualified on November 13.

[3] Wright was elected speaker on June 11, 1781, to replace Bruff who was absent because of illness. When Bruff returned on June 14, Wright withdrew, "being much indisposed," and Bruff was reelected speaker.

[4] The Committee on Public Taxes was created in the second session to "enquire into and report the state of the public taxes under the act passed last session (October 1780) for raising the supplies for the present year and more particularly the specific taxes, and the rate of exchange between specie and bills of credit fixed in the respective counties from time to time by the commissioners of the tax."

GENERAL ASSEMBLY OF 1781–1782

Thomas Sim Lee, governor

FIRST SESSION: November 5, 1781–January 22, 1782
SECOND SESSION: April 25–June 15, 1782

SENATE

WESTERN SHORE
George Plater, president
Thomas Stone
Charles Carroll of
  Carrollton
John Smith
James McHenry
Daniel Carroll
Charles Carroll, Barrister
Richard Barnes

Benedict Edward Hall

EASTERN SHORE
Matthew Tilghman
John Henry
Robert Goldsborough

William Hindman
Josiah Polk
Edward Lloyd

HOUSE OF DELEGATES

ST. MARY'S
Uriah Forrest
John Allen Thomas
Edmund Plowden
James Mills

KENT
John Cadwalader
William Stevenson
James Lloyd
Marmaduke Tilden

ANNE ARUNDEL
John Hall
Nicholas Worthington
Brice T. B. Worthington
William Brogden

CALVERT
William Fitzhugh
Samuel Chew
Michael Taney
William Allein

CHARLES
Gerard Blackstone Causin
John Dent (R–2)
Daniel Jenifer
Michael Jenifer Stone
Samuel Hanson, of Samuel
  (E–2)

BALTIMORE
Thomas Cockey Deye,
  speaker
Charles Ridgely, of William
Samuel Worthington
John Beale Howard

TALBOT
John Gibson
James Hindman
Howes Goldsborough
  (DNS, R–1)
William Maynadier
Hugh Sherwood (E–1)

SOMERSET
John Winder
Henry Waggaman
Thomas King
Josiah Dashiell

DORCHESTER
James Shaw
Thomas Firmin Eccleston
Levin Kirkman
John Smoot (DNS, R–1)

CECIL
Archibald Job
Samuel Miller
Benjamin Brevard

William Rowland

ANNAPOLIS
Allen Quynn
Samuel Chase

PRINCE GEORGE'S
Josias Beall (DNS, R–2)
Walter Bowie
George Fraser Hawkins
Thomas Duckett
Rinaldo Johnson (E–2)

QUEEN ANNE'S
Turbutt Wright
James Kent
John Seney
Edward DeCoursey

WORCESTER
Henry Dennis
William Morris
Joseph Dashiell
Samuel Handy

FREDERICK
Thomas Beatty
John Hanson (DNS, R–1)
Samuel Duvall
David Shriver
Thomas Johnson (E–1,
  DNS, R–1)

William Murdock Beall
  (E–2)

HARFORD
John Taylor
Benjamin Bradford Norris
William Smithson
John Love

CAROLINE
William Whitely
Hugh McBryde
Richard Mason (DNS)
William Hopper

BALTIMORE TOWN
Henry Wilson
David McMechen

WASHINGTON
John Stull
John Barnes
Thomas Sprigg
James Chapline

MONTGOMERY
Edward Burgess
Charles Greenbury Griffith
William Bayly
Laurence O'Neale

Committee Service

ELECTIONS AND PRIVILEGES
N. Worthington (1, 2)
Quynn (1, 2)
McMechen (1, 2)
Gibson (1)
Ridgely, of William (1)
Taylor (2)
Winder (2)

GRIEVANCES AND COURTS OF
JUSTICE
B. Worthington (1, 2)
J. Hall (1, 2)
Dent (1)
M. J. Stone (1)
Bayly (1, 2)

Quynn (2)
Thomas (2)
Morris (2)
Waggaman (2)
Beatty (2)

CLAIMS
Forrest (1, 2)
Wilson (1, 2)
Duckett (1, 2)
Allein (1)
Brogden (1)
J. Hindman (1, 2)
Bowie (1)
Stevenson (1)
W. M. Beall (2)
B. Worthington (2)

Eccleston (2)
McBryde (2)

MANUFACTORIES
Job (1)
Duvall (1)
S. Worthington (1, 2)
Wilson (1, 2)
Stull (1, 2)
Shriver (1, 2)
Cadwalader (1)
Waggaman (2)
Jenifer (2)

LAWS TO EXPIRE
Quynn (1, 2)
J. Lloyd (1)

N. Worthington (1, 2)
Seney (2)
Jenifer (2)

PUBLIC TAXES
Kent (1)
Brogden (1)
J. Lloyd (1)
Griffith (1)
Duckett (1, 2)
Hawkins (1, 2)
Job (1)
Handy (2)
Josiah Dashiell (2)
N. Worthington (2)

EXECUTIVE COUNCIL

November 21, 1781–November 15, 1782

John Hoskins Stone   James Brice   Jeremiah Townly Chase
Samuel Turbutt Wright   Benjamin C. Stoddert

GENERAL ASSEMBLY OF 1782–1783

William Paca, governor

FIRST SESSION: November 4, 1782–January 15, 1783
SECOND SESSION: April 21–June 1, 1783

SENATE

WESTERN SHORE
George Plater, president 1 [1]
Thomas Stone
Charles Carroll of
  Carrollton, president 2 [1]
John Smith
James McHenry
Daniel Carroll (DNS)
Charles Carroll, Barrister
  (D–2)
Richard Barnes
Benedict Edward Hall

Samuel Hughes (E–2)

EASTERN SHORE
Matthew Tilghman,
  president 1, 2 [1]
John Henry

Robert Goldsborough
  (R–2)
William Hindman
Josiah Polk (DNS)
Edward Lloyd

HOUSE OF DELEGATES

ST. MARY'S
Uriah Forrest
Thomas Bond
Philip Key
Athanasius Ford

KENT
Thomas Smyth, Jr.
John Cadwalader
James Pearce
James Lloyd

ANNE ARUNDEL
Brice T. B. Worthington
Nicholas Worthington
John Hall
William Brogden

CALVERT
William Fitzhugh
Samuel Chew
Edward Reynolds
John Weems, Jr.

CHARLES
George Dent
William Wilkinson
Michael Jenifer Stone
William Courts

BALTIMORE
Thomas Cockey Deye,
  speaker
Charles Ridgely, of William
Samuel Worthington
John Cradock

TALBOT
Hugh Sherwood, of
  Huntington
James Hindman
John Roberts, Jr.
Woolman Gibson, Jr.

SOMERSET
John Done
Gillis Polk (DNS)
Henry Jackson
John Stewart

DORCHESTER
James Shaw
Robertson Stevens
Levin Kirkman
John Smoot

CECIL
Archibald Job
Samuel Miller
Benjamin Brevard

William Rowland

ANNAPOLIS
Allen Quynn
Samuel Chase

PRINCE GEORGE'S
Thomas Duckett
Walter Bowie
Jeremiah Magruder
George Fraser Hawkins

QUEEN ANNE'S
James Kent
John Seney
Clement Sewell
Edward DeCoursey

WORCESTER
Joseph Dashiell
Henry Dennis
William Morris
Nehemiah Holland

FREDERICK
David Shriver
Thomas Ogle
Samuel Duvall
Peter Mantz (DNS, R–1)
Thomas Beatty (E–1)

HARFORD
John Taylor
Benjamin Bradford Norris
Ignatius Wheeler, Jr.
William Smithson

CAROLINE
William Hopper
Philemon Downes (DNS,
  R–1)
Hugh McBryde (DNS)
Charles Daffin (DNS)
William Keene (E–1)

BALTIMORE TOWN
William Fell
David McMechen

WASHINGTON
John Stull
John Barnes
James Chapline
Thomas Sprigg

MONTGOMERY
Edward Burgess
Charles Greenbury Griffith
Laurence O'Neale
Benjamin Edwards

Committee Service

ELECTIONS AND PRIVILEGES
Dashiell (1)
N. Worthington (1, 2)
Cradock (1)
Quynn (1, 2)
McMechen (1, 2)
S. Duvall (2)
Chew (2)

**GRIEVANCES AND COURTS OF
JUSTICE**
B. Worthington (1, 2)

S. Chase (1, 2)
Fell (1, 2)
J. Hall (1, 2)
Kent (1, 2)

CLAIMS
J. Hindman (1, 2)
Brogden (1, 2)
Stewart (1)
Sewall (1)
Done (1)

Bond (1, 2)
S. Worthington (1)
Duckett (2)
Reynolds (2)
Jackson (2)
Key (2)

LAWS TO EXPIRE
Quynn (1, 2)
N. Worthington (1, 2)
Ogle (1, 2)

MANUFACTORIES
McMechen (1, 2)
Job (1, 2)
Dashiell (1)
Magruder (1, 2)
Stewart (1)
Forrest (2)
Ridgely, of William (2)
S. Chase (2)
Jackson (2)

EXECUTIVE COUNCIL

November 16, 1782–November 23, 1783

Benjamin C. Stoddert   Gabriel Duvall   Jeremiah Townly Chase
James Brice   John Hoskins Stone

[1] Tilghman was elected president on December 24, 1782, to replace Plater who was unable to attend. Charles Carroll of Carrollton was elected president on May 22, 1783, to replace Tilghman, who was indisposed.

GENERAL ASSEMBLY OF 1783

William Paca, governor

November 3–December 26, 1783

SENATE

WESTERN SHORE
George Plater
Thomas Stone (DNS)
Charles Carroll of
    Carrollton, president [1]
John Smith

James McHenry
Daniel Carroll, president [1]
Richard Barnes [1]
Benedict Edward Hall
Samuel Hughes

EASTERN SHORE
Matthew Tilghman
    (DNS, R)
John Henry
William Hindman
Josiah Polk (DNS)

Edward Lloyd
John Cadwalader (E, Dcl)
Robert Goldsborough (E,
    DNS)
William Perry (E)

HOUSE OF DELEGATES

ST. MARY'S
William Somerville
John DeButts
Edmund Plowden
Philip Key

KENT
Peregrine Lethrbury
William Stevenson
Robert Maxwell
James Brown Dunn

ANNE ARUNDEL
Brice T. B. Worthington
Nicholas Worthington
John Hall
Nicholas (Maccubbin)
    Carroll [2]

CALVERT
John Grahame
Levin Mackall
Thomas Harwood III
William Ireland

CHARLES
Frances Ware
Josias Hawkins
Samuel Hanson, Jr.

John Dent, of John

BALTIMORE
Thomas Cockey Deye,
    speaker
Charles Ridgely, of William
John Stevenson
Charles Ridgely

TALBOT
James Hindman
Woolman Gibson (DNS)
John Roberts
Edward Harris

SOMERSET
Henry Jackson
John Done (DNS)
John Winder (DNS, R)
Gillis Polk

DORCHESTER
James Shaw
Daniel Sulivane
Levin Kirkman (DNS)
Thomas Firmin Eccleston
    (DNS, R)
Gustavus Scott (E)

CECIL
Archibald Job
Samuel Miller
William Rowland
Benjamin Brevard

ANNAPOLIS
Allen Quynn
Samuel Chase (DNS)

PRINCE GEORGE'S
Walter Bowie (DNS)
Thomas Duckett
George Digges
Jeremiah Magruder

QUEEN ANNE'S
John Seney
Clement Sewell
James Kent
Edward DeCoursey

WORCESTER
Nehemiah Holland
William Morris
Henry Dennis (DNS)
Joseph Dashiell (DNS)

FREDERICK
Thomas Beatty
David Shriver

Nathan Hammond
Thomas Ogle

HARFORD
Benjamin Bradford Norris
John Love
John Taylor (DNS)
Ignatius Wheeler, Jr.

CAROLINE
William Hopper
William Keene
Thomas Hughlett
Thomas Hardcastle (DNS)

BALTIMORE TOWN
John Sterett
David McMechen

WASHINGTON
John Stull (DNS)
James Chapline (DNS)
Nicholas Swingle
John Jeremiah Jacob

MONTGOMERY
Laurence O'Neale
Benjamin Edwards
Edward Burgess (DNS)
Thomas Sprigg Wooton

Committee Service

ELECTIONS AND PRIVILEGES
B. Worthington
Seney
N. Worthington
Quynn
J. Hindman

GRIEVANCES AND COURTS OF
JUSTICE
Ware
Ridgely, of William
J. Hall
Key
J. Hindman

CLAIMS
J. Hindman
Digges
Sterett
Key
Duckett
Hawkins

Hammond

LAWS TO EXPIRE
Quynn
N. Worthington
T. Ogle

EXECUTIVE COUNCIL [3]

November 24, 1783–November 24, 1784

Jeremiah Townly Chase (R)   Gabriel Duvall (R)   James Brice (R, E, Dcl)
John Hoskins Stone   Benjamin Ogle (Dcl)   John Davidson (E)
Charles Wallace (E)   Samuel Turbutt Wright (E)   Aquila Paca (E)

[1] Barnes was elected president on December 23, 1783, to replace Daniel Carroll who was indisposed, but Barnes declined to accept the position. Charles Carroll of Carrollton was then chosen.
[2] In accordance with conditions specified in the will of his uncle, Charles Carroll, Barrister, Nicholas Maccubbin changed his surname to Carroll by Act of Assembly.
[3] Chase, Duvall, Brice, Stone, and Ogle were elected to the Council on November 24, 1783. Ogle, however, declined to accept, and both Chase and Brice resigned during December. On December 26, 1783, Governor Paca wrote to the General Assembly suggesting that since the Council had only two remaining members, not a quorum, the Assembly should select the necessary replacements. Accordingly, on that date, the legislature elected Davidson, Wallace, and Wright. When Duvall resigned in July 1784, the Council reelected Brice to fill the vacancy. When Brice declined to serve again, Paca was elected in August 1784.

GENERAL ASSEMBLY OF 1784

William Paca, governor

November 1, 1784–January 22, 1785

SENATE

WESTERN SHORE
George Plater, president [1]
Thomas Stone
Charles Carroll of
    Carrollton

John Smith, president [1]
James McHenry
Daniel Carroll
Richard Barnes
Benedict Edward Hall
Samuel Hughes

EASTERN SHORE
John Henry
William Hindman
Josiah Polk (DNS, D)
Edward Lloyd

Robert Goldsborough (Dcl)
William Perry
William Hemsley (E, Dcl)
George Gale (E)
James Lloyd (E, DNS)

HOUSE OF DELEGATES

ST. MARY'S
Philip Key
John DeButts
Edmund Plowden
Athanasius Ford (DNS)

KENT
Peregrine Lethrbury
John Scott
Richard Graves (Ds, E) [2]
John Cadwalader

ANNE ARUNDEL
John Hall
Brice T. B. Worthington
Nicholas Worthington
Nicholas (Maccubbin)
    Carroll

CALVERT
John Grahame
Michael Taney
John Weems, Jr.
Alexander Frazier

CHARLES
Francis Ware
George Dent
Josias Hawkins (DNS)

Samuel Hanson

BALTIMORE
Thomas Cockey Deye,
    speaker
Charles Ridgely, of William
Charles Ridgely
John Stevenson

TALBOT
James Hindman
Edward Harris
John Roberts
John Gibson III

SOMERSET
George Gale (R)
John Dashiell
Richard Waters, Jr.
Arnold Elzey

DORCHESTER
James Shaw
Gustavus Scott
James Steele
Thomas Firmin Eccleston
    (DNS)

CECIL
Samuel Miller

Benjamin Brevard
Archibald Job
John Oglivie

ANNAPOLIS
Allen Quynn
Samuel Chase

PRINCE GEORGE'S
Walter Bowie
George Digges
Rinaldo Johnson
Erasmus Gantt

QUEEN ANNE'S
Robert Wright
Edward DeCoursey
John Seney
Clement Sewell

WORCESTER
Joshua Townshend
Peter Chaille
William Morris (DNS)
Joseph Dashiell

FREDERICK
Thomas Beatty
Thomas Gantt
John D. Cary

David Shriver

HARFORD
Benjamin Bradford Norris
John Love
James Bond
Ignatius Wheeler, Jr.

CAROLINE
Thomas Hardcastle
Thomas Hughlett
Henry Downes
William Wheatly (DNS)

BALTIMORE TOWN
John Sterett
David McMechen

WASHINGTON
John Stull
John Cellars
Nicholas Swingle
Thomas Hart (DNS)

MONTGOMERY
Benjamin Edwards
Thomas Cramphin
Laurence O'Neale
Thomas Sprigg Wooton

Committee Service

ELECTIONS AND PRIVILEGES
N. Worthington
Quynn
R. Wright
Joseph Dashiell
Fraizer

GRIEVANCES AND COURTS
OF JUSTICE
Ware
N. Carroll
J. Hall
Key
E. Gantt

CLAIMS
J. Scott
Digges
Job
Key
Johnson
DeButts

Grahame
J. Hindman

LAWS TO EXPIRE
Quynn
N. Worthington
McMechen

EXECUTIVE COUNCIL

November 25, 1784–November 17, 1785

Charles Wallace   Aquila Paca   John Davidson
John Hoskins Stone   Samuel Turbutt Wright

[1] Smith was elected president on January 13, 1785, to replace Plater who had a leave of absence.
[2] Graves was declared ineligible for election after a report was delivered that indicated he had not resigned his commission as a field officer until after the election. He was discharged on November 24, was reelected, and again qualified on December 11, 1784.

GENERAL ASSEMBLY OF 1785

William Smallwood, governor

November 7, 1785–March 12, 1786

SENATE

WESTERN SHORE
George Plater, president [1]
Thomas Stone
Charles Carroll of
    Carrollton

John Smith
James McHenry (DNS, R)
Daniel Carroll, president [1]
Richard Barnes
Benedict Edward Hall

Samuel Hughes
Daniel Bowley (E)

EASTERN SHORE
John Henry
William Hindman (DNS)

Edward Lloyd
William Perry
George Gale
James Lloyd

HOUSE OF DELEGATES

ST. MARY'S
Philip Key
Thomas Bond
William Somerville
John DeButts

KENT
Peregrine Lethrbury
Robert Maxwell
Richard Graves
James Pearce

ANNE ARUNDEL
Brice T. B. Worthington
Nicholas Worthington
John Hall
Nicholas (Maccubbin)
    Carroll

CALVERT
John Grahame
Michael Taney
Thomas Gantt, Jr.
Alexander Frazier

CHARLES
John Courts Jones
Zephaniah Turner
George Dent, Jr.

John Hoskins Stone

BALTIMORE
Thomas Cockey Deye,
    speaker
Charles Ridgely, of William
John Stevenson
Charles Ridgely

TALBOT
John Roberts
Pollard Edmondson
Howes Goldsborough
John Bracco

SOMERSET
John Gale
John Dashiell
Richard Waters, Jr.
William Adams

DORCHESTER
Henry Waggaman
William Ennalls Hooper
Levin Kirkman
Henry Ennalls

CECIL
Jeremiah Baker
John Oglivie

Samuel Miller
Nathaniel Ramsay

ANNAPOLIS
Allen Quynn
Samuel Chase

PRINCE GEORGE'S
Walter Bowie
Fielder Bowie
Robert Bowie
George Digges

QUEEN ANNE'S
Clement Sewell
John Seney
Joshua Seney
George Jackson

WORCESTER
John Pope Mitchell
William Purnell
Joseph Dashiell
Peter Chaille

FREDERICK
Abraham Faw
John D. Cary
John Beatty
Mountjoy Bayly

HARFORD
Benjamin Bradford Norris
John Love
James Bond
Ignatius Wheeler, Jr.

CAROLINE
Thomas Hughlett
William Whitely
Matthew Driver
Henry Downes

BALTIMORE TOWN
John Sterett
David McMechen

WASHINGTON
John Stull
John Cellars
Jacob Funk
Henry Schnebeley (DNS)

MONTGOMERY
Thomas Sprigg Wooton
Thomas Beall, of George
Laurence O'Neale
Thomas Cramphin

Committee Service

ELECTIONS AND PRIVILEGES
N. Worthington
B. Worthington
John Seney
Quynn
Ramsay

GRIEVANCES AND COURTS OF
JUSTICE
N. Carroll

Joseph Dashiell
Bracco
Ridgely, of William
S. Chase
B. Worthington
McMechen

CLAIMS
Turner
Beall

Sewell
Digges
Ramsay
Faw
Sterett
Goldsborough
Ridgely, of William
Grahame

LAWS TO EXPIRE
N. Worthington

Quynn
S. Chase

MANUFACTORIES
Joseph Dashiell
DeButts
Bracco
B. Worthington
Taney

EXECUTIVE COUNCIL [2]

November 18, 1785–November 30, 1786

Jeremiah Townly Chase   James Brice   Gabriel Duvall (R)
John Kilty   Samuel Turbutt Wright   William Paca (E, R)

[1] Carroll was elected president on January 18, 1786, to replace Plater, who had a leave of absence.
[2] Duvall resigned from the Executive Council on April 20, 1786, because of his opinion that the "late Act to vest certain Powers in the Governor and Council, is repugnant to the Constitution and Form of Government of this State. . . ." William Paca, who was elected on April 27 to replace Duvall, resigned on November 4, 1786, in order to take his seat in the House on November 6, 1786.

GENERAL ASSEMBLY OF 1786–1787

William Smallwood, governor

FIRST SESSION: November 6, 1786–January 20, 1787
SECOND SESSION: April 10–May 26, 1787

SENATE

WESTERN SHORE
Thomas Stone
Charles Carroll of
  Carrollton
Thomas Johnson (Dcl)
Richard Barnes (Dcl)
George Plater, president 1,
  2 [1]
John Hall
John Smith, president 1 [1]
Daniel Carroll, president 2 [1]
Richard Ridgely

Samuel Hughes (E–1)
Benjamin C. Stoddert (E–1,
  Dcl)
William Harrison (E–1)
EASTERN SHORE
John Henry

George Gale
Edward Lloyd
William Hemsley
William Paca (Dcl)
William Perry
Peregrine Tilghman (E–1)

HOUSE OF DELEGATES

ST. MARY'S
Samuel Abell, Jr.
John DeButts
Uriah Forrest (Ds–1) [2]
James Hopewell
Zachariah Forrest (E–2)

KENT
Isaac Perkins
Richard Miller
Josiah Johnson
Robert Wright

ANNE ARUNDEL
Richard Harwood
Nicholas Worthington
Samuel Chase
Brice T. B. Worthington

CALVERT
Michael Taney
William Fitzhugh, Jr.
John Grahame
Thomas Gantt, Jr.

CHARLES
George Dent
Zephaniah Turner
William Hanson McPherson

John Hoskins Stone

BALTIMORE
Thomas Cockey Deye,
  speaker
Samuel Owings
Edward Cockey
Charles Ridgely

TALBOT
John Roberts
Hugh Sherwood
John Stevens
John Gibson

SOMERSET
John Gale
William Adams
Gillis Polk
John Stewart

DORCHESTER
James Shaw
William Ennalls Hooper
Archibald Patison
James Steele

CECIL
Richard Bond
Michael Wallace
William Matthews

Benjamin Bravard

ANNAPOLIS
Allen Quynn
Thomas Jennings (R–1,
  E–1)

PRINCE GEORGE'S
Walter Bowie
Fielder Bowie
Robert Bowie
George Digges

QUEEN ANNE'S
John Seney
Joshua Seney
George Jackson
William Paca

WORCESTER
John Pope Mitchell
William Purnell
Josiah Mitchell
Jenkins Henry [3]

FREDERICK
Abraham Faw
Peter Mantz
Thomas Johnson
Mountjoy Bayly

HARFORD
Benjamin Bradford Norris
James Bond
John Love
Ignatius Wheeler

CAROLINE
Thomas Loockerman
Philip Walker
Thomas Goldsborough
  (DNS)
Thomas Hardcastle

BALTIMORE TOWN
Jesse Hollingsworth
David McMechen

WASHINGTON
John Cellars
Jacob Funk
John Stull
Richard Cromwell

MONTGOMERY
Laurence O'Neale
Edward Burgess
William Holmes
John Haymond Nichols

Committee Service

ELECTIONS AND PRIVILEGES
Paca (1, 2)
T. Johnson (1, 2)
McMechen (1, 2)
Quynn (1, 2)
John Seney (1, 2)

GRIEVANCES AND COURTS OF
JUSTICE
Jennings (1, 2)

Harwood (1, 2)
U. Forrest (1)
F. Bowie (1)
Wallace (1)
Paca (1, 2)
Z. Forrest (2)
S. Chase (2)
Dent (2)

CLAIMS
Jackson (1)
Turner (1, 2)
Hollingsworth (1, 2)
Stewart (1)
Faw (1, 2)
Gibson (1)
U. Forrest (1)
DeButts (1)
J. Johnson (1)

Patison (2)
Owings (2)
Digges (2)
Perkins (2)

LAWS TO EXPIRE
N. Worthington (1, 2)
Quynn (1, 2)
Joshua Seney (1)
McMechen (2)

EXECUTIVE COUNCIL

December 1, 1786–November 22, 1787

James Brice   Jeremiah Townly Chase   James Hindman
John Kilty   John Davidson

[1] Smith was elected president on January 8, 1787, to replace Plater, who had a leave of absence. Plater was reelected president for the second session, but was granted another leave of absence on May 20, 1787, and Carroll was chosen to replace him.
[2] Forrest was declared ineligible at the time of election "for the want of residence." He was discharged on January 15.
[3] It is presumed that the full name of this delegate was Francis Jenkins Henry.

GENERAL ASSEMBLY OF 1787–1788

William Smallwood, governor

FIRST SESSION: November 5–December 17, 1787
SECOND SESSION: May 12–27, 1788

SENATE

WESTERN SHORE
Thomas Stone (D–1)
Charles Carroll of
  Carrollton
George Plater,
  president 1, 2 [1]

John Hall
John Smith, president 2 [1]
Daniel Carroll, president 2 [1]
Richard Ridgely
Samuel Hughes
William Harrison (DNS)

Richard Potts (E–1, Dcl)
Thomas Johnson (E–2,
  DNS)

EASTERN SHORE
John Henry

George Gale
Edward Lloyd
William Hemsley
William Perry
Peregrine Tilghman

HOUSE OF DELEGATES

ST. MARY'S [2]
Samuel Abell, Jr.
George Thomas (Ds–2) [2]
Philip Key (Ds–2) [2]
Uriah Forrest

KENT
Richard Miller
Jeremiah Nichols
Josiah Johnson (DNS)
Philip Reed

ANNE ARUNDEL
Richard Harwood
Nicholas Worthington
Brice T. B. Worthington
James Carroll

CALVERT
Michael Taney
John Grahame
William Fitzhugh, Jr.
Thomas Gantt

CHARLES
George Dent
John Parnham
William Hanson McPherson
Henry Henley Chapman

BALTIMORE
Thomas Cockey Deye,
  speaker
Harry Dorsey Gough
Edward Cockey
Charles Ridgely

TALBOT
John Roberts
Hugh Sherwood, of
  Huntington
James Tilghman
William Hayward, Jr.

SOMERSET
John Gale
John Stewart
Gillis Polk
William Adams

DORCHESTER
James Shaw
Archibald Patison
Moses Lecompte
James Steele

CECIL
Benjamin Bravard
Richard Bond

William Matthews
Samuel Miller

ANNAPOLIS
Allen Quynn
Gabriel Duvall

PRINCE GEORGE'S
David Craufurd
Fielder Bowie
Walter Bowie
George Digges

QUEEN ANNE'S
John Seney
Joshua Seney
John Brown
George Jackson

WORCESTER
John Selby Purnell
John Pope Mitchell
William Purnell
Francis Jenkins Henry

FREDERICK
Thomas Sim Lee (DNS,
  R–2)
Thomas Johnson
Abraham Faw

Richard Potts

HARFORD
John Love
Aquila Scott
Benjamin Bradford Norris
Ignatius Wheeler

CAROLINE
Thomas Loockerman
Henry Downes
Philip Walker
Thomas Hughlett

BALTIMORE TOWN
Samuel Chase
David McMechen

WASHINGTON
Jacob Funk
Andrew Bruce
John Cellars
Ignatius Taylor

MONTGOMERY
Laurence O'Neale
Edward Burgess
William Holmes
Charles Greenbury Griffith

Committee Service

ELECTIONS AND PRIVILEGES
Quynn (1, 2)
Harwood (1)
T. Johnson (1)
Dent (1)
Joshua Seney (1)
Faw (2)
Norris (2)
B. Worthington (2)
John Seney (2)

GRIEVANCES AND COURTS OF
JUSTICE
N. Worthington (1)
John Seney (1)
Taney (1)
Faw (1)
Patison (1)
Duvall (1, 2)
T. Johnson (1)
Joshua Seney (1)
McMechen (1)

C. Ridgely (2)
O'Neale (2)
B. Worthington (2)
Quynn (2)

LAWS TO EXPIRE
N. Worthington (1, 2)
J. Carroll (1)
Quynn (1, 2)
Duvall (2)

CLAIMS
Jackson (1)

Faw (1, 2)
Craufurd (1, 2)
Digges (1, 2)
J. Tilghman (1, 2)
Patison (1)
Dent (1)
Grahame (1)
Loockerman (1, 2)
John Seney (2)
Forrest (2)
Nichols (2)
Holmes (2)

EXECUTIVE COUNCIL

November 23, 1787–November 10, 1788

Jeremiah Townly Chase
John Davidson
James Brice
Benjamin Harrison
John Kilty

[1] Carroll was elected president on May 15, 1788, to replace Plater, who was indisposed. Carroll was absent on May 24 and Smith was chosen. He resigned the following day, however, and Plater was returned to the presidency for the remainder of the session.

[2] Charges of "treating" were brought against all four of the St. Mary's County delegates. Thomas and Key were declared unduly elected on May 20, 1788.

GENERAL ASSEMBLY OF 1788

Thomas Johnson, governor (Dcl) [1]

John Eager Howard, governor [1]

November 3–December 23, 1788

SENATE

WESTERN SHORE
Charles Carroll of
  Carrollton
George Plater, president [2]
John Hall

John Smith
Daniel Carroll, president [2]
Richard Ridgely
Samuel Hughes
William Harrison (DNS)
Thomas Johnson (Dcl)

James Carroll (E)

EASTERN SHORE
John Henry
George Gale
Edward Lloyd (R)

William Hemsley (DNS)
William Perry
Peregrine Tilghman
Nicholas Hammond (E)

HOUSE OF DELEGATES

ST. MARY'S
Uriah Forrest
Samuel Abell
Charles Chilton
George Thomas

KENT
William Tilghman
Richard Miller
Philip Reed
Cornelius Comegys

ANNE ARUNDEL
Richard Harwood
John Frances Mercer
Jeremiah Townly Chase
Nicholas Worthington

CALVERT
Thomas Gantt
Alexander Frazier
William Fitzhugh, Jr.
Thomas Blake

CHARLES
John Parnham
George Dent
Henry Henley Chapman
William Hanson McPherson

BALTIMORE
Thomas Cockey Deye,
  speaker
Charles Ridgely
Charles Ridgely, of William
Edward Cockey

TALBOT
Hugh Sherwood, of
  Huntington
James Tilghman, Jr.
David Kerr
Samuel Chamberlaine

SOMERSET
John Stewart
Gillis Polk
John Gale (DNS)
Henry Waggaman

DORCHESTER
William Vans Murray
James Shaw
Moses Lecompte
James Steele

CECIL
Richard Bond
Samuel Miller
William Matthews

Benjamin Bravard

ANNAPOLIS
Allen Quynn
Gabriel Duvall

PRINCE GEORGE'S
David Craufurd
Walter Bowie
George Digges
Robert Bowie (Ds) [3]
Fielder Bowie (E) [3]

QUEEN ANNE'S
John Seney
James Tilghman
James Hollyday
Clement Sewell

WORCESTER
John Selby Purnell
Benjamin Dennis
William Purnell
James Houston

FREDERICK
Richard Potts
Abraham Faw
John McPherson
John Gwinn

HARFORD
Benjamin Bradford Norris
Aquila Scott
William Pinkney
John Lee Webster (DNS, R)
Abraham Jarrett (E)

CAROLINE
Peter Edmondson
Charles Emory
Thomas Mason
Zabdiel Potter (DNS, R)
William Banckes (E)

BALTIMORE TOWN
James McHenry
John Coulter

WASHINGTON
Thomas Sprigg
Henry Shryock
Ignatius Taylor
John Lynn

MONTGOMERY
Jeremiah Crabb
Thomas Cramphin
Laurence O'Neale
William Hammond Dorsey

Committee Service

ELECTIONS AND PRIVILEGES
Seney
Forrest
Potts
Faw
Dent

GRIEVANCES AND COURTS OF JUSTICE
Shaw
Worthington
J. Tilghman
Stewart
Faw

CLAIMS
Faw
Chilton
Ridgely, of William
Digges
Shaw
Stewart

Sewell

LAWS TO EXPIRE
Worthington
Quynn
Mercer

EXECUTIVE COUNCIL

November 11, 1788–November 16, 1789

James Brice   John Davidson   William Hindman
Josias Carvil Hall   John Kilty

[1] Johnson was chosen governor by joint ballot of the Senate and House on November 10, 1788. Notice that he declined to accept the appointment was received by the Senate on November 20, and after taking a new ballot John Eager Howard was declared governor on November 21. Six days later he was qualified and assumed office.

[2] Carroll was elected president on December 16, 1788, to replace Plater, who had been granted a leave of absence.

[3] A remonstrance, received from Fielder Bowie on November 4, 1788, claimed that Robert Bowie was collector of the taxes at the time of his election, and therefore ineligible. Robert Bowie was discharged on November 12, and a new election was called. On November 28 Fielder Bowie was qualified as the newly elected delegate from Prince George's County.

GENERAL ASSEMBLY OF 1789

John Eager Howard, governor

November 2–December 25, 1789

SENATE

WESTERN SHORE
Charles Carroll of
  Carrollton
George Plater (DNS)
John Hall

John Smith, president [1]
Daniel Carroll, president [1]
Richard Ridgely
Samuel Hughes
William Harrison (DNS, D)

James Carroll
Daniel Bowley (E)

EASTERN SHORE
John Henry (DNS)
George Gale

William Hemsley (DNS)
William Perry
Peregrine Tilghman
Nicholas Hammond

HOUSE OF DELEGATES

ST. MARY'S
Henry James Carroll
Zachariah Forrest
Richard Barnes
James Hopewell

KENT
William Tilghman
Matthew Tilghman
John Moore
Peregrine Lethrbury (DNS)

ANNE ARUNDEL
Nicholas Worthington
John Griffith Worthington
Brice T. B. Worthington
Richard Harwood

CALVERT
Alexander Frazier
Thomas Gantt
Peregrine Freeland
John Somerville

CHARLES
George Dent, speaker
John Parnham
William Craik
William Hanson McPherson

BALTIMORE
Charles Ridgely
James Gittings
Charles Ridgely, of William
Richard Owings

TALBOT
Hugh Sherwood, of
  Huntington
James Tilghman, Jr.
Edward Lloyd (DNS)
David Kerr

SOMERSET
Tubman Lowes
John Stewart
John Gale
Levin Winder

DORCHESTER
William Vans Murray
James Shaw
Moses Lecompte
James Steele

CECIL
William Matthews
Nathaniel Ramsay
  (DNS, R)

Edward Oldham
Richard Bond
Henry Hollingsworth (E)

ANNAPOLIS
Allen Quynn
Gabriel Duvall

PRINCE GEORGE'S
Robert Bowie
Walter Bowie
Thomas Clark
George Digges

QUEEN ANNE'S
John Seney
James O'Bryon
James Tilghman
John Brown (DNS)

WORCESTER
John Selby Purnell
Benjamin Dennis
Isaac Houston
Benjamin F. A. C. Dashiell

FREDERICK
Abraham Faw
Joshua Dorsey
David Shriver

Mountjoy Bayly

HARFORD
Benjamin Bradford Norris
William Pinkney
John Lee Webster (DNS)
John Love

CAROLINE
William Banckes
William Whitely
Charles Emory
Thomas Mason

BALTIMORE TOWN
Samuel Sterett
James McHenry

WASHINGTON
Henry Shryock
John Stull
Adam Ott
John Lynn

MONTGOMERY
Edward Burgess
Jeremiah Crabb
Laurence O'Neale
Uriah Forrest

Committee Service

ELECTIONS AND PRIVILEGES
Craik
B. Worthington
Seney
U. Forrest
C. Ridgely, of William

GRIEVANCES AND COURTS OF
JUSTICE
Pinkney

Quynn
Seney
Stewart
O'Neale

CLAIMS
M. Tilghman

Stewart
Banckes
Faw
C. Ridgely, of William
Sterett
B. Worthington
J. Tilghman, Jr.

LAWS TO EXPIRE
Faw
Quynn
U. Forrest
Dorsey
N. Worthington
Duvall

EXECUTIVE COUNCIL

November 17, 1789–November 8, 1790

John Kilty   James Brice   John Davidson
William Hindman   Randolph Brandt Latimer

[1] Smith was elected president on December 7, 1789, to replace Carroll who had been granted a leave of absence.

Biographies

ABBOTT, JOHN (?–?). BORN: probably in England. IMMIGRATED: by 1631, probably as a servant or employee of Cloberry & Company. RESIDED: on Kent Island. PRIVATE CAREER. SOCIAL STATUS AND ACTIVITIES: probably left the colony in the 1640s after Ingle's Rebellion. OCCUPATIONAL PROFILE: indentured servant or employee of Cloberry & Company, 1631; laborer, 1633; planter. PUBLIC CAREER. LEGISLATIVE SERVICE: Assembly, Kent County, 1640. LOCAL OFFICE: justice, Kent County, 1645/46. WEALTH DURING LIFETIME. LAND AT FIRST ELECTION: 40 acres; patented an additional 200 acres in 1644.

ABELL, SAMUEL (ca. 1677–1762). BORN: in 1675 or 1678 in St. Mary's County; elder son. NATIVE: third generation. RESIDED: on Beaverdam Manor, St. Mary's County. FAMILY BACKGROUND. FATHER: Samuel Abell (?–1698), son of Capt. Robert Abell (1628–?). MOTHER: Ann. BROTHER: John (1680–1746). MARRIED ca. 1704 Winifred Hall (?–1754). CHILDREN. SONS: Samuel, Jr. (ca. 1719–1777); John (ca. 1721–?). PRIVATE CAREER. EDUCATION: literate. RELIGIOUS AFFILIATION: Anglican. OCCUPATIONAL PROFILE: planter. PUBLIC CAREER. LEGISLATIVE SERVICE: Lower House, St. Mary's County, 1745. WEALTH DURING LIFETIME. LAND AT FIRST ELECTION: at least 196 acres of manor land in St. Mary's County held under lease from the proprietor. SIGNIFICANT CHANGES IN LAND BETWEEN FIRST ELECTION AND DEATH: leased an additional 76 acres of Beaverdam Manor, St. Mary's County, in 1762. WEALTH AT DEATH. DIED: in 1762 in St. Mary's County. PERSONAL PROPERTY: TEV, £217.3.3 current money (including 4 slaves); FB, £170.17.8. LAND: leases on ca. 272 acres in St. Mary's County.

ABELL, SAMUEL, JR. (1755–ca. 1801). BORN: on January 13, 1755, in St. Andrew's Parish, St. Mary's County; second son. NATIVE: fifth generation. RESIDED: in Lower Resurrection Hundred, St. Mary's County. FAMILY BACKGROUND. FATHER: Samuel Abell, Jr. (ca. 1719–1777), son of *Samuel Abell* (ca. 1677–1762). MOTHER: Eleanor Bryan. BROTHERS: Philip (1741–1772); Robert (1757–1802), a member of the Constitutional Convention from Kentucky in 1788; and Abner (1759–?). SISTERS: Mary (?–1815), who married Ignatius Abell; Dorothy, who married (first name unknown) Winsor; Winifred, who married Benjamin Morgan; Alethia, who married (first name unknown) Spalding; and Eleanor. MARRIED Mary (?–1813). CHILDREN. Probably none who survived. PRIVATE CAREER. EDUCATION: literate. RELIGIOUS AFFILIATION: Anglican. SOCIAL STATUS AND ACTIVITIES: Esq., by 1785. OCCUPATIONAL PROFILE: probably a planter; owned water mills inherited from his father. PUBLIC CAREER. LEGISLATIVE SERVICE: Lower House, St. Mary's County, 1786–1787, 1787–1788, 1788. LOCAL OFFICES: sheriff, St. Mary's County, 1782–1785, 1794–1797; tobacco inspector, Leonardtown warehouse, St. Mary's County, in office 1786–at least 1788; justice, St. Mary's County, 1792–1794, 1797–1801. WEALTH DURING LIFETIME. PERSONAL PROPERTY: 12 slaves, 1790; 11 slaves, 1794; 10 slaves, 1796 and 1801; 4 oz. plate, 1801. LAND AT FIRST ELECTION: 351 acres of manor land in St. Mary's County leased before the Revolution and purchased by Abell as confiscated British property in 1782. SIGNIFICANT CHANGES IN LAND BETWEEN FIRST ELECTION AND DEATH: probably purchased 61 acres in St. Mary's County shortly before his death. WEALTH AT DEATH. DIED: inventory filed in December 1801 in St. Mary's County. PERSONAL PROPERTY: TEV, at least $1,840.41 current money (including 7 slaves and 4 oz. plate). LAND: probably 412 acres in St. Mary's County.

ADAIR, ROBERT (?–1768). BORN: in Calvert County, of age by 1745. NATIVE: at least second generation. RESIDED: in Baltimore Town, by 1751. FAMILY BACKGROUND. FATHER: Alexander Adair (?–1740), a surgeon, of Calvert and Kent counties. MOTHER: Christian (?–1766), daughter of Thomas Sterling, of Calvert County. SISTERS: Cassandra, who married John Moore, of Kent County; Elizabeth. MARRIED Martha. PRIVATE CAREER. EDUCATION: literate. RELIGIOUS AFFILIATION: Protestant. SOCIAL STATUS AND ACTIVITIES: Gent., 1750; Mr. and Esq. at death. OCCUPATIONAL PROFILE: merchant. PUBLIC CAREER. LEGISLATIVE SERVICE: Lower House, Baltimore County, 1768 (election of entire county delegation voided on June 14, 1768, because of "treating of voters"). LOCAL OFFICES: St. James' Parish Vestry, Baltimore County, in office 1755–1758; churchwarden, St. Paul's Parish, Baltimore County, in office 1764–1765, 1768–1769; sheriff, Baltimore County, 1764–at least 1766; justice, Baltimore County, 1752–1767 (quorum, 1754–1767); commissioner to build Baltimore County courthouse, appointed 1768; commissioner, Baltimore Town, in office 1768. WEALTH DURING LIFETIME. LAND AT FIRST ELECTION: at least 800 acres in Baltimore and Kent counties, plus 2 lots in Baltimore Town. WEALTH AT DEATH. DIED: on

October 22, 1768, in Baltimore Town. LAND: at least 800 acres in Baltimore and Kent counties, plus 2 lots in Baltimore Town.

ADAMS, HENRY (?–1686). BORN: probably in England. IMMIGRATED: in 1639 as an indentured servant to *Thomas Greene* (?–ca. 1651/52). RESIDED: in St. Mary's County; Port Tobacco, Charles County, by 1650. MARRIED by 1658 Mary (1637–?), daughter of John Cockshutt and wife Jane (1612–?); stepdaughter of *Robert Clarke* (ca. 1611–1664). Her half brother was *Ignatius Causine* (ca. 1642–1695). Her sister was Jane, who married *Thomas Mathews* (ca. 1622–1675/76). CHILDREN. Probably died without progeny. PRIVATE CAREER. EDUCATION: literate. RELIGIOUS AFFILIATION: Catholic. SOCIAL STATUS AND ACTIVITIES: Mr. by 1658; first appointment to the bench followed his marriage. OCCUPATIONAL PROFILE: servant, free by 1647; probably worked for Margaret Brent in 1647; planter, 1649; merchant. PUBLIC CAREER. LEGISLATIVE SERVICE: Lower House, Charles County, 1661, 1663, 1671–1674/75 (Accounts 2; Laws 3), 1676–1682, 1682–1684. LOCAL OFFICES: justice, Charles County, 1658–1665, 1667–1685 (quorum, 1667–1685); sheriff, Charles County, 1665–1666. STANDS ON PUBLIC/PRIVATE ISSUES: probably forced into temporary exile during Ingle's Rebellion, returning ca. 1647. WEALTH DURING LIFETIME. LAND AT FIRST ELECTION: claimed rights to 50 acres in 1654; acquired at least 600 acres through his marriage. WEALTH AT DEATH. DIED: will probated on July 4, 1686. PERSONAL PROPERTY: TEV, £569.15.7 sterling (including 1 slave, 5 servants, and 28 books). LAND: 800 acres.

ADAMS, JOHN (?–?). BORN: by 1730 in Somerset County. NATIVE: second generation. RESIDED: in Wicomico District, Somerset County. FAMILY BACKGROUND. FATHER: Rev. Alexander Adams (ca. 1679–1769), who immigrated from England in 1704 and served as rector of Stepney Parish, Somerset County from 1704 to 1769. MOTHER: Sarah, daughter of Samuel Horsey and wife Ann. BROTHERS: James Alexander (?–by 1741); Rev. Alexander, Jr. (ca. 1725–1767), who was ordained in London, England, on December 21, 1748, and was rector of St. James Parish at Herring Creek, Anne Arundel County from 1748 to 1767 and who married on May 19, 1745, Sarah Jones (?–ca. 1782); *William Adams* (?–1795); George (?–by 1801); Samuel (?–by 1796), who married Rebecka Whittington; Stephen (?–by 1801); Andrew, who married in 1759 Mary Whittingham; and Henry Smith

(1739–probably by 1769). NIECE: (first name unknown) Adams, who married *William Horsey* (ca. 1745–1786). MARRIED on February 14, 1760, Sarah Piper, widow of Clement Dashiell. CHILDREN. SONS: John (1760–?); William (1765–?). STEPDAUGHTER: Ann Dashiell (1751–1778), who married William Dixon. PRIVATE CAREER. EDUCATION: literate. RELIGIOUS AFFILIATION: Anglican. OCCUPATIONAL PROFILE: probably a planter; obtained the right to build a water mill, 1763. PUBLIC CAREER. LEGISLATIVE SERVICE: Lower House, Somerset County, 1762–1763 (Grievances 2), 1765–1766 (Grievances 2, 3), 1771; Conventions, Somerset County, 6th–8th, 1775–1776 (did not attend the 7th Convention). LOCAL OFFICES: justice, Somerset County, 1766–at least 1777 (quorum, 1768–at least 1777); justice, Court of Oyer and Terminer and Gaol Delivery, Somerset County, commissioned 1772; justice, Orphans' Court, Somerset County, commissioned 1777; commissioner of tax, Somerset County, 1777–at least 1783; judge, court of appeals, appointed under the Act to Procure Troops for the American Army, Somerset County, appointed 1778. MILITARY SERVICE: captain, by 1763. WEALTH DURING LIFETIME. PERSONAL PROPERTY: inherited £239.16.6 from his father, 1774; assessed value £1,065.0.0, including 19 slaves, 1783. LAND AT FIRST ELECTION: 1,022 acres in Somerset County (185 acres were a gift from his father; 837 acres by patent). SIGNIFICANT CHANGES IN LAND BETWEEN FIRST ELECTION AND DEATH: owned 1,746 acres in Somerset County, 1783. WEALTH AT DEATH. DIED: after 1783, possibly by 1796; size of estate unknown.

ADAMS (ADDAMS), PETER (?–1785). RESIDED: in Great Choptank Hundred, Caroline County. FAMILY BACKGROUND. BROTHER: William Adams (?–by 1788), of Caroline County. OTHER KINSHIP: William Adams, Jr., and Anne Adams are listed as his nearest kin in his inventory. PRIVATE CAREER. EDUCATION: literate. OCCUPATIONAL PROFILE: possibly a merchant. PUBLIC CAREER. LEGISLATIVE SERVICE: Convention, Caroline County, 5th, 1775. MILITARY SERVICE: captain, militia, elected by the battalion on January 2, 1776; captain, Smallwood Maryland Regiment, 1776; major, Seventh Maryland Regiment, 1777; lieutenant colonel, 1777; lieutenant colonel-commandant, First Maryland Regiment, 1779, transferred to Third Maryland Regiment in 1781 and served until 1783. In 1781 William Smallwood wrote to Gov. Thomas Sim Lee complaining that Col. Adams was "commonly activated by avarice and invincible obstinancy," and that he refused to obey orders. WEALTH DURING LIFETIME. SIGNIFICANT CHANGES IN LAND BETWEEN FIRST ELECTION AND DEATH: in September 1782 he purchased two lots on Monocacy Manor in Frederick County, one containing 182 acres and the other 133 acres, which had been sold as confiscated British property. In November 1782 he wrote the intendant complaining that the lots he had purchased did not agree with the description given of them at the time of the auction. Adams claimed he had been deceived and his request that the sale be voided was granted with respect to the 133-acre tract; purchased 14 acres in Caroline County, 1783. WEALTH AT DEATH. DIED: will probated on September 5, 1785, in Caroline County. PERSONAL PROPERTY: TEV, at least £908.12.6 current money (including 1 slave and books), received by his brother William Adams, the executor and sole legatee, and "in no way accounted for." LAND: 14 acres in Caroline County; possibly still owned 182 acres in Frederick County. As an officer, Col. Adams was entitled to 400 acres west of Fort Cumberland, Allegany County.

ADAMS, THOMAS (ca. 1611–1641/42). BORN: ca. 1611, probably in England. IMMIGRATED: by 1636 as a free adult. RESIDED: in Kent County. PRIVATE CAREER. EDUCATION: literate. OCCUPATIONAL PROFILE: bookkeeper for Cloberry & Company, 1636; Indian trader. PUBLIC CAREER. LEGISLATIVE SERVICE: Assembly, Kent County, 1640–1641. LOCAL OFFICE: justice, Kent County, 1640/41. STANDS ON PUBLIC/PRIVATE ISSUES: censured by the Assembly in October 1640 "for some indecent speeches touching the Lord Proprietor." WEALTH DURING LIFETIME. LAND AT FIRST ELECTION: had surveyed 1,000 acres. WEALTH AT DEATH. DIED: by March 26, 1642; size of estate unknown.

ADAMS, WILLIAM (?–1795). BORN: in Somerset County. NATIVE: second generation. RESIDED: District 1, Wicomico Hundred, Somerset County. FAMILY BACKGROUND. FATHER: Rev. Alexander Adams (ca. 1679–1769), rector of Stepney Parish, Somerset County from 1704 to 1769, immigrated from England in 1704. MOTHER: Sarah, daughter of Samuel Horsey and wife Ann. BROTHERS: James Alexander (?–by 1741); Rev. Alexander, Jr. (ca. 1725–1767), who was ordained in London, England, on December 21, 1748, and was rector of St. James Parish at Herring Creek, Anne Arundel County from 1748 to 1767 and who married on May 19, 1745, Sarah Jones (?–ca. 1782); *John*

Adams (?–?); George (?–by 1801); Samuel (?–by 1796), who married in 1756 Rebecka Whittington; Stephen (?–by 1801); Andrew, who married in 1759 Mary Whittingham; and Henry Smith (1739–probably by 1769). NIECE: (first name unknown) Adams, who married *William Horsey* (ca. 1745–1786). MARRIED first, by 1763 Leah (?–probably by 1773). MARRIED second, Ann (?–ca. 1801), who subsequently married by February 1797 William Cottman. CHILDREN. None surviving. PRIVATE CAREER. EDUCATION: literate. RELIGIOUS AFFILIATION: Anglican. SOCIAL STATUS AND ACTIVITIES: Gent., 1783; Esq. at death. OCCUPATIONAL PROFILE: probably a planter; owned a mill. PUBLIC CAREER. LEGISLATIVE SERVICE: Lower House, Somerset County, 1762–1763 (Arms and Ammunition 2), 1765–1766 (Arms and Ammunition 2, 4), 1770 (elected to the 3rd session to fill vacancy); Conventions, Somerset County, 6th–8th, 1775–1776 (did not attend the 7th Convention); Lower House, Somerset County, 1785, 1786–1787, 1787–1788. LOCAL OFFICES: justice, Somerset County, 1763–1775; Maryland Senate elector, Somerset County, elected 1786. WEALTH DURING LIFETIME. PERSONAL PROPERTY: inherited £239.16.7 from his father, 1774. LAND AT FIRST ELECTION: at least 929 acres in Somerset County (at least 200 acres were a gift from his father in 1750). SIGNIFICANT CHANGES IN LAND BETWEEN FIRST ELECTION AND DEATH: sold 200 acres in Somerset County in 1763. Patented a 879-acre tract in Somerset County in 1764, but had divided and sold all of it by 1783. Inherited at least 393 acres in Somerset County from his father's estate, 1769. Patented 1 acre in Salisbury, Somerset County (later became part of Wicomico County) with *William Horsey* (ca. 1745–1786) in 1771. In 1771 and 1773 he executed bonds to convey 700 acres in Somerset County, plus a 25-acre tract in that county that he had patented in 1772. Purchased 3 lots in Annapolis in 1772 and built a large brick house attributed to architect William Buckland. The house and 2 lots were leased out for 12 years in 1786. Adams purchased ca. 62 acres in Somerset County in 1783 and was assessed that year for a total of 437 acres in Somerset County. In 1792 he purchased land on Great Devil's Island (now Deal Island in Somerset County) to which he added 139 acres of vacant land and patented it in 1793 into a 558-acre tract. WEALTH AT DEATH. DIED: in 1795 in Somerset County. PERSONAL PROPERTY: TEV, £3,966.17.8, plus $1,669.53; FB, £3,817.14.0, plus $1,312.68. LAND: 1,015 acres in Somerset County, plus a dwelling house and lot in Princess Anne, Somerset County, and 3 lots, plus a large brick house in Annapolis. ADDITIONAL COMMENTS: His principal heirs were his two brothers Stephen and Andrew, and the children and grandchildren of his deceased brothers George, Alexander, and Samuel.

ADDISON, JOHN (?–ca. 1705/6). BORN: in Westmoreland, England; younger son. IMMIGRATED: in 1674 as a free adult from England. RESIDED: in St. Mary's County; Charles County, by 1687; Prince George's County, after 1695. FAMILY BACKGROUND. FATHER: probably Rev. Launcelot Addison, M.A. BROTHERS: Thomas; Henry, both merchants at Whitehaven, Cumberland, England; probably Launcelot, chaplain to King Charles II; and Anthony, rector of Abingdon and chaplain to the Duke of Marlborough. MARRIED by 1677 Rebecca (?–1726), widow of *Thomas Dent* (ca. 1630–1676); daughter of Rev. William Wilkinson. Her sister was Elizabeth, who married *William Hatton* (?–1712). CHILDREN. SONS: *Thomas Addison* (1679–1727), who married first, Elizabeth, daughter of *Thomas Tasker* (?–1700), and second, Elinor (1689–1761), daughter of *Walter Smith* (?–1711). STEPSONS: *William Dent* (ca. 1660–1704); Thomas Dent; *Peter Dent* (ca. 1665–1710/11); and George Dent (?–1702). STEPDAUGHTERS: Margaret Dent; Barbara Dent (1676–?), who married *Thomas Brooke* (ca. 1659–1730/31). PRIVATE CAREER. EDUCATION: literate. RELIGIOUS AFFILIATION: Anglican. SOCIAL STATUS AND ACTIVITIES: member of a socially ascending family in England; Gent., ca. 1670; Esq., after 1692; established a powerful political family in Prince George's County. OCCUPATIONAL PROFILE: merchant; Indian trader; planter; the ship, *Liverpool Merchant*, of which he owned a share, was condemned and its cargo seized for violation of the Navigation Acts, 1679–1682. PUBLIC CAREER. LEGISLATIVE SERVICE: Associators' Convention, Charles County, 1689–1692; Grand Committee of Twenty, 1690–1692; Upper House, 1692–1693 (Accounts 1; Laws 1), 1694–1697 (Accounts 1; Laws 7), 1697/98–1700, 1701–1704, 1704–1705 (died before the 4th session). OTHER PROVINCIAL OFFFICES: Council, 1692–1705; justice, Provincial Court, 1692–1694; judge, Court of Chancery, 1693; associate chancellor, 1696; associate commissary general, 1699–1700. LOCAL OFFICES: justice, Charles County, 1687–1692; coroner, Charles County, 1691; Piscattaway (King George's) Parish Vestry, Charles County, 1693–1705. MILITARY SERVICE: captain, Charles County, 1689–1694; colonel, Charles and Prince George's counties, 1694–1705. STANDS ON PUBLIC/PRIVATE ISSUES: his active support of the revolution of 1689 led to

his first provincial offices. WEALTH DURING LIFETIME. LAND AT FIRST ELECTION: at least 3,289 acres. WEALTH AT DEATH. DIED: between November 1705 and April 1706. PERSONAL PROPERTY: TEV, £1,840.0.1 sterling (including 14 slaves and 1 servant), plus a balance of just under £1,000 sterling in the hands of several London merchants. LAND: 6,478.5 acres.

ADDISON, JOHN (1713–1764). BORN: on September 16, 1713, in St. John's Parish, Prince George's County; probably eldest son. NATIVE: third generation. RESIDED: in King George's Parish, Prince George's County. FAMILY BACKGROUND. FATHER: *Thomas Addison* (1679–1727), son of *John Addison* (?–ca. 1705/6). MOTHER: Elinor (Eleanor) (1689–1761), daughter of *Walter Smith* (?–1711). HALF UNCLES: *William Dent* (ca. 1660–1704); *Peter Dent* (ca. 1665–1710/11). AUNTS: Lucy Smith (1688–1770), who married *Thomas Brooke* (1683–1744); Anne Smith (1694–1759), who married second, *Thomas Trueman Greenfield* (1682–1733); and Rebecca Smith (1696–1737), who married *Daniel Dulany* (1685–1753). HALF AUNT: Barbara Dent (1676–1764), who married *Thomas Brooke* (ca. 1659–1730/31). BROTHERS: Thomas (1715–1770); Henry (1717–1789); and Anthony (?–1753). SISTER: Ann (1711/12–1753), who married *William Murdock* (?–1769). HALF SISTERS: Rebecca (1703–?), who married first, *James Bowles* (?–ca. 1727/28), and second, *George Plater* (1695–1755); Elinor (1705–?), who married fourth, *Corbin Lee* (?–1774). FIRST COUSINS: *Richard Brooke* (1716–1783); Eleanor Brooke (1718–?), who married *Samuel Beall* (ca. 1713–ca. 1778); *Daniel Dulany, Jr.* (1722–1797); *Walter Dulany* (?–1773); Margaret Dulany, who married first, *Alexander Hamilton* (1712–1756), and second, *William Murdock* (?–1769); and Marianne Greenfield, who married *John Stoddert* (?–1767). NEPHEW: *Addison Murdock* (1731–1793). NIECE: Eleanor Murdock, who married *Benjamin Hall, of Francis* (?–1803). ADDITIONAL COMMENTS: his father's first wife was Elizabeth (1686–1706/7), daughter of *Thomas Tasker* (?–1700). MARRIED Susannah Wilkinson (?–1774). CHILDREN. SONS: Thomas, Jr. (?–1774), who married Rebecca, daughter of *Walter Dulany* (?–1773); John, who married Nancy, daughter of *Samuel Hanson* (1716–1794). DAUGHTERS: Eleanor, who married Rev. Jonathan Boucher (1737/38–1804), Anglican clergyman, noted tutor, outspoken Loyalist; Ann, who married Overton Carr, of Virginia. PRIVATE CAREER. EDUCATION: literate. RELIGIOUS AFFILIATION: Anglican, St. John's Parish, Prince

George's County; King George's Parish, Prince George's County. OCCUPATIONAL PROFILE: probably a planter. PUBLIC CAREER. LEGISLATIVE SERVICE: Lower House, Prince George's County, 1745 (Arms and Ammunition), 1745/46–1748 (Arms and Ammunition Cv 1, 1–3, 4; Laws 3), 1749–1751 (Arms and Ammunition Cv-3; Aggrievances Cv-3), 1751–1754 (Arms and Ammunition 1–6; Grievances 1–6), 1754–1757 (Arms and Ammunition 1–4; Grievances 1–6). LOCAL OFFICES: ranger (from Seneca Creek downwards to the limits of the county), Prince George's County, commissioned 1739; King George's Parish Vestry, Prince George's County, in office 1739–1742, 1747–1750, 1753–1756, and 1759–1762. MILITARY SERVICE: captain, by 1747; colonel, by 1760. WEALTH DURING LIFETIME. LAND AT FIRST ELECTION: at least 4,825 acres in Prince George's County (4,526 acres were the remainder of lands inherited from his father). WEALTH AT DEATH. DIED: will probated on November 16, 1764, in Prince George's County. PERSONAL PROPERTY: TEV, £2,362.18.2 current money, plus 25,660 pounds of tobacco (including 47 slaves, 290 oz. good plate, 27 oz. sorry plate, and books); FB, £638.7.1, plus 23,571 pounds of tobacco. LAND: 4,825 acres in Prince George's County.

ADDISON, THOMAS (1679–1727). BORN: in 1679 in St. Mary's County; only son. NATIVE: second generation. RESIDED: in St. Mary's County; Charles County, by 1687; St. Elizabeth's, Oxon Hill Creek, Prince George's County, after 1696. FAMILY BACKGROUND. FATHER: *John Addison* (?–ca. 1705/6). MOTHER: Rebecca Dent. HALF BROTHERS: *William Dent* (ca. 1660–1704); *Peter Dent* (ca. 1665–1710/11); George Dent (?–by 1702); and Thomas Dent. HALF SISTERS: Margaret Dent; Barbara Dent (1676–1764), who married *Thomas Brooke* (ca. 1659–1730/31). MARRIED first, on April 21, 1701, Elizabeth (1686–1706/7), daughter of *Thomas Tasker* (?–1700). Her brothers were John (?–1711), who married Eleanor, daughter of *Thomas Brooke* (ca. 1659–1730/31); Thomas (?–1696), who married Clare, daughter of *Nicholas Sewall* (ca. 1655–1737); and *Benjamin Tasker* (ca. 1690–1768). MARRIED second, in June 1709 Eleanor (1688–1761), daughter of *Walter Smith* (?–1711). Her brothers were Richard (?–1732); Walter Smith (ca. 1692–1734). Her sisters were Lucy (1688–1770), who married *Thomas Brooke* (1683–1744); Anne (1694–1759), who married first, Francis Wilkinson, and second, *Thomas Trueman Greenfield* (1682–1733); Rebecca (1696–1737), who married *Daniel Dulany* (1685–1753);

Elizabeth; and Mary. Her first cousins were *Walter Smith* (ca. 1693–1748); Barbara Smith (1693–1764), who married first, *Thomas Holdsworth* (ca. 1692–1718), and second, *Benjamin Mackall* (1675–1761). CHILDREN. SONS: *John Addison* (1713–1764), who married Susannah Wilkinson; Thomas (1715–1770); Henry (1717–1789), who married Rachel, daughter of *Daniel Dulany* (1685–1753); and Anthony (?–1753). DAUGHTERS: Rebecca (1703–?), who married first, *James Bowles* (?–ca. 1727/28), and second, *George Plater* (1695–1755); Elinor (1705–?), who married first, Bennett Lowe (?–1722), son of *Henry Lowe* (?–1717), second, Richard Smith (?–1732), son of *Walter Smith* (?–1711), third, Posthumous Thornton, and fourth, *Corbin Lee* (?–1774); and Ann (1711/12–1753), who married *William Murdock* (?–1769). PRIVATE CAREER. EDUCATION: literate. RELIGIOUS AFFILIATION: Anglican. SOCIAL STATUS AND ACTIVITIES: second generation councilor; his father's high status brought early preferment and patronage; he was one of the few men to be appointed to the Council without prior service in the Assembly. OCCUPATIONAL PROFILE: surveyor; planter; merchant. PUBLIC CAREER. LEGISLATIVE SERVICE: Upper House, 1710–1711 (first sat in the 3rd session), 1712–1714, 1715, 1716–1718, 1719–1721/22, 1722–1724, 1725–1726 (died before the 4th session). OTHER PROVINCIAL OFFICES: deputy naval officer, Potomac, 1697; Council, 1708–1727; justice, Provincial Court, 1714–1727. LOCAL OFFICES: surveyor, Prince George's County, 1696–1697; justice, Prince George's County, 1704–1705; Piscattaway (King George's) Parish Vestry, Prince George's County, 1704–1727; sheriff, Prince George's County, 1705–1707/8. MILITARY SERVICE: lieutenant colonel, by 1713; colonel, 1714–1727. WEALTH DURING LIFETIME. LAND AT FIRST ELECTION: 800 acres when appointed a justice in 1704; at least 8,294 acres in 1706 after his father's death. WEALTH AT DEATH. DIED: will probated on June 28, 1727. PERSONAL PROPERTY: TEV, £5,722.11.8 (including 71 slaves and 3 servants); FB, £5,369.18.8. LAND: 14,000–15,000 acres.

AISQUITH, THOMAS (?–1761). NATIVE: second generation. RESIDED: in St. Mary's Hundred, St. Mary's County. FAMILY BACKGROUND. FATHER: *William Aisquith* (?–1719). MOTHER: Elizabeth. BROTHERS: William (?–ca. 1741); George. SISTER: Elizabeth. MARRIED first, by 1724 Ann, widow of Adam Bell (?–1718); daughter of Hugh Hopewell (?–1690). Her mother or stepmother was Ann, who subsequently married John Duckworth. Her brothers were *Richard Hopewell* (?–ca. 1745); Francis; Hugh; and Joseph. MARRIED second, Elinor (Eleanor), who subsequently married Robert Watts. CHILDREN. SONS: George; John. ADDITIONAL COMMENTS: His wife was pregnant when Aisquith made his will in December 1760. PRIVATE CAREER. EDUCATION: literate. RELIGIOUS AFFILIATION: Anglican. SOCIAL STATUS AND ACTIVITIES: Mr., 1729. OCCUPATIONAL PROFILE: probably a planter; probably engaged in mercantile activities, because his inventory mentioned "goods in the store" and he and his brother George patented a 4-acre tract called "Thomas & George & Company." His father was also a merchant. Officeholder. PUBLIC CAREER. LEGISLATIVE SERVICE: Lower House, St. Mary's County, 1738, 1739–1741. LOCAL OFFICES: justice, St. Mary's County, 1723–1761 (quorum, 1736–1761); deputy commissary, St. Mary's County, 1724–1761; All Faith's Parish Vestry, St. Mary's County, elected 1729. MILITARY SERVICE: called colonel, by 1760. WEALTH DURING LIFETIME. LAND AT FIRST ELECTION: 750 acres in St. Mary's County (at least 200 acres inherited from his father). WEALTH AT DEATH. DIED: will probated on March 5, 1761, in St. Mary's County. PERSONAL PROPERTY: TEV, £1,911.7.11 (including 26 slaves, 1 servant, 64 oz. 17 dwt. 15 gr. plate, and books); FB, £1,888.1.7. LAND: 733 acres in St. Mary's County.

AISQUITH, WILLIAM (?–1719). IMMIGRATED: by 1677 as a free adult. RESIDED: in St. Mary's County. MARRIED Elizabeth. CHILDREN. SONS: *Thomas Aisquith* (?–1761); William (?–ca. 1741), who married Susannah; and George. DAUGHTER: Elizabeth. PRIVATE CAREER. EDUCATION: literate. RELIGIOUS AFFILIATION: Protestant. SOCIAL STATUS AND ACTIVITIES: in the province twelve years before obtaining his first minor office; Gent., by 1693. OCCUPATIONAL PROFILE: merchant; planter. PUBLIC CAREER. LEGISLATIVE SERVICE: Lower House, St. Mary's County, 1704–1707 (Elections and Privileges 4). LOCAL OFFICES: common councilman, St. Mary's City, 1689, 1694; justice, St. Mary's County, 1693–1696, 1708–1710; clerk, St. Mary's County, 1698–1705; deputy commissary, St. Mary's County, 1705–1710. MILITARY SERVICE: lieutenant, 1691; major, 1704–1706; lieutenant colonel, 1706–1708; colonel, 1708. WEALTH DURING LIFETIME. LAND AT FIRST ELECTION: 700–900 acres. WEALTH AT DEATH. DIED: by June 8, 1719. PERSONAL PROPERTY: TEV, £314.17.6; FB, £205.1.2. LAND: 700–900 acres.

ALEXANDER, AMOS (1729–1780). BORN: in 1729 in Cecil County. NATIVE: third generation. RESIDED: in Cecil County. FAMILY BACKGROUND. FATHER: James Alexander (1693–1779), a yeoman, son of Joseph Alexander and wife Abigail McKnitt. MOTHER: Margaret (?–by 1745), a cousin of her husband, daughter of John McKnitt. STEPMOTHER: Abigail. BROTHERS: Theophilus (1714–1768), a blacksmith who married Catherine; Hezekiah (1728–1801), who moved to North Carolina, studied law, and married Mary Sample (Temple); Josiah; Ezekial; and John McKnitt (1733–1817), who moved to North Carolina, became a tailor and surveyor, and married ca. 1760 Jane Bane. SISTERS: Jemima, who married (first name unknown) Sharp; Elizabeth, who married (first name unknown) Semple; Abigail, who married (first name unknown) Bradley; and Margaret, who married (first name unknown) McCoy. MARRIED Sarah Sharp. CHILDREN. SONS: Walter (?–by 1779), who married Priscilla; James; Amos; and Mark. DAUGHTERS: Rachel; Ruth; Mary, who married John Evans, son of Robert Evans, owner of the rolling mill on Big Elk Creek, Cecil County; Dorea; Sarah; and Margaret. PRIVATE CAREER. EDUCATION: literate. RELIGIOUS AFFILIATION: Presbyterian, elder of Rock Church, Cecil County. SOCIAL STATUS AND ACTIVITIES: Esq., 1779. OCCUPATIONAL PROFILE: cooper, 1768; mill owner. PUBLIC CAREER. LEGISLATIVE SERVICE: Lower House, Cecil County, 1777–1778. LOCAL OFFICE: justice, Cecil County, commissioned 1774, 1777, and 1778. MILITARY SERVICE: a colonel during the Revolution in the Continental service in John Patterson's Brigade of Wagons under the direction of Col. Francis Wade, Esq.; deputy quartermaster general, Delaware, from November 29, 1779, to at least February 1780. WEALTH DURING LIFETIME. LAND AT FIRST ELECTION: 110 acres in Cecil County. WEALTH AT DEATH. DIED: between February 16 and May 1, 1780, of wounds received in the war; buried at Head of Christiana Creek, Delaware. PERSONAL PROPERTY: TEV, £1,735.2.0 current money (including 5 slaves, books, and mills); FB, £1,212.17.10. LAND: at least 110 acres in Cecil County. His wife was charged with 247 acres in Cecil County on the 1783 tax assessment.

ALEXANDER, MARK (?–by 1797). BORN: by 1731 in Cecil County; fifth son. NATIVE: at least third generation. RESIDED: in Baltimore Town, by 1756; lived with his sister Mary Cox in Baltimore Town from ca. 1770 to 1790. FAMILY BACKGROUND. FATHER: Moses Alexander (?–1762), of Cecil County. BROTHERS: Nathaniel; Abraham;

James (?–1779); Zebulon; Moses; and Daniel. SIS-TERS: Priscilla, who married (first name unknown) White; Ruth, who married (first name unknown) Dysart (Dizard); and Mary (?–1790), who married James Cox (?–1777), a tailor, of Baltimore Town. MARRIED never. CHILDREN. Died without progeny. PRIVATE CAREER. EDUCATION: literate. RELIGIOUS AFFILIATION: Presbyterian. SOCIAL STATUS AND ACTIVITIES: Mr., 1765; Esq., 1779; Gent., 1785. OCCUPATIONAL PROFILE: merchant, of Baltimore Town, owned a warehouse and later a store near the public wharf; also owned a schooner and was involved in the wheat trade in the 1770s. PUBLIC CAREER. LEGISLATIVE SERVICE: Lower House, Baltimore Town, 1779–1780 (Manufactories 1, 2), 1780–1781 (Manufactories 1, 2). LOCAL OFFICE: Committee of Correspondence, Baltimore Town, in office 1774. MILITARY SERVICE: Baltimore Town Militia, 1778. WEALTH DURING LIFETIME. PERSONAL PROPERTY: £300 in Continental certifi-cates, ca. 1783. ADDITIONAL COMMENTS: He was heavily in debt by 1783 when he filed a petition as an insolvent debtor. Alexander owed £3,000 to *Daniel Dulany, Jr.* (1722–1797) and *Charles Car-roll of Carrollton* (1737–1832) as executors of Ro-bert Montgomery, of Philadelphia, Pennsylvania, and Rev. William Thompson, of Cecil County. Alexander was jailed for at least two months in 1787 as an insolvent debtor. In 1790 his sister Mary Cox made provision in her will granting Al-exander an annual income of £35. LAND AT FIRST ELECTION: at least 450 acres in Baltimore and Cecil counties, 90 acres in Chester County, Penn-sylvania, plus 1 lot and parts of 2 other lots in Baltimore Town. SIGNIFICANT CHANGES IN LAND BETWEEN FIRST ELECTION AND DEATH: sold 1 lot in Baltimore Town to his sister Mary Cox in return for money to pay his major credi-tors, 1784; the remainder of his land was turned over to the sheriff to pay his other debts. Al-though Alexander held two mortgages and several unpatented certificates for land after that, they and all of his other real property were in the con-trol of his trustee by 1787 under the terms of his insolvency petition. WEALTH AT DEATH. DIED: prior to April 1797; size of estate unknown.

ALEXANDER, ROBERT (1740–1805). BORN: in 1740 in Cecil County; only child. NATIVE: second generation. RESIDED: in Baltimore Town, 1762 until the fall of 1776; on his plantation near the Village of Elk in Cecil County from late 1776 until September 1777 when he followed the British forces to Philadelphia, Pennsylvania; moved to New York City, 1778; in London, England, 1784–

1805. FAMILY BACKGROUND. FATHER: William Alexander (?–1745), a merchant, who immigrated from Scotland to Antigua, West Indies, before 1732; in Cecil County, Maryland by 1735. STEPFA-THERS: John Mackey, Esq. (?–ca. 1749); George Catto, Gent. (?–1780), of Cecil County. MOTHER: Araminta (?–1765), widow of both Col. *Ephraim Augustus Herman* (1683–1734/35) and Col. Jo-seph Young (?–1737), of Cecil County. HALF BROTHER: Ephraim Augustine Herman (1734–1751). HALF SISTER: Elizabeth Young. STEPSIS-TERS: Catherine Herman; Mary Herman; Mary Young; and Milcah Young. MARRIED Isabella (?–1822), daughter of Alexander Lawson (?–1761), a merchant of Baltimore County, and wife Dorothy Smith (1719–?). Her brother was Alexander Law-son (?–1798), who married Elizabeth Brown. Her sisters were Susanna (1743–1798), who married *Andrew Buchanan* (ca. 1733–1786); Rebecca (?–1759), who married *Lloyd Buchanan* (1729–ca. 1762); Mary (Polly), who marred Robert Christie, Jr.; Dorothy (?–1752); Elizabeth (?–1752); and Margaret (?–1752); the last three drowned while ice-skating on a pond at their father's ironworks. CHILDREN. SONS: William, a lawyer, who married in 1795 Margaret Partridge, of Cecil County; Law-son (ca. 1768–1828), a lawyer; Robert (?–by 1798); Henry, who married Esther Johnson; and Andrew (?–1797). DAUGHTER: Araminta (1773–1854), who married in 1796 Solomon Betts. PRIVATE CAREER. EDUCATION: studied law in Annapolis, probably with *Stephen Bordley* (ca. 1710–1764). RELIGIOUS AFFILIATION: Anglican, St. Paul's Parish, Baltimore County. SOCIAL STATUS AND ACTIVI-TIES: Gent., 1761. OCCUPATIONAL PROFILE: law-yer, admitted to the following courts: Annapolis Mayor's Court in January 1761; Cecil County in March 1761; Baltimore County in June 1761; Pro-vincial Court in April 1762; Frederick County in March 1763; Anne Arundel County in August 1765; Court of Chancery by February 1768; Har-ford County in March 1774. Farmer, 1765–1777. PUBLIC CAREER. LEGISLATIVE SERVICE: Conven-tions, Baltimore County, 1st, 1774, 4th, 1775, 5th, 1775, 6th–8th, 1775–1776 (did not attend the 7th and 8th conventions). OTHER STATE OFFICE: 1st Council of Safety, Western Shore, 1775. LOCAL OFFICES: St. Paul's Parish Vestry, Baltimore County, in office 1768–1771; commissioner, Baltimore Town, in office 1768; Committee of Ob-servation, Baltimore Town, elected 1774. OUT OF STATE SERVICE: delegate, Continental Congress, 1775–1776 (elected on December 9, 1775, to fill vacancy, but did not attend until January 1776; reelected in May 1776 and July 1776; no record of attendance after May 15, 1776). Served in various advisory positions to the British commanders in Philadelphia and New York, 1777–1783. Prepared "an Account of the State of the Country about Wilmington" (Delaware) for General Sir William Howe, ca. 1778, and an account of the "State of the Country of South Carolina" for General Sir Henry Clinton, ca. 1779; also wrote for Clinton in 1780 the well-researched and persuasive "Remarks on the Peninsula or Eastern Shore of Maryland," which advocated the British capture of the supply-rich Delmarva peninsula. A member of the board established by the British "to direct and control operations of Associated Loyalists," June 1781 to November 1782. Represented Maryland Loyalists in their claims for relief by the British government, 1784–?. STANDS ON PUBLIC/PRIVATE ISSUES: Initially a supporter of American complaints against the British, Alexander became a Loyalist and fled Maryland in September 1777. After the war, in a memorial to the British Loyalist Claims Commission, he stated that he was of the opinion "that British subjects of America were not subject to taxation by the British Parliament and that Maryland subjects were expressedly free thereof by Charter." However, he was "opposed to every measure of violence and to taking up arms." After refusing to take the patriot oath of fidelity renouncing allegiance to the British sovereign, Alexander withdrew from politics, and in August 1777 when the British army under General Howe landed near his home at Head of Elk, Cecil County, Alexander offered Howe his support and assistance. Leaving behind his wife and six children, Alexander followed the British to Philadelphia, Pennsylvania. It is unlikely that he ever saw his family again. He was outlawed for high treason by the Maryland General Court in May 1780. WEALTH DURING LIFETIME. PERSONAL PROPERTY: Alexander's property was seized and inventoried by the Maryland commissioners of confiscated British property in April 1781. At that time he was listed as owning 44 slaves, 22 of whom were confiscated, and a law library of 63 titles (106 volumes). Alexander claimed ownership of 28 slaves and a law library of 240 volumes in his memorial to the British Loyalist Claims Commission. His confiscated property was sold in 1782. The following year Isabella Alexander's property was valued at £785.10.0, including 17 slaves and 4 oz. plate. ANNUAL INCOME: law practice estimated to be worth over £450 sterling per year, 1771–1776. LAND AT FIRST ELECTION: probably 1,167 acres in Cecil County, plus title to 4 lots in the Village of Elk (later called Elkton) that he had leased out during his development of the town in the 1760s. All of this land was the residue of a deed of gift from his mother and stepfather George Catto, received ca. 1760, which conveyed to Alexander the land held for him from his father's estate, but did not include 100 acres that Alexander claimed he had given to Catto in 1765. SIGNIFICANT CHANGES IN LAND BETWEEN FIRST ELECTION AND DEATH: 900 acres, or two-thirds of Alexander's land, were confiscated by the Maryland government and sold in 1782. His wife Isabella petitioned the Maryland legislature in 1781 asking that land be reserved for her children. The General Assembly allowed her and the children the "mansion house" and 363 acres of land in 1784. In his memorial to the British Loyalist Claims Commission Alexander claimed to have lost 1,563 acres in Cecil County divided into three large farms with dwelling houses, good barns, and outbuildings that produced wheat, Indian corn, and livestock worth about £600 current money per annum. ADDITIONAL COMMENTS: After 1782 Alexander held title to no real or personal property in Maryland. In order to receive compensation from the British government for remaining loyal to the British crown, he valued his combined real and personal losses at £9,756 sterling and £450 sterling per annum. He received £5,459 sterling and £220 sterling per annum in compensation. Alexander left behind £814.18.7 current money in debts, which was collected from the proceeds of the sales of his confiscated property. WEALTH AT DEATH. DIED: in November 1805 at his apartment in Norfolk Street, Strand, London, England.

ALLEIN (ALLEN), WILLIAM (ca. 1742–ca. 1802). BORN: ca. 1742 in Anne Arundel County; probably youngest son. NATIVE: at least second generation. RESIDED: in Anne Arundel County until at least 1759; at "Newington," Calvert County, 1777–ca. 1802, formerly the home of his father-in-law. FAMILY BACKGROUND. FATHER: Benjamin Allein (?–1748), of Anne Arundel County, an innkeeper, who ran the ferryboat at Pig Point, Anne Arundel County. MOTHER: Mary (?–1752). GUARDIAN: Samuel Roundell, from 1752 until at least 1759. BROTHERS: James (by 1730–?); John Zachariah (by 1730–?); Benjamin (by 1730–?); Thomas; Joseph; and Prindowell, a minor in 1752, who married on June 7, 1766, Elizabeth Brown. SISTER: Ann, who married Capt. Philip Allingham. MARRIED by 1771 Sarah Weems (ca. 1754–ca. 1804), daughter of Roger Wheeler (?–1763), a merchant of Calvert County, and wife Susannah Weems (?–by 1763); granddaughter of

James Weems (ca. 1707–1781). Her uncle was *John Weems* (1737–1813). Her aunts were Sarah Weems (?–1763), who married *Samuel Chew* (1737–1790); Margaret Weems (?–1783), who married second, *Joseph Sprigg* (1732–1800). Her sisters were Mary Heighe (Hughe) (ca. 1750–?), who married John Brooke; Elizabeth (ca. 1752–?), who married Levin Ballard; and Ann Weems (ca. 1761–?), who became the ward of her brother-in-law William Allein in 1771 and who subsequently married Daniel Kent (?–by 1835). Her first cousin was Margaret Weems, who married *Levin Mackall* (1760–?). Her paternal grandmother as well as her maternal step-grandmother was Mary Crompton Wheeler Weems (?–1769). ADDITIONAL COMMENTS: Her maternal grandfather *James Weems* (?–1781) also became her paternal stepgrandfather when he married Mary Wheeler. CHILDREN. SONS: William, Jr. (ca. 1772–?); George W. (?–by 1835). DAUGHTERS: Mary D.; Priscilla H., who resided in the District of Columbia by April 1812. PRIVATE CAREER. EDUCATION: literate. RELIGIOUS AFFILIATION: Anglican, owned a pew in All Saints' Parish Church, Calvert County, 1794. SOCIAL STATUS AND ACTIVITIES: Gent., 1781; Esq., 1781. OCCUPATIONAL PROFILE: merchant; planter. It is possible that by the time of William's marriage, ca. 1771, he had been an apprentice in the Wheeler family's mercantile business. PUBLIC CAREER. LEGISLATIVE SERVICE: Conventions, Calvert County, 6th–8th, 1775–1776; Lower House, Calvert County, 1777, 1781–1782 (Claims 1). OTHER STATE OFFICE: Patuxent Association, in office 1781. LOCAL OFFICES: justice, Calvert County, commissioned 1773, 1777, and 1782; sheriff, Calvert County, 1785–1788. WEALTH DURING LIFETIME. PERSONAL PROPERTY: in 1777 he offered his plantation for sale, which included a large seven-room dwelling house and an outbuilding, a gristmill, and ca. 9 slaves, all of which he probably acquired through marriage, except perhaps one or two slaves. Assessed value £380.15.0, including 7 slaves and 30 oz. plate, 1782; owned 11 slaves that he mortgaged to Wallace, Johnson & Muir, 1785. At the time of William's petition for insolvency on March 20, 1794, his inventory included household furniture, farm equipment and livestock, a gristmill, a snuff mill, 4 slaves, and books. On May 13, 1801, a schedule of personal property attached to a petition requesting release from insolvency indicated that many items were encompassed in the 1794 inventory, including slaves. ADDITIONAL COMMENTS: At a public sale of his personal property in 1794, 11 out of 12 lots were purchased by his son William, Jr.; the last lot was purchased by

Elizabeth Ballard, his sister-in-law, accounting perhaps for the repetition in the 1801 inventory. LAND AT FIRST ELECTION: at least 531 acres in Calvert County, formerly owned by his father-in-law, Roger Wheeler, and of which his wife held sole title to 240 acres. SIGNIFICANT CHANGES IN LAND BETWEEN FIRST ELECTION AND DEATH: charged with 578 acres in Calvert County in 1783, the additional acreage all being previously shown as belonging to Roger Wheeler's heirs (including a gristmill and a snuff mill); 305 acres (exclusive of the gristmill) were mortgaged in 1785 to Wallace, Johnson & Muir, Annapolis merchants, to whom he was indebted for £2,120.13.9. Following his petition for insolvency in 1794, the 305 mortgaged acres were sold to Wallace, Johnson & Muir at a public sale, but William's wife was able to keep the title to her 240 acres. Her brother-in-law, Daniel Kent, became a trustee under court order for the 240-acre tract in 1799, and was ordered by the General Assembly to hold the land for his sister-in-law's benefit. WEALTH AT DEATH. DIED: ca. 1802 in Calvert County, probably insolvent. LAND: his wife, Sarah Weems Allein, retained her interest in her 240-acre patrimony until her death in 1804, and in 1813 it was sold by their daughters Mary and Priscilla.

ALLEN, FRANCIS (?–1745). BORN: of age by 1715. RESIDED: in Somerset County (later became part of Worcester County). MARRIED first, (name unknown). MARRIED second, probably by 1718 Mary, widow of both Rev. James Hindman (?–1713) and Hugh Eccleston, Jr. (?–by 1717); daughter of *Jacob Lookerman* (1652–1730). Her brothers were Jacob, Jr. (1678–1731); *Govert Lookerman* (ca. 1681–1728); Thomas (?–ca. 1714); John (1686–1760); and Nicholas (1697–1771). CHILDREN. SONS: John (?–ca. 1738); Francis (ca. 1715–?), a planter, who married Mary, widow of William Brady; *William Allen* (?–1792); Joseph; and Moses. STEPSON: *Jacob Hindman* (by 1713–1766). DAUGHTERS: Eleanor; Mary, who married in 1759 Rev. John Rosse, of Snow Hill, Worcester County; and Elizabeth. PRIVATE CAREER. EDUCATION: literate. RELIGIOUS AFFILIATION: Protestant. SOCIAL STATUS AND ACTIVITIES: Gent., 1722. OCCUPATIONAL PROFILE: planter; attorney, admitted to the following courts: Somerset County by May 1717; Provincial Court in April 1723; Talbot County in March 1723/24; Dorchester County by August 1728. PUBLIC CAREER. LEGISLATIVE SERVICE: Lower House, Somerset County, 1732–1734 (Laws 1–Cv). OTHER PROVINCIAL OFFICE: deputy collector of Pocomoke, sworn 1724 and 1729. LO-

CAL OFFICES: clerk of Indictments, Somerset County, sworn 1718 and 1728, Talbot County, sworn March 1723/24 and March 1738/39; acting deputy clerk, Somerset County, in office in March 1722/23; sheriff, Somerset County, 1725–1728. **WEALTH DURING LIFETIME. LAND AT FIRST ELECTION:** 871 acres in Somerset County, by 1734. **WEALTH AT DEATH. DIED:** will probated on May 17, 1745, in Worcester County. **PERSONAL PROPERTY:** TEV, at least £296.18.7 (including 1 slave, 86 law books, and other titles). **ADDITIONAL COMMENTS:** his wife deeded 13 slaves to her children a year after Allen's inventory had been taken. **LAND:** at least 933 acres and 1 lot in Worcester and Somerset counties.

ALLEN, JOHN (?–by 1678). **BORN:** probably in England. **IMMIGRATED:** by 1670 as a free adult from London. **RESIDED:** in Charles County. **PRIVATE CAREER. EDUCATION:** literate. **SOCIAL STATUS AND ACTIVITIES:** Gent. on first appearance in the records; perhaps he was the "Jack Allen," master of a ship trading to Maryland in 1663, who conveyed messages from Charles Calvert to Cecilius Calvert. **OCCUPATIONAL PROFILE:** merchant, of London, England, 1669/70; merchant; planter; owned a water mill and smith shop. **PUBLIC CAREER. LEGISLATIVE SERVICE:** Lower House, Charles County, 1676 (died before the 2nd session). **LOCAL OFFICE:** sheriff, Charles County, 1672–1674. **WEALTH DURING LIFETIME. LAND AT FIRST ELECTION:** ca. 1,050 acres. **WEALTH AT DEATH. DIED:** prior to August 1678. **LAND:** ca. 1,050 acres.

ALLEN, THOMAS (?–1648). **BORN:** probably in England. **IMMIGRATED:** in 1633/34 as an indentured servant to *Leonard Calvert* (ca. 1606–1647). **RESIDED:** in St. Mary's County; Kent County, 1637/38. **CHILDREN. SONS:** Thomas; William; and Robert. **PRIVATE CAREER. EDUCATION:** literate. **RELIGIOUS AFFILIATION:** Protestant. **OCCUPATIONAL PROFILE:** indentured servant, 1633/34; planter, by 1637/38. **PUBLIC CAREER. LEGISLATIVE SERVICE:** Assembly, Kent County, 1640, present 1647/48. **LOCAL OFFICE:** justice, Kent County, 1637/38. **WEALTH DURING LIFETIME. LAND AT FIRST ELECTION:** 60 acres. **WEALTH AT DEATH. DIED:** between April 23 and August 17, 1648. **PERSONAL PROPERTY:** TEV, 5,393 pounds of tobacco (including 1 servant).

ALLEN, WILLIAM (?–1792). **BORN:** probably in Somerset County, of age by 1745; younger son. **NATIVE:** at least second generation. **RESIDED:** in

Worcester County; Talbot County, 1778; Worcester County, 1779–1792; Dorchester County, 1785. **FAMILY BACKGROUND. FATHER:** *Francis Allen* (?–1745). **MOTHER:** Mary, widow of first, Rev. James Hindman (?–1713), and second, Hugh Eccleston, Jr. (?–by 1717); daughter of *Jacob Lookerman* (1652–1730). **UNCLE:** *Govert Lookerman* (ca. 1681–1728). **BROTHERS:** Joseph; Moses. **HALF BROTHERS:** John (?–ca. 1738); Francis (ca. 1715–by 1744). **STEPBROTHER:** *Jacob Hindman* (by 1713–1766). **SISTERS:** Eleanor; Mary; and Elizabeth. **FIRST COUSIN:** Sarah Lookerman, who married *Joseph Cox Gray* (?–1764). **HALF OR STEPNEPHEW:** *Peter Chaille* (?–1802). **STEPNEPHEWS:** *James Hindman* (1741–1830); *William Hindman* (1743–1822). **STEPNIECE:** Elizabeth Hindman (?–by 1788), who married *William Perry* (1746–1799). **MARRIED** Patience, daughter of Thomas Marshall. **CHILDREN.** Probably died without progeny. **PRIVATE CAREER. EDUCATION:** literate. **RELIGIOUS AFFILIATION:** Anglican. **SOCIAL STATUS AND ACTIVITIES:** Gent., 1750; Esq., 1765. **OCCUPATIONAL PROFILE:** attorney, admitted to the Somerset County Court in November 1747; planter. **PUBLIC CAREER. LEGISLATIVE SERVICE:** Lower House, Worcester County, 1762–1763 (Elections 1, 2; Public Offices 1, 2; Accounts 2), 1765–1766 (Grievances 3, 4), 1768–1770 (Grievances 1, 2, 4), 1771. **LOCAL OFFICES:** sheriff, Somerset County, 1755–1758; Coventry Parish Vestry, Somerset and Worcester counties, in office 1763; justice, Worcester County, by 1764–at least 1775 (quorum, by 1764–at least 1775); justice, Court of Oyer and Terminer and Gaol Delivery, Worcester County, commissioned 1766, 1770, and 1771; visitor, Eden School, Worcester County, in office 1771. **MILITARY SERVICE:** recorded as being delinquent when required for militia service, 1782. **STANDS ON PUBLIC/PRIVATE ISSUES:** requested in 1779 that three slaves be manumitted immediately after his death. **WEALTH DURING LIFETIME. PERSONAL PROPERTY:** 13 slaves and a gristmill, 1766; assessed value £466.0.0, including 13 slaves, 1783; 50 slaves, 1790. **LAND AT FIRST ELECTION:** 1,504 acres in Worcester County (inherited more than 576 acres from his father, including lot 9 in Snow Hill, Worcester County). **SIGNIFICANT CHANGES IN LAND BETWEEN FIRST ELECTION AND DEATH:** purchased 6,069 acres in Worcester County and sold more than 1,272 acres, plus lot 9 in Snow Hill, Worcester County, 1763–1792. **WEALTH AT DEATH. DIED:** will probated on July 17, 1792, in Worcester County. He requested that he be buried next to his wife in Talbot County. **PERSONAL PROPERTY:** TEV, £2,672.1.10 current money; FB,

£2,369.18.6. ADDITIONAL COMMENTS: mentioned at least 14 slaves and law books in his will. LAND: probably ca. 6,301 acres in Worcester County. ADDITIONAL COMMENTS: His principal heirs were *Peter Chaille* (?–1802), his nephew William Davis, and other children of his brothers and sisters.

ANDROS, EDMUND (1637–1713/14). BORN: on December 6, 1637, in Guernsey, England; second son. IMMIGRATED: in 1693 on his first visit to Maryland. RESIDED: never a permanent resident. FAMILY BACKGROUND. FATHER: a Guernsey gentleman in the household of King Charles I. PRIVATE CAREER. EDUCATION: literate. RELIGIOUS AFFILIATION: Anglican. SOCIAL STATUS AND ACTIVITIES: a member of an old aristocratic family; made a knight in 1678; a landgrave in Carolina in the early 1670s with a 48,000-acre estate; made two trips to Maryland between September 1693 and July 1694 to oversee governmental affairs. OCCUPATIONAL PROFILE: military officer and colonial bureaucrat. PUBLIC CAREER. PROVINCIAL OFFICE: acting governor, September 25, 1693–July 26, 1694. ADDITIONAL COMMENTS: his assumption of Maryland's government in 1693 was an improper act based on the misreading of his commission; later he was forced to return the salary he had claimed for nine months' service. OUT OF COLONY SERVICE: officer in the West Indies, 1666–1668; governor, New York, 1674–1681; governor, Dominion of New England, 1684–1689; governor, Virginia, 1692–1698; lieutenant governor, Guernsey, England, 1704–1706. WEALTH AT DEATH. DIED: on February 27, 1713/14, in London, England; size of estate unknown.

ARCHER, JOHN (1741–1810). BORN: on May 5, 1741, probably in Cecil County; only surviving child. NATIVE: second generation. RESIDED: New Castle, Delaware, 1767–1769; near Churchville, Spesutia Hundred, Harford County. FAMILY BACKGROUND. FATHER: Thomas Archer (?–1772), who immigrated from County Donegal, Ireland, and became an agent for an ironworks in Cecil County; later moved to Baltimore County. MOTHER: Elizabeth, daughter of (first name unknown) Stevenson. John Archer had four brothers and sisters who died in infancy of malignant fevers. MARRIED in 1766 Catherine, daughter of Thomas Harris, of Harford County. Her brother was Robert, of Cumberland County, Pennsylvania, a physician. CHILDREN. SONS: Thomas; Robert Harris; John; James; all of whom became doctors; George Washington, who died while studying medicine; Stevenson (1786–1848), a lawyer, member of the Maryland House of Delegates from 1809 to 1811, member of the U.S. House of Representatives from 1811 to 1817 and from 1819 to 1821, U.S. judge for the Mississippi Territory appointed in 1817, associate justice of the Court of Appeals of Maryland from 1824 to 1844 and chief justice from 1844 until death, who married Pamela Hays; plus four other children who died young. PRIVATE CAREER. EDUCATION: Nottingham Academy, Cecil County; College of New Jersey (later became Princeton University), 1760; M.A., 1763; Philadelphia College of Medicine, 1768. ADDITIONAL COMMENTS: Archer received the first degree in medicine offered by an American school. RELIGIOUS AFFILIATION: Presbyterian; studied theology in preparation for the ministry and was an elder in the Churchville Presbyterian Church, Harford County. SOCIAL STATUS AND ACTIVITIES: Esq., 1783; one of the founders of the Medical and Chirurgical Faculty of Maryland, 1799. ADDITIONAL COMMENTS: he suffered from a severe chronic throat ailment throughout his adult life, which precluded public speaking and forced him to use a voice trumpet. OCCUPATIONAL PROFILE: a physician, who began his practice in New Castle, Delaware, 1767–1769; continued to practice in Harford County from 1769 until his death; from about 1785 he taught medicine at his home, "Medical Hall" . PUBLIC CAREER. LEGISLATIVE SERVICE: Convention, Harford County, 9th 1776; Lower House, Harford County, 1777, 1779–1780. LOCAL OFFICES: Committee of Correspondence, Harford County, elected 1774; Committee of Observation, Harford County, elected 1776; justice, Harford County, 1777–at least 1793; justice, Orphans' Court, Harford County, 1779–at least 1784; subscription officer, Continental Loan Office, Harford County, appointed 1779; judge, Court of Appeals for Tax Assessment, Harford County, appointed 1786; Maryland Senate elector, Harford County, elected 1811. MILITARY SERVICE: captain, Lower Crosswoods Company, Harford County Militia, elected 1774; 2nd major, Upper Battalion, Harford County Militia, appointed 1779; served as a volunteer aide-de-camp to Gen. Anthony Wayne at the Battle of Stony Point, 1779; captain, Continental Army, 1779; major, Continental Army, 1779. OUT OF STATE OFFICES: presidential elector, Maryland, 1796, 1800; representative, U.S. Congress, 1801–1803, 1803–1805, 1805–1807; a Democrat. STANDS ON PUBLIC/PRIVATE ISSUES: signed the Bush Declaration on March 22, 1775. In his will he absolved the debts of his insolvent patients and provided for the manumission of his slaves. WEALTH DURING LIFE-

TIME. PERSONAL PROPERTY: assessed value £476.0.0, including 8 slaves and 15 oz. plate, 1783; 7 slaves, 1790. LAND AT FIRST ELECTION: 450 acres in Harford County (inherited from his father). SIGNIFICANT CHANGES IN LAND BETWEEN FIRST ELECTION AND DEATH: during the late 1780s and early 1800s he purchased about 350 acres in Harford County adjoining his home plantation; received a number of mortgages as payment or security for debts owed to him. WEALTH AT DEATH. DIED: on September 28, 1810, at "Medical Hall," Harford County. PERSONAL PROPERTY: TEV, $58,070.80 (including stock in Baltimore City and Washington, D.C. banks, roads, insurance, and U.S. certificates); FB, $58,038.10. LAND: his home plantation consisted of 807 acres, plus he had an additional 260 acres in Harford County; he may also have owned property in Cumberland County, Pennsylvania.

ASHMAN, GEORGE (?–ca. 1699/1700). BORN: in England. IMMIGRATED: in 1678, probably as a redemptioner from London. RESIDED: in Baltimore County. FAMILY BACKGROUND. BROTHERS: John; James. MARRIED by 1685/86 Elizabeth, widow of William Cromwell (?–1683). CHILDREN. SON: John. STEPSONS: Thomas Cromwell; Philip Cromwell; and William Cromwell. DAUGHTERS: Charity; Elizabeth. PRIVATE CAREER. EDUCATION: literate. RELIGIOUS AFFILIATION: Anglican. SOCIAL STATUS AND ACTIVITIES: probably a servant (redemptioner) on arrival; no title as late as the first reference after his marriage; his appointment to a justiceship followed his marriage; Gent. in 1696. OCCUPATIONAL PROFILE: probably a servant, 1678; planter. PUBLIC CAREER. LEGISLATIVE SERVICE: Lower House, Baltimore County, 1692–1693, 1696–1697 (elected to the 6th session), 1697/98–1699 (Aggrievances 1; died before the 4th session). LOCAL OFFICES: overseer of highways, Baltimore County, 1684; justice, Baltimore County, 1686–1699/1700 (quorum, 1692–1699/1700); Patapsco Vestry, Baltimore County, 1693–1696. MILITARY SERVICE: colonel at death. WEALTH DURING LIFETIME. PERSONAL PROPERTY: £150.14.3, plus 5 servants through his marriage; 3 slaves and 6 servants in 1692; 3 slaves and 4 servants in 1694; 2 slaves and 5 servants in 1695. LAND AT FIRST ELECTION: 300 acres from his wife's dower; patented another 572 acres in 1695. WEALTH AT DEATH. DIED: will probated on February 23, 1699/1700. PERSONAL PROPERTY: TEV, £415.6.2 sterling (including 5 slaves and 5 servants); FB, £278.8.0. LAND: over 618 acres (2 plantations).

ASHMEAD, SAMUEL (?–ca. 1779). IMMIGRATED: probably, if so by 1766. RESIDED: in Baltimore County (later became part of Harford County). FAMILY BACKGROUND. Probably related to Joseph Ashmead (?–ca. 1787), of Annapolis, an innkeeper. MARRIED Ruth. CHILDREN. SON: John (by 1757–?), an insolvent debtor in 1801. PRIVATE CAREER. EDUCATION: literate. OCCUPATIONAL PROFILE: miller; owned a gristmill, by 1769. PUBLIC CAREER. LEGISLATIVE SERVICE: Convention, Harford County, 5th, 1775. LOCAL OFFICE: justice, Harford County, appointed 1778. WEALTH DURING LIFETIME. LAND AT FIRST ELECTION: 400 acres in Harford County, mortgaged, 1769; 1 lot on Fells Point, Baltimore Town. SIGNIFICANT CHANGES IN LAND BETWEEN FIRST ELECTION AND DEATH: obtained a release on his mortgaged land shortly before his death. WEALTH AT DEATH. DIED: between October 24, 1778, and January 13, 1779, in Harford County. LAND: 400 acres in Harford County; probably 1 lot on Fells Point, Baltimore Town.

BAIRD (BAYARD, BEARD), WILLIAM (ca. 1732–1792). BORN: ca. 1732. RESIDED: in Upper District, Frederick County (later became part of Washington County); resided in Elizabeth Town (later called Hagerstown), Washington County, by 1790 until death. MARRIED by 1784 Margaret (?–1800), widow of John Reynolds. CHILDREN. SON: William, Jr. (ca. 1767–?), resided in Elizabeth Hundred, Frederick County (later became part of Washington County); moved to Westmoreland County, Pennsylvania, by 1794; he possibly married in 1785 Dorothy Camrey. STEPSONS: Joseph Reynolds; William McKee Reynolds; Thomas Reynolds; and John Reynolds. DAUGHTERS: Esther, who married Joseph Little; Fanny; Peggy; and Ruth, who married (first name unknown) Wallace. STEPDAUGHTERS: Betsy Reynolds; Mary Reynolds, who married Joseph Clarke; and Sarah Reynolds, who married Edward A. Thomas. PRIVATE CAREER. EDUCATION: literate. SOCIAL STATUS AND ACTIVITIES: Mr., 1775; Esq., 1780. OCCUPATIONAL PROFILE: probably a planter; land speculator. PUBLIC CAREER. LEGISLATIVE SERVICE: Conventions, Frederick County, 6th–8th, 1775–1776. LOCAL OFFICES: Committee of Observation, Frederick County, 1775; collector of gold and silver coin, Frederick County, appointed 1776; coroner, Washington County, 1777–1792. MILITARY SERVICE: major, 1754. WEALTH DURING LIFETIME. PERSONAL PROPERTY: 6 slaves, 1790. LAND AT FIRST ELECTION: 802 acres in Frederick County. SIGNIFICANT CHANGES IN LAND BE-

TWEEN FIRST ELECTION AND DEATH: he apparently gave land in Frederick County (later became part of Washington County) to his son, William, Jr. WEALTH AT DEATH. DIED: in May 1792 in Washington County. PERSONAL PROPERTY: TEV, at least £603.7.0 current money (including 5 slaves and 23 books). LAND: 2 houses and 2 lots in Elizabeth Town (later called Hagerstown), Washington County; at least 1,250 acres in Kentucky; 1,000 acres in Virginia, and additional land in North Carolina.

BAKER, FRANCIS (?–?). BORN: probably in Cecil County, of age by 1760. NATIVE: third or fourth generation. RESIDED: in Cecil County; Talbot County, 1760; Harford County, 1786 until at least 1788; possibly in Pennsylvania, with his son Henry. FAMILY BACKGROUND. FATHER: *Henry Baker* (ca. 1710–1768). MOTHER: Elizabeth. UNCLE: *Nathan Baker* (?–?). BROTHERS: *Jeremiah Baker* (ca. 1748–1813); Henry (?–1780); Jethro (?–1777); and Samuel (?–by 1766). MARRIED by 1765 Frances, an only child, daughter of Harris Clayland (?–by 1740/41), of Talbot County, a planter, and wife Elizabeth; stepdaughter of Joseph Atkinson, a Quaker. CHILDREN. SONS: Samuel (by 1765–1786), died without progeny; Henry Clayland (by 1768–?), of Philadelphia, Pennsylvania by 1788, a lieutenant in the Maryland Line, married by 1790 Sarah. Possibly other children. PRIVATE CAREER. EDUCATION: literate. SOCIAL STATUS AND ACTIVITIES: Gent., 1765. OCCUPATIONAL PROFILE: planter, 1760; merchant, 1767; farmer, 1774; owned a schooner and seines used for trawling, 1771. PUBLIC CAREER. LEGISLATIVE SERVICE: Conventions, Talbot County, 4th, 1775, 5th, 1775, 6th, 1775 (elected, but did not attend; discharged on December 11, 1775, for a "breach of the continental association"). ADDITIONAL COMMENTS: In 1775 Baker was discharged from the conventions for violating the nonimportation agreements. He had loaned an old fishing net for trawling to a British captain in 1773. The captain promised to bring Baker a new seine from England on his next voyage. By June 1775 when the captain brought Baker his net, there was a ban on the importation of all British goods. Baker petitioned the Talbot County Committee of Observation for permission to keep the net, but the decision was unanimous that he send it back. Baker delivered the net to the ship, but made arrangements to reclaim it later that night. He was caught in this act to which he ultimately confessed, claiming he was "tempted by Poverty, and not by Will." Though his name was not published as an enemy, he was barred from

holding any future office of trust. By June 1776, however, this part of the sentence had been rescinded. LOCAL OFFICE: Committee of Observation, Talbot County, elected 1775. MILITARY SERVICE: 1st lieutenant of a company of militia in Talbot County belonging to the Fourth Militia, commissioned May 1776, resigned August 1776; buyer of cattle, salt, barreled beef and pork for the Continental Army, 1778; one of fifty-six persons drafted to raise two battalions of militia to reinforce the American Army, Talbot County, 1781. WEALTH DURING LIFETIME. PERSONAL PROPERTY: 12 slaves, 1 bay schooner, livestock, 1771 (mortgaged in 1771; released from mortgage, 1774); 9 slaves, 1776; assessed value £915.0.0, including 16 slaves and 12 oz. plate, 1783; 21 slaves, livestock, farm untensils, household furniture, and other property mortgaged in 1788 and sold in 1789 for £1,000 current money. LAND AT FIRST ELECTION: 569 acres in Talbot County (500 acres through his first marriage, 69 acres by purchase, all of which was mortgaged in 1771, but reclaimed by 1774). SIGNIFICANT CHANGES IN LAND BETWEEN FIRST ELECTION AND DEATH: gave the 500 acres in Talbot County acquired through his marriage to his son Henry by deed of gift, 1781; purchased 213 acres in Cecil County and patented 34 acres in Talbot County, by 1783; along with his sons he sold the 500-acre tract plus 120 additional acres in Talbot County, 1785; purchased 580 acres in Harford County and 555 acres in York County, Pennsylvania, 1785–1786; mortgaged 1,349 acres in Cecil and Harford counties, and York County, Pennsylvania, being most if not all his lands, 1788; gave his son Henry power of attorney and apparently defaulted on his mortgage payments, 1789; *Thomas Sim Lee* (1745–1819), from whom Baker had purchased his Harford County land on bond, was at that time making arrangements to take possession of Baker's land in York County, Pennsylvania, in order to secure payment. Continuously in and out of debt, he bought land only by mortgaging that which he already owned. At his death Baker probably had nothing left after all the mortgage payments were met by his son.

BAKER, HENRY (ca. 1710–1768). BORN: ca. 1710, probably in Cecil County. NATIVE: at least second generation. RESIDED: at "New Cormough" plantation, Cecil County. FAMILY BACKGROUND. FATHER: Nathan Baker (?–1729), of Cecil County, merchant; son of Henry Baker (?–ca. 1700), a Quaker, who immigrated in 1684 to Bucks County, Pennsylvania, from Lancashire, England, became a large landowner and was a burgess for

Bucks County, Pennsylvania, in 1685, 1687, 1688, 1690, and 1698. MOTHER: Sarah, daughter of Jeremiah Collet, of Chester, Pennsylvania. BROTHERS: Jeremiah; *Nathan Baker* (?–?). SISTER: Mary, who married Job Ruston. MARRIED Elizabeth. CHILDREN. SONS: *Jeremiah Baker* (ca. 1748–1813); Henry (?–1780); Jethro (?–1777), of Millford Hundred, Cecil County; *Francis Baker* (?–?); and Samuel (?–by 1766), who died without progeny in Dublin, Ireland. PRIVATE CAREER. RELIGIOUS AFFILIATION: Anglican, St. Mary Anne's Parish, Cecil County. SOCIAL STATUS AND ACTIVITIES: Gent., 1763. OCCUPATIONAL PROFILE: merchant, in partnership with Robert Craig, by 1765. PUBLIC CAREER. LEGISLATIVE SERVICE: Lower House, Cecil County, 1750–1751 (elected to the 2nd session to fill vacancy), 1754–1757, 1757–1758, 1758–1761 (Arms and Ammunition Cv 1, 1, Cv 2), 1762–1763, 1765–1766, 1768 (died before the 2nd session). LOCAL OFFICES: justice, Cecil County, 1741–at least 1744; St. Mary Anne's Parish Vestry, Cecil County, in office 1743–1746, 1751–1754, and 1754–1760. WEALTH DURING LIFETIME. PERSONAL PROPERTY: owned one-half interest in the brigantine *Polly,* valued at £1,300.0.0 current money, 1766. LAND AT FIRST ELECTION: 1,222 acres in Cecil County and in Pennsylvania. SIGNIFICANT CHANGES IN LAND BETWEEN FIRST ELECTION AND DEATH: acquired ca. 3,961 additional acres in Cecil County and in Pennsylvania, plus 2 lots in Charlestown, Cecil County, 1752–1767; mortgaged ca. 500 acres in Cecil County as indemnification against escaping court jurisdiction in a lawsuit brought against him by *Charles Carroll, Sr.* (1702–1782); he sold at least 1,784 acres in Cecil County and in Pennsylvania. WEALTH AT DEATH. DIED: in July 1768 in Cecil County. PERSONAL PROPERTY: TEV, £911.7.5 gold currency (including 12 slaves and 1 servant); FB, estate overpaid £37.19.10 as calculated. LAND: ca. 3,000 acres in Cecil County, as shown in debt books, of which ca. 500 acres were mortgaged. ADDITIONAL COMMENTS: his estate at death was heavily in debt to his business partner Robert Craig and was the subject of lengthy litigation.

BAKER, JEREMIAH (ca. 1748–1813). BORN: ca. 1748. NATIVE: at least third generation. RESIDED: at "Clayfall," Cecil County. FAMILY BACKGROUND. FATHER: *Henry Baker* (ca. 1710–1768). UNCLE: *Nathan Baker* (?–?). BROTHERS: Henry (?–1780); Jethro (?–1777); *Francis Baker* (?–?); and Samuel (?–by 1766). MARRIED first, on December 14, 1769, Hannah Thackey. MARRIED second, on February 8, 1793, Rebecca Mauldin, who subsequently married by 1817 Samuel Hogg. CHILDREN. SONS: Francis (1774–by 1817); Henry, who married Eliza Jane Adair; Jeremiah (?–1835), who married Mary Campbell, who subsequently married by 1838 (first name unknown) Logan. DAUGHTERS: Elizabeth (1776–by 1817), who married (first name unknown) Oyleby; Sarah (1778–?), who married Isaac Watson; Mary Anne; and Charlotte. PRIVATE CAREER. EDUCATION: literate. RELIGIOUS AFFILIATION: Anglican, St. Mary Anne's Parish, Cecil County. SOCIAL STATUS AND ACTIVITIES: Esq., 1790. OCCUPATIONAL PROFILE: farmer. PUBLIC CAREER. LEGISLATIVE SERVICE: Lower House, Cecil County, 1785. LOCAL OFFICES: North Elk Parish Vestry, Cecil County, elected 1773 and 1774; purchasing agent, Cecil County, appointed 1779; justice, Cecil County, 1782–at least 1800; justice, Orphans' Court, Cecil County, 1782–1786; commissioner of tax, Cecil County, 1782–1785. MILITARY SERVICE: captain of a company of Cecil County Militia belonging to the Thirtieth Battalion, commissioned July 1776. WEALTH DURING LIFETIME. LAND AT FIRST ELECTION: 500 acres in Cecil County. SIGNIFICANT CHANGES IN LAND BETWEEN FIRST ELECTION AND DEATH: required to sell 400 acres in Cecil County at public auction in 1790 as the result of a decision of the Chancery Court regarding his father's estate, which was indebted to Robert Craig, his father's former business partner; he repurchased part of this tract in 1810. WEALTH AT DEATH. DIED: by June 1813; buried at St. Mary Anne's Cemetery, North East, Cecil County. PERSONAL PROPERTY: TEV, $3,409.76 (including 7 slaves); FB, $2,589.46. LAND: possibly 369 acres in Cecil County.

BAKER, JOHN (?–ca. 1730/31). BORN: in St. Mary's County; probably oldest son. NATIVE: second generation. RESIDED: in St. Mary's County. FAMILY BACKGROUND. FATHER: John Baker (?–by 1687), who immigrated as a servant, but was free by 1673. He became an innholder and was sheriff of St. Mary's County from 1685 to 1686. MOTHER: Elizabeth Bateman (?–1712). MARRIED by 1706 Ann, daughter of Thomas Courtney. She subsequently married William Thompson. CHILDREN. SON: John. PRIVATE CAREER. EDUCATION: literate. RELIGIOUS AFFILIATION: Protestant. SOCIAL STATUS AND ACTIVITIES: Gent., by 1700. PUBLIC CAREER. LEGISLATIVE SERVICE: Lower House, St. Mary's County, 1702–1704 (elected to the 3rd session), 1715 (Elections), 1716–1718 (Elections and Privileges 1), 1721–1721/22 (elected to the 4th session to fill vacancy). LOCAL OFFICE: justice, St. Mary's County, sitting 1699/1700. MILITARY SERVICE: captain, 1717; colonel, by 1726. WEALTH AT DEATH. DIED: by March 5, 1730/31. PERSONAL PROPERTY: TEV, £256.11.0 (including 3 servants); FB, estate overpaid £14.12.0.

BAKER, NATHAN (?–?). BORN: of age by 1743. NATIVE: at least second generation. RESIDED: in Charlestown, Cecil County, 1775. FAMILY BACKGROUND. FATHER: Nathan Baker (?–1729), of Cecil County, merchant; son of Henry Baker (?–ca. 1700), a Quaker, who immigrated in 1684 to Bucks County, Pennsylvania, from Lancashire, England, became a large landowner and was a burgess for Bucks County, Pennsylvania, in 1685, 1687, 1688, 1690, and 1698. MOTHER: Sarah, daughter of Jeremiah Collet, of Chester, Pennsylvania. BROTHERS: *Henry Baker* (ca. 1710–1768); Jeremiah. SISTER: Mary, who married Job Ruston. NEPHEWS: *Jeremiah Baker* (ca. 1748–1813); *Francis Baker* (?–?). MARRIED on January 12, 1736/37, Joyce Yardley. CHILDREN. DAUGHTER: Elizabeth. PRIVATE CAREER. EDUCATION: literate. RELIGIOUS AFFILIATION: Anglican, St. Mary Anne's Parish, Cecil County. SOCIAL STATUS AND ACTIVITIES: Gent., 1759. OCCUPATIONAL PROFILE: a miller, in partnership with Jethro Browne, 1748–1765. PUBLIC CAREER. LEGISLATIVE SERVICE: Lower House, Cecil County, 1763 (elected to the 2nd session to fill vacancy). LOCAL OFFICES: justice, Cecil County, 1741–at least 1758 (quorum, 1754–at least 1758); churchwarden, St. Mary Anne's Parish, Cecil County, in office 1743; St. Mary Anne's Parish Vestry, Cecil County, in office 1748–1751, 1755–1758, 1761–1764, and 1765; justice, Court of Oyer and Terminer and Gaol Delivery, Cecil County, commissioned 1750 and 1759. MILITARY SERVICE: captain, by 1755. WEALTH DURING LIFETIME. PERSONAL PROPERTY: inherited a gristmill on the Northeast River, Cecil County, in 1754 from his deceased business partner, Jethro Browne, as well as half of Browne's estate. LAND AT FIRST ELECTION: probably 193 acres in Cecil County, plus one-half of the real estate of his business partner. WEALTH AT DEATH. DIED: after 1778; size of estate unknown.

BAKER, WILLIAM (ca. 1749–1812). BORN: ca. 1749. NATIVE: at least second generation. RESIDED: in Frederick County, 1774–1776; Montgomery County, 1778; Prince George's County, 1779; Alexandria, Virginia, 1787; "The Lodge," Prince George's County, 1790–1807; Georgetown, D.C., 1812. MARRIED first, by 1778 Mildred Hanson (ca. 1746–by 1796), daughter of *Samuel Hanson* (1716–1794). Her brothers were *Samuel Hanson, of Samuel* (ca. 1752–1830); Thomas Hawkins Hanson (1750–1810). Her sisters were Chloe, who married *George Lee* (ca. 1736–?); Sarah; Nancy; Eleanor, who married *Henry Henley Chapman* (?–1821); Anne; and Elizabeth. MARRIED second, by 1796 (name unknown). CHILDREN. SONS: Samuel Hanson (1773–?); Philip Thomas (1775–?); and William, Jr. (1782–?). DAUGHTERS: Nancy (1777–?); Chloe (1784–?); and Eleanor (1785–1796). PRIVATE CAREER. EDUCATION: trained as a doctor. RELIGIOUS AFFILIATION: Protestant. OCCUPATIONAL PROFILE: physician; land speculator. PUBLIC CAREER. LEGISLATIVE SERVICE: Convention, Frederick County, 1st, 1774 (appointed, but did not attend); Lower House, Prince George's County, 1796. LOCAL OFFICES: Committee of Observation, Frederick County, elected 1775; justice, Montgomery County, commissioned 1778, Prince George's County, 1788–at least 1792, 1799–at least 1800. STANDS ON PUBLIC/PRIVATE ISSUES: manumitted one female slave in 1796, because she had borne him "a numerous family." WEALTH DURING LIFETIME. PERSONAL PROPERTY: assessed value £752.0.10, including 33 slaves and 34 oz. plate, 1793; assessed value £285.2.1, including 9 slaves and 24 oz. plate, 1807. SIGNIFICANT CHANGES IN LAND BETWEEN FIRST ELECTION AND DEATH: purchased 6,417 acres in Prince George's County and Franklin County, Georgia, including 707 acres of confiscated British property, 1775–1801; sold 5,730 acres by 1801, 4,600 acres of this was in Franklin County, Georgia, and comprised 4 large tracts. WEALTH AT DEATH. DIED: in 1812 in Georgetown, D.C.; size of estate unknown.

BALDRIDGE, THOMAS (?–ca. 1655). BORN: probably in England. IMMIGRATED: probably in 1635, definitely by 1637, possibly as an indentured servant. RESIDED: in St. Mary's County; moved to Virginia by 1650. FAMILY BACKGROUND. BROTHER: James (?–1654), who married Dorothy (?–1662). MARRIED Grace, who subsequently married Maj. John Tew. CHILDREN. SONS: James (?–1664), who married Elizabeth; William. PRIVATE CAREER. RELIGIOUS AFFILIATION: Protestant. SOCIAL STATUS AND ACTIVITIES: possibly arrived as a servant, certainly of low social status; his role in Ingle's Rebellion probably accounts for his removal to Virginia. OCCUPATIONAL PROFILE: possibly a servant; planter. PUBLIC CAREER. LEGISLATIVE SERVICE: Assembly, present 1637/38, St. Michael's Hundred, St. Mary's County, 1640–

1641, present 1641/42. LOCAL OFFICES: sheriff and coroner, St. Mary's County, 1638/39–1641. MILITARY SERVICE: sergeant, 1638/39. OUT OF COLONY SERVICE: justice, Northumberland County, Virginia, probably 1652–1653, Westmoreland County, Virginia, 1653–1654; captain, by 1650; major at death. STANDS ON PUBLIC/PRIVATE ISSUES: a commander of the rebel forces during Ingle's Rebellion. WEALTH DURING LIFETIME. LAND AT FIRST ELECTION: no evidence of any. WEALTH AT DEATH. DIED: an inventory of his estate was taken in 1655. LAND: at least 840 acres owned with his brother in Northumberland County, Virginia.

BALDWIN, JOHN (?–1752). BORN: probably in Anne Arundel County; eldest son. NATIVE: at least third generation. RESIDED: in Cecil County by 1729. FAMILY BACKGROUND. FATHER: John Baldwin (?–1715), of Anne Arundel County. MOTHER: Hester. BROTHERS: Thomas; James (?–by 1725). SISTERS: Catharine (1705–1733), who married by 1725 Charles Griffith (1693–1771); Mary, who married by 1725 Robert Lusby. NIECE: Catherine Griffith (1732–1793), who married *Nicholas Worthington* (1734–1793). MARRIED by 1728 Mary, widow of John Thompson, daughter of *William Dare* (?–1719). ADDITIONAL COMMENTS: possibly married second, by 1743 Mary, daughter of Dominick Carroll. CHILDREN. DAUGHTERS: Hester Thompson; Catherine, who married in 1750/51 George Milligan, a merchant, of Chestertown, Kent County; Mary Knight. PRIVATE CAREER. EDUCATION: literate. RELIGIOUS AFFILIATION: Anglican. SOCIAL STATUS AND ACTIVITIES: Gent., 1718; Mr., 1745. OCCUPATIONAL PROFILE: possibly a planter. PUBLIC CAREER. LEGISLATIVE SERVICE: Lower House, Cecil County, 1749 (election voided on June 6, 1749, when the Lower House judged that the election was not free). LOCAL OFFICES: justice, Cecil County, in office 1723–1727, 1734–at least 1751 (quorum, 1734–at least 1751); sheriff, Cecil County, 1727–1730, 1736–1739; North Sassafras Parish Vestry, Cecil County, in office ca. 1728, 1732–1733; justice, Court of Oyer and Terminer and Gaol Delivery, Cecil County, commissioned 1742 and 1749. MILITARY SERVICE: captain, by 1736; major, by 1740; colonel, by 1752. WEALTH DURING LIFETIME. LAND AT FIRST ELECTION: 675 acres in Anne Arundel and Cecil counties, and 2 lots in Cecil County (280 acres from his wife's dower); he had been very active in buying and selling land prior to his first election. WEALTH AT DEATH. DIED: will probated on August 15, 1752, in Cecil County. LAND: ca.

666 acres in Anne Arundel and Cecil counties, plus 3 lots in Cecilton, Cecil County, and 1 lot in Fredericktown, Cecil County.

BALLARD, CHARLES (ca. 1670–ca. 1724/25). BORN: ca. 1670 in Somerset County; younger son. NATIVE: second generation. RESIDED: in Manokin Hundred, Somerset County. FAMILY BACKGROUND. FATHER: Charles Ballard (?–1682), who immigrated in 1665, was both literate and a merchant, and who served as a justice of Somerset County from 1670 to 1676 and from 1676 to 1682. MOTHER: Sarah, widow of both John Elzey and Thomas Jordan, whose fourth husband was *Stephen Luffe* (?–1693). BROTHERS: Henry (1666–1697); Jarvis (?–1765). SISTERS: Sarah (1668–?), who married Randall Revell, son of *Randall Revell* (ca. 1611–1686/87); Elizabeth, who married first, John King, second, Thomas Wilson, and third, *Peter Dent* (ca. 1665–1710/11). MARRIED Eleanor, daughter of *Robert King* (?–1697). Her brother was *Robert King* (1689–1755). Her sister was Mary (1674–1744), who married first, *Francis Jenkins* (ca. 1650–1710), second, Rev. John Henry (?–1717), and third, Rev. John Hampton (?–1720/21). CHILDREN. SONS: Henry; Charles. DAUGHTERS: Sarah; Anna; Isabella; Alice; and Elizabeth. PRIVATE CAREER. EDUCATION: literate. RELIGIOUS AFFILIATION: Protestant, probably a Presbyterian. SOCIAL STATUS AND ACTIVITIES: Gent., by 1694. OCCUPATIONAL PROFILE: planter. PUBLIC CAREER. LEGISLATIVE SERVICE: Lower House, Somerset County, 1715. LOCAL OFFICES: justice, Somerset County, 1699–1724/25; coroner, Somerset County, 1705, 1711–1713. MILITARY SERVICE: captain, 1701; major, by 1722/23. WEALTH DURING LIFETIME. LAND AT FIRST ELECTION: ca. 1,200 acres. WEALTH AT DEATH. DIED: between November 1724 and January 21, 1724/25. PERSONAL PROPERTY: TEV, £683.10.2 (including 17 slaves and books). LAND: over 600 acres.

BANCKES (BANKS, BANCKS), WILLIAM (?–1806). BORN: probably in Queen Anne's County, of age by 1776; oldest, and possibly only, son. NATIVE: at least second generation. RESIDED: in Queen Anne's County; Caroline County, 1776. FAMILY BACKGROUND. FATHER: William Banckes (?–1766), of Queen Anne's County; a merchant who probably declared insolvency in 1763. MOTHER: Deborah, daughter of John Hawkins (?–ca. 1745), of Queen Anne's County, and wife Deborah Grundy Pemberton (?–1749). HALF UNCLE: *Grundy Pemberton* (?–1768). OTHER KINSHIP:

Elizabeth F. Clifton and Deborah Bordley are listed as kin in his inventory. PRIVATE CAREER. EDUCATION: literate. SOCIAL STATUS AND ACTIVITIES: Gent. OCCUPATIONAL PROFILE: farmer. PUBLIC CAREER. LEGISLATIVE SERVICE: Lower House, Caroline County, 1788 (elected to the Assembly to fill vacancy), 1789 (Claims). LOCAL OFFICES: sheriff, Caroline County, elected 1785; justice, Caroline County, commissioned 1793 and 1794. WEALTH DURING LIFETIME. PERSONAL PROPERTY: assessed value £53.0.0, 1783; 1 slave, 1798. LAND AT FIRST ELECTION: 699 acres in Caroline County (419 acres from his father; 280 acres by purchase). SIGNIFICANT CHANGES IN LAND BETWEEN FIRST ELECTION AND DEATH: sold nearly all of his land in 1804 to John Fisher, who later became the administrator of his estate. WEALTH AT DEATH. DIED: in 1806 in Caroline County. LAND: inventory lists his worth as $40.00, which was the annual rent due on a piece of property he had under a 90-year lease.

BANKS, RICHARD (ca. 1612–ca. 1667). BORN: ca. 1612, probably in England. IMMIGRATED: in 1641/42 as a free adult. RESIDED: in St. Mary's County. MARRIED in 1652 Margaret, widow of Richard Hatton. Her brother- in-law was *Thomas Hatton* (?–1654/55). CHILDREN. STEPSONS: *William Hatton* (?–1712), who married first, Elizabeth, daughter of Rev. William Wilkinson, and second, Mary; Richard, who married by 1674 Ann (1659–?), daughter of *John Price* (ca. 1607–1660/61). STEPDAUGHTERS: Elinor (1642–1725), who married first, *Thomas Brooke* (1632–1676), and second, *Henry Darnall* (ca. 1645–1711); Mary, who married *Zachary Wade* (ca. 1627–1678); Elizabeth, who married first, *Luke Gardiner* (1622–1674), and second, *Clement Hill* (?–1708); and Barbara, who married *James Johnson* (?–?). PRIVATE CAREER. EDUCATION: literate. RELIGIOUS AFFILIATION: Protestant. OCCUPATIONAL PROFILE: held a 200-acre plantation in partnership with William Wright, 1641/42; planter. PUBLIC CAREER. LEGISLATIVE SERVICE: Assembly, present 1647/48 (Defense), St. Mary's County, 1649 (Accounts); Parliamentary Commission, 1652. OTHER PROVINCIAL OFFICE: justice, Provincial Court, 1652. LOCAL OFFICE: justice, St. Mary's County, 1658–1660. MILITARY SERVICE: lieutenant, 1648–1658; captain, 1658–1660. STANDS ON PUBLIC/- PRIVATE ISSUES: initially supported the Puritan government in 1652, but later fought against it; supported Fendall's Rebellion in 1660, for which he lost his offices. WEALTH DURING LIFETIME. LAND AT FIRST ELECTION: ca. 200 acres. WEALTH AT DEATH. DIED: ca. 1667. LAND: probably 400 acres.

BANNING, HENRY (ca. 1736–1818). BORN: ca. 1736 at "Isthmus," opposite Oxford, Talbot County. NATIVE: at least second generation. RESIDED: in Talbot County; Mill Hundred, Talbot County, 1776. FAMILY BACKGROUND. FATHER: William Banning (?–by 1746). MOTHER: Jane (?–1767); the St. Michael's Parish Vestry ordered Jane and Nicholas Goldsborough to appear on charges of lewdness and incontinence, but they refused, 1744. STEPFATHER: Nicholas Goldsborough (1704–1756). STEPUNCLES: *Charles Goldsborough* (1707–1767); *William Goldsborough* (1709–1760); and *John Goldsborough* (1711–1778). BROTHERS: Jeremiah (1733–ca. 1798), a merchant and mariner, appointed in 1777 as the naval officer of the Seventh District, colonel in the Thirty-eighth Battalion, Talbot County Militia in 1777, justice of Talbot County from 1778 to at least 1789, justice of the Orphans' Court of Talbot County from 1779 to at least 1789, commissioner of tax in Talbot County from 1779 to 1782, a member of the Constitution Ratification Convention from Talbot County in 1788; Anthony (ca. 1740–1787), of Chestertown, Kent County; and Andrew. OTHER KINSHIP: his stepgrandfather was *Robert Goldsborough* (1660–1746). MARRIED first, (name unknown). MARRIED second, by 1789 Araminta (ca. 1750–1807), who died of a "bilious fever" at "Woodly," Talbot County. CHILDREN. SONS: Anthony; Thomas; and John Wesley (?–1823). DAUGHTERS: Jane, who married (first name unknown) Parrott; Ann, who married James Earle Denny (?–ca. 1802); (first name unknown), who married John Kersey. PRIVATE CAREER. EDUCATION: literate. RELIGIOUS AFFILIATION: Anglican; Methodist, 1808. ADDITIONAL COMMENTS: Banning gave the ground in Talbot County where Sardis Methodist Chapel was built for a Methodist meeting and a schoolhouse "for the encouragement of religion and learning," 1808. SOCIAL STATUS AND ACTIVITIES: Esq., 1783. OCCUPATIONAL PROFILE: planter, 1786; shipwright, 1788; farmer, 1800. PUBLIC CAREER. LEGISLATIVE SERVICE: Lower House, Talbot County, 1777 (discharged on February 12, 1777, for serving as a field officer at the time of first election; reelected and seated; Manufactories 1), 1779–1780. LOCAL OFFICES: St. Michael's Parish Vestry, Talbot County, elected 1768, 1775, 1776, 1783, and 1784; justice, Talbot County, 1774–at least 1778; judge for the special election of delegates to the convention whose duty it was to frame a constitution for Maryland, Talbot County, appointed 1776; justice, Orphans' Court, Talbot County, appointed 1778; judge, Second Election District, Talbot County, appointed 1800. MILITARY SERVICE: captain, Thirty-eighth Battalion, Talbot County Militia, by May 1776; discharged from the Lower House for serving as a field officer, February 12, 1777; captain, Oxford Company, Thirty-eight Battalion, Talbot County Militia, commissioned April 1778, still serving in December 1779. STANDS ON PUBLIC/PRIVATE IS-SUES: manumitted twelve slaves, 1786; manumitted nine slaves in his will, 1818. WEALTH DURING LIFETIME. PERSONAL PROPERTY: 15 slaves, 1776; assessed value £884.1.8, including 11 slaves and 20 oz. plate, 1783; assessed value £396.6.8, 1793; assessed value £375.5.10, including 3 slaves, 1798; assessed value £384.3.4, 1800; assessed value £402.5.0, 1804; assessed value $1,265.00, 1813; assessed value $811.00, 1817. LAND AT FIRST ELECTION: 208 acres in Talbot County (inherited from stepfather, then resurveyed). SIGNIFICANT CHANGES IN LAND BETWEEN FIRST ELECTION AND DEATH: purchased at least 777 acres in Talbot, Caroline, and Queen Anne's counties between 1784 and 1816; sold 110 acres, partly in Queen Anne's County and partly in Caroline County, 1793; listed in tax assessments as owning 558 acres in Caroline County, 1798. WEALTH AT DEATH. DIED: on Wednesday, August 19, 1818, in Talbot County. PERSONAL PROPERTY: TEV, at least $4,753.65, plus $1,200.13 debts owed to him (including 5 slaves, 1 servant, 30 shares in the Farmers Bank, 30 shares in the Bank of Caroline County, and books). LAND: at least 892 acres in Talbot and Caroline counties; possibly 558 additional acres in Caroline County.

BARBER, LUKE (?–1668). BORN: probably in England. IMMIGRATED: in 1654/55 as a free adult from England. RESIDED: in Newtown, St. Mary's County. MARRIED Elizabeth, who subsequently married in 1669 John Bloomfield (?–1692). CHILDREN. SONS: Luke; Edward (?–1694); and Thomas. DAUGHTERS: Mary; Elizabeth, married *Joshua Guibert* (?–1713); and Ann. PRIVATE CAREER. EDUCATION: literate; probably well educated. RELIGIOUS AFFILIATION: almost certainly Protestant. SOCIAL STATUS AND ACTIVITIES: arrived with high status; apparently returned briefly to England in 1655; transported thirteen servants by 1659; usually called "Doctor." OCCUPATIONAL PROFILE: servant in the household of Oliver Cromwell prior to 1654/55; doctor; planter. PUBLIC CAREER. LEGISLATIVE SERVICE: Upper House, 1658 (did not attend), 1659/60. OTHER PROVIN-

CIAL OFFICES: Council, 1656–1660; justice, Provincial Court, 1656–1660; deputy Governor, 1657–1657/58. STANDS ON PUBLIC/PRIVATE ISSUES: provided important testimony to Oliver Cromwell in 1655 against the Parliamentary Commissioners and was sympathetic to proprietary party; he was rewarded with an appointment to Council. His position on Fendall's Rebellion in 1659/60 is unclear because he left the Assembly before the actual overthrow of proprietary government, but was not reappointed to the Council after the rebellion. WEALTH DURING LIFETIME. LAND AT FIRST ELECTION: 2,000 acres. WEALTH AT DEATH. DIED: by November 1668. PERSONAL PROPERTY: £196.6.4 sterling (including 82 books in English, as well as 50 in Latin and 43 in French), plus his will mentioned £200.0.0 in England; FB, £159.1.9. LAND: 2,000 acres ("Micham Hall" and "Lukeland").

BARNES, ABRAHAM (?–ca. 1778). IMMIGRATED: between 1740 and 1744 from Virginia. ADDITIONAL COMMENTS: immigrated to Virginia from England. RESIDED: in St. Mary's County. MARRIED first, Mary Elizabeth (1715–1739), daughter of *Robert King* (1689–1755); granddaughter of *Robert King* (?–1697); niece of Mary King (1674–1744), who married first, *Francis Jenkins* (ca. 1650–1710), Eleanor King, who married *Charles Ballard* (ca. 1670–ca. 1724/25), Sarah Covington (1683–1755), who married first, *Edward Lloyd* (1670–1718/19), and second, *James Hollyday* (1696–1747), and Elizabeth Covington, who married *Benjamin Wailes* (?–ca. 1729). Her brothers were Robert (?–1752); Nehemiah (?–1766). Her first cousins were *Robert Jenkins Henry* (ca. 1712–1766); *John Henry* (ca. 1714–1781); *Edward Lloyd* (1711–1770); *Richard Lloyd* (1717–1786); *James Hollyday* (1722–1786); and *Henry Hollyday* (ca. 1725–1789). Her nephew was *Thomas King* (?–?). MARRIED second, by 1743 Elizabeth, daughter of *John Rousby* (1685–1744); granddaughter of *John Rousby* (?–1685/86); half niece of both *Walter Smith* (ca. 1693–1748) and Barbara Smith (1693–1764), who married first, *Thomas Holdsworth* (ca. 1692–1718), and second, *Benjamin Mackall* (1675–1761). Her brother was John (1728–1750/51). Her stepbrother was *George Plater* (1695–1755). Her sisters were Anne (1721–1769), who married *Edward Lloyd* (1711–1770); Gertrude, who married *Robert Jenkins Henry* (ca. 1712–1766). Her half first cousins were Mary Holdsworth (1713–?), who married *Benson Bond* (1710–1750); Betty Holdsworth (1715–?), who married *James Heighe* (?–1757); *Benjamin Mack-*

all, Jr. (ca. 1723–1795), and Barbara Mackall, who married *William Wilkinson* (?–1755). Her nephew was *Edward Lloyd* (1744–1796). Her nieces were Elizabeth Lloyd (1741/42–?), who married *John Cadwalader* (1741/42–1786); Elizabeth Rousby, who married *George Plater* (1735–1792). CHILDREN. SONS: *John Barnes* (ca. 1743–1800); *Richard Barnes* (?–1804). DAUGHTER: Mary King, who married Thomson Mason (1733–1785), of Virginia, a lawyer and the brother of George Mason (1725–1792), of "Gunston Hall," Virginia. PRIVATE CAREER. EDUCATION: literate. RELIGIOUS AFFILIATION: Anglican, St. Andrew's Church, St. Mary's County. SOCIAL STATUS AND ACTIVITIES: Gent., 1747. OCCUPATIONAL PROFILE: merchant, Leonardtown, St. Mary's County; land speculator. PUBLIC CAREER. LEGISLATIVE SERVICE: Lower House, St. Mary's County, 1745 (Bills of Credit), 1745/46–1748 (Bills of Credit 1–3, 4), 1749–1751 (election voided on June 10, 1749; reelected to the 2nd session and seated; Bills of Credit Cv–3), 1751–1754 (Bills of Credit 1–6); Convention, St. Mary's County, 1st, 1774. ADDITIONAL COMMENTS: Barnes, with other St. Mary's County delegates, was dismissed in 1749 for being improperly elected, having used a great quantity of liquor to influence the electorate. LOCAL OFFICES: justice, St. Mary's County, 1739–at least 1755 (quorum, 1753–at least 1755); St. Andrew's Parish Vestry, St. Mary's County, in office 1753–1761, 1767–1770; churchwarden, St. Andrew's Parish, St. Mary's County, elected 1770; trustee, St. Mary's County Free School, in office 1772; chairman, Committee of Observation, St. Mary's County, elected ca. 1775; commissioner of tax, St. Mary's County, appointed 1777. MILITARY SERVICE: major, by 1751; colonel, by 1756. OUT OF COLONY SERVICE: Maryland delegate to the Albany Congress, 1754. STANDS ON PUBLIC/PRIVATE ISSUES: favored the proprietary party from the beginning of his legislative career. WEALTH DURING LIFETIME. LAND AT FIRST ELECTION: 2,446 acres in St. Mary's County, 1753 (at least 1,086 acres by purchase or patent). SIGNIFICANT CHANGES IN LAND BETWEEN FIRST ELECTION AND DEATH: purchased or patented at least 697 acres in St. Mary's County between 1758 and 1774; sold 63 acres in St. Mary's County, 1795; acquired 4,923 acres in Frederick County (later became part of Washington County), by 1773. WEALTH AT DEATH. DIED: probably at Leonardtown, St. Mary's County; will probated on January 13, 1778, in St. Mary's County. PERSONAL PROPERTY: size of estate unknown. LAND: 8,702 acres in St. Mary's and Washington counties, plus 14 lots in Leonardtown, St. Mary's County, 1774. ADDITIONAL COMMENTS: In 1764 Abraham gave his son *John Barnes* (ca. 1743–1800) enough goods to go into trade. By 1773 John was deeply in debt, caused, according to Abraham, by his being obstinate and rejecting all his father's advice. Consequently, Barnes left all of his estate to his other son *Richard Barnes* (?–1804).

BARNES, JOHN (ca. 1743–1800). BORN: ca. 1743, probably in St. Mary's County. NATIVE: second generation. RESIDED: in St. Mary's County; Washington County, 1777; lived at "Mont Pelier," Washington County, a tract belonging to his brother *Richard Barnes* (?–1804), which Richard formed from land inherited from his father. FAMILY BACKGROUND. FATHER: *Abraham Barnes* (?–ca. 1778), who married first, Mary Elizabeth King (1715–1739). MOTHER: Elizabeth, daughter of *John Rousby* (1685–1744). AUNTS: Anne Rousby (1721–1769), who married *Edward Lloyd* (1711–1770); Gertrude Rousby, who married *Robert Jenkins Henry* (ca. 1712–1766). BROTHER: *Richard Barnes* (?–1804). HALF SISTER: Mary King. FIRST COUSINS: *Edward Lloyd* (1744–1796); Elizabeth Lloyd (1741/42–?), who married *John Cadwalader* (1741/42–1786); Elizabeth Rousby, who married *George Plater* (1735–1792). PRIVATE CAREER. EDUCATION: literate. SOCIAL STATUS AND ACTIVITIES: Esq., 1783. OCCUPATIONAL PROFILE: merchant, in partnership with Thomas Howe Ridgate, of Port Tobacco, Charles County, in the firm of Barnes & Ridgate. PUBLIC CAREER. LEGISLATIVE SERVICE: Convention, St. Mary's County, 4th, 1775 (elected, but did not attend); Lower House, Washington County, 1777–1778 (Claims 2), 1778–1779 (Laws to Expire 2; Grievances 3), 1779–1780, 1780–1781 (elected to the 1st session to fill vacancy), 1781–1782, 1782–1783, 1795. LOCAL OFFICES: justice, Washington County, 1777–1800 (chief justice, 1791–1800); justice, Orphans' Court, Washington County, 1778–at least 1785. MILITARY SERVICE: called colonel at time of death. WEALTH DURING LIFETIME. PERSONAL PROPERTY: assessed value £163.6.8, including 20 oz. plate, Washington County, 1783. LAND AT FIRST ELECTION: no evidence of land found. ADDITIONAL COMMENTS: in 1764 his father gave John a sufficient quantity of goods to begin in trade. By 1773 John was in a London jail for insolvency, his firm of Barnes & Ridgate having gone bankrupt, and his partner Thomas Howe Ridgate having fled England. When John's father wrote his will in June 1773 he left nothing more to John. *Abraham Barnes* (?–ca. 1778) called his son careless and obstinate. John had lost all that his father had given him, and then proceeded to bind his father as a security with Hanbury & Co., merchants in London, England, and others. John was so excessively in debt that it was beyond the capacity of his father to meet the obligations. **WEALTH AT DEATH.** DIED: in June 1800 in Washington County. PERSONAL PROPERTY: TEV, £1,972.18.1 specie (including 13 oz. plate); FB, £1,558.6.3. LAND: none found; lived on his brother's estate, "Mont Pelier," Washington County.

BARNES, RICHARD (?–1804). NATIVE: second generation. RESIDED: in Leonardtown, St. Mary's County. **FAMILY BACKGROUND.** FATHER: *Abraham Barnes* (?–ca. 1778), who married first, Mary Elizabeth King (1715–1739). MOTHER: Elizabeth, daughter of *John Rousby* (1685–1744). AUNTS: Anne Rousby (1721–1769), who married *Edward Lloyd* (1711–1770); Gertrude Rousby, who married *Robert Jenkins Henry* (ca. 1712–1766). BROTHER: *John Barnes* (ca. 1743–1800). HALF SISTER: Mary King. FIRST COUSINS: *Edward Lloyd* (1744–1796); Elizabeth Lloyd (1741/42–?), who married *John Cadwalader* (1741/42–1786); Elizabeth Rousby, who married *George Plater* (1735–1792). MARRIED probably never. CHILDREN. Died without progeny. **PRIVATE CAREER.** EDUCATION: literate. RELIGIOUS AFFILIATION: Anglican. SOCIAL STATUS AND ACTIVITIES: Gent., 1779; Esq., 1783. OCCUPATIONAL PROFILE: planter. **PUBLIC CAREER.** LEGISLATIVE SERVICE: Lower House, St. Mary's County, 1773–1774 (Accounts 1, Cv); Conventions, St. Mary's County, 3rd, 1774, 4th, 1775, 5th, 1775, 6th–8th, 1775–1776, 9th, 1776 (Loan Office); Lower House, St. Mary's County, 1777–1778 (Grievances 1–3), 1789; Senate, Western Shore, Term of 1776–1781: 1778–1779 (elected on November 20, 1778, to fill vacancy; qualified on December 11, 1778), 1779–1780, 1780–1781, Term of 1781–1786: 1781–1782, 1782–1783, 1783 (elected president on December 23, 1783, but declined to accept), 1784, 1785, Term of 1786–1791: 1786 (declined to serve on November 30, 1786). OTHER STATE OFFICE: Constitution Ratification Convention, St. Mary's County, 1788. LOCAL OFFICES: justice, St. Mary's County, at least by 1772–1778 (quorum, at least by 1772–1778; "desires to be left out," 1778); justice, Orphans' Court, St. Mary's County, commissioned 1777, commissioned 1778 ("desires to be left out"); county lieutenant, St. Mary's County, appointed 1777; churchwarden, All Faith's Parish, St. Mary's County, in office 1780–1781; All Faith's Parish Vestry, St. Mary's County, in office 1786–

1790. MILITARY SERVICE: called colonel, by 1780. STANDS ON PUBLIC/PRIVATE ISSUES: voted for Federalist candidates in 1789 and 1790; in his will he manumitted all of his slaves, numbering between 300 and 400, to be effective three years after his death provided "they behave themselves." **WEALTH DURING LIFETIME.** PERSONAL PROPERTY: assessed value £2,633.0.0, including 40 slaves, Washington County, 1783; 209 slaves, St. Mary's County, 1790; assessed value £5,846.18.9, including 224 slaves and 284 oz. plate, Lower Newton, St. George's, and St. Inigoes hundreds, St. Mary's County, 1793; assessed value £6,270.8.9, including 235 slaves and 316 oz. plate, Lower Newton, St. George's, and St. Inigoes hundreds, St. Mary's County, 1801; assessed value £3,542.6.8, including 181 slaves and 8 oz. plate, Washington County, 1804. LAND AT FIRST ELECTiON: 30 acres in Frederick County. SIGNIFICANT CHANGES IN LAND BETWEEN FIRST ELECTION AND DEATH: inherited 8,702 acres in St. Mary's and Washington counties from his father, 1778; patented 748 acres in St. Mary's and Washington counties between 1784 and 1803. ADDITIONAL COMMENTS: Barnes was his father's sole heir, 1778; Barnes's brother *John Barnes* (ca. 1743–1800) lived with him at "Mont Pelier" in Washington County. **WEALTH AT DEATH.** DIED: on April 29, 1804, in Leonardtown, St. Mary's County. PERSONAL PROPERTY: requested no appraisal of his estate. LAND: 9,427 acres in Washington and St. Mary's counties. ADDITIONAL COMMENTS: his principal heir was his nephew John Thomson Mason.

BARTON, WILLIAM (ca. 1605–early 1680s). BORN: ca. 1605, probably in England. IMMIGRATED: by 1654 as a free adult with his wife and two children. RESIDED: in St. Mary's County; may have moved to Charles County in the late 1660s. CHILDREN. SON: William (?–1717), a justice of Charles County from 1672 to 1696 and from 1704 to 1709, who married Margaret, widow of William Hungerford and daughter of William Smoote. DAUGHTER: Margaret. **PRIVATE CAREER.** RELIGIOUS AFFILIATION: Protestant. SOCIAL STATUS AND ACTIVITIES: no title on arrival; Gent., by the late 1650s. OCCUPATIONAL PROFILE: mariner; planter. **PUBLIC CAREER.** LEGISLATIVE SERVICE: Lower House, St. Mary's County, 1659/60 (election voided), 1661. LOCAL OFFICES: justice, St. Mary's and Potomac (St. Mary's County), 1655–probably 1658 (quorum), St. Mary's County, 1658–1668 (quorum). STANDS ON PUBLIC/PRIVATE ISSUES: rewarded by Lord Baltimore in 1656 for his loyalty, probably for his services in the Battle of the Severn. WEALTH DURING LIFETIME. LAND AT FIRST ELECTION: a freeholder on St. Clement's Manor, 1657; 500 acres in 1661. WEALTH AT DEATH. DIED: in the early 1680s. LAND: at least 600 acres.

BARTON, WILLIAM (1667/68–1705). BORN: on February 27, 1667/68, in Charles County; oldest surviving son. NATIVE: third generation. RESIDED: in Calvert County; Charles County; Prince George's County, after 1695. FAMILY BACKGROUND. FATHER: William Barton (?–1717), son of *William Barton* (ca. 1605–early 1680s); a justice of Charles County from 1672 to 1709 and a militia captain, but he never held provincial office. MOTHER: Ann (ca. 1640–?), widow of William Hungerford. BROTHER: William Barton (1662–by 1667/68). SISTERS: Grace (1659–died young); Elizabeth (1671/72–?). MARRIED Sarah (?–by 1739), widow of Basil Waring; daughter of Richard Marsham. She subsequently married by 1709 James Haddock, and finally Rev. William Brogden. CHILDREN. STEPSONS: Basil Waring, who married Martha, daughter of *Thomas Greenfield* (ca. 1649–1715); Marsham Waring. DAUGHTERS: Sarah (?–1733), who married first, by 1713 *Samuel Perrie* (?–1729), and second, Patrick Andrew; Katherine, who married Capt. John Murdock. PRIVATE CAREER. EDUCATION: literate. RELIGIOUS AFFILIATION: Anglican. SOCIAL STATUS AND ACTIVITIES: he was a third generation justice; his family was very active in negotiations with the Indians on matters of trade and defense. OCCUPATIONAL PROFILE: Indian trader; merchant; planter. PUBLIC CAREER. LEGISLATIVE SERVICE: Lower House, Prince George's County, 1696–1697 (elected to the 5th session; Laws 7), 1697/98–1698 (resigned after the 2nd session to become sheriff), 1704–1705 (died before the 4th session). LOCAL OFFICES: St. Paul's Parish Vestry, Calvert County, 1693–1696; justice, Calvert County, 1694–1695/96, Prince George's County, 1695/96–1699 (quorum), 1702–1705 (chief justice, 1704–1705); sheriff, Prince George's County, 1699–1702, Charles County, 1704/5–1705 (served the remaining term of his deceased cousin, Thomas Smoote). MILITARY SERVICE: major, 1695/96–1703; lieutenant colonel, 1703–1705. WEALTH DURING LIFETIME. LAND AT FIRST ELECTION: at least 2,243 acres. WEALTH AT DEATH. DIED: between October 23 and November 6, 1705. PERSONAL PROPERTY: TEV, £1,718.6.10 sterling (including 19 slaves); FB, £1,036.7.2. LAND: 2,493 acres.

BATEMAN, JOHN (?–1663). BORN: in England. IMMIGRATED: in 1658 or 1659 as a free adult with his wife from London, England. RESIDED: in Calvert County. MARRIED ca. 1649 Mary (?–1666/67), daughter of Margaret Perry. Her brother was *Richard Perry* (?–?). CHILDREN. DAUGHTER: Mary, a minor living in England when her mother died. PRIVATE CAREER. EDUCATION: literate. RELIGIOUS AFFILIATION: probably a Protestant. SOCIAL STATUS AND ACTIVITIES: enjoyed high status on his arrival in Maryland; brought eight servants with him; he quickly achieved appointment to the Council. OCCUPATIONAL PROFILE: haberdasher in London in the 1650s; factor for Henry Scarburgh, merchant of London; entrepreneur. PUBLIC CAREER. LEGISLATIVE SERVICE: Upper House, 1661, 1662, 1663 (died before the 2nd session). OTHER PROVINCIAL OFFICES: Council, 1660–1663; justice, Provincial Court, 1660–1663. WEALTH DURING LIFETIME. PERSONAL PROPERTY: his wife's dower amounted to £500; Bateman obligated himself to provide her £2,000 from his estate if he predeceased her. LAND AT FIRST ELECTION: over 2,900 acres. WEALTH AT DEATH. DIED: will probated on December 3, 1663. PERSONAL PROPERTY: TEV, 142,606 pounds of tobacco (including 12 servants, 5 of whom were blacks), with 89,000 pounds of the tobacco representing the value of his land; FB, 31,534 pounds of tobacco. LAND: over 2,900 acres.

BATHURST, EDWARD (?–1709). BORN: probably in England. IMMIGRATED: in 1694 as a free adult. RESIDED: in Kent County. MARRIED in 1697 after eloping with Rose Blakiston, daughter of John Tucker and wife Rose. She was the wife of Ebenezer Blakiston (1658–1709), nephew of *Nehemiah Blakiston* (?–1693). Her sister was Sarah, who married William Fitzhugh, of Virginia. ADDITIONAL COMMENTS: Rose was much mistreated by Blakiston during their marriage, and tried to commit suicide in the 1680s. PRIVATE CAREER. RELIGIOUS AFFILIATION: Protestant. SOCIAL STATUS AND ACTIVITIES: Gent. in 1709. ADDITIONAL COMMENTS: In 1694 Bathurst accused *Elias King* (?–1706/7) and Mary Tilden of incontinent living. Bathurst's career was undoubtedly hampered by his elopement with Rose Blakiston, for which he was found guilty and fined 1,400 pounds of tobacco in 1700. OCCUPATIONAL PROFILE: probably the same Edward Bathurst, a merchant of London, England, mentioned in Maryland records before 1694; an agent for Micajah Perry and his partners, 1693; merchant. PUBLIC CAREER. LEGISLATIVE SERVICE: Lower House, Kent County,

1708B (excused from attendance due to illness; died before the 2nd session of 1708B–1711 Assembly). **WEALTH DURING LIFETIME. LAND AT FIRST ELECTION**: over 50 acres. **WEALTH AT DEATH. DIED**: by August 20, 1709. PERSONAL PROPERTY: TEV, £293.0.11 sterling. LAND: over 50 acres.

BAXTER, JAMES (?–1763). BORN: of age by 1747. NATIVE: possibly, if so, at least second generation. RESIDED: in Cecil County. **MARRIED** Elizabeth. **CHILDREN**. SONS: *William Baxter* (?–1773); Joseph. DAUGHTERS: Elizabeth, who married Thomas Jones, of Baltimore County; Grace, who married (first name unknown) Smith; Mary Waugh (1742/43–?), who married (first name unknown) Thomas; and Rachel (1745–?), who probably married in 1771 Baruch Williams. **PRIVATE CAREER**. EDUCATION: literate. RELIGIOUS AFFILIATION: Anglican, St. Mary Ann's Parish, Cecil County. OCCUPATIONAL PROFILE: merchant. **PUBLIC CAREER**. LEGISLATIVE SERVICE: Lower House, Cecil County, 1750–1751 (elected to the 2nd session to fill vacancy; Bills of Credit 3). LOCAL OFFICES: justice, Cecil County, 1747–1763 (quorum, 1757–1763); St. Mary Anne's Parish Vestry, Cecil County, in office 1748–1751 and 1755; justice, Court of Oyer and Terminer and Gaol Delivery, Cecil County, commissioned 1749, 1750, 1752, and 1759. MILITARY SERVICE: colonel, 1763. **WEALTH DURING LIFETIME. LAND AT FIRST ELECTION**: 275 acres in Cecil County. SIGNIFICANT CHANGES IN LAND BETWEEN FIRST ELECTION AND DEATH: acquired 577 acres in Cecil County, 1754–1761; guardian of 607 acres in Queen Anne's County for John Role's heirs, ca. 1754–1758; sold original 275-acre tract in 1760. **WEALTH AT DEATH. DIED**: on February 24, 1763, probably in Cecil County. PERSONAL PROPERTY: TEV, £1,791.14.8 current money (including 19 slaves); FB, £619.8.3. LAND: 577 acres in Cecil County.

BAXTER, WILLIAM (?–1773). BORN: in Cecil County, of age by 1764; eldest son. NATIVE: at least second generation. RESIDED: in Cecil County. **FAMILY BACKGROUND. FATHER**: *James Baxter* (?–1763). MOTHER: Elizabeth. BROTHER: Joseph. SISTERS: Elizabeth, who married Thomas Jones, of Baltimore County; Grace, who married (first name unknown) Smith; Mary Waugh (1742/43–?), who married (first name unknown) Thomas; and Rachel (1745–?), who probably married Baruch Williams. **CHILDREN**. Probably died without progeny. **PRIVATE CAREER**. EDUCATION: literate. RELIGIOUS AFFILIATION: Anglican. OCCUPATIONAL PROFILE: probably a planter. **PUBLIC CAREER**. LEGISLATIVE

SERVICE: Lower House, Cecil County, 1768–1770, 1771. LOCAL OFFICES: sheriff, Cecil County, by 1762–1763; North Elk Parish Vestry, Cecil County, in office 1764–1767; justice, Cecil County, by 1764–at least 1769 (quorum, 1768–at least 1769). **WEALTH DURING LIFETIME. LAND AT FIRST ELECTION**: at least 270 acres in Cecil County, plus possibly 107 additional acres (all inherited from his father). **WEALTH AT DEATH. DIED**: between March and June 1773 in Cecil County. PERSONAL PROPERTY: TEV, £453.10.9 (including 3 slaves, 22 books, and china). LAND: at least 270 acres, plus possibly 107 additional acres, all in Cecil County.

BAYARD, PETER (1702–1766). BORN: on July 10, 1702, in North Sassafras Parish, Cecil County; eldest son. NATIVE: third generation. RESIDED: in Bohemia, Cecil County. **FAMILY BACKGROUND. FATHER**: Samuel Bayard (1675–1721), son of Petrus Bayard (?–1699, died in New York), and wife Blandina Kierstede. MOTHER: Susanna (?–1750), daughter of Lege de Bouchelle and wife Anna Margaretta Couda; Susanna, who was well educated, could write and speak Latin, French, and Dutch, as well as English. BROTHERS: Samuel (1705–?), who married in 1729 Francina, daughter of *Francis Mauldin* (?–1734/35); James (Jacobus) (1708–?), a merchant. SISTER: Anna Marya (1700–?), who married in May 1738 Dr. Sluyter Bouchelle. OTHER KINSHIP: his father's first wife was Elizabeth Sluyter. **MARRIED** Susanna Richardson (?–1766), whose family resided near Wilmington, Delaware. **CHILDREN**. DAUGHTERS: Susanna, who married Jonathan Smith, of Philadelphia, Pennsylvania; Elizabeth (?–1763), who married Rev. John Rogers, an intimate friend and advisor of Gen. George Washington; and Nansey (Ann), who married (first name unknown) Scott. **PRIVATE CAREER**. EDUCATION: literate. RELIGIOUS AFFILIATION: Anglican, St. Stephen's Church, North Sassafras Parish, Cecil County. SOCIAL STATUS AND ACTIVITIES: Gent., 1745. OCCUPATIONAL PROFILE: farmer, 1724; merchant, 1742. **PUBLIC CAREER**. LEGISLATIVE SERVICE: Lower House, Cecil County, 1745/46–1748, 1749 (election voided on June 6, 1749, when the Lower House judged that the election was not valid). LOCAL OFFICES: St. Stephen's Church Vestry, North Sassafras Parish, Cecil County, elected 1726; churchwarden, St. Stephen's Church, North Sassafras Parish, Cecil County, 1734–1735; justice, Cecil County, 1744–at least 1757 (quorum, 1756–at least 1757); justice, Court of Oyer and Terminer and Gaol Delivery, Cecil County, commissioned

1752. MILITARY SERVICE: captain, by 1739; colonel, by 1756. WEALTH DURING LIFETIME. LAND AT FIRST ELECTION: 600 acres in Delaware (inherited from his father), plus 150 acres of leasehold land in Cecil County. Probably managed an additional 868 acres that his father bequeathed to Peter's underage brothers, the control of which he relinquished after they became of age. WEALTH AT DEATH. DIED: will probated on November 26, 1766, in Cecil County. PERSONAL PROPERTY: TEV, at least £920.9.10 current money (including 9 slaves and books). LAND: 600 acres on Bombay Hook Island, Delaware; 150 acres of leasehold land on Bohemia Manor, Cecil County.

BAYLEY, GODFREY (?–ca. 1670/71). BORN: in England. IMMIGRATED: in 1658 as a free adult from London, England. RESIDED: in Baltimore County. FAMILY BACKGROUND. Rose, probably the widow of John Scotcher. CHILDREN. DAUGHTERS: Elizabeth, who married *George Warner* (by 1657–1703); Rosamund. PRIVATE CAREER. EDUCATION: literate. SOCIAL STATUS AND ACTIVITIES: brought five others and some capital with him on his arrival in the colony; Gent., by late 1658. OCCUPATIONAL PROFILE: factor for John Bayspoole, of London, England; merchant; planter. PUBLIC CAREER. LEGISLATIVE SERVICE: Lower House, Baltimore County, 1659/60. LOCAL OFFICE: justice, Baltimore County, 1664–1664/65. STANDS ON PUBLIC/PRIVATE ISSUES: supported Fendall's Rebellion, but was pardoned in 1661. WEALTH DURING LIFETIME. LAND AT FIRST ELECTION: ca. 400 acres. WEALTH AT DEATH. DIED: will probated on January 5, 1670/71. PERSONAL PROPERTY: TEV, £306.6.0 sterling; FB, 19,723 pounds of tobacco. LAND: unspecified acreage valued at 40,000 pounds of tobacco.

BAYLY (BAILEY, BAILLIE, BAYLEY), MOUNTJOY (1755–1836). BORN: in 1755 in Virginia. IMMIGRATED: first generation from Virginia; may have been of Scottish origin. RESIDED: in Frederick Town, Frederick County, 1785. FAMILY BACKGROUND. FATHER: William Bayly (1715–1782), of Fairfax County, Virginia. MOTHER: Mary, daughter of Wade Hampton, of South Carolina. BROTHERS: Pierce (1742–1800), of Loudoun County, Virginia, who married Mary Payne; *William Bayly* (ca. 1742–1824); Samuel (ca. 1749–?); Joseph (ca. 1752–1789), who married Elizabeth; Tarpley (1756–?), of Berkeley County, Virginia; and Robert (1759–?). SISTERS: Sarah (ca. 1745–ca. 1785), who married Robert Rogers (?–1786); Nancy, who married in 1762 John Singleton; and

Betty, who married Robert Boggess. MARRIED by 1784 Elizabeth (1760–1832), daughter of *Christopher Edelin* (?–ca. 1786). Her sisters were Eleanor (1762–?), who married Capt. *John Lynn* (1760–1813); Rebecca (1765–?). CHILDREN. SONS: Benjamin (1783–1836); Richard (1785–?). DAUGHTERS: Eleanor, who married (first name unknown) Hanson; Elizabeth, who married (first name unknown) Eaton. PRIVATE CAREER. EDUCATION: literate. RELIGIOUS AFFILIATION: Presbyterian. SOCIAL STATUS AND ACTIVITIES: Gent., 1799, charter member of the Society of Cincinnati. OCCUPATIONAL PROFILE: probably a planter; officeholder. PUBLIC CAREER. LEGISLATIVE SERVICE: Lower House, Frederick County, 1785, 1786–1787, 1789, 1790, 1793. LOCAL OFFICES: auctioneer, Frederick County, 1780. MILITARY SERVICE: captain, Seventh Maryland Regiment, 1776, resigned 1778; major, 1789; brigadier general, Ninth Brigade (upper part of Frederick County), Maryland Militia, 1794–1795 (resigned). OUT OF STATE SERVICE: sergeant-at-arms of the U.S. Senate, November 6, 1811–December 9, 1833. WEALTH DURING LIFETIME. PERSONAL PROPERTY: 10 slaves, 1790. LAND AT FIRST ELECTION: none found in Maryland; may have inherited his father's land in Virginia, 1782. SIGNIFICANT CHANGES IN LAND BETWEEN FIRST ELECTION AND DEATH: purchased 670 acres in Frederick County, including 347 acres of confiscated British property; sold 192 acres, including 5 lots (3 in Frederick Town, Frederick County), 1785–1805. Entitled to 200 acres in Allegany County for service during the Revolutionary War. WEALTH AT DEATH. DIED: in 1836; buried in the Congressional Cemetery, Washington, D.C. LAND: possibly ca. 478 acres in Frederick County.

BAYLY (BAILEY, BAYLEY), WILLIAM (ca. 1742–1824). BORN: ca. 1742 in Virginia; second son. IMMIGRATED: from Virginia, first generation. RESIDED: in Frederick County, 1773; Georgetown, Montgomery County, 1787; Prince George's County, 1788; St. Mary's County, 1809; Washington County, 1810. FAMILY BACKGROUND. FATHER: William Bayly (1715–1782), of Fairfax County, Virginia. MOTHER: Mary, daughter of Wade Hampton, of South Carolina. BROTHERS: Pierce (1742–1800), of Loudoun County, Virginia, who married Mary Payne; Samuel (ca. 1749–?); Joseph (ca. 1752–1789), who married Elizabeth; *Mountjoy Bayly* (1755–1836); Tarpley (1756–?), of Berkeley County, Virginia; and Robert (1759–?). SISTERS: Sarah (ca. 1745–ca. 1785), who married Robert Rogers (?–1786); Nancy, who married in

1762 John Singleton; and Betty, who married Robert Boggess. MARRIED on June 25, 1769, Susannah Fraser (?-by 1800), daughter of *John Hawkins, Jr.* (1713-1757). Her brothers were Giles Blizzard (1732-?); John Stone (1734-ca. 1764); *George Fraser Hawkins* (ca. 1741-1785); and Alexander Thomas. Her sister was Elizabeth Lawrence. Her stepsister was Rebeckah Covington, who married *Benjamin Mackall, Jr.* (ca. 1723-1795). CHILDREN. SONS: Robert (1773-?); Samuel (ca. 1774-?); and William (ca. 1776-?). DAUGHTERS: Rebecca, who married first, (possibly Walter) Mackall, and second, in 1814 Rev. Walter D. Addison; Anisia Mariah, who married Philip Thomas Baker; Priscilla; Sarah, who married (first name unknown) Hebb; and Mary. PRIVATE CAREER. EDUCATION: literate. RELIGIOUS AFFILIATION: uncertain, but wife's father was an Anglican minister. SOCIAL STATUS AND ACTIVITIES: Gent., 1788; Esq., 1793. OCCUPATIONAL PROFILE: merchant, in partnership with *William Deakins, Jr.* (?-1798), 1788; probably a farmer, by 1800; surveyor. PUBLIC CAREER. LEGISLATIVE SERVICE: Convention, Frederick County, 9th, 1776 (election voided on August 15, 1776, because the Frederick County election judges were appointed by a county commission contrary to the resolves of the 8th Convention; subsequently reelected and seated); Lower House, Montgomery County, 1777-1778, 1778-1779 (Claims 2; Elections 3), 1779-1780, 1780-1781 (Grievances 1, 2), 1781-1782 (Grievances 1, 2). LOCAL OFFICES: Committee of Correspondence, Frederick County, 1774-1775; Committee of Observation, Frederick County, 1775; committee to collect money to buy arms, Frederick County, 1775; deputy surveyor, Montgomery County, 1777; justice, Prince George's County, 1799-at least 1800. MILITARY SERVICE: captain, Twenty-ninth Militia Battalion, Montgomery County, by 1777. WEALTH DURING LIFETIME. PERSONAL PROPERTY: 34 slaves, 1790; sued by *Charles Carroll of Carrollton* (1737-1832) for using false bidding techniques to lower the price of land sold at auction to pay the debts of *George Fraser Hawkins* (ca. 1741-1785), 1793; 37 slaves, household furnishings, livestock, and slaves were sold to pay debts, 1800. LAND AT FIRST ELECTION: 466 acres in Frederick and Montgomery counties, plus 1 lot in Georgetown, Montgomery County (249 acres was his wife's dower). SIGNIFICANT CHANGES IN LAND BETWEEN FIRST ELECTION AND DEATH: he bought 2,640 acres in Georgia, as well as land in and around Georgetown, Montgomery County, with his business partner, 1780-1797; sold much of his real property in 1797 to settle debts owed,

with his greatest creditor being *Philip Key* (1750-1820). WEALTH AT DEATH. DIED: on March 9, 1824, near Bladensburg, Prince George's County, probably at "Blue Plains," his dwelling plantation. PERSONAL PROPERTY: 30 shares in the Bank of Washington. LAND: 240 acres in Prince George's County.

BAYNE (BEAN, BEANE), JOHN (ca. 1662-1701). BORN: ca. 1662, probably in Charles County; first son. NATIVE: second generation. RESIDED: in Charles County; St. Mary's County. FAMILY BACKGROUND. FATHER: *Walter Bayne* (?-1670). MOTHER: Elinor. BROTHER: Thomas. SISTERS: Edith; Elinor, who married first, *John Stone* (ca. 1648-1697), second, Hugh Tears, and third, *John Beale, of Lawson* (ca. 1674-1751); and Elizabeth. STEPNIECE: Elizabeth Teares, who married *William Middleton* (1686-1769). MARRIED by 1687 Ann (?-1702/3), widow of Thomas Gerard; daughter of Richard Hawkins or William Smallwood. CHILDREN. SONS: Ellsworth, who married Catherine, daughter of *Gerard Fowke* (1662/63-ca. 1734/35); Walter. DAUGHTER: Anne, who married *Thomas Dent* (1685-1725). PRIVATE CAREER. EDUCATION: literate. RELIGIOUS AFFILIATION: Protestant. SOCIAL STATUS AND ACTIVITIES: second generation burgess; Gent., by 1686. OCCUPATIONAL PROFILE: innkeeper; planter; possibly a merchant. PUBLIC CAREER. LEGISLATIVE SERVICE: Lower House, St. Mary's County, 1694-1696 (resigned after the 5th session to become sheriff). LOCAL OFFICES: justice, St. Mary's County, 1692-1694, 1694-1696 (quorum, 1694-1696), Charles County, 1698-1700 or 1701 (quorum); deputy commissary, St. Mary's County, 1693; sheriff, St. Mary's County, 1694, Charles County, 1696-1698; surveyor, St. Mary's County, 1695. MILITARY SERVICE: captain, St. Mary's County by 1693/94-1696, Charles County, 1696-1700 or 1701. WEALTH DURING LIFETIME. LAND AT FIRST ELECTION: 1,450 acres inherited from his father. WEALTH AT DEATH. DIED: will probated on October 25, 1701, in Charles County. Bayne probably died while on a trip to England. PERSONAL PROPERTY: TEV, £1,067.13.6 sterling (including 17 slaves and 18 servants). LAND: 2,450 acres.

BAYNE (BEAN, BEANE), WALTER (?-1670). BORN: in England. IMMIGRATED: in 1641 as a free adult from Virginia. RESIDED: in St. Mary's County; Charles County after 1658. ADDITIONAL COMMENTS: immigrated to Virginia in the mid-1630s, probably as a servant; came to Maryland with a man servant to join his brother, probably upon completion of his own indenture. FAMILY BACKGROUND. BROTHER: Ralph (?–1655), who was transported by *Leonard Calvert* (ca. 1606–1647) as indentured servant in 1634 and who owned 1,500 acres by the time of his death. OTHER KINSHIP: his stepgrandaughter was Elizabeth Teares, who married *William Middleton* (1686–1769). MARRIED Elinor (Helene) (?–1701). CHILDREN. SONS: *John Bayne* (ca. 1662–1701), who married by 1687 Ann (?–1702/3), widow of Thomas Gerard (?–1686); Thomas. DAUGHTERS: Edith, who married Matthew Hill; Elinor, who married first *John Stone* (ca. 1648–1697), second, Hugh Tears, and third, *John Beale, of Lawson* (ca. 1674–1751); and Elizabeth. PRIVATE CAREER. EDUCATION: illiterate. RELIGIOUS AFFILIATION: Protestant. SOCIAL STATUS AND ACTIVITIES: Gent., by the mid-1650s. OCCUPATIONAL PROFILE: probably a servant, 1630s; planter, by 1643; merchant. PUBLIC CAREER. LEGISLATIVE SERVICE: Assembly, present 1641/42, St. George's Hundred, St. Mary's County, 1650–1650/51 (Laws 1). LOCAL OFFICES: justice, St. Mary's County, 1655–1658, Charles County, 1660–1667. STANDS ON PUBLIC/PRIVATE ISSUES: probably a supporter of Lord Baltimore against Fendall's Rebellion in 1660. WEALTH DURING LIFETIME. LAND AT FIRST ELECTION: ca. 700 acres in 1650. WEALTH AT DEATH. DIED: will probated on May 28, 1670. PERSONAL PROPERTY: TEV, £399.9.0 sterling (including 3 slaves and 6 servants). LAND: 2,800 acres.

BEALE, JOHN (?–1734). BORN: of age in 1707; probably only son. NATIVE: probably second generation. RESIDED: in Annapolis and on his plantation, "Norwood's Beale," in Anne Arundel County. FAMILY BACKGROUND. FATHER: probably *Thomas Beale* (?–1713). MOTHER: Elizabeth. SISTER: Elizabeth, who married Rev. Henry Jennings, rector of William and Mary Parish in St. Mary's County from 1706 to 1714. MARRIED on August 19, 1708, Elizabeth (1688–1753), daughter of Andrew Norwood (?–1701), of Anne Arundel County, and wife Elizabeth Howard. Her brother was Andrew. Her sisters were Ann; Hannah; and (first name unknown). CHILDREN. SON: Thomas (1714–1717). DAUGHTERS: Elizabeth (1711–?), who married first, in 1729 William Nicholson, a merchant, and second, Richard Dorsey; Ann (1716/17–?), who married Thomas Rutland. WARDS: Andrew Norwood, Jr.; John Howard (ca. 1709–1805); and *Vachel Denton* (ca. 1696–1752). PRIVATE CAREER. EDUCATION: literate. RELIGIOUS AFFILIATION: Protestant. SOCIAL STATUS AND ACTIVITIES: Mr., by 1717; Gent., by 1719; Esq., by

1727. OCCUPATIONAL PROFILE: probably a planter; officeholder. PUBLIC CAREER. LEGISLATIVE SERVICE: Lower House, Annapolis, 1718 (elected to the 3rd session to fill vacancy; Accounts 3), 1719 (Accounts 1; discharged for accepting an appointment as clerk of the Council between the 1st and 2nd sessions), Anne Arundel County, 1722–1724 (Accounts 1–3), 1725–1727 (Accounts 1–4; Aggrievances 1–4), 1728–1731 (Accounts 1–5; Aggrievances 1–5), 1732–1734 (Accounts 1–Cv; Aggrievances 1–Cv; discharged during convention for accepting an office "of trust and profit" from the government). OTHER PROVINCIAL OFFICES: clerk, Secretary's Office and Provincial Court, 1707–1718; register, Chancery Court, 1708–1709; clerk, Council, 1719–1721; commissioner, Paper Currency Office, appointed 1733. LOCAL OFFICES: clerk, Anne Arundel County, 1711–1734; St. Anne's Parish Vestry, Anne Arundel County, in office 1713–1720, 1727–1730; alderman, Annapolis, 1714–at least 1726; clerk, Court of Oyer and Terminer and Gaol Delivery, Anne Arundel County, commissioned 1720; deputy commissary, Anne Arundel County, 1720–1734; trustee of public schools, Anne Arundel County, period of service unknown. WEALTH DURING LIFETIME. LAND AT FIRST ELECTION: 640 acres in Anne Arundel County, plus 1 lot in Annapolis. SIGNIFICANT CHANGES IN LAND BETWEEN FIRST ELECTION AND DEATH: acquired an additional 1,138 acres in Anne Arundel and Baltimore counties; gave 150 acres in Anne Arundel County to son-in-law William Nicholson in 1731. WEALTH AT DEATH. DIED: between March 5 and May 9, 1734, in Anne Arundel County. PERSONAL PROPERTY: TEV, £1,558.14.8 (including 13 slaves and books); FB, estate overpaid £344.8.11. LAND: ca. 1,628 acres in Anne Arundel and Baltimore counties, plus 3 lots in Annapolis; after his death his land was sold to pay his debts.

BEALE, JOHN, OF LAWSON (ca. 1674–1751). BORN: ca. 1674, probably in Anne Arundel County; only son. NATIVE: second generation. RESIDED: in Charles County; Prince George's County. FAMILY BACKGROUND. FATHER: John Beale (?–1675/76), who immigrated in 1670. MOTHER: Joane Lawson Reid Mounten (?–1675), widow of Robert Tyler (?–1673). HALF BROTHERS: George Reid; Peter Mounten; and *Robert Tyler* (ca. 1671–1738). HALF SISTER: Elizabeth Tyler. MARRIED first, Sarah Pierce (?–ca. 1700), granddaughter of Thomas Sprigg (1630–1704). MARRIED second, by late 1700 Elinor, widow of both *John Stone* (ca. 1648–1697) and Hugh Tears;

daughter of *Walter Bayne* (?–1670). Her brother was *John Bayne* (ca. 1662–1701). MARRIED third, Johanna Catherine (?–1751). CHILDREN. SONS: John (1700–1754); Richard, of Essex County, Virginia. PRIVATE CAREER. EDUCATION: literate. RELIGIOUS AFFILIATION: Protestant, but refused to serve as a churchwarden of Durham Parish, Charles County, 1703. SOCIAL STATUS AND ACTIVITIES: perhaps raised in a Sprigg household as was his half brother, *Robert Tyler* (ca. 1671–1738). OCCUPATIONAL PROFILE: planter. PUBLIC CAREER. LEGISLATIVE SERVICE: Lower House, Charles County, 1708A. LOCAL OFFICE: justice, Charles County, 1714–1715. WEALTH DURING LIFETIME. LAND AT FIRST ELECTION: ca. 942 acres. WEALTH AT DEATH. DIED: will probated on April 27, 1751. PERSONAL PROPERTY: TEV, £50.10.8 (including 2 slaves, 1 servant, and books); FB, estate overpaid £0.15.0.

BEALE, NINIAN (ca. 1625–1717/18). BORN: ca. 1625 in Fifeshire, Scotland. IMMIGRATED: in 1655 from Barbados as an indentured servant to *Richard Hall* (?–1688). RESIDED: in Calvert County; Prince George's County after 1695. FAMILY BACKGROUND. FATHER: James Beale. MARRIED in 1668 Ruth, daughter of Richard Moore. CHILDREN. SONS: Ninian (1669–by 1717/18); Charles (1672–1740); John (1674–?); Thomas; and George (1695–1780), who married Elizabeth (1699–1748), daughter of *Thomas Brooke* (ca. 1659–1730/31). DAUGHTERS: Hester (Esther), who married *Joseph Belt* (ca. 1680–1761); Mary; Rachel; and Sarah (?–1734), who married *Samuel Magruder* (1654–1711). PRIVATE CAREER. EDUCATION: literate. RELIGIOUS AFFILIATION: Presbyterian; was a ruling elder on the Western Shore. SOCIAL STATUS AND ACTIVITIES: cornet; he became a political prisoner upon being captured at the Battle of Dunbar in Scotland in 1650; he was transported first to Barbados, and then to Maryland; Gent., by the 1690s; called "an honest Cavalier" in 1700. OCCUPATIONAL PROFILE: servant, free by 1667; planter; surveyor; mill owner; land speculator. PUBLIC CAREER. LEGISLATIVE SERVICE: Associators' Convention, Calvert County, 1689–1692; Lower House, Prince George's County, 1696–1697 (elected to the 5th session), 1697/98–1700 (Laws 2). LOCAL OFFICES: deputy surveyor, Calvert County, 1680–1685; town officer, Mount Calvert Town, Calvert County, 1686; sheriff, Calvert County, 1692–1694. MILITARY SERVICE: lieutenant, by 1668; captain, 1676–1689; major, 1689–1692; colonel, 1692–1698. STANDS ON PUBLIC/PRIVATE ISSUES: he was a very strong supporter and active participant in the revolution of 1689. WEALTH DURING LIFETIME. LAND AT FIRST ELECTION: ca. 4,000 acres; during his lifetime Beale surveyed 21,833 acres for himself, of which 8,198 was subsequently patented by others. WEALTH AT DEATH. DIED: between January 15 and February 28, 1717/18. PERSONAL PROPERTY: TEV, £87.13.5; FB, estate overpaid £171.15.6. LAND: 2,117 acres; he had given his children 2,820 acres before his death.

BEALE, THOMAS (?–1713). BORN: probably in England. IMMIGRATED: ca. 1667 as an indentured servant from Exon or Topsham, England. RESIDED: in St. Mary's County. MARRIED possibly Elizabeth. CHILDREN. SON: John. PRIVATE CAREER. EDUCATION: illiterate. RELIGIOUS AFFILIATION: Protestant. SOCIAL STATUS AND ACTIVITIES: first minor office did not come until he had been in the colony for approximately twenty years. OCCUPATIONAL PROFILE: indentured servant in 1667, free by 1672; planter; innkeeper in the 1680s; merchant. PUBLIC CAREER. LEGISLATIVE SERVICE: Lower House, St. Mary's County, 1697/98–1700, 1701–1704, 1704–1707. LOCAL OFFICES: alderman, St. Mary's City, 1689, 1694; William and Mary Parish Vestry, St. Mary's County, 1693–1696; justice, St. Mary's County, 1694–1713 (quorum, 1697–1713). MILITARY SERVICE: captain, 1704; major, 1706. WEALTH AT DEATH. DIED: will probated on May 25, 1713. PERSONAL PROPERTY: TEV, £344.19.10 sterling (including 9 slaves).

BEALL, JOSHUA (ca. 1719–ca. 1796). BORN: ca. 1719 in Prince George's County; third son. NATIVE: third generation. RESIDED: in St. John's or Prince George's Parish, Prince George's County. FAMILY BACKGROUND. FATHER: Capt. Charles Beall (1672–1740), son of *Ninian Beale* (ca. 1625–1717/18). MOTHER: Mary Wolstad. AUNTS: Esther Beall, who married *Joseph Belt* (ca. 1680–1761); Sarah Beall, who married *Samuel Magruder* (1654–1711). BROTHERS: Charles; Ninian (?–by 1753), who married Suzanna. SISTERS: Mary; Rachel. FIRST COUSINS: *Thomas Beall, of George* (1735–1819); *John Magruder* (1694–1750). MARRIED first, by 1748 Eleanor Smith (?–by 1776), daughter of James Greenfield (?–1734) and wife Eleanor; granddaughter of Thomas Smith, of Calvert County. Her sisters were Sarah, who married John Prigg; Mary, who married (first name unknown) Brooke; Elizabeth, who married (first name unknown) Skinner. MARRIED second, on February 3, 1787, Elizabeth, widow of Basil Waring (?–1776); probably the daughter of Benjamin Belt (?–1773). CHILDREN. SON: George (ca. 1746–

?), who married Ann. DAUGHTER: Amelia (ca. 1748–?), who married Gen. Rezin Beall. PRIVATE CAREER. EDUCATION: literate. RELIGIOUS AFFILIATION: Presbyterian; manager of a lottery for the building fund of the Bladensburg Presbyterian Church, Prince George's County, 1790. SOCIAL STATUS AND ACTIVITIES: Gent., by 1776. OCCUPATIONAL PROFILE: planter. PUBLIC CAREER. LEGISLATIVE SERVICE: Conventions, Prince George's County, 1st, 1774, 2nd–3rd, 1774, 4th, 1775, 5th, 1775. LOCAL OFFICES: justice, Prince George's County, 1751–1759, 1762–1787 (resigned); sheriff, Prince George's County, 1759–1762; justice, Court of Oyer and Terminer and Gaol Delivery, Prince George's County, commissioned 1771 and 1772; justice, Orphans' Court, Prince George's County, 1777–at least 1787. MILITARY SERVICE: captain, Prince George's County troops at Fort Frederick and Fort Duquesne, 1756–1758; colonel, Prince George's County Militia, appointed 1775; resigned from Upper Battalion, Prince George's County Militia, 1776. WEALTH DURING LIFETIME. PERSONAL PROPERTY: 20 slaves, 1776. LAND AT FIRST ELECTION: at least 2,048 acres in Prince George's County (inherited from his father and brothers), plus possibly 135 acres in Prince George's County (acquired through his marriage). SIGNIFICANT CHANGES IN LAND BETWEEN FIRST ELECTION AND DEATH: sold 54 acres in Prince George's County in small parcels between 1776 and 1790. WEALTH AT DEATH. DIED: will probated on February 17, 1796, in Prince George's County. PERSONAL PROPERTY: TEV, £1,682.10.3 current money (including 14 slaves and more than 12 books); FB, £1,180.1.4 current money. LAND: probably ca. 2,000 acres in Prince George's County.

BEALL, JOSIAH (?–1768). BORN: of age by 1747; younger son. NATIVE: third generation. RESIDED: in Frederick County. FAMILY BACKGROUND. FATHER: John Beall (?–1742), son of Alexander Beall (?–1744). MOTHER: Verlinda (?–1745), daughter of *Samuel Magruder* (1654–1711). UNCLE: *John Magruder* (1694–1750). BROTHERS: *Samuel Beall* (ca. 1713–ca. 1778); Basil, who married Lucy; John, who married Mary, daughter of Peter Dent; and Clement (?–by 1794), who married Priscilla. SISTERS: Sarah (?–1779), who married by 1742 James Offutt; Rebecca, who married her first cousin *Nathan Magruder* (ca. 1718–1786); Lucy; Hannah; and Verlinda. FIRST COUSINS: *Nathan Magruder* (ca. 1718–1786); *Zadock Magruder* (1730–1811). CHILDREN. At least seven, including SONS: Thaddeus (ca. 1745–1808), who married

Amelia (ca. 1747–after 1809), daughter of *Samuel Beall* (ca. 1713–ca. 1778); Josiah (?–1805), who married Elizabeth Brooke. DAUGHTERS: Lucy (?–1799); Verlinda (?–by 1799), who married Thomas Beall (1744–1823), son of *Samuel Beall* (ca. 1713–ca. 1778). PRIVATE CAREER. EDUCATION: literate. RELIGIOUS AFFILIATION: Anglican. SOCIAL STATUS AND ACTIVITIES: Mr., 1754; Gent., 1763. OCCUPATIONAL PROFILE: planter, 1741, 1757; agent for Hartly & Sons, of Whitehaven, England, 1763–1768. PUBLIC CAREER. LEGISLATIVE SERVICE: Lower House, Frederick County, 1754–1757 (Bills of Credit 1–6). LOCAL OFFICES: tobacco inspector, Rock Creek warehouse, Frederick County, 1748–1750; coroner, Frederick County, 1748; sheriff, Frederick County, 1752–1753; justice, Frederick County, 1763–at least 1767. WEALTH DURING LIFETIME. LAND AT FIRST ELECTION: 400 acres in Prince George's and Frederick counties (300 acres inherited from his father; 100 acres by personal acquisition). SIGNIFICANT CHANGES IN LAND BETWEEN FIRST ELECTION AND DEATH: patented 107 acres in Frederick County, 1763; bought 2 partial lots in Georgetown, Frederick County, 1767. WEALTH AT DEATH. DIED: administration bond granted on October 6, 1768, in Frederick County. PERSONAL PROPERTY: TEV, £507.8.10 current money (including 9 slaves, 4 books, and plate); FB, £187.5.0. LAND: 482 acres in Frederick County.

BEALL, JOSIAS (ca. 1725–1803). BORN: ca. 1725. NATIVE: third generation. RESIDED: at "Strife," near Piscataway, Prince George's County. FAMILY BACKGROUND. FATHER: John Beall (?–ca. 1757), son of James Beall (?–1725). MOTHER: Elizabeth, daughter of *John Fendall* (1674–1734). FIRST COUSINS: *Philip Richard Fendall* (?–?); Sarah Fendall (ca. 1732–1793), who married *Thomas Contee* (ca. 1729–1811); and *Samuel Hanson, Jr.* (?–1817). MARRIED first, ca. 1760 Millicent (1733–1772), daughter of Robert Bradley and wife Ann, of Prince George's County; granddaughter of *Robert Bradley* (?–1724). MARRIED second, in common law marriage, Ann (1750–1781), daughter of John Boswell and wife Elizabeth. Ann resided with Josias from 1774 until her death. CHILDREN. SONS: John Bradley (1760–?); Josias Fendall (1762–ca. 1816), who married in 1804 Ann Middleton Marlowe; James Alexander (1765–?), who married in 1787 Ann Mitchell; Robert Augustus (1767–?), who married Elizabeth; Benjamin Bradley (1771–?); and David Fendall (1775–?). DAUGHTERS: (first name unknown) (1764–1764); Ann Fendall (1768–?); Anna (1777–

by 1803); and Ann Elizabeth (1781–?). PRIVATE CAREER. RELIGIOUS AFFILIATION: Protestant. SOCIAL STATUS AND ACTIVITIES: Gent., 1786. OCCUPATIONAL PROFILE: planter. PUBLIC CAREER. LEGISLATIVE SERVICE: Lower House, Prince George's County, 1758–1761 (Bills of Credit 1, Cv 2, 2, Cv 3), 1762–1763 (Bills of Credit 1, 2; Grievances 2), 1765–1766 (Bills of Credit 2, 4; Public Offices 3), 1768–1770 (Claims 1, 2, 4; Public Offices 2; Grievances 4), 1771 (Claims; Grievances), 1773–1774 (Claims 1, Cv, 2; Laws to Expire 1, Cv, 2; Grievances 1, Cv, 2, 3); Conventions, Prince George's County, 2nd, 1774, 4th, 1775 (elected, but did not attend), 5th, 1775, 6th–8th, 1775–1776 (Manufactories 8th); Lower House, Prince George's County, 1778–1779 (Laws to Expire 2; Tax Commissioners 3), 1779–1780 (speaker 1–3), 1781–1782 (elected, but did not attend; resigned during the 2nd session). LOCAL OFFICES: trustee, Charlotte Hall, appointed 1774. WEALTH DURING LIFETIME. PERSONAL PROPERTY: paid taxes on at least £100, 1756; paid taxes on at least £300, 1757; 21 slaves, 1776; assessed value £1,076.7.5, including 42 slaves and 107 oz. plate, 1793–1794; assessed value £1,266.1.8, including 49 slaves and 107 oz. plate, 1802. LAND AT FIRST ELECTION: 297 acres in Prince George's County (all by purchase). SIGNIFICANT CHANGES IN LAND BETWEEN FIRST ELECTION AND DEATH: he inherited 1,632 acres in Prince George's County plus 1,142 acres in Frederick County from his father and his uncle James Beall between 1768 and 1772. He purchased 266 acres in Prince George's County between 1774 and 1795. He also purchased 311 acres in Charles County, 1788–1792. He sold at least 700 acres, including 100 acres in Frederick County in 1768 and 600 acres in Prince George's County in 1788. WEALTH AT DEATH. DIED: will probated on March 12, 1803, in Prince George's County. LAND: at least 2,721 acres (ca. 1,268 acres in Prince George's County, 1,142 acres in Montgomery County, and 311 acres in Charles County).

BEALL, SAMUEL (ca. 1713–ca. 1778). BORN: ca. 1713; eldest son. NATIVE: third generation. RESIDED: at "Kelly's Purchase," Frederick County (later became part of Washington County). FAMILY BACKGROUND. FATHER: John Beall (?–1742), son of Alexander Beall (?–1744). MOTHER: Verlinda (?–1745), daughter of *Samuel Magruder* (1654–1711). UNCLE: *John Magruder* (1694–1750). BROTHERS: *Josiah Beall* (?–1768); Basil, who married Lucy; John, who married Mary, daughter of Peter Dent; and Clement (?–by 1794), who married Priscilla. SISTERS: Sarah (?–by 1779), who

married by 1742 James Offutt; Rebecca, who married her first cousin *Nathan Magruder* (ca. 1718–1786); Lucy; Hannah; and Verlinda. FIRST COUSINS: *Nathan Magruder* (ca. 1718–1786); *Zadock Magruder* (1730–1811). MARRIED ca. 1734 Eleanor (1718–?), daughter of *Thomas Brooke* (1683–1744); granddaughter of both *Thomas Brooke* (ca. 1659–1730/31) and *Walter Smith* (?–1711); niece of Ann Smith (1694–1759), who married second, *Thomas Trueman Greenfield* (1682–1733), Elinor Smith, who married *Thomas Addison* (1679–1727), Rebecca Smith, who married *Daniel Dulany* (1685–1753), Sarah Brooke (?–1724), who married first, *William Dent* (ca. 1660–1704) and second, *Philip Lee* (ca. 1681–1744), and Priscilla Brooke, who married *Thomas Gantt* (?–1765). Her brothers were Thomas (1706–1749); Walter (1707–1740/41); Nathaniel (1712–?); *Richard Brooke* (1716–1783); Isaac (1722–1756); Daniel (1726–1735); Charles (1727–1727); Robert (1728–1777); and Rev. Clement (1730–1800). Her sisters were Mary (1709–?); Anna (1711–?); Lucy (1714–1718); Rachel (1719–1789); Lucy (1721–?); Rebecca (1722–?); and Elizabeth (1724–1794). Her first cousins were *John Addison* (1713–1764); *Richard Lee* (ca. 1707–1787); *Arthur Lee* (?–1760); *Francis Lee* (?–1749); *Thomas Gantt* (ca. 1710–1785); *Fielder Gantt* (?–1807); *Edward Gantt* (?–by 1783); Ann Addison (1711/12–?), who married *William Murdock* (?–1769); probably Ann Gantt, who married *John Brome* (1703–1748); *Daniel Dulany, Jr.* (1722–1797); *Walter Dulany* (?–1773); Margaret Dulany, who married first, *Alexander Hamilton* (1712–1756), and second, *William Murdock* (?–1769); and Marianne Greenfield, who married *John Stoddert* (?–1767). CHILDREN. SONS: Samuel; Richard, who married Sarah Brooke; Walter, who married Rebecca Tanyhill; Thomas (1744–1823), who founded Cumberland, Maryland; Brooke (?–1796), who married Margaret Johns; Isaac, who married Margery White; Daniel, who married Martha Peyton; Basil, who married Ariana Beall; and Jeremiah (?–by 1777). DAUGHTERS: Verlinda, who married William Dent; Amelia (ca. 1747–after 1809), who married Thaddeus Beall (ca. 1745–1808), son of *Josiah Beall* (?–1768); Eleanor; Ann; Rebecca; and Frances. PRIVATE CAREER. EDUCATION: literate. RELIGIOUS AFFILIATION: Anglican. OCCUPATIONAL PROFILE: planter, 1755; steward of Conegocheaque Manor, 1762; ironmaster, 1765. On October 31, 1765 an agreement was executed among Beall and his three partners, *Joseph Chapline* (1707–ca. 1769), David Ross, and Richard Henderson, of Prince George's County, for the purpose of purchasing land in Frederick County, particulary on the Antietam and Potomac rivers, in order to erect an ironworks, a furnace, and forges. **PUBLIC CAREER.** LEGISLATIVE SERVICE: Conventions, Frederick County, 4th, 1775 (elected, but did not attend), 5th, 1775, 9th, 1776 (Manufactories); Lower House, Washington County, 1777 (Elections 1; Loan Office 1; Manufactories 2; Grievances 2). LOCAL OFFICES: Prince George's Parish Vestry, Frederick County, 1749; sheriff, Frederick County, 1753–1756, 1759–1762; collector of land tax, Frederick County, 1759; public school visitor, Frederick County, 1763; justice, Frederick County, 1763–at least 1775 (quorum, 1768–at least 1775), Washington County, commissioned 1777; justice, Court of Oyer and Terminer and Gaol Delivery, Frederick County, commissioned 1770, 1772, and 1773; justice, Orphans' Court, Washington County, commissioned 1777. MILITARY SERVICE: colonel, 1761, 1763–at least 1776. **WEALTH DURING LIFETIME.** LAND AT FIRST ELECTION: 3,863 acres in Prince George's and Frederick counties (at least 139 acres inherited from father, the remainder by purchase and patent). In 1755 he leased out 120 acres. **WEALTH AT DEATH.** DIED: will probated on January 10, 1778, in Washington County. PERSONAL PROPERTY: TEV, at least £2,572.15.5 current money (including 13 slaves and a gristmill). LAND: At least 1,020 acres in Frederick, Prince George's, Washington, and Montgomery counties, plus 1 lot in Georgetown, D.C. Samuel and his partners had many small tracts resurveyed into one large parcel of 8,025 acres owned by the Frederick Forge, 1772; one-fourth share of this ironworks was owned by Samuel at his death.

BEALL, THOMAS, OF GEORGE (1735–1819). BORN: in 1735, probably in Prince George's County; younger son. NATIVE: third generation. RESIDED: on lot 72, Georgetown, D.C. **FAMILY BACKGROUND.** FATHER: Col. George Beall (1695–1780), son of *Ninian Beale* (ca. 1625–1717/18). MOTHER: Elizabeth (1699–1748), daughter of Col. *Thomas Brooke* (ca. 1659–1730/31). HALF UNCLE: *Thomas Brooke* (1683–1744). AUNT: Jane Brooke (?–1779), who married *Alexander Contee* (ca. 1691–1740). HALF AUNTS: Sarah Brooke, who married first, *William Dent* (ca. 1660–1704), and second, *Philip Lee* (ca. 1681–1744); Priscilla Brooke, who married *Thomas Gantt* (?–1765). BROTHER: George (1729–1807), who married first, Anna, and second, Elizabeth. SISTER: Elizabeth, who married (first name unknown) Evans. FIRST COUSINS: *John Contee* (1722–ca. 1796); *Thomas Contee* (ca. 1729–1811); and Jane Contee (1728–

1812), who married *John Hanson, Jr.* (1721–1783). ADDITIONAL COMMENTS: his father was previously married. MARRIED by 1775 Nancy, granddaughter of John Orme (?–1758), of Prince George's County, a minister, and wife Ruth. **CHILDREN.** DAUGHTERS: Elizabeth, who married George C. Washington (?–1854), great-nephew of Gen. George Washington (1731/32–1799); Harriet Ann, her twin sister, who married Maj. John Peter. **PRIVATE CAREER.** EDUCATION: literate. RELIGIOUS AFFILIATION: Presbyterian. SOCIAL STATUS AND ACTIVITIES: Gent., 1780. OCCUPATIONAL PROFILE: probably a planter. **PUBLIC CAREER.** LEGISLATIVE SERVICE: Lower House, Montgomery County, 1785 (Claims), 1800. LOCAL OFFICES: auctioneer, Montgomery County, commissioned 1780; justice, Montgomery County, 1780–at least 1785, commissioned 1800. **WEALTH DURING LIFETIME.** PERSONAL PROPERTY: assessed value £1,300.0.0, including 8 slaves, 1783; assessed value £680.0.0, including 15 slaves, 1793–1797; assessed value £510.0.0, including 15 slaves, 1798–1812. LAND AT FIRST ELECTION: at least 3,124 acres in Montgomery County (308 acres, plus at least 1 lot in Georgetown, D.C., received from his father). SIGNIFICANT CHANGES IN LAND BETWEEN FIRST ELECTION AND DEATH: tax lists from 1793 to 1813 show ownership of 2,550 acres in Montgomery County, of which 420 acres were held in partnership with two other people; purchased 174 acres in Lexington, Kentucky in 1812; also held land in Jefferson County, Virginia; owned 40 lots in Georgetown, D.C., 1798. **WEALTH AT DEATH.** DIED: on October 5, 1819, in Georgetown, D.C.; buried in the Presbyterian Cemetery, Georgetown, D.C.; his body was later moved to "Oakhill," Georgetown, D.C. LAND: at least 2,130 acres in Montgomery County, plus 420 acres in Montgomery County held in partnership with two other people, plus 40 lots in Georgetown, D.C., 174 acres in Lexington, Kentucky, and unknown acreage in Jefferson County, Virginia.

BEALL, WILLIAM MURDOCK (ca. 1742–1823). BORN: ca. 1742; second son. NATIVE: probably third generation. RESIDED: in Frederick Town, Frederick County. **FAMILY BACKGROUND.** FATHER: Nathaniel Beall, Gent. (?–1757), planter. MOTHER: Ann, daughter of Rev. George Murdock (?–1761), of Prince George's County. BROTHERS: George, who married in 1757 Elizabeth Turner; Elisha (1745–1838). SISTERS: Elizabeth; Mary. MARRIED Mary (1743–1810). **CHILDREN.** SONS: William Murdock, Jr. (?–by 1813), who married Frances. DAUGHTERS: Mary Ann (1772–1817), never married; Rebecca (1776–1807), who married Thomas P. Willson (1768–1832). **PRIVATE CAREER. EDUCATION**: literate. **RELIGIOUS AFFILIATION**: Anglican. **SOCIAL STATUS AND ACTIVITIES**: Gent., 1790. **OCCUPATIONAL PROFILE**: farmer; merchant, by 1785. **PUBLIC CAREER. LEGISLATIVE SERVICE**: Lower House, Frederick County, 1778–1779 (Grievances 1; Tax Commissioners 1; Claims 2, 3), 1782 (elected to the 2nd session of the 1781–1782 Assembly to fill vacancy; Claims 2). **LOCAL OFFICES**: justice, Frederick County, 1777–at least 1794; judge, court of appeals, appointed under the Act to Procure Troops for the American Army, Frederick County, appointed 1778; justice, Orphans' Court, Frederick County, 1779–at least 1793; commissioner of tax, Frederick County, 1782–at least 1792. **STANDS ON PUBLIC/PRIVATE ISSUES**: manumitted many slaves in his will and expressed concern about their welfare. **WEALTH DURING LIFETIME. LAND AT FIRST ELECTION**: 1,939 acres in Frederick, Montgomery, and Washington counties (131 acres inherited from his father). **SIGNIFICANT CHANGES IN LAND BETWEEN FIRST ELECTION AND DEATH**: purchased 5,205 acres in Frederick County; sold 1,057 acres in Frederick and Washington counties, 1778–1801; held additional land in Virginia and New York. **WEALTH AT DEATH. DIED**: on November 5, 1823, in Frederick Town, Frederick County. **LAND**: at least 1,407 acres in Frederick County and 2,050 acres in New York, plus 4 lots in Frederick Town, Frederick County, and 2 lots in Washington, D.C.

BEARD, RICHARD (?–1681). **IMMIGRATED**: in 1650 as a free adult with his wife and two children, probably from Virginia. **RESIDED**: in South River Hundred, Anne Arundel County. **ADDITIONAL COMMENTS**: probably lived in Virginia from at least 1646 until his migration to Maryland, during which period he married and had two children. **MARRIED** ca. 1646 Rachel, daughter of Edward Robins (1602–by 1646), a merchant of Accomack County, Virginia. Her sister was Elizabeth, who married *William Burgess* (ca. 1622–1686/87). **CHILDREN. SONS**: Richard (ca. 1648–1703), a justice of Anne Arundel County from 1679 to ca. 1692, who made the first map of Annapolis and who married Susannah (?–1708); John (?–1678). **DAUGHTERS**: Rachel (?–after 1724), who married first, Neale Clarke (?–1676), second, John Stimpson (?–by 1692), third, Robert Proctor (?–by 1695), fourth, Richard Kilburne (?–by 1698), and fifth, Thomas Freeborne (?–1713); Rebecca, who married (first name unknown) Nicholson; and Ruth, who married John Gaither,

of Virginia. **PRIVATE CAREER. EDUCATION**: illiterate. **RELIGIOUS AFFILIATION**: Protestant; Quaker by 1657. **OCCUPATIONAL PROFILE**: boatwright; planter. **PUBLIC CAREER. LEGISLATIVE SERVICE**: Lower House, Anne Arundel County, 1662, 1663–1664, 1666 (Laws). **STANDS ON PUBLIC/PRIVATE ISSUES**: summoned for service on a grand jury of the Provincial Court in 1660, but he refused to swear the required oath; presented a petition with others in 1674 to obtain relief for Quakers from swearing oaths; his religious beliefs undoubtedly account for his failure to hold offices other than that of burgess. **WEALTH DURING LIFETIME. LAND AT FIRST ELECTION**: ca. 1,500 acres. **WEALTH AT DEATH. DIED**: will probated on August 10, 1681. **PERSONAL PROPERTY**: TEV, 19,067 pounds of tobacco (including 1 servant). **LAND**: over 1,485 acres.

BEATTY, CHARLES (ca. 1736–1804). **BORN**: ca. 1736; second son. **NATIVE**: at least third generation. **RESIDED**: in Frederick County (later became part of Montgomery County); Georgetown, Montgomery County, 1783; Georgetown, "Washington County," District of Columbia, by 1802. **FAMILY BACKGROUND. FATHER**: *Thomas Beatty* (?–1768). **MOTHER**: Mary. **BROTHERS**: *Thomas Beatty* (ca. 1735–1815); James. **SISTERS**: Susanna; Sarah. **MARRIED** first, by 1771 (possibly his cousin) Martha Middagh (ca. 1736–1790). Her brother was John Middagh. Her sisters were Mary, who married (first name unknown) Rickey; Susannah, who married (first name unknown) Johnson. **MARRIED** second, by 1801 Verlinda. **CHILDREN. SONS**: John Middagh; Charles Asfordley; Thomas Johnson; and Randle Hulse Cradock. **DAUGHTER**: Mary Franckenfeld. **PRIVATE CAREER. EDUCATION**: literate. **RELIGIOUS AFFILIATION**: Protestant. **SOCIAL STATUS AND ACTIVITIES**: Gent., 1770. **OCCUPATIONAL PROFILE**: merchant; partner in land transactions with *George Fraser Hawkins* (ca. 1741–1785), ca. 1770; partner in a mill with Barnard O'Neill, of St. Mary's County, and *William Deakins, Jr.* (?–1798), 1778; partner in land transactions with *William Deakins, Jr.* (?–1798), ca. 1783; surveyor. **PUBLIC CAREER. LEGISLATIVE SERVICE**: Lower House, Frederick County, 1771, 1773–1774; Conventions, Frederick County, 2nd–3rd, 1774, 4th, 1775, 5th, 1775, 6th–8th, 1775–1776. **LOCAL OFFICES**: Committee of Observation, Frederick County, elected 1775; county lieutenant, Frederick County, appointed 1777; judge, Court of Appeals for Tax Assessment, Montgomery County, commissioned 1786. **MILITARY SERVICE**: colonel, by 1776; deputy quartermaster general of the Continental Army, by 1778. STANDS ON PUB-LIC/PRIVATE ISSUES: signed along with other Frederick County delegates an address to *Charles Carroll of Carrollton* (1737–1832) thanking him for the stand he took in opposition to Gov. Robert Eden's Fee Bill proclamation, 1773. WEALTH DURING LIFETIME. LAND AT FIRST ELECTION: 2,248 acres in Frederick County, which included a half interest in 208 acres held with *George Fraser Hawkins* (ca. 1741–1785). SIGNIFICANT CHANGES IN LAND BETWEEN FIRST ELECTION AND DEATH: owned 3,474 acres (including the partnership in 208 acres) in Frederick County, by 1773; Beatty was very active in patenting, resurveying, buying, and selling tracts. Due to the creation of several new counties from Frederick County during the period between 1773 and 1798, some of the tracts he owned were possibly overlooked when Beatty was assessed in 1798. Also, some of the tracts may ultimately have been incorporated into Washington, D.C. He owned at least 1,820 acres, including 115 lots in Frederick, Montgomery, Prince George's, and Allegany counties, and Georgetown and Washington, D.C., 1798; patented 248 acres in Prince George's County between 1801 and 1802; sold 305 acres in Frederick County between 1802 and 1804. WEALTH AT DEATH. DIED: between August 18 and November 21, 1804, in Montgomery County. PERSONAL PROPERTY: TEV, £630.16.6 current money (including 13 slaves); FB, estate overpaid £512.5.10. LAND: at least 1,763 acres, including 115 lots in Frederick, Montgomery, Prince George's, and Allegany counties, and Georgetown and Washington, D.C.

BEATTY (BEATIE, BEATY), JOHN (?–1811). BORN: probably in Frederick County. NATIVE: possibly; if so, second generation. RESIDED: in Frederick County; Cumberland Town, Allegany County. FAMILY BACKGROUND. FATHER: possibly Robert Beatty. UNCLE: possibly *Thomas Beatty* (?–1768). MARRIED on December 21, 1799, Ann Beall. CHILDREN. SONS: William Beall; Thomas Beall; Otho Beall; Lewis; Henry Grosh; and John Elie. DAUGHTERS: Louisa Eleanor; Eliza; and Priscilla. PRIVATE CAREER. EDUCATION: literate. OCCUPATIONAL PROFILE: probably a planter. PUBLIC CAREER. LEGISLATIVE SERVICE: Lower House, Frederick County, 1779–1780, 1785. LOCAL OFFICES: sheriff, Allegany County, commissioned 1790, 1791, and 1800; justice, Allegany County, 1795–at least 1800. WEALTH DURING LIFETIME. PERSONAL PROPERTY: 3 slaves, 1800. LAND AT FIRST ELECTION: 166 acres in Frederick County. SIGNIFICANT CHANGES IN LAND BETWEEN FIRST ELECTION

AND DEATH: patented 1,658 acres in Allegany County, and purchased 4 lots in Cumberland Town, Allegany County, 1793–1795. WEALTH AT DEATH. DIED: between October 22 and November 25, 1811, in Allegany County. PERSONAL PROPERTY: TEV, $2,855.29 current money (including china, silver, and a Bible); FB, $1,548.85. LAND: possibly 1,758 acres in Allegany County, plus 4 lots in Cumberland Town, Allegany County. IDENTIFICATION PROBLEMS. There were five men named John Beatty during this time period. Information on family background is scarce and it is very difficult in many instances to differentiate the references to John Beatty. Thus the link between the legislator and the John Beatty identified here is tentative.

BEATTY, THOMAS (?–1768). BORN: probably in Monocacy, Prince George's County. NATIVE: probably, if so second generation. RESIDED: in Frederick County. FAMILY BACKGROUND. MOTHER: Susanna (?–ca. 1745). BROTHERS: Robert; William; John; Edward (?–1755); and Jaime (James). SISTERS: Agness; Martha, who married Capt. John Midaugh (Midday). NEPHEW: possibly *John Beatty* (?–1811). MARRIED Mary. CHILDREN. SONS: *Thomas Beatty* (ca. 1735–1815); James; and *Charles Beatty* (ca. 1736–1804). DAUGHTERS: Susanna, who married Nathan Maynard; Sarah. PRIVATE CAREER. EDUCATION: literate; provided for the education of his minor children in his will. RELIGIOUS AFFILIATION: Protestant. SOCIAL STATUS AND ACTIVITIES: Mr., 1753; Gent., 1762. OCCUPATIONAL PROFILE: yeoman. PUBLIC CAREER. LEGISLATIVE SERVICE: Lower House, Frederick County, 1757–1758, 1762–1763. LOCAL OFFICES: justice, Prince George's County, 1739–1747, Frederick County, 1748–at least 1763 (quorum, 1748–at least 1763); justice, Court of Oyer and Terminer and Gaol Delivery, Frederick County, commissioned 1762, 1764, 1765, and 1766. WEALTH DURING LIFETIME. LAND AT FIRST ELECTION: at least 529 acres in Frederick County. SIGNIFICANT CHANGES IN LAND BETWEEN FIRST ELECTION AND DEATH: sold 145 acres and patented at least 1,100 acres in Frederick County, plus he purchased a mill in partnership with two other people, between 1757 and 1768. WEALTH AT DEATH. DIED: between February 1768, and April 8, 1768, in Frederick County. PERSONAL PROPERTY: TEV, £859.4.7 current money (including 4 slaves and 1 servant); FB, £571.7.11. LAND: possibly ca. 1,484 acres in Frederick County.

BEATTY, THOMAS (ca. 1735–1815). BORN: ca. 1735; eldest son. NATIVE: at least third generation. RESIDED: probably in Creagerstown, Frederick County. FAMILY BACKGROUND. FATHER: *Thomas Beatty* (?–1768). MOTHER: Mary. BROTHERS: *Charles Beatty* (ca. 1736–1804); James. SISTERS: Susanna; Sarah. MARRIED Jane (?–1788). CHILDREN. SON: Maj. Thomas, Jr. (ca. 1759–1815), of Georgetown, D.C., who married Anna. DAUGHTERS: Catherine (?–by 1810), who married John Ritchie; Henrietta, who married Rev. William Parkinson, living in New York by 1810. PRIVATE CAREER. EDUCATION: literate. RELIGIOUS AFFILIATION: Baptist, member of the Baptist Church of Jesus Christ, Frederick Town, Frederick County; wife was a member of the Evangelical Reformed Church, Frederick County. SOCIAL STATUS AND ACTIVITIES: Esq., 1790. OCCUPATIONAL PROFILE: farmer, 1772; possibly a merchant. PUBLIC CAREER. LEGISLATIVE SERVICE: Lower House, Frederick County, 1781 (elected to the 2nd session of the 1780–1781 Assembly to fill vacancy), 1781–1782 (Grievances 2), 1782–1783 (elected to the 1st session to fill vacancy), 1783, 1784, 1790. LOCAL OFFICES: sheriff, Frederick County, commissioned 1777 (ineligible before October 1779), elected 1785–out of office by 1788; collector of tax, Frederick County, commissioned 1778 and 1779; commissioner of tax, Frederick County, appointed 1792 and 1798. WEALTH DURING LIFETIME. PERSONAL PROPERTY: owned 8 slaves, 1790. LAND AT FIRST ELECTION: ca. 1,360 acres in Frederick County, plus 2 lots in Georgetown, Montgomery County. SIGNIFICANT CHANGES IN LAND BETWEEN FIRST ELECTION AND DEATH: owned at least 2,200 acres in Frederick County, plus 2 lots in Creagerstown, 1798; also received ground rents from 114 lots in Creagerstown. WEALTH AT DEATH. DIED: on December 31, 1815, in Creagerstown, Frederick County. PERSONAL PROPERTY: TEV, $12,449.48 (including 13 slaves and sundry books), plus $2,264.43 received for land sold after his death; FB, $4,777.40. LAND: owned land in Tennessee, as well as in Allegany and Frederick counties, and at least 8 lots in Creagerstown, at least 2 lots in Georgetown, and at least 2 lots in Washington, D.C.

BECKLER, EDWARD (?–?). IMMIGRATED: on Kent Island by 1637/38. RESIDED: in Kent County. PRIVATE CAREER. RELIGIOUS AFFILIATION: probably a Protestant. SOCIAL STATUS AND ACTIVITIES: does not appear in the records of the colony after the Assembly of 1637/38. OCCUPATIONAL PROFILE: planter. PUBLIC CAREER. LEGISLATIVE SERVICE: Assembly, Kent County, 1637/38. STANDS ON PUBLIC/PRIVATE ISSUES: arrest warrant issued for him, *John Boteler* (ca. 1601–1642), and Thomas Smith on December 30, 1637, to answer accusations of sedition, piracy, and murder.

BELT, JOSEPH (ca. 1680–1761). BORN: ca. 1680 in Anne Arundel County; second son. NATIVE: probably third generation. RESIDED: at "Chelsea," Prince George's County. FAMILY BACKGROUND. FATHER: John Belt (?–1698), of Anne Arundel County. STEPFATHER: John Lamb, a merchant. MOTHER: Elizabeth. BROTHERS: John, of Baltimore County, a Quaker, who married Lucy, daughter of Benjamin Lawrence; Benjamin (1682–1773); and Jeremiah (1698–?), who married Mary, daughter of *John Wight* (?–1705). SISTERS: Elizabeth; Charity; and Sarah, who married in 1718 Thomas Harwood, of Anne Arundel County. HALF SISTER: Margaret Lamb (ca. 1702–?). MARRIED first, by 1706 Hester (Esther), daughter of *Ninian Beale* (ca. 1625–1717/18). Her brothers were Ninian (1669–by 1717/18); Charles (1672–1740); John (1674–?); Thomas; and George (1695–1780). Her sisters were Mary; Rachel; and Sarah (?–1734), who married *Samuel Magruder* (1654–1711). Her nephews were *Joshua Beall* (ca. 1719–ca. 1796); *Thomas Beall, of George* (1735–1819); and *John Magruder* (1694–1750). MARRIED second, by 1737 Margery (?–1783), widow of Thomas Sprigg (?–1725); daughter of *John Wight* (?–1705). Her brother or half brother was John. Her half brother was *Thomas Gantt* (?–1765). Her sisters were Mary; Feilder. CHILDREN. SONS: John (ca. 1707–?), who married in 1727/28 Margery Queen; Joseph, Jr. (1717–1761), who married his stepsister Anne Sprigg; Capt. Tobias (1720–1785), who married Mary Gordon (?–1795); Jeremiah (1724–1784), who married in 1746 his stepsister Mary Sprigg (1723–?); James (1726–?); and Humphrey. STEPSONS: *Thomas Sprigg* (1715–1781), who married Elizabeth (1721/22–1789), daughter of Richard Galloway (1691–1741) and wife Sophia Richardson; John Sprigg (1716–?); and *Edward Sprigg* (?–?). DAUGHTERS: Anne (1708/9–?), who married first, in 1724 Thomas Claggett, and second, Ignatius Perry; Rachel (1711–?), who married *Osborn Sprigg* (1707–1749/50); Mary (1722–?), who married, first, *Edward Sprigg* (1697–1751), and second, Thomas Pindell; Margery, who married first, (first name unknown) Lyles, and second, (first name unknown) Perry. STEPDAUGHTERS: Anne Sprigg, who married her stepbrother Joseph Belt, Jr. (1717–1761); Mary Sprigg (1723–?), who married in 1746 her stepbrother Jeremiah Belt (1724–1784). **PRIVATE CAREER.** EDUCATION: literate. RELIGIOUS AFFILIATION: Anglican, Queen Anne's Parish, Prince George's County. SOCIAL STATUS AND ACTIVITIES: Gent., by 1726. OCCUPATIONAL PROFILE: merchant; probably also a planter. **PUBLIC CAREER.** LEGISLATIVE SERVICE: Lower House, Prince George's County, 1725–1727 (Aggrievances 1–4), 1728–1731 (Aggrievances 1–5), 1732–1734 (Aggrievances 1–Cv), 1734/35–1737 (Aggrievances 1, Cv, 2–4). OTHER PROVINCIAL OFFICE: justice, Provincial Court, 1732–at least 1734. LOCAL OFFICES: Queen Anne Parish Vestry, Prince George's County, in office 1714–1717, 1726–1729, 1740–1743, 1746–1749; justice, Prince George's County, 1715/16–at least 1729 (quorum, 1720–at least 1729); churchwarden, Queen Anne Parish, Prince George's County, 1724–1725; justice, Court of Oyer and Terminer and Gaol Delivery, Prince George's County, commissioned 1721, 1725/26, 1729, and 1734. MILITARY SERVICE: lieutenant colonel, by 1725; colonel, by 1726. **WEALTH DURING LIFETIME.** LAND AT FIRST ELECTION: 1,010 acres in Prince George's and Baltimore counties (250 acres inherited from his father; 760 acres by patent). SIGNIFICANT CHANGES IN LAND BETWEEN FIRST ELECTION AND DEATH: purchased or patented at least 2,118 acres in Prince George's and Frederick counties between 1726 and 1755; sold at least 836 acres in Prince George's and Baltimore counties between 1738 and 1745; gave 200 acres in Prince George's County to his godson, 1740; an additional 437 acres in Prince George's County may have come from Belt's second marriage. **WEALTH AT DEATH.** DIED: on June 26, 1761, in Prince George's County; his death was "supposed to be occassioned by Grief for the Death of his Son Joseph, Jr. a few Weeks before." PERSONAL PROPERTY: TEV, £2,538.12.3 current money (including 33 slaves, 83 oz. silver, and books); FB, £999.6.7. LAND: 2,861 acres in Frederick and Prince George's counties.

BENNETT, RICHARD (ca. 1608–1675). BORN: ca. 1608 in England. IMMIGRATED: in 1648 as a free adult with his family from Virginia. RESIDED: on the Severn River, Anne Arundel County; returned to Virginia, ca. 1652. ADDITIONAL COMMENTS: in Virginia by 1628 to manage his uncle's plantation. **FAMILY BACKGROUND.** UNCLE: Edward Bennett, a London merchant and director of the Virginia Company, 1621. MARRIED by 1638 Ann, widow of John Utie (?–by 1638). **CHILDREN.** SON: *Richard Bennett* (ca. 1639–1667), who married Henrietta Maria (1647–1697), daughter of *James Neale* (ca. 1615–1684). STEPSONS: John Utie; *Nathaniel Utie* (ca. 1635–ca. 1675/76); and *George Utie* (?–1678). DAUGHTERS: Elizabeth, who married Charles Scarborough; Ann (?–by 1694), who married first, Theodorick Bland (?–1671), and second, *St. Leger Codd* (ca. 1634–ca. 1707/8). **PRIVATE CAREER.** EDUCATION: literate. RELIGIOUS AFFILIATION: Protestant; Puritan. SOCIAL STATUS AND ACTIVITIES: he led a migration of religious dissenters from Virginia to Maryland and received a grant from Lord Baltimore for settlement on the Severn River which they named Providence, 1648; after 1652, he resided at his plantation on the Nassemond River in Virginia. OCCUPATIONAL PROFILE: merchant; planter. **PUBLIC CAREER.** PROVINCIAL OFFICE: commissioner of Parliament for Maryland, 1651–1657/58. OUT OF COLONY OFFICES: burgess, Virginia, 1629–1631; Virginia Council, 1642, 1660; commissioner of Parliament for Virginia, 1651–1660; governor of Virginia, 1652–1655; major general of the Virginia Militia, 1666. STANDS ON PUBLIC/PRIVATE ISSUES: leader of the Puritan and anti-royal factions in Virginia and Maryland during the 1640s and 1650s; returned to England to oppose Lord Baltimore's claim to Maryland, 1655. **WEALTH AT DEATH.** DIED: will probated on April 12, 1675; size of estate unknown.

BENNETT, RICHARD (ca. 1639–1667). BORN: ca. 1639 in Virginia; only son. IMMIGRATED: by 1663 as a free adult from Virginia. RESIDED: in Baltimore County. **FAMILY BACKGROUND.** FATHER: *Richard Bennett* (ca. 1608–1675). MOTHER: Anne, widow of John Utie (?–by 1638). HALF BROTHERS: John Utie; *Nathaniel Utie* (ca. 1635–ca. 1675/76); and *George Utie* (?–1678). SISTERS: Elizabeth, who married Charles Scarborough; Ann (?–by 1694), who married first, Theodorick Bland, and second, *St. Leger Codd* (ca. 1634–ca. 1707/8). OTHER KINSHIP: his great-uncle was Edward Bennett, a London merchant and director of the Virginia Company, 1621. MARRIED Henrietta Maria (1647–1697), daughter of *James Neale* (ca. 1615–1684). She subsequently married in 1669 *Philemon Lloyd* (1646–1685). Her brothers were James, who married first, Elizabeth, daughter of *William Calvert* (ca. 1642/43–1682), and second, Elizabeth, daughter of Capt. John Lord, of Virginia; Anthony, who married first, Elizabeth, daughter of *Thomas Turner* (?–ca. 1662/63), and second, Elizabeth, daughter of *William Digges* (ca. 1650–1697). Her sisters were Jane, who married William Boreman, son of *William Boreman* (ca. 1630–1709); Dorothy. **CHILDREN.** SON: Richard (1667–

1749), who married Elizabeth (1682–1740), daughter of *John Rousby* (?–1685/86). DAUGHTER: Susanna (1666–1714), who married first, *John Darnall* (?–1684), and second, ca. 1686 *Henry Lowe* (?–1717). PRIVATE CAREER. EDUCATION: literate; attended Harvard College, 1655. RELIGIOUS AFFILIATION: Protestant, but married a Catholic. OCCUPATIONAL PROFILE: planter. PUBLIC CAREER. LEGISLATIVE SERVICE: Lower House, Baltimore County, 1663–1664. LOCAL OFFICE: justice, Baltimore County, 1665–1667 (Quorum). WEALTH DURING LIFETIME. LAND AT FIRST ELECTION: patented 1,650 acres in 1664; patented an additional 600 acres in 1665. WEALTH AT DEATH. DIED: will probated on May 6, 1667. LAND: over 2,000 acres.

BENSON, EDMOND (1687–1734). BORN: on June 4, 1687, in Talbot County; second son. NATIVE: second generation. RESIDED: in Anne Arundel County, by 1716. FAMILY BACKGROUND. FATHER: Capt. James Benson (?–1709), of St. Michael's River, Talbot County, a physician. MOTHER: Margaret, immigrated as a servant, free by 1679. BROTHERS: James (1684/85–?); *Perry Benson* (1694–1751); and Nicholas (1699–1775), who married Rachel. SISTERS: Margaret (1682/83–?); Ann (1689–?), who married James Spencer, Jr.; Elizabeth (1691–?); and Mary (1702–?), who married James Parrott. NEPHEW: *James Benson* (?–1792). MARRIED on August 15, 1714, Hannah (1678–1752), widow of *Charles Hammond* (ca. 1670–1713); daughter of Philip Howard; granddaughter of Matthew Howard, of Anne Arundel County, who immigrated in 1649, and wife Ruth Baldwin; niece of *Cornelius Howard* (?–1680), Elizabeth Howard, who married *Henry Ridgeley* (?–1710), and Mary Howard, who married *John Hammond* (1643–1707). Her first cousins were *Matthew Howard* (ca. 1675–1750); Sarah Howard, who married first, *John Worthington* (1650–1701), and second, *John Brice* (?–1713); *Charles Hammond* (ca. 1670–1713); *Thomas Hammond* (?–ca. 1724/25); and *John Hammond* (ca. 1665–1742/43). CHILDREN. STEPSONS: *Charles Hammond* (1692/93–1772); John Hammond (?–1755), who married Ann, daughter of *Edward Dorsey* (?–1705); Rezin Hammond (ca. 1713–1739); Nathaniel Hammond (1708–1762), who married Anne Welsh; and *Philip Hammond* (1697–1760). STEPDAUGHTERS: Hamutel Hammond, who married Charles Worthington; Ruth Hammond, who married first, Peaslee Ingram, and second, *Thomas Franklin* (ca. 1706–1787). PRIVATE CAREER. EDUCATION: literate. RELIGIOUS AFFILIATION: Angli-

can. SOCIAL STATUS AND ACTIVITIES: Gent., 1716. OCCUPATIONAL PROFILE: planter. PUBLIC CAREER. LEGISLATIVE SERVICE: Lower House, Anne Arundel County, 1719–1721/22 (Laws 1, 3, 4). LOCAL OFFICES: justice, Anne Arundel County, 1716–at least 1723; justice, Court of Oyer and Terminer and Gaol Delivery, Anne Arundel County, commissioned 1716, 1717, 1718, and 1720; St. Anne's Parish Vestry, Anne Arundel County, in office 1722–1725. WEALTH DURING LIFETIME. PERSONAL PROPERTY: mortgaged 12 slaves, livestock, silver, and household goods to a London merchant to cover debt of £600 sterling in 1724. LAND AT FIRST ELECTION: 200 acres in Anne Arundel and Talbot counties (50 acres in Talbot County inherited from his father) and a certificate of survey on 667 acres in Baltimore County. SIGNIFICANT CHANGES IN LAND BETWEEN FIRST ELECTION AND DEATH: bought 150 acres in Anne Arundel County from the estate of *Charles Hammond* (ca. 1670–1713) and patented it into a 197-acre tract in 1722. Gave his brother Nicholas all of his Talbot County land in 1724. Three years later he placed all of his land, 1,035 acres, in Anne Arundel and Baltimore counties into a trust for the support of his wife. Benson purchased 447 acres in Anne Arundel County in 1727. WEALTH AT DEATH. DIED: in 1734 in Anne Arundel County. LAND: 447 acres in Anne Arundel County.

BENSON, JAMES (?–1792). BORN: on the north side of the St. Michael's River, Talbot County, of age by 1750; only son. NATIVE: third generation. RESIDED: on the north side of the St. Michael's River, Talbot County. FAMILY BACKGROUND. FATHER: *Perry Benson* (1694–1751). MOTHER: Rebecca, widow of Michael Russell. UNCLE: *Edmond Benson* (1687–1734). HALF BROTHERS: William Russell; Thomas Russell. SISTERS: Rebecca; Margaret; and Ann. HALF SISTERS: Sarah Russell; Elizabeth Russell; and Mary Russell. MARRIED in August 1748 Hannah, daughter of William Ratcliffe (?–1741), of Queen Anne's County, and wife Hannah. Her sisters were Mary, who married by 1740 Thomas Hackett; Jane; Frances; and Elizabeth. CHILDREN. SONS: Perry; James; William; and Robert. DAUGHTERS: Margaret, who married Dr. Edward White; Rebecca; Elizabeth; Charlotte; and Anne. PRIVATE CAREER. EDUCATION: literate. RELIGIOUS AFFILIATION: Anglican, St. Michael's Parish, Talbot County; Methodist, 1781. SOCIAL STATUS AND ACTIVITIES: Mr., 1750; Gent., 1772. OCCUPATIONAL PROFILE: planter; agreed to build an addition to St. Michael's Parish Church and to make pews for the addition, 1761. **PUBLIC CAREER**. **LEGISLATIVE SERVICE**: Convention, Talbot County, 5th, 1775; Lower House, Talbot County, 1777, 1777–1778 (resigned on March 4, 1778, to attend to his business affairs). **LOCAL OFFICES**: churchwarden, St. Michael's Parish, Talbot County, elected 1750; tobacco inspector, St. Michael's River, Talbot County, appointed 1751, 1753, 1756, 1766, and 1774; St. Michael's Parish Vestry, Talbot County, elected 1756, 1769, and 1775; justice, Talbot County, appointed 1778 (did not qualify); commissioner of tax, Talbot County, 1779–1782. **MILITARY SERVICE**: captain, Thirty-eighth Battalion, Talbot County Militia, 1776. **STANDS ON PUBLIC/PRIVATE ISSUES**: manumitted three slaves, 1781. **WEALTH DURING LIFETIME**. **PERSONAL PROPERTY**: assessed value £808.5.0, including 12 slaves and 3 oz. plate, 1783. **LAND AT FIRST ELECTION**: 372 acres in Talbot County (134 acres from his father; 200 acres by purchase). **ADDITIONAL COMMENTS**: obtained 192 acres in Queen Anne's County through his marriage by 1754, but sold it all in 1760. **WEALTH AT DEATH**. **DIED**: will probated on March 6, 1792, in Talbot County. **PERSONAL PROPERTY**: size of estate unknown; no inventories or accounts were recorded; his will mentioned slaves and livestock. **LAND**: 373 acres in Talbot County.

BENSON, PERRY (1694–1751). **BORN**: on April 1, 1694, in St. Michael's Parish, Talbot County; third son. **NATIVE**: second generation. **RESIDED**: on the north side of the St. Michael's River, Talbot County. **FAMILY BACKGROUND**. **FATHER**: Capt. James Benson (?–1709), who immigrated in 1674 from England, resided on St. Michael's River, Talbot County, a chirurgeon. **MOTHER**: Margaret, immigrated as a servant, free by 1679. **BROTHERS**: James (1684/85–?); *Edmond Benson* (1687–1734); and Nicholas (ca. 1699–?), who married in 1722 Rachel (1701–1775). **SISTERS**: Margaret (1682/83–?); Ann (1689–?), who married James Spencer, Jr.; Elizabeth (1691–?), who married (first name unknown) Harrison; and Mary (1702/3–?), who married James Parrott. **MARRIED** by 1719 Rebecca, widow of Michael Russell. **CHILDREN**. **SON**: *James Benson* (?–1792). **STEPSONS**: William Russell; Thomas Russell. **DAUGHTERS**: Rebecca; Margaret; and Ann. **STEPDAUGHTERS**: Sarah Russell, who married by 1728 William Dawson; Elizabeth Russell, who married by 1728 William Edwards; and Mary Russell. **PRIVATE CAREER**. **EDUCATION**: literate. **RELIGIOUS AFFILIATION**: Anglican, St. Michael's Parish, Talbot County. **SOCIAL STATUS AND ACTIVITIES**: Gent., 1731. **OCCUPATIONAL**

PROFILE: carpenter, 1715; planter, 1743. **PUBLIC CAREER**. **LEGISLATIVE SERVICE**: Lower House, Talbot County, 1732–1734. **LOCAL OFFICES**: justice, Talbot County, 1732–1751 (quorum, 1739–1751); St. Michael's Parish Vestry, Talbot County, elected 1742, 1744, and 1750; coroner, Talbot County, commissioned 1743; tobacco inspector, Thomas Bruff's Landing, St. Michael's River, Talbot County, appointed 1748 and 1749 (refused to serve). **WEALTH DURING LIFETIME**. **LAND AT FIRST ELECTION**: 96 acres in Talbot County (all by patent); also held 740 acres in Talbot County for the heirs of his wife's first husband. **ADDITIONAL COMMENTS**: Benson had received 220 acres in Talbot County by deed of gift from his brother in 1731, but he sold it all before his first election. **SIGNIFICANT CHANGES IN LAND BETWEEN FIRST ELECTION AND DEATH**: patented 740 acres in Talbot County with John Valiant in 1733, but sold or gave away all of it before his death; purchased and patented 232 acres in Talbot County, 1741, 1749–1750. **WEALTH AT DEATH**. **DIED**: on September 24, 1751, in Talbot County. **PERSONAL PROPERTY**: at least 2 slaves mentioned in will. **LAND**: 328 acres in Talbot County.

BERRY, JAMES (?–1666). **IMMIGRATED**: in 1652/53 as a free adult with his wife and children from Virginia. **RESIDED**: in Calvert County. **ADDITIONAL COMMENTS**: in Accomack County, Virginia, by 1636 when he received a patent for 350 acres for transporting himself, his wife, and five other individuals. **MARRIED** by 1636 Elizabeth. **CHILDREN**. **SONS**: *William Berry* (ca. 1636–1691), who married first, Naomi (?–1663), daughter of *Richard Preston* (?–ca. 1669/70), and second, in 1669 Margaret (?–1688), widow of Richard Preston (?–by 1669) and daughter of *Thomas Marsh* (ca. 1615–1656/57); Roger. **DAUGHTER**: Martha. **PRIVATE CAREER**. **EDUCATION**: literate. **RELIGIOUS AFFILIATION**: Protestant, probably a Quaker. **SOCIAL STATUS AND ACTIVITIES**: no title on arrival in Maryland; Mr., by 1655. **OCCUPATIONAL PROFILE**: planter. **PUBLIC CAREER**. **LEGISLATIVE SERVICE**: Assembly, Patuxent (Calvert County), 1654. **LOCAL OFFICE**: justice, Patuxent (Calvert County), 1655. **STANDS ON PUBLIC/PRIVATE ISSUES**: fined in 1655 and probably lost his court commission for supporting the proprietary governor William Stone against the Parliamentary Commissioners. **WEALTH DURING LIFETIME**. **LAND AT FIRST ELECTION**: probably 400 acres in Maryland and 600 acres in Virginia; sold his land in Virginia in 1655 and patented another 900 acres in Maryland in 1658. WEALTH AT DEATH. DIED: in 1666; size of estate unknown.

BERRY, WILLIAM (ca. 1636–1691). BORN: ca. 1636, possibly in Virginia; first son. IMMIGRATED: in 1652/53 as a minor with his family from Virginia. RESIDED: in Calvert County; Talbot County at the time of his death. FAMILY BACKGROUND. FATHER: *James Berry* (?–1666). MOTHER: Elizabeth. BROTHER: Roger. SISTER: Martha. MARRIED first, Naomi (?–1663), daughter of *Richard Preston* (?–ca. 1669/70). Her brothers were Richard (?–by 1669); James, and Samuel. Her sisters were Margaret; Rebecca; and Sarah, who married *William Ford* (?–1678/79). MARRIED second, in 1669 Margaret (?–1688), widow of Richard Preston (?–by 1669); daughter of *Thomas Marsh* (ca. 1615–1656/57). Her brother was *Thomas Marsh* (ca. 1643–1679). Her sisters were Elizabeth (?–1684); Sarah (?–1688). CHILDREN. SONS: William (?–1693), of Pennsylvania, who married first, Nancy, and second, by 1691 Mary; James, who married first, in 1686 Sarah Wilchurch, and second, in 1691 Elizabeth Pitt; and Thomas (1678–?), who married in 1699 Sarah Godard. STEPSON: Samuel Preston. DAUGHTER: Rebecca, who married in 1686 James Ridley. PRIVATE CAREER. EDUCATION: literate. RELIGIOUS AFFILIATION: Quaker. SOCIAL STATUS AND ACTIVITIES: second generation burgess; Mr., by 1657. OCCUPATIONAL PROFILE: planter. PUBLIC CAREER. LEGISLATIVE SERVICE: Lower House, Calvert County, 1674–1674/75 (elected to the 3rd session; Laws 3, 4). LOCAL OFFICE: justice, Calvert County, 1669/70. STANDS ON PUBLIC/PRIVATE ISSUES: very active in 1674, 1676, and 1681, in petitioning the Assembly to exempt Quakers from having to take oaths. WEALTH DURING LIFETIME. LAND AT FIRST ELECTION: over 500 acres. WEALTH AT DEATH. DIED: will probated on May 16, 1691. PERSONAL PROPERTY: at least 2 black servants. LAND: ca. 2,000 acres.

BESSON, THOMAS (ca. 1617–1679). BORN: ca. 1617 in England. IMMIGRATED: in 1649 as a free adult with his family from Virginia. ADDITIONAL COMMENTS: transported to Virginia in 1638 by Robert Freeman, a merchant. RESIDED: in Anne Arundel County. MARRIED Hester, widow of Henry Caplin. She subsequenly married by 1680 Thomas Sutton. CHILDREN. SONS: Thomas; William; and John. DAUGHTERS: Anne, who married *Nicholas Gassaway* (1634–1691/92); Martha. PRIVATE CAREER. EDUCATION: literate. RELIGIOUS AFFILIATION: Protestant, probably a Puritan. SO-

CIAL STATUS AND ACTIVITIES: no title on arrival in Maryland. OCCUPATIONAL PROFILE: planter. PUBLIC CAREER. LEGISLATIVE SERVICE: Assembly, Providence (Anne Arundel County), 1657; Lower House, Anne Arundel County, 1666. LOCAL OFFICE: justice, Anne Arundel County, 1658–1668. MILITARY SERVICE: captain, 1661. WEALTH DURING LIFETIME. LAND AT FIRST ELECTION: 800 acres in 1658. WEALTH AT DEATH. DIED: will probated on April 29, 1679. PERSONAL PROPERTY: TEV, £80.18.0 sterling; FB, £43.8.0. LAND: 3 tracts of unspecified acreage.

BIGGER, JOHN (ca. 1654–1714). BORN: ca. 1654, certainly by 1657, in Calvert County. NATIVE: second generation. RESIDED: in Calvert County. FAMILY BACKGROUND. FATHER: John Bigger (ca. 1634–ca. 1673), who immigrated in 1652 as an indentured servant and became a planter with over 3,000 acres. MOTHER: Ann, who subsequently married James Rumsey. BROTHER: James Bigger. SISTER: Mary, who married James Stockley (?–1676), son of *Woodman Stockley* (?–ca. 1663). MARRIED Ann, daughter of Dr. James Trueman and wife Ann Storer; niece of *Thomas Trueman* (ca. 1625–1685). Her stepbrother was *Robert Skinner* (?–1713). Her half brothers were Clark Skinner; William Skinner; and *Adderton Skinner* (ca. 1677–1756). Her sisters were Mary, who married *Thomas Hollyday* (ca. 1661–1702/3); Martha, who married *Thomas Greenfield* (ca. 1649–1715); and Elizabeth. Her stepsister or half sister was Mary Skinner. CHILDREN. DAUGHTER: Ann, who married first, William Head, and second, James Gibson. PRIVATE CAREER. EDUCATION: literate. RELIGIOUS AFFILIATION: Protestant. SOCIAL STATUS AND ACTIVITIES: closely related by marriage to the powerful Skinner, Greenfield, and Hollyday families. OCCUPATIONAL PROFILE: planter. PUBLIC CAREER. LEGISLATIVE SERVICE: Lower House, Calvert County, 1692–1693. OTHER PROVINCIAL OFFICE: justice, Provincial Court, 1699–1702. LOCAL OFFICES: justice, Calvert County, 1692–1699, 1705–1706 (quorum); trustee, King William's School, 1696. MILITARY SERVICE: captain, 1690–1694; major, 1694–1695; lieutenant colonel, 1695–1700; colonel, 1700–still serving in 1707. STANDS ON PUBLIC/PRIVATE ISSUES: an active supporter of the revolution of 1689, which brought him his first political offices. WEALTH DURING LIFETIME. LAND AT FIRST ELECTION: at least 1,450 acres. WEALTH AT DEATH. DIED: will probated in November 1714. PERSONAL PROPERTY: TEV, £1,584.8.3 sterling (including 32 slaves and 5 servants); FB, £1,359.8.11. LAND: 3,096 acres.

BIGGS, SETH (?–1708). BORN: probably in Bristol, England. IMMIGRATED: in 1680 as a free adult from Bristol. RESIDED: briefly in Calvert County before moving to Anne Arundel County. FAMILY BACKGROUND. SISTER: Sarah, who married William Webb. MARRIED Mary, who subsequently married by 1710 Dr. William Lock. PRIVATE CAREER. EDUCATION: literate. RELIGIOUS AFFILIATION: Anglican. SOCIAL STATUS AND ACTIVITIES: arrived with capital and mercantile connections. OCCUPATIONAL PROFILE: merchant of Bristol, 1679; merchant in Maryland, probably in partnership with *William Holland* (?–1732) and others. PUBLIC CAREER. PROVINCIAL OFFICES: justice, Provincial Court, 1702–1704, 1705–1706; Council, 1708. LOCAL OFFICES: justice, Anne Arundel County, 1694–1702; St. James' Parish Vestry, Anne Arundel County, 1695–1708; deputy commissary, Anne Arundel County, 1697. WEALTH DURING LIFETIME. PERSONAL PROPERTY: owned the ship *Providence Galley*, 1708. LAND: 2,500–3,000 acres, by 1708. WEALTH AT DEATH. DIED: buried on August 2, 1708. PERSONAL PROPERTY: TEV, £1,481.4.3 sterling (including 21 slaves and 2 servants); much of his estate was in the hands of Isaac Milner, a London merchant. LAND: 2,500–3,000 acres.

BILLINGSLEY, FRANCIS (?–1695). IMMIGRATED: in 1652 as a free adult with his wife and son. RESIDED: in Calvert County. FAMILY BACKGROUND. BROTHER: Thomas (?–1674); probably John (?–by 1659), a major. MARRIED Susannah. CHILDREN. SONS: James (?–by 1664/65), who married Susannah, daughter of *Richard Ewen* (?–1660); John (?–by 1695). DAUGHTER: Rebecca (1677–?), who married in 1690 Abraham Birkhead. PRIVATE CAREER. EDUCATION: literate. RELIGIOUS AFFILIATION: Quaker. SOCIAL STATUS AND ACTIVITIES: no title on arrival in the colony; acquired a servant in 1653 and another in 1657. OCCUPATIONAL PROFILE: planter. PUBLIC CAREER. LEGISLATIVE SERVICE: Lower House, Calvert County, 1678–1682 (elected to the 2nd session). LOCAL OFFICE: constable, Clifts, Calvert County, 1654. STANDS ON PUBLIC/PRIVATE ISSUES: active in the effort by the Quakers to receive a dispensation from taking legally required oaths in the 1670s and the 1680s. WEALTH DURING LIFETIME. LAND AT FIRST ELECTION: 1,250 acres. WEALTH AT DEATH. DIED: on August 10, 1695. PERSONAL PROPERTY: TEV, £139.13.10 sterling (including an

unspecified number of Negroes and servants). LAND: 1,250 acres.

BIRCKHEAD (BIRKHEAD, BURKHEAD, BURKETT, BRICKHEAD), CHRISTOPHER (by 1740–1788). BORN: between 1730 and 1740 in Talbot County. NATIVE: fourth generation. RESIDED: in Talbot County; Third District, Talbot County, 1783. FAMILY BACKGROUND. FATHER: Christopher Birckhead (?–by 1740). MOTHER: Ann (?–1758), daughter of William Harrison (?–1719), of Talbot County, a planter. STEPFATHERS: Samuel Sharp (1713/14–1748); William Brooke (?–1754/55); and Daniel Powell. BROTHER: Solomon (?–ca. 1753). HALF BROTHERS: Peter Sharp (1746–1768), who married Hannah; William Harrison Brooke (?–1771). SISTERS: Ann (1730–by 1768), who married William Troth, Jr.; Rachel (by 1740–1818), who married first, Philip McManus, and second, in 1765 *Pollard Edmondson* (ca. 1718–1794). MARRIED his stepniece, either Lucretia, Mary, or Ann, one of three daughters of *Pollard Edmondson* (ca. 1718–1794); stepdaughter of Rachel Birckhead McManus (by 1740–1818); granddaughter of *John Edmondson* (1692–1743); niece of Ann Dickinson (?–ca. 1774), who married *Samuel Bowman* (?–1768). Her brothers were James (?–ca. 1774), who married Rachel Leeds Bozman; Pollard. Her first cousins were *Philip Walker* (?–1791); Elizabeth Walker (?–1783), who married *Henry Dickinson* (?–1789); Ann Walker Mein Hindman (?–by 1787), who married third, *Henry Dickinson* (?–1789). MARRIED second, Henrietta (?–1791), daughter of (first name unknown) Trippe. Her brother was Capt. William Trippe. CHILDREN. SONS: Solomon, of Cambridge, Dorchester County, a physician; Christopher (?–1799); James (?–ca. 1800); John Trippe (?–1796); William (ca. 1775–?); Levin; Edward; and Henry. DAUGHTER: Ann (?–1791), never married. PRIVATE CAREER. EDUCATION: literate. RELIGIOUS AFFILIATION: Anglican; his parents were Quakers. SOCIAL STATUS AND ACTIVITIES: Gent., 1758. OCCUPATIONAL PROFILE: planter. PUBLIC CAREER. LEGISLATIVE SERVICE: Lower House, Talbot County, 1779–1780. LOCAL OFFICES: churchwarden, St. Peter's Parish, Talbot County, elected 1766; county lieutenant, Talbot County, appointed 1777; justice, Talbot County, 1777–1779 (did not qualify); justice, Orphans' Court, Talbot County, appointed 1777; St. Peter's Parish Vestry, Talbot County, elected 1779. JURY SERVICE: grand jury, Talbot County, 1765. MILITARY SERVICE: colonel, Fourth Battalion, Talbot County Militia, 1776. STANDS ON PUBLIC/PRIVATE ISSUES: manumitted thirty slaves to be set free after various terms of service, 1788. **WEALTH DURING LIFETIME. PERSONAL PROPERTY**: assessed value £1,081.6.8, including 25 slaves and 86 oz. plate, 1783. **LAND AT FIRST ELECTION**: 1,736 acres in Talbot and Caroline counties (1,636 acres inherited from his family; 100 acres by purchase). **WEALTH AT DEATH. DIED**: between March 3 and July 18, 1788, in Talbot County. **PERSONAL PROPERTY**: TEV, £1,710.2.1 current money (including 29 slaves, probably the same ones who were manumitted after various terms of service in 1788, 84 oz. plate, and books); FB, £552.16.2. **LAND**: 1,736 acres in Talbot and Caroline counties.

BISHOP, HENRY (?–by 1644/45). **BORN**: probably in England. **IMMIGRATED**: in 1634 as an indentured servant. **RESIDED**: in St. Mary's County. **PRIVATE CAREER. EDUCATION**: illiterate. **RELIGIOUS AFFILIATION**: probably a Catholic; close association with the Jesuits. **OCCUPATIONAL PROFILE**: servant, free writ 1637/38; planter; partner with Simon Demibiel, 1640. **PUBLIC CAREER. LEGISLATIVE SERVICE**: Assembly, Mattapanient Hundred, St. Mary's County, 1638/39, present 1641/42, Mattapanient Hundred, St. Mary's County, 1642A. **WEALTH AT DEATH. DIED**: by 1644/45; size of estate unknown.

BISHOP, SMITH (?–1783). **BORN**: of age by 1771. **RESIDED**: in Acquango Hundred, Worcester County. **MARRIED** ca. 1771 Hannah (?–1807), daughter of James Stewart (?–1763). **CHILDREN. DAUGHTERS**: Elizabeth; Esther; and Sarah. **PRIVATE CAREER. EDUCATION**: literate. **OCCUPATIONAL PROFILE**: physician. **PUBLIC CAREER. LEGISLATIVE SERVICE**: Conventions, Worcester County, 3rd, 1774, 6th–8th, 1775–1776 (did not attend the 7th Convention), 9th, 1776 (election voided on August 15, 1776, because voter qualifications had not been ascertained as prescribed by the 8th Convention resolves; reelected and seated); Lower House, Worcester County, 1777. **WEALTH DURING LIFETIME. PERSONAL PROPERTY**: 9 slaves, 1771. **LAND AT FIRST ELECTION**: 1,060 acres in Worcester County (wife's dower), and 1 lot in Snow Hill, Worcester County. **WEALTH AT DEATH. DIED**: administration bond taken, August 1783 in Worcester County. **PERSONAL PROPERTY**: TEV, at least £947.18.9 current money (including 15 slaves). **LAND**: 1,060 acres in Worcester County, and one and one-third lots in Snow Hill, Worcester County.

BISHOP, WILLIAM (?–1685). **BORN**: probably in England. **IMMIGRATED**: in 1663 as a free adult.

RESIDED: in Kent County; Talbot County, after 1675. **FAMILY BACKGROUND. BROTHERS**: Richard; John. **SISTER**: Joan, who married Gregory Salter. **PRIVATE CAREER. EDUCATION**: literate. **SOCIAL STATUS AND ACTIVITIES**: Gent. on arrival. **OCCUPATIONAL PROFILE**: planter; merchant. **PUBLIC CAREER. LEGISLATIVE SERVICE**: Lower House, Kent County, 1671–1674/75. **LOCAL OFFICES**: justice, Kent County, 1669–1670, Talbot County, 1675/76–1685. **WEALTH DURING LIFETIME. LAND AT FIRST ELECTION**: 200 acres by 1672. **WEALTH AT DEATH. DIED**: will probated on May 9, 1685. **PERSONAL PROPERTY**: TEV, £478.3.9 sterling, plus 74,068 pounds of tobacco (including 14 servants). **LAND**: over 1,400 acres.

BLACKISTON (BLAKISTON, BLACKISTONE, BLAKISTONE), EBENEZER (ca. 1684–ca. 1746/47). **BORN**: ca. 1684; elder son. **NATIVE**: probably second generation. **RESIDED**: in Kent County. **FAMILY BACKGROUND. FATHER**: Ebenezer Blakiston (ca. 1650–1709), probably immigrated in 1668 with his father, George Blakiston (?–1669); militia captain in 1689; justice of Cecil County in 1691, 1697–1698, and 1702; sheriff of Cecil County in 1691; Protestant. **MOTHER**: Elizabeth James. **BROTHER**: *William Blackiston* (?–1737). **SISTER**: Anna Blakiston. **OTHER KINSHIP**: his second cousin was *Nehemiah Blakiston* (?–1693); his third cousin was *Nathaniel Blakiston* (ca. 1663–1722). **MARRIED** by 1712/13 Sarah, daughter of Thomas Joce (?–1712/13). She subsequently married John Garrett. Her brothers were Nicholas (?–1734); Thomas. **CHILDREN. DAUGHTER**: Rosamond, who married by 1748 William Wilmer. **PRIVATE CAREER. EDUCATION**: literate. **RELIGIOUS AFFILIATION**: Anglican, St. Paul's Parish, Kent County. **SOCIAL STATUS AND ACTIVITIES**: Gent., 1720. **OCCUPATIONAL PROFILE**: planter. **PUBLIC CAREER. LEGISLATIVE SERVICE**: Lower House, Kent County, 1724 (elected to the 3rd session to fill vacancy), 1727 (elected to the 4th session to fill vacancy), 1728–1731, 1732–1734. **LOCAL OFFICES**: justice, Kent County, 1733–at least 1744; justice, Court of Oyer and Terminer and Gaol Delivery, Kent County, commissioned 1740; coroner, Kent County, appointed 1740. **MILITARY SERVICE**: captain, 1724; major, 1745. **WEALTH DURING LIFETIME. LAND AT FIRST ELECTION**: 775 acres in Kent County. **SIGNIFICANT CHANGES IN LAND BETWEEN FIRST ELECTION AND DEATH**: purchased 1 lot in Chestertown, Kent County, 1730–1735; assumed the administration of 550 acres in Kent County as guardian for his nephew Pascoa Joce from 1734 to at least 1742. WEALTH AT DEATH. DIED: by January 19, 1746/47, in Kent County. PERSONAL PROPERTY: TEV, £1,013.11.8 current money (including 11 slaves, books, and plate); FB, £991.16.3. LAND: owned 775 acres in Kent County.

BLACKISTON (BLAKISTON, BLACKISTONE, BLAKISTONE), WILLIAM (?–1737).

BORN: of age by 1712; younger son. NATIVE: probably second generation. RESIDED: in Kent County. FAMILY BACKGROUND. FATHER: Ebenezer Blakiston (ca. 1650–1709), immigrated in 1668 with his father George Blackiston (?–1669); justice of Cecil County in 1691, 1697–1698, and 1702; militia captain in 1689; sheriff of Cecil County in 1691; Protestant. MOTHER: Elizabeth James. BROTHER: *Ebenezer Blackiston* (ca. 1684–ca. 1746/47). SISTER: Anna Blakiston. OTHER KINSHIP: his second cousin was *Nehemiah Blakiston* (?–1693); his third cousin was *Nathaniel Blakiston* (ca. 1663–1722). MARRIED by 1711 Ann, daughter of Robert Park (?–1708) and wife Mary; stepdaughter of Robert Dunn (1674–1729), of Kent County, vestryman of St. Paul's Parish, Kent County. Her stepbrothers were *Robert Dunn* (1693–1745); William (?–1728), who married Martha Miller; and James (1699–died young). Her sister was Elizabeth (?–1760), who married first, Charles Ringgold, and second, Philip Davis (?–1749). Her stepsisters were Jane (1701–?); Mary. CHILDREN. SONS: Ebenezer; William (of age by 1721). DAUGHTERS: Mary (1711/12–?); Ann, who married (first name unknown) Miller; Hanna; and Rose. OTHER CHILDREN: unborn child mentioned in his will. PRIVATE CAREER. EDUCATION: literate. RELIGIOUS AFFILIATION: Protestant. SOCIAL STATUS AND ACTIVITIES: Gent., 1712; Mr. at death. OCCUPATIONAL PROFILE: planter. PUBLIC CAREER. LEGISLATIVE SERVICE: Lower House, Kent County, 1722–1724. WEALTH DURING LIFETIME. LAND AT FIRST ELECTION: 100 acres in Kent County (by purchase). WEALTH AT DEATH. DIED: will probated on May 10, 1737, in Kent County. PERSONAL PROPERTY: TEV, £333.12.0 current money (including 12 slaves and 1 servant); FB, £327.10.0. LAND: 100 acres in Kent County.

BLADEN, THOMAS (1698–1780).

BORN: in 1698 in Maryland; eldest son. NATIVE: second generation. RESIDED: in England from at least 1712 until 1742; Annapolis, Anne Arundel County, 1742–1747; England, 1747 until death. FAMILY BACKGROUND. FATHER: *William Bladen* (1670–1718). MOTHER: Anne, daughter of Garrett Van Swearin-gen and wife Mary Smith. SISTER: Anne, who married *Benjamin Tasker* (ca. 1690–1768). NEPHEW: *Benjamin Tasker, Jr.* (1720/21–1760). NIECES: Ann Tasker (?–1816), who married *Samuel Ogle* (1694–1752); Rebecca Tasker (1724–?), who married *Daniel Dulany, Jr.* (1722–1797). MARRIED on July 14, 1737, Barbara, daughter of Sir Theodore Janssen (ca. 1658–1748), immigrated from France to England in 1680, naturalized in 1685, became a baronet in 1714, and wife Williamsa (?–1731); granddaughter of Sir Robert Henley, M.P. Her brothers included Abraham (?–1765); Henry (?–1766); Stephen Theodore (?–1777), lord mayor of London; and William (?–ca. 1740/41), principal secretary of Maryland from February 1732/33 until death. Her sisters were Mary (?–1748), who married *Charles Calvert, 5th Lord Baltimore* (1699–1751); and others whose names are unknown. Her nephews were *Frederick Calvert, 6th Lord Baltimore* (1731/32–1771); *Benedict Calvert* (ca. 1724–1788). Her niece was Caroline Calvert, who married *Robert Eden* (1741–1784). CHILDREN. DAUGHTERS: Harriet (?–1821), who married on March 3, 1767, William Anne Capel, fourth earl of Essex (1732–1799); Barbara, who married on August 31, 1773, Gen. Henry St. John (1738–1818). PRIVATE CAREER. EDUCATION: attended schools in England. RELIGIOUS AFFILIATION: Anglican; mother's family was Catholic. SOCIAL STATUS AND ACTIVITIES: Gent., 1720; Esq., 1744; a member of a family prominent in both England and Maryland. OCCUPATIONAL PROFILE: officeholder; land speculator. PUBLIC CAREER. PROVINCIAL OFFICES: governor, 1742–1746/47 (commissioned April 1742, sworn in August 1742; dismissed from office by October 1746 because he was "tactless and quarrelsome"; served until his successor was sworn in March 1746/47); surveyor general, Western Shore, 1742–1746; chancellor, 1742–1746/47. MILITARY SERVICE: colonel, period of service unknown. OUT OF COLONY SERVICE: M.P., Steyning, England, 1727–1734, Ashburton, Devonshire, England, 1735–1741. WEALTH DURING LIFETIME. LAND AT FIRST ELECTION: at least 6,955 acres in Charles, Baltimore, and Cecil counties (remaining from at least 16,000 acres in those counties, plus additional acreage in Anne Arundel and Queen Anne's counties that were inherited from his father; sold 8,870 acres, 1720–1724). SIGNIFICANT CHANGES IN LAND BETWEEN FIRST ELECTION AND DEATH: received warrants for ca. 7,400 acres in Prince George's and Frederick counties. He patented 854 acres of these warrants himself, but sold the certificates for 3,691 acres to others who patented them. The certificates for 2,814 acres remained unpatented. While in Maryland Bladen sold at least 6,850 acres inherited from his father, plus about 1,000 acres in Frederick and Anne Arundel counties that he had obtained by patent and purchase. WEALTH AT DEATH. DIED: in 1780 in England. LAND: 80 acres in Charles County and land in Baltimore County that was confiscated by the state in 1782; holdings in England are unknown.

BLADEN, WILLIAM (1670–1718). BORN: in 1670 in London or Yorkshire, England; eldest son. IMMIGRATED: in 1690 as a free adult from London, England. RESIDED: in St. Mary's County; Annapolis, Anne Arundel County, by the mid-1690s. FAMILY BACKGROUND. FATHER: Nathaniel Bladen, Esq., of Hemsworth, Yorkshire, England; a barrister who attended Lincoln's Inn. MOTHER: Isabella (?–1691), daughter of Sir William Fairfax (1609–1644), of Steeton, Yorkshire, England, a cousin of Sir Thomas Fairfax (1612–1671). BROTHERS: Francis; Martin (ca. 1680–1746), who was comptroller of the mint in 1714, M.P. for Hampshire from 1715 to 1734, for Maldon, Essex from 1734 to 1741, and for Portsmouth from 1741 to 1746, a Lord of Trade from 1717 to 1746, and a director of the Royal African Company from 1717 to 1726. MARRIED first, Letitia, daughter of Judge Dudley Loftus, vicar general of Ireland. MARRIED second, in 1695/96 Ann, daughter of Garrett Van Swearingen and wife Mary. CHILDREN. SONS: *Thomas Bladen* (1698–1780), who married Barbara, daughter of Sir Theodore Janssen, Bart. (ca. 1658–1748); Christopher; William; and Martin. DAUGHTERS: Ann, who married in 1711 *Benjamin Tasker* (ca. 1690–1768); Priscilla. PRIVATE CAREER. EDUCATION: literate; admitted to the Inner Temple in 1687. RELIGIOUS AFFILIATION: Anglican. SOCIAL STATUS AND ACTIVITIES: a member of a prominent English family; his education quickly brought him profitable clerkships and legal business; he was hired in 1692 by Gov. Lionel Copley to handle all of his business and legal affairs. OCCUPATIONAL PROFILE: placeman; lawyer, admitted to the following courts: Provincial Court in 1693; Cecil County in 1693/94; Prince George's County in 1696; Anne Arundel County by 1703. Contractor; merchant. PUBLIC CAREER. LEGISLATIVE SERVICE: Lower House, Annapolis, 1708A (election voided). OTHER PROVINCIAL OFFICES: clerk, Lower House, 1695–1698; register of the Admiralty Court, 1698–still serving in 1703; clerk, Council, 1698–1716; naval officer, Annapolis, 1698/99–1718; clerk, Prerogative Office, 1699–1700; secretary of Maryland, 1701; deputy auditor

and surveyor general of customs, 1703–1715; attorney general, 1704–1718; commissary general, 1708–1718. LOCAL OFFICES: clerk, St. Mary's County, 1695–1698; clerk of Indictments, Prince George's County, 1696; surveyor of Annapolis, 1697–1718; St. Anne's Parish Vestry, Anne Arundel County, 1704. MILITARY SERVICE: colonel at death. STANDS ON PUBLIC/PRIVATE ISSUES: actively sought permanent appointment as secretary of the colony in 1701 and years following, and led the opposition to Sir *Thomas Lawrence* (ca. 1645–1714), the incumbent secretary. WEALTH DURING LIFETIME. PERSONAL PROPERTY: part owner of the ship *Tryon*, of London, England, 1699. ANNUAL INCOME: as clerk of the Council, one of his many patronage positions, he received 12,000 pounds of tobacco a year. LAND AT FIRST ELECTION: at least 6,000 acres. WEALTH AT DEATH. DIED: on August 7, 1718. PERSONAL PROPERTY: TEV, £2,106.14.1 (including 26 slaves, 9 servants, a printing press, and books, including 48 law titles); FB, £1,646.1.2. LAND: at least 15,745 acres.

BLAKE, THOMAS (?–?). BORN: in Calvert County, of age in 1753. NATIVE: third generation. RESIDED: First District, Calvert County. FAMILY BACKGROUND. FATHER: Richard Blake (?–ca. 1764), son of Capt. Thomas Blake and wife Jane Sutton Isaac. MOTHER: Susanna Nicols. MARRIED by June 1766, probably Barbara Bond, widow of William Hamilton Smith. CHILDREN. SON: Thomas Blake, who possibly married Elizabeth, daughter of *James Heighe* (?–1757). PRIVATE CAREER. EDUCATION: literate. RELIGIOUS AFFILIATION: Anglican. SOCIAL STATUS AND ACTIVITIES: Mr., 1788; Esq., 1788. OCCUPATIONAL PROFILE: probably a planter. PUBLIC CAREER. LEGISLATIVE SERVICE: Lower House, Calvert County, 1788. LOCAL OFFICES: churchwarden, All Saints' Parish, Calvert County, in office 1753; All Saints' Parish Vestry, Calvert County, in office 1761; commissioner of tax, Calvert County, 1779–at least 1783; justice, Calvert County, in office 1781 and 1794. WEALTH DURING LIFETIME. PERSONAL PROPERTY: assessed value £850.3.4, including 20 slaves and 16 oz. plate, 1783. LAND AT FIRST ELECTION: 767 acres in Calvert County (545 acres inherited from his father; 222 acres probably by personal acquisition). WEALTH AT DEATH. DIED: probably in Calvert County, after 1795; size of estate unknown.

BLAKISTON, NATHANIEL (ca. 1663–1722). BORN: ca. 1663 in England; first son. IMMIGRATED: in 1698 as a free adult. RESIDED: in Annapolis, Anne Arundel County; returned to England in 1702, where he lived in Northumberland and Middlesex counties. **FAMILY BACKGROUND.** **FATHER:** John Blakiston (1633–1701/2), of Newcastle, England; a barrister and judge of the Admiralty Court; son of John Blakiston (1603–1650), M.P. for Newcastle, England, from 1641 to 1650. **MOTHER:** Phoebe, daughter of William Johnson, of Kibblesworth, Durham, England. **UNCLES:** *Nehemiah Blakiston* (?–1693); Sir Nathaniel Johnson (1645–1713), who was governor of the Leeward Islands from 1686 to 1689 and governor of South Carolina from 1703 to 1709. **BROTHERS:** William (1665–1665); Robert (1673–?). **SISTERS:** Jane (1668–1671); Sarah (1678–1680); and Margaret, who married Maj. Edward Nott, of Kingston, Surrey, England, the deputy governor of Virginia from 1705 to 1706. **MARRIED** first, Thomasine (?–1697), widow of Sir Timothy Thornhill, first baronet of Barbados; daughter of Sir Robert Legard, of Yorkshire, England, a master in Chancery. **MARRIED** second, Mary. **CHILDREN.** **SON:** Nathaniel. **DAUGHTER:** Rachel. **PRIVATE CAREER.** **EDUCATION:** literate. **RELIGIOUS AFFILIATION:** Anglican. **SOCIAL STATUS AND ACTIVITIES:** a member of a prominent English family that was well connected in the colonial bureaucracy; arrived in Maryland as governor. **OCCUPATIONAL PROFILE:** colonial bureaucrat; member of the Merchant Adventurers' Company of London, 1698. **PUBLIC CAREER.** **PROVINCIAL OFFICES:** governor, 1698–1702; chancellor, 1699–1702; agent for Maryland in England, 1702–1709, 1713–1721. **OUT OF COLONY SERVICE:** lieutenant governor of Montserrat, 1689–1695; agent for Virginia in England, 1706–1722; M.P. for Mitchell, Cornwall, England, 1715–1722. **WEALTH DURING LIFETIME.** **ANNUAL INCOME:** his salary as governor of Maryland was at least £1,700 per annum with an additional allowance of £30 for rent; his salary as Maryland's agent in England was £120 per annum. **WEALTH AT DEATH.** **DIED:** in 1722 in England; size of estate unknown.

BLAKISTON (BLACKISTON), NEHEMIAH (?–1693). **BORN:** in England, probably in the Newcastle area; fourth son. **IMMIGRATED:** in 1668 as a free adult from England. **RESIDED:** St. Mary's County. **FAMILY BACKGROUND.** **FATHER:** John Blakiston (1603–1650), of Northumberland, England, who was an M.P. for Newcastle, England, from 1641 to 1650. **UNCLE:** George Blakiston, who immigrated in 1668 with his nephew. **MARRIED** in 1669 Elizabeth (?–1716), daughter of *Thomas Gerard* (1608–1673). She subsequently married Ralph Rymer and finally, *Joshua Guibert* (?–1713). Her brothers were Thomas (?–1686); Justin-

ian (?–1688); and John. Her sisters were Susannah, who married first, *Robert Slye* (ca. 1628–1670/71), and second, *John Coode* (ca. 1648–1708/9); Frances; Temperance; and Mary, who married *Kenelm Cheseldyne* (1640–1708). **CHILDREN.** **SON:** John (?–1724), who married Anne, daughter of *Joshua Guibert* (?–1713). **DAUGHTERS:** Susanna, who married first, Thomas Hatton, grandson of *Thomas Hatton* (?–1654/55), and second, (first name unknown) Attaway; Rebecca; and Mary, who married *Matthew Mason* (ca. 1689–ca. 1728/29). **PRIVATE CAREER.** **EDUCATION:** literate. **RELIGIOUS AFFILIATION:** Anglican. **SOCIAL STATUS AND ACTIVITIES:** younger son of a prominent English family, which aided him in obtaining colonial patronage; soon after his arrival in the colony he married into a prominent and controversial Maryland family; Gent., by 1673. **OCCUPATIONAL PROFILE:** planter; attorney, admitted to the following courts: Court of Chancery in the 1670s; Provincial Court in 1677; St. Mary's County in 1677; Charles County by 1678/69. Placeman. **PUBLIC CAREER.** **LEGISLATIVE SERVICE:** Associators' Convention, St. Mary's County, 1689–1692 (speaker 4, 5, 6); Grand Committee of Twenty, 1690–1692 (president after August 1690); Upper House, 1692–1693. **OTHER PROVINCIAL OFFICES:** surveyor and comptroller general, 1682/83–1684/85; acting king's attorney, 1684/85; collector of Patuxent, 1684/85–1685; collector of North Potomac, 1685–1693; Council, 1691–1693; justice, Provincial Court, 1691–1693 (chief justice, 1691–1692); chancellor and commissary general, 1692–1693. **LOCAL OFFICES:** justice, St. Mary's County, 1689–1692 (quorum); coroner, 1689–1692; King and Queen Parish Vestry, St. Mary's County, 1693. **MILITARY SERVICE:** captain, 1689–1692; colonel, 1692–1693. **STANDS ON PUBLIC/PRIVATE ISSUES:** as customs collector he was often at odds with the proprietary establishment in the late 1680s and he registered protests against the government in England; with brothers-in-law *John Coode* (ca. 1648–1708/9) and *Kenelm Cheseldyne* (1640–1708) he was a prominent leader in the revolution of 1689, which overthrew Lord Baltimore's government; he became head of the interim government when Coode and Cheseldyne left for England in the late summer of 1690; in 1692 he became chief confidant and ally of the new royal governor *Lionel Copley* (1648–1693), and fought unsuccessfully for control of the government after Copley's death in the fall of 1693; he was involved in extensive conflicts with *Edward Randolph* (1632–1703), surveyor general of customs, in 1692–1693 over Blakiston's alleged corruption and embezzlement of royal revenue, for which he was later criminally charged; he was dismissed from all of his offices on October 2 and 3, 1693; he died much indebted to the crown for customs fees previously collected but not paid to the government, which led to extended controversy and litigation over the settlement of his estate. WEALTH DURING LIFETIME. LAND AT FIRST ELECTION: ca. 550 acres. WEALTH AT DEATH. DIED: in December 1693. PERSONAL PROPERTY: TEV, £1,586.2.0 sterling (including 14 slaves, 4 servants, and numerous books); FB, estate overpaid £14.3.5. LAND: ca. 550 acres.

BLANCKENSTEIN (BLAKISTON), WILLIAM (1660–by 1721). BORN: in 1660 at "Hofstein." IMMIGRATED: in 1678 as an indentured servant to *William Dare* (?–1719). RESIDED: in Cecil County; St. Mary's County, by the mid-1680s. PRIVATE CAREER. EDUCATION: literate. RELIGIOUS AFFILIATION: Protestant. SOCIAL STATUS AND ACTIVITIES: naturalized by an Act of the Assembly, 1682; Gent., by 1684; went to England in 1692, with no mention of him found thereafter in Maryland records. OCCUPATIONAL PROFILE: servant, free by 1681/82; planter; Indian trader. PUBLIC CAREER. LEGISLATIVE SERVICE: Associators' Convention, St. Mary's City, 1689–1692. OTHER PROVINCIAL OFFICE: agent to New York on Indian affairs, 1690–1691. LOCAL OFFICES: alderman, St. Mary's City, 1689; probably a justice, St. Mary's County, 1692. WEALTH DURING LIFETIME. LAND AT FIRST ELECTION: over 1,200 acres. WEALTH AT DEATH. DIED: by 1721. LAND: over 1,200 acres. ADDITIONAL COMMENTS: land escheated for want of heirs, 1721.

BLAY, EDWARD (ca. 1653–1713). BORN: ca. 1653 in Anne Arundel County; first son. NATIVE: second generation. RESIDED: in Anne Arundel County; Cecil County, by 1685; Kent County, by 1707. FAMILY BACKGROUND. FATHER: William Blay (?–ca. 1661), who was probably transported to Virginia as a servant in 1636, but was in Maryland by 1652 when he surveyed 600 acres in Anne Arundel County. MARRIED first, Barbara, daughter of Josias Lanham. MARRIED second, by 1695 Anne (?–1712/13), widow of Robert Burnan. CHILDREN. SON: *William Blay* (ca. 1681–1716), who married Isabella, daughter of *William Pearce* (ca. 1641–1720/21). PRIVATE CAREER. EDUCATION: literate. RELIGIOUS AFFILIATION: Anglican. SOCIAL STATUS AND ACTIVITIES: Gent., by 1697. OCCUPATIONAL PROFILE: planter; merchant. PUBLIC CAREER. LEGISLATIVE SERVICE: Lower House, Cecil County, 1697 (elected to the 7th session), 1704–1707, Kent County, 1712–1713 (died before

the 3rd session). LOCAL OFFICES: justice, Cecil County, 1685–1687, 1690–1692, 1694–1702 (quorum, 1702), Kent County, 1693 (refused to take the required oath), 1707–1713 (chief justice, 1708–1713); Shrewsbury Parish Vestry, Cecil County, 1695–1696, 1704–1709, 1712. MILITARY SERVICE: captain, by 1696; lieutenant colonel, by 1707. WEALTH DURING LIFETIME. LAND AT FIRST ELECTION: probably over 1,000 acres. WEALTH AT DEATH. DIED: in November 1713. PERSONAL PROPERTY: TEV, £1,318.17.10 sterling (including 15 slaves); balance in London of £394.16.1. LAND: over 1,000 acres.

BLAY, WILLIAM (ca. 1681–1716). BORN: ca. 1681 in Cecil County, of age by 1702; only son. NATIVE: third generation. RESIDED: in Cecil County; Kent County, by 1702. FAMILY BACKGROUND. FATHER: *Edward Blay* (ca. 1653–1713). MOTHER: probably Barbara, daughter of Josias Lanham. STEPMOTHER: probably Anne (?–1712/13), widow of Robert Burnan. MARRIED Isabella, daughter of *William Pearce* (ca. 1641–1720/21). She subsequently married by 1722 John Johnson. Her brothers were *Daniel Pearce* (1677–1727); William, Jr. (?–1703); and Benjamin (1683–1734), who married Mary, widow of *John Hynson* (ca. 1670–1708). Her sisters were Elizabeth, who married *Henry Ward* (?–1734); Sarah. CHILDREN. SONS: Edward (1707–?); William (1714–?). DAUGHTERS: Rachel (1703–?), who married first, in 1724 *Edward Scott* (?–1725), second, by 1727 John Brown, and third, Aquila Paca, son of *Aquila Paca* (early 1670s–1721); Catherine, who married John Tilden; and Isabella, who married Robert Wetherhead. PRIVATE CAREER. EDUCATION: literate. RELIGIOUS AFFILIATION: Anglican. SOCIAL STATUS AND ACTIVITIES: second generation burgess; did not become a justice or burgess until after his father's death; Mr. at death. OCCUPATIONAL PROFILE: planter. PUBLIC CAREER. LEGISLATIVE SERVICE: Lower House, Kent County, 1714 (elected to the 4th session), 1715. LOCAL OFFICES: Shrewsbury Parish Vestry, Kent County, 1710–1711, 1715–1716; justice, Kent County, 1714–1716. WEALTH DURING LIFETIME. LAND AT FIRST ELECTION: ca. 1,000 acres. WEALTH AT DEATH. DIED: by September 25, 1716. PERSONAL PROPERTY: TEV, £1,620.17.0 (including 19 slaves); FB, £1,429.9.8. LAND: probably 2,600 acres.

BLOUNT (BLUNT), WILLIAM (?–?). IMMIGRATED: in 1642 as a free adult. RESIDED: in Kent County, St. Mary's County; left Maryland in 1643. PRIVATE CAREER. EDUCATION: literate. SO-

CIAL STATUS AND ACTIVITIES: Esq. on arrival; apparently left Maryland between April 10 and May 1, 1643, and did not return. PUBLIC CAREER. LEGISLATIVE SERVICE: Assembly, special writ 1642A, probably a special writ 1642B (did not attend). OTHER PROVINCIAL OFFICES: Council, 1642–1643; justice, Provincial Court, 1642–1643. MILITARY SERVICE: captain, 1642–1643; commander, St. Mary's County Militia, 1642.

BLUNT, RICHARD (ca. 1621–1669). BORN: probably in England. IMMIGRATED: in 1649 as a free adult. RESIDED: in Kent County. MARRIED Ann. CHILDREN. SONS: Samuel; Richard; Josias; Robert; and Thomas. DAUGHTERS: April; Grace; and Rebecca. PRIVATE CAREER. EDUCATION: illiterate. SOCIAL STATUS AND ACTIVITIES: not called Mr. prior to holding office. OCCUPATIONAL PROFILE: planter. PUBLIC CAREER. LEGISLATIVE SERVICE: Lower House, Kent County, 1662, 1666, 1669. LOCAL OFFICES: sheriff, Kent County, 1662; justice, Kent County, 1666–1669. WEALTH DURING LIFETIME. LAND AT FIRST ELECTION: 330 acres, 1650; 530 acres by 1669. WEALTH AT DEATH. DIED: on September 16, 1669. PERSONAL PROPERTY: TEV, 43,629 pounds of tobacco; FB, 27,190 pounds of tobacco. LAND: 530 acres.

BOARMAN, HENRY (?–1800). BORN: of age by 1772; only son. NATIVE: at least second generation. RESIDED: in Bryan Town Hundred, Charles County. FAMILY BACKGROUND. FATHER: James Boarman. MOTHER: Mary Pile (?–1791). SISTER: Elizabeth, who married Edward Boarman (?–by 1800). MARRIED Theresa (?–1801), daughter of Richard Edelen (?–1803) and wife Sarah Harrison. Her brothers were Richard, Jr.; Philip; and Samuel. Her sisters were Rachel, who married (first name unknown) Gardner; Jane, who married (first name unknown) Mudd; Dorothy, who married (first name unknown) Gardner; Elizabeth; and Araminta. CHILDREN. Died without progeny. PRIVATE CAREER. EDUCATION: literate. RELIGIOUS AFFILIATION: wife bequeathed money to the Catholic archbishop of Baltimore. OCCUPATIONAL PROFILE: probably a planter. PUBLIC CAREER. LEGISLATIVE SERVICE: Lower House, Charles County, 1780 (elected, but did not attend; resigned on November 2, 1780). LOCAL OFFICE: Committee of Observation, Charles County, elected 1775. MILITARY SERVICE: 1st lieutenant, Third Maryland Battalion of the Flying Camp, July–December 1776; captain, Twelfth Battalion, Charles County Militia, commissioned 1777. WEALTH DURING LIFETIME. PERSONAL PROPERTY: assessed value

£477.0.0, including 11 slaves; 17 slaves, 1790; inherited 9 slaves from his mother, 1791; 35 slaves, 1798. LAND AT FIRST ELECTION: 436 acres in Charles County, 1783. WEALTH AT DEATH. DIED: in June 1800 in Bryan Town Hundred, Charles County. PERSONAL PROPERTY: TEV, $5,976.80 (including 37 slaves and 30 books). LAND: 280 acres in Charles County, 1798; disposition of his estate was contested by his sister's family, 1801–1819.

BOND, BENSON (1710–1750). BORN: on September 25, 1710, in Calvert County; second son. NATIVE: at least second generation. RESIDED: in Calvert County. FAMILY BACKGROUND. FATHER: Richard Bond (?–1719), of Calvert County. MOTHER: Elizabeth (?–1725), widow of Benjamin Chew (?–1700), of Anne Arundel County. BROTHERS: Richard (1707–?); Thomas (1713–?); John (1715–?); and Phineas (1717–?). HALF BROTHER: Samuel Chew (by 1700–?). SISTER: Sarah (1708–?). HALF SISTERS: Mary Chew (by 1700–?); Elliz Chew (by 1700–?). MARRIED Mary (1713–?), daughter of *Thomas Holdsworth* (ca. 1692–1718); stepdaughter of *Benjamin Mackall* (1675–1761); niece of *Walter Smith* (ca. 1693–1748); half niece of *John Rousby* (1685–1744); stepniece of Ann Mackall (1661–?), who married *Robert Skinner* (?–1713). Her half brother was *Benjamin Mackall, Jr.* (ca. 1723–1795). Her sisters were Betty (1715–?), who married *James Heighe* (?–1757); Rebeka (1716–?); and Ann (1719–?). Her half sister was Barbara Mackall (1722–?), who married *William Wilkinson* (?–1755). Her half first cousins were Ann Rousby (1721–1769), who married *Edward Lloyd* (1711–1770); Elizabeth Rousby, who married *Abraham Barnes* (?–ca. 1778); and Gertrude Rousby (?–ca. 1770), who married *Robert Jenkins Henry* (ca. 1712–1766). Her half nephew was *William Mackall Wilkinson* (1752–1799). CHILDREN. SONS: Richard; Thomas. DAUGHTERS: Elizabeth; Barbary (Barbara). PRIVATE CAREER. EDUCATION: literate. RELIGIOUS AFFILIATION: uncertain, but the Bond family is listed in early Quaker records. SOCIAL STATUS AND ACTIVITIES: Gent., 1749; Mr. at death. OCCUPATIONAL PROFILE: possibly a planter. PUBLIC CAREER. LEGISLATIVE SERVICE: Lower House, Calvert County, 1749–1750 (died before the 3rd session). WEALTH DURING LIFETIME. LAND AT FIRST ELECTION: inherited unspecified acreage in Calvert County from his father in 1719, possibly more than 200 acres. WEALTH AT DEATH. DIED: in July 1750 in Calvert County. PERSONAL PROPERTY: TEV, £1,542.6.11 (including 2 slaves); FB, £441.17.11. LAND: more than 200 acres in Calvert County.

BOND, JACOB (ca. 1725–1780). BORN: ca. 1725 in Baltimore County; youngest son. NATIVE: fourth generation. RESIDED: in Baltimore County (later became part of Harford County). FAMILY BACKGROUND. FATHER: Thomas Bond (?–1755), of Baltimore County; son of *Peter Bond* (?–1718). MOTHER: Ann, daughter of (first name unknown) Robisson (Robertson), of Anne Arundel County. BROTHERS: Thomas (1703–1788), who married Elizabeth Scott (1705–?); Peter; William; John, who married Alesanna Webster; and Joshua (?–1768), who married Ann Partridge. SISTERS: Sarah, who married first William Fell (?–1746), and second, Greenbury Dorsey. NEPHEWS: *Thomas Bond, of Thomas* (?–1800); *William Bond, of Joshua* (ca. 1747–1788); and *James Bond* (ca. 1757–1803). NIECE: Ann, who married second, *James Giles* (1749/50–?). MARRIED on December 28, 1747, Frances (?–by 1776), daughter of Dr. Buckler Partridge (?–by 1757), of Baltimore County, and wife Jane (?–1761). Her brothers were William (?–by 1765); Daubeney Buckler (?–1769). Her sisters were Ann, who married Joshua Bond (?–1768); Elizabeth, who married Height Sollers. Her nephews were *William Bond, of Joshua* (ca. 1747–1788); *James Bond* (ca. 1757–1803). CHILDREN. SONS: Jacob (1750–1804); Dennis (1760–?); and Ralph (1763–?). DAUGHTERS: Sarah, who married Bernard Preston; Priscilla (1759–?); Martha (1766–?); Charlotte (1767–?); and Ann. PRIVATE CAREER. EDUCATION: literate. RELIGIOUS AFFILIATION: his father, son Jacob, and at least two of his brothers were Quakers. OCCUPATIONAL PROFILE: planter; owned extensive orchards. PUBLIC CAREER. LEGISLATIVE SERVICE: Conventions, Harford County, 1st, 1774, 9th, 1776; Lower House, Harford County, 1777 (Grievances 2), 1777–1778. LOCAL OFFICES: Committee of Observation, Harford County, 1774–1776; coroner, Harford County, appointed 1775. WEALTH DURING LIFETIME. PERSONAL PROPERTY: 21 slaves, 1776. LAND AT FIRST ELECTION: at least 1,048 acres in Harford County (700 acres inherited from his father in 1755; 20 acres inherited from his brother Joshua in 1768; remainder probably purchased). SIGNIFICANT CHANGES IN LAND BETWEEN FIRST ELECTION AND DEATH: purchased about 250 acres of land in Harford County from his cousin Thomas in 1779. WEALTH AT DEATH. DIED: between October 2 and November 30, 1780, in Harford County. PERSONAL PROPERTY: TEV, at least £1,979.11.3 current money (including 25 slaves,

carpenter's tools, and surveying instruments). LAND: ca. 1,358 acres in Harford County and rights to an unknown amount of vacant land adjoining the tracts he owned. IDENTIFICATION PROBLEMS. Jacob Bond, Jr. (1750–1804) was old enough and wealthy enough to be a legislator. The legislative journals do not refer to the legislator as "Jr." For this reason and because there was no indication of public service for Jacob, Jr., his father was selected as the legislator.

BOND, JAMES (ca. 1757–1803). BORN: ca. 1757 in Baltimore County; youngest son. NATIVE: fifth generation. RESIDED: in Bush River Lower Hundred, Harford County. FAMILY BACKGROUND. FATHER: Joshua Bond (?–1768), of Baltimore County, son of Thomas Bond (?–1755) and wife Ann Robisson (Robertson). MOTHER: Ann, daughter of Dr. Buckler Partridge (?–by 1757), of Baltimore County, and wife Jane (?–1761). UNCLE: *Jacob Bond* (ca. 1725–1780). BROTHERS: *William Bond, of Joshua* (ca. 1747–1788); Buckler, who married Mary Standsbury; and Thomas, who died a minor. SISTERS: Sarah (ca. 1746–?), who married Israel Morris; Ann (?–1784); Mary (ca. 1752–?); Elizabeth (ca. 1760–?); and Amelia (Pamela), who married William Wilson. FIRST COUSINS: *Thomas Bond, of Thomas* (?–1800); Ann, who married second, *James Giles* (1749/50–?); Catherine Fell (by 1746–by 1795), who married *Thomas Bond, of Thomas* (?–1800). OTHER KINSHIP: his great-grandfather was *Peter Bond* (?–1718). CHILDREN. NATURAL DAUGHTERS: Sophia Moore; Ann (Nancy) Moore; and Amelia (Pamela) Moore; all three were the children of Susan Moore and were minors in 1806. PRIVATE CAREER. EDUCATION: literate. RELIGIOUS AFFILIATION: had a strong Quaker background; his two sisters married Quakers. SOCIAL STATUS AND ACTIVITIES: Esq., 1803. ADDITIONAL COMMENTS: testimony given in a Chancery Court case after his death described Bond as a heavy drinker and gambler by the early 1790s. OCCUPATIONAL PROFILE: merchant, in partnership with his brother, *William Bond, of Joshua* (ca. 1747–1788), by 1774, importing goods from London; by 1787 the firm was indebted to Alexander and Benjamin Contee, Prince George's County merchants, for over £1,658 sterling. PUBLIC CAREER. LEGISLATIVE SERVICE: Lower House, Harford County, 1784, 1785, 1786–1787, 1793, 1794, 1795, 1797, 1799. MILITARY SERVICE: lieutenant, Harford County Company, Flying Camp, by 1776. WEALTH DURING LIFETIME. PERSONAL PROPERTY: assessed value £265.13.0, including 5 slaves and 24 oz. plate, 1783. LAND AT FIRST

ELECTION: 316 acres in Harford County, plus 1 lot in Bel Air, Harford County (250 acres inherited from his father in 1768; ca. 66 acres obtained as a result of the death of his brother Thomas). SIGNIFICANT CHANGES IN LAND BETWEEN FIRST ELECTION AND DEATH: purchased 500 acres, plus 5 lots in Bel Air, Harford County, from his brother *William Bond, of Joshua* (ca. 1747–1788). Two years later, just before the Contees received a judgment for recovery of the 1787 debt owed them by the Bonds' mercantile firm, James deeded his entire holdings of ca. 800 acres, plus 6 lots in Bel Air, Harford County, to his brother Buckler. Although the land was deeded back to James in 1797 or 1798 to "remove any objection that might be made. . .to his eligibility as a Representative of Harford in the House of Delegates," the deed was not recorded and was later destroyed. Buckler and James sold 1 lot and 47 acres in the early 1800s, but Buckler retained legal title to the remaining property, claiming that James was in no condition to handle it himself and might lose it through gambling. WEALTH AT DEATH. DIED: will probated on July 1, 1803, in Harford County. PERSONAL PROPERTY: TEV, £544.14.8 (including books); FB, estate overpaid £144.16.8. LAND: none in his own name, but James's children won a suit in the Chancery Court against their uncle Buckler giving them the right to part of the land devised to them by their father.

BOND, PETER (?–1718). BORN: probably in Anne Arundel County, of age by 1699; eldest son. NATIVE: second generation. RESIDED: Baltimore County. FAMILY BACKGROUND. FATHER: Peter Bond (?–1705), who immigrated by 1675 to Anne Arundel County (later became part of Baltimore County), a planter. STEPFATHER: Philip Washington, of Baltimore County, a planter. MOTHER: Alice, who separated from Philip Washington by 1708 when Peter gave a £100 sterling bond that he would support her. BROTHERS: Thomas; John; and William. MARRIED Elinor, who subsequently married by 1719 Hill Savage. CHILDREN. SONS: Richard; William; Thomas (?–1756), who married Ann Robison; Peter, who married Esther Butterworth; John; and Benjamin. PRIVATE CAREER. EDUCATION: literate. RELIGIOUS AFFILIATION: Protestant. SOCIAL STATUS AND ACTIVITIES: Mr. at death. OCCUPATIONAL PROFILE: planter, by 1708; had a mill on the Patapsco River at the time of his death. PUBLIC CAREER. LEGISLATIVE SERVICE: Lower House, Baltimore County, 1716–1717 (died before the 3rd session). LOCAL OFFICES: justice, Baltimore County, 1715–1717; justice, Court of Oyer and Terminer and Gaol Delivery, Baltimore County, appointed 1715. WEALTH DURING LIFETIME. LAND AT FIRST ELECTION: 645 acres in Baltimore County (301 acres inherited from his father in 1705; 243 acres held jointly with William Hamilton; 223 acres on the Patapsco River by personal acquisition). SIGNIFICANT CHANGES IN LAND BETWEEN FIRST ELECTION AND DEATH: sold the 243 acres that he held jointly with Hamilton, patented 200 acres, and inherited 100 acres from Stephen Gill, thus increasing his holdings on the Patapsco River between Gwynn's Falls and Jones' Falls to ca. 533 acres. WEALTH AT DEATH. DIED: between February 28, 1717/18, and April 23, 1718, in Baltimore County. PERSONAL PROPERTY: TEV, £244.4.7 current money, plus 12,221 pounds of tobacco (including 2 slaves, 2 servants, 1 pair of millstones recently shipped from England, and goods ordered from Europe); FB, £63.15.11. LAND: probably 834 acres in Baltimore County. ADDITIONAL COMMENTS: income at death included 500 pounds of tobacco received as rent on a leased plantation.

BOND, RICHARD (1728–1819). BORN: on October 4, 1728, in St. Mary Anne's Parish, Cecil County. NATIVE: second generation. RESIDED: in East Nottingham Hundred, Cecil County; immigrated to Virginia, 1799 (later became part of West Virginia). FAMILY BACKGROUND. FATHER: Samuel Bond (1692–1783). MOTHER: Ann Sharples (1708–1786). SISTERS: Sarah (1729–?), who married (first name unknown) Howell; Margaret (1732–?), who married (first name unknown) Davis; and Susannah, who married (first name unknown) Davis. MARRIED Mary. CHILDREN. SONS: Samuel, who married in 1778 Elizabeth McVea; Abel, who married in 1790 Elizabeth, daughter of Thomas Booth (?–1773); and Richard, Jr. (1754–1820). PRIVATE CAREER. EDUCATION: literate. RELIGIOUS AFFILIATION: Anglican. SOCIAL STATUS AND ACTIVITIES: Esq., 1783. OCCUPATIONAL PROFILE: farmer, 1774; established gun factory, 1776. PUBLIC CAREER. LEGISLATIVE SERVICE: Lower House, Cecil County, 1777, 1786–1787, 1787–1788, 1788, 1789, 1790, 1791–1792, 1793, 1794, 1795. LOCAL OFFICES: justice, Cecil County, 1777–1782, 1786–at least 1795; sheriff, Cecil County, 1782–1785; collector of tax, Cecil County, gave security bond in 1784. STANDS ON PUBLIC/PRIVATE ISSUES: In 1788, Bond, along with his fellow Cecil County delegates, objected to the commission of *Patrick Ewing* (?–1819), as justice of Cecil County. Nevertheless, Ewing's commission was confirmed by the governor and council.

WEALTH DURING LIFETIME. PERSONAL PROP-
ERTY: assessed value £202.0.0, including 3 slaves,
1783. LAND AT FIRST ELECTION: at least 200
acres in Cecil County. SIGNIFICANT CHANGES IN
LAND BETWEEN FIRST ELECTION AND DEATH:
ca. 530 acres inherited in 1781 and 1783; 127 acres
of vacant land added to a patent resurvey, 1783;
376 acres purchased, 1790–1793; 963 acres sold,
1792–1799 (over 600 acres of this was disposed of
in 1799). WEALTH AT DEATH. DIED: January 14,
1819, in Virginia (later became part of West Virginia); size of estate unknown.

BOND, THOMAS (?–ca. 1797). BORN: in St.
Mary's County, of age by 1760. NATIVE: at least
third generation. RESIDED: in Upper Resurrection
Hundred, St. Mary's County. FAMILY BACK-
GROUND. FATHER: Capt. John Bond (?–1760), son
of Zachariah Bond (?–ca. 1716). MOTHER:
Elizabeth, daughter of John Attaway (?–1732), of
St. Mary's County. UNCLE: *Zachariah Bond* (?–ca.
1776). BROTHERS: Gerard (?–1789), died without
progeny; Samuel; John; Richard; and William.
SISTERS: Susannah, who married (first name unknown) Bates; Elizabeth, who married (first name
unknown) Jordan; Margaret, who married (first
name unknown) Sothoron. FIRST COUSIN: (first
name unknown) Bond, who married *Henry Greenfield Sothoron* (ca. 1732–1793). MARRIED by 1757
Cecelia (?–ca. 1797), widow of Dr. John Key (?–
1755), son of *Philip Key* (1696/97–1764); daughter
of Dr. Gustavus Brown (?–1762); stepdaughter of
Margaret; niece of Anne Brown Claggett Horner,
who married third, *Samuel Hanson* (1716–1794).
Her brother was Richard. Her sisters were Sarah,
who married (first name unknown) Scott; Mary,
who married (first name unknown) Throkeld;
Elizabeth, who married (first name unknown)
Wallace; Jane, who married (first name unknown)
Campbell; and Anne, who married (first name unknown) Claggett. CHILDREN. SONS: Peregrine;
Thomas; and John. STEPSON: *Philip Key* (1750–
1820). DAUGHTERS: Cecelia, who married (first
name unknown) Gardiner; Elizabeth, who married
(first name unknown) Briscoe. STEPDAUGHTER:
Susannah Gardiner Key. PRIVATE CAREER. EDU-
CATION: literate. RELIGIOUS AFFILIATION: Angli-
can, All Faiths Parish, St. Mary's County. SOCIAL
STATUS AND ACTIVITIES: Mr., by 1767; Esq., by
death. OCCUPATIONAL PROFILE: planter; owned a
mill in St. Clement's Hundred, St. Mary's County.
PUBLIC CAREER. LEGISLATIVE SERVICE: Lower
House, St. Mary's County, 1773–1774 (Bills of
Credit 1, Cv, 2, 3), 1782–1783 (Claims 1, 2), 1785,
1790, 1791–1792. LOCAL OFFICES: justice, St.

Mary's County, in office 1764–1773, 1778–at least
1792; justice, Court of Oyer and Terminer and
Gaol Delivery, St. Mary's County, commissioned
1768 and 1772; justice, Orphans' Court, St.
Mary's County, 1778–at least 1786; commissioner
of tax, St. Mary's County, 1779–at least 1785.
MILITARY SERVICE: called major, period of service
unknown. WEALTH DURING LIFETIME. PERSONAL
PROPERTY: 12 slaves, 1790; assessed value £97.0.0,
including 2 slaves and plate, 1793. He petitioned
as an insolvent debtor in 1794. LAND AT FIRST
ELECTION: 765 acres in St. Mary's County (438
acres inherited from his father, 1760; 7 acres by
patent, 1758). SIGNIFICANT CHANGES IN LAND
BETWEEN FIRST ELECTION AND DEATH: owned
494 acres in 1793, but listed only 340 acres in insolvency petition in 1794, all in St. Mary's
County. WEALTH AT DEATH. DIED: inventory
dated December 12, 1797, St. Mary's County.
PERSONAL PROPERTY: TEV, £312.17.1 current
money; FB, £283.17.10. LAND: at least 140 acres
in St. Mary's County.

BOND, THOMAS, OF THOMAS (?–1800).
BORN: in Baltimore County, of age by 1770; eldest
son. NATIVE: fifth generation. RESIDED: at "Isle of
Caprea," Baltimore County (later became part of
Harford County). FAMILY BACKGROUND. FATHER:
Thomas Bond (1703–1788), of Harford County; a
farmer; son of Thomas Bond (?–1755) and wife
Ann Robisson (Robertson). MOTHER: Elizabeth
(1705–?), daughter of *Daniel Scott* (?–1744/45).
UNCLE: *Jacob Bond* (ca. 1725–1780). BROTHER:
Daniel (?–by 1787). SISTERS: Ann, who married
William Clemments, of Charles County; Elizabeth
(?–by 1787), who married (first name unknown)
Howard; Hannah, who married first, Zacheus On-
ion, and second, William Maccomas; Martha
(1747–?), who married (first name unknown)
Smith; and Sarah (?–by 1787), who married (first
name unknown) Howard. FIRST COUSINS: *William
Bond, of Joshua* (ca. 1747–1788); *James Bond* (ca.
1757–1803); and Ann, who married second, *James
Giles* (1749/50–?); *Aquila Scott* (1756–?); *James
McComas* (1735–1791); Elizabeth Scott, who married *William Smithson* (ca. 1744–1809). MARRIED
by 1771 his first cousin Catherine (by 1746–by
1795), daughter of William Fell (?–1746) and wife
Sarah; granddaughter of Thomas Bond (?–1755).
Her brother was Edward (1736–1763), who married Ann Bond. Her sisters were Janet, who married (first name unknown) Few; Ann, who married
(first name unknown) Day; and Margaret. Her
nephew was *William Fell* (1759–1786). CHILDREN.
SONS: Fell; Edward; and Thomas. DAUGHTERS:

Sally; Achsah; Patty; Elizabeth, who married (first name unknown) Gibson; Peggy, who married John Hambleton; and Hannah, who married (first name unknown) Allen. PRIVATE CAREER. EDUCATION: literate. RELIGIOUS AFFILIATION: Anglican; family background Quaker. SOCIAL STATUS AND ACTIVITIES: Esq., 1771. OCCUPATIONAL PROFILE: planter. PUBLIC CAREER. LEGISLATIVE SERVICE: Lower House, Harford County, 1774 (elected to the 3rd session in the first Harford County delegation); Conventions, Harford County, 1st, 1774, 3rd, 1774, 5th, 1775, 6th–8th, 1775–1776; Lower House, Harford County, 1777. LOCAL OFFICES: justice, Harford County, 1774–1800 (quorum, 1793–1800); justice, Orphans' Court, Harford County, 1777, 1784–at least 1794; judge, court of appeals, appointed under the Act to Procure Troops for the American Army, Harford County, appointed 1778. STANDS ON PUBLIC/PRIVATE ISSUES: directed that his slaves be manumitted under conditions specified in his will. WEALTH DURING LIFETIME. PERSONAL PROPERTY: assessed value £1,670.10 current money, including 16 slaves and 18 oz. plate, 1783. LAND AT FIRST ELECTION: 952 acres in Harford and Baltimore counties, plus 1 lot in Baltimore Town (at least 200 acres inherited from his grandfather in 1755; 422 acres and 1 lot in Baltimore Town acquired through his marriage). SIGNIFICANT CHANGES IN LAND BETWEEN FIRST ELECTION AND DEATH: in the early 1780s he sold his wife's lot in Baltimore Town and leased 4 lots on Fells Point, Baltimore Town. He inherited about 919 acres in Baltimore and Harford counties from his father in 1788. In two transactions in 1794 and 1795 Bond sold 1,275 acres in Harford and Baltimore counties and the 4 lots on Fells Point, which comprised the bulk of his estate, to his son Fell. Shortly before his death he sold another 96 acres of his home plantation in Harford County. WEALTH AT DEATH. DIED: buried on September 3, 1800, in St. John's Parish Cemetery, Harford County. LAND: probably 480 acres in Harford County.

BOND, WILLIAM, OF JOSHUA (ca. 1747–1788). BORN: ca. 1747 in Baltimore County; eldest son. NATIVE: fifth generation. RESIDED: in Bush River Lower Hundred, Harford County. FAMILY BACKGROUND. FATHER: Joshua Bond (?–1768), of Baltimore County; son of Thomas Bond (?–1755) and wife Ann Robisson (Robertson). MOTHER: Ann, daughter of Dr. Buckler Partridge (?–by 1757), of Baltimore County, and wife Jane (?–1761). UNCLE: *Jacob Bond* (ca. 1725–1780). BROTHERS: Buckler, who married Mary Stands-

bury; Thomas, who died a minor; and *James Bond* (ca. 1757–1803). SISTERS: Sarah (ca. 1746–?), who married Israel Morris; Ann (?–1784); Mary (ca. 1752–?); Elizabeth (ca. 1760–?); and Amelia (Pamela), who married William Wilson. FIRST COUSINS: *Thomas Bond, of Thomas* (?–1800); Ann, who married second, *James Giles* (1749/50–?); Catherine Fell, who married *Thomas Bond, of Thomas* (?–1800). OTHER KINSHIP: his great-grandfather was *Peter Bond* (?–1718). CHILDREN. Died without progeny. PRIVATE CAREER. EDUCATION: literate. RELIGIOUS AFFILIATION: had a strong Quaker background; his two sisters married Quakers. SOCIAL STATUS AND ACTIVITIES: Esq., 1783. OCCUPATIONAL PROFILE: a merchant, in partnership with his brother *James Bond* (ca. 1757–1803) by 1774, importing goods from London; by 1787 the firm was indebted to Alexander and William Contee, Prince George's County merchants, for over £1,658 sterling. PUBLIC CAREER. LEGISLATIVE SERVICE: Lower House, Harford County, 1778–1779 (Laws to Expire 2, 3). LOCAL OFFICES: justice, Harford County, 1777–at least 1782; justice, Orphans' Court, Harford County, appointed 1782. WEALTH DURING LIFETIME. PERSONAL PROPERTY: assessed value £156.13.4, including 4 oz. plate, 1783. LAND AT FIRST ELECTION: 370 acres in Harford County (inherited 250 acres from his father in 1768; 120 acres acquired as the result of the death of his younger brother Thomas). SIGNIFICANT CHANGES IN LAND BETWEEN FIRST ELECTION AND DEATH: in the early 1780s he purchased 250 acres in Harford County, plus 5 lots in Bel Air, Harford County. Just before his death Bond deeded his entire holdings to his brother *James Bond* (ca. 1757–1803), probably to secure it against his creditors. WEALTH AT DEATH. DIED: will probated on October 21, 1788, in Harford County. PERSONAL PROPERTY: TEV, at least £195.17.1, including a still and 10 beehives. LAND: none in his own name. ADDITIONAL COMMENTS: his principal heirs were his brothers.

BOND, ZACHARIAH (?–ca. 1776). BORN: in St. Mary's County before 1716, probably of age by 1733. NATIVE: at least second generation. RESIDED: in St. Mary's County. FAMILY BACKGROUND. FATHER: Zachariah Bond (?–1716). STEPFATHER: probably George Haskins. MOTHER: Ann. BROTHERS: Thomas (?–1740); Capt. John (?–1760), who married Elizabeth Attaway. SISTERS: Elizabeth, who married (first name unknown) Tennison. NEPHEW: *Thomas Bond* (?–ca. 1797). MARRIED Margaret. CHILDREN. At least one, a daughter who married *Henry Greenfield Sothoron* (ca.

1732–1793). **PRIVATE CAREER. EDUCATION**: literate. **RELIGIOUS AFFILIATION**: Anglican. **OCCUPATIONAL PROFILE**: planter; owned mills. **PUBLIC CAREER. LEGISLATIVE SERVICE**: Lower House, St. Mary's County, 1745, 1745/46–1748, 1749–1751 (election voided on June 10, 1749, because of illegal conduct of the sheriff at the election; reelected and seated; Bills of Credit Cv–3), 1751–1754 (Bills of Credit 1–6). **LOCAL OFFICES**: justice, St. Mary's County, 1746–at least 1764 (quorum, 1761–at least 1764); justice, Court of Oyer and Terminer and Gaol Delivery, St. Mary's County, commissioned 1768; trustee, St. Mary's County Free School, in office 1772. **MILITARY SERVICE**: captain, by 1758; major, by 1768. **WEALTH DURING LIFETIME. LAND AT FIRST ELECTION**: probably 200 acres in St. Mary's County. **SIGNIFICANT CHANGES IN LAND BETWEEN FIRST ELECTION AND DEATH**: purchased 162 acres in St. Mary's County in the 1750s and patented an additional 1,011 acres in St. Mary's County in 1768. **WEALTH AT DEATH. DIED**: will probated on February 1, 1776, in St. Mary's County. **LAND**: probably ca. 1,500 acres in St. Mary's County.

BOOTHBY, EDWARD (?–1698). **IMMIGRATED**: by 1685 as a free adult. **RESIDED**: in St. Mary's County; Spesutia Hundred, Baltimore County, by 1691. **MARRIED** in 1693/94 Elizabeth, widow of both *Nathaniel Utie* (ca. 1635–ca. 1675/76) and *Henry Johnson* (?–1690/91); daughter of John Carter, Esq., of Lancaster County, Virginia. **CHILDREN. STEPSON**: Joseph Johnson. **DAUGHTER**: Frances. **PRIVATE CAREER. EDUCATION**: literate. **RELIGIOUS AFFILIATION**: Protestant. **SOCIAL STATUS AND ACTIVITIES**: a very active attorney in the Baltimore County Court in 1691; Gent., by 1696. **OCCUPATIONAL PROFILE**: placeman; attorney, admitted to the Baltimore County Court in the early 1690s. **PUBLIC CAREER. LEGISLATIVE SERVICE**: Lower House, Baltimore County, 1692–1693 (Laws 1; Aggrievances 2), 1694–1697 (Laws 3–8). **OTHER PROVINCIAL OFFICES**: clerk, Secretary's Office and Provincial Court, 1686–1687/88; agent to Pennsylvania on Indian affairs, 1697. **LOCAL OFFICES**: deputy commissary, Baltimore County, serving in 1693; justice, Baltimore County, 1694–1698 (quorum). **WEALTH DURING LIFETIME. PERSONAL PROPERTY**: 2 slaves, 1694 and 1696; 1 slave in a household of 7 taxables, 1695. **LAND AT FIRST ELECTION**: ca. 700 acres; patented 900 additional acres in 1695. **WEALTH AT DEATH. DIED**: on December 12, 1698. **PERSONAL PROPERTY**: TEV, £755.13.2 sterling (including 1 slave and 4 ser-

vants); FB, estate overpaid £1.0.0. **LAND**: ca. 1,600 acres.

BORDLEY, JAMES (?–ca. 1793). **BORN**: of age by 1769. **IMMIGRATED**: probably. **RESIDED**: on a farm on a branch of Corsica Creek, Queen Anne's County. **MARRIED** by May 1769 Mary Ann (1742–?), widow of Philemon Charles Blake (?–1765), of Queen Anne's County; daughter of *William Hopper* (1707–1772); stepdaughter of Sarah Dockery Hopper; niece of both Anne Wright, who married *Edward Oldham* (1709–1773) and *Thomas Wright* (?–ca. 1784). Her brother was *William Hopper* (by 1747–1806). Her half sister was Elizabeth Hopper (1739–1806), who married *Joseph Nicholson, Jr.* (?–1786). Her first cousins were Ann Oldham (?–by 1794), who married *Joshua Clarke* (?–1781); Elizabeth Oldham (?–by 1776), who married *William Hopper* (by 1747–1806); Hannah Oldham (?–1828), who married *Nicholas Martin* (1743–ca. 1808); and *Samuel Turbutt Wright* (1749–1810). **CHILDREN. SONS**: James; William Hopper, who married Deborah, daughter of John Fisher; and John Wesley. **STEPSONS**: Philemon Charles Blake (ca. 1763–?); William Hopper Blake (ca. 1764–?). **DAUGHTERS**: Alice, who married Christopher Cox; Ann; and Maria. **PRIVATE CAREER. EDUCATION**: literate. **RELIGIOUS AFFILIATION**: Anglican; probably converted to Methodism. **SOCIAL STATUS AND ACTIVITIES**: Gent., by 1774. **OCCUPATIONAL PROFILE**: probably a planter. **PUBLIC CAREER. LEGISLATIVE SERVICE**: Lower House, Queen Anne's County, 1777, 1778–1779 (Grievances 1; Tax Commissioners 1; Manufactories 1). **LOCAL OFFICES**: St. Paul's Parish Vestry, Queen Anne's County, in office 1769, 1781–1783; register, St. Paul's Parish Vestry, Queen Anne's County, in office 1771; justice, Queen Anne's County, 1773–at least 1786; Committee of Correspondence, Queen Anne's County, elected 1774; justice, Orphans' Court, Queen Anne's County, 1778–at least 1786. **MILITARY SERVICE**: captain of a company of Queen Anne's County Militia of the Twentieth Battalion, 1776. **STANDS ON PUBLIC/-PRIVATE ISSUES**: refused to acknowledge the validity of appointments of militia officers by the Convention, 1776. Bordley manumitted all of his slaves after various terms of service between 1785 and 1792 and gave one of his slaves an acre of ground, rent free for life. **WEALTH DURING LIFETIME. PERSONAL PROPERTY**: assessed value £1,252.0.0, including 21 slaves and at least 12 oz. plate, 1783. **LAND AT FIRST ELECTION**: 852 acres in Queen Anne's County (all by purchase). **SIGNIFICANT CHANGES IN LAND BETWEEN FIRST ELEC-**

TION AND DEATH: bought at least 224 additional acres in Queen Anne's County between 1779 and 1785. WEALTH AT DEATH. DIED: will probated on February 5, 1793, in Queen Anne's County. PERSONAL PROPERTY: TEV, £749.1.3 current money (including 2 Negroes and 7 other servants with various terms of service remaining, 30 oz. plate, and books); FB, £372.6.2. LAND: 1,090 acres in Queen Anne's County.

BORDLEY, JOHN BEALE (1726/27–1804). BORN: on February 11, 1726/27, in Annapolis, Anne Arundel County; youngest son. NATIVE: second generation. RESIDED: in Joppa Town, Baltimore County, in the 1750s; Baltimore Town, 1766; "The Vineyards," Wye Island, Queen Anne's County, 1770; Philadelphia, Pennsylvania, 1791 until death. FAMILY BACKGROUND. FATHER: *Thomas Bordley* (ca. 1683–1726). STEPFATHER: *Edmund Jennings* (?–1756). MOTHER: Ariana (1690–1741), widow of *James Frisby* (1684–1719); daughter of *Matthias Vanderheyden* (?–1729). HALF UNCLE: *Henry Ward* (?–1734). AUNTS: Francina Vanderheyden, who married second, *Charles Hynson* (1692–1748); Augustina Vanderheyden (?–1775), who married *James Harris* (1682–1743). BROTHERS: Thomas (ca. 1724–1748); Matthias (1725–1756). HALF BROTHERS, PATERNAL: *Stephen Bordley* (ca. 1710–1764); William (1714–1762); John (?–1718); and John (1721–1761). HALF BROTHERS, MATERNAL: Peter Jennings (1729–by 1737); Edmund Jennings (1731–1819); and (first name unknown) Jennings (?–by 1737). HALF SISTERS, PATERNAL: Elizabeth (1716/17–1789); Margaret (1719–by 1726/27); and Mary (1722–1722). HALF SISTERS, MATERNAL: Sarah Frisby (1714–1782); Ariana Margaret Frisby (1717–?), who married *William Harris* (1704–1748); Francesca Augustina Frisby (1719–1766); and Ariana Jennings (1730–?). FIRST COUSIN: *Matthias Harris* (1718–1773). ADDITIONAL COMMENTS: his father's first wife was Rachel Beard (?–1722). MARRIED first, in 1751 Margaret (?–1773), daughter of Samuel Chew (ca. 1704–1736/37) and wife Henrietta Maria Lloyd (?–1765); stepdaughter of *Daniel Dulany* (1685–1753); granddaughter of *Philemon Lloyd* (ca. 1674–1732/33). Her brothers were *Samuel Chew* (by 1734–1786); Bennett (?–1793), who married Anna Maria, daughter of *Edward Tilghman* (1713–1786); and Philemon Lloyd (?–1770). Her stepbrothers were *Daniel Dulany, Jr.* (1722–1797); *Walter Dulany* (?–1773). Her sisters were Henrietta Maria (1731–1762), who married *Edward Dorsey* (1718–1760); Ann Mary (?–1774), who married *William Paca* (1740–1799).

Her stepsister was Margaret Dulany, who married first, *Alexander Hamilton* (1712–1756), and second, *William Murdock* (?–1769). Her niece was Henrietta Maria Chew (1759–1847), who married *Benjamin Galloway* (1752–1831). MARRIED second, on October 8, 1776, Sarah Fishbourne, widow of John Mifflin, of Philadelphia, Pennsylvania. CHILDREN. SONS: Matthias, of Wye Island, Queen Anne's County; John, of Kent County, a farmer. STEPSON: John F. Mifflin, of Philadelphia, Pennsylvania. DAUGHTERS: Henrietta Maria, who married John Ross, of Bladensburg, Prince George's County; Elizabeth, who married James Gibson, of Philadelphia, Pennsylvania. PRIVATE CAREER. EDUCATION: had approximately two years of schooling under Rev. Charles Peale in Chestertown, Kent County; studied law under his half brother *Stephen Bordley* (ca. 1710–1764) in Annapolis from 1744 to 1749. RELIGIOUS AFFILIATION: Anglican. SOCIAL STATUS AND ACTIVITIES: Esq. at death; member of the Tuesday Club in Annapolis in the 1750s; elected to the American Philosophical Society, 1783; founded the Philadelphia Society for Promoting Agriculture, 1785. ADDITIONAL COMMENTS: When Bordley was ten years old his mother Ariana departed for England with her third husband *Edmund Jennings* (?–1756), leaving Bordley in the care of his uncle *Charles Hynson* (1692–1748) and his wife Francina Vanderheyden. Bordley read extensively in the natural sciences and philosophy, and enjoyed mathematics and landscape painting in his leisure time. He published many books and pamphlets, among which were *A Summary View of Courses of Crops in the Husbandry of England and Maryland* (Philadelphia, 1784), *Yellow Fever* (Philadelphia, 1793), *Money, Coins, Weights and Measures* (1789), *National Credit and Character* (1790), and *Essays and Notes on Husbandry and Rural Affairs* (Philadelphia, 1799; 2nd ed., Philadelphia, 1801). He also wrote on diet, conservation, lead poisoning, and was an experimental agriculturalist, amateur mathematician, and animal breeder. He ran a self-sufficient farm with livestock, brick kilns, a brew house, and a windmill. He produced his own salt, gunpowder, and fabric. OCCUPATIONAL PROFILE: lawyer, 1750 until approximately 1770, admitted to the following courts: Cecil County by March 1757, also Harford and Baltimore counties. Merchant, 1751; planter and agronomist from approximately 1770, when his first wife inherited Wye Island, Queen Anne's County; officeholder, 1753–1775. PUBLIC CAREER. LEGISLATIVE SERVICE: Upper House, 1768–1770, 1771, 1773–1774. OTHER PROVINCIAL/STATE OFFICES: judge, Provincial

Court, 1766–1776 (quorum, 1766 and 1773); judge, Admiralty Court, 1767–1776; judge, Assize Court, Western Shore, 1767–1768; judge, Assize Court, Eastern Shore, appointed 1768; commissioner to run a boundary line between Maryland and Delaware, appointed 1768; Council, 1768–at least 1774 (appointed and qualified on May 24, 1768); 1st Council of Safety, Eastern Shore, 1775 (declined); judge, General Court, appointed 1777. LOCAL OFFICES: clerk, Baltimore County, 1753–1775 (resigned); commissioner, Baltimore Town, in office 1768. OUT OF STATE SERVICE: appointed by President Washington as a commissioner to receive subscriptions to the Bank of the United States, 1791. STANDS ON PUBLIC/PRIVATE ISSUES: opposed jailing debtors; against intemperance; condemned slavery on three points: first, because it was contrary to Lockeian principles of equality; second, because it was often accompanied by a "scandalous lack of decency"; and third, because it was not good for agriculture because a farmer became a "slave to his slaves." Bordley manumitted many of his own slaves or bound them out as apprentices. After he declined to serve on the Council of Safety on August 29, 1775, he said that "The few who realy [*sic*] know my Sentiments, my Principles, Feelings will not doubt of my Fidelity to the interests of my country; and that, as an individual, in such sorts as is within the reach of my talents every power will be exerted to that end." Although he retired from politics, he continued to support the Revolution. WEALTH DURING LIFE-TIME. PERSONAL PROPERTY: assessed value £6,044.6.8, including 162 slaves and 314 oz. plate, Queen Anne's, Talbot, and Kent counties, 1783; 128 slaves, Queen Anne's County, 1790. LAND AT FIRST ELECTION: 8,498 acres in Baltimore, Frederick, Kent, and Anne Arundel counties (inherited at least 1,874 acres from his father, and at least 4,463 acres from his brothers). SIGNIFICANT CHANGES IN LAND BETWEEN FIRST ELECTION AND DEATH: acquired at least 1,400 acres of land that his wife had inherited from her brother in Queen Anne's County through his first marriage, 1770; owned a total of at least 8,497 acres in Anne Arundel, Cecil, Harford, Kent, Montgomery, and Queen Anne's counties, plus 5 lots in Annapolis, 1783; there is evidence that Bordley gave large portions of his estate to his sons John and Matthias between 1783 and his death. Between 1783 and his death he also signed several "deeds of intent to sell" for large tracts in Harford and Montgomery counties and instructed that these deeds be confirmed by his executors. WEALTH AT DEATH. DIED: on January 26, 1804, in Philadelphia, Pennsylva-

nia. LAND: acreage could not be determined, but Bordley owned at least 1,500 acres in Maryland, plus lands on Bear Creek and in Chester County, Pennsylvania, lots in Baltimore City and Annapolis, and a stable and house on Union Street, Philadelphia, Pennsylvania.

BORDLEY, STEPHEN (ca. 1710–1764). BORN: ca. 1710 in Annapolis, Anne Arundel County; eldest son. NATIVE: second generation. RESIDED: in Annapolis, where he lived with his sister Elizabeth in the family home, now called the Bordley-Randall House. FAMILY BACKGROUND. FATHER: *Thomas Bordley* (ca. 1683–1726). MOTHER: Rachel (?–1722), daughter of Richard Beard (ca. 1648–1703), a surveyor; granddaughter of *Richard Beard* (?–1681). STEPMOTHER: Ariana (1690–1741), widow of *James Frisby* (1684–1719); daughter of *Matthias Vanderheyden* (?–1729). She subsequently married *Edmund Jennings* (?–1756). STEP-AUNTS: Francina Vanderheyden, who married second, *Charles Hynson* (1692–1748); Augustina Vanderheyden (?–1775), who married *James Harris* (1682–1743). BROTHERS: William (1714–1762); John (?–1718); and John (1721–1761). HALF BROTHERS: Thomas (ca. 1724–1748); Matthias (1725–1756); and *John Beale Bordley* (1726/27–1804). STEPBROTHERS: Peter Jennings (1729–by 1737); Edmund Jennings (1731–1819); and (first name unknown) Jennings (?–by 1737). SISTERS: Elizabeth (1716/17–1789); Margaret (1719–by 1726/27); and Mary (1722–1722). STEP-SISTERS: Sarah Frisby (1714–1782); Ariana Margaret Frisby (1717–?), who married *William Harris* (1704–1748); Francesca Augustina Frisby (1719–1766); and Ariana Jennings (1730–?). MARRIED never. PRIVATE CAREER. EDUCATION: attended school in Blackheath, London, England; served law apprenticeship in London, England; admitted to the Inner Temple in November 1729 and returned to Maryland in 1733. RELIGIOUS AFFILIATION: Anglican, St. Anne's Parish, Anne Arundel County. SOCIAL STATUS AND ACTIVITIES: Hon., at death; member of the Tuesday Club, Annapolis. OCCUPATIONAL PROFILE: lawyer, admitted to the following courts: Anne Arundel County in June 1733; Prince George's County in June 1733; Baltimore County in August 1733; Provincial Court in October 1739; Court of Chancery by October 1741; Frederick County in March 1748/49; Kent County by March 1753; trained apprentices in his Annapolis law office. PUBLIC CAREER. LEGISLATIVE SERVICE: Lower House, Annapolis, 1745 (Laws), Anne Arundel County, 1749–1751 (Laws Cv-3), Annapolis, 1754–1756 (Laws 1–4; discharged at the beginning of the 5th session for serving as attorney general and naval officer of the Port of Annapolis since the close of the 4th session); Upper House, 1759–1761 (appointed before the 2nd convention), 1762–1763. OTHER PROVINCIAL OFFICES: naval officer, Annapolis, 1755–1762; attorney general, 1756–1763; Council, 1759–1764 (appointed and qualified on April 4, 1759); commissary general, 1762–1764. LOCAL OFFICES: churchwarden, St. Anne's Parish, Anne Arundel County, elected April 1734 (left province by August 1734); St. Anne's Parish Vestry, Anne Arundel County, 1742–1745; common councilman, Annapolis, 1754–1755, 1757–1760; alderman, Annapolis, 1760–1763; mayor, Annapolis, 1761 (elected to fill vacancy), 1764. WEALTH DURING LIFETIME. LAND AT FIRST ELECTION: 1,710 acres in Annapolis and Anne Arundel County, including lots in Annapolis (the remainder of 1,810 acres and lots inherited from his father). SIGNIFICANT CHANGES IN LAND BETWEEN FIRST ELECTION AND DEATH: controlled 1 lot in Annapolis for his sister Elizabeth by 1753; sold 1,340 acres in Anne Arundel County, 1759; administered 2,057 acres in Kent County, which his brother John left to his half brother *John Beale Bordley* (1726/27–1804) between 1762 and 1764. WEALTH AT DEATH. DIED: on Thursday evening, December 6, 1764, at his home in Annapolis; in the summer of 1763 he had suffered a stroke, and by the fall of 1764 he was virtually an invalid. PERSONAL PROPERTY: requested no appraisal of his estate; in his will, he mentioned that his debts were small and few; had an extensive library of law and miscellaneous titles. LAND: 370 acres in Annapolis and Anne Arundel County, including lots in Annapolis.

BORDLEY, STEPHEN (ca. 1734–1771). BORN: ca. 1734 in St. Paul's Parish, Kent County; eldest son. NATIVE: third generation. RESIDED: in Chestertown, Kent County. FAMILY BACKGROUND. FATHER: Thomas Bordley (?–1752), of Kent County; son of immigrant, Rev. Stephen Bordley, of Kent County. MOTHER: Ann Miller. BROTHERS: William (1741–?); Arthur (1743–?); and Thomas (?–1749). SISTERS: Sarah; Mary (1746–?). OTHER KINSHIP: his great-uncle was *Thomas Bordley* (ca. 1683–1726); his second cousins were *Stephen Bordley* (ca. 1710–1764) and *John Beale Bordley* (1726/27–1804). MARRIED by 1768 possibly Hannah, daughter of Thomas Bowers, yeoman, of Kent County. CHILDREN. Probably died without progeny. PRIVATE CAREER. EDUCATION: trained as a lawyer. RELIGIOUS AFFILIATION: Anglican, Chester Parish, Kent County. SOCIAL STATUS

AND ACTIVITIES: Gent., 1764. OCCUPATIONAL PROFILE: lawyer, admitted to the following courts: Annapolis Mayor's Court in 1753; Provincial Court in October 1756; Queen Anne's County in November 1757; Kent County by March 1759; Cecil County by June 1760. PUBLIC CAREER. LEGISLATIVE SERVICE: Lower House, Kent County, 1768–1770 (Grievances 1–3; Public Offices 1; Elections 3), 1771 (elected, but died before attending). LOCAL OFFICE: clerk of Indictments, Cecil County, in office 1760. WEALTH DURING LIFETIME. LAND AT FIRST ELECTION: 1,305 acres in Kent County. SIGNIFICANT CHANGES IN LAND BETWEEN FIRST ELECTION AND DEATH: disposed of interest in 1,134 acres and purchased an additional 229 acres in Kent County, plus 1.5 lots in Chestertown, Kent County. WEALTH AT DEATH. DIED: administration bond filed on September 20, 1771, in Kent County. PERSONAL PROPERTY: TEV, £830.1.7 current money (including 7 slaves and 56 books); FB, £357.13.7. LAND: probably ca. 400 acres in Kent County, plus 1.5 lots in Chestertown, Kent County.

BORDLEY, THOMAS (ca. 1683–1726). BORN: ca. 1683 in Yorkshire, England; youngest son. IMMIGRATED: in 1694 as a minor with his brother from England. RESIDED: in Kent County; Annapolis, Anne Arundel County, by 1704. FAMILY BACKGROUND. FATHER: Rev. Stephen Bordley, who received an M.A. from Cambridge University in 1689; prebendary of St. Paul's, London, England. BROTHER: Rev. Stephen Bordley (ca. 1675–1709), a rector in Maryland from 1694 to 1709, who married Anne, daughter of *John Hynson* (?–1705). SISTERS: Mary; Elizabeth. MARRIED first, in December 1708 Rachel (?–1722), daughter of Richard Beard (ca. 1648–1703), of Annapolis. MARRIED second, in September 1723 Ariana (1690–1741), who died in England after a smallpox inoculation, widow of *James Frisby* (1684–1719); daughter of *Matthias Vanderheyden* (?–1729). She subsequently married *Edmund Jennings* (?–1756). Her half brother was *Henry Ward* (?–1734). Her sisters were Jane; Francina; and Augustina, who married *James Harris* (1682–1743). CHILDREN. SONS: *Stephen Bordley* (ca. 1710–1764); William (1714–1762), of Cecil County, who married (first name unknown) Pearce; John; Thomas; Mathias; and *John Beale Bordley* (1726/27–1804), who married first, ca. 1750 Margaret (?–1773), daughter of Samuel Chew, and second, in 1776 Sarah Mifflin, of Philadelphia. DAUGHTER: Elizabeth. PRIVATE CAREER. EDUCATION: literate; studied law in Annapolis.

RELIGIOUS AFFILIATION: Anglican; his grandfather, father, and brother were Anglican clergymen. SOCIAL STATUS AND ACTIVITIES: he visited England on several occasions, most importantly in 1715; he was a close ally of Gov. John Hart, who bestowed considerable patronage on him; he was a patron of the poet Ebenezer Cooke, who wrote "An Elegy on the Death of Thomas Bordley, Esq." OCCUPATIONAL PROFILE: placeman, by 1703–1721; became a leading lawyer in the colony, admitted to the following courts: Provincial Court in 1704; Anne Arundel County Court in 1709; Court of Chancery by 1712; Prince George's County Court in 1712. PUBLIC CAREER. LEGISLATIVE SERVICE: Lower House, Annapolis, 1708B–1711 (Accounts 2–4), Anne Arundel County, 1715 (Laws), Annapolis, 1716–1718 (Laws 1–3), 1719 (Laws 1; appointed to Council between the 1st and 2nd sessions); Upper House, 1720–1721 (appointed by the 2nd session; discharged by the 5th session); Lower House, Anne Arundel County, 1722–1724 (Laws 1; Aggrievances 3); 1725–1726 (Laws 1–3: Aggrievances 1–3; died before the 4th session). OTHER PROVINCIAL OFFICES: clerk, Secretary's Office and Provincial Court, 1703–1707; clerk, Committees of the Lower House, 1704, 1706, 1714; clerk, Prerogative Office, 1708–1712; surveyor general, Western Shore, 1717–1718; attorney general, 1718–1721; commissary general, 1718–1721; Council, April 1720–September 1721. LOCAL OFFICES: clerk, Anne Arundel County, 1703–1708; St. Anne's Parish Vestry, Anne Arundel County, 1712–1715, 1718–1722; recorder, Annapolis, 1721–1726. STANDS ON PUBLIC/PRIVATE ISSUES: acquitted in 1704 by the Lower House of a charge of contempt for his refusal while clerk of Anne Arundel County to release the county's book of laws; removed from the Anne Arundel County clerkship in 1708 by *Philemon Lloyd* (ca. 1674–1732/33), for which Bordley went to court in an attempt to regain the office; he became a leader of the popular or "country" party against the proprietary interests in the early 1720s; he incurred the anger of Charles Calvert in 1721, which brought his dismissal from the Council; he espoused publicizing the action of the Assembly by printing the legislative proceedings; he edited *The Charter of Maryland, Together with the Debates and Proceedings of the. . . Assembly. . .1722, 1723, 1724* (Philadelphia, 1725), and was instrumental in bringing the printer William Parks to Annapolis in 1726. WEALTH DURING LIFETIME. LAND AT FIRST ELECTION: at least 500 acres. WEALTH AT DEATH. DIED: on October 11, 1726, in England. PERSONAL PROPERTY: FB, £3,179.14.8 sterling,

£1,964.17.3 current money (including 19 slaves, 6 servants, and 100 law books). LAND: over 7,500 acres.

BOREMAN (BOARMAN), WILLIAM (ca. 1630–1709). BORN: probably in England. IMMIGRATED: by 1645 as a free adult. RESIDED: in St. Mary's County. MARRIED first, by 1651 Sarah (?–ca. 1669). MARRIED second, Mary, daughter of *Thomas Mathews* (ca. 1622–1675/76). MARRIED third, Mary, daughter of *John Jarbo* (1619–1674/75). She subsequently married by 1712 John Sanders. CHILDREN. SONS: William, Jr. (1654–1720), a justice of St. Mary's County from 1679 to 1689, who married first, Jane, daughter of *James Neale* (ca. 1615–1684), and second, Mary, daughter of *Joseph Pile* (?–1692); Francis Ignatius; John Baptiste (1687–?), who married Elizabeth Edelen; and Benedict Leonard (1687–?), who married Ann. DAUGHTERS: Mary, who married first, John Gardiner, son of *Luke Gardiner* (1622–1674), and second, Gerard Slye (1654–by 1703), son of *Robert Slye* (ca. 1628–1670/71); Anne, who married Leonard Brooke (?–1718), son of *Baker Brooke* (1628–1678/79); Elizabeth, who married (first name unknown) Hammersly; Clare, who married first, Richard Brooke, and second, Richard Shirbin; Mary, who married Robert Greene, son of *Thomas Greene* (?–ca. 1651/52); and Sarah, who married first, Thomas Mathews (?–1676/77), son of *Thomas Mathews* (ca. 1622–1675/76), and second, Thomas Mudd. PRIVATE CAREER. EDUCATION: literate. RELIGIOUS AFFILIATION: Catholic. SOCIAL STATUS AND ACTIVITIES: low status on arrival; no land until the late 1650s; Gent., by 1665. OCCUPATIONAL PROFILE: a mariner in the 1640s; planter; Indian trader; land speculator. PUBLIC CAREER. LEGISLATIVE SERVICE: Lower House, St. Mary's County, 1671–1674/75 (Laws 4). LOCAL OFFICES: justice, St. Mary's County, 1663/64–1664, 1666–1668, 1675/76–1679 (quorum, 1675/76–1679); coroner, St. Mary's County, 1671; sheriff, St. Mary's County, 1679–1683. MILITARY SERVICE: captain, 1661; major, by 1676. STANDS ON PUBLIC/PRIVATE ISSUES: closely allied with the Calverts; fined 1,000 pounds of tobacco in 1656 for supporting the Calverts at the Battle of the Severn; rewarded for his support with extensive patronage in the 1660s. WEALTH DURING LIFETIME. LAND AT FIRST ELECTION: ca. 3,000 acres, 1671; 5,117 acres by 1673; 6,050 acres by 1675. WEALTH AT DEATH. DIED: by July 11, 1709. PERSONAL PROPERTY: TEV, £332.4.0 sterling (including 8 slaves and 1 servant); FB, £273.10.10. LAND: probably 7,500 acres.

BOTELER (BUTLER), JOHN (ca. 1601–1642). BORN: ca. 1601, probably in Kent, England. IMMIGRATED: in 1635 as a free adult. RESIDED: on Kent Island. FAMILY BACKGROUND. FATHER: John Boteler, of Roswell, Essex, England. MOTHER: Jane Elliott. UNCLE: Capt. Nathaniel Boteler, governor of Bermuda and of Providence Island. BROTHER: Thomas Boteler, who married Joan Mountstephen. SISTER: Elizabeth (ca. 1611–after 1668), who married in 1635 *William Claiborne* (1600–ca. 1677). PRIVATE CAREER. RELIGIOUS AFFILIATION: probably a Protestant. OCCUPATIONAL PROFILE: planter. PUBLIC CAREER. LEGISLATIVE SERVICE: Assembly, special writ, 1638/39 (apparently never attended). LOCAL OFFICES: justice, Kent County, 1639/40. MILITARY SERVICE: captain, 1638. STANDS ON PUBLIC/PRIVATE ISSUES: he was a leader of Claiborne's forces on Kent Island, 1638; he was captured by Leonard Calvert's men, and was later urged by Calvert to join the proprietary party. WEALTH DURING LIFETIME. LAND AT FIRST ELECTION: surveyed 200 acres, 1640. WEALTH AT DEATH. DIED: ca. April 1642; size of estate unknown.

BOUGHTON, RICHARD (?–1706). IMMIGRATED: in 1666 as a free adult, possibly from Virginia. RESIDED: in Nanjemoy, Charles County. FAMILY BACKGROUND. FATHER: possibly either Thomas Boughton, armiger of Bilton, Warwickshire, England, who attended Gray's Inn in 1647/48, or Richard Boughton, of Lewes, Sussex, England. UNCLE: *William Stone* (ca. 1603–ca. 1659/60). MARRIED first, in 1667 Verlinda (?–by 1694), widow of Thomas Burdett; daughter of Rev. William Cotton, of Lower Accomack County, Virginia. MARRIED second, by March 1694 Honor. CHILDREN. SON: Samuel. DAUGHTERS: Katherine; Verlinda; and Mary. PRIVATE CAREER. EDUCATION: literate; had clerical skills; may have attended Gray's Inn or Lincoln's Inn. RELIGIOUS AFFILIATION: Protestant. SOCIAL STATUS AND ACTIVITIES: may have been distantly related to the proprietary family; early preferment seems to have come from his education and family connections, but he failed to maintain his position; Gent., 1666/67; accused of dishonesty and temporarily lost his positions in 1669. OCCUPATIONAL PROFILE: placeman; attorney, admitted to the following courts: Provincial Court in 1666/67; Charles County in 1670. PUBLIC CAREER. LEGISLATIVE SERVICE: Lower House, Charles County, 1669 (Aggrievances). OTHER PROVINCIAL OFFICES: Council, 1666–1666/67; justice, Provincial Court, 1666; secretary and judge of Probate, 1666–

1667; clerk, Upper House, 1674–1676. LOCAL OFFICES: clerk, Charles County, 1667–1669, 1682–1689/90, Anne Arundel County, 1674–1682; registrar, Nanjemoy Parish, Charles County, 1700; deputy commissary, Charles County, 1704. STANDS ON PUBLIC/PRIVATE ISSUES: opposition to the revolution of 1689 brought his dismissal from the Charles County clerkship and virtually terminated his political career. WEALTH DURING LIFETIME. ANNUAL INCOME: in February 1670/71 he was in debtor's prison. His debts included money owed for drinks consumed at his first wedding. LAND AT FIRST ELECTION: no evidence of landownership while a burgess or councilor. SIGNIFICANT CHANGES IN LAND BETWEEN FIRST ELECTION AND DEATH: patented 950 acres in 1679, but he sold it in 1684; acquired 100 acres in 1684, which he sold in 1690; took a 21-year lease on 400 acres in 1684. WEALTH AT DEATH. DIED: in 1706. PERSONAL PROPERTY: TEV, £16.4.4 sterling, plus 1,420 pounds of tobacco.

BOWIE, ALLEN, JR. (1737–1803). BORN: in 1737 in Prince George's County; probably eldest son. NATIVE: third generation. RESIDED: at the "Hermitage," Lower District, Frederick County (later became part of Montgomery County). FAMILY BACKGROUND. FATHER: John Bowie, Jr. (1708–1753), of "Thorpeland," Prince George's County; son of John, the immigrant. STEPFATHER: Thomas Cramphin (?–1783). MOTHER: Elizabeth Pottinger (?–by 1777). UNCLE: *William Bowie* (1721–1791). BROTHERS: James; Rev. John (1744–?), who married Margaret Dallas. HALF BROTHERS: William Bowie, Jr., who married Rachel Pottinger; Robert Cramphin; Basil Cramphin; and Richard Cramphin (1760–?). STEPBROTHER: *Thomas Cramphin, Jr.* (ca. 1740–ca. 1831). HALF SISTER: Mary Bowie, who married James Magruder. STEPSISTER: Ruth Cramphin (1742–1812). FIRST COUSINS: *Walter Bowie* (1748–1810); *Robert Bowie* (ca. 1750–1818); and *Fielder Bowie* (ca. 1745–1794). ADDITIONAL COMMENTS: Bowie's father John had previously married Mary (?–by 1735), daughter of William Offet and wife Mary. MARRIED in 1766 his stepsister Ruth (1742–1812), daughter of Thomas Cramphin (?–1783) and wife Mary Jackson. Her brother was *Thomas Cramphin, Jr.* (ca. 1740–ca. 1831). CHILDREN. SONS: Thomas (1767–?), of Bladensburg, Prince George's County; John (?–1825), who inherited the "Hermitage," his father's dwelling plantation, and who served as a physician in the War of 1812, he never married; Washington (1776–1826), a godson of George Washington (1731/32–1799) and a merchant in Georgetown, D.C., who married in 1799 Margaret Crable (?–1840), widow of Thomas Johns Chew; Allen (1778–1782); and Richard. DAUGHTERS: Elizabeth (1772–?), who married Thomas Davis; Mary (1774–1800); and Hannah (1780–1782). **PRIVATE CAREER. EDUCATION**: literate. RELIGIOUS AFFILIATION: Anglican, Prince George's Parish, Montgomery County. OCCUPATIONAL PROFILE: planter; a merchant, in partnership with his stepbrother *Thomas Cramphin, Jr.* (ca. 1740–ca. 1831) and Richard Wooten under the name "Allen Bowie and Company." The firm had substantial financial resources that the partners utilized principally in loaning money and dealing in real estate during the Revolution. **PUBLIC CAREER**. LEGISLATIVE SERVICE: Convention, Frederick County, 1st, 1774. LOCAL OFFICES: justice, Montgomery County, commissioned 1777, 1785, 1788, and 1794–at least 1800; commissioner of tax, Montgomery County, 1785–1786, 1798; Levy Court, Montgomery County, 1799–1800. MILITARY SERVICE: captain, 1776; colonel, 1780. **WEALTH DURING LIFETIME. PERSONAL PROPERTY**: 30 slaves, 1790. LAND AT FIRST ELECTION: 1,489 acres in Frederick County (603 acres inherited from his father; 350 acres belonged to his brother James, but were under his control in 1769; 537 acres by personal acquisition). ADDITIONAL COMMENTS: his father, John Bowie, Jr., purchased 2,000 acres in Frederick County in 1747, naming the plantation the "Hermitage" after an old land grant. He built a brick dwelling on the tract for his son Allen, who was then a minor. His father continued living at "Thorpeland" until his death. Part of the tract on which the "Hermitage" was built was devised to Allen, who moved there when he came of age. SIGNIFICANT CHANGES IN LAND BETWEEN FIRST ELECTION AND DEATH: purchased 2,035 acres and sold 167 acres in Montgomery County, 1778–1794. **WEALTH AT DEATH**. DIED: in May 1803; buried in Prince George's Parish, Montgomery County. LAND: owned 1,869 acres in Montgomery County in 1794; no other land transactions found after that date.

BOWIE, FIELDER (ca. 1745–1794). BORN: ca. 1745 at "Brookridge," near Nottingham, Prince George's County; elder son. NATIVE: third generation. RESIDED: in the town of Nottingham, Prince George's County. **FAMILY BACKGROUND. FATHER**: Allen Bowie, Sr., Gent. (1719–1783), justice of the peace in Prince George's County from 1752 to 1754; inspector of tobacco, Marlborough warehouse in 1757; son of John Bowie, Sr. (ca. 1688–1759). MOTHER: Priscilla (?–1747), widow of Capt.

William Finch, a mariner and London shipowner. STEPMOTHER: Ann (1718–1779), daughter of Rev. John Fraser (?–1742), rector of King George's Parish, Prince George's County, and wife Ann Blyzard. UNCLE: *William Bowie* (1721–1791). STEPUNCLE: *George Fraser* (?–1764). STEPAUNT: Susannah Fraser, who married *John Hawkins, Jr.* (1713–1757). HALF BROTHER, PATERNAL: John Fraser Bowie. HALF SISTERS, PATERNAL: Susannah Fraser Bowie (1749–?), who married Matthew Eversfield (1742–1798), son of Rev. John Eversfield (ca. 1701–1780); Priscilla Bowie (1750–1786), who married *Thomas Duckett* (1744–1806); and Anne Bowie (1751–1782), who married Lt. John Smith Brookes. HALF SISTER, MATERNAL: Phoebe Finch, who married Mordecai Smith (1737–?), of Calvert County, son of Nathan Smith and wife Cassandra. FIRST COUSINS: *Allen Bowie, Jr.* (1737–1803); *Walter Bowie* (1748–1810); and *Robert Bowie* (ca. 1750–1818). MARRIED ca. 1765 Elizabeth Clagett (1745–1794), who was buried at "Brookridge," Prince George's County; daughter of Rev. John Eversfield (ca. 1701–1780), who immigrated from England in 1728, was the rector of St. Paul's Parish, Prince George's County from 1728 to 1780, and an outspoken Tory whose property was confiscated during the Revolution, but was ultimately returned to him and his wife Eleanor Clagett; granddaughter of Richard Clagett, Sr. (ca. 1681–1752) and wife Deborah Dorsey. Her brothers were John (1731–?), who was educated for the ministry at Oxford University, England, but died on his return voyage to America, leaving a widow and one daughter; Matthew (1742–1798), who married Susanna Fraser (1749–?), daughter of Allen Bowie, Sr. (1719–1783); Charles (1750–ca. 1815), a physician, who married in 1785 Elizabeth, daughter of Thomas Gantt, of Calvert County; and William (1753–?), who died young. Her sisters were Eleanor (1733–?), who married William Eversfield, of England; Mary (ca. 1739–?), who married Benjamin Brooke, Jr.; and Deborah (1748–?), who married Benjamin Berry. **CHILDREN. SONS**: Allen (ca. 1768–1795), who married Sarah Chew; Thomas Contee (1771–1813), who married Mary Mackall (1776–1825), daughter of *Robert Bowie* (ca. 1750–1818); Eversfield (1773–1815), who married Elizabeth Lane; and John Fraser, Jr. (1781–1823), who married Mary Calvert. DAUGHTERS: Priscilla (1776–1810), never married; Elizabeth Susannah (1785–1824), who married Joseph Howard, Jr. (1786–1839). **PRIVATE CAREER. EDUCATION**: educated at Rev. John Eversfield's school near Nottingham, Prince George's County. RELIGIOUS AFFILIATION: Anglican, St. Paul's Parish,

Prince George's County. OCCUPATIONAL PROFILE: planter and merchant; in business in Nottingham, Prince George's County, with *Thomas Contee* (ca. 1729–1811) in a firm that engaged in the European tobacco trade and the importation of large quantities of goods. They advertised the firm's dissolution on April 1, 1775. Bowie applied for a license to operate the Nottingham Ferry in 1788 and owned a store in Nottingham, Prince George's County, at the time of his death. PUBLIC CAREER. LEGISLATIVE SERVICE: Lower House, Prince George's County, 1785, 1786–1787 (Grievances 1), 1787–1788, 1788 (elected to the Assembly to fill vacancy), 1790. OTHER STATE OFFICE: Constitution Ratification Convention, Prince George's County, 1788. LOCAL OFFICES: register, St. Paul's Parish, Prince George's County, in office 1767; Committee for inspection for armed resistance, Prince George's County, 1775; justice, Prince George's County, 1777–1794 (chief justice, 1793–1794); St. Paul's Parish Vestry, Prince George's County, in office 1779, 1782, 1785–1788; justice, Orphans' Court, Prince George's County, 1782–at least 1790; Maryland Senate elector, Prince George's County, elected 1786. MILITARY SERVICE: captain, Nottingham Company, Prince George's County Militia, promoted from 1st lieutenant, 1776. WEALTH DURING LIFETIME. PERSONAL PROPERTY: 60 slaves, 1790; mortgaged 60 slaves, plus all of his household furniture, plate, livestock, plantation utensils, a chariot, and a sulky between 1789 and 1792. LAND AT FIRST ELECTION: at least 1,752 acres, plus 1 lot and a partnership in another lot, and one undivided fifth part of 526 acres, all in Prince George's County (at least 561 acres, the remainder of at least 661 acres inherited or received by deed of gift from his father; 262 acres through his marriage, but all sold before first election; 1,471 acres, plus 1 lot and a partnership in another lot, and one undivided fifth part of 526 acres by purchase, but 280 acres of this purchased land had been sold before his first election). SIGNIFICANT CHANGES IN LAND BETWEEN FIRST ELECTION AND DEATH: sold 130 acres in Prince George's County, 1789; purchased 2 lots in Nottingham, Prince George's County, 1790; sold at least 975 acres in Prince George's County to his son Allen, 1791; Bowie mortgaged and remortgaged several of his tracts as security for his various debts between 1790 and 1792. WEALTH AT DEATH. DIED: in September 1794 in Prince George's County; buried at "Brookridge," Prince George's County. PERSONAL PROPERTY: TEV, £3,749.14.7 current money (including 38 slaves, 115 oz. plate, and books, all of which in addition

to the remainder of his personal property Bowie had mortgaged before his death); FB, estate overpaid £110.7.3. LAND: 543 acres, plus 3 lots, a partnership in another lot, and one undivided fifth part of 526 acres, all in Prince George's County. After Bowie's death his creditors went before the Chancery Court where it was determined that his personal property was insufficient to pay his debts. The court ordered that 155 acres plus 2 lots be sold to settle Bowie's accounts.

BOWIE, ROBERT (ca. 1750–1818). BORN: in March ca. 1750 at "Mattaponi," Prince George's County; second son. NATIVE: third generation. RESIDED: in the town of Nottingham, Prince George's County; had a summer home at "Mattaponi," Prince George's County. FAMILY BACKGROUND. FATHER: *William Bowie* (1721–1791). MOTHER: Margaret (1726/27–1804), daughter of *Osborn Sprigg* (1707–1749/50). HALF UNCLES: *Joseph Sprigg* (1736–1800); *Osborn Sprigg* (ca. 1741–1815); and *Thomas Sprigg* (1747–1809). BROTHERS: *Walter Bowie* (1748–1810); William Sprigg (1751–1809); and Osborn (?–1806). SISTERS: Elizabeth (1746–?); Ann (1765–?); and Margaret (1765–?). FIRST COUSINS: *Allen Bowie, Jr.* (1737–1803); *Fielder Bowie* (ca. 1745–1794). MARRIED ca. 1773 Priscilla (1758–1823), with whom, according to tradition, he eloped; daughter of *James John Mackall* (1717–1772); granddaughter of *John Mackall* (1669–1739); niece of *Samuel Hance* (by 1732–?). Her brothers were *John Mackall* (1740–1799); *Benjamin Mackall IV* (1745–by 1810); James (1747–ca. 1837); Richard (1749–?); and *Thomas Mackall* (1751–1799). Her sisters were Susannah (ca. 1737–?), who married *Thomas Gantt, Jr.* (?–1808); Mary (1742–?), who married *Edward Reynolds* (?–?); Elizabeth (ca. 1743–?); Sarah (1752–?); Ann (1753–?); Margaret (1755–1799); and Barbary (Barbara) (1755–?). CHILDREN. SONS: James John (1785–1809), who was killed in a duel; Robert William (1787–1848), who was a member of the Whig party, served four terms in the Maryland House of Delegates and three terms in the Maryland Senate, was three times a member of the governor's council, a presidential elector in 1821 and 1837, and who married in 1818 Catherine (1800–1867), daughter of Isaac Lansdale and wife Catherine Brooke; and Robert H. (?–died young). DAUGHTERS: Mary Mackall (1776–1825), who married first, in 1794 Turner Wooton, and second, Thomas Contee Bowie (1771–1813), son of *Fielder Bowie* (ca. 1745–1794); Elizabeth Margaret (1780–1854), who married in 1800 John Waring, Jr. (?–1815); Margaret Anne (1783–1850), who married in 1804 Dr. Reverdy Ghiselin (ca. 1765–1823); and Caroline (?–died young). WARD: John H. Waring. PRIVATE CAREER. EDUCATION: educated at Rev. John Eversfield's school, near Nottingham, Prince George's County; a student of Rev. Craddock in Baltimore County. RELIGIOUS AFFILIATION: Anglican. SOCIAL STATUS AND ACTIVITIES: Gent., by 1781; Esq., by 1787. OCCUPATIONAL PROFILE: planter, by 1773; merchant, by 1785. PUBLIC CAREER. LEGISLATIVE SERVICE: Lower House, Prince George's County, 1785, 1786–1787, 1788 (discharged on November 11, 1788, for serving as county tax collector at the time of his election and thereafter), 1789, 1790, 1801, 1802, 1803; Senate, Western Shore, Term of 1806–1811: 1809 (elected on June 5, 1809, to fill vacancy in the 1808–1809 Assembly), 1809, 1810. OTHER STATE OFFICE: governor, 1803–1806, 1811–1812. LOCAL OFFICES: member of a committee appointed by the citizens of Nottingham, Prince George's County, to see that resolutions of the Continental Congress were carried into effect, November 1774; commissary for horses, Prince George's County, appointed 1781; sheriff, Prince George's County, 1782 (elected, but was not commissioned); St. Paul's Parish Vestry, Prince George's County, in office 1783, 1787, 1816–1818; justice, Prince George's County, 1784–1802; collector of tax, Prince George's County, appointed 1787; justice, Orphans' Court, Prince George's County, 1790–at least 1796; commissioner of tax, Prince George's County, appointed 1792 and 1798; justice, Levy Court, Prince George's County, 1795–1796, 1798–1802, 1806–1809; Maryland Senate elector, Prince George's County, elected 1796. ADDITIONAL COMMENTS: during his first three terms as governor, the Bank Stock controversy with England was finally settled, the National Road opened, an act was passed prohibiting the immigration of free Negroes into the state, and the size of the Baltimore City delegation in the House of Delegates was increased. MILITARY SERVICE: appointed to enroll a company of minutemen, Prince George's County, 1775; commissioned 1st lieutenant, Prince George's County Militia, 1776; commissioned captain, Second Battalion, Maryland Flying Artillery, June 1776; major, Prince George's County Militia, appointed 1794; brigadier general, Fourth Brigade (Prince George's County and the lower part of Montgomery County), Maryland Militia, 1801–1804; major general, First Division, Maryland Militia, commissioned 1812. OUT OF STATE OFFICE: presidential elector, 1808 (for James Madison). STANDS ON PUBLIC/PRIVATE ISSUES: Bowie was a Democratic

Republican in the early 1800s. He was known as a radical Democrat and was a strong advocate of war against England by 1808. While in the legislature, Bowie strongly advocated the establishment of St. John's College in Annapolis. During his term as governor from 1811 to 1812, a staunchly Federalist newspaper, the *Federal Republican,* edited by Alexander Contee Hanson (1786–1819), published a strong editorial condemning the war with England and the Republicans' handling of it. An angry mob destroyed the newspaper building and its contents on June 22, 1812, and several persons were killed. Bowie was urged to investigate the incident and was accused of shielding the criminals who were never caught. The opposition, aroused by the riot, worked against Bowie and the Republicans, which cost him the race for governor in 1812. WEALTH DURING LIFETIME. PERSONAL PROPERTY: 42 slaves, 1790; assessed value £1,532.5.0, including 51 slaves and 90 oz. plate, 1796; assessed value at least $7,528.00, including 83 slaves and 180 oz. plate, 1817. LAND AT FIRST ELECTION: 806 acres in Prince George's County (433 acres as a gift from his father; 373 acres by purchase). SIGNIFICANT CHANGES IN LAND BETWEEN FIRST ELECTION AND DEATH: inherited a one-half acre lot in Nottingham, Prince George's County, from his father, 1791; inherited 414 acres in Prince George's County from his father's estate upon the death of his mother, 1804; acquired 1,288 additional acres in Prince George's County between 1786 and 1818, of which at least 675 acres were purchased. WEALTH AT DEATH. DIED: on January 8, 1818, at "Mattaponi," Prince George's County; buried in the family graveyard at "Mattaponi." PERSONAL PROPERTY: TEV, $52,513.68 (including 82 slaves, 276 oz. plate, and books); FB, $4,801.84. LAND: 2,508 acres in Prince George's County, plus 2 lots in Nottingham and part of a lot in Upper Marlboro, Prince George's County.

BOWIE, WALTER (1748–1810). BORN: in 1748 in Mattaponi Hundred, Prince George's County. NATIVE: third generation. RESIDED: at "Locust Grove," Prince George's County. FAMILY BACKGROUND. FATHER: *William Bowie* (1721–1791). MOTHER: Margaret (1726/27–1804), daughter of *Osborn Sprigg* (1707–1749/50) and wife Elizabeth. HALF UNCLES: *Joseph Sprigg* (1736–1800); *Osborn Sprigg* (ca. 1741–1815); and *Thomas Sprigg* (1747–1809). BROTHERS: *Robert Bowie* (ca. 1750–1818); William Sprigg (1751–1809); and Osborn (?–1806). SISTERS: Elizabeth (1746–?); Ann (1765–?); and Margaret (1765–?). OTHER KINSHIP: his great-uncle was *Edward Sprigg* (1697–1751); his great-aunt was Priscilla Sprigg, who married *Ralph Crabb* (?–1733). MARRIED on May 16, 1771, Mary (1747–1812), daughter of Benjamin Brookes (?–1787) and wife Mary Townley; stepdaughter of Sarah Johnson. Her brothers were Maj. Benjamin, who married in 1785 Margaret (1765–?), daughter of *William Bowie* (1721–1791); John Smith, who married first, Ann Bowie, and second, (first name unknown) Harwood. CHILDREN. SONS: William (1776–?), who married in 1802 Kitty Duckett; Daniel (1777–?); and Walter, Jr. (1785–?), who married in 1812 Amelia Margaret Weems. DAUGHTERS: Margaret (1772–1797), who married in 1792 Isaac Duckett; Elizabeth (1781–?), who married in 1803 Thomas Brooke; and Juliet Matilda (1788–?), who married in 1812 James B. Brookes. PRIVATE CAREER. EDUCATION: attended Rev. John Eversfield's school, common schools in Annapolis, and Craddock's school in Baltimore County. RELIGIOUS AFFILIATION: Anglican. SOCIAL STATUS AND ACTIVITIES: Gent., 1800; horse racer. OCCUPATIONAL PROFILE: planter; merchant, owned the firm of Walter Bowie & Company of Bladensburg, Prince George's County. The company shipped tobacco to England and imported goods from England and India. PUBLIC CAREER. LEGISLATIVE SERVICE: Conventions, Prince George's County, 2nd–3rd, 1774, 4th, 1775, 5th, 1775, 9th, 1776 (election voided on August 15, 1776, because the freemen illegally appointed election judges after the ones officially appointed failed to act; reelected and seated); Lower House, Prince George's County, 1777, 1777–1778, 1778–1779 (Elections 2; Grievances 3), 1781–1782 (Claims 1), 1782–1783, 1783 (elected, but did not attend), 1784, 1785, 1786–1787, 1787–1788, 1788, 1789, 1790, 1791–1792, 1792, 1793, 1794, 1795, 1796, 1797; Senate, Western Shore, Term of 1801–1806: 1801 (did not serve), 1802 (did not serve; probably declined). OTHER STATE OFFICES: associate justice, First District, appointed 1791, resigned 1792. LOCAL OFFICE: Maryland Senate elector, Prince George's County, elected 1786, 1791, and 1801. OUT OF STATE OFFICE: representative, U.S. Congress, 1802–1803 (elected to fill vacancy; seated on March 24, 1802), 1803–1805. STANDS ON PUBLIC/PRIVATE ISSUES: a leader in the affair that resulted in the burning of the *Peggy Stewart,* 1774. WEALTH DURING LIFETIME. LAND AT FIRST ELECTION: 674 acres in Prince George's County (529 acres from his father). SIGNIFICANT CHANGES IN LAND BETWEEN FIRST ELECTION AND DEATH: purchased considerable additional property during the 1790s, all in Prince George's

County. WEALTH AT DEATH. DIED: on November 9, 1810, intestate, in Prince George's County, after a long illness. He was buried on his plantation "Locust Grove," Prince George's County. PERSONAL PROPERTY: TEV, $24,984.60 current money (including 71 slaves, 75 oz. plate, and books); FB, estate overpaid $2,961.19. LAND: 2,359 acres in Prince George's County. ADDITIONAL COMMENTS: his annual income at death included rents totaling $774.18. He owed almost $10,000, with his largest creditors being the Farmers Bank, *Charles Carroll of Carrollton* (1737–1832), *Robert Bowie* (ca. 1750–1818), Charles Ridgely, and John Turnbull.

BOWIE, WILLIAM (1721–1791). BORN: in 1721 at "Brooke Ridge," near Nottingham, Prince George's County; fourth son. NATIVE: second generation. RESIDED: at "Brooke Reserve" (later called "Mattaponi"), Prince George's County. FAMILY BACKGROUND. FATHER: John Bowie, Sr., Gent. (ca. 1688–1759), who probably immigrated from Scotland ca. 1706. MOTHER: Mary, daughter of James Mulliken. BROTHERS: John, Jr. (1708–1753), who married first, Mary Offet, and second, Elizabeth Pottinger; James (1714–1744); Allen (1719–1783), who married first, Priscilla Finch (?–1747), and second, Anne Fraser (1718–1779); and Thomas (1723–?), who married first, Esther (1730–?), daughter of *Osborn Sprigg* (1707–1749/50), and second, Hannah, daughter of *Philip Lee* (ca. 1681–1744). SISTERS: Eleanor (1709–?), who married first, Benjamin Brookes, second, Edward Clagett, and third, (first name unknown) Skinner; Mary (1726–?), who married William Beanes, Jr. NEPHEWS: *Allen Bowie, Jr.* (1737–1803); *Fielder Bowie* (ca. 1745–1794). MARRIED ca. 1745 Margaret (1726/27–1804), daughter of *Osborn Sprigg* (1707–1749/50); stepdaughter of Rachel Belt (1711–?); granddaughter of *Thomas Sprigg* (ca. 1670–by 1739); stepgranddaughter of *Joseph Belt* (ca. 1680–1761); niece of both *Edward Sprigg* (1697–1751) and Priscilla Sprigg, who married *Ralph Crabb* (?–1733). Her half brothers were *Joseph Sprigg* (1736–1800); *Osborn Sprigg* (ca. 1741–1815); and *Thomas Sprigg* (1747–1809). Her first cousins were *Thomas Sprigg* (1715–1781); *Edward Sprigg* (1723–1758); *Henry Wright Crabb* (1722/23–1764); *Edward Sprigg* (?–?); and *Francis King* (1724/25–1771). CHILDREN. SONS: *Walter Bowie* (1748–1810); *Robert Bowie* (ca. 1750–1818); William Sprigg (1751–1809), who was commissioned a captain in the Fourth Battalion of the Maryland Line in January 1777 and was severely wounded at the Battle of Germantown on October

4, 1777. The injury forced him to resign his commission on December 15, 1777, and kept him an invalid for many years. William became involved in mercantile activities and owned a store in Upper Marlboro, Prince George's County by 1788, but his health seemed to keep him from making the business a success. In 1800 William petitioned the Assembly as an insolvent debtor and when he died in 1809 he owned no land of his own. William married in 1781 Elizabeth, widow of John Clark Sprigg (?–1781) and daughter of Benjamin Brookes, Sr. (?–1787). Osborn Sprigg (?–1806). DAUGHTERS: Elizabeth (1746–?), who married Walter Smith, of Calvert County; Ann (1765–?), who married Philemon Lloyd Chew, of Calvert County; and Margaret Sprigg (1765–?), who married Maj. Benjamin Brookes, Jr., son of Benjamin Brookes, Sr. (?–1787). PRIVATE CAREER. EDUCATION: literate; a subscriber to St. John's College, Annapolis, at death. RELIGIOUS AFFILIATION: Anglican. SOCIAL STATUS AND ACTIVITIES: Gent., by 1759; Esq., by 1785. OCCUPATIONAL PROFILE: planter, by 1744. PUBLIC CAREER. LEGISLATIVE SERVICE: Conventions, Prince George's County, 1st, 1774, 2nd–3rd, 1774, 4th, 1775 (elected, but did not attend), 5th, 1775. LOCAL OFFICES: tobacco inspector, Nottingham, Prince George's County, appointed 1753; churchwarden, St. Paul's Parish, Prince George's County, period of service unknown; St. Paul's Parish Vestry, Prince George's County, period of service unknown; justice, Prince George's County, 1759–at least 1761; Committee of Correspondence, Prince George's County, elected 1774; Committee of Observation, Prince George's County, elected 1775; commissioner of tax, Prince George's County, 1777–at least 1783; committee to raise supplies for the army, Prince George's County, appointed 1778; judge, Court of Appeals for Tax Assessment, Prince George's County, appointed 1786 (declined). JURY SERVICE: foreman, grand jury, in office 1764 and 1766. MILITARY SERVICE: captain, by 1760. WEALTH DURING LIFETIME. LAND AT FIRST ELECTION: 2,540 acres in Prince George's and Charles counties (402 acres were the remainder of 612 acres acquired from his father through deeds of gift and inheritance; at least 1,731 acres by purchase; and 89 acres, the remainder of 112 acres patented before his first election). ADDITIONAL COMMENTS: Before his first election William transferred 432 acres by deed of gift to his son *Robert Bowie* (ca. 1750–1818). This acreage was composed partially of William's inherited land and partially of land he had purchased. SIGNIFICANT CHANGES IN LAND BETWEEN FIRST ELEC-

TION AND DEATH: transferred by deed of gift 695 acres in Charles County to his son William, 1782; transferred by deed of gift 1 acre in Prince George's County to his son *Robert Bowie* (ca. 1750–1818), 1785. WEALTH AT DEATH. DIED: between March 15 and April 9, 1791, in Prince George's County. PERSONAL PROPERTY: TEV, £2,451.16.0 current money (including 45 slaves, 98 oz. plate, and 4 books); FB, £104.10.11. LAND: 1,845 acres in Prince George's County.

BOWLES, JAMES (?–ca. 1727/28). BORN: in England; only son. IMMIGRATED: probably in 1699 as a free adult. RESIDED: in Charles County; St. Mary's County by 1700. FAMILY BACKGROUND. FATHER: Tobias Bowles (?–1727), a sugar and tobacco merchant of London and Deal, England, who was nominated for the governorship of Maryland after death of his uncle, *John Seymour* (1649–1709). SISTERS: (first name unknown), who married Henry Alexander Primrose; (first name unknown), who married Capt. John Underdowne; and Jane. MARRIED first, by 1718 Jane, daughter of *Henry Lowe* (?–1717); niece of *Nicholas Lowe* (ca. 1662–1714). Her brothers were *Henry Lowe* (?–1721); Bennett (?–1722); *Nicholas Lowe* (?–1728); and Thomas. Her sisters were Ann; Elizabeth; Henrietta Maria; Dorothy; Mary; and Susannah Maria. MARRIED second, Rebecca (1703–?), daughter of *Thomas Addison* (1679–1727) and wife Elizabeth Tasker (1686–1706/7); stepdaughter of Eleanor (1689–1761), daughter of *Walter Smith* (?–1711); granddaughter of both *John Addison* (?–ca. 1705/6) and *Thomas Tasker* (?–1700); niece of *Benjamin Tasker* (ca. 1690–1768). Her half brothers were *John Addison* (1713–1764); Henry; Thomas; and Anthony. Her sister was Elinor. Her half sister was Ann, who married *William Murdock* (?–1769). CHILDREN. DAUGHTERS: Elinor, who married William Gooch, son of Gov. William Gooch, of Virginia; Mary, who married William Armistead; and Jane, who married Rev. Thomas Price. PRIVATE CAREER. EDUCATION: literate, probably had considerable schooling. RELIGIOUS AFFILIATION: Anglican. SOCIAL STATUS AND ACTIVITIES: apparently came to Maryland to settle the estate of Capt. Anthony Bowles and to serve as his father's agent in the colony; married the daughters of two of the wealthiest and most politically powerful men on the lower Western Shore. OCCUPATIONAL PROFILE: merchant; planter. PUBLIC CAREER. LEGISLATIVE SERVICE: Lower House, St. Mary's County, 1710–1711 (elected to the 3rd session); Upper House, 1720–1721/22 (appointed to the 3rd session), 1722–1724, 1725–1727. OTHER PROVINCIAL OFFICES: collector of North Potomac, 1710–1718; Council, 1720–1727/28. LOCAL OFFICE: justice, St. Mary's County, 1709–?. WEALTH DURING LIFETIME. LAND AT FIRST ELECTION: at least 1,300 acres. WEALTH AT DEATH. DIED: will probated on January 3, 1727/28. PERSONAL PROPERTY: TEV, £5,086.17.7 (including 40 slaves); FB, £4,828.6.4. LAND: over 2,000 acres, plus property in England.

BOWLES, JOHN (ca. 1616–1676). BORN: ca. 1616. IMMIGRATED: in 1661 as a free adult. RESIDED: in Charles County. FAMILY BACKGROUND. BROTHER: Edward Bowles (ca. 1598–1659), who immigrated in 1650, was an illiterate justice of St. Mary's County in 1655, and owned 200 acres at the time of his death. MARRIED in 1663 Margery (1633–ca. 1676), widow of William Batten. PRIVATE CAREER. EDUCATION: illiterate. RELIGIOUS AFFILIATION: Protestant. SOCIAL STATUS AND ACTIVITIES: Mr., 1662. OCCUPATIONAL PROFILE: planter. PUBLIC CAREER. LEGISLATIVE SERVICE: Lower House, Charles County, 1669, 1671–1674/75. LOCAL OFFICE: justice, Charles County, 1670–1676. WEALTH DURING LIFETIME. LAND AT FIRST ELECTION: 1,000 acres by 1673; at least 1,750 acres by 1675. WEALTH AT DEATH. DIED: will probated on April 25, 1676. LAND: 1,750 acres.

BOWLEY, DANIEL (1745–1807). BORN: in 1745 in Baltimore County; only child. NATIVE: at least second generation. RESIDED: in Baltimore Town and at "Finley," Baltimore County. FAMILY BACKGROUND. FATHER: Daniel Bowley (?–1745), of Baltimore County, a merchant. MOTHER: Elizabeth (?–1793), daughter of *Darby Lux* (ca. 1698–1750). UNCLES: *Darby Lux* (?–1795); *William Lux* (ca. 1730–1778). MARRIED Ann (?–1793). CHILDREN. SONS: William Lux (1783–1855), who married in 1809 Mary Hollins; Francis Russell; Samuel Hughes (after 1787–?); and Daniel (?–1793). DAUGHTERS: five, including Ann Lux, who married in 1798 Henry Thompson; Sarah Stewart, who married in 1805 Charles Wirgman; Rebecca Maria (after 1787–?); and Elizabeth (1791–?), who married William Hollins. PRIVATE CAREER. EDUCATION: literate. RELIGIOUS AFFILIATION: Anglican, pewholder at St. Paul's Church, Baltimore City. SOCIAL STATUS AND ACTIVITIES: Mr., 1777; Esq., 1786. OCCUPATIONAL PROFILE: merchant by 1770, in partnership with his uncle *William Lux* (ca. 1730–1778). Owned a wharf on the harbor in Baltimore Town; active in land development in Baltimore Town; owned a privateer during the Revolution. PUBLIC CAREER. LEGISLATIVE SERVICE: Senate, Western Shore, Term of 1781–1786: 1785 (elected on January 7, 1786, to fill vacancy in the 1785 Assembly; qualified on January 11, 1786), Term of 1786–1791: 1789 (elected on November 20, 1789, to fill vacancy; qualified on December 9, 1789), 1790, Term of 1791–1796: 1791–1792 (elected to fill vacancy; qualified on April 3, 1792), 1792 (did not serve), 1793 (resigned on November 26, 1793). LOCAL OFFICES: St. Paul's Church Vestry, Baltimore Town, in office 1775–1777, 1779–1781, 1784–1785; Committee to Execute Circulation of Paper Money, Baltimore County, in office 1781; commissioner, Baltimore Town, 1781–1796; warden, port of Baltimore, appointed 1783; commissioner of tax, Baltimore County, 1783–1786. WEALTH DURING LIFETIME. PERSONAL PROPERTY: assessed value in Baltimore County £1,022.0.0, including 18 slaves and merchandize in Baltimore Town, 1783; 18 slaves, 1790. ANNUAL INCOME: ground rents of £28 sterling per annum on lots in Baltimore Town, 1783. LAND AT FIRST ELECTION: 382 acres in Baltimore County, ca. 9 lots in Baltimore Town, plus 1,400 acres in Monongahela County, Virginia. SIGNIFICANT CHANGES IN LAND BETWEEN FIRST ELECTION AND DEATH: inherited one-third interest in ca. 3,000 acres in Anne Arundel, Harford, and Baltimore counties, plus 40 acres in Baltimore Town from *Thomas Harrison* (?–1782) in 1782. By 1795 Bowley had purchased the rights of Harrison's other two devisees. Much of the Harrison land had already been sold or leased by that time, but Bowley soon sold the remainder except for many of the lots in Baltimore Town. From the late 1780s until his death he concentrated on the development of his Baltimore Town lots, (Harrison's and those he acquired alone), most of them on Philpot's Hill, the York Turnpike, and in the harbor area around "Bowley's Wharf." WEALTH AT DEATH. DIED: buried on November 14, 1807, in St. Paul's Church Cemetery, Baltimore City. PERSONAL PROPERTY: TEV, $8,920.52 current money (including 25 slaves and shares of stock in the York Turnpike Road and the Frederick Road); FB, $88.53. A Chancery Court case in 1808 allowed a debt of £3,986.11.3, plus interest from 1807 that Bowley owed to *Daniel Dulany, Jr.* (1722–1797) to be charged against Bowley's estate and directed that a portion of his land be sold to satisfy Dulany's claim. LAND: 2,623 acres in Baltimore County, 190 acres in Frederick County, 326 lots (of which ca. 150 were undeveloped) in Baltimore City, plus one-half share of 25 lots in Baltimore City, and 1,400 acres in Monongahela

County, Virginia. ADDITIONAL COMMENTS: income at death included ground rents totaling $3,512.00 per annum on land leased from ca. 1790 to 1807.

BOWMAN, SAMUEL (?–1768). BORN: of age by 1743/44. IMMIGRATED: by 1743/44 from Whitehaven, Cumberland County, England. RESIDED: in Talbot County; Kingstown, Talbot County, 1765. FAMILY BACKGROUND. SISTER: Jane, of Cumberland County, England. MARRIED on November 30, 1751, Ann (?–ca. 1774), daughter of James Dickinson (?–1738) and wife Hannah Coale. Her brother was William Dickinson, who married Mary Anne (ca. 1715–1775), daughter of *Thomas Bozman* (ca. 1693–1752). Her sisters were Elizabeth (?–by 1756), who married first, Anthony Richardson, and second, Rev. Philip Walker (?–1776), a merchant; Mary (?–by 1765), who married in 1738 *Pollard Edmondson* (ca. 1718–1794). Her nephew was *Philip Walker* (?–1791). Her nieces were Elizabeth Walker (?–1783), who married *Henry Dickinson* (?–1789); Ann Walker Mein Hindman (?–by 1787), who married third, *Henry Dickinson* (?–1789); and (first name unknown) Edmondson, who married *Christopher Birckhead* (by 1740–1788). CHILDREN. SONS: Samuel (1758–?), who married in 1791 Sarah Tyler, a Quaker; James (1759–?); and Joseph (1760–?). DAUGHTERS: Elizabeth (1752–1753); Mary (1754–1754); Ann (1756–?), a twin; Hannah (1756–1756), a twin; and Jane (1762–?). PRIVATE CAREER. EDUCATION: literate. RELIGIOUS AFFILIATION: Anglican, St. Peter's Parish, Talbot County. SOCIAL STATUS AND ACTIVITIES: Gent., 1744. ADDITIONAL COMMENTS: in his will he requested that his two eldest sons be sent to Whitehaven, England, or somewhere in that vicinity after his death for their "improvement." OCCUPATIONAL PROFILE: merchant. PUBLIC CAREER. LEGISLATIVE SERVICE: Lower House, Talbot County, 1758–1761. WEALTH DURING LIFETIME. LAND AT FIRST ELECTION: 636 acres in Talbot and Queen Anne's counties (286 acres acquired through his marriage; 350 acres by purchase). SIGNIFICANT CHANGES IN LAND BETWEEN FIRST ELECTION AND DEATH: purchased 83 acres in Talbot County, 1767. WEALTH AT DEATH. DIED: between August 27 and September 16, 1768, in Talbot County. PERSONAL PROPERTY: TEV, £3,741.12.2 current money (including 14 slaves, 1 servant, 71 oz. plate, 32 oz. old silver, books, and store goods); FB, £1,483.6.2. LAND: 719 acres in Talbot and Queen Anne's counties.

BOYD, JOHN (1737–1790). BORN: in 1737, possibly in Pennsylvania. IMMIGRATED: ca. 1761, probably from Pennsylvania. RESIDED: in Baltimore Town. FAMILY BACKGROUND. SISTERS: Martha Stewart; Jane Culberson; Mary Stelle; Ann Lloyd; and Elizabeth Smith. MARRIED on May 8, 1777, Ann (ca. 1747–1833), widow of John Little (?–1774), an innholder of Baltimore Town. Her sister was Mary Priery. CHILDREN. STEPDAUGHTER: Mary Little. PRIVATE CAREER. EDUCATION: College of New Jersey (later Princeton University), A.B. 1757; A.M. 1760. RELIGIOUS AFFILIATION: Presbyterian, member of the First Presbyterian Church, Baltimore Town, by 1766. SOCIAL STATUS AND ACTIVITIES: founding member of the Medical Society of Baltimore, 1789. OCCUPATIONAL PROFILE: physician, established a drugstore in Baltimore Town by 1764. Later took as a business partner Dr. Miles Littlejohn (1758–1815). PUBLIC CAREER. LEGISLATIVE SERVICE: Conventions, Baltimore County, 2nd–3rd, 1774. LOCAL OFFICE: Committee of Correspondence, Baltimore Town, elected 1774. STANDS ON PUBLIC/PRIVATE ISSUES: provided in his will for the manumission of his slaves. WEALTH DURING LIFETIME. SIGNIFICANT CHANGES IN LAND BETWEEN FIRST ELECTION AND DEATH: acquired 153 acres in Baltimore County, plus 5 lots in Baltimore Town, 1780–1789, and at the same time took out leases on 2 additional lots in Baltimore Town. Leased out 53 acres in Baltimore County and at least 5 lots in Baltimore Town, and sold his leases on the 2 additional lots in Baltimore Town. WEALTH AT DEATH. DIED: on February 4, 1790, in Baltimore Town. PERSONAL PROPERTY: directed in his will that no inventory or accounts be made because he owed no debts. An inventory made in April 1801 totaled £5,133.0.11 current money. LAND: 153 acres in Baltimore County, plus 5 lots in Baltimore Town; 53 acres of the land in Baltimore County and the 5 lots in Baltimore Town were leased out.

BOZMAN (BOSMAN), JOHN (1650–1716). BORN: in 1650 in Virginia; probably oldest son. IMMIGRATED: by 1663 as a minor with his father from Virginia. RESIDED: in Manokin Hundred, Somerset County. FAMILY BACKGROUND. FATHER: William Bozman (?–1664/65), who was in Virginia by 1649. MOTHER: Bridget (?–1660). STEPMOTHER: Eleanor, widow of Alexander Maddox, of Northampton County, Virginia. BROTHERS: William (1655–?); George (1659–1701). STEPBROTHER: *Lazarus Maddox* (ca. 1656–1716/17). SISTERS: Bridget (1653–after 1709), who married George

Betts; Anne (1657–?), who married George Downes; Katherine, who married John Nelson; and Mary. MARRIED by 1670/71 Blandina Risdon (?–1727). CHILDREN. SONS: William (1674/75–?); John (1679–1743); George; Risdon; *Thomas Bozman* (ca. 1693–1752), who married first, in 1715 Mary (1691–?), widow of both Rev. John Allen (?–1708) and Rev. William Glen (?–1713) and daughter of *Nicholas Lowe* (ca. 1662–1714), and second, in 1735/36 Elizabeth, widow of Jonathan Taylor and daughter of (first name unknown) Sherwood. DAUGHTERS: Mary (1670/71–by 1716), who married in 1686 Marcy Fountaine; Naomi (1672/73–by 1716); Bridget (1677–died in infancy); Bridget (1687–1759); and Ann (?–1751). PRIVATE CAREER. EDUCATION: literate. RELIGIOUS AFFILIATION: Protestant. OCCUPATIONAL PROFILE: planter. PUBLIC CAREER. LEGISLATIVE SERVICE: Lower House, Somerset County, 1692–1693 (elected to fill vacancy in the 1st session), 1694–1697, 1697/98–1700, 1701–1704. OTHER PROVINCIAL OFFICES: naval officer, Pocomoke, 1698–1705, justice, Provincial Court, 1705–1706. LOCAL OFFICES: justice, Somerset County, 1694–1705, 1713–1716 (quorum, 1694–1705; chief justice, 1713–1716); coroner, Somerset County, 1705, 1711/12, 1713; sheriff, Somerset County, 1707–1710. WEALTH DURING LIFETIME. LAND AT FIRST ELECTION: at least 400 acres. WEALTH AT DEATH. DIED: will probated on September 26, 1716. PERSONAL PROPERTY: TEV, £230.2.5 (including 5 slaves, 1 servant, and books). LAND: 4 tracts of unspecified acreage; he had given at least 400 acres to his two sons in 1711.

BOZMAN (BOSMAN), THOMAS (ca. 1693–1752).

BORN: ca. 1693, probably in Somerset County. NATIVE: third generation. RESIDED: in Somerset County; Oxford Neck, Talbot County, ca. 1715. FAMILY BACKGROUND. FATHER: *John Bozman* (1650–1716). MOTHER: Blandina Risdon (?–1727). BROTHERS: William (1674/75–?); John (1679–1743); George; and Risdon. SISTERS: Mary (1670/71–by 1716); Naomi (1672/73–by 1716); Bridget (1677–died in infancy); Bridget (1687–1759); and Ann (?–1751). MARRIED on May 27, 1715, Mary (1691–?), widow of both Rev. John Allen (?–1708) and Rev. William Glen (?–1713), who had accidentally shot and killed her first husband, Rev. John Allen, while they were hunting wild turkeys; daughter of *Nicholas Lowe* (ca. 1662–1714). Her brothers were Nicholas (1697–1745), who married Margaret; Vincent (ca. 1702–?); and Henry (ca. 1702–1704). Her sisters were Dorothy (1700–?), who married first, Francis Har-

rison (?–1722), and second, Joseph Eason; Sarah, who married first, (first name unknown) Long, and second, (first name unknown) Pattison; Elizabeth, who married William Wood; and Prudence (1695–?), who married (first name unknown) Price. MARRIED second, on January 20, 1735/36, Elizabeth Sherwood, widow of Jonathan Taylor. CHILDREN. SONS: John (?–1767), who married in 1754 Lucretia Leeds; Thomas (ca. 1717–?), who was lost at sea. STEPSONS: Nicholas Glen (1710–?); John Glen (1712–?); and Thomas Taylor (?–by 1747). DAUGHTERS: Mary Anne (ca. 1715–1775), who married first, William Dickinson, and second, Thomas Loveday; Prudence (ca. 1720–?), who married John Sherwood (?–1745); Sarah (ca. 1721–?), who married in 1739 Elijah Skillington; (first name unknown), who married Robert Harwood; Mary Memorial; Elizabeth (1728–1729); and Elizabeth, who married first, in 1755 Rev. John Belchier, who was already married and who deserted her, and second, in 1756 Rev. Thomas Bacon, rector of St. Peter's Parish, Talbot County. STEPDAUGHTERS: Elizabeth Allen (ca. 1708–?), who married in 1732 *William Thomas* (1705–1767); Rachel Taylor, who married *James Dickinson* (ca. 1726–1787). PRIVATE CAREER. EDUCATION: literate. RELIGIOUS AFFILIATION: Anglican, St. Peter's Parish, Talbot County; his second wife was a Quaker. SOCIAL STATUS AND ACTIVITIES: Gent., 1720. OCCUPATIONAL PROFILE: probably a planter; officeholder. PUBLIC CAREER. LEGISLATIVE SERVICE: Lower House, Talbot County, 1723–1724 (elected to the 2nd session to fill vacancy; Elections 2). OTHER PROVINCIAL OFFICE: surveyor and searcher, Oxford, at least by 1741–1752. LOCAL OFFICES: St. Peter's Parish Vestry, Talbot County, in office 1717–1720, 1728–1731, 1736–1739, 1743–1746; sheriff, Talbot County, in office 1720, 1721, 1725–1728, 1731, 1732, and 1733; commissioner, Talbot County Free School, in office 1723; deputy commissary, Talbot County, in office 1724–1734; justice, Talbot County, 1725–1751 (quorum, 1734–1751); visitor, Talbot County Free School, in office 1727; receiver, baliff, and collector of quitrents, Talbot County, appointed January 1733/34; justice, Court of Oyer and Terminer and Gaol Delivery, Talbot County, commissioned 1741. MILITARY SERVICE: colonel, 1746. WEALTH DURING LIFETIME. LAND AT FIRST ELECTION: at least 350 acres in Talbot County (all by purchase or patent). SIGNIFICANT CHANGES IN LAND BETWEEN FIRST ELECTION AND DEATH: controlled 400 acres in Talbot County for his stepson John Glen from ca. 1719 to ca. 1744; controlled at least 727 acres in Talbot and Dorchester counties for his Taylor stepchildren from ca. 1735/36 to ca. 1744; at least 1,853 acres in Talbot and Dorchester counties by purchase or patent between 1726 and 1749; sold 461 acres in Talbot County between 1748 and 1752. WEALTH AT DEATH. DIED: between May 5 and July 21, 1752, in Talbot County. PERSONAL PROPERTY: at least 14 slaves mentioned in his will. LAND: 1,762 acres in Talbot and Dorchester counties.

BRACCO, JOHN (?–1794). BORN: of age by 1748. RESIDED: at "Bracco," Queen Anne's County, by 1748; Miles River, Talbot County, by 1761. FAMILY BACKGROUND. OTHER KINSHIP: a Thomas Bracco signed John Bracco's inventory as a next of kin. MARRIED by 1753 Elizabeth, daughter of Nathaniel Beall and wife Elizabeth Brooke; granddaughter of Roger Brooke (1673–1718), of Prince George's County, and wife Elizabeth Hutchins. Her sisters were Ann, a minor in 1757; Priscilla. Her first cousins were *Richard Bennett Carmichael* (1753–1824); Elizabeth Brooke Carmichael, who married *John Lambert Wilmer* (1747–1799); and *Richard Brooke* (1736–1788). CHILDREN. SONS: John (ca. 1763–1794), of Queen Anne's County, a surgeon, who married Henrietta Nicholson; James (?–by 1794), who was appointed register of wills of Talbot County in 1785 after his father resigned, and who married Ann. DAUGHTER: Priscilla, who married James Booker. PRIVATE CAREER. EDUCATION: literate. RELIGIOUS AFFILIATION: Protestant. SOCIAL STATUS AND ACTIVITIES: Gent., 1752; Esq., 1783. OCCUPATIONAL PROFILE: planter, 1753; merchant, 1761. PUBLIC CAREER. LEGISLATIVE SERVICE: Lower House, Queen Anne's County, 1754–1757 (Bills of Credit 2, 4–6), 1757–1758 (Bills of Credit 1, Cv, 2; Grievances 1, Cv, 2), Talbot County, 1777 (elected to fill vacancy, but did not attend; resigned on March 13, 1777, upon his appointment as register of wills and commissioner of the peace of Talbot County), 1785 (Grievances; Manufactories). LOCAL OFFICES: St. John's Parish Vestry, Queen Anne's County, in office 1752–1755, 1757–1760; justice, Queen Anne's County, 1754–1756, Talbot County, by 1769–at least 1789 (quorum, 1774–at least 1789); St. Michael's Parish Vestry, Talbot County, in office 1763, 1770–1773, 1773–1776, 1776–1779, and 1787; tobacco inspector, Miles River, Talbot County, in office 1766–1768; deputy commissary, Talbot County, in office 1771–1777; Committee of Observation, Talbot County, elected ca. 1774; loan officer, Continental Loan Office, Talbot County, appointed 1777; commissioner of tax, Talbot County, appointed 1777; register of

wills, Talbot County, 1777–1785; justice, Court of Oyer and Terminer and Gaol Delivery, Talbot County, commissioned 1778; judge, court of appeals, appointed under the Act to Procure Troops for the American Army, Talbot County, appointed 1778; justice, Orphans' Court, Queen Anne's County, appointed 1789 and 1791. WEALTH DURING LIFETIME. PERSONAL PROPERTY: assessed value £1,050.18.9, including 34 slaves and 3 oz. plate, Talbot and Queen Anne's counties, 1783; 25 slaves, 1790. LAND AT FIRST ELECTION: 1,399 acres in Queen Anne's County (all by patent). SIGNIFICANT CHANGES IN LAND BETWEEN FIRST ELECTION AND DEATH: mortgaged 622 acres in Queen Anne's County, 1767; owned a total of 1,348 acres in Talbot and Queen Anne's counties, 1783; mortgaged 400 acres in Talbot County, 1789; deeded 622 acres in Queen Anne's County as a gift to his son John, 1792, but he retained a life estate in it. WEALTH AT DEATH. DIED: between July 29 and November 13, 1794, in Talbot County. PERSONAL PROPERTY: TEV, £1,813.0.11 current money (including 32 slaves and books); FB, £676.2.3. LAND: 400 acres in Talbot County which were sold to pay a debt of £2,498.9.1 that Bracco owed to *James Lloyd Chamberlaine* (1732–1783).

BRADFORD, JOHN (?–1725/26). BORN: probably in Leicestershire, England. IMMIGRATED: by 1701 as a free adult. RESIDED: in Prince George's County. FAMILY BACKGROUND. FATHER: John Bradford, of Leicestershire, England. SISTER: Mary Jones. MARRIED first, by 1706 Ann, daughter of John Gant; stepdaughter of *John Wight* (?–1705). MARRIED second, ca. 1712 Joyce, widow of James Butler. Her brother was James Carroll. CHILDREN. SONS: William (1713–?); John. PRIVATE CAREER. EDUCATION: literate. RELIGIOUS AFFILIATION: Anglican. SOCIAL STATUS AND ACTIVITIES: Gent., by 1706; in England in 1709; his second marriage brought him considerable wealth. OCCUPATIONAL PROFILE: planter; land developer; factor for John Hyde, of London, England; merchant. PUBLIC CAREER. LEGISLATIVE SERVICE: Lower House, Prince George's County, 1708A, 1708B–1711 (Accounts 1, 3, 4), 1715 (Accounts), 1716–1718 (Accounts 1–3). LOCAL OFFICES: justice, Prince George's County, 1711–1718, 1724–1725/26; King George's Parish Vestry, Prince George's County, 1712–1718, 1724–1725/26. MILITARY SERVICE: captain, 1708–1714; major, 1714–1722; colonel, 1722–1725/26. WEALTH DURING LIFETIME. LAND AT FIRST ELECTION: 452 acres in 1706; began to purchase large tracts in 1710.

WEALTH AT DEATH. DIED: by late March 1725/26. PERSONAL PROPERTY: TEV, £1,957.8.0 (including 40 slaves and 4 servants); FB, £250.4.6. LAND: ca. 14,070 acres, of which 4,500 acres were jointly owned with *Daniel Dulany* (1685–1753).

BRADLEY (BRADLY), ISAAC (?–ca. 1795). RESIDED: in Caroline County, 1774; Sussex County, Delaware, by 1775. FAMILY BACKGROUND. FATHER: William Bradley (?–ca. 1784), of Dorchester County, who died in Delaware. BROTHERS: William (?–ca. 1814); Joseph (?–by 1814); and Jacob (?–ca. 1775), of Caroline County. SISTERS: Nancy (?–by 1784), who married Charles Brown; Mary, who married (first name unknown) Bannister; and Betty, who married (first name unknown) Freeny. MARRIED in March 1781 Elizabeth Casson (?–by 1798). CHILDREN. SONS: probably Henry; probably Joshua. DAUGHTER: Polly, who married (first name unknown) Wilson. PRIVATE CAREER. EDUCATION: literate. SOCIAL STATUS AND ACTIVITIES: Esq., by 1775. PUBLIC CAREER. LEGISLATIVE SERVICE: Convention, Caroline County, 1st, 1774. OUT OF STATE SERVICE: Council of Safety, Sussex County, Delaware, appointed 1775; Convention, Sussex County, Delaware, elected on August 19, 1776 (this convention met on September 11, 1776, for the purpose of "ordaining and declaring the future form of Government of that State."); justice, Sussex County, Delaware, appointed 1784. WEALTH AT DEATH. DIED: ca. 1795 in Sussex County, Delaware. LAND: 100 acres in Caroline County; probably had land in Delaware as well.

BRADLEY, ROBERT (?–1724). BORN: probably in England. IMMIGRATED: by 1693 as a free adult. RESIDED: in Prince George's County. FAMILY BACKGROUND. BROTHER: Benjamin Bradley, a merchant of London, England. MARRIED Sarah, (1677–?), daughter of *Richard Hall* (?–1688). Her brothers were *Elisha Hall* (1663–ca. 1716/17); Joseph (1665–1705); *Benjamin Hall* (1667–1721); and Aaron (1669–1704). Her sisters were Rachel (1671–1730), who married *Walter Smith* (?–1711); Elizabeth (1673–1743); and Lucia (1675–?), who married *John Smith* (?–1738). CHILDREN. SON: Robert, a justice of Prince George's County from 1729 to 1731/32, who married (first name unknown), daughter of Clement Hill, nephew and heir of *Clement Hill* (?–1708). PRIVATE CAREER. EDUCATION: literate. RELIGIOUS AFFILIATION: Presbyterian. SOCIAL STATUS AND ACTIVITIES: he had important mercantile connections; he was prosecuted in 1694 for violating the Navigation Acts, but was acquitted. OCCUPATIONAL PROFILE: factor for Edward and Dudley Carleton, merchants in England; merchant; shipowner. PUBLIC CAREER. LEGISLATIVE SERVICE: Lower House, Prince George's County, 1701–1704 (Accounts 1–3, 5), 1706–1707 (elected to the 4th session), 1708A, 1708B–1711 (speaker, 1–4). OTHER PROVINCIAL OFFICE: justice, Provincial Court, 1709–1714. LOCAL OFFICES: justice, Prince George's County, 1695/96–1709 (quorum, 1697–1709; chief justice, 1705–1709); coroner, Prince George's County, 1696–1707; St. Paul's Parish Vestry, Prince George's County, 1704. WEALTH DURING LIFETIME. LAND AT FIRST ELECTION: at least 100 acres. WEALTH AT DEATH. DIED: in 1724. PERSONAL PROPERTY: gave all of his personal property to his son before his death. LAND: gave 870 acres to his son before his death.

BRADNOX (BRADNOCKS, BRODNOX), THOMAS (ca. 1599–1661). BORN: ca. 1599, probably in England. IMMIGRATED: on Kent Island, by 1637/38. RESIDED: in Kent County. MARRIED Mary (?–1674), who subsequently married ca. 1664 John Vicaris (?–ca. 1669), and finally, Francis Pine (?–by 1674). CHILDREN. Died without progeny. PRIVATE CAREER. EDUCATION: illiterate. RELIGIOUS AFFILIATION: Protestant. SOCIAL STATUS AND ACTIVITIES: in 1642 he had the third highest assessment of seventy-one men on Kent Island; Mr., by 1647/48; Gent., by 1652/53; usually owned at least two or three servants, whom he notoriously mistreated; he was one of the most disreputable men in the colony; raised Francis Mauldin (?–1710/11) for six years before Mauldin's mother reclaimed him in 1659/60. OCCUPATIONAL PROFILE: planter. PUBLIC CAREER. LEGISLATIVE SERVICE: Assembly, Kent County, 1637/38, present 1647/48. LOCAL OFFICES: justice, Kent County, 1647–1653, 1658–1661; sheriff, Kent County, 1653. MILITARY SERVICE: commander's mate, Kent County, 1641; captain and commander of all the forces on Kent Island, 1658. WEALTH DURING LIFETIME. LAND AT FIRST ELECTION: acquired with William Brantwell legal control over 2,000 acres in 1640; sold 200 acres in 1661. WEALTH AT DEATH. DIED: between October 20 and December 25, 1661. PERSONAL PROPERTY: no value given in his inventory; 4 servants; 3 horses, 64 hogs, 34 cattle. LAND: 1,900 acres.

BRAINTHWAITE, WILLIAM (?–ca. 1649/50). BORN: probably in England. IMMIGRATED: by 1637/38 as a free adult. RESIDED: in Kent County; St. Mary's County, by 1643. FAMILY BACKGROUND. FATHER: probably Robert Brainthwaite, secretary to Sir Richard Weston, who was probably a son of Edward Brainthwaite, who married a member of the Calvert family. MOTHER: probably Ann, daughter of Francis Carter, chief clerk of His Majesty's Rolls. BROTHER: probably Robert Brainthwaite of Carlingill, Westmoreland, England, who married Elizabeth, sister of Sir Thomas Burton, of Brampton, England. COUSIN: *Leonard Calvert* (ca. 1606–1647). MARRIED Eleanor Stephenson, a former servant brought to Virginia in 1645 by Edmund Plowden, from whom she fled to Maryland. PRIVATE CAREER. EDUCATION: literate; probably well educated. RELIGIOUS AFFILIATION: almost certainly a Catholic. SOCIAL STATUS AND ACTIVITIES: probably Gent. on arrival, certainly by 1638; called a "kinsman" by *Cecilius Calvert, 2nd Lord Baltimore* (1605–1675), in 1638. OCCUPATIONAL PROFILE: Indian trader, 1639. PUBLIC CAREER. LEGISLATIVE SERVICE: Assembly, present 1637/38. PROVINCIAL OFFICES: Treasury Commission, 1643, Council, 1644 (no record of service other than his oath taken on November 2, 1644). LOCAL OFFICES: commander, Kent Isle, 1638–1639/40, 1644/45; justice, Kent County, 1639/40–1640; commander, St. Mary's County, 1643–1644. MILITARY OFFICE: captain, 1640. WEALTH AT DEATH. DIED: by February 1649/50; size of estate unknown.

BRANDT, RANDOLPH (?–ca. 1698/99). IMMIGRATED: in 1674 as a free adult with his wife and children, probably from Barbados. RESIDED: in Charles County. FAMILY BACKGROUND. BROTHERS: Charles; Jacob. MARRIED Mary. CHILDREN. SONS: Jacob; Randolph; Charles; and Marcus, of Barbados. DAUGHTERS: Elizabeth, who married Joseph Bullitt; Mary, who married James Lattimore; Margaret, who married Francis Hammersley; and Judith. NATURAL DAUGHTER: Anne, the daughter of Susannah Skeens. PRIVATE CAREER. EDUCATION: literate. RELIGIOUS AFFILIATION: Catholic. SOCIAL STATUS AND ACTIVITIES: Mr. at first appearance in the records; Gent. at death. OCCUPATIONAL PROFILE: placeman; planter; kept books for Humphrey Warren, Jr. (1665–1695), son of *Humphrey Warren* (ca. 1632–ca. 1670/71) in the 1680s. PUBLIC CAREER. LEGISLATIVE SERVICE: Lower House, Charles County, 1681–1682 (elected to the 3rd session). LOCAL OFFICES: clerk, Charles County, 1676–1682; deputy surveyor, Charles County, 1679–1684. MILITARY SERVICE: captain, by 1678. WEALTH DURING LIFETIME. LAND AT FIRST ELECTION: 500 acres of improved land in Barbados (inherited from his father); probably over 1,000 acres in Maryland. WEALTH AT DEATH. DIED: will probated on February 10, 1698/99. PERSONAL PROPERTY: TEV, £241.4.8 sterling, plus 9,055 pounds of tobacco (including 5 slaves and 3 servants). LAND: ca. 2,070 acres, plus 500 acres in Barbados.

BRANNOCK (BRONNACK), JOHN (ca. 1669–1741). BORN: ca. 1669; probably eldest son. NATIVE: probably, if so probably second generation. RESIDED: in Dorchester County. FAMILY BACKGROUND. FATHER: Edmond Brannock (?–ca. 1703), of Dorchester County, planter. BROTHERS: Thomas (ca. 1674–1744/45), planter, who married Frances; David (under 21-years of age in 1701); and Edmond (?–by 1718), who married Rebecca. SISTERS: Mary; Jane, who married (first name unknown) Jones; and Elizabeth. MARRIED by 1709 Margaret (?–1751), a Quaker, widow of Anthony Lecompte (?–1705), of Dorchester County, planter. CHILDREN. STEPSONS: Nehemiah Lecompte (ca. 1698–?); Anthony Lecompte (under 18-years of age in 1704/5). DAUGHTER: Ann, who married first, Robert Spedden (?–1742), and second, Joseph Pain. STEPDAUGHTER OR DAUGHTER: Margaret, who married (first name unknown) Matthews. PRIVATE CAREER. EDUCATION: literate. RELIGIOUS AFFILIATION: Protestant. SOCIAL STATUS AND ACTIVITIES: Gent., 1702. OCCUPATIONAL PROFILE: sawyer, 1694; planter; attorney, admitted to the following courts: Court of Appeals by 1715; Dorchester County by 1717. ADDITIONAL COMMENTS: as an attorney of Dorchester County, Brannock was accused of having forged a summons in the king's name, 1715. PUBLIC CAREER. LEGISLATIVE SERVICE: Lower House, Dorchester County, 1716–1718, 1719–1721/22 (Laws 1), 1728–1731, 1732–1734, 1738, 1739–1740 (died before the 3rd session). WEALTH DURING LIFETIME. PERSONAL PROPERTY: sold 6 slaves, 1 manservant, livestock, and other personal property to his brother Thomas to pay his debts, 1709. ADDITIONAL COMMENTS: A petition was submitted to the Lower House in 1732 by John Anderson, coroner of Dorchester County, stating that John Brannock, a member of the Lower House, had been arrested and confined by him until Brannock could appear in court to satisfy a person who had recovered a judgment against him. Brannock was alleged to have escaped from custody. After hearing both parties, the House rejected Anderson's petition. In 1738 Brannock, again a member of the Lower House, entered a complaint against *Peter Taylor* (1680–ca. 1747/48), the sheriff of Dorchester County, alleging that *Edmund Jennings* (?–1756) had turned over to Taylor some bonds that Brannock owed to Jennings. Brannock had offered to pay the fees due to Taylor, and in fact had payed him some tobacco, but Taylor incarcerated him anyway to the great detriment of Brannock's person and fortune. The Lower House reprimanded both Taylor and his undersheriff for their tactics in collecting debts before any demands had been made by the obligators on the bonds, terming their treatment of many debtors in Dorchester County, including Brannock, "illegal, cruel and inhuman." LAND AT FIRST ELECTION: 118 acres in Dorchester County (by patent). ADDITIONAL COMMENTS: Prior to his first election to office, Brannock had purchased and/or patented 1,048 acres in Dorchester County in his own right, and 1,200 acres in partnership with *John Lecompte* (ca. 1662–1705) between 1691 and 1706. He sold 400 acres of this land in 1706, and he sold all but 118 acres of the remainder of his land, including the tract patented with Lecompte to his brother, Thomas, to pay his large number of debts in 1709. SIGNIFICANT CHANGES IN LAND BETWEEN FIRST ELECTION AND DEATH: patented 100 acres in Dorchester County, 1732. Henry Hill obtained the 118-acre tract in Dorchester County as a result of a court judgment in his favor for a debt Brannock owed him, 1734. WEALTH AT DEATH. DIED: between April 8 and May 27, 1741, in Dorchester County. PERSONAL PROPERTY: TEV, £409.3.2 current money (including books). His inventory also listed 7 slaves, 1 manservant, and other personal property, but these had been sold to Brannock's brother in 1709. They were repurchased by Brannock's widow in 1742. FB, estate overpaid £103.11.6. LAND: 100 acres in Dorchester County, however, Brannock made bequests of 400 additional acres, even though they were among the tracts he had sold to his brother in 1709 to pay his debts. ADDITIONAL COMMENTS: In 1742 Brannock's widow bought back at least 530 acres of the Dorchester County land her husband had sold his brother, Thomas, in 1709. Brannock and his brother may have had an unwritten agreement concerning the land, which provided for John's heirs to regain possession of it after his debts were paid.

BRENT, FULKE (?–1656). BORN: in the late 1590s in Gloucestershire, England; probably oldest son. IMMIGRATED: in 1638 as a free adult. RESIDED: in St. Mary's County; returned to England, ca. 1642. FAMILY BACKGROUND. FATHER: Richard Brent, of Stoke and Addington, England, the sheriff of Gloucestershire, England, in 1614. MOTHER: Elizabeth, daughter of Giles Reed, Lord of Tusburie and Witten. BROTHERS: *Giles Brent* (1600–ca.

1671/72); George (1602–1671), who married Marianna, daughter of Sir John Peyton, of Doddington, England; Richard; William; and Edward (?–1625). SISTERS: Margaret (1601–1671); Mary (?–1658); Catherine; Elizabeth; Eleanor; Jane; and Anne. PRIVATE CAREER. EDUCATION: literate; entered Oxford University, 1613; Middle Temple, London, England, 1615. RELIGIOUS AFFILIATION: Catholic. SOCIAL STATUS AND ACTIVITIES: high status on arrival; Mr. on first appearance in Maryland records; returned to England temporarily in 1638/39 and returned with his sisters. OCCUPATIONAL PROFILE: probably a planter. PUBLIC CAREER. LEGISLATIVE SERVICE: Assembly, special writ 1638/39, 1640–1641 (attended only the 2nd session), 1641/42. WEALTH AT DEATH. DIED: in 1656; size of estate unknown.

BRENT, GEORGE (?–1782). BORN: of age by 1776. RESIDED: west of Licking Creek, Fort Frederick Hundred, Frederick County (later became part of Washington County). FAMILY BACKGROUND. May have been related to the Brent family of Virginia. MARRIED Charity, who subsequently married in 1783 John Read (Ried). CHILDREN. SON: Thomas. DAUGHTER: Elizabeth, who married by 1803 (first name unknown) Grayham. PRIVATE CAREER. OCCUPATIONAL PROFILE: probably a planter. PUBLIC CAREER. LEGISLATIVE SERVICE: Conventions, Frederick County, 7th–8th, 1776 (did not attend the 8th Convention). LOCAL OFFICES: justice, Frederick County, 1773–at least 1775; Committee of Observation, Frederick County, 1775. MILITARY SERVICE: referred to as an American officer who was out of the army in 1781. WEALTH DURING LIFETIME. SIGNIFICANT CHANGES IN LAND BETWEEN FIRST ELECTION AND DEATH: purchased more than 100 acres in Washington County, 1779. WEALTH AT DEATH. DIED: administration bond dated June 27, 1782, in Washington County. PERSONAL PROPERTY: TEV, £1,050.9.10 current money (including 12 slaves, considerable livestock, and 20 oz. plate); FB, £808.3.11. LAND: ca. 386 acres.

BRENT, GILES (1600–ca. 1671/72). BORN: in 1600 in Gloucestershire, England; probably second son. IMMIGRATED: in 1638 as a free adult. RESIDED: in St. Mary's and Kent counties; moved to Stafford County, Virginia, ca. 1649. FAMILY BACKGROUND. FATHER: Richard Brent, of Stoke and Addington, England, the sheriff of Gloucestershire, England, in 1614. MOTHER: Elizabeth, daughter of Giles Reed, Lord of Tusburie and Witten. BROTHERS: *Fulke Brent* (?–1656); George

(1602–1671), who married Marianna, daughter of Sir John Peyton, of Doddington, England; Richard; William; and Edward (?–1625). SISTERS: Margaret (1601–1671); Mary (?–1658); Catherine; Elizabeth; Eleanor; Jane; and Anne. MARRIED first, Kittamaquund, daughter of the Emperor of the Piscattaway Indians. MARRIED second, Frances, widow of Jeremiah Harrison (?–by 1654), of York County, Virginia. Her brother was Thomas Whitgreaves, of Staffordshire, England. CHILDREN. SONS: Giles (1652–1679), who married Mary, daughter of George Brent and wife Marianna Peyton; Richard (?–died young). DAUGTHER: Mary, who married John Fitzherbert, brother of *Edward Fitzherbert* (?–?). PRIVATE CAREER. EDUCATION: literate, probably well educated. RELIGIOUS AFFILIATION: Catholic. SOCIAL STATUS AND ACTIVITIES: Mr. on arrival, and was accorded special social and political distinctions immediately; his marriage to an Indian princess fostered his hopes of some political power but greatly alarmed the proprietary interests. OCCUPATIONAL PROFILE: planter. PUBLIC CAREER. LEGISLATIVE SERVICE: Assembly, special writ 1638/39, special writ 1640–1641 (also Kent County, 1640), special writ 1641/42 (Aggrievances), special writ 1642A, special writ 1642B (Laws), special writ 1647/48 (Accounts). OTHER PROVINCIAL OFFICES: Council, 1638–1644 (suspended briefly, 1642), 1647–1649; treasurer, 1639–1643; commander, Kent Isle, 1639/40–1642; acting governor and lieutenant general, 1643–1644. STANDS ON PUBLIC/PRIVATE ISSUES: an opponent of the proprietary prerogatives in the Assembly, 1642; suspended briefly from the Council in 1642 on the charge of disaffection to Lord Baltimore and was removed from the commandership of Kent Isle; found innocent by a jury of charges brought by John Lewger that Brent had caused the failure of an expedition against the Susquehannah Indians and that he was guilty of contempt and other misdemeanors, 1642; issued a controversial order for the seizure of Richard Ingle's ship, 1643/44; dismissed Lewger from the Council, 1644; a warrant was issued for Brent's arrest for "crimes against the dignity and dominion" of the lord proprietor, 1644/45; seized during Ingle's Rebellion and carried to England, 1645; eventually broke completely with Lord Baltimore in the late 1640s after his temporary reinstatement to the Council. WEALTH DURING LIFETIME. LAND AT FIRST ELECTION: 1,063 acres, 1638; acquired an additional 1,000 acres, Kent Fort Manor, in 1640, which he later transferred to his sister; over 1,518 acres in Virginia, 1654. WEALTH AT DEATH. DIED: will probated on February 16, 1671/72. LAND: probably over 1,500 acres.

BRETTON (BRITTON), WILLIAM (?–ca. 1672). BORN: probably in England. IMMIGRATED: in 1637/38 as a free adult with his wife and child. RESIDED: in Newtown, St. Mary's County; Charles County, by 1668. MARRIED first, Mary, daughter of Thomas Nabbs. MARRIED second, in 1651 Temperance Jay. CHILDREN. SON: William, Jr. (ca. 1633–?). DAUGHTER OR STEPDAUGHTER: Mary, who married William Thompson (?–1660). PRIVATE CAREER. EDUCATION: literate; extensive clerical skills. RELIGIOUS AFFILIATION: Catholic. SOCIAL STATUS AND ACTIVITIES: Gent. on arrival; brought three servants with him; his clerical skills led to quick and profitable patronage in a series of clerkships. OCCUPATIONAL PROFILE: placeman; planter. PUBLIC CAREER. LEGISLATIVE SERVICE: Assembly, present 1637/38, present 1641/42, special writ 1642A, present 1647/48 (Defense), St. Mary's County, 1649. OTHER PROVINCIAL OFFICES: clerk, Assembly, 1637/38–1650; clerk, Council, by 1638–1647; clerk, Secretary's Office and Provincial Court, 1647–1652, 1657/58–1660; clerk, Lower House, 1650–1650/51, 1661–1666. LOCAL OFFICES: justice, St. Mary's County, 1658–1668; coroner, St. Mary's County, 1669–1670. WEALTH DURING LIFETIME. LAND AT FIRST ELECTION: acquired "Little Brittaine," 750 acres, in 1640, and another 100 acres in 1649; sold both tracts in 1668. WEALTH AT DEATH. DIED: ca. 1672; size of estate unknown.

BREVARD (BRAVARD), BENJAMIN (?–1793). BORN: probably in Cecil County, of age by 1757. NATIVE: probably, if so, at least second generation. RESIDED: in Back Creek Hundred, Cecil County. FAMILY BACKGROUND. FATHER: probably John Brevard, of Cecil County, one of the founders and elders of the Broad Creek Presbyterian Church, Cecil County. BROTHER: probably Dr. Ephraim Brevard, who immigrated to North Carolina along with other Cecil County families by 1775; chairman of the North Carolina committee that drafted the Mecklenberg declaration of independence in 1775. MARRIED Rebecca (?–1802). CHILDREN. SONS: Joshua (?–by 1806); Adam; and Benjamin. DAUGHTERS: Rachel (?–by 1799), who married in 1788 William Taylor; Rebecca, who married in 1796 Nicholas Chambers; and Clarissa, who married in 1800 David Culbertson. PRIVATE CAREER. EDUCATION: literate. RELIGIOUS AFFILIATION: probably a Presbyterian. OCCUPATIONAL PROFILE: farmer; perhaps also a surveyor, because surveying instruments and a book on this subject were mentioned in his will. **PUBLIC CAREER. LEGISLATIVE SERVICE:** Convention, Cecil County, 9th, 1776; Lower House, Cecil County, 1781–1782, 1782–1783, 1783, 1784, 1786–1787, 1787–1788, 1788. **STANDS ON PUBLIC/PRIVATE ISSUES:** Brevard, along with his fellow Cecil County delegates, objected to the commission of *Patrick Ewing* (?–1819) as justice of Cecil County in 1788. Nevertheless, Ewing's commission was confirmed. In 1789 Brevard manumitted one slave, ca. 14 years of age, to take effect in 1796. **WEALTH DURING LIFETIME. PERSONAL PROPERTY:** assessed value £197.16.8, including 2 oz. plate, 1783; 1 slave, 1790. **LAND AT FIRST ELECTION:** ca. 340 acres in Cecil County and Delaware. **WEALTH AT DEATH. DIED:** will probated on March 27, 1793, in Cecil County. **PERSONAL PROPERTY:** requested no appraisal of his estate. **LAND:** home plantation, consisting of probably ca. 300 acres including adjoining land in Cecil County and Delaware.

BREWER, JOHN (?–ca. 1663/64). **BORN:** probably in England. **IMMIGRATED:** by the late 1640s as an indentured servant. **RESIDED:** in Anne Arundel County. **MARRIED** Elizabeth (?–1668). **CHILDREN. SON:** John. **PRIVATE CAREER. SOCIAL STATUS AND ACTIVITIES:** free by 1658, when he claimed rights for completion of his service as an indentured servant and for transporting three individuals in 1652 and another one in 1657. **OCCUPATIONAL PROFILE:** indentured servant; planter. **PUBLIC CAREER. LEGISLATIVE SERIVCE:** Lower House, Anne Arundel County, 1661. **LOCAL OFFICE:** justice, Anne Arundel County, 1658–1663/64. **WEALTH DURING LIFETIME. LAND AT FIRST ELECTION:** 400 acres. **WEALTH AT DEATH. DIED:** ca. 1663/64. **LAND:** over 466 acres.

BRICE, BENEDICT (1749–1786). **BORN:** on April 1, 1749 in Annapolis, Anne Arundel County; fourth surviving son. **NATIVE:** third generation. **RESIDED:** in Annapolis, Anne Arundel County; Kent County, Delaware, and Caroline County alternately after 1771, with probate being registered in both counties. **FAMILY BACKGROUND. FATHER:** John Brice (1705–1766), a resident of Annapolis who was chief justice of Maryland, an alderman of Annapolis, a judge of Assize for the Western Shore, and clerk of Anne Arundel County Court; he was the son of *John Brice* (?–1713). **MOTHER:** Sarah (1714–1782), daughter of *James Frisby* (1684–1719) and wife Ariana Vanderheyden (1690–?); stepdaughter of both *Thomas Bordley* (ca. 1683–1726) and *Edmund Jennings* (?–

1756); granddaughter of *Matthias Vanderheyden* (?–1729). **HALF UNCLE:** *John Beale Bordley* (1726/27–1804). **AUNTS:** Ariana Margaret Frisby (1717–?), who married *William Harris* (1704–1748); Anne Brice (1708–1765), who married *Vachel Denton* (ca. 1696–1752); and Rachel Brice (1711–1786), who married *Philip Hammond* (1697–1760). **BROTHERS:** John (1737–1737); *John Brice* (1738–1820); *James Brice* (1746–1801); and Edmund (?–1784), who married in September 1783 Harriet Woodward. **SISTERS:** Ariana, who married Dr. David Ross (?–by 1779); Sarah, who married Richard Henderson; Anne; Margaret Augustina, who married William Sydebotham; and Elizabeth, who married first, Lloyd Dulany (1742–1782), son of *Daniel Dulany* (1685–1753), and second, ca. 1785 Walter Dulany, son of *Walter Dulany* (?–1773). **FIRST COUSINS:** *William Stevenson* (1739–1785); *John Hammond* (1735–1784); *Rezin Hammond* (1745–1809); and *Matthias Hammond* (1740–1786). **MARRIED** in January 1775 Mary (1755–1796), daughter of *John Goldsborough* (1711–1778) and wife Ann Turbutt (1715–1766); stepdaughter of Mary Skinner Loockerman; granddaughter of both *Robert Goldsborough* (1660–1746) and *Foster Turbutt* (1679–1720/21); niece of *Charles Goldsborough* (1707–1767), *William Goldsborough* (1709–1760), Sarah Turbutt (1706–?), who married *Nicholas Goldsborough* (ca. 1689–1766), and Elizabeth Turbutt (1708–?), who married *Tench Francis* (1701–1758). Mary Goldsborough Brice subsequently married in August 1787 Dr. James Cook (?–1794). Her brothers were Robert (ca. 1736–1770); John (1740–1803); Greenbury (1742–1829); Charles (1744–1774); and William (1759–1794). Her sisters were Elizabeth (ca. 1735–ca. 1786), who married second *Benson Stainton* (?–ca. 1781); Anne (1751–1781); and Henrietta Maria (ca. 1753–1839). Her first cousins were *Robert Goldsborough IV* (1740–1798); *William Goldsborough* (1750/51–1801); *Howes Goldsborough* (1747–1797); *Robert Goldsborough* (1733–1788); Elizabeth Greenberry Goldsborough (1731–1820), who married *William Ennalls* (?–1785); *Thomas Goldsborough* (ca. 1728–1793); Ann Goldsborough (1732–?), who married *Edward Oldham* (1709–1773); and Ann Francis (1727–?), who married *James Tilghman* (1716–1793) Her niece was Margaret Campbell (ca. 1766–1789), who married *John Henry, Jr.* (ca. 1750–1798). **CHILDREN. DAUGHTER:** Sarah (1776–?), who married Andrew Price. **PRIVATE CAREER. EDUCATION:** literate. **SOCIAL STATUS AND ACTIVITIES:** Gent., 1771. **OCCUPATIONAL PROFILE:** farmer, 1783; merchant, 1784; owned stores in

Greensboro, Caroline County. PUBLIC CAREER. LEGISLATIVE SERVICE: Convention, Caroline County, 3rd, 1774. OUT OF STATE SERVICE: Boston Relief Committee, Kent County, Delaware, elected on August 14, 1775; 2nd lieutenant, Infantry, Eighth or Dover Regiment, Delaware Militia, period of service unknown. WEALTH DURING LIFETIME. LAND AT FIRST ELECTION: one-quarter interest in 477 acres in Cecil County (the residue of sales from at least 819 acres inherited from his father); probably owned land in Kent County, Delaware. SIGNIFICANT CHANGES IN LAND BETWEEN FIRST ELECTION AND DEATH: sold the remainder of his land in Cecil County that he inherited from his father, 1777; owned at least 1,500 acres in Kent County, Delaware, which he advertised for sale in 1777. WEALTH AT DEATH. DIED: administration bond granted on July 11, 1786, in Caroline County. PERSONAL PROPERTY: TEV, £1,179.18.5 current money (including 3 slaves, 57 oz. plate, and books); FB, estate overpaid £177.6.9. LAND: lot 6 in Greensboro, Caroline County; probably also owned land in Kent County, Delaware.

BRICE, JAMES (1746–1801). BORN: on August 26, 1746, in Annapolis, Anne Arundel County. NATIVE: third generation. RESIDED: in the Brice House, a large townhouse he built between 1767 and 1775, in Annapolis. FAMILY BACKGROUND. FATHER: John Brice (1705–1766); clerk of Anne Arundel County from 1734 to 1765; justice of the Provincial Court from 1741 to probably 1766; judge of the Assize of the Western Shore from 1754 to 1766; son of *John Brice* (?–1713). MOTHER: Sarah (1714–1782), daughter of *James Frisby* (1684–1719) and wife Ariana (1690–?); stepdaughter of both *Thomas Bordley* (ca. 1683–1726) and *Edmund Jennings* (?–1756); granddaughter of *Matthias Vanderheyden* (?–1729). HALF UNCLE: *John Beale Bordley* (1726/27–1804). AUNTS: Ariana Margaret Frisby (1717–?), who married *William Harris* (1704–1748); Anne Brice (1708–1765), who married *Vachel Denton* (ca. 1696–1752); and Rachel Brice (1711–1786), who married *Philip Hammond* (1697–1760). BROTHERS: John (?–died in infancy); *John Brice* (1738–1820); *Benedict Brice* (1749–1786); and Edmund (?–1784), who married in 1783 Harriet Woodward. SISTERS: Ariana, who married Dr. David Ross (?–by 1779); Sarah, who married Richard Henderson; Anne; Margaret Augustina, who married William Sydebotham; and Elizabeth, who married first, Lloyd Dulany (1742–1782), son of *Daniel Dulany* (1685–1753), and second, ca. 1785 Walter Dulany,

son of *Walter Dulany* (?–1773). FIRST COUSINS: *William Stevenson* (1739–1785); *John Hammond* (1735–1784); *Rezin Hammond* (1745–1809); and *Matthias Hammond* (1740–1786). MARRIED in 1781 Julianna (ca. 1764–1837), daughter of *Thomas Jennings* (ca. 1736–1796). Her brothers were Thomas; George; William; John; Daniel; Horner; and Horatio. Her sisters were Ann (?–by 1839), who married *Nicholas (Maccubbin) Carroll* (1750/51–1812); Elizabeth. CHILDREN. SONS: James Frisby; Thomas Jennings; and John. DAUGHTERS: Julianna (1782–?), who married in 1808 John Stephen (?–1844); Sarah Ann (1783–1784); and Anne Carroll (1785–?). PRIVATE CAREER. RELIGIOUS AFFILIATION: Anglican, St. Anne's Parish, Anne Arundel County. SOCIAL STATUS AND ACTIVITIES: Gent., 1771. ADDITIONAL COMMENTS: manager of a lottery to build a new dock for Annapolis, 1772; member of a committee to supervise the building of St. John's College, Annapolis, and hiring of a professor for it, 1789; manager of a lottery to fund completion of St. Anne's Church, Annapolis, 1790. OCCUPATIONAL PROFILE: lawyer, admitted to the following courts: Baltimore County in 1765; Frederick County in 1765; Prince George's County in 1765. Planter. PUBLIC CAREER. STATE OFFICES: Executive Council, 1777 (elected on April 16, 1777, to fill vacancy, but declined to serve), 1777–1778 (elected on November 25, 1777, to fill vacancy), 1778–1779, 1779–1780, 1780–1781, 1781–1782, 1782–1783, 1783 (resigned on December 26, 1783, because he could not "consistently act any longer as one of the Council"; reelected on July 29, 1784, but declined to serve saying he could not "with any degree of consistency accept. . ."), accepted the office 1785–1786, 1786–1787, 1787–1788, 1788–1789, 1789–1790, 1791–1792, 1792–1793, 1793–1794, 1794–1795, 1795–1796, 1798–1799; acting governor, 1792 (following the death of George Plater). LOCAL OFFICES: commissioner of tax, Anne Arundel County, 1777–1779; county lieutenant, Anne Arundel County, appointed 1777; alderman, Annapolis, 1780–1782, 1784–1787, 1789–1792; mayor, Annapolis, 1782–1783, 1788–1789; St. Anne's Parish Vestry, Anne Arundel County, 1783–1787; treasurer, Annapolis, 1784–1801; Maryland Senate elector, Annapolis, elected 1786 and 1791; common councilman, Annapolis, 1793–1801. MILITARY SERVICE: colonel, 1779. STANDS ON PUBLIC/PRIVATE ISSUES: On May 30, 1774 he signed a protest that appeared in the *Maryland Gazette* against a resolution of some Anne Arundel County patriots to prohibit lawyers from suing Maryland residents for debts owed to

British creditors. WEALTH DURING LIFETIME. PERSONAL PROPERTY: assessed value £1,613.13.4, including 28 slaves and 160 oz. plate, 1783. LAND AT FIRST ELECTION: ca. 1,700 acres in Anne Arundel and Cecil counties, plus 2 lots in Annapolis (inherited ca. 1,000 acres in Cecil County and Annapolis lots from his father, 1766; purchased ca. 700 acres in Anne Arundel County in 1771). WEALTH AT DEATH. DIED: on July 11, 1801, in Anne Arundel County. PERSONAL PROPERTY: TEV, £7,291.3.11 (including 51 slaves and plate); FB, £624.10.6 prior to the distribution of property to his widow and children. His land was sold to pay debts and legacies. LAND: ca. 1,700 acres in Anne Arundel and Cecil counties, plus 2 lots and a large house in Annapolis.

BRICE, JOHN (?–1713). BORN: probably in England. IMMIGRATED: probably in 1696 as a free adult. ADDITIONAL COMMENTS: he may have been native born; a John Brice patented land in 1664 that was later owned by the burgess, John Brice. He may only appear in the records in 1696 when he came of age. Perhaps his father returned to England. RESIDED: in Anne Arundel County. FAMILY BACKGROUND. BROTHER: Thomas, of London, England. SISTER: Elizabeth Butcher, of Northampton, England. MARRIED by 1703 Sarah (?–1726), widow of *John Worthington* (1650–1701); daughter of Matthew Howard (ca. 1640–1692/93) and wife Sarah Dorsey; niece of *Cornelius Howard* (?–1680), Elizabeth Howard, who married *Henry Ridgeley* (?–1710), and Mary Howard, who married *John Hammond* (1643–1707). Her brothers were *Matthew Howard* (ca. 1675–1750); Samuel; and John. Her first cousins were *Charles Hammond* (ca. 1670–1713); *Thomas Hammond* (?–ca. 1724/25); *John Hammond* (ca. 1665–1742/43); and Hannah Howard, who married first, *Charles Hammond* (ca. 1670–1713), and second, *Edmond Benson* (1687–1734). CHILDREN. SON: John (1705–1766), who married Sarah, daughter of *James Frisby* (1684–1719). STEPSONS: John Worthington; *Thomas Worthington* (ca. 1691–1753); William Worthington; and Charles Worthington. DAUGHTERS: Ann (1708–1765), who married in 1721 *Vachel Denton* (ca. 1696–1752); Rachel (1711–1781), who married *Philip Hammond* (1697–1760). STEPDAUGHTER: Sarah Worthington, who married in 1711 Nicholas Ridgely. PRIVATE CAREER. EDUCATION: literate. RELIGIOUS AFFILIATION: Anglican. SOCIAL STATUS AND ACTIVITIES: his first public office came after his marriage to the widow Worthington. OCCUPATIONAL PROFILE: planter; factor and agent for Benjamin Halsey &

Company, of England, 1706; merchant. PUBLIC CAREER. LEGISLATIVE SERVICE: Lower House, Anne Arundel County, 1709 (election to the 2nd session voided). LOCAL OFFICES: justice, Anne Arundel County, 1702–1708, 1709–1713 (quorum, 1705–1708, 1709–1713); coroner, Anne Arundel County, 1704. WEALTH DURING LIFETIME. LAND AT FIRST ELECTION: over 2,500 acres. WEALTH AT DEATH. DIED: in December 1713. PERSONAL PROPERTY: TEV, £4.496.14.11 sterling (including 10 slaves). LAND: over 2,543 acres.

BRICE, JOHN (1738–1820). BORN: in September 1738 in Annapolis, Anne Arundel County; eldest surviving son. NATIVE: third generation. RESIDED: on Prince George Street, Annapolis. FAMILY BACKGROUND. FATHER: John Brice (1705–1766); clerk of Anne Arundel County from 1734 to 1765; justice of the Provincial Court from 1741 to probably 1766; judge of the Assize of the Western Shore from 1754 to 1766; son of *John Brice* (?–1713). MOTHER: Sarah (1714–1782), daughter of *James Frisby* (1684–1719) and wife Ariana (1690–?); stepdaughter of both *Thomas Bordley* (ca. 1683–1726) and *Edmund Jennings* (?–1756); granddaughter of *Matthias Vanderheyden* (?–1729). HALF UNCLE: *John Beale Bordley* (1726/27–1804). AUNTS: Ariana Margaret Frisby (1717–?), who married *William Harris* (1704–1748); Anne Brice (1708–1765), who married *Vachel Denton* (ca. 1696–1752); Rachel Brice (1711–1786), who married *Philip Hammond* (1697–1760). BROTHERS: John (?–died in infancy); *James Brice* (1746–1801); *Benedict Brice* (1749–1786); and Edmund (?–1784), who married in 1783 Harriet Woodward. SISTERS: Ariana, who married Dr. David Ross (?–by 1779); Sarah, who married Richard Henderson; Anne; Margaret Augustina, who married William Sydebotham; and Elizabeth, who married first, Lloyd Dulany (1742–1782), son of *Daniel Dulany* (1685–1753), and second, ca. 1785 Walter Dulany, son of *Walter Dulany* (?–1773). FIRST COUSINS: *William Stevenson* (1739–1785); *John Hammond* (1735–1784); *Rezin Hammond* (1745–1809); and *Matthias Hammond* (1740–1786). MARRIED on October 30, 1766, at St. Margaret's Church, Anne Arundel County, Mary Clare (1749–1806), daughter of Nicholas Maccubbin (1709–1787) and wife Mary Clare; granddaughter of *Charles Carroll* (1691–1755); niece of *Charles Carroll, Barrister* (1723–1783). Her brothers were *Nicholas (Maccubbin) Carroll* (1750/51–1812); John Henry (1754–?); Charles (1756–?), who married Sarah Allen; *James (Maccubbin) Carroll* (1761–1832); and Samuel (1763–

by 1784). Her sister was Susanna (1757–?), who married Nicholas Lingan. CHILDREN. SONS: Nicholas; Edmund (?–1822), who married in 1818 Charlotte Elizabeth Moss (?–1823); Henry; and John, who married Sarah Lane. DAUGHTER: Margaretta Clare, who married in 1807 Clement Smith. PRIVATE CAREER. EDUCATION: entered Clare College, Cambridge University, England, in November 1757; admitted to the Middle Temple in November 1757. RELIGIOUS AFFILIATION: Anglican, St. Anne's Parish, Anne Arundel County. SOCIAL STATUS AND ACTIVITIES: Gent., 1766. OCCUPATIONAL PROFILE: lawyer, admitted to the Annapolis Mayor's Court in 1761; merchant with store in Annapolis in partnership with Thomas Harwood III from 1769 to 1778; planter. PUBLIC CAREER. LEGISLATIVE SERVICE: Lower House, Annapolis, 1777 (Claims 2), 1777–1778 (Grievances 1, 2; Laws to Expire 1–3; Loan Office 1), 1778–1779 (Claims 1, 2; resigned on July 22, 1779). OTHER STATE OFFICE: Executive Council, 1779–1780. LOCAL OFFICES: Committee of Observation, Anne Arundel County, elected 1774 and 1775; clerk, Anne Arundel County, 1765–at least 1777; churchwarden, St. Anne's Parish, Anne Arundel County, in office 1767–1768; justice, Anne Arundel County, in office 1777, 1778, 1782–at least 1805; justice, Orphans' Court, Anne Arundel County, 1777–1790; alderman, Annapolis, in office 1780, 1782, 1783, 1785, 1789, 1791, and 1792 (resigned); mayor, Annapolis, 1780–1781; commissioner of tax, Anne Arundel County, 1783–1798. WEALTH DURING LIFETIME. PERSONAL PROPERTY: £500.0.0 sterling and books inherited from his father in 1766; received £2,052.0.0 current money as his share of the business when the partnership with Thomas Harwood III was dissolved in 1778; 4 slaves and their children inherited from his mother in 1782; assessed value £1,807.18.4, including 30 slaves and 229 oz. plate, 1783. LAND AT FIRST ELECTION: 313 acres in Anne Arundel County and 1 lot in Annapolis (all from his father by gift or inheritance). Brice probably also controlled the 987 acres in Anne Arundel County in which his mother held a life estate under the terms of his father's will. SIGNIFICANT CHANGES IN LAND BETWEEN FIRST ELECTION AND DEATH: received title to his mother's 987 acres in Anne Arundel County, plus 1 lot in Annapolis, when she died in 1782. Brice consolidated his Anne Arundel County land into large tracts under three patents in 1809 and 1812. He gave one of these tracts, 365 acres, to his son Edmund in 1812. WEALTH AT DEATH. DIED: between April 22 and July 26, 1820, in Annapolis. Buried in St. Paul's

Church Cemetery in Baltimore City. PERSONAL PROPERTY: TEV, $1,080.67 (including $300.00 in the bank and $210.00 in his pocket). The bulk of his personal property had probably been given to his children before his death. LAND: ca. 1,000 acres in Anne Arundel County, plus 2 lots in Annapolis.

BRISCOE, PHILIP (?–ca. 1724/25). IMMIGRATED: origins uncertain, but in Maryland by 1684 as a free adult. RESIDED: in St. Mary's County; Charles County by 1696. FAMILY BACKGROUND. Perhaps a descendant of Dr. John Briscoe, of Cumberland, England, who had come to Maryland with Leonard Calvert in 1634. MARRIED first, Mary Foster. MARRIED second, Susannah, daughter of Edward Swan. CHILDREN. SONS: John (1678–1734), who married Eleanor, probably the daughter of *Samuel Williamson* (1658–1729); Philip, who married Susannah, daughter of Ralph Williamson; Edward (1685–1726), who married Susannah, daughter of Gerard Slye (1654–by 1703); George (?–1733); and James. DAUGHTERS: Sarah; Judith (?–1738), who married first, Charles Ashcom, and second, Thomas Brooke (1706–1749), son of *Thomas Brooke* (1683–1744); Susannah; and Ann. PRIVATE CAREER. EDUCATION: literate. RELIGIOUS AFFILIATION: Anglican. OCCUPATIONAL PROFILE: planter. PUBLIC CAREER. LEGISLATIVE SERVICE: Lower House, Charles County, 1699–1700 (elected to the 3rd session). LOCAL OFFICES: justice, St. Mary's County, by 1691/92–1696, Charles County, 1696–1708/9; King and Queen Parish Vestry, St. Mary's County, 1693–1696. WEALTH DURING LIFETIME. LAND AT FIRST ELECTION: at least 280 acres. WEALTH AT DEATH. DIED: will probated on January 29, 1724/25. PERSONAL PROPERTY: TEV, £671.19.9 (including 14 slaves and numerous books); FB, £490.7.2. LAND: over 600 acres.

BROGDEN, WILLIAM (1742/43–1824). BORN: on March 8, 1742/43, in All Hallow's Parish, Anne Arundel County; eldest son. NATIVE: at least third generation. RESIDED: at "Rowdown," Rhode River Hundred, Anne Arundel County. FAMILY BACKGROUND. FATHER: Rev. William Brogden (1710–1770), born in Calvert County, an Anglican minister ordained in 1735, rector of Dorchester Parish in Dorchester County from 1735/36 to 1737, All Hallow's Parish in Anne Arundel County from 1739 to 1751, Queen Anne Parish in Prince George's County from 1751 until death. He married first, Sarah, widow of Basil Waring, *William Barton* (1667/68–1705), and Col. James

Haddock, an attorney in Prince George's County; daughter of Richard Marsham. MOTHER: Elizabeth Chapman. BROTHERS: John Lestrange (1744–1782); Samuel; and Richard. SISTERS: Rebecca (1746–1760); Elizabeth, who married in 1778 Thomas Walker. STEPSISTER: Sarah Barton (?–1733), who married *Samuel Perrie* (?–1729). STEPNEPHEW: *William Murdock* (?–1769). MARRIED on December 19, 1795, Margaret (by 1766–after 1829), daughter of James McCullock (?–1766), of Baltimore County, a merchant, and his wife Mary (?–1794). Her maternal grandfather was James Dick (?–1782), of Anne Arundel County, a merchant. Her brother was James (?–by 1829). Her sister was Elizabeth (?–by 1829). CHILDREN. SONS: William, who married in 1828 Mary Stevenson, of Baltimore City; James; and David M., who married in 1827 Margaret Sellman. DAUGHTER: Mary (?–1826), who never married. PRIVATE CAREER. EDUCATION: probably studied with his father who was schoolmaster of the Prince George's County school during the 1750s. RELIGIOUS AFFILIATION: Anglican, All Hallow's Parish, Anne Arundel County. OCCUPATIONAL PROFILE: planter; merchant. PUBLIC CAREER. LEGISLATIVE SERVICE: Lower House, Anne Arundel County, 1780–1781 (discharged on November 11, 1780, for having served as a field officer at the time of his election; reelected to the 1st session and seated; Grievances 1; Claims 2), 1781–1782 (Claims 1; Public Taxes 1), 1782–1783 (Claims 1, 2), 1792, 1793, 1794, 1796, 1797, 1798, 1799. LOCAL OFFICES: justice, Anne Arundel County, commissioned 1773 and 1777; purchasing agent, Anne Arundel County, appointed 1779; All Hallow's Parish Vestry, Anne Arundel County, in office 1813–ca. 1815. MILITARY SERVICE: captain, South River Militia Company, Anne Arundel County, by 1776; major, by 1780. WEALTH DURING LIFETIME. PERSONAL PROPERTY: 40 slaves, 1776; assessed value £2,356.19.4, including 41 slaves and 119 oz. plate, 1783; 45 slaves, 1790; 48 slaves, 1798. LAND AT FIRST ELECTION: ca. 536 acres in Anne Arundel County (ca. 386 acres inherited from his father and 150 acres of confiscated British property purchased in 1780). SIGNIFICANT CHANGES IN LAND BETWEEN FIRST ELECTION AND DEATH: The same tract which he had inherited from his father was appraised as containing 473 acres in 1798. WEALTH AT DEATH. DIED: on September 12, 1824, at "Rowdown" in Anne Arundel County. PERSONAL PROPERTY: TEV, at least $13,030.12 (including 52 slaves). LAND: probably ca. 625 acres in Anne Arundel County.

BROME (BROOME), JOHN (1703–1748). BORN: on September 2, 1703, in Christ Church Parish, Calvert County; eldest son. NATIVE: third generation. RESIDED: in Calvert County; probably lived on his father's plantation, "Island Neck." FAMILY BACKGROUND. FATHER: *John Broome* (1676–ca. 1738/39). MOTHER: Anne (?–1761), daughter of *Henry Hooper* (ca. 1643–1720). UNCLE: *Henry Hooper* (ca. 1687–1767). AUNT: Mary Hooper Hicks (?–ca. 1757), who married *John Rider* (1686–1739/40). HALF AUNT: Mary Hooper (1674–1745), who married *Henry Ennalls* (1675–1734). BROTHERS: Henry; Thomas. SISTERS: Ann; Mary (1707–?); Margaret; Elizabeth; and Sarah. FIRST COUSINS: *Henry Hooper, Jr.* (ca. 1727–1790); *Henry Travers* (?–1765); and Dorothy Rider (1725–by 1781), who married *John Henry* (ca. 1714–1781). OTHER KINSHIP: his second cousins were *John Henry, Jr.* (ca. 1750–1798); *Francis Jenkins Henry* (?–1796); Charlotte Henry, who married *William Winder, Jr.* (?–1808); and Dorothy (Dolly) Henry, who married *Isaac Henry* (?–ca. 1802). MARRIED by 1750, probably Ann, daughter of *Thomas Gantt* (?–1765); stepgranddaughter of both *Thomas Hollyday* (ca. 1661–1702/3) and *John Wight* (?–1705); niece of both *Thomas Brooke* (1683–1744) and Sarah Brooke, who married first, *William Dent* (ca. 1660–1704), and second, *Philip Lee* (ca. 1681–1744); half niece of Jane Brooke, who married *Alexander Contee* (ca. 1691–1740). Her brothers were *Thomas Gantt* (ca. 1710–1785); *Edward Gantt* (?–by 1783); *Fielder Gantt* (?–1807); and George (?–1779). Her sisters were Priscilla; Elizabeth. Her first cousins were *Richard Brooke* (1716–1783); Eleanor Brooke, who married *Samuel Beall* (ca. 1713–ca. 1778); *Richard Lee* (ca. 1707–1787); *Arthur Lee* (?–1760); and *Francis Lee* (?–1749). Her nephews were *Erasmus Gantt* (?–?); *Thomas Gantt* (?–ca. 1802). Her nieces were Rachel Gantt, who married *Richard Brooke* (1716–1783); Sarah Gantt, who married *Osborn Sprigg* (ca. 1741–1815); and Ann Gantt, who married *Thomas Harwood III* (by 1757–by 1805). CHILDREN. SONS: Col. John (1727–1797), a lawyer and captain in the Calvert County Militia from 1754 to 1758, who received land in Western Maryland and Virginia for his services in the French and Indian War. John married Mary, sister of *John Mackall* (1738–1813) and granddaughter of *James Mackall* (1671–1717). Henry (1730–1772), who married Ann, daughter of William Dawkins; Thomas; and Alexander. DAUGHTERS: Niece Pattison; Mary (1731–?). PRIVATE CAREER. EDUCATION: literate. RELIGIOUS AFFILIATION: Anglican, Christ Church, Christ Church Parish, Calvert County.

SOCIAL STATUS AND ACTIVITIES: Mr., 1742. OC-
CUPATIONAL PROFILE: planter. PUBLIC CAREER.
LEGISLATIVE SERVICE: Lower House, Calvert
County, 1740–1741 (elected to the 1st session to
fill vacancy), 1742–1744, 1745, 1745/46–1748.
LOCAL OFFICES: sheriff, Calvert County, in office
1725; justice, Calvert County, 1731–at least 1736
(quorum, 1734–at least 1736); land commissioner,
Calvert County, period of service unknown;
trustee and visitor of a school, Calvert County,
period of service unknown. MILITARY SERVICE:
colonel, period of service unknown. WEALTH DUR-
ING LIFETIME. LAND AT FIRST ELECTION: inherited part of his father's dwelling plantation and 1
other tract both of unspecified acreage, 1738/39.
WEALTH AT DEATH. DIED: ca. September 1748 in
Calvert County. PERSONAL PROPERTY: TEV,
£73.12.4 sterling, £1,520.11.3 current money; FB,
estate overpaid £116.4.4 sterling, £1,255.17.2 current money.

BROOKE, BAKER (1628–1678/79). BORN: in
1628 in England; first son. IMMIGRATED: in 1650
as a young adult with his father and siblings. RE-
SIDED: in Calvert County. FAMILY BACKGROUND.
FATHER: *Robert Brooke* (1602–1655). MOTHER:
Mary (?–1634), daughter of Thomas Baker, Esq., a
barrister; granddaughter of Sir Thomas Engham,
of Goodneston, Kent, England. STEPMOTHER:
Mary Mainwaring (?–1663). BROTHER: *Thomas
Brooke* (1632–1676). HALF BROTHERS: *Charles
Brooke* (1636–1671); Roger (1637–1700); Robert
(1639–1667); John (1640–1677); William (1643–?);
Francis (1648–1671); Basil (?–1651, died in in-
fancy); and Henry (1655–1672). SISTERS: Mary
(1630–by 1650); Barbara (1634–by 1650). HALF
SISTERS: Mary (1642–?); Ann (1645–?); and
Elizabeth (1655–?), who married Richard Smith
(?–1714), son of *Richard Smith* (?–ca. 1690). MAR-
RIED in 1664 Anne, daughter of *Leonard Calvert*
(ca. 1606–1647); niece of *Cecilius Calvert, 2nd
Lord Baltimore* (1605–1675). She subsequently
married both Henry Brent (?–1693) and Richard
Marsham (?–1713). Her brother was *William Calvert* (ca. 1642/43–1682). CHILDREN. SONS: Baker
(?–1698), who married Catherine; Charles (?–
1698); and Leonard (?–1718), who married Ann,
daughter of *William Boreman* (ca. 1630–1709).
DAUGHTER: Mary (?–1763), who married Raphael
Neale (1683–1743), son of Anthony Neale. PRI-
VATE CAREER. EDUCATION: literate; he probably
had considerable schooling. RELIGIOUS AFFILIA-
TION: Protestant, but he converted to Roman Catholicism, probably at the time of his marriage.
SOCIAL STATUS AND ACTIVITIES: he was Mary-

land's first second generation councilor; his earliest offices came soon after his father's death; his
religious conversion and marriage to the proprietor's niece reestablished the family as one of the
most powerful in the colony. OCCUPATIONAL PRO-
FILE: planter. PUBLIC CAREER. LEGISLATIVE SER-
VICE: Upper House, special writ 1658, 1659/60,
1661, 1662, 1663–1664, 1666, 1669, 1671–1674/75
(Accounts 1, 2; Laws 1, 2), 1676–1678 (died before the 3rd session). OTHER PROVINCIAL OF-
FICES: Council, 1658–1678/79; justice, Provincial
Court, 1658–1678/79; deputy governor, 1669–
1670; surveyor general, 1671–1678/79. WEALTH
DURING LIFETIME. LAND AT FIRST ELECTION:
owned 2,100 acres and controlled 4,000 acres of
deceased father's land. WEALTH AT DEATH. DIED:
will probated in March 1678/79. PERSONAL PROP-
ERTY: TEV, 135,126 pounds of tobacco (equiva-
lent to £709.8.2) (including 2 slaves, 5 servants,
and books); FB, 109,582 pounds of tobacco.
LAND: over 3,500 acres.

BROOKE, CHARLES (1636–1671). BORN: in
1636 in England; third son. IMMIGRATED: in 1650
as a minor with his father and siblings. RESIDED:
in Calvert County. FAMILY BACKGROUND. FA-
THER: *Robert Brooke* (1602–1655). MOTHER: Mary
(?–1663), daughter of Roger Mainwaring, the dean
of Worcester and bishop of St. David's. BROTH-
ERS: Roger (1637–1700); Robert (1639–1667);
John (1640–1677); William (1643–?); Francis
(1648–1671); Basil (?–1651, died in infancy); and
Henry (1655–1672). HALF BROTHERS: *Baker
Brooke* (1628–1678/79); *Thomas Brooke* (1632–
1676). SISTERS: Mary (1642–?); Ann (1645–?); and
Elizabeth (1655–?), who married Richard Smith
(?–1714), son of *Richard Smith* (?–ca. 1690). HALF
SISTERS: Mary (1630–by 1650); Barbara (1634–by
1650). MARRIED never. CHILDREN. Died without
progeny. PRIVATE CAREER. EDUCATION: literate;
probably attended Harvard College and headed
the class in 1651. RELIGIOUS AFFILIATION: probably a Protestant. SOCIAL STATUS AND ACTIVITIES:
second generation provincial officeholder; member
of a very prominent political family. OCCUPA-
TIONAL PROFILE: planter. PUBLIC CAREER. LEGIS-
LATIVE SERVICE: Lower House, Calvert County,
1671 (died before the 3rd session). LOCAL OF-
FICES: justice, Calvert County, 1661–1665, 1671
(quorum, 1664–?); sheriff, Calvert County, 1665–
1666; keeper of weights and measures, Calvert
County, 1671. WEALTH DURING LIFETIME. LAND
AT FIRST ELECTION: over 5,000 acres. WEALTH AT
DEATH. DIED: will probated on December 15,
1671. PERSONAL PROPERTY: TEV, 24,278 pounds

of tobacco (including 3 servants). LAND: over 5,000 acres.

BROOKE, JOHN (by 1646–1692/93). BORN: by 1646, probably in Yorkshire, England; only son. IMMIGRATED: in 1654 as a minor with his parents from Virginia. RESIDED: in Calvert County; Dorchester County by 1671. FAMILY BACKGROUND. FATHER: *Michael Brooke* (?–ca. 1663/64). STEPFATHER: *Henry Trippe* (1632–1697/98). MOTHER: Frances. MARRIED first, by 1679 Katherine, widow of Robert Stevens. MARRIED second, Judith (?–1693). CHILDREN. DAUGHTERS: Mary, who married *Joseph Ennalls* (?–1709); Ann, who married first, *Thomas Cooke* (?–1692/93), and second, John Stevens, son of *John Stevens* (?–1692). PRIVATE CAREER. EDUCATION: literate. RELIGIOUS AFFILIATION: Protestant. SOCIAL STATUS AND ACTIVITIES: second generation burgess. OCCUPATIONAL PROFILE: physician; planter. PUBLIC CAREER. LEGISLATIVE SERVICE: Lower House, Dorchester County, 1681–1682 (elected to the 3rd session), 1682–1684, 1686–1688; Associators' Convention, Dorchester County, 1689–1692; Grand Committee of Twenty, 1690–1692; Lower House, Dorchester County, 1692 (died before the 2nd session). OTHER PROVINCIAL OFFICE: justice, Provincial Court, 1691–1692. LOCAL OFFICES: justice, Dorchester County, 1671–1674, 1676–1693 (quorum, 1679–1693); town officer of Yarmouth, Dorchester County, 1686; deputy commissary, Dorchester County, 1692. STANDS ON PUBLIC/PRIVATE ISSUES: supported the Protestant Associators' revolution of 1689. WEALTH DURING LIFETIME. LAND AT FIRST ELECTION: over 500 acres. WEALTH AT DEATH. DIED: between January 24 and March 21, 1692/93. LAND: 850 acres, plus 2 tracts of unspecified acreage.

BROOKE, MICHAEL (?–ca. 1663/64). BORN: in Yorkshire, England. IMMIGRATED: in 1654 as a free adult with his wife and son from Virginia. RESIDED: in Calvert County. FAMILY BACKGROUND. FATHER: John Brooke, of Yorkshire, England. MARRIED Frances, who subsequently married in 1665 *Henry Trippe* (1632–1697/98). CHILDREN. SON: *John Brooke* (by 1646–1692/93), who married first, Katherine, widow of Robert Stevens, and second, Judith (?–1693). PRIVATE CAREER. EDUCATION: literate. RELIGIOUS AFFILIATION: Protestant, probably a Puritan. SOCIAL STATUS AND ACTIVITIES: transported two servants on his arrival; Mr., 1655. OCCUPATIONAL PROFILE: attorney, 1657/58; planter. PUBLIC CAREER. LEGISLATIVE SERVICE: Parliamentary Commission, 1655–

1657/58; Assembly, Patuxent (Calvert County), 1657; Lower House, Calvert County, 1658, 1659/60. OTHER PROVINCIAL OFFICES: justice, Provincial Court, 1655–1657/58. LOCAL OFFICE: justice, Patuxent (Calvert County), 1655–1661. STANDS ON PUBLIC/PRIVATE ISSUES: his religious beliefs probably accounted for his move from Virginia and his immediate assumption of high office under the Puritan government of Maryland, 1654; he probably supported Fendall's Rebellion, 1659/60–1660, and lost his justiceship as a consequence. WEALTH DURING LIFETIME. LAND AT FIRST ELECTION: rights to 200 acres; 350 acres by 1662. WEALTH AT DEATH. DIED: by February 2, 1663/64. PERSONAL PROPERTY: TEV, 21,015 pounds of tobacco. LAND: 500–1,000 acres.

BROOKE, RICHARD (1716–1783). BORN: on June 2, 1716, in Prince George's County; fourth son. NATIVE: fifth generation. RESIDED: at "Brookfield," Prince George's County. FAMILY BACKGROUND. FATHER: *Thomas Brooke* (1683–1744). MOTHER: Lucy, daughter of *Walter Smith* (?–1711). AUNTS: Ann Smith (1694–1759), who married second, *Thomas Trueman Greenfield* (1682–1733); Elinor Smith, who married *Thomas Addison* (1679–1727); Rebecca Smith, who married *Daniel Dulany* (1685–1753); Sarah Brooke (?–1724), who married first, *William Dent* (ca. 1660–1704), and second, *Philip Lee* (ca. 1681–1744); and Priscilla Brooke, who married *Thomas Gantt* (?–1765). BROTHERS: Thomas (1706–1749); Walter (1707–1740/41); Nathaniel (1712–?); Isaac (1722–1756); Daniel (1726–1735); Charles (1727–1727); Robert (1728–1777); and Rev. Clement (1730–1800). SISTERS: Mary (1709–?); Anna (1711–?); Lucy (1714–1718); Eleanor (1718–?), who married ca. 1734 Col. *Samuel Beall* (ca. 1713–ca. 1778); Rachel (1719–1789); Lucy (1721–?); Rebecca (1722–?); and Elizabeth (1724–1794). FIRST COUSINS: *John Addison* (1713–1764); Ann Addison (1711/12–?), who married *William Murdock* (?–1769); *Richard Lee* (ca. 1707–1787); *Arthur Lee* (?–1760); *Francis Lee* (?–1749); *Daniel Dulany, Jr.* (1722–1797); *Walter Dulany* (?–1773); Margaret Dulany, who married first, *Alexander Hamilton* (1712–1756), and second, *William Murdock* (?–1769); Marianne Greenfield, who married *John Stoddert* (?–1767); *Thomas Gantt* (ca. 1710–1785); *Fielder Gantt* (?–1807); *Edward Gantt* (?–by 1783); and probably Ann Gantt, who married *John Brome* (1703–1748). MARRIED on November 1, 1767, Rachel (?–1793), daughter of *Thomas Gantt* (ca. 1710–1785); granddaughter of both *Thomas Gantt* (?–1765) and *John Smith* (?–1738); niece of

Edward Gantt (?–by 1783), *Fielder Gantt* (?–1807), Sarah Smith, who married *Joseph Hall* (ca. 1701–?), Tabitha Smith (ca. 1690–1769), who married *Thomas Sheredine* (1699–1752), and probably Ann Gantt, who married *John Brome* (1703–1748). Her brothers were *Thomas Gantt, Jr.* (?–1808); John (1740–?); and Dr. Edward (1741–1837), who died in Kentucky. Her half brother was *Erasmus Gantt* (?–?). Her half sister was Sarah, who married in 1799 *Osborn Sprigg* (ca. 1741–1815). Her first cousins were Dr. *Thomas Gantt* (?–ca. 1802); Ann Gantt, who married *Thomas Harwood III* (by 1757–by 1805); and *Upton Sheredine* (1740–1800). CHILDREN. SON: Frederick Thomas (1770–?). DAUGHTER: Sarah (1772–1849), who married Samuel Harper. PRIVATE CAREER. EDUCATION: literate. RELIGIOUS AFFILIATION: Anglican, St. Paul's Parish, Prince George's County. ADDITIONAL COMMENTS: in 1745 Dr. Brooke wrote to the president of His Majesty's Council, complaining that the lord proprietor unduly favored the Catholics in the province. OCCUPATIONAL PROFILE: physician; he was a well-known proponent of inoculation as a means of preventing smallpox. PUBLIC CAREER. LEGISLATIVE SERVICE: Conventions, Prince George's County, 2nd, 1774, 4th, 1775 (elected, but did not attend), 5th, 1775. STANDS ON PUBLIC/PRIVATE ISSUES: prior to 1771 he made voyages to England for "the good of the country." In his will written in 1771 he requested that the General Assembly and Provincial Court become his trustees because the personal expenditures involved in these trips, as well as other family expenses, exceeded the value of his land. WEALTH DURING LIFETIME. LAND AT FIRST ELECTION: 322 acres in Prince George's County (a dwelling plantation inherited from his father). WEALTH AT DEATH. DIED: on July 13, 1783, in Prince George's County. PERSONAL PROPERTY: TEV, £1,476.0.5 current money (including 16 slaves, medical instruments, and medicines); FB, £1,386.1.0. LAND: 322 acres in Prince George's County, his dwelling plantation. ADDITIONAL COMMENTS: he stated in his will that if all of his legatees died, his estate was to become a college endowment.

BROOKE, RICHARD (1736–1788). BORN: in 1736 in Prince George's County; third son. NATIVE: fifth generation. RESIDED: at "Fair Hill," Frederick County (later became part of Montgomery County). FAMILY BACKGROUND. FATHER: James Brooke (1705–1784). MOTHER: Deborah, eldest daughter of Richard Snowden and wife Eliza Coale (1692–ca. 1713). HALF AUNTS: Margaret

Snowden (1726–1793), who married *John Contee* (1722–ca. 1796); Anne Snowden, who married *Henry Wright Crabb* (1722/23–1764). BROTHERS: James (1730/31–1767), who married Hannah Janney; Roger (1734–1790), who married Mary Matthews; Basil (1738–1794), who married Elizabeth Hopkins; and Thomas (1744/45–1789). SISTER: Elizabeth (1740/41–?), who married Thomas Pleasants. FIRST COUSINS: *Richard Bennett Carmichael* (1753–1824); *Richard Thomas* (ca. 1728–1806); *Evan Thomas* (1738/39–1826); Elizabeth Brooke Carmichael, who married *John Lambert Wilmer* (1747–1799); and Elizabeth Beall, who married *John Bracco* (?–1794). MARRIED in 1758 Jane Lynn (?–1774). CHILDREN. SON: Roger (?–by 1791). DAUGHTER: Ann (1773–by 1816), who married ca. 1789 *William Hammond Dorsey* (1764–ca. 1819). PRIVATE CAREER. EDUCATION: literate. RELIGIOUS AFFILIATION: Quaker; the Brooke family had been Catholic, but Richard's father became a Protestant. OCCUPATIONAL PROFILE: probably a planter. PUBLIC CAREER. LEGISLATIVE SERVICE: Conventions, Frederick County, 1st, 1774, 2nd–3rd, 1774, 4th, 1775, 5th, 1775. LOCAL OFFICES: Committee of Observation, Frederick County, elected 1775; commissioner of tax, Montgomery County, 1777–at least 1779, 1782–at least 1785; purchasing agent, Montgomery County, commissioned 1779. MILITARY SERVICE: colonel, Revolutionary War. WEALTH DURING LIFETIME. PERSONAL PROPERTY: assessed value £628.16.6, including 13 slaves and 32 oz. plate, 1783. LAND AT FIRST ELECTION: 4,999 acres in Frederick and Montgomery counties (2,495 acres were a gift from his father). SIGNIFICANT CHANGES IN LAND BETWEEN FIRST ELECTION AND DEATH: received one-sixth of his father's real estate by bequest, 1784. WEALTH AT DEATH. DIED: will probated on June 11, 1788, in Montgomery County; buried at "Fair Hill," Frederick County. PERSONAL PROPERTY: TEV, £2,607.4.2 current money (including 21 slaves); FB, £1,789.7.4. LAND: 4,579 acres in Frederick and Montgomery counties.

BROOKE, ROBERT (1602–1655). BORN: in 1602 in London, England; third son. IMMIGRATED: in 1650 as a free adult with his wife and ten children. RESIDED: in Calvert County. FAMILY BACKGROUND. FATHER: Thomas Brooke (1561–1612), who was a barrister at the Inner Temple, and who served as an M.P. for Whitchurch, England, from 1604 to 1611. MOTHER: Susan, daughter of Sir Thomas Foster, a judge of Common Pleas; sister of Sir Robert Foster, a justice of the King's Bench. BROTHERS: Thomas (1599–1665); Richard;

William; Humphrey; and Charles. SISTERS: Susan; Elizabeth; and Frances. MARRIED first, in 1627 Mary (?–1634), daughter of Thomas Baker, Esq., barrister; granddaughter of Sir Thomas Engham, of Goodneston, Kent, England. MARRIED second, in 1635 Mary (?–1663), daughter of Roger Mainwaring, the dean of Worcester and bishop of St. David's. CHILDREN. SONS: *Baker Brooke* (1628–1678/79), who married Anne, daughter of *Leonard Calvert* (ca. 1606–1647); *Thomas Brooke* (1632–1676), who married Elinor (1642–1725), daughter of Richard Hatton; *Charles Brooke* (1636–1671); Roger (1637–1700), who married first, Dorothy, daughter of *James Neale* (ca. 1615–1684), and second, Mary Wolseley, grandaughter of Sir Thomas Wolseley; Robert (1639–1667), who married Elizabeth, daughter of William Thompson; John (1640–1677), who married Rebecca Isaac; William (1643–?); Francis (1648–1671); Basil (?–1651, died in infancy); and Henry (1655–1672). DAUGHTERS: Mary (1630–by 1650); Barbara (1634–by 1650); Mary (1642–?); Ann (1645–?), who married Christopher Beans; and Elizabeth (1655–?), who married Richard Smith (?–1714), son of *Richard Smith* (?–ca. 1690). PRIVATE CAREER. EDUCATION: B.A., Wadham College, Oxford University, 1620; M.A., 1624. RELIGIOUS AFFILIATION: Protestant. SOCIAL STATUS AND ACTIVITIES: in exchange for an agreement to transport forty persons to Maryland, Brooke was to receive from Cecilius Calvert a manor of 2,000 acres for every ten persons; he arrived with a Council commission; brought twenty-eight servants with him; he established a very prominent political family, the first to have third and fourth generations members holding provincial offices. OCCUPATIONAL PROFILE: called "minister" in 1634; planter. PUBLIC CAREER. LEGISLATIVE SERVICE: Upper House, 1650–1650/51 (did not serve); Parliamentary Commission, 1652–1653. OTHER PROVINCIAL OFFICES: Council, 1649–1654; justice, Provincial Court, 1650–1654. LOCAL OFFICE: commander, Charles County, 1650–1654. STANDS ON PUBLIC/-PRIVATE ISSUES: Brooke's cooperation with the Bennett-Claiborne Puritan faction from 1652 to 1654 brought him the displeasure of Lord Baltimore and the loss of his proprietary offices. WEALTH DURING LIFETIME. LAND AT FIRST ELECTION: 8,000 acres. WEALTH AT DEATH. DIED: on July 20, 1655. LAND: 8,000 acres.

BROOKE, THOMAS (1632–1676). BORN: in 1632 in England; second son. IMMIGRATED: in 1650 as a minor with father and siblings. RESIDED: in Calvert County. FAMILY BACKGROUND. FATHER: *Robert Brooke* (1602–1655). MOTHER: Mary (?–1635), daughter of Thomas Baker, Esq., barrister; granddaughter of Sir Thomas Engham, of Goodneston, Kent, England. STEPMOTHER: Mary Mainwaring (?–1663). BROTHER: *Baker Brooke* (1628–1678/79). HALF BROTHERS: *Charles Brooke* (1636–1671); Roger (1637–1700); Robert (1639–1667); John (1640–1677); William (1643–?); Francis (1648–1671); Basil (?–1651, died in infancy); and Henry (1655–1672). SISTERS: Mary (1630–by 1650); Barbara (1634–by 1650). HALF SISTERS: Mary (1642–?); Ann (1645–?); and Elizabeth (1655–?), who married Richard Smith (?–1714), son of *Richard Smith* (?–ca. 1690). MARRIED Elinor (1642–1725), daughter of Richard Hatton and wife Margaret; niece of *Thomas Hatton* (?–1654/55). She subsequently married *Henry Darnall* (ca. 1645–1711). Her brothers were *William Hatton* (?–1712); Richard. Her sisters were Mary, who married *Zachary Wade* (ca. 1627–1678); Elizabeth, who married first, *Luke Gardiner* (1622–1674), and second, *Clement Hill* (?–1708); and Barbara, who married *James Johnson* (?–?). CHILDREN. SONS: *Thomas Brooke* (ca. 1659–1730/31), who married first, Ann, and second, Barbara (1676–1754), daughter of *Thomas Dent* (ca. 1630–1676); Robert (1663–1714), a Jesuit priest; Ignatius (1670–1751), a Jesuit priest; Matthew (1672–1703), a Jesuit priest; and Clement (1676–1737), who married Jane, daughter of *Nicholas Sewall* (ca. 1655–1737). DAUGHTERS: Elinor, who married first, Philip Darnall (1671–1705), son of *Henry Darnall* (ca. 1645–1711), and second, William Digges, son of *William Digges* (ca. 1650–1697); Mary, who married first, James Bowling (1636–1693), second, *Benjamin Hall* (1667–1721), and third, Henry Witham. PRIVATE CAREER. EDUCATION: literate; he probably had considerable schooling. RELIGIOUS AFFILIATION: raised as a Protestant but converted to Roman Catholicism. SOCIAL STATUS AND ACTIVITIES: second generation provincial officeholder; father and brother served on the Council and another brother was a burgess. OCCUPATIONAL PROFILE: planter. PUBLIC CAREER. LEGISLATIVE SERVICE: Lower House, Calvert County, 1663–1664, 1666, 1671–1674/75 (Accounts 2; Laws 4), 1676 (Accounts 1; died before the 2nd session). LOCAL OFFICES: justice, Calvert County, 1661–1666, 1667–1668, 1669/70–1674, 1675/76–1676 (quorum, 1669/70–1674, 1675/76–1676); sheriff, Calvert County, 1666–1667, 1668–1669. MILITARY SERVICE: captain, 1658; major, 1660/61. WEALTH DURING LIFETIME. LAND AT FIRST ELECTION: 3,000 acres (inherited 2,000 acres from his father). WEALTH AT

DEATH. DIED: will probated on December 29, 1676. PERSONAL PROPERTY: TEV, 95,910 pounds of tobacco (including 10 slaves and 10 servants). LAND: 7,742 acres.

BROOKE, THOMAS (ca. 1659–1730/31). BORN: ca. 1659 in Calvert County; eldest son. NATIVE: third generation. RESIDED: in Calvert County; Prince George's County after 1695. FAMILY BACKGROUND. FATHER: *Thomas Brooke* (1632–1676), son of *Robert Brooke* (1602–1655). STEPFATHER: *Henry Darnall* (ca. 1645–1711). MOTHER: Elinor (1642–1725), daughter of Richard Hatton and wife Margaret. UNCLES: *Baker Brooke* (1628–1678/79); *Charles Brooke* (1636–1671); *William Hatton* (?–1712); *Zachary Wade* (ca. 1627–1678); *Luke Gardiner* (1622–1674); *Clement Hill* (?–1708); and *James Johnson* (?–?). BROTHERS: Robert (1663–1714); Ignatius (1670–1751); Matthew (1672–1703); and Clement (1676–1737). STEPBROTHER: Philip Darnall (1671–1705). HALF BROTHER: Henry Darnall (1682–1759). SISTERS: Mary, who married second, *Benjamin Hall* (1667–1721); Elinor. HALF SISTERS: Mary Darnall (1678–1742); Ann Darnall (1680–1749); Elizabeth Darnall (?–1704). FIRST COUSIN: *Richard Gardiner* (?–1687). MARRIED first, Ann. MARRIED second, Barbara (1676–1754), daughter of *Thomas Dent* (ca. 1630–1676); stepdaughter of *John Addison* (?–ca. 1705/6). Her brothers were *William Dent* (ca. 1660–1704); Thomas; *Peter Dent* (ca. 1665–1710/11); and George (?–by 1703). Her half brother was *Thomas Addison* (1679–1727). Her sister was Margaret. CHILDREN. SON: *Thomas Brooke* (1683–1744), who married in 1706 Lucy, daughter of *Walter Smith* (?–1711); Nathaniel; John; Benjamin; Baker; and Thomas (1717–1768), who never married. DAUGHTERS: Elinor, who married first, in 1705 John Tasker, son of *Thomas Tasker* (?–1700), and second, Charles Sewall, son of *Nicholas Sewall* (ca. 1655–1737); Sarah (?–1724), who married first, *William Dent* (ca. 1660–1704), and second, *Philip Lee* (ca. 1681–1744); Priscilla, who married *Thomas Gantt* (?–1765); Jane (?–1779), who married *Alexander Contee* (ca. 1691–1740); Rebecca (?–1763), who married John Howard (?–1742); Mary (?–1758), who married Dr. Patrick Sim (?–1740); Elizabeth (1699–1748), who married George Beale (1695–1780), son of *Ninian Beale* (ca. 1625–1717/18); and Lucy, who married Thomas Hodgkin. PRIVATE CAREER. EDUCATION: literate. RELIGIOUS AFFILIATION: probably raised as a Catholic, but an Anglican by 1691. SOCIAL STATUS AND ACTIVITIES: first third generation provincial officeholder in colony; Esq., by 1691. OCCUPATIONAL PROFILE: planter. PUBLIC CAREER. LEGISLATIVE SERVICE: Upper House, 1692–1693, 1694–1697, 1697/98–1700, 1701–1704, 1704–1707; Lower House, Prince George's County, 1708A (absent the entire session); Upper House, 1716–1718, 1719–1721/22, 1722 (dismissed by the 2nd session). OTHER PROVINCIAL OFFICES: Council, 1691–1708, 1715/16–1722, (president, 1715/16–1722; last attended on October 20, 1722; discharged); justice, Provincial Court, 1693–1694; deputy secretary, 1694–1696; commissary general, 1699–1706, 1722–1727; surveyor general, 1720. LOCAL OFFICES: justice, Calvert County, 1685–1689 (quorum, 1686–1689); St. Paul's Parish Vestry, Calvert County, 1693–1697. STANDS ON PUBLIC/PRIVATE ISSUES: probably opposed the revolution of Protestant Associators in 1689, when he was removed from his justiceship; nominated by Lord Baltimore to become a member of the first royal Council in 1690, and he was probably appointed in an effort to mollify the proprietor after his loss of the colony; dismissed from all offices by Gov. John Seymour in 1708 as a result of close Catholic ties—his three brothers were Jesuits and *Henry Darnall* (ca. 1645–1711) was his stepfather—and for poor Council attendance, although his attendance had been very regular prior to Seymour's governorship; he was restored to the Council after the colony reverted to proprietary control in 1715; the precise reason for his second dismissal from the Council in 1722 is unclear. WEALTH DURING LIFETIME. LAND AT FIRST ELECTION: at least 6,011 acres in 1689; 9,517 acres by 1696; 7,393 acres in 1706. WEALTH AT DEATH. DIED: on January 7, 1730/31. PERSONAL PROPERTY: TEV, £1,374.0.0 (including proceeds of the sale of land; and 36 slaves, 17 of whom were mortgaged); FB, estate overpaid £355.3.0; LAND: most of his acreage was heavily mortgaged at the time of his death.

BROOKE, THOMAS (1683–1744). BORN: in 1683 in Calvert County; first son. NATIVE: fourth generation. RESIDED: in Calvert County; "Brookfield," Prince George's County, after 1695. FAMILY BACKGROUND. FATHER: *Thomas Brooke* (ca. 1659–1730/31). MOTHER: Ann. STEPMOTHER: Barbara (1676–1754), daughter of *Thomas Dent* (ca. 1630–1676); sister of *William Dent* (ca. 1660–1704). HALF BROTHERS: Nathaniel; John; Benjamin; Baker; and Thomas (1717–1768), who never married. SISTERS: Elinor, who married first, John Tasker (?–1711), son of *Thomas Tasker* (?–1700), and second, Charles Sewall, son of *Nicholas Sewall* (ca. 1655–1737); Sarah (?–1724), who married first, *William Dent* (ca. 1660–1704), and second, *Philip Lee* (ca. 1681–1744); and Priscilla, who married *Thomas Gantt* (?–1765). HALF SISTERS: Jane (?–1779), who married *Alexander Contee* (ca. 1691–1740); Rebecca (?–1763), who married John Howard (?–1742); Mary (?–1758), who married Dr. Patrick Sim (?–1740); Elizabeth, who married George Beale (1695–1780), son of *Ninian Beale* (ca. 1625–1717/18); and Lucy, who married Thomas Hodgkin. NEPHEWS: *Thomas Gantt* (ca. 1710–1785); *Fielder Gantt* (?–1807); and *Edward Gantt* (?–by 1783). NIECE: probably Ann Gantt, who married *John Brome* (1703–1748). MARRIED in 1706 Lucy (1688–1770), daughter of *Walter Smith* (?–1711). Her brothers were Richard (?–1733) and Walter (ca. 1692–1734). Her sisters were Elinor, who married *Thomas Addison* (1679–1727); Rebecca, who married *Daniel Dulany* (1685–1753); Elizabeth; Mary; Ann (1694–1759), who married second, *Thomas Trueman Greenfield* (1682–1733). Her first cousins were *Walter Smith* (ca. 1693–1748); Barbara Smith (1693–1764), who married first, *Thomas Holdsworth* (ca. 1692–1718), and second, *Benjamin Mackall* (1675–1761). Her nephews were *Daniel Dulany, Jr.* (1722–1797); *Walter Dulany* (?–1773); and *John Addison* (1713–1764). Her nieces were Margaret Dulany, who married first, *Alexander Hamilton* (1712–1756), and second, *William Murdock* (?–1769); Ann Addison (1711/12–?), who married *William Murdock* (?–1769); and Marianne Greenfield, who married *John Stoddert* (?–1767). CHILDREN. SONS: Thomas (1706–1749), who married first, Judith (?–1738), widow of Charles Ascom and daughter of *Philip Briscoe* (?–ca. 1724/25), and second, Sarah (1715–?), daughter of George Mason (1660–1716), of Virginia; Walter (1707–1740/41); Nathaniel (1712–?); *Richard Brooke* (1716–1783), who married Rachel (?–1793), daughter of Col. *John Smith* (?–1738); Isaac (1722–1756); Daniel (1726–1735); Charles (1727–died the same year); Robert (1728–1777); and Clement (1730–1800). DAUGHTERS: Mary (1709–?), who married Peter Dent; Anne (1711–?), who married (first name unknown) Harris; Lucy (1714–1718); Eleanor (1718–?), who married *Samuel Beall* (ca. 1713–ca. 1778); Rachel (1719–1789); Lucy (1721–?), who married John Estep, of Charles County; Rebecca (1722–?); and Elizabeth (1724–1794). PRIVATE CAREER. EDUCATION: literate. RELIGIOUS AFFILIATION: Anglican. SOCIAL STATUS AND ACTIVITIES: first fourth generation provincial officeholder in Maryland; his great-grandfather *Robert Brooke* (1602–1655) immigrated in 1650 and established very prominent family; Thomas Brooke suffered severe economic

misfortunes, and only his son *Richard Brooke* (1716–1783) held public office. OCCUPATIONAL PROFILE: planter. PUBLIC CAREER. LEGISLATIVE SERVICE: Lower House, Prince George's County, 1712–1714 (Accounts 2–4). LOCAL OFFICES: justice, Prince George's County, 1706–1708/9; deputy commissary, Prince George's County, 1721/22–1727; clerk, St. Mary's County, 1728–1740; sheriff, Prince George's County, 1731–1734. WEALTH DURING LIFETIME. LAND AT FIRST ELECTION: heir-at-law to his father's estate, but no land in his own name. WEALTH AT DEATH. DIED: on December 28, 1744. PERSONAL PROPERTY: TEV, £504.18.6 (including 5 slaves mortgaged). LAND: at least 979 acres.

BROOKES, FRANCIS (ca. 1608–by 1658/59). BORN: ca. 1608, probably in England. IMMIGRATED: by 1635, probably as an indentured servant. RESIDED: in Kent County; St. Mary's County, by 1650. MARRIED first, (name unknown). MARRIED second, Ann (?–1653), daughter of Elizabeth Boulton, of Middlesex, England, who immigrated in 1649 or 1650 as governess for the children of *William Mitchell* (?–1658). MARRIED third, by 1656 Mary. ADDITIONAL COMMENTS: accused in 1656 of beating his wife Mary and causing her to have a stillborn child. CHILDREN. SON: Francis (ca. 1635–1667/68). PRIVATE CAREER. EDUCATION: illiterate. RELIGIOUS AFFILIATION: probably a Protestant. SOCIAL STATUS AND ACTIVITIES: probably an indentured servant to *William Claiborne* (1600–ca. 1677); Mr. and Gent. after 1647. OCCUPATIONAL PROFILE: probably an indentured servant or low-wage laborer for Cloberry & Company; miller in the late 1630s; planter. PUBLIC CAREER. LEGISLATIVE SERVICE: Assembly, present 1647/48; Lower House, St. Mary's Hundred, St. Mary's County, 1650. LOCAL OFFICE: justice, Kent County, 1647–1647/48. STANDS ON PUBLIC/PRIVATE ISSUES: granted 100 acres in Kent County in 1651 for supporting Lord Baltimore during Ingle's Rebellion. WEALTH DURING LIFETIME. LAND AT FIRST ELECTION: probably 200 acres. WEALTH AT DEATH. DIED: by January 20, 1658/59. LAND: probably 450 acres.

BROOME (BROME), JOHN (1676–ca. 1738/39). BORN: in 1676 in Calvert County; oldest son. NATIVE: second generation. RESIDED: in Calvert County. FAMILY BACKGROUND. FATHER: John (?–by 1688/89), an innholder and merchant as well as a planter who owned 2,750 acres. MOTHER: Winifred Margaret, who subsequently married in 1699 Henry Fernley. MARRIED Anne

(?–1761), daughter of *Henry Hooper* (ca. 1643–1720) and wife Mary Woolford; niece of *Roger Woolford* (1670–1730), *William Holland* (?–1732), *Thomas Ennalls* (?–1718), and *Govert Lookerman* (ca. 1681–1728). Her brothers were Richard; John (?–1754); Roger; *Henry Hooper* (ca. 1687–1767); Thomas; and James (1703–1789). Her sisters were Mary (1674–1745), who married *Henry Ennalls* (1675–1734); Priscilla; Elizabeth, who married *Matthew Travers* (ca. 1672–1742); Rebecca; Mary (?–ca. 1757), who married second, *John Rider* (1686–1739/40); Rosannah; and Sarah. **CHILDREN.** SONS: *John Brome* (1703–1748), who probably married Ann, daughter of *Thomas Gantt* (?–1765); Henry; and Thomas. DAUGHTERS: Ann, who married (first name unknown) Travers; Mary (1707–?); Margaret, who married Daniel Rawlings; Elizabeth, who married Joshua Sedgewick; and Sarah, who married Samuel Askcom. **PRIVATE CAREER.** EDUCATION: literate. RELIGIOUS AFFILIATION: Anglican. OCCUPATIONAL PROFILE: planter. **PUBLIC CAREER.** LEGISLATIVE SERVICE: Lower House, Calvert County, 1712–1713 (resigned after the 2nd session to become sheriff). LOCAL OFFICE: sheriff, Calvert County, 1713/14–1717. **WEALTH DURING LIFETIME.** LAND AT FIRST ELECTION: at least 550 acres inherited from his father. **WEALTH AT DEATH.** DIED: will probated on January 26, 1738/39. PERSONAL PROPERTY: TEV, £941.11.6 current money (including 15 slaves); FB, £690.9.10. LAND: 1,150 acres, plus 3 tracts of unspecified acreage.

BROUGHE, WILLIAM (?–1651). BORN: in England or Holland. IMMIGRATED: in 1636 as a free adult. RESIDED: in St. Mary's County. **MARRIED** Sarah, who subsequently married in 1652 William Scott. **CHILDREN.** Died without progeny. **PRIVATE CAREER.** EDUCATION: probably literate. RELIGIOUS AFFILIATION: Protestant. SOCIAL STATUS AND ACTIVITIES: low to middling social status; acquired land by 1642; held no titles; made a trip to Holland shortly before his death. OCCUPATIONAL PROFILE: planter. **PUBLIC CAREER.** LEGISLATIVE SERVICE: Assembly, present 1637/38, St. Clement's Hundred, St. Mary's County, 1642A, present 1642B; Lower House, Newtown Hundred, St. Mary's County, 1650–1650/51 (Accounts 1). **WEALTH DURING LIFETIME.** LAND: 200 acres, which he sold before his death. **WEALTH AT DEATH.** DIED: will probated on December 5, 1651. PERSONAL PROPERTY: TEV, 6,704 pounds of tobacco.

BROWN, EDWARD (?–1716). BORN: probably in Kent County. NATIVE: probably second or third generation. RESIDED: in Kent County; "of Kent Island," Queen Anne's County, by 1707. **FAMILY BACKGROUND.** FATHER: probably either Edward Brown, who immigrated as a servant in 1655, married in 1668 Sarah, daughter of Morgan Williams (?–1685), and served as constable of Upper Hundred of Kent Island from 1669/70 to 1670; or Morgan Brown (1669–by 1705), son of Edward Brown. **MARRIED** Mary. **CHILDREN.** SONS: John (?–1723), who married Catherine; Matthew. DAUGHTERS: Mary; Rachel; and Sarah. **PRIVATE CAREER.** EDUCATION: literate. RELIGIOUS AFFILIATION: Protestant. SOCIAL STATUS AND ACTIVITIES: Mr., 1706; Gent., 1715. OCCUPATIONAL PROFILE: planter. **PUBLIC CAREER.** LEGISLATIVE SERVICE: Lower House, Queen Anne's County, 1715. LOCAL OFFICE: justice, Queen Anne's County, 1715/16 (quorum). **WEALTH AT DEATH.** DIED: will probated on June 9, 1716. PERSONAL PROPERTY: TEV, £413.16.4 current money (including 4 slaves and 1 servant); FB, £344.4.9.

BROWN, JAMES (?–1770). NATIVE: probably, if so second generation. RESIDED: in Dorchester County. **FAMILY BACKGROUND.** FATHER: Thomas Brown (?–ca. 1713), of Dorchester County. STEPFATHER: Thomas Smith (?–1727), of Dorchester County. MOTHER: Roseannah. BROTHERS: John (?–1767), who married Mary Anderton; Thomas; and Charles. **MARRIED** by 1713 Sarah, widow of William Clarkson (?–1706), of Dorchester County, planter. **CHILDREN.** SONS: John (?–1768); Thomas (?–by 1769), who married Elizabeth; and James, Jr., who married Sarah. STEPSONS: William Clarkson; Thomas Clarkson, who married Mary; Robert Clarkson; and Richard Clarkson. DAUGHTERS: Mary (?–ca. 1769), who married Edward Newton; (first name unknown), who married (first name unknown) Handley; Sarah, who married John Edwards; and Margery (?–by 1761), who married first, Thomas Kennerly, second, Benjamin Wheland, and third, John Gibbs. OTHER CHILDREN: a stepchild, (first name and sex unknown) Clarkson. **PRIVATE CAREER.** EDUCATION: literate. SOCIAL STATUS AND ACTIVITIES: Gent., 1728. OCCUPATIONAL PROFILE: husbandman, 1718; planter, 1767. **PUBLIC CAREER.** LEGISLATIVE SERVICE: Lower House, Dorchester County, 1734/35–1737. LOCAL OFFICES: land commissioner, Dorchester County, appointed 1728; justice, Dorchester County, commissioned 1736 and 1737. MILITARY SERVICE: captain, by 1758. **WEALTH DURING LIFETIME.** LAND AT FIRST ELECTION: 1,050 acres in Dorchester County (inherited 100 acres from his stepfather, but sold it to his brother before his election; purchased 650 acres and· patented 250 acres). SIGNIFICANT CHANGES IN LAND BETWEEN FIRST ELECTION AND DEATH: patented 200 acres in Dorchester County between 1741 and 1748; sold 350 acres in Dorchester County to his sons and one stepson between 1760 and 1765; sold 105 acres in Dorchester County between 1765 and 1768. WEALTH AT DEATH. DIED: will probated on May 3, 1770, in Dorchester County. PERSONAL PROPERTY: TEV, £322.5.8 current money (including 8 slaves and books); FB, ·£255.9.4. LAND: at least 694 acres in Dorchester County.

BROWN (BROWNE), JOHN (?–1793). BORN: in Queen Anne's County, of age by 1750. NATIVE: at least second generation. RESIDED: in Upper District Hundred, Queen Anne's County. FAMILY BACKGROUND. FATHER: James Brown (?–ca. 1756), of Queen Anne's County, a planter. MOTHER: Sarah. BROTHERS: James; Joel; William (1741–?); and Samuel (1744–?). SISTERS: Elizabeth; Hesther (Easter), who married Andrew Hall; Sarah; Ann (1746–?); and Rebecca (1751–?). MARRIED on January 13, 1757, Catherine, daughter of William Carmichael (?–1769), who immigrated from Scotland, a merchant, and wife Elizabeth; stepdaughter of Ann Brooke (1712–ca. 1754); stepgranddaughter of Roger Brooke (1673–1718), of Prince George's County, and wife Elizabeth Hutchins. Her brothers were Walter; James (?–1778), a ship's captain, who married Selitia Emory; and William (?–1795), of Chestertown, Kent County, an attorney. Educated in Edinburgh, Scotland, William served as secretary to the commission in Paris comprised of Silas Deane, Benjamin Franklin, and Arthur Lee, which attempted to persuade France to aid the colonies, ca. 1775. He also served as a delegate to the Continental Congress from 1778 to 1779, as secretary to John Jay, minister to Spain, ca. 1780, and as chargé d'affaires in Madrid, Spain in 1782. Unpaid for years, and with his fortune depleted, William died in Madrid in 1795. He married first, (first name unknown) Stirling, daughter of an Episcopal rector of Queen Anne's County, and second, Antonia Reynon, of Spain; she and their daughter Alphonsa came to live near Chestertown, Kent County, after William's death. Catherine's half or stepbrother was *Richard Bennett Carmichael* (1753–1824). Her sisters were Ann; Elizabeth, who married Samuel Thompson; and Margaret (ca. 1741–1767), who married Arthur Holt. Her stepsister was Elizabeth Brooke, born before her mother's marriage to William Car-

michael, then adopted by him and who married *John Lambert Wilmer* (1747–1799). CHILDREN. DAUGHTER: Sarah (1757–?). PRIVATE CAREER. EDUCATION: literate. RELIGIOUS AFFILIATION: Anglican, St. Luke's Parish, Queen Anne's County. OCCUPATIONAL PROFILE: farmer. PUBLIC CAREER. LEGISLATIVE SERVICE: Lower House, Queen Anne's County, 1773–1774; Conventions, Queen Anne's County, 1st, 1774, 3rd, 1774, 5th, 1775; Lower House, Queen Anne's County, 1778–1779 (Grievances 1; Tax Commissioners 1; Claims 3), 1779–1780 (Grievances 2, 3), 1787–1788, 1789 (elected, but did not attend), 1790 (elected, but did not attend). LOCAL OFFICES: churchwarden, St. Luke's Parish, Queen Anne's County, in office 1752 and 1769; justice, Queen Anne's County, 1756–1793 (quorum, 1763–1793); St. Luke's Parish Vestry, Queen Anne's County, in office 1762–1768, 1772–1773, 1783–1785; commissioner of surveys, Queen Anne's County, in office 1766; Committee of Correspondence, Queen Anne's County, elected 1774; justice, Orphans' Court, Queen Anne's County, in office 1777–1780, 1786–at least 1791; commissioner of tax, Queen Anne's County, in office 1777, 1782–at least 1792; judge, court of appeals, appointed under the Act to Procure Troops for the American Army, Queen Anne's County, appointed 1778. MILITARY SERVICE: captain, by 1756. WEALTH DURING LIFETIME. PERSONAL PROPERTY: assessed value £1,923.0.0, including 49 slaves and 108 oz. plate, 1783. LAND AT FIRST ELECTION: 884 acres in Queen Anne's County (received 298 acres from his father's estate; patented 186 acres and purchased 400 acres). SIGNIFICANT CHANGES IN LAND BETWEEN FIRST ELECTION AND DEATH: owned a total of 1,145 acres in Queen Anne's County, 1783. WEALTH AT DEATH. DIED: will probated on March 14, 1793, in Queen Anne's County. PERSONAL PROPERTY: he mentioned 16 slaves in his will. LAND: 1,137 acres in Queen Anne's County.

BROWN (BROWNE), MATTHEW (?–?). IMMIGRATED: probably. RESIDED: in Somerset County, April 1773; Dorchester County by June 1774. PRIVATE CAREER. EDUCATION: literate. SOCIAL STATUS AND ACTIVITIES: Esq., 1776. OCCUPATIONAL PROFILE: lawyer, admitted to the following courts: Charles County in November 1772 (sworn in as "Matthias Brown"); Dorchester County in March 1773; Prince George's County in March 1773; Provincial Court in April 1773; Caroline County in November 1775. PUBLIC CAREER. LEGISLATIVE SERVICE: Conventions, Dorchester County, 1st, 1774, 3rd, 1774, 4th, 1775. LOCAL OFFICE: clerk of

Indictments, Caroline County, appointed 1775. STANDS ON PUBLIC/PRIVATE ISSUES: The Council of Safety issued a permit to Matthew Brown "to pass from any Sea-Port Town in this Province, to Europe with his Baggage" on June 23, 1776; possibly a Loyalist.

BROWN, NICHOLAS (ca. 1608–1655). BORN: ca. 1606, probably in England. IMMIGRATED: by 1638 as a free adult from Virginia. ADDITIONAL COMMENTS: in Virginia by 1634. RESIDED: in Kent County. FAMILY BACKGROUND. BROTHER: Robert Brown, a "waterman," of London, England. PRIVATE CAREER. EDUCATION: illiterate. RELIGIOUS AFFILIATION: Protestant. OCCUPATIONAL PROFILE: planter. PUBLIC CAREER. LEGISLATIVE SERVICE: Assembly, Kent County, 1638/39. LOCAL OFFICE: justice, Kent County, 1648–1654/55. WEALTH DURING LIFETIME. LAND AT FIRST ELECTION: under 500 acres. WEALTH AT DEATH. DIED: buried on July 21, 1655. PERSONAL PROPERTY: TEV, 16,587 pounds of tobacco, plus livestock and other items perhaps worth as much as £50. LAND: 200 acres, plus another plantation of unspecified acreage.

BROWN (BROWNE), RICHARD (?–?). IMMIGRATED: in 1648 as a free adult with his wife. RESIDED: in St. Mary's County; moved to Virginia, 1654. PRIVATE CAREER. SOCIAL STATUS AND ACTIVITIES: Mr. on arrival; no other evidence of public service except jury duty, 1648/49. PUBLIC CAREER. LEGISLATIVE SERVICE: Assembly, St. Mary's County, 1649 (Accounts). WEALTH DURING LIFETIME. LAND AT FIRST ELECTION: rights to 200 acres.

BROWNE, DAVID (?–1697). BORN: probably in Scotland. IMMIGRATED: in 1670 as a free adult from Scotland. RESIDED: in Somerset County. MARRIED by 1672 Winifred, widow of Capt. William Thorne. CHILDREN. Died without progeny. PRIVATE CAREER. EDUCATION: literate; possibly attended Glasgow University. RELIGIOUS AFFILIATION: Presbyterian. SOCIAL STATUS AND ACTIVITIES: Gent., by 1686. OCCUPATIONAL PROFILE: merchant; planter. PUBLIC CAREER. LEGISLATIVE SERVICE: Associators' Convention, Somerset County, 1689–1692; Grand Committee of Twenty, 1690–1692; Upper House, 1692–1693 (Laws 2), 1694–1697 (did not attend the 8th session). OTHER PROVINCIAL OFFICES: Council, 1691–1697; justice, Provincial Court, 1693–1694. LOCAL OFFICES: justice, Somerset County, 1672/73–1692 (quorum, 1679/80–1692); coroner, Somerset County, 1688–1692. MILITARY SERVICE: captain, 1679/80–1690;

colonel, 1690–1697. STANDS ON PUBLIC/PRIVATE ISSUES: active supporter of the revolution of 1689, which brought him his first provincial offices. WEALTH DURING LIFETIME. LAND AT FIRST ELECTION: 1,780 acres. WEALTH AT DEATH. DIED: will probated on September 17, 1697. PERSONAL PROPERTY: TEV, £1,838.1.6 sterling (including 4 slaves and 4 servants). LAND: 980 acres.

BROWNE, JAMES (1640–1675). BORN: in Salem, Massachusetts. IMMIGRATED: perhaps by 1663/64, certainly by 1667, as a free adult, probably with his wife and children from New England. RESIDED: in Baltimore County; "Farley," Cecil County, ca. 1675. ADDITIONAL COMMENTS: came to Maryland in connection with his father's business. FAMILY BACKGROUND. FATHER: John Browne (?–1685), a merchant of Salem, Massachusetts, who had trade associations with Maryland for many years, and who sold 1,676 acres on the Sassafras River in 1663/64. MARRIED in 1664 Hannah, daughter of Henry Bartholomew. CHILDREN. SONS: Bartholomew (1669–?); James (1675–?). DAUGHTERS: Elizabeth (1671–?); Hannah (1673–?). PRIVATE CAREER. RELIGIOUS AFFILIATION: Protestant. OCCUPATIONAL PROFILE: partner with father; merchant; storekeeper. PUBLIC CAREER. LEGISLATIVE SERVICE: Lower House, Baltimore County, 1671–1675 (no evidence he ever sat; left for a voyage to New England before the 1st session). WEALTH DURING LIFETIME. LAND AT FIRST ELECTION: over 1,900 acres. WEALTH AT DEATH. DIED: committed suicide on November 12, 1675. PERSONAL PROPERTY: 143,744 pounds of tobacco, plus a cargo of goods from England and New England probably worth at least £191. LAND: over 1,900 acres.

BRUCE, ANDREW (?–1815). BORN: probably in Maryland, of age in 1765. NATIVE: at least second generation. RESIDED: in Frederick County; Washington County; "Mt. Pleasant," Allegany County. FAMILY BACKGROUND. BROTHER: possibly *Normand Bruce* (?–1811). MARRIED Barbara (?–by 1814), daughter of William Murdock (?–1815); granddaughter of Rev. George Murdock, rector of Prince George's Parish, Prince George's County in 1726. Her brothers were William (?–ca. 1825), a merchant of London, England; Benjamin, of Frederick County; and *George Murdock* (ca. 1742–1805). Her first cousin was *William Murdock Beall* (ca. 1742–1823). CHILDREN. SONS: at least eight, including Normand Murdock; William; Andrew; George; and Charles. DAUGHTERS: Susannah; Margaret, who married (first name unknown)

Cresap; and Helen. **PRIVATE CAREER. EDUCATION**: literate. **SOCIAL STATUS AND ACTIVITIES**: Gent., 1802. **OCCUPATIONAL PROFILE**: attorney, admitted to the following courts: Frederick County in March 1765; Prince George's County in June 1765. Planter. **PUBLIC CAREER. LEGISLATIVE SERVICE**: Lower House, Washington County, 1787–1788. **LOCAL OFFICES**: Committee of Observation, Frederick County, elected 1775; justice, Washington County, 1777–1789, Allegany County, 1790–at least 1800; commissioner of tax, Washington County, 1777–at least 1779, Allegany County, appointed 1792; justice, Orphans' Court, Allegany County, appointed 1802. **WEALTH DURING LIFETIME. PERSONAL PROPERTY**: assessed value £187.0.0, including 3 slaves, 1783. **LAND AT FIRST ELECTION**: 2,056 acres in Washington and Frederick counties, plus 1 leased lot in Cumberland, Washington County. **SIGNIFICANT CHANGES IN LAND BETWEEN FIRST ELECTION AND DEATH**: acquired by purchase and patent 4,925 acres in Frederick, Washington, and Allegany counties, 1788–1805. Included in this total are 9 fifty-acre lots in Wills Town Hundred, Allegany County. In 1805, 6 of these lots were added to a 440-acre tract he already owned, and he combined this with a 451-acre vacancy to form his dwelling plantation. He sold a total of 1,403 acres in Washington, Frederick, and Allegany counties (1,060 acres of this was comprised of 1 large tract), 1793–1798. **WEALTH AT DEATH. DIED**: at "Mt. Pleasant," Wills Town Hundred, Allegany County; will probated on April 1, 1815. **LAND**: probably ca. 5,578 acres in Frederick, Washington, and Allegany counties. His will mentioned 900 acres in Hardy County, Virginia (later became part of West Virginia).

BRUCE, NORMAND (?–1811). **BORN**: in Scotland. **IMMIGRATED**: in 1748 as a freeman from Scotland. **RESIDED**: in St. Mary's County, 1748–1765; Bruceville, Big Pipe Creek, Frederick County, 1765–1811. **FAMILY BACKGROUND. BROTHER**: possibly *Andrew Bruce* (?–1815). **MARRIED** on November 19, 1761, Susanna Gardiner (1742–1811), daughter of *Philip Key* (1696/97–1764). Her brothers were Capt. Richard Ward Key (?–1765); *Edmund Key* (?–1766); Dr. John Key (?–1755); Francis Key (1731/32–1770); *Thomas Key* (?–1772); and Philip Barton Key (?–1756). Her nephews were *Philip Key* (1750–1820); *John Ross Key* (1754–1821). **CHILDREN. SON**: Charles, who first resided in the Middle District, Frederick County, but in early life left to live in the West Indies. **DAUGHTER**: Elizabeth Key, who

married John Scott. **PRIVATE CAREER. EDUCATION**: literate. **RELIGIOUS AFFILIATION**: Anglican. **SOCIAL STATUS AND ACTIVITIES**: Esq., 1761; Gent., 1768; married into a very prominent family with extensive landholdings in the colony. **OCCUPATIONAL PROFILE**: landlord; mill owner. **PUBLIC CAREER. LEGISLATIVE SERVICE**: Lower House, Frederick County, 1780 (elected, but did not attend; resigned on November 9, 1780). **LOCAL OFFICES**: sheriff, St. Mary's County, 1761–1764, Frederick County, 1768–1771; justice, Frederick County, commissioned 1768 and 1773–at least 1777; Committee of Observation, Frederick County, elected 1774; justice, Orphans' Court, Frederick County, commissioned 1777; commissioner of tax, Frederick County, 1777–at least 1779; purchasing agent, Frederick County, appointed 1779; subscription officer, Continental Loan Office, Frederick County, appointed 1779. **MILITARY SERVICE**: colonel, 1776; commanded a battalion of the Flying Camp. **WEALTH DURING LIFETIME. PERSONAL PROPERTY**: 24 slaves, 1790. **LAND AT FIRST ELECTION**: 20,648 acres in Frederick, Montgomery, Prince George's and Washington counties (his wife inherited at least 1,399 acres from her father). His father-in-law owned 5,000 acres in Frederick County, which was a factor in inducing Bruce and his wife to move from St. Mary's County to Frederick County. **SIGNIFICANT CHANGES IN LAND BETWEEN FIRST ELECTION AND DEATH**: patented 3,016 acres in Frederick and Montgomery counties, 1783–1796. **WEALTH AT DEATH. DIED**: will probated on August 5, 1811, in Frederick County. **LAND**: probably ca. 24,000 acres in Frederick, Montgomery, Prince George's, and Washington counties.

BRUFF, WILLIAM (ca. 1741–1802). **BORN**: ca. 1741 in Talbot County; probably eldest son. **NATIVE**: at least second generation. **RESIDED**: in Queen Anne's County, 1764; Island Hundred, Queen Anne's County, 1778; Baltimore Town, 1795. **FAMILY BACKGROUND. FATHER**: Richard Bruff (?–1760), of Talbot County. **MOTHER**: Rachel, widow of (name unknown). **BROTHER**: Richard. **STEPBROTHER**: Jonathan (surname unknown). **SISTERS**: Mary; Lucy; Rachel; and Rebecca. **MARRIED** first, by 1765 Catherine (1743–?), daughter of Maj. Nathan Wright (?–1767) and wife Mary (?–1773); stepdaughter of (first name unknown) Bruff; granddaughter of *Charles Wright* (?–1720); niece of *Robert Norrest Wright* (?–ca. 1746/47). Her brothers were *Turbutt Wright* (ca. 1741–1783); Robert (1756–?). Her sister was Mary (1746–1754). **MARRIED** second, by 1794 Catherine, widow of Nicholas Jones (?–1791), of Baltimore County; she moved to Dorchester County after Bruff's death. CHILDREN. SON: William, Jr. PRIVATE CAREER. EDUCATION: literate. RELIGIOUS AFFILIATION: Anglican; Methodist. SOCIAL STATUS AND ACTIVITIES: Gent., 1770; Esq., 1778. OCCUPATIONAL PROFILE: planter; merchant, 1762; merchant in partnership with *Richard Tilghman Earle* (1728/29–1788) and his brother James Earle, in the firm of Richard T. Earle & Co., which was in existence from 1772 to 1775; merchant in Baltimore City, in partnership with Daniel Chambers, in the firm of Chambers & Bruff, 1799; merchant in Baltimore City, in partnership with William Bruff, Jr., in the firm of William Bruff & Son, by 1802, at which time they liquidated all their assets to pay their creditors. PUBLIC CAREER. LEGISLATIVE SERVICE: Convention, Queen Anne's County, 9th, 1776 (election voided on August 16, 1776, because the freemen of Queen Anne's County appointed the election judges contrary to the resolves of the 8th Convention; reelected and seated); Lower House, Queen Anne's County, 1777 (Claims 1, 2; Grievances 1; Elections 2), 1777–1778 (resigned on October 31, 1777; reelected to the 2nd session; Elections 2; Grievances 2, 3; Claims 2, 3), 1778–1779 (Manufactories 1; Claims 1), 1779–1780 (Grievances 1–3; Tax Commissioners 1, 2), 1780–1781 (speaker 1, 2; resigned as speaker on June 11, 1781, when "indisposed"; reappointed on June 14, 1781). OTHER STATE OFFICE: Special Council for the Eastern Shore (in case of invasion it was empowered to act in place of the governor and Council), appointed 1780. LOCAL OFFICES: Committee of Correspondence, Queen Anne's County, elected 1774; justice, Queen Anne's County, commissioned 1777, 1778, 1779, 1780 (did not qualify); justice, Orphans' Court, Queen Anne's County, commissioned 1777 and 1778; St. Luke's Parish Vestry, Queen Anne's County, in office 1784; board of trustees, Methodist Church, Queen Anne's County, elected 1794; commission to build a courthouse and jail, Queen Anne's County, period of service unknown. STANDS ON PUBLIC/PRIVATE ISSUES: manumitted seven slaves between 1785 and 1797. WEALTH DURING LIFETIME. PERSONAL PROPERTY: assessed value £587.0.0, including 24 slaves and 30 oz. plate, 1783; 10 slaves, 1790; sold 8 slaves and 1 servant, part of the assets of William Bruff & Son, to pay debts, 1802. LAND AT FIRST ELECTION: 815 acres in Queen Anne's County (365 acres through first marriage, 450 acres by purchase). SIGNIFICANT CHANGES IN LAND BETWEEN FIRST ELECTION AND DEATH:

owned a total of 1,138 acres in Queen Anne's County, 1783; at least 211 acres in Baltimore County, plus 2 lots in Baltimore City through his second marriage, by 1794; placed a tract of unknown acreage in Cecil County, 200 acres in Queen Anne's County, and a lot and house in Baltimore City in trust for his wife between 1794 and 1801; owned a total of 659 acres in Queen Anne's County, plus 1,116 sq. ft. in Baltimore City, 1798; sold 652 acres in Baltimore and Queen Anne's counties, plus a wharf and building on Fell's Point, Baltimore City, plus 570 acres on the Sciota River, Northwest Territory, all the real property assets of William Bruff & Son, to pay debts, 1802. WEALTH AT DEATH. DIED: between July 21 and November 13, 1802, in Baltimore City. LAND: all lands, except those held in trust for his wife, had been sold to pay the debts of William Bruff & Son.

BUCHANAN, ANDREW (ca. 1733–1786). BORN: ca. 1733 in Baltimore County; second son. NATIVE: second generation. RESIDED: in Baltimore County. FAMILY BACKGROUND. FATHER: Dr. *George Buchanan* (ca. 1697–1750). MOTHER: Eleanor Rogers (?–1758). BROTHERS: *Lloyd Buchanan* (1729–ca. 1762); Archibald (1736–1785); George (1739–?); James (1744–1783); and William (1748–?). SISTERS: Eleanor (1732–?); Elizabeth (1742–?), who married *James Gittings* (1735–ca. 1823). MARRIED on July 20, 1760, Susanna (1743–1798), daughter of Alexander Lawson (?–1760), a merchant, and wife Dorothy Smith (1719–?); granddaughter of Walter Smith (ca. 1692–1734), of "Hall's Craft," Calvert County, Her brother was Alexander (?–1798), who married in 1763 Elizabeth Brown. Her sisters were Isabella (?–1822), who married *Robert Alexander* (1740–1805); Mary (Polly), who married Robert Christie, Jr.; Rebecca (?–1759), who married *Lloyd Buchanan* (1729–ca. 1762); Dorothy (?–1752); Elizabeth (?–1752); and Margaret (?–1752). Dorothy, Elizabeth, and Margaret all drowned while ice skating on the pond at their father's ironworks. CHILDREN. SONS: George; Andrew; Alexander Pitt; Archibald; Lloyd; and James. DAUGHTERS: Eleanor (?–died as a minor); Dorothy, who married Benjamin Lowndes; Elizabeth, who married David C. Stewart; and Susannah, who married Thomas Johnston, Jr. PRIVATE CAREER. EDUCATION: literate. RELIGIOUS AFFILIATION: Anglican, St. Paul's Parish, Baltimore County. SOCIAL STATUS AND ACTIVITIES: Mr., 1761; Gent., 1782. OCCUPATIONAL PROFILE: a merchant, with a store on Calvert Street, Baltimore Town. PUBLIC CAREER. LEGISLATIVE SERVICE: Conventions, Baltimore

County, 1st, 1774 (appointed, but did not attend), 4th, 1775 (elected, but did not attend); Senate, Western Shore, Term of 1776–1781: 1779 (elected on July 21, 1779, to fill a vacancy in the 1778–1779 Assembly; declined to serve on July 24, 1779). LOCAL OFFICES: St. Paul's Parish Vestry, Baltimore Town, in office 1762–1765, 1767–1770; commissioner, Baltimore Town, 1768–1781; justice, Baltimore County, 1769–1786 (quorum, 1772–1786); one of several citizens who purchased land to build a public market house in Baltimore Town, in office 1771; justice, Court of Oyer and Terminer and Gaol Delivery, Baltimore County, commissioned 1772; Committee of Observation, Baltimore Town, elected 1774; trustee for the poor, Baltimore County, in office 1775; county lieutenant, Baltimore County, appointed 1777; commissioner of tax, Baltimore County, 1777–at least 1783; justice, Orphans' Court, Baltimore County, 1777–1786; subscription officer, Continental Loan Office, Baltimore County, appointed 1779. MILITARY SERVICE: brigadier general, Maryland Militia, 1776. WEALTH DURING LIFETIME. PERSONAL PROPERTY: inherited 1 slave from his father, 1750; inherited 2 slaves from his father-in-law, 1761; assessed value £1,422.12.0, including 29 slaves and 90 oz. plate, 1783. LAND AT FIRST ELECTION: 1,297 acres in Baltimore County (378 acres inherited from his father, 1750; 100 acres through his marriage), plus ca. 9 lots in Baltimore Town. SIGNIFICANT CHANGES IN LAND BETWEEN FIRST ELECTION AND DEATH: speculated on lots in Baltimore Town by buying lots and then leasing them whole or in smaller parcels, retaining the ground rents. WEALTH AT DEATH. DIED: on March 12, 1786, in Baltimore County. PERSONAL PROPERTY: included a warehouse and store in Baltimore Town; requested that no appraisal of his estate be made. LAND: at least 1,194 acres in Baltimore County and ca. 8 lots in Baltimore Town, with houses on at least 3 of them.

BUCHANAN, GEORGE (ca. 1697–1750). BORN: ca. 1697, probably in Scotland. IMMIGRATED: ca. 1723 from Scotland. RESIDED: in Baltimore County. MARRIED by 1726 Eleanor (?–1758), daughter of Nicholas Rogers (?–1720) and wife Eleanor, who subsequently married (first name unknown) Harris. Her brothers were William; Nicholas (?–1758), a merchant. Her sisters were Sarah; Mary; Elizabeth (1715–1777); and Catherine. CHILDREN. SONS: *Lloyd Buchanan* (1729–ca. 1762); *Andrew Buchanan* (ca. 1733–1786); Archibald (1736–1785), a merchant, who married Sarah Brooke Lee (?–1811), sister of *Thomas Sim Lee*

(1745–1819); George (1739–?); James (1744–1783); and William (1748–?). DAUGHTERS: Eleanor (1732–?), who married Richard Croxall; Elizabeth (1742–?), who married *James Gittings* (1735–ca. 1823). PRIVATE CAREER. EDUCATION: literate. RELIGIOUS AFFLILIATION: Protestant. SOCIAL STATUS AND ACTIVITIES: Gent., 1726. OCCUPATIONAL PROFILE: physician; probably owned a small store in Baltimore Town at the time of his death. PUBLIC CAREER. LEGISLATIVE SERVICE: Lower House, Baltimore County, 1745 (Accounts), 1745/46–1748 (Accounts Cv 1, 1–3, 4), 1749 (Accounts Cv, 1; died before the 2nd session). LOCAL OFFICES: commissioner, Baltimore County, appointed to purchase the land upon which Baltimore Town was to be built, 1729; commissioner, Baltimore Town, 1745–1750; justice, Baltimore County, 1732–at least 1749 (quorum, 1741–at least 1749); justice, Court of Oyer and Terminer and Gaol Delivery, Baltimore County, appointed 1746 and 1748. WEALTH DURING LIFETIME. LAND AT FIRST ELECTION: ca. 2,000 acres in Baltimore County (200 acres through marriage). SIGNIFICANT CHANGES IN LAND BETWEEN FIRST ELECTION AND DEATH: purchased 78 acres in Baltimore County, plus 1 lot in Baltimore Town, 1745–1746; gave 150 acres in Baltimore County to his son *Lloyd Buchanan* (1729–ca. 1762), 1749. WEALTH AT DEATH. DIED: on April 25, 1750, in Baltimore County; buried in Druid Hill Cemetery. PERSONAL PROPERTY: TEV, £4,490.1.10 current money (including 18 slaves, 2 servants, and books); FB, £3,935.2.0. LAND: ca. 1,900 acres in Baltimore County, plus 1 lot in Baltimore Town.

BUCHANAN, LLOYD (1729–ca. 1762). BORN: in 1729 in Baltimore County; eldest son. NATIVE: second generation. RESIDED: in Baltimore County. FAMILY BACKGROUND. FATHER: Dr. *George Buchanan* (ca. 1697–1750). MOTHER: Eleanor Rogers (?–1758). BROTHERS: *Andrew Buchanan* (ca. 1733–1786); Archibald (1736–1785); George (1739–?); James (1744–1783); and William (1748–?). SISTERS: Eleanor (1732–?); Elizabeth (1742–?), who married *James Gittings* (1735–ca. 1823). MARRIED Rebecca (?–1759, died in childbirth), daughter of Alexander Lawson (?–1760), a merchant, and wife Dorothy Smith. Her brother was Alexander (?–1798), who married in 1763 Elizabeth Brown. Her sisters were Isabella (?–ca. 1822), who married *Robert Alexander* (1740–1805); Mary (Polly), who married Robert Christie, Jr.; Susanna (1743–1798), who married *Andrew Buchanan* (ca. 1733–1786); Dorothy (?–1752); Elizabeth (?–1752); and Margaret (?–1752). Dorothy, Elizabeth, and Margaret all drowned while ice skating on the pond at their father's ironworks. **CHILDREN.** DAUGHTER: Eleanor (1757–1812), who married Nicholas Rogers (1753–1822). **PRIVATE CAREER.** EDUCATION: literate. RELIGIOUS AFFILIATION: Protestant. OCCUPATIONAL PROFILE: lawyer, admitted to the following courts: Charles County by August 1753; Provincial Court in September 1753; Baltimore County by March 1754; Frederick County in March 1755; Anne Arundel County by November 1755; Court of Chancery by July 1759. **PUBLIC CAREER.** LEGISLATIVE SERVICE: Lower House, Baltimore County, 1751–1754 (election of county delegation voided on December 12, 1751, because of the illegal actions of the sheriff; reelected to the 2nd session and seated), 1754–1755 (discharged during the 3rd session for serving as clerk of Indictments in the Baltimore County Court). LOCAL OFFICES: clerk of Indictments, Baltimore County, in office 1755. **WEALTH DURING LIFETIME.** LAND AT FIRST ELECTION: 728 acres in Baltimore County, plus 1 lot in Baltimore Town (all from his father by gift or inheritance). SIGNIFICANT CHANGES IN LAND BETWEEN FIRST ELECTION AND DEATH: purchased 242 acres in Baltimore County, 1758–1760; added 75 acres to his home plantation by patent, 1760. **WEALTH AT DEATH.** DIED: will probated on January 21, 1762, in Baltimore County. PERSONAL PROPERTY: requested no appraisal of his estate. LAND: 1,045 acres in Baltimore County, plus at least 1 lot in Baltimore Town.

BUCHANAN, ROBERT (ca. 1737–1799). BORN: ca. 1737. RESIDED: in Chester Parish, Kent County. MARRIED by March 1764 Mary, daughter of John Kennard, of Kent County; granddaughter of *Philip Kennard* (?–ca. 1739/40). Her sister was Ann. Her other relatives included greatgrandfather *Philip Kennard* (?–1732). **CHILDREN.** SONS: Robert, Jr.; James. DAUGHTERS: Harriet; Anna Maria; and Mary, who married Dr. William Blay Tilden. **PRIVATE CAREER.** EDUCATION: literate. RELIGIOUS AFFILIATION: Anglican, Chester Parish, Kent County. SOCIAL STATUS AND ACTIVITIES: Gent., 1765. OCCUPATIONAL PROFILE: probably a planter. **PUBLIC CAREER.** LEGISLATIVE SERVICE: Lower House, Kent County, 1765–1766 (Bills of Credit 2), 1768–1770 (Claims 1; Public Offices 2; Grievances 3), 1771, 1773–1774 (Public Offices 1); Conventions, Kent County, 6th–8th, 1775–1776. LOCAL OFFICES: Chester Parish Vestry, Kent County, elected 1767, 1769, 1786, and 1787; commissioner of tax, Kent County, appointed 1777, 1790, and 1792. **WEALTH DURING**

LIFETIME. LAND AT FIRST ELECTION: 1,097 acres in Kent County (all from wife's dower). SIGNIFICANT CHANGES IN LAND BETWEEN FIRST ELECTION AND DEATH: purchased 815 acres in Kent and Queen Anne's counties, plus 1 lot in Chestertown, Kent County, by 1771–1797; sold 268 acres in Kent County, 1796–1797. **WEALTH AT DEATH.** DIED: will probated on September 27, 1799, in Kent County. PERSONAL PROPERTY: TEV, £2,683.9.7 current money (including 36 slaves); FB, estate overpaid £24.11.11. LAND: 995 acres in Kent and Queen Anne's counties, and 1 lot in Chestertown, Kent County, plus several tracts in his will with unspecified acreage.

BUCHANAN, WILLIAM (1732–1804). BORN: on August 10, 1732, in Carlisle, Cumberland County, Pennsylvania; younger son. IMMIGRATED: in 1759 from Pennsylvania. RESIDED: in Baltimore Town. **FAMILY BACKGROUND.** FATHER: Robert Buchanan (1697–1748), of Carlisle, Pennsylvania; immigrated in 1720 from Ireland. MOTHER: Janet (Jane) Boyd (?–1799). BROTHER: James (1731–1751). SISTERS: Mary (1729–1782), who married *John Smith* (1718–1794); Elizabeth (1733–1784), who married in 1752 William Smith (1728–1814); Margaret (1736–?), who married Maj. (first name unknown) Galbraith. NIECE: Janet Smith (1752–1812), who married *Josias Carvil Hall* (1746–1814). MARRIED Esther (?–by 1810), daughter of Samuel Smith (1693–1784), a merchant of Baltimore Town, who immigrated in 1759 from Carlisle, Pennsylvania, and wife Sidney Gamble (?–1759). Her brother was *John Smith* (1718–1794). **CHILDREN.** Thirteen, including SONS: Robert (1751–ca. 1783); Samuel (1752–1758); William (1762–1815), who resided in France and married Mary Emelia Louise Merven; John Smith (1766–?); James A. (1768–1840), who married in 1793 Elizabeth Calhoun; and Boyd (1772–by 1804). DAUGHTERS: Sidney (1753–?); Janet (1756–died as a minor); Mary (1757–?), who married in 1787 Rev. Patrick Allison (1740–1802); Margaret (Peggy) (1758–?); Janet (1764–by 1804); and Elizabeth Esther (1774–by 1804). **PRIVATE CAREER.** EDUCATION: literate. RELIGIOUS AFFILIATION: Presbyterian; member of a committee to build the First Presbyterian Church, Baltimore Town, 1764–1781; elder, First Presbyterian Church, Baltimore Town, elected 1781. SOCIAL STATUS AND ACTIVITIES: Esq., 1774; Gent., 1793. OCCUPATIONAL PROFILE: merchant, in partnership with *John Smith* (1718–1794). The firm traded in goods from the Far East and the West Indies. **PUBLIC CAREER.** LEGISLATIVE SERVICE: Conventions, Baltimore County, 2nd–3rd, 1774, 5th,

1775. LOCAL OFFICES: justice, Baltimore County, 1772–at least 1778 (quorum, 1774–at least 1778); Committee of Observation, Baltimore Town, elected 1775. MILITARY SERVICE: deputy commissary general of purchases, commissioned 1777; commissary general of purchases, 1777–1778 (resigned). WEALTH DURING LIFETIME. PERSONAL PROPERTY: assessed value of at least £1,265.0.0, including at least 20 slaves and 102 oz. plate, 1783. LAND AT FIRST ELECTION: ca. 600 acres in Baltimore County, plus at least 2 lots in Baltimore Town. SIGNIFICANT CHANGES IN LAND BETWEEN FIRST ELECTION AND DEATH: developed Baltimore Town lots and leased them either as a whole or in smaller parcels; purchased land in Baltimore County, 1780; owned ca. 2,600 acres in Baltimore County, 1783. In the late 1790s he sold almost one-half of his Baltimore County land and later patented more acreage within Baltimore Town. WEALTH AT DEATH. DIED: on September 19, 1804, in Baltimore County. LAND: ca. 1,600 acres in Baltimore County, plus ca. 9 lots in Baltimore Town (with 1 wharf, 5 warehouses, and 1 three-story brick dwelling). ADDITIONAL COMMENTS: income at death included ground rents on 12 additional lots in Baltimore Town.

BURFORD, THOMAS (?–1686/87). IMMIGRATED: by 1679 as a free adult with his family. RESIDED: in Charles County. MARRIED Anne (?–1700). CHILDREN. SON: Thomas, Jr. (?–1697), who married Margery, widow of Humphrey Warren, Jr. (1665–1695) and daughter of John Cage. DAUGHTERS: Elizabeth, who married James Cottrill; Jane, who married Richard Dodd; and Ann (?–ca. 1717), who married first, Robert Doyne (?–1689), second, ca. 1694 George Plater (ca. 1664–1707), and third, by 1709 *John Rousby* (1685–1744). PRIVATE CAREER. EDUCATION: literate; probably with considerable legal training. RELIGIOUS AFFILIATION: Protestant. SOCIAL STATUS AND ACTIVITIES: Gent. on arrival. OCCUPATIONAL PROFILE: lawyer, one of the most able and active in seventeenth-century Maryland, who was admitted to the following courts: Provincial Court in 1679; Charles County by at least 1679. Planter. PUBLIC CAREER. LEGISLATIVE SERVICE: Lower House, Charles County, 1682–1684 (Trade 2; Laws 3), 1686 (died before the 2nd session). OTHER PROVINCIAL OFFICE: attorney general, 1681–1686/87. LOCAL OFFICE: justice, Charles County, 1685–1686/87. WEALTH DURING LIFETIME. LAND AT FIRST ELECTION: ca. 968 acres. WEALTH AT DEATH. DIED: will probated on March 24, 1686/87. PERSONAL PROPERTY: TEV,

£202.0.11 sterling (including 2 slaves, 1 servant, and 21 law titles, plus other books). LAND: ca. 968 acres.

BURGESS, EDWARD (ca. 1733–1809). BORN: ca. 1733 in Anne Arundel County; fourth son. NATIVE: fourth generation. RESIDED: in Anne Arundel County; Frederick County (later became part of Montgomery County), 1773. FAMILY BACKGROUND. FATHER: John Burgess (1696–1774), of Anne Arundel County, son of Edward Burgess (ca. 1655–1723) and wife Sarah Chew. MOTHER: Jane MacElfresh (?–1733). STEPMOTHER: Matilda Sparrow (?–by 1773). BROTHERS: William (1721–by 1773); John, who married Sarah Dorsey; and Joseph, who married Elizabeth Dorsey. HALF BROTHERS: Samuel (?–by 1773); West; Caleb; and Benjamin. SISTERS: Ann; Sarah, who married (first name unknown) Disney; and Mary. HALF SISTERS: Mary, who married (first name unknown) Ansby; Anna; Elizabeth; and Susannah. OTHER KINSHIP: his great-grandfather was *William Burgess* (ca. 1622–1686/87). MARRIED by 1767 Mary (?–by 1797), daughter of Thomas Davis (?–1749) and wife Elizabeth Gaither. Her brothers were Thomas; Amos (?–1797). Her sisters were Elizabeth (Betsy), who married first, John Welsh (?–1795), and second, (first name unknown) Norwood; Sarah, who married Henry Griffith, son of *Henry Griffith* (ca. 1720–1794). CHILDREN. SONS: Edward, Jr. (?–1824), died without progeny; John (?–by 1816); Ephraigm, of Allegany County; and Thomas, who left Maryland. DAUGHTERS: Elizabeth; Ann (Nancy); Jane; Margaret, who married Ninian Clagett; Sally (Sarah), who married Daniel Hook and left Maryland; and Mary, who married John Sheckles and left Maryland. PRIVATE CAREER. EDUCATION: literate. SOCIAL STATUS AND ACTIVITIES: Gent., 1773; Esq., 1790. OCCUPATIONAL PROFILE: planter. PUBLIC CAREER. LEGISLATIVE SERVICE: Lower House, Montgomery County, 1777, 1777–1778, 1778–1779 (Claims 1; Laws to Expire 2; Tax Commissioners 3), 1779–1780 (Claims 1–3), 1781–1782, 1782–1783, 1783 (elected, but did not serve), 1786–1787, 1787–1788, 1789, 1790, 1795. LOCAL OFFICES: justice, Frederick County, 1773–at least 1775, Montgomery County, 1777–at least 1792; justice, Orphans' Court, Montgomery County, 1777–at least 1790 (quorum, by 1790); Maryland Senate elector, Montgomery County, 1786. MILITARY SERVICE: captain, First Maryland Battalion of the Flying Camp, 1776. WEALTH DURING LIFETIME. PERSONAL PROPERTY: assessed value £234.2.6, including 3 slaves, 1783; assessed value £613.0.0, including 19 slaves and 6 oz. plate, 1793; assessed value £402.0.0, including 16 slaves and 6 oz. plate, 1804; assessed value £386.17.6, including 15 slaves and 6 oz. plate, 1808. Sold slaves and chattel to secure debt of £800 sterling to *Thomas Contee* (ca. 1729–1811). LAND AT FIRST ELECTION: probably 846 acres in Montgomery County (231 acres acquired through marriage). SIGNIFICANT CHANGES IN LAND BETWEEN FIRST ELECTION AND DEATH: purchased almost 1,200 acres in Montgomery and Frederick counties between 1779 and 1790. By 1791 Burgess was being sued for a debt by *Thomas Contee* (ca. 1729–1811) and lost at least 1,444 acres in Montgomery and Frederick counties, which were attached and sold by court order between 1792 and 1798. Burgess himself sold 71 acres in 1793. In 1806 Burgess contracted to buy back 1,138 acres of the 1,444 acres sold by court order; however, although he had the use of the land, he never paid for it and did not obtain title to it. WEALTH AT DEATH. DIED: in December 1809. PERSONAL PROPERTY: TEV, $427.30 current money (including books); FB, estate overpaid $64.68. LAND: possibly 478 acres in Montgomery County.

BURGESS, WILLIAM (ca. 1622–1686/87). BORN: ca. 1622 in England, probably Wiltshire. IMMIGRATED: in 1650 as a free adult with his wife and children from Virginia. RESIDED: in Anne Arundel County. FAMILY BACKGROUND. BROTHERS: probably Joseph Burgess (?–1672), "late of Maryland," and living in Wiltshire, England, in 1672; Samuel; Jeremiah; Isaac; and Daniel. SISTERS: probably Elizabeth Parker; Mary; and Anne. MARRIED first, Elizabeth, daughter of Edward Robbins (1602–?), a merchant of Virginia. Her sister was Rachel, who married *Richard Beard* (?–1681). MARRIED second, Sophia, widow of *Richard Ewen* (?–1660). MARRIED third, Ursulah, who subsequently married Dr. Mordecai Moore. CHILDREN. SONS: Edward, a justice of Anne Arundel County from 1674 to 1689, who married Sarah, daughter of *Samuel Chew* (ca. 1630–1676/77); George, who married Katherine, widow of Henry Stockett; William, who married Ann, widow of John Watkins, and daughter of *Nicholas Gassaway* (1634–1691/92); John; Joseph; Benjamin, who married Jane Buchanan; and Charles, who married Elizabeth Thomas. DAUGHTERS: Susannah, who married *Nicholas Sewall* (ca. 1655–1737), son of *Henry Sewall* (?–1665), and stepson of *Charles Calvert, 3rd Lord Baltimore* (1637–1714/15); Anne (1680–?), who married Thomas Sparrow; and Susannah (1684–?), who married John Mitch-

ell. PRIVATE CAREER. EDUCATION: literate. RELIGIOUS AFFILIATION: Protestant; perhaps a Quaker in 1658 when he refused to take an oath. SOCIAL STATUS AND ACTIVITIES: one of the Puritans who moved from Virginia to Anne Arundel County in 1650; became a councilor after his daughter's marriage to Lord Baltimore's stepson. OCCUPATIONAL PROFILE: planter; merchant. PUBLIC CAREER. LEGISLATIVE SERVICE: Lower House, Anne Arundel County, 1659/60, 1669 (Aggrievances), 1671–1674/75 (Laws 3; Accounts 3), 1676–1682 (Accounts 1, 3); Upper House, 1682–1684 (Trade 1; Accounts 3), 1686 (died before the 2nd session). OTHER PROVINCIAL OFFICES: Council, 1682–1686/87; justice, Provincial Court, 1682–1686/87; Board of Governors, 1684–1686/87. LOCAL OFFICES: justice, Anne Arundel County, 1658 (refused to take the required oath), 1663/64–1682 (president, 1674–1682); sheriff, Anne Arundel County, 1663–1664. MILITARY SERVICE: lieutenant, by 1660; captain, by 1664; major, by 1675; colonel, 1676–1686/87. STANDS ON PUBLIC/PRIVATE ISSUES: he was pardoned for his participation in Fendall's Rebellion because of his role in restoring Lord Baltimore's government, 1660/61. WEALTH DURING LIFETIME. LAND AT FIRST ELECTION: at least several plantations. WEALTH AT DEATH. DIED: on January 24, 1686/87. PERSONAL PROPERTY: TEV, £3,934.5.4 sterling (including 12 slaves, 13 servants, and 2 stores). LAND: over 7,280 acres.

BURLE, ROBERT (ca. 1610–1676). BORN: ca. 1610, probably in England. IMMIGRATED: in 1649 as a free adult with his wife and two children from Virginia. RESIDED: in Anne Arundel County. MARRIED first, Mary. MARRIED second, (name unknown). CHILDREN. SONS: Robert (?–by 1676); Stephen (?–1683/84), who married Blanche; John (?–by 1676); and Thomas. DAUGHTERS: Rebecca; Susanna; and Mary. PRIVATE CAREER. EDUCATION: literate. RELIGIOUS AFFILIATION: Protestant. SOCIAL STATUS AND ACTIVITIES: no title on arrival in the colony, but brought three servants with him; had migrated to Virginia by 1639. OCCUPATIONAL PROFILE: planter. PUBLIC CAREER. LEGISLATIVE SERVICE: Lower House, Anne Arundel County, 1662, 1666. ADDITIONAL COMMENTS: pardoned by the Assembly in 1662 for writing "mutinous and seditious" expressions in a paper addressed to members of that body. LOCAL OFFICES: justice, Anne Arundel County, 1658–1668, 1674–1676 (quorum, 1661–1668, 1674–1676). WEALTH DURING LIFETIME. LAND AT FIRST ELECTION: 1,150 acres in 1662. WEALTH AT

DEATH. DIED: will probated on June 27, 1676. PER-
SONAL PROPERTY: TEV, 15,884 pounds of tobacco
(including 3 servants); FB, 1,103 pounds of tobacco. LAND: 750 acres.

CADWALADER (CADWALLADER), JOHN
(1741/42–1786). BORN: on January 10, 1741/42, in
Philadelphia, Pennsylvania; elder son. NATIVE: at
least second generation in Pennsylvania. RESIDED:
maintained a residence in Philadelphia until at
least 1770; maintained a residence in Talbot
County where his wife's relatives lived; Kent
County. FAMILY BACKGROUND. FATHER: Dr.
Thomas Cadwalader (ca. 1707–1799), of Pennsylvania; educated abroad; lay preacher; studied with
John Jones in Philadelphia. MOTHER: Hannah,
daughter of Thomas Lambert, Jr. BROTHER: Lambert (1743–1823). SISTER: Mary, who married Philemon Dickinson. MARRIED first, in October 1768
Elizabeth (Betsy) (1742–?), daughter of *Edward
Lloyd* (1711–1770); granddaughter of both *Edward Lloyd* (1670–1718/19) and *John Rousby*
(1685–1744); stepgranddaughter of *James Hollyday* (1696–1747); niece of *Richard Lloyd* (1717–
1786), Elizabeth Rousby, who married *Abraham
Barnes* (?–ca. 1778), and Gertrude Rousby, who
married *Robert Jenkins Henry* (ca. 1712–1766).
Her brothers were *Edward Lloyd* (1744–1796);
Richard Bennett (1750–1787). Her sister was Henrietta Maria (1746/47–?). Her first cousins were
James Lloyd (1745–1820); *John Barnes* (ca. 1743–
1800); *Richard Barnes* (?–1804); and Elizabeth
Rousby, who married *George Plater* (1735–1792).
MARRIED second, in 1779 Williamina, daughter of
Dr. Phineas Bond, of Philadelphia, Pennsylvania,
one of the founders of the College of Philadelphia
(later the University of Pennsylvania) and wife
Williamina Moore. Her brother was Phineas Bond
(1749–1815), lawyer, and British consul from 1786
to 1813 in Philadelphia. CHILDREN. SONS: Thomas
(1779–1841), lawyer, brigadier general in 1814;
John. DAUGHTERS: Maria (?–1810), who married
Samuel Ringgold (?–1829); Elizabeth; Ann; and
Fanny, who married first, David Montague, and
second, Lord Erskine. PRIVATE CAREER. EDUCA-
TION: attended the University of Pennsylvania in
1757. RELIGIOUS AFFILIATION: Anglican, Shrewsbury Parish, Kent County. SOCIAL STATUS AND
ACTIVITIES: Gent., 1770; Esq., 1772. OCCUPA-
TIONAL PROFILE: merchant, in business with his
brother, Lambert; planter; landlord. PUBLIC CA-
REER. LEGISLATIVE SERVICE: Lower House, Kent
County, 1777–1778 (elected, but did not attend;
resigned on March 1, 1778), 1780 (elected to the
2nd session of the 1779–1780 Assembly to fill va-

cancy), 1780–1781, 1781–1782 (Manufactories 1),
1782–1783, 1784; Senate, Eastern Shore, Term of
1781–1786: 1783 (elected on November 24, 1783,
to fill vacancy; declined to serve on November 26,
1783). LOCAL OFFICE: Committee of Correspondence, Queen Anne's County, 1774. MILITARY
SERVICE: captain, Silk Stocking Company, Philadelphia Militia, before the Revolution; colonel,
regiment of the Pennsylvania Militia, 1776; brigadier general, Continental Army, February 1777
(declined); brigadier general, Pennsylvania Militia,
April 1777–to close of the war; brigadier general,
Continental Army and commander of the cavalry
in the service of the U.S., 1778 (declined). ADDI-
TIONAL COMMENTS: Cadwalader cooperated with
Gen. George Washington in the capture of the
Hessians at Trenton in 1776. He was present as a
volunteer at the Battles of Brandywine and Germantown in 1777, and the Battle of Monmouth in
1778. At Washington's request, he assisted in the
organization of the militia on Maryland's Eastern
Shore in 1777. In 1778 Cadwalader fought a duel
with Thomas Conway, a leader of a group of men,
both in and out of Congress, who sought the removal of George Washington as commander in
chief. OUT OF STATE SERVICE: Philadelphia Committee of Safety, elected ca. 1775; Orphans' Court,
Philadelphia; Provincial Congress, Philadelphia;
trustee, University of Pennsylvania, 1779–1786.
WEALTH DURING LIFETIME. PERSONAL PROP-
ERTY: assessed value £4,236.0.0, including 102
slaves and 312 oz. plate, 1783. LAND AT FIRST
ELECTION: 4,119 acres in Queen Anne's, Kent, and
Talbot counties (3,909 acres devised to wife
Elizabeth; 87 acres wife's dower; 123 acres by purchase from his father-in-law *Edward Lloyd* (1711–
1770). WEALTH AT DEATH. DIED: on February 11,
1786, in Shrewsbury Parish, Kent County. PER-
SONAL PROPERTY: TEV, £5,883.12.6 current
money (including at least 100 household and quar-
ter slaves, 101 books, 492 oz. plate, 1 sailboat, and
1 skiff); FB, £2,708.4.10. LAND: 3,942 acres in
Kent and Talbot counties, plus unspecified acreage in New Jersey.

CALDER, JAMES (ca. 1695–1755). BORN: ca.
1695. IMMIGRATED: ca. 1727. RESIDED: on lot 7,
Chestertown, Kent County. MARRIED Katherine
Murray. Her brother was Dr. William Murray, of
Dorchester County. CHILDREN. SONS: James (?–
1766), who married Mary; Alexander. DAUGH-
TERS: Sarah, who married James Nichols, of Ches-
tertown, Kent County, lawyer; Ann. PRIVATE CA-
REER. EDUCATION: trained as a lawyer. RELIGIOUS
AFFILIATION: Protestant. OCCUPATIONAL PRO-

FILE: lawyer, admitted to the following courts: Cecil County by 1727; Talbot County by November 1727; Queen Anne's County by March 1729; Kent County by June 1731; Provincial Court by October 1732; Court of Chancery by 1748. Planter. PUBLIC CAREER. LEGISLATIVE SERVICE: Lower House, Kent County, 1739–1741 (Laws Cv–3; Aggrievances 3), 1742–1744 (Laws 1, 2). LOCAL OFFICE: deputy commissary, Kent County, in office 1748–1755. WEALTH DURING LIFETIME. LAND AT FIRST ELECTION: 45 acres in Kent County, plus 2 lots in Chestertown, Kent County. SIGNIFICANT CHANGES IN LAND BETWEEN FIRST ELECTION AND DEATH: acquired 3,731 acres in Kent County (2,900 acres by deed of gift from Richard Bennett), and sold 45 acres in Kent County, 1740–1754; bought 1 water lot in Chestertown, Kent County, and sold 3 lots and deeded another lot as a gift to his daughter and son-in-law, 1751. WEALTH AT DEATH. DIED: will probated on April 22, 1755, in Kent County. PERSONAL PROPERTY: TEV, £1,058.0.2 current money (including 15 slaves and 78 oz. silver); FB, £273.10.9. LAND: 802 acres in Kent County.

CALDWELL, JOHN (?–1747). BORN: of age by 1712. NATIVE: probably second generation. RESIDED: in Somerset County, probably in Salisbury. FAMILY BACKGROUND. FATHER: John Caldwell (?–by 1717/18), who owned land and possibly resided in Sussex County, Delaware; illiterate. MOTHER: Gennett. BROTHER: Robert (?–by 1717/18), who married Margaret. MARRIED Mary. CHILDREN. SONS: Joshua, of age by 1731, who was the sheriff of Somerset County from 1731 to 1734, a justice of Somerset County from 1745 to 1756 (quorum, 1751–1756), and who married Elizabeth; John (?–1775), a mariner, who married Mary; and Samuel (?–by 1775), a minor in 1747, who was apprenticed to Robert Mills. DAUGHTERS: Mary, who married William Venables; Sarah, who married Joseph Seroggen. PRIVATE CAREER. EDUCATION: literate. RELIGIOUS AFFILIATION: probably Presbyterian. SOCIAL STATUS AND ACTIVITIES: Gent., 1719. OCCUPATIONAL PROFILE: shingler, 1713; involved in extensive land speculation, ca. 1713 to ca. 1739; contracted to shingle the State House, make dormer windows, lay the platform and build a handsome cupola and good flagstaff for the building in 1721, for which he was paid £150.0.0 sterling; owned one-fourth of a sloop and mills (possibly sawmills) at the time of his death. PUBLIC CAREER. LEGISLATIVE SERVICE: Lower House, Somerset County, 1719–1721/22, 1732–1734. LOCAL OFFICES: overseer of the road,

Wicomico Hundred, Somerset County, appointed 1725; justice, Somerset County, by 1725–1733 (quorum, 1725–1733); commissioner to purchase land and to lay out a town at the head of the Wicomico River, Somerset County, 1732. WEALTH DURING LIFETIME. LAND AT FIRST ELECTION: ca. 2,300 acres in Somerset County (ca. 800 acres inherited from his father and brother; ca. 1,500 acres by purchase). SIGNIFICANT CHANGES IN LAND BETWEEN FIRST ELECTION AND DEATH: obtained over 1,600 additional acres in Somerset County, but disposed of over 2,500 acres in Somerset County; between ca. 1713 and ca. 1739 he was involved in extensive land speculation, which is not included in the figures given above. WEALTH AT DEATH. DIED: between July 11 and August 19, 1747, in Somerset County. PERSONAL PROPERTY: TEV, at least £449.1.6 (including 5 slaves, books, one-fourth part of sloop, part of a cargo aboard a sloop, and 4,000 feet of plank). LAND: ca. 1,000 acres in Somerset County with mills (possibly sawmills), plus a house and lot, probably in Salisbury.

CALVERT, BENEDICT (ca. 1724–1788). BORN: ca. 1724 in England; an illegitimate son who was known in childhood as Benedict Swingate. IMMIGRATED: in 1742 from England; sent by his father and placed under the care of Dr. *George Steuart* (1700–ca. 1784), of Annapolis. RESIDED: in Annapolis, Anne Arundel County, 1742; "Mt. Airy," Prince George's County, by 1765. FAMILY BACKGROUND. FATHER: *Charles Calvert, 5th Lord Baltimore* (1699–1751). MOTHER: (name unknown). HALF BROTHER: *Frederick Calvert, 6th Lord Baltimore* (1731/32–1771). HALF SISTERS: Frances Dorothy (1734–1736); Caroline, who married *Robert Eden* (1741–1784); and Louisa, who married John Browning, Esq. HALF NEPHEW: *Henry Harford* (ca. 1759–1834). MARRIED on April 27, 1748, Elizabeth (1730–1798), daughter of *Charles Calvert* (?–1733/34). Her guardians were *George Plater* (1695–1755) and Onorio Razolini. Her brother was Charles (1723–1724). Her sister was Ann (1726–by 1748). CHILDREN. SONS: Charles (1756–1774), who died at Eton, England; Edward Henry (1766–1846), who married Elizabeth Biscoe (Briscoe); George (1768–1838), who married Rosalie Stier; John; William; Philip (?–died young); Leonard (?–died young); Cecilius (?–died young); and Robert. DAUGHTERS: Rebecca (1749–?); Eleanor (1753–1811), who married first, on February 3, 1774, Col. John Parke Custis (?–1781), stepson of George Washington (1731/32–1799), and second, in 1783 Dr. David Stuart, of Virginia; Elizabeth, who married on June 15,

1780, Dr. Charles Steuart, of Annapolis, son of *George Steuart* (1700–ca. 1784); and Ariana (1763–1784). PRIVATE CAREER. EDUCATION: literate. RELIGIOUS AFFILIATION: Anglican. SOCIAL STATUS AND ACTIVITIES: Esq.; Hon., 1748. OCCUPATIONAL PROFILE: planter, who managed over 20,000 acres of land; probably a merchant in the firm of Benedict Calvert & Company; officeholder. PUBLIC CAREER. LEGISLATIVE SERVICE: Upper House, 1748 (appointed before the 4th session), 1749–1751, 1751–1754, 1754–1757 (Bills of Credit–Paper Currency 6), 1757–1758, 1758–1761 (Bills of Credit–Paper Currency 1, Cv 3), 1762–1763 (Bills of Credit–Paper Currency 2), 1765–1766 (Bills of Credit–Paper Currency 2, 4), 1768–1770 (Claims–Bills of Credit 1–4), 1771 (Claims–Bills of Credit), 1773–1774 (Claims–Bills of Credit 1, Cv, 2, 3). OTHER PROVINCIAL OFFICES: collector, Patuxent, 1745–1775; Council, 1747/48–1776 (appointed and qualified on March 8, 1747/48); judge, Land Office, 1775–1777 (commissioned jointly with George Steuart, who returned to Scotland in 1775). LOCAL OFFICE: common councilman, Annapolis, 1755–1765 (resigned). STANDS ON PUBLIC/PRIVATE ISSUES: A letter dated May 13, 1777, from Thomas Johnson to Calvert regarding turning over the Land Office to a new judge stated "you declined giving up office." Calvert apparently thought that he could keep his job as register, but the Assembly ousted him and chose Samuel George Peale in his place. Calvert did not sign the Oath of Fidelity of 1778, but remained in Maryland, probably at "Mt. Airy," during the Revolution. His property was not confiscated. WEALTH DURING LIFETIME. PERSONAL PROPERTY: his wife Elizabeth was the sole survivor and heir of Gov. *Charles Calvert* (?–1733/34), and as such her husband was given charge of Calvert's estate on September 10, 1748. LAND AT FIRST ELECTION: unspecified acreage on the Patuxent River in Prince George's County given to him by his father. SIGNIFICANT CHANGES IN LAND BETWEEN FIRST ELECTION AND DEATH: He acquired through marriage 1,962 acres in Anne Arundel and Prince George's counties, plus 2 lots in Annapolis, 1748. He patented 260 additional acres in Anne Arundel County in 1750, and acquired an 874-acre tract in Frederick County by 1753. He patented 606 acres in Prince George's County, plus 4,095 acres in Frederick County with 4 others, 1761–1768. By 1770 he had acquired an additional 1,991 acres in Frederick County jointly with *Thomas Johnson* (1732–1819), which was resurveyed in 1772 for 7,715 acres. He acquired 12,201 acres in Prince George's and Frederick counties, plus 1 lot in Upper Marlboro, by 1772. He sold 470 acres in Anne Arundel County, 1762–1769, and 1,172 acres in Prince George's County by 1772. WEALTH AT DEATH. DIED: on January 9, 1788; buried under the chancel of St. Thomas Church, Croom, Prince George's County. LAND: at least 18,026 acres in Prince George's, Frederick, Montgomery, and Anne Arundel counties, plus 2 lots in Annapolis, 1 lot in Upper Marlboro, and 2 lots in Bladensburg. Not included in this amount is Anne Arundel Manor, which he stated in his will was devised to him by *Charles Calvert, 5th Lord Baltimore* (1699–1751). The acreage of Anne Arundel Manor was unspecified because of court litigation to clear the title.

CALVERT, BENEDICT LEONARD (1700–1732). BORN: on September 20, 1700, in England; second son. IMMIGRATED: in July 1727. RESIDED: in Surrey, England; in Annapolis, Anne Arundel County, 1727 until death. FAMILY BACKGROUND. FATHER: *Benedict Leonard Calvert, 4th Lord Baltimore* (1679–1715). STEPFATHER: Christopher Crewe. GUARDIAN: Francis North, 2nd baron of Guilford. MOTHER: Lady Charlotte Lee (?–1721). BROTHERS: *Charles Calvert, 5th Lord Baltimore* (1699–1751); *Edward Henry Calvert* (1701–1730); and Cecilius (1702–1765). SISTERS: Charlotte (1702–1744); Jane (1703–?); Barbara (1704–died young); and Anne. ADDITIONAL COMMENTS: His parents were divorced in 1705. PRIVATE CAREER. EDUCATION: studied under Thomas Hearne at Christ Church College, Oxford University; trained in historical writing and intended to write a history of Maryland. RELIGIOUS AFFILIATION: Anglican. SOCIAL STATUS AND ACTIVITES: Esq.; Hon.; tour of the European continent as a young man included stays in France and Italy. ADDITIONAL COMMENTS: Calvert apparently had great difficulty adjusting to Maryland's climate and suffered ill health during most of his residence in the province. While in Maryland, Calvert carefully researched the history of the province and in 1729 wrote a long letter to his brother *Charles Calvert, 5th Lord Baltimore* (1699–1751) setting forth his conclusions and recommendations for improving relations between the proprietor and the citizens of the colony. OCCUPATIONAL PROFILE: placeman. PUBLIC CAREER. PROVINCIAL OFFICES: governor, 1726/27–1731 (commissioned March 1726/27; sworn in July 1727); chancellor, 1726/27–1731. LOCAL OFFICES: St. Anne's Parish Vestry, Anne Arundel County, 1730–1732. OUT OF COLONY SERVICE: M.P., Harwich, England, 1726. STANDS ON PUBLIC/PRIVATE ISSUES: supported his family's paternal attitude toward the province in the face of increasing demands by Marylanders for more power, particularly in regard to the proprietor's right to veto legislation enacted by the General Assembly. WEALTH AT DEATH. DIED: on June 1, 1732, at sea on his way back to England. PERSONAL PROPERTY: TEV, £315.11.5 sterling, £325.16.9 current money (including 1 slave and 2 servants); FB, £54.1.4 sterling, £125.0.3 current money. Bequeathed one-third of his personal estate to King William School in Annapolis "for the encouragement and education of the youth."

CALVERT, BENEDICT LEONARD, 4TH LORD BALTIMORE (1679–1715). BORN: in 1679 in Maryland; oldest surviving son. NATIVE: second generation. RESIDED: in St. Mary's County; England after 1684. FAMILY BACKGROUND. FATHER: *Charles Calvert, 3rd Lord Baltimore* (1637–1714/15). MOTHER: Jane Lowe Sewall (?–1700). BROTHERS: *Cecilius Calvert* (1667–1681); Charles (1680–1733). HALF BROTHER: *Nicholas Sewall* (ca. 1655–1737). SISTERS: Clare (1670–by 1694); Anne (1673–1713). HALF SISTERS: Jane Sewall; Elizabeth Sewall; Anne Sewall; and Mary Sewall. MARRIED in 1698/99 Charlotte (?–1721), daughter of Edward Henry Lee (1663–1716), earl of Lichfield, and wife Charlotte Fitzroy. Divorced in 1705, Charlotte subsequently married in 1719 Christopher Crewe. CHILDREN. SONS: *Charles Calvert, 5th Lord Baltimore* (1699–1751); *Benedict Leonard Calvert* (1700–1732); *Edward Henry Calvert* (1701–1730), who married Margaret Lee; and Cecilius (1702–1765), principal secretary of Maryland, who served jointly with Thomas Beake from January 1729/30 to February 1732/33, and alone from 1751 until death. DAUGHTERS: Charlotte (1702–1744), who married Thomas Brerewood; Jane (1703–?), who married in 1720 John Hyde, of Kingston Isle, Berkshire, England; Barbara (1704–?); and Anne. PRIVATE CAREER. EDUCATION: literate, probably had extensive schooling. RELIGIOUS AFFILIATION: Catholic, converted to Anglicanism in 1713. SOCIAL STATUS AND ACTIVITIES: close associate of Francis North, lord Guilford, who as a member of the Board of Trade and a prominent Tory, aided in obtaining the restoration of the proprietary government and became guardian of Charles Calvert, 5th Lord Baltimore, in 1715. ADDITIONAL COMMENTS: his mother-in-law, Charlotte Fitzroy, was the natural daughter of King Charles II. OCCUPATIONAL PROFILE: lord proprietor of Maryland, 1714/15–1715. PUBLIC CAREER. OUT OF COLONY SERVICE: M.P., (Tory), Harwich, Essex, England, 1714–1715. STANDS ON PUBLIC/-

PRIVATE ISSUES: his conversion to Protestantism was an important condition leading to the restoration of the colony to Calvert family as a proprietary colony. WEALTH DURING LIFETIME. PERSONAL PROPERTY: given £600 a year by his father at the time of marriage, he was nevertheless often in financial straits. He was dependent on Queen Anne for support after his divorce, because his fathering of illegitimate children by his housekeeper and his religious conversion caused a break with his father. Calvert received an annual pension of £300 and an estimated £1,500 in arrears of customs duties from Maryland, 1713/14–1714/15. His father claimed to have paid a considerable amount of his son's debts and was paying for the education of his grandchildren. WEALTH AT DEATH. DIED: on April 16, 1715, at Epsom, Surrey, England; size of estate unknown.

CALVERT, CECILIUS, 2ND LORD BALTIMORE (1605–1675). BORN: on August 8, 1605, in Kent County, England; first son. RESIDED: in England, never immigrated to Maryland. FAMILY BACKGROUND. FATHER: Sir George Calvert, 1st Lord Baltimore (1578/79–1632). MOTHER: Anne (1579–1622), daughter of George Mynne. BROTHERS: *Leonard Calvert* (ca. 1606–1647); George (1613–1634); Francis; Henry; and John (1618–1618/19). HALF BROTHER: *Philip Calvert* (1626–1682). SISTERS: Anne, who married William Peasley; Dorothy; Elizabeth; Grace (1614–?), who married in 1631/32 Sir Robert Talbot, of Carton, England; and Helen (1615–1655), who married James Talbot, of Ballyconnell, Ireland. MARRIED in 1627/28 Anne (?–1649), daughter of Sir Thomas Arundell, of Wardour, England. CHILDREN. SONS: George (1634–1636); *Charles Calvert, 3rd Lord Baltimore* (1637–1714/15), who married first, ca. 1650 Mary, daughter of Ralph Darnall, of Loughton, Herefordshire, England, second, in 1666 Jane (?–1700), widow of *Henry Sewall* (?–1665) and daughter of Vincent Lowe, of Denby, England, third, in 1701 Mary Thorpe (?–1710), and fourth, Margaret (?–1731), daughter of Thomas Charleton, of Hexham, Northumberland, England. DAUGHTERS: Anne; Mary (1630–1663), who married ca. 1650 Sir William Blakiston, of Gibside, Durham, England; and Elizabeth. PRIVATE CAREER. EDUCATION: literate; entered Trinity College, Oxford University, 1621. RELIGIOUS AFFILIATION: Catholic. SOCIAL STATUS AND ACTIVITIES: succeeded his father as Lord Baltimore in 1632 and settled Maryland, the charter for which George Calvert had first obtained from the king. OCCUPATIONAL PROFILE: colonial investor and entrepreneur. PUBLIC CAREER. PROVINCIAL OF-FICE: proprietor of Maryland, 1632–1675. OUT OF COLONY SERVICE: M.P., 1634. STANDS ON PUB-LIC/PRIVATE ISSUES: became increasingly disenchanted with the Jesuits and their adherents in the late 1630s and early 1640s; skillfully lobbied in England with the merchant community and Puritan government to save his colony during the years of the English Civil War and Commonwealth government; shrewdly distributed patronage in colony to maintain support among Protestants as well as Catholics; active promoter of religious toleration. WEALTH AT DEATH. DIED: on November 30, 1675, in Middlesex, England; size of estate unknown.

CALVERT, CECILIUS (1667–1681). BORN: in 1667 in St. Mary's County; first son. NATIVE: second generation. RESIDED: in St. Mary's County. FAMILY BACKGROUND. FATHER: *Charles Calvert, 3rd Lord Baltimore* (1637–1714/15). MOTHER: Jane Lowe Sewall (?–1700). BROTHER: *Benedict Leonard Calvert, 4th Lord Baltimore* (1679–1715). HALF BROTHER: *Nicholas Sewall* (ca. 1655–1737). SISTERS: Clare (1670–by 1694); Anne (1673–1731). HALF SISTERS: Jane Sewall; Elizabeth Sewall; Anne Sewall (?–1693); and Mary Sewall (?–1693/94). PRIVATE CAREER. RELIGIOUS AFFILIA-TION: Catholic. SOCIAL STATUS AND ACTIVITIES: son and heir of the proprietor; died before he came of age. PUBLIC CAREER. PROVINCIAL OFFICES: lieutenant general and governor, 1676–1679; held these offices nominally, with real power being executed by Deputy Governors *Jesse Wharton* (?–1676) and *Thomas Notley* (1634–1679) and his father, Lord Baltimore. WEALTH AT DEATH. DIED: in 1681; size of estate unknown.

CALVERT, CHARLES, 3RD LORD BALTIMORE (1637–1714/15). BORN: on August 27, 1637, in England; oldest surviving son. IMMI-GRATED: in 1661 as a free adult with his wife. RE-SIDED: in St. Mary's County; returned to England, 1684. FAMILY BACKGROUND. FATHER: *Cecilius Calvert, 2nd Lord Baltimore* (1605–1675). MOTHER: Anne (?–1649), daughter of Sir Thomas Arundell, of Wardour, England. UNCLES: *Philip Calvert* (1626–1682); *Leonard Calvert* (ca. 1606–1647). BROTHER: George (1634–1636). SISTERS: Anne; Mary (1630–1663); and Elizabeth. FIRST COUSINS: *William Calvert* (ca. 1642/43–1682); *George Talbot* (?–?); and *William Talbot* (?–1691). MARRIED first, ca. 1650 Mary, daughter of Ralph Darnall, of Loughton, Herefordshire, England. MARRIED second, in 1666 Jane (?–1700), widow of

Henry Sewall (?–1665); daughter of Vincent Lowe, of Denby, England. Her brothers were *Vincent Lowe* (?–1692); Nicholas; Henry (?–1700), and John (1616–?). Her sisters were Dorothy; Grace; Anne; and Mary. MARRIED third, in 1701 Mary Thorpe (?–1710). MARRIED fourth, Margaret (?–1731), daughter of Thomas Charleton, of Hexham, Northumberland, England. She subsequently married in 1718 Lawrence Eliot. CHILDREN. SONS: *Cecilius Calvert* (1667–1681); *Benedict Leonard Calvert, 4th Lord Baltimore* (1679–1715), who married in 1698 Charlotte, daughter of Edward Henry Lee (1663–1716); and Charles (1680–1733). STEPSON: *Nicholas Sewall* (ca. 1655–1737), who married Susanna, daughter of *William Burgess* (ca. 1622–1686/87). DAUGHTERS: Clare (1670–by 1694), who married in 1690 Edward Maria Somersett; Anne (1673–1731), who married first, in 1694 Edward Maria Somersett, and second, William Parton, of Hoxton, Gloucestershire, England. STEPDAUGHTERS: Jane Sewall, who married *Philip Calvert* (1626–1682); Elizabeth Sewall, who married first, *Jesse Wharton* (?–1676), and second, *William Digges* (ca. 1650–1697); Anne Sewall (?–1693), who married first, *Benjamin Rozer* (?–1681), and second, *Edward Pye* (?–1696); and Mary Sewall (?–1693/94), who married first, William Chandler (1652–1685), son of *Job Chandler* (?–1659), and second, George Brent. PRIVATE CA-REER. EDUCATION: literate, probably had extensive schooling. RELIGIOUS AFFILIATION: Catholic. SO-CIAL STATUS AND ACTIVITIES: arrived as governor and heir-apparent to the proprietorship of the colony; married the widow of his close friend *Henry Sewall* (?–1665), who immigrated with him; established a residence at Mattapany. OCCUPATIONAL PROFILE: placeman; colonial entrepreneur. PUBLIC CAREER. PROVINCIAL OFFICES: receiver general, 1660; governor, 1661–1675; secretary, 1665–1666, 1667–1669, 1673–1673/74; collector of Patuxent, 1673–1675/76; proprietor of Maryland, 1675–1714/15 (without governing rights, 1689–1714/15). STANDS ON PUBLIC/PRIVATE ISSUES: expressed frequent discontent in the 1660s and the 1670s with the caliber and social standing of the Council; often at odds with his uncle *Philip Calvert* (1626–1682) and the latter's protéegée, *Henry Coursey* (ca. 1629–1695); continued his father's policy of religious toleration, and in particular reached accommodation in the 1680s with the Quakers; fashioned a close circle of political leaders, almost exclusively Catholics, who were usually bound to him by blood kinship or marriage, especially in the case of his Sewall stepchildren; his struggles with William Penn over the northern boundary of Maryland and attacks against the colony's charter finally necessitated his return to England in 1684; his deputies lacked Calvert's ability to defuse attacks and govern smoothly; Calvert lost his colony in the royal settlement following the Glorious Revolution, during which he was charged with outlawry and treason, charges that were later dropped; he made many unsuccessfull efforts to regain the colony in the subsequent twenty-five years; he broke off relations with his son *Benedict Leonard Calvert, 4th Lord Baltimore* (1679–1715) upon the latter's conversion to Protestantism. WEALTH AT DEATH. DIED: on February 20, 1714/15; estate size unknown.

CALVERT, CHARLES (?–1733/34). IMMIGRATED: in 1720. RESIDED: in Annapolis, Anne Arundel County. FAMILY BACKGROUND. AUNT: Margaret, who married Henry Lazenby, of Anne Arundel County. MARRIED on November 21, 1722, Rebecca (1706–1734/35), daughter of John Gerard (1678–1715), of Prince George's County, a merchant and planter, and wife Elizabeth. CHILDREN. SON: Charles (1723–1723/24). DAUGHTERS: Ann (1726–by 1748); Elizabeth (1729/30–1798), who married *Benedict Calvert* (ca. 1724–1788) and was a goddaughter of *Benedict Leonard Calvert* (1700–1732). PRIVATE CAREER. EDUCATION: literate. RELIGIOUS AFFILIATION: Anglican, St. Anne's Parish, Anne Arundel County. SOCIAL STATUS AND ACTIVITIES: Esq., 1722; Hon., 1722. OCCUPATIONAL PROFILE: placeman; took the position as chancellor in 1725 stating that he wished to better provide for his family. PUBLIC CAREER. LEGISLATIVE SERVICE: Upper House, 1727 (appointed before the 4th session), 1728–1731, 1732–1733 (died before the convention). OTHER PROVINCIAL OFFICES: governor, 1719/20–1727 (commissioned February 1719/20; presided over the Assembly, October 1720); chancellor, 1720, 1725–1727; surveyor general, Eastern Shore, 1720–1726; surveyor general, Western Shore, 1726–1733/34; Council, 1727–1733/34 (qualified on July 12, 1727; president, 1730–1733/34); commissary general, 1727–1728, 1730–1733/34. LOCAL OFFICE: St. Anne's Parish Vestry, Anne Arundel County, in office 1721–1728. MILITARY SERVICE: probably an ensign, First Grenadier Guards, by 1709; captain, by 1720. WEALTH DURING LIFETIME. SIGNIFICANT CHANGES IN LAND BETWEEN FIRST ELECTION AND DEATH: patented ca. 1,200 acres in Prince George's and Anne Arundel counties in 1724 (acquired 918 acres of this through his marriage). Held 2 mortgages that were forfeited, which yielded him 150 acres in Anne Arundel County, plus 1 lot and a house in Annapolis. Purchased at least 100 additional acres in Anne Arundel County, plus 1 lot and 10 acres in Annapolis. Shortly before his death he took out a warrant for 5,000 acres. WEALTH AT DEATH. DIED: on February 2, 1733/34, in Annapolis. PERSONAL PROPERTY: TEV, £151.3.11 gold, £1,288.18.0 sterling, £2,984.13.11 current money (including 577 oz. plate, family portraits, and a fiddle, flutes, and music books); FB, £69.4.2 gold, £1,217.3.4 sterling, £2,245.15.10 current money. LAND: 1,962 acres in Anne Arundel and Prince George's counties, plus 2 lots and a house in Annapolis and a warrant for 5,000 acres. IDENTIFICATION PROBLEMS. *Charles Calvert, 3rd Lord Baltimore* (1637–1714/15), granted 1,000 acres of manor land to a Charles Calvert Lazenby in 1701. Lazenby sold the land in 1709, shortly before a Charles Calvert began his career in the First Grenadier Guards. Sources indicate that *Charles Calvert* (?–1733/34) and Charles Calvert Lazenby may have been the same man.

CALVERT, CHARLES, 5TH LORD BALTIMORE (1699–1751). BORN: on September 29, 1699, in England; eldest son. IMMIGRATED: in December 1732. RESIDED: in England; in Maryland from December 1732 until July 1733 when he returned to England. FAMILY BACKGROUND. FATHER: *Benedict Leonard Calvert, 4th Lord Baltimore* (1679–1715). STEPFATHER: Christopher Crewe. MOTHER: Lady Charlotte Lee (?–1721). BROTHERS: *Benedict Leonard Calvert* (1700–1732); *Edward Henry Calvert* (1701–1730); and Cecilius (1702–1765). SISTERS: Charlotte (1702–1744); Jane (1703–?); Barbara (1704–died young); and Anne. ADDITIONAL COMMENTS: His parents were divorced in 1705. MARRIED in 1730 Mary (?–1748), daughter of Sir Theodore Janssen (ca. 1658–1748), who immigrated from France to England in 1680, was naturalized in 1685, and became a baronet in 1714, and wife Williamsa (?–1731); granddaughter of Sir Robert Henley, M.P. Her brothers included Abraham (?–1765); Henry (?–1766); Stephen Theodore (?–1777), lord mayor of London; and William (?–ca. 1740/41), principal secretary of Maryland from February 1732/33 until death. Her sisters included Barbara, who married *Thomas Bladen* (1698–1780). CHILDREN. SONS: *Frederick Calvert, 6th Lord Baltimore* (1731/32–1771); Charles (1737–died young). NATURAL SON: *Benedict Calvert* (ca. 1724–1788). DAUGHTERS: Frances Dorothy (1734–1736); Louisa, who married John Browning (?–1792); and Caroline, who married *Robert Eden* (1741–1784). PRIVATE CA-

REER. EDUCATION: literate. RELIGIOUS AFFILIA-
TION: Catholic, converted to Anglican. SOCIAL
STATUS AND ACTIVITIES: fellow of the Royal Society. ADDITIONAL COMMENTS: Thomas Carlyle
(1795–1881) described Calvert "as something of a
fool, to judge by the face of him in portraits, and
by some of his doings in the world," but a modern
historian credits him as being "a careful and fairly
successful administrator." OCCUPATIONAL PRO-
FILE: proprietor of Maryland, 1715–1751. PUBLIC
CAREER. PROVINCIAL OFFICES: governor, 1732–
1733; chancellor, 1732–1733. OUT OF COLONY
SERVICE: cofferer to H.R.H. Frederick, Prince of
Wales; lord of the Admiralty, 1741; M.P., Surrey,
England. WEALTH DURING LIFETIME. As proprietor Calvert's private income included duties enacted by the provincial legislature for his benefit,
such as a 14 pence sterling per ton duty on shipping, plus up to £10,000 sterling per year in land
revenues. Calvert owned all unpatented land in
Maryland. He personally owned twenty-one manors in various locations in the colony, plus reserves
around each manor to prevent encroachment by
patentees. Manor and reserved lands totaled at
least 103,000 acres. By 1751 manor lands
amounted to ca. 111,500 acres. WEALTH AT
DEATH. DIED: on April 24, 1751; size of estate unknown.

CALVERT, EDWARD HENRY (1701–1730).
BORN: on August 31, 1701, in England; third son.
IMMIGRATED: ca. 1728. RESIDED: in England; An-
napolis, Anne Arundel County. FAMILY BACK-
GROUND. FATHER: *Benedict Leonard Calvert, 4th
Lord Baltimore* (1679–1715). STEPFATHER: Christopher Crewe. MOTHER: Lady Charlotte Lee (?–
1721). BROTHERS: *Charles Calvert, 5th Lord
Baltimore* (1699–1751); *Benedict Leonard Calvert*
(1700–1732); and Cecilius (1702–1765). SISTERS:
Charlotte (1702–1744); Jane (1703–?); Barbara
(1704–died young); and Anne. NEPHEWS: *Frederick
Calvert, 6th Lord Baltimore* (1731/32–1771); *Benedict Calvert* (ca. 1724–1788). NIECE: Caroline Calvert, who married *Robert Eden* (1741–1784). ADDI-
TIONAL COMMENTS: His parents were divorced in
1705. MARRIED Margaret Lee, who subsequently
married James Fitzgerald, Esq. CHILDREN. Died
without progeny. PRIVATE CAREER. EDUCATION:
literate. RELIGIOUS AFFILIATION: Anglican. SO-
CIAL STATUS AND ACTIVITIES: Esq.; Hon. OCCU-
PATIONAL PROFILE: assisted in the administration
of his family's provincial affairs. PUBLIC CAREER.
LEGISLATIVE SERVICE: Upper House, 1728–1729
(did not attend the 1st session; died before the 3rd
session). OTHER PROVINCIAL OFFICES: Council,

1728–1730 (appointed on June 19, 1728; qualified
on February 6, 1728/29; president 1728/29–1730);
commissary general, 1728/29–1730 (commissioned
June 1728; sworn February 1728/29; died in office, 1730). WEALTH DURING LIFETIME. LAND:
none in his own name in the province; probably
lived with relatives or rented a furnished house in
Annapolis. WEALTH AT DEATH. DIED: on April 24,
1730, in Annapolis. PERSONAL PROPERTY: TEV,
at least £388.19.0 current money (including 1 servant, 157 oz. plate, and a violin).

**CALVERT, FREDERICK, 6TH LORD
BALTIMORE** (1731/32–1771). BORN: on February 6, 1731/32, in England; only surviving legiti-
mate son. RESIDED: in England and on the European continent; never visited Maryland. FAMILY
BACKGROUND. FATHER: *Charles Calvert, 5th Lord
Baltimore* (1699–1751). GUARDIANS: Arthur Ons-
low, speaker of the House of Commons; John
Sharpe, Esq. (?–1756), brother of *Horatio Sharpe*
(1718–1790); Hon. Cecilius Calvert (1702–1765);
Hugh Hammersley, Esq. (?–1789), principal secre-
tary of Maryland from 1765 to 1776. MOTHER:
Mary Janssen (?–1748). UNCLES: *Benedict Leonard
Calvert* (1700–1732); *Edward Henry Calvert*
(1701–1730). AUNT: Barbara Janssen, who married
Thomas Bladen (1698–1780). BROTHER: Charles
(1737–died in infancy). HALF BROTHER: *Benedict
Calvert* (ca. 1724–1788). SISTERS: Frances Dorothy
(1734–1736); Louisa; and Caroline, who married
Robert Eden (1741–1784). MARRIED on March 9,
1753, Lady Diana (1732–1758), daughter of
Scroop Egerton, duke of Bridgewater. CHILDREN.
NATURAL SON: by Hester Whalen, of Ireland,
Henry Harford (ca. 1759–1834). NATURAL
DAUGHTERS: by Hester Whalen, Frances Mary
Harford (ca. 1760–1822), who married William
Frederick Wyndham (1763–1828); by Elizabeth
Dawson, of Lincolnshire, England, twins, Sophia
Hales (1765–?) and Elizabeth Hales (1765–?); by
Elizabeth Hope, of Munster, Germany, Charlotte
Hope (1770–?). PRIVATE CAREER. EDUCATION:
literate. RELIGIOUS AFFILIATION: Anglican. ADDI-
TIONAL COMMENTS: Modern historians have
noted that he "took little part in the government
of his province" and characterized him as "a dis-
solute, but generous man." He was the author of
*Tour in the East in the Years 1763 and 1764 with
Remarks on the City of Constantinople and the
Turks, Also Select Pieces of Oriental Wit, Poetry
and Wisdom* , *Gaudia Poetica Latina, Anglica, et
Gallica Lingua composita* , and *Caelestes et Inferi* .
In 1768 he was tried in England on a charge of
raping a young woman, but he was acquitted.

Against the wishes of his family, he devised the province of Maryland to *Henry Harford* (ca. 1759–1834), subject to the payment of £20,000 to be divided between his sisters, Louisa and Caroline. OCCUPATIONAL PROFILE: proprietor of Maryland, 1751–1771. **WEALTH DURING LIFETIME.** As proprietor Calvert's private income included duties enacted by the provincial legislature for his benefit, such as a 14 pence sterling per ton duty on shipping, plus up to £10,000 sterling per year in land revenues. He owned all unpatented land in Maryland. Calvert held as his personal fiefdom manors in various counties totaling at least 111,500 acres in 1751, plus reserves around each manor. Calvert appointed a commission in 1766 to sell his manors and reserves. About 50,000 acres were sold by 1771 (ca. 25,000 acres from the manors and ca. 25,000 acres of the 45,000-acre Baltimore Reserves). In 1768, ca. 10,700 acres of manor land in Frederick County were given to John Morton Jordan (?–1771), one of the agents for the sale of the proprietary lands. By 1771 the manor and reserve lands, including 121,000 acres on the western frontier of the province, totaled ca. 245,000 acres. **WEALTH AT DEATH.** DIED: on September 4, 1771, in Naples, Italy; buried at Epsom, Surrey, England; size of estate unknown.

CALVERT, LEONARD (ca. 1606–1647). BORN: ca. 1606 in England; second son. IMMIGRATED: in 1633/34 as a free adult. RESIDED: in St. Mary's County. **FAMILY BACKGROUND.** FATHER: Sir George Calvert, 1st Lord Baltimore (1578/79–1632). MOTHER: Anne (1579–1622), daughter of George Mynne. BROTHERS: *Cecilius Calvert, 2nd Lord Baltimore* (1605–1675); George (1613–1634); Francis; Henry; and John (1618–1618/19). HALF BROTHER: *Philip Calvert* (1626–1682). SISTERS: Anne; Dorothy; Elizabeth; Grace (1614–?); and Helen (1615–1655). MARRIED possibly Anne Brent. **CHILDREN.** SON: *William Calvert* (ca. 1642/43–1682), who married in 1661/62, Elizabeth, daughter of *William Stone* (ca. 1603–ca. 1659/60). DAUGHTER: Anne (1644–ca. 1714), who married first in 1664, *Baker Brooke* (1628–1678/79), second, ca. 1680, Henry Brent (?–1693), and third, Richard Marsham (?–1713). **PRIVATE CAREER.** EDUCATION: literate, probably had considerable schooling. RELIGIOUS AFFILIATION: Catholic. SOCIAL STATUS AND ACTIVITIES: sailed to Maryland as governor with the first two ships of immigrants, 1633; returned to England in 1641/42 and 1643/44, during which time he fathered his two children, who were probably illegitimate. OCCCUPATIONAL PROFILE: placeman;

planter; engaged in some trade with the Indians. PUBLIC CAREER. PROVINCIAL OFFICES: governor, 1633–1647. OUT OF COLONY SERVICE: prothonotary and keeper of writs in Connaught and Thomond, Ireland, 1621. STANDS ON PUBLIC/PRIVATE ISSUES: Calvert had a very difficult task in the initial years of settlement of steering a middle ground between the demands of various groups in colony, especially the Jesuits, and his responsibilities as chief executive officer for his brother; he was generally more lenient to special interest groups in Maryland than his brother wished. **WEALTH DURING LIFETIME.** LAND AT FIRST ELECTION: 3,000 acres in 1634. **WEALTH AT DEATH.** DIED: on June 11, 1647. LAND: patents or certificates for ca. 9,000 acres.

CALVERT, PHILIP (1626–1682). BORN: in 1626 in England; youngest son. IMMIGRATED: in 1656 as a free adult with his wife. RESIDED: at "Pope's Freehold," St. Mary's County until 1679; "St. Peter's," St. Mary's County after 1679. **FAMILY BACKGROUND.** FATHER: Sir George Calvert, 1st Lord Baltimore (1578/79–1632). MOTHER: Joan. HALF BROTHERS: *Cecilius Calvert, 2nd Lord Baltimore* (1605–1675); *Leonard Calvert* (ca. 1606–1647); George (1613–1634); Francis; Henry; and John (1618–1618/19). HALF SISTERS: Anne; Dorothy; Elizabeth; Grace (1614–?); and Helen (1615–1655). MARRIED first, by 1656 Anne, daughter of Sir Thomas Wolseley, of Wolseley, Staffordshire, England, and wife Helen Broughton. MARRIED second, in 1681 Jane, daughter of *Henry Sewall* (?–1665) and wife Jane Lowe; stepdaughter of *Charles Calvert, 3rd Lord Baltimore* (1637–1714/15). Her brother was *Nicholas Sewall* (ca. 1655–1737). Her sisters were Elizabeth, who married first, *Jesse Wharton* (?–1676), and second, *William Digges* (ca. 1650–1697); Anne, who married first, *Benjamin Rozer* (?–1681), and second, *Edward Pye* (?–1696); and Mary (?–1693/94), who married first, William Chandler (1652–1685), son of *Job Chandler* (?–1659), and second, George Brent. **CHILDREN.** Died without progeny. **PRIVATE CAREER.** EDUCATION: literate, probably had considerable schooling. RELIGIOUS AFFILIATION: Catholic. SOCIAL STATUS AND ACTIVITIES: arrived with commissions as councilor and secretary; very influential member of the proprietary family; his twenty-five years on the Council was a rare example of longevity in that office for seventeenth-century Maryland. OCCUPATIONAL PROFILE: placeman; planter. PUBLIC CAREER. LEGISLATIVE SERVICE: Upper House, 1658, 1659/60, 1661, 1662, 1663–1664, 1666, 1669 (Aggrievances),

1671–1674/75, 1676–1682, 1682 (died before the 2nd session). OTHER PROVINCIAL OFFICES: Council, 1656–1660, 1661–1682 (president, 1656–1660, 1661–1682); justice, Provincial Court, 1656–1660, 1661–1682; secretary, 1656–1660; treasurer and receiver general, 1659–1660; governor, 1660–1661; chancellor, 1660–1682; deputy governor, 1669; commissary general, 1672–1682. LOCAL OFFICE: mayor, St. Mary's City, 1668–1671. STANDS ON PUBLIC/PRIVATE ISSUES: his arrival in colony in 1656 was the first time since 1647 that Lord Baltimore had a trusted family member and advisor in the colony; over the next thirty-six years, Calvert provided important stability and leadership, although he often incurred the displeasure of his nephew, Charles Calvert, after the latter arrived to supersede Philip as governor in 1661. WEALTH DURING LIFETIME. LAND AT FIRST ELECTION: 4,700 acres by 1660, which he sold or surrendered by 1664; acquired 1,900 acres in 1664, and an additional 2,000 acres in 1670. WEALTH AT DEATH. DIED: in late December 1682. PERSONAL PROPERTY: an extensive library of nearly 100 books. LAND: over 3,900 acres.

CALVERT, WILLIAM (ca. 1642/43–1682). BORN: ca. 1642/43 in England; perhaps illegitimate. IMMIGRATED: in 1661 as a free adult from England. RESIDED: in St. Mary's County. FAMILY BACKGROUND. FATHER: *Leonard Calvert* (ca. 1606–1647). MOTHER: possibly Anne Brent. UNCLE: *Philip Calvert* (1626–1682). UNCLE AND GUARDIAN: *Cecilius Calvert, 2nd Lord Baltimore* (1605–1675). SISTER: Anne (1644–ca. 1714), who married first, *Baker Brooke* (1628–1678/79), second, Henry Brent (?–1693), and third, Richard Marsham (?–1713). FIRST COUSIN: *Charles Calvert, 3rd Lord Baltimore* (1637–1714/15). MARRIED in 1661/62 Elizabeth, daughter of *William Stone* (ca. 1603–ca. 1659/60). Her brothers were Thomas (ca. 1635–1676); Charles; Richard (?–1767); and *John Stone* (ca. 1648–1697). Her sisters were Mary; Catherine. CHILDREN. SONS: Charles (1662–1733), who married first, Mary, daughter of Robert Howson, of Stafford County, Virginia, and second, Barbara, daughter of Martin Kirke; William (1666–?); George (1668–after 1739), who married Elizabeth Doyne; and Richard (1670–1718). DAUGHTER: Elizabeth, who married in 1681 James Neale (1650–1727), son of *James Neale* (ca. 1615–1684). PRIVATE CAREER. EDUCATION: literate, had considerable schooling. RELIGIOUS AFFILIATION: Catholic. SOCIAL STATUS AND ACTIVITIES: second generation provincial officeholder; Esq. on arrival; received extensive preferment as a member of the proprietary family. OCCUPATIONAL PROFILE: placeman; planter. PUBLIC CAREER. LEGISLATIVE SERVICE: Lower House, St. Mary's County, 1663–1664, 1666; Upper House, special writ 1669 (Aggrievances), 1671–1674/75, 1676–1682 (died during the 4th session). OTHER PROVINCIAL OFFICES: attorney general, 1666–1669; secretary and judge of Probate, 1669–1670, 1673/74–1682; Council, 1669–1682; justice, Provincial Court, 1669–1682. LOCAL OFFICES: alderman, St. Mary's City, 1668–1671. MILITARY SERVICE: colonel, by 1679; commander of foot, St. Mary's County, 1681. WEALTH DURING LIFETIME. LAND AT FIRST ELECTION: at least 9,000 acres inherited from his father. WEALTH AT DEATH. DIED: on May 26, 1682; drowned while trying to ford the swollen Wicomico River. PERSONAL PROPERTY: TEV, £981.2.2 sterling (including 12 slaves, 8 servants, 28 books, and 1 sloop); FB, 8,044 pounds of tobacco. LAND: ca. 1,400 acres.

CAMPBELL (CAMELL, CAMBELL), JOHN (1634–1695). BORN: in 1634, probably in England. IMMIGRATED: ca. 1651 as an indentured servant to Dr. *John Wade* (?–1658). RESIDED: at Poplar Hill, St. Mary's County. MARRIED Catherine. CHILDREN. SONS: Thomas; Richard; and James. DAUGHTERS: Faith, who married Henry Taylor; Rachel, who married John Russell; and Dorothy. PRIVATE CAREER. EDUCATION: illiterate. RELIGIOUS AFFILIATION: Anglican. SOCIAL STATUS AND ACTIVITIES: arrived as a servant: held no title until his first militia office in 1681; his illiteracy probably accounted for his removal from the justiceship in 1692; his sons held no public office. OCCUPATIONAL PROFILE: indentured servant, ca. 1651–1656; planter. PUBLIC CAREER. LEGISLATIVE SERVICE: Associators' Convention, St. Mary's County, 1689–1692; Lower House, St. Mary's County, 1692–1693. LOCAL OFFICES: justice, St. Mary's County, 1689–1692; William and Mary Parish Vestry, St. Mary's County, 1693–1695. MILITARY SERVICE: captain, 1681–1689; major, 1689–1695. STANDS ON PUBLIC/PRIVATE ISSUES: his important role in military affairs during the revolution of 1689 were rewarded by civil offices and by promotion in the militia. WEALTH DURING LIFETIME. LAND AT FIRST ELECTION: ca. 580 acres. WEALTH AT DEATH. DIED: will probated on November 4, 1695. PERSONAL PROPERTY: TEV, £218.18.7 sterling (including 2 servants). LAND: ca. 580 acres.

CAMPBELL (CAMBELL), WALTER (1665–1738). BORN: in 1665, probably in Dumbarton,

Scotland. IMMIGRATED: by 1689/90 as a free adult. RESIDED: in Dorchester County. FAMILY BACKGROUND. UNCLE: William Campbell, a merchant of Dumbarton, Scotland. MARRIED first, by 1701 Susannah. MARRIED second, by 1731 Elizabeth, daughter of William Robson. Her sisters were Hagar, who married *John Meekins* (ca. 1674–1734); Jane, who married *Tobias Pollard* (ca. 1669–1749). PRIVATE CAREER. EDUCATION: illiterate. RELIGIOUS AFFILIATION: Presbyterian. SOCIAL STATUS AND ACTIVITIES: Gent., by 1697; perhaps he was transferred from his justiceship to a shrievalty in 1695 by Gov. Francis Nicholson because of his illiteracy. OCCUPATIONAL PROFILE: planter; merchant. PUBLIC CAREER. LEGISLATIVE SERVICE: Lower House, Dorchester County, 1697/98–1700 (Aggrievances, 1–4), 1708B–1711. LOCAL OFFICES: justice, Dorchester County, 1693–1695, 1700–1734 (quorum, 1694–1695, 1700–1734); sheriff, Dorchester County, 1695–1698. MILITARY SERVICE: officer, 1696. WEALTH DURING LIFETIME. LAND AT FIRST ELECTION: 463 acres. WEALTH AT DEATH. DIED: will probated on April 13, 1738. PERSONAL PROPERTY: TEV, £644.8.10 current money (including 15 slaves); FB, £383.0.5. LAND: over 1,100 acres.

CAMPBELL, ZACHARIAH (?–1777). BORN: probably in Glasgow, Scotland, of age by 1767. IMMIGRATED: by 1767 from Virginia. RESIDED: in Vienna, Dorchester County. FAMILY BACKGROUND. BROTHER: Capt. James (?–ca. 1782), commander of the brigantine of war *Sturdy Beggar,* 1777. MARRIED by 1767 Mary (ca. 1745–1779), daughter of Levin Hicks (?–1753) and wife Mary Hooper Ennalls; granddaughter of both Levin Hicks (?–1731) and wife Mary Hooper (?–ca. 1757), and *Henry Hooper* (ca. 1687–1767); stepgranddaughter of *John Rider* (1686–1739/40); niece of *Henry Hooper, Jr.* (ca. 1727–1790), Ann Hicks (?–1773), who married *Henry Travers* (?–1765); stepniece of Dorothy Rider (1725–?), who married *John Henry* (ca. 1714–1781). Her brother was Levin (1748–?), who never married. Her first cousin was *William Ennalls Hooper* (?–1795) CHILDREN. SON: Levin Hicks (ca. 1774–?). DAUGHTERS: Ann (ca. 1778–?); Elizabeth, who married Richard Henry Handy (ca. 1772–?); Mary (?–by 1796), who married David Smith; and Isabella, who married by 1796 David Smith, her brother-in-law. PRIVATE CAREER. EDUCATION: literate. SOCIAL STATUS AND ACTIVITIES: Gent., 1776. OCCUPATIONAL PROFILE: probably a planter. PUBLIC CAREER. LEGISLATIVE SERVICE: Convention, Dorchester County, 3rd, 1774. OTHER STATE OFFICE:

naval officer, Sixth District, appointed 1777. LOCAL OFFICES: collector of blankets, clothing, and other necessities for the American Army, Nanticoke Hundred, Dorchester County, appointed 1777. MILITARY SERVICE: captain, Transquakin Company, Dorchester County Militia, commissioned 1776. WEALTH DURING LIFETIME. PERSONAL PROPERTY: 13 slaves, 1776. LAND AT FIRST ELECTION: 308 acres in Dorchester County (255 acres through marriage; 50 acres by purchase; 3 acres by patent). SIGNIFICANT CHANGES IN LAND BETWEEN FIRST ELECTION AND DEATH: acquired 585 acres in Dorchester County (inherited by his wife after her brother died without progeny), by 1776. WEALTH AT DEATH. DIED: between February and August 1777. PERSONAL PROPERTY: size of estate unknown. LAND: 893 acres in Dorchester County.

CARLINE, HENRY (ca. 1608–?). IMMIGRATED: in 1651 as a free adult with his wife. RESIDED: in Kent County. MARRIED Rachel, who subsequently married William Head. PRIVATE CAREER. EDUCATION: illiterate. RELIGIOUS AFFILIATION: converted to Quakerism in 1658. SOCIAL STATUS AND ACTIVITIES: Mr. on arrival; brought two servants with him; no record of him as being in Maryland after 1664. OCCUPATIONAL PROFILE: planter. PUBLIC CAREER. LEGISLATIVE SERVICE: Lower House, Kent County, 1663–1664. LOCAL OFFICES: justice, Kent County, 1654/55–1655/56; sheriff, Kent County, 1656–1657. WEALTH AT DEATH. LAND: at least 188 acres.

CARMICHAEL, RICHARD BENNETT (1753–1824). BORN: in 1753 in Queen Anne's County; his mother was pregnant with him when she married Carmichael. NATIVE: second generation. RESIDED: in Queen Anne's County; lived part of each year in Wilmington, Delaware, by 1813. FAMILY BACKGROUND. STEPFATHER OR POSSIBLY FATHER: William Carmichael (?–1769), immigrated from Scotland, died at Roundtop, near the Chester River, Queen Anne's County; a merchant. MOTHER: Ann (1712–ca. 1754), daughter of Roger Brooke (1673–1718), of Prince George's County, and wife Elizabeth Hutchins. STEPBROTHERS OR HALF BROTHERS: Walter; James (?–1778), a ship's captain, who married Selitia Emory Kirby; William (?–1795), of Chestertown, Kent County, an attorney, who was educated in Edinburgh, Scotland. He was a diplomat who served in Paris as secretary to the commissioners Silas Deane, Benjamin Franklin, and Arthur Lee, who were attempting to persuade France to aid the colonies, ca. 1775; delegate to the Continental Congress from 1778 to 1779; secretary to John Jay, minister to Spain, ca. 1780; chargé d'affaires in Madrid in 1782. He married first, (first name unknown) Stirling, daughter of an Episcopal rector of Queen Anne's County, and second, Antonia Reynon, of Spain. Unpaid for years, and his fortune depleted, William died in Madrid in 1795. His widow and daughter Alphonsa came to live near Chestertown, Kent County, after William's death. SISTER: Elizabeth Brooke, born before her mother's marriage to Carmichael and then adopted by him, who married *John Lambert Wilmer* (1747–1799). STEPSISTERS OR HALF SISTERS: Catherine, who married *John Brown* (?–1793); Ann; Elizabeth, who married Samuel Thompson; and Margaret (ca. 1741–1767), who married Arthur Holt. FIRST COUSINS: Elizabeth Beall, who married *John Bracco* (?–1794); *Richard Brooke* (1736–1788). MARRIED on Sunday evening, March 6, 1774, Kitty (also called Katherine), daughter of Dr. William Murray (1708–1769), a native of Scotland living in Chestertown, Kent County, and wife Ann. Kitty's brothers were William, of Anne Arundel County, a physician; Alexander; and James (ca. 1741–1819), of Annapolis, a physician, who married in 1773 Sarah Ennalls Maynadier Nevett (1751–1837). Her sisters were Elizabeth; Ann; and Sarah. CHILDREN. SON: William (1775–1853). DAUGHTERS: Ann, who married in 1798 Henry Hollyday (1771–1850), son of *Henry Hollyday* (ca. 1725–1789); Katherine; Elizabeth (?–by 1820); and Sarah. PRIVATE CAREER. EDUCATION: literate. RELIGIOUS AFFILIATION: Anglican. OCCUPATIONAL PROFILE: probably a planter. PUBLIC CAREER. LEGISLATIVE SERVICE: Lower House, Queen Anne's County, 1778–1779. LOCAL OFFICES: justice, Queen Anne's County, commissioned 1777 and 1785; St. Paul's Parish Vestry, Queen Anne's County, in office 1783 and 1789; judge, Court of Appeals for Tax Assessment, Queen Anne's County, appointed 1786. MILITARY SERVICE: captain, Twentieth Battalion, Queen Anne's County Militia, 1780–1781. STANDS ON PUBLIC/PRIVATE ISSUES: manumitted all of his slaves in his will. WEALTH DURING LIFETIME. PERSONAL PROPERTY: assessed value £1,455.0.0, including 35 slaves and 24 oz. plate, 1783; 61 slaves, 1798. LAND AT FIRST ELECTION: approximately 900 acres in Queen Anne's County (all inherited from his mother to whom they had been devised by Richard Bennett, Esq., of Queen Anne's County, who died in 1749). SIGNIFICANT CHANGES IN LAND BETWEEN FIRST ELECTION AND DEATH: owned a total of 875 acres in Queen Anne's

County, 1783; owned a total of 858 acres in Queen Anne's County, 1798. WEALTH AT DEATH. DIED: on February 13, 1824, in Queen Anne's County. PERSONAL PROPERTY: the administration bond on his estate was $40,000. LAND: at least 858 acres in Queen Anne's County.

CARROLL, CHARLES (1691–1755). BORN: in 1691 in Ireland. IMMIGRATED: ca. 1715 as a free adult. RESIDED: in Annapolis, Anne Arundel County; traveled to England, 1734–1735. FAMILY BACKGROUND. FATHER: Charles Carroll, baron of Ely-O'Carroll, son of Daniel Carroll. MOTHER: Clare, daughter of O'Connor Dunn and wife Jane Bermingham, of Ireland. BROTHER: John. SISTER: Dorothy. OTHER KINSHIP: a distant cousin of *Charles Carroll, Sr.* (1702–1782). MARRIED first, Dorothy, daughter of Charles Blake (?–1732), of Talbot County, and wife Henrietta Maria Lloyd (1673–1702); granddaughter of *Philemon Lloyd* (1646–1685); niece of *Edward Lloyd* (1670–1718/19), *Philemon Lloyd* (ca. 1674–1732/33), *James Lloyd* (1679/80–1723), Anna Maria Lloyd (1676–1748), who married *Richard Tilghman* (1672/73–1738/39), and Margaret Lloyd (1683–?), who married *Matthew Tilghman Ward* (ca. 1676–1741). Her brothers were John S.; Philemon. Her sister was Henrietta Maria, who married (first name unknown) Stringfellow. Her first cousins were *Edward Lloyd* (1711–1770); *Richard Lloyd* (1717–1786); Henrietta Maria Lloyd (?–1766), who married second, *Daniel Dulany* (1685–1753); Mary Tilghman (1702–1736), who married *James Earle, Jr.* (ca. 1694–1739); Henrietta Maria Tilghman (1707–1771), who married first, *George Robins* (1697–1742), and second, *William Goldsborough* (1709–1760); Anna Maria Tilghman (1709–1763), who married first, *William Hemsley* (1703–1736), and second, *Robert Lloyd* (ca. 1712–1770); *William Tilghman* (1711–1782); *Edward Tilghman* (1713–1786); *James Tilghman* (1716–1793); *Matthew Tilghman* (1717/18–1790); Anne Lloyd (1723–1794), who married *Matthew Tilghman* (1717/18–1790); Henrietta Maria Lloyd (ca. 1711–1748), who married *Samuel Chamberlaine* (1698–1773); *Robert Lloyd* (ca. 1712–1770); and Margaret Lloyd (1714–ca. 1785), who married *William Tilghman* (1711–1782). MARRIED second, by 1751 Ann, possibly the daughter of George Plater and wife Ann Burford Doyne Plater; possibly stepdaughter of *John Rousby* (1685–1744). Her brother was possibly *George Plater* (1695–1755). CHILDREN. SONS: *Charles Carroll, Barrister* (1723–1783); John Henry (1732–1754). DAUGHTER: Mary Clare, who married in 1747, Nicholas Maccubbin (1709–1784), of Annapolis, a merchant. **PRIVATE CAREER.** EDUCATION: received medical training in Great Britain before immigration. RELIGIOUS AFFILIATION: Catholic in early life, became an Anglican; member of St. Anne's Church, Annapolis. His will stated: "I declare that I am in communion with the Church of England." OCCUPATIONAL PROFILE: physician; practiced medicine in Annapolis for several years after immigration, then turned to mercantile activity. Traded with merchants in Barbados; owned a shipyard on the Patapsco River, which built ships that were sold in England; experimented in the manufacturing of hemp. He owned and operated iron furnaces in Baltimore County, and was one of the five founding partners of the Baltimore Ironworks Company, established in 1731. Acted for many years as the manager of the Baltimore Ironworks negotiating with contractors and workmen. Tension and bickering between the partners was detrimental to the project, and other partners accused Carroll of profiting at their expense. Land speculator; financier; planter. **PUBLIC CAREER.** LEGISLATIVE SERVICE: Lower House, Annapolis, 1738 (Laws; Aggrievances), Anne Arundel County, 1739–1741 (Laws Cv–3; Aggrievances Cv–3), 1742–1744 (Laws 1, 2; Aggrievances 1, 2), 1745 (Laws; Aggrievances), 1745/46–1748 (Laws Cv 1, 1–3, 4; Aggrievances Cv 1, 1–3, 4), 1749–1751 (Laws Cv–3; Aggrievances Cv–3), 1751–1754 (Laws 1–6; Grievances 1–6), 1754–1755 (Laws 1–3; Grievances 1–3; died before the 4th session). OTHER PROVINCIAL OFFICE: agent to provision 500 men for an expedition against the Spanish Indies, appointed under the first Supply Act in July of 1740. LOCAL OFFICES: churchwarden, St. Anne's Parish, Anne Arundel County, in office 1739–1740; St. Anne's Parish Vestry, Anne Arundel County, 1740–1743, 1748–1751. STANDS ON PUBLIC/PRIVATE ISSUES: quoted as saying in 1751, "Planting will not do without some other Business or Professions." Believed that the British government should aid American industry with subsidies to stimulate the development of its resources. He was particularly interested in the iron industry, and in 1733 wrote a memorandum for the directors of the Baltimore Ironworks Company describing how Parliament should encourage that industry, most specifically by lowering the tariffs on bar iron exported from America. Traveled to London in 1734–1735 in a futile attempt to gain support on this issue. Also traveled widely through the back country of Maryland, Virginia, and Pennsylvania, and favored the development of Maryland's western lands. **WEALTH DURING LIFETIME.** PERSONAL PROPERTY: owned 2 warehouses on the dock in Annapolis, which were destroyed by fire in 1746. Valued his estate at £13,000.0.0 sterling (including land, slaves, and loans that were predominately bonds and mortgages, which totaled £818.0.0 sterling and £4,000.0.0 current money), 1754. A modern historian points out that Carroll usually surpassed his anticipated profit of 400 percent on speculative land transactions, yet he sometimes lacked cash and was forced to borrow. LAND AT FIRST ELECTION: 6,632 acres in Baltimore, Prince George's, Frederick, and Anne Arundel counties, plus 10 lots in Annapolis (all by personal acquisition and remaining from a total of 11,202 acres in Baltimore County and 200 acres in Frederick County patented between 1720 and 1738). SIGNIFICANT CHANGES IN LAND BETWEEN FIRST ELECTION AND DEATH: patented an additional 8,567 acres in Baltimore County in the 1740s and 568 acres there in the 1750s, plus 181 acres in Anne Arundel County in the 1750s. By a deed in 1751 (but originally agreed upon in 1746), Carroll sold 8,200 acres in Baltimore County. He then turned his attention to Frederick County, where he patented over 28,000 acres in the 1750s. According to a modern study of his speculation in western Maryland lands, Carroll took out warrants or patents in his name and immediately resold them to men who had neither the benefits of his efficient messenger service between Annapolis and the Frederick County Land Office nor the agents to take care of the surveying and paperwork in Frederick County. Between 1730 and 1755 he obtained warrants on 91 tracts in Frederick County totaling 31,529 acres, patented 83 tracts there totaling 28,480 acres, and bought 13 tracts in Frederick County totaling 3,049 acres. He sold 57 of these tracts, totaling 22,781 acres. **WEALTH AT DEATH.** DIED: on September 29, 1755, at his home in Annapolis. PERSONAL PROPERTY: stated in his will that his debts were few. LAND: probably at least 15,000 acres in Anne Arundel, Prince George's, Baltimore, and Frederick counties, plus 11 lots in Annapolis.

CARROLL, CHARLES, SR. (1702–1782). BORN: on April 2, 1702, in Annapolis, Anne Arundel County; second surviving son. NATIVE: second generation. RESIDED: in Annapolis and at "Doughoregan Manor," Anne Arundel County. **FAMILY BACKGROUND.** FATHER: Charles Carroll (1660–1720), of Annapolis, who immigrated in 1688 as attorney general of Maryland. MOTHER: Mary (1678–1742), daughter of Col. *Henry Darnall* (ca. 1645–1711) and wife Eleanor Hatton

Brooke (1642–1725), widow of *Thomas Brooke* (1632–1676). HALF UNCLE: *Thomas Brooke* (ca. 1659–1730/31). HALF AUNT: Mary Brooke, who married second, *Benjamin Hall* (1667–1721). BROTHERS: Charles (1695–1695); Charles (1696–1696); Henry (1697–1719), died at sea on a voyage home from school in England; and Daniel (1707–1734), who married Ann Rozer (1710–1764), who subsequently married *Benjamin Young* (?–1754). SISTERS: Eleanor (1699–1699); Bridget (1701–1701); Mary (1711–?); and Eleanor (1712–1734). NIECE: Eleanor Carroll, who married *Daniel Carroll* (1730–1796). OTHER KINSHIP: a distant cousin of *Charles Carroll* (1691–1755). MARRIED on February 15, 1757, Elizabeth (1709–1761), daughter of Clement Brooke (ca. 1676–1737) and wife Jane (?–1761); granddaughter of both *Thomas Brooke* (1632–1676) and *Nicholas Sewall* (ca. 1655–1737); niece of *Thomas Brooke* (ca. 1659–1730/31) and Mary Brooke, who married second, *Benjamin Hall* (1667–1721). Her brothers were Henry; Joseph; Nicholas; Charles; William; and Clement, Jr. (?–1732). **CHILDREN. SON:** *Charles Carroll of Carrollton* (1737–1832). **PRIVATE CAREER. EDUCA-**TION: College of St. Omer, France, left after obtaining a philosophy degree, but before entering the Middle Temple in England because his father's death in 1720 required his return to Maryland. RELIGIOUS AFFILIATION: Catholic. SOCIAL STATUS AND ACTIVITIES: Esq., 1774. ADDITIONAL COM-MENTS: in 1757 Gov. *Horatio Sharpe* (1718–1790) described him as "a sensible man, who has read much and is well acquainted with the constitution and strength of these American colonies." OCCU-PATIONAL PROFILE: planter, with several large estates under cultivation; original partner in the Baltimore Ironworks Company; moneylender. **PUBLIC CAREER. STATE OFFICE:** Executive Council, 1777 (elected, but declined to serve due to advanced age). STANDS ON PUBLIC/PRIVATE ISSUES: thought of himself as a "provident and tender father." Considered moving to Louisiana under a grant from the French in 1756 to escape the "envy and malice" caused by discrimination against Roman Catholics in Maryland. Bitter toward the proprietor for his harsh treatment of Carroll's father and other Catholics; said of the proprietor in 1760 that "the family of the Proprietary have sacrificed us, abandoned their friends. . .they have no principle at all." Opposed the legal tender bill of 1777. **WEALTH DURING LIFETIME. PERSONAL** PROPERTY: said in 1756, "There is but one man in the Province whose fortune equals mine." In 1757 Gov. *Horatio Sharpe* (1718–1790) estimated Carroll's fortune at £30,000–£40,000. Carroll's own evaluation of his assets in 1764 was: one-fifth interest in the Baltimore Ironworks Company at £10,000; 285 slaves at an average of £30 each, equalling £8,550; cattle, horses, livestock, and equipment totaling £1,000; plate at £600; debts due him as of 1762, £24,230. Much of Carroll's personal wealth was derived from lending money at interest for which he received bonds or mortgages on land and/or personal property. ANNUAL INCOME: £400.0.0 sterling from the Baltimore Ironworks Company; ca. £1,800.0.0 from land, 1764. LAND AT FIRST ELECTION: at least 22,228 acres in Anne Arundel, St. Mary's, Prince George's, Queen Anne's, and Frederick counties (most inherited from his father). SIGNIFICANT CHANGES IN LAND BETWEEN FIRST ELECTION AND DEATH: *Charles Carroll of Carrollton* (1737–1832) took increased control of his father's land as his father advanced in age. **WEALTH AT DEATH.** DIED: on May 30, 1782, as a result of a fall from the porch of his mansion in Annapolis. PERSONAL PROPERTY: assessed value £12,864.0.0, including 434 slaves and 362 oz. plate, 1783. LAND: at least 13,538 acres in Anne Arundel and Talbot counties, 28 lots in Annapolis, 2 lots owned with his son in Bath, Virginia (Berkley Springs, West Virginia), plus perhaps 3,000 acres in Frederick County.

CARROLL, CHARLES, BARRISTER (1723–1783). BORN: on March 22, 1723, in Annapolis, Anne Arundel County; elder son. NATIVE: second generation. RESIDED: in Portugal and England, 1734–1746; Annapolis, 1746–1751; England, 1751–1755; Annapolis, 1755 until death; spent much of this last period at his estate "Mt. Clare" outside of Baltimore Town, but always styled himself "of Annapolis" in official records. **FAMILY BACKGROUND. FATHER:** *Charles Carroll* (1691–1755). MOTHER: Dorothy Blake. STEPMOTHER: Ann. BROTHER: John Henry (1732–1754). SISTER: Mary Clare. NEPHEWS: *Nicholas (Maccubbin) Carroll* (1750/51–1812); *James (Maccubbin) Carroll* (1761–1832). NIECE: Mary Clare Maccubbin (1749–1806), who married *John Brice* (1738–1820). MARRIED on June 23, 1763, Margaret (1742–1817), daughter of *Matthew Tilghman* (1717/18–1790); grandddaughter of *James Lloyd* (1679/80–1723); niece of *William Tilghman* (1711–1782), *Edward Tilghman* (1713–1786), *James Tilghman* (1716–1793), *Robert Lloyd* (ca. 1712–1770), Mary Tilghman (1702–1736), who married *James Earle, Jr.* (ca. 1694–1739), Anna Maria Tilghman (1709–1763), who married first, *William Hemsley* (1703–1736), and second, *Robert*

Lloyd (ca. 1712–1770), Henrietta Maria Tilghman (1707–1771), who married first, *George Robins* (1697–1742), and second, *William Goldsborough* (1709–1760), Henrietta Maria Lloyd (ca. 1711–1748), who married *Samuel Chamberlaine* (1698–1773), and Margaret Lloyd (1714–ca. 1785), who married *William Tilghman* (1711–1782). Her brothers were Matthew Ward (1743–1753); Lloyd (1749–1811), who married his first cousin Henrietta Maria (1763–1796), daughter of *James Tilghman* (1716–1793); and Richard (1746/47–1805). Her sister was Anna Maria (1755–1843), who married her first cousin Tench Tilghman (1744–1786), son of *James Tilghman* (1716–1793). Her first cousins were *Michael Earle* (1722–1787); *Richard Tilghman Earle* (1728/29–1788); Anna Maria Earle, who married *Thomas Ringgold* (1715–1772); Henrietta Maria Earle, who married *William Hemsley* (1736/37–1812); *Peregrine Tilghman* (ca. 1741–1807); *James Tilghman* (1743–1809); Margaret Robins (1734–1808), who married *William Hayward* (?–1791); Henrietta Maria Robins (1736–1791), who married *James Lloyd Chamberlaine* (1732–1783); Anna Maria Robins (1732–1806), who married *Henry Hollyday* (ca. 1725–1789); *William Hemsley* (1736/37–1812); *Richard Tilghman* (1740–1809); *Matthew Tilghman* (1760–ca. 1801); *William Tilghman* (1756–1827); *James Tilghman, Jr.* (ca. 1748–1796); *James Lloyd Chamberlaine* (1732–1783); Anne Chamberlaine, who married *Richard Tilghman Earle* (1728/29–1788); *Samuel Chamberlaine* (1742–1811); Deborah Lloyd, who married *Peregrine Tilghman* (ca. 1741–1807); and Henrietta Maria Lloyd (?–1822), who married *William Hayward, Jr.* (ca. 1758–1834). CHILDREN. Twins who died in infancy. PRIVATE CAREER. EDUCATION: attended the English school at Bairro Alto, Lisbon, Portugal, and Eton College; admitted to Clare College, Cambridge University in January 1741/42; admitted to the Middle Temple in 1751 to study law. RELIGIOUS AFFILIATION: Anglican, St. Anne's Parish, Annapolis; joined the congregation of St. Paul's Church, Baltimore County in 1769. SOCIAL STATUS AND ACTIVITIES: Esq., 1755; interested in racehorses; maintained a bowling green. ADDITIONAL COMMENTS: when in Maryland, suffered from annual "fever and ague" which modern historians have identified as malaria. Traveled to Boston in 1762 to escape the summer heat. OCCUPATIONAL PROFILE: businessman; planter. Although Carroll was trained as a lawyer and called himself "Barrister," he apparently never practiced the profession. He was active in the business of the Baltimore Ironworks Company and his own business endeavors, which included flour mills in Baltimore County that he established in the late 1750s. He had considerable rental property in addition to his own large working plantations in Baltimore County, and he maintained a warehouse and wharf on the dock at Annapolis. PUBLIC CAREER. LEGISLATIVE SERVICE: Lower House, Anne Arundel County, 1756–1757 (elected to the 4th session to fill vacancy; Laws 4; Grievances 4), 1757–1758 (Elections 1, Cv, 2; Grievances 1, Cv, 2; Public Offices 1, Cv, 2), 1758–1761 (Elections Cv 1, 1, Cv 2, 2, 3, Cv 3; Grievances Cv 1, 1, Cv 2, 2, 3, Cv 3; Public Offices Cv 1, 1, Cv 2, 2, 3, Cv 3); Conventions, Anne Arundel County, 1st, 1774, 2nd–3rd, 1774, 4th, 1775, 5th, 1775, 6th–8th, 1775–1776 (president, 7th), 9th, 1776 (Elections; resigned on August 27, 1776, because the opinions of his constituents concerning the establishment of a state government were "incompatible with good government and the public peace and happiness."); Senate, Western Shore, Term of 1776–1781: 1777, 1777–1778, 1778–1779, 1779–1780, 1780–1781, Term of 1781–1786: 1781–1782, 1782–1783 (died before the 2nd session). OTHER STATE OFFICES: Councils of Safety, Western Shore, 1st, 1775, 2nd, 1776, 3rd, 1776, 4th, 1776; judge, General Court, appointed 1777 (declined). LOCAL OFFICES: St. Anne's Parish Vestry, Anne Arundel County, sworn 1762; St. Paul's Parish Vestry, Baltimore County, 1779–1782. OUT OF STATE SERVICES: delegate, Continental Congress, 1776–1777 (elected in November 1776). STANDS ON PUBLIC/PRIVATE ISSUES: credited with framing Maryland's declaration of independence adopted on July 3, 1776. WEALTH DURING LIFETIME. PERSONAL PROPERTY: *Charles Carroll* (1691–1755) valued his son's land, slaves, and livestock at about £2,000.0.0 sterling, ca. 1751. Upon his father's death in 1755, Carroll inherited a one-fifth share in the Baltimore Ironworks Company. This share was valued at £10,000.0.0 sterling and yielded an annual income of no less than £400.0.0 sterling in 1764. Personal property in Anne Arundel and Baltimore counties (not including "Mt. Clare") was valued at £3,225.16.8, including 72 slaves and 50 oz. plate, 1783. ADDITIONAL COMMENTS: Supported Charles Willson Peale's art studies in London, England, in the 1760s with money and letters of advice and introduction. Owned an extensive library; ordered books and monthly book reviews to be sent from London. Interested in horticulture and agronomy, he maintained an orangery and ornamental garden at "Mt. Clare." LAND AT FIRST ELECTION: at least 19,000 acres in Anne Arundel, Baltimore,

Prince George's, and Frederick counties, plus 10 lots in Annapolis (all inherited from or gifts from his father). SIGNIFICANT CHANGES IN LAND BETWEEN FIRST ELECTION AND DEATH: sold nearly 700 acres in Anne Arundel County and 2 lots in Annapolis before 1774. Most of his land transactions, however, were carried on in Frederick County. In the seven years between 1756 and 1763, he acquired, mostly by patents, 1,753 acres in Frederick County and sold 2,674 acres for a net loss of 921 acres; but during the next seven years he acquired 5,018 acres in Frederick County (including patents for 3,767 acres in 1766) and sold 3,384 acres for a net gain of 1,634 acres. He did not acquire additional land in Frederick County after 1770, but he sold at least 3,527 acres, most of which were in tracts of less than 200 acres. WEALTH AT DEATH. DIED: on March 23, 1783, at "Mt. Clare," Baltimore County. PERSONAL PROPERTY: requested that no inventory be returned and no accounts be made. LAND: at least 15,000 acres in Anne Arundel, Baltimore, Frederick, and possibly Prince George's counties, plus 7 lots in Annapolis. In his will, written in 1781, Carroll named his nephews, *Nicholas (Maccubbin) Carroll* (1750/51–1812) and *James (Maccubbin) Carroll* (1761–1832) as his principal heirs, with the condition that they legally take his surname.

CARROLL, CHARLES, OF CARROLLTON

(1737–1832). BORN: on September 19, 1737, in Annapolis, Anne Arundel County; only child. NATIVE: third generation. RESIDED: in Annapolis and "Doughoregan Manor," Anne Arundel County; main residence in Baltimore City about 1800. For about the last fifteen years of his life Carroll spent the winters with the Catons at their Lombard Street house in Baltimore City, and the summers at "Doughoregan Manor." FAMILY BACKGROUND. FATHER: *Charles Carroll, Sr.* (1702–1782). MOTHER: Elizabeth Brooke (1709–1761). FIRST COUSIN: Eleanor Carroll, who married *Daniel Carroll* (1730–1796). MARRIED on June 5, 1768, Mary (Molly) (1749–1782), daughter of Henry Darnall, Jr. (ca. 1725–1772), of Prince George's County, and wife Rachel (ca. 1731/32–1781); granddaughter of Clement Brooke, Jr. (?–1732). CHILDREN. SON: Charles (1775–1825), of "Homewood," Baltimore County, who married in 1800 Harriet (1775–1861), daughter of Benjamin Chew, chief justice of Pennsylvania. DAUGHTERS: Elizabeth (1769–1769); Mary (Polly) (1770–1846), who married in 1786 Richard Caton (1763–1845); Louisa Rachel (1772–1772); Anne Brooke (1776–died young); Catherine (ca. 1778–1861), who married

in 1801 Robert Goodloe Harper (1765–1825); and Elizabeth (1780–1783). ADDITIONAL COMMENTS: son Charles's wife was the sister of Peggy Chew, who married *John Eager Howard* (1752–1827). PRIVATE CAREER. EDUCATION: Jesuit academy at Bohemia Manor, Cecil County, 1747; College of St. Omer, France, 1749–1753; College of French Jesuits, Rheims, France, 1754; College of Louis-le-Grand, Paris, France, 1755–1757; studied civil law at Bourges, France, 1757–February 1759; completed degree in Civil Law, Paris, France, February–August 1759; studied law in Middle Temple, London, England, 1759–September 1764. RELIGIOUS AFFILIATION: Catholic. SOCIAL STATUS AND ACTIVITIES: Esq., by 1795. ADDITIONAL COMMENTS: Carroll's close relationship with his father *Charles Carroll, Sr.* (1702–1782) is chronicled in their voluminous correspondence extending from Carroll's school days in France until his father's death. In 1776 John Adams described Carroll as a "complete master of the French language; yet a warm, a firm, a zealous supporter of the rights of America, in whose cause he has hazarded his all." OCCUPATIONAL PROFILE: planter, who closely supervised the management of his large landed estate; partner in the Baltimore Ironworks Company; landlord; moneylender. Subscribed £1,000.0.0 to the Potomac Company, ca. 1772; proprietor of the Susquehanna Canal in 1783. Interested in Alum Works Company in the 1820s. Member of the board of directors of the Baltimore & Ohio Railroad; turned the first spade of dirt for the cornerstone of the railway on July 4, 1828. PUBLIC CAREER. LEGISLATIVE SERVICE: Conventions, Anne Arundel County, 2nd–3rd, 1774, 4th, 1775, 5th, 1775, 6th–8th, 1775–1776 (did not attend the 7th Convention), Annapolis, 9th, 1776 (Loan Office); Senate, Western Shore, Term of 1776–1781: 1777, 1777–1778, 1778–1779, 1779–1780, 1780–1781, Term of 1781–1786: 1781–1782, 1782–1783 (elected president on May 22, 1783), 1783 (elected president on December 23, 1783), 1784, 1785, Term of 1786–1791: 1786–1787, 1787–1788, 1788, 1789, 1790, Term of 1791–1796: 1791–1792, 1792, 1793, 1794, 1795, Term of 1796–1801: 1796, 1797, 1798, 1799, 1800. OTHER STATE OFFICES: Committee of Correspondence, appointed 1774; 1st Council of Safety, Western Shore, 1775. LOCAL OFFICES: Committee of Observation, Annapolis and Anne Arundel County, elected 1774 and 1775; common councilman, Annapolis, 1780–1783, 1785 (resigned); alderman, Annapolis, 1784–1785 (resigned). OUT OF STATE SERVICE: accompanied Benjamin Franklin, *Samuel Chase* (1741–1811), and Rev. John Carroll on an expedition to Canada to enlist Canadian support for the Revolution, 1776; delegate, Continental Congress, 1776 (elected in July 1776), 1777–1778 (elected in February 1777 and December 1777), 1780 (elected in November 1780, but did not attend; resigned on January 3, 1781); senator, U.S. Congress, 1789–1791, 1791–1792 (resigned on November 30, 1792); nominated by George Washington to be one of three commissioners to treat with the western Indians, 1793, but declined because of advanced age. STANDS ON PUBLIC/PRIVATE ISSUES: opposed the Stamp Act, and spoke of the possibility of armed conflict, 1765. Writing as "First Citizen," he carried on a public debate with "Antilon," *Daniel Dulany, Jr.* (1722–1797), in the *Maryland Gazette*, January–July, 1773. Carroll opposed the proclamation of Gov. *Robert Eden* (1741–1784) setting fees for civil officers and supported his position with careful legal reasoning. His stand brought him a popular following and he was generally considered to have won the argument. Signed the Declaration of Independence in August 1776. Consistently opposed Maryland's confiscation of Loyalist properties as being impolitic, uncivilized, adding to the difficulties in making peace, financially unsound, and promoting speculation and corruption. Protested a bill in May 1783 concerning admission and qualification standards for lawyers, intended as retribution for suspected Toryism and monopolizing by members of the legal profession. Opposed to emitting paper money as proposed by *Samuel Chase* (1741–1811), 1787. Supporter of the ratification of the U.S. Constitution, 1787–1788. While in the U.S. Senate, he opposed the use of titles for the president and high government officials, 1789. Advocated a site on the Potomac River as the permanent seat of Congress, 1790. Introduced a bill in the Maryland Senate for gradual abolition of slavery, 1797. Opposed Thomas Jefferson and the Democrats, 1800. Opposed war with England in 1812 on the grounds that England was fighting to rid Europe of Napoleon Bonaparte. Supported Andrew Jackson in the 1820s. Elected president of the American Colonization Society, 1830. Used his fortune to support education; contributed to the fund which enabled artist Charles Willson Peale to study in London, 1767; supported St. John's College, Annapolis, 1790–1803; member of the first public library in Baltimore Town, 1795; and gave money and land to St. Charles College, Anne Arundel County. WEALTH DURING LIFETIME. PERSONAL PROPERTY: Carroll was generally regarded by his contemporaries as one of the wealthiest men in the colonies. John Adams estimated

Carroll's annual income at £10,000 sterling and "increasing" in 1774. Two years later Adams wrote that his fortune was "perhaps the largest in America," from £150,000 to £200,000 sterling. Senator William Maclay called Carroll "the richest man in the Union" in 1789. A part of Carroll's personal fortune was land based. He received substantial rents from his leased land, principally the Carrollton plantation in Frederick County and the lots in Baltimore City which he had developed and rented out. By 1804 the latter were yielding $2,500 per year. The Doughoregan Manor plantation in northern Anne Arundel County consistently produced a profit, which in 1819 amounted to $6,900 per year. In 1768 Carroll estimated that he would inherit from his father over 300 slaves with an average value of about £30 sterling each; and in 1783, shortly after his father's death, Carroll was assessed as owning 453 slaves on his Anne Arundel County properties (416 on "Doughoregan Manor"). During the next twenty years Carroll tried to reduce his slave holdings, and by 1800 there were only 182 slaves at "Doughoregan Manor." However, this number increased again in the years before his death. The assessed value of Carroll's personal property in Anne Arundel and Talbot counties was £12,946, including the 453 slaves noted above and 1,652 oz. plate, 1783. Although his land was important to Carroll and he carefully directed its management until just a few months before he died, the bulk of his income was derived from investments. Prior to the Revolution Carroll joined his father in operating virtually as colonial bankers. They had nearly £30,000 sterling lent out on interest in 1768. Twenty years later that principal had grown to £85,000 sterling, or an estimated $375,000 including accruing interest. In 1798 the principal was £128,705 sterling and in 1804 it was £143,000 sterling. The last figure accounted for 46 percent of Carroll's "monied estate" and represented a heavy investment in high-yield bank stocks and U.S. government securities with which he had replaced the private mortgages and bonds of the earlier period. Also in 1804 Carroll began investing in British securities. Ten years later he held £6,150 sterling in five percent British naval stock. Before his death Carroll sold his British holdings and invested the profits in the Bank of Montreal, Canada. Throughout his life Carroll acted to increase his monied estate to the greatest extent consistent with its security. He was determined to pass on to his children the fruits of his father's labors suitably expanded by his own efforts. From the date of his children's marriages each received from Carroll about $10,000 per year in gifts and annuities. LAND AT FIRST ELECTION: ca. 11,788 acres in Baltimore and Anne Arundel counties, plus 12,700 acres in Frederick County (most as gifts from his father). SIGNIFICANT CHANGES IN LAND BETWEEN FIRST ELECTION AND DEATH: inherited his father's property of at least 16,000 acres in Anne Arundel and Talbot counties, plus 28 lots in Annapolis and 2 lots owned jointly with his father in Bath, Virginia (Berkley Springs, West Virginia). Assessment of property in Annapolis, including 19 houses and 1.5 acres with improvements, was $9,000.00, 1819. Carroll owned at least 28,000 acres in Pennsylvania by 1820 and a resurvey of "Doughoregan Manor" totaled 13,361 acres. Carroll also absorbed the real property of his children, usually as security for debts which he had assumed for them. He controlled the Harper and Caton estates in Baltimore County, their townhouses in Baltimore City, and 45,000 acres of land in Pennsylvania and New York which Harper and Caton had acquired through speculation. WEALTH AT DEATH. DIED: on November 14, 1832; buried at "Doughoregan Manor." PERSONAL PROPERTY: TEV, $1,460,004.86 (including 259 slaves, plate valued at $6,203.00, 75 books, a gristmill, sawmill, chapel, stocks and bonds in roads, banks, the Baltimore & Ohio Railroad, the Georgetown Bridge Company, and a gold mine in North Carolina, and loans to Maryland, Pennsylvania, and the United States); FB, $680,250.14 before distributions, but including some interest and dividends received as late as 1855. LAND: ca. 57,000 acres in Anne Arundel, Baltimore, Frederick, and Talbot counties, plus lots in Annapolis and Baltimore City, and land in New York State and Pennsylvania.

CARROLL, DANIEL (1730–1796). BORN: on July 22, 1730, in Upper Marlboro, Prince George's County; eldest surviving son. NATIVE: at least second generation. RESIDED: referred to alternately as being from Prince George's and Frederick counties throughout the 1750s and 1760s; Northwest Hundred, Frederick County, 1776; Rock Creek Parish, Forest Glen, Montgomery County, 1777–1796. FAMILY BACKGROUND. FATHER: Daniel Carroll (1696–1751), of Prince George's County, a prosperous merchant, son of Kean Carroll, of Ireland. MOTHER: Eleanor Darnall (1709–1796), educated in France, held much of her husband's property in her own name through her long widowhood. BROTHERS: Henry (?–drowned as a child); John (1735–1815), appointed head of the Roman Catholic Church of America on November 25, 1784;

appointed bishop, 1789; founded Georgetown University, Washington, D.C., 1789; appointed archbishop, 1808. SISTERS: Ann (Nancy) (1733–1804), who married Robert Brent (?–1780), of Stafford County, Virginia; Eleanor, who married William Brent; Mary (1742–?), who married Notley Young; and Elizabeth (1743–after 1796). NIECE: Catherine Brent, who married *George Digges* (ca. 1742–1792). MARRIED his cousin Eleanor (?–1763), daughter of Daniel Carroll of "Duddington Manor" (1707–1734) and wife Ann Rozier; stepdaughter of *Benjamin Young* (?–1754), a lawyer and relative of Lord Baltimore; niece of *Charles Carroll, Sr.* (1702–1782), of Annapolis. Her brother was Charles, of Duddington (1729–?). Her sister was Mary, who married Ignatius Digges. Her first cousin was *Charles Carroll of Carrollton* (1737–1832). CHILDREN. SON: Daniel (1752–1790), who married Elizabeth Digges. DAUGHTER: Mary (1754–?), who married Col. Patrick Sim. PRIVATE CAREER. EDUCATION: attended Bohemia Academy, Cecil County; attended the Jesuit College of St. Omer in France, 1742–1748. RELIGIOUS AFFILIATION: Catholic. SOCIAL STATUS AND ACTIVITIES: Gent., 1750; Esq., 1765; a mason, admitted to Lodge No. 16, 1780. OCCUPATIONAL PROFILE: planter; merchant. PUBLIC CAREER. LEGISLATIVE SERVICE: Senate, Western Shore, Term of 1781–1786: 1781–1782, 1782–1783 (elected, but did not serve), 1783 (president, but replaced in this capacity on December 23, 1783, because of illness), 1784, 1785 (elected president on January 18, 1786, to replace George Plater), Term of 1786–1791: 1786–1787 (elected president on May 21, 1787, to replace George Plater), 1787–1788 (elected president on May 15, 1788, to replace George Plater; served as president until May 24, 1788), 1788 (elected president on December 16, 1788, to replace George Plater), 1789 (president, but replaced in this capacity on December 7, 1789, after requesting a leave of absence), 1790. OTHER STATE OFFICE: Executive Council, 1777–1778, 1778–1779, 1779–1780, 1780–1781. OUT OF STATE SERVICE: delegate, Continental Congress, 1781–1783 (elected on January 16, 1781, to fill vacancy; reelected in November 1781 and November 1782; chosen chairman, September 9 and November 3, 1783, during absence of the president); Federalist delegate, Constitutional Convention, 1789–1791; representative, U.S. Congress, 1789–1791; appointed by George Washington to survey the District of Columbia; first Board of Commissioners, District of Columbia, appointed in 1791 (resigned in 1795 due to poor health). STANDS ON PUBLIC/PRIVATE ISSUES: signer of the Articles of

Confederation, 1781; a strong supporter of the Federal Constitution; he favored the electoral college, a national census, and an open economy; he opposed export taxes. **WEALTH DURING LIFETIME.** PERSONAL PROPERTY: 12 slaves, 5 servants, plus control of 46 slaves belonging to his mother who resided with him, 1776; combined assessed value with his mother £2,285.0.0, including 47 slaves and 100 oz. plate, 1783; assessed value alone £793.0.0, including 17 slaves and 183 oz. plate, 1796. LAND AT FIRST ELECTION: at least 7,607 acres in Frederick and Prince George's counties (3,850 acres inherited from his father and devised to him by his brother, John), plus several lots in Upper Marlboro, Prince George's County. SIGNIFICANT CHANGES IN LAND BETWEEN FIRST ELECTION AND DEATH: acquired an additional 611 acres in Montgomery County, 1778–1794; deeded 778 acres as a gift to his son and sold 263 acres in Montgomery County, 1778–1794; acquired 627 acres in Prince George's County in 1796, probably at the death of his mother. **WEALTH AT DEATH.** DIED: on May 7, 1796, in Rock Creek, Montgomery County. PERSONAL PROPERTY: TEV, at least £2,802.3.2 (including 32 slaves). This figure incorporates the TEV of his mother, who shared his residence and predeceased him by 4 months. LAND: probably ca. 7,804 acres in Montgomery, Frederick, and Prince George's counties.

CARROLL, HENRY JAMES (ca. 1767–ca. 1814). BORN: ca. 1767, probably in St. Mary's County; eldest son. NATIVE: at least second generation. RESIDED: at "Susquehana Point," St. Mary's County; "Kingston Hall," Somerset County, ca. 1792. **FAMILY BACKGROUND.** FATHER: Capt. Henry Carroll (1727–1775), a mariner. STEPFATHER: George Biscoe. MOTHER: Araminta, daughter of Mary Thompson, of St. Mary's County, and heiress of *John Rousby* (1685–1744). BROTHERS: probably Michael; probably John Charles. SISTERS: Julian; Margaret; and Harriot. MARRIED on July 26, 1792, Elizabeth Barnes (1770–1826), daughter of Capt. *Thomas King* (?–?); granddaughter of *Robert King* (1689–1755). Her other relatives included great-grandfather *Robert King* (?–1697); great-aunts Mary King (1674–?), who married *Francis Jenkins* (ca. 1650–1710) and Eleanor King, who married *Charles Ballard* (ca. 1670–ca. 1724/25). **CHILDREN.** SONS: Thomas (1793–1873), governor of Maryland in 1830, who married Juliana Stevenson, of Baltimore County; Henry James; and Charles C. DAUGHTER: Elizabeth Mary. **PRIVATE CAREER.** EDUCATION: literate. RELIGIOUS AFFILIATION: Catholic; his

wife's family was Presbyterian. OCCUPATIONAL PROFILE: probably a planter. **PUBLIC CAREER.** LEGISLATIVE SERVICE: Lower House, St. Mary's County, 1789, 1790, 1791–1792, Somerset County, 1794, 1795, 1803. LOCAL OFFICES: justice, Somerset County, 1795–at least 1800; Maryland Senate elector, Somerset County, elected 1806 and 1811. MILITARY SERVICE: major, by 1802; inspector, Tenth Brigade (Somerset and Worcester counties), Maryland Militia, 1802–1809. **WEALTH DURING LIFETIME.** PERSONAL PROPERTY: assessed value £5,490.0.0, including 58 slaves and 180 oz. plate, 1813. LAND AT FIRST ELECTION: probably none. His father's land was in the name of his stepfather on the assessment of 1793, and Henry was listed as owning no land. SIGNIFICANT CHANGES IN LAND BETWEEN FIRST ELECTION AND DEATH: inherited 170 acres of his father's land in St. Mary's County, by 1801; acquired 1,600 acres through his wife's inheritance in Somerset County, 1802. **WEALTH AT DEATH.** DIED: ca. 1814; his inventory was recorded on September 9, 1814, in Somerset County. PERSONAL PROPERTY: TEV, $15,227.06 current money (including 58 slaves and 180 oz. plate); FB, $3,971.64. LAND: at least 1,597 acres in Somerset and St. Mary's counties.

CARROLL, JAMES (MACCUBBIN) (1761–1832). BORN: on December 8, 1761, in St. Anne's Parish, Anne Arundel County; fourth son. NATIVE: at least fourth generation. RESIDED: in Annapolis until at least 1787; Baltimore County until death. **FAMILY BACKGROUND.** FATHER: Nicholas Maccubbin (1709–1787), of Annapolis, a merchant; son of Zachariah Maccubbin and wife Susanna Nicholson. MOTHER: Mary Clare, daughter of *Charles Carroll* (1691–1755). UNCLE: *Charles Carroll, Barrister* (1723–1783). BROTHERS: *Nicholas (Maccubbin) Carroll* (1750/51–1812), who married Ann (?–by 1839), daughter of *Thomas Jennings* (ca. 1736–1796); John Henry (1754–?); Charles (1756–?), who married Sarah Allen; and Samuel (1763–by 1784). SISTERS: Mary Clare (1749–1806), who married *John Brice* (1738–1820); Susanna (1757–?), who married Nicholas Lingan. MARRIED in December 1787 Sophia (1772–1816), daughter of *Harry Dorsey Gough* (ca. 1745–1808) and wife Prudence Carnan (?–1822); niece of Charles Ridgely, of "Hampton" (1760–1829), governor of Maryland, 1816–1819. **CHILDREN.** SONS: James, Jr.; Charles Ridgely; Harry Dorsey (1793–?), who married Elizabeth Ridgely (1797–1828); and John Gough (1811–1817). DAUGHTER: Prudence Gough. **PRIVATE CAREER.** EDUCATION: literate. RELIGIOUS AFFILIA-

TION: Anglican. SOCIAL STATUS AND ACTIVITIES: Mr., 1783; Esq., 1791. ADDITIONAL COMMENTS: In accordance with conditions specified in the will of his uncle *Charles Carroll, Barrister* (1723–1783), James changed his surname to "Carroll" by act of the Assembly, 1783. OCCUPATIONAL PROFILE: planter; owned mills on his "Mt. Clare" property in Baltimore County. PUBLIC CAREER. LEGISLATIVE SERVICE: Lower House, Anne Arundel County, 1787–1788 (Laws to Expire 1); Senate, Western Shore, Term of 1786–1791: 1788 (elected on November 12, 1788 to fill vacancy; qualified on November 20, 1788), 1789, 1790; Lower House, Baltimore County, 1796, 1797 (speaker; resigned on November 13, 1797), 1798, 1799. OTHER STATE OFFICE: associate justice, Third District Court, February 1792–May 1792 (resigned). LOCAL OFFICES: justice, Baltimore County, 1795–at least 1800; St. Paul's Parish Vestry, Baltimore County, in office 1803–1813. WEALTH DURING LIFETIME. LAND AT FIRST ELECTION: 1,289 acres in Anne Arundel County and 1 lot in Annapolis (inherited from his father, 1787), plus rights to ca. 1,000 acres in Baltimore County ("Mt. Clare," inherited from his uncle subject to his aunt's life estate in the property). SIGNIFICANT CHANGES IN LAND BETWEEN FIRST ELECTION AND DEATH: received the rights to a large number of lots and buildings in Baltimore City through his wife's inheritance as the only child of her father, 1808. Also inherited ca. 400 acres in Baltimore City from his mother-in-law, 1822. Cleared his title to "Mt. Clare" and patented it in his own name, 1812. Shortly before his death, Carroll made agreements to sell his Anne Arundel County land. WEALTH AT DEATH. DIED: on January 27, 1832, probably at "Mt. Clare," Baltimore County. PERSONAL PROPERTY: TEV, $10,569.41 current money (including 19 slaves); FB, $3,660.24 current money. LAND: ca. 1,400 acres in Baltimore County and Baltimore City, including city lots leased out to others.

CARROLL, NICHOLAS (MACCUBBIN)

(1750/51–1812). BORN: on March 1, 1750/51, in St. Anne's Parish, Anne Arundel County; eldest son. NATIVE: at least fourth generation. RESIDED: at the "Carroll Mansion," on Green Street in Annapolis. FAMILY BACKGROUND. FATHER: Nicholas Maccubbin (1709–1787), of Annapolis, merchant; son of Zachariah Maccubbin and wife Susanna Nicholson. MOTHER: Mary Clare, daughter of *Charles Carroll* (1691–1755). UNCLE: *Charles Carroll, Barrister* (1723–1783). BROTHERS: John Henry (1754–?); Charles (1756–?), who married

Sarah Allen; *James (Maccubbin) Carroll* (1761–1832); and Samuel (1763–by 1784). SISTERS: Mary Clare (1749–1806), who married *John Brice* (1738–1820); Susanna (1757–?), who married Nicholas Lingan. MARRIED on October 30, 1783, Ann (?–by 1839), daughter of *Thomas Jennings* (ca. 1736–1796) and wife Julianna. Her brothers were Thomas; George; William; John; Daniel; Horner; and Horatio. Her sisters were Julianna (ca. 1764–1837), who married *James Brice* (1746–1801); Elizabeth. CHILDREN. SONS: Nicholas; Thomas H. (1796–1849); and John H. (?–1856), who married Matilda E. Hollingsworth. DAUGHTERS: Mary Clare, who married Robert Traill Spence; Ann, who married William Temple Thomson Mason. PRIVATE CAREER. EDUCATION: literate. RELIGIOUS AFFILIATION: Anglican, St. Anne's Parish, Anne Arundel County. SOCIAL STATUS AND ACTIVITIES: Esq., 1784. ADDITIONAL COMMENTS: in accordance with conditions specified in the will of his uncle *Charles Carroll, Barrister* (1723–1783), Nicholas changed his surname to "Carroll" by an act of the Assembly, 1783. OCCUPATIONAL PROFILE: planter. PUBLIC CAREER. LEGISLATIVE SERVICE: Lower House, Anne Arundel County, 1778 (elected to the 3rd session of the 1777–1778 Assembly to fill vacancy), 1778–1779 (Grievances 1; Claims 2; Tax Commissioners 3), 1779–1780 (Laws to Expire 2, 3), 1780–1781, 1783, 1784 (Grievances), 1785 (Grievances). OTHER STATE OFFICES: Constitution Ratification Convention, Annapolis, 1788; associate justice, Third District Court, appointed 1791. LOCAL OFFICES: common councilman, Annapolis, 1780–at least 1781; justice, Anne Arundel County, 1779–1780 ("will not continue"); alderman, Annapolis, 1783–1784, 1786–1789, 1792–1801; mayor, Annapolis, 1784–1785, 1790–1791; visitor, St. John's College, Annapolis, in office 1790. WEALTH DURING LIFETIME. PERSONAL PROPERTY: Anne Arundel County property valued at £1,296.0.0, including 20 slaves, 1783. LAND AT FIRST ELECTION: none in his own name, but probably managed 930 acres in Anne Arundel County belonging to his father. SIGNIFICANT CHANGES IN LAND BETWEEN FIRST ELECTION AND DEATH: by his will in 1783 *Charles Carroll, Barrister* (1723–1783) made Nicholas heir to all his property (except about 1,000 acres in Baltimore County), totaling 4,370 acres in Anne Arundel and Baltimore counties, plus 6.5 lots in Annapolis, 2 lots in Elk Ridge, Anne Arundel County, and a share of the land belonging to the Baltimore Ironworks Company. Most of the property was subject to his aunt's dower rights. In 1787 his father devised him the 970 acres in Anne Arundel County, as well as 1,049 acres in Kent County. During the 1780s and the 1790s Carroll developed his uncle's lots along Green Street in Annapolis, renting them for long terms with the stipulation that the leasee build a substantial house. **WEALTH AT DEATH. DIED:** on May 22, 1812, in Annapolis. **PERSONAL PROP-ERTY:** TEV, $67,114.80 current money (including 110 slaves, books, and plate); FB, $40,203.78, before payments of $40,287.90 to his heirs, 1815–1839. **LAND:** 7,378 acres in Baltimore, Anne Arundel, and Kent counties, plus lots in Annapolis and Elk Ridge, Anne Arundel County, and 2,280 acres as his part of the Baltimore Ironworks Company land. Total value of land $222,033.73; ground rents received on lots and houses in Annapolis were £68.3.4 current money per annum.

CARVILE, JOHN (ca. 1670–1709). **BORN:** ca. 1670 in St. Mary's County; first son. **NATIVE:** second generation. **RESIDED:** in St. Mary's County; Cecil County, by 1689; Kent County after 1707. **FAMILY BACKGROUND. FATHER:** Thomas Carvile (?–1717), who was transported by *Thomas Trueman* (ca. 1625–1685) in 1669, possibly from Virginia. An illiterate planter, he was highly critical of the Calverts in the 1680s and sided with *John Coode* (ca. 1648–1708/9). He acquired 800 acres in Kent County in 1682/83. **MOTHER:** Mary (?–by 1700). **MARRIED** by 1689 Mary (?–1738), daughter of James Phillips and wife Susannah. She subsequently married by 1718 Richard Smithers. Her brother was *James Phillips* (?–1720). Her sister was Martha, who married *Aquila Paca* (early 1670s–1721). **CHILDREN. SON:** John. **DAUGHTERS:** Averilla, who married in 1717 Edward Hall (1697–1738), son of *John Hall* (ca. 1658–1737); Blanche, who married Parker Hall (1707–1756), son of *John Hall* (ca. 1658–1737); Phoebe, who married Charles Hynson (1713–1782), son of Thomas Hynson; and Susannah, who married (possibly John) Johnson. **PRIVATE CAREER. EDUCATION:** literate. **RELIGIOUS AFFILIATION:** Protestant. **SOCIAL STATUS AND ACTIVITIES:** moved to Cecil County about the time of marriage; probably lived at "Carvile Hall," which still stands today. **OCCUPATIONAL PROFILE:** planter. **PUBLIC CAREER. LEGISLATIVE SERVICE:** Lower House, Cecil County, 1697/98–1699 (resigned after the 3rd session to become sheriff), Kent County, 1708A, 1708B (died before the 2nd session of 1708B–1711 Assembly). **LOCAL OFFICES:** sheriff, Cecil County 1694–1696, 1700–1702; justice, Cecil County, 1697–1700 (quorum, 1697/98–1700), Kent County, 1707–1709 (quorum). **WEALTH DURING LIFETIME. LAND AT FIRST ELECTION:** over 800 acres. **WEALTH AT DEATH. DIED:** will probated on September 5, 1709. **PERSONAL PROPERTY:** TEV, £1,027.15.7 sterling. **LAND:** over 1,600 acres.

CARVILE, ROBERT (ca. 1636–by 1705). **BORN:** ca. 1636, probably in England. **IMMIGRATED:** in 1669 as a free adult. **RESIDED:** in St. Mary's County. **MARRIED** by 1676 Johanna, daughter of Alexander D'Hinozossa (ca. 1630–ca. 1670), the Dutch governor of the Delaware River settlement, who was in Maryland by 1664. **CHILDREN. DAUGHTER:** Margaret (?–by 1721), who married Cecil Butler. **PRIVATE CAREER. EDUCATION:** literate. **RELIGIOUS AFFILIATION:** Catholic. **SOCIAL STATUS AND ACTIVITES:** Gent. on arrival; considerable legal skills and one of the most active attorneys in the province; last appeared in Maryland records in 1697. **OCCUPATIONAL PROFILE:** lawyer, admitted to the following courts: Court of Chancery in 1669; Provincial Court in 1669. He was disbarred for "scandalous speeches" against the proprietor in 1684, but was readmitted that same year. **PUBLIC CAREER. LEGISLATIVE SERVICE:** Lower House, St. Mary's City, 1674–1674/75 (elected to the 3rd session; Laws 3), 1676–1682 (Accounts 2, 4; Laws 2), 1682–1684 (Trade, chairman 1; Elections and Privileges 2; Laws 2). **OTHER PROVINCIAL OFFICES:** clerk, Lower House, 1669, 1671; register and examiner in Chancery, 1669; attorney general, April–October 1688. **LOCAL OFFICES:** recorder, St. Mary's City, in office 1674; justice, St. Mary's County, 1688–1689 (quorum). **STANDS ON PUBLIC/PRIVATE ISSUES:** the Lower House insisted that Carvile be summoned to attend the Assembly because of his valuable role as legislator, 1676; he verbally attacked the proprietary government, 1683/84; as a Catholic, he was excluded from public office after 1689 and temporarily excluded from practicing law. **WEALTH DURING LIFETIME. LAND AT FIRST ELECTION:** 1,050 acres. **WEALTH AT DEATH. DIED:** by October 1705, probably long before. **LAND:** 500 acres.

CARY (CAREY), JOHN DOW (?–?). **BORN:** in Frederick County, of age by 1779; probably eldest surviving son. **NATIVE:** probably third generation. **RESIDED:** in Frederick County; possibly out of state after 1798. **FAMILY BACKGROUND. FATHER:** John Cary (?–1777), a physician who resided in Frederick Town, Frederick County. **MOTHER:** Mary. **BROTHERS:** Robert Turner; William; David; and Jacob (?–by 1773). **SISTERS:** Betsy; Nelly (?–by 1773). **MARRIED** perhaps, but name of wife unknown. **CHILDREN.** Perhaps one son, name unknown. **PRIVATE CAREER.** EDUCATION: trained as a physician. OCCUPATIONAL PROFILE: physician, 1781; planter, 1784. **PUBLIC CAREER.** LEGISLATIVE SERVICE: Lower House, Frederick County, 1784, 1785. MILITARY SERVICE: sergeant, Maryland Militia, 1777; ensign, Second Maryland Regiment, 1781; 2nd lieutenant, 1781, resigned April 1783. **WEALTH DURING LIFETIME.** LAND AT FIRST ELECTION: 1 lot in Frederick Town, Frederick County; a house in Baltimore Town, Baltimore County (from his father's will). SIGNIFICANT CHANGES IN LAND BETWEEN FIRST ELECTION AND DEATH: acquired at least 1,665 acres in Maryland and Virginia; he and his brothers deeded their interest in their father's estate in trust to George French and Jacob Young, on August 8, 1791, and then Cary sought relief as an insolvent debtor from the Assembly, which was granted on December 30, 1791. **WEALTH AT DEATH.** DIED: date unknown; alive in 1800 when he received a warrant for 200 acres of federal land to which he was entitled for his service as a lieutenant in the Continental Army.

CASSON, HENRY (?–ca. 1788). RESIDED: in Queen Anne's County (later became part of Caroline County). MARRIED in October 1739 Esther, daughter of Thomas Baynard (?–1731), of Queen Anne's County, a merchant and Quaker, and wife Esther Pratt, a Quaker. Her brothers were John Pratt (?–ca. 1747), a Quaker, who married in 1730 Elizabeth, widow of Richard Fisher; Thomas, who married in 1746 Hannah Nicholson; and Nathan, who married Sarah. Her sisters were Rachel, who married in 1734 William Willson; Deborah, who married first, in 1739 Jeffrey Horner, and second, Hawkins Downes (?–1756). Her niece was Margaret Baynard, who married second, *Matthew Driver* (1740–1798). ADDITIONAL COMMENTS: Esther had a first cousin, George Pratt, orphan of her uncle Thomas Pratt, who was adopted by her mother, thereby legally becoming her brother. **CHILDREN.** SONS: John; James; Thomas; and possibly Henry, Jr. (?–1777), who married Elizabeth. DAUGHTER: Esther, who married *Matthew Driver* (1740–1798). There may have been other children. **PRIVATE CAREER.** EDUCATION: literate. RELIGIOUS AFFILIATION: Anglican, St. John's Parish, Queen Anne's County. SOCIAL STATUS AND ACTIVITIES: Gent., by 1743. ADDITIONAL COMMENTS: In his will, Casson directed his executor to employ some proper person "to correct and prepare my main works for the press and to get them printed. . . ." OCCUPATIONAL PROFILE: merchant. **PUBLIC CAREER.** LEGISLATIVE SERVICE: Lower House, Queen Anne's County, 1754–1757 (Arms and Ammunition 5, 6; Bills of Credit 5). LOCAL OFFICES: justice, Queen Anne's County, 1741–at least 1749; churchwarden, St. Paul's Parish, Queen Anne's County, in office 1747; St. John's Parish Vestry, Queen Anne's County, in office 1752 and 1758; Committee of Correspondence, Queen Anne's County, ca. 1774; judge, court of appeals, appointed under the Act to Procure Troops for the American Army, Caroline County, appointed 1778. MILITARY SERVICE: captain, by 1776. **WEALTH DURING LIFETIME.** PERSONAL PROPERTY: assessed value £298.0.0, including 6 slaves and 8 oz. plate, 1783. LAND AT FIRST ELECTION: 1,515 acres in Queen Anne's and Dorchester counties (all acquired by purchase or patent). SIGNIFICANT CHANGES IN LAND BETWEEN FIRST ELECTION AND DEATH: gave 241 acres in Queen Anne's County by deed of gift to his son John, 1768. **WEALTH AT DEATH.** DIED: will probated on January 29, 1788, in Caroline County. PERSONAL PROPERTY: TEV, £283.0.11 current money (including 5 slaves, 16 oz. plate, and books); FB, estate overpaid £198.9.10. LAND: at least 1,303 acres in Caroline County.

CASWELL, RICHARD (1685–1755). BORN: in 1685 in London, England. IMMIGRATED: in 1712 to Baltimore County. RESIDED: in Joppa, Baltimore County, until 1747 when he moved with his family to Johnston County, North Carolina. MARRIED on January 12, 1723, Christian (1704–1787), daughter of Richard Dallam (?–1714) and wife Elizabeth (Betty), who subsequently married William Smith, Gent. (?–1731), of Calvert County and later Baltimore County. Dallam immigrated to Calvert County by May 1701, was a lawyer, clerk of the Lower House from 1708 to 1713, and deputy commissary of Calvert County in 1713. Christian was the granddaughter of William Martin, of Calvert County. Her brothers were Richard (1708–ca. 1765), who married Frances Wallis (1711–?); William (1706–1761), who married Elizabeth Johnson. Her half brother was *William Smith* (?–?). Her half sister was Elizabeth, who married *John Paca* (1712–1785). Her nephew was *Richard Dallam* (1743–1820). Her half nephews were *Aquila Paca* (1738–1788); *William Paca* (1740–1799). **CHILDREN.** SONS: William (1726–1755), who moved to North Carolina in 1746 and died on shipboard returning to Maryland; Richard (1729–1789), a lawyer, member of the North Carolina House of Delegates from 1754 to 1771, delegate to the Continental Congress from 1774 to 1776, governor of North Carolina from 1776 to

1780, and from 1784 to 1787, member of the North Carolina Senate from 1782 to 1784; Martin (1733–1789); Joseph (stillborn 1736); Benjamin (1737–1792); Joseph Winston (1739–1761); and Samuel (1742–1785). DAUGHTERS: Elizabeth (1724–1725); Mary (1731–?); Christian (1737–1758); and Ann (1742–1784). PRIVATE CAREER. EDUCATION: literate. RELIGIOUS AFFILIATION: Anglican. SOCIAL STATUS AND ACTIVITIES: Gent., Mr. OCCUPATIONAL PROFILE: merchant. PUBLIC CAREER. LEGISLATIVE SERVICE: Lower House, Baltimore County, 1738, 1739–1741 (Bills of Credit Cv–3), 1742–1744 (Bills of Credit 1). LOCAL OFFICES: deputy sheriff, Baltimore County, in office 1724; justice, Baltimore County, 1735–at least 1744 (quorum, 1739–1744); coroner, Baltimore County, in office 1736. MILITARY SERVICE: captain, troop of horses, Gunpowder Hundred, Baltimore County, qualified 1735. WEALTH DURING LIFETIME. LAND AT FIRST ELECTION: 528 acres in Baltimore County. SIGNIFICANT CHANGES IN LAND BETWEEN FIRST ELECTION AND DEATH: between 1745 and 1746 he sold his 528 acres in Baltimore County to his brother-in-law William Dallam and moved to North Carolina where he received a warrant for 400 acres in Johnston County in 1747. By 1751 Caswell had been granted warrants for an additional 250 acres in Johnston County. WEALTH AT DEATH. DIED: on April 24, 1755, at his home, "Newington-on-the-Hill," Johnston County, North Carolina (now near Kinston, Lenoir County, North Carolina).

CAUSIN (CAUSEEN, CAUSEENE, CAWSEENE, COSSIN, CAWSEEN, CAUSINE), GERARD BLACKSTONE (?–?). BORN: probably at "Causin Manor," Charles County, of age by 1769. NATIVE: fourth generation. RESIDED: in Charles County. FAMILY BACKGROUND. FATHER: John Causeen (1690–1751), son of *Ignatius Causine* (ca. 1642–1695). GUARDIANS: first, William Causin (?–1753), after 1753 William Sands and Roger Smith. MOTHER: (first name unknown), daughter of John Sanders. BROTHERS: William (?–1753); Josias (?–1769). MARRIED Jane Pope (ca. 1746–1803). CHILDREN. SONS: Nicholas; Nathaniel Pope, who married in 1808 Elizabeth, daughter of *John Hoskins Stone* (by 1750–1804). DAUGHTER: Rose, who married Luke Francis Matthews. PRIVATE CAREER. EDUCATION: literate. SOCIAL STATUS AND ACTIVITIES: Gent., 1790. OCCUPATIONAL PROFILE: planter. PUBLIC CAREER. LEGISLATIVE SERVICE: Lower House, Charles County, 1780–1781, 1781–1782. LOCAL OFFICE: commissioner of tax, Charles County, 1783–at least 1790. WEALTH DURING

LIFETIME. PERSONAL PROPERTY: 75 slaves, 1790; 68 slaves, 1798. LAND AT FIRST ELECTION: 709 acres in Charles County by 1769. SIGNIFICANT CHANGES IN LAND BETWEEN FIRST ELECTION AND DEATH: sold at least 759 acres to satisfy his creditors, 1791. Declared bankruptcy in 1790, giving Alexander Hamilton, a Prince George's County attorney, power to sell all of his land and 39 slaves to pay off his creditors (debts dating from 1784 totaled £4,444.2.7). WEALTH AT DEATH. DIED: after 1800; size of estate unknown.

CAUSINE, IGNATIUS (ca. 1642–1695). BORN: ca. 1642 in Charles County; first son. NATIVE: second generation. RESIDED: in Charles County. FAMILY BACKGROUND. FATHER: Nicholas (ca. 1608–by 1658), who immigrated by 1639 from France. MOTHER: Jane (1612–?), widow of John Cockshutt. She subsequently married *Robert Clarke* (ca. 1611–1664). BROTHER: Nicholas (1651–?). HALF SISTERS: Jane Cockshutt, who married *Thomas Mathews* (ca. 1622–1675/76); Mary Cockshutt, who married *Henry Adams* (?–1686). MARRIED Jane. CHILDREN. SONS: Ignatius (1682–?); John (1690–1751); and William (1692/93–?). DAUGHTER: Jane (1682–?). PRIVATE CAREER. EDUCATION: literate. RELIGIOUS AFFILIATION: Catholic. OCCUPATIONAL PROFILE: planter. PUBLIC CAREER. LEGISLATIVE SERVICE: Lower House, Charles County, 1671–1674/75. OTHER PROVINCIAL OFFICES: coroner, Charles County, 1670; justice, Charles County, 1672–1689 (quorum, by 1687). MILITARY SERVICE: captain, by 1676. STANDS ON PUBLIC/PRIVATE ISSUES: as a Catholic, he lost all of his offices after the revolution of 1689. WEALTH DURING LIFETIME. LAND AT FIRST ELECTION: 1,070 acres. WEALTH AT DEATH. DIED: will probated on June 11, 1695. PERSONAL PROPERTY: TEV, £129.6.6 sterling (including 2 servants). LAND: 1,070 acres.

CAUTHER, JAMES (?–by 1643). BORN: probably in England. IMMIGRATED: by 1637/38. RESIDED: in St. Mary's County. MARRIED never. CHILDREN. Died without progeny. PRIVATE CAREER. EDUCATION: illiterate. OCCUPATIONAL PROFILE: planter, 1637/38; fur trader with the Indians. PUBLIC CAREER. LEGISLATIVE SERVICE: Assembly, present 1637/38, St. Michael's Hundred, St. Mary's County, 1638/39. MILITARY SERVICE: commander, 1643. WEALTH DURING LIFETIME. LAND AT FIRST ELECTION: owned a plantation, 1641. WEALTH AT DEATH. DIED: by December 1643; size of estate unknown.

CELLARS (CELLAR, CELLER, CELLERS, SELLARS), JOHN (?–1818). BORN: of age by 1768. NATIVE: possibly, if so, second generation. RESIDED: in Frederick County (later became part of Washington County), by 1768. FAMILY BACKGROUND. FATHER: possibly John Keller, Sr. BROTHER: probably George (?–1828), of Washington County. MARRIED by 1777 Susannah. CHILDREN. Probably died without progeny. PRIVATE CAREER. EDUCATION: literate. SOCIAL STATUS AND ACTIVITIES: Gent., 1778; Esq., 1790. OCCUPATIONAL PROFILE: farmer. PUBLIC CAREER. LEGISLATIVE SERVICE: Lower House, Washington County, 1784, 1785, 1786–1787, 1787–1788, 1790, 1791–1792, 1796, 1798, 1799, 1800, 1801. LOCAL OFFICES: justice, Washington County, 1777–at least 1800; justice, Orphans' Court, Washington County, commissioned 1781 and 1782; commissioner of tax, Washington County, appointed 1782. WEALTH DURING LIFETIME. PERSONAL PROPERTY: assessed value £18.0.0, 1783; assessed value £184.0.0, including 2 slaves, 1804. LAND AT FIRST ELECTION: ca. 216 acres in Washington County, plus 1 lot in Elizabeth Town (later called Hagerstown), Washington County. SIGNIFICANT CHANGES IN LAND BETWEEN FIRST ELECTION AND DEATH: he resurveyed and enlarged the 216 acres into a 275-acre tract, 1787; sold 41 acres in Washington County in 6 small tracts ranging from 2 to 15 acres, 1787–1807; owned 254 acres in Washington County, 1804. WEALTH AT DEATH. DIED: in 1818 in Washington County. PERSONAL PROPERTY: TEV, $1,804.58 current money (including 1 slave and 8 books); FB, $1,330.21. LAND: probably ca. 247 acres in Washington County, plus 1 lot in Elizabeth Town (later called Hagerstown), Washington County.

CHAILLE, PETER (?–1802). BORN: probably in Somerset County, of age by 1753. NATIVE: third generation. RESIDED: in Acquango Hundred, Worcester County. FAMILY BACKGROUND. FATHER: Moses Chaillé (?–1763), of Snow Hill, Worcester County; son of Dr. Pierre Chaillé, a Huguenot who immigrated from France, ca. 1710. MOTHER: Mary. HALF OR STEPUNCLE: *William Allen* (?–1792). SISTER: Mary, who married (first name unknown) Johnson. MARRIED first, by 1753 Comfort, daughter of Joseph Houston, Sr. MARRIED second, by 1797 Scarborough, widow of *Nehemiah Holland* (?–1788). CHILDREN. SONS: Moses; Zachariah. DAUGHTERS: Mary, who married Robert Done (?–1785); Henrietta, who married in 1801 Anthony Bacon; Margaret; and Comfort, who married (first name unknown) Long. PRIVATE

CAREER. EDUCATION: literate; an original subscriber to the establishment of Washington College, Kent County. RELIGIOUS AFFILIATION: Protestant. SOCIAL STATUS AND ACTIVITIES: Esq., 1785. ADDITIONAL COMMENTS: contributed £750 paper money to the common fund to bolster the credit of the Maryland state treasury, 1776. OCCUPATIONAL PROFILE: planter. PUBLIC CAREER. LEGISLATIVE SERVICE: Lower House, Worcester County, 1762–1763 (Public Offices 1, 2), 1765–1766, 1771, 1773–1774; Conventions, Worcester County, 1st, 1774, 3rd, 1774, 5th, 1775, 6th–8th, 1775–1776, 9th, 1776 (election voided on August 15, 1776, because voter qualifications had not been ascertained as prescribed by the 8th Convention resolves; reelected and seated); Lower House, Worcester County, 1777 (Grievances 1), 1777 (elected to the 1777–1778 Assembly, but did not attend; resigned on October 31, 1777), 1778–1779 (Tax Commissioners 3), 1779–1780 (Grievances 3), 1784, 1785, 1790. OTHER STATE OFFICES: Constitution Ratification Convention, Worcester County, 1788; associate justice, Fourth District, appointed and resigned 1791. LOCAL OFFICES: Committee of Observation, Worcester County, in office 1776; justice, Worcester County, 1779–1786 (resigned); justice, Orphans' Court, Worcester County, 1779–1786 (resigned); commissary for purchases, Worcester County, appointed 1780; commissary for horses, Worcester County, appointed 1781; commissary for clothing, Worcester County, appointed 1781; Maryland Senate elector, Worcester County, elected 1791. MILITARY SERVICE: captain, by 1762; colonel, First Battalion, Worcester County Militia, elected 1776. WEALTH DURING LIFETIME. PERSONAL PROPERTY: assessed value £800.0.0, including 12 slaves and 42 oz. plate, 1783; 22 slaves, 1790; as a principal heir of *William Allen* (?–1792), he inherited two-thirds of a one-sixth share in Allen's personal estate, 1792. LAND AT FIRST ELECTION: 475 acres in Worcester County (147 acres from his father, 328 acres by personal acquisition). SIGNIFICANT CHANGES IN LAND BETWEEN FIRST ELECTION AND DEATH: inherited 641 acres in Worcester County, plus lots in Snow Hill, Worcester County, from his father, 1763; resurveyed a tract he owned at first election for a net gain of 189 acres in Worcester County, 1768; sold 130 acres in Worcester County, 1773–1783; owned a total of 930 acres in Worcester County, 1783; sold 737 acres in Worcester County in 1797; deeded several tracts to his son-in-law to pay his many debts, 1802. WEALTH AT DEATH. DIED: in 1802, probably in Worcester County.

PERSONAL PROPERTY: TEV, at least $479.14. LAND: he left instructions for unspecified acreage to be sold for payment of his debts.

CHAIRES (CHAIRS, CHEARES), JOHN (?–1728/29).

BORN: of age by 1717; eldest son. NATIVE: at least second generation. RESIDED: in Queen Anne's County. FAMILY BACKGROUND. FATHER: John Chaires (?–ca. 1718), of Queen Anne's County. STEPFATHER: (first name unknown) Collins. MOTHER: Catherine (?–by 1730). BROTHERS: Joseph; Thomas; and James. SISTERS: Hannah, who married (first name unknown) Ellis; Catherine (?–by 1730). MARRIED Mary, who subsequently married *Solomon Clayton* (1685–1739). CHILDREN. SONS: John (?–1747), who married Margaret; Thomas; and James. PRIVATE CAREER. EDUCATION: literate. RELIGIOUS AFFILIATION: Anglican, St. Paul's Parish,. Queen Anne's County, and later St. Luke's Parish, Queen Anne's County. OCCUPATIONAL PROFILE: probably a planter. PUBLIC CAREER. LEGISLATIVE SERVICE: Lower House, Queen Anne's County, 1722–1724, 1725–1727. LOCAL OFFICE: Old Chester Church Vestry, St. Paul's Parish, Queen Anne's County, 1725–1728. WEALTH DURING LIFETIME. LAND AT FIRST ELECTION: at least 350 acres in Queen Anne's County. WEALTH AT DEATH. DIED: between January 15 and February 4, 1728/29, in Queen Anne's County. PERSONAL PROPERTY: TEV, £312.0.1 (including 2 slaves, 5 servants, and books); FB, £207.15.10. LAND: at least 350 acres in Queen Anne's County.

CHAMBERLAINE, JAMES LLOYD (1732–1783).

BORN: on October 10, 1732, in Oxford, Talbot County; second son. NATIVE: second generation. RESIDED: in Talbot County; "Peach Blossom," Talbot County, 1771. FAMILY BACKGROUND. FATHER: *Samuel Chamberlaine* (1698–1773). MOTHER: Henrietta Maria (ca. 1711–1748), daughter of *James Lloyd* (1679/80–1723). UNCLE: *Robert Lloyd* (ca. 1712–1770). AUNTS: Margaret Lloyd (1714–ca. 1785), who married *William Tilghman* (1711–1782); Ann Lloyd (ca. 1723–1794), who married *Matthew Tilghman* (1717/18–1790). BROTHERS: Thomas (1731–1764); *Samuel Chamberlaine* (1742–1811); Richard; and Robert Lloyd. SISTERS: Anne (1734–1786), who married *Richard Tilghman Earle* (1728/29–1788); Henrietta Maria (1739–1777). FIRST COUSINS: *Richard Tilghman* (1740–1809); Margaret Tilghman (1742–1817), who married *Charles Carroll, Barrister* (1723–1783); Deborah Lloyd, who married *Peregrine Tilghman* (ca. 1741–1807); and

Henrietta Maria Lloyd (?–1822), who married *William Hayward, Jr.* (ca. 1758–1834). NEPHEW: *Samuel Earle* (1756–1790). NIECE: Henrietta Maria Nicols (1761–1818), who married *Samuel Earle* (1756–1790). MARRIED on May 16, 1757, Henrietta Maria (1736–1791), daughter of *George Robins* (1697–1742); stepdaughter of *William Goldsborough* (1709–1760); granddaughter of both *Thomas Robins* (1672–1721) and *Richard Tilghman* (1672/73–1738/39); niece of *William Tilghman* (1711–1782), *Edward Tilghman* (1713–1786), *James Tilghman* (1716–1793), *Matthew Tilghman* (1717/18–1790), Mary Tilghman (1702–1736), who married *James Earle, Jr.* (ca. 1694–1739), and Anna Maria Tilghman (1709–1763), who married first, *William Hemsley* (1703–1736), and second, *Robert Lloyd* (ca. 1712–1770); half niece of Elizabeth Robins (1710–1746), who married *William Goldsborough* (1709–1760). Her brother was Thomas (1740–1762). Her sisters were Anna Maria (ca. 1732–1804), who married *Henry Hollyday* (ca. 1725–1789); Margaret (1734–1808), who married *William Hayward* (?–1791); Susanna (1738–?); and Elizabeth (1742–by 1764). Her first cousins were *Richard Tilghman* (1740–1809); *Michael Earle* (1722–1787); *Richard Tilghman Earle* (1728/29–1788); *Peregrine Tilghman* (ca. 1741–1807); *James Tilghman* (1743–1809); *William Tilghman* (1756–1827); *Matthew Tilghman* (1760–ca. 1801); *James Tilghman, Jr.* (ca. 1748–1796); *William Hemsley* (1736/37–1812); Margaret Tilghman (1742–1817), who married *Charles Carroll, Barrister* (1723–1783); Anna Maria Earle (1725–1795), who married *Thomas Ringgold* (1715–1772); Henrietta Maria Earle (1730–1767), who married *William Hemsley* (1736/37–1812); Deborah Lloyd, who married *Peregrine Tilghman* (ca. 1741–1807); Anna Maria Tilghman, who married *William Hemsley* (1736/37–1812); and Elizabeth Tilghman, who married *James Lloyd* (1745–1820). Her nephew was *James Hollyday* (1758–1807). Her nieces were Henrietta Maria Hollyday (1750–1832), who married *Samuel Chamberlaine* (1742–1811); Anna Maria Hollyday (1756–?), who married *George Gale* (1756–1815); and Rebecca Hollyday (1762–?), who married *Nicholas Hammond* (1758–1830). CHILDREN. SONS: Samuel (?–1784), died without progeny; Robins (?–1773), died young; and Robins (1773–1808), an insolvent debtor by 1804, who married Mary, daughter of Charles Crookshanks, a merchant of Baltimore County. DAUGHTERS: Henrietta Maria (?–1804), who married *William Hayward, Jr.* (ca. 1758–1834); Margaret, who married Col. John Hughes. PRIVATE CAREER. EDUCATION: literate.

RELIGIOUS AFFILIATION: Anglican. SOCIAL STA-
TUS AND ACTIVITIES: Gent., 1756; Esq., 1759;
Hon., 1776. OCCUPATIONAL PROFILE: merchant,
1769; amassed a fortune through commercial ventures; owned a privateer during the Revolution.
PUBLIC CAREER. LEGISLATIVE SERVICE: Lower
House, Talbot County, 1771 (Grievances; Accounts), 1773–1774 (Grievances 1, Cv, 2, 3; Accounts 1, Cv, 2, 3); Conventions, Talbot County,
4th, 1775, 5th, 1775, 6th–8th, 1775–1776 (Claims
7th, 8th), 9th, 1776; Lower House, Talbot County,
1780–1781 (Grievances 1; resigned on May 25,
1781). OTHER STATE OFFICES: one of four commissioners sent by the Convention of Maryland to
New York and New Jersey to offer bounty for
enlistment of soldiers in the Flying Camp, appointed 1776; 5th Council of Safety, Eastern
Shore, 1777 (appointed on January 3, 1777, to fill
vacancy, but declined to serve). LOCAL OFFICES:
St. Michael's Parish Vestry, Talbot County,
elected 1757 (refused to serve), 1765; sheriff, Talbot County, 1758–1761; commissioner of tax, Talbot County, 1777–1779; St. Peter's Parish Vestry,
Talbot County, elected 1779 and 1780. MILITARY
SERVICE: brigadier general, upper district of the
Eastern Shore, 1776. WEALTH DURING LIFETIME.
LAND AT FIRST ELECTION: 3,716 acres in Talbot
and Queen Anne's counties, and 3 lots in Oxford,
Talbot County (773 acres and 3 lots in Oxford
received by deed of gift from his father; 1,633
acres, plus part of 136 additional acres through his
marriage; 1,310 acres by purchase and patent),
plus control of 1,927 acres in Talbot County for
his nephew Thomas Chamberlaine. SIGNIFICANT
CHANGES IN LAND BETWEEN FIRST ELECTION
AND DEATH: inherited at least 393 additional
acres in Talbot County from his father, 1773.
WEALTH AT DEATH. DIED: between November and
December 1783 in Talbot County. PERSONAL
PROPERTY: assessed value £3,552.0.0, including 77
slaves and 450 oz. plate, 1783. LAND: 4,010 acres
in Talbot and Caroline counties, plus 5 lots in Talbot County; plus he still controlled 1,927 acres in
Talbot County for his nephew Thomas Chamber-
laine, and he also controlled 1,013 acres in Talbot
County for his nephews Henry and Samuel Nicols.

CHAMBERLAINE, SAMUEL (1698–1773).
BORN: on May 18, 1698, at "Sanghall" on the Dee
River, Cheshire, England; third son. IMMIGRATED:
ca. 1721/22 from Liverpool, England. RESIDED: in
Oxford, Talbot County, 1722/23; "Plain Deal-
ing," Tred Avon River, Talbot County, 1735.
FAMILY BACKGROUND. FATHER: Thomas Cham-
berlaine (1658–1757), of Liverpool, England; a

merchant and shipowner who traded with Oxford,
Talbot County; son of Richard Chamberlaine, a
merchant. MOTHER: Ann Penketh. STEPMOTHER:
(first name unknown) Heyling. BROTHERS: John
(1690–1721), a ship's master, who married Margaret Clay, of Yorkshire, England; Thomas, who
never married and died at age 20. HALF BROTH-
ERS: Richard; William; and Joseph, who married
in 1740 Ann Prescott (?–1775). MARRIED first, in
1721 Mary (?–1726), daughter of *Robert Ungle*
(1670/71–1726). MARRIED second, in 1729 Henrietta Maria (ca. 1711–1748), daughter of *James
Lloyd* (1679/80–1723); stepdaughter of Rev. Edward Fottrell; granddaughter of *Philemon Lloyd*
(1646–1685); niece of *Edward Lloyd* (1670–
1718/19), *Philemon Lloyd* (ca. 1674–1732/33),
Anna Maria Lloyd (ca. 1676–1748), who married
Richard Tilghman (1672/73–1738/39), Margaret
Lloyd, who married *Matthew Tilghman Ward* (ca.
1676–1741); half niece of Susanna Bennett (1666–
1714), who married first, *John Darnall* (?–1684),
and second, *Henry Lowe* (?–1717). Her brothers
were *Robert Lloyd* (ca. 1712–1770); James
(1716/17–1768); and Philemon (1721–died
young). Her sisters were Margaret (1714–ca.
1785), who married *William Tilghman* (1711–
1782); Deborah (1719–?); and Anne (ca. 1723–
1794), who married *Matthew Tilghman* (1717/18–
1790). Her first cousins were *Edward Lloyd* (1711–
1770); *Richard Lloyd* (1717–1786); *William Tilghman* (1711–1782); *Edward Tilghman* (1713–1786);
Matthew Tilghman (1717/18–1790); *James Tilghman* (1716–1793); Henrietta Maria Lloyd (?–
1766), who married second, *Daniel Dulany* (1685–
1753); Mary Tilghman (1702–1736), who married
James Earle, Jr. (ca. 1694–1739); Henrietta Maria
Tilghman (1707–1771), who married first, *George
Robins* (1697–1742), and second, *William Goldsborough* (1709–1760); and Anna Maria Tilghman
(1709–1763), who married first, *William Hemsley*
(1703–1736), and second, *Robert Lloyd* (ca. 1712–
1770). Her nephew was *Richard Tilghman* (1740–
1809). Her nieces were Margaret Tilghman (1742–
1817), who married *Charles Carroll, Barrister*
(1723–1783); Deborah Lloyd, who married *Peregrine Tilghman* (ca. 1741–1807); and Henrietta
Maria Lloyd (?–1822), who married *William Hayward, Jr.* (ca. 1758–1834). CHILDREN. SONS: Col.
Thomas (1731–1764), who married Susanna
(1738–?), daughter of *George Robins* (1697–1742);
James Lloyd Chamberlaine (1732–1783); *Samuel
Chamberlaine* (1742–1811); Richard; and Robert
Lloyd, who died at the age of 11. DAUGHTERS:
Henrietta Maria (1739–1777), who married in
1760 William Nicols (1730–1774); Anne (1734–

1786), who married *Richard Tilghman Earle* (1728/29–1788). PRIVATE CAREER. EDUCATION: literate. RELIGIOUS AFFILIATION: Anglican. SOCIAL STATUS AND ACTIVITIES: Gent., 1726; Esq., 1756; Hon., 1769. OCCUPATIONAL PROFILE: acted as supercargo (factor) on the ship *Squire,* 1719; a merchant in Liverpool, England, 1718/19–1722/23; acquired the business of Messrs. Ratchdale, Norris & Co., of Liverpool, England, in partnership with his father and widowed sister-in-law, Margaret Clay Chamberlaine, 1723; planter and merchant, 1726; officeholder. PUBLIC CAREER. LEGISLATIVE SERVICE: Lower House, Talbot County, 1728–1731 (Accounts 1–5); Upper House, 1739–1741 (appointed during the convention, but did not attend until the 1st session), 1742–1744, 1745, 1745/46–1748 (Bills of Credit–Paper Currency 3), 1749–1751 (Bills of Credit–Paper Currency 1), 1751–1754, 1754–1757 (Bills of Credit–Paper Currency 3, 4), 1757–1758 (Bills of Credit–Paper Currency 1, Cv, 2), 1758–1761 (Bills of Credit–Paper Currency 2, 3), 1762–1763 (Bills of Credit–Paper Currency 1), 1765–1766 (Bills of Credit–Paper Currency 2), 1768 (resigned before the 2nd session). OTHER PROVINCIAL OFFICES: Council, 1739–1769 (nominated on June 2, 1739; qualified on April 22, 1740; resigned on June 22, 1769); commissioner to supervise the survey defining the territorial limits of Maryland, 1739; naval officer, Pocomoke, commissioned 1740 and 1742, Oxford, 1754–1768 (resigned in favor of his son Samuel). LOCAL OFFICES: justice, Talbot County, 1723–at least 1738 (quorum, 1732–at least 1738); St. Peter's Parish Vestry, Talbot County, elected 1725. WEALTH DURING LIFETIME. PERSONAL PROPERTY: executed a deed of gift of 15 slaves to his son *Samuel Chamberlaine* (1742–1811), 1762. LAND AT FIRST ELECTION: 220 acres and 14 lots in Talbot County (10 lots in Oxford by deed of gift from his first father-in-law; 220 acres and 4 lots in Oxford by purchase). SIGNIFICANT CHANGES IN LAND BETWEEN FIRST ELECTION AND DEATH: acquired 5,893 acres in Talbot County by purchase or patent between 1729 and 1772; disposed of 3,150 acres in Talbot County between 1729 and 1772, of which at least 120 acres were sold and 1,941 acres, plus all lots in Oxford, were given by deeds of gift to three of his sons. WEALTH AT DEATH. DIED: on April 29, 1773, at his home in Talbot County. PERSONAL PROPERTY: TEV, £5,067.11.8 current money (including 54 slaves, at least 335 oz. plate, and books); FB, £1,350.5.10. LAND: 2,962 acres in Talbot County.

CHAMBERLAINE, SAMUEL (1742–1811). BORN: on August 23, 1742, at "Plain Dealing," Tred Avon River, Talbot County; third son. NATIVE: second generation. RESIDED: in Talbot County; "Bonfield," near Oxford, Talbot County, 1773. FAMILY BACKGROUND. FATHER: *Samuel Chamberlaine* (1698–1773). MOTHER: Henrietta Maria (ca. 1711–1748), daughter of *James Lloyd* (1679/80–1723). UNCLE: *Robert Lloyd* (ca. 1712–1770). AUNTS: Margaret Lloyd (1714–ca. 1785), who married *William Tilghman* (1711–1782); Anne Lloyd (ca. 1723–1794), who married *Matthew Tilghman* (1717/18–1790). BROTHERS: Thomas (1731–1764); *James Lloyd Chamberlaine* (1732–1783); Richard; and Robert. SISTERS: Henrietta Maria (1739–1777); Anne (1734–1786), who married *Richard Tilghman Earle* (1728/29–1788). FIRST COUSINS: *Richard Tilghman* (1740–1809); Margaret Tilghman (1742–1817), who married *Charles Carroll, Barrister* (1723–1783); Deborah Lloyd, who married *Peregrine Tilghman* (ca. 1741–1807); and Henrietta Maria Lloyd (?–1822), who married *William Hayward, Jr.* (ca. 1758–1834). NEPHEW: *Samuel Earle* (1756–1790). NIECES: Henrietta Maria Chamberlaine (?–1804), who married *William Hayward, Jr.* (ca. 1758–1834); Henrietta Maria Nicols (1761–1818), who married *Samuel Earle* (1756–1790). MARRIED on January 15, 1772, Henrietta Maria (1750–1832), daughter of *Henry Hollyday* (ca. 1725–1789); granddaughter of both *James Hollyday* (1696–1747) and *George Robins* (1697–1742); stepgranddaughter of *William Goldsborough* (1709–1760); niece of *James Hollyday* (1722–1786), Margaret Robins (1734–1808), who married *William Hayward* (?–1791); and Henrietta Maria Robins (1736–1791), who married *James Lloyd Chamberlaine* (1732–1783); half niece of both *Edward Lloyd* (1711–1770) and *Richard Lloyd* (1717–1786). Her brothers were Henry (?–died young); *James Hollyday* (1758–1807); Thomas (1760–1823); and Henry (1771–1850). Her sisters were Sarah (1753–?); Anna Maria (1756–?), who married *George Gale* (1756–1815); Rebecca (1762–by 1812), who married *Nicholas Hammond* (1758–1830); Elizabeth (1768–?); and Margaret (1774–?). Her first cousin was Henrietta Maria Chamberlaine (?–1804), who married *William Hayward, Jr.* (ca. 1758–1834). CHILDREN. SONS: James Lloyd (1785–1844), who married in 1818 his first cousin Anna Maria, daughter of *Nicholas Hammond* (1758–1830); Henry (1787–?), who married in 1811 his first cousin Henrietta Maria Elizabeth, daughter of *George Gale* (1756–1815); Samuel (1790–1828), who married in 1814 Ariana Worthington Davis; and Richard Lloyd (1792–1831). DAUGHTERS: Anna Maria (1774–1836), who married in 1797 John Goldsborough, Jr., an attorney; Henrietta Maria (1776–1804); Marion (1778–1807); Sarah Hollyday (1781–1820), who married in 1801 John Leeds Kerr (1781–1844), son of *David Kerr* (1749–1814); and Harriet Rebecca (1783–?), who married in 1813 her first cousin Levin Gale (1784–1834), son of *George Gale* (1756–1815). PRIVATE CAREER. EDUCATION: literate. RELIGIOUS AFFILIATION: Anglican, St. Peter's Parish, Talbot County. OCCUPATIONAL PROFILE: farmer; officeholder. PUBLIC CAREER. LEGISLATIVE SERVICE: Lower House, Talbot County, 1778 (elected to the 2nd session of the 1777–1778 Assembly to fill vacancy, but did not attend; resigned on April 11, 1778, to attend to family and private business matters), 1788. OTHER PROVINCIAL OFFICE: naval officer, Oxford, 1768–1777 (succeeded his father who resigned in his favor). LOCAL OFFICES: justice, Talbot County, commissioned 1778 (did not qualify); judge, court of appeals, appointed under the Act to Procure Troops for the American Army, Talbot County, appointed 1778; commissioner of tax, Talbot County, 1779–at least 1798; trustee of the poor, Talbot County, in office 1787 and 1793; St. Peter's Parish Vestry, Talbot County, in office 1788–1789, 1790–1793, 1797, 1805, 1807; judge of elections, Third District, Talbot County, in office 1800; trustee of the academy at Easton, Talbot County, in office 1800. STANDS ON PUBLIC/PRIVATE ISSUES: Historians have identified Chamberlaine as a religious zealot. His religious fervor manifested itself in bitter attacks on Quakers and Methodists in the press, in letters, and in verbal debates. WEALTH DURING LIFETIME. PERSONAL PROPERTY: received 15 slaves by deed of gift from his father, 1762; assessed value £2,493.6.0, including 66 slaves and 317 oz. 15 dwt. 12 gr. plate, 1783; assessed value £2,287.3.4, including 72 slaves and 241 oz. plate, 1804. LAND AT FIRST ELECTION: 2,576 acres, plus lots in Oxford, Talbot County (all inherited or received as gifts from his father). SIGNIFICANT CHANGES IN LAND BETWEEN FIRST ELECTION AND DEATH: resurveyed 4 of the tracts he owned at first election for a net loss of 92 acres in Talbot County, 1783; purchased or patented 253 acres in Talbot County between 1787 and 1803; sold at least 33 acres in Talbot County, 1809. WEALTH AT DEATH. DIED: on May 30, 1811, at "Bonfield," Talbot County. PERSONAL PROPERTY: requested no appraisal of his estate. LAND: 2,561 acres in Talbot County, plus 11 lots in Oxford, Talbot County.

CHANDLER, JOB (?–1659). IMMIGRATED: in 1651 as a free adult with his wife from Accomack County, Virginia. RESIDED: in Port Tobacco, Charles County. FAMILY BACKGROUND. FATHER: Edward (?–1650), a draper of Ware, Herefordshire, England. MOTHER: Elizabeth. BROTHERS: Edward; Noah; Daniel; and Richard, a merchant of London. SISTERS: Susan; Mary; Sarah; Rebecca; and Martha. MARRIED first, Anne, daughter of Adam Thorowgood (1602–1641), of Lower Norfolk County, Virginia, and wife Sarah Offley (1609–?); stepdaughter of *Francis Yardley* (ca. 1624–by 1655). She subsequently married in 1661 *Gerard Fowke* (1625–1669). Her sister, (first name unknown), married Simon Oversee. CHILDREN. SONS: Richard (1651–1697); William (1652–1685), a colonel, who married Mary, daughter of *Henry Sewall* (?–1665), and stepdaughter of *Charles Calvert, 3rd Lord Baltimore* (1637–1714/15). DAUGHTER: Anne. PRIVATE CAREER. EDUCATION: literate. RELIGIOUS AFFILIATION: Protestant. OCCUPATIONAL PROFILE: merchant; planter. PUBLIC CAREER. LEGISLATIVE SERVICE: Parliamentary Commission, 1652–1653; Lower House, Potomac (St. Mary's County), 1654 (declined to sit because of his oath to Lord Baltimore); Upper House, 1658 (did not attend). OTHER PROVINCIAL OFFICES: Council, 1651–1659; justice, Provincial Court, 1651–1653, 1657/58–1659; receiver general, 1651–1659. STANDS ON PUBLIC/PRIVATE ISSUES: his important ties to Puritan merchants led to his proprietary appointments; he loyally defended Lord Baltimore against Puritan opposition. WEALTH DURING LIFETIME. LAND AT FIRST ELECTION: 2,400 acres by 1652; acquired 2,150 additional acres by 1654. SIGNIFICANT CHANGES IN LAND BETWEEN FIRST ELECTION AND DEATH: he began disposing of his land in the late 1650s. WEALTH AT DEATH. DIED: in April 1659. LAND: 2,550 acres.

CHAPLINE (CHAPLAIN), JAMES (1750–by 1829). BORN: on September 28, 1750, in All Saints' Parish, Frederick County; third son. NATIVE: fourth generation. RESIDED: in Washington County; Jefferson County, Ohio, by 1813. FAMILY BACKGROUND. FATHER: *Joseph Chapline* (1707–ca. 1769). MOTHER: Ruhamah (?–1796), daughter of Rev. William Williams (?–1759), of Frederick County. BROTHERS: William Williams (1742–1804); *Joseph Chapline* (1746–1821); and Jeremiah (1756–?). SISTERS: Ruhamah (1743/44–1748); Deborah (1746–?), twin sister of Joseph; Jane (1748–1754); Ruhamah (1752–?); Sarah (1754–1834); Jean (Jane) (1758–1838); and Theodosha (1760–?). MARRIED by December 4, 1798, Catherine. **CHILDREN**. SONS: Joseph; Heros; Atlas; and Cyrus. DAUGHTERS: Althea, who married William Wallace; Rowena, who married John Miser. **PRIVATE CAREER**. EDUCATION: literate. RELIGIOUS AFFILIATION: his father was an Anglican. OCCUPATIONAL PROFILE: probably a planter. **PUBLIC CAREER**. LEGISLATIVE SERVICE: Lower House, Washington County, 1779–1780, 1780–1781, 1781–1782, 1782–1783, 1783 (elected, but did not attend). LOCAL OFFICE: commissioner of tax, Washington County, appointed 1786. **WEALTH DURING LIFETIME**. PERSONAL PROPERTY: assessed value £1,721.13.0, including 6 slaves and 4 oz. plate, 1783. LAND AT FIRST ELECTION: 1,628 acres in Washington County (over 853 acres inherited from his father); also controlled ca. 550 acres in Washington County that his brother William had conveyed to him in trust in 1773 because of William's heavy indebtedness. James sold 244 acres of this, including 1 mill, and leased out a farm, ca. 1777; he kept the rents and profits himself and never settled the trust according to the terms of the agreement with his brother. SIGNIFICANT CHANGES IN LAND BETWEEN FIRST ELECTION AND DEATH: acquired at least 1,168 additional acres in Washington County, by 1783, and purchased 2 small tracts (ca. 71 acres), 1797–1798; leased out 325 acres, 1793–1796; mortgaged more than 400 acres, 1794–1821; sold 2,606 acres, 1786–1824, all in Washington County. ADDITIONAL COMMENTS: He became involved in a lengthy court dispute over land with his brothers William and *Joseph Chapline* (1746–1821), which began in 1790 and was not settled until 1832. During the course of the litigation, he obtained an act for the relief of insolvent debtors from the General Assembly, 1802. On August 19, 1805, the Chancery Court ordered that all of his remaining real estate, which was not already mortgaged, be sold. **WEALTH AT DEATH**. DIED: by December 1829 in Jefferson County, Ohio; a Court of Chancery declared that no administration was necessary since "he left no personal or other estate."

CHAPLINE (CHAPLAIN, CHAPLAINE, CHAPLIN), JOSEPH (1707–ca. 1769).

BORN: on September 7, 1707, in Queen Anne Parish, Prince George's County; eldest son. NATIVE: fifth generation in the colonies, third generation in Maryland. RESIDED: at "Forest," his father's plantation in Prince George's County, 1729–1738; established a large plantation in the Antietam Valley (later became part of Frederick County), 1738. **FAMILY BACKGROUND**. FATHER: William Chapline (1686–1752), son of William Chapline (1659–ca. 1717), of Dorchester County, and wife Susannah Kimball. MOTHER: Elizabeth Travers. BROTHERS: William (1709–?); Moses (1717–1762), who married Jeanette Caton. SISTERS: Mary (1712–?); Anna (1714–?). OTHER KINSHIP: his second cousin was *Matthew Travers* (ca. 1672–1742). MARRIED on October 22, 1741, Ruhamah (?–1796), daughter of Rev. William Williams, Gent. (?–1759), a Welsh Presbyterian minister. Her sisters were Sarah, who married William Price, a lawyer; Jane, who married Col. Benjamin Chambers, the founder of Chambersburg, Pennsylvania. **CHILDREN**. SONS: William Williams (1742–1804); *Joseph Chapline* (1746–1821), twin to Deborah; *James Chapline* (1750–by 1829); and Jeremiah (1756–?). DAUGHTERS: Ruhamah (1743/44–1748); Deborah (1746–?), who married in 1783 John Thomson, son of a Presbyterian minister, Samuel Thomson, of Pennsylvania; Jane (1748–1754); Ruhamah (1752–?), who married in 1785 Capt. Alexander Thomson (1753–1815), son of Rev. Samuel Thomson; Sarah (1754–1834); Jean (Jane) (1758–1838); and Theodosha (1760–?), who married (first name unknown) Hays. **PRIVATE CAREER**. EDUCATION: trained as a lawyer. RELIGIOUS AFFILIATION: Anglican, All Saints' Parish, Frederick County, during the 1750s; his father-in-law, Rev. William Willaims, a Welsh Presbyterian minister, became the resident divine on Chapline's estate after being expelled from his own church for an unknown offense; Chapline persuaded him to become an Anglican. SOCIAL STATUS AND ACTIVITIES: Mr., 1739. OCCUPATIONAL PROFILE: practiced law in Annapolis, 1729–ca. 1738; planter, 1738; owned a share of the Ohio Company, which was formed for the purpose of trading with the Indians and was in operation from 1749 until 1779; engaged in building an ironworks with Col. Samuel Beall & Co. **PUBLIC CAREER**. LEGISLATIVE SERVICE: Lower House, Frederick County, 1749–1751, 1751–1754, 1754–1757, 1757–1758, 1758–1761 (Arms and Ammunition 3, Cv 3), 1762–1763, 1765–1766, 1768 (died before 2nd session). LOCAL OFFICES: justice, Prince George's County, 1739–1748, Frederick County, 1748–at least 1750 (quorum, 1748–at least 1750); trustee, Frederick County Free School, 1763. **WEALTH DURING LIFETIME**. LAND AT FIRST ELECTION: at least 2,175 acres, possibly as much as 4,729 acres in Frederick County. SIGNIFICANT CHANGES IN LAND BETWEEN FIRST ELECTION AND DEATH: he received 4,500 acres, plus a tract of 6,352 acres all adjacent to his existing estate, by 1764 from Gov. Horatio Sharpe in appreciation for financing and supporting the construction of Fort Frederick, Frederick County;

received 635 acres near Shepherdstown, Virginia, from Lord Fairfax. WEALTH AT DEATH. DIED: between December 23, 1768, and January 12, 1769, in Frederick County. PERSONAL PROPERTY: TEV, £3,043.4.3 current money (including 4 slaves and books); FB, £2,247.16.2. LAND: at least 6,385 acres in Frederick County, probably as much as 15,000 acres in Frederick County and Virginia.

CHAPLINE (CHAPLAIN, CHAPLAINE, CHAPLIN), JOSEPH (1746–1821). BORN: on September 9, 1746, in All Saints' Parish, Frederick County; second son. NATIVE: sixth generation in the colonies, fourth generation in Maryland. RESIDED: at "Mt. Pleasant," near Sharpsburg, Frederick County (later became part of Washington County). FAMILY BACKGROUND. FATHER: *Joseph Chapline* (1707–ca. 1769). MOTHER: Ruhamah Williams (?–1796). BROTHERS: William Williams (1742–1804); *James Chapline* (1750–by 1829); and Jeremiah (1756–?). SISTERS: Ruhamah (1743/44–1748); Deborah (1746–?), his twin sister; Jane (1748–1754); Ruhamah (1752–?); Sarah (1754–1834); Jean (Jane) (1758–1838); and Theodosha (1760–?). MARRIED in 1770 Mary Ann Christiana Abigail Furgeson (?–1823), of Frederick Town, Frederick County. Her brother was John W. Furgeson (?–by 1822). CHILDREN. Died without progeny. PRIVATE CAREER. EDUCATION: literate; possibly trained as a lawyer. RELIGIOUS AFFILIATION: Lutheran. OCCUPATIONAL PROFILE: pursued a legal career in Frederick Town in his early years; member of the Ohio Company, which later became the Potomac Company, but resigned in 1796 when the venture no longer appeared profitable. PUBLIC CAREER. LEGISLATIVE SERVICE: Conventions, Frederick County, 2nd–3rd, 1774, 4th, 1775 (elected, but did not attend), 5th, 1775; Lower House, Washington County, 1780–1781. LOCAL OFFICES: Committee of Observation, Frederick County, elected 1775; justice, Washington County, 1777–at least 1789; commissioner of tax, Washington County, commissioned 1777, 1779, and 1783; judge, court of appeals, appointed under the Act to Procure Troops for the American Army, Washington County, appointed 1778; subscription officer, Continental Loan Office, Washington County, appointed 1779; justice, Orphans' Court, Washington County, 1781–at least 1789. MILITARY SERVICE: captain, 1776; organized Sharpsburg Select Militia. WEALTH DURING LIFETIME. PERSONAL PROPERTY: assessed value £413.11.8, including 1 slave and 5 oz. plate, Washington County, 1783; assessed value £548.10.0, including 14 slaves and 54 oz. plate, Washington County, 1804. LAND AT

FIRST ELECTION: 3,159 acres in Frederick County (2,605 acres inherited from his father). He also owned part of 2,386 acres in Frederick County, which he and his brothers inherited jointly from their father. SIGNIFICANT CHANGES IN LAND BETWEEN FIRST ELECTION AND DEATH: patented 1,795 acres in Washington and Frederick counties, between 1775 and 1795; resurveyed 2,605 acres of the lands he inherited from his father in Washington County, for a net loss of 30 acres, 1791; owned a total of 400 acres in Frederick County, 1798; owned a total of 2,249 acres in Washington County, 1804; patented 13 acres in Washington County, 1811; sold 1,000 acres, plus lots in Sharpsburg, Washington County, to his nephew John Jones Hays, 1821. WEALTH AT DEATH. DIED: in September 1821 at "Mt. Pleasant," near Sharpsburg, Washington County. PERSONAL PROPERTY: TEV, $6,847.19 (including 18 slaves and books); FB, $169.55. LAND: probably ca. 1,660 acres in Washington and Frederick counties. ADDITIONAL COMMENTS: his widow brought suit against his nephew, John J. Hays, in 1821 claiming that the second will written by her husband in April of that year was composed when he was incompetent. Her charge that her husband had been fraudulently influenced by his nephew was decided against her by an Orphans' Court jury in 1822.

CHAPMAN, HENRY HENLEY (?–1821). BORN: of age by 1782. NATIVE: at least second generation. RESIDED: in Charles County; Annapolis, Anne Arundel County, 1818; Georgetown, D.C., 1819. FAMILY BACKGROUND. FATHER: John Chapman (?–ca. 1801), of Charles County; extensive landowner. MOTHER: Catharine. BROTHER: Samuel. SISTERS: Barbara Anna; Sarah (?–1792). MARRIED first, ca. 1782 Eleanor (?–1796), youngest daughter of *Samuel Hanson* (1716–1794). Her brothers were Thomas (1750–1810); Samuel (1752–1830). Her sisters were Chloe (ca. 1743–?), who married *George Lee* (ca. 1736–?); Mildred (ca. 1746–by 1796), who married *William Baker* (ca. 1749–1812); Sarah (ca. 1750–?); Nancy; Anne; and Elizabeth. MARRIED second, in 1799 Mary, daughter of John Davidson (?–1794), of Annapolis, a merchant. CHILDREN. At least eleven, including SON: John Henley (ca. 1801–1814). DAUGHTER: Anne Hanson (?–1796). PRIVATE CAREER. EDUCATION: literate. SOCIAL STATUS AND ACTIVITIES: Esq., 1795; a member of the Society of Cincinnati, ca. 1782. OCCUPATIONAL PROFILE: lawyer. PUBLIC CAREER. LEGISLATIVE SERVICE: Lower House, Charles County, 1787–1788, 1788, 1791–1792, 1792, 1796, 1797, 1798 (speaker), 1799 (speaker),

1800, 1801, 1802, 1803, 1804, 1805, 1806, 1808–1809, 1809, 1814 (speaker), 1815 (speaker). OTHER STATE OFFICE: Executive Council, 1816–1817, 1818–1819. LOCAL OFFICES: justice, Charles County, commissioned 1789, 1791, and 1793; associate justice, First District, Charles County, appointed May 1792–resigned September 1792; Maryland Senate elector, Charles County, in office 1796, 1801, 1811. MILITARY SERVICE: ensign, Second Maryland Regiment, 1781; lieutenant, 1782; continued service in the Maryland Battalion until November 1783; major, by 1821. WEALTH DURING LIFETIME. PERSONAL PROPERTY: 7 slaves, 1790; 16 slaves, 1798. SIGNIFICANT CHANGES IN LAND BETWEEN FIRST ELECTION AND DEATH: received as a gift from father 558 acres in Charles County, 1793; inheritance from father, acreage unknown, ca. 1801; purchased and patented 706 acres in Charles County, 1807–1816. WEALTH AT DEATH. DIED: prior to December 1821 in Georgetown, D.C. PERSONAL PROPERTY: TEV, $12,125.70 (including 56 slaves); FB, $9,436.61. LAND: at least 1,164 acres in Charles County, plus lots in Annapolis, and the right to four military lots (200 acres) in Allegany County (now Garrett County).

CHASE, JEREMIAH (?–1755). BORN: in England, of age by October 1743; younger son. IMMIGRATED/NATIVE: arrived in 1734 with his father, probably as a minor, from England. RESIDED: in Charles County, by 1749. FAMILY BACKGROUND. FATHER: Rev. Richard Chase (?–1742), of St. Andrew's, London, England; educated at Cambridge University; immigrated in 1734. An Anglican clergyman, he was appointed chaplain to *Charles Calvert, 5th Lord Baltimore* (1699–1751) on March 25, 1734; served as rector of St. Margaret's Church, Westminster Parish, Anne Arundel County from 1734 to 1734/35, of All Hallow's Parish, Anne Arundel County from 1734/35 to 1737, of Christ Church, Calvert County from 1737 to 1742, and of Port Tobacco Parish, Charles County from 1742 to death. On April 25, 1735 Commissary Jacob Henderson, who was charged with superintending the conduct of the clergy, wrote to the bishop of London that Chase was a man of "much levity, no learning, and supposed to be a free thinker, or deist. He gives himself great liberties in ridiculing religion and that set of people highly caress and admire him." Richard Chase was the son of Samuel Chase, freeman of London, England, and a member of the Honorable Company of Tylers and Brickmakers and the owner of considerable property in Westminster and Maidenhead, England. MOTHER: Margaret Frances, daughter of Jeremiah Townley, of London, England, a merchant. BROTHER: Richard (?–1757), a lawyer. FIRST COUSIN: *Samuel Chase* (1741–1811). NEPHEW: *Jeremiah Townly Chase* (1748–1828). MARRIED Judith (?–1790), daughter of William Dent (1706–1757) and wife Anne Warren; granddaughter of *Thomas Dent* (1685–1725). Her brothers were *Warren Dent* (?–1794); George, who married first, Rose Townshend Knox (?–1794), and second, in 1796 Elizabeth Harrison Knox. Her sisters were Eleanor, who married *John Jordan* (?–1763); Mary, who married Rev. William Dowie (Bowie?); Ann, who married Samuel Briscoe; Grace, who married Robert Harrison; and Rebecca, who married *William Harrison* (?–1789). Her niece was Mary Hanson Briscoe, who married *Michael Jenifer Stone* (1747–1812). CHILDREN. Died without progeny. PRIVATE CAREER. EDUCATION: literate. RELIGIOUS AFFILIATION: Protestant. SOCIAL STATUS AND ACTIVITIES: Gent., by 1749; Esq., at death. OCCUPATIONAL PROFILE: a lawyer, admitted to the following courts: Provincial Court in October 1743; Charles County by June 1744; Prince George's County in March 1746; Court of Chancery by December 1753. PUBLIC CAREER. LEGISLATIVE SERVICE: Lower House, St. Mary's County, 1754–1755 (Laws 1, 2; died before the 3rd session). LOCAL OFFICES: clerk and cryer, Court of Oyer and Terminer and Gaol Delivery, Charles County, commissioned 1743. WEALTH DURING LIFETIME. LAND AT FIRST ELECTION: 278 acres in Charles County (all by purchase). WEALTH AT DEATH. DIED: on April 2, 1755, as a result of poisoning at a gentleman's house while on a journey for the Baltimore Assizes. On January 10, 1755 William Stratton, one of Chase's servants, gave his master some boiled milk and bread that had been mixed with poisonous herbs and powders. Chase immediately became ill and died on April 2. Stratton and two slaves were convicted of the crime and sentenced to death. Another slave was convicted of conspiring to murder Chase. PERSONAL PROPERTY: TEV, £2,897.11.3 sterling, plus £1,489.0.6 current money and 88,660 pounds of tobacco (including 5 slaves, 1 servant, 339 oz. 18 dwt. 12 gr. plate, and books); FB, £2,706.7.11 sterling, plus £1,373.17.2 current money and 33,989 pounds of tobacco. LAND: 278 acres in Charles County. ADDITIONAL COMMENTS: his principal heirs were his wife Judith and his brother Richard.

CHASE, JEREMIAH TOWNLY (TOWNLEY) (1748–1828). BORN: on May 23, 1748, in St. Paul's

Parish, Baltimore County; only son. NATIVE: third generation. RESIDED: in Annapolis, Anne Arundel County, at least 1767–ca. 1773; Baltimore County, ca. 1773–1779; Annapolis, 1779 until death. FAMILY BACKGROUND. FATHER: Richard Chase, Gent. (?–1757), son of Rev. Richard Chase (?–ca. 1742), chaplain to *Charles Calvert, 5th Lord Baltimore* (1699–1751), rector of Westminster Parish and All Hallow's Parish in Anne Arundel County and Christ Church in Calvert County; immigrated in 1734. GUARDIAN: his great-uncle Rev. Thomas Chase (1700–1779), rector of St. Paul's Parish, Baltimore County, from 1745 to 1779. MOTHER: Catherine (?–by 1757). UNCLE: *Jeremiah Chase* (?–1755). SISTER: Frances Hatton, who married Richard Moale (1739–1786), son of *John Moale* (?–1740). OTHER KINSHIP: his second cousin was *Samuel Chase* (1741–1811). MARRIED on June 24, 1779, Hester (?–1823), daughter of Thomas Baldwin, Gent., of Anne Arundel County, and wife Agnes. Her sisters were Anne, who married *Samuel Chase* (1741–1811); Rebecca. CHILDREN. SON: Richard Moale (?–ca. 1840), who married Mary Marriott (?–1836). DAUGHTERS: Frances Townly (ca. 1780–1857), who married Richard Loockerman (ca. 1782–1834); Hester Ann (1791–1875); Matilda (ca. 1786–1829), who married Thomas Chase (1774–1826), son of *Samuel Chase* (1741–1811); and Catherine, who married Richard Crabb. PRIVATE CAREER. EDUCATION: his early education was provided by his guardian Rev. Thomas Chase; probably studied law in Annapolis under *Samuel Chase* (1741–1811). RELIGIOUS AFFILIATION: Anglican. SOCIAL STATUS AND ACTIVITIES: Esq., by 1788; Hon., by 1798. OCCUPATIONAL PROFILE: lawyer, admitted to the Anne Arundel County Court in August 1771; prosecutor, Annapolis Mayor's Court, 1772–1773. Appeared as an attorney in Anne Arundel County Court over 500 times between 1772 and 1773, and 1783 and 1791 (no appearances between 1773 and 1783), with the bulk of his cases occurring between 1783 and 1789; his most active year was 1787. He frequently appeared for *Samuel Chase* (1741–1811) in the 1780s. PUBLIC CAREER. LEGISLATIVE SERVICE: Conventions, Baltimore County, 4th 1775, 5th, 1775, 6th–8th, 1775–1776, Baltimore Town, 9th, 1776; Lower House, Baltimore Town, 1777 (Elections 1, 2; Grievances 1; Laws to Expire 1; Manufactories 1), 1777–1778 (Elections 1, 2; Laws to Expire 1), 1778–1779 (Manufactories 1; Elections 2; Tax Commissioners 3), Anne Arundel County, 1788. OTHER STATE OFFICES: Executive Council, 1779–1780, 1780–1781, 1781–1782, 1782–1783, 1783 (resigned on

December 12, 1783), 1785–1786, 1786–1787, 1787–1788; Constitution Ratification Convention, Anne Arundel County, 1788; judge, General Court, 1789–1805; chief judge, Third Judicial District and of the Court of Appeals, 1806–1826 (resigned). LOCAL OFFICES: Committee of Correspondence, Baltimore County, elected 1774; Committee of Observation, Baltimore Town, elected 1774; common councilman, Annapolis, elected 1781; alderman, Annapolis, 1781–1791; mayor, Annapolis, 1783–1784; Maryland Senate elector, Anne Arundel County, elected 1796. OUT OF STATE SERVICE: delegate, Continental Congress, 1783–1784 (elected on December 9, 1783, to fill vacancy). STANDS ON PUBLIC/PRIVATE ISSUES: opposed ratification of the U.S. Constitution, 1788. WEALTH DURING LIFETIME. PERSONAL PROPERTY: assessed value £425.0.0, including 8 slaves and 132 oz. plate, 1783; assessed value of Annapolis property $2,335.00, including 8 slaves and 500 oz. plate, 1819, and $1,760.00, including 8 slaves and 500 oz. plate, 1821. He was awarded £576.14.1 current money by the Chancery Court as his father's share of the estate of *Jeremiah Chase* (?–1755), 1787. ADDITIONAL COMMENTS: he held several mortgages, usually on land, as security for bonds signed by *Samuel Chase* (1741–1811), *Luther Martin* (1744–1826), and others. LAND AT FIRST ELECTION: probably none. SIGNIFICANT CHANGES IN LAND BETWEEN FIRST ELECTION AND DEATH: In 1778 Chase began purchasing small tracts of land in or adjacent to Baltimore Town, which would later be subdivided into lots and sold separately. His major holdings were on Whetstone Point; some of this land was confiscated British property that Chase bought in 1781, while other portions of it were obtained by mortgage foreclosures and later by purchase. He bought most of the land in Baltimore County and Baltimore Town before 1790 and sold or leased it by 1815. In the mid-1820s Chase was again active in Baltimore County land transactions, but he sold most of the acreage before his death. The majority of Chase's real property was located in Anne Arundel County, principally on Annapolis Neck and in the northwestern part of the county, which is now Howard County. With *Samuel Chase* (1741–1811), he purchased over 1,600 acres in the latter area, of which 580 acres were patented in 1786. The following year J. T. Chase bought Samuel Chase's interest in this tract. He repatented most of the acreage in 1800, and much of it was sold by 1825. In 1798 Chase began buying land on Annapolis Neck with a 690-acre purchase from *Benjamin Ogle* (1748/49–1809). Over the next three decades he enlarged his holdings there to almost 1,100 acres, 795 acres of which he patented into "Bellemont" in 1817. In 1815 he bought 542 acres in Anne Arundel County as a gift for his daughter Catherine Crabb and her husband. The Crabbs deeded 235 acres of this property back to Chase in 1824. From at least 1789 until his death, Chase lived in the "elegant" house of *Matthias Hammond* (1740–1786) in Annapolis. He rented the house and its 4 accompanying lots until he purchased the property in 1811. Chase also bought 2 Annapolis lots in 1795 and had a one-third interest in a 15-acre tract within that city, 1815–1822. WEALTH AT DEATH. DIED: on May 11, 1828, in Annapolis. PERSONAL PROPERTY: TEV, $20,754.19 current money (including 9 slaves, 530 oz. plate, 144 law titles and other books at his Annapolis residence, and 38 shares valued at $100 per share in the Bank of Columbia); FB, $1,468.92, insufficient to pay debts and legacies. LAND: at least 21 acres in Baltimore County and 12 lots on Whetstone Point, Baltimore City, plus a one-third interest in 2 lots in Baltimore City. Probably 1,700 acres in Anne Arundel County, plus at least 6 lots in Annapolis, plus a mortgage on 1,000 acres in Caroline County owned by Richard Loockerman.

CHASE, SAMUEL (1741–1811). BORN: on April 17, 1741, at his mother's home near Princess Anne, Somerset County; eldest son. NATIVE: second generation. RESIDED: in Baltimore County, 1745–1759; Annapolis, 1759–ca. 1786; as state agent for the recovery of Maryland bank stock, Chase lived in London, England, from September 1783 until August 1784; in Baltimore City in his house at the corner of Eutaw and Lexington streets, ca. 1786 until death. FAMILY BACKGROUND. FATHER: Rev. Thomas Chase (ca. 1703–1779), born in England, educated at St. John's and Sidney Sussex colleges, Cambridge University. Immigrated to the West Indies to practice medicine. Returned to England and was ordained as an Anglican priest in February 1739. Immigrated in 1739 to become rector of Somerset Parish, Somerset County, from May 1739 to February 1744/45. Rector of St. Paul's Parish, Baltimore County, from 1745 to 1779. MOTHER: Matilda (?–by 1744), daughter of Thomas Walker (?–1744), of Somerset County, a planter and innkeeper, and wife Sarah Maddox. STEPMOTHER: Ann (?–1772), daughter of Thomas Birch, chirurgeon and male midwife of England. HALF BROTHERS: Thomas (ca. 1765–1773); George; Russell Birch; and Richard. HALF SISTERS: Anne; Elizabeth. FIRST COUSIN: *Jeremiah Chase* (?–1755). OTHER KINSHIP: his second cousin was *Jeremiah Townly Chase* (1748–1828). MARRIED first, on May 2, 1762, Ann (?–1776), daughter of Thomas Baldwin, Gent., (?–1762), of Anne Arundel County, who died soon after his imprisonment for debt, and wife Agnes. Her sisters were Hester (?–1823), who married *Jeremiah Townly Chase* (1748–1828); Rebecca. MARRIED second, in 1784 Hannah Kitty Giles (?–1848). CHILDREN. SONS: Thomas (1764–1765); Samuel (1773–1841); and Thomas (1774–1826), who married in 1816 Matilda (ca. 1786–1829), daughter of *Jeremiah Townly Chase* (1748–1828). DAUGHTERS: Matilda (1763–?), who married in 1787 Henry Ridgely (1753–1811), lawyer and judge; Nancy (1768–1770); Fanny (1770–1771); Ann (Nancy) (1771–1852); Elizabeth (after 1784–?), who married first, George Dugan, and second, (first name unknown) Cole; and Mary (after 1784–?), who married in 1808 William B. Barney. ADDITIONAL COMMENTS: Chase was guardian to his young half brothers and half sisters after his father's death. His move to Baltimore County in 1786 was said to have been caused by the need for greater income to support his family. PRIVATE CAREER. EDUCATION: received a classical education from his father; studied law in Annapolis under *John Hall* (1729–1797). RELIGIOUS AFFILIATION: Anglican, St. Anne's Parish, Anne Arundel County and St. Paul's Parish, Baltimore County. Delegate to diocesan convention, 1794, 1801. SOCIAL STATUS AND ACTIVITIES: Esq., 1769; Gent., 1779; member of the Forensic Club, Annapolis, 1761, expelled in 1762 for "extremely irregular and indecent" behavior. ADDITIONAL COMMENTS: in 1790 *Alexander Contee Hanson* (1749–1806) said "that vile as Chase has been held by most of the better kind of his fellow citizens, he has been the mover of almost every thing this state has to boast of—Strange, inconsistent man!" Late in life, Chase wrote "A Course of Law and Literary Study," a five-year course of training for his law students. OCCUPATIONAL PROFILE: lawyer, admitted to the following courts: Annapolis Mayor's Court in 1761; Anne Arundel, Baltimore, Frederick, and Prince George's counties in 1763; Provincial Court in 1765; Chancery Court by 1768; Charles County in 1772. Chase was involved with *Allen Quynn* (ca. 1726–1803) and others in a saltworks on the West River, Anne Arundel County, 1777–1778. Quynn was a close associate with Chase in several ventures and handled Chase's business affairs when he was away from Annapolis in the 1770s and 1780s. Partner with *Thomas Dorsey* (?–1790) in the mercantile firm of John Dorsey & Co. from May 1778 until ca. December 1780. By 1789 the other partners in the company were insolvent; the partnership owed £42,000 when dissolved and had assets of less than £5,000. In partnership with *John Sterett* (1750/51–1787), *Charles Ridgely* (1733–1790), *Benjamin Nicholson* (?–1792), *Darby Lux* (?–1795), and others in the purchase and operation of the Nottingham Ironworks Company, bought as confiscated property, 1782. Later Chase owned a wharf on the west side of Jones Falls, Baltimore City, and had a lumberyard built on the wharf in 1806 that dealt mainly in barrel staves. He had a "mud machine" built in 1809, and a device described as a "mud and pile driving machine with equipment" was valued at $750.00 in his inventory at death. PUBLIC CAREER. LEGISLATIVE SERVICE: Lower House, Annapolis, 1765–1766 (Grievances 2, 3; Public Offices 2, 3; Laws to Expire 2, 3), Anne Arundel County, 1768–1770 (Grievances 2, 3; Public Offices 1; Laws to Expire 3, 4), 1771 (Elections; Grievances; Laws to Expire), 1773–1774 (Elections 1, Cv; Laws to Expire 1, Cv, 3); Conventions, Anne Arundel County, 1st, 1774, 2nd–3rd, 1774, 4th, 1775, 5th, 1775, 6th–8th, 1775–1776 (did not attend the 7th Convention), 9th, 1776 (Elections; resigned on August 27, 1776, because the opinions of his constituents concerning the establishment of a state government were "incompatible with good government and the public peace and happiness" ; subsequently he was reelected and seated); Lower House, Annapolis, 1777, 1777 (Grievances 1; resigned from the 1777–1778 Assembly on November 22, 1777), 1779 (elected to the 3rd session of the 1778–1779 Assembly to fill vacancy; Elections 3), 1779–1780 (Elections 1–3), 1780–1781, 1781–1782, 1782–1783 (Grievances 1, 2; Manufactories 2), 1783 (elected, but did not attend), 1784, 1785 (Grievances; Laws to Expire), Anne Arundel County, 1786–1787 (Grievances 2), Baltimore Town, 1787–1788; Senate, Western Shore, Term of 1791–1796: 1791 (did not serve; probably declined). OTHER PROVINCIAL/STATE OFFICES: His long public career included the following positions: Provincial Committee of Correspondence, in office 1773–1775; 1st Council of Safety, Western Shore, 1775; agent for the recovery of Maryland bank stock from England, appointed 1783; Potomac River Commission, in office 1784–1785; Constitution Ratification Convention, Anne Arundel County, 1788; judge, General Court, 1791–1796 (resigned). LOCAL OFFICES: prosecutor, Mayor's Court, Annapolis, appointed 1761; justice, Anne Arundel County, commissioned 1764 (quorum) and 1779 ("desires to be left out"); common councilman,

Annapolis, elected 1766; St. Anne's Parish Vestry, Anne Arundel County, in office 1770–1773, 1774, and 1779; alderman, Annapolis, 1773–1779; recorder, Annapolis, in office ca. 1773–1786; churchwarden, St. Anne's Parish, Anne Arundel County, 1774–1775; Committee of Observation, Annapolis and Anne Arundel County, elected 1774 and 1775; Committee of Correspondence, Annapolis and Anne Arundel County, elected 1774; justice, Orphans' Court, Anne Arundel County, commissioned 1779; Maryland Senate elector, Anne Arundel County, elected 1786; chief justice, Court of Oyer and Terminer and Gaol Delivery, Baltimore Town, 1788–1789 (resigned), 1792–at least 1794; commissioner, Baltimore Town, 1788–1796. OUT OF STATE SERVICE: delegate, Continental Congress, 1774–1778 (elected in June 1774, December 1774, April 1775, August 1775, May 1776, July 1776, November 1776, February 1777, and December 1777), 1781 (elected in November 1781, but did not attend; resigned on May 31, 1782), 1783 (elected in November 1783, but did not attend), 1784 (elected in December 1784, but did not attend). Journeyed to Canada with *Charles Carroll of Carrollton* (1737–1832), Benjamin Franklin, and Rev. John Carroll on a congressional mission to enlist Canadian support for the revolt against Great Britain, 1776. Associate justice, U.S. Supreme Court, 1796–1811. Chase was impeached by the House of Representatives in 1804 for his supposedly improper judicial behavior during the Fries and Callender trials in 1800 and while instructing a grand jury in New Castle, Delaware, in 1800, and for his partisan remarks in his capacity as associate justice before a Baltimore grand jury in 1803. He was acquitted by the Senate on March 1, 1805. Among Chase's defense lawyers were Robert Goodloe Harper, Philip Barton Key, and *Luther Martin* (1744–1826). The defense argued that any action which was not indictable was also not impeachable. Of the eight articles of impeachment Chase was judged guilty on three by only a two vote majority in each case. Chase's impeachment is thought by some historians to have been the opening move in a Republican attempt to purge the Supreme Court of Federalists. STANDS ON PUBLIC/PRIVATE ISSUES: Chase took a leading role against the Annapolis government in a despute over alleged violations of the city charter and the government's denial of the citizens' rights, 1763. Admitted leader of opposition to the Stamp Act, 1765. Opposed the poll tax for the support of the Anglican clergy in Maryland, 1772–1774. Joined *Baker Johnson* (1747–1811), *William Paca* (1740–1799), and *Thomas*

Johnson (1732–1819) in the successful defense of *Joseph Hanson Harrison* (?–1785) in a test case concerning the Fee Bill, 1773. Supported *Charles Carroll of Carrollton* (1737–1832) in his newspaper debate with *Daniel Dulany, Jr.* (1722–1797), 1773. Signer of the Declaration of Independence, August 2, 1776. Opposed ratification of the Federal Constitution, 1788. WEALTH DURING LIFETIME. PERSONAL PROPERTY: received a £125.0.0 legacy from his grandfather, 1770. Property in Annapolis valued at £969.13.4, including 5 slaves and 268 oz. plate, 1783. In 1789 he declared himself privately indebted for £2,000, even after having mortgaged all of his personal property; his assets were "good debts," estimated at about £1,200.0.0, plus "some fees"; at that time he agreed to convey to *Thomas Dorsey* (?–1790) £600 current money, plus £3,400 worth of property, as his share of the debts of John Dorsey & Co. Received £643.15.0 current money, plus costs as his commission as agent for the recovery of Maryland's bank stock in England, 1811 (this was about one-half the amount he had requested). ANNUAL INCOME: lawyer's fees estimated at ca. £374.0.0, 1765. LAND AT FIRST ELECTION: 2,886 acres in Anne Arundel, Frederick, and Dorchester counties (1,318 acres by patent; 1,568 acres by purchase, 1763–1765), plus one-half interest in 5,449 acres in Frederick County by patents with *Thomas Johnson* (1732–1819) in 1764 and one-half interest in 1,660 acres in Frederick County by patent with *William Paca* (1740–1799) in 1764. Most of this land was acquired by speculating in proclamation warrants and by buying land from people unable to pay quitrents on their patents. SIGNIFICANT CHANGES IN LAND BETWEEN FIRST ELECTION AND DEATH: continued to speculate, especially on land in Frederick County, by patents and purchases until 1776, obtaining an additional 6,000 acres by 1774. In 1769 sold *William Paca* (1740–1799) his share of the land held with him, plus some of the land patented with *Thomas Johnson* (1732–1819). Bought a lot in Annapolis in 1769, and began to build an impressive brick house, but was overextended and forced to sell the lot and unfinished house to *Edward Lloyd* (1744–1796) in 1771. Sold 559 acres in Dorchester County, and about 500 acres in Frederick County, 1771. Sold additional land in Frederick County, including more of the land patented with *Thomas Johnson* (1732–1819) in 1779. Invested heavily in acreage in Anne Arundel County with *Jeremiah Townly Chase* (1748–1828) in 1780, and began buying confiscated British property with notes secured by *Jeremiah Townly Chase* (1748–1828)

and *Allen Quynn* (ca. 1726–1803) in 1781. By the mid-1780s Chase was in severe financial difficulties and had to mortgage the confiscated British property, plus 3,500 additional acres of land in Anne Arundel County to *Jeremiah Townly Chase* (1748–1828) and *Allen Quynn* (ca. 1726–1803). He sold over 1,100 acres in Anne Arundel County to pay a debt owed to *John Beale Bordley* (1726/27–1804); sold his share of the land bought with *Jeremiah Townly Chase* (1748–1828) to pay debts owed to him; and conveyed over 500 acres in Anne Arundel County to pay debts owed *Allen Quynn* (ca. 1726–1803), and to secure further credit from him. Upon a petition from Chase in 1787, the state agreed to void his purchase of the confiscated British property, and in 1795 *Jeremiah Townly Chase* (1748–1828) and *Allen Quynn* (ca. 1726–1803) were able to release the mortgage. During the 1780s while he was selling land in other areas, Chase was acquiring land in Baltimore Town, and for the next ten years he continued to sell land in Frederick County while concentrating on the development of his holdings in Baltimore Town. He sold at least 10 lots and leased at least 23 others between 1801 and 1810. Shortly before his death, Chase conveyed at least 15 lots in Baltimore City to his sons and 21 acres to *Jeremiah Townly Chase* (1748–1828). WEALTH AT DEATH. DIED: on June 19, 1811, in Washington, D.C.; buried at Old St. Paul's Cemetery, Baltimore City. PERSONAL PROPERTY: TEV, $14,866.01 current money (including 15 slaves, 1 share in Washington Tontine, plus leases held on 26 acres on Whetstone Point valued at $80.00 and 5 acres in Baltimore City valued at $4,620.00); FB, estate overpaid $1,740.62 with additional debts filed later in Chancery Court litigation. LAND: 1 lot and 2.75 acres, including "Chase's Wharf," and 6 acres on Whetstone Point, Baltimore City, plus ground rent on at least 10 lots in Baltimore City and possibly as much as 2,500 acres in Anne Arundel, Baltimore, and Frederick counties. ADDITIONAL COMMENTS: income at time of death included $1,177.00 per year from ground rents, plus his $769.29 salary from the U.S. government.

CHESELDYNE, KENELM (1640–1708). BORN: in 1640 at Brauston Manor, Lincolnshire, England; second son. IMMIGRATED: in 1669 as a free adult. RESIDED: on the Eastern Shore; St. Mary's County, by 1677. FAMILY BACKGROUND. FATHER: Kenelm Cheseldyne (1603–1677), vicar of Blaxham, of Lincolnshire, England. MOTHER: Grace Dryden. MARRIED first, in 1669 Bridget Faulkner. MARRIED second, by 1677 Mary, daughter of

Thomas Gerard (1608–1673). Her brothers were Thomas (?–1686); Justinian (?–1688); and John. Her sisters were Susannah, who married first, *Robert Slye* (ca. 1628–1670/71), and second, *John Coode* (ca. 1648–1708/9); Frances; Temperance; and Elizabeth, who married first, *Nehemiah Blakiston* (?–1693), second, Ralph Rymer, and third, *Joshua Guibert* (?–1713). CHILDREN. SONS: Kenelm Cheseldyne (1683–1719), who married Mary Phippard. DAUGHTERS: Mary (1678–?), who married first, *James Hay* (?–by 1717/18), and second, George Fobes; Susannah (1680–1730), who married *Thomas Trueman Greenfield* (1682–1733); and Dryden (1687–1760), who married first, *Henry Peregrine Jowles* (1681–1720), and second, John Fobes. PRIVATE CAREER. EDUCATION: literate; extensive legal training. RELIGIOUS AFFILIATION: Anglican. SOCIAL STATUS AND ACTIVITIES: Gent. on arrival; one of the leading attorneys in Maryland; his second marriage brought him into a prominent, but controversial, family. OCCUPATIONAL PROFILE: practiced law in England before emigration; a lawyer, admitted to the following courts: Provincial Court in 1670; Court of Chancery in the 1670s. Planter. PUBLIC CAREER. LEGISLATIVE SERVICE: Lower House, St. Mary's City, 1676–1682 (Accounts 2; Security and Defense 2; Laws 2), 1686–1688 (speaker 2), Associators' Convention, 1689–1690 (speaker 1, 2; went to England before the 3rd session); Lower House, St. Mary's County, 1692–1693 (speaker 1, 2), 1694–1697 (speaker 5–8), 1701–1704 (Laws 1, 2, chairman 2); Upper House, 1704–1707, 1708A. OTHER PROVINCIAL OFFICES: attorney general, 1676–1681; agent to England, 1690–1692; commissary general, 1693–1699 (dismissed in 1697 for drunkenness and negligence, but continued to serve); Council, 1704–1708; justice, Provincial Court, 1708. LOCAL OFFICES: recorder, St. Mary's City, 1685–1690; justice, St. Mary's County, 1689–1690, 1692–1694, 1694/95–1697, 1698–1704 (quorum; president, 1694/95–1697, 1698–1704); William and Mary Parish Vestry, St. Mary's County, 1693–1696. STANDS ON PUBLIC/PRIVATE ISSUES: his relationship with *John Coode* (ca. 1648–1708/9) probably led to proprietary disfavor and loss of the attorney general's office in 1681; he became an opponent of the proprietary establishment and a leader in the revolution of 1689; represented the Protestant Associators' government before the colonial authorities in England, 1690–1691. WEALTH DURING LIFETIME. LAND AT FIRST ELECTION: had patented at least 1,334 acres; with his second wife's land, which included 3 plantations, he had over 3,800 acres. WEALTH AT

DEATH. DIED: will probated on December 18, 1708. PERSONAL PROPERTY: TEV, £259.9.6 sterling (including 12 slaves and law books). LAND: at least 683 acres, excluding his wife's inheritance.

CHESELDYNE, KENELM, (1683–1719). BORN: in 1683 in St. Mary's County; only son. NATIVE: second generation. RESIDED: in St. Mary's County. FAMILY BACKGROUND. FATHER: *Kenelm Cheseldyne* (1640–1708). MOTHER: Mary, daughter of *Thomas Gerard* (1608–1673). UNCLES: *Nehemiah Blakiston* (?–1693); *John Coode* (ca. 1648–1708/9); *Robert Slye* (ca. 1628–1670/71); and *Joshua Guibert* (?–1713). SISTERS: Mary (1678–?), who married first, *James Hay* (?–by 1717/18), and second, George Fobes; Susannah (1680–1730), who married *Thomas Trueman Greenfield* (1682–1733); and Dryden (1687–1760), who married first, *Henry Peregrine Jowles* (1681–1720), and second, John Fobes. MARRIED Mary, probably the widow of William Phippard; daughter of John Brown. She subsequently married Hugh Collins. CHILDREN. SONS: Kenelm; Kalius; and Cyrenius. PRIVATE CAREER. EDUCATION: literate. RELIGIOUS AFFILIATION: Anglican. SOCIAL STATUS AND ACTIVITIES: third generation burgess through his maternal grandfather; held no office after 1715 when he was charged with "incontinency," cohabiting with a lewd woman, Mary Phippard, whom he married sometime thereafter; his sons held no office. OCCUPATIONAL PROFILE: planter. PUBLIC CAREER. LEGISLATIVE SERVICE: Lower House, St. Mary's County, 1712–1714. LOCAL OFFICE: sheriff, St. Mary's County, 1709–1711. WEALTH DURING LIFETIME. LAND AT FIRST ELECTION: over 2,500 acres. WEALTH AT DEATH. DIED: will probated on May 29, 1719. PERSONAL PROPERTY: TEV, £972.7.1 (including 8 slaves); FB, £465.2.9. LAND: over 2,500 acres.

CHESLEY, ROBERT (?–1768). RESIDED: at "Vineyard," St. Mary's County. FAMILY BACKGROUND. BROTHERS: probably John, Esq. (?–1767), of St. Mary's County, a justice of St. Mary's County from 1727 to 1764; probably Thomas (?–1761). MARRIED by 1735 Ann, daughter of *Thomas Waughop* (?–1735). CHILDREN. SONS: Robert; John. DAUGHTERS: Susannah; Ann; Mary; and Elizabeth. PRIVATE CAREER. EDUCATION: literate. RELIGIOUS AFFILIATION: Protestant. SOCIAL STATUS AND ACTIVITIES: Gent., 1768; Esq., 1768. OCCUPATIONAL PROFILE: probably a planter. PUBLIC CAREER. LEGISLATIVE SERVICE: Lower House, St. Mary's County, 1742–1744. LOCAL OFFICES: justice, St. Mary's County, 1739–

1747, 1752–at least 1761 (quorum, 1753–at least 1761); sheriff, St. Mary's County, 1748–1751; justice, Court of Oyer and Terminer and Gaol Delivery, St. Mary's County, commissioned 1755 and 1761. MILITARY SERVICE: captain, by 1763. WEALTH DURING LIFETIME. LAND AT FIRST ELECTION: 523 acres in St. Mary's County, 1753, plus 2 lots in Leonardtown, St. Mary's County (probably all by purchase). SIGNIFICANT CHANGES IN LAND BETWEEN FIRST ELECTION AND DEATH: purchased 365 additional acres in St. Mary's County, 1759–1765; sold 130 acres in St. Mary's County in 1766. WEALTH AT DEATH. DIED: will probated on March 11, 1768, in St. Mary's County. PERSONAL PROPERTY: TEV, £3,433.6.7 current money (including 35 slaves, 1 servant, plate, and books); FB, estate overpaid £13.13.8. LAND: 758 acres in St. Mary's County, plus 2 lots in Leonardtown, St. Mary's County.

CHEW, SAMUEL (ca. 1630–1676/77). BORN: in 1630 in Virginia. IMMIGRATED: by 1659 as a free adult with his wife from Virginia. RESIDED: in Anne Arundel County. FAMILY BACKGROUND. FATHER: John Chew (?–by 1688), who immigrated to Virginia in 1621 or 1622 with his wife and three servants, and who became a prosperous merchant. He served as a member of the Virginia House of Burgesses, 1623–1624, 1627, 1642–1643, 1644. MOTHER: Sarah. BROTHER: Joseph. MARRIED in 1658 Ann, daughter of William Ayres, of Nansemond County, Virginia. CHILDREN. SONS: Samuel (ca. 1660–1718), a justice of Anne Arundel County in 1685, who married first in 1682 Anne (?–1702), and second, in 1704 Elizabeth (?–1709/10), widow of William Coale and daughter of *Thomas Thurston* (ca. 1622–1693); Joseph (1662/63–1704/5), who married first, (name unknown), and second, Elizabeth, daughter of Henry Hanslap; Nathaniel; William (?–1709/10); Benjamin (1671–1700), who married in 1692 Elizabeth Benson; John (?–1696/97); and Caleb (?–1688). DAUGHTERS: Sarah (?–1740), who married after 1676 Edward Burgess, son of *William Burgess* (ca. 1622–1686/87); and Anne (?–1699/1700). PRIVATE CAREER. EDUCATION: literate. RELIGIOUS AFFILIATION: Quaker, perhaps convinced by George Fox. SOCIAL STATUS AND ACTIVITIES: his father was a prominent merchant and officeholder in Virginia; Samuel became a leader of the Quaker community in Maryland. OCCUPATIONAL PROFILE: merchant; planter. PUBLIC CAREER. LEGISLATIVE SERVICE: Lower House, Anne Arundel County, 1661; Upper House, 1671–1674/75 (Accounts 1), 1676 (died before the 2nd session).

OTHER PROVINCIAL OFFICES: Council, 1669–1676/77; justice, Provincial Court, 1669–1676/77. LOCAL OFFICES: sheriff, Anne Arundel County, 1663–1664; justice, Anne Arundel County, 1665–1669 (quorum, 1668–1669). MILITARY SERVICE: colonel, 1675–1676/77. WEALTH DURING LIFETIME. LAND AT FIRST ELECTION: over 1,000 acres. WEALTH AT DEATH. DIED: on March 15, 1676/77. LAND: over 2,000 acres.

CHEW, SAMUEL (by 1734–1786). BORN: between ca. 1727 and 1734; eldest son. NATIVE: sixth generation. RESIDED: in Herring Bay, Anne Arundel County; on Kent Island, Queen Anne's County, after 1785. FAMILY BACKGROUND. FATHER: Samuel Chew (ca. 1704–1736/37). STEPFATHER: *Daniel Dulany* (1685–1753). MOTHER: Henrietta Maria (?–1765), daughter of *Philemon Lloyd* (ca. 1674–1732/33). BROTHERS: Philemon (?–1770); Bennett (?–1793), who married in 1763 Anna Maria, daughter of *Edward Tilghman* (1713–1786). HALF BROTHERS: Lloyd Dulany (1742–ca. 1782); Richard Dulany (?–died in infancy). STEPBROTHERS: *Daniel Dulany, Jr.* (1722–1797); *Walter Dulany* (?–1773); and Dennis Dulany (1730–1779). SISTERS: Henrietta Maria (1731–1762), who married *Edward Dorsey* (1718–1760); Margaret (?–1773), who married *John Beale Bordley* (1726/27–1804); Ann Mary (1736–1774), who married in 1763 *William Paca* (1740–1799). STEPSISTERS: Rebecca Dulany, who married first, James Paul Heath (?–1746), and second, William Hedges; Rachel Dulany, who married first, William Knight, and second, Rev. Henry Addison; Margaret Dulany, who married first, Dr. *Alexander Hamilton* (1712–1756), and second, *William Murdock* (?–1769); and Mary Dulany. STEPNEPHEW: *James Heath* (?–1766). MARRIED by 1759 Elizabeth (1729–1807), widow of Richard Snowden, Jr. (?–1753), of Prince George's County; daughter of John Croley (Crowley) (?–1749), of Prince George's County, and wife Miriam (?–1767), who subsequently married (first name unknown) Richardson. CHILDREN. SONS: Samuel Lloyd (1756–1796), who married in 1777 Dorothy Harrison (1758–1791); John Croley (by 1767–by 1786). DAUGHTERS: Henrietta Maria (1759–1847), who married in 1775 *Benjamin Galloway* (1752–1831); Elizabeth (1765–?), who married in 1781 Peregrine Fitzhugh (1759–1810) and who died in New York; and Ann (after 1770–?), who died in New York. PRIVATE CAREER. RELIGIOUS AFFILIATION: Anglican; his wife was a Quaker. SOCIAL STATUS AND ACTIVITIES: Gent., 1759; Esq., 1779. OCCUPATIONAL PROFILE: planter. PUBLIC CA-

REER. LEGISLATIVE SERVICE: Conventions, Anne Arundel County, 1st, 1774, 2nd, 1774. LOCAL OFFICES: St. James' Parish Vestry, Anne Arundel County, in office 1755–1758, 1759–1761, 1763, 1770, and 1771; justice, Anne Arundel County, in office, 1757–1777 (quorum, 1762–1777). STANDS ON PUBLIC/PRIVATE ISSUES: Rev. Bennett Allen challenged Chew to a duel because Chew supported the Dulany family in opposing Allen's desire to hold both St. Anne's and St. James' parishes in 1767. Chew accepted, saying, "I am determined that only one of us shall live to tell the tale." Allen withdrew his challenge because of bad weather and the "informality" of the arrangements. WEALTH DURING LIFETIME. PERSONAL PROPERTY: assessed value £3,721.2.4, including 97 slaves and 196 oz. plate, Anne Arundel, Calvert, and Montgomery counties, 1783. LAND AT FIRST ELECTION: probably 8,975 acres in Anne Arundel, Calvert, and Frederick counties (900 acres in Anne Arundel County devised by his father; 1,410 acres in Anne Arundel and Calvert counties obtained from his brother Philemon in accordance with the terms of their mother's will, 1766; 3,159 acres in Frederick County obtained through marriage; ca. 3,332 acres in Frederick County, half of which was inherited from his father and half conveyed by his brother Philemon, 1766; 125 acres in Anne Arundel County by purchase). SIGNIFICANT CHANGES IN LAND BETWEEN FIRST ELECTION AND DEATH: gave each daughter a one-third interest in his 3,332 acres in Frederick County (by then Washington County), 1781–1782; his wife's land in Frederick County (by then Montgomery County) was reduced to 1,400 acres, partly because of the terms of her first husband's will, by 1783; bought 2,150 acres on Kent Island, Queen Anne's County in 1785; apparently mortgaged most of his land in Anne Arundel and Calvert counties to *Charles Carroll of Carrollton* (1737–1832) prior to his death. WEALTH AT DEATH. DIED: will probated on July 29, 1786, in Queen Anne's County. PERSONAL PROPERTY: TEV, £2,769.6.0 current money, plus $8,303.95 (including at least 66 slaves and 82 oz. plate); FB, £0.0.8, plus $638.11. His estate was not settled until 1811. LAND: probably 4,730 acres in Anne Arundel, Calvert, and Queen Anne's counties.

CHEW, SAMUEL (1737–1790). BORN: in 1737 in Anne Arundel County; eldest son. NATIVE: sixth generation. RESIDED: in Calvert County. FAMILY BACKGROUND. FATHER: Samuel Chew (1709–1749), who died in London, England. STEPFATHER: Richard Chew (1716–1769). MOTHER: Sarah

Loch (1721–1791), daughter of Dr. William Loch (?–1732) and his wife Sarah Harrison Lane. BROTHERS: John Lane, who married in 1787 Mary Wilson; William (1746–1801), who married Elizabeth, daughter of *Thomas Reynolds* (?–1778). HALF BROTHERS: Samuel (1755–1785); Richard; Philemon; and Locke. SISTER: Elizabeth, who married first, (first name unknown) Smith, and second, (first name unknown) Sprigg. HALF SISTERS: Sarah; Mary, who married first, *Alexander Hamilton Smith* (?–ca. 1785), and second, *William Lyles* (?–1790). MARRIED first, in 1763 Sarah (?–1763), daughter of *James Weems* (ca. 1707–1781) and his wife Sarah Parker Stoddert. Her half–uncle was *James John Mackall* (1717–1772). Her brothers were William Loch (?–1783); James; and *John Weems* (1737–1813). Her sisters were Susannah, who married Roger Wheeler (?–1763); Margaret (?–1783), who married first (first name unknown) Elzey, and second, *Joseph Sprigg* (1732–1800). Her first cousin was *John Weems* (1727–1794). Her niece was Sarah Wheeler (ca. 1754–ca. 1804), who married *William Allein* (ca. 1742–ca. 1802). MARRIED second, Priscilla, daughter of Rev. Samuel Clagett and wife Elizabeth Gantt. CHILDREN. SONS: Samuel (1763–1820), who died in Kentucky; John Hamilton (1771–1830); and Thomas John (?–by 1794). PRIVATE CAREER. EDUCATION: literate. RELIGIOUS AFFILIATION: Protestant; the Loch and Chew family backgrounds were strongly Quaker. OCCUPATIONAL PROFILE: planter. PUBLIC CAREER. LEGISLATIVE SERVICE: Convention, Calvert County, 5th, 1775; Lower House, Calvert County, 1777–1778 (elected to the 1st session to fill vacancy), 1778–1779 (Tax Commissioners 3), 1781–1782, 1782–1783 (Elections 2). LOCAL OFFICES: justice, Calvert County, 1761–1790 (quorum, 1769–1790); justice, Orphans' Court, Calvert County, 1777–at least 1789; commissioner of tax, Calvert County, 1777–1779. WEALTH DURING LIFETIME. PERSONAL PROPERTY: assessed value £1,252.0.0, including 38 slaves and 42 oz. plate, 1783. LAND AT FIRST ELECTION: 1,140.5 acres in Calvert County (1,006 acres inherited from his father in 1749). SIGNIFICANT CHANGES IN LAND BETWEEN FIRST ELECTION AND DEATH: owned 1,115 acres in Calvert County, plus 5 lots in Lower Marlboro, Calvert County, 1783. WEALTH AT DEATH. DIED: on February 20, 1790, Calvert County. LAND: probably 1,115 acres in Calvert County, plus 5 lots in Lower Marlboro, Calvert County.

CHILTON, CHARLES (?–1824). BORN: probably in St. Mary's County. NATIVE: at least second generation. RESIDED: in Harvey Hundred, St. Mary's County. FAMILY BACKGROUND. FATHER: Stephen Chilton (?–ca. 1773), of St. Mary's County. MOTHER: Ann. BROTHERS: Stephen (?–1776); George; Thomas; John; and William (?–by 1796). SISTERS: Ann, who married by 1770 (first name unknown) Leigh; Elizabeth, who married Dr. (first name unknown) Coleman, of Virginia. PRIVATE CAREER. EDUCATION: literate. RELIGIOUS AFFILIATION: Anglican, St. Andrew's Parish, St. Mary's County. SOCIAL STATUS AND ACTIVITIES: Esq. at death. OCCUPATIONAL PROFILE: probably a planter; owned two water mills by 1821. PUBLIC CAREER. LEGISLATIVE SERVICE: Lower House, St. Mary's County, 1788 (Claims). OTHER STATE OFFICES: Constitution Ratification Convention, St. Mary's County, 1788; associate justice, First District Court, appointed 1792 (did not qualify). LOCAL OFFICES: justice, St. Mary's County, appointed 1791 and 1792; St. Andrew's Parish Vestry, St. Mary's County, in office 1791–1793, 1796, 1806–1809, 1812, 1819–1824. STANDS ON PUBLIC/PRIVATE ISSUES: in his will he manumitted all of his slaves unless they were too old to support themselves. Several received money and equipment, and provision was made for the maintenance of those who could not become self-supporting. WEALTH DURING LIFETIME. PERSONAL PROPERTY: 6 slaves, 1790; assessed value £603.0.0, including 9 slaves and 3.5 oz. plate, 1793; 9 slaves, 20 oz. plate, and 2 water mills, 1821. LAND AT FIRST ELECTION: probably 513 acres in St. Mary's County. SIGNIFICANT CHANGES IN LAND BETWEEN FIRST ELECTION AND DEATH: purchased 686 acres, patented 103 acres, and sold 513 acres all in St. Mary's County by 1821. WEALTH AT DEATH. DIED: will probated on April 20, 1824, in St. Mary's County. PERSONAL PROPERTY: TEV, at least $2,279.38 (including 10 slaves and books). LAND: 790 acres in St. Mary's County.

CHRISTISON, WENLOCK (?–1679). IMMIGRATED: by 1670 as a free adult, probably from Barbados. RESIDED: in Talbot County. MARRIED first, Mary. MARRIED second, by 1672 Elizabeth (?–1697), widow of Robert Harwood; daughter of John Gary; stepdaughter of *Peter Sharpe* (?–1671/72). She subsequently married William Dixon. Her brother was *William Sharpe* (ca. 1655–1699). CHILDREN. STEPSONS: Samuel Harwood; Peter Harwood; and John Harwood. DAUGHTERS: Elizabeth (1673–?); Mary, who married John Dine. PRIVATE CAREER. EDUCATION: literate. RELIGIOUS AFFILIATION: Quaker; active in

missionary work in New England and Barbados in the 1660s. OCCUPATIONAL PROFILE: planter. PUBLIC CAREER. LEGISLATIVE SERVICE: Lower House, Talbot County, 1676–1678 (Accounts 2; Security and Defense 2; Laws 2; died before the 3rd session). WEALTH DURING LIFETIME. LAND AT FIRST ELECTION: over 300 acres (received grant of land from future Sharpe in-laws, 1670). WEALTH AT DEATH. DIED: will probated on May 20, 1679. LAND: over 300 acres.

CLAGETT, THOMAS (1677–1732). BORN: in 1677 in Calvert County; probably first son. NATIVE: second generation. RESIDED: in Calvert County; Mount Calvert Hundred, Prince George's County, by 1699. FAMILY BACKGROUND. FATHER: Thomas Clagett, probably the son of Edward Clagett and wife Margaret, who was the daughter of Sir Thomas Adams, mayor of London, England; immigrated from England by 1670, became a militia captain, owned over 2,000 acres of land, and opposed the revolution of 1689. MOTHER: Sarah Patterson, of London, England. BROTHER: Charles, who married Maudlin (1697–?), daughter of *Thomas Howe* (?–1720/21). MARRIED ca. 1700 Mary Keene, widow of Richard Hooper (?–1693). CHILDREN. SONS: Thomas (?–1738), justice of Prince George's County from 1733 to 1738, who married first, Ann Belt, and second, Ann Wheeler Fogg; Richard; Charles; and John (1713–1790), who married Sarah Magruder. DAUGHTERS: Elizabeth, who married (first name unknown) Prather; Sarah; Martha; Margaret; and Anne. PRIVATE CAREER. EDUCATION: literate. RELIGIOUS AFFILIATION: Protestant, probably an Anglican. OCCUPATIONAL PROFILE: planter. PUBLIC CAREER. LEGISLATIVE SERVICE: Lower House, Prince George's County, 1712 (resigned after the 1st session to become sheriff). LOCAL OFFICES: constable, Prince George's County, 1705–1706; justice, Prince George's County, 1706–1709, 1710–1713, 1716–1719; sheriff, Prince George's County, 1713–1716, 1719–1722. MILITARY SERVICE: captain, by 1709–1717. WEALTH DURING LIFETIME. LAND AT FIRST ELECTION: 500–800 acres (inherited 800 acres from his father). WEALTH AT DEATH. DIED: in 1732. PERSONAL PROPERTY: TEV, £502.9.7 (including 14 slaves); FB, £244.2.1. LAND: at least 1,670 acres.

CLAGETT, THOMAS (1740/41–1792). BORN: on February 12, 1740/41, in Prince George's Parish, Prince George's County; eldest son. NATIVE: fourth generation. RESIDED: in Piscataway, Prince George's County. FAMILY BACKGROUND. FATHER:

John Clagett (1713–1790), son of *Thomas Clagett* (1677–1732). MOTHER: Sarah, daughter of Capt. Alexander Magruder. BROTHERS: Alexander (1744–1821); Richard (1746–?); William (1748–1792), who married Harriet Sothoron; David (1749–?); Nathaniel (1751–1809); John (1752–?); Hezekiah (1754–1832); Horatio (1756–1815), of London, England; Walter (1763–?), who married Martha Williams; and Zadock. SISTERS: Mary (1742–?); Annie, who married John Chesley. MARRIED on October 11, 1768, Mary Meek (ca. 1746–1809), daughter of Enoch Margruder (?–1786) and wife Meek Wade. Mary Meek Clagett subsequently married *Thomas Duckett* (1744–1806). Her brother was Dennis. Her sisters were Nancy Coombs, who married (first name unknown) Burgess; Elioner, who married (first name unknown) Burgess; Sarah, who married (first name unknown) Lyles; and Ann, who married (first name unknown) Lowe. CHILDREN. SONS: Judson Magruder (1769–1800), who married Caroline Hesselius; Thomas (1773–?); Hector (1776–died young); Hector (1780–?); and Hannibal (1782–1809). DAUGHTERS: Mary (1771–1816), who married first, in 1789 Patrick McEldery, and second, Jacob Duckett; Elizabeth (1778–?), who married in 1794 Henry Addison; Sarah Magruder (1780–?), who married in 1800 Upton Bruce. PRIVATE CAREER. EDUCATION: literate. RELIGIOUS AFFILIATION: Anglican, Piscataway Parish, Prince George's County. SOCIAL STATUS AND ACTIVITIES: Gent., by 1779. OCCUPATIONAL PROFILE: merchant; had an accounting house in Piscataway, Prince George's County. PUBLIC CAREER. LEGISLATIVE SERVICE: Lower House, Prince George's County, 1780–1781 (Claims 1, 2). LOCAL OFFICES: justice, Prince George's County, 1773–1792 (chief justice, by 1791); justice, Orphans' Court, Prince George's County, 1777–1782 ("desires to be left out"); purchasing agent, Prince George's County, appointed 1778 and 1779; subscription officer, Continental Loan Office, Prince George's County, appointed 1779. WEALTH DURING LIFETIME. PERSONAL PROPERTY: 16 slaves, 1776; 40 slaves, 1790. LAND AT FIRST ELECTION: 500 acres in Prince George's County, plus 8 acres in Piscataway (all by personal acquisition), plus 308 acres in Prince George's County in his wife's name. SIGNIFICANT CHANGES IN LAND BETWEEN FIRST ELECTION AND DEATH: purchased 82 acres in Prince George's County in 1784 and ca. 300 acres in 1790 and 1791. Clagett acquired 914 acres in Prince George's County shortly before his death. WEALTH AT DEATH. DIED: on December 27, 1792, in Prince George's County. PERSONAL PROPERTY: TEV,

£3,627.6.2 current money (including at least 31 slaves, ca. 250 oz. plate, and 14 books); FB, £328.18.4. LAND: probably 1,766 acres in Prince George's County, plus lots in Piscataway, Prince George's County. IDENTIFICATION PROBLEMS. There are at least two other men by this name of age in 1780 in Prince George's County: Thomas Clagett, Sr. (?–ca. 1790), who was illiterate and died with an inventory valued at £702.0.0, and Thomas Clagett (1750–1790), son of Thomas Clagett, planter, who married Sarah White in 1785. Identification has been made on the basis of age, wealth, and political activity.

CLAIBORNE, WILLIAM (1600–ca. 1677). BORN: in 1600 in Crayford Parish, Kent, England; second son. IMMIGRATED: on Kent Island in 1627, but never settled permanently in Maryland. ADDITIONAL COMMENTS: brought three servants with him when he migrated to Virginia in 1621; he arrived in Virginia as a provincial officer and began acquisition of land in 1624; he led an expedition up the Chesapeake Bay in 1627 and established a trading base on Kent Island, which he actively developed in the next decade; he returned to England 1630–1631 and 1647–1650. FAMILY BACKGROUND. FATHER: Thomas Clayborne (ca. 1557–1607), of Kent, England, the mayor of King's Lynn, Norfolk, England in 1592, and a merchant; son of Thomas Clayborne (?–1581), the mayor of King's Lynn, Norfolk, England in 1573, and a merchant. MOTHER: Sara (?–1627), widow of Roger James, a brewer of London, England; daughter of John Smith, a brewer of Southwark, England. BROTHER: Thomas (1599–?). HALF BROTHERS: Sir Roger James; John James. SISTERS: Sara; Katherine; and Blanche. HALF SISTERS: Sara James; Margaret James. MARRIED by 1635 Elizabeth Boteler (ca. 1611–after 1668), daughter of John Boteler, of Roswell, Essex, England, and wife Jane Elliott; niece of Capt. Nathaniel Boteler, governor of Bermuda and Providence Island. Her brothers were *John Boteler* (ca. 1601–1642); Thomas Boteler. CHILDREN. SONS: William (1636–?), a burgess of New Kent County, Virginia, from 1660 to 1676, who married Elizabeth Wilkes; Thomas (1647–1681), who married Sarah, daughter of Samuel Fenn; Leonard (ca. 1649–?), who moved to Jamaica; and John. DAUGHTER: Jane (1638–?), who married ca. 1658 Thomas Brereton, of Northumberland, Virginia. PRIVATE CAREER. EDUCATION: literate; admitted to Pembroke College, Cambridge University, 1617. RELIGIOUS AFFILIATION: Protestant. OCCUPATIONAL PROFILE: placeman; merchant, by 1631, with a one-sixth interest in a joint stock venture with William Cloberry and Maurice Thompson for trading operations in the Chesapeake Bay; planter. **PUBLIC CAREER. PROVINCIAL OFFICE**: commissioner of Parliament for Maryland, 1651–1657/58. **OUT OF COLONY OFFICES**: Virginia: surveyor, 1621; Council, 1624–1660 (deputy governor, 1652–1660); secretary, 1626–1634, 1652–1661; commander of Kent Isle, 1631; treasurer, 1642–by 1650; general and chief commander of Virginia forces, 1644; commissioner of Parliament for Virginia, 1651–1660; colonel, by 1653. **STANDS ON PUBLIC/PRIVATE ISSUES**: battled with the proprietary forces from 1634 to the 1660s for control of Kent Island; he was the most persistent opponent of Lord Baltimore's claims in the Chesapeake Bay area. **WEALTH DURING LIFETIME. LAND**: over 1,600 acres in Virginia; patented over 20,600 acres during his lifetime. **WEALTH AT DEATH. DIED**: ca. 1677; size of estate unknown.

CLARK (CLARKE), THOMAS (ca. 1760–1796). **BORN**: ca. 1760 in Prince George's County; elder son. **NATIVE**: third generation. **RESIDED**: in Prince George's County; Georgetown, Montgomery County, by 1794. **FAMILY BACKGROUND. FATHER**: Charles Clark (?–1767), son of Thomas Clark (?–1766), of Prince George's County, a lawyer, and wife Amy Rivers, of Calvert County. **STEPFATHER**: *Osborn Sprigg* (ca. 1741–1815). **MOTHER**: Martha (?–1778), widow of William Hamilton (?–1759), of Prince George's County, a merchant who was killed by an accidental discharge of a gun; daughter of David Craufurd (?–1749), of Upper Marlboro, Prince George's County, a merchant, and wife Mary (?–1794). **UNCLE**: *David Craufurd* (ca. 1738–1801). **BROTHER**: David (?–1792), a physician, who married in 1788 Eleanor, daughter of *Benjamin Hall, of Francis* (?–1803). **HALF SISTER**: Wilhemina Hamilton (ca. 1759–?), who married in 1780 Edward Nicholls. **FIRST COUSIN**: Margaret Lee Clark (?–ca. 1794), who married *John Rogers* (1723–1789). **MARRIED** on December 21, 1781, Ann (1762–1809), daughter of *Benjamin Hall, of Francis* (?–1803); granddaughter of *William Murdock* (?–1769); niece of *Addison Murdock* (1731–1793). Her brothers were William Murdock (1759–ca. 1792); Henry Lowe (1761–1817). Her sisters were Eleanor (1768–?); Catherine (1778–?). **CHILDREN. SONS**: Thomas; Benjamin Hall, who married in 1809 Eleanor, daughter of Joseph White Clagett, and wife Eleanor Digges; and Charles Thomas (ca. 1787–1819), a midshipman and lieutenant in the U.S. Navy, who married in 1817 Susanna (1796–1846), daughter of Charles Adams, granddaughter of President John Adams.

DAUGHTERS: Martha Craufurd; Anna Maria (?–1823). **PRIVATE CAREER. EDUCATION**: literate. **SOCIAL STATUS AND ACTIVITIES**: Gent., by 1793. **OCCUPATIONAL PROFILE**: merchant. **PUBLIC CAREER. LEGISLATIVE SERVICE**: Lower House, Prince George's County, 1789, 1790, 1791–1792, 1792, 1794. **LOCAL OFFICE**: justice, Orphans' Court, Prince George's County, appointed 1791, resigned 1792. **WEALTH DURING LIFETIME. PERSONAL PROPERTY**: received £232.14.4 from his father's estate, 1778; received £289.0.0 on a judgment against his stepfather *Osborn Sprigg* (ca. 1741–1815) for ten years worth of rents on part of the lands he had inherited from his father, ca. 1788; 28 slaves, 1790; assessed value £254.10.0, including 8 slaves and 54 oz. plate, 1794. **LAND AT FIRST ELECTION**: 647 acres in Prince George's County (527 acres inherited from his father; 120 acres by purchase). **SIGNIFICANT CHANGES IN LAND BETWEEN FIRST ELECTION AND DEATH**: purchased an additional 105 acres in Prince George's County, 1790, but disposed of 35 acres of it by 1796. **WEALTH AT DEATH. DIED**: in 1796 in Georgetown, Montgomery County. **PERSONAL PROPERTY**: TEV, £1,602.0.3 current money (including 4 slaves, 2 servants, books, silver, and 51 shares of Columbia Bank stock); FB, estate overpaid £1,099.16.2. **LAND**: at least 717 acres in Prince George's County, and 1 lot in Georgetown, Montgomery County. Clark, however, had made an agreement with Benjamin Berry in March 1795 to exchange at least 527 acres of this land, plus £500, for 800 acres in Prince George's County that Berry owned. A few days later Clark made an agreement to sell the 800 acres to Benjamin Stoddert. After Clark's death, the Chancery Court ordered his widow to release her dower and agree to the aforesaid sales. She was also to pay Berry £571.3.1 current money out of Clark's personal estate, part of which Clark had originally agreed to pay and part of which was to account for a deficiency in the acreage sold.

CLARKE, DANIEL (ca. 1633–1702). **BORN**: ca. 1633. **IMMIGRATED**: by 1665 as a free adult from Virginia, probably from Isle of Wight County. **RESIDED**: in Talbot County; Dorchester County, by late 1669. **MARRIED** in 1691 Katherine (?–before 1702). **PRIVATE CAREER. EDUCATION**: literate. **RELIGIOUS AFFILIATION**: probably a Protestant. **SOCIAL STATUS AND ACTIVITIES**: no title on first appearance in Maryland records; Mr., 1669. **OCCUPATIONAL PROFILE**: planter. **PUBLIC CAREER. LEGISLATIVE SERVICE**: Lower House, Talbot County, 1669, Dorchester County, 1671–1674/75 (Joint

Committee of Laws 3), 1686–1688. LOCAL OF-FICES: deputy surveyor, Dorchester County, 1669; justice, Dorchester County, 1671–1674 (quorum); sheriff, Dorchester County, 1674–1676. ADDI-TIONAL COMMENTS: he was sued by Stephen Gray and convicted on a charge of assault committed while he was sheriff, which probably accounts for his failure to hold an appointive office after 1676. WEALTH DURING LIFETIME. LAND AT FIRST ELECTION: ca. 300 acres. WEALTH AT DEATH. DIED: will probated on December 1, 1702. PER-SONAL PROPERTY: TEV, £149.16.2 sterling (in-cluding 3 servants).

CLARKE, GEORGE (ca. 1692–1753). BORN: ca. 1692. IMMIGRATED: his family was exiled from Scotland for its support of the Stuart cause; he possibly immigrated as a child with his parents. RESIDED: probably in Poplar Hill Hundred, St. Mary's County. MARRIED Susannah Attaway, who subsequently married by 1756 John Black. CHIL-DREN. SON: John Attaway, who married Hannah. DAUGHTERS: Susannah Mackall, who married John Somerville; Hannah Key Ellen (Elenor); Ann, who married William Chesley; and Sarah (after 1730–?). PRIVATE CAREER. EDUCATION: lit-erate. RELIGIOUS AFFILIATION: Protestant. OCCU-PATIONAL PROFILE: probably a planter. PUBLIC CAREER. LEGISLATIVE SERVICE: Lower House, St. Mary's County, 1719–1721/22. LOCAL OFFICES: justice, St. Mary's County, in office 1727–1728, 1732–1753 (quorum, 1736–1753); sheriff, St. Mary's County, 1729–1732. MILITARY SERVICE: captain, by 1731; called colonel at the time of his death. WEALTH DURING LIFETIME. LAND AT FIRST ELECTION: at least 392 acres, possibly as much as 492 acres patented in St. Mary's County in 1720. SIGNIFICANT CHANGES IN LAND BE-TWEEN FIRST ELECTION AND DEATH: purchased at least 1,063 acres, and possibly 1,163 acres in St. Mary's County, 1735–1738; purchased an addi-tional 50 acres in St. Mary's County, by 1753; sold 100 acres, 1736. WEALTH AT DEATH. DIED: will probated in July 1753 in St. Mary's County. PERSONAL PROPERTY: TEV, £1,145.4.0 current money (including 23 slaves); FB, £1,075.5.1. LAND: ca. 1,334 acres in St. Mary's County.

CLARKE, GILBERT (ca. 1654–1700). BORN: ca. 1654 in Charles County; probably first son. NA-TIVE: probably second generation, possibly third generation. RESIDED: in St. Mary's County; Charles County, by 1689. FAMILY BACKGROUND. FATHER: John Clarke. MOTHER: probably Conyers. MARRIED Fantale. CHILDREN. Died without prog-

eny. PRIVATE CAREER. EDUCATION: literate. RELI-GIOUS AFFILIATION: Protestant. SOCIAL STATUS AND ACTIVITIES: Gent., by 1684. OCCUPATIONAL PROFILE: ordinary keeper; planter. PUBLIC CA-REER. LEGISLATIVE SERVICE: Associators' Conven-tion, St. Mary's City, 1689 (resigned after the 1st session to become sheriff). LOCAL OFFICES: under-sheriff, St. Mary's County, 1684–1686 (convicted of falsifying a writ); councilman, St. Mary's City, in office in 1685; sheriff, Charles County, 1689–1691; Nanjemoy Parish Vestry, Charles County, 1693–1696. ADDITIONAL COMMENTS: found guilty of extortion while sheriff in 1691, and held only the position of vestryman after his conviction. STANDS ON PUBLIC/PRIVATE ISSUES: he was active in the revolution of 1689 and was a prominent figure in first session of the Associators' Conven-tion. WEALTH DURING LIFETIME. LAND AT FIRST ELECTION: ca. 1,328 acres. WEALTH AT DEATH. DIED: late in 1700. PERSONAL PROPERTY: TEV, £84.5.0 sterling (including 4 servants). IDENTIFI-CATION PROBLEMS. Some confusion exists regard-ing his origins; there were three men named John Clarke in Charles County in the second half of the seventeenth century; one was the son of *Robert Clarke* (ca. 1611–1664), but circumstantial evi-dence suggests he was not the father of Gilbert.

CLARKE (CLARK), JOSHUA (?–1781). BORN: probably in Queen Anne's County; a minor in 1747; only son. NATIVE: at least second generation. RESIDED: in Queen Anne's County; Talbot County, 1759; Queen Anne's County (later be-came part of Caroline County), 1768; Tuckahoe Hundred, Caroline County, 1775. FAMILY BACK-GROUND. FATHER: Joshua Clarke (?–by 1741), of Queen Anne's County, planter. STEPFATHERS: John Baynard (?–1747), of Queen Anne's County, a planter and Quaker; Henry Feddeman (?–1764), of Queen Anne's County, planter. MOTHER: Elizabeth. HALF BROTHERS: Philip Feddeman; Henry Feddeman. STEPBROTHER: Thomas Bay-nard (?–1753), of Talbot County, planter. SISTERS: Hannah, who married first, her stepbrother Thomas Baynard (?–1753), and second, Henry Thompson; Rachel, who married (first name un-known) Dudley; Rebecca; and Lydia (?–by 1781), who married Henry Costin (?–by 1777). STEPSIS-TERS: Margaret Baynard (?–by 1777), who married first, John Casson (?–ca. 1761), of Dorchester County, and second, in 1762 *Matthew Driver* (1740–1798); Rachel Baynard. NIECES: Elizabeth Baynard (1748–1809), who married second, *Phile-mon Downes* (ca. 1741–ca. 1796); Margaret Bay-nard (1752–by 1788), who married *Henry Downes* (ca. 1748–1816). MARRIED by 1764 Anne (?–by 1794), daughter of *Edward Oldham* (1709–1773) and wife Ann Wright (?–by 1754); stepdaughter of Ann Goldsborough (1732–?); granddaughter of *John Oldham* (?–1729); stepgranddaughter of *Nicholas Goldsborough* (ca. 1689–1766); niece of Hannah Oldham (1702–1759), who married *James Edge* (ca. 1710–1757), *Thomas Wright* (?–ca. 1784), and Mary Anne Wright (?–1747), who married *William Hopper* (1707–1772); stepniece of *Thomas Goldsborough* (ca. 1728–1793). Anne subsequently married by 1785 Robert Williams. Her sisters were Hannah (?–1828), who married *Nicholas Martin* (1743–ca. 1808); Elizabeth (?–by 1776), who married *William Hopper* (by 1747–1806); and Mary (?–by 1772). Her first cousins were *William Hopper* (by 1747–1806); Mary Ann Hopper (1742–by 1792), who married second, *James Bordley* (?–ca. 1793); and *Samuel Turbutt Wright* (1749–1810). ADDITIONAL COMMENTS: by 1759 Anne and her sister Elizabeth were living with their aunt Hannah Oldham Edge from whom they inherited the lands of their uncle *James Edge* (ca. 1710–1757). CHILDREN. SONS: Joshua, who married in 1791 Ann, daughter of William Coursey, of Queen Anne's County, and wife Ann; Edward Oldham (?–ca. 1808), who probably never married; and Phillip (?–ca. 1809), who never married. DAUGHTERS: Ann; Elizabeth; Mary; and Margaret. PRIVATE CAREER. EDUCATION: literate. RELIGIOUS AFFILIATION: Anglican. SOCIAL STATUS AND ACTIVITIES: Gent., 1759; Esq., 1769. OCCUPATIONAL PROFILE: merchant. PUBLIC CAREER. LEGISLATIVE SERVICE: Conventions, Caroline County, 3rd, 1774, 4th, 1775, 5th, 1775, 6th–8th, 1775–1776 (did not attend the 7th and 8th Conventions). LOCAL OFFICES: justice, Queen Anne's County, 1768–1773, Caroline County, 1774–1777, 1778 (commissioned, but did not qualify), 1793–at least 1800; churchwarden and vestryman, Tuckahoe Chapel, St. John's Parish, Queen Anne's County (later became part of Caroline County), 1769; Committee of Correspondence, Queen Anne's County, 1774; justice, Orphans' Court, Caroline County, commissioned 1777. WEALTH DURING LIFETIME. LAND AT FIRST ELECTION: 3,986 acres in Queen Anne's, Talbot, and Dorchester counties, plus 2 lots, probably in Talbot County (918 acres from his father; 2,999 acres, plus 2 lots through his marriage, at least 2,000 acres of which were given to his wife in 1759 by her aunt, Hannah Edge, widow of James Edge; 2 acres by purchase). SIGNIFICANT CHANGES IN LAND BETWEEN FIRST ELECTION AND DEATH: purchased 32 acres in Talbot County, 1775; purchased 345 acres in Queen Anne's County, part of the estate of his brother-in-law Henry Costin, which Clarke was authorized to sell by virtue of a court decree, 1777; sold 81 acres of his wife's lands in Caroline County, 1780. WEALTH AT DEATH. DIED: between January and February 1781 in Caroline County. PERSONAL PROPERTY: TEV, £2,253.14.4 current money (including 31 slaves and books); FB, £1,436.8.5. LAND: 4,280 acres in Caroline, Talbot, and Queen Anne's counties.

CLARKE (CLARK), PHILIP (?–1699). IMMIGRATED: by 1686. RESIDED: in St. Mary's County. MARRIED by 1686 Hannah, daughter of George Mackall and wife Ann. Her sister was Jane, who married *John Watson* (ca. 1649–1699). CHILDREN. SONS: George; Philip; and Rozer. DAUGHTERS: two, first names unknown. PRIVATE CAREER. EDUCATION: literate. RELIGIOUS AFFILIATION: Protestant. SOCIAL STATUS AND ACTIVITIES: may be the Philip Clarke who was transported in 1676 as indentured servant, but there is no definite proof of the connection; it was charged in 1698 that "from working at the Howe hoe, he had presumed to take upon him that noble profession of the Law" ; Mr., by 1692/93. OCCUPATIONAL PROFILE: lawyer, admitted to the following courts: Provincial Court in 1691; Court of Chancery by 1696; also claimed to have practiced in several county courts in the 1690s. Planter. PUBLIC CAREER. LEGISLATIVE SERVICE: Lower House, St. Mary's County, 1692–1693 (Laws 1; Elections and Privileges 1), 1694–1697 (Laws 5–8, probably chairman 6, 8), 1697/98–1698 (chairman, Grand Committee of Lower House 1; Laws, probably chairman 1; died before the 3rd session). OTHER PROVINCIAL OFFICES: naval officer, Potomac, 1694–1696; justice, Provincial Court, July–December 1696 (quorum; dismissed). LOCAL OFFICES: justice, St. Mary's County, 1689–by 1694; alderman, St. Mary's City, 1694. STANDS ON PUBLIC/PRIVATE ISSUES: dismissed from the Provincial Court in 1696 for his support of *John Coode* (ca. 1648–1708/9); alleged coconspirator against Gov. Francis Nicholson in 1696–1698; called by Nicholson "one of the great Incendiarys in the house of Delegates," 1698; wrote the act of religion in 1698 and led Lower House opposition to the governor; jailed for six months for his defamation of Nicholson, and the question of releasing Clarke and his seating at the October 1698 session of the Assembly became a major issue. WEALTH DURING LIFETIME. LAND AT FIRST ELECTION: 2 plantations of unspecified acreage. WEALTH AT DEATH. DIED: by June 29,

1699. PERSONAL PROPERTY: TEV, £285.13.2 sterling (including 5 slaves, 4 servants, and books). LAND: 2 plantations of unspecified acreage.

CLARKE (CLERK, CLARK), ROBERT (ca. 1611–1664). BORN: ca. 1611, probably in England. IMMIGRATED: in 1637 as an indentured servant of Father Thomas Copley, a Jesuit priest. RESIDED: in St. Mary's County. MARRIED first, (name unknown). MARRIED second, by November 1654 Winifred, widow of both *Thomas Greene* (?–ca. 1651/52) and Nicholas Harvey. MARRIED third, in 1656 Jane (1612–?), widow of both John Cockshutt and Nicholas Causine. CHILDREN. SONS: John (?–1686), who married Ann; Robert (1652–1698); and Thomas (1654–?). STEPSONS: *Ignatius Causine* (ca. 1642–1695); *Leonard Greene* (?–1688); Thomas Greene; Robert Greene, who married Mary, daughter of *William Boreman* (ca. 1630–1709); and Francis Greene. DAUGHTER: Mary. STEPDAUGHTERS: Jane, who married *Thomas Mathews* (ca. 1622–1675/76); Mary, who married *Henry Adams* (?–1686). PRIVATE CAREER. EDUCATION: literate; had clerical skills. RELIGIOUS AFFILIATION: Catholic. SOCIAL STATUS AND ACTIVITIES: Gent., by 1638; his Council appointment probably followed his marriage to the widow of Thomas Greene, a councilor and often acting governor; his loyal service to the proprietary family brought repeated patronage and upward mobility; he was frequently reported to be in financial difficulties. OCCUPATIONAL PROFILE: servant, free by 1638; placeman; planter. PUBLIC CAREER. LEGISLATIVE SERVICE: Assembly, present 1637/38, present 1638/39, present 1641/42, special writ 1642A, present 1642B, present 1647/48, St. Mary's County, 1649; Upper House, special writ 1650 (Laws, dismissed during the 1st session); Upper House, 1658, 1659/60, 1661, 1662, 1663 (died before the 2nd session). OTHER PROVINCIAL OFFICES: deputy surveyor general, 1639/40–1648; surveyor general, 1648–1661; temporary clerk, Provincial Court, 1648; clerk, Council, 1647–1653/54; Council, 1653/54–1654, 1658–1664; justice, Provincial Court, 1653/54–1654, 1658–1664. STANDS ON PUBLIC/PRIVATE ISSUES: spokesman for the Jesuits, 1637/38; consistent supporter of proprietary interests. WEALTH DURING LIFETIME. LAND AT FIRST ELECTION: acquired 1,000 acres in 1652. WEALTH AT DEATH. DIED: in July 1664. PERSONAL PROPERTY: TEV, 10,462 pounds of tobacco (£70.12.4). LAND: probably 1,150 acres.

CLARKSON, ROBERT (?–1666). BORN: probably in England. IMMIGRATED: by 1657, probably as a free adult. RESIDED: in Middle Neck Hundred, Anne Arundel County. MARRIED Milcah, who subsequently married in 1666 *Richard Hill* (ca. 1640–1700). CHILDREN. SON: Robert (?–ca. 1686). DAUGHTERS: Elizabeth; Mary, who married first, Thomas Francis, and second, *Samuel Young* (1662–1736). PRIVATE CAREER. EDUCATION: literate. RELIGIOUS AFFILIATION: Protestant; Quaker by 1657. OCCUPATIONAL PROFILE: planter. PUBLIC CAREER. LEGISLATIVE SERVICE: Lower House, Anne Arundel County, 1659/60. STANDS ON PUBLIC/PRIVATE ISSUES: he was fined for refusing to bear arms, 1662. WEALTH DURING LIFETIME. LAND AT FIRST ELECTION: probably 200–500 acres. WEALTH AT DEATH. DIED: will probated on May 22, 1666. PERSONAL PROPERTY: TEV, 78,100 pounds of tobacco. LAND: 1,000 acres.

CLAYTON, SOLOMON (1685–1739). BORN: in 1685, probably in Maryland; second son. NATIVE: probably, if so, second generation. RESIDED: in Talbot County; Queen Anne's County, after 1707. FAMILY BACKGROUND. FATHER: William Clayton (ca. 1655–1721), who was illiterate and served on the St. Paul's Parish Vestry, Queen Anne's County from 1707 to 1721. STEPMOTHER: Joan (?–1730). BROTHER: *William Clayton* (ca. 1682–1728/29). SISTERS: Rachel (?–1749), who married William Finney (?–ca. 1723), son of *William Finney* (ca. 1637–1696); Alice, who married *Edward Wright* (?–1740/41); and Margaret, who married Thomas Kemp. MARRIED first, by 1714/15 Rachel (?–1729), daughter of Edward Smith (?–1700) and wife Ann Sheppard Marshall. MARRIED second, in November 1729 Mary, widow of *John Chaires* (?–1728/29). CHILDREN. SONS: William; Edward; Solomon; and Charles. STEPSONS: John Chaires; Thomas Chaires; and James Chaires. DAUGHTERS: Rachel, who married William Coursey (1703–1769), son of *Henry Coursey* (1662–1707); Mary, who married William Clayton, son of *William Clayton* (ca. 1682–1728/29). PRIVATE CAREER. EDUCATION: literate. RELIGIOUS AFFILIATION: Anglican. SOCIAL STATUS AND ACTIVITIES: Mr., 1723; Gent., 1726; Esq., 1729. OCCUPATIONAL PROFILE: planter; merchant. PUBLIC CAREER. LEGISLATIVE SERVICE: Lower House, Queen Anne's County, 1715, 1732–1734, 1738, 1739 (died before the 1st session). LOCAL OFFICES: St. Paul's Parish Vestry, Queen Anne's County, 1707, 1723–1727, 1728; justice, Queen Anne's County, 1722–1735 (quorum, 1729/30–1735). WEALTH DURING LIFETIME. PERSONAL PROPERTY: owned one-half of the 30-ton brigantine, *Charming Molly* in 1732 and at death; one-half of a 13-ton sloop in 1738 and at death; one-half of a 6-ton shallop, 1739; all of these vessels held in partnership with his brother *William Clayton* (ca. 1682–1728/29). LAND AT FIRST ELECTION: at least 200 acres; over 1,400 acres by 1732. WEALTH AT DEATH. DIED: on September 13, 1739. PERSONAL PROPERTY: TEV, £2,695.12.11 current money (including 31 slaves, 4 servants, and books); FB, £894.12.5. LAND: ca. 1,700 acres.

CLAYTON, WILLIAM (ca. 1682–1728/29). BORN: ca. 1682, probably in Queen Anne's County; elder son. NATIVE: probably second generation. RESIDED: in Talbot County, by 1710/11. FAMILY BACKGROUND. FATHER: William Clayton (ca. 1655–1721), of Queen Anne's County. STEPMOTHER: Joane (Joan) (?–1730), widow of Robert Gough (?–1705). BROTHER: *Solomon Clayton* (1685–1739). STEPBROTHERS: Joseph Gough; William Gough; Robert Gough; and John Gough. SISTERS: Rachel (?–1749), who married Capt. William Finney (?–ca. 1723), son of *William Finney* (ca. 1637–1696); Alice, who married *Edward Wright* (?–1740/41); and Margaret, who married Thomas Kemp (?–ca. 1727). NIECE: Margaret Finney (?–by 1767), who married first, *John Edmondson* (1692–1743), and second, *William Thomas* (1705–1767). MARRIED Katharine (?–1735), widow of both David Blaney (?–1699) and William Alderne (?–1701/2). CHILDREN. SON: William (ca. 1710–1740/41), who married Mary, daughter of *Solomon Clayton* (1685–1739). STEPDAUGHTER: Susanna Blaney, who married by 1724 William Edmondson. PRIVATE CAREER. EDUCATION: literate. RELIGIOUS AFFILIATION: Anglican, Wye Church, St. Paul's Parish, Queen Anne's County. SOCIAL STATUS AND ACTIVITIES: Mr., 1719; Gent., 1722. OCCUPATIONAL PROFILE: planter, 1708; merchant, 1718. PUBLIC CAREER. LEGISLATIVE SERVICE: Lower House, Talbot County, 1720–1721/22 (elected to the 3rd session to fill vacancy). LOCAL OFFICES: justice, Talbot County, 1710–at least 1727 (quorum, 1723–at least 1727); St. Paul's Parish Vestry, Queen Anne's County, in office 1717–1723. WEALTH DURING LIFETIME. LAND AT FIRST ELECTION: 1,848 acres in Dorchester, Talbot, and Queen Anne's counties (150 acres from his father; 1,698 acres by purchase). SIGNIFICANT CHANGES IN LAND BETWEEN FIRST ELECTION AND DEATH: purchased at least 950 acres in Talbot and Queen Anne's counties between 1723 and 1724. WEALTH AT DEATH. DIED: administrative bond filed on March 19, 1728/29 in Talbot County. PERSONAL PROPERTY: TEV, £3,027.12.8 current money (including 42 slaves, 8

white indentured servants, 25 oz. plate, and books); FB, £2,954.15.10. LAND: at least 2,798 acres in Dorchester, Talbot, and Queen Anne's counties.

COCKEY, EDWARD (1731–ca. 1795). BORN: on December 20, 1731, in St. Thomas Parish, Baltimore County; fifth son. NATIVE: third generation. RESIDED: in St. Thomas Parish, Back River Upper Hundred, Baltimore County. FAMILY BACKGROUND. FATHER: Capt. John Cockey (1681–1746), of Baltimore County. MOTHER: Elizabeth (1685–1780), daughter of William Slade (?–1731). STEPFATHER: Rev. Charles Baker. BROTHERS: William (1718–1756), who married Constant Ashman; Thomas (1724–?), who married Prudence Gill; Joshua (1726–1765), who married Charcilla Cockey Deye (1731–1806), sister of *Thomas Cockey Deye* (ca. 1728–1807); John (1729–1746); and Peter (1734–by 1749). SISTERS: Susanna (1714–?), who married Thomas Gist, son of *Richard Gist* (1683–1741); Mary (1716–?), who married Joshua Owings, brother of *Samuel Owings* (1702–1775); and Sarah (1721–ca. 1807), who married Thomas Boone. MARRIED on June 19, 1753, Eleanor Pindell (?–1795). CHILDREN. SONS: Joshua (1755–?); William (1758–?); and Thomas. DAUGHTER: Urath (1754–?). PRIVATE CAREER. EDUCATION: literate. RELIGIOUS AFFILIATION: Anglican, St. Thomas Parish, Baltimore County. OCCUPATIONAL PROFILE: planter; surveyor. PUBLIC CAREER. LEGISLATIVE SERVICE: Lower House, Baltimore County, 1786–1787, 1787–1788, 1788. OTHER STATE OFFICE: Constitution Ratification Convention, Baltimore County, 1788. LOCAL OFFICES: churchwarden, St. Thomas Parish, Baltimore County, 1755; justice, Baltimore County, 1777–at least 1794; sheriff, Baltimore County, at least 1778–1779 (resigned); St. Thomas Parish Vestry, Baltimore County, 1782–1784; judge, Court of Appeals for Tax Assessment, Baltimore County, appointed 1786 (declined). WEALTH DURING LIFETIME. PERSONAL PROPERTY: assessed value £402.0.0, including 4 slaves and 8 oz. plate, 1783; 6 slaves, 1790. LAND AT FIRST ELECTION: 200 acres in Baltimore County (ca. 170 acres inherited from his father), plus a 100-acre leasehold in Baltimore County. WEALTH AT DEATH. DIED: will probated in February 1795 in Baltimore County. PERSONAL PROPERTY: TEV, £790.7.2 current money (including 5 slaves, books, and 218 silver dollars); FB, £725.11.6 prior to final distribution. LAND: 200 acres in Baltimore County and 100 acres of leased land in Baltimore

County, which Cockey's inventory described as "worth nothing."

CODD, ST. LEGER (ca. 1634–ca. 1707/8). BORN: ca. 1634 in Kent, England; first son. IMMIGRATED: by 1688 as a free adult with his family from Virginia. RESIDED: in Cecil County. FAMILY BACKGROUND. FATHER: William Codd, Esq. (1604–1653), of Pelicans, Kent, England. MOTHER: Mary (1613–?), daughter of Sir Warham St. Leger, of Ulcombe, Kent, England. MARRIED first, (first name unknown), probably the daughter of Richard Parrott, of Lancaster County, Virginia. MARRIED second, Anne (?–by 1694), widow of Theodorick Bland (?–1671); daughter of *Richard Bennett* (ca. 1608–1675). Her brother was *Richard Bennett* (ca. 1639–1667). Her half brothers were *Nathaniel Utie* (ca. 1635–ca. 1675/76); *George Utie* (?–1678). Her sister was Elizabeth. MARRIED third, by 1694 Anne, widow of both Benjamin Randall and *Joseph Wickes* (ca. 1620–1692); daughter of *Thomas Hynson* (1620–ca. 1667/68). Her brothers were *John Hynson* (?–1705); Thomas (?–1679); and *Charles Hynson* (1663–1711). Her sister was Grace. CHILDREN. SONS: James, who inherited family lands in England; Berkeley, who settled in Delaware; *St. Leger Codd* (?–1730), who married in 1700 Mary, daughter of *Hans Hanson* (ca. 1647–1704). DAUGHTERS: Beatrix; Mary, who married (first name unknown) Paddison. PRIVATE CAREER. EDUCATION: literate, attended Gray's Inn, London, England, 1656. RELIGIOUS AFFILIATION: Anglican. SOCIAL STATUS AND ACTIVITIES: in Virginia and holding high office by 1671; in England in 1684, when he petitioned the Privy Council for protection from arrest arising from a suit brought against him by Sarah Bland; probably settled in Maryland soon thereafter in the area where the Bennetts and Uties, relatives of his second wife, had made their homes; he quickly became a leading figure in Cecil County. OCCUPATIONAL PROFILE: planter. PUBLIC CAREER. LEGISLATIVE SERVICE: Lower House, Cecil County, 1692 (Aggrievances; dismissed from the 1st session for his earlier opposition to the Associators' Convention), 1694–1697, 1701–1704. OTHER PROVINCIAL OFFICE: justice, Provincial Court, 1694–1697 (quorum; did not serve due to "Infirmities of body"). LOCAL OFFICES: justice, Cecil County, 1688–1689 (chief justice, October 1688–1689). MILITARY SERVICE: colonel, 1688–1689, 1694–1707/8. OUT OF COLONY SERVICE: colonel, Virginia Militia, by 1671; justice, 1677; burgess, elected for both Northumberland and Lancaster counties, Virginia, 1680. STANDS ON PUBLIC/PRIVATE ISSUES: a strong opponent of the Protestant Associators' revolution of 1689; nominated by Lord Baltimore for appointment to the first royal Council in 1691, but was not commissioned. WEALTH AT DEATH. DIED: will probated on February 9, 1707/8. PERSONAL PROPERTY: TEV, £556.6.10 sterling; FB, £533.9.10. LAND: unspecified acreage, but substantial holdings in Maryland, Lancaster County, Virginia, and England.

CODD, ST. LEGER (?–1730). BORN: in the 1670s in Virginia; third son. IMMIGRATED: by 1688 as a minor with father. RESIDED: in Cecil County; Kent County, by 1712. FAMILY BACKGROUND. FATHER: *St. Leger Codd* (ca. 1634–ca. 1707/8). MOTHER: Anne Bennett Bland, daughter of *Richard Bennett* (ca. 1608–1675). STEPMOTHER: Anne, widow of *Joseph Wickes* (ca. 1620–1692); daughter of *Thomas Hynson* (1620–ca. 1667/68). UNCLES: *Richard Bennett* (ca. 1639–1667); *Nathaniel Utie* (ca. 1635–ca. 1675/76); *George Utie* (?–1678); *John Hynson* (?–1705); and *Charles Hynson* (1663–1711). HALF BROTHERS: James; Berkeley. SISTERS: Beatrix; Mary. MARRIED in 1700 Mary (?–1730), daughter of *Hans Hanson* (ca. 1647–1704). CHILDREN. DAUGHTERS: Anne, who married by 1732 James Stout, of Kent County; Beatrix, who married in 1734 Gideon Pearce, Jr.; and Mary, who married Benjamin Hopkins (?–by 1736). PRIVATE CAREER. EDUCATION: literate. RELIGIOUS AFFILIATION: Anglican. SOCIAL STATUS AND ACTIVITIES: second generation burgess; a court case in 1729 established that he had married Mary Hanson against his father's advice, that she had been guilty of many "enormities," that he had built himself a separate house in 1721, and that they had not lived together since that time; the court required him to pay her £10 annually for her support; admonished by St. Paul's Parish Vestry, Kent County, in 1728 for seeing a married woman. OCCUPATIONAL PROFILE: planter. PUBLIC CAREER. LEGISLATIVE SERVICE: Lower House, Kent County, 1712–1714 (Elections and Privileges 1–4), 1715 (Elections and Privileges), 1716–1718 (Accounts 1–3), 1719–1721/22 (Accounts 1–5; Aggrievances 1). OTHER PROVINCIAL OFFICE: justice, Provincial Court, 1722–1730 (quorum, 1726–1730); judge, Court of Assize, Oyer and Terminer and Gaol Delivery, Eastern Shore, commissioned 1727. LOCAL OFFICES: justice, Kent County, 1714–1715/16, 1720; St. Paul's Parish Vestry, Kent County, 1715–1717; justice, Court of Oyer and Terminer and Gaol Delivery, Talbot County, 1728, Anne Arundel County, 1728. MILITARY SERVICE: captain, by 1714–1730. WEALTH DURING

LIFETIME. PERSONAL PROPERTY: inherited ca. £300 from his father and £250 from his brother; received £80 through his marriage. LAND AT FIRST ELECTION: probably ca. 300 acres, inherited from father. WEALTH AT DEATH. DIED: by April 3, 1730. PERSONAL PROPERTY: TEV, £779.15.7 current money (including 9 slaves, 2 servants, and 34 books); FB, £693.15.10. LAND: at least 250–300 acres.

COLEGATE, RICHARD (?–ca. 1721/22). BORN: in England. IMMIGRATED: in 1697 as a free adult, probably from London, England. RESIDED: in Baltimore County. MARRIED by 1707 Rebecca, possibly the daughter of *William Harbert* (?–1718) and wife Elinor Pattison (?–1743). She subsequently married in 1722 James Powell. CHILDREN. SONS: Richard; John; Thomas, who married Cassandra Cockey Deye (?–by 1777), sister of *Thomas Cockey Deye* (ca. 1728–1807); and Benjamin. DAUGHTERS: Temperance; Prudence, who married John Talbott; and Patience, who married William Buckner. PRIVATE CAREER. EDUCATION: literate. RELIGIOUS AFFILIATION: Anglican. SOCIAL STATUS AND ACTIVITIES: Mr., by 1710; Gent., by 1715. ADDITIONAL COMMENTS: his children were all minors when he died; his sons held no known provincial offices. OCCUPATIONAL PROFILE: factor for Thomas Yoakley & Pettett, London merchants, 1697; merchant, 1701–1721/22; planter. PUBLIC CAREER. LEGISLATIVE SERVICE: Lower House, Baltimore County, 1707 (elected to the 5th session), 1708A (Elections and Privileges), 1708B–1711, 1712–1714 (election voided for the 1st session; reelected to the 2nd session; Laws 1, 3, 4), 1715 (Laws), 1716–1718 (Laws 1–3), 1719–1721 (Elections and Privileges 1–4; Aggrievances 1; Laws 2, 3; died before the 5th session). LOCAL OFFICES: justice, Baltimore County, by 1703–1721/22; deputy commissary, Baltimore County, 1713; land commissioner, Baltimore County, appointed 1718. MILITARY SERVICE: captain, by 1706; major, 1716; colonel at death. WEALTH DURING LIFETIME. LAND AT FIRST ELECTION: over 1,300 acres; over 2,500 acres by 1715. WEALTH AT DEATH. DIED: will probated on February 16, 1721/22. PERSONAL PROPERTY: TEV, £3,792.17.8 (including 18 slaves); FB, £1,195.13.11. LAND: over 5,000 acres.

COLLINS, SAMUEL (ca. 1647–1707/8). BORN: ca. 1647. IMMIGRATED: in 1678 as a free adult. RESIDED: in Pocomoke Hundred, Somerset County. MARRIED first, in 1680 Margaret Hodson. MARRIED second, Elizabeth. CHILDREN. SONS: Samuel (1683/84–ca. 1713/14), who married

Katherine; John (1689–ca. 1708/9), who married Mary. DAUGHTERS: Sarah (1681–?), who married (first name unknown) Clifton; Anne (1687–ca. 1713/14), who married (first name unknown) Adams; and Mary (1692–1713). PRIVATE CAREER. EDUCATION: literate. RELIGIOUS AFFILIATION: Protestant. SOCIAL STATUS AND ACTIVITIES: held no known offices except one term as a burgess; his sons held no known offices. OCCUPATIONAL PROFILE: bricklayer; planter. PUBLIC CAREER. LEGISLATIVE SERVICE: Lower House, Somerset County, 1697/98–1700. WEALTH AT DEATH. DIED: will probated on March 9, 1707/8. LAND: 1,023 acres, plus 2 tracts of unspecified acreage.

COLVILL (COLVIL), THOMAS (ca. 1688–1766). BORN: ca. 1688. IMMIGRATED: after 1708 from London, England. RESIDED: in Cecil County until ca. 1755; Fairfax County, Virginia, 1755–1766. FAMILY BACKGROUND. FATHER: Richard Colvill, Esq. (1665–?), of London, England, a member of the Inner Temple. MOTHER: Frances (1680–?), daughter of Thomas Carter (1634–ca. 1688), alderman of York, England. BROTHER: John (?–1755), of Fairfax County, Virginia, who was in considerable debt to his brother Thomas at the time of his death. MARRIED Frances. CHILDREN. Probably died without progeny. PRIVATE CAREER. EDUCATION: literate. RELIGIOUS AFFILIATION: Protestant. SOCIAL STATUS AND ACTIVITIES: Gent., 1737. OCCUPATIONAL PROFILE: merchant; owned a storehouse in Shrewsbury Parish, Kent County, 1730. PUBLIC CAREER. LEGISLATIVE SERVICE: Lower House, Cecil County, 1738 (Bills of Credit), 1739–1741 (Bills of Credit Cv–3; Laws 1–3), 1742–1744 (Bills of Credit 1, 2; Laws 1, 2), 1745 (Bills of Credit; Laws), 1750–1751 (elected to the 2nd session to fill vacancy; Bills of Credit 2, 3). LOCAL OFFICES: justice, Cecil County, 1730–at least 1751 (quorum, 1732–at least 1751); justice, Court of Oyer and Terminer and Gaol Delivery, Cecil County, commissioned 1742, 1749, 1750, and 1752. MILITARY SERVICE: captain, by 1730; colonel, by 1739. WEALTH DURING LIFETIME. LAND AT FIRST ELECTION: 290 acres in Cecil County. SIGNIFICANT CHANGES IN LAND BETWEEN FIRST ELECTION AND DEATH: leased an additional 400 acres in Cecil County, 1744. WEALTH AT DEATH. DIED: ca. October 1766 at "Clish," near Alexandria, Virginia; size of estate unknown. George Washington (1731/32–1799) was named as one of the executors of his estate, which was not settled until 1793.

COMEGYS, CORNELIUS (ca. 1758–1817). BORN: ca. 1758. NATIVE: probably fourth generation. RESIDED: in George Town Cross Roads, Kent County. FAMILY BACKGROUND. Although information on immediate family background is uncertain, it is known that the original immigrant and great-great-grandfather of the legislator, also named Cornelius (?–1708), arrived in America in 1652 and settled near Jamestown, Virginia. He moved his family to Chestertown, Kent County, in 1661 to escape the persecution of the Puritans in Virginia. MARRIED by September 29, 1780, Sophia Charlotte, widow of (first name unknown) Massey; daughter of Peregrine Brown (?–1777). Her brother was Peregrine Brown, Jr. CHILDREN. DAUGHTER: Anna Maria (?–1857), who married on April 3, 1804, Dr. Edward Scott. PRIVATE CAREER. EDUCATION: literate. SOCIAL STATUS AND ACTIVITIES: Gent., 1805; Esq., 1805. OCCUPATIONAL PROFILE: planter, 1780; merchant, partner in firm of Comegys & Vansant, 1800. PUBLIC CAREER. LEGISLATIVE SERVICE: Lower House, Kent County, 1788, 1790, 1797, 1806. OTHER STATE OFFICE: clerk, Treasury Department, assigned duty of preparing and signing Continental currency, appointed 1778. LOCAL OFFICE: justice, Kent County, 1803–at least 1810. MILITARY SERVICE: sergeant, Flying Camp, 1776; reenlisted as an ensign under George Washington. WEALTH DURING LIFETIME. PERSONAL PROPERTY: assessed value £50.0.0, including 3 slaves and 3 oz. plate, 1783; assessed value, including real property, $2,983.00, 1806. LAND AT FIRST ELECTION: at least 1,049 acres in Kent County (almost all from his wife's dower). SIGNIFICANT CHANGES IN LAND BETWEEN FIRST ELECTION AND DEATH: purchased 460 acres in Kent County, 1788–1800. He then divided the land into one-half- to ten-acre lots, eventually selling seventeen of them. WEALTH AT DEATH. DIED: in 1817 in Kent County. PERSONAL PROPERTY: TEV, at least $1,345.98 current money; assessed value of combined real and personal property, $2,045.00. LAND: ca. 589 acres in Kent County.

CONNER, PHILIP (ca. 1615–1660). BORN: ca. 1615, probably in England. IMMIGRATED: by 1636 as a free adult. RESIDED: in Kent County. MARRIED Mary, widow of John Philips. She subsequently married by 1667 John Wright. CHILDREN. SON: Philip (ca. 1653–1703), a justice of Kent County from 1680 to 1685, and in 1694. DAUGHTER: Sarah (?–1666). PRIVATE CAREER. EDUCATION: literate. RELIGIOUS AFFILIATION: Protestant. SOCIAL STATUS AND ACTIVITIES: no title on arrival; Mr., by 1647. OCCUPATIONAL PROFILE: planter. PUBLIC CAREER. LEGISLATIVE SERVICE:

Assembly, present 1641/42, present 1647/48, Kent County, 1649 (Accounts); Lower House, Kent County, 1658. LOCAL OFFICE: justice, Kent County, 1647–1660. MILITARY SERVICE: commander, 1652–1658. STANDS ON PUBLIC/PRIVATE ISSUES: apparently cooperated with the Parliamentary Commissioners; continued as a justice, but was removed from his military post after the proprietary party regained control of the government in 1658. WEALTH DURING LIFETIME. LAND AT FIRST ELECTION: 100 acres in 1640; acquired 500 additional acres in 1658. WEALTH AT DEATH. DIED: by August 7, 1660. PERSONAL PROPERTY: included 4 servants. LAND: 600 acres.

CONTEE, ALEXANDER (ca. 1691–1740). BORN: ca. 1691 in Barnstaple, Devonshire, England. IMMIGRATED: ca. 1703. RESIDED: in Charles County to ca. 1720; in Prince George's County thereafter. FAMILY BACKGROUND. FATHER: Peter Contee (?–ca. 1714), of Barnstaple, Devonshire, England, a physician. MOTHER: Catherine. STEPMOTHER: Francis, widow of Capt. William Hopkins. UNCLE: *John Contee* (?–1708). BROTHER: John (?–ca. 1712). HALF BROTHER: Peter. STEPBROTHER: Andrew Hopkins (ca. 1690–?). OTHER KINSHIP: his great-nephew was *Thomas Sim Lee* (1745–1819). MARRIED ca. 1721 Jane (?–1779), daughter of Col. *Thomas Brooke* (ca. 1659–1730/31); granddaughter of *Thomas Dent* (ca. 1630–1676). Her brothers were Nathaniel; John; Benjamin; Baker; and Thomas (1717–1768). Her half brother was *Thomas Brooke* (1683–1744). Her sisters were Mary (?–1758); Rebecca (?–1763); Elizabeth; and Lucy. Her half sisters were Sarah (?–1724), who married first, *William Dent* (ca. 1660–1704), and second, *Philip Lee* (ca. 1681–1744); Priscilla Brooke, who married *Thomas Gantt* (?–1765). Her nephews were *Thomas Beall, of George* (1735–1819); *Joseph Sim* (?–1793). CHILDREN. SONS: *John Contee* (1722–ca. 1796); Alexander, Jr. (1724–1732); Peter (1726–ca. 1779); Col. *Thomas Contee* (ca. 1729–1811); Alexander (1734–1744); and Theodore (1736–1764), who married Elizabeth Skinner (ca. 1743–?), who subsequently married *John Lee Webster* (ca. 1735–1795). DAUGHTERS: Jane (1728–1812), who married in 1747 *John Hanson, Jr.* (1721–1783); Catherine (1732–1831), who married John Harrison; Grace (1738–?), who married (first name unknown) Hollyday; Barbara (1741–1796), who married in 1772 John Reed Magruder. PRIVATE CAREER. EDUCATION: literate; attended school in Barnstaple, England. RELIGIOUS AFFILIATION: Anglican. SOCIAL STATUS AND ACTIVITIES: Gent. OCCUPATIONAL PROFILE:

officeholder, 1717–1740; attorney, admitted to Charles County Court in 1720; planter, 1729–1730; merchant, 1730. **PUBLIC CAREER.** LEGISLATIVE SERVICE: Lower House, Charles County, 1720–1721/22 (elected to the 3rd session to fill vacancy; Laws 3–5). LOCAL OFFICES: deputy commissary, Charles County, in office 1716–out of office by 1721; clerk, Charles County, 1717–1720, Prince George's County, 1720–1740; recommended by the court to be clerk of Indictments, Charles County, 1721. **WEALTH DURING LIFETIME.** LAND AT FIRST ELECTION: 427 acres in Prince George's and Charles counties (inherited from his uncle, 1708). SIGNIFICANT CHANGES IN LAND BETWEEN FIRST ELECTION AND DEATH: sold 250 acres in Charles County, 1726; acquired 458 acres (his wife's dower) in Prince George's County, 1726; patented 2,921 acres in Charles County, 1727–1737; leased 200 acres in Charles County, 1729–1730. **WEALTH AT DEATH.** DIED: on December 24, 1740, in Prince George's County; buried at "The Valley," Brookefield, Prince George's County. PERSONAL PROPERTY: TEV, £1,613.2.11 sterling, plus £3,827.19.8 current money (including 32 slaves, 2 servants, books, and clerk's writing equipment). LAND: at least 2,598 acres in Charles and Prince George's counties.

CONTEE, JOHN (?–1708). BORN: in Barnstable, Devonshire, England. IMMIGRATED: ca. 1699 as a free adult with a kinsman from England. RESIDED: in Charles County. **FAMILY BACKGROUND.** FATHER: probably Peter Contee, son of Adolphe de Conti, a Huguenot who immigrated to England from France during the reign of Louis XIII; he was lord mayor of London, England, in 1643, and sheriff of Middlesex, England. MOTHER: Grace. BROTHER: Peter Contee (?–ca. 1714), of Barnstable, England, physician. SISTER: Agnes Contee Berry. NEPHEW: *Alexander Contee* (ca. 1691–1740), who married Jane, daughter of *Thomas Brooke* (ca. 1659–1730/31). MARRIED first, in 1703 Charity (?–1703), widow of *John Courts* (1655/56–1702); daughter of *Robert Henley* (ca. 1617–1684). MARRIED second, ca. June 1704 Mary Townley (?–by 1725). She subsequently married both *Philemon Hemsley* (1670–1719) and Capt. William Rogers of Annapolis. Her sisters were Frances, who married James Wotton, of Wiltshire, England; Judith, who married John Bruce. Her first cousin was Gov. *John Seymour* (1649–1709), with whom she immigrated in 1704. **CHILDREN.** STEPSONS: *John Courts* (1691/92–1747/48); Henley Courts; Charles Courts; and William Courts. STEPDAUGHTERS: Ann Courts (1693–?), who married John

Rogers; and Charity Courts (1680–1711), who married first Bayne Smallwood, son of *James Smallwood* (ca. 1639–ca. 1714/15), and second, in 1710 *Daniel Dulany* (1685–1753). **PRIVATE CAREER.** EDUCATION: literate. RELIGIOUS AFFILIATION: Anglican. SOCIAL STATUS AND ACTIVITIES: Contee arrived with important mercantile connections. Two marriages within a year brought important family connections and control of the substantial estate of *John Courts* (1655/56–1702). His second marriage to Mary Townley, a favorite cousin of Gov. Seymour, was reported by a contemporary to have been responsible for his appointments to office. OCCUPATIONAL PROFILE: factor for Sir John Rogers, of Plymouth, England, 1699; merchant; planter. **PUBLIC CAREER.** LEGISLATIVE SERVICE: Lower House, Charles County, 1705–1707 (elected to the 3rd session; Laws 4, 5). OTHER PROVINCIAL OFFICES: commissary general and judge of probate (joint appointment, 1704–1706; sole appointment, 1706–1708); naval officer, Pocomoke, 1705–1708; Council, 1708. LOCAL OFFICES: justice, Charles County, 1704–1708 (quorum, 1705–1708); William and Mary Parish Vestry, Charles County, 1705. MILITARY SERVICE: major, 1704/5–1705/6; colonel, 1705–1708. **WEALTH DURING LIFETIME.** LAND AT FIRST ELECTION: ca. 2,500 acres, plus 1,000 acres he held for the orphans of *John Courts* (1655/56–1702). **WEALTH AT DEATH.** DIED: by August 3, 1708. PERSONAL PROPERTY: TEV, £2,252.17.8 sterling (including 13 slaves). LAND: ca. 3,697 acres. ADDITIONAL COMMENTS: Depositions taken in 1725 at the request of *Alexander Contee* (ca. 1691–1740) revealed that the "pretended will" of John Contee, which was confirmed by Act of Assembly in 1708 and which named Mary, his wife, sole executrix, had actually been written by *Philip Lynes* (1649–1709), a person "Very Officious to Oblige The said Mary," and that Contee had refused to sign it. An Act of Assembly passed in 1725 repealed this earlier act, stating it had passed both Houses through "perjury" and "other means too shocking to be transmitted to posterity."

CONTEE, JOHN (1722–ca. 1796). BORN: in 1722 near Nottingham, Prince George's County; eldest son. NATIVE: second generation. RESIDED: at "Ranelagh," Prince George's County. **FAMILY BACKGROUND.** FATHER: *Alexander Contee* (ca. 1691–1740). MOTHER: Jane (?–1779), daughter of *Thomas Brooke* (ca. 1659–1730/31) and wife Barbara Dent (1676–1754). HALF UNCLE: *Thomas Brooke* (1683–1744). HALF AUNTS: Priscilla Brooke, who married *Thomas Gantt* (?–1765); Sarah Brooke (?–1724), who married first, *William Dent* (ca. 1660–1704), and second, *Philip Lee* (ca. 1681–1744). BROTHERS: Alexander (1724–1732); Peter (1726–ca. 1779); *Thomas Contee* (ca. 1729–1811); Alexander (1734–1744); and Theodore (1734–1764). SISTERS: Jane (1728–1812), who married *John Hanson, Jr.* (1721–1783); Catherine (1732–1831); Grace; and Barbara (1741–1796). FIRST COUSIN: *Thomas Beall, of George* (1735–1819). NEPHEW: *Alexander Contee Hanson* (1749–1806). NIECE: Jane Contee Hanson (1747–1781), who married *Philip Thomas* (1747–1815). OTHER KINSIP: his maternal great-grandfather was *Thomas Dent* (ca. 1630–1676). MARRIED ca. 1744 Margaret (1726–1793), daughter of Richard Snowden, the younger (?–1763), of Anne Arundel County, an ironmaster and owner of the Patuxent Ironworks, and wife Elizabeth Thomas (?–1775); granddaughter of Samuel Thomas (ca. 1655–?) and wife Mary Hutchins. Her brothers were Richard (1719/20–1753), who married Elizabeth, the only daughter of John Crowley and wife Miriam, and who died without progeny; Thomas (ca. 1722–?), who married Mary (?–1770), daughter of Henry Wright; Samuel (1728–1801), who married Elizabeth (?–1790), daughter of *Philip Thomas* (1693/94–1762); and John, who married Rachel, daughter of Richard Hopkins. Her sisters were Ann, who married *Henry Wright Crabb* (1722/23–1764); Elizabeth, who married Joseph Cowman. Her nephews were *Richard Crabb* (?–1780); *Jeremiah Crabb* (1760–1800). CHILDREN. SON: Richard Alexander (1753–?), who married first, in 1785 Mary (1768–1787), daughter of *David Craufurd* (ca. 1738–1801), and second, Elizabeth Gassaway, daughter of Gassaway Rawlings, of Anne Arundel County. Richard was declared insane in 1799. DAUGHTERS: Elizabeth (1746–1827), who married James Keith, of Virginia; Jane; Anne (1758–?), who married in 1779 Dennis Magruder, Sr.; and Mary, who married in 1785 Alexander W. Magruder. PRIVATE CAREER. EDUCATION: literate. RELIGIOUS AFFILIATION: Anglican, Queen Anne Parish, Prince George's County. SOCIAL STATUS AND ACTIVITIES: Esq., by 1763. OCCUPATIONAL PROFILE: probably a planter. PUBLIC CAREER. LEGISLATIVE SERVICE: Conventions, Prince George's County, 4th, 1775 (elected, but did not attend), 5th, 1775; Lower House, Prince George's County, 1777–1778 (Claims 1, 2; Loan Office 1). OTHER STATE OFFICE: Executive Council, 1777 (elected on February 14, 1777, but declined to serve in a letter dated February 24, 1777, citing the smallpox epidemic in Annapolis as his reason). LOCAL OFFICES: justice, Prince George's County,

1746–at least 1766 (quorum, 1752–at least 1766); churchwarden, Queen Anne Parish, Prince George's County, elected 1747; Queen Anne Parish Vestry, Prince George's County, in office 1748–1750, 1754–1760; justice, Court of Oyer and Terminer and Gaol Delivery, Prince George's County, commissioned 1759 and 1766; Committee of Correspondence, Prince George's County, elected 1774 and 1775; Committee of Observation, Prince George's County, elected 1775; commissioner of tax, Prince George's County, appointed 1779, 1782, 1783, 1785, 1786, and 1790 (declined). WEALTH DURING LIFETIME. PERSONAL PROPERTY: 17 slaves, 1790; assessed value £756.13.11, including 18 slaves and 219 oz. plate, 1793; assessed value £584.13.11, including 14 slaves and 219 oz. plate, 1794. LAND AT FIRST ELECTION: 2,955 acres in Charles, Prince George's, and Frederick counties (inherited 1,164 acres from his father, but sold it before his first election; obtained another 1,757 acres from his father's estate, but disposed of 584 acres of it before his first election; 500 acres through his marriage; at least 1,262 acres by purchase). SIGNIFICANT CHANGES IN LAND BETWEEN FIRST ELECTION AND DEATH: transferred by deeds of gift to his children land totaling 2,185 acres in Prince George's, Charles, and Montgomery (originally Frederick) counties, 1783–1794. WEALTH AT DEATH. DIED: will probated on January 12, 1796, in Prince George's County. PERSONAL PROPERTY: size of estate unknown. LAND: 769 acres in Prince George's County.

CONTEE, THOMAS (ca. 1729–1811). BORN: ca. 1729 at "Brookefield," Prince George's County; fourth son. NATIVE: second generation. RESIDED: at "Brookefield," Prince George's County; Charles County, by 1761; Prince George's County, by 1763; Charles County, by 1764; Prince George's County, by 1771; Baltimore County, by 1785; Prince George's County, by 1790 until death. FAMILY BACKGROUND. FATHER: *Alexander Contee* (ca. 1691–1740). MOTHER: Jane (?–1779), daughter of *Thomas Brooke* (ca. 1659–1730/31). HALF UNCLE: *Thomas Brooke* (1683–1744). HALF AUNTS: Priscilla Brooke, who married *Thomas Gantt* (?–1765); Sarah Brooke (?–1724), who married first, *William Dent* (ca. 1660–1704), and second, *Philip Lee* (ca. 1681–1744). BROTHERS: *John Contee* (1722–ca. 1796); Alexander (1724–1732); Peter (1726–ca. 1779); Alexander (1734–1744); and Theodore (1736–1764). SISTERS: Jane (1728–1812), who married *John Hanson, Jr.* (1721–1783); Catherine (1732–1831); Grace; and Barbara (1741–1796).

FIRST COUSIN: *Thomas Beall, of George* (1735–1819). NEPHEW: *Alexander Contee Hanson* (1749–1806). NIECE: Jane Contee Hanson (1747–1781), who married *Philip Thomas* (1747–1815). OTHER KINSHIP: his maternal great-grandfather was *Thomas Dent* (ca. 1630–1676). MARRIED ca. 1755 Sarah (ca. 1732–1793), daughter of Benjamin Fendall (?–1764), of Charles County, and wife Eleanor Lee (1710–1759); stepdaughter of Priscilla (ca. 1714–1763); granddaughter of both *John Fendall* (1674–1734) and *Philip Lee* (ca. 1681–1744); niece of *Richard Lee* (ca. 1707–1787), *Arthur Lee* (?–1760), and *Francis Lee* (?–1749); half niece of both *Corbin Lee* (?–1774) and *George Lee* (ca. 1736–?); stepniece of Hannah Sewall, who married second, *Joseph Sprigg* (1736–1800). Her brothers were *Philip Richard Fendall* (?–?); John; Benjamin; Rev. Henry, rector of Durham Parish, Charles County from 1767 to 1775; and Samuel. Her first cousins were *Josias Beall* (ca. 1725–1803); *Samuel Hanson, Jr.* (?–1817); *Philip Thomas Lee* (1738–1778); *Thomas Sim Lee* (1745–1819); *Richard Potts* (1753–1808); Sarah Lettice Lee (?–1761), who married *Philip Richard Fendall* (?–?); Hannah Lee (?–ca. 1763), who married *George Plater* (1735–1792), and Alice Lee (?–1789), who married *John Weems* (1737–1813). Sarah Fendall Contee died at "Brookefield," Prince George's County. CHILDREN. SONS: Alexander (ca. 1755–1810), who was a merchant and never married; Rev. Benjamin (1755–1815), a merchant and lawyer, born at "Brookefield," near Nottingham, Prince George's County, served as a lieutenant and captain in the Third Maryland Battalion during the Revolution, served as a delegate to the Continental Congress from 1787 to 1788 and as a representative to the U.S. Congress from 1789 to 1791, declared insolvency due to "mishaps in trade" by 1799, ordained as an Anglican minister in 1803, served as pastor of the Port Tobacco Church, Charles County, presiding judge of Charles County Orphans' Court at death, he married in 1794 Sarah Russell (ca. 1767–1810), daughter of *Philip Thomas Lee* (1738–1778). ADDITIONAL COMMENTS: Alexander and Benjamin were partners in London in a merchantile business, ca. 1784, with stores in Nottingham, Queen Anne, and Upper Marlboro, Prince George's County. DAUGHTERS: Eleanor Lee (1758–1787), who married Dr. Michael Wallace (1749–1794), of Elkton, Cecil County; Jane (1761–1825), who married in 1782 William Worthington, of Anne Arundel County; and Sarah, who married (first name unknown) Slater. **PRIVATE CAREER.** EDUCATION: literate. RELIGIOUS AFFILIATION: Anglican, St. Paul's Parish,

Prince George's County. SOCIAL STATUS AND ACTIVITIES: Esq., by 1758. ADDITIONAL COMMENTS: Contee was sent to Philadelphia, Pennsylvania, to confer with the Continental Congress about the organization of the army and the general plans for defense. OCCUPATIONAL PROFILE: merchant, by 1764; attorney in fact for William Molleson, of London, England, merchant, by 1766; in business in Nottingham, Prince George's County, with *Fielder Bowie* (ca. 1745–1794) in a firm engaged in the tobacco trade with Europe and the importation of large quantities of goods until the firm advertised its dissolution in 1775; had the management of a store at Pig Point, Prince George's County, ca. 1772–1775; agent for his sons Alexander and Benjamin, London merchants, for their stores in Nottingham, Queen Anne, and Upper Marlboro, Prince George's County, ca. 1784; attorney in fact for both John Yerbury & Company and John Walker, of London, merchant, by 1785; probably also a planter. **PUBLIC CAREER.** LEGISLATIVE SERVICE: Lower House, Prince George's County, 1769–1770 (elected to the 2nd session to fill vacancy; Claims 3, 4), 1771 (Claims), 1773–1774 (Accounts 1; Claims Cv, 2, 3); Conventions, Prince George's County, 4th, 1775, 5th, 1775, 6th–8th, 1775–1776 (Claims 6th–8th); Senate, Western Shore, Term of 1776–1781: 1777, 1777–1778, 1778 (did not serve; resigned on November 20, 1778). OTHER STATE OFFICE: 5th Council of Safety, Western Shore, 1776–1777 (elected on November 11, 1776, to fill vacancy). LOCAL OFFICES: St. Paul's Parish Vestry, Prince George's County, 1755–1758, 1770–1774, 1779–1780, 1782 (excused from service), 1793–1796, 1798–1800, 1802, 1804–1806; sheriff, Prince George's County, 1757; justice, Prince George's County, in office 1757, 1794–1801; receiver or collector of land tax, Prince George's County, gave bond 1757; collector of excise, Prince George's County, gave bond 1757; churchwarden, St. Paul's Parish, Prince George's County, in office 1758, 1775, 1777, and 1792; justice, Charles County, 1764–1769; trustee from Prince George's County for Charlotte Hall Free School, St. Mary's County, which served Prince George's, Charles, and St. Mary's counties; Committee of Observation, Prince George's County, elected 1775; Levy Court, Upper Marlboro, Prince George's County, 1795–1796; election official, First District, Prince George's County, appointed 1801; associate justice, First District Court, Prince George's County, 1802–1805. MILITARY SERVICE: major, militia, by 1776; lieutenant colonel, First District Militia, ca. 1776. **WEALTH DURING LIFETIME. PERSONAL**

PROPERTY: 25 slaves, 1790; assessed value £835.0.0, including 21 slaves and 64 oz. plate, 1810. LAND AT FIRST ELECTION: at least 649 acres in Prince George's and Charles counties, plus 1 lot in Nottingham, Prince George's County (inherited at least 1 lot in Nottingham, Prince George's County, from his father; purchased at least 498 acres, plus another 2 acres in partnership with James Swann). SIGNIFICANT CHANGES IN LAND BETWEEN FIRST ELECTION AND DEATH: acquired 599 acres in Prince George's County and 387 acres in Charles County probably by inheritance from his mother, 1779; gave 811 acres in Charles County to his son by deed of gift in 1782, but repurchased it in 1790 and sold it in 1793; purchased 417 acres in Baltimore County, 1793; purchased 1,430 acres in Montgomery and Frederick counties from Edward Burgess, against whom Contee had obtained a court judgment in 1793, but sold 1,359 acres of it in 1806; by 1810 he disposed of the 599 acres in Prince George's County that he probably inherited from his mother; acquired 567 additional acres in that county by 1810; acquired 4,833 acres in Kentucky by 1811. WEALTH AT DEATH. DIED: in January 1811 in Prince George's County; buried at "Brookefield," Prince George's County. PERSONAL PROPERTY: TEV, $9,167.75 (including 19 slaves, books, and silver); FB, $1,884.42; there were still debts outstanding against the estate in 1821, including a judgment obtained by James Allston for the Union Bank of Maryland amounting to over $12,000. LAND: 1,082 acres in Prince George's, Baltimore, and Frederick counties, 4 lots in Prince George's and Montgomery counties, plus 4,833 acres in Kentucky.

COODE, JOHN (ca. 1648–1708/9). BORN: ca. 1648 in Penryn, Cornwall, England; second son. IMMIGRATED: in 1672 as a free adult. RESIDED: in St. Mary's County. FAMILY BACKGROUND. FATHER: John Coode (1622–1713), a lawyer. MOTHER: Grace (?–1694), daughter of Thomas Robins, of Glasney College. BROTHERS: Thomas (1642–1685); William (1652–1716). MARRIED first, in 1674 Susannah (?–by 1683), widow of *Robert Slye* (ca. 1628–1670/71); daughter of *Thomas Gerard* (1608–1673). Her brothers were Thomas (?–1686); Justinian (?–1688); and John. Her sisters were Frances; Temperance; Elizabeth (?–1716), who married first, *Nehemiah Blakiston* (?–1693), second, Ralph Rymer, and third, *Joshua Guibert* (?–1713); and Mary, who married *Kenelm Cheseldyne* (1640–1708). MARRIED second, by 1685 Elizabeth, who subsequently married by 1710 Wil-

liam Hook. CHILDREN. SONS: John, Jr. (?–1718), the sheriff of St. Mary's County from 1704 to 1707; William (1679–?), the sheriff of St. Mary's County from 1707 to 1709; and Richard. STEPSON: Gerard Slye (1654–by 1703). DAUGHTERS: Winnifred; Anne; and Mary, who married *Justinian Jordan* (ca. 1686–1749). PRIVATE CAREER. EDUCATION: literate; Exeter College, Oxford University, England, 1664–1666, "literatus." RELIGIOUS AFFILIATION: Anglican, took orders as a priest in England, ca. 1669; he was an atheist in later life. SOCIAL STATUS AND ACTIVITIES: descended from a distinguished English family with a long tradition in the law; Gent. on arrival; attained much wealth and political power through his marriage to Susannah Slye; had a controversial career in politics; his sons held no provincial offices. OCCUPATIONAL PROFILE: Anglican priest, Penryn, Cornwall, England, ca. 1669–1672, "turned out" in 1672; some minor officiating as a priest during his initial years in Maryland; planter. PUBLIC CAREER. LEGISLATIVE SERVICE: Lower House, St. Mary's County, 1676–1682 (Accounts 2; Security and Defense 2; Laws 2), 1688 (elected to the 2nd session); Associators' Convention, St. Mary's County, 1689–1690 (went to England before the 3rd session); Lower House, St. Mary's County, 1696 (elected to the 7th session; dismissed on the grounds that he was ineligible because he was a former priest), 1708A (election voided), 1708B (dismissed from 1708B–1711 Assembly on the grounds that he was ineligible as a former priest). OTHER PROVINCIAL OFFICES: commander in chief (acting chief executive), 1689–1690; naval officer, North Potomac, 1689–1690; agent to England, 1690–1692. LOCAL OFFICES: justice, St. Mary's County, 1676–1681 (dismissed), 1689–1690 (quorum, 1677–1681, 1689–1690; president, 1679–1681); coroner, St. Mary's County, 1678; King and Queen Parish Vestry, St. Mary's County, 1693–1696; sheriff, St. Mary's County, 1694–1696. MILITARY SERVICE: captain, 1676–1681, 1689–1694; lieutenant colonel, 1694–1696. STANDS ON PUBLIC/PRIVATE ISSUES: involved in four rebellions (1681, 1689, 1693, 1696–1698), one of which was successful in 1689; always unable to work cooperatively for any appreciable length of time under any government; he lost all his offices in 1681 and 1696 for opposition to government; convicted for blasphemy, 1699. WEALTH DURING LIFETIME. LAND AT FIRST ELECTION: controlled at least 1,000 acres that belonged to his wife and stepchildren from the estate of *Robert Slye* (ca. 1628–1670/71). WEALTH AT DEATH. DIED: between February 27, 1708/9, and March 28, 1709. PERSONAL PROPERTY: TEV, £259.13.8 sterling (including 7 slaves). LAND: over 1,000 acres.

COOKE, THOMAS (?–1692/93). BORN: probably in London, England. IMMMIGRATED: in 1679, but returned to England; resettled in Maryland by 1683 as a free adult. RESIDED: in Dorchester County. FAMILY BACKGROUND. FATHER: almost certainly Sir Andrew Cooke, a London merchant who came to Maryland in 1661, patented 1,000 acres, and returned to England. BROTHERS: Edward; probably Andrew (?–1711). NEPHEW: probably Ebenezer Cooke, author of *The Sot-weed Factor* and other poems. MARRIED Ann, daughter of *John Brooke* (by 1646–1692/93); granddaughter of *Michael Brooke* (?–ca. 1663/64). She subsequently married John Stevens, son of *John Stevens* (?–1692). Her sister was Mary, who married *Joseph Ennalls* (?–1709). CHILDREN. SONS: Babington; John. DAUGHTERS: Ann; Mary. PRIVATE CAREER. EDUCATION: literate. RELIGIOUS AFFILIATION: Protestant. SOCIAL STATUS AND ACTIVITIES: Gent. upon arrival. OCCUPATIONAL PROFILE: a merchant of London, England; 1676/77; an ordinary keeper, 1691; merchant; planter. PUBLIC CAREER. LEGISLATIVE SERVICE: Associators' Convention, Dorchester County, 1689–1691 (resigned after the 5th session to become sheriff). LOCAL OFFICES: clerk, Dorchester County, 1686 (during the illness of the incumbent); sheriff, Dorchester County, 1691–1692/93. STANDS ON PUBLIC/PRIVATE ISSUES: supported the revolution of Protestant Associators in 1689. WEALTH DURING LIFETIME. LAND AT FIRST ELECTION: over 616 acres. WEALTH AT DEATH. DIED: between January 25 and March 7, 1692/93. PERSONAL PROPERTY: TEV, £208.7.1 sterling (2 slaves and 1 servant). LAND: over 616 acres.

COPLEY, LIONEL (1648–1693). BORN: in 1648 in Wadsworth, Yorkshire, England; first son. IMMIGRATED: in 1692 as a free adult with his family. RESIDED: in St. Mary's City. FAMILY BACKGROUND. FATHER: Lionel Copley (1607–1675), of Wadsworth, England. MOTHER: Frisalina (?–1696), widow of John Wheeler, of London, England; daughter of George Ward, of Capethorne, England. BROTHER: William (1654–died young). SISTERS: Anne, who married John Crofts, of York, England; Castilianca, who married first, in 1675 John Beckworth, Esq., and second, Rev. Thomas Mauleverea. MARRIED in 1676 Ann (1660–1692/93), daughter of Sir Philip Boteler, of Watton Woodhall, Hertfordshire, England. CHILDREN.

SONS: Lionel, who became Sir Lionel, of Sprotsborough; John. DAUGHTER: Ann, who married in 1696 Isaac Milner, of London, England. PRIVATE CAREER. EDUCATION: literate; matriculated at Brasenose College, Oxford University, England, 1665. RELIGIOUS AFFILIATION: Anglican. SOCIAL STATUS AND ACTIVITIES: arrived in Maryland as governor; history of strong anti-Catholic activity in the army; protéegée of Thomas Osborne, earl of Danby. OCCUPATIONAL PROFILE: military officer and royal placeman. PUBLIC CAREER. PROVINCIAL OFFICES: governor, 1691–1693; chancellor, 1692. OUT OF COLONY SERVICE: captain in King's Regiment, 1676; lieutenant governor of Hull, England, 1681–1690. STANDS ON PUBLIC/PRIVATE ISSUES: his partisanship and avarice as governor helped create serious rifts among members of the first royal Council, three members of which he suspended; he opposed the activities of *Edward Randolph* (1632–1703) and Sir *Thomas Lawrence* (ca. 1645–1714), two other royal placemen in Maryland and discriminated against the supporters of Lord Baltimore. WEALTH AT DEATH. DIED: on September 12, 1693. PERSONAL PROPERTY: indebted to crown in the amount of £480. LAND: 20 acres and 2 lots in St. Mary's City, plus a family estate in England.

CORNWALEYS (CORNWALLIS), THOMAS (ca. 1605–1675/76). BORN: ca. 1605 in Norfolk, England; probably second son. IMMIGRATED: in 1633/34 as a free adult. RESIDED: at "Cornwaleys Crosse Manor," St. Mary's County; resettled permanently in England, 1659. FAMILY BACKGROUND. FATHER: Sir William Cornwaleys, probably son of Sir Charles Cornwaleys (?–1629), ambassador to Spain from 1605 to 1610. MOTHER: probably Catherine, daughter of Sir Philip Parker, of Ewarton, Suffolk, England. UNCLE: probably Francis Cornwaleys, who married Katherine Arundell, niece of Lady Anne Baltimore. MARRIED first, by 1638 (name unknown). MARRIED second, in 1654 Penelope (?–still alive in 1688), daughter of John Wiseman, of Terrells Hall, Essex, England. CHILDREN. SONS: William (ca. 1659–ca. 1679), probably clerk of the Prerogative Office from 1678 to 1679; Thomas (1661–1731), of Ewarton, Suffolk, England. DAUGHTER: Frances, who married Samuel Richardson. PRIVATE CAREER. EDUCATION: literate, probably well educated. RELIGIOUS AFFILIATION: Catholic. SOCIAL STATUS AND ACTIVITIES: came from an English family of high status; he was the most important investor in Maryland in the 1630s who was not an immediate member of the Calvert family; one of the first adventurers, he transported at least seventy-one servants between 1643 and 1651; he often returned to England over the next two decades. OCCUPATIONAL PROFILE: entrepreneur; actively engaged in the tobacco trade, Indian trade (licensed in 1637), and retail provisions trade; built the colony's first mill; a large investor in land. PUBLIC CAREER. LEGISLATIVE SERVICE: Assembly, special writ 1637/38 (Laws), special writ 1638/39, special writ 1641/42 (Aggrievances), special writ 1642A (Laws, chairman), special writ 1642B (Laws); Lower House, St. Inigoe's Hundred, St. Mary's County, 1658. OTHER PROVINCIAL OFFICES: commissioner of the colony, 1633–1637; Council, 1637–1642, 1657; deputy governor, 1638; justice, Provincial Court, sat 1658. MILITARY SERVICE: chief military officer in Maryland in the 1630s and 1640s; captain of an expedition against the Indians, 1643. STANDS ON PUBLIC/PRIVATE ISSUES: champion of the Assembly having legislative initiative, 1637/38, and a frequent opponent of proprietary spokesmen in other early assemblies; an advocate of limits on the duration of laws, 1642; an outspoken opponent of proprietary efforts to limit the rights of the Catholic church, especially those of the Jesuits; he refused to take the oath as councilor, 1642; aided Richard Ingle's escape, 1643/44, "to declare his [Cornwaleys's] affection to the Parliament"; within a year he was called the "chiefe Agent for Settling Popish faction in Maryland" by Ingle and his associates; he was impeached for aiding Ingle, 1643/44; opposed the cultivation of tobacco. WEALTH DURING LIFETIME. PERSONAL PROPERTY: 20 servants in 1659. LAND AT FIRST ELECTION: 6,000 acres by 1640; 11,200 acres by 1658; sold two manors, "Cornwaleys Crosse" and "St. Elizabeth's" in 1661. WEALTH AT DEATH. DIED: will probated on March 4, 1675/76; size of estate unknown.

COSDEN (COSTIN, COSTINE, COSTON), ALPHONSO (ca. 1696–1738).

BORN: probably ca. 1696 in Calvert County. NATIVE: third generation. RESIDED: in Calvert County; Cecil County, by 1733. FAMILY BACKGROUND. FATHER: Alphonso Cosden (ca. 1676–1696), of Calvert County, son of Thomas Cosden (1635–1683), who immigrated in 1668 to St. Mary's County. GUARDIAN: Christopher Bean. MARRIED Elizabeth, who subsequently married in 1739 Bartlet Smith. CHILDREN. Nine, including SONS: Alphonso (1720–1748), whose guardian was *Benjamin Pearce* (1711/12–1756); Easalin. DAUGHTER: Alifera, who married in 1743 Benjamin Terry. PRIVATE CAREER. EDUCATION: literate. RELIGIOUS AFFILIA-

TION: Anglican, North Sassafras Parish, Cecil County. SOCIAL STATUS AND ACTIVITIES: Mr., 1719. OCCUPATIONAL PROFILE: probably a planter. PUBLIC CAREER. LEGISLATIVE SERVICE: Lower House, Cecil County, 1738 (elected, but did not serve; died before the convention). WEALTH DURING LIFETIME. LAND AT FIRST ELECTION: 370 acres in Cecil County (inherited at least 1,500 acres, and possibly as much as 2,540 acres, from his father and grandfather, all of which he sold by 1736). WEALTH AT DEATH. DIED: ca. May 1738 in Cecil County. PERSONAL PROPERTY: TEV, £407.18.10 current money (including 4 slaves, 1 servant, books, and sea charts); FB, £257.9.3. LAND: 370 acres in Cecil County. ADDITIONAL COMMENTS: income from his plantation was estimated to be 900 pounds of tobacco annually.

COULTER, JOHN (1751–1823).

BORN: in 1751 in Ireland. IMMIGRATED: in 1772 from Ireland. RESIDED: in Baltimore Town. MARRIED on February 2, 1788, Mary (Polly) McCaskey. CHILDREN. SON: probably Henry S. PRIVATE CAREER. EDUCATION: literate. RELIGIOUS AFFILIATION: Presbyterian, member of the Second Presbyterian Church, Baltimore Town. SOCIAL STATUS AND ACTIVITIES: Esq., 1787. OCCUPATIONAL PROFILE: physician, began practice in Baltimore Town, 1772. PUBLIC CAREER. LEGISLATIVE SERVICE: Lower House, Baltimore Town, 1788. OTHER STATE OFFICE: Constitution Ratification Convention, Baltimore Town, 1788. LOCAL OFFICES: justice, Baltimore County, 1783–1787 (resigned); justice, Orphans' Court, Baltimore County, appointed 1785 (declined); special commissioner, Baltimore Town, in office 1793; trustee for Potter's Field (Baltimore Town cemetery for the poor), in office 1794. MILITARY SERVICE: surgeon, Maryland ship *Defence*, in office 1776; surgeon, Military Hospitals, Baltimore Town, in office 1776. STANDS ON PUBLIC/PRIVATE ISSUES: Federalist candidate for the convention to ratify the federal Constitution, 1788; said to favor ratification of the Constitution prior to acceptance of amendments. WEALTH DURING LIFETIME. PERSONAL PROPERTY: 4 slaves, 1790. LAND AT FIRST ELECTION: 3 lots in Baltimore Town, including 1 containing 100 acres and 1 lot leased out. SIGNIFICANT CHANGES IN LAND BETWEEN FIRST ELECTION AND DEATH: active speculator in Baltimore City lots. WEALTH AT DEATH. DIED: on May 24, 1823, in Baltimore City. PERSONAL PROPERTY: TEV, $9,654.69 current money (including 2 slaves); FB, $766.13. LAND: at least 4 lots in Baltimore City.

COURSEY, HENRY (ca. 1629–1695). BORN: ca. 1629, probably in Ireland. IMMIGRATED: in 1649 as a free adult with his brothers from Virginia. RESIDED: briefly in St. Mary's County; Calvert County, by 1651; the Eastern Shore by the late 1650s. FAMILY BACKGROUND. FATHER: Henry Coursey. BROTHERS: John (?–1661), the sheriff of Kent County in 1657; *William Coursey* (?–1685); and James, of Lincoln's Inn, Middlesex, England. SISTERS: Jane; Catherine; Ann, who married Tristram Thomas; and Juliana, who married John Russell (?–1660). MARRIED first, in 1658 Mary, widow of Richard Harris (?–1657). MARRIED second, Elizabeth (?–1702), widow of Simon Carpenter (?–1670). CHILDREN. SONS: Thomas (?–1700/1), who married in 1699 Ann Harris; *Henry Coursey* (1662–1707), who married Elizabeth (?–1728), daughter of Elizabeth Desmyniers, of Dublin, Ireland; James (?–1714); and John (?–1713), who married Mary, daughter of Michael Turbutt. DAUGHTER: Jane (?–1696). STEPDAUGHTERS: Ann (?–ca. 1709), who married Michael Earle (?–1709); Mary, who married John Lillingston (?–1709). PRIVATE CAREER. EDUCATION: literate; probably well educated; had clerical skills. RELIGIOUS AFFILIATION: Protestant. SOCIAL STATUS AND ACTIVITIES: Mr. on arrival; Gent., by 1658; Esq., by 1660; protégé of *Philip Calvert* (1626–1682), who first appointed Coursey to provincial office and defended him against attacks from the governor and the proprietor. OCCUPATIONAL PROFILE: placeman; attorney, 1651; planter. PUBLIC CAREER. LEGISLATIVE SERVICE: Upper House, 1661, 1662 (excused from attendance), 1663–1664, 1666, 1669 (Aggrievances), 1678–1682 (appointed before the 2nd session, but first sat at the 3rd session; Accounts 3), 1682–1684, special writ 1686 (speaker); Lower House, Talbot County, 1694–1695 (died before the 4th session). OTHER PROVINCIAL OFFICES: clerk, Secretary's Office, by 1652–1656/57; clerk, Council, by 1654–1659/60; secretary and judge of Probate, 1660–1661; Council, 1660–1670, 1676–1684 (president, 1682–1684); justice, Provincial Court, 1660–1670, 1676–1689 (chief justice, 1683–1689); surveyor and comptroller general, 1673–prior to June 23, 1680; agent to New York on Indian affairs, 1678, 1681. LOCAL OFFICE: justice, Calvert County, 1658. MILITARY SERVICE: colonel, by 1677–1689; commander of foot, Cecil and Kent counties, 1681. STANDS ON PUBLIC/PRIVATE ISSUES: a leading provincial figure in matters relating to Indian affairs, he negotiated many treaties with area Indians. Although he rendered valuable service to the Calverts, Coursey was never well-liked by *Charles Calvert, 3rd Lord Baltimore* (1637–1714/15), who often removed Coursey from office to make room for other favorites and who omitted Coursey from the Council in 1684. Calvert later chastized his councilors for their favoritism to Coursey, especially for having him sit as speaker of the Upper House in 1686. Nevertheless, when Catholicism excluded most of the proprietary circle from eligibility for office after 1689, Calvert recommended Coursey to become governor in 1690. Coursey was called a Jacobite in 1692. WEALTH DURING LIFETIME. LAND AT FIRST ELECTION: ca. 2,100 acres. WEALTH AT DEATH. DIED: by October 3, 1695. PERSONAL PROPERTY: TEV, £1,667.17.1 sterling (including 15 slaves and 1 servant). LAND: ca. 3,225 acres.

COURSEY, HENRY (1662–1707). BORN: on May 24, 1662, on the Eastern Shore; probably a second son. RESIDED: in Talbot County. FAMILY BACKGROUND. FATHER: *Henry Coursey* (ca. 1629–1695). MOTHER: Mary Harris. UNCLE: *William Coursey* (?–1685). BROTHERS: Thomas (?–1700/1); James (?–1714); and John (?–1713). SISTER: Jane (?–1696). STEPSISTERS: Ann (?–ca. 1709); Mary. FIRST COUSIN: *William Coursey* (?–ca. 1717/18). MARRIED Elizabeth (?–1729), daughter of Elizabeth Desmyniers, of Dublin, Ireland. CHILDREN. SONS: Henry (1693–?); Otho; and William (1703–1769), who married Rachel, daughter of *Solomon Clayton* (1685–1739). DAUGHTERS: Araminta; Elizabeth, who married *William Cumming* (ca. 1696–1752); Juliana; and Mary. PRIVATE CAREER. EDUCATION: literate; probably educated in England. RELIGIOUS AFFILIATION: Protestant. SOCIAL STATUS AND ACTIVITIES: second generation burgess; Gent. on coming of age in 1682. OCCUPATIONAL PROFILE: agent of Robert Morris, a mason and mariner of Middlesex, England, 1682; attorney; merchant. PUBLIC CAREER. LEGISLATIVE SERVICE: Lower House, Talbot County, 1704–1706 (Laws 2; died before the 5th session). LOCAL OFFICE: justice, Talbot County, 1685–1689. STANDS ON PUBLIC/PRIVATE ISSUES: refused to serve under the Protestant Associators' government, 1689; testified in England on behalf of Lord Baltimore against the rebels, 1690; recommended for appointment to the Council, 1707. WEALTH DURING LIFETIME. LAND AT FIRST ELECTION: probably at least 1,675 acres inherited from his father. WEALTH AT DEATH. DIED: by May 29, 1707. PERSONAL PROPERTY: TEV, £392.7.0 sterling (including 2 slaves and law and medical books).

COURSEY, WILLIAM (?–1685). BORN: probably in Ireland; younger son. IMMIGRATED: in 1649, probably as a minor with his brothers from Virginia. RESIDED: in St. Mary's County; Calvert County, by 1651; Kent County by 1661; Talbot County, by 1662. FAMILY BACKGROUND. FATHER: Henry Coursey. BROTHERS: John (?–1661), the sheriff of Kent County in 1657; *Henry Coursey* (ca. 1629–1695); and James, of Lincoln's Inn, Middlesex, England. SISTERS: Jane; Catherine; Ann; and Juliana. MARRIED ca. 1664 Elizabeth. CHILDREN. SON: *William Coursey* (?–ca. 1717/18), who married by 1694 Elizabeth (1658/59–1726), widow of *Vincent Lowe* (?–1692) and daughter of Seth Foster (?–1674/75). PRIVATE CAREER. EDUCATION: literate. RELIGIOUS AFFILIATION: Protestant. SOCIAL STATUS AND ACTIVITIES: Mr. on arrival; benefitted from the political prominence achieved by his brother *Henry Coursey* (ca. 1629–1695). OCCUPATIONAL PROFILE: planter. PUBLIC CAREER. LEGISLATIVE SERVICE: Lower House, Talbot County, 1666 (Laws). LOCAL OFFICES: acting sheriff, Calvert County, 1658–1659; justice, Kent County, 1661 (quorum), Talbot County, 1661/62–1667, 1670–1674, 1679–1685 (quorum); sheriff, Talbot County, 1667–1669, 1674–1679. MILITARY SERVICE: major, by 1679. WEALTH DURING LIFETIME. LAND AT FIRST ELECTION: ca. 1,800 acres. WEALTH AT DEATH. DIED: by August 12, 1685. PERSONAL PROPERTY: TEV, £363.8.4 sterling plus 4,000 pounds of tobacco, (including 1 slave and 2 servants). LAND: ca. 3,000 acres.

COURSEY, WILLIAM (?–ca. 1717/18). BORN: after 1664 in Talbot County; only son. NATIVE: second generation. RESIDED: in Talbot County; Queen Anne's County after 1707. FAMILY BACKGROUND. FATHER: *William Coursey* (?–1685). MOTHER: Elizabeth. UNCLE: *Henry Coursey* (ca. 1629–1695). FIRST COUSIN: *Henry Coursey* (1662–1707). MARRIED by 1694 Elizabeth (1658/59–1726), widow of *Vincent Lowe* (?–1692); daughter of Seth Foster (?–1674/75). Her half brother was *John Hawkins* (ca. 1657–1717). CHILDREN. Died without progeny. PRIVATE CAREER. EDUCATION: literate, probably educated in England. RELIGIOUS AFFILIATION: Anglican. SOCIAL STATUS AND ACTIVITIES: second generation burgess; in England at time of his father's death, 1685; Gent., by 1694. OCCUPATIONAL PROFILE: planter. PUBLIC CAREER. LEGISLATIVE SERVICE: Lower House, Talbot County, 1696–1697 (elected to the 7th session) 1702 (election to the 3rd session voided); Upper House, 1704 (appointed by the 5th session), 1704–1707, 1708A, 1708B–1711, 1712–1714 (absent the

1st and 2nd sessions), 1715, 1716–1717 (died before the 3rd session). OTHER PROVINCIAL OFFICE: Council, 1703/4–1717/18. LOCAL OFFICES: justice, Talbot County, 1694–1703/4 (quorum); St. Paul's Parish Vestry, Talbot County, 1694–1699/1700. MILITARY SERVICE: major, by 1707; colonel, 1707–1717/18. STANDS ON PUBLIC/PRIVATE ISSUES: opposed the revolution of Protestant Associators in 1689; achieved first offices under Gov. Francis Nicholson. WEALTH DURING LIFETIME. LAND AT FIRST ELECTION: ca. 5,000 acres; 1,500 acres from his wife's dower. WEALTH AT DEATH. DIED: will probated on February 3, 1717/18. PERSONAL PROPERTY: TEV, £449.16.3 (including 8 slaves). LAND: over 3,000 acres; probably over 5,000 acres.

COURTS, JOHN (1655/56–1702). BORN: in 1655/56 in Charles County; first son. NATIVE: second generation. RESIDED: in Charles County. FAMILY BACKGROUND. FATHER: John Courts, Sr. (?–1702), who immigrated in 1639 as an indentured servant, but later became a substantial landowner. MOTHER: Margaret, who immigrated by 1649 as an indentured servant. BROTHER: Hugh. SISTER: Margaret (1665/66–?). NATURAL SISTER: Elizabeth (1663–?), who married *James Keech* (ca. 1651–1708/9). MARRIED Charity (?–1703), daughter of *Robert Henley* (ca. 1617–1684). She subsequently married *John Contee* (?–1708). CHILDREN. SONS: *John Courts* (1691/92–1747/48), who married Elizabeth; Henley (?–ca. 1712); Charles; and William. DAUGHTERS: Ann (1693–?), who married John Rogers; Charity (1680–1711), who married first, Bayne Smallwood (?–1709), son of *James Smallwood* (ca. 1639–ca. 1714/15), and second, in 1710 *Daniel Dulany* (1685–1753). PRIVATE CAREER. EDUCATION: literate. RELIGIOUS AFFILIATION: Anglican. SOCIAL STATUS AND ACTIVITIES: his marriage brought upward social mobility, with first offices coming shortly after his father-in-law's death. OCCUPATIONAL PROFILE: wheelwright; planter; merchant. PUBLIC CAREER. LEGISLATIVE SERVICE: Associators' Convention, Charles County, 1689–1692; Grand Committee of Twenty, 1690–1692; Upper House, 1692–1693, 1694–1697, 1697/98–1700, 1701–1702 (died before the 4th session). OTHER PROVINCIAL OFFICES: Council, 1691–1702; joint commissary general, 1699–1700. LOCAL OFFICES: justice, Charles County, 1685–1692; coroner, Charles County, 1692; William and Mary Parish Vestry, Charles County, 1693–1697. MILITARY SERVICE: captain, 1689–1695; colonel, 1695–1702. STANDS ON PUBLIC/PRIVATE ISSUES: His active role in the revolution of 1689 promoted him into office on the provincial level. WEALTH DURING LIFETIME. LAND AT FIRST ELECTION: over 1,000 acres (he acquired a substantial estate from his father-in-law). WEALTH AT DEATH. DIED: by November 1702. PERSONAL PROPERTY: TEV, £1,815.11.2 sterling (including 30 slaves and 6 servants). LAND: 2,260 acres.

COURTS, JOHN (1691/92–1747/48). BORN: on March 3, 1691/92, at "Pyckyawaxon," Charles County. NATIVE: third generation. RESIDED: in "Pyckyawaxon," Charles County. FAMILY BACKGROUND. FATHER: *John Courts* (1655/56–1702). STEPFATHER: *John Contee* (?–1708). MOTHER: Charity (?–1703), daughter of *Robert Henley* (ca. 1617–1684). BROTHERS: Henley (?–ca. 1712); Charles; and William (?–1758). SISTERS: Ann (1693–?); Charity (1680–1711), who married second, *Daniel Dulany* (1685–1753). MARRIED Elizabeth. CHILDREN. SONS: William (?–1758), who married Elizabeth; John; and *Robert Hendly Courts* (?–1774). DAUGHTERS: Ann; Charity, who married (first name unknown) Adams; Mary Ann, who married (probably John) Martin; and Elizabeth, who married (probably Charles) Jones. PRIVATE CAREER. EDUCATION: literate. RELIGIOUS AFFILIATION: Protestant. SOCIAL STATUS AND ACTIVITIES: Mr., 1747/48. OCCUPATIONAL PROFILE: probably a planter. PUBLIC CAREER. LEGISLATIVE SERVICE: Lower House, Charles County, 1722–1724, 1725–1727, 1728–1731, 1732–1734, 1734/35–1737, 1738, 1739–1741, 1744 (elected to the 2nd session to fill vacancy), 1745 (Elections), 1745/46–1747 (died before the 4th session). WEALTH DURING LIFETIME. LAND AT FIRST ELECTION: at least 1,007 acres in Charles, Prince George's, and Calvert counties (307 acres inherited from his father, 1703; 500 acres inherited from his father's estate after the death of his brother Henley; at least 200 acres inherited from his stepfather). WEALTH AT DEATH. DIED: between January 16 and January 29, 1747/48, in Charles County, of pleurisy, having claimed recovery from the disease twenty-nine times before. PERSONAL PROPERTY: TEV, £2,933.1.11 current money (including 57 slaves, 1 servant, and 11 books); FB, £1,538.11.4. LAND: at least 1,707 acres in Charles, Calvert, and Prince George's counties, plus lots in Nottingham, Prince George's County, in partnership with *Daniel Dulany* (1685–1753).

COURTS, ROBERT HENDLY (?–1774). BORN: of age by 1762; probably third son. NATIVE: fourth generation. RESIDED: in East Hundred, Charles County. FAMILY BACKGROUND. FATHER: *John Courts* (1691/92–1747/48), son of *John Courts*

(1655/56–1702). MOTHER: Elizabeth. BROTHERS William (?–1758); John. SISTERS: Ann; Charity; Mary Ann; and Elizabeth. NEPHEW: *William Courts* (ca. 1753–1792). MARRIED Elizabeth (?–1779). CHILDREN. SONS: John; Robert Henley (?–1810); George; and Daniel. DAUGHTERS: Anne; Betty. PRIVATE CAREER. EDUCATION: literate. RELIGIOUS AFFILIATION: Protestant. SOCIAL STATUS AND ACTIVITIES: Gent., 1762. OCCUPATIONAL PROFILE: planter. PUBLIC CAREER. LEGISLATIVE SERVICE: Lower House, Charles County, 1770 (elected to the 3rd session to fill vacancy), 1773 (died before the 3rd session). WEALTH DURING LIFETIME. LAND AT FIRST ELECTION: 750 acres in Charles County (650 acres inherited from his father in 1748, 100 acres by personal acquisition). SIGNIFICANT CHANGES IN LAND BETWEEN FIRST ELECTION AND DEATH: purchased 142 acres in Charles County. WEALTH AT DEATH. DIED: in 1774 in Charles County. PERSONAL PROPERTY: TEV, £1,505.19.2 current money (including 33 slaves and a parcel of books); FB, £475.17.8. LAND: 892 acres in Charles County.

COURTS, WILLIAM (ca. 1753–1792). BORN: ca. 1753 in Charles County; probably second son. NATIVE: fifth generation. RESIDED: in Charles County. FAMILY BACKGROUND. FATHER: William Courts (?–1758), son of *John Courts* (1691/92–1747/48). MOTHER: Elizabeth (ca. 1758–?). UNCLE: *Robert Hendly Courts* (?–1774). BROTHERS: John; Richard Henly. MARRIED Elizabeth. CHILDREN. SON: William. DAUGHTER: one, name unknown. PRIVATE CAREER. EDUCATION: literate. RELIGIOUS AFFILIATION: Protestant. SOCIAL STATUS AND ACTIVITIES: Esq., 1792. OCCUPATIONAL PROFILE: probably a planter. PUBLIC CAREER. LEGISLATIVE SERVICE: Lower House, Charles County, 1782–1783. JURY SERVICE: impaneled to serve on Grand Inquest, Charles County, 1781; foreman, grand jury, Charles County, 1786. WEALTH DURING LIFETIME. LAND AT FIRST ELECTION: 1,240 acres in Charles County (200 acres inherited from his father, 1758). SIGNIFICANT CHANGES IN LAND BETWEEN FIRST ELECTION AND DEATH: sold 139 acres in Charles County, 1786. WEALTH AT DEATH. DIED: on September 28, 1792, in Charles County. PERSONAL PROPERTY: TEV, £2,345.3.0 current money (including 35 slaves); FB, estate overpaid £137.2.2. LAND: 1,100 acres in Charles County.

COVINGTON (COVENTON), THOMAS (?–1708/9). BORN: probably in Talbot County, of age by 1695; only surviving son. NATIVE: second generation. RESIDED: in Talbot County; Kent County, by 1695. **FAMILY BACKGROUND. FATHER**: Nehemiah (?–1681), a planter. **MOTHER**: Ann, who subsequently married by 1682 Philip Hopkins. **MARRIED** by 1699 Rachel, who subsequently married by 1710 Robert Hannan. **CHILDREN**. Probably died without progeny. **PRIVATE CAREER. EDUCATION**: literate. **RELIGIOUS AFFILIATION**: Anglican. **OCCUPATIONAL PROFILE**: planter. **PUBLIC CAREER. LEGISLATIVE SERVICE**: Lower House, Kent County, 1708A, 1708B (died before the 2nd session of 1708B–1711 Assembly). **LOCAL OFFICE**: St. Paul's Parish Vestry, Kent County, 1708–1708/9. **WEALTH DURING LIFETIME. LAND AT FIRST ELECTION**: at least 300 acres (purchased in 1695). **WEALTH AT DEATH. DIED**: buried on January 24, 1708/9. **PERSONAL PROPERTY**: TEV, £178.1.3 sterling. **LAND**: at least 300 acres.

COX, JOHN (1741–1785). **BORN**: in 1741, probably in Cecil County; only surviving son. **NATIVE**: fourth generation. **RESIDED**: in Sassafras Neck, Cecil County. **FAMILY BACKGROUND. FATHER**: John Cox (1704–1755), of Cecil County. **MOTHER**: Susannah (surname was possibly Ward) (?–1766). **SISTERS**: Rebecca; Hester (1743–?); Rosamond; and Sophia (?–by 1766). **MARRIED** Rebecca (?–1794). **CHILDREN. SONS**: John (1761–?); Benjamin (1763–?), who married Margaret; Thomas (1765–?); Samuel (1774–?); George; and Elija. **DAUGHTERS**: Sophia (1768–?), who married (first name unknown) Miller; Rebecca; and Alice. **PRIVATE CAREER. EDUCATION**: literate. **RELIGIOUS AFFILIATION**: Anglican, St. Stephen's Parish, Cecil County. **SOCIAL STATUS AND ACTIVITIES**: Esq. at death; subscribed £20 to the establishment of Washington College, Chestertown, Kent County, 1783. **OCCUPATIONAL PROFILE**: farmer. **PUBLIC CAREER. LEGISLATIVE SERVICE**: Convention, Cecil County, 5th, 1775. **LOCAL OFFICES**: Committee of Observation, Cecil County, elected 1775; justice, Cecil County, 1777–1785; militia recruiting officer, Cecil County, in office 1777–1778; appointed "to carry out the Act to prohibit for a limited time the exportation of Indian Corn etc. by land," Cecil County, 1780. **MILITARY SERVICE**: lieutenant colonel, Sassafras Battalion, Cecil County Militia, commissioned 1778. **WEALTH DURING LIFETIME. PERSONAL PROPERTY**: assessed value £820.0.0, including 14 slaves and 3.5 oz. plate, 1783. **LAND AT FIRST ELECTION**: 900 acres in Cecil County (including 642.5 acres inherited from his father, 257 acres by purchase). **SIGNIFICANT CHANGES IN LAND BETWEEN FIRST ELECTION AND DEATH**: probably sold or deeded as a gift ca. 200 acres in Cecil County, 1775–1783. **WEALTH AT DEATH.**

DIED: will probated on June 23, 1785, in Cecil County. **PERSONAL PROPERTY**: TEV, at least £1,164.16.6 current money (including 11 slaves and 1 servant). **LAND**: his dwelling plantation, containing at least 700 acres on Sassafras Neck, Cecil County.

COXE, JAMES (?–?). **IMMIGRATED**: in 1649 as a free adult, probably from Virginia. **RESIDED**: in Anne Arundel County. **PRIVATE CAREER. RELIGIOUS AFFILIATION**: probably a Protestant. **SOCIAL STATUS AND ACTIVITIES**: transported two others with him on his arrival in the colony; Mr. on first appearance in the records, 1650; disappeared from the records in 1651. **PUBLIC CAREER. LEGISLATIVE SERVICE**: Lower House, Providence (Anne Arundel County), 1650–1650/51 (speaker; Accounts 1). **WEALTH DURING LIFETIME. LAND AT FIRST ELECTION**: rights to 300 acres.

CRABB, HENRY WRIGHT (1722/23–1764). **BORN**: on January 16, 1722/23, in Queen Anne Parish, Prince George's County; second son. **NATIVE**: at least second generation. **RESIDED**: in Frederick County. **FAMILY BACKGROUND. FATHER**: *Ralph Crabb* (?–1733). **MOTHER**: Priscilla, daughter of Col. *Thomas Sprigg* (ca. 1670–by 1739). **UNCLES**: *Edward Sprigg* (1697–1751); *Osborn Sprigg* (1707–1749/50). **BROTHERS**: Thomas; Ralph; Jeremiah; and John. **SISTERS**: Sarah; Margaret. **FIRST COUSINS**: *Edward Sprigg* (?–?); *Edward Sprigg* (1723–1758); *Thomas Sprigg* (1715–1781); *Thomas Sprigg* (1747–1809); *Joseph Sprigg* (1736–1800); Margaret Sprigg (1726/27–1804), who married *William Bowie* (1721–1791); *Osborn Sprigg* (1741–1815); and *Francis King* 1724/25–1771). **MARRIED** Ann, daughter of Richard Snowden (?–1763), an ironmaster and ironworks owner of Anne Arundel County, and wife Elizabeth (?–1775); granddaughter of Samuel Thomas (ca. 1655–?) and wife Mary Hutchins; niece of *Philip Thomas* (1693/94–1762). Her brothers were Richard (1719/20–1753), who died without progeny, and who married Elizabeth, only daughter of John Crowley and wife Miriam; Thomas (ca. 1722–?), who married Mary (?–1770), daughter of Henry Wright; Samuel (1728–1801), who married Elizabeth (?–1790), daughter of *Philip Thomas* (1693/94–1762); and John, who married Rachel, daughter of Richard Hopkins. Her sisters were Margaret, (1726–1793), who married *John Contee* (1722–ca. 1796); Elizabeth, who married Joseph Cowman. **CHILDREN. SONS**: *Richard Crabb* (?–1780); Ralph; John; and *Jeremiah Crabb* (1760–1800). **DAUGHTER**: Elizabeth. **PRIVATE CAREER. EDUCATION**: literate. **RELIGIOUS**

AFFILIATION: Protestant. SOCIAL STATUS AND ACTIVITIES: Gent., 1757; Mr., 1764. OCCUPATIONAL PROFILE: probably a planter. PUBLIC CAREER. LEGISLATIVE SERVICE: Lower House, Frederick County, 1749–1751 (Arms and Ammunition 1), 1751–1754 (Arms and Ammunition 1–6), 1754–1757 (Arms and Ammunition 1–4; Bills of Credit 5), 1758–1761. LOCAL OFFICE: justice, Frederick County, 1750–at least 1754. MILITARY SERVICE: captain, 1751. WEALTH DURING LIFETIME. LAND AT FIRST ELECTION: at least 292 acres in Frederick County. SIGNIFICANT CHANGES IN LAND BETWEEN FIRST ELECTION AND DEATH: owned 4,510 acres in Frederick County, 1754–1758; sold 1,011 acres in Frederick County, 1758. WEALTH AT DEATH. DIED: will probated on June 12, 1764, in Frederick County. LAND: 3,518 acres in Frederick County.

CRABB, JEREMIAH (1760–1800). BORN: in 1760 in Frederick County. NATIVE: at least third generation. RESIDED: near Rockville, Montgomery County. FAMILY BACKGROUND. FATHER: *Henry Wright Crabb* (1722/23–1764). MOTHER: Ann Snowden. AUNT: Margaret Snowden (1726–1793), who married *John Contee* (1722–ca. 1796). BROTHERS: *Richard Crabb* (?–1780); Ralph; and John. SISTER: Elizabeth. HALF FIRST COUSINS: *Richard Brooke* (1736–1788); *Richard Thomas* (ca. 1728–1806); and *Evan Thomas* (1738/39–1826). OTHER KINSHIP: his great-uncle was *Philip Thomas* (1693/94–1762). MARRIED Elizabeth Ridgely (1764–1828), daughter of *Charles Greenbury Griffith* (1744–1792). CHILDREN. SONS: Charles Henry; Richard. DAUGHTERS: Elizabeth Ridgely (?–1821), who married Thomas Worthington Howard; Sarah Griffith; Ann Snowden, who married Richard J. Orme; Matilda; Emeline; and Lydia Ridgely. PRIVATE CAREER. EDUCATION: literate. SOCIAL STATUS AND ACTIVITIES: Esq., 1795. OCCUPATIONAL PROFILE: planter. PUBLIC CAREER. LEGISLATIVE SERVICE: Lower House, Montgomery County, 1788, 1789, 1790, 1791–1792, 1792, 1793. LOCAL OFFICE: associate justice, 5th District Court, Montgomery County, 1791–1792 (resigned). MILITARY SERVICE: 2nd lieutenant, Fourth Maryland Regiment, 1776; 1st lieutenant, Fourth Maryland Regiment, 1777–1778 (resigned); brigadier general, Seventh Brigade (lower part of Frederick County and upper part of Montgomery County), Maryland Militia, 1794–1800. OUT OF STATE SERVICE: representative, U.S. Congress, 1795–1796 (resigned). WEALTH DURING LIFETIME. PERSONAL PROPERTY: assessed value £397.18.6, including 10 slaves and 7.5 oz. plate,

1783; 20 slaves, 1790; as an only child his wife inherited all of her father's estate, assessed value £1,278.0.0, including 22 slaves and 16 oz. plate, 1792; 41 slaves, 1793; 36 slaves, 1798. LAND AT FIRST ELECTION: at least 2,435 acres, possibly as much as 3,035 acres in Frederick County (later became part of Montgomery County) (600 acres inherited from his father). SIGNIFICANT CHANGES IN LAND BETWEEN FIRST ELECTION AND DEATH: acquired an additional 1,598 acres in Montgomery County, of which 1,200 acres were his wife's inheritance, 1792–1800; sold 1,429 acres in Montgomery County, of which 1,131 acres were his wife's land, 1793–1798. WEALTH AT DEATH. DIED: on February 19, 1800, in Montgomery County. PERSONAL PROPERTY: TEV, £4,001.17.5 current money (including 35 slaves, plate, and books); FB, £1,103.8.9. LAND: probably ca. 2,604 acres, possibly as much as 3,204 acres, in Montgomery County.

CRABB, RALPH (?–1733/34). BORN: of age by 1716. RESIDED: in Prince George's County. FAMILY BACKGROUND. BROTHER: Edward. OTHER KINSHIP: probably related to *Thomas Crabb* (?–1719/20). MARRIED on August 22, 1716, Priscilla, daughter of *Thomas Sprigg* (ca. 1670–by 1739); granddaughter of Edward Mariartee and wife Honor. Her uncle was *Daniel Mariartee* (ca. 1676–1726/27). Her brothers were Thomas; *Edward Sprigg* (1697–1751); and *Osborn Sprigg* (1707–1749/50). Her sisters were Margaret; Eleanor. Her first cousin was *John Smith Prather* (1706–1763). Her nephews were *Edward Sprigg* (?–?); *Edward Sprigg* (1723–1758); *Thomas Sprigg* (1715–1781); *Thomas Sprigg* (1747–1809); *Joseph Sprigg* (1736–1800); *Osborn Sprigg* (ca. 1741–1815); and *Francis King* (1724/25–1771). Her niece was Margaret Sprigg (1726/27–1804), who married *William Bowie* (1721–1791). CHILDREN. SONS: Thomas (1719–?); *Henry Wright Crabb* (1722/23–1764); Ralph (1724–?); Jeremiah (1728–?); and John (1731–?). DAUGHTERS: Sarah (1717–?), who married on December 5, 1734, Robert Magruder; Margaret (1720–?), who married in 1735 William Hilleary; and Ellinor (1726–?). PRIVATE CAREER. EDUCATION: literate. RELIGIOUS AFFILIATION: Anglican. SOCIAL STATUS AND ACTIVITIES: Mr., 1718; Gent., 1721. OCCUPATIONAL PROFILE: merchant, 1718. PUBLIC CAREER. LEGISLATIVE SERVICE: Lower House, Prince George's County, 1719–1721/22 (Elections 1–5), 1722–1724 (Elections 1–3), 1725–1727 (Elections 1–3; Aggrievances 4), 1728–1731 (Elections 1–5), 1732–1733 (Elections 1, 2; died before the convention). LOCAL

OFFICES: Queen Anne Parish Vestry, Prince George's County, in office 1716–1719, 1722–1723, 1725–1726, 1731–1734; justice, Prince George's County, 1719–ca. 1733 (quorum, 1727–ca. 1733); justice, Court of Oyer and Terminer and Gaol Delivery, commissioned 1729; churchwarden, Queen Anne Parish, Prince George's County, in office 1730–1731. WEALTH DURING LIFETIME. LAND AT FIRST ELECTION: 194 acres in Prince George's County (all by purchase). SIGNIFICANT CHANGES IN LAND BETWEEN FIRST ELECTION AND DEATH: purchased an additional 1,234 acres in Prince George's County, and possibly as much as 1,534 acres, 1723–1725; patented 470 acres in Prince George's County in 1723. WEALTH AT DEATH. DIED: will probated on March 8, 1733/34, in Prince George's County. PERSONAL PROPERTY: TEV, £978.15.4 (including 14 slaves, 159.5 oz. plate, and books); FB, £772.12.4. LAND: ca. 2,040 acres in Prince George's County.

CRABB, RICHARD (?–1780). BORN: in Frederick County. NATIVE: at least third generation. RESIDED: in Montgomery County. FAMILY BACKGROUND. FATHER: *Henry Wright Crabb* (1722/23–1764). MOTHER: Ann Snowden. AUNT: Margaret Snowden (1726–1793), who married *John Contee* (1722–ca. 1796). BROTHERS: *Jeremiah Crabb* (1760–1800); Ralph; and John. SISTER: Elizabeth. HALF FIRST COUSINS: *Richard Brooke* (1736–1788); *Richard Thomas* (ca. 1728–1806); and *Evan Thomas* (1738/39–1826). OTHER KINSHIP: his great-uncle was *Philip Thomas* (1693/94–1762). PRIVATE CAREER. EDUCATION: literate. OCCUPATIONAL PROFILE: probably a planter. PUBLIC CAREER. LEGISLATIVE SERVICE: Lower House, Montgomery County, 1777, 1777–1778, 1778–1779 (Elections 3). WEALTH DURING LIFETIME. LAND AT FIRST ELECTION: one-fourth interest in ca. 2,850 undivided acres in Montgomery County (devised to him by his father). WEALTH AT DEATH. DIED: in 1780 in Montgomery County. PERSONAL PROPERTY: TEV, £1,034.18.6 current money (including 15 slaves and books); FB, estate overpaid £23.10.6. LAND: probably a one-fourth interest in ca. 2,850 acres in Montgomery County.

CRABB, THOMAS (?–1719/20). IMMIGRATED: by 1700 as a free adult. RESIDED: in Charles County. FAMILY BACKGROUND. His origins are ambiguous, but perhaps he was related to William Crabb, who was a merchant of Bristol, England, in 1683, and *Ralph Crabb* (?–1733/34). MARRIED Elizabeth, who subsequently married Randolph Morris. CHILDREN. DAUGHTERS: Elizabeth; Mar-

garet; and Jane, who married Charles Somersett Smith. PRIVATE CAREER. EDUCATION: literate. RELIGIOUS AFFILIATION: Anglican. OCCUPATIONAL PROFILE: merchant. PUBLIC CAREER. LEGISLATIVE SERVICE: Lower House, Charles County, 1708B–1711. LOCAL OFFICES: justice, Charles County, 1708–1719/20 (quorum, 1712/13–1719/20); All Faiths Parish Vestry, St. Mary's County, 1709–1711. MILITARY SERVICE: captain, 1708–1717; major, 1717–1719; colonel, 1719–1719/20. WEALTH DURING LIFETIME. LAND AT FIRST ELECTION: 780 acres. WEALTH AT DEATH. DIED: will probated on March 8, 1719/20. PERSONAL PROPERTY: TEV, £1,053.0.10 (including 12 slaves and 3 servants); FB, £891.3.8. LAND: 1,210 acres.

CRADOCK, JOHN (ca. 1749–1794). BORN: on January 25, ca. 1749, in St. Thomas Parish, Baltimore County; second son. NATIVE: second generation. RESIDED: at "Bloomsbury," Baltimore County. FAMILY BACKGROUND. FATHER: Rev. Thomas Cradock (1718–1770), born in Wolverhamp, Bedfordshire, England; educated at Oxford University; immigrated in 1744 from England; first rector of St. Thomas Parish, Baltimore County in 1745; brother of John Cradock (ca. 1708–1778), archbishop of Dublin and chaplain to John, fourth duke of Bedford (1710–1771). MOTHER: Katherine (ca. 1728–1795), daughter of John Risteau and wife Katherine. UNCLE: *George Risteau* (?–1792). BROTHERS: Arthur (1747–1769), a minister; Thomas (1732–1821), a physician. SISTER: Ann (1755–?), who married Charles Walker. MARRIED in 1776 Ann (1760–1809), daughter of John Worthington and wife Mary Todd. Her sisters were Eleanor; Hannah; Elizabeth Mary, who married Edward Carvil Tolley; and Margaret (1767–?), who married William Laman, of Allegany County. CHILDREN. SON: Arthur (1782–1821), a physician. DAUGHTERS: Mary (1778–?), who married in 1797 Stephen Cromwell; Katherine (1779–?), who married in 1818 Dr. Thomas Cradock Walker; Elizabeth (1784–?); and Ann (1786–?), who married (first name unknown) Bosley, of Kentucky. PRIVATE CAREER. EDUCATION: attended his father's school for boys and later studied medicine in Philadelphia. RELIGIOUS AFFILIATION: Anglican, St. Thomas Parish, Baltimore County; a delegate to the diocesan conventions in Maryland, 1784–1789. OCCUPATIONAL PROFILE: physician; began his practice in Baltimore County, 1768. PUBLIC CAREER. LEGISLATIVE SERVICE: Convention, Baltimore County, 5th, 1775; Lower House, Baltimore County, 1782–1783 (Elections 1). LOCAL OFFICES: Committee of

Observation, Baltimore County, in office 1774 and 1775; justice, Baltimore County, 1774–1794; St. Thomas Parish Vestry, Baltimore County, 1775–1789. MILITARY SERVICE: major, Second Maryland Battalion, Flying Camp, July to December 1776. WEALTH DURING LIFETIME. PERSONAL PROPERTY: assessed value £763.10.0, including 7 slaves and 43 oz. plate, 1783. LAND AT FIRST ELECTION: 349 acres in Baltimore County (inherited from his father in 1770). SIGNIFICANT CHANGES IN LAND BETWEEN FIRST ELECTION AND DEATH: from 1786 through the 1790s Cradock was heavily in debt and was finally forced to mortgage his main estate of 338 acres in Baltimore County shortly before his death to secure a debt of £2,400 current money. WEALTH AT DEATH. DIED: on October 4, 1794, in Baltimore County. PERSONAL PROPERTY: TEV, £770.18.10 current money (including 7 slaves); FB, estate overpaid £26.2.2. LAND: ca. 400 acres in Baltimore County (338 acres of which were mortgaged).

CRAIK, WILLIAM (1761–?). BORN: on October 3, 1761, near Port Tobacco, Charles County; probably only son. NATIVE: second generation. RESIDED: in Charles County; Baltimore County; Frederick County, 1793. FAMILY BACKGROUND. FATHER: Dr. James Craik (1731–1814), graduated from the University of Edinburgh; emigrated from Scotland; accompanied George Washington on an expedition against the French and Indians in 1754, and was with Edward Braddock in 1755. He was director-general of the hospital at the seige of Yorktown in 1781. After the Revolution he was invited by Washington to settle near Mount Vernon. Craik served as Washington's physician; he died in Fairfax County, Virginia, on February 6, 1814. MOTHER: Marianne Ewell (1739–1815), originally from Prince William County, Virginia. MARRIED on November 9, 1796, in Allegany County to Hannah Hall. PRIVATE CAREER. EDUCATION: literate, attended Delamere (Delameve?) school in Frederick County. SOCIAL STATUS AND ACTIVITIES: Esq., 1790. OCCUPATIONAL PROFILE: lawyer, practiced in Port Tobacco, Charles County, and Leonardtown, St. Mary's County. PUBLIC CAREER. LEGISLATIVE SERVICE: Lower House, Charles County, 1789 (Elections), 1790, 1791–1792. OTHER STATE OFFICES: Constitution Ratification Convention, Charles County, 1788; chief justice, Fifth Judicial District of Maryland, 1793–1796, 1801–1802. OUT OF STATE SERVICE: representative, U.S. Congress, 1796–1797 (elected to fill vacancy; seated on December 5, 1796), 1797–1799, 1799–1801. WEALTH DURING LIFETIME. PER-

SONAL PROPERTY: owned 23 slaves, 1790. SIGNIFICANT CHANGES IN LAND BETWEEN FIRST ELECTION AND DEATH: patented and purchased 264 acres in Charles County, 1793 and 1796. WEALTH AT DEATH. DIED: prior to 1814; size of estate unknown.

CRAMPHIN (CRAMPPIN), THOMAS, JR. (ca. 1740–ca. 1831). BORN: on January 26, ca. 1740, in Prince George's Parish, Prince George's County; eldest son. NATIVE: at least third generation. RESIDED: at the "Hermitage," Lower District, Frederick County (later became part of Montgomery County). FAMILY BACKGROUND. FATHER: Thomas Cramphin, Sr. (1715–1783), son of Henry Cramphin (?–1746), of Prince George's County, an innkeeper. MOTHER: Mary Jackson. STEPMOTHER: Elizabeth Pottinger, widow of John Bowie, Jr. SISTER: Ruth (1742–?), who married in 1776 her stepbrother *Allen Bowie, Jr.* (1737–1803). HALF BROTHERS: Basil; Robert; and Richard Pottinger (1760–1806), of Bladensburg, Prince George's County, never married. STEPBROTHERS: *Allen Bowie, Jr.* (1737–1803); James Bowie; and John Bowie (1744–?), who married Margaret Dallas. MARRIED never. CHILDREN. Died without progeny. PRIVATE CAREER. EDUCATION: literate. RELIGIOUS AFFILIATION: Anglican. OCCUPATIONAL PROFILE: planter. PUBLIC CAREER. LEGISLATIVE SERVICE: Conventions, Frederick County, 1st, 1774, 4th, 1775, 5th, 1775; Lower House, Montgomery County, 1778–1779, 1779–1780 (Claims 1–3), 1780–1781 (Claims 1, 2), 1784, 1785, 1788. OTHER STATE OFFICE: Constitution Ratification Convention, Montgomery County, 1788. LOCAL OFFICES: Committee of Observation, Frederick County, elected 1774 and 1775; justice, Montgomery County, commissioned 1777; commissioner of tax, Montgomery County, commissioned 1783, in office 1792–at least 1798; Prince George's Parish Vestry, Montgomery County, by 1790–1792, 1792–at least 1796; justice, Orphans' Court, Montgomery County, commissioned 1791, 1794, and 1797. STANDS ON PUBLIC/PRIVATE ISSUES: attended the protest meeting at Hungerford Tavern, Rockville, Montgomery County, on June 11, 1774, which denounced Great Britain and recommended breaking off all commerce with the mother country. WEALTH DURING LIFETIME. PERSONAL PROPERTY: assessed value £2,097.0.0, including 30 slaves, 1783; assessed value £10,521.0.0, including 104 slaves, 1813; assessed value £11,069.3.0, including 155 slaves, 1820; assessed value in the 4th district only, $4,565.33 including 48 slaves and 56 oz. plate, 1826; assessed value $13,021.00, including 214 slaves and 73 oz. plate, 1831. LAND AT FIRST ELECTION: 1,978 acres in Frederick, Prince George's, and Montgomery counties (427 acres inherited from his father). SIGNIFICANT CHANGES IN LAND BETWEEN FIRST ELECTION AND DEATH: patented 2,324 acres in Montgomery County, 1775–1788; owned 5,182 acres in Montgomery County in 1813; owned 5,913 acres in Montgomery County in 1820. ADDITIONAL COMMENTS: gained substantial wealth by investing in mortgages and bonds. WEALTH AT DEATH. DIED: ca. 1831, in Montgomery County. PERSONAL PROPERTY: TEV, $68,140.86 current money (including 245 slaves on 5 plantations, china, and paintings); FB, $50,474.43. LAND: 6,132 acres in Montgomery County.

CRAUFURD (CRANFORD, CRAUFORD, CRAWFORD), DAVID (ca. 1738–1801). BORN: ca. 1738 in Prince George's County; only son. NATIVE: at least second generation. RESIDED: in Upper Marlboro, Prince George's County. FAMILY BACKGROUND. FATHER: David Crawford (?–1749), of Upper Marlboro, Prince George's County, a merchant. MOTHER: Mary (?–1794). SISTERS: Mary, who married (first name unknown) Parker; Martha (?–1778), who married first, William Hamilton (?–1759), a merchant, who was killed by an accidental discharge of a gun, second, Charles Clark (?–1767), and third, *Osborn Sprigg* (ca. 1741–1815). NEPHEW: *Thomas Clark* (ca. 1760–1796). MARRIED by 1764 Sarah (ca. 1749–1780), daughter of Nathaniel Offutt; granddaughter of William Offutt. CHILDREN. SONS: David; Nathaniel (by 1764–?). DAUGHTERS: Mary (ca. 1768–1787), who married Richard Alexander Contee (1753–?), son of *John Contee* (1722–ca. 1796); Sarah (1771–1832), who died in Washington, D.C., and who married Richard Forrest (ca. 1768–1828), postmaster of Georgetown, D.C., in 1797, and one of eight clerks of the Department of State appointed by President Thomas Jefferson; Martha (1777–1796), who married in 1794 George Walker. PRIVATE CAREER. EDUCATION: literate. RELIGIOUS AFFILIATION: Anglican. SOCIAL STATUS AND ACTIVITIES: Gent., by 1773; Esq., by 1787. ADDITIONAL COMMENTS: Crauford gave £1,000 current money and 21 hogsheads of tobacco to help finance the Continental Army, 1780. OCCUPATIONAL PROFILE: clerk and bookkeeper for *Stephen West* (1727–1790) between January 1757 and December 1758; a merchant, with a store in Upper Marlboro, Prince George's County. After the Revolution, Crauford, with John Read Ma-

gruder and occasionally *Gabriel Duvall* (1752–1844) held powers of attorney from various London merchants, including John Stephenson and William Dawes, for transactions involving their properties and creditors in the United States. PUBLIC CAREER. LEGISLATIVE SERVICE: Conventions, Prince George's County, 2nd–3rd, 1774, 4th, 1775, 5th, 1775; Lower House, Prince George's County, 1777, 1779–1780 (Claims 1, 3), 1780–1781 (Claims 1, 2; Elections 1, 2), 1787–1788 (Claims 1, 2), 1788. LOCAL OFFICES: justice, Prince George's County, 1761–1789 (quorum, at least by 1769–1789); St. Paul's Parish Vestry, Prince George's County, in office 1767–1770, 1782–1785, 1789–1792, and 1795; Committee of Correspondence, Prince George's County, elected 1774; Committee of Observation, Prince George's County, elected 1775; justice, Orphans' Court, Prince George's County, 1777–1790; subscription officer, Continental Loan Office, Prince George's County, appointed 1777 and 1779; commissioner of tax, Prince George's County, 1786–at least 1798; associate justice, First District Court, Prince George's County, appointed 1790–1791; Maryland Senate elector, Prince George's County, elected 1791 and 1796. MILITARY SERVICE: captain, by 1776. WEALTH DURING LIFETIME. PERSONAL PROPERTY: assessed value £1,210.0.0, including 28 slaves, Montgomery County, 1783; gave 25 slaves to son Nathaniel, 1785; 50 slaves, Prince George's County, 1790; assessed value £1,100.0.0, including 36 slaves, Montgomery County, 1798; assessed value £1,592.7.6, including 40 slaves and 158 oz. plate, Prince George's County, 1800; gave 4 slaves to granddaughter Sarah Forrest, 1800. LAND AT FIRST ELECTION: 2,891 acres in Prince George's and Frederick counties, plus 2 lots each in Upper Marlboro and Carrollsburg, Prince George's County (688 acres in Prince George's County was the remainder of 737 acres inherited from his father; 1,940 acres in Prince George's and Frederick counties acquired through his marriage; 263 acres in Prince George's and Frederick counties plus 4 lots by purchase). SIGNIFICANT CHANGES IN LAND BETWEEN FIRST ELECTION AND DEATH: Crauford patented 691 acres of his wife's land in Frederick County (later became Montgomery County) with adjoining vacant land into a 900-acre tract in 1775. He sold his 150 acres in Montgomery County (formerly Frederick County) in 1777; and in the same year he and his wife formed a trust giving their son Nathaniel the rest of her inheritance, a 1,294-acre tract in Prince George's County, but reserving a life estate in the property. In 1785 Crauford deeded 800 acres of this tract, including the "mansion house," outright to Nathaniel. Crauford sold several small tracts totaling 172 acres in Prince George's County, 1776–1781. He acquired by purchase or patent 384 acres in Prince George's and Montgomery counties, 1782–1801, as well as additional lots in Upper Marlboro, Prince George's County, Georgetown, Montgomery County, and Washington, D.C. In 1787 he gave his granddaughter Sarah Contee one-half of a lot in Upper Marlboro on which a house was being built. **WEALTH AT DEATH. DIED:** between May 10 and May 27, 1801, in Prince George's County. **LAND:** ca. 2,000 acres in Montgomery and Prince George's counties, plus 11 lots in Upper Marlboro, Prince George's County, 4 lots in Washington, D.C., and possibly 1 lot in Georgetown, D.C.

CRAWFORD (CRANFORD), JAMES (?–1699).

IMMIGRATED: ca. 1675 as a indentured servant from England. **RESIDED:** in Calvert County. **MARRIED** by 1696 Katherine. **PRIVATE CAREER. EDUCATION:** literate; studied law in George Parker's office. **RELIGIOUS AFFILIATION:** Protestant. **SOCIAL STATUS AND ACTIVITIES:** arrived as a servant to George Parker; Gent. by 1688; his experience in Parker's office led to a prosperous legal career. **OCCUPATIONAL PROFILE:** indentured servant, free by 1678; lawyer, admitted to the following courts: Prerogative Court by 1684; Provincial Court in 1694; Anne Arundel County by 1694; Calvert County by 1694; Prince George's County in 1696. Planter. **PUBLIC CAREER. LEGISLATIVE SERVICE:** Lower House, Calvert County, 1696–1697 (elected to the 5th session; Laws 7), 1697/98–1699 (Laws, 1–3; died during the 3rd session). **STANDS ON PUBLIC/PRIVATE ISSUES:** opposed the revolution of 1689; a controversial attorney, he was disbarred from practice in August 1697 for an alleged dishonest administration of an estate; he was supported by the Assembly, however, and readmitted to the bar soon after. **WEALTH DURING LIFETIME. LAND AT FIRST ELECTION:** over 1,725 acres. **WEALTH AT DEATH. DIED:** on July 13, 1699; he was killed when struck by lightning at the State House. **PERSONAL PROPERTY:** TEV, £787.18.0 sterling (including 9 slaves, 3 servants, and 21 law books); FB, £51.18.0. **LAND:** 1,725 acres.

CRESAP, THOMAS (ca. 1703–1788).

BORN: ca. 1703 in Skipton, Yorkshire, England. **IMMIGRATED:** ca. 1718. **RESIDED:** in Baltimore County, 1727; Prince George's County (later became part of Washington County), ca. 1737; Western Maryland (later became part of Allegany County), ca. 1740. **FAMILY BACKGROUND. BROTHER:** Robert Cresap, of London, England. **SISTER:** Ann Dobson, of London, England. **MARRIED** first, by 1727 Hannah Johnson. **MARRIED** second, by 1783 Margaret. **CHILDREN. SONS:** Daniel (1727/28–?); Thomas (1732/33–1756), killed by an Indian; and Capt. Michael (1742–1775). **DAUGHTERS:** Elizabeth (1736/37–?); Sarah (1740–?). **PRIVATE CAREER. EDUCATION:** literate, self taught. **RELIGIOUS AFFILIATION:** Protestant. **SOCIAL STATUS AND ACTIVITIES:** Gent., 1749; Esq., 1751. **OCCUPATIONAL PROFILE:** planter, 1735; fur trader and surveyor, ca. 1737; merchant, 1783. His home and trading post at Old Town lay on the trail that the Iroquois followed in their wars with the Southern Indians. He acted as Maryland's agent in dealing with the Cherokees and Iroquois, and often advised Virginia's Governor Dinwiddie on Indian affairs. He was respected by both whites and Indians from Canada to the Carolinas. A founder of the Ohio Company in 1749, Cresap and his associates were instrumental in opening a road, sixty miles in length, between the Potomac and the Ohio rivers. **PUBLIC CAREER. LEGISLATIVE SERVICE:** Lower House, Frederick County, 1757–1758 (Accounts 1, Cv, 2; Arms and Ammunition 1, Cv, 2); 1758–1761 (Accounts Cv 1, 1, Cv 2, 3, Cv 3; Arms and Ammunition Cv 1, 1, Cv 2, 3, Cv 3), 1762–1763 (Arms and Ammunitions 2), 1765–1766 (Arms and Ammunition 2; Grievances 2, 3), 1768–1770 (Arms and Ammunition 1–3; Grievances 1). **LOCAL OFFICES:** justice, Prince George's County, 1739–1748 (quorum, 1741–1748), Frederick County, 1748–at least 1775 (quorum, 1748–at least 1775); deputy surveyor, Prince George's County, commissioned 1747; justice, Court of Oyer and Terminer and Gaol Delivery, Frederick County, commissioned 1751 and 1775; Committee of Observation, Frederick County, elected 1774 and 1775. **MILITARY SERVICE:** captain, ca. 1732; colonel, 1749. **STANDS ON PUBLIC/PRIVATE ISSUES:** By 1729 he had established a farm on Maryland's disputed northern border with Pennsylvania under lenient terms offered by Lord Baltimore. Supported by the proprietary government, which made him a local magistrate and captain of militia, Cresap stubbornly asserted Maryland sovereignty in the area. His aggressive defiance of Pennsylvania authority escalated the controversy into armed conflict, the Conojacular War, and earned him the respect of influential Maryland officials. The Pennsylvanians viewed him as the "Maryland Monster." **WEALTH DURING LIFETIME. PERSONAL PROPERTY:** home burned by Pennsylvanians in

1737; insolvent ca. 1739 when a large shipment of his furs was taken by the French. LAND AT FIRST ELECTION: 3,727 acres in Baltimore, Prince George's, and Frederick counties, plus one-twentieth, or 25,000 acres, of a 500,000-acre grant on the Ohio River that he received as a founder of the Ohio Company in 1749. SIGNIFICANT CHANGES IN LAND BETWEEN FIRST ELECTION AND DEATH: sold 1,505 acres in Frederick and Washington counties, 1760–1783; deeded as a gift 25,000 acres (his share of the Ohio Company) to his son Daniel and his grandsons James and Michael in 1783. WEALTH AT DEATH. DIED: letters of administration granted on April 26, 1788, to Margaret Cresap, but will was not probated until January 21, 1790, in Allegany County. LAND: at least 1,210 acres in Maryland, Virginia, and Pennsylvania.

CROMWELL, RICHARD (1749–1802). BORN: on December 30, 1749, in St. Thomas Parish, Baltimore County; youngest son. NATIVE: fourth generation. RESIDED: in Baltimore County; Washington County, ca. 1780. FAMILY BACKGROUND. FATHER: Joseph Cromwell (1707–1769). MOTHER: Comfort (1710–1787), daughter of *John Dorsey* (ca. 1682–?) and wife Comfort Stimpson. UNCLE: *John Hammond Dorsey* (1718–1774). BROTHERS: Philomen (?–1767); Nathan (1731–1813), who married Phoebe; Joseph (1741–1782), who married Anne Orrick; and Stephen (1747–1783), a member of the Baltimore County Committee of Observation and a major in the Gunpowder Upper Battalion, Baltimore County. SISTERS: Ruth (1738–?), who married Ezekiel Towson; Chloe (1746–1823), who married Capt. John Cockey; and Comfort. OTHER KINSHIP: his great-uncle was *Richard Gist* (1683–1741). MARRIED on February 4, 1772, Rachel (1748–1806), daughter of William Cockey and wife Constance (Constant) Ashman; granddaughter of both John Cockey and wife Elizabeth Slade, and John Ashman and wife Constance Wilmott. CHILDREN. SONS: William (1773–1809); Oliver (1775–1857), who died in St. Louis, Missouri; Richard (1777–?), who married Susan McLaughlin; Philomen (1780–1804); Nathan (1785–?), an adjutant in the First Maryland Regiment during the War of 1812; John Cockey (1787–?); Stephen (1790–?); and Joseph Frederick (1792–?). DAUGHTERS: Constant (1782–1851); Chloe (1783–?). PRIVATE CAREER. EDUCATION: literate. RELIGIOUS AFFILIATION: Anglican. SOCIAL STATUS AND ACTIVITIES: Mr., 1788; Gent., 1791; Esq., 1794. OCCUPATIONAL PROFILE: farmer, 1775. PUBLIC CAREER. LEGISLATIVE SERVICE: Lower House,

Washington County, 1786–1787, 1792, 1795, 1800, 1802. LOCAL OFFICES: Committee of Observation, Baltimore County, elected 1775; justice, Baltimore County, 1777–1780 (moved residence), Washington County, 1791–at least 1800. MILITARY SERVICE: 1st lieutenant, Baltimore County Militia, 1777; captain, 1780. WEALTH DURING LIFETIME. PERSONAL PROPERTY: assessed value £784.0.0, including 11 slaves and 1 oz. plate, 1783. LAND AT FIRST ELECTION: ca. 1,811 acres in Washington, Baltimore, and Anne Arundel counties, plus 1 lot in Baltimore East Hundred, Baltimore County (ca. 400 acres inherited from his father; purchased 590 acres of confiscated British property). SIGNIFICANT CHANGES IN LAND BETWEEN FIRST ELECTION AND DEATH: acquired by purchase and patent 1,127 acres in Washington County, 1791–1802. WEALTH AT DEATH. DIED: on December 25, 1802; buried in St. Anne's Churchyard, Annapolis. His funeral was attended by members of both houses of the legislature and a "large concourse of respectable citizens. . . ." PERSONAL PROPERTY: TEV, £3,034.4.0 (including 12 slaves and more than 6 books); FB, £2,703.11.0. LAND: probably ca. 2,938 acres in Washington, Baltimore, and Anne Arundel counties.

CROOKE, ROBERT (?–1697) BORN: probably in England. IMMIGRATED: by 1665 as an indentured servant to *Thomas Howell* (?–1675). RESIDED: in Cecil County. MARRIED never. CHILDREN. Died without progeny. PRIVATE CAREER. EDUCATION: illiterate. RELIGIOUS AFFILIATION: Anglican. OCCUPATIONAL PROFILE: servant, 1665; a planter, who also engaged in some mercantile activity. PUBLIC CAREER. LEGISLATIVE SERVICE: Lower House, Cecil County, 1692–1693 (elected to the 1st session to fill vacancy). LOCAL OFFICES: North Sassafras Parish Vestry, Cecil County, 1693–1697; justice, Cecil County, 1694–1697. MILITARY SERVICE: officer, 1696. STANDS ON PUBLIC/PRIVATE ISSUES: opposed the revolution of 1689. WEALTH DURING LIFETIME. LAND AT FIRST ELECTION: 4 tracts of unspecified acreage. WEALTH AT DEATH. DIED: will probated on June 9, 1697. PERSONAL PROPERTY: TEV, £414.7.0 sterling (including 1 slave and 6 servants); £176.2.6 in debts owed to his estate. LAND: 4 tracts, 1 containing at least 100 acres.

CUMMING (COMMINGS, CUMMINGS), WILLIAM (ca. 1696–1752). BORN: ca. 1696. IMMIGRATED: arrested ca. 1716 as a Jacobite rebel in Lancaster, Great Britain, and transported to Maryland on the ship *Friendship* from Belfast, Ireland. He was sold as a servant first to Thomas Macnemara and then to *Thomas Bordley* (ca. 1683–1726). RESIDED: in Annapolis, Anne Arundel County. MARRIED first, on January 21, 1719/20, Elizabeth, daughter of *Henry Coursey* (1662–1707); granddaughter of *Henry Coursey* (ca. 1629–1695). Her brothers were Henry (1693–?); Otho; and William (1703–1769). Her sisters were Araminta; Juliana; and Mary. Her nephew was *Edward DeCoursey* (ca. 1759–1827). Her niece was Sarah Coursey, who married *Robert Wright* (1752–1826). MARRIED second, by 1742/43 Margaret Thomas (?–1804). CHILDREN. SONS: William (baptised on February 28, 1719/20–died young); Alexander (1721–1774), of Frederick and Baltimore counties; William (1724–1793), of Annapolis, in Frederick County by July 1751, a planter and attorney who was fined £25 during the Revolution by the Frederick County justices for allegedly drinking to His Majesty's health; Henry (1726–1768), of St. Botolph Aldgate Parish, London, England, a mariner; James; and David (?–1796), of Anne Arundel County. DAUGHTERS: Elizabeth, who married (first name unknown) Hamilton; Mary (1742/43–?), who married John Dorsey (?–1815), son of John Dorsey and wife Elizabeth; Margaret; and Araminta (?–1824), of Frederick County, who married in 1800 Capt. Ely Dorsey (?–1821), son of Ely Dorsey and wife Deborah. PRIVATE CAREER. EDUCATION: literate; while a servant to Macnemara and *Thomas Bordley* (ca. 1683–1726) Cummings said he had obtained some knowledge of the law. RELIGIOUS AFFILIATION: Anglican, St. Anne's Parish, Anne Arundel County. SOCIAL STATUS AND ACTIVITIES: servant, ca. 1716. OCCUPATIONAL PROFILE: lawyer, admitted to the following courts: Anne Arundel County in March 1718/19 (he was fined 100 pounds of tobacco during March 1721/22 for nonattendance in court); Prince George's County in March 1718/19; Baltimore County in August 1719 (his petition to be admitted was rejected, but no reason was given); Court of Chancery by July 1720; Provincial Court ca. 1722 or 1723 (he was fined 100 pounds of tobacco in October 1726 for nonattendance in court); Prince George's County in November 1725 (took new oath required by law); Prerogative Court in March 1725/26; St. Mary's County by June 1729; Calvert County by August 1741; Frederick County by March 1748/49. PUBLIC CAREER. LEGISLATIVE SERVICE: Lower House, Annapolis, 1732–1734 (Laws 1–Cv; Accounts Cv). OTHER STATE OFFICES: clerk, Lower House, July 1731 (served for Michael Macnemara); clerk, High Court of Appeals and Errors, commissioned 1733.

LOCAL OFFICES: clerk of Indictments, Prince George's County, sworn 1720 and 1727; common councilman, Annapolis, elected 1721; churchwarden, St. Anne's Parish, Anne Arundel County, 1721–1722; St. Anne's Parish Vestry, Anne Arundel County, 1732–1735; alderman, Annapolis, by 1740–1752. WEALTH DURING LIFETIME. PERSONAL PROPERTY: executed a deed of trust to his son William transferring all his real and personal property for the benefit of his creditors in 1751, including 117 law books, 40 slaves, 1 black and 3 white servants, and silver plate. LAND AT FIRST ELECTION: 778 acres in Anne Arundel and Prince George's counties, plus 3 lots in Annapolis (all by purchase or patent, including a one-half interest in 660 acres in Prince George's County patented with James Edmondston). SIGNIFICANT CHANGES IN LAND BETWEEN FIRST ELECTION AND DEATH: gave 4,609 acres in Anne Arundel and Frederick counties, plus 3 lots in Annapolis, by deed of trust to his son William to be sold for the benefit of his creditors in 1751, this being the total of his real property; Cumming even offered to "surrender his body which is Old Exausted [*sic*] and Impaired to Satisfy his Creditors if required"; he requested only that his son redeem the mortgage he had taken out on his dwelling house and outhouses in Annapolis from *Philip Hammond* (1697–1760). WEALTH AT DEATH. DIED: on March 11, 1752, of an apoplectic fit near Lower Marlboro, Calvert County, on his return from St. Mary's County. PERSONAL PROPERTY: TEV, £411.2.5 current money (including 7 slaves, 2 servants, law books and other books, 70 oz. plate, and a Tuesday Club medal). All of his personal property, however, had previously been given by deed of trust to his son in 1751 to be sold for the benefit of his creditors; FB, £89.5.1. LAND: all of his real estate had been given by deed of trust in 1751 to his son to be sold for the benefit of his creditors; by 1770 some of Cumming's creditors still had not been paid. ADDITIONAL COMMENTS: in 1770 Alexander Cumming, eldest son and heir-at-law of William, petitioned the legislature for damages he felt were due him as a result of the quartering of some of the king's forces in his father's house in Annapolis in 1754. The premises were left in a ruinous and shattered condition, and had since been appraised and sold at a lower price for the benefit of his father's creditors. Alexander's petition was rejected by the Lower House, which stated that there appeared to be creditors of William Cumming who had not yet received payment.

CURRER (CURRIER), WILLIAM (ca. 1739–1784). BORN: on February 28, ca. 1739, in St. Mary Anne's Parish, Cecil County; third son. NATIVE: at least second generation. RESIDED: in Cecil County. FAMILY BACKGROUND. FATHER: John Currer. MOTHER: Sarah. BROTHERS: Thomas (ca. 1724–?); Michael (ca. 1727–?); and John (ca. 1747–?). SISTERS: Mary (1722–?); Elizabeth (ca. 1729–?); Sarah (ca. 1731–?); and Catharine (ca. 1733–?). MARRIED on July 17, 1774, Mary, daughter of Empson Bird (?–1787) and wife Susanna. Mary subsequently married John Harford, of Montgomery County. Her brothers were George; Thomas, who was underage in 1786. Her sisters were Margaret, who married (first name unknown) Gordon; Susanna. CHILDREN. DAUGHTER: Sarah (1775–by 1783). PRIVATE CAREER. EDUCATION: literate. RELIGIOUS AFFILIATION: Anglican, St. Mary Anne's Parish, Cecil County. SOCIAL STATUS AND ACTIVITIES: Esq., 1779. OCCUPATIONAL PROFILE: innholder, 1770; probably a planter. PUBLIC CAREER. LEGISLATIVE SERVICE: Conventions, Cecil County, 5th, 1775, 6th–8th, 1775–1776 (elected to the 6th Convention, but did not attend). LOCAL OFFICE: North Elk Parish Vestry, Cecil County, in office 1779–1782. WEALTH DURING LIFETIME. PERSONAL PROPERTY: assessed value £568.0.0, including 7 slaves and 40 oz. plate, 1783. LAND AT FIRST ELECTION: ca. 486 acres in Cecil County (129 acres possibly inherited from his uncle). SIGNIFICANT CHANGES IN LAND BETWEEN FIRST ELECTION AND DEATH: sold 129 acres in Cecil County in 1775; he acquired an additional 379 acres in Cecil County by 1783. WEALTH AT DEATH. DIED: will probated on March 17, 1784, in Cecil County. PERSONAL PROPERTY: TEV, at least £568.0.0 current money (including 7 slaves and 40 oz. plate). LAND: possibly ca. 736 acres in Cecil County.

DAFFIN, CHARLES (?–1794). BORN: in St. Mary's County, of age by 1775. NATIVE: at least second generation. RESIDED: in St. Mary's County; Dorchester County, June 1775; Bay Hundred, Talbot County, December 1775; Caroline County, 1778; River District, Caroline County, 1783. FAMILY BACKGROUND. FATHER: George Daffin (?–probably by 1758), of St. Mary's County. MOTHER: Susannah, widow of William Aisquith (?–ca. 1741), son of *William Aisquith* (?–1719). BROTHERS: *Joseph Daffin* (?–1796); John; and George. HALF BROTHERS: William Aisquith (?–1804); Thomas Aisquith (ca. 1740–ca. 1770). HALF SISTERS: Mary Aisquith (?–by 1770), who married (first name unknown) Piercy; Ann Aisquith, who

married Nicholas Sherwood; and Susannah Aisquith, who married David Hellen. MARRIED in 1775 Mabel (?–1796), widow of both (first name unknown) Ridgway and Risdon Bozman (?–1774); daughter of Philip Sherwood (?–ca. 1789), of Talbot County. Her brother was Nicholas. Her sisters were Frances, who married John Stevens; Deborah, who married Joseph Yates; and Elizabeth, who married Theophilus Marshall. CHILDREN. SONS: Capt. Thomas B., who married Rebecca (?–1812), daughter of *Henry Dickinson* (?–1789); Joseph G., who married Elizabeth; and Charles (?–by 1801, in his minority). STEPSON: William Ridgway. DAUGHTER: Susannah, who married Francis J. Wilson, of Queen Anne's County. STEPDAUGHTER: Sarah Ridgway (?–1798), who married *William Ennalls Hooper* (?–1795). PRIVATE CAREER. EDUCATION: literate. OCCUPATIONAL PROFILE: merchant. PUBLIC CAREER. LEGISLATIVE SERVICE: Lower House, Caroline County, 1779–1780, 1782–1783 (elected, but did not attend). LOCAL OFFICES: justice, Caroline County, 1779–at least 1785 (out of the county), commissioned 1793 and 1794; justice, Orphans' Court, Caroline County, 1781–at least 1785. WEALTH DURING LIFETIME. PERSONAL PROPERTY: 26 slaves, 1776; assessed value £1,165.0.0, including 20 slaves and 60 oz. plate, 1783; 37 slaves, 1790; paid a debt of £754.0.0 owed by the estate of his wife's former husband who had been cosecurity on an unpaid bond, thereby attaining the right to collect from the other two securities or their heirs. LAND AT FIRST ELECTION: 1,052 acres in Caroline and Talbot counties (771 acres through his marriage, 281 acres by purchase), plus a 99-year lease in Dorchester County, acreage unknown, held with his brother *Joseph Daffin* (?–1796). SIGNIFICANT CHANGES IN LAND BETWEEN FIRST ELECTION AND DEATH: held the same 99-year lease, but in his name only, 1786; acquired an additional 373 acres in Talbot County through his marriage, by 1783; purchased or resurveyed at least 218 acres in Caroline, Dorchester, and Talbot counties between 1786 and 1791; sold at least 12 acres in Dorchester County between 1787 and 1790. WEALTH AT DEATH. DIED: administration bond granted November 19, 1794, in Caroline County. PERSONAL PROPERTY: TEV, £2,283.16.9 current money (including 30 slaves and books); FB, £145.2.5. LAND: at least 1,496 acres in Talbot, Caroline, and Dorchester counties.

DAFFIN, JOSEPH (?–1796). BORN: probably in St. Mary's County, of age by 1775. NATIVE: at least second generation. RESIDED: in Dorchester

County, 1775; Transquakin Hundred, Dorchester County, 1776. **FAMILY BACKGROUND. FATHER**: George Daffin, of St. Mary's County. **MOTHER**: Susannah, widow of William Aisquith (?–ca. 1741), of St. Mary's County. **BROTHERS**: *Charles Daffin* (?–1794); John, who probably died without progeny; and George, who died without progeny. **HALF BROTHERS**: William Aisquith (?–1804), of Baltimore County; Thomas Aisquith (ca. 1740–ca. 1770), who died without progeny. **HALF SISTERS**: Mary Aisquith (?–by 1770), who married (first name unknown) Piercy; Ann Aisquith, who married Nicholas Sherwood; and Susannah Aisquith, who married David Hellen. **MARRIED** in 1775 Elinor (ca. 1738–1793), daughter of Col. Joseph Ennalls (1702–1759) and wife Mary; granddaughter of *Joseph Ennalls* (?–1709); niece of *William Ennalls* (?–1731), *Bartholomew Ennalls* (ca. 1700–1783), Elizabeth Ennalls (?–by 1739), who married *Charles Goldsborough* (1707–1767), and Mary Ennalls, who married *Henry Hooper* (ca. 1687–1767). Her brothers were *John Ennalls* (by 1746–1778); *William Ennalls* (?–1785). Her sisters were Mary (?–by 1766), who married David Murray; Ann (Nancy) (1750–1803), who married Thomas Muse; and Elizabeth. Her first cousins were *Joseph Ennalls* (ca. 1745–1779); *Henry Hooper, Jr.* (ca. 1727–1790); *Robert Goldsborough* (1733–1788); Mary Ennalls, who married *Ennalls Hooper* (?–ca. 1763); Ann Ennalls (ca. 1729–by 1790), who married *Henry Hooper, Jr.* (ca. 1727–1790); and Elizabeth Greenberry Goldsborough (ca. 1731–1820), who married *William Ennalls* (?–1785). **CHILDREN**. Died without progeny. **PRIVATE CAREER. EDUCATION**: literate. **RELIGIOUS AFFILIATION**: Anglican, Great Choptank Parish, Dorchester County. **SOCIAL STATUS AND ACTIVITIES**: Gent., 1778; Esq., 1786. **OCCUPATIONAL PROFILE**: merchant, in partnership with his brother *Charles Daffin* (?–1794), by 1775. **PUBLIC CAREER. LEGISLATIVE SERVICE**: Lower House, Dorchester County, 1777–1778, 1793. **LOCAL OFFICES**: Committee of Observation, Dorchester County, elected 1775; justice, Dorchester County, ca. 1783–1788 (did not qualify in 1788); trustee for the poor, Dorchester County, appointed 1785 (refused to serve); justice, Orphans' Court, Dorchester County, 1786–1788 (did not qualify in 1788); Great Choptank Parish Vestry, Dorchester County, in office 1788–1790, 1790–1792, 1795. **MILITARY SERVICE**: captain, by 1776; major, by 1786; colonel, by 1795. **STANDS ON PUBLIC/PRIVATE ISSUES**: manumitted several slaves in his will, requesting that those slave families not manumitted be kept as closely connected as possible.

WEALTH DURING LIFETIME. PERSONAL PROPERTY: 40 slaves, 1776; assessed value £1,883.11.8, including 43 slaves and 35 oz. plate, 1783. **LAND AT FIRST ELECTION**: 644 acres in Dorchester County (all acquired through marriage). **SIGNIFICANT CHANGES IN LAND BETWEEN FIRST ELECTION AND DEATH**: purchased 150 acres in St. Mary's County, date unknown; acquired 800 additional acres in Dorchester County, which his wife inherited from her brother *John Ennalls* (by 1746–1778), ca. 1780. At his wife's death Daffin became heir to one-fourth part of 11,009 acres in Dorchester County, which he would have inherited through the Ennalls family after the death of his sister-in-law, Elizabeth Greenberry Goldsborough Ennalls (1731–1820). Elizabeth outlived him, however, and he never obtained actual possession of this land. **WEALTH AT DEATH. DIED**: will probated on June 27, 1796, in Dorchester County. **PERSONAL PROPERTY**: size of estate unknown. **LAND**: 1,601 acres in Dorchester and St. Mary's counties, plus a lot in Cambridge and a water lot in Vienna, Dorchester County. **ADDITIONAL COMMENTS**: Daffin appears to have been a man of colorful language. In explaining why he did not leave more land to a nephew who already had a large estate, he told his executor that he did not "think it worthwhile to greese a fat Sow in the Arse." In his will Daffin manumitted several slaves, bequeathing them to themselves and the devil, the prince of darkness, or the Knight of LaMancha. Daffin even provided an expense account for one of the slaves to be used during his journeys through the plutonian regions. This apparently was a ruse to ensure that no other person would interfere with their freedom.

DALLAM, RICHARD (1743–1820). **BORN**: on September 24, 1743, in St. John's Parish, Baltimore County; second of three surviving sons. **NATIVE**: third generation. **RESIDED**: in Baltimore County (later became Harford County); Abingdon, Harford County, until ca. 1807 when he moved to Logan County, Kentucky. **FAMILY BACKGROUND. FATHER**: Maj. William Dallam (ca. 1706–1761), of Baltimore County; son of Richard Dallam (?–1714), a lawyer of Calvert County who immigrated by May 1701, served as clerk of the Lower House from 1708 to 1713 and deputy commissary of Calvert County in 1713, and who married Elizabeth (Betty), daughter of William Martin, of Calvert County. Elizabeth Martin Dallam subsequently married William Smith, Gent. (?–1731), of Calvert County and later of Baltimore County. **MOTHER**: Elizabeth (?–1748), daughter of (first name unknown) Johnson. HALF UNCLE: *William Smith* (?–?). AUNT: Christian Dallam (1704–1787), who married *Richard Caswell* (1685–1755). HALF AUNT: Elizabeth Smith, who married *John Paca* (1712–1785). BROTHERS: Josias (1739–1744); William (1741–1742); William (1742–1774); and Josias William (1747–1820), who married first, Sarah (1749–?), daughter of *William Smith* (?–?) and second, Henrietta. HALF COUSINS: *Aquila Paca* (1738–1788); *William Paca* (1740–1799). MARRIED on May 16, 1765, his half cousin Frances (?–ca. 1787), daughter of *John Paca* (1712–1785); granddaughter of *Aquila Paca* (early 1670s–1721); niece of *William Smith* (?–?); half niece of Christian Dallam (1704–1787), who married *Richard Caswell* (1685–1755). Her brothers were *Aquila Paca* (1738–1788); *William Paca* (1740–1799). Her sisters were Mary (1733–?); Elizabeth (1742–1758); Martha (1743/44–1826); and Susannah. MARRIED second, by 1794 Margaret (?–by 1804). CHILDREN. SONS: John Josias Middlemore (1770–?), who married Frances, daughter of *Aquila Paca* (1738–1788); William S. PRIVATE CAREER. EDUCATION: literate. RELIGIOUS AFFILIATION: Anglican, St. George's Parish, Harford County; possibly converted to Methodism by 1784 and was a trustee of the "Preaching House" in Abingdon, Harford County. SOCIAL STATUS AND ACTIVITIES: Esq.; Gent. OCCUPATIONAL PROFILE: merchant; land developer in Harford County. ADDITIONAL COMMENTS: owned a gun manufactory in partnership with James May, Harford County, 1776. PUBLIC CAREER. LEGISLATIVE SERVICE: Lower House, Harford County, 1774 (elected to the 3rd session in the first Harford County delegation); Conventions, Harford County, 1st, 1774, 3rd, 1774, 5th, 1775, 6th–8th, 1775–1776. LOCAL OFFICES: St. George's Parish Vestry, Baltimore County, in office 1768–1771; commissioner, Harford County, appointed 1773; collector of gold and silver coin, Harford County, appointed 1776; county lieutenant, Harford County, 1777–at least 1781; purchasing agent, Harford County, appointed 1779; commissary for purchases, Harford County, appointed 1780; militia receiver ("to receive and provide quarters and necessaries for. . . recruits"), Harford County, appointed 1781. MILITARY SERVICE: quartermaster, Upper Battalion, Harford County Militia, 1776; colonel, Harford County Militia, by 1782. STAND ON PUBLIC/PRIVATE ISSUES: signed the Bush Declaration on March 22, 1775. WEALTH DURING LIFETIME. PERSONAL PROPERTY: assessed value £834.5.0, including 25 slaves, 1783; 12 slaves, 1798. ADDITIONAL COMMENTS: Although he was a promoter of "Richard Dallam's Land and Cash Lottery," ca. 1792, Dallam and his brother shared the first prize of one square mile of land in Harford County. LAND AT FIRST ELECTION: at least 1,728 acres in Harford County, plus 1 lot in Baltimore Town (at least 1,050 acres inherited from his father and 225 acres devised to him by Frances Middlemore in 1759). SIGNIFICANT CHANGES IN LAND BETWEEN FIRST ELECTION AND DEATH: in the early 1780s he received over 66 acres in Harford County, 5 lots in Abingdon, and other lots in "Washington," Harford County, by right of his wife Frances (title confirmed to Richard alone in 1787), and sold a lot in Baltimore Town. Upon the death of *John Paca* (1712–1785), he inherited jointly with *Aquila Paca* (1738–1788) at least 20 additional lots in Abingdon. Purchased 790 acres in Harford County in 1786. Over the next 20 years Dallam sold most of the Abingdon lots and divided the 790 acres into smaller parcels, which he sold in more than fourteen transactions. After 1790 he purchased or patented about 200 acres in Harford County and sometime before 1807 he and his brother Josias William purchased land in Logan County, Kentucky. By 1807 Dallam was living in Kentucky, although he returned to Harford County briefly that year to complete the sale of the estate of *Aquila Paca* (1738–1788), for which he was trustee. Dallam had conveyed 640 acres in Harford County to his son William in 1804, and in 1812 he deeded most of the rest of his Harford County holdings to his son John J. M. Both sons were also residing in Kentucky. By 1814 he had divested himself of all his Maryland land. He was assessed for 16,487 acres in ten counties in Kentucky in 1810, but was bound to convey 777 acres of this to his brother Josias William before 1815. WEALTH AT DEATH. DIED: on June 27, 1820, in Butler County, Kentucky PERSONAL PROPERTY: TEV, at least $989.88.

DARE, NATHANIEL (?–1742). BORN: in Calvert County; only known son. NATIVE: probably third generation. RESIDED: in Calvert County. FAMILY BACKGROUND. FATHER: probably Nathaniel Dare (?–1699), son of James Dare, who immigrated in 1670 and became a substantial landowner. MOTHER: probably Elizabeth, widow of Thomas Binkes (?–1685) and daughter of Thomas Cleverley (?–1686). SISTER: Amy, who married (first name unknown) Battson. MARRIED Mary (?–1748). CHILDREN. SONS: Gideon (?–1757), a justice of Calvert County from 1727 to 1731; Cleverley. DAUGHTERS: Althea, who married first, *Walter Smith* (ca. 1693–1748), and second, Rev. George

Cook, rector of Christ Church Parish, Calvert County, from 1749/50 to 1761., Regia, who married (first name unknown) Broome; and Diana, who married Charles Clagett. **PRIVATE CAREER.** EDUCATION: literate. RELIGIOUS AFFILIATION: Protestant. OCCUPATIONAL PROFILE: planter. **PUBLIC CAREER.** LEGISLATIVE SERVICE: Lower House, Calvert County, 1708A, 1708B–1711, 1716–1718. **WEALTH DURING LIFETIME.** LAND AT FIRST ELECTION: at least 675 acres and probably considerable additional acreage. **WEALTH AT DEATH.** DIED: will probated on July 14, 1742. LAND: over 2,294 acres.

DARE, WILLIAM (?–1719). BORN: in England. IMMIGRATED: by 1675 as a free adult from Dorchester, England. RESIDED: in Calvert County; Cecil County, by 1681. MARRIED by 1689 Margaret. **CHILDREN.** SON: *William Dare* (?–ca. 1721/22). DAUGHTER: Mary, who married John Thompson, son of *John Thompson* (?–1701); Margaret (?–1718), who married in 1707 *Roger Larramore* (?–1721). **PRIVATE CAREER.** EDUCATION: literate. RELIGIOUS AFFILIATION: Protestant. SOCIAL STATUS AND ACTIVITIES: migrated to settle the affairs of John Parker, a factor for a firm in Dorset, England; returned to England briefly, but resettled in Maryland by 1677, bringing eight others with him; Gent., by 1684. OCCUPATIONAL PROFILE: factor to William Twiss and John West, mercers of Dorset, England, 1670; mercer of Dorset, England, 1672; merchant; planter. **PUBLIC CAREER.** LEGISLATIVE SERVICE: Lower House, Cecil County, 1686–1688; Associators' Convention, Cecil County, 1689 (no record of attendance after the 1st session); Lower House, Cecil County, 1692 (dismissed from the 1st session for failure to provide security for good behavior), 1704–1707, 1712–1714. LOCAL OFFICES: justice, Cecil County, 1681–1689, 1694–1698, 1708–1715 (quorum, 1685–1689, 1694–1698, 1708–1715). STANDS ON PUBLIC/PRIVATE ISSUES: opposed the revolution of 1689 and was not returned to public office until the tenure of Gov. Francis Nicholson. **WEALTH DURING LIFETIME.** LAND AT FIRST ELECTION: at least 1,950 acres and probably 700 additional acres. **WEALTH AT DEATH.** DIED: will probated on August 13, 1719. PERSONAL PROPERTY: TEV, £225.17.10 sterling (including 7 slaves and books). LAND: 2,070 acres.

DARE, WILLIAM (?–ca. 1721/22). BORN: probably in Cecil County. NATIVE: second generation. RESIDED: in Cecil County. **FAMILY BACKGROUND.** FATHER: *William Dare* (?–1719). SISTERS: Mary, who married John Thompson, son of *John Thompson* (?–1701); Margaret (?–1718), who married in 1707 *Roger Larramore* (?–1721). **CHILDREN.** DAUGHTERS: Catherine, who was underage at the time of her father's death and was placed in the care of her aunt, Mary Dare Thompson; Margaret, also underage at the time of her father's death and who was placed in care of a family friend, Capt. *Benjamin Pearce* (1711/12–1756); and Mary, also underage at the time of her father's death. **PRIVATE CAREER.** EDUCATION: literate. RELIGIOUS AFFILIATION: Anglican. SOCIAL STATUS AND ACTIVITIES: Mr., 1715; Gent., 1719. OCCUPATIONAL PROFILE: merchant. **PUBLIC CAREER.** LEGISLATIVE SERVICE: Lower House, Cecil County, 1719–1720 (appointed sheriff between the 3rd and 4th sessions). LOCAL OFFICES: undersheriff, Cecil County, appointed 1716; justice, Cecil County, 1720–1721; sheriff, Cecil County, commissioned 1721. **WEALTH DURING LIFETIME.** LAND AT FIRST ELECTION: ca. 1,050 acres in Cecil County (all inherited from his father). SIGNIFICANT CHANGES IN LAND BETWEEN FIRST ELECTION AND DEATH: sold 150 acres in Cecil County, 1719. **WEALTH AT DEATH.** DIED: will probated on February 24, 1721/22, in Cecil County. PERSONAL PROPERTY: TEV, £324.11.6 current money (including 5 slaves, 1 servant, and books); FB, estate overpaid £198.10.5. LAND: 900 acres in Cecil County.

DARNALL, HENRY (ca. 1645–1711). BORN: ca. 1645 in Hertfordshire, England. IMMIGRATED: by 1664 as a free adult. RESIDED: in Calvert County. **FAMILY BACKGROUND.** FATHER: Philip Darnall (1604–?), secretary to Sir George Calvert, 1st Lord Baltimore. MOTHER: Mary Calvert, sister of Lord Talbot. BROTHER: *John Darnall* (?–1684). SISTER: Elizabeth. COUSIN: *Charles Calvert, 3rd Lord Baltimore* (1637–1714/15). MARRIED first, name unknown. MARRIED second, Elinor (1642–1725), widow of *Thomas Brooke* (1632–1676); daughter of Richard Hatton and wife Margaret; stepdaughter of *Richard Banks* (ca. 1612–ca. 1667); niece of *Thomas Hatton* (?–1654/55). Her brothers were *William Hatton* (?–1712); Richard. Her sisters were Mary, who married *Zachary Wade* (ca. 1627–1678); Elizabeth, who married first, *Luke Gardiner* (1622–1674), and second, *Clement Hill* (?–1708); and Barbara, who married *James Johnson* (?–?). **CHILDREN.** SONS: Philip (1671–1705), who married Elinor, daughter of *Thomas Brooke* (1632–1676); Henry (1682–1759), who married Ann, daughter of *William Digges* (ca. 1650–1697). STEPSONS: *Thomas Brooke* (ca. 1659–1730/31), who married first, Ann, and second, Barbara

(1676–1754), daughter of *Thomas Dent* (ca. 1630–1676); Robert (1663–1714); Ignatius (1670–1751); Matthew (1672–1703); and Clement (1676–1737), who married Jane, daughter of *Nicholas Sewall* (ca. 1655–1737). DAUGHTERS: Mary (1678–1742), who married in 1693 Charles Carroll; Ann (1680–1749), who married in 1696 Clement Hill, nephew and heir of *Clement Hill* (?–1708); and Elizabeth (?–1704), who married in 1699 Edward Digges (?–1714), son of *William Digges* (ca. 1650–1697). STEPDAUGHTERS: Mary, who married first, James Bowling, second, *Benjamin Hall* (1667–1721), and third, Henry Withan; Elinor, who married first, Philip Darnall (1671–1705), and second, William Digges, son of *William Digges* (ca. 1650–1697). PRIVATE CAREER. EDUCATION: literate; probably had considerable schooling. RELIGIOUS AFFILIATION: Catholic. SOCIAL STATUS AND ACTIVITIES: he was related to the proprietary family; he arrived with high social and political status and after 1689 he served as the primary agent for Lord Baltimore. OCCUPATIONAL PROFILE: placeman; planter; merchant. PUBLIC CAREER. LEGISLATIVE SERVICE: Lower House, Calvert County, 1674 (elected to the 3rd session; resigned during the session to become sheriff); Upper House, 1681–1682 (appointed by the 3rd session), 1682–1684 (Laws 3), 1686–1688. OTHER PROVINCIAL OFFICES: Council, 1679–1689; justice, Provincial Court, 1679–1689; joint chancellor and commissary general, 1682/83–1685; Board of Deputy Governors, 1684–1689; Land Council, 1684–1689; rent roll keeper, 1684–1689; receiver general, 1684–1711; principal keeper of forest and chief ranger, 1684; chancellor, 1685–1689. LOCAL OFFICE: sheriff, Calvert County, 1674–1679. MILITARY SERVICE: captain, by 1676–1679; lieutenant colonel, 1679–1681; colonel, 1681–1689. STANDS ON PUBLIC/PRIVATE ISSUES: he was a leading supporter of the proprietary establishment against the rebels in 1689; his Catholicism prevented him from holding public office after 1689, but he remained the primary agent in the colony for the proprietary interests until his death. WEALTH DURING LIFETIME. LAND AT FIRST ELECTION: over 1,000 acres; patented 10,717 acres between 1680 and 1688, and another 25,068 acres between 1690 and 1705. ANNUAL INCOME: granted with William Digges one-third of all seizures of vessels in 1684. WEALTH AT DEATH. DIED: on June 17, 1711. PERSONAL PROPERTY: TEV, £3,505.3.3 sterling (including 105 slaves). LAND: over 26,000 acres.

DARNALL, JOHN (?–1684). BORN: probably in Hertfordshire, England; younger son. IMMIGRATED: probably by 1672, as a free adult with his kinsmans. RESIDED: in Calvert County; Anne Arundel County. FAMILY BACKGROUND. FATHER: Philip Darnall (1604–?), secretary to Sir George Calvert, 1st Lord Baltimore. MOTHER: Mary Calvert, sister of Lord Talbot. BROTHER: *Henry Darnall* (ca. 1645–1711), who married Elinor (1642–1725), widow of *Thomas Brooke* (1632–1676); daughter of Richard Hatton. SISTER: Elizabeth. FIRST COUSIN: *Charles Calvert, 3rd Lord Baltimore* (1637–1714/15). MARRIED Susanna Maria, daughter of *Richard Bennett* (ca. 1639–1667) and wife Henrietta Maria; stepdaughter of *Philemon Lloyd* (1646–1685); granddaughter of both *Richard Bennett* (ca. 1608–1675) and *James Neale* (ca. 1615–1684). Susanna Maria Bennett Darnall subsequently married by 1686 *Henry Lowe* (?–1717). Her half brothers were *Edward Lloyd* (1670–1718/19); *Philemon Lloyd* (ca. 1674–1732/33); and *James Lloyd* (1679/80–1723). CHILDREN. DAUGHTER: Henrietta (?–by 1704). PRIVATE CAREER. EDUCATION: literate; he had clerical skills. RELIGIOUS AFFILIATION: Catholic. SOCIAL STATUS AND ACTIVITIES: because he was related to the proprietary family and his brother was an influential councilor, Darnall enjoyed profitable patronage. OCCUPATIONAL PROFILE: placeman; planter. PUBLIC CAREER. LEGISLATIVE SERVICE: Upper House, 1683–1684 (appointed by the 2nd session; Laws 3). OTHER PROVINCIAL OFFICES: Council, 1682/83–1684; justice, Provincial Court, 1682/83–1684; joint secretary, 1682/83–1684; Board of Deputy Governors, 1684. LOCAL OFFICE: clerk, Calvert County, 1673–1684. WEALTH DURING LIFETIME. LAND AT FIRST ELECTION: patented 4,000 acres, 1683–1684. WEALTH AT DEATH. DIED: on December 14, 1684. PERSONAL PROPERTY: TEV, £1,159.14.10 sterling (including 10 slaves and 10 servants); FB, £226.12.0. LAND: at least 1,950 acres, plus land in Virginia and England.

DASHIELL, BENJAMIN FREDERICK AUGUSTUS CAESAR (1763–1820). BORN: on May 22, 1763, in Wicomico Hundred, Worcester County; second son. NATIVE: fifth generation. RESIDED: in Worcester County; Somerset County (later became part of Wicomico County), probably by 1792. FAMILY BACKGROUND. FATHER: *Joseph Dashiell* (1736–ca. 1787). MOTHER: Martha Bluett. STEPMOTHER: Susannah (?–1792). UNCLE: *Thomas Dashiell* (1733–1771). HALF UNCLE: *George Dashiell* (1743–?). BROTHER: William Pitt (1761–?). SISTERS: Martha Bluett (1759–?); Eleanor Matilda (1765–?). FIRST COUSIN: *Josiah Dashiell* (1746–1784). MARRIED Henrietta (1757–1791). CHIL-

DREN. SON: Theodore Gunby (?–1855); in 1812 an act was passed to change the name of Theodore Gunby, of Somerset County, to Theodore Gunby Dashiell. DAUGHTERS: Elizabeth Leah, who married John Upshur Dennis; Henrietta Ann (1791–1791). PRIVATE CAREER. EDUCATION: class of 1784, Washington College, Chestertown, Kent County. SOCIAL STATUS AND ACTIVITIES: Esq., 1798; fifth generation legislator; member of the Freemasons, 1804. OCCUPATIONAL PROFILE: lawyer. PUBLIC CAREER. LEGISLATIVE SERVICE: Lower House, Worcester County, 1789, Somerset County, 1792, 1797, 1800, 1802, 1803. MILITARY SERVICE: served in a company of the Wicomico Battalion, Somerset County Militia, by 1780. WEALTH DURING LIFETIME. PERSONAL PROPERTY: assessed value £510.0.0, including 9 slaves and 58 oz. plate, 1793; assessed value $3,520.00, including 44 slaves and 44 oz. plate, 1817. LAND AT FIRST ELECTION: probably 226 acres in Somerset and Worcester counties. SIGNIFICANT CHANGES IN LAND BETWEEN FIRST ELECTION AND DEATH: purchased unspecified acreage in Somerset County, 1799; purchased 600 acres in Somerset County, 1800; purchased 2 lots in Princess Anne, Somerset County, 1807. WEALTH AT DEATH. DIED: on April 5, 1820, in Somerset County; buried at "Dashiell Lott Farm," Somerset County. LAND: 922.5 acres in Somerset County and 2 lots in Princess Anne, Somerset County.

DASHIELL, GEORGE (1690/91–1748). BORN: on January 31, 1690/91, in Somerset County; eldest son. NATIVE: third generation. RESIDED: in Somerset County. FAMILY BACKGROUND. FATHER: *Thomas Dashiell* (1666–ca. 1756), son of *James Dashiell* (ca. 1634–1697). MOTHER: Elizabeth Mitchell (1670–?). BROTHERS: Thomas (1700–by 1765); Henry (1702/3–1756); Charles (1705–1765); John (1711/12–1736); and Levin (1711/12–1795). SISTERS: Priscilla (1688/89–?); Betty (1693/94–1762); Isabell (1695–?); Jane (1698–?); Anne (1707–?), who married *Isaac Handy* (?–1762); and Sarah (1709–?). FIRST COUSIN: *William Winder* (1714/15–1792). NEPHEWS: *John Handy* (ca. 1724–1756); *Isaac Handy* (1743–ca. 1774); and *John Dashiell* (ca. 1740–1817), a possible legislator. NIECE: Priscilla Handy (?–by 1748/49), who married *Benjamin Handy* (?–ca. 1763). MARRIED first, Betty (?–1739). MARRIED second, on September 10, 1740, Elizabeth (?–ca. 1749), widow of James Fairfax, of Northampton County, Virginia. Her nearest relatives were Isack and Jacob Marshall. CHILDREN. SONS: Arthur (1715–1741); Capt. Clement (1720–1756), a mariner, who mar-

ried Sarah, daughter of Capt. William Piper; Louther (1722–1765), who married Anna, daughter of Capt. William Piper; Isaac (1726–?), who married Henrietta Scarburgh; *Thomas Dashiell* (1733–1771); *Joseph Dashiell* (1736–ca. 1787); Benjamin (1738/39–ca. 1758), died without progeny; and *George Dashiell* (1743–?). DAUGHTER: Eleanor (1730–?), who married John Martin. PRIVATE CAREER. EDUCATION: literate. RELIGIOUS AFFILIATION: Anglican, Stepney Parish, Somerset County (later became part of Wicomico County). OCCUPATIONAL PROFILE: planter; attorney, admitted to the Somerset County Court in June 1713. PUBLIC CAREER. LEGISLATIVE SERVICE: Lower House, Somerset County, 1719–1721/22 (Laws 1; Elections 5), 1724 (elected to the 3rd session to fill vacancy), 1725–1727 (Aggrievances 1), 1728–1731, 1732–1734, 1734/35–1737 (Accounts 1, Cv, 2–4), 1745/46–1748 (Accounts Cv 1, 1–3, 4; Elections Cv 1, 1–3, 4). LOCAL OFFICES: clerk of Indictments, Somerset County, appointed 1726; justice, Somerset County, 1734–1748 (quorum, 1740–1748); justice, Court of Oyer and Terminer and Gaol Delivery, Somerset County, commissioned 1736. MILITARY SERVICE: captain, militia, by 1725; major, militia, by 1733/34; colonel, militia, by 1736. WEALTH DURING LIFETIME. LAND AT FIRST ELECTION: surveyed 116 acres in Somerset County, but no patent had been issued prior to his first election. SIGNIFICANT CHANGES IN LAND BETWEEN FIRST ELECTION AND DEATH: patented 2,124 acres in Somerset and Worcester counties between 1723 and 1745; received a deed of gift of unspecified acreage in Somerset County from his father, 1731; purchased 275 acres in Somerset County between 1734 and 1745; gave 900 acres in Somerset County by deeds of gift to two of his sons, Clement and Louther, in 1742. WEALTH AT DEATH. DIED: on November 7, 1748, in Somerset County. PERSONAL PROPERTY: TEV, £233.15.1 gold and silver currency and £1,951.15.8 current money (including 35 slaves, 310 oz. 12 dwt. 7 gr. silver plate, books, and 1 bay sloop); FB, £112.10.8 gold and silver currency and £1,215.12.6 current money. LAND: at least 1,549 acres in Somerset and Worcester counties.

DASHIELL, GEORGE (1743–?). BORN: on August 28, 1743, in Somerset County; youngest of eight sons. NATIVE: fourth generation. RESIDED: in Wicomico Hundred, Somerset County, until the 1790s; Worcester County, until the early 1800s. FAMILY BACKGROUND. FATHER: Col. *George Dashiell* (1690/91–1748), son of *Thomas Dashiell* (1666–ca. 1756). MOTHER: Elizabeth (?–ca. 1749), widow of James Fairfax, of Northampton County, Virginia. AUNT: Anne Dashiell (1707–?), who married *Isaac Handy* (?–1762). HALF BROTHERS: Arthur (1715–1741); Capt. Clement (1720–1756); Louther (1722–1765); Isaac (1726–?); *Thomas Dashiell* (1733–1771); *Joseph Dashiell* (1736–ca. 1787); and Benjamin (1738/39–ca. 1758). HALF SISTER: Eleanor (1730–?). FIRST COUSINS: *John Handy* (ca. 1724–1756); *Isaac Handy* (1743–ca. 1774); and *John Dashiell* (ca. 1740–1817), a possible legislator. HALF NEPHEW: *Benjamin F. A. C. Dashiell* (1763–1820). HALF NIECE: Henney Dashiell (1758–ca. 1784), who married *Josiah Dashiell* (1746–1784). OTHER KINSHIP: his father's first wife was Betty (?–1739). MARRIED first, on August 6, 1760, Rose (Arosy), daughter of Maddox Fisher, of Northampton County, Virginia. MARRIED second, by 1803 Sally Dennis. CHILDREN. SONS: James Fairfax (1761–?); Tubman (1763–?); John (1765–?); Josiah (1768–?); Dr. Robert (1769–1814), who practiced medicine in Isle of Wight and Nansemond counties, Virginia; Rev. George (1770–1852); Fisher (ca. 1774–1812), a member of the Virginia House of Delegates from 1804 to 1812, of Nansemond County, Virginia; William D. (1780–?), of Isle of Wight County, Virginia. PRIVATE CAREER. EDUCATION: literate. RELIGIOUS AFFILIATION: Anglican. SOCIAL STATUS AND ACTIVITIES: Gent., 1768; fourth generation legislator. OCCUPATIONAL PROFILE: probably a planter. PUBLIC CAREER. LEGISLATIVE SERVICE: Conventions, Somerset County, 1st, 1774, 3rd, 1774, 4th, 1775, 5th, 1775, 6th–8th, 1775–1776. LOCAL OFFICES: sheriff, Somerset County, 1770–1773; justice, Somerset County, commissioned 1775 and 1777; county lieutenant, Somerset County, appointed 1777; judge, Court of Appeals for Tax Assessment, Somerset County, commissioned 1786. WEALTH DURING LIFETIME. PERSONAL PROPERTY: inherited £171.13.0 from his mother in 1752. LAND AT FIRST ELECTION: 499 acres in Somerset County (435 acres inherited from his father; 64 acres by purchase); may also have had land in Virginia obtained through inheritance and dower. WEALTH AT DEATH. DIED: probably after 1805; size of estate unknown.

DASHIELL (DASHIEL, DASHIELD), JAMES (ca. 1634–1697). BORN: ca. 1634 in Edinburgh, Scotland. IMMIGRATED: in 1663/64 with his wife and son from Northumberland County, Virginia. RESIDED: in Somerset County. MARRIED in 1659 Ann, daughter of Edward Cannon. CHILDREN. SONS: James (ca. 1660–1708/9), a justice of Somerset County from 1699 to 1708/9, who married

first, by 1690 Mary (1667–?), daughter of Sampson Waters, and second, in 1698 Isabel (1675–?), daughter of George Mitchell; *Thomas Dashiell* (1666–ca. 1756), who married in 1686 Elizabeth (1670–?), daughter of George Mitchell; George (1669–1733), who married in 1694 Priscilla Mitchell; and Robert (1677–1718), who married ca. 1700 Sarah Haste. DAUGHTERS: Katherine (1672–1696), who married in 1692/93 William Jones; Jane (1675–?), who married in 1696 John Winder. PRIVATE CAREER. EDUCATION: literate. RELIGIOUS AFFILIATION: Protestant. OCCUPATIONAL PROFILE: planter. PUBLIC CAREER. LEGISLATIVE SERVICE: Lower House, Somerset County, 1676–1682. OTHER PROVINCIAL OFFICE: customs officer, 1692. LOCAL OFFICE: justice, Somerset County, 1672/73–1697 (quorum, by 1692–1697). STANDS ON PUBLIC/PRIVATE ISSUES: signed a memorial in 1680 stating that Lord Baltimore was not partial to Catholics. WEALTH DURING LIFETIME. LAND AT FIRST ELECTION: 1,000 acres. WEALTH AT DEATH. DIED: will probated on August 31, 1697. PERSONAL PROPERTY: TEV, £232.1.7 sterling (including 6 servants). LAND: 1,000 acres.

DASHIELL, JOHN (?–?). BORN: of age by 1783, probably in Somerset County; elder son. NATIVE: fifth generation. RESIDED: in Nanticoke Hundred, Somerset County. FAMILY BACKGROUND. FATHER: Winder Dashiell (1718–1781), son of James Dashiell (1690–1737) and wife Bridget Winder. MOTHER: Ann. BROTHER: Winder (ca. 1757–?). SISTERS: Ann (1753–?); Sarah; and Bridget. FIRST COUSIN: *John Dashiell* (1757–1818), a possible legislator. OTHER KINSHIP: his third cousin was *John Dashiell* (ca. 1740–1817), a possible legislator. MARRIED by 1786 Ann (Nancy). PRIVATE CAREER. EDUCATION: literate. RELIGIOUS AFFILIATION: probably Anglican. OCCUPATIONAL PROFILE: planter. PUBLIC CAREER. LEGISLATIVE SERVICE: Lower House, Somerset County, 1784, 1785. *See* statement in Identification Problems section. WEALTH DURING LIFETIME. PERSONAL PROPERTY: assessed value £45.0.0, including 1 slave, 1783. LAND AT FIRST ELECTION: 188 acres in Somerset County (all inherited from his father). SIGNIFICANT CHANGES IN LAND BETWEEN FIRST ELECTION AND DEATH: resurveyed a tract in Somerset County that he had inherited from his father for a net gain of 17.5 acres in 1786; sold 190 acres in Somerset County, 1786–1787. WEALTH AT DEATH. PERSONAL PROPERTY: size of estate unknown. IDENTIFICATION PROBLEMS. There were three men named John Dashiell who were eligible to represent Somerset County in the 1784 and

1785 assemblies. It was not possible to positively identify which of these three was the delegate. Therefore, three biographical profiles have been included, and the same legislative service assigned to each. See also *John Dashiell* (ca. 1740–1817) and *John Dashiell* (1757–1818).

DASHIELL, JOHN (ca. 1740–1817). BORN: March 24, ca. 1740, probably in Somerset County; only son. NATIVE: fourth generation. RESIDED: in Monie Hundred, Somerset County. FAMILY BACK-GROUND. FATHER: Levin Dashiell (1711/12–ca. 1795), son of *Thomas Dashiell* (1666–ca. 1756). MOTHER: Bridget (?–1796). UNCLE: *George Da-shiell* (1690/91–1748). AUNT: Ann Dashiell (1707–1762), who married *Isaac Handy* (?–1762). SIS-TERS: Sarah (1745–?), who married John Evans (1750–?); Anne (1742–?), who married John Jones; Priscilla (1736–?), who married William Jones; and Elizabeth (1738–?), who married first, Thomas Jones, and second, Arnold Ballard. FIRST COUS-INS: *John Handy* (ca. 1724–1756); *Isaac Handy* (1743–ca. 1774); Priscilla Handy (?–by 1748/49), who married *Benjamin Handy* (?–ca. 1763); *Thomas Dashiell* (1733–1771); *Joseph Dashiell* (1736–ca. 1787); and *George Dashiell* (1743–?). OTHER KINSHIP: his third cousins were *John Da-shiell* (1757–1818), a possible legislator, and *John Dashiell* (?–?), a possible legislator. MARRIED on December 29, 1762, Elizabeth, a minor in 1753, daughter of Rodger Killet (Kellet) (?–1748), and wife Eunice (?–1753). Her guardian after 1753 was Sarah Henry, a cousin of her mother. Her brother was Robert, a minor in 1753. CHILDREN. SONS: Levin (1767–?), who married Priscilla Evans Da-shiell; John (1769–ca. 1825), who married Mary; and Robert Killet Washington (1789–1854), who married Eleanor Leatherbury (1792–1831). DAUGHTERS: Eunice (1770–?), who married Wil-liam Jones; Leah Washington, never married; and Sarah Anne. PRIVATE CAREER. EDUCATION: liter-ate. RELIGIOUS AFFILIATION: Anglican, Manye (Monye) Church, Somerset Parish, Somerset County. He rented a pew with his son John in 1799. OCCUPATIONAL PROFILE: probably a planter. PUBLIC CAREER. LEGISLATIVE SERVICE: Lower House, Somerset County, 1784, 1785. *See* statement in Indentification Problems section. LO-CAL OFFICE: collector of tax, Somerset County, 1780; churchwarden, Somerset Parish, Somerset County, 1780, 1800; Somerset Parish Vestry, Som-erset County, 1781, 1788–1792, 1795–1797; com-missioner of tax, Somerset County, 1788, 1798. MILITARY SERVICE: 1st lieutenant, Monie Com-pany, Princess Anne Battalion, Somerset County

Militia, commissioned 1777. WEALTH DURING LIFETIME. PERSONAL PROPERTY: assessed value £840.0.0, including 27 slaves and 48 oz. plate, 1783; assessed value £1,050.0.0, including 60 slaves and 48 oz. plate, 1793; 48 slaves, 1798; as-sessed value $2,675.00, including 33 slaves and 24 oz. plate, 1817. LAND AT FIRST ELECTION: 100 acres in Somerset County (all through marriage). SIGNIFICANT CHANGES IN LAND BETWEEN FIRST ELECTION AND DEATH: inherited 935 acres in Somerset County from his father, 1785; 275 acres of this inherited land was charged to his son John, Jr., in a tax assessment, by 1798; purchased 115.25 acres in Somerset County, by 1817. WEALTH AT DEATH. DIED: will probated on October 6, 1817, in Somerset County. PERSONAL PROPERTY: TEV, $11,148.55 (including 34 slaves and books); FB, $4,027.74. LAND: 875.25 acres in Somerset County. IDENTIFICATION PROBLEMS. There were three men named John Dashiell who were eligible to represent Somerset County in the 1784 and 1785 assemblies. It was not possible to positively identify which of these three was the delegate. Therefore, three biographical profiles have been included, and the same legislative service assigned to each. See also *John Dashiell* (1757–1818) and *John Dashiell* (?–?).

DASHIELL, JOHN (1757–1818). BORN: on Au-gust 11, 1757, in Stepney Parish, Somerset County; fourth son. NATIVE: fifth generation. RE-SIDED: in Stepney Parish, Somerset County. FAM-ILY BACKGROUND. FATHER: Jesse Dashiell (1716–1778), son of James Dashiell (1690–1737) and wife Bridget Winder. MOTHER: Susanna Townsend (1722–1785). BROTHERS: James (1740–ca. 1796), who married Sarah Evans; Benjamin (1745/46–?), never married; Jesse (1752–?), died young; and Isaac (1759–?). SISTERS: Sarah (1741/42–before 1778), who married (first name unknown) Purti-man; Rebecka (1744–?), who married (first name unknown) Whithier; Susanna (1747/48–?), never married; Bridget (1755–ca. 1781), who married John Shiles; and Elizabeth (1762–?), who married John Jones (1757–?). FIRST COUSIN: *John Dashiell* (?–?), a possible legislator. OTHER KINSHIP: his third cousin was *John Dashiell* (ca. 1740–1817), a possible legislator. MARRIED by 1795 Eleanor (?–1821), daughter of Priscilla Dashiell. CHILDREN. At least three children including SON: George. DAUGHTERS: Eleanor T., who married first, by 1815 (first name unknown) Savage, and second, by 1820 (first name unknown) Wailes; Betsey (Elizabeth), who married (first name unknown) Dashiell. PRIVATE CAREER. EDUCATION: literate.

RELIGIOUS AFFILIATION: Anglican, Stepney Parish, Somerset County. OCCUPATIONAL PROFILE: probably a planter. PUBLIC CAREER. LEGISLATIVE SERVICE: Lower House, Somerset County, 1784, 1785. *See* statement in Identification Problems section. LOCAL OFFICES: Stepney Parish Vestry, Somerset County, 1803–1808; churchwarden, Stepney Parish, Somerset County, 1810, 1815, 1816. MILITARY SERVICE: captain, by 1798; major, by 1804. WEALTH DURING LIFETIME. PERSONAL PROPERTY: assessed value £250.0.0, including 6 slaves, 1793; 11 slaves, 1798; assessed value $1,615.00, including 13 slaves and 10 oz. plate, 1817. LAND AT FIRST ELECTION: no evidence of landownership. SIGNIFICANT CHANGES IN LAND BETWEEN FIRST ELECTION AND DEATH: purchased at least 1,045 acres in Somerset County, 1790–1815; sold 100 acres in Somerset County, 1795. WEALTH AT DEATH. DIED: will probated on April 15, 1818, in Somerset County. PERSONAL PROPERTY: size of estate unknown; his will mentioned a grain mill, sawmill, and 12 slaves. LAND: 1,042 acres in Somerset County. IDENTIFICATION PROBLEMS. There were three men named John Dashiell who were eligible to represent Somerset County in the 1784 and 1785 assemblies. It was not possible to positively identify which of these three was the delegate. Therefore, three biographical profiles have been included, and the same legislative service assigned to each. See also *John Dashiell* (ca. 1740–1817) and *John Dashiell* (?–?).

DASHIELL, JOSEPH (1736–ca. 1787). BORN: in 1736 in Somerset County; sixth son. NATIVE: fourth generation. RESIDED: in Somerset County; Wicomico Hundred, Worcester County, by 1765. FAMILY BACKGROUND. FATHER: *George Dashiell* (1690/91–1748), son of *Thomas Dashiell* (1666–ca. 1756). MOTHER: Betty (?–1739). STEPMOTHER: Elizabeth (?–ca. 1749), widow of James Fairfax, of Northampton County, Virginia. AUNT: Anne Dashiell (1707–?), who married *Isaac Handy* (?–1762). BROTHERS: Arthur (1715–1741); Clement (1720–1756); Louther (1722–1765); Isaac (1726–?); *Thomas Dashiell* (1733–1771); and Benjamin (1738/39–ca. 1758). HALF BROTHER: *George Dashiell* (1743–?). FIRST COUSINS: *John Handy* (ca. 1724–1756); *Isaac Handy* (1743–ca. 1774); and *John Dashiell* (ca. 1740–1817), a possible legislator. NEPHEW: *Josiah Dashiell* (1746–1784). OTHER KINSHIP: his great-grandfather was *James Dashiell* (ca. 1634–1697); his second cousin was *William Winder* (1714/15–1792). MARRIED first, on May 18, 1757, Martha, daughter of (first name unknown) Bluett and wife Eleanor (?–1798). MAR-

RIED second, by 1774 Susannah. CHILDREN. SONS: William Pitt; *Benjamin F. A. C. Dashiell* (1763–1820). DAUGHTERS: Martha Bluett (1759–?); Eleanor Matilda, who married (first name unknown) Handy. PRIVATE CAREER. EDUCATION: literate. RELIGIOUS AFFILIATION: Anglican, Stepney Parish, Somerset County. SOCIAL STATUS AND ACTIVITIES: Esq., 1769; fourth generation legislator. OCCUPATIONAL PROFILE: mariner, 1759; planter, 1760; owned mills. PUBLIC CAREER. LEGISLATIVE SERVICE: Lower House, Worcester County, 1768–1770; Conventions, Worcester County, 6th–8th, 1775–1776; Lower House, Worcester County, 1780–1781 (Grievances 1, 2), 1781–1782, 1782–1783 (Elections 1; Manufactories 1), 1783 (elected, but did not attend), 1784 (Elections), 1785 (Grievances; Manufactories). LOCAL OFFICES: justice, Worcester County, 1766–1774, probably 1775–1782 (records missing), 1783–1787; county lieutenant, Worcester County, appointed 1777; commissary for purchases, Worcester County, 1778–1780; justice, Orphans' Court, Worcester County, commissioned 1786 and 1787. MILITARY SERVICE: captain, by 1757; lieutenant colonel, First Battalion, Worcester County Militia, by 1776; colonel, by 1777. STANDS ON PUBLIC/PRIVATE ISSUES: subscriber to Washington College, Chestertown, Kent County. WEALTH DURING LIFETIME. PERSONAL PROPERTY: inherited £310.1.6 from his brother, Benjamin, 1762; assessed value £1,300.10.0, including 32 slaves, 1783. LAND AT FIRST ELECTION: 911 acres in Worcester and Somerset counties (63.5 acres inherited from his father, 847 acres by purchase). SIGNFICANT CHANGES IN LAND BETWEEN FIRST ELECTION AND DEATH: owned 1,245 acres in Worcester County, 1774; owned 1,841 acres in Worcester County, 1783; charged with an additional 764 acres for Haste Handy and 385 acres for Moses Claywell Smith, all in Worcester County, 1783. WEALTH AT DEATH. DIED: administration bond taken in February 1787 in Worcester County. PERSONAL PROPERTY: TEV, £2,044.2.3 (including 29 slaves, 41 oz. plate, 23 books, and a sloop); FB, £703.7.5. LAND: probably 1,841 acres in Worcester County.

DASHIELL, JOSIAH (1746–1784). BORN: on October 12, 1746, in Stepney Parish, Somerset County; elder son. NATIVE: fifth generation. RESIDED: in Wicomico Hundred, Somerset County. FAMILY BACKGROUND. FATHER: Capt. Clement Dashiell (1720–1756), son of *George Dashiell* (1690/91–1748). MOTHER: Sarah, daughter of Capt. William Piper. GUARDIAN: his uncle, Louther Dashiell (1722–1765). UNCLES: *Thomas*

Dashiell (1733–1771); *Joseph Dashiell* (1736–ca. 1787). HALF UNCLE: *George Dashiell* (1743–?). BROTHER: Clement (1748–died young). SISTERS: Mary (1741–?), who married (first name unknown) Jones; Sarah (1744–1788), who never married; (first name unknown) (1751–1778), who married William Dixon. FIRST COUSIN: *Benjamin F. A. C. Dashiell* (1763–1820). OTHER KINSHIP: his great-grandfather was *Thomas Dashiell* (1666–ca. 1756); his second cousin was *John Handy* (ca. 1724–1756); his third cousin was *William Winder* (1714/15–1792). MARRIED his first cousin Henney (1758–ca. 1787), daughter of *Thomas Dashiell* (1733–1771); granddaughter of *George Dashiell* (1690/91–1748); niece of *Joseph Dashiell* (1736–ca. 1787); half niece of *George Dashiell* (1743–?). Her brothers were George (1759–probably died young); William (1763–?). Her sisters were Patience (1761–?); Jane (1765–?). Her first cousin was *Benjamin F. A. C. Dashiell* (1763–1820). Her other relatives included second cousin *John Handy* (ca. 1724–1756) and third cousin *William Winder* (1714/15–1792). CHILDREN. Died without progeny. PRIVATE CAREER. EDUCATION: literate. RELIGIOUS AFFILIATION: Anglican, Stepney Parish, Somerset County. PUBLIC CAREER. LEGISLATIVE SERVICE: Lower House, Somerset County, 1779–1780, 1781–1782 (Public Taxes 2). LOCAL OFFICES: sheriff, Somerset County, in office 1773–1775; justice, Somerset County, 1778–1784. MILITARY SERVICE: captain, Whitehaven Company, Salisbury Battalion, Somerset County Militia, commissioned 1777. WEALTH DURING LIFETIME. PERSONAL PROPERTY: assessed value £582.0.0, including 12 slaves and 17 oz. plate, 1783. LAND AT FIRST ELECTION: 450 acres in Somerset County (inherited from his father). WEALTH AT DEATH. DIED: between April 3 and June 9, 1784. PERSONAL PROPERTY: TEV, £1,404.1.6 (including 13 slaves, 17 oz. plate, and half ownership of a sloop); FB, £623.1.2. LAND: 440 acres in Somerset County, 1783. ADDITIONAL COMMENTS: stated in his will, drawn in 1784, that neither his uncle *George Dashiell* (1743–?) nor any of his uncle's descendants were to receive anything from his estate.

DASHIELL (DASHIEL, DASHIELD), THOMAS (1666–ca. 1756). BORN: on April 23, 1666, in Somerset County; second son. NATIVE: second generation. RESIDED: in Wicomico Hundred, Somerset County. FAMILY BACKGROUND. FATHER: *James Dashiell* (ca. 1634–1697). MOTHER: Ann. BROTHERS: James (ca. 1660–1708/9); George (1669–1733); and Robert (1677–1718). SISTERS:

Katherine (1672–1696); Jane (1675–?). MARRIED in 1686 Elizabeth (1670–?), daughter of George Mitchell and wife Isabell. CHILDREN. SONS: *George Dashiell* (1690/91–1748); Thomas (1700–by 1765), who married in 1722 Jean Collier; Henry (1702/3–1756), who married in 1725 Jane; Charles (1705–1765); John (1711/12–1736); and Levin (1711/12–ca. 1795), who married in 1738 Bridget. DAUGHTERS: Priscilla (1688/89–?); Betty (1693/94–1762), who married John West; Isabell (1695–?); Jane (1698–?), who married first, John Handy, and second, Thomas Gillis; Ann (1707–1762), who married in 1726 *Isaac Handy* (?–1762); and Sarah (1709–?), who married George Irving. PRIVATE CAREER. EDUCATION: literate. RELIGIOUS AFFILIATION: Protestant. SOCIAL STATUS AND ACTIVITIES: second generation provincial officeholder. OCCUPATIONAL PROFILE: planter. PUBLIC CAREER. LEGISLATIVE SERVICE: Lower House, Somerset County, 1715, 1716 (resigned after the 2nd session to become sheriff). LOCAL OFFICES: constable, Wicomico Hundred, Somerset County, 1694–1695; justice, Somerset County, 1708–probably 1710, 1715/16–1716; sheriff, Somerset County, probably 1710–1713, 1716–1719. WEALTH DURING LIFETIME. LAND AT FIRST ELECTION: at least 750 acres. WEALTH AT DEATH. DIED: will probated on February 17, 1756, in Somerset County. PERSONAL PROPERTY: TEV, £1,372.4.1 current money; FB, estate overpaid £1.15.2. LAND: 600 acres, plus 2 tracts of unspecified acreage.

DASHIELL (DASHIEL, DASHIELD), THOMAS (1733–1771). BORN: in 1733 in Somerset County; fifth son. NATIVE: fourth generation. RESIDED: in Stepney Parish, Wicomico Hundred, Somerset County. FAMILY BACKGROUND. FATHER: *George Dashiell* (1690/91–1748), son of *Thomas Dashiell* (1666–ca. 1756). MOTHER: Betty (?–1739). STEPMOTHER: Elizabeth (?–ca. 1749), widow of James Fairfax, of Northampton County, Virginia. AUNT: Anne Dashiell (1707–?), who married *Isaac Handy* (?–1762). BROTHERS: Arthur (1715–1741); Capt. Clement (1720–1756); Louther (1722–1765); Isaac (1726–?); *Joseph Dashiell* (1736–ca. 1787); and Benjamin (1738/39–ca. 1758). HALF BROTHER: *George Dashiell* (1743–?). SISTER: Eleanor (1730–?). FIRST COUSINS: *John Handy* (ca. 1724–1756); Priscilla Handy (?–by 1748/49), who married *Benjamin Handy* (?–ca. 1763); *Isaac Handy* (1743–ca. 1774); and *John Dashiell* (ca. 1740–1817), a possible legislator. OTHER KINSHIP: his second cousin was *William Winder* (1714/15–1792). MARRIED on May 8, 1757, Anne Guibert. CHILDREN. SONS: George (1759–?), probably died young; William (1763–?), who married Mary Nichols. DAUGHTERS: Henney (1758–ca. 1787), who married *Josiah Dashiell* (1746–1784); Patience (1761–?); and Jane (1765–?), who married William Cottman. PRIVATE CAREER. EDUCATION: literate. RELIGIOUS AFFILIATION: Anglican, Stepney Parish, Somerset County. SOCIAL STATUS AND ACTIVITIES: Gent., 1758; fourth generation legislator. OCCUPATIONAL PROFILE: probably a planter. PUBLIC CAREER. LEGISLATIVE SERVICE: Lower House, Somerset County, 1768–1770. LOCAL OFFICES: sheriff, Somerset County, 1764–1767; visitor for a free school that was to be erected for Somerset and Worcester counties (to be named Eden School), appointed 1770. WEALTH DURING LIFETIME. LAND AT FIRST ELECTION: 426 acres in Somerset County (probably all inherited). WEALTH AT DEATH. DIED: between May 13 and August 26, 1771, in Somerset County. PERSONAL PROPERTY: TEV, £1,564.12.3 current money (including 13 slaves); FB, £1,447.10.6. LAND: ca. 426 acres in Somerset County.

DAVIDSON, JOHN (1754–1807). BORN: on June 21, 1754. IMMIGRATED: probably, if so, probably from another colony before 1776. RESIDED: in Anne Arundel County; in Annapolis, Anne Arundel County, from the late 1790s until at least 1801; lived in the Adams-Kilty House on Charles Street, Annapolis. MARRIED on October 2, 1796, Anne Marie Luthall (Lutrell) (ca. 1775–1815), daughter of Thomas Grason (?–by 1786). Her first cousin was probably William Grason (ca. 1788–1868), governor of Maryland from 1839 to 1842. CHILDREN. SONS: John Thomas (?–1821), lieutenant, Eleventh Regiment, U.S. Artillery, who died in St. Augustine, Florida; Pinkney (1803–1821), who died as a cadet at the U.S. Military Academy, West Point, New York. DAUGHTER: Ann Janette, who married in 1821 William Montgomery Waters. PRIVATE CAREER. EDUCATION: literate. RELIGIOUS AFFILIATION: Anglican, St. Anne's Parish, Annapolis. SOCIAL STATUS AND ACTIVITIES: Esq., by 1784; Gent., by 1786. ADDITIONAL COMMENTS: played the violin at Annapolis parties; director of the Washington Tontine Company, 1806. OCCUPATIONAL PROFILE: land speculator; owned a privateer during the Revolution; officeholder. PUBLIC CAREER. STATE OFFICES: naval officer, Third District, appointed 1777; Executive Council, 1783–1784, 1784–1785, 1786–1787, 1787–1788, 1788–1789, 1789–1790, 1790–1791, 1791–1792, 1792–1793, 1793–1794, 1794–1795, 1795–1796, 1796–1797, 1797–1798, 1798–1799, 1799–1800, 1800–1801. LOCAL OFFICES: common councilman, An-napolis, 1797–1799; churchwarden, St. Anne's Parish, Anne Arundel County, in office, 1797; St. Anne's Parish Vestry, Anne Arundel County, in office 1798–1801; alderman, Annapolis, in office 1799, 1801–1805 (resigned); mayor, Annapolis, 1799–1800. MILITARY SERVICE: 2nd lieutenant, Allen's Independent Maryland Company, 1776; captain, Second Maryland Regiment, 1776; major, Fifth Maryland Regiment, 1781–1783 (retired); brigadier general, Eighth Brigade (Calvert and Anne Arundel counties), Maryland Militia, 1794–1795 (resigned). WEALTH DURING LIFETIME. LAND AT FIRST ELECTION: at least 2,000 acres in Anne Arundel and Baltimore counties. SIGNIFICANT CHANGES IN LAND BETWEEN FIRST ELECTION AND DEATH: purchased 829 acres of confiscated British property in Baltimore County in the 1780s and took out certificates of survey, but sold the land before patenting it. Sold most of his other Baltimore County land in 1786, and bought 235 acres in Montgomery County and a small amount of acreage in Allegany County between 1794 and 1796. Acquired 250 acres in Queen Anne's County by marriage, 1796. Took out certificates of survey on more than 10,500 acres in Washington and Allegany counties in 1797. Was entitled to 400 acres in Allegany County for his service in the Revolution. WEALTH AT DEATH. DIED: on February 2, 1807, in Baltimore County; buried in Annapolis with full military honors. PERSONAL PROPERTY: TEV, £1,622.10.8 current money (including 3 slaves, books, and paintings); FB, estate overpaid £520.10.4. LAND: probably 522 acres in Anne Arundel, Montgomery, and Allegany counties, and at least 7,500 acres in unpatented certificates, plus houses leased out in Annapolis, Georgetown, and Washington, D.C.

DAVIS, JOHN (?–1779). BORN: before 1710 when he is described as a minor, probably in Queen Anne's County. NATIVE: at least second generation. RESIDED: in Wye Hundred, Queen Anne's County. FAMILY BACKGROUND. FATHER: John Davis (?–1710), of Queen Anne's County, planter. MOTHER: Anne. BROTHER: Thomas (?–1745), of Queen Anne's County, who married Elizabeth. SISTERS: Ann; Mary; Rebeccah; and Hester. OTHER KINSHIP: his brothers-in-law were Matthew Williams and Daniel Walker. MARRIED first, before 1745 (name unknown). MARRIED second, by 1761 Margaret, widow of John Alley (?–1756), of Queen Anne's County. CHILDREN. SONS: Thomas, of age by 1750; probably John, Jr. (?–1790), who married by 1761 his probable stepsister Katherine Alley. STEPSONS: John Alley, of age by 1761; William

Alley (?–by 1761); James Alley (?–by 1761); and Thomas Alley. STEPDAUGHTERS: Katherine Alley, who married by 1761 her probable stepbrother John Davis, Jr.; Sarah Alley (?–by 1761), who married Thomas Wiggens; Mary Alley; Martha Alley; and Loverain Alley. PRIVATE CAREER. EDUCATION: literate. RELIGIOUS AFFILIATION: Protestant. SOCIAL STATUS AND ACTIVITIES: Gent., by 1750. OCCUPATIONAL PROFILE: probably a planter. PUBLIC CAREER. LEGISLATIVE SERVICE: Lower House, Queen Anne's County, 1749–1751. MILITARY SERVICE: captain, by 1776. WEALTH DURING LIFETIME. PERSONAL PROPERTY: 9 slaves, 1776. LAND AT FIRST ELECTION: 370 acres in Queen Anne's County (220 acres from his father; 150 acres by purchase). SIGNIFICANT CHANGES IN LAND BETWEEN FIRST ELECTION AND DEATH: purchased 70 acres in Queen Anne's County, 1750. WEALTH AT DEATH. DIED: administration bond dated October 26, 1779, in Queen Anne's County. PERSONAL PROPERTY: TEV, at least £638.18.5 current money (including 10 slaves and books). LAND: at least 440 acres in Queen Anne's County; may have owned 300 additional acres in Queen Anne's County in partnership with two other men.

DAVIS, THOMAS (?–?). IMMIGRATED: by 1683. RESIDED: in Kent County. PRIVATE CAREER. EDUCATION: literate. RELIGIOUS AFFILIATION: Protestant. SOCIAL STATUS AND ACTIVITIES: probably the man who was a merchant-attorney for Edward and Dudley Carleton, merchants of London, England, in 1688; no mention of him in the colony's records after 1689. OCCUPATIONAL PROFILE: planter; probably a factor. PUBLIC CAREER. LEGISLATIVE SERVICE: Associators' Convention, Kent County, 1689–perhaps 1692. JURY SERVICE: foreman, grand jury, Kent County, 1686. STANDS ON PUBLIC/PRIVATE ISSUES: supported the revolution of 1689. WEALTH DURING LIFETIME. LAND AT FIRST ELECTION: at least 100 acres, patented in 1683.

DEAKINS, WILLIAM, JR. (?–1798). BORN: in Prince George's County, of age by 1765. NATIVE: third generation. RESIDED: in Georgetown, Frederick County (later became part of Montgomery County and then Washington, D.C.). FAMILY BACKGROUND. FATHER: William Deakins, Sr. (1720–1800), of Prince George's County, a large landowner and the son of John Deakins, an immigrant from England. MOTHER: possibly Ann, daughter of Francis Marbury (?–1734), of Prince George's County. BROTHERS: Leonard; Col. Fran-

cis. SISTER: (first name unknown), who married Paul Hoye, of Washington County. MARRIED Jane Johns, widow of Nicholas Greenbury Ridgley. Her brother was Thomas Johns. CHILDREN. STEPDAUGHTER: Elizabeth Ridgley (by 1771–?), who married by 1797 John Threkield. PRIVATE CAREER. EDUCATION: literate. RELIGIOUS AFFILIATION: his father was Anglican. OCCUPATIONAL PROFILE: merchant, in partnership with his brother Francis in the firm of William Deakins & Co.; incorporator of the Georgetown Bridge Company and the Bank of Columbia; partner in a mill with Barnard O'Neill and *Charles Beatty* (ca. 1736–1804), 1778; partner in land transactions with *Charles Beatty* (ca. 1736–1804). PUBLIC CAREER. LEGISLATIVE SERVICE: Conventions, Frederick County, 4th, 1775, 5th, 1775. OTHER STATE OFFICE: Constitution Ratification Convention, Montgomery County, 1788. LOCAL OFFICES: justice, Frederick County, 1772–at least 1775, Montgomery County, April 1777–March 1778, commissioned November 1778 and November 1779 (refused to serve); Committee of Observation, Frederick County, elected 1774 and 1775; justice, Orphans' Court, Montgomery County, commissioned 1778 and 1779 (refused to qualify); subscription officer, Continental Loan Office, Montgomery County, appointed 1779. MILITARY SERVICE: colonel, 1789. OUT OF STATE SERVICE: treasurer, Board of Commissioners, Washington, D.C., 1793. STANDS ON PUBLIC/PRIVATE ISSUES: supported establishment of the Federal City in Georgetown, Montgomery County. WEALTH DURING LIFETIME. PERSONAL PROPERTY: assessed value £588.0.0, including 9 slaves and 56 oz. plate, 1783. LAND AT FIRST ELECTION: probably 2,681 acres in Frederick County. SIGNIFICANT CHANGES IN LAND BETWEEN FIRST ELECTION AND DEATH: in partnership with brother Francis, as William Deakins & Co., acquired 1,058 acres in Montgomery County, by 1795. WEALTH AT DEATH. DIED: on March 3, 1798, in Georgetown, D.C. PERSONAL PROPERTY: TEV, at least £2,261.11.10 (including 10 slaves, 33 books, and a large quantity of plate and china). LAND: 1,064 acres in the District of Columbia, Prince George's and Montgomery counties, plus possible acreage in Washington and Allegany counties; 64 lots in the District of Columbia, plus possibly 8 dwelling houses; 1 lot in Hamburgh, Prince George's County.

DEBUTTS, JOHN (?–1796). IMMIGRATED: from County Sligo, Ireland. RESIDED: at "Trent Place" on the Patuxent River, St. Mary's County. FAMILY BACKGROUND. FATHER: probably Richard De-

Butts. BROTHER: Samuel, (?–1813), a physician who resided at Mt. Welby, Prince George's County. SISTERS: Margaret, who married (first name unknown) Armstrong; Catherine, who married (first name unknown) Ralph; and Sarah, who married (first name unknown) Powell. MARRIED Margaret Trueman (?–1798), daughter of Margaret Somerville. Her sister was Susannah, who married *George Fraser Hawkins* (ca. 1741–1785). CHILDREN. Died without progeny. PRIVATE CAREER. RELIGIOUS AFFILIATION: Anglican, St. Andrew's Parish, St. Mary's County, 1773–1786, and All Faiths Parish, St. Mary's County, 1792 to death. SOCIAL STATUS AND ACTIVITIES: Mr., 1773; Esq., 1784. OCCUPATIONAL PROFILE: probably a planter. PUBLIC CAREER. LEGISLATIVE SERVICE: Conventions, St. Mary's County, 3rd, 1774, 4th, 1775 (elected, but did not attend); Lower House, St. Mary's County, 1783, 1784 (Claims), 1785 (Manufactories), 1786–1787 (Claims 1). OTHER STATE OFFICE: associate justice, First District, 1791–at least 1793. LOCAL OFFICES: justice, St. Mary's County, 1772–1774 (no records 1775–1778), 1779–at least 1789; St. Andrew's Parish Vestry, St. Mary's County, in office 1773–1780, 1781–1786; justice, Orphans' Court, St. Mary's County, 1779–at least 1789; churchwarden, St. Andrew's Parish, St. Mary's County, in office 1780–1781 and 1781–1786; commissioner of tax, St. Mary's County, appointed 1782 and 1783; All Faiths Parish Vestry, St. Mary's County, in office 1791. WEALTH DURING LIFETIME. PERSONAL PROPERTY: 34 slaves, 1790; assessed value £766.0.0, including 28 slaves and plate, 1793. LAND AT FIRST ELECTION: 750 acres in St. Mary's County (450 acres inherited from other family members). SIGNIFICANT CHANGES IN LAND BETWEEN FIRST ELECTION AND DEATH: owned 4,031 acres in St. Mary's County, 1793. WEALTH AT DEATH. DIED: between March 20 and May 10, 1796, at "Trent Place," St. Mary's County. PERSONAL PROPERTY: TEV, £6,996.10.4 current money (including 41 slaves, 35 books, and more than 80 gallons of wine and whiskey); FB, £6,415.8.1. LAND: 4,031 acres in St. Mary's County in 1793, as well as unspecified acreage in Virginia and County Sligo, Ireland.

DECOURSEY (COURSEY, COURCEY, CORCEY), EDWARD (ca. 1759–1827). BORN: ca. 1759, probably in Queen Anne's County; second son. NATIVE: fourth generation. RESIDED: on Wye Neck, Queen Anne's County. FAMILY BACKGROUND. FATHER: Col. William Coursey (1703–1769), of Queen Anne's County, son of *Henry Coursey* (1662–1707). MOTHER: Rachel, daughter of *Solomon Clayton* (1685–1739). AUNT: Elizabeth Coursey, who married *William Cumming* (ca. 1696–1752). BROTHER: Henry (?–ca. 1815). HALF BROTHER: William. SISTERS: Mary, who married (first name unknown) Downs; Rachel; and Sarah, who married *Robert Wright* (1752–1826). ADDITIONAL COMMENTS: his father had a previous wife (name unknown). MARRIED in December 1786 Ann (1762–?), daughter of William Nicols (1730–1774), of Kent County, and wife Henrietta Maria Lloyd Chamberlaine (1739–1777); granddaughter of both Rev. Henry Nicols (1687–ca. 1749), rector of St. Michael's Parish in Talbot County from 1708 to 1749, and wife Dorothy Elizabeth Rowle, and *Samuel Chamberlaine* (1698–1773); niece of *James Lloyd Chamberlaine* (1732–1783), *Samuel Chamberlaine* (1742–1811), and Anne Chamberlaine (1734–1786), who married *Richard Tilghman Earle* (1728/29–1788). Her brothers were Samuel (1770–?), who married first, (first name unknown) Blake, and second, Elizabeth Smyth; Henry (1764–1810), who married in 1786 Elizabeth Robins (1765–1814). Her sister was Henrietta Maria (1761–?), who married first, *Samuel Earle* (1756–1790), and second, Charles Blake (?–1798). Her first cousins were Henrietta Maria Chamberlaine (?–1804), who married *William Hayward, Jr.* (ca. 1758–1834); *Samuel Earle* (1756–1790). CHILDREN. SONS: William Henry (?–1848), who married Elizabeth, daughter of Henry Notley Rozier; Edward (ca. 1791–1822). DAUGHTER: Henrietta. PRIVATE CAREER. EDUCATION: literate. RELIGIOUS AFFILIATION: Anglican, Chester Church, St. Paul's Parish, Queen Anne's County. SOCIAL STATUS AND ACTIVITIES: Gent., 1778; Esq., 1779; subscriber to Washington College, Chestertown, Kent County; member of the Society of Cincinnati. OCCUPATIONAL PROFILE: probably a planter; director, Easton branch of the Farmer's Bank of Maryland, 1811–1812. PUBLIC CAREER. LEGISLATIVE SERVICE: Lower House, Queen Anne's County, 1781–1782, 1782–1783, 1783, 1784. LOCAL OFFICES: Chester Church Vestry, St. Paul's Parish, Queen Anne's County, elected 1792, 1798, 1799, 1800, 1805, 1806, and 1808; trustee for the poor, Queen Anne's County, in office 1795–1798. MILITARY SERVICE: 3rd lieutenant, Veazy's Independent Maryland Regiment, 1776; wounded and taken prisoner at the Battle of Long Island, 1776; major, by 1794. WEALTH DURING LIFETIME. PERSONAL PROPERTY: assessed valued £5,086.0.0, including 20 slaves, 1783; 45 slaves, 1798; deeded at least 24 slaves as a gift to son William Henry, 1822. LAND AT FIRST ELEC-

TION: 1,509 acres in Queen Anne's County (1,115 acres from his father; 394 acres by purchase). SIGNIFICANT CHANGES IN LAND BETWEEN FIRST ELECTION AND DEATH: made a deed of gift of part of his home estate on Wye Neck, Queen Anne's County, to his son William Henry, 1822; deeded 600 acres in Queen Anne's County, plus 11 slaves, a library of books, and plate to his son William Henry in return for an annual rent of $200.00, 1824. WEALTH AT DEATH. DIED: on April 8, 1827, probably in Queen Anne's County. PERSONAL PROPERTY: size of estate unknown; probably had deeded everything to his only surviving son before his death. LAND: probably all of his real property deeded to his son before his death. ADDITIONAL COMMENTS: In his will he requested that his descendants resume the spelling of the family name as "DeCoursey," instead of "Coursey," the "De" having been dropped "to efface the mark of their being of French descent."

DENNIS, BENJAMIN (?–1808). BORN: of age by 1768. RESIDED: in Acquango Hundred, Worcester County. MARRIED possibly Leza. CHILDREN. SONS: Benjamin; James; and Whetty (Wheatley). DAUGHTERS: Leah, who married James Fooks, son of Thomas Fooks; Sarah, who married (first name unknown) Atkinson; Ann, who married John Johnson, son of Benjamin Johnson; and Betsy. PRIVATE CAREER. EDUCATION: literate. OCCUPATIONAL PROFILE: carpenter, 1789; owned two-thirds of a vessel, 1789; mill owner. PUBLIC CAREER. LEGISLATIVE SERVICE: Lower House, Worcester County, 1788, 1789, 1790, 1791–1792, 1792. LOCAL OFFICE: justice, Worcester County, 1791–at least 1800. MILITARY SERVICE: captain of a company belonging to the Wicomico Battalion, Worcester County Militia, commissioned 1776. WEALTH DURING LIFETIME. PERSONAL PROPERTY: assessed value £188.7.4, including at least 4 slaves, 1783; owned 7 slaves, 1790. LAND AT FIRST ELECTION: possibly ca. 850 acres in Worcester County. SIGNIFICANT CHANGES IN LAND BETWEEN FIRST ELECTION AND DEATH: obtained over 1,260 acres in Worcester County through purchase, patent, and several patent resurveys, which he deeded to his children between 1802 and 1808, reserving a life estate for himself. WEALTH AT DEATH. DIED: between July 29 and August 26, 1808, in Worcester County. LAND: at least 865 acres, plus a life estate in over 1,260 acres in Worcester County.

DENNIS, HENRY (?–1785). BORN: probably at "Beverly" on the Pocomoke River, Worcester

County, of age by 1774; second son, but eldest surviving son by 1777. NATIVE: probably fifth generation. RESIDED: in Pitts Creek Hundred, Worcester County. FAMILY BACKGROUND. FATHER: *Littleton Dennis* (ca. 1728–1774), son of *John Dennis* (1704–1767). MOTHER: Susanna Upshur (1733–1784). UNCLE: *John Dennis, Jr.* (ca. 1724–1782). BROTHERS: James (?–by 1777); Littleton; and John. SISTERS: Elizabeth; Sarah. FIRST COUSIN: *Samuel Handy* (1751/52–1828). MARRIED on November 23, 1783, Ann, daughter of Capt. John Purnell (?–ca. 1761), and wife Euphame Arbuckle (1734–?); granddaughter of *John Purnell* (?–1755), and of Gen. William Arbuckle (1689–1751), of Virginia; niece of *William Purnell* (?–1777), a possible legislator, *Zadock Purnell* (?–1805), *Thomas Purnell, of John* (?–1796), and Arralantar Purnell (?–1782), who married *Thomas Robins* (?–1766). Her brother was *William Purnell* (?–1798). Her first cousin was *John Purnell Robins* (?–1780). Ann subsequently married by 1793 William Polk. CHILDREN. SON: Littleton (1784–?). PRIVATE CAREER. EDUCATION: literate. RELIGIOUS AFFILIATION: Anglican, Rehobeth Church, Coventry Parish, Worcester County. SOCIAL STATUS AND ACTIVITIES: Esq. at death. OCCUPATIONAL PROFILE: merchant, partner with Zedekiah Whalley; owned mill lands; owned a privateer during the Revolution. PUBLIC CAREER. LEGISLATIVE SERVICE: Lower House, Worcester County, 1779–1780, 1780–1781, 1781–1782, 1782–1783, 1783 (elected, but did not attend). LOCAL OFFICES: Coventry Parish Vestry, Somerset and Worcester counties, elected 1781 and 1784; militia recruiter, Worcester County, in office 1781. MILITARY SERVICE: 1st lieutenant, Snow Hill Battalion, Worcester County Militia, commissioned 1777. WEALTH DURING LIFETIME. PERSONAL PROPERTY: inherited law books from his father, 1774; assessed value £513.0.0, including 13 slaves, 1783. LAND AT FIRST ELECTION: over 2,850 acres in Worcester County (inherited from his father), plus 116 acres in Accomack County, Virginia. WEALTH AT DEATH. DIED: ca. July 1, 1785, in Worcester County. PERSONAL PROPERTY: TEV, at least £2,833.3.11 (including 25 slaves); FB, estate overpaid £358.16.10. LAND: ca. 3,214 acres in Worcester County, plus 116 acres in Accomack County, Virginia.

DENNIS, JOHN (1704–1767). BORN: on August 12, 1704, in Somerset County. NATIVE: probably third generation. RESIDED: in Pocomoke Hundred, Somerset County. FAMILY BACKGROUND. FATHER: John Dennis (1676/77–1744/45). MOTHER: Sarah

(?–1732), daughter of Col. Southey Littleton (1645–1679). STEPMOTHER: Elizabeth Day. BROTHERS: Valentine; Lazarus (?–1754); Wheatley; Solomon; and Daniel. MARRIED on November 10, 1724, Mary (?–1768), daughter of William Purnell. CHILDREN. SONS: *John Dennis, Jr.* (ca. 1724–1782); *Littleton Dennis* (ca. 1728–1774). DAUGHTERS: Sarah, who married Thomas Hollbrook; Leah, who married Rev. James Robertson (?–1767); Mary, who married first, in 1737 Samuel Handy (?–1755), and second, (first name unknown) Pollett. PRIVATE CAREER. EDUCATION: literate. RELIGIOUS AFFILIATION: Anglican. SOCIAL STATUS AND ACTIVITIES: Gent., 1729. OCCUPATIONAL PROFILE: innholder, 1725; owner and master of sloops, 1734–1739; part owner of a sloop with William Lane, 1748/49; ship's captain. PUBLIC CAREER. LEGISLATIVE SERVICE: Lower House, Somerset County, 1745, 1745/46–1746 (appointed sheriff before the 3rd session), 1754–1757. LOCAL OFFICES: sheriff, Somerset County, 1746–1749, 1758–1761; coroner, Somerset County, commissioned 1745; justice, Somerset County, 1746–at least 1763 (quorum, 1751–at least 1763); Coventry Parish Vestry, Somerset and Worcester counties, in office 1748. WEALTH DURING LIFETIME. PERSONAL PROPERTY: owned a 15-ton sloop, 1734; owned a 30-ton sloop, 1736; owned a 30-ton sloop, 1739; owned half-interest in a 35-ton sloop, 1748/49. LAND AT FIRST ELECTION: ca. 900 acres in Somerset and Worcester counties. SIGNIFICANT CHANGES IN LAND BETWEEN FIRST ELECTION AND DEATH: deeded ca. 700 acres in Somerset County to his son, 1755. WEALTH AT DEATH. DIED: will probated on September 2, 1767, in Somerset County. PERSONAL PROPERTY: TEV, at least £480.3.0 current money (including 8 slaves). LAND: 287 acres in Somerset County.

DENNIS, JOHN, JR. (ca. 1724–1782). BORN: ca. 1724 in Somerset County; probably elder son. NATIVE: probably fourth generation. RESIDED: in Worcester County. FAMILY BACKGROUND. FATHER: *John Dennis* (1704–1767). MOTHER OR POSSIBLY STEPMOTHER: Mary Purnell (?–1768). BROTHER OR POSSIBLY HALF BROTHER: *Littleton Dennis* (ca. 1728–1774). SISTERS OR POSSIBLY HALF SISTERS: Sarah; Leah; and Mary. NEPHEWS: *Henry Dennis* (?–1785); *Samuel Handy* (1751/52–1828). MARRIED Anna Maria (?–by 1781). CHILDREN. SONS: John; Robert (ca. 1751–?). PRIVATE CAREER. EDUCATION: literate. RELIGIOUS AFFILIATION: Anglican, St. Martin's Church, Worcester Parish, Worcester County. OCCUPATIONAL PROFILE: planter, 1758; built a water mill, 1762; owned a sawmill and gristmill, 1766. PUBLIC CAREER. LEGISLATIVE SERVICE: Lower House, Worcester County, 1754–1755 (appointed sheriff before the 4th session). LOCAL OFFICES: sheriff, Worcester County, 1755–1758; justice, Somerset County, commissioned 1746, 1747, 1748, and 1762; justice, Worcester County, in office 1751–1755, 1764–1782 (quorum, 1754–1755, 1764–1782); Coventry Parish Vestry, Worcester and Somerset counties, in office 1763; justice, Court of Oyer and Terminer and Gaol Delivery, Worcester County, commissioned 1766; justice, Orphans' Court, Worcester County, 1777–1782; subscription officer, Continental Loan Office, Worcester County, appointed 1779. MILITARY SERVICE: captain, by 1758. WEALTH DURING LIFETIME. PERSONAL PROPERTY: 13 slaves included in a deed of trust, 1766. LAND AT FIRST ELECTION: 250 acres in Worcester County (by purchase). SIGNIFICANT CHANGES IN LAND BETWEEN FIRST ELECTION AND DEATH: 250 acres mortgaged and lost, 1755; owned at least 2,243 acres obtained through patents and purchases by 1766; because of heavy indebtedness, a deed of trust was executed to his creditors involving 2,243 acres in 1766, but he apparently was able to retain ownership; sold ca. 850 acres by 1774; all land was probably in Worcester County. ADDITIONAL COMMENTS: his brother or half brother *Littleton Dennis* (ca. 1728–1774) inherited all of his father's estate. WEALTH AT DEATH. DIED: will probated on June 6, 1782, in Worcester County. PERSONAL PROPERTY: 11 slaves; requested no appraisal of his estate. LAND: at least 1,200 acres in Worcester County, plus one and one-half lots in Snow Hill, Worcester County.

DENNIS, LITTLETON (ca. 1728–1774). BORN: on February 3, ca. 1728, in Somerset County; younger son. NATIVE: probably fourth generation. RESIDED: in Somerset County; Worcester County, by 1759. FAMILY BACKGROUND. FATHER: *John Dennis* (1704–1767). MOTHER: Mary Purnell (?–1768). BROTHER OR POSSIBLY HALF BROTHER: *John Dennis, Jr.* (ca. 1724–1782). SISTERS OR POSSIBLY HALF SISTERS: Sarah; Leah; and Mary. NEPHEW: *Samuel Handy* (1751/52–1828). MARRIED on August 12, 1754, Susanna (1733–1784), daughter of Abel Upshur (?–1754) and wife Rachel Revell. CHILDREN. SONS: James (?–by 1777); *Henry Dennis* (?–1785); Littleton (1765–1833), who married Elizabeth Upshur (1769–1819); and John. DAUGHTERS: Elizabeth, who married John Teackle, of Accomack County, Virginia; Sarah. PRIVATE CAREER. EDUCATION: literate. SOCIAL STATUS AND ACTIVITIES: Gent., 1759; Esq., 1772.

OCCUPATIONAL PROFILE: planter; attorney, admitted to the following courts: Somerset County in August 1749; Worcester County by June 1769. He was also engaged in mercantile activity and directed his executors to sell and dispose "of every matter I have in Trade"; in partnership with *Josiah Polk* (?–1784) and *Gillis Polk* (?–1793) in the building of a sawmill and gristmill at the head of the Wicomico River. PUBLIC CAREER. LEGISLATIVE SERVICE: Lower House, Somerset County, 1771 (Grievances), 1773–1774 (elected, but did not attend). ADDITIONAL COMMENTS: Littleton Dennis had extensive landholdings in both Somerset and Worcester counties, and although his actual residence was probably in Worcester County, his acreage in Somerset County was sufficient to qualify him for election from that county. LOCAL OFFICES: prosecutor of his lordship's pleas, Somerset County, appointed 1753; deputy commissary, Somerset County, sworn 1763; Coventry Parish Vestry, Somerset and Worcester counties, in office 1763, 1767, 1774. WEALTH DURING LIFETIME. LAND AT FIRST ELECTION: 4,925 acres in Somerset and Worcester counties, plus 232 acres in Somerset and Worcester counties held jointly with other people (at least 1,190 acres obtained from his father and at least 3,445 acres by patent or purchase). SIGNIFICANT CHANGES IN LAND BETWEEN FIRST ELECTION AND DEATH: purchased 550 acres in 1772 and sold 600 acres in 1773, all in Worcester County. WEALTH AT DEATH. DIED: on May 6, 1774, in Worcester County. PERSONAL PROPERTY: TEV, at least £10,270.19.7 current money (including 51 slaves, 171 oz. 8 dwt. 8 gr. plate, law books, other books, two-thirds interest in a schooner, and 2 sloops). LAND: 4,875 acres in Somerset and Worcester counties, plus 232 acres in Somerset and Worcester counties owned jointly with other people.

DENT, GEORGE (1690–1754). BORN: on September 27, 1690, at "Nanjemoy," Charles County; second surviving son. NATIVE: third generation. RESIDED: in Charles County. FAMILY BACKGROUND. FATHER: *William Dent* (ca. 1660–1704), son of *Thomas Dent* (ca. 1630–1676). MOTHER: Elizabeth (?–1698/99), daughter of *Gerard Fowke* (1625–1669). STEPMOTHER: Sarah, daughter of *Thomas Brooke* (ca. 1659–1730/31). She subsequently married *Philip Lee* (ca. 1681–1744), son of Richard Lee II, of Virginia. BROTHERS: *Thomas Dent* (1685–1725); William (1687–1695); Gerard (?–died young); Peter (1694–?); and Philip (?–died young). SISTERS: Elizabeth (1688–1699); Anne (1692–?); and Elizabeth (1699–?). MARRIED in

1713 Anne (?–1764), daughter of *William Harbert* (?–1718). CHILDREN. SONS: *George Dent* (?–1785); *John Dent, of George* (ca. 1733–1809). DAUGHTERS: Elizabeth, who married first, William Penn, and second, *Richard Harrison* (?–1780); Ann, who married first, Gilbert Ireland, and second, Maj. (first name unknown) Sweeney; Sarah; Rebecca (1714–died young); Letty (Letitia), who married first, Kenelm Truman Stoddert, and second, Peter DeJean; Mary, who married Gerard Alexander; Eleanor, who married first, John Blakiston, second, Alexander McFarland (McParling), and third, Dr. James Bayard; Margaret, who married Kenelm Truman Greenfield; and Rebecca (1735–1770), who married *Thomas Hanson Marshall* (1731–1801). PRIVATE CAREER. EDUCATION: literate. RELIGIOUS AFFILIATION: Anglican, member of Christ Church, Nanjemoy, Charles County. SOCIAL STATUS AND ACTIVITIES: Gent., 1719; Esq., 1730; Hon., 1730; OCCUPATIONAL PROFILE: planter. PUBLIC CAREER. LEGISLATIVE SERVICE: Lower House, Charles County, 1719–1721/22, 1722–1724 (Laws 1–3), 1725–1727 (Laws 1–4). OTHER PROVINCIAL OFFICES: justice, Provincial Court, 1728–1735, 1738–1754 (quorum, 1732–1735, 1738–1754; chief justice, 1754); judge, Assize Court, Western Shore, 1733–1735, 1738– at least 1740, 1747–at least 1749. LOCAL OFFICES: justice, Charles County, 1715–at least 1728 (quorum, 1728); justice, Court of Oyer and Terminer and Gaol Delivery, Charles County, commissioned 1718, 1720, 1731, 1733, 1734, 1743, 1744, 1745, and 1750; sheriff, Charles County, 1735–1738; school visitor, Charles County, dates of service unknown; William and Mary Parish Vestry, St. Mary's County, dates of service unknown. MILITARY SERVICE: captain, militia, 1726; called "colonel," by 1737. WEALTH DURING LIFETIME. LAND AT FIRST ELECTION: at least 1,566 acres in Charles County (1,066 acres inherited from his father, at least 500 acres from his wife's dower). SIGNIFICANT CHANGES IN LAND BETWEEN FIRST ELECTION AND DEATH: acquired 843 acres in Charles and Prince George's counties, 1724–1737. WEALTH AT DEATH. DIED: on May 12, 1754, in Charles County. PERSONAL PROPERTY: TEV, at least £714.7.9 (including 23 slaves). LAND: 2,955 acres in Charles and Prince George's counties.

DENT, GEORGE (?–1785). BORN: on his father's plantation near Pope's Creek, Charles County, of age by 1750. NATIVE: fourth generation. RESIDED: on a plantation on Pope's Creek, Charles County. FAMILY BACKGROUND. FATHER: *George Dent* (1690–1754), son of *William Dent* (ca. 1660–

1704). MOTHER: Anne (?–1764), daughter of *William Harbert* (?–1718). BROTHER: *John Dent, of George* (ca. 1733–1809). SISTERS: Elizabeth, who married second, *Richard Harrison* (?–1780); Ann; Sarah; Rebecca (1714–died young); Letty (Letitia); Mary; Eleanor; Margaret; and Rebecca (1735–1770), who married *Thomas Hanson Marshall* (1731–1801). MARRIED between 1746 and 1751 Eleanor, daughter of *Henry Holland Hawkins* (1683–1751); granddaughter of both *Henry Hawkins* (?–1699) and *Thomas Greenfield* (ca. 1649–1715); niece of *Thomas Trueman Greenfield* (1682–1733). Her brothers were Samuel; Henry; and *Josias Hawkins* (ca. 1735–1789). Her sisters were Elizabeth; Martha Portase; Jane; Susannah; and Ruth. Her first cousins were *Thomas Greenfield* (ca. 1715–1774); Marianne Greenfield, who married *John Stoddert* (?–1767); and *Francis Waring* (1715–1769). CHILDREN. SONS: Henry; George, who married Elizabeth Yates. DAUGHTERS: Elander (Eleanor) (?–1819), a spinster; Joanna (Johanna) Greenfield; Jane (?–1827), a spinster; Mary, who married first, Henry Alexander Ashton, and second, Johannis Storke; and Anne, who married Dr. *John Parnham* (ca. 1748–1813). PRIVATE CAREER. EDUCATION: literate. RELIGIOUS AFFILIATION: Protestant; his father was an Anglican. SOCIAL STATUS AND ACTIVITIES: Esq., 1781; fourth generation legislator. OCCUPATIONAL PROFILE: probably a planter. PUBLIC CAREER. LEGISLATIVE SERVICE: Lower House, Charles County, 1757–1758 (Arms and Ammunition Cv, 2), 1758–1761 (Arms and Ammunition 2), 1762–1763 (Accounts 1, 2), 1765–1766 (Accounts 2, 4), Conventions, Charles County, 2nd, 1774, 4th, 1775 (elected, but did not attend), 5th, 1775 (elected, but did not attend). LOCAL OFFICES: sheriff, Charles County, 1753–1756; justice, Charles County, 1757–at least 1774 (quorum, 1766–at least 1774); justice, Court of Oyer and Terminer and Gaol Delivery, Charles County, 1773; judge, court of appeals, appointed under the Act to Procure Troops for the American Army, Charles County, appointed 1778; trustee, Charlotte Hall School, 1778. MILITARY SERVICE: captain, 1757. WEALTH DURING LIFETIME. PERSONAL PROPERTY: assessed value £2,104.10.0, including 43 slaves and 16 oz. plate, 1783. LAND AT FIRST ELECTION: 1,886 acres in Charles County (1,786 acres inherited from his father). SIGNIFICANT CHANGES IN LAND BETWEEN FIRST ELECTION AND DEATH: in April 1781 his home in Charles County was burned by the British. In May 1781, as part of the act to raise supplies for that year, Dent was exempted from paying his taxes because

of the losses he had sustained at the hands of the British. WEALTH AT DEATH. DIED: between September 12 and December 31, 1785, in Charles County. LAND: He was charged with 1,383 acres in Charles County in 1783. His will, two years later, mentioned only 300 acres, but stated that he had already provided for his daughters.

DENT, GEORGE (ca. 1758–1813). BORN: ca. 1758 at "Clarks Inheritance" on Mattawoman Creek, Pomonkey Hundred, Charles County; probably elder son. NATIVE: fifth generation. RESIDED: in Pomonkey Hundred, Charles County, 1778; plantation near Augusta, Georgia, 1802 until death. FAMILY BACKGROUND. FATHER: *John Dent, of George* (ca. 1733–1809), son of *George Dent* (1690–1754). MOTHER: Sarah (?–1795), daughter of Thomas Marshall and wife Elizabeth Bishop (1735–?). UNCLE: *George Dent* (?–1785). AUNT: Elizabeth Dent (?–1781), who married *Richard Harrison* (?–1780). BROTHER: Thomas Marshall (1761–1823). SISTERS: Ann Herbert (1756–1813); Elizabeth (1754–died young). MARRIED Anne Magruder, daughter of James Truman (?–1789) and wife Elizabeth Gordon (?–ca. 1807). CHILDREN. SONS: John Herbert (1782–?), who married Elizabeth Anne Harry; James Truman (1790–?), who married Catherine Anne Cooper; George Columbus (1792–1815), who died in a duel; and Dennis (1796–?), who married Martha Beall. DAUGHTERS: Sarah Marshall (1783–?), who married first, Edward Briscoe, and second, (first name unknown) Fendall; Elizabeth Truman (1786–1789); Maria (1788–?), who married John Neilson; and Mary Ann, (?–died young). PRIVATE CAREER. EDUCATION: literate. RELIGIOUS AFFILIATION: Anglican, St. John's Parish, Piscataway, Charles County. SOCIAL STATUS AND ACTIVITIES: Gent., 1789; fifth generation legislator. OCCUPATIONAL PROFILE: possibly a planter. PUBLIC CAREER. LEGISLATIVE SERVICE: Lower House, Charles County, 1782–1783, 1784, 1785, 1786–1787 (Grievances 2), 1787–1788 (Elections 1; Claims 1), 1788 (Elections), 1789 (speaker), 1790 (speaker); Senate, Western Shore, Term of 1791–1796: 1791–1792 (president 2), 1792 (president; resigned on December 21, 1792). LOCAL OFFICES: justice, Charles County, 1774–at least 1795; justice, Orphans' Court, Charles County, commissioned 1778 and 1779; subscription officer, Charles County, 1779. MILITARY SERVICE: 1st lieutenant, Third Maryland Battalion, Flying Camp, 1776; 1st lieutenant, Charles County Militia, commissioned 1778, then promoted to captain and assigned to the Twenty-sixth Battalion. OUT

OF STATE SERVICE: representative, U.S. Congress, 1793–1795, 1795–1797, 1797–1799, 1799–1801; nominated as marshal of Washington, D.C., 1801; he expected to receive the post of U.S. treasurer because of his ardent support of Thomas Jefferson in the 1801 election; when disappointed in his failure to receive the post, he moved to Georgia in 1802. WEALTH DURING LIFETIME. PERSONAL PROPERTY: assessed value £1,167.10.0, including 39 slaves and 16 oz. plate, 1783. LAND AT FIRST ELECTION: 1,863 acres in Charles County (580 acres inherited from his father). SIGNIFICANT CHANGES IN LAND BETWEEN FIRST ELECTION AND DEATH: sold 580 acres of his land and 243 acres of his wife's land, 1802. WEALTH AT DEATH. DIED: on December 2, 1813, on his plantation near Augusta, Georgia, as a result of being thrown from a horse; size of estate unknown.

DENT, JOHN, OF GEORGE (ca. 1733–1809). BORN: ca. 1733 in Pomonkey Hundred, Durham Parish, Charles County. NATIVE: fourth generation. RESIDED: at "Clarks Inheritance," Charles County, 1758; in Pomonkey Hundred, Charles County, 1778. FAMILY BACKGROUND. FATHER: *George Dent* (1690–1754), son of *William Dent* (ca. 1660–1704). MOTHER: Anne (?–1764), daughter of *William Harbert* (?–1718). UNCLE: *Thomas Dent* (1685–1725). BROTHERS: *George Dent* (?–1785). SISTERS: Elizabeth, who married second, *Richard Harrison* (?–1780); Ann; Sarah; Rebecca (1714–died young); Letty (Letitia); Mary; Eleanor; Margaret; and Rebecca (1735–1770), who married *Thomas Hanson Marshall* (1731–1801). MARRIED on February 27, 1753/54, Sarah (1735–1795), daughter of Thomas Marshall and wife Elizabeth Bishop, of Prince George's County. Her brother was *Thomas Hanson Marshall* (1731–1801). CHILDREN. SONS: *George Dent* (ca. 1758–1813); Thomas Marshall (1761–1823), who married Anne Magruder. DAUGHTERS: Elizabeth (1754–died young); Ann Herbert (1756–1813), who married *William Mackall Wilkinson* (1752–1799). PRIVATE CAREER. EDUCATION: literate. RELIGIOUS AFFILIATION: Protestant. SOCIAL STATUS AND ACTIVITIES: Esq., 1784; fourth generation legislator. OCCUPATIONAL PROFILE: probably a planter. PUBLIC CAREER. LEGISLATIVE SERVICE: Conventions, Charles County, 1st, 1774, 2nd–3rd, 1774, 4th, 1775, 5th, 1775, 9th, 1776; Lower House, Charles County, 1781 (elected to the 2nd session to fill vacancy; Elections 2), 1781–1782 (Grievances 1; resigned on May 7, 1782). LOCAL OFFICES: justice, Charles County, 1764–at least 1799 (quorum, 1794–at least 1799); justice, Orphans' Court,

Charles County, 1777–at least 1789; King George's Parish Vestry, Prince George's County, elected 1775, in office 1784–1786. MILITARY SERVICE: brigadier general, Lower District, Western Shore, 1776; held same rank in Flying Camp, 1776. WEALTH DURING LIFETIME. PERSONAL PROPERTY: assessed value £966.0.0, including 19 slaves and 55 oz. plate, 1783; 24 slaves, 1798. LAND AT FIRST ELECTION: 1,280 acres in Charles County (1,000 acres acquired by deed of gift from his parents at the time of his marriage). SIGNIFICANT CHANGES IN LAND BETWEEN FIRST ELECTION AND DEATH: devised 580 acres in Charles County to son *George Dent* (ca. 1758–1813) in 1785. WEALTH AT DEATH. DIED: will probated on August 24, 1809, in Charles County. LAND: ca. 498 acres in Pomonkey Hundred, Charles County.

DENT, JOHN, OF JOHN (?–1799). BORN: at "Dents Inheritance," Newport Hundred, Charles County, of age by 1777. NATIVE: fourth generation. RESIDED: in Trinity Parish, Bryan Town Hundred, Charles County, 1778. The tract "Dents Inheritance" was the seat of the branch of the Dent family descended from John Dent I, grandfather of *John Dent of John* (?–1799). FAMILY BACKGROUND. FATHER: John Dent (by 1733–1791), of Newport Hundred, Charles County. MOTHER: Mary Blackman. BROTHERS: Bennett (?–1779), died without progeny; Hatch, who married twice, leaving a widow named Elizabeth. SISTERS: Mary; Sarah Clark; Tabitha, who married Walter Moreland; and Anne, who married Charles Davis. MARRIED Mary. CHILDREN. SON: John Shelton (1792–?). DAUGHTER: Priscilla, who married John Brewer Dent. PRIVATE CAREER. EDUCATION: literate. RELIGIOUS AFFILIATION: Anglican, Trinity Parish, Charles County. OCCUPATIONAL PROFILE: probably a planter. PUBLIC CAREER. LEGISLATIVE SERVICE: Lower House, Charles County, 1783. WEALTH DURING LIFETIME. PERSONAL PROPERTY: assessed value £263.0.0, including 5 slaves, 1783; 4 slaves, 1798. LAND AT FIRST ELECTION: 250 acres in Charles County. WEALTH AT DEATH. DIED: between January 16 and November 4, 1799; will probated in Charles County. PERSONAL PROPERTY: TEV, £374.0.9 current money (including 3 slaves); FB, £182.5.8. LAND: 198 acres in Charles County.

DENT, PETER (ca. 1665–1710/11). BORN: ca. 1665 in St. Mary's County; third son. NATIVE: second generation. RESIDED: in St. Mary's County; Somerset County, by 1686. FAMILY BACKGROUND. FATHER: *Thomas Dent* (ca. 1630–1676). STEPFA-

THER: *John Addison* (?–ca. 1705/6). MOTHER: Rebecca Wilkinson (?–1726). BROTHERS: *William Dent* (ca. 1660–1704); Thomas; and George (?–by 1702). HALF BROTHER: *Thomas Addison* (1679–1727). SISTERS: Margaret; Barbara (1676–1754), who married *Thomas Brooke* (ca. 1659–1730/31). MARRIED first, ca. February 1703/4 Elizabeth, widow of both John King and Thomas Wilson; daughter of Charles Ballard. Her brother was *Charles Ballard* (ca. 1670–ca. 1724/25). MARRIED second, Jane Pittman, daughter of *Joseph Gray* (?–1724). She subsequently married John Scott. CHILDREN. DAUGHTER: Rebecca. PRIVATE CAREER. EDUCATION: literate; had clerical skills. RELIGIOUS AFFILIATION: Protestant. SOCIAL STATUS AND ACTIVITIES: second generation burgess. OCCUPATIONAL PROFILE: attorney, admitted to the Somerset County Court in 1689; placeman; storekeeper in the early 1690s. PUBLIC CAREER. LEGISLATIVE SERVICE: Lower House, Somerset County, 1701/2–1704 (elected to the 2nd session). OTHER PROVINCIAL OFFICE: assistant clerk, Lower House, 1692. LOCAL OFFICES: clerk of Indictments, Somerset County, 1692; clerk, Somerset County, 1696/97–1705; deputy commissary, Somerset County, 1700–1708. MILITARY SERVICE: officer, 1696. STANDS ON PUBLIC/PRIVATE ISSUES: supported the revolution of Protestant Associators in 1689. WEALTH DURING LIFETIME. LAND AT FIRST ELECTION: probably ca. 700 acres (had inherited 1,086 acres equally with brother George in 1676; patented 200 acres in 1689). WEALTH AT DEATH. DIED: between February 25 and March 7, 1710/11. PERSONAL PROPERTY: TEV, £644.5.8 sterling (including 4 slaves, 1 servant, and books). LAND: probably ca. 700 acres.

DENT, THOMAS (ca. 1630–1676). BORN: ca. 1630 in Yorkshire, England; younger son. IMMIGRATED: by 1658 as a free adult from England. RESIDED: in St. Mary's County. FAMILY BACKGROUND. FATHER: Peter Dent, of Gisborough, Yorkshire, England. MARRIED Rebecca (?–1726), daughter of Rev. William Wilkinson. She subsequently married by February 1676/77 *John Addison* (?–ca. 1705/6). Her sister was Elizabeth, who married *William Hatton* (?–1712). CHILDREN. SONS: *William Dent* (ca. 1660–1704), who married first, Elizabeth (?–1698/99), daughter of *Gerard Fowke* (1625–1669), and second, Sarah, daughter of *Thomas Brooke* (ca. 1659–1730/31); Thomas; *Peter Dent* (ca. 1665–1710/11), who married first, Elizabeth, widow of both John King and Thomas Wilson, and daughter of Charles Ballard (?–1682), and second, Jane Pittman, daughter of *Joseph*

Gray (?–1724); and George (?–by 1702). DAUGHTERS: Margaret, who married in 1681 Edmund Howard (?–1713); Barbara (1676–1754), who married *Thomas Brooke* (ca. 1659–1730/31). PRIVATE CAREER. EDUCATION: literate. RELIGIOUS AFFILIATION: Anglican. SOCIAL STATUS AND ACTIVITIES: Gent. on arrival; entered rights for transporting at least seventy-five persons, 1658–1676. OCCUPATIONAL PROFILE: merchant; planter. PUBLIC CAREER. LEGISLATIVE SERVICE: Lower House, St. Mary's County, 1669, 1674–1674/75 (elected to the 3rd session; Laws 3; Accounts 3). LOCAL OFFICES: justice, St. Mary's County, by 1661–1664, ca. 1665–1676 (quorum); sheriff, St. Mary's County, 1664–1665; coroner, St. Mary's County, 1669; alderman, St. Mary's City, 1673. WEALTH DURING LIFETIME. LAND AT FIRST ELECTION: at least 850 acres. WEALTH AT DEATH. DIED: between March 28 and April 21, 1676. PERSONAL PROPERTY: TEV, £596.8.0 sterling (including 6 slaves, 8 servants, and books). LAND: 1,083 acres, plus 3 plantations of unspecified acreage.

DENT, THOMAS (1685–1725). BORN: in 1685 in Charles County; first son. NATIVE: third generation. RESIDED: in Charles County. FAMILY BACKGROUND. FATHER: *William Dent* (ca. 1660–1704), son of *Thomas Dent* (ca. 1630–1676). MOTHER: Elizabeth (?–1698/99), daughter of *Gerard Fowke* (1625–1669). STEPMOTHER: Sarah, daughter of *Thomas Brooke* (ca. 1659–1730/31). UNCLES: *Peter Dent* (ca. 1665–1710/11); *Gerard Fowke* (1662/63–1734/35); and *Thomas Addison* (1679–1727). BROTHERS: William (1687–1695); Gerard (?–died young); *George Dent* (1690–1754), who married Anne, daughter of *William Harbert* (?–1718); Peter (1694–1757); and Philip (?–died young). SISTERS: Elizabeth (1688–1699); Anne (1692–?); and Elizabeth (1699–?), who married Richard Tarvin. OTHER KINSHIP: *John Addison* (1713–1764); *Thomas Brooke* (1683–1744). MARRIED by 1705 Anne, daughter of *John Bayne* (ca. 1662–1701); granddaughter of *Walter Bayne* (?–1670); niece of both *John Stone* (ca. 1648–1697) and *John Beale, of Lawson* (ca. 1674–1751). CHILDREN. SONS: Thomas (?–1750), who married Elizabeth Cove, of Stafford County, Virginia; and William (1706–1757), who married Anne, daughter of John Warren, of Wicomico Hundred, Charles County, and wife Judith Townley. PRIVATE CAREER. EDUCATION: literate. RELIGIOUS AFFILIATION: Anglican. OCCUPATIONAL PROFILE: planter. PUBLIC CAREER. LEGISLATIVE SERVICE: Lower House, Charles County, 1715 (Accounts; Laws), 1716–1718 (Laws 1; Aggrievances 1–3). LOCAL OFFICES:

clerk, Prince George's County, 1702–1708/9; justice, Charles County, 1706–1711; sheriff, Charles County, 1711–1714. MILITARY SERVICE: captain from at least 1708. WEALTH DURING LIFETIME. LAND AT FIRST ELECTION: inherited over 2,000 acres from his father and his wife brought him an additional 700 acres; he began selling land in 1707 to pay off debts; exact acreage in 1715 is unknown, but it was probably over 1,500 acres. WEALTH AT DEATH. DIED: in 1725. PERSONAL PROPERTY: probably penniless because of gambling debts; committed to debtor's prison in 1722.

DENT, WARREN (?–1794). BORN: at "Guyther" (his father's dwelling plantation, also sometimes called "Friendship"), Charles County, of age by 1772; eldest son. NATIVE: fifth generation. RESIDED: at "Friendship," Nanjemoy Creek, Charles County. FAMILY BACKGROUND. FATHER: William Dent (1706–1757), son of *Thomas Dent* (1685–1725). MOTHER: Anne, daughter of John Warren and wife Judith Townley. BROTHER: George, who married first, Rose Townshend Knox (?–1794), and second, in 1796 Elizabeth Harrison Knox. SISTERS: Eleanor, who married *John Jordan* (?–1763); Judith, who married *Jeremiah Chase* (?–1755); Mary, who married Rev. William Dowie; Ann, who married Samuel Briscoe; Grace, who married Robert Harrison; and Rebecca, who married *William Harrison* (?–1789). NIECE: Mary Hanson Briscoe, who married *Michael Jenifer Stone* (1747–1812). MARRIED never. CHILDREN. Died without progeny. PRIVATE CAREER. EDUCATION: literate. RELIGIOUS AFFILIATION: Anglican, Durham Parish, Charles County. SOCIAL STATUS AND ACTIVITIES: Gent., 1781; Mr., 1786; Esq., 1789. OCCUPATIONAL PROFILE: merchant, 1786; probably also a planter. PUBLIC CAREER. LEGISLATIVE SERVICE: Lower House, Charles County, 1778–1779, 1779–1780, 1780–1781 (Claims 1). LOCAL OFFICES: justice, Charles County, 1771–1794; Committee of Observation, Charles County, elected 1774; Durham Parish Vestry, Charles County, elected 1775 and 1776, in office 1779–1788; commissioner of tax, Charles County, appointed 1777; justice, Orphans' Court, Charles County, commissioned 1779 and 1787 ("refuses to act"); judge, Court of Appeals for Tax Assessment, Charles County, 1786. STANDS ON PUBLIC/PRIVATE ISSUES: manumitted two slaves in his will, one to be freed immediately after his death and the second five years later. WEALTH DURING LIFETIME. PERSONAL PROPERTY: assessed value £970.0.0, including 13 slaves, 1 servant, and 124 oz. plate, 1783; 34 slaves, 1790. LAND AT FIRST ELECTION: 2,011 acres in Charles County (inherited 1,857 acres from his father in 1757, 154 acres through personal acquisition). WEALTH AT DEATH. DIED: on October 24, 1794, at his seat in Charles County. PERSONAL PROPERTY: TEV, at least $978.35 (including 5 slaves and books). LAND: mentioned 313 acres in Charles County in his will. His brother George, under the terms of their father's will, received all the 1,857 acres in Maryland that Warren had inherited.

DENT, WILLIAM (ca. 1660–1704). BORN: ca. 1660 in Charles County; first son. NATIVE: second generation. RESIDED: in Nanjemoy, Charles County. FAMILY BACKGROUND. FATHER: *Thomas Dent* (ca. 1630–1676). MOTHER: Rebecca (?–1726), daughter of Rev. William Wilkinson. She subsequently married in 1676/77 *John Addison* (?–ca. 1705/6). UNCLE: *William Hatton* (?–1712). BROTHERS: Thomas; *Peter Dent* (ca. 1665–1710/11); and George (?–1702). HALF BROTHER: *Thomas Addison* (1679–1727). SISTERS: Margaret; Barbara (1676–1754); who married *Thomas Brooke* (ca. 1659–1730/31). MARRIED first, in 1684/85 Elizabeth (?–1698/99), daughter of *Gerard Fowke* (1625–1669). Her brother was *Gerard Fowke* (1662/63–ca. 1734/35). MARRIED second, Sarah (?–1724), daughter of *Thomas Brooke* (ca. 1659–1730/31); granddaughter of *Thomas Brooke* (1632–1676). She subsequently married *Philip Lee* (ca. 1681–1744), son of Richard Lee, of Virginia. Her brother was *Thomas Brooke* (1683–1744). Her half brothers were Benjamin; John; Thomas (1717–1768); Nathaniel; and Baker. Her sisters were Eleanor; Priscilla, who married *Thomas Gantt* (?–1765). Her half sisters were Elizabeth; Mary; Rebecca; Jane, who married *Alexander Contee* (ca. 1691–1740); and Lucy. Her nephews were *Thomas Gantt* (ca. 1710–1785); *Fielder Gantt* (?–1807); *Edward Gantt* (?–by 1783); and *Richard Brooke* (1716–1783). Her nieces were Eleanor Brooke, who married *Samuel Beall* (ca. 1713–ca. 1778); probably Ann Gantt, who married *John Brome* (1703–1748). CHILDREN. SONS: *Thomas Dent* (1685–1725), who married in 1705 Anne (?–1725), daughter of *John Bayne* (ca. 1662–1701); William (1687–1695); Gerard (?–died young); *George Dent* (1690–1754), who married Anne, daughter of *William Harbert* (?–1718); Peter (1694–?); and Philip (?–died young). DAUGHTERS: Elizabeth (1688–1699); Anne (1692–?); and Elizabeth (1699–?), who married Richard Tarvin. PRIVATE CAREER. EDUCATION: literate; studied law under *Thomas Burford* (?–1686/87). RELIGIOUS AFFILIATION: Anglican. SOCIAL STATUS

AND ACTIVITIES: second generation burgess; Gent. on coming of age; he enjoyed considerable patronage from Gov. Francis Nicholson, who was possibly a kinsman. OCCUPATIONAL PROFILE: prominent lawyer, admitted to the following courts: Charles County in 1682/83; Provincial Court in 1684/85. Planter; merchant. PUBLIC CAREER. LEGISLATIVE SERVICE: Lower House, Charles County, 1692–1693 (Laws, chairman 1; Aggrievances, chairman 2), 1694–1697 (Laws 3–5, 7, 8, probably chairman 3–5); Upper House, 1698 (special writ 2); Lower House, Charles County, 1701–1704 (Laws, chairman 1–3; speaker 4), 1704 (speaker 1; died before the 2nd session). OTHER PROVINCIAL OFFICES: clerk, Lower House, 1686–1688; solicitor general, 1688–1689, 1694; naval officer, North Potomac (joint appointment, 1694–1696, sole appointment, 1696–1704); deputy attorney general, 1694–1698; Council, attended meetings in 1698, but was never officially commissioned; attorney general, 1698–1704; advocate, Court of Admiralty, 1698; commissary general, 1704. LOCAL OFFICES: clerk of Indictments, Charles County, 1685; Nanjemoy Parish Vestry, Charles County, 1696–1697; justice, Charles County, 1700–1704 (president). MILITARY SERVICE: major, 1696–1704; lieutenant colonel, 1704; colonel, 1704. WEALTH DURING LIFETIME. LAND AT FIRST ELECTION: over 2,171 acres. WEALTH AT DEATH. DIED: in November 1704. PERSONAL PROPERTY: TEV, £3,023.19.1 sterling (including 34 slaves, 7 servants, 153 books, considerable silver plate, a sloop, and merchandise worth £300); FB, £783.9.3. LAND: 6,000 acres.

DENTON, VACHEL (ca. 1696–1752). BORN: ca. 1696. NATIVE: at least second generation. RESIDED: in Annapolis, Anne Arundel County, by 1722; Anne Arundel County, by 1742. FAMILY BACKGROUND. FATHER: Henry Denton, Gent. (?–1698), of St. Mary's County, clerk of St. Mary's County from 1692 to 1695, clerk of the Lower House from 1692 to 1693, clerk of the Council from 1693 to 1698, appointed first register of the Admiralty Court in 1694, and naval officer of Annapolis from 1696 to 1698. GUARDIANS: *Thomas Beale* (?–1713); *John Beale* (?–1734). MOTHER: Mary, who subsequently married Andrew Price, of Queen Anne's County. She left Vachel in the care of his guardians. MARRIED in 1721 Anne (1708–1765), daughter of *John Brice* (?–1713); niece of *Matthew Howard* (ca. 1675–1750). Her brother was John (1705–1766), who married Sarah, daughter of *James Frisby* (1684–1719). Her half brother was *Thomas Worthington* (ca. 1691–1753). Her sister was Rachel (1711–1786), who married *Philip Hammond* (1697–1760). Her nephews were *John Hammond* (1735–1784); *Rezin Hammond* (1745–1809); *Matthias Hammond* (1740–1786); *John Brice* (1738–1820); *James Brice* (1746–1801); and *Benedict Brice* (1749–1786). Her half nephews were *Samuel Worthington* (1734–1815); *Brice T. B. Worthington* (1727–1794); and *Nicholas Worthington* (1734–1793). CHILDREN. No surviving children. PRIVATE CAREER. EDUCATION: literate. RELIGIOUS AFFILIATION: Anglican. SOCIAL STATUS AND ACTIVITIES: Mr., 1715; Esq., 1727; Gent., 1726 until death. OCCUPATIONAL PROFILE: officeholder; merchant. PUBLIC CAREER. LEGISLATIVE SERVICE: Lower House, Annapolis, 1725–1727 (Laws 1–4), Anne Arundel County, 1734/35–1737 (Accounts 1, Cv, 2–4), 1738 (Accounts; Laws), 1739–1741 (Accounts Cv–3; Laws Cv–3). OTHER PROVINCIAL OFFICES: clerk, Secretary's Office and Provincial Court, 1718–1732; register in Chancery, 1718–1720 (resigned); clerk, Prerogative Office, 1721–1723 (resigned). LOCAL OFFICES: justice, Anne Arundel County, in office 1717; alderman, Annapolis, in office by 1720–1721, 1723–at least 1730; mayor, Annapolis, 1722–1723; churchwarden, St. Anne's Parish, Anne Arundel County, in office 1723; St. Anne's Parish Vestry, Anne Arundel County, 1724–1727, 1733–1736. WEALTH DURING LIFETIME. LAND AT FIRST ELECTION: probably 2,459 acres in Dorchester, Cecil, and Anne Arundel counties (1,904 acres in Dorchester and Cecil counties inherited from his father; probably 555 acres in Anne Arundel County acquired through his marriage). SIGNFICANT CHANGES IN LAND BETWEEN FIRST ELECTION AND DEATH: sold 400 acres in Dorchester County in 1726; purchased 2 lots in Annapolis and 662 acres in Anne Arundel and Baltimore counties, 1727–1728; sold 280 acres in Baltimore and Anne Arundel counties, 1737–1742, and in 1747 put his remaining 938 acres in Anne Arundel County and 4 lots in Annapolis under the trusteeship of *Alexander Hamilton* (1712–1756) for his heirs, reserving a life estate in the land for himself and his wife; probably sold 1,000 acres in Cecil County before his death. ADDITIONAL COMMENTS: held a number of mortgages, especially during the 1730s, and as early as 1729 he was accepting goods to cancel debts owed to him. WEALTH AT DEATH. DIED: will probated on August 25, 1752, in Anne Arundel County. PERSONAL PROPERTY: TEV, £10.17.0 gold, £139.16.0 sterling, £1,486.8.0 current money (including 21 slaves and 1 servant); FB, £9.11.2 gold, £110.15.9 sterling, £1,411.14.2 current money; however, his estate was still liable for a

£1,800 note held by *Philip Hammond* (1697–1760) since 1740, which Hammond collected after ligitation. LAND: probably 1,438 acres in Anne Arundel and Dorchester counties. ADDITIONAL COMMENTS: Denton named as his principal heirs *Rezin Hammond* (1745–1809), Denton Hammond, and Ann Hammond, the children of *Philip Hammond* (1697–1760).

DEYE (DYE, DIE), THOMAS COCKEY (ca. 1728–1807). BORN: on January 27, ca. 1728; only son. NATIVE: at least second generation. RESIDED: at "Taylor's Hall," Back River Upper Hundred, Baltimore County. FAMILY BACKGROUND. FATHER: probably Col. Thomas Cockey (1677–1737), of Anne Arundel County, who married in 1700 Elizabeth (?–1738), widow of Richard Moss (?–1700) and daughter of *John Hammond* (1643–1707). In his will Col. Thomas Cockey named a daughter Elizabeth, who married Thomas John Hammond, and mentioned that Penelope Deye was living at "Taylor's Hall" in Baltimore County. The Deye children are named as his principal heirs. MOTHER: Penelope Deye (?–1784), of Baltimore County, gentlewoman. SISTERS: Charlotte Cockey Deye, who married Thomas Ford; Charcilla Cockey Deye (1731–1806), who married Joshua Cockey (1729–1764), brother of *Edward Cockey* (1731–ca. 1795); Cassandra Cockey Deye (?–by 1777), who married Thomas Colegate, son of *Richard Colegate* (?–ca. 1721/22). HALF SISTER: possibly Elizabeth Cockey, who married Thomas John Hammond. CHILDREN. Died without progeny. PRIVATE CAREER. EDUCATION: literate. RELIGIOUS AFFILIATION: Anglican, St. Thomas Parish, Baltimore County. SOCIAL STATUS AND ACTIVITIES: Gent., 1754; Esq., 1774. OCCUPATIONAL PROFILE: planter. PUBLIC CAREER. LEGISLATIVE SERVICE: Lower House, Baltimore County, 1757–1758, 1758–1761 (Arms and Ammunition Cv 1, 1, Cv 2, 2), 1762–1763, 1765–1766, 1768–1770 (election voided on June 14, 1768, because of "treating" of voters at the election; reelected to the 3rd session to fill vacancy), 1771 (Accounts), 1773–1774 (Accounts 1, Cv, 2, 3; Arms and Ammunition 2, 3; Grievances 2, 3); Conventions, Baltimore County, 1st, 1774, 2nd–3rd, 1774, 4th, 1775, 5th, 1775 (elected, but did not attend), 9th, 1776; Lower House, Baltimore County, 1777, 1777–1778 (Elections 3), 1778–1779 (Elections 1), 1779–1780 (Elections 1, 3), 1780–1781 (Elections 1), 1781–1782 (speaker 1, 2), 1782–1783 (speaker 1, 2), 1783 (speaker), 1784 (speaker), 1785 (speaker), 1786–1787 (speaker 1, 2), 1787–1788 (speaker 1, 2), 1788 (speaker), 1791–1792, 1792. LOCAL OF-

FICE: churchwarden, St. Thomas Parish, Baltimore County, in office 1755. MILITARY SERVICE: captain, Baltimore County Militia, by 1776. STANDS ON PUBLIC/PRIVATE ISSUES: provided for the manumission of his slaves in his will. WEALTH DURING LIFETIME. PERSONAL PROPERTY: inherited livestock and at least 10 slaves from Col. Thomas Cockey, 1737; assessed value £1,481.0.0, including 28 slaves and 19 oz. plate, 1783; 40 slaves, 1790. LAND AT FIRST ELECTION: at least 2,700 acres in Baltimore County (2,500 acres inherited from Col. Thomas Cockey in 1737). SIGNIFICANT CHANGES IN LAND BETWEEN FIRST ELECTION AND DEATH: 3,119.5 acres in Baltimore County, 1783 (280 acres inherited from his mother in 1784); acquired a total of more than 2,500 acres by purchase and approximately 1,700 acres through resurveys and patents; sold only about 100 acres, all in Baltimore County; also acquired 1,315 acres in Anne Arundel County. WEALTH AT DEATH. DIED: on May 7, 1807; buried at "Taylor's Hall," Baltimore County. PERSONAL PROPERTY: TEV, $29,180.18 (including 14 slaves and more than 76 books); FB, $25,751.27 (before payment of legacies and distribution to heirs). LAND: at least 7,300 acres in Baltimore County; 1,315 acres in Anne Arundel County. ADDITIONAL COMMENTS: among those named as his principal heirs were the children of his sister Charcilla.

DICKINSON (DICKENSON), HENRY (?–1789). BORN: probably in Talbot County, of age by 1768. NATIVE: third generation. RESIDED: probably in Talbot County; Dorchester County (later became part of Caroline County), 1768; Lower Choptank District, Caroline County. FAMILY BACKGROUND. FATHER: Charles Dickinson (?–1779), of Dorchester and Caroline counties; a merchant; son of John Dickinson (ca. 1633–1718). MOTHER: Sophia, daughter of Daniel Richardson (?–1722), of Talbot County; granddaughter of *William Richardson* (?–1698). BROTHER: *John Dickinson* (ca. 1726–1789). SISTERS: Sidney, who married Thomas Lockerman; Margaret, who married *Philip Walker* (?–1791). FIRST COUSIN: *William Richardson* (1735–1825). MARRIED first, by 1774 Elizabeth (?–1783), daughter of Rev. Philip Walker (?–1776), of Caroline County, the rector of St. Mary's Whitechapel Parish (Anglican) in Caroline County from 1756 to 1767, and wife Elizabeth Dickinson Richardson (?–by 1756); granddaughter of James Dickinson (?–1738) and wife Hannah Coale; niece of both Mary Dickinson (?–by 1765), who married *Pollard Edmondson* (ca. 1718–1794) and Ann Dickinson (?–ca. 1774), who married

Samuel Bowman (?–1768). Her brother was *Philip Walker* (?–1791). Her sister was Ann (see below for details). Her first cousin was (first name unknown) Edmondson, who married *Christopher Birckhead* (by 1740–1788). MARRIED second, in January 1784 Ann (?–by 1787), widow of both Andrew Mein and Edward Hindman (?–1781), son of *Jacob Hindman* (by 1713–1766); daughter of Rev. Philip Walker (?–1776) and wife Elizabeth Dickinson Richardson. MARRIED third, in March 1787 Deborah (ca. 1748–1805), daughter of William Perry (?–1750), an immigrant who resided in Talbot County and was a planter and merchant, and wife Anne Fleaharty (?–by 1751). Her brother was *William Perry* (1746–1799). Her natural sister was Sarah, who was born before her parents' marriage, and married first, by 1764 Alexander Frazier, and second, Thomas Noel. CHILDREN. SONS: Charles; Philip (?–ca. 1789), died of consumption; and Henry (ca. 1789–?). STEPSON: Andrew Mein. DAUGHTERS: Elizabeth, who married in June 1790 William Richardson (?–1831), son of *William Richardson* (1735–1825); Rebecca (?–1812), who married Capt. Thomas B. Daffin, son of *Charles Daffin* (?–1794). PRIVATE CAREER. EDUCATION: literate. RELIGIOUS AFFILIATION: Anglican, Hunting Creek Parish, probably Caroline County. SOCIAL STATUS AND ACTIVITIES: Gent., 1770; Esq., 1783. OCCUPATIONAL PROFILE: planter. PUBLIC CAREER. LEGISLATIVE SERVICE: Conventions, Caroline County, 3rd, 1774, 4th, 1775, 5th, 1775, 6th–8th, 1775–1776, 9th, 1776; Lower House, Caroline County, 1777 (Loan Office 1), 1777–1778. OTHER STATE OFFICE: treasurer, Eastern Shore, 1779–1789. LOCAL OFFICES: receiver of alienation fines, Dorchester County, by 1768–at least 1771; trustee to erect a ballroom for the use and benefit of the subscribers, Dorchester County, 1770; Committee of Observation, Caroline County, 1776; loan officer, Continental Loan Office, Caroline County, appointed 1777; justice, Caroline County, 1779–at least 1782, commissioned 1783 (but "will not qualify"), 1786–1788; justice, Orphans' Court, Caroline County, commissioned 1782, 1783, 1785 (but "will not qualify"), and 1788; judge, Court of Appeals for Tax Assessment, Caroline County, 1786. MILITARY SERVICE: colonel, 1776. WEALTH DURING LIFETIME. PERSONAL PROPERTY: assessed value £1,243.0.0, including 34 slaves and 112 oz. plate, 1783. LAND AT FIRST ELECTION: 1,424 acres in Caroline County (254 acres from his father, 1,000 acres by purchase). SIGNIFICANT CHANGES IN LAND BETWEEN FIRST ELECTION AND DEATH: inherited additional land at his father's death, 1779; acquired 383 acres through his

third marriage, 1787. WEALTH AT DEATH. DIED: in November 1789 in Caroline County. PERSONAL PROPERTY: TEV, £8,570.6.6 current money (including 82 slaves, books, and plate); FB, £8,046.18.2. LAND: at least 3,202 acres in Caroline County.

DICKINSON (DICKENSON, DICKERSON, DICKASON), JAMES (ca. 1726–1787). BORN: ca. 1726. IMMIGRATED: probably; possibly from Cumberland County, England. RESIDED: in Talbot County, 1743/44; Third District, Talbot County, 1783. FAMILY BACKGROUND. NEPHEW: John Singleton (1750–1819), who married first, Bridget (1744–1774), daughter of *Nicholas Goldsborough* (ca. 1689–1766), and second, Anna Goldsborough (1764–1825), granddaughter of *Nicholas Goldsborough* (ca. 1689–1766), and niece of his first wife Bridget. MARRIED on August 10, 1748, Rachel (?–by 1785), daughter of Jonathan Taylor (?–by 1735), of Talbot County, and wife Elizabeth Sherwood, a Quaker; stepdaughter of *Thomas Bozman* (ca. 1693–1752); stepgranddaughter of *John Bozman* (1650–1716). Her brother was Thomas (?–by 1747), who died as a minor. CHILDREN. SON: (first name unknown) (?–by 1785). PRIVATE CAREER. EDUCATION: literate. RELIGIOUS AFFILIATION: Anglican, St. Peter's Parish, Talbot County. SOCIAL STATUS AND ACTIVITIES: Gent., 1750; Esq., 1754. OCCUPATIONAL PROFILE: merchant. PUBLIC CAREER. LEGISLATIVE SERVICE: Lower House, Talbot County, 1768–1770 (Accounts 1–3; Claims 1, 2, 4). LOCAL OFFICES: St. Peter's Parish Vestry, Talbot County, in office 1750–1753, 1759–1763, 1766; sheriff, Talbot County, 1752–1755; justice, Talbot County, 1756–at least 1775 (quorum, 1770–at least 1775). STANDS ON PUBLIC/PRIVATE ISSUES: manumitted six slaves, 1781; in his will Dickinson ordered that his nephew manumit all of his remaining slaves, binding the children as apprentices in useful trades, 1787. WEALTH DURING LIFETIME. PERSONAL PROPERTY: owned a schooner, 1772; assessed value £1,346.4.8, including 20 slaves and 125 oz. plate, 1783. LAND AT FIRST ELECTION: 1,117 acres in Talbot and Dorchester counties (all through his marriage); probably also owned land in Cumberland County, England. SIGNIFICANT CHANGES IN LAND BETWEEN FIRST ELECTION AND DEATH: sold 267 acres in Dorchester County, 1769; resurveyed 300 acres and patented it as a 449-acre tract in Talbot County, 1774; sold 150 acres in Talbot County, 1781; purchased 121 acres in Talbot County in 1781, and sold all but 41 acres of it, by 1783; owned a total of 844 acres in Talbot County, 1783; purchased 27 acres in Talbot County, 1785; sold 5 acres in Talbot County, 1787. WEALTH AT DEATH. DIED: will probated on December 18, 1787, in Talbot County. LAND: 866 acres in Talbot County, plus lands in Cumberland County, England. ADDITIONAL COMMENTS: His principal heir was his nephew John Singleton.

DICKINSON (DICKENSON), JOHN (ca. 1726–1789). BORN: ca. 1726, probably in Talbot County. NATIVE: third generation. RESIDED: in Talbot County; Transquakin Hundred, Dorchester County, by 1774. FAMILY BACKGROUND. FATHER: Charles Dickinson (?–1779), of Dorchester and Caroline counties, merchant, son of John Dickinson (ca. 1633–1718) and wife Rebackah. MOTHER: Sophia, daughter of Daniel Richardson (?–1722), of Talbot County. BROTHER: *Henry Dickinson* (?–1789). SISTERS: Sidney, who married Thomas Lockerman; Margaret (Peggy), who married *Philip Walker* (?–1791). FIRST COUSIN: *William Richardson* (1735–1825). OTHER KINSHIP: his great-grandfather was *William Richardson* (?–1698). MARRIED on March 30, 1758, Ann, daughter of *Henry Trippe* (?–1744); granddaughter of *Henry Trippe* (?–ca. 1723/24); niece of Elizabeth Trippe, who married second, *Bartholomew Ennalls* (ca. 1700–1783), and Mary Trippe (?–1782), who married *Jacob Hindman* (by 1713–1766). Her brother was Henry (?–ca. 1770). Her sisters were Mary Emerson (ca. 1739–1811), who married *Robert Goldsborough IV* (1740–1798); Sarah; and Elizabeth. Her first cousins were *James Hindman* (1741–1830); *William Hindman* (1743–1822); and Elizabeth Hindman (?–by 1788), who married *William Perry* (1746–1799). CHILDREN. SONS: Charles (1759–by 1789); Henry (1760–1827), of Cambridge, Dorchester County, who married in 1809 Ann (1790–1842), daughter of Maj. John Hooper; Philip (1762–by 1789); John (?–by 1810), who died without progeny; Granby (?–by 1810), who died without progeny; and James (ca. 1774–by 1810), who died without progeny. DAUGHTER: Sophia (?–by 1810), who married in 1796 Stanley Byass Lockerman. PRIVATE CAREER. EDUCATION: literate. RELIGIOUS AFFILIATION: Anglican; preceding generations of his family were Quakers. OCCUPATIONAL PROFILE: probably a planter. PUBLIC CAREER. LEGISLATIVE SERVICE: Conventions, Dorchester County, 3rd, 1774, 4th, 1775. LOCAL OFFICES: sheriff, Dorchester County, 1764–1767; justice, Dorchester County, 1770–1789 (quorum, 1773–1789); commissioner, Dorchester County, in office 1773; chairman, Committee of Observation, Dorchester County, 1776; justice, Orphans' Court,

Dorchester County, 1777–1787 (refused to qualify in 1787); justice, Court of Oyer and Terminer and Gaol Delivery, Dorchester County, commissioned 1781; judge, Court of Appeals for Tax Assessment, Dorchester County, appointed 1786. MILITARY SERVICE: colonel, Dorchester County Militia, 1775–at least 1778. WEALTH DURING LIFETIME. PERSONAL PROPERTY: 40 slaves, 1776; assessed value £2,127.10.0, including 61 slaves and 102 oz. plate, Dorchester, Caroline, and Talbot counties, 1783. LAND AT FIRST ELECTION: 502 acres in Dorchester and Talbot counties (359 acres through marriage, plus 143 acres by purchase); also controlled 650 acres for his son Henry and 132 acres as executor of his brother-in-law's estate. SIGNIFICANT CHANGES IN LAND BETWEEN FIRST ELECTION AND DEATH: inherited approximately 1,188 acres in Caroline County from his father, 1779. WEALTH AT DEATH. DIED: on June 8, 1789, probably in Dorchester County. PERSONAL PROPERTY: size of estate unknown. LAND: 1,493 acres in Caroline, Dorchester, and Talbot counties.

DIGGES, GEORGE (ca. 1742–1792). BORN: ca. 1742 in Prince George's County; fourth son. NATIVE: fourth generation. RESIDED: at "Warburton Manor," Prince George's County. FAMILY BACKGROUND. FATHER: William Digges (1713–1783), of "Warburton Manor," Prince George's County; son of Charles Digges (?–1744), of "Warburton Manor," Prince George's County, and wife Susannah Maria Lowe. MOTHER: Anne (?–1757), daughter of George Attwood and wife Ann Petre. BROTHERS: Charles (1740–1769), of Upper Marlboro, Prince George's County, who was sent to Europe to be educated, became a merchant in partnership with Thomas Philpot, of London, England, and who died in Dumfries, Virginia; Francis (?–died young); Thomas Attwood (ca. 1741–1821), a scholar and diplomat who was sent to Europe to be educated, spent much of his youth in London, England, became a confidential representative to the Court of St. James, and died in Washington, D.C.; Henry, who never married and who died at sea; and Joseph (?–ca. 1776), a doctor, who died at Teneri in the Canary Islands. SISTERS: Teresa (1744–?), who married Ralph Foster; Susanah (1748–?), who died young; Ann (1750–1804), who never married; Mary (1751–ca. 1761); Elizabeth (1753–1843), who married Daniel Carroll of Rock Creek (1752–1790), son of *Daniel Carroll* (1730–1796); and Jane (Jean) (1755–1825), who married in June 1779 Col. John Fitzgerald, of Alexandria, Virginia. OTHER KINSHIP: his great-grandfather was *William Digges* (ca. 1650–1697). MARRIED

Catherine (ca. 1773–1835), daughter of Robert Brent (?–1780), of Aquia, Stafford County, Virginia, and wife Anne Carroll (1733–1804); niece of *Daniel Carroll* (1730–1796). Her brother was Robert (1764–?), the first mayor of Washington, D.C., from 1802 to 1812, who married in 1787 Mary, the youngest daughter of Notley Young. Catherine died in Washington, D.C., and was buried in the churchyard of St. John's Catholic Church, Carroll Chapel, Forest Glen, Maryland. **CHILDREN**. SON: William Dudley (1790–1830), who married Eleanor (Norah) (ca. 1791–1864), daughter of Daniel Carroll of Duddington (1764–1849), and wife Anne Brent; both William and Norah were buried in the churchyard of St. John's Catholic Church, Forest Glen, Maryland. DAUGHTER: Anna Maria (ca. 1792–1865), who married in June 1811 the Hon. Robert LeRoy Livingston, a representative to Congress from New York between 1809 and 1812. Anna Maria died in New York City and was buried in the churchyard of St. John's Catholic Church, Forest Glen, Maryland. **PRIVATE CAREER**. EDUCATION: literate; his father sent him and his two older brothers to Europe for an education. RELIGIOUS AFFILIATION: Catholic. SOCIAL STATUS AND ACTIVITIES: Gent., 1769; Esq. at death. ADDITIONAL COMMENTS: Digges sailed for London in 1763 and was in London again in 1775 where he spent three years with his brother Thomas. Digges was one of the men responsible for raising subscriptions for St. John's College, ca. 1785, personally contributing £100 to the school. His home at "Warburton Manor," later the site of Fort Washington, was directly across the Potomac River from Mount Vernon. George Washington's diaries record frequent visits between the two families. OCCUPATIONAL PROFILE: probably a planter. **PUBLIC CAREER**. LEGISLATIVE SERVICE: Lower House, Prince George's County, 1783 (Claims), 1784 (Claims), 1785 (Claims), 1786–1787 (Claims 2), 1787–1788 (Claims 1, 2), 1788 (Claims), 1789. OTHER STATE OFFICE: Constitution Ratification Convention, Prince George's County, 1788. LOCAL OFFICE: Committee of Inspection, Prince George's County, elected 1775. **WEALTH DURING LIFETIME. PERSONAL PROPERTY**: 105 slaves, 1790. LAND AT FIRST ELECTION: 8,229 acres in Prince George's, Charles, and Montgomery counties (all inherited from his father). SIGNIFICANT CHANGES IN LAND BETWEEN FIRST ELECTION AND DEATH: sold 165 acres in Prince George's County, 1787; purchased 2 lots in Georgetown, Montgomery County, 1787, 1791; sold 809 acres in Charles County, 1788. **WEALTH AT DEATH. DIED**: on November 18, 1792,

at "Warburton Manor," Prince George's County. PERSONAL PROPERTY: TEV, £4,819.19.9 current money (including 48 slaves, books, plate, and a picture of George Washington). LAND: at least 6,572 acres in Prince George's, Charles, and Montgomery counties, plus 2 lots in Georgetown, Montgomery County.

DIGGES, JOHN (?–1783). BORN: probably in St. Mary's County, of age by 1770; eldest son. NATIVE: fourth generation. RESIDED: out of the province, 1769; St. Mary's County, 1770; Charles County, 1775. **FAMILY BACKGROUND. FATHER**: Edward Digges (?–1769), of St. Mary's County; son of John Digges, Gent., of Frederick County. MOTHER: Mary, daughter of Raphael Neale and wife Mary, of St. Mary's County. BROTHER: Edward (?–1799), deaf-mute. SISTERS: Elizabeth (?–1787), who married Wilfred Neale; Elianor (?–1779), who married Bernard O'Neale; Mary, (?–died young); and Ann (?–1796), a deaf-mute. OTHER KINSHIP: his great-grandfather was *William Digges* (ca. 1650–1697). ADDITIONAL COMMENTS: his grandfather, John Digges, was a Catholic with large landholdings in Frederick County. MARRIED Ann Hammersley (?–1805). Her brother was Henry Hammersley. Her sister was Elizabeth, who married (first name unknown) Lewellin. **CHILDREN**. SON: Edward (1774–?). DAUGHTER: Jane. **PRIVATE CAREER**. EDUCATION: literate. OCCUPATIONAL PROFILE: planter. **PUBLIC CAREER**. LEGISLATIVE SERVICE: Lower House, Charles County, 1778–1779, 1779–1780. LOCAL OFFICE: justice, Charles County, 1779–1783. **WEALTH DURING LIFETIME. PERSONAL PROPERTY**: assessed value £752.0.0, including 13 slaves and 20 oz. plate, 1783. LAND AT FIRST ELECTION: at least 312 acres in Charles County, probably 300 acres in Frederick County. **WEALTH AT DEATH. DIED**: between May 26 and August 18, 1783, in the First District, Charles County. PERSONAL PROPERTY: TEV, £1,457.3.3 current money (including 14 slaves, over 6 books, and 20 oz. plate); FB, £908.5.11. LAND: 632 acres in Charles and Frederick counties.

DIGGES, WILLIAM (ca. 1650–1697). BORN: ca. 1650, probably in England, but possibly in Virginia; oldest son. IMMIGRATED: in 1679 as a free adult from Virginia. RESIDED: in St. Mary's County; returned to Virginia after 1689. ADDITIONAL COMMENTS: probably spent most of his youth in London where his father lived in the late 1650s and 1660s; held his first public office in Virginia in 1671. **FAMILY BACKGROUND. FATHER**:

Edward Digges (ca. 1621–1675/76), son of Sir Dudley Digges (1583–1639), who immigrated to Virginia in 1650, served as councilor in 1654 and by 1670–1675/76, was governor of Virginia from 1655 to 1658, Virginia's agent in England in 1658, and a member of the Council for Foreign Plantations from 1661 to 1664. MOTHER: Elizabeth Page. BROTHER: Dudley (1665–1710), a burgess from Warwick County, Virginia, in 1695/96, who served on the Virginia Council in 1698. SISTERS: Mary; Ann. MARRIED ca. 1679 Elizabeth, widow of *Jesse Wharton* (?–1676); daughter of *Henry Sewall* (?–1665) and wife Jane Lowe; stepdaughter of *Charles Calvert, 3rd Lord Baltimore* (1637–1714/15). Her brother was *Nicholas Sewall* (ca. 1655–1737). Her sisters were Jane, who married *Philip Calvert* (1626–1682); Anne, who married first, *Benjamin Rozer* (?–1681), and second, *Edward Pye* (?–1696); and Mary. CHILDREN. SONS: Edward (?–1714), who married in 1699 Elizabeth (?–1704), daughter of *Henry Darnall* (ca. 1645–1711); William, who married Elinor, widow of Philip Darnall (1671–1705) and daughter of *Thomas Brooke* (ca. 1659–1730/31); John; Dudley; Charles, married Susannah Maria, daughter of *Henry Lowe* (?–1717); and Nicholas. DAUGHTERS: Jane; Elizabeth, who married Anthony Neale, son of *James Neale* (ca. 1615–1684); Ann, who married Henry Darnall (1682–1759), son of *Henry Darnall* (ca. 1645–1711); and Mary. PRIVATE CAREER. EDUCATION: literate, probably had extensive schooling. RELIGIOUS AFFILIATION: Protestant, but his wife was Catholic. SOCIAL STATUS AND ACTIVITIES: appointed to the Maryland Council immediately after his marriage to the proprietor's stepdaughter; he was the only Protestant on the governor's Council in 1689. OCCUPATIONAL PROFILE: merchant; planter. PUBLIC CAREER. LEGISLATIVE SERVICE: Upper House, 1681–1682 (appointed by the 3rd session), 1682–1684 (Accounts 1–3), 1686–1688 (Accounts, chairman 2). OTHER PROVINCIAL OFFICES: Council, 1679/80–1689; justice, Provincial Court, 1679/80–1689; joint chancellor and commissary general, 1682/83–1685; Board of Deputy Governors, 1684–1689; joint collector of Patuxent, 1684–1685; Land Council, 1684; joint secretary, 1685–1689. MILITARY SERVICE: colonel, 1679–1689. OUT OF COLONY SERVICE: justice, York County, Virginia, 1671; sheriff, York County, Virginia, 1679; captain of horse, 1674. STANDS ON PUBLIC/PRIVATE ISSUES: rejected the appeal of Protestants in 1689 to lead the resistance against the proprietor, whom he subsequently defended against the rebel Protestant Associators; resumed his residence in Virginia after the rebellion of 1689 and his plantation there became a refuge for some of his Catholic colleagues and relatives from Maryland; brought before the Virginia Council on charges of plotting to restore King James II, 1693. WEALTH DURING LIFETIME. LAND AT FIRST ELECTION: had considerable acreage in Virginia; had ca. 4,000 acres in Maryland, which he began to sell in 1692. WEALTH AT DEATH. DIED: will probated on July 24, 1697. PERSONAL PROPERTY: TEV, £798.8.7 sterling (including 29 slaves and books). LAND: over 3,000 acres.

DIXON, AMBROSE (?–1687). IMMIGRATED: by 1661/62 as a free adult from Northampton County, Virginia. RESIDED: in Annemesex Hundred, Somerset County. ADDITIONAL COMMENTS: he was living in Virginia by 1645, where he patented 600 acres of land in Northampton County with *Stephen Horsey* (ca. 1620–1671), probably in 1652. MARRIED by 1652 Mary, widow of Henry Peddington (?–1647). CHILDREN. SON: *Thomas Dixon* (?–1720), who married first, Christiana Potter, and second, Susanna. DAUGHTERS: Elizabeth (?–1687), who married Robert Dukes; Sarah, who married Edward Beauchamp; Grace, who married John Richards; Mary, who married Thomas Cottingham; Alice (1663/64–?), who married Henry Potter; and Hannah (1666–1667). PRIVATE CAREER. EDUCATION: illiterate. RELIGIOUS AFFILIATION: Quaker; religious persecution drove him to Maryland, where his home became an important meeting place for Quakers. OCCUPATIONAL PROFILE: caulker; planter; innkeeper, 1670. PUBLIC CAREER. LEGISLATIVE PROFILE: Lower House, Somerset County, 1671 (did not sit). LOCAL OFFICE: surveyor of highways, Somerset County, 1666. WEALTH DURING LIFETIME. LAND AT FIRST ELECTION: 550 acres. WEALTH AT DEATH. DIED: buried on April 12, 1687. PERSONAL PROPERTY: TEV, £326.3.0 sterling (including 11 slaves and 1 servant). LAND: 550 acres.

DIXON, THOMAS (?–1720). BORN: in Northampton County, Virginia; only son. IMMIGRATED: by 1661/62 as a minor with his parents from Virginia. RESIDED: in Annemesex Hundred, Somerset County. FAMILY BACKGROUND. FATHER: *Ambrose Dixon* (?–1687). MOTHER: Mary. SISTERS: Elizabeth (?–1687); Sarah; Grace; Mary; Alice (1663/64–?); and Hannah (1666–1667). MARRIED first, in 1672 Christiana Potter. MARRIED second, Susanna. CHILDREN. SONS: Ambrose (1673–?); Thomas (1677/78–1747); and William (1686–?). DAUGHTERS: Adria (1675–?); Mary (1683–?); Diana; Grace; Christiana; Abigail; and Alice, who married Henry Toadvine. PRIVATE CAREER. EDUCATION: illiterate. RELIGIOUS AFFILIATION: Anglican. SOCIAL STATUS AND ACTIVITIES: second generation burgess. OCCUPATIONAL PROFILE: planter. PUBLIC CAREER. LEGISLATIVE SERVICE: Lower House, Somerset County, 1694–1697. LOCAL OFFICES: justice, Somerset County, 1694–1704 (quorum); Coventry Parish Vestry, Somerset County, 1695. MILITARY SERVICE: captain, by 1697. WEALTH DURING LIFETIME. LAND AT FIRST ELECTION: probably 1,200 acres. WEALTH AT DEATH. DIED: will probated on May 5, 1720. PERSONAL PROPERTY: TEV, £430.17.9 (including 11 slaves).

DOCKWRA (DOCURA), THOMAS (?–1719). IMMIGRATED: by 1708. RESIDED: in Annapolis, Anne Arundel County. MARRIED Mary. CHILDREN. SON: John (before 1695–ca. 1738), who married Salome, widow of James Robinson (?–ca. 1716). PRIVATE CAREER. EDUCATION: literate. RELIGIOUS AFFILIATION: Protestant. SOCIAL STATUS AND ACTIVITIES: origins unknown; apparently a protéegée of Charles Carroll, the Settler. OCCUPATIONAL PROFILE: tanner; contractor; house builder. PUBLIC CAREER. LEGISLATIVE SERVICE: Lower House, Annapolis, 1712–1714. STANDS ON PUBLIC/PRIVATE ISSUES: tried to avoid payment of the poll tax for support of the established church, 1708. WEALTH DURING LIFETIME. LAND AT FIRST ELECTION: lots, houses, and a tanyard in Annapolis. WEALTH AT DEATH. DIED: by September 16, 1719. LAND: lots, houses, and a tanyard in Annapolis.

DOLLAHYDE (DALLAHIDE, DALLAHYDE), FRANCIS (?–1720 or 1721). BORN: probably in England. IMMIGRATED: in 1680 as an indentured servant to *Nicholas Gassaway* (1634–1691/92). RESIDED: in Anne Arundel County; Baltimore County, by 1695. MARRIED first, Providence. MARRIED second, Sarah, who probably subsequently married by 1721/22 William Greves. PRIVATE CAREER. EDUCATION: literate. RELIGIOUS AFFILIATION: Protestant. SOCIAL STATUS AND ACTIVITIES: first evidence of landownership, 1694. OCCUPATIONAL PROFILE: servant, 1680; planter. PUBLIC CAREER. LEGISLATIVE SERVICE: Lower House, Baltimore County, 1704–1707 (Elections and Privileges 1; resigned during the 5th session to become sheriff), 1715, 1716–1718, 1719–1720 (died before the 4th session). LOCAL OFFICES: justice, Baltimore County, 1701–1707, 1709–1720; sheriff, Baltimore County, 1707–1709; justice, Court of

Oyer and Terminer and Gaol Delivery, Baltimore County, appointed 1715 and 1718; coroner, Baltimore County, appointed 1717; land commissioner, Baltimore County, appointed 1718. MILITARY SERVICE: captain, 1714/15. WEALTH DURING LIFETIME. LAND AT FIRST ELECTION: ca. 481 acres. WEALTH AT DEATH. DIED: between October 20, 1720 and July 1721. LAND: ca. 550 acres.

DONE, JOHN (ca. 1747–1831). BORN: ca. 1747 in Somerset County; eldest son. NATIVE: at least second generation. RESIDED: in Somerset County; Worcester County; Annapolis, Anne Arundel County. FAMILY BACKGROUND. FATHER: John Done (?–1772), a physician. STEPFATHER: David Wilson, of Somerset County. MOTHER: Sarah, daughter of William Waters (?–ca. 1781). BROTHERS: Robert (?–ca. 1785), a lawyer, who married Mary, daughter of *Peter Chaille* (?–1802); William. MARRIED first, Sarah, daughter of John Rigley. MARRIED second, Patience, daughter of Esme Bayly and wife Sarah. CHILDREN. Eighteen children including SON: Col. William (1792–1830). DAUGHTERS: Sarah Martin, eldest; Juliet Henrietta; Leah Bayly; and Elizabeth Bayly. PRIVATE CAREER. EDUCATION: literate. RELIGIOUS AFFILIATION: Anglican. SOCIAL STATUS AND ACTIVITIES: Gent., 1829; a Freemason; subscriber to Washington College, Chestertown, Kent County. ADDITIONAL COMMENTS: he was one of several trustees who purchased a tract for the purpose of erecting a schoolhouse, 1804; deeded to an unmarried daughter a parcel of land for the erection of a school or seminary in Somerset County, 1816. OCCUPATIONAL PROFILE: attorney, admitted to the following courts: Somerset County in November 1769; Worcester County in November 1769. Planter. PUBLIC CAREER. LEGISLATIVE SERVICE: Conventions, Worcester County, 1st, 1774, 6th–8th, 1775–1776; Lower House, Somerset County, 1780–1781 (elected, but did not attend), 1782–1783 (Claims 1), 1783 (elected, but did not attend). OTHER STATE OFFICES: Constitution Ratification Convention, Worcester County, 1788; chief justice, Fourth District, 1791–1799 (resigned), 1812–1814 (resigned); judge, General Court, 1799–1805; associate judge, Fourth District, 1806–1812; judge, Court of Appeals, 1812–1814. LOCAL OFFICES: sheriff, Worcester County, 1773–1775; Committee of Observation, Worcester County, in office 1776; clerk, Worcester County, appointed 1777; Maryland Senate elector, Worcester County, elected 1786, Somerset County, elected 1791; Somerset Parish Vestry, Somerset County, in office 1791–1809; justice of the peace, Somerset County, in office 1794 and 1801; judge, Somerset County, in office 1799. MILITARY SERVICE: colonel, Princess Anne Battalion, Somerset County Militia, commissioned 1781. OUT OF STATE SERVICE: presidential elector, 1796 (for John Adams). WEALTH DURING LIFETIME. PERSONAL PROPERTY: assessed value £602.8.0, including 12 slaves and 18 oz. plate, 1783. ANNUAL INCOME: law fees for practice in Somerset County and Worcester County courts totaled £25.15.0 current money and 66,569 pounds of tobacco in 1785. LAND AT FIRST ELECTION: 555 acres in Somerset County (by deed of gift from his mother and brother). SIGNIFICANT CHANGES IN LAND BETWEEN FIRST ELECTION AND DEATH: sold 300 acres in Somerset County between 1785 and 1803; owned 4 lots in Princess Anne, Somerset County, but he sold 2 of these lots and leased out 2 other lots, 1797–1829. WEALTH AT DEATH. DIED: in October 1831 in Annapolis. PERSONAL PROPERTY: assessed value £659.0.0, including 3 slaves and 29 oz. plate, 1831. He sold several slaves to an unmarried daughter for $300.00, 1827–1829; he sold many more slaves for $4,000.00 in 1831.

DORSEY, EDWARD (?–1705). BORN: probably in Virginia; first son. IMMIGRATED: in 1649 as a minor with his parents and siblings from Virginia. RESIDED: in Anne Arundel County; Baltimore County, by 1700. FAMILY BACKGROUND. FATHER: Edward Dorsey (?–1659), who immigrated to Virginia by 1642 from Middlesex, England, and settled in Lower Norfolk County; he was a Quaker by 1657. BROTHERS: *John Dorsey* (ca. 1645–1714/15); Joshua (?–1688); and probably Samuel. NEPHEW: *John Dorsey* (ca. 1682–?). MARRIED first, ca. 1670 Sarah, daughter of Nicholas Damaris Wyatt. MARRIED second, Margaret, daughter of John Larkin. She subsequently married John Isaac (or Israel). CHILDREN. SONS: Edward (?–died young); Joshua, who married Ann, daughter of Henry Ridgely (1669–1699/1700); John, who married Honor Elder; Samuel; Nicholas, who married Frances Hughes; Benjamin; Larkin; Francis; and Edward. DAUGHTERS: Sarah, who married John Petticoate; Hannah, who married Joseph Howard (1676–1736), son of *Cornelius Howard* (?–1680); and Anne, who married John Hammond (?–1755), son of *Charles Hammond* (ca. 1670–1713). PRIVATE CAREER. EDUCATION: literate. RELIGIOUS AFFILIATION: Protestant. SOCIAL STATUS AND ACTIVITIES: recommended for a position on the Council in 1689 and 1696/97, but he was never commissioned; his sons held no public office higher than county justice. OCCUPATIONAL PRO-

FILE: planter; merchant; contractor. PUBLIC CAREER. LEGISLATIVE SERVICE: Lower House, Anne Arundel County, 1694–1697 (probably Laws 6), Baltimore County, 1701–1704 (Laws 2), 1704–1705 (Elections and Privileges, chairman 1; Aggrievances, chairman 2; died before the 4th session). OTHER PROVINCIAL OFFICE: judge, Court of Chancery, 1694–1696. LOCAL OFFICES: justice, Anne Arundel County, 1679–1685, 1686–1689, Baltimore County, by 1701–1705. MILITARY SERVICE: captain, 1686–1687; major, 1687–1689, 1694–1702; colonel, by 1704–1705. STANDS ON PUBLIC/PRIVATE ISSUES: his strong support of Lord Baltimore in 1689 brought his dismissal from his justiceship and militia commission after the overthrow of the proprietary government; he testified against the Protestant Associators in England, 1690; he was accused of being a Jacobite, 1692. WEALTH DURING LIFETIME. LAND AT FIRST ELECTION: over 1,000 acres. WEALTH AT DEATH. DIED: will probated on December 31, 1705. PERSONAL PROPERTY: TEV, £721.9.8 sterling (including 13 slaves and 2 servants); FB, £573.8.11. LAND: over 1,247 acres.

DORSEY, EDWARD (1718–1760). BORN: in September 1718 in Anne Arundel County; sixth of eight sons. NATIVE: fourth generation. RESIDED: maintained a house in Annapolis and a residence at his plantation, "Dorsey," in Anne Arundel County. FAMILY BACKGROUND. FATHER: Caleb Dorsey, Gent. (1683–1742), of Anne Arundel County. MOTHER: Elinor (1683–1752), daughter of Richard Warfield and wife Eleanor Brown. BROTHERS: Basil (1705–1763), twin to Achsah, who married Sarah Worthington; John (1708–?), who married Elizabeth Dorsey; Caleb (1710–?), who married Priscilla Hill; Samuel (1712–1739), never married; Richard (1714–?), who married Elizabeth Beale, widow of William Nicholson; Joshua (1720–1744), never married; and Thomas Beal (1727–?), who married Ann Worthington. SISTERS: Achsah (1705–?), who married first, Amos Woodward, and second, Edward Fatterell; Sophia (1707–?), who married Thomas Gough; Elinor (1715/16–?), who married first, Thomas Todd, and second, William Lynch; Deborah (1722–?), who married second, Ely Dorsey; and Mary (1725–ca. 1787), who married *John Ridgely* (?–1771). NEPHEWS: *Harry Dorsey Gough* (ca. 1745–1808); *Thomas Dorsey* (?–1790); and *Charles Ridgely, of John* (?–ca. 1787). NIECES: Achsah Dorsey, who married *Ephraim Howard* (1745–1788); Rebecca Dorsey, who married *Charles Ridgely* (1733–1790); Eleanor Dorsey, who married *John Hall* (1729–1797); Eleanor Dorsey, who married *Upton Sheredine* (1740–1800); Deborah Ridgely (1749–1817), who married *John Sterett* (1750/51–1787); Mary Ridgely (?–1804), who married *Benjamin Nicholson* (?–1792); and Mary Dorsey (?–1816), who married *John Weems* (1727–1794). MARRIED on February 18, 1748, Henrietta Maria (1730–1762), daughter of Samuel Chew (ca. 1704–1736/37) and wife Henrietta Maria Lloyd (?–1765); stepdaughter of *Daniel Dulany* (1685–1753); granddaughter of *Philemon Lloyd* (ca. 1674–1732/33). Her brothers were *Samuel Chew* (by 1734–1786); Bennett (?–1793), who married Anna Maria, daughter of *Edward Tilghman* (1713–1786); and Philemon Lloyd (?–1770). Her stepbrothers were *Daniel Dulany, Jr.* (1722–1797); *Walter Dulany* (?–1773). Her sisters were Margaret (?–1773), who married *John Beale Bordley* (1726/27–1804); Ann Mary (?–1774), who married *William Paca* (1740–1799). Her stepsister was Margaret Dulany, who married first, Dr. *Alexander Hamilton* (1712–1756), and second, *William Murdock* (?–1769). Her niece was Henrietta Maria Chew (1759–1847), who married *Benjamin Galloway* (1752–1831). CHILDREN. DAUGHTERS: Henrietta Maria (1754–1766); Elinor (?–by 1766). PRIVATE CAREER. EDUCATION: trained as a lawyer. RELIGIOUS AFFILIATION: Anglican, St. Anne's Parish, Anne Arundel County. SOCIAL STATUS AND ACTIVITIES: Esq., 1753. OCCUPATIONAL PROFILE: lawyer, admitted to the following courts: Anne Arundel County in November 1742; Prince George's County in November 1742; Provincial Court by April 1747; Court of Chancery by May 1747; Frederick County in March 1748/49. Planter; owned one-third share of an ironworks with Alexander Lawson and Caleb Dorsey. PUBLIC CAREER. LEGISLATIVE SERVICE: Lower House, Frederick County, 1757–1758 (Grievances 1, Cv, 2; Public Offices 1, Cv, 2), 1758–1760 (Elections Cv 1, 1, Cv 2, 2; Grievances Cv 1, 1, Cv 2, 2; Public Offices Cv 1, 1, Cv 2, 2; died during the 3rd session). LOCAL OFFICE: clerk of indictments, Anne Arundel County, commissioned 1744. WEALTH DURING LIFETIME. LAND AT FIRST ELECTION: at least 14,531 acres in Anne Arundel, Baltimore, and Frederick counties, plus 3 lots and a house in Annapolis. SIGNIFICANT CHANGES IN LAND BETWEEN FIRST ELECTION AND DEATH: accumulated through patent and purchase 2,288 acres in Anne Arundel and Frederick counties, 1757–1760. WEALTH AT DEATH. DIED: between May 5 and October 16, 1760, in Newport, Rhode Island; he was returning home from New England where he had gone for his health. PERSONAL PROP-

ERTY: TEV, £13,607.10.1 current money (including 72 slaves, 3 servants, one-half share in 3 servants and 8 slaves, one-third share in 23 servants and 22 slaves, law books, and other books); FB, £8,487.5.0. LAND: ca. 16,800 acres in Frederick, Anne Arundel, and Baltimore counties.

DORSEY, JOHN (ca. 1645–1714/15). BORN: ca. 1645 in Lower Norfolk County, Virginia; second son. IMMIGRATED: in 1649 as a minor with his parents and siblings. RESIDED: in Anne Arundel County; Baltimore County, by 1704. FAMILY BACKGROUND. FATHER: Edward Dorsey (?–ca. 1659), who immigrated to Virginia by 1642 from Middlesex, England, and settled in Lower Norfolk County; he was a Quaker by 1657. BROTHERS: *Edward Dorsey* (?–1705); Joshua (?–1688); and probably Samuel. NEPHEW: *John Dorsey* (ca. 1682–?). MARRIED Pleasance Ely. CHILDREN. SONS: Edward Dorsey (ca. 1677–1701); Caleb (1683–1742), who married in 1704 Eleanor, daughter of Richard Warfield. DAUGHTER: Deborah, who married first, Charles Ridgely (by 1680–1705), son of Robert Ridgely (?–1681), and second, Richard Clagett (1681–1752). PRIVATE CAREER. EDUCATION: literate. RELIGIOUS AFFILIATION: Protestant. SOCIAL STATUS AND ACTIVITIES: he was more prosperous and somewhat less controversial than his brother *Edward Dorsey* (?–1705); his sons held no provincial offices. OCCUPATIONAL PROFILE: planter; merchant. PUBLIC CAREER. LEGISLATIVE SERVICE: Lower House, Anne Arundel County, 1692–1693, 1701–1704 (Aggrievances 1); Upper House, 1711 (appointed by the 4th session), 1712–1714. OTHER PROVINCIAL OFFICE: Council, 1710/11–1714/15. LOCAL OFFICE: justice, Anne Arundel County, 1694–ca. 1698. MILITARY SERVICE: captain, by 1695–1714/15. STANDS ON PUBLIC/PRIVATE ISSUES: like his brother, he probably opposed the revolution of 1689; gained his first appointive office from Gov. Francis Nicholson, who was sympathetic to proprietary supporters. WEALTH DURING LIFETIME. LAND AT FIRST ELECTION: 1,242 acres by 1692; 2,484 acres by 1696. WEALTH AT DEATH. DIED: between January 18 and March 22, 1714/15. PERSONAL PROPERTY: TEV, £2,752.11.1 sterling (including 17 slaves). LAND: probably ca. 5,000 acres.

DORSEY, JOHN (ca. 1682–?). BORN: ca. 1682 in Anne Arundel County; only child. NATIVE: second generation. RESIDED: in Baltimore County, after 1707; left the province ca. 1727. FAMILY BACKGROUND. FATHER: Joshua Dorsey (?–1688), of Anne Arundel County, who immigrated from Virginia with his family. STEPFATHER: Thomas Blackwell (?–1700), of Anne Arundel County, a carpenter and an innholder. MOTHER: Sarah, daughter of Lawrence Richardson and wife Elizabeth. UNCLES: *Edward Dorsey* (?–1705); *John Dorsey* (ca. 1645–1714/15). MARRIED on August 22, 1702, Comfort (ca. 1684–ca. 1747), daughter of John Stimpson, Gent. (?–by 1692), of Anne Arundel County, and wife Rachel (?–after 1724), widow of Neale Clarke (?–1676); stepdaughter of Robert Proctor (?–by 1695), Richard Kilburne (?–by 1698), and Thomas Freeborne (?–1713); granddaughter of *Richard Beard* (?–1681). Her brother was John (?–by 1718). Her sister was Rachel (?–1748/49), who married first, *Charles Greenberry* (1672–1713), and second, *Charles Hammond* (1692/93–1772). Her niece was Ann Hammond (1716–?), who married second, *William Govane* (1716/17–1768). CHILDREN. SONS: Joshua (1711–by 1784), who married Flora Fitzsimmons; Greenbury (1711–?), who married Mary Belt; Vincent (?–1753), who married Sarah Day; and *John Hammond Dorsey* (1718–1774). DAUGHTERS: Sarah (?–died young); Venetia (?–died young); Comfort (1710–?), who married Joseph Cromwell; Sarah (?–by 1788), who married Alexander Cromwell and died in Edgecombe County, North Carolina; and Venetia, who married Woodquist Cromwell. PRIVATE CAREER. EDUCATION: apprenticed to *William Dent* (ca. 1660–1704), a lawyer, ca. 1698. RELIGIOUS AFFILIATION: Anglican. SOCIAL STATUS AND ACTIVITIES: Gent., by 1708; Esq., by 1715. OCCUPATIONAL PROFILE: planter; surveyor, laid out Joppa Town, Baltimore County. PUBLIC CAREER. LEGISLATIVE SERVICE: Lower House, Baltimore County, 1721/22 (elected to the 5th session to fill vacancy). LOCAL OFFICES: sheriff, Baltimore County, 1713–1715; justice, Baltimore County, 1716–at least 1727 (quorum, 1727); justice, Court of Oyer and Terminer and Gaol Delivery, Baltimore County, commissioned 1718 and 1722; deputy surveyor, Baltimore County, commissioned 1720; "committee for laying the county levy," Baltimore County, appointed 1721; coroner, Baltimore County, in office 1722; commissioner, Baltimore County, by 1724. MILITARY SERVICE: captain, Baltimore County Militia, by 1717; colonel, by 1724. WEALTH DURING LIFETIME. PERSONAL PROPERTY: gave livestock, books, and musical instruments to his son Greenbury at the time of his marriage, 1726. A chancery case in 1733 described Dorsey as having a lower court judgment against him for £70.13.7 sterling and 8,713 pounds of tobacco that was owed to John Stokes, sheriff of Baltimore County from 1718 to 1721, and accused

Dorsey of leaving Maryland ca. 1727 "in a private and clandestine manner" to escape payment. Comfort Dorsey, his wife, denied that Dorsey left secretly, but other witnesses refuted her statement. Stokes's widow wanted Dorsey's land sold to pay his debts, but John Hammond proved his ownership and the case was dismissed in 1737. LAND AT FIRST ELECTION: ca. 1,150 acres in Baltimore County (probably inherited 598 acres, at least 148 from his stepfather; 559 acres through his marriage). SIGNIFICANT CHANGES IN LAND BETWEEN FIRST ELECTION AND DEATH: patented 1,145 acres and purchased 815 acres in Baltimore County between 1720 and 1725; sold 198 acres in Baltimore County during this period. By March 1726 Dorsey and his family were living with John Hammond, of Cecil County, to whom Dorsey deeded his dwelling plantation a few months later. Testimony in the 1733 Chancery Court case stated that the transfer to Hammond was made to protect the property from Dorsey's creditors and Hammond's will devised the land back to Dorsey's family. Dorsey mortgaged 1,725 acres in Baltimore County in August 1726 and January 1726/27. Soon after that he left Maryland, possibly for the Carolinas.

DORSEY, JOHN (1734–1779). BORN: on July 3, 1734, in Anne Arundel County; eldest son. NATIVE: at least fourth generation. RESIDED: in Upper Fork Hundred or Bearground Hundred, Anne Arundel County. FAMILY BACKGROUND. FATHER: Michael Dorsey (1712–1776), son of John Dorsey and wife Honor Elder. MOTHER: Ruth, daughter of Lancelot Todd and wife Elizabeth. BROTHERS: Lancelot (1742–?), who married Sarah Warfield; Michael, who married Honor Howard. SISTERS: Elizabeth (1735–?), who married John Burgess; Sarah (1739–?), who married Richard Berry, of Prince George's County; Ruth (1743–?), who married Ely Dorsey; Honor Elder (1737–?), who married John Elder; Anne Elder; and Lydia, who married (first name unknown) Talbott. MARRIED by 1771 Anne (1740–1795), daughter of Philemon Dorsey (1714–1772) and wife Catherine (1723–ca. 1751); stepdaughter of Rachel Lawrence; granddaughter of Henry Ridgely; niece of *Henry Ridgely* (1728–1791), Elizabeth Ridgely, who married *Thomas Dorsey* (?–1790), Anne Ridgely, who married *Brice T. B. Worthington* (1727–1794), and Sarah Ridgely, who married *Charles Greenbury Griffith* (1744–1792). Her brother was Philemon (1743/44–1806). Her half brother was *Joshua Dorsey* (?–1818). Her sisters were Elizabeth (1742–?), who married William Ridgely; Catherine (1745–

1804), who married Benjamin Warfield; Sarah, who married Vachel Warfield; and Amelia (1749–?), who married Samuel Biggs (?–1814). CHILDREN. SONS: Philemon; Vachel, who married Anne Poole; and Michael, who married in 1796 in Frederick County, Elizabeth Poole. DAUGHTERS: Catherine, who married Charles Warfield; Ruth, who married in 1788 Gassaway Watkins; Eleanor, who married in 1785 Basil Burgess; and Elizabeth (?–ca. 1789). PRIVATE CAREER. EDUCATION: literate. SOCIAL STATUS AND ACTIVITIES: Mr., by 1773. OCCUPATIONAL PROFILE: planter. PUBLIC CAREER. LEGISLATIVE SERVICE: Convention, Anne Arundel County, 5th, 1775. LOCAL OFFICE: Committee of Observation, Annapolis and Anne Arundel County, elected 1774 and 1775. MILITARY SERVICE: colonel, Elk Ridge Battalion, Anne Arundel County Militia, by 1776. WEALTH DURING LIFETIME. LAND AT FIRST ELECTION: 860 acres in Anne Arundel County (150 acres inherited from his grandfather, John Dorsey, and 231 acres acquired through his marriage). WEALTH AT DEATH. DIED: between January 28 and March 9, 1779, in Anne Arundel County. PERSONAL PROPERTY: TEV, £2,536.0.3 current money; FB, £2,042.5.2 (before distribution). LAND: 893 acres in Anne Arundel County.

DORSEY, JOHN HAMMOND (1718–1774). BORN: in 1718 in Baltimore County; youngest son. NATIVE: third generation. RESIDED: in Baltimore County. FAMILY BACKGROUND. FATHER: *John Dorsey* (ca. 1682–?). MOTHER: Comfort (ca. 1684–ca. 1747). AUNT: Rachel Stimpson (?–1748/49), who married first, *Charles Greenberry* (1672–1713), and second, *Charles Hammond* (1692/93–1772). BROTHERS: Joshua (1711–by 1784); Greenbury (1711–?); and Vincent (?–1753). SISTERS: Sarah (?–died young); Venetia (?–died young); Comfort (1710–?); Sarah (?–by 1788); and Venetia. FIRST COUSIN: Ann Hammond (1716–?), who married second, *William Govane* (1716/17–1768). NEPHEW: *Richard Cromwell* (1749–1802). MARRIED in 1742 Frances, daughter of John Watkins (?–1743), of Anne Arundel County, and wife Mary (?–1768). Her brothers were John; Stephen; and Nicholas. Her sisters were Anne, who married Samuel Smith; Sarah, who married first, (first name unknown) Gassaway, and second, (first name unknown) Keene; Mary; Hester, who married (first name unknown) Lane; and Jean (Jane), who married Anthony Smith. CHILDREN. SONS: John Hammond, Jr. (1744–1748); Stephen (1747–1749); John Hammond, Jr. (1754–?), who married Ann Maxwell; and Stephen (1758–?), who married

Rachel Ewing. DAUGHTERS: Mary Hammond (1749–?), who married John Hammond Cromwell; Rebecca (1752–?), who married John Lane; and Frances (1756–?). PRIVATE CAREER. EDUCATION: literate. RELIGIOUS AFFILIATION: Anglican. St. John's Parish, Baltimore County. SOCIAL STATUS AND ACTIVITIES: Mr., by 1766; Gent., by 1770. OCCUPATIONAL PROFILE: planter; kept a "publick house," ca. 1748; merchant, by 1764. PUBLIC CAREER. LEGISLATIVE SERVICE: Lower House, Baltimore County, 1757–1758, 1758–1761 (Arms and Ammunition Cv 1, 1, Cv 2, 2; Public Offices Cv 3), 1762–1763. LOCAL OFFICES: St. John's Parish Vestry, Baltimore County, in office 1747–1748 (discharged for keeping a "publick house") and 1762–1765; justice, Baltimore County, commissioned 1753. MILITARY SERVICE: captain, by 1756. WEALTH DURING LIFETIME. LAND AT FIRST ELECTION: 687 acres in Baltimore and Cecil counties (27 acres in Cecil County by patent, 1746; 99 acres in Baltimore County by purchase, 1744–1748; 561 acres inherited from John Hammond in 1739, which was part of Dorsey's father's home plantation which had been sold to Hammond in 1726 probably to keep it from being attached for payment of his father's debts. SIGNIFICANT CHANGES IN LAND BETWEEN FIRST ELECTION AND DEATH: purchased 204 acres in Baltimore County and 1 lot in Joppa Town, Baltimore County; leased 255 acres in Baltimore County in 1765, of which he relinquished 176 acres in 1773; conveyed 303 acres in Baltimore County to his son, 1771. WEALTH AT DEATH. DIED: in 1774 in Baltimore County. PERSONAL PROPERTY: TEV, £1,361.12.8 current money (including 15 slaves); FB, £1,067.7.7 (after first account). Testamentary proceedings mention a large number of creditors with money due from the estate. LAND: 588 acres in Baltimore and Cecil counties, and 1 lot in Joppa Town, Baltimore County, plus probably a lease on 79 acres in Baltimore County.

DORSEY, JOSHUA (?–1818). BORN: in Anne Arundel County, of age by 1771; younger son. NATIVE: at least second generation. RESIDED: in Frederick County. FAMILY BACKGROUND. FATHER: Capt. Philemon Dorsey (1714–1772), resided in Elkridge, Anne Arundel County, a district surveyor, and the son of Joshua Dorsey. Philemon married first, in 1738/39 Catherine (?–ca. 1750), daughter of Col. Henry Ridgely. MOTHER: Rachel. HALF BROTHER: Philemon (1743/44–?). HALF SISTERS: Ann (1740–1795), who married *John Dorsey* (1734–1779); Elizabeth, who married William Ridgley, son of William Ridgley; Catherine (1745–1804), who married Benjamin Warfield; Sarah (1747–?), who married Vachel Warfield; Amelia, who married Samuel Riggs; Henrietta (?–1798), who married William Hobbs; and Ariana, who married Samuel Owings. **MARRIED** Jane Kennedy, of Philadelphia, Pennsylvania. **CHILDREN. DAUGHTER:** Elizabeth, who married Dr. Thomas W. Johnson. **PRIVATE CAREER. EDUCATION:** trained as a lawyer. **RELIGIOUS AFFILIATION:** Anglican, All Saints' Parish, Frederick County. **SOCIAL STATUS AND ACTIVITIES:** Esq., 1796. **OCCUPATIONAL PROFILE:** lawyer, admitted to the Frederick County bar in 1785. **PUBLIC CAREER. LEGISLATIVE SERVICE:** Lower House, Frederick County, 1789 (Laws to Expire), 1792. **OTHER STATE OFFICE:** clerk, Senate, elected 1783, resigned 1789. **LOCAL OFFICES:** churchwarden, Queen Caroline Parish, Anne Arundel County, elected 1776; justice, Frederick County, in office 1796; Maryland Senate elector, Frederick County, elected 1796. **WEALTH DURING LIFETIME. PERSONAL PROPERTY:** assessed value £380.0.0, including 2 slaves in Upper Fork and Bearground hundreds, Anne Arundel County, 1783. **LAND AT FIRST ELECTION:** 420 acres in Anne Arundel County (inherited from his father). **SIGNIFICANT CHANGES IN LAND BETWEEN FIRST ELECTION AND DEATH:** purchased 257 acres in Frederick County, plus 1 lot in Frederick Town, Frederick County, 1801. **WEALTH AT DEATH. DIED:** will probated on November 28, 1818, in Frederick County. **LAND:** possibly 677 acres in Anne Arundel and Frederick counties, plus 1 lot in Frederick Town.

DORSEY, THOMAS (?–1790). **BORN:** in Anne Arundel County, of age by 1762; second son. **NATIVE:** fifth generation. **RESIDED:** in Huntington Hundred, Anne Arundel County. **FAMILY BACKGROUND. FATHER:** Basil Dorsey (1704–1763), of Anne Arundel County, a planter. **MOTHER:** Sarah (1715/16–?), daughter of *Thomas Worthington* (ca. 1691–1753) and wife Elizabeth Ridgely. **UNCLES:** *Edward Dorsey* (1718–1760); *Brice T. B. Worthington* (1727–1794); and *Nicholas Worthington* (1734–1793). **AUNT:** Mary Dorsey (1725–ca. 1787), who married *John Ridgely* (?–1771). **BROTHERS:** Caleb (1734–1763); Dennis (?–1788). **SISTERS:** Sarah, who married John Burgess; Ariana, who married Thomas Sollers; Eleanor, who married *Upton Sheredine* (1740–1800); and Elizabeth, who married Ephraim Howard Jr., of Frederick County. **FIRST COUSINS:** *Harry Dorsey Gough* (ca. 1745–1808); Achsah Dorsey (1746–1799), who married

Ephraim Howard (1745–1788); Rebecca Dorsey (1739–1812), who married *Charles Ridgely* (1733–1790); Eleanor Dorsey (ca. 1739–1805), who married *John Hall* (1729–1797); Mary Dorsey (?–1816), who married *John Weems* (1727–1794); *Charles Ridgely, of John* (?–ca. 1787); Deborah Ridgely (1749–1817), who married *John Sterett* (1750/51–1787); Mary Ridgely (?–1804), who married *Benjamin Nicholson* (?–1792); *John G. Worthington* (1764–1797); and Catherine Worthington (1761–1814), who married *Baker Johnson* (1747–1811). **MARRIED** first, Elizabeth, daughter of Col. Henry Ridgely (?–1750) and wife Elizabeth Warfield; niece of Elizabeth Ridgely (?–1734), who married *Thomas Worthington* (ca. 1691–1753). Her brothers were Greenberry (1726–?); *Henry Ridgely* (1728–1791); Nicholas (?–died young); Benjamin (1732–?); Joshua (1734–?); Charles G. (1735–?); Thomas (1740–?); and Nicholas G. (1742–?). Her sisters were Catherine (1723–ca. 1751), who married Philemon Dorsey (1714–1772); Anne (1725–?), who married *Brice T. B. Worthington* (1727–1794); and Sarah (1745–?), who married *Charles Greenbury Griffith* (1744–1792). Her niece was Anne Dorsey (1740–1795), who married *John Dorsey* (1734–1779). **MARRIED** second, on June 21, 1761, Elizabeth (1745–1815), daughter of Judge Nicholas Ridgely, of Delaware. **CHILDREN. SONS:** Daniel (1757–?), who married Eleanor Dorsey; Archibald; Theodore, who married Elizabeth Dorsey; and Nicholas. **DAUGHTERS:** Mary, who married in 1788 in Baltimore County Samuel Norwood; Elizabeth Ridgely, who married Benjamin Berry; Juliet, who married in 1801 in Baltimore County William Hawkins; Harriet, who married in 1803 in Baltimore County John Berry; and Matilda, who married in 1814 in Baltimore County John Sullivan. **PRIVATE CAREER. EDUCATION:** literate. **RELIGIOUS AFFILIATION:** Anglican, Queen Caroline Parish, Anne Arundel County. **SOCIAL STATUS AND ACTIVITIES:** Gent., by 1763; Esq., by 1777. **OCCUPATIONAL PROFILE:** planter, 1763; merchant; land speculator. **PUBLIC CAREER. LEGISLATIVE SERVICE:** Conventions, Anne Arundel County, 1st, 1774, 2nd–3rd, 1774, 5th, 1775. **LOCAL OFFICES:** Queen Caroline Parish Vestry, Anne Arundel County, in office 1762; justice, Anne Arundel County, 1768–1778 (appointed, but did not qualify in 1778); Committee of Observation, Annapolis and Anne Arundel County, elected 1774 and 1775; commissioner of tax, Anne Arundel County, 1777–1782; purchasing agent, Anne Arundel County, appointed 1778. **MILITARY SERVICE:** colonel, Elk Ridge Battalion, Anne Arundel County Militia, by 1777. **WEALTH DUR-**

ING LIFETIME. PERSONAL PROPERTY: assessed value £1,160.0.0, including 27 slaves and 48 oz. plate, Anne Arundel County, 1783. LAND AT FIRST ELECTION: at least 15,657 acres in Anne Arundel and Frederick counties, plus 1 lot in Annapolis (10,649 acres in Frederick County and 1 lot in Annapolis inherited from his uncle Edward Dorsey; most of his land in Anne Arundel County was inherited from his father). SIGNIFICANT CHANGES IN LAND BETWEEN FIRST ELECTION AND DEATH: About 1778 Dorsey formed a mercantile partnership with John Dorsey, *Samuel Chase* (1741–1811), and later, Luke Wheeler. They dealt in state bonds as early as 1781 and by Dorsey's death the firm owed the state over £15,000 current money. The partnership also had dealings with Evelyn Pierpont, of Virginia and Delaware, to whom Dorsey mortgaged property in 1784. By 1789 Dorsey's company had property worth less than £5,000 current money and owed more than £42,000 in debts. Dorsey signed a statement with Chase on November 19, 1789, saying that he had paid or secured £30,000 of the company's debt and was insolvent (as were John Dorsey and Luke Wheeler). Chase agreed to turn over his property to Dorsey, but had not done so by Dorsey's death. Sold ca. 8,700 acres in Anne Arundel and Frederick counties, plus 1 lot in Annapolis, and mortgaged his remaining land, 1784–1789; purchased and patented ca. 20,000 acres in Kentucky, date unknown. WEALTH AT DEATH. DIED: will probated on October 30, 1790, in Anne Arundel County. PERSONAL PROPERTY: TEV, £5,071.15.1 current money; FB, estate overpaid £10,157.11.3. LAND: probably none with clear title in Maryland, but he had nearly 20,000 acres in Kentucky. ADDITIONAL COMMENTS: In his will Dorsey stated that he had lost a "liberal fortune" by "indiscretion and ill-judged confidence."

DORSEY, WILLIAM HAMMOND (1764–ca. 1819). BORN: on February 12, 1764, at "Oaklands," in the Elkridge section of Anne Arundel or Baltimore counties; fourth son. NATIVE: at least third generation. RESIDED: in Georgetown, D.C., and Montgomery County. FAMILY BACKGROUND. FATHER: Col. John Dorsey (ca. 1736–1810), amassed a fortune from iron deposits on Curtis Creek in Anne Arundel County, which enabled him to establish John Dorsey & Co. in Baltimore Town; eventually his company became insolvent and he lost practically all of his former wealth. MOTHER: Mary (ca. 1738–?), daughter of Col. William Hammond and wife Elizabeth Hughes. BROTHERS: Robert (1758–1841); Larkin (1760–?),

a captain in the Revolution who died in the West Indies; Alexander (1762–1813); Walter (1771–?), a merchant, who married Hopewell, daughter of Vernon Hebb, of St. Mary's County; John E. (1773–?), a merchant, who married Margaret, widow of (first name unknown) Hudson; and Clement (1773–1848), a major in the militia from 1812 to 1818, judge of the Fifth Circuit Court of Maryland, who married first, Priscilla, daughter of Vernon Hebb, of St. Mary's County, and second, Decandia, widow of Henry Smith and daughter of Henry Ireland and wife Susannah Reeder. SISTERS: Elizabeth (1766–?), who married Edward Dorsey; Sarah (1768–1846). MARRIED first, in 1789 Ann (ca. 1773–by 1815), daughter of *Richard Brooke* (1736–1788). MARRIED second, by 1815 Rosetta. CHILDREN. SONS: Robert E. (?–1876), a physician, who married on July 20, 1826, Sarah Duvall; Richard Brooke (1790–?), who married his first cousin Anne, daughter of Clement Dorsey; James M. (1798–1808); and William Hammond (1800–?), who married on October 31, 1825, Susan Robertson. DAUGHTERS: Anne (1792–died young); Maria A. (1794–?), who married William Johnson. PRIVATE CAREER. EDUCATION: literate. SOCIAL STATUS AND ACTIVITIES: Esq., 1798. OCCUPATIONAL PROFILE: ironmaster; joint partner in the Etna Furnace with his brothers Walter and John. Heavily in debt, the business was sold for $102,697.70 in 1813. PUBLIC CAREER. LEGISLATIVE SERVICE: Lower House, Montgomery County, 1788; Senate, Western Shore, Term of 1796–1801: 1796, 1797, 1798, 1799, 1800. OUT OF STATE SERVICE: judge, Orphans' Court, Washington, D.C., appointed 1801. WEALTH DURING LIFETIME. PERSONAL PROPERTY: 18 slaves, 1790; assessed value £593.0.0, including 15 slaves, 1798–1812; assessed value £483.5.0, including 3 slaves, 1813. SIGNIFICANT CHANGES IN LAND BETWEEN FIRST ELECTION AND DEATH: acquired at least 4,500 acres in Montgomery County through his marriage in 1789. Between 1794 and 1802 he sold or mortgaged all except ca. 500 acres. Purchased 792 acres in Montgomery County (592 acres of this between 1813 and 1816) and sold 246 acres between 1815 and 1818; the sale of the ironworks owned by him and his two brothers included 5,810 acres in Anne Arundel and Baltimore counties, 1813. WEALTH AT DEATH. DIED: administration bond granted on January 24, 1819, in Montgomery County. PERSONAL PROPERTY: TEV, $13,031.31 (including 3 slaves, more than 48 books, and plate); FB, $10,481.23. LAND: probably ca. 1,050 acres in Montgomery County.

DOUGLASS, JOHN (ca. 1636–ca. 1678/79). BORN: ca. 1636, probably in England. IMMIGRATED: in 1659 as a free adult. RESIDED: in Charles County. MARRIED Sarah Bouls, possibly a daughter of John Bouls. She subsequently married Ralph Smith. CHILDREN. SONS: John; Robert (?–1694), who married Mary, widow of Richard Beaumont; Charles (?–1703); Joseph; and Benjamin. DAUGHTERS: Elizabeth (1673–?); Sarah. PRIVATE CAREER. EDUCATION: literate. SOCIAL STATUS AND ACTIVITIES: no title upon arrival; sons held no offices. OCCUPATIONAL PROFILE: planter. PUBLIC CAREER. LEGISLATIVE SERVICE: Lower House, Charles County, 1676–1678 (Accounts 1; Defense 2; died before the 3rd session). LOCAL OFFICE: justice, Charles County, 1672–1678. MILITARY SERVICE: captain, 1675; major and colonel, 1676. WEALTH DURING LIFETIME. LAND AT FIRST ELECTION: over 450 acres; acquired Cold Spring Manor, 1,050 acres, in 1677. WEALTH AT DEATH. DIED: between December 14, 1678, and January 27, 1678/79. LAND: 1,600 acres.

DOUGLASS (DOUGLAS), WILLIAM (?–1782). BORN: possibly in Pennsylvania, of age by 1763. IMMIGRATED: by 1763, possibly from Kent County, Delaware. RESIDED: in Caernarvon Township, Lancaster County, Pennsylvania; possibly Kent County, Delaware; Worcester County, 1763; Dorchester County (later became part of Caroline County), 1771; Great Choptank Hundred, Caroline County, 1778. MARRIED Sarah, who subsequently married by March 1785 William Carpenter, Sr., of Kent County, Delaware. CHILDREN. SON: James (?–ca. 1799), of Kent County, Delaware; possibly others. PRIVATE CAREER. EDUCATION: literate. SOCIAL STATUS AND ACTIVITIES: Gent., 1763. OCCUPATIONAL PROFILE: ironmaster, in partnership with Jonathan Vaughan and six Pennsylvania businessmen in the Nanticoke Forge and Deep Creek Furnace, ca. 1763. This ironworks was the first to be formed in Worcester County. It was a large operation with ca. 7,000 acres of land on the Eastern Shore plus sawmills, gristmills, water mills, corn mills, coal, slaves, servants, and merchandise which was shipped directly to England. When the Revolution broke out the Chesapeake Bay was blockaded and business was suspended. The ironworks never recovered from this interruption and the operation was not resumed after the war. The ironworks' property, however, remained in the hands of the company until an act of the legislature was passed in 1802 to divide it among the heirs of the original owners. The furnace tract and other lands on Deep Creek went to Douglass's grandsons. He was also a partner with John Douglass, of Chester County, Pennsylvania, in a waterworks and a small forge from ca. 1770 to 1776, when the partnership was dissolved. PUBLIC CAREER. LEGISLATIVE SERVICE: Lower House, Caroline County, 1777, 1777–1778 (Manufactories 3). LOCAL OFFICES: commissioner of tax, Caroline County, commissioned 1779; commissary of horses, Caroline County, commissioned 1781 (but "refused to act being in a bad state of health"). WEALTH DURING LIFETIME. LAND AT FIRST ELECTION: held partnership with seven other people in ca. 7,000 acres in Worcester and Dorchester counties, and in Sussex County, Delaware; a partner, with one other person, in ca. 1,600 acres in Caroline County. SIGNIFICANT CHANGES IN LAND BETWEEN FIRST ELECTION AND DEATH: bought out his partner's interest in the ca. 1,600 acres in Caroline County between 1776 and 1782. WEALTH AT DEATH. DIED: in 1782 in Caroline County. PERSONAL PROPERTY: TEV, £1,469.5.7 (including 8 slaves, 10 oz. plate, and books); FB, £1,289.6.9. LAND: 1,517 acres in Caroline County, plus his part of ca. 7,000 acres in Worcester and Dorchester counties, and in Sussex County, Delaware, belonging to the Deep Creek Ironworks.

DOWNES (DOWNS), HENRY (ca. 1748–1816). BORN: ca. 1748, probably in Queen Anne's County; younger son. NATIVE: at least third generation. RESIDED: in Queen Anne's County (later became part of Caroline County); Hillsborough, Caroline County. FAMILY BACKGROUND. FATHER: Henry Downes (1707–by 1772), of Queen Anne's County, son of John Downes (?–1707), of Talbot County. MOTHER: Frances Noble (?–by 1775). BROTHER: *Philemon Downes* (ca. 1741–ca. 1796). FIRST COUSIN: Henrietta Downes (1739–1812), who married *Thomas Hardcastle* (ca. 1737–1808). MARRIED first, by 1769 Margaret (1752–by 1788), daughter of Thomas Baynard (?–1753), of Talbot County, a planter who died as a minor under 21 years of age, and wife Hannah Clarke; stepdaughter of Henry Thompson; niece of both *Joshua Clarke* (?–1781) and Margaret Baynard (?–by 1777), who married second *Matthew Driver* (1740–1798). Her sisters were Elizabeth (1748–1809), who married first, John Tillotson, Jr. (?–by 1777), and second, *Philemon Downes* (ca. 1741–ca. 1796); Lydia (1750–by 1769). Her first cousin was Elizabeth Driver (by 1777–?), who married *Peter Edmondson* (ca. 1753–1819). MARRIED second, in November 1788 Margaret Green. CHILDREN. DAUGHTERS: Elizabeth (?–by 1816), who married

Francis Sellers (?–1804), merchant; (first name unknown) (?–by 1816), who married Henry Nichols (?–1831); possibly other children; probably no surviving children at the time of his death. PRIVATE CAREER. EDUCATION: literate. RELIGIOUS AFFILIATION: Methodist Episcopal, 1797. SOCIAL STATUS AND ACTIVITIES: trustee for *William Hopper* (by 1747–1806) and *James Kent* (ca. 1738–1805), insolvent debtors; his will mentioned "my old respectable master," *Richard Tilghman Earle* (1728/29–1788). OCCUPATIONAL PROFILE: planter, 1774; farmer, 1779. PUBLIC CAREER. LEGISLATIVE SERVICE: Lower House, Caroline County, 1777, 1777–1778 (elected, but did not attend; resigned on March 3, 1778 to "attend to private affairs"), 1784, 1785, 1787–1788, 1790. LOCAL OFFICES: justice, Caroline County, commissioned 1777, 1778, 1783 ("will not qualify"), 1785, and 1786, in office 1791, 1797, 1801–1806; sheriff, Caroline County, in office 1778, elected 1779; purchasing agent, Caroline County, 1779; subscription officer, Continental Loan Office, Caroline County, appointed 1779; justice, Orphans' Court, Caroline County, commissioned 1783 ("will not qualify") and 1785 ("did not qualify"); commissioner of tax, Caroline County, appointed 1783; judge, Court of Appeals for Tax Assessment, Caroline County, appointed 1786; associate justice, Fourth District, Caroline County, commissioned 1791, 1793; president, Hillsborough School, Caroline County, at his death, a post that then passed to his grandson Henry Downes Sellers. MILITARY SERVICE: 2nd major, Twenty-eighth Battalion, commissioned January 1776; resigned commission to become adjutant under Col. Federman, April 1776. STANDS ON PUBLIC/PRIVATE ISSUES: manumitted three slaves, 1803; inventory mentioned freeing some additional slaves after a period of years, 1816. WEALTH DURING LIFETIME. PERSONAL PROPERTY: assessed value £283.0.0, including 5 slaves, 1783; 5 slaves, 1790; 13 slaves, 1798. LAND AT FIRST ELECTION: 253 acres in Caroline County (137 acres through his marriage, 116 acres by purchase). SIGNIFICANT CHANGES IN LAND BETWEEN FIRST ELECTION AND DEATH: a further partition of his first wife's inherited land brought the total acreage he acquired through marriage to 214 acres, 1784; 200 acres of first wife's land were given by deed of gift to their daughter, 1784; purchased at least 1,614 acres in Caroline, Queen Anne's, and Talbot counties between 1792 and 1814; sold at least 205 acres in Caroline County between 1808 and 1813. WEALTH AT DEATH. DIED: on December 4, 1816, in Hillsborough, Caroline County. PERSONAL PROPERTY: TEV, $5,611.78 (including

11 slaves, 1 servant, books, and 2 shares of Bank of Baltimore stock); FB, $2,946.40. LAND: at least 1,394 acres in Talbot, Caroline, and Queen Anne's counties, plus houses and lots in Hillsborough, Caroline County, and Centreville, Queen Anne's County.

DOWNES (DOWNS), PHILEMON (ca. 1741–ca. 1796). BORN: ca. 1741, probably in Queen Anne's County; elder son. NATIVE: at least third generation. RESIDED: in Queen Anne's County; in Baltimore County, 1778–1779; in Caroline County, ca. 1780. FAMILY BACKGROUND. FATHER: Henry Downes (1707–by 1772), of Queen Anne's County, son of John Downes (?–1707), of Talbot County. MOTHER: Frances Noble (?–by 1775). BROTHER: *Henry Downes* (ca. 1748–1816). FIRST COUSIN: Henrietta Downes (1739–1812), who married *Thomas Hardcastle* (ca. 1737–1808). MARRIED first, by 1776 Mary (?–by 1779), widow of Jacob Seth (?–1773), of Queen Anne's County. MARRIED second, in August 1780 Elizabeth (1748–1809), widow of John Tillotson, Jr. (?–by 1777), of Caroline County; daughter of Thomas Baynard (?–1753), of Talbot County, a planter who died a minor under 21-years of age, and wife Hannah Clarke; stepdaughter of Henry Thompson; niece of both *Joshua Clarke* (?–1781) and Margaret Baynard (?–by 1777), who married second, *Matthew Driver* (1740–1798). Her sisters were Lydia (1750–by 1769); Margaret (1752–by 1788), who married *Henry Downes* (ca. 1748–1816). Her first cousin was Elizabeth Driver (by 1777–?), who married *Peter Edmondson* (ca. 1753–1819). CHILDREN. SONS: Philemon; Henry. STEPSONS: Thomas Baynard Tillotson; John Tillotson. DAUGHTER: Mary. PRIVATE CAREER. EDUCATION: literate. OCCUPATIONAL PROFILE: farmer. PUBLIC CAREER. LEGISLATIVE SERVICE: Lower House, Caroline County, 1782 (elected, but did not attend; resigned on November 13, 1782), 1795. LOCAL OFFICES: sheriff, Queen Anne's County, 1773–1775; justice, Queen Anne's County, commissioned 1778 (moved to Baltimore County), 1779 (moved to Baltimore County), Caroline County, 1781–at least 1795; subscription officer, Continental Loan Office, Queen Anne's County, appointed 1779; justice, Orphans' Court, Caroline County, 1782–at least 1792. JURY SERVICE: foreman, grand jury, Eastern Shore, 1792. WEALTH DURING LIFETIME. PERSONAL PROPERTY: assessed value £671.0.0, including 14 slaves and 32 oz. plate, 1783; 6 slaves, 1790. LAND AT FIRST ELECTION: 394 acres in Caroline County (all acquired through his marriage to his second wife). SIGNIFICANT CHANGES

IN LAND BETWEEN FIRST ELECTION AND DEATH: deeds of gift to stepson totaling 124 acres, 1784, 1794. WEALTH AT DEATH. DIED: will probated on January 23, 1796, in Caroline County. PERSONAL PROPERTY: TEV, at least £1,103.1.10 (including at least 5 slaves); FB, £382.10.9. LAND: 268 acres in Caroline County.

DRAPER, LAWRENCE (?–1713). BORN: probably in England. IMMIGRATED: ca. 1676 as a free adult. RESIDED: in Anne Arundel County; Baltimore County, by 1704. MARRIED Elizabeth. CHILDREN. SON: Lawrence. DAUGHTER: Mary, who married Robert Lissby. PRIVATE CAREER. EDUCATION: literate. RELIGIOUS AFFILIATION: Anglican. SOCIAL STATUS AND ACTIVITIES: transported two others with him on his arrival in the colony. OCCUPATIONAL PROFILE: planter. PUBLIC CAREER. LEGISLATIVE SERVICE: Lower House, Anne Arundel County, 1701/2–1704 (elected to the 2nd session). LOCAL OFFICES: Middle Neck Parish Vestry, Anne Arundel County, 1693–1696; justice, Anne Arundel County, 1702–1703, Baltimore County, by 1705/6, sitting in 1709. MILITARY SERVICE: officer, 1697; captain, by 1701/2. WEALTH DURING LIFETIME. LAND AT FIRST ELECTION: at least 250 acres. WEALTH AT DEATH. DIED: will probated on August 5, 1713. PERSONAL PROPERTY: TEV, £345.8.4 sterling.

DRIVER, MATTHEW (1740–1798). BORN: on August 30, 1740, in Dorchester County; younger son. NATIVE: at least third generation. RESIDED: on James Island, Dorchester County, 1740–1742; Ingrams Creek, Dorchester County (later became part of Caroline County), 1742; Bridgetown Hundred, Caroline County, 1776. FAMILY BACKGROUND. FATHER: Matthew Driver, Sr. (1707–by 1776), planter; son of Matthew Driver (?–1714) and wife Levina Pattison; stepson of Moses Lecompte. MOTHER: Renness (?–ca. 1777). BROTHER: Christopher, who married in 1775 Sarah Ringgold. SISTERS: Anna Nancy; Rennis, who married first, James Pritchett, and second, James Lecompt; and Leviney, who possibly married (first name unknown) Fountain. MARRIED on January 12, 1762, Margaret (?–by 1777), widow of John Casson (?–ca. 1761), of Dorchester County; daughter of John Pratt Baynard (?–1747), of Queen Anne's County, planter, and wife Elizabeth Fisher; stepdaughter of Elizabeth Clarke; niece of Esther Baynard, who married *Henry Casson* (?–ca. 1788). Her brother was Thomas (?–1753), of Talbot County, a planter who married his stepsister Hannah Clarke. Her stepbrother was *Joshua Clarke* (?–1781). Her

sister was Rachel. Her first cousin was Esther Casson, who married *Matthew Driver* (1740–1798). Her nieces were Elizabeth Baynard (1748–1809), who married second, *Philemon Downes* (ca. 1741–ca. 1796); Margaret Baynard (1752–by 1788), who married *Henry Downes* (ca. 1748–1816). MARRIED second, on January 21, 1777, Esther, daughter of *Henry Casson* (?–ca. 1788) and wife Esther Baynard. Her brothers were John; James; Thomas; and probably Henry (?–1777). Her first cousin was Margaret Baynard (?–by 1777), who married second, *Matthew Driver* (1740–1798). CHILDREN. SONS: Joshua (1767–?); Henry; and Matthew. STEPSONS: Robert Casson; John Casson; Ferdinando Casson; and Myers Casson. DAUGHTERS: Margaret, who married in 1782 William Robinson; Elizabeth, who married in 1791 *Peter Edmondson* (ca. 1753–1819); Ann, who married by 1807 James M. Broome, of Baltimore City, attorney; and Esther. STEPDAUGHTER: Elizabeth Casson. STEPCHILD: one child, sex unknown (?–1776, died in infancy). PRIVATE CAREER. EDUCATION: literate. ADDITIONAL COMMENTS: founder and supporter of Washington College, Chestertown, Kent County, 1782. OCCUPATIONAL PROFILE: planter, 1764; farmer, 1774; owned a sawmill which he rented out, and a gristmill. PUBLIC CAREER. LEGISLATIVE SERVICE: Lower House, Caroline County, 1778 (elected, but did not attend; discharged on October 28, 1778, for serving as a field officer at time of election), 1779–1780, 1780–1781, 1785. OTHER STATE OFFICE: Constitution Ratification Convention, Caroline County, 1788. LOCAL OFFICES: justice, Caroline County, 1774–at least 1796 (heads list by 1789); chairman, Committee of Observation, Caroline County, 1775; commissioner of tax, Caroline County, commissioned 1777, in office 1782–at least 1785; justice, Orphans' Court, Caroline County, 1778–at least 1797 (heads list by 1789). MILITARY SERVICE: captain, Fourteenth Militia Battalion, 1775; major, Second East Battalion, 1776; commander, Fourteenth Militia Battalion, 1776; president, Caroline County Court for a court-martial proceeding; lieutenant colonel, Fourteenth Militia Battalion, 1777; colonel, Fourteenth Militia Battalion, 1778. WEALTH DURING LIFETIME. PERSONAL PROPERTY: 21 slaves, 1776; assessed value £949.0.0, including 18 slaves and 30 oz. plate, 1783; 24 slaves, 1790. LAND AT FIRST ELECTION: 967 acres in Caroline and Dorchester counties (160 acres from his father 557 acres through his first marriage, 250 acres by purchase and patent), plus control of an additional 469 acres in Dorchester County belonging to his stepson. SIGNIFICANT CHANGES IN LAND BETWEEN FIRST ELECTION AND DEATH: acquired 903 acres in Caroline County through his second marriage, ca. 1788; purchased or patented at least 1,382 acres in Caroline County between 1785 and 1797; sold 263 acres in Caroline County between 1786 and 1796. WEALTH AT DEATH. DIED: on July 23, 1798, in Caroline County. PERSONAL PROPERTY: included 23 slaves, plate, and a sawmill mentioned in his will. LAND: 3,000 acres in Caroline County.

DUCKETT, THOMAS (1744–1806). BORN: on March 26, 1744, in Queen Anne Parish, Prince George's County. NATIVE: third generation. RESIDED: in Prince George's County. FAMILY BACKGROUND. FATHER: Richard Duckett (1704/5–1788), son of Richard Duckett (1675–1754), an immigrant, and wife Charity Jacob. MOTHER: Elizabeth Williams (1719–1798). BROTHERS: Richard; Baruch (ca. 1745–1810); Isaac, who married Margaret (1772–1797), daughter of *Walter Bowie* (1748–1810); Jacob; and Richard Jacob. SISTERS: Eleanor (1737–?), who married (first name unknown) Lyles; Charity, who married in 1757 Thomas Boyd; Elizabeth (ca. 1741–?); Martha, who married (first name unknown) Hall; Ann, who married (first name unknown) Hall; and Rachel, who married first, (first name unknown) Williams, and second, (first name unknown) Turner. MARRIED first, by 1772 Priscilla Fraser (1750–1786), daughter of Allen Bowie, Sr., Gent. (1719–1783) and wife Ann Fraser (1718–1779); granddaughter of both John Bowie, Sr. (ca. 1688–1759) and Rev. John Fraser (?–1742), who was rector of King George's Parish, Prince George's County, and wife Ann Blyzard; niece of *William Bowie* (1721–1791), *George Fraser* (?–1764), and Susannah Fraser, who married *John Hawkins, Jr.* (1713–1757). Her brother was John Fraser. Her half brother was *Fielder Bowie* (ca. 1745–1794). Her sisters were Susannah Fraser (1749–?), who married Matthew Eversfield; Anne (1751–1782), who married Lt. John Smith Brookes. Her first cousins were *Allen Bowie, Jr.* (1737–1803); *Walter Bowie* (1748–1810); *Robert Bowie* (ca. 1750–1818); *George Fraser Hawkins* (ca. 1741–1785); and Susannah Fraser Hawkins, who married *William Bayly* (ca. 1742–1824). MARRIED second, on January 7, 1796, Mary Meek (ca. 1746–1809), widow of *Thomas Clagett* (1740/41–1792), daughter of Enoch Magruder (?–1786) and wife Meek Wade. Her brother was Dennis. Her sisters were Nancy Coombs, who married (first name unknown) Burgess; Elioner, who married (first name unknown) Burgess; Sarah, who married (first name un-

known) Lyles; and Ann, who married (first name unknown) Lowe. CHILDREN. SONS: Allen Bowie (ca. 1775–1809), an associate judge of the Circuit Court of Washington, D.C. at death, who married in 1799 Margaret, daughter of Joseph Howard; John Bowie (ca. 1776–1805), clerk of the Maryland House of Delegates at death; Dr. Richard (ca. 1778–1854), of Milford, Prince George's County; Thomas, who sailed from Baltimore for the West Indies and was lost at sea, 1806. STEPSONS: Judson Magruder Clagett (1769–1800), who married Caroline Hesselius; Thomas Clagett (1773–?); Hector Clagett (1776–?), who died young; Hector Clagett (1780–?); and Hannibal Clagett (1782–1809). DAUGHTERS: Anne Fraser (1772–1808), who married Thomas F. Brooke and died in Allegany County; Susannah, who married Daniel Rawlings. STEPDAUGHTERS: Mary Clagett (1771–1816), who married first, in 1789 Patrick McEldery, and second, Jacob Duckett; Elizabeth Clagett (1778–?), who married in 1794 Henry Addison; and Sarah Magruder Clagett (1780–?), who married in 1800 Upton Bruce. PRIVATE CAREER. EDUCATION: literate. SOCIAL STATUS AND ACTIVITIES: Gent., by 1778. OCCUPATIONAL PROFILE: merchant, planter. PUBLIC CAREER. LEGISLATIVE SERVICE: Lower House, Prince George's County, 1780–1781 (Manufactories 1, 2; Claims 2), 1781–1782 (Claims 1, 2; Public Taxes 1, 2), 1782–1783 (Claims 2), 1783 (Claims); Senate, Western Shore, Term of 1801–1806: 1802 (elected on November 18, 1802, to fill vacancy), 1803, 1804, 1805, Term of 1806–1811: 1806 (died during the Assembly). LOCAL OFFICES: sheriff, Prince George's County, 1777–1779; assessor of the property tax, Prince George's County, in office 1778; collector of supplies for the army, Prince George's County, appointed 1779; judge, Court of Appeals for Tax Assessment, Prince George's County, appointed 1786; justice, Prince George's County, 1788–1792; associate justice, First District Court, Prince George's County, 1793–1802. JURY SERVICE: foreman, grand jury, Prince George's County, 1776. WEALTH DURING LIFETIME. PERSONAL PROPERTY: 35 slaves, 1790; assessed value £1,207.0.0, including 34 slaves and 18 oz. plate, 1796; assessed value £1,584.0.0, including 43 slaves and 96 oz. plate, 1806. LAND AT FIRST ELECTION: 360 acres in Prince George's County (all by purchase). SIGNIFICANT CHANGES IN LAND BETWEEN FIRST ELECTION AND DEATH: purchased at least 370 acres in Prince George's County between 1783 and 1789; sold 40 acres in Prince George's County, 1785; acquired 309 acres in Prince George's County through his second marriage, 1796. ADDI-

TIONAL COMMENTS: Duckett and Samuel Tyler were indebted to the firm of Wallace, Johnson, & Muir, Annapolis merchants, for £2,300.0.0 sterling, and in order to secure payment of this debt they mortgaged a total of 1,090 acres in Prince George's County to the firm in 1789. WEALTH AT DEATH. DIED: on December 2, 1806, in Prince George's County. PERSONAL PROPERTY: TEV, £6,235.11.3 (including 49 slaves and 97 oz. plate); FB, £4,649.7.0. LAND: 929 acres in Prince George's County.

DULANY, BENJAMIN TASKER (1752–1816). BORN: in 1752 in Annapolis; younger son. NATIVE: third generation. RESIDED: in Frederick County until 1777; Alexandria, Fairfax County, Virginia, 1777 until death. FAMILY BACKGROUND. FATHER: *Daniel Dulany, Jr.* (1722–1797). MOTHER: Rebecca (1724–1822), daughter of *Benjamin Tasker* (ca. 1690–1768) and wife Anne Bladen. UNCLES: *Walter Dulany* (?–1773); *Benjamin Tasker, Jr.* (1720/21–1760). AUNTS: Ann Tasker (1723–1817), who married *Samuel Ogle* (1694–1752); Margaret Dulany, who married first, *Alexander Hamilton* (1712–1756), and second, *William Murdock* (?–1769). BROTHER: Daniel (1750–1824), a barrister, Lincoln's Inn, London, England. SISTER: Ann (Nancy) (?–1828), who married on April 21, 1784, William Delasserre, divorced by May 1800 when she petitioned for a change of name for herself and her daughter Rebecca. FIRST COUSIN: *James Heath* (?–1766). OTHER KINSHIP: his great-grandfather was *William Bladen* (1670–1718); his great-uncle was *Thomas Bladen* (1698–1780). MARRIED in February 1773 Elizabeth, daughter of Daniel French (?–by 1773), of "Claremont," Virginia, and wife Penelope Manly; goddaughter of George Washington (1731/32–1799). CHILDREN. Six sons and six daughters, including DAUGHTER: Elizabeth, who married Joseph Forrest. PRIVATE CAREER. EDUCATION: literate; studied at the Rev. Jonathan Boucher's school. RELIGIOUS AFFILIATION: Protestant. SOCIAL STATUS AND ACTIVITIES: Esq., 1773. OCCUPATIONAL PROFILE: planter. PUBLIC CAREER. LEGISLATIVE SERVICE: Convention, Frederick County, 1st, 1774 (appointed, but did not attend). LOCAL OFFICES: clerk, Frederick County, commissioned 1773–out of office by May 1777; Committee of Correspondence, Frederick County, 1774. OUT OF STATE SERVICE: justice, Fairfax County, Virginia, 1787, 1801; trustee, Alexandria Academy, Alexandria, Fairfax County, Virginia. WEALTH DURING LIFETIME. PERSONAL PROPERTY: wife's dowry amounted to £20,000, 1773. LAND AT FIRST ELECTION: 3,058 acres in

Frederick County and a house in Frederick Town, Frederick County (acquired through deeds of gift from his father before his marriage). SIGNIFICANT CHANGES IN LAND BETWEEN FIRST ELECTION AND DEATH: acquired 2 lots in Frederick Town, Frederick County, by 1782; sold at least 229 acres in Frederick County, 1778–1786, plus 2 lots in Frederick Town, Frederick County, 1783. WEALTH AT DEATH. DIED: in 1816 in Virginia; size of estate unknown.

DULANY (DELANEY), DANIEL (1685–1753). BORN: in 1685 in Queen's County, Ireland. IMMIGRATED: in 1703 as an indentured servant with his older brothers William and Joseph from Queen's County, Ireland. Col. George Plater (ca. 1664–1709) purchased his three-year indenture and employed him as a clerk in his law office. RESIDED: in Port Tobacco, Charles County, 1703–ca. 1713; Nottingham Town, Mattapany Hundred, Prince George's County, ca. 1713–1720; Annapolis, Anne Arundel County, 1720–1753. FAMILY BACKGROUND. FATHER: Thomas Dulany, of Queen's County, Ireland. BROTHERS: William; Joseph. MARRIED first, in 1710 Charity (1680–1711), widow of Bayne Smallwood, son of *James Smallwood* (ca. 1639–ca. 1714/15); daughter of *John Courts* (1655/56–1702); stepdaughter of *John Contee* (?–1708); granddaughter of *Robert Henley* (ca. 1617–1684); niece of Elizabeth Courts (1663–?), who married *James Keech* (ca. 1651–1708/9). Her brothers were *John Courts* (1691/92–1747/48); Charles; and William. Her sister was Ann (1693–?). Her first cousins were *Walter Smith* (ca. 1693–1748); Barbara Smith (1693–1764), who married first, *Thomas Holdsworth* (ca. 1692–1718), and second, *Benjamin Mackall* (1675–1761). Her nephew was *Robert Hendly Courts* (?–1774). MARRIED second, in 1717 Rebecca (ca. 1695–1737), daughter of *Walter Smith* (?–1711); granddaughter of both *Richard Smith* (?–ca. 1690) and Richard Hall (?–1688), a prominent Quaker. Her brothers were Richard (?–1732); Walter (ca. 1692–1734). Her sisters were Lucy (1688–1770), who married *Thomas Brooke* (1683–1744); Eleanor (1690–1761), who married *Thomas Addison* (1679–1727); Elizabeth; Ann (1694–1759), who married second, *Thomas Trueman Greenfield* (1682–1733); and Mary. Her nephews were *Richard Brooke* (1716–1783); *John Addison* (1713–1764). Her nieces were Eleanor Brooke, who married *Samuel Beall* (ca. 1713–ca. 1778); Ann Addison (1711/12–1753), who married *William Murdock* (?–1769); and Marianne Greenfield, who married *John Stoddert* (?–1767). MARRIED third, in September 1738 Henrietta Maria (?–1766), widow of Samuel Chew (1704–1736/37); daughter of *Philemon Lloyd* (ca. 1674–1732/33); granddaughter of *Philemon Lloyd* (1646–1685); niece of *James Lloyd* (1679/80–1723), *Edward Lloyd* (1670–1718/19), Anna Maria Lloyd, who married *Richard Tilghman* (1672/73–1738/39), and Margaret Lloyd (1683–?), who married *Matthew Tilghman Ward* (ca. 1676–1741); half niece of Susannah Bennett (1666–1714), who married first, *John Darnall* (?–1684) and second, *Henry Lowe* (?–1717). Her first cousins were *Robert Lloyd* (ca. 1712–1770); Henrietta Maria Lloyd (ca. 1711–1748), who married second, *Samuel Chamberlaine* (1698–1773); Margaret Lloyd (1714–?), who married *William Tilghman* (1711–1782); Ann Lloyd (1723–1794), who married *Matthew Tilghman* (1717/18–1790); *Edward Lloyd* (1711–1770); *Richard Lloyd* (1717–1786); *William Tilghman* (1711–1782); *Edward Tilghman* (1713–1786); *James Tilghman* (1716–1793); *Matthew Tilghman* (1717/18–1790); Henrietta Maria Tilghman (1707–1771), who married first, *George Robins* (1697–1742), and second, *William Goldsborough* (1709–1760); Anna Maria Tilghman (1709–1763), who married first, *William Hemsley* (1703–1736), and second, *Robert Lloyd* (ca. 1712–1770); Mary Tilghman (1702–1736), who married *James Earle, Jr.* (ca. 1694–1739); Dorothy Blake, who married *Charles Carroll* (1691–1755). Henrietta Marie Lloyd Chew Dulany's other relatives included great-grandfathers *Edward Lloyd* (ca. 1620–1696) and *James Neale* (ca. 1615–1684); and second cousins *Michael Earle* (1722–1787) and *Richard Tilghman Earle* (1728/29–1788). CHILDREN. SONS: *Daniel Dulany, Jr.* (1722–1797); Dennis (1730–1779), the clerk of Kent County from 1754 to 1777, who died unmarried, leaving his estate to Mary, widow of his brother Walter; *Walter Dulany* (?–1773); Richard (?–died young); Lloyd (1742–1782), who married Elizabeth, daughter of John Brice and wife Sarah Frisby. Lloyd died in London, England, of wounds received in a duel with Rev. Bennett Allen, former rector of St. Anne's Parish, Anne Arundel County. His widow later married Maj. Walter Dulany, Jr., son of his half brother *Walter Dulany* (?–1773). STEPSONS: Philemon Lloyd Chew (?–1770); Bennett Chew (?–1793), who married Anna Maria, daughter of *Edward Tilghman* (1713–1786); and *Samuel Chew* (by 1734–1786). DAUGHTERS: Rebecca, who married first, James Paul Heath (?–1746), and second, William Hedges, of Cecil County, planter; Rachel, who married first, on November 7, 1741, William Knight, and second, Rev. Henry Addison; Margaret, who married

first, *Alexander Hamilton* (1712–1756), and second, *William Murdock* (?–1769); and Mary. STEPDAUGHTERS: Henrietta Maria Chew (1731–1762), who married *Edward Dorsey* (1718–1760); Margaret Chew (?–1773), who married *John Beale Bordley* (1726/27–1804); and Ann Mary Chew (1736–1774), who married *William Paca* (1740–1799). PRIVATE CAREER. EDUCATION: University of Dublin; law clerk in the office of Col. George Plater; admitted to Gray's Inn, London, England, on February 20, 1716/17. RELIGIOUS AFFILIATION: Anglican, St. Anne's Parish, Anne Arundel County. SOCIAL STATUS AND ACTIVITIES: Mr., 1722; Esq., 1731; Hon., at time of death. OCCUPATIONAL PROFILE: servant/law clerk; planter; officeholder; lawyer, admitted to the following courts: Charles County in August 1709 and sworn in again in March 1709/10; Prince George's County in June 1710; Provincial Court by July 1711; Anne Arundel County in June 1712; Baltimore County in November 1719; Court of Appeals; Chancery Court; Calvert County; St. Mary's County. A land speculator, who invested in warrants that he held until the demand for plantations in the unsettled back country justified the expenses of surveying the land. He was a founder of the Baltimore Ironworks Company, along with *Benjamin Tasker* (ca. 1690–1768), *Charles Carroll* (1691–1755), *Charles Carroll, Sr.* (1702–1782), and Daniel Carroll, of Duddington. His initial investment of £700 in 1731 increased in value to £10,000 by the time of his death. A moneylender by 1730, he was in the loan business on a large scale, dealing in all three types of money, sterling, current money, and tobacco. Most of his debtors were small tradesmen and planters. Dulany also invested in the slave trade, which offered the attraction of double profits, first on the sale of the slaves, and second on loans made to the planters who purchased them. PUBLIC CAREER. LEGISLATIVE SERVICE: Lower House, Annapolis, 1722–1724 (Laws 1–3), Anne Arundel County, 1727 (elected to the 4th session to fill vacancy; Laws 4), 1728–1731 (Laws 1–5), 1732–1734 (Laws 1–Cv; discharged during the convention for accepting an office "of trust and profit" from the government), 1734/35–1737 (elected speaker of the 1st session, but declined for reasons of health; Laws 1, Cv, 2–4), 1738 (elected for both Anne Arundel County and Annapolis, he chose to represent Anne Arundel County; Laws), Annapolis, 1739–1741 (Laws Cv–3), 1742 (Laws 1; appointed to the Council during the 1st session); Upper House, 1742–1744 (appointed during the 1st session), 1745, 1745/46–1748, 1749–1751, 1751–1753 (died before the 4th session). OTHER PROVINCIAL OFFICES: collector of North Potomac, May 1718–January 1718/19; commissary general, 1721 (commissioned jointly with William Holland and Thomas Addison), 1722–1724 (commissioned jointly with William Holland, Thomas Addison, and Thomas Brooke), 1734–1753; attorney general, 1721–1725, 1734–1744; judge, Court of Vice-Admiralty, appointed 1733; agent and receiver general, 1733–1734; Council, 1742–1753 (qualified on September 25, 1742). LOCAL OFFICES: clerk of Indictments, Charles County, appointed 1710; common councilman, Annapolis, elected 1721; St. Anne's Parish Vestry, Anne Arundel County, 1721–1724, 1735 (elected, but did not serve). STANDS ON PUBLIC/PRIVATE ISSUES: In the early years of his public career he was the leader of the country party, espousing the people's cause in the controversy over English statutes affecting the American colonies. In 1728 he published *The Right of the Inhabitants of Maryland to the Benefit of the English Laws.* In 1732 he concluded that the people were entitled to all the benefits of English statutes. Eventually, however, he left the country party to take a place in the proprietary establishment. WEALTH DURING LIFETIME. ANNUAL INCOME: in the 1750s the annual net profit from his investment in the Baltimore Ironworks Company was £400 sterling. LAND AT FIRST ELECTION: ca. 15,340 areas in surveyed tracts and 19,000 acres in warrants in Baltimore, Anne Arundel, Kent, Prince George's, and possibly Calvert counties (all by personal acquisition). By 1720 he converted 6,000 acres of his Baltimore County and Eastern Shore properties into leaseholds, forming a partnership with *John Bradford* (?–1725/26) for locating and surveying unclaimed lands. SIGNIFICANT CHANGES IN LAND BETWEEN FIRST ELECTION AND DEATH: acquired ca. 37,120 acres in Frederick County between 1724 and 1746. He divided 5,000 acres of this land into tracts ranging from 100 to 300 acres, which he then sold for less than they had cost him in order to encourage settlement. After 1739 he actively engaged in selling tracts in the Monocacy and Antietam valleys in Frederick County to German, Scottish, and Welsh immigrants. He sold 1,800 acres, of which more than 600 acres were near his old residence in Prince George's County, in the mid-1720s; he seemed disposed at this time to sell his property in the more settled parts of Prince George's County as he increased his acquisitions to the west and north. In 1745 he surveyed 340 lots, which he named Frederick Town. He leased some lots of land for 1 shilling a year for the first 21 years, and

2 shillings annually thereafter, payable to himself and his heirs in perpetuity. Other lots in the town were sold in fee simple for £4 to £5 for each half acre. WEALTH AT DEATH. DIED: on December 5, 1753; buried next to his second wife Rebecca at St. Anne's Church Cemetery in Annapolis. PERSONAL PROPERTY: TEV, at least £10,921.9.8 current money (including 187 slaves, 98 books, 2,594 oz. plate, and more than 563 gallons of wine). This does not include one of his largest assets, money out on loan. LAND: ca. 10,000 acres in Kent, Baltimore, Anne Arundel, Frederick, and Queen Anne's counties were divided among his heirs. He also controlled 1,585 acres in Anne Arundel County, which went to his stepchildren, the heirs of Samuel Chew.

DULANY (DULANEY), DANIEL, JR. (1722–1797). BORN: on June 28, 1722, in St. Anne's Parish, Annapolis, Anne Arundel County; eldest son. NATIVE: second generation. RESIDED: in Annapolis, 1722–1776; "Hunting Ridge," Baltimore County, 1776–1781; Baltimore Town, 1781–1797. FAMILY BACKGROUND. FATHER: *Daniel Dulany* (1685–1753). MOTHER: Rebecca (ca. 1695–1737), daughter of *Walter Smith* (?–1711) and wife Rachel Hall. STEPMOTHER: Henrietta Maria (?–1766), widow of Samuel Chew (1704–1736/37); daughter of *Philemon Lloyd* (ca. 1674–1732/33). AUNTS: Lucy Smith (1688–1770), who married *Thomas Brooke* (1683–1744); Eleanor Smith (1690–1761), who married *Thomas Addison* (1679–1727); and Anne Smith (1694–1759), who married second, *Thomas Trueman Greenfield* (1682–1733). BROTHERS: *Walter Dulany* (?–1773); Dennis (1730–1779). HALF BROTHERS: Lloyd (1742–1782); Richard (1745–died in infancy). STEPBROTHERS: *Samuel Chew* (by 1734–1786); Philemon Lloyd Chew (?–1770); and Bennett Chew (?–1793). SISTERS: Rebecca; Rachel; Margaret, who married first, Dr. *Alexander Hamilton* (1712–1756), and second, *William Murdock* (?–1769); and Mary. STEPSISTERS: Henrietta Maria Chew (1731–1762), who married *Edward Dorsey* (1718–1760); Margaret Chew (?–1773), who married *John Beale Bordley* (1726/27–1804); and Ann Mary Chew (1736–1774), who married *William Paca* (1740–1799). FIRST COUSINS: *Richard Brooke* (1716–1783); Eleanor Brooke, who married *Samuel Beall* (ca. 1713–ca. 1778); *John Addison* (1713–1764); Rebecca Addison (1703–?), who married first, *James Bowles* (?–ca. 1727/28), and second, *George Plater* (1695–1755); Eleanor Addison (1705–?), who married fourth, *Corbin Lee* (?–1774); Ann Addison (1711/12–1753), who married *William*

Murdock (?–1769); and Marianne Greenfield, who married *John Stoddert* (?–1767). NEPHEW: *James Heath* (?–1766). OTHER KINSHIP: his great-grandfather was *Richard Smith* (?–ca. 1690). MARRIED on September 16, 1749, Rebecca (1724–1822), daughter of *Benjamin Tasker* (ca. 1690–1768); granddaughter of *William Bladen* (1670–1718); niece of *Thomas Bladen* (1698–1780). Her brothers were *Benjamin Tasker, Jr.* (1720/21–1760); and four others who died young. Her sisters were Ann (1723–1817), who married *Samuel Ogle* (1694–1752); Elizabeth (1726–?); and Frances. Her nephew was *Benjamin Ogle* (1748/49–1809). Her niece was Mary Ogle, who married *John Ridout* (1732–1797). CHILDREN. SONS: Daniel (1750–1824), who closed his law practice and sailed for London, England, in 1774. As a result, his extensive properties in the province were confiscated during the Revolution. He later became a barrister of Lincoln's Inn, London, England; *Benjamin Tasker Dulany* (1752–1816). DAUGHTER: Ann (?–1828), who married on April 21, 1784, William Delasserre; divorced by May 1800, when she petitioned for a change of surname for herself and her daughter Rebecca. PRIVATE CAREER. EDUCATION: completed Eton, 1738; entered Clare College, Cambridge University, in January 1739 as a pensioner; entered Middle Temple, 1742; called to the bar in 1746, a form of recognition rarely accorded a colonist. RELIGIOUS AFFILIATION: Anglican, St. Anne's Parish, Annapolis. SOCIAL STATUS AND ACTIVITIES: member of a prominent and affluent family. OCCUPATIONAL PROFILE: lawyer, admitted to the following courts: Provinical Court in October 1747; Anne Arundel County in November 1747; Prince George's County in November 1747; Court of Chancery by December 1747; Frederick County in March 1748/49. Retired from active practice in 1763; planter. Daniel and his brother *Walter Dulany* (?–1773) jointly held one share in the Baltimore Ironworks Company, which they had inherited from their father, and they controlled another share held by the Tasker family. The Carroll family, which owned three shares, frequently combined to outvote the Dulanys. There was a history of ill-feelings between the Dulany and the Carroll families that worsened over time. PUBLIC CAREER. LEGISLATIVE SERVICE: Lower House, Frederick County, 1749 (election voided on June 8, 1749), 1751–1754 (Laws 1–6), Annapolis, 1756–1757 (elected to the 5th session to fill vacancy); Upper House, 1757–1758, 1758–1761, 1762–1763, 1765–1766, 1768–1770, 1771, 1773–1774. OTHER PROVINCIAL OFFICES: commissary general, commissioned jointly with *Benjamin*

Tasker (ca. 1690–1768), in 1754, resigned 1756, commissioned again in 1759, resigned 1761; Council, 1757–1776 (appointed and qualified on June 12, 1757); secretary of Maryland, sworn 1761, recommissioned 1773, office abolished 1776; commissioner for the sale of proprietary manors and reserved lands, 1766–1771. LOCAL OFFICES: justice, Frederick County, in office at least by 1749–out of office by 1751 (quorum, at least 1749–1751); recorder, Annapolis, 1754–1765; mayor, Annapolis, 1764–1765. STANDS ON PUBLIC/PRIVATE ISSUES: argued against the Stamp Act, but was opposed to the actions of the Sons of Liberty; under the pseudonym "Antilon," he debated *Charles Carroll of Carrollton* (1737–1832) in a series of newspaper articles concerning the Fee Bill controversy, 1773; espoused neutrality during the Revolution. WEALTH DURING LIFETIME. PERSONAL PROPERTY: 6 slaves, 1790; as part of their one share of the Baltimore Ironworks, he and his brother *Walter Dulany* (?–1773) had an interest in the company's furnaces, forges, slaves, indentured servants, and the sloop *Baltimore.* LAND AT FIRST ELECTION: 14,000 acres in Frederick County, plus 170 town lots in Frederick Town, Frederick County (deed of gift from his father, 1748); owned one-half share, or a ten percent interest, in the Baltimore Ironworks, which comprised 20,000 acres in Baltimore County. SIGNIFICANT CHANGES IN LAND BETWEEN FIRST ELECTION AND DEATH: controlled 2,150 acres in Kent and Frederick counties as guardian of his half brother Lloyd, 1752; sold 3,300 acres composed of farmsteads, consisting of 50-acre to 300-acre lots for cash or on credit, plus 144 lots in Frederick Town, Frederick County, 1769; deeded all of his remaining real property to his sons, except for 3,000 acres, 1772–1775. WEALTH AT DEATH. DIED: on March 17, 1797, in Baltimore City; buried at St. Paul's Church, Baltimore City. LAND: ca. 3,000 acres in Frederick and Anne Arundel counties.

DULANY, WALTER (?–1773). BORN: of age by 1743; second son. NATIVE: second generation. RESIDED: in Annapolis, Anne Arundel County. FAMILY BACKGROUND. FATHER: *Daniel Dulany* (1685–1753). MOTHER: Rebecca (ca. 1695–1737), daughter of *Walter Smith* (?–1711). STEPMOTHER: Henrietta Maria (?–1766), widow of Samuel Chew (1704–1736/37); daughter of *Philemon Lloyd* (ca. 1674–1732/33). AUNTS: Lucy Smith (1688–1770), who married *Thomas Brooke* (1683–1744); Eleanor Smith (1690–1761), who married *Thomas Addison* (1679–1727); and Ann Smith (1694–1759), who married second, *Thomas Trueman Greenfield*

(1682–1733). BROTHERS: *Daniel Dulany, Jr.* (1722–1797); Dennis (1730–1779). HALF BROTHERS: Lloyd (1742–1782); Richard (?–died in infancy). STEPBROTHERS: *Samuel Chew* (by 1734–1786); Philemon Lloyd Chew (?–1770); Bennett Chew (?–1793). SISTERS: Rebecca; Rachel; Margaret, who married first, Dr. *Alexander Hamilton* (1712–1756), and second, *William Murdock* (?–1769); and Mary. STEPSISTERS: Henrietta Maria Chew (1731–1762), who married *Edward Dorsey* (1718–1760); Margaret Chew (?–1773), who married *John Beale Bordley* (1726/27–1804); and Ann Mary Chew (1736–1774), who married *William Paca* (1740–1799). FIRST COUSINS: *Richard Brooke* (1716–1783); Eleanor Brooke, who married *Samuel Beall* (ca. 1713–ca. 1778); *John Addison* (1713–1764); Ann Addison (1711/12–1753), who married *William Murdock* (?–1769); and Marianne Greenfield, who married *John Stoddert* (?–1767). NEPHEWS: *Benjamin Tasker Dulany* (1752–1816); *James Heath* (?–1766). MARRIED ca. 1745 Mary, daughter of Richard Grafton, a wealthy landowner and merchant of New Castle, Delaware. CHILDREN. SONS: Daniel, of Walter (?–1783), who was living in London by 1781; Walter, Jr., who married ca. 1785 Elizabeth Brice, widow of his half uncle Lloyd Dulany (1742–1782); and Grafton (?–1778). DAUGHTERS: Rebecca, who married first, in 1767 Thomas Addison, Jr., and second, Thomas Hanson (1750–1810), son of *Samuel Hanson* (1716–1794); Mary, who married (first name unknown) Fitzhugh; Margaret, who married ca. 1771 Rev. John Montgomery; and Catherine, who married (first name unknown) Belt. PRIVATE CAREER. EDUCATION: literate; apprenticed to a merchant in Philadelphia, Pennsylvania, 1735. RELIGIOUS AFFILIATION: Anglican, St. Anne's Parish, Anne Arundel County. SOCIAL STATUS AND ACTIVITIES: Gent., 1747; Esq., 1764; member of the Tuesday Club. OCCUPATIONAL PROFILE: merchant; investor; contractor; officeholder; controlled his father's share of the Baltimore Ironworks Company jointly with his brother *Daniel Dulany, Jr.* (1722–1797) until 1759 when he sold his interest to his brother Daniel; handled the sale of the indentures of German immigrants for his father, 1752; served as contractor for public buildings and a wharf in Annapolis, 1763–1766. PUBLIC CAREER. LEGISLATIVE SERVICE: Lower House, Annapolis, 1745/46–1748, 1749–1751 (Laws Cv–3; discharged from the 2nd session for serving as deputy commissary of Anne Arundel County; reelected to the 2nd session and seated), 1751–1754 (Bills of Credit 1–6), 1754–1757 (Bills of Credit 1–6), 1757–1758 (Bills of Credit 1, Cv, 2), 1758–1761

(Bills of Credit Cv 1, 1, Cv 2, 2, 3, Cv 3), 1762–1763 (Bills of Credit 1, 2; Grievances 1, 2), 1765 (discharged on September 24, 1765, for serving as naval officer of the Patuxent; reelected to the 2nd session; Bills of Credit 2; Grievances 2; reelection voided on November 12, 1765, for serving as mayor of Annapolis at the time of his election); Upper House, 1768–1770 (Claims-Bills of Credit 1–4), 1771 (Claims-Bills of Credit), 1773. OTHER PROVINCIAL OFFICES: naval officer, Patuxent, 1765–1767 (resigned); commissary general, 1767–1773; Council, 1767–1773 (appointed and qualified on February 11, 1767). LOCAL OFFICES: deputy commissary, Anne Arundel County, 1749–1754; churchwarden, St. Anne's Parish, Anne Arundel County, in office 1749–1750, 1764–ca. 1765; St. Anne's Parish Vestry, Anne Arundel County, in office 1751–1754, ca. 1765–1768; common councilman, Annapolis, 1756–1764; alderman, Annapolis, in office 1764–1765, 1767; mayor, Annapolis, 1766–1767 (elected September 1765 and in office by October 1765). WEALTH DURING LIFETIME. ANNUAL INCOME: estimated gross income per year as commissary general £1,000, 1767–1769. ADDITIONAL COMMENTS: he borrowed heavily from at least 1770 until his death. His principal creditors included *John Cadwalader* (1741/42–1786), Upton Scott, and Osgood Hanbury & Company, of London, merchants. LAND AT FIRST ELECTION: none in his own name, but probably controlled 5,258 acres in Baltimore County that was formally deeded to him by his father as a gift in 1747. SIGNIFICANT CHANGES IN LAND BETWEEN FIRST ELECTION AND DEATH: received an additional 363 acres in Baltimore County, plus at least 1 lot, warehouses, and land on the dock in Annapolis as gifts from his father, 1747–1748. Lost 294 acres in a resurvey of his Baltimore County land in 1750. Inherited 1,231 acres in Baltimore and Anne Arundel counties under the terms of his father's will in 1753. Purchased 12.5 lots in Annapolis, 1753–1759. In 1765 Walter and his brother *Daniel Dulany, Jr.* (1722–1797) patented 1,950 acres in Frederick County in individual tracts of between 50 and 200 acres each. This was a part of the acreage for which their father had received warrants, but which he had not patented. Purchased 1,250 acres and sold 363 acres in Baltimore County in 1767. Purchased 1,126 acres in Anne Arundel County shortly before his death. WEALTH AT DEATH. DIED: on September 20, 1773, in Annapolis. PERSONAL PROPERTY: TEV, £6,260.6.6 current money (including ca. 58 slaves, 412 oz. plate, a harpsichord, and 51 books); FB, estate overpaid

£768.2.5. Dulany's estate was not settled until 1800. Debts paid by his administrator included £3,041.13.7 to *John Cadwalader* (1741/42–1786). LAND: 8,571 acres in Anne Arundel and Baltimore counties and 14.5 lots in Annapolis, plus 1,950 acres in Frederick County held jointly with *Daniel Dulany, Jr.* (1722–1797). After his father's death Daniel Dulany, of Walter mortgaged 6,544 acres in Anne Arundel and Baltimore counties and the "mansion house" with adjacent lots in Annapolis to Osgood Hanbury & Company to secure a debt of £9,121.13.7 sterling that Walter owed the company at the time of his death.

DUNN (DUNNE), JAMES BROWN (1751–1788).

BORN: on May 9, 1751, in Kent County; eldest of seven sons. NATIVE: fifth generation. RESIDED: in Upper Langford's Bay Hundred, Kent County. FAMILY BACKGROUND. FATHER: James Dunn (1728–?), son of *Robert Dunn* (1693–1745). MOTHER: Martha Ann. STEPMOTHER: Elizabeth. HALF BROTHERS: Hezekiah (1757–?); Robert (1759–?); James (1764–?); Michael (1766–?); Daruns (1767–?); and Curtis (1769–?). HALF SISTERS: Ann (1754–?); Elizabeth (1756–?); and Rebecca (1761–?). MARRIED Elizabeth, who subsequently married Gideon Comegys. CHILDREN. SONS: James Lorain; Thomas; and James. DAUGHTERS: Martha Ann Brown; Mary Ann; Anne Elizabeth; Anne; and Rebecca. PRIVATE CAREER. EDUCATION: literate. RELIGIOUS AFFILIATION: Anglican, St. Paul's Parish, Kent County. SOCIAL STATUS AND ACTIVITIES: Gent., 1783. OCCUPATIONAL PROFILE: planter. PUBLIC CAREER. LEGISLATIVE SERVICE: Lower House, Kent County, 1783. LOCAL OFFICE: St. Paul's Parish Vestry, Kent County, in office 1780. WEALTH DURING LIFETIME. PERSONAL PROPERTY: assessed value £613.0.0, including 14 slaves and 24 oz. plate, 1783. LAND AT FIRST ELECTION: 384 acres in Kent County. WEALTH AT DEATH. DIED: between June 6 and November 7, 1788, in Kent County. PERSONAL PROPERTY: TEV, £897.6.4 current money (including 11 slaves, 21 oz. plate, and books); FB, estate overpaid £163.10.1. LAND: probably 384 acres in Kent County.

DUNN, ROBERT (ca. 1630–1676).

BORN: ca. 1630, probably in England. IMMIGRATED: in 1649 as a free adult. RESIDED: in Kent County. MARRIED Jane (Joan), stepdaughter of William Elliot. She subsequently married Anthony Workman. CHILDREN. SON: Robert (1674–1729), who married Mary, daughter of *William Harris* (ca. 1644–1712). DAUGHTERS: Susanna; Joan; Rebecca; and Alice. PRIVATE CAREER. EDUCATION: literate. RELIGIOUS AFFILIATION: converted to Quakerism, 1658. SOCIAL STATUS AND ACTIVITIES: not called Mr. on first appearance in the records; his son became an Anglican vestryman, but held no major public office. OCCUPATIONAL PROFILE: planter. PUBLIC CAREER. LEGISLATIVE SERVICE: Lower House, Kent County, 1663–1664, 1669. LOCAL OFFICES: justice, Kent County, 1664–1673 (president, 1669–1673); keeper of weights and measures, Kent County, 1671; sheriff, Kent County, 1673–1676. WEALTH DURING LIFETIME. LAND AT FIRST ELECTION: 200 acres; 700 acres by 1669. WEALTH AT DEATH. DIED: on May 12, 1676. PERSONAL PROPERTY: TEV, 60,661 pounds of tobacco (including 1 slave, 1 servant, books, and various debts owed the estate totaling 12,197 pounds of tobacco); FB, 36,790 pounds of tobacco. LAND: 750 acres.

DUNN, ROBERT (1693–1745).

BORN: in 1693 in Kent County. NATIVE: third generation. RESIDED: in St. Paul's Parish, Kent County. FAMILY BACKGROUND. FATHER: Robert Dunn (1674–1729), of Kent County; vestryman of St. Paul's Parish, Kent County; son of *Robert Dunn* (ca. 1630–1676). MOTHER: Mary (?–1709), daughter of *William Harris* (ca. 1644–1712). STEPMOTHER: Mary, widow of Robert Park (?–1708). UNCLE: *James Harris* (1682–1743). BROTHERS: William (?–1728), who married Martha, daughter of Michael Miller (1675–1738); James (1699–died young). SISTERS: Jane (1701–?); Mary. STEPSISTERS: Elizabeth Park (?–1760), who married first, in 1705 Charles Ringgold, and second, Philip Davis (?–1749); Ann Park, who married by 1711 *William Blackiston* (?–1737). MARRIED first, Ann (1698–?), daughter of Michael Miller (1675–1738) and wife Martha Wickes; granddaughter of both *Joseph Wickes* (ca. 1620–1692) and *Michael Miller* (ca. 1644–1699). MARRIED second, Martha (?–1746). CHILDREN. SONS: James (1728–?), who married first, Martha Ann, and second, Elizabeth; Darius (1731–?); and Hezekiah (1734–?). DAUGHTERS: Martha; Rebecca (1726–?), who married by 1744 Joseph Wickes. PRIVATE CAREER. EDUCATION: probably literate. RELIGIOUS AFFILIATION: Anglican, St. Paul's Church, St. Paul's Parish, Kent County. SOCIAL STATUS AND ACTIVITIES: Gent., 1745; Mr., 1747. OCCUPATIONAL PROFILE: probably a planter. PUBLIC CAREER. LEGISLATIVE SERVICE: Lower House, Kent County, 1722–1724. LOCAL OFFICES: churchwarden, St. Paul's Parish, Kent County, in office 1725; justice, Kent County, 1735–at least 1743 (quorum, 1738–at least 1743). MILITARY

SERVICE: captain, 1724. **WEALTH DURING LIFE-TIME.** LAND AT FIRST ELECTION: 93 acres in Kent County (by purchase). SIGNIFICANT CHANGES IN LAND BETWEEN FIRST ELECTION AND DEATH: acquired 1,257 acres in Kent County (500 devised from father), 1729–1742. **WEALTH AT DEATH.** DIED: in 1745 in Kent County. PERSONAL PROPERTY: TEV, £2,295.6.0 current money (including 29 slaves, 55 oz. plate, 26 books, and additional law titles); FB, £2,046.4.7. LAND: 1,350 acres in Kent County.

DURAND, WILLIAM (?–1672). BORN: probably in England. IMMIGRATED: in 1648/49 as a free adult with his wife and daughter from Virginia. RESIDED: in Broad Neck Hundred, Anne Arundel County; Talbot County, probably after 1668. ADDITIONAL COMMENTS: in Virginia by 1635; he received a patent for 800 acres on the Rappahannock River in 1642, but was banished from Virginia in 1648 for his role as a leading elder of the nonconforming Puritans and lost his land there. **MARRIED** Alice. **CHILDREN.** DAUGHTERS: Alice; Elizabeth, who married *Samuel Withers* (?–1671). **PRIVATE CAREER.** EDUCATION: literate. RELIGIOUS AFFILIATION: Protestant; Quaker by 1656. SOCIAL STATUS AND ACTIVITIES: he brought seven others with him to Maryland; Gent. on arrival; he was temporarily out of the province in 1655/56; at the time of his death he was a widower planning to marry Elizabeth Ayler. OCCUPATIONAL PROFILE: planter. **PUBLIC CAREER.** LEGISLATIVE SERVICE: Assembly, Providence (Anne Arundel County) 1654; Parliamentary Commission, 1654–probably 1657/58 (no record of service after 1655). OTHER PROVINCIAL OFFICES: secretary of the province, 1654–1657/58; justice, Provincial Court, 1654–1657/58. (no record of service after 1655); clerk, Assembly, 1654. **WEALTH DURING LIFETIME.** LAND AT FIRST ELECTION: at least 800 acres. **WEALTH AT DEATH.** DIED: will probated on December 6, 1672. PERSONAL PROPERTY: TEV, 21,849 pounds of tobacco (including 1 servant); FB, 9,378 pounds of tobacco. LAND: at least 300 acres.

DURHAM, SAMUEL (ca. 1728–ca. 1787). BORN: ca. 1728 in Baltimore County (later became Harford County); eldest son. NATIVE: probably fourth generation. RESIDED: in Bush River Lower Hundred, Harford County. **FAMILY BACKGROUND.** FATHER: Samuel Durham (?–1772), of Baltimore County, a planter. MOTHER: Elinor (ca. 1703–?), daughter of Thomas Smithson (?–ca. 1732) and wife Ann. BROTHERS: Joshua (ca. 1733–?), who

married Sarah Thompson; Mordecai (1734–1778); Daniel (1736–by 1772); John (1738–by 1772); and Aquilla (ca. 1746–?). SISTERS: Hannah (1740–?); Sarah, who married first, Thomas Thompson, and second, (first name unknown) Ramsey. **MARRIED** his first cousin Ann (ca. 1738–?), daughter of Thomas Smithson (?–1795) and wife Mary. Her brothers were Nathaniel; Thomas (?–by 1795); Archibald; Daniel; and *William Smithson* (ca. 1744–1809). Her sisters were Margaret Baslin; Cassandra Green; Elizabeth Durham; and Sarah Durham. **CHILDREN.** SONS: Samuel, Jr. (ca. 1765–?); Thomas (ca. 1768–?); Aquila (ca. 1770–?); Lloyd (ca. 1771–?); Lee (ca. 1774–?); and Joseph. DAUGHTERS: Mary (ca. 1756–by 1786); Susannah (ca. 1759–?); Elinor (ca. 1761–?); and Charlotte. **PRIVATE CAREER.** EDUCATION: literate. OCCUPATIONAL PROFILE: planter. **PUBLIC CAREER.** LEGISLATIVE SERVICE: Convention, Harford County, 5th, 1775. JURY SERVICE: grand jury, Harford County, 1774; petit jury, Harford County, 1783. MILITARY SERVICE: private, Company No. 11, Harford County Militia, enrolled 1775. **WEALTH DURING LIFETIME.** PERSONAL PROPERTY: 8 slaves, 1 white servant, 1776; assessed value £412.16.8, including 8 slaves and 2 oz. plate, 1783. LAND AT FIRST ELECTION: 273 acres in Harford County (248 acres from his father by gift and bequest). **WEALTH AT DEATH.** DIED: between July 6, 1786, and February 27, 1787, in Harford County. PERSONAL PROPERTY: TEV, at least £787.0.0 current money (including 13 slaves, plate, books, and a still with equipment). LAND: 273 acres in Harford County.

DUVALL, GABRIEL (1752–1844). BORN: on December 6, 1752, in Prince George's County; sixth child, second son. NATIVE: fourth generation. RESIDED: in Annapolis, Anne Arundel County, from at least 1777 until at least 1802, when he moved to Washington, D.C., and "Marietta," Prince George's County. **FAMILY BACKGROUND.** FATHER: Benjamin Duvall (1719–ca. 1801), son of Benjamin Duvall (?–1774). MOTHER: Susanna (1717/18–1794), daughter of Edward Tyler and wife Elizabeth Duvall. BROTHERS: Benjamin (1746–?), who married ca. 1772 Jemima Taylor; Edward (1755–1780); Isaac (1757–1781); and William (1762–died young). SISTERS: Elizabeth (1744–1777), who married ca. 1770 William Clarke; Susanna (1746–1807), who married first, in 1770 William Higgins, and second, Joseph R. Hodges; Delilah (1747–1839); Sarah (1751–?), who married Amos Simpson; and Sophia (1760–died young). FIRST COUSIN: *Samuel Duvall* (1748–1811). OTHER

KINSHIP: his great-grandfathers were Mareen Duvall (?–1694), of "Middle Plantation," Prince George's County, and *Robert Tyler* (ca. 1671–1738). MARRIED probably on July 24, 1787, Mary (ca. 1762–1790), daughter of Capt. Robert Bryce (?–ca. 1771), of Annapolis, and wife Frances Wilson. Her brother was John (1771–1805). MARRIED second, on May 5, 1795, Jane (1757–1834), daughter of Capt. James Gibbon, of Philadelphia, Pennsylvania. CHILDREN. SON: Edmund Bryce (1790–1831), who married Augusta Caroline McCausland (1798–1832). DAUGHTER: possibly Polly (by 1794–?). PRIVATE CAREER. EDUCATION: studied law. RELIGIOUS AFFILIATION: Anglican; maintained pews in St. Anne's Church, Annapolis, and at his parish (probably Queen Anne Parish) in Prince George's County. SOCIAL STATUS AND ACTIVITIES: Esq. OCCUPATIONAL PROFILE: lawyer, admitted to the following courts: Prince George's County in 1778; Annapolis Mayor's Court by 1781; Anne Arundel County by 1783. Appeared in the Anne Arundel County Court almost 600 times between 1783 and 1792. Maintained his practice in Prince George's County until at least 1823. Officeholder. In 1808 Duvall helped to organize the Columbia Manufacturing Company, a cotton factory in Washington, D.C. PUBLIC CAREER. LEGISLATIVE SERVICE: Lower House, Annapolis, 1787–1788 (Grievances 1, 2; Laws to Expire 2), 1788, 1789 (Laws to Expire), 1790, 1791–1792, 1792, 1793. OTHER STATE OFFICES: clerk, 4th–9th Conventions, 1775–1776; clerk, Council of Safety, in office 1776; clerk, Lower House, appointed 1777; clerk, Commission for the Sale of Confiscated British Property, appointed February 1781; Commission for the Sale of Confiscated British Property, appointed July 1781–resigned November 1782 but attended property sales as commissioner until November 1785; Executive Council, 1782–1783, 1783–1784 (resigned on July 2, 1784), 1785–1786 (resigned on April 20, 1786, because of his opinion that ". . .the late Act to vest certain Powers in the Governor and Council, is repugnant to the Constitution and Form of Government of this State. . ."); judge, General Court, 1796–1802 (resigned); chancellor and judge, Land Office, appointed 1806 (refused); chief judge, First District Court, appointed 1806 (refused); judge, Court of Appeals, appointed 1806 (declined). LOCAL OFFICES: prosecutor, Mayor's Court, Annapolis, in office 1781–1784; recorder, Annapolis, 1788–1801; Board of Visitors and Governors, St. John's College, Annapolis, in office 1792–1802; alderman, Annapolis, in office 1798; Maryland Senate elector, Annapolis, elected 1801. MILITARY SERVICE:

major, Anne Arundel County Militia, appointed 1794. OUT OF STATE SERVICE: representative, U.S. Congress, 1794–1795 (elected to fill vacancy; seated on November 11, 1794), 1795–1796 (resigned on March 28, 1796, to become judge of the General Court of Maryland); offered position as chief judge of the District of Columbia, 1801 (declined); first comptroller of the U.S. Treasury, December 15, 1802–November 21, 1811; associate justice, U.S. Supreme Court, 1811–1835 (appointed on November 15, 1811, by President James Madison; resigned on January 15, 1835, because of deafness). ADDITIONAL COMMENTS: Thomas Jefferson wrote to Duvall in 1802 expressing his "sincere esteem and high consideration" of him, noting he had "so much merited the public confidence." Although John Quincy Adams remembered Duvall as a "feeble individual" domineered by William Pinkney, John Marshall praised him upon his resignation from the Supreme Court for "the fidelity with which he discharged the part which had devolved" on him, for his "private virtues," and the "purity of his public life." STANDS ON PUBLIC/PRIVATE ISSUES: publicly defended Thomas Jefferson in 1800 against the charge that he had fled from Richmond before the British advance during the Revolution. Described Jefferson as "the Friend of the People" prior to the presidential election of 1800. WEALTH DURING LIFETIME. PERSONAL PROPERTY: assessed value £90.0.0, Annapolis, 1783; at least 8 slaves, Prince George's County, 1798. LAND AT FIRST ELECTION: probably none. SIGNIFICANT CHANGES IN LAND BETWEEN FIRST ELECTION AND DEATH: prior to 1798 Duvall's father gave him the 660 acres in Prince George's County that the family had owned for at least two generations and on which stood the Duvall home, "Marietta." Duvall also owned a large brick dwelling in Annapolis in 1798. Shortly before his death, Duvall sold a tract of land that he owned on the South River in Anne Arundel County and purchased a three-fifths interest in 197 acres in Prince George's County. WEALTH AT DEATH. DIED: on March 6, 1844, at "Marietta," Prince George's County; interred in the family burial ground on the estate. PERSONAL PROPERTY: TEV, $54,208.96 current money (including 36 slaves, 271 oz. plate, a law library of 528 volumes and an additional 400 volumes on other subjects, and bank stock valued at $14,260.00); FB, $41,863.89, not including legacies of $14,250.45. LAND: ca. 800 acres in Prince George's County. ADDITIONAL COMMENTS: His principal heirs were his sister Sarah Simpson and his grandchildren Marcus, Edmund, Mary Frances, and Gabriella Augusta Duvall.

DUVALL, SAMUEL (1748–1811). BORN: on December 24, 1748, in Rock Creek Parish, Frederick County; eldest son. NATIVE: fourth generation. RESIDED: in Frederick Town, Frederick County, 1788 until death. FAMILY BACKGROUND. FATHER: Capt. William Duvall, Gent. (1723–1810), son of Benjamin Duvall (before 1700–1774). MOTHER: Priscilla Prewitt. BROTHERS: William (1750–1826), who married Mary Prather; Prewitt Duvall (1752–?), who joined the British navy; and Col. Mareen Duvall (1767–1852), who married first, Rachel Howard, and second, Polly Chambers. SISTER: Sophia (1755–?), who married Henry Bayne. FIRST COUSIN: *Gabriel Duvall* (1752–1844). MARRIED on January 21, 1774, Priscilla Ann (1756–1836), daughter of John Dawson and wife Martha Anne Marbury (1714–?). CHILDREN. SONS: Hampden, died without progeny; Algernon Sidney, died without progeny; Grafton (1780–1841), who resided in Frederick County, was a physician and a member of the Executive Council of Maryland, elected December 1819 and December 1820. Grafton married in 1804 Elizabeth Whitaker Hawkins (1785–1831). PRIVATE CAREER. EDUCATION: literate. RELIGIOUS AFFILIATION: Anglican, All Saints' Parish, Frederick County. SOCIAL STATUS AND ACTIVITIES: Mr., 1782; Gent., 1788; Esq., 1790. OCCUPATIONAL PROFILE: surveyor. PUBLIC CAREER. LEGISLATIVE SERVICE: Lower House, Frederick County, 1781–1782 (Manufactories 1); 1782–1783 (Elections 2). LOCAL OFFICES: deputy surveyor, Frederick County, 1783–1811; All Saints' Vestry, Frederick County, 1811 (elected, but did not serve). MILITARY SERVICE: helped organize volunteer troop of light dragoons, Frederick County, 1781. WEALTH DURING LIFETIME. PERSONAL PROPERTY: 2 slaves, 1790. SIGNIFICANT CHANGES IN LAND BETWEEN FIRST ELECTION AND DEATH: purchased 2,000 acres in Frederick County, 1784; purchased and sold approximately 3,700 acres in Frederick County, 1784–1802; owned one-half lot in Cumberland, Allegany County, 1793. WEALTH AT DEATH. DIED: on January 17, 1811, in Frederick County. PERSONAL PROPERTY: TEV, £414.12.4 current money (including 1 slave); FB, estate overpaid £284.3.0.

EARLE, JAMES, SR. (?–1734). BORN: probably in Talbot County, of age by 1709. NATIVE: second generation. RESIDED: at "Heathworth," Queen Anne's County. FAMILY BACKGROUND. FATHER: James Earle (1631–1684), of Talbot County, immigrated in 1683 from Ireland. STEPFATHER: (name unknown). MOTHER: Rhoda (ca. 1640–1714). BROTHERS: John; Michael (?–1709), a lawyer, who married first, Sarah Stevens (?–1688), and second, Anne Carpenter (?–ca. 1709); and Joseph (?–1740). SISTER: Lana, who married Christopher Denny. Eight other brothers and sisters, names unknown. NEPHEW: *James Earle, Jr.* (ca. 1694–1739). NIECE: Elizabeth Earle (ca. 1694–?), who married *William Turbutt* (1683/84–1739). MARRIED Anne. CHILDREN. SONS: John, of Ogletown, Queen Anne's County, until 1734, then "Heathworth," Queen Anne's County, a contractor and builder, who married Martha, daughter of Thomas Ringgold; James, a sea captain, who married in 1737 Ann Scott. DAUGHTERS: Elizabeth; Ann; Rhodah, who married Thomas Whittington; and Margaret, who married Christopher Cox. PRIVATE CAREER. EDUCATION: literate. RELIGIOUS AFFILIATION: Protestant. SOCIAL STATUS AND ACTIVITIES: Gent. at death. OCCUPATIONAL PROFILE: probably a planter. PUBLIC CAREER. LEGISLATIVE SERVICE: Lower House, Queen Anne's County, 1719–1721/22 (Accounts 2–5). LOCAL OFFICES: justice, Queen Anne's County, 1715–at least 1730; St. Paul's Parish Vestry, Queen Anne's County, in office 1722–1726; visitor, Queen Anne's County Free School, in office 1723; St. Luke's Parish Vestry, Queen Anne's County, in office 1728/29–1731 and 1734. WEALTH DURING LIFETIME. LAND AT FIRST ELECTION: 760 acres in Queen Anne's County (at least 700 acres by purchase). SIGNIFICANT CHANGES IN LAND BETWEEN FIRST ELECTION AND DEATH: purchased 1,180 acres in Queen Anne's County, between 1720 and 1727. WEALTH AT DEATH. DIED: between May 29 and June 18, 1734, in Queen Anne's County. PERSONAL PROPERTY: TEV, £970.8.9 current money (including 15 slaves, plate, law books, and other books); FB, £756.8.6. LAND: 1,856 acres in Queen Anne's County, plus 1 lot in Ogletown, Queen Anne's County.

EARLE, JAMES, JR. (ca. 1694–1739). BORN: on February 17, ca. 1694, in Talbot County; a twin and eldest son. NATIVE: third generation. RESIDED: in Queen Anne's County; "Corsica," Queen Anne's County, built after his first marriage. FAMILY BACKGROUND. FATHER: Michael Earle (?–1709), a lawyer, who married first, Sarah Stevens (?–1688), by whom he had no issue; son of James Earle (1631–1684), of Talbot County, who immigrated in 1683 from Ireland. GUARDIAN: *Richard Tilghman* (1672/73–1738/39). MOTHER: Anne (?–ca. 1709), daughter of Symon Carpenter (?–1670) and wife Elizabeth (?–1702); stepdaughter of *Henry Coursey* (ca. 1629–1695). UNCLE: *James Earle, Sr.* (?–1734). STEPUNCLE: *Henry Coursey* (1662–1707). BROTHERS: (first name unknown), died the day after birth; Carpenter (1697–1728), who married Mary Thomas. SISTER: Elizabeth (ca. 1694–?), his twin, who married *William Turbutt* (1683/84–1739). FIRST COUSIN: Jane Lillingston (?–by 1746), who married first, *John Wells* (?–1714), and second, *Thomas Hammond* (1693–?). NIECES: Anna Maria Turbutt, who married *Edward Tilghman* (1713–1786); Elizabeth Turbutt (?–ca. 1760), who married *Thomas Harris* (?–1760). MARRIED first, on October 12, 1721, Mary (1702–ca. 1736), daughter of *Richard Tilghman* (1672/73–1738/39); granddaughter of *Philemon Lloyd* (1646–1685); niece of *Edward Lloyd* (1670–1718/19), *Philemon Lloyd* (ca. 1674–1732/33), *James Lloyd* (1679/80–1723), Rebecca Tilghman (?–1725), who married *Simon Wilmer* (ca. 1656–1699), and Margaret Lloyd (1683–1747), who married *Matthew Tilghman Ward* (ca. 1676–1741); half niece of Susanna Bennett (1664–1714), who married first, *John Darnall* (?–1684), and second, *Henry Lowe* (?–1717). Her brothers were Philemon (1704–ca. 1724); Richard (1705–1768); *William Tilghman* (1711–1782); *Edward Tilghman* (1713–1786); *James Tilghman* (1716–1793); and *Matthew Tilghman* (1717/18–1790). Her sisters were Henrietta Maria (1707–1771), who married first, *George Robins* (1697–1742) and second, *William Goldsborough* (1709–1760); Anna Maria (1709–1763), who married first, *William Hemsley* (1703–1736) and second, *Robert Lloyd* (ca. 1712–1770). Her first cousins were *Matthew Tilghman Ward* (ca. 1676–1741); *Lambert Wilmer* (1682–1732); *Simon Wilmer* (1686–1737); *Edward Lloyd* (1711–1770); *Richard Lloyd* (1717–1786); *Robert Lloyd* (ca. 1712–1770); Henrietta Maria Lloyd Chew (?–1765), who married second, *Daniel Dulany* (1685–1753); Henrietta Maria Lloyd (ca. 1711–1748), who married *Samuel Chamberlaine* (1698–1773); Margaret Lloyd (1714–ca. 1785), who married *William Tilghman* (1711–1782); and Ann Lloyd (ca. 1723–1794), who married *Matthew Tilghman* (1717/18–1790). Her nephews were *William Hemsley* (1736/37–1812); *Richard Tilghman* (1740–1809); *Matthew Tilghman* (1760–ca. 1801); *James Tilghman* (1743–1809); *Peregrine Tilghman* (ca. 1741–1807); *James Tilghman, Jr.* (ca. 1748–1796); *William Tilghman* (1756–1827). Her nieces were Deborah Lloyd, who married *Peregrine Tilghman* (ca. 1741–1807); Margaret Tilghman (1742–1817), who married *Charles Carroll, Barrister* (1723–1783); Anna Maria Tilghman, who mar-

ried *William Hemsley* (1736/37–1812); Elizabeth Tilghman, who married *James Lloyd* (1745–1820); Anna Maria Robins (1732–1806), who married *Henry Hollyday* (ca. 1725–1789); Margaret Robins (1734–1808), who married *William Hayward* (?–1791); and Henrietta Maria Robins (1736–1791), who married *James Lloyd Chamberlaine* (1732–1783). MARRIED second, on November 6, 1738, Sarah, widow of Edward Chetham (?–1736), of Queen Anne's County; daughter of John Crapp, of Philadelphia, Pennsylvania, and wife Susanna Berd. CHILDREN. SONS: *Michael Earle* (1722–1787); Richard (1727–1728), who died of pleurisy; *Richard Tilghman Earle* (1728/29–1788); Joseph (1732–1732); James (1734–1810), who married Eleanor (?–1779), daughter of Dominick Carroll (?–ca. 1737), of Cecil County, and wife Mary; and *Joseph Earle* (1739–1777). STEPSONS: James Chetham; Edward Chetham. DAUGHTERS: Anna Maria (1725–1795), who married *Thomas Ringgold* (1715–1772); Henrietta Maria (1730–1767), who married *William Hemsley* (1736/37–1812). STEPDAUGHTERS: Hannah Chetham, who married in 1752 Edward Clayton; Suzannah Chetham (1736–?). PRIVATE CAREER. EDUCATION: literate. RELIGIOUS AFFILIATION: Anglican, Old Chester Church, St. Paul's Parish, Queen Anne's County. SOCIAL STATUS AND ACTIVITIES: Esq., 1731. OCCUPATIONAL PROFILE: lawyer; apprenticed to *Wornell Hunt* (?–by 1728/29), an Anne Arundel County lawyer, by his guardian *Richard Tilghman* (1672/73–1738/39); authorized to practice law in Talbot, Kent, Cecil, and Queen Anne's counties on November 5, 1714; appeared in the following courts: Queen Anne's County in June 1715; Cecil County in June 1715, but in March 1716/17 he was fined 100 pounds of tobacco for nonattendance; Talbot County in August 1715; Provincial Court in April 1717. PUBLIC CAREER. LEGISLATIVE SERVICE: Lower House, Queen Anne's County, 1721–1721/22 (elected to the 4th session to fill vacancy; Laws 4, 5). LOCAL OFFICES: clerk of Indictments, Talbot County, appointed 1718, Queen Anne's County, appointed 1718; St. Luke's Parish Vestry, Queen Anne's County, in office 1734; sheriff, Queen Anne's County, 1730–1733; deputy commissary, Queen Anne's County, 1733–1739; visitor, Queen Anne's County Free School, 1734–1739. MILITARY SERVICE: captain, troop of horse, Queen Anne's County, elected 1732. WEALTH DURING LIFETIME. LAND AT FIRST ELECTION: 500 acres in Queen Anne's and Cecil counties (500 acres from his father; 285 acres inherited from his mother, which had been sold before his first election). SIGNIFICANT CHANGES IN

LAND BETWEEN FIRST ELECTION AND DEATH: patented 350 acres in Queen Anne's County, but sold 150 acres between 1723 and 1727; controlled 400 acres in Queen Anne's County which belonged to his father-in-law *Richard Tilghman* (1672/73–1738/39), by 1734, to which his father-in-law left actual title to James's son, *Richard Tilghman Earle* (1728/29–1788) in 1738/39. WEALTH AT DEATH. DIED: between May 19 and July 9, 1739, in Queen Anne's County. PERSONAL PROPERTY: TEV, £8.3.7 Maryland gold, £56.1.5 sterling, £70.19.1 Virginia current money, £2.17.0 Boston current money, £2.16.6 Pennsylvania and New Jersey current money, £2,703.16.0 Maryland paper money (including 27 slaves, 8 servants, 105 oz. 10 dwt. 12 gr. plate, 1 dwt. 13 gr. old silver, law and other books); debts, £103.0.1 Maryland gold, £70.13.0 sterling, £16.5.5 Pennsylvania and New Jersey current money, £323.7.1 Maryland paper money; FB not calculated, because conversion could not be made. LAND: 700 acres in Queen Anne's and Cecil counties, plus control of 400 acres for his son *Richard Tilghman Earle* (1728/29–1788).

EARLE, JOSEPH (1739–1777). BORN: in 1739 in Queen Anne's County; fourth son. NATIVE: fourth generation. RESIDED: in Georgetown, Kent County, by 1769; Queen Anne's County. FAMILY BACKGROUND. FATHER: *James Earle, Jr.* (ca. 1694–1739). MOTHER: Sarah Crapp Chetham. HALF BROTHERS: James (1734–1810); *Richard Tilghman Earle* (1728/29–1788); *Michael Earle* (1722–1787); James Chetham; and Edward Chetham. HALF SISTERS: Ann Maria (1725–1795), who married *Thomas Ringgold* (1715–1772); Henrietta Maria (1730–1767), who married *William Hemsley* (1736/37–1812); Hannah Chetham; and Suzannah Chetham (1736–?). HALF NEPHEW: *Samuel Earle* (1756–1790). MARRIED Ann (1746–?), daughter of Rev. Richard Harrison (?–1763), rector of St. Luke's Parish, Queen Anne's County from 1742 to 1763, and his wife Charlotte. Her brothers were John (1747–?); William (1749–1751); William (1752–?); and Richard Everingham (1761–?), who married in 1790 Sarah Thompson. Her sisters were Mary (1755–?); Charlotte (1757–by 1763). CHILDREN. SONS: George W. (?–died young); William (?–died young). PRIVATE CAREER. EDUCATION: trained as a lawyer. RELIGIOUS AFFILIATION: Anglican, St. Luke's Parish, Queen Anne's County. SOCIAL STATUS AND ACTIVITIES: Esq., 1776. OCCUPATIONAL PROFILE: lawyer, admitted to the following courts: Kent County by March 1764; Queen Anne's County in March 1764; Provincial Court in September 1765; Cecil County by March 1769. PUBLIC CAREER. LEGISLATIVE SERVICE: Conventions, Kent County, 1st, 1774, 3rd, 1774, 4th, 1775, 5th, 1775, 9th, 1776. LOCAL OFFICE: Committee of Correspondence, Kent County, in office 1774. MILITARY SERVICE: lieutenant colonel of a battalion from the Eastern Shore, elected 1776. STANDS ON PUBLIC/PRIVATE ISSUES: on January 26, 1776, Earle wrote to *James Hollyday* (1722–1786) that he preferred a constitutional settlement of the difficulties between the colonies and Great Britain until he read Thomas Paine's *Common Sense*, which convinced him that separation was essential if liberty was to be preserved. He felt that the Maryland Convention should ensure the protection of every man's right to his personal beliefs. WEALTH DURING LIFETIME. PERSONAL PROPERTY: his wife inherited £78.11.5 current money from her father's estate, 1763. WEALTH AT DEATH. DIED: in 1777 in Queen Anne's County. PERSONAL PROPERTY: TEV, at least £1,103.9.3 current money (including 10 slaves and law books). LAND: no evidence of any landownership.

EARLE, MICHAEL (1722–1787). BORN: on October 19, 1722, in Queen Anne's County; eldest son. NATIVE: fourth generation. RESIDED: in Queen Anne's County; Fredericktown, Cecil County, by 1752. FAMILY BACKGROUND. FATHER: *James Earle, Jr.* (ca. 1694–1739). MOTHER: Mary (1702–ca. 1736), daughter of *Richard Tilghman* (1672/73–1738/39). STEPMOTHER: Sarah Crapp Chetham. UNCLES: *William Tilghman* (1711–1782); *Edward Tilghman* (1713–1786); *James Tilghman* (1716–1793); and *Matthew Tilghman* (1717/18–1790). AUNTS: Elizabeth Earle (ca. 1694–?), who married *William Turbutt* (1683/84–1739); Henrietta Maria Tilghman (1707–1771), who married first, *George Robins* (1697–1742), and second, *William Goldsborough* (1709–1760); and Anna Maria Tilghman (1709–1763), who married first, *William Hemsley* (1703–1736), and second, *Robert Lloyd* (ca. 1712–1770). BROTHERS: Richard (1727–1728); *Richard Tilghman Earle* (1728/29–1788); Joseph (1732–1732); and James (1734–1810). HALF BROTHER: *Joseph Earle* (1739–1777). STEPBROTHERS: James Chetham; Edward Chetham. SISTERS: Anna Maria (1725–1795), who married *Thomas Ringgold* (1715–1772); Henrietta Maria (1730–1767), who married *William Hemsley* (1736/37–1812). STEPSISTERS: Hannah Chetham; Suzannah Chetham (1736–?). FIRST COUSINS: *William Hemsley* (1736/37–1812); *Richard Tilghman* (1740–1809); *Matthew Tilghman* (1760–ca. 1801); *James Tilghman* (1743–1809); *Peregrine Tilghman* (ca. 1741–1807); *James Tilghman, Jr.* (ca. 1748–1796); *William Tilghman* (1756–1827); Deborah Lloyd, who married *Peregrine Tilghman* (ca. 1741–1807); Margaret Tilghman (1742–1817), who married *Charles Carroll, Barrister* (1723–1783); Anna Maria Tilghman, who married *William Hemsley* (1736/37–1812); Elizabeth Tilghman, who married *James Lloyd* (1745–1820); Anna Maria Robins (1732–1806), who married *Henry Hollyday* (ca. 1725–1789); Margaret Robins (1734–1808), who married *William Hayward* (?–1791); Henrietta Maria Robins (1736–1791), who married *James Lloyd Chamberlaine* (1732–1783); Anna Maria Turbutt, who married *Edward Tilghman* (1713–1786), and Elizabeth Turbutt (?–ca. 1760), who married *Thomas Harris* (?–1760). NEPHEW: *Thomas Ringgold* (1744–1776). OTHER KINSHIP: his great-grandfather was *Philemon Lloyd* (1646–1685). MARRIED Mary, eldest daughter of Dominick Carroll (?–ca. 1737) and wife Mary; stepdaughter of John Baldwin. Her sisters were Juliana, who married *Edward Tilghman* (1713–1786); Eleanor (?–1779), who married James Earle (1734–1810); Anastatia, who married Henry Ward Pearce; and Susanna (?–by 1759). CHILDREN. Probably died without progeny. PRIVATE CAREER. EDUCATION: literate. RELIGIOUS AFFILIATION: Anglican. SOCIAL STATUS AND ACTIVITIES: Mr., 1749; Gent., 1749; a member of the Tuesday Club. OCCUPATIONAL PROFILE: commander of a merchant ship, 1744; merchant, 1753. PUBLIC CAREER. LEGISLATIVE SERVICE: Lower House, Cecil County, 1751–1754, 1754–1757 (Bills of Credit 1–6), 1757–1758 (Bills of Credit 1, Cv, 2), 1758–1761 (Bills of Credit Cv 1, 1, Cv 2, 2, 3), 1762–1763 (Bills of Credit 1, 2), 1765–1766 (Bills of Credit 2, 4; Accounts 4). LOCAL OFFICES: sheriff, Cecil County, 1748–1751; deputy commissary, Cecil County, 1749–1757; justice, Cecil County, commissioned 1751 and 1754; North Sassafrass Parish Vestry, Cecil County, in office 1763–1765. WEALTH DURING LIFETIME. PERSONAL PROPERTY: assessed value £1,158.0.0, including 24 slaves and 1,166 oz. plate, 1783. LAND AT FIRST ELECTION: 1,065 acres in Frederick and Cecil counties (at least 405 acres from wife's dower and 660 acres by purchase). SIGNIFICANT CHANGES IN LAND BETWEEN FIRST ELECTION AND DEATH: purchased an additional 692 acres in Cecil County and sold 1,056 acres in Cecil and Frederick counties, 1755–1769; owned a total of 631 acres in Cecil County, 1783. WEALTH AT DEATH. DIED: will probated on December 19, 1787, in Cecil County. PERSONAL PROPERTY: TEV, £1,821.16.1 current money (including 26 slaves and 35 books); FB, £1,177.2.8. LAND: ca. 631 acres in Cecil County. ADDITIONAL COMMENTS: his principal heirs were his brothers *Richard Tilghman Earle* (1728/29–1788) and James (1734–1810); his nephews James Earle and Michael Earle; and his niece, Henrietta Earle.

EARLE, RICHARD TILGHMAN (1728/29–1788). BORN: on February 10, 1728/29, in Queen Anne's County; third son. NATIVE: fourth generation. RESIDED: at "Earle's Beginning Rectified," Queen Anne's County. FAMILY BACKGROUND. FATHER: *James Earle, Jr.* (ca. 1694–1739). MOTHER: Mary (1702–ca. 1736), daughter of *Richard Tilghman* (1672/73–1738/39). STEPMOTHER: Sarah Crapp Chetham. UNCLES: *William Tilghman* (1711–1782); *Edward Tilghman* (1713–1786); *James Tilghman* (1716–1793); and *Matthew Tilghman* (1717/18–1790). AUNTS: Elizabeth Earle (ca. 1694–?), who married *William Turbutt* (1683/84–1739); Henrietta Maria Tilghman (1707–1771), who married first, *George Robins* (1697–1742), and second, *William Goldsborough* (1709–1760); and Anna Maria Tilghman (1709–1763), who married first, *William Hemsley* (1703–1736), and second, *Robert Lloyd* (ca. 1712–1770). BROTHERS: *Michael Earle* (1722–1787); Richard (1727–1728); Joseph (1732–1732); and James (1734–1810). HALF BROTHER: *Joseph Earle* (1739–1777). STEP-BROTHERS: James Chetham; Edward Chetham. SISTERS: Anna Maria (1725–1795), who married *Thomas Ringgold* (1715–1772); Henrietta Maria (1730–1767), who married *William Hemsley* (1736/37–1812). STEPSISTERS: Hannah Chetham; Suzannah Chetham (1736–?). FIRST COUSINS: *William Hemsley* (1736/37–1812); *Richard Tilghman* (1740–1809); *Matthew Tilghman* (1760–ca. 1801); *James Tilghman* (1743–1809); *Peregrine Tilghman* (ca. 1741–1807); *James Tilghman, Jr.* (ca. 1748–1796); *William Tilghman* (1756–1827); Deborah Lloyd, who married *Peregrine Tilghman* (ca. 1741–1807); Margaret Tilghman (1742–1817), who married *Charles Carroll, Barrister* (1723–1783); Anna Maria Tilghman, who married *William Hemsley* (1736/37–1812); Elizabeth Tilghman, who married *James Lloyd* (1745–1820); Anna Maria Robins (1732–1806), who married *Henry Hollyday* (ca. 1725–1789); Margaret Robins (1734–1808), who married *William Hayward* (?–1791); Henrietta Maria Robins (1736–1791), who married *James Lloyd Chamberlaine* (1732–1783); Anna Maria Turbutt, who married *Edward Tilghman* (1713–1786); and Elizabeth Turbutt (?–ca. 1760), who married *Thomas Harris* (?–1760). NEPHEW: *Thomas Ringgold* (1744–1776). OTHER

KINSHIP: his great-grandfather was *Philemon Lloyd* (1646–1685). MARRIED on February 1, 1755, Ann (1734–1786), daughter of *Samuel Chamberlaine* (1698–1773); granddaughter of *James Lloyd* (1679/80–1723); niece of *Robert Lloyd* (ca. 1712–1770), Margaret Lloyd (1714–ca. 1785), who married *William Tilghman* (1711–1782), and Anne Lloyd (ca. 1723–1794), who married *Matthew Tilghman* (1717/18–1790). Her brothers were Thomas (1731–1764); *James Lloyd Chamberlaine* (1732–1783); *Samuel Chamberlaine* (1742–1811); Richard; and Robert Lloyd, who died at eleven years of age. Her sister was Henrietta Maria (1739–1777). Her first cousins were *Richard Tilghman* (1740–1809); Margaret Tilghman (1742–1817), who married *Charles Carroll, Barrister* (1723–1783); and Deborah Lloyd, who married *Peregrine Tilghman* (ca. 1741–1807). Her nieces were Henrietta Maria Chamberlaine (?–1804), who married *William Hayward, Jr.* (ca. 1758–1834); Henrietta Maria Nicols (1761–1818), who married *Samuel Earle* (1756–1790). CHILDREN. SONS: *Samuel Earle* (1756–1790); James (1764–1790); Richard Tilghman (1767–1843), who served in the Maryland General Assembly in 1796 and from 1808 to 1809, was a member of the executive council from 1804 to 1805, and a judge of the Court of Appeals from 1809 to 1834; Thomas (1771–?), who married Henrietta Maria (1779–1821), daughter of *William Hemsley* (1736/37–1812). DAUGHTERS: Mary (1760–by 1785), who married Dr. John Hindman; Henrietta Maria (1761–1828), who married first, Solomon Clayton, and second, Samuel W. Thomas; Ann (1762–1782); Margaret (1765–1795), who married Philip Feddeman; Deborah (1769–1790), who married Charles Wright; and Suzanna (1773–1795). PRIVATE CAREER. EDUCATION: literate. RELIGIOUS AFFILIATION: Anglican. SOCIAL STATUS AND ACTIVITIES: Mr., 1756; Gent., 1761; Esq., 1780. OCCUPATIONAL PROFILE: merchant, in partnership with his brother James Earle and *William Bruff* (ca. 1741–1802), in the firm of Richard Tilghman Earle & Co. The partnership was in existence from 1772 to 1775; the firm kept a store at Chester Mill in Queen Anne's County and sold large quantities of goods on credit; after the dissolution of the firm Richard continued to operate the store himself until 1776; probably also a planter. PUBLIC CAREER. LEGISLATIVE SERVICE: Lower House, Queen Anne's County, 1771 (Accounts), 1773–1774 (Accounts 1, Cv, 2, 3); Conventions, Queen Anne's County, 1st, 1774, 4th, 1775, 5th, 1775, 6th–8th, 1775–1776 (Claims 6th–8th; Manufactories 8th); Lower House, Queen Anne's County, 1777–1778

(Loan Office 1; Grievances 2; Claims 2), 1779–1780 (Elections 2; Tax Commissioners 2). OTHER STATE OFFICE: Special Council of the Eastern Shore, appointed 1780. LOCAL OFFICES: clerk, Court of Oyer and Terminer and Gaol Delivery, Queen Anne's County, commissioned 1751; St. Paul's Parish Vestry, 1756–1759, 1764–1784; churchwarden, St. Paul's Parish, Queen Anne's County, in office 1759; visitor, Queen Anne's County Free School, in office 1770 and 1782; commissioner of tax, Queen Anne's County, 1777–at least 1790. WEALTH DURING LIFETIME. PERSONAL PROPERTY: assessed value £2,128.10.0, including 35 slaves and 196 oz. plate, Queen Anne's County, 1783. LAND AT FIRST ELECTION: 3,210 acres in Queen Anne's County (400 acres inherited from his grandfather Richard Tilghman, which he then resurveyed into a 517-acre tract; 554 acres by patent; at least 2,020 acres by purchase); controlled 800 acres in Dorchester County for his wife to whom the land was apparently entailed; he had no authority to dispose of it and always referred to it as his wife's land. SIGNIFICANT CHANGES IN LAND BETWEEN FIRST ELECTION AND DEATH: owned 600 acres in Delaware, by 1785. WEALTH AT DEATH. DIED: will probated on March 24, 1788, in Queen Anne's County. PERSONAL PROPERTY: TEV, £2,143.16.8 current money (including 39 slaves, 176 oz. plate, and 12 books); FB, estate overpaid £5,956.1.4. LAND: at least 3,311 acres in Queen Anne's and Caroline counties; 600 acres in Delaware; his wife still owned 800 acres in Caroline County. ADDITIONAL COMMENTS: Earle died very much in debt, and subject to numerous court judgments. His estate was declared insolvent, and his son Richard Tilghman Earle, Jr., sold 3,058 acres of his father's land in Queen Anne's and Caroline counties between 1815 and 1818 to satisfy the remaining creditors.

EARLE, SAMUEL (1756–1790). BORN: on February 3, 1756, probably in Queen Anne's County; eldest son. NATIVE: fifth generation. RESIDED: in Queen Anne's County; Kent County, by 1785; "Needwood," near Centreville, Queen Anne's County, 1788 until death. FAMILY BACKGROUND. FATHER: *Richard Tilghman Earle* (1728/29–1788), son of *James Earle, Jr.* (ca. 1694–1739). MOTHER: Ann Chamberlaine (1734–1786). UNCLES: *James Lloyd Chamberlaine* (1732–1783); *Samuel Chamberlaine* (1742–1811); and *Michael Earle* (1722–1787). HALF UNCLE: *Joseph Earle* (1739–1777). AUNTS: Anna Maria Earle (1725–1795), who married *Thomas Ringgold* (1715–1772); Henrietta Maria Earle (1730–1767), who married *William Hemsley* (1736/37–1812). BROTHERS: James (1764–1790); Richard Tilghman (1767–1843); and Thomas Chamberlaine (1771–?). SISTERS: Mary (1760–by 1785); Henrietta Maria (1761–1828); Ann (1762–1782); Margaret (1765–1795); Deborah (1769–1790); and Suzanna (1773–1795). FIRST COUSINS: *Thomas Ringgold* (1744–1776); Henrietta Maria Chamberlaine (?–1804), who married *William Hayward, Jr.* (ca. 1758–1834); and Henrietta Maria Nicols (1761–1818). MARRIED his first cousin Henrietta Maria (1761–1818), daughter of William Nicols (1730–1774), of Kent County, and wife Henrietta Maria Chamberlaine (1739–1777); granddaughter of both Rev. Henry Nicols (1687–ca. 1749) and *Samuel Chamberlaine* (1698–1773); niece of *James Lloyd Chamberlaine* (1732–1783), *Samuel Chamberlaine* (1742–1811), and Ann Chamberlaine (1734–1786), who married first, *Richard Tilghman Earle* (1728/29–1788), and second, Charles Blake (?–1798). Her brothers were Samuel (1770–?), who married first, (first name unknown) Blake, and second, Elizabeth Smyth; Henry (1764–1810), who married in 1786 Elizabeth Robins (1765–1814). Her sister was Ann (1762–?), who married *Edward DeCoursey* (ca. 1759–1827). Her first cousin was Henrietta Maria Chamberlaine (?–1804), who married *William Hayward, Jr.* (ca. 1758–1834). CHILDREN. SON: William Nicols (ca. 1782–1824), who never married. DAUGHTERS: Anne; Henrietta Maria (called Maria), who married in 1807 Turbutt Harris, son of *Edward Harris* (ca. 1757–ca. 1837). PRIVATE CAREER. EDUCATION: literate. SOCIAL STATUS AND ACTIVITIES: Gent., 1779. OCCUPATIONAL PROFILE: lawyer, practiced in Georgetown, Kent County, from the end of the war until his death. PUBLIC CAREER. LEGISLATIVE SERVICE: Lower House, Queen Anne's County, 1780–1781. MILITARY SERVICE: private, in the Minute Company that marched from Queen Anne's County, February 3, 1776; ensign, Queen Anne's County Militia, by June 1776; ensign, Capt. Dean's Company, Fourth Maryland Battalion, Flying Camp, July–December 1776. WEALTH DURING LIFETIME. PERSONAL PROPERTY: assessed value £205.0.0, including 2 slaves and 40 oz. plate, 1783. LAND AT FIRST ELECTION: 298 acres in Queen Anne's County (deed of gift from his father). SIGNIFICANT CHANGES IN LAND BETWEEN FIRST ELECTION AND DEATH: land he had received from his father was returned to his father by a deed of gift, 1785; received 500 acres in Caroline County through his wife, 1786; as heir to his mother Samuel received 800 acres in Caroline County, 1786; purchased a lot in Georgetown, Kent County, 1787; inherited 619 acres in Queen Anne's County from his father in 1788, but his father made the bequest contingent on Samuel's deeding the 800 acres he had inherited from his mother to his brother, Thomas, when he came of age. WEALTH AT DEATH. DIED: in the spring of 1790, at "Needwood," Queen Anne's County. PERSONAL PROPERTY: TEV, £2,590.2.9 current money (including 30 slaves, 6 servants, 128 law and other books, and 208 oz. 5 dwt. plate); FB, £219.19.7. LAND: 500 acres in Caroline County, plus 1 lot in Georgetown, Kent County; also inherited 800 acres in Caroline County from his mother and 619 acres in Queen Anne's County from his father on the condition that he transfer the 800 acres to his brother, Thomas; possessed and occupied both tracts until his death and made no recorded conveyance to his brother.

ECCLESTON, HUGH (?–1710/11). IMMIGRATED: by 1688 as a free adult, perhaps from Virginia. RESIDED: in Dorchester County. MARRIED Elizabeth, probably the sister of Thomas Skinner, of Dorchester County. CHILDREN. SONS: Hugh (?–by 1717), who married Mary, widow of Rev. James Hindeman and daughter of *Jacob Lookerman* (1652–1730); John (?–1758), a justice and colonel of Dorchester County, who married Dorothy (ca. 1714–1759), daughter of Andrew Skinner; and Thomas. DAUGHTERS: Margaret, who married Bazell Nowell; Mary; Rachel; Sarah; and Elizabeth. PRIVATE CAREER. EDUCATION: literate; he had clerical skills. RELIGIOUS AFFILIATION: Anglican. SOCIAL STATUS AND ACTIVITIES: Gent., by 1693. OCCUPATIONAL PROFILE: placeman; planter. PUBLIC CAREER. LEGISLATIVE SERVICE: Lower House, Dorchester County, 1701–1704 (Elections and Privileges 1), 1704–1707 (Laws 3, 4), 1708A (Accounts), 1708B–1710 (Elections and Privileges 3; died before the 4th session). LOCAL OFFICE: clerk, Dorchester County, 1691–1710/11 (suspended briefly in 1692). WEALTH DURING LIFETIME. LAND AT FIRST ELECTION: at least 1,440 acres. WEALTH AT DEATH. DIED: in 1710/11. PERSONAL PROPERTY: TEV, £488.15.6 sterling (including 7 slaves and 1 servant). LAND: ca. 1,800 acres.

ECCLESTON, THOMAS FIRMIN (ca. 1738–1785). BORN: ca. 1738, probably in Dorchester County. NATIVE: third generation. RESIDED: in Transquakin Hundred, Dorchester County. FAMILY BACKGROUND. FATHER: Col. John Eccleston (?–1758), of Dorchester County, son of *Hugh Eccleston* (?–1710/11). MOTHER: Dorothy (ca. 1714–1759), daughter of Andrew Skinner. BROTHER:

Hugh (?–by 1778), who married Elizabeth, daughter of John Trippe and wife Anne. SISTERS: Rachel, who never married; Dorothy, who married Joseph Richardson. MARRIED on April 15, 1782, Milcah, widow of Robert Pitt, of Virginia; daughter of Rev. Thomas Airey (1701–1765), rector of Christ Church, Great Choptank Parish, Cambridge, Dorchester County from 1728–1765, and wife Milcah Hill Gale; granddaughter of Henry Hill, of Anne Arundel and Dorchester counties, mariner. She may have subsequently married Thomas Martin, of Talbot County, by 1788. Her brother was Thomas Hill, who married Mary. Her half sister was Mary Gale (ca. 1734–by 1790), who married *Samuel Wilson* (1735–1790). ADDITIONAL COMMENTS: Milcah's father, Rev. Thomas Airey, had previously married Elizabeth Pitt. Her mother had previously married *John Gale* (?–ca. 1744). CHILDREN. SON: Thomas John Hugh (1785–1868), who married in 1806 Sarah Ennalls, daughter of Col. John Hooper. STEPSON: Samuel Wilson Pitt (ca. 1771–1805), who married Mary. DAUGHTER: Leah (?–1803), who married Govert Haskins, of Baltimore County, merchant. PRIVATE CAREER. EDUCATION: literate. SOCIAL STATUS AND ACTIVITIES: Gent., 1779. OCCUPATIONAL PROFILE: probably a planter. PUBLIC CAREER. LEGISLATIVE SERVICE: Lower House, Dorchester County, 1778–1779 (Claims 1, 3), 1779–1780 (Claims 1–3; Tax Commissioners 2), 1780 (elected, but did not attend; resigned on November 1, 1780), 1781–1782 (Claims 2), 1783 (elected, but did not attend; resigned on November 19, 1783), 1784 (elected, but did not attend). LOCAL OFFICES: justice, Dorchester County, 1777–1785; justice, Orphans' Court, Dorchester County, 1780–1785. MILITARY SERVICE: lieutenant, Cambridge Blues Company, Dorchester County Militia, ca. 1775. WEALTH DURING LIFETIME. PERSONAL PROPERTY: 15 slaves, 1776; assessed value £907.3.4, including 15 slaves and 40 oz. plate, 1783. LAND AT FIRST ELECTION: 1,744 acres in Dorchester County (inherited at least 1,138 acres from his father; patented 550 acres). WEALTH AT DEATH. DIED: between late April and November 8, 1785, in Dorchester County. PERSONAL PROPERTY: TEV, at least £3,418.13.6 current money (including 19 slaves and 37 books). LAND: 1,688 acres in Dorchester County.

EDELIN (EDELEN, EDELINE), CHRISTOPHER (?–ca. 1786).

BORN: probably in Prince George's County, of age by 1753; younger son. NATIVE: at least third generation. RESIDED: in Frederick Town, Frederick County. FAMILY BACKGROUND. FATHER: Christopher Edelen, Sr. (?–1771), of Prince George's County. MOTHER: Jane. BROTHERS: John; Richard. SISTERS: Ann, who married (first name unknown) Gomer; Elizabeth, who married by 1770 (first name unknown) Wheeler; and Catherine. MARRIED on July 24, 1754, Rebecca, daughter of George Johnson. CHILDREN. SON: Christopher. DAUGHTERS: Elizabeth (1760–?), who married *Mountjoy Bayly* (1755–1836); Eleanor (1762–?), who married *John Lynn* (1760–1813); and Rebecca (1765–?), who married John Hodge Bayard. PRIVATE CAREER. EDUCATION: literate. RELIGIOUS AFFILIATION: Anglican, All Saints' Parish, Frederick County. SOCIAL STATUS AND ACTIVITIES: Gent., 1753; Esq., 1781. OCCUPATIONAL PROFILE: merchant. PUBLIC CAREER. LEGISLATIVE SERVICE: Convention, Frederick County, 9th, 1776; Lower House, Frederick County, 1777, 1777–1778 (Elections 1; Manufactories 3). LOCAL OFFICES: Committee of Observation, Frederick County, elected 1775; judge of elections, Middle District, Frederick County, appointed 1776; justice, Frederick County, commissioned 1777 and 1778; justice, Orphans' Court, Frederick County, commissioned 1778; sheriff, Frederick County, in office 1778–1779; tax collector, Frederick County, in office 1780 and 1781; commissary for clothing, Frederick County, appointed 1781; commissary for horses, Frederick County, in office in 1782. WEALTH DURING LIFETIME. PERSONAL PROPERTY: assessed value £128.10.0, 1778; assessed value £200.0.0, including 5 slaves and 12 oz. plate, 1782. LAND AT FIRST ELECTION: 566 acres in Frederick and Prince George's counties, plus 1 lot in Georgetown, Montgomery County (all by personal acquisition). SIGNIFICANT CHANGES IN LAND BETWEEN FIRST ELECTION AND DEATH: sold 323 acres and bought 1 lot in Hamburgh, Prince George's County, 1779–1783. WEALTH AT DEATH. DIED: ca. 1786, in Frederick County. PERSONAL PROPERTY: TEV, at least £232.6.9 (including 4 slaves); his personal property sold to pay his debts; the state collected the balance of Edelin's estate in payment for money he collected but never remitted as the Frederick County tax collector. LAND: at least 130 acres in Frederick County, which was sold to pay his debts.

EDEN, JOHN (ca. 1728–1775).

BORN: ca. 1728. RESIDED: in St. Mary's County. MARRIED first, Mary (?–by 1763), daughter of *James Mills* (?–1764). Her brothers were John; *James Mills* (ca. 1734–1791). Her sister was Elizabeth. MARRIED second, Betty (?–by 1799), widow of John Rogers; daughter of Dr. Daniel Jenifer (?–1729) and wife

Elizabeth Mason; stepdaughter of both John Theobolds and Robert Whythill; granddaughter of both Daniel of St. Thomas Jenifer (?–1730) and wife Elizabeth Ashcom (?–ca. 1734), and Robert Mason (?–ca. 1697) and wife Susanna (?–ca. 1716). Her brothers were *Daniel Jenifer* (?–1795); *Daniel of St. Thomas Jenifer* (1723–1790). Her sisters were Elizabeth, who married Col. Daniel Stone; Ann, who married Josias Adams; and Mary, who married Robert Christie, of London, England. Her nephews were *John Hoskins Stone* (by 1750–1804); *Michael Jenifer Stone* (1747–1812). CHILDREN. SONS: James (ca. 1749–1777), who died without progeny; John, Jr. (?–1785); Townshend (ca. 1756–1787); and Thomas (by 1759–1780). DAUGHTER: Ann Nappier, who married (first name unknown) Llewellyn. PRIVATE CAREER. EDUCATION: literate. RELIGIOUS AFFILIATION: Anglican, King and Queen Parish, St. Mary's County. SOCIAL STATUS AND ACTIVITIES: Mr., 1759; Esq., at death. OCCUPATIONAL PROFILE: probably a merchant; planter. PUBLIC CAREER. LEGISLATIVE SERVICE: Lower House, St. Mary's County, 1768–1770 (Claims 1, 3). LOCAL OFFICES: sheriff, St. Mary's County, 1758–1761; justice, St. Mary's County, 1764–at least 1773; justice, Court of Oyer and Terminer and Gaol Delivery, St. Mary's County, commissioned 1768 and 1771; trustee, St. Mary's County Free School, in office 1772. WEALTH DURING LIFETIME. LAND AT FIRST ELECTION: 2,126 acres in St. Mary's and Frederick counties (1,876 acres by purchase; a moiety of 500 acres patented in Frederick County with his brother-in-law James Mills). SIGNIFICANT CHANGES IN LAND BETWEEN FIRST ELECTION AND DEATH: inherited 81 acres in St. Mary's County from his father-in-law in 1764, but he did not receive the land until ca. 1773; he purchased 347 additional acres in St. Mary's County, 1773. WEALTH AT DEATH. DIED: on July 1, 1775, in St. Mary's County. PERSONAL PROPERTY: TEV, £1,932.14.2 (including 23 slaves, more than 31 books, and many luxury items); FB, £1,030.9.9. LAND: 2,452 acres in St. Mary's and Frederick counties, plus 2 lots in Carrollsburgh, Prince George's County.

EDEN, ROBERT (1741–1784). BORN: on September 14, 1741, in England; second son. IMMIGRATED: on June 5, 1769, as governor. RESIDED: in Annapolis, Anne Arundel County, from 1769 until May 28, 1774; England; Annapolis, from November 8, 1774 to June 24, 1776; England; Annapolis, from the summer of 1783 to death. FAMILY BACKGROUND. FATHER: Sir Robert Eden (ca. 1712–1755), 3rd baronet of West Auckland.

MOTHER: Mary (?–1794), daughter of William Davison, Esq., of Beamish, Durham County, England. BROTHERS: John (1740–1812), 4th baronet of West Auckland, M.P., Durham County, England, from 1774 to 1790, who married first, Catherine Thompson (?–1766), and second, Dorothea Johnson (?–1792); William (1744–1814), 1st baron of Auckland, 1789, Lord Auckland of West Auckland, 1793, barrister-at-law, M.P. for Woodstock from 1774 to 1784, M.P. for Duncannon, Ireland, from 1781 to 1783, M.P. for Heytesbury from 1784 to 1793, peace commissioner to America, 1778, who married Eleanor Elliot (?–1818); Thomas (?–1805), a ship's captain in the tobacco trade between Maryland and England and a founder of the mercantile firm of T. Eden & Company, who married Mariana Jones; Morton (1752–1830), 1st baron Henley of Chardstock, Dorset, England, who married Elizabeth Henley (?–1821), daughter of the 1st earl of Northington. SISTERS: three, including Catherine, who married in 1770 John Moore (1730–1805), archbishop of Canterbury. MARRIED on April 26, 1765, Caroline, daughter of *Charles Calvert, 5th Lord Baltimore* (1699–1751); niece of Barbara Janssen, who married *Thomas Bladen* (1698–1780). Her brother was *Frederick Calvert, 6th Lord Baltimore* (1731/32–1771). Her half brother was *Benedict Calvert* (ca. 1724–1788). Her sister was Louisa. Her nephew was *Henry Harford* (ca. 1759–1834). CHILDREN. SONS: Frederick Morton (1766–1808), 2nd baronet of Maryland, an author and economist, who married in 1792 Ann, daughter of James Paul Smith, of London, England; William Thomas (1768–1851), a major general. DAUGHTER: Catherine (1770–1835). PRIVATE CAREER. EDUCATION: received a classical education; a contemporary of Eden's said of him "Few equalled him in letter writing." RELIGIOUS AFFILIATION: Anglican. SOCIAL STATUS AND ACTIVITIES: Esq., 1771; created 1st baronet of Maryland in October 1776; leader of Annapolis society during his term as governor; supported the theatre in Annapolis; an honorary member of the Homony Club; owned a stable of racehorses. ADDITIONAL COMMENTS: the will of his brother-in-law *Frederick Calvert, 6th Lord Baltimore* (1731/32–1771) named Eden as one of four executors to administer the province of Maryland until *Henry Harford* (ca. 1759–1834) came of age. Although the proprietorship was effectively ended by the American victory in the War for Independence, Eden returned to Maryland with Harford in 1783 to help him seek compensation for property that had been confiscated by the state. OCCUPATIONAL PROFILE: officeholder. PUB-

LIC CAREER. PROVINCIAL OFFICES: governor, 1768–1776 (commissioned in 1768; arrived in Maryland in 1769; left the province for England in May 1774, but returned in November 1774; sailed for England in 1776); surveyor general of the Western Shore, 1771–1776; commissioner for the sale of proprietary manors and reserved lands, commissioned 1771. MILITARY SERVICE: in England, lieutenant fireworker in the Royal Regiment of Artillery, 1757; ensign, The Coldstream Guards, 1758; active duty in Germany with The Coldstream Guards, 1760; lieutenant and captain in The Coldstream Guards, 1762; applied for a lieutenant colonel's brevet, but was denied, 1770; in Maryland, commander in chief of all provincial forces. WEALTH DURING LIFETIME. PERSONAL PROPERTY: Eden was granted £100 per year by his father-in-law from the time of his marriage until his appointment as governor. He was given £800 current money by the General Assembly in 1769. While governor, his estimated annual income was £3000–4,000 per year. After his return to England in 1776, Eden's personal property in Maryland was confiscated, but 8 slaves confiscated in 1781 as Eden's property were later found to have been conveyed to a creditor for payment of a debt. In an Estate Act of 1781 passed by the British Parliament, £17,500 was awarded to Eden and his wife in a settlement of litigation over the proprietorship. By 1791 his creditors had made claims of £3,132.2.4 current money against the estate. All except £834.8.2 in debts incurred after 1776 were allowed. LAND AT FIRST ELECTION: probably none in Maryland, except ca. 388 acres in Anne Arundel County, given to his wife by her father before 1771. SIGNIFICANT CHANGES IN LAND BETWEEN FIRST ELECTION AND DEATH: In 1769, Eden purchased the "Capitol Mansion House" and grounds in Annapolis previously tenanted by Gov. Horatio Sharpe, but he mortgaged it immediately for the entire £1,000 purchase price. The mortgage was released by 1775. One of Eden's largest creditors, *William Fitzhugh* (ca. 1722–1798), apparently took the ca. 388 acres of land in Anne Arundel County in payment for Eden's debts to him. Eden also owned 1 lot in Carrollsburgh, Prince George's County, which was confiscated in 1781 along with his lands in Annapolis. WEALTH AT DEATH. DIED: on September 2, 1784, in Annapolis, of dropsy. Buried at old St. Margaret's Parish Church, Anne Arundel County; his body was later removed to St. Anne's Churchyard, Annapolis. PERSONAL PROPERTY: estate appraised by the General Assembly at £2,745.15.0 current money; £356.5.10 remained after payments to his creditors by 1794, with a claim of an additional £559.13.2 outstanding as of that date. LAND: none in Maryland. ADDITIONAL COMMENTS: income at death was at least £800 from a pension allowed him by the British government.

EDGE, JAMES (ca. 1710–1757). BORN: ca. 1710. IMMIGRATED: probably; probably from England. RESIDED: in Mill Hundred, Talbot County. MARRIED by 1746 Hannah (1702–1759), widow of Capt. Tamberlaine Davis (?–1735), of Talbot County, a mariner; eldest daughter of *John Oldham* (?–1729). Her brother was *Edward Oldham* (1709–1773). Her sisters were Elizabeth (1704–by 1765); Mary (1707–?); and Martha. Her nieces were Ann Oldham (?–by 1794), who married *Joshua Clarke* (?–1781); Elizabeth Oldham (?–by 1776), who married *William Hopper* (by 1747–1806); and Hannah Oldham (?–1828), who married *Nicholas Martin* (1743–ca. 1808). CHILDREN. STEPDAUGHTER: Frances Davis. PRIVATE CAREER. EDUCATION: literate. RELIGIOUS AFFILIATION: Anglican, St. Michael's Parish, Talbot County. SOCIAL STATUS AND ACTIVITIES: Gent., 1739. OCCUPATIONAL PROFILE: merchant, agent and factor for Richard Gildart, Esq., of Liverpool, England. PUBLIC CAREER. LEGISLATIVE SERVICE: Lower House, Talbot County, 1754–1756 (Accounts 1–5; Bills of Credit 1–5; died before the 6th session). LOCAL OFFICES: justice, Talbot County, 1741–at least 1756 (quorum, 1749–at least 1756); St. Michael's Parish Vestry, Talbot County, in office 1743, 1750, 1756–1757. WEALTH DURING LIFETIME. PERSONAL PROPERTY: his wife received all of the real and personal estate of her first husband, whose TEV was at least £1,610.13.9 current money (including 20 slaves and a brigantine called *Hannah & Frances*), 1735; his wife bound herself to pay £600 current money to her daughter by her first husband when she became 21 years of age or married, 1739. LAND AT FIRST ELECTION: 3,843 acres in Talbot and Dorchester counties, plus 1 lot in Oxford, Talbot County (303 acres were the residue of 623 acres of the land acquired through his marriage; 3,540 acres, plus 1 lot, by purchase and patent). WEALTH AT DEATH. DIED: in January 1757; buried at Christ Church, St. Michael's, Talbot County. LAND: 3,843 acres in Talbot and Dorchester counties. ADDITIONAL COMMENTS: Edge left all of his real and personal estate to his wife, who in turn left nearly all of her estate, as well as her own, to her two nieces, Ann and Elizabeth Oldham, both of whom married legislators.

EDMONDSON (EDMUNDSON, EDMON-STON, EDMONSON), JOHN (1692–1743). BORN: in December 1692, probably in Talbot County; probably eldest son. NATIVE: third generation. RESIDED: in Talbot County. FAMILY BACKGROUND. FATHER: James Edmondson (1670–1702), son of *John Edmundson* (?–1697/98). STEPFATHER: Jacob Loockerman, Gent. (1678–1731), of Talbot County; son of *Jacob Lookerman* (1652–1730). MOTHER: Magdalen (1679–1739), daughter of *John Stevens* (?–1692). UNCLE: *Thomas Edmondson* (?–ca. 1721/22). BROTHERS: James (?–by 1731); William, who married Susanna Blaney, stepdaughter of *William Clayton* (ca. 1682–1728/29). SISTER: Sarah, who married in 1718 Howell Powell. FIRST COUSIN: Sarah Stevens, who married *Thomas Woolford* (ca. 1699–ca. 1750/51). MARRIED by 1718 Margaret (?–by 1729), daughter of *Tobias Pollard* (ca. 1669–1749); granddaughter of *John Pollard* (?–1702); niece of Hager Robson, who married *John Meekins* (ca. 1674–1734). MARRIED second, by 1730 Margaret (?–by 1767), daughter of Capt. William Finney (?–ca. 1723) and wife Rachel Clayton (?–1749); granddaughter of *William Finney* (ca. 1637–1696); niece of *William Clayton* (ca. 1682–1728/29), *Solomon Clayton* (1685–1739), and Alice Clayton, who married *Edward Wright* (?–1740/41). Margaret Finney Edmondson subsequently married by 1762 *William Thomas* (1705–1767). Her brothers were William; Vincent. Her sister was Katherine, who married Dr. John Jackson. CHILDREN. SONS: *Pollard Edmondson* (ca. 1718–1794); John; James (?–by 1747), who married Ann; and Samuel (?–1751). DAUGHTERS: Elizabeth, who married Hugh Hopewell; Rachel, who married William Hanson, of Talbot County, a merchant. PRIVATE CAREER. EDUCATION: literate. RELIGIOUS AFFILIATION: Anglican, St. Peter's Parish, Talbot County. His parents were Quakers. SOCIAL STATUS AND ACTIVITIES: Gent., 1729. OCCUPATIONAL PROFILE: planter. PUBLIC CAREER. LEGISLATIVE SERVICE: Lower House, Talbot County, 1728–1731, 1732–1734, 1734/35–1737. LOCAL OFFICE: St. Peter's Parish Vestry, Talbot County, in office 1724, 1729–1732. WEALTH DURING LIFETIME. LAND AT FIRST ELECTION: 2,524 acres in Talbot and Dorchester counties (2,356 acres inherited from his father; 168 acres by patent). WEALTH AT DEATH. DIED: in July 1743 in Talbot County. PERSONAL PROPERTY: TEV, £1,112.6.11 current money (including 13 slaves, 4 servants, and books); FB, £316.4.11. LAND: at least 2,340 acres in Talbot County.

EDMONDSON (EDMUNDSON, EDMUNSON), PETER (ca. 1753–1819). BORN: ca. 1753, probably in Dorchester County; possibly only son. NATIVE: fourth generation. RESIDED: in Great Choptank Hundred, Caroline County, 1778; Talbot County, 1795. FAMILY BACKGROUND. FATHER: Peter Sharpe Edmondson (1702–after 1784), son of William Edmondson (1677–1702), a merchant, and wife Sarah Sharpe (?–1702). OTHER KINSHIP: his great-grandfather was *John Edmundson* (?–1697/98). MARRIED on May 5, 1791, Elizabeth (by 1777–?), daughter of *Matthew Driver* (1740–1798); stepdaughter of Esther Casson; stepgranddaughter of *Henry Casson* (?–ca. 1788); stepniece of *Joshua Clarke* (?–1781). Her brother was Joshua (1767–?). Her sister was Margaret. Her first cousins were Elizabeth Baynard Tillotson (1748–1809), who married second, *Philemon Downes* (ca. 1741–ca. 1796); Margaret Baynard (1752–by 1788), who married *Henry Downes* (ca. 1748–1816). CHILDREN. DAUGHTERS: Maria (?–1817), who married Dr. John Rogers; Rachel, who married Alexander Hands, Esq.; and Elizabeth. PRIVATE CAREER. EDUCATION: literate. SOCIAL STATUS AND ACTIVITIES: Gent., 1782; Esq., 1789. OCCUPATIONAL PROFILE: farmer. PUBLIC CAREER. LEGISLATIVE SERVICE: Lower House, Caroline County, 1788. OTHER STATE OFFICE: Constitution Ratification Convention, Caroline County, 1788. LOCAL OFFICES: sheriff, Caroline County, elected 1782, appointed January 1791, elected October 1791; collector of tax, Caroline County, 1783–at least 1785; justice, Caroline County, 1786–at least 1791; justice, Orphans' Court, Caroline County, 1786–at least 1789; trustee to build schoolhouse, Talbot County, 1799. STANDS ON PUBLIC/PRIVATE ISSUES: manumitted several slaves in his will. WEALTH DURING LIFETIME. PERSONAL PROPERTY: 14 slaves, 1790; 25 slaves, 1798; his wife's inheritance, which was received in 1798, consisted of £1,000 in £100 annual payments. LAND AT FIRST ELECTION: 804 acres in Caroline County (457 acres from his father, 347 acres by purchase). SIGNIFICANT CHANGES IN LAND BETWEEN FIRST ELECTION AND DEATH: inherited the remainder of Andrew Mein's estate, which he resurveyed for 423 acres in Talbot County, 1792–1797. WEALTH AT DEATH. DIED: on Tuesday, October 21, 1819, at Dover Bridge, Talbot County. PERSONAL PROPERTY: will mentioned 38 slaves (all but 2 to be manumitted after a period of years), capital stock in the Bank of Caroline, and stock in the Dover Bridge. His executors did not return an inventory or an account. LAND: 2,600 acres in Caroline and Talbot counties.

EDMONDSON, POLLARD (ca. 1718–1794). BORN: ca. 1718 in Talbot County; eldest son. NATIVE: fourth generation. RESIDED: in Dorchester County, 1742; Talbot County from 1743 to death; taxed in the Third District, Talbot County, in 1783. FAMILY BACKGROUND. FATHER: *John Edmondson* (1692–1743). MOTHER: Margaret (?–by 1729), daughter of *Tobias Pollard* (ca. 1669–1749). STEPMOTHER: Margaret Finney (?–by 1767). BROTHERS: John; James (?–by 1747). HALF BROTHER: Samuel (?–1751). SISTER: Elizabeth. HALF SISTER: Rachel. MARRIED first, on March 5, 1738, Mary (?–by 1765), daughter of James Dickinson (?–1738) and wife Hannah Coale. Her brother was William, who married Mary Anne (ca. 1715–1775), daughter of *Thomas Bozman* (ca. 1693–1752). Her sisters were Elizabeth (?–by 1756), who married first, Anthony Richardson, and second, Rev. Philip Walker (?–1776), a merchant; Ann (?–ca. 1774), who married *Samuel Bowman* (?–1768). Her nephew was *Philip Walker* (?–1791). Her nieces were Elizabeth Walker (?–1783), who married *Henry Dickinson* (?–1789); Ann Walker Mein Hindman (?–by 1787), who married third, *Henry Dickinson* (?–1789). MARRIED second, ca. October 1765 Rachel (by 1740–1818), widow of Philip McManus; daughter of Christopher Birckhead (?–by 1740) and wife Ann Harrison (?–1758); stepdaughter of Samuel Sharp (1713/14–1748), William Brooke (?–1754/55), and Daniel Powell. Her brothers were *Christopher Birckhead* (by 1740–1788); Solomon (by 1740–ca. 1753). Her sister was Ann (1730–by 1768), who married William Troth, Jr. CHILDREN. SONS: James (?–ca. 1774), who married Rachel Leeds Bozman; Pollard, appointed 3rd lieutenant of the Fourth Independent Company of Regulars in January 1776, but resigned in March 1776; Horatio (by 1771–1810), who married Charlotte Leeds Thomas; and John (ca. 1773–1841). DAUGHTERS: Lucretia; Ann; Mary; one of the preceding three married *Christopher Birckhead* (by 1740–1788); Lucretia (1766–1826), who married in 1786 Capt. Severn Teackle (?–by 1794); Harriott, who married Richard Trippe; and Sarah, who married by 1790 *Edward Harris* (ca. 1757–ca. 1837). STEPDAUGHTERS: Elizabeth McManus; Margaret McManus; and Ann McManus. PRIVATE CAREER. EDUCATION: literate. RELIGIOUS AFFILIATION: Anglican, St. Peter's Parish, Talbot County. SOCIAL STATUS AND ACTIVITIES: Gent., 1743; Esq., 1777. OCCUPATIONAL PROFILE: probably a planter. PUBLIC CAREER. LEGISLATIVE SERVICE: Lower House, Talbot County, 1751–1754, 1754–1757, 1757–1758 (Accounts 1), 1758–1761, 1762–1763 (Elections 1,

2), 1765–1766 (Elections 2, 4; Arms and Ammunition 2); Conventions, Talbot County, 6th–8th, 1775–1776, 9th, 1776; Lower House, Talbot County, 1785. LOCAL OFFICES: St. Peter's Parish Vestry, Talbot County, in office 1745, 1746–1748, 1750–1756, 1758, 1760–1762; Maryland Senate elector, Talbot County, elected 1791. MILITARY SERVICE: colonial troop of horse, Talbot County Militia, 1748. WEALTH DURING LIFETIME. PERSONAL PROPERTY: assessed value £1,650.0.0, including 39 slaves and 27 oz. plate, 1783; 40 slaves, 1790. LAND AT FIRST ELECTION: 2,244 acres in Queen Anne's, Dorchester, and Talbot counties (inherited 1,296 acres from his father and 661 acres from his maternal grandfather; 287 acres acquired through his first marriage). WEALTH AT DEATH. DIED: between September 16 and October 28, 1794, in Talbot County. PERSONAL PROPERTY: requested no appraisal of his estate. LAND: at least 2,051 acres in Talbot, Dorchester, and Queen Anne's counties.

EDMONDSON (EDMUNDSON, EDMONDSTON), THOMAS (?–ca. 1721/22). BORN: probably between 1677 and 1684 in Talbot County; fourth son. NATIVE: second generation. RESIDED: in Talbot County. FAMILY BACKGROUND. FATHER: *John Edmundson* (?–1697/98). MOTHER: Sarah, daughter of *William Parker* (?–1673/74). BROTHERS: John (1666–1687); James (1670–1702); William (1677–1702); and Samuel (1684–1704). STEPBROTHER: possibly Abraham Morgan (he may have been a natural brother or a brother-in-law). SISTERS: Sarah (1665–?); Grace (1668–?); Henrietta Maria (1671–?); Martha (1673–?); and Elizabeth (?–1709). NEPHEW: *John Edmondson* (1692–1743). MARRIED on August 7, 1699, Mary (?–1742), widow of Robert Grasum (Grason, Greason) (?–1698), a merchant of Stockton, England, and Talbot County; kinswoman of Robert Grundy (?–1720). CHILDREN. STEPSON: Joshua Greason. DAUGHTERS: Sarah, who married (first name unknown) Hopkins; Ann, who married John Tibballs. PRIVATE CAREER. EDUCATION: literate. RELIGIOUS AFFILIATION: he was married in a Quaker Meeting House; his father was a Quaker. SOCIAL STATUS AND ACTIVITIES: Gent., 1704. OCCUPATIONAL PROFILE: planter. PUBLIC CAREER. LEGISLATIVE SERVICE: Lower House, Talbot County, 1719–1721/22. WEALTH DURING LIFETIME. LAND AT FIRST ELECTION: at least 234 acres in Talbot County (probably inherited from his father and brother). Edmondson may have owned additional acreage inherited from his father and brothers, but the exact amount could not be determined. SIGNIF-

ICANT CHANGES IN LAND BETWEEN FIRST ELEC-
TION AND DEATH: sold 234 acres in Talbot
County between 1719 and 1720; purchased 700
acres in Dorchester County, 1720/21. ADDI-
TIONAL COMMENTS: inherited ca. 2,200 acres in
Talbot County from his father, but sold it to his
brother before his first election. WEALTH AT
DEATH. DIED: between December 28, 1721, and
February 13, 1721/22, probably in Talbot County.
LAND: at least 700 acres in Dorchester County.

EDMUNDSON (EDMONDSON), JOHN (?–
1697/98). BORN: probably in Ireland. IMMI-
GRATED: in 1658 from Barbados as an indentured
servant to John Horne, a merchant of London,
England. RESIDED: in Calvert County; Talbot
County after 1664. MARRIED Sarah, daughter of
William Parker (?–1673/74). CHILDREN. SONS:
John (1666–1687), who married Susannah (1673–
1685), daughter of Bryan Omealey; James (1670–
1702), who married in 1691 Magdalen (?–1739),
daughter of *John Stevens* (?–1692); William (1677–
1702), a justice of Talbot County in 1701, who
married Sarah (?–1702), daughter of *William
Sharpe* (ca. 1655–1699); *Thomas Edmondson* (?–
ca. 1721/22), who married in 1699 Mary Grason;
and Samuel (1684–1704). STEPSON, NATURAL
SON, OR SON-IN-LAW: Abraham Morgan. DAUGH-
TERS: Sarah (1665–?), who married William Johnson, of Radcliffe, England; Grace (1668–?); Henrietta Maria (1671–?); Martha (1673–?); and
Elizabeth (?–1709), who married in 1695 William
Stevens, Jr. PRIVATE CAREER. EDUCATION: literate. RELIGIOUS AFFILIATION: Quaker. SOCIAL STA-
TUS AND ACTIVITIES: helped to establish a library
at Third Haven, Talbot County. OCCUPATIONAL
PROFILE: indentured servant, who was free by
1663 when he served as John Horne's attorney in
the Provincial Court; owned a corn mill in the
1660s, which he sold by 1671; a merchant from
1664 until his death (served as a factor for Andrew Cooke, of England, 1677, and later for Josias
Beale and Thomas Legge); called John Edmundson & Co., 1689 (a firm trading with Barbados);
one of the most active land speculators in Maryland and Delaware, buying and selling over 68,000
acres. PUBLIC CAREER. LEGISLATIVE SERVICE:
Lower House, Talbot County, 1676–1682 (Accounts 3; Trade 5), 1686–1688, Associators' Convention, Talbot County, 1689–1692; Grand Committee of Twenty, 1690–1692; Lower House,
Talbot County, 1692 (dismissed from the 1st session, because as a Quaker would not subscribe to
the required oaths), 1694 (dismissed from the 1st
session, because as a Quaker would not subscribe

to the required oaths). OTHER PROVINCIAL OF-
FICE: justice, Provincial Court, 1691–1692.
STANDS ON PUBLIC/PRIVATE ISSUES: strong lob-
byist in the 1680s for dispensation of oaths for
Quakers; active supporter of the Protestant Associators' revolution in 1689, but lost his eligibility
for offices with the establishment of the royal government; he was the object of much controversy in
the Talbot County elections of 1692 and 1694,
because the freeholders insisted on returning him
as a delegate. WEALTH DURING LIFETIME. PER-
SONAL PROPERTY: owned the ship *Holly Merchant,* 1689. LAND AT FIRST ELECTION: had patented over 12,000 acres. WEALTH AT DEATH.
DIED: will probated on March 9, 1697/98. PER-
SONAL PROPERTY: TEV, £387.13.3 sterling (including 18 slaves). LAND: over 7,450 acres.

EDWARDS, BENJAMIN (1753–1829). BORN: on
August 12, 1753, in Stafford County, Virginia.
IMMIGRATED: ca. 1777 from Virginia. RESIDED: in
Montgomery County, ca. 1777–ca. 1800; Nelson
County, Kentucky, ca. 1800–1829. MARRIED by
1775 Margaret, daughter of Ninian Beall, Gent.
(?–1790), of Montgomery County. Her brothers
were Andrew (?–by 1777), who never married;
Charles (?–by 1790), who married Tabitha Beall.
Her sisters were Susannah, who married Alexander Catlett; Eleanor, who married Zachariah Offutt; Ruth, who married Charles Gassaway; Mary,
who married John Watkins, Jr.; and Rachel, who
married Hardage Lane. CHILDREN. Probably five
sons and five daughters, including SON: Ninian
(1775–1833), who studied medicine and law; was
elected to the Kentucky legislature; served as a
judge of the General Court, Circuit Court, Court
of Appeals, and chief justice of Kentucky; was
appointed governor of Illinois by President Madison in 1809; elected to the U.S. Senate from Illinois, 1818–1824; elected governor of Illinois in
1826. PRIVATE CAREER. EDUCATION: literate. RE-
LIGIOUS AFFILIATION: obtained a tract from his
brother-in-law for "a Society of Christians called
Baptists"; his wife's father donated land to the
Baptists out of "natural love, good will and affection." OCCUPATIONAL PROFILE: planter, by 1784;
merchant in Georgetown, Montgomery County,
1790. PUBLIC CAREER. LEGISLATIVE SERVICE:
Lower House, Montgomery County, 1782–1783,
1783, 1784. OTHER STATE OFFICE: Constitution
Ratification Convention, Montgomery County,
1788. LOCAL OFFICES: trustee of the poor, Montgomery County, in office 1789; associate justice,
Circuit Court, Montgomery County, appointed
1793. OUT OF STATE SERVICE: representative, U.S.

Congress, 1795 (elected to fill vacancy; seated on January 2, 1795). WEALTH DURING LIFETIME. PERSONAL PROPERTY: assessed value £840.0.0, including 17 slaves, 1783; assessed value £521.0.0, including 16 slaves and 14 oz. plate, 1793; assessed value £416.0.0, including 11 slaves and 14 oz. plate, 1797; 13 slaves, Kentucky, 1800; 14 slaves, Kentucky, 1811; 16 slaves, Kentucky, 1812. LAND AT FIRST ELECTION: 976 acres in Montgomery County (700 acres from wife's dower, plus 276 acres that his wife inherited from her brother). SIGNIFICANT CHANGES IN LAND BETWEEN FIRST ELECTION AND DEATH: purchased 2,009 acres in Maryland and Kentucky, 1784–1812; sold 906 acres in Montgomery County, 1784–1812. WEALTH AT DEATH. DIED: on November 13, 1829, in Elkton, Kentucky; buried on his estate in Elkton, Kentucky. LAND: owned ca. 2,985 acres in 1812, of which ca. 1,061 acres were in Kentucky and the remainder in Montgomery County.

ELLIOTT, WILLIAM (?–1756). BORN: of age by 1713; eldest son. NATIVE: at least second generation. RESIDED: on Kent Island, Queen Anne's County. FAMILY BACKGROUND. FATHER: William Elliott (?–1713), of Kent Island, Queen Anne's County; a carpenter. MOTHER: Elizabeth. BROTHERS: Thomas; Henry; John, a cooper; Joseph; and Benjamin. SISTER: Elizabeth. MARRIED Mary. CHILDREN. SON: John. DAUGHTERS: Elizabeth, who married Thomas Elliott Hutchings; (first name unknown), who married Matthew Griffith. PRIVATE CAREER. EDUCATION: literate. RELIGIOUS AFFILIATION: Anglican, Christ Church Parish, Kent Island, Queen Anne's County. SOCIAL STATUS AND ACTIVITIES: Mr., 1722; Gent., 1725. OCCUPATIONAL PROFILE: planter. PUBLIC CAREER. LEGISLATIVE SERVICE: Lower House, Queen Anne's County, 1722–1724, 1725–1727, 1728–1731, 1732–1734, 1734/35–1737. LOCAL OFFICES: justice, Queen Anne's County, 1732–at least 1734 (quorum, 1734); coroner, Queen Anne's County, appointed 1739; reader, Christ Church Parish, Queen Anne's County, license granted 1747. MILITARY SERVICE: captain, by 1727. WEALTH DURING LIFETIME. LAND AT FIRST ELECTION: at least 220 acres in Queen Anne's County (220 acres from his father). WEALTH AT DEATH. DIED: between April 1 and April 22, 1756, in Queen Anne's County. PERSONAL PROPERTY: TEV, £858.19.5 current money (including 21 slaves, 1 servant, 12 oz. 13 dwt. 10 gr. silver, and books); FB, £811.13.3. LAND: 220 acres in Queen Anne's County.

ELTONHEAD, WILLIAM (ca. 1616–1655). BORN: ca. 1616 in Eltonhead, Lancastershire, England; first son. IMMIGRATED: in 1643, apparently returned to England and reimmigrated in 1648 as a free adult. RESIDED: in Calvert or St. Mary's counties. FAMILY BACKGROUND. FATHER: John Eltonhead, of Middle Temple, England. MOTHER: Elizabeth, daughter of John Osbaldeston. UNCLE: Edward Eltonhead, of Henham, Essex, England, a master in Chancery in 1658. BROTHER: Richard Eltonhead, Esq., of Eltonhead, Lancastershire, England. SISTER: Jane, who married first, Robert Moryson, of Kecoughtan, Virginia, and second, in 1649 *Cuthbert Fenwick* (1614–1655). MARRIED by 1649 Jane (1617–1659), widow of both Thomas Smith and Philip Taylor (ca. 1610–?). CHILDREN. STEPSON: Thomas Taylor (ca. 1643–1696), the sheriff of Dorchester County in 1669 and a justice (quorum) of Dorchester County by 1679, who married Frances. PRIVATE CAREER. EDUCATION: literate; admitted to St. John's College, Cambridge University, 1631; admitted to the Middle Temple, London, England, 1632/33. RELIGIOUS AFFILIATION: probably a Protestant. SOCIAL STATUS AND ACTIVITIES: brought six men servants, one maid, and one boy with him when he immigrated to Maryland; in partnership with his uncle Edward Eltonhead to transport 100 persons to Maryland for a grant of 10,000 acres; probably recruited by *Cecilius Calvert, 2nd Lord Baltimore* (1605–1675), in an effort to attract influential Protestants to Maryland; often returned to England and rarely served as a councilor. OCCUPATIONAL PROFILE: planter. PUBLIC CAREER. LEGISLATIVE SERVICE: Upper House, 1650–1650/51 (appointed, but did not serve). PROVINCIAL OFFICE: Council, 1649–1655. STANDS ON PUBLIC/PRIVATE ISSUES: supported Lord Baltimore against the Parliamentary Commissioners. WEALTH DURING LIFETIME. LAND AT FIRST ELECTION: a 2,000-acre manor, 1649 (probably held land in partnership with his uncle). WEALTH AT DEATH. DIED: on March 25, 1655, when captured and executed at the Battle of the Severn. PERSONAL PROPERTY: TEV, 14,202 pounds of tobacco (including 2 servants). LAND: 1,130 acres.

ELZEY, ARNOLD (ca. 1758–1818). BORN: ca. 1758, probably in Somerset County. NATIVE: at least second generation. RESIDED: in Somerset County; Baltimore County, 1779; Princess Anne Hundred, Somerset County, 1783; Washington, D.C., 1801. FAMILY BACKGROUND. FATHER: possibly Arnold Elzey, Gent. (ca. 1724–?). MARRIED by 1796 Henrietta (?–1835), daughter of Ephraim

Wilson (1726–1778) and wife Mary; granddaughter of *David Wilson* (1704–1750); niece of *Samuel Wilson* (1735–1790). Her brother was David, said to be mentally incompetent in 1777. Her sister was Peggy. **CHILDREN.** DAUGHTER: Elizabeth M. PRIVATE CAREER. EDUCATION: A.B., College of New Jersey (later became Princeton University), 1775. RELIGIOUS AFFILIATION: Anglican, Somerset Parish, Somerset County. SOCIAL STATUS AND ACTIVITIES: member of the American Whig Society, 1775; a founder of the Medical and Chirurgical Faculty of Maryland, 1799; vice president of the Medical Society of the District of Columbia. OCCUPATIONAL PROFILE: a physician. PUBLIC CAREER. LEGISLATIVE SERVICE: Lower House, Somerset County, 1784. LOCAL OFFICE: Somerset Parish Vestry, Somerset County, elected 1792, 1795, out of office by 1797. MILITARY SERVICE: surgeon, Twenty-third Regiment, Maryland Militia, served from 1794–1800; garrison surgeon's mate, U.S. Army Fifth District, appointed 1814; post surgeon, Washington, D.C., appointed in 1816. WEALTH DURING LIFETIME. PERSONAL PROPERTY: assessed value £315.0.0, including 8 slaves, 1783; assessed value £460.0.0, including 17 slaves, 1793. LAND AT FIRST ELECTION: possibly ca. 775 acres in Somerset County obtained through his marriage, but the date of his marriage is unknown. SIGNIFICANT CHANGES IN LAND BETWEEN FIRST ELECTION AND DEATH: assessed for 817 acres in Somerset County, 1793; purchased at least 137 acres in Somerset County, plus 1 lot in Princess Anne, Somerset County, 1795; sold more than 1,006 acres in Somerset County, plus 1 lot in Princess Anne, Somerset County, 1796 to 1808. WEALTH AT DEATH. DIED: on June 6, 1818, in Washington, D.C.; size of estate unknown.

EMERSON (EMMERSON, EMORSON, EMBERSON, EMERTON), THOMAS (?–1720). BORN: probably in Talbot County, of age by 1688; only son. NATIVE: at least third generation. RESIDED: in Talbot County. FAMILY BACKGROUND. FATHER: Thomas Emerson (?–1686), of Wye River, Talbot County; a cooper, 1669; a planter, 1676. STEPFATHER: Isaac Winchester (?–ca. 1695), of Talbot County. MOTHER: Katherine, daughter of Philip Stevenson, of Talbot County. STEPBROTHER: Isaac Winchester. STEP OR HALF SISTERS: Sarah Winchester; Rebecca Winchester. MARRIED Mary (?–by 1713), daughter of John Sargeant (?–1698), of Talbot County, and wife Mary (?–1711), of Queen Anne's County. Her sisters were Elizabeth (?–1708), who married Nicholas Goldsborough (1662–1705); Katherine, who mar-

ried first, by 1711 (first name unknown) Bowdell, and second, by 1713 Matthew Erickson; Priscilla, who married (first name unknown) Brewin; possibly also (first name unknown), who married (first name unknown) Gibson. Her stepnephew was *Nicholas Goldsborough* (ca. 1689–1766). CHILDREN. SONS: Thomas; Philip (ca. 1712–1755), who married Sarah (?–1755), daughter of *Henry Trippe* (?–ca. 1723/24). DAUGHTERS: Katherine (ca. 1703–?), who married Thomas Hammond; Elizabeth; and Mary. PRIVATE CAREER. EDUCATION: literate. SOCIAL STATUS AND ACTIVITIES: Mr., 1701; Gent., 1713. OCCUPATIONAL PROFILE: possibly a merchant; probably a planter. PUBLIC CAREER. LEGISLATIVE SERVICE: Lower House, Talbot County, 1716–1718, 1719 (Aggrievances 1; died before the 2nd session). LOCAL OFFICES: justice, Talbot County, 1706–at least 1719 (quorum, 1707–at least 1719); justice, Court of Oyer and Terminer and Gaol Delivery, Talbot County, commissioned 1716 and 1718. MILITARY SERVICE: major, 1716. WEALTH DURING LIFETIME. LAND AT FIRST ELECTION: at least 1,532 acres in Talbot and Queen Anne's counties (520 acres inherited from his father; 200 acres, plus one-third of 200 additional acres, through his marriage; 746 acres by purchase). WEALTH AT DEATH. DIED: in April 1720 in Talbot County. PERSONAL PROPERTY: TEV, £1,271.7.7 current money (including 18 slaves, 2 servants, and goods in his store); FB, £739.14.1. LAND: at least 1,660 acres in Talbot and Queen Anne's counties.

EMORY (EMERY, EMMERY, EMMORY), CHARLES (ca. 1750–1811). BORN: ca. 1750, probably in Queen Anne's County; younger son, second son to be named Charles. NATIVE: third generation. RESIDED: in Queen Anne's County; Tuckahoe Hundred, Queen Anne's County, 1778; Caroline County, 1786; Talbot County, 1796. FAMILY BACKGROUND. FATHER: John Emory (?–1763), of Queen Anne's County, a planter and the deputy surveyor of Queen Anne's County in 1743. MOTHER: Ann (?–1774). BROTHERS: Arthur, who married Sophia; James (?–1772); John; Thomas; William; and Charles, the elder. SISTERS: Sophia, who married John Fisher; Sarah, who married William Durding; Rebeccah, who married Caleb Clemonds; Elizabeth, who married William Emory; and Ann. MARRIED first, by 1774 Littilen. MARRIED second, by 1792 Elizabeth. MARRIED third, by 1795 Frances (?–1810), daughter of Elijah Bishop (?–ca. 1783), of Queen Anne's County, and wife Deborah Hawkins (ca. 1755–by 1792); stepdaughter of *Joshua Seney* (1756–1798); stepgranddaughter of *John Seney* (?–1795). Her brother was Dr. William Smith Bishop (?–by 1809). CHILDREN. SON: John Martin Groome, who served in the Fourth Maryland Regiment during the War of 1812, and married first, in 1812 Harriot Downes (?–1814), and second, in 1818 Ann North, daughter of Col. North, of Philadelphia, Pennsylvania. DAUGHTERS: Mary Eliza Bishop, who married in 1827 John Chamberlaine Goldsborough; Anna Maria, who married in 1812 Gideon Davis, of Centreville, Queen Anne's County; and Sophia Frances. PRIVATE CAREER. EDUCATION: literate. RELIGIOUS AFFILIATION: Methodist; father held a pew in Wye Chapel (Anglican), Queen Anne's County. SOCIAL STATUS AND ACTIVITIES: Gent., 1792; Esq., 1803. OCCUPATIONAL PROFILE: planter; surveyor. PUBLIC CAREER. LEGISLATIVE SERVICE: Lower House, Caroline County, 1788, 1789, 1791–1792. OTHER STATE OFFICE: examiner general, Eastern Shore, 1796–1810 (resigned). LOCAL OFFICES: deputy surveyor, Caroline County, 1794; surveyor, Caroline County, 1800; Maryland Senate elector, Talbot County, 1801. STANDS ON PUBLIC/PRIVATE ISSUES: manumitted two slaves, 1785; manumitted six slaves, 1807. WEALTH DURING LIFETIME. PERSONAL PROPERTY: 4 slaves, 1770, 1772 (gifts from his mother); 3 slaves, 1798. LAND AT FIRST ELECTION: 147 acres in Caroline and Queen Anne's counties (100 acres from his father, of which 90 acres had been sold before his first election; 137 acres by purchase). SIGNIFICANT CHANGES IN LAND BETWEEN FIRST ELECTION AND DEATH: acquired leases on 3 lots in Easton, Talbot County, and acquired an additional 1,216 acres between 1790 and 1810 (gained 900 acres in Anne Arundel County, plus one-third part of 206 acres in Queen Anne's County, through his third marriage; purchased 218 acres in Talbot County; gained 30 acres on a resurvey of part of the Caroline County land he owned at the time of his first election). Sold at least 353 acres in Talbot, Caroline, and Queen Anne's counties between 1795 and 1810; sold one-third part of 206 acres, 1806; gave his daughters 900 acres in Anne Arundel County and 2 lots in Easton, Talbot County, retaining a life estate for himself and his wife, 1810. WEALTH AT DEATH. DIED: on Friday, February 1, 1811, in Easton, Talbot County, after a long illness. PERSONAL PROPERTY: TEV, at least $705.66 (including books and surveyor's instruments). LAND: at least 42 acres and a lease on 1 lot in Talbot County, plus a life estate in 900 acres and leases on 2 lots in Anne Arundel and Talbot counties.

ENNALLS (ENNOLDS, ENNALS), BARTHOLOMEW (1643–1688). BORN: in 1643. IMMIGRATED: by 1668 as a free adult with his wife and children from York County, Virginia. RESIDED: in Dorchester County. MARRIED by 1661/62 Mary, widow of Francis Heyward, of York County, Virginia. CHILDREN. SONS: *Thomas Ennalls* (?–1718), who married Elizabeth (1664/65–1739), daughter of *Roger Woolford* (?–ca. 1701/2); William, who married Anne Warren; *Joseph Ennalls* (?–1709), who married Mary, daughter of *John Brooke* (by 1646–1692/93); *Henry Ennalls* (1675–1734), who married Mary (1674–1745), daughter of *Henry Hooper* (ca. 1643–1720); and Bartholomew. STEPSONS: Francis Heyward; and John Heyward, who married Sarah, daughter of *Henry Hooper* (ca. 1643–1720). DAUGHTERS: Mary, who married John Foster; Elizabeth (1664/65–1739), who married *Roger Woolford* (1670–1730). PRIVATE CAREER. EDUCATION: literate. RELIGIOUS AFFILIATION: Protestant. SOCIAL STATUS AND ACTIVITIES: in Virginia by 1661; no title on arrival in Maryland; proved his rights in 1669 for transporting eleven people, including four servants from Virginia; purchased 2,000 acres from *John Edmundson* (?–1697/98) for a sloop and 1,000 pounds of tobacco in 1668; established a politically active family, with three sons serving in the Assembly. OCCUPATIONAL PROFILE: planter; merchant. PUBLIC CAREER. LEGISLATIVE SERVICE: Lower House, Dorchester County, 1676–1682 (Accounts 3), 1682–1684 (Trade 2). LOCAL OFFICES: justice, Dorchester County, 1671–1674 (dismissed for refusing to take the required oath, 1674), 1679–1688 (quorum, 1685–1688). STANDS ON PUBLIC/PRIVATE ISSUES: refused to take the required oath as justice in 1674 because of a complaint against the court clerk, Edward Savage. WEALTH DURING LIFETIME. LAND AT FIRST ELECTION: over 2,145 acres; acquired an additional 2,156 acres in 1681. WEALTH AT DEATH. DIED: will probated on June 20, 1688. PERSONAL PROPERTY: TEV, £991.0.3 sterling (including 21 slaves, 9 books, and £176 in goods in Barbados and en route from England). LAND: ca. 4,300 acres.

ENNALLS, BARTHOLOMEW (ca. 1700–1783). BORN: ca. 1700 in Dorchester County. NATIVE: third generation. RESIDED: at "Fort Neck," Transquakin Hundred, Dorchester County. FAMILY BACKGROUND. FATHER: *Joseph Ennalls* (?–1709), son of *Bartholomew Ennalls* (1643–1688). MOTHER: Mary, daughter of *John Brooke* (by 1646–1692/93). UNCLES: *Thomas Ennalls* (?–1718); *Henry Ennalls* (1675–1734). AUNTS:

Elizabeth Ennalls, who married *Roger Woolford* (1670–1730); Ann Brooke, who married first, *Thomas Cooke* (?–1692/93). BROTHERS: *William Ennalls* (?–1731); Joseph (1702–1759); Thomas (?–1753); and Henry (?–1734). SISTERS: Elizabeth (?–by 1739), who married *Charles Goldsborough* (1707–1767); Mary, who married *Henry Hooper* (ca. 1687–1767). FIRST COUSIN: *Thomas Woolford* (ca. 1699–ca. 1750/51). NEPHEWS: *Joseph Ennalls* (ca. 1745–1779); *William Ennalls* (?–1785); *John Ennalls* (by 1746–ca. 1778); *Henry Hooper, Jr.* (ca. 1727–1790); and *Robert Goldsborough* (1733–1788). NIECES: Mary Ennalls, who married *Ennalls Hooper* (?–ca. 1763); Ann Ennalls (ca. 1729–by 1790), who married *Henry Hooper, Jr.* (ca. 1727–1790); Elinor Ennalls (ca. 1738–1793), who married *Joseph Daffin* (?–1796); and Elizabeth Greenberry Goldsborough (ca. 1731–1820), who married *William Ennalls* (?–1785). MARRIED first, by 1725 Mary Smith. MARRIED second, by 1735 Elizabeth, widow of William Taylor (?–1730); daughter of *Henry Trippe* (?–ca. 1723/24); stepdaughter of John Eccleston; granddaughter of *Henry Trippe* (1632–1697/98); half niece or stepniece of *John Brooke* (by 1646–1692/93). Her brothers were Edward (?–1772); *Henry Trippe* (?–1744); and John. Her sisters were Sarah (?–1755); Mary (?–1782), who married *Jacob Hindman* (by 1713–1766). Her nephews were *James Hindman* (1741–1830); *William Hindman* (1743–1822). Her nieces were Elizabeth Hindman (?–by 1788), who married *William Perry* (1746–1799); Mary Emerson Trippe (ca. 1739–1811), who married *Robert Goldsborough IV* (1740–1798); Ann Trippe, who married *John Dickinson* (ca. 1726–1789). CHILDREN. SONS: Joseph (1735–?), who resided in North Carolina by 1785; Henry (1739–?); William (1741–?); and Bartholomew (1746–?), who married first, in 1789 Sally Hooper, and second, Nancy Keene. DAUGHTERS: Mary; Sarah; Elizabeth; Ann (1737–?); and Leath (Leah) (1743–?). STEPDAUGHTER: Mary Taylor. PRIVATE CAREER. EDUCATION: literate. RELIGIOUS AFFILIATION: Protestant. SOCIAL STATUS AND ACTIVITIES: Gent., by 1736. OCCUPATIONAL PROFILE: mariner, 1718; probably also a planter. PUBLIC CAREER. LEGISLATIVE SERVICE: Lower House, Dorchester County, 1738, 1739–1741, 1742–1744, 1745 (Elections), 1745/46–1748 (Elections Cv 1, 1-3, 4). LOCAL OFFICES: justice, Dorchester County, by 1734–at least 1743 (quorum, 1734–at least 1743); sheriff, Dorchester County, 1749–1752; deputy commissary, Dorchester County, in office 1753–1755. MILITARY SERVICE: captain, by 1730; major, 1748; called colonel, 1776. WEALTH DURING LIFETIME.

PERSONAL PROPERTY: 27 slaves, 1776. LAND AT FIRST ELECTION: 659 acres in Dorchester County; also controlled 324 acres in Dorchester County for his stepdaughter, Mary Taylor. ADDITIONAL COMMENTS: Bartholomew inherited 300 acres in Dorchester County from his uncle, *Thomas Ennalls* (?–1718). A few months later, in November 1718, Bartholomew exchanged this inherited land for 600 acres that his brother *William Ennalls* (?–1731) owned in Dorchester County. This land comprised the bulk of his acreage at first election. SIGNIFICANT CHANGES IN LAND BETWEEN FIRST ELECTION AND DEATH: acquired 2,050 acres in Dorchester County by purchase or patent between 1747 and 1769; sold 569 acres in Dorchester County between 1749 and 1764. WEALTH AT DEATH. DIED: in 1783, probably in Dorchester County. PERSONAL PROPERTY: assessed value £1,357.10.10, including 25 slaves and 2.5 oz. plate, 1783; also paid taxes on 14 slaves for various other people, 1783. LAND: 1,590 acres in Dorchester County; not known if he still controlled 324 acres in Dorchester County for his stepdaughter.

ENNALLS (ENNOLDS, ENNALS), HENRY (1675–1734). BORN: in 1675 in Dorchester County; younger son. NATIVE: second generation. RESIDED: in Dorchester County. FAMILY BACKGROUND. FATHER: *Bartholomew Ennalls* (1643–1688). MOTHER: Mary Heyward. BROTHERS: *Thomas Ennalls* (?–1718), who married Elizabeth (1664/65–1739), daughter of *Roger Woolford* (?–ca. 1701/2); William; *Joseph Ennalls* (?–1709), who married Mary, daughter of *John Brooke* (by 1646–1692/93); and Bartholomew. HALF BROTHERS: Francis Heyward; John Heyward. SISTERS: Elizabeth (1664/65–1739), who married *Roger Woolford* (1670–1730); Mary. MARRIED Mary (1674–1745), daughter of *Henry Hooper* (ca. 1643–1720). Her brothers were Richard; John (?–1754); Roger; *Henry Hooper* (ca. 1687–1767); Thomas; and James (1703–1789). Her sisters were Priscilla; Elizabeth, who married *Matthew Travers* (ca. 1672–1742); Rebecca; Ann (1687–1767), who married *John Broome* (1676–ca. 1738/39); Mary, who married first, Levin Hicks (?–1731), son of *Thomas Hicks* (1659–1722), and second, *John Rider* (1686–1739/40); and Rosannah, who married John Hudson, Quartus (?–1751), son of *John Hudson* (1653–1730) and wife Sarah. CHILDREN. SONS: Henry (?–1770), who married Margaret; Thomas, who married Ann, daughter of Andrew Skinner; Bartholomew (?–by 1752); and Joseph (1709–1756), who married Mary (?–ca. 1772), widow of Thomas Haskins and daughter of *Govert Lookerman* (ca.

1681–1728). DAUGHTERS: Sarah (1697–1742), who married Dr. William Murray (1692–1763); Elizabeth, who married (first name unknown) Feddeman; and Rebecca, who married John Caile. PRIVATE CAREER. EDUCATION: literate. RELIGIOUS AFFILIATION: Protestant. SOCIAL STATUS AND ACTIVITIES: second generation burgess; first elected to the Assembly after the death of his brother *Joseph Ennalls* (?–1709), but the reason for his brief legislative tenure is unknown. OCCUPATIONAL PROFILE: planter. PUBLIC CAREER. LEGISLATIVE SERVICE: Lower House, Dorchester County, 1712–1714. LOCAL OFFICES: justice, Dorchester County, by 1700–1734 (chief justice, ca. 1722–1734). MILITARY SERVICE: captain, by 1702; major, by 1723; colonel, by 1731–1734. WEALTH DURING LIFETIME. LAND AT FIRST ELECTION: at least 3 tracts inherited from his father. WEALTH AT DEATH. DIED: between March 21, 1733/34, and May 1, 1734. PERSONAL PROPERTY: TEV and FB £789.9.12 current money (including 16 slaves and a parcel of law and divinity books). LAND: 3,570 acres, plus part of a 517-acre tract held in partnership with Jacob Lookerman.

ENNALLS, HENRY (ca. 1741–by 1788). BORN: ca. 1741 in Dorchester County; younger son. NATIVE: fourth generation. RESIDED: in Upper District, Dorchester County. FAMILY BACKGROUND. FATHER: Dr. Joseph Ennalls (1709–1756), son of *Henry Ennalls* (1675–1734). MOTHER: Mary (?–ca. 1772), widow of Thomas Haskins (?–1735); daughter of *Govert Lookerman* (ca. 1681–1728) and wife Sarah Woolford. AUNT: Sarah Lookerman (?–by 1745), who married *Joseph Cox Gray* (?–1764). BROTHER: *Thomas Ennalls* (?–by 1783). HALF BROTHERS: William Haskins (1729–1779), who married in 1759 Sarah (?–1786), daughter of Rev. Thomas Airey (1701–1765) and wife Elizabeth Pitt; Joseph Haskins (1731–?), who married in 1759 Sarah, daughter of Thomas Ennalls (?–1746) and wife Ann Skinner. SISTERS: Mary (1738–?), who married in 1765 James Sulivane (1737–?), son of *Daniel Sulivane* (ca. 1708–by 1783); Margaret (?–by 1795), who married *William Maynadier* (1747–1795); Rebecca (?–by 1767); and Henrietta. HALF SISTER: Elizabeth Haskins (1733–1805), who married in 1754 Hall Caile. FIRST COUSIN: *James Murray* (?–1784). NIECE: Sarah Ennalls (1761–1842), who married *Henry Waggaman* (1753–1809). OTHER KINSHIP: his second cousin was *Henry Ennalls* (?–ca. 1803). MARRIED by 1775 Ann, a minor in 1753, daughter of William Smith (?–ca. 1752), of Dorchester County, and wife Sophia. Her brothers were

Thomas (?–1775), who married Sophia Griffith (?–1775); William. PRIVATE CAREER. EDUCATION: literate. SOCIAL STATUS AND ACTIVITIES: Gent., by 1774. OCCUPATIONAL PROFILE: planter. PUBLIC CAREER. LEGISLATIVE SERVICE: Lower House, Dorchester County, 1785. *See* statement in Identification Problem section. LOCAL OFFICE: justice, Dorchester County, 1773. WEALTH DURING LIFETIME. PERSONAL PROPERTY: assessed value £1,135.11.8, including 27 slaves and 23 oz. plate, 1783. LAND AT FIRST ELECTION: 787 acres in Dorchester County (359 acres inherited from his father; at least 228 acres by purchase); also had control over 1,227 acres in Dorchester County for the heirs of his wife's brother. WEALTH AT DEATH. DIED: by February 2, 1788, probably in Dorchester County. LAND: 787 acres in Dorchester County; not known whether he still controlled the land for Smith's heirs. IDENTIFICATION PROBLEMS. There were two men named Henry Ennalls living in Dorchester County during the term of legislative service. Both were from prominent families, both had considerable real and personal estates, and both had legislative connections within their families. There were no identifying characteristics or titles given in the minutes of the Lower House for 1785, which might have helped in discovering which man served. Therefore, biographical sketches are included for both.

ENNALLS, HENRY (?–ca. 1803). BORN: in Dorchester County, a minor in 1769; elder son. NATIVE: fifth generation. RESIDED: near Cambridge, Dorchester County. FAMILY BACKGROUND. FATHER: Henry Ennalls, Jr. (ca. 1723–1760), of Dorchester County, son of Thomas Ennalls (?–1746), of Great Choptank, Dorchester County, and wife Ann Skinner. Henry Ennalls, Jr., was also known as Henry Ennalls, Ferry. STEPFATHER: (first name unknown) Keene. GUARDIAN: his uncle, Joseph Ennalls (?–by 1797). MOTHER: Mary, daughter of Thomas Nevett (?–by 1760), of Dorchester County, a merchant, and wife Sarah Rider (1710–?); stepdaughter of both William Fishwick and Robert Darnall; granddaughter of *John Rider* (1686–1739/40). BROTHER: Thomas. SISTERS: Catherine, who married (first name unknown) Bruff; Mary, who married George Ward; Ann (?–by 1803), who married Richard Bassett (1745–1815), of Delaware, a lawyer. Bassett was a member of the Delaware Senate in 1782, a member of the Delaware House of Representatives in 1786, a U.S. senator from 1789 to 1793, chief justice of the Court of Common Pleas in Delaware from 1793 to 1799, governor of Delaware from 1799 to 1801, and was appointed a judge of the U.S. Circuit Court in 1801. OTHER KINSHIP: his second cousin was *Henry Ennalls* (ca. 1741–by 1788). MARRIED on June 1, 1785, Sarah (ca. 1758–by 1832), daughter of *Robert Goldsborough* (1733–1788); granddaughter of *Charles Goldsborough* (1707–1767); niece of Elizabeth Greenberry Goldsborough (ca. 1731–1820), who married *William Ennalls* (?–1785). Her brothers were Charles (ca. 1756–ca. 1759); Charles (1761–1801); Robert (ca. 1766–1790); John (by 1766–?); William; Richard; and Howes. Her sisters were Rebecca (ca. 1757–?), who married *Howes Goldsborough* (1747–1797); Elizabeth; and Rachel (?–1811). Sarah Goldsborough Ennalls subsequently married in 1804 Robert North Carnan (?–1836), of Baltimore County. CHILDREN. Died without progeny. PRIVATE CAREER. EDUCATION: literate. RELIGIOUS AFFILIATION: Anglican; converted to Methodism, ca. 1790. ADDITIONAL COMMENTS: Ennalls wrote a letter detailing the sad state of the Anglican church, ca. 1788. SOCIAL STATUS AND ACTIVITIES: Gent., by 1781; Esq., by 1793. OCCUPATIONAL PROFILE: probably a planter. PUBLIC CAREER. LEGISLATIVE SERVICE: Lower House, Dorchester County, 1785. *See* statement in Identification Problem section. LOCAL OFFICE: Great Choptank Parish Vestry, Dorchester County, 1788–1790. STANDS ON PUBLIC/PRIVATE ISSUES: manumitted seven slaves in 1790. WEALTH DURING LIFETIME. PERSONAL PROPERTY: assessed value £162.0.0, including 2 slaves, 1783. LAND AT FIRST ELECTION: approximately 3,732 acres in Dorchester County, plus 1.5 lots in Cambridge, Dorchester County (500 acres were remaining from at least 896 acres inherited from his father; 332 acres were originally inherited by his brother, but were listed under Henry's name in the tax lists of 1783). SIGNIFICANT CHANGES IN LAND BETWEEN FIRST ELECTION AND DEATH: his wife inherited a proportional share in her father's real and personal estate, ca. 1788, but the exact acreage is unknown; Ennalls and his wife began selling her rights to her father's estate, by 1790; he sold much land between 1785 and 1803, often without mentioning the tract name on the acreage conveyed. WEALTH AT DEATH. DIED: between February 11, 1802, and June 28, 1803, probably in Dorchester County. LAND: exact acreage unknown; at least 746 acres of his land in Dorchester County were sold after his death to pay his large number of debts. IDENTIFICATION PROBLEMS. There were two men named Henry Ennalls living in Dorchester County during the term of legislative service. Both were from prominent families, both had considerable real and

personal estates, and both had legislative connections within their families. There were no identifying characteristics or titles given in the minutes of the Lower House for 1785, which might have helped in discovering which man served. Therefore, biographical sketches are included for both.

ENNALLS, JOHN (by 1746–ca. 1778). BORN: between 1736 and 1746 in Dorchester County; younger son. NATIVE: fourth generation. RESIDED: in Transquakin Hundred, Dorchester County. FAMILY BACKGROUND. FATHER: Col. Joseph Ennalls (1702–1759), son of *Joseph Ennalls* (?–1709). MOTHER: Mary. UNCLES: *Bartholomew Ennalls* (ca. 1700–1783); *William Ennalls* (?–1731). AUNTS: Elizabeth Ennalls (?–by 1739), who married *Charles Goldsborough* (1707–1767); Mary Ennalls, who married *Henry Hooper* (ca. 1687–1767). BROTHER: *William Ennalls* (?–1785). SISTERS: Mary (?–by 1766), who married David Murray; Elinor (ca. 1738–1793), who married *Joseph Daffin* (?–1796); Elizabeth; and Ann (Nancy) (1750–1803), who married Thomas Muse (?–1776), of Virginia. FIRST COUSINS: *Joseph Ennalls* (ca. 1745–1779); *Henry Hooper, Jr.* (ca. 1727–1790); *Robert Goldsborough* (1733–1788); Mary Ennalls, who married *Ennalls Hooper* (?–ca. 1763); Ann Ennalls (ca. 1729–by 1790), who married *Henry Hooper, Jr.* (ca. 1727–1790); Elizabeth Greenberry Goldsborough (ca. 1731–1820), who married *William Ennalls* (?–1785). MARRIED never. PRIVATE CAREER. EDUCATION: literate. RELIGIOUS AFFILIATION: Protestant. SOCIAL STATUS AND ACTIVITIES: Esq. at death. OCCUPATIONAL PROFILE: probably a planter. PUBLIC CAREER. LEGISLATIVE SERVICE: Lower House, Dorchester County, 1773–1774; Conventions, Dorchester County, 1st, 1774, 4th, 1775, 6th–8th, 1775–1776 (did not attend the 8th Convention), 9th, 1776. LOCAL OFFICES: superintendent to collect clothing and blankets to supply the Maryland troops, Dorchester County, appointed 1777; commissioner of tax, Dorchester County, commissioned 1777. MILITARY SERVICE: lieutenant colonel, Second Battalion, Lower Eastern Shore Militia at Cambridge, by July 1776; colonel, Nineteenth Battalion, Dorchester County Militia, commissioned October 1776. WEALTH DURING LIFETIME. PERSONAL PROPERTY: 38 slaves, 1776. LAND AT FIRST ELECTION: at least 3,792 acres in Dorchester County (all inherited from his father). SIGNIFICANT CHANGES IN LAND BETWEEN FIRST ELECTION AND DEATH: patented 338 acres in Dorchester County, 1774. WEALTH AT DEATH. DIED: will probated on February 16, 1778, in Dorchester County. PERSONAL PROP-

ERTY: size of estate unknown. LAND: at least 4,130 acres in Dorchester County, which John left to his two sisters Anne Muse and Elinor Daffin, wife of *Joseph Daffin* (?–1796), and to Anne Muse's two children.

ENNALLS (ENNOLDS, ENNALS), JOSEPH

(?–1709). BORN: almost certainly in Dorchester County; second or third son. NATIVE: second generation. RESIDED: in Dorchester County. FAMILY BACKGROUND. FATHER: *Bartholomew Ennalls* (1643–1688). MOTHER: Mary Heyward. BROTHERS: *Thomas Ennalls* (?–1718), who married Elizabeth (1664/65–1739), daughter of *Roger Woolford* (?–ca. 1701/2); William; *Henry Ennalls* (1675–1734), who married Mary, daughter of *Henry Hooper* (ca. 1643–1720); and Bartholomew. HALF BROTHERS: Francis Heyward; and John Heyward. SISTERS: Elizabeth (1664/65–1737), who married *Roger Woolford* (1670–1730); and Mary. MARRIED by 1692/93 Mary, daughter of *John Brooke* (by 1646–1692/93). Her sister was Ann, who married first, *Thomas Cooke* (?–1692/93), and second, John Stevens, son of *John Stevens* (?–1692). CHILDREN. SONS: *William Ennalls* (?–1731), who married Anne; *Bartholomew Ennalls* (ca. 1700–1783), who married first, Mary Smith, and second, Elizabeth, widow of William Taylor and daughter of *Henry Trippe* (?–ca. 1723/24); Thomas (?–by 1753); Henry (?–1734), who married Elizabeth Beckwith; and Joseph (1702–1759). DAUGHTERS: Elizabeth, who married *Charles Goldsborough* (1707–1767); Mary, who married *Henry Hooper* (ca. 1687–1767). PRIVATE CAREER. EDUCATION: literate. RELIGIOUS AFFILIATION: Protestant. SOCIAL STATUS AND ACTIVITIES: second generation burgess; first elected after his brother *Thomas Ennalls* (?–1718) was promoted from the Lower House to the Upper House. OCCUPATIONAL PROFILE: planter. PUBLIC CAREER. LEGISLATIVE SERVICE: Lower House, Dorchester County, 1704–1707, 1708A, 1708B (died before the 2nd session of 1708B–1711 Assembly). LOCAL OFFICES: justice, Dorchester County, 1702–1709; deputy surveyor, Dorchester County, 1707. WEALTH DURING LIFETIME. LAND AT FIRST ELECTION: over 650 acres. WEALTH AT DEATH. DIED: in 1709. PERSONAL PROPERTY: TEV, £640.3.2 sterling (including 8 slaves and 1 servant); FB, £628.1.5. LAND: over 650 acres.

ENNALLS, JOSEPH

(ca. 1745–1779). BORN: ca. 1745 in Dorchester County; probably eldest son. NATIVE: fourth generation. RESIDED: in Transquakin Hundred, Dorchester County. FAMILY BACK-

GROUND. FATHER: Capt. Thomas Ennalls (?–1753), son of *Joseph Ennalls* (?–1709). STEPFATHER: James Hodson (?–1768). MOTHER: Anne. UNCLES: *William Ennalls* (?–1731); *Bartholomew Ennalls* (ca. 1700–1783). AUNTS: Elizabeth Ennalls (?–by 1739), who married *Charles Goldsborough* (1707–1767); Mary Ennalls, who married *Henry Hooper* (ca. 1687–1767). BROTHERS: William; Thomas III (?–ca. 1788), a merchant, who married Anne. HALF BROTHERS OR STEPBROTHERS: James Hodson; John Hodson; and Henry Hodson. HALF SISTER OR STEPSISTER: Elizabeth Hodson. FIRST COUSINS: *William Ennalls* (?–1785); *John Ennalls* (by 1746–ca. 1778); *Henry Hooper, Jr.* (ca. 1727–1790); *Robert Goldsborough* (1733–1788); Elinor Ennalls (ca. 1738–1793), who married *Joseph Daffin* (?–1796); Elizabeth Greenberry Goldsborough (ca. 1731–1820), who married *William Ennalls* (?–1785); Mary Ennalls, who married *Ennalls Hooper* (?–ca. 1763); and Ann Ennalls (ca. 1729–by 1790), who married *Henry Hooper, Jr.* (ca. 1727–1790). MARRIED first, ca. 1765 Mary (?–ca. 1773), daughter of Edward Trippe, Jr. (?–ca. 1756) and wife Anne (?–by 1756); granddaughter of Edward Trippe (?–ca. 1752) and wife Mary. Her mother's first husband was John Trippe (?–by 1746), of Dorchester County. MARRIED second, by 1779 Sarah Heron. CHILDREN. SONS: Thomas (?–ca. 1791), probably never married; William; Joseph; John; and possibly Henry. DAUGHTERS: Elizabeth, who married (first name unknown) Millis; Anne, who married by 1792 William Whittington. PRIVATE CAREER. EDUCATION: literate. SOCIAL STATUS AND ACTIVITIES: Gent., by 1769; Esq., by 1778. OCCUPATIONAL PROFILE: planter. PUBLIC CAREER. LEGISLATIVE SERVICE: Convention, Dorchester County, 9th, 1776. LOCAL OFFICES: sheriff, Dorchester County, elected 1777; justice, Dorchester County, commissioned 1777; collector of clothing for soldiers, Dorchester County, appointed 1778. MILITARY SERVICE: lieutenant colonel, Upper Battalion, Dorchester County Militia, commissioned 1776; colonel, Upper Battalion, Dorchester County Militia, 1778–1779. WEALTH DURING LIFETIME. PERSONAL PROPERTY: 18 slaves, 1776. LAND AT FIRST ELECTION: 1,742 acres in Dorchester County (217 acres probably inherited from his father; 116 acres inherited from his stepfather; 1,675 acres through his first marriage, 282 acres of which were released in a land division with his wife's half sister; 23 acres by patent). WEALTH AT DEATH. DIED: on November 10, 1779, probably in Dorchester County. PERSONAL PROPERTY: size of estate unknown. LAND: 1,742 acres in Dorchester County.

ENNALLS (ENNOLDS, ENNALS), THOMAS (?–1718). BORN: probably ca. 1663, probably in York County, Virginia; eldest son. IMMIGRATED: by 1668 as a minor with his parents from Virginia. RESIDED: in Dorchester County. FAMILY BACKGROUND. FATHER: *Bartholomew Ennalls* (1643–1688). MOTHER: Mary Heyward. BROTHERS: William; *Joseph Ennalls* (?–1709), who married Mary, daughter of *John Brooke* (by 1646–1692/93); *Henry Ennalls* (1675–1734), who married Mary, daughter of *Henry Hooper* (ca. 1643–1720); and Bartholomew. HALF BROTHERS: Francis Heyward; John Heyward. SISTERS: Elizabeth, who married *Roger Woolford* (1670–1730); Mary. MARRIED Elizabeth (1664/65–1739), daughter of *Roger Woolford* (?–ca. 1701/2). She subsequently married *William Holland* (?–1732). Her brother was *Roger Woolford* (1670–1730). Her sister was Sarah, who married *Govert Lookerman* (ca. 1681–1728). CHILDREN. Died without progeny. PRIVATE CAREER. EDUCATION: literate. RELIGIOUS AFFILIATION: Protestant. SOCIAL STATUS AND ACTIVITIES: second generation burgess. OCCUPATIONAL PROFILE: mariner, 1689; planter; merchant, trading with Madeira. PUBLIC CAREER. LEGISLATIVE SERVICE: Lower House, Dorchester County, 1692–1693, 1694–1697, 1697/98–1700 (Laws 4), 1701–1702 (Laws 1; appointed to the Council before the 4th session); Upper House, 1703–1704 (appointed by the 4th session, but never sat), 1704–1707, 1708A, 1708B–1711 (did not attend the 1st or 3rd sessions), 1712–1714 (did not attend the 1st or 4th sessions), 1715, 1716–1718. OTHER PROVINCIAL OFFICE: Council, 1703–1718. LOCAL OFFICE: justice, Dorchester County, 1690–1703 (quorum, 1694–1703). MILITARY SERVICE: captain, 1690; lieutenant colonel, by 1700; colonel, by 1701/2–1718. WEALTH DURING LIFETIME. LAND AT FIRST ELECTION: at least 2,864 acres inherited from his father. WEALTH AT DEATH. DIED: by October 21, 1718. PERSONAL PROPERTY: TEV, £4,661.17.11 current money (including 38 slaves and 3 servants). LAND: ca. 5,000 acres.

ENNALLS, THOMAS (?–by 1783). BORN: in Dorchester County, of age by 1757; elder son. NATIVE: fourth generation. RESIDED: in Dorchester County. FAMILY BACKGROUND. FATHER: Dr. Joseph Ennalls (1709–1756), son of *Henry Ennalls* (1675–1734). MOTHER: Mary (?–ca. 1772), widow of Thomas Haskins (?–1735); daughter of *Govert Lookerman* (ca. 1681–1728) and wife Sarah Woolford. AUNT: Sarah Lookerman (?–by 1745), who married *Joseph Cox Gray* (?–1764). BROTHER: *Henry Ennalls* (ca. 1741–by 1788). HALF BROTH-

ERS: William Haskins (1729–1779), who married in 1759 Sarah (?–1786), daughter of Rev. Thomas Airey (1701–1765) and wife Elizabeth Pitt; Joseph Haskins (1731–?), who married in 1759 Sarah, daughter of Thomas Ennalls (?–1746) and wife Ann Skinner. SISTERS: Mary (1738–?), who married in 1765 James Sulivane (1737–?), son of *Daniel Sulivane* (ca. 1708–by 1783); Margaret (?–by 1795), who married *William Maynadier* (1747–1795); Rebecca (?–by 1767); and Henrietta. HALF SISTER: Elizabeth Haskins (1733–1805), who married in 1754 Hall Caile. FIRST COUSIN: *James Murray* (?–1784). MARRIED by 1761 Mary, daughter of *Daniel Sulivane* (ca. 1708–by 1783); stepgranddaughter of *Peter Taylor* (1680–ca. 1747/48). Her brothers were James (1737–?); *Daniel Sulivane* (ca. 1748–1799). CHILDREN. DAUGHTER: Sarah (1761–1842), who married *Henry Waggaman* (1753–1809). PRIVATE CAREER. EDUCATION: literate. SOCIAL STATUS AND ACTIVITIES: Gent., by 1776. OCCUPATIONAL PROFILE: mariner. PUBLIC CAREER. LEGISLATIVE SERVICE: Conventions, Dorchester County, 3rd, 1774, 4th, 1775, 5th, 1775. MILITARY SERVICE: captain, by 1766; colonel, Lower Battalion, Dorchester County Militia, commissioned, 1776. WEALTH DURING LIFETIME. LAND AT FIRST ELECTION: at least 1,002 acres in Dorchester County (at least 200 acres inherited from his father; 500 acres by deed of gift from an uncle or great-uncle; 302 acres by patent). WEALTH AT DEATH. DIED: between March 1776 and 1783, probably in Dorchester County; size of estate unknown. ADDITIONAL COMMENTS: in the tax assessment of 1783 his widow was charged with 945 acres in Dorchester County and an assessed personal property value of £248.0.0, including 4 slaves.

ENNALLS, WILLIAM (?–1731). BORN: in Dorchester County, of age by 1710; eldest son. NATIVE: third generation. RESIDED: in Dorchester County. FAMILY BACKGROUND. FATHER: *Joseph Ennalls* (?–1709), son of *Bartholomew Ennalls* (1643–1688). MOTHER: Mary, daughter of *John Brooke* (by 1646–1692/93). UNCLES: *Thomas Ennalls* (?–1718); *Henry Ennalls* (1675–1734). AUNTS: Elizabeth Ennalls, who married *Roger Woolford* (1670–1730); Ann Brooke, who married first, *Thomas Cooke* (?–1692/93). BROTHERS: *Bartholomew Ennalls* (ca. 1700–1783); Joseph (1702–1759); Thomas (?–1753); and Henry (?–1734). SISTERS: Elizabeth (?–by 1739), who married *Charles Goldsborough* (1707–1767); Mary, who married *Henry Hooper* (ca. 1687–1767). FIRST COUSIN: *Thomas Woolford* (ca. 1699–ca. 1750/51). NEPH-

EWS: *Joseph Ennalls* (ca. 1745–1779); *William Ennalls* (?–1785); *John Ennalls* (by 1746–ca. 1778); *Henry Hooper, Jr.* (ca. 1727–1790); and *Robert Goldsborough* (1733–1788). NIECES: Elinor Ennalls (ca. 1738–1793), who married *Joseph Daffin* (?–1796); Elizabeth Greenberry Goldsborough (ca. 1731–1820), who married *William Ennalls* (?–1785). MARRIED by 1720 Anne. CHILDREN. DAUGHTERS: Mary, who married *Ennalls Hooper* (?–ca. 1763); Ann (ca. 1729–by 1790), who married *Henry Hooper, Jr.* (ca. 1727–1790); and Betty, who married John Hicks. PRIVATE CAREER. EDUCATION: literate. RELIGIOUS AFFILIATION: Anglican. SOCIAL STATUS AND ACTIVITIES: Gent., by 1718. OCCUPATIONAL PROFILE: merchant, by 1717; yeoman, by 1717. PUBLIC CAREER. LEGISLATIVE SERVICE: Lower House, Dorchester County, 1728–1731 (discharged during the 1st session for "undue election" ; reelected to the 2nd session and seated). MILITARY SERVICE: lieutenant colonel, by 1725; colonel, by 1728. WEALTH DURING LIFETIME. LAND AT FIRST ELECTION: 7,980 acres in Dorchester County (3,037 acres inherited from his uncle; 1,109 acres inherited from his father, but sold to his brothers before first election; at least 4,674 acres by purchase or patent). ADDITIONAL COMMENTS: In 1718 William exchanged 600 acres of the lands in Dorchester County he had inherited from his father for 300 acres that his brother *Bartholomew Ennalls* (ca. 1700–1783) owned in the same county. This transaction is reflected in the total acreage he owned at first election. Ennalls and *John Rider* (1686–1739/40) claimed land which by treaty had been granted to the Nanticoke Indians. In 1723 the Lower House noted that Ennalls and Rider had molested the Indians and had not permitted them to cultivate any part of the disputed land. No further reference was found to Ennalls's claim, although Rider's was successfully resolved in favor of his heirs, who ultimately received 1,664 acres in Dorchester County. SIGNIFICANT CHANGES IN LAND BETWEEN FIRST ELECTION AND DEATH: purchased at least 1,485 acres in Dorchester and Kent counties between 1728 and 1731. WEALTH AT DEATH. DIED: between October 7 and December 5, 1731, in Dorchester County. PERSONAL PROPERTY: TEV, £2,989.15.7 current money (including 47 slaves, 1 servant, books, several articles of gold and silver plate valued at £159.11.0, and fifteen-sixteenths of the brigantine *Mary Anne*); plus 7,275 pounds of pork, 24,418 pounds of tobacco, 1,000 shingles, and 32 barrels of corn, as calculated; FB, £2,740.17.7 current money, plus 7,275 pounds of pork, 21,194 pounds of tobacco, 1,000 shingles, and 24 barrels of corn. LAND: 9,618 acres in Dorchester and Kent counties.

ENNALLS, WILLIAM (?–1785). BORN: in Dorchester County, of age by 1749; elder son. NATIVE: fourth generation. RESIDED: in Dorchester County. FAMILY BACKGROUND. FATHER: Col. Joseph Ennalls (1702–1759), son of *Joseph Ennalls* (?–1709). MOTHER: Mary. UNCLES: *Bartholomew Ennalls* (ca. 1700–1783); *William Ennalls* (?–1731). AUNTS: Elizabeth Ennalls (?–by 1739), who married *Charles Goldsborough* (1707–1767); Mary Ennalls, who married *Henry Hooper* (ca. 1687–1767). BROTHER: *John Ennalls* (by 1746–ca. 1778). SISTERS: Mary (?–by 1766), who married David Murray; Elinor (ca. 1738–1793), who married *Joseph Daffin* (?–1796); Elizabeth; and Ann (Nancy) (1750–1803), who married Thomas Muse (?–1776), of Virginia. FIRST COUSINS: *Joseph Ennalls* (ca. 1745–1779); *Henry Hooper, Jr.* (ca. 1727–1790); *Robert Goldsborough* (1733–1788); Mary Ennalls, who married *Ennalls Hooper* (?–ca. 1763); and Ann Ennalls (ca. 1729–by 1790), who married *Henry Hooper, Jr.* (ca. 1727–1790). MARRIED by 1761 his first cousin Elizabeth (Betty) Greenberry (ca. 1731–1820), daughter of *Charles Goldsborough* (1707–1767) and wife Elizabeth Ennalls (?–by 1739); stepdaughter of Elizabeth Dickinson (1723–?); granddaughter of both *Robert Goldsborough* (1660–1746) and *Joseph Ennalls* (?–1709); niece of *William Goldsborough* (1709–1760), *John Goldsborough* (1711–1778), *William Ennalls* (?–1731), *Bartholomew Ennalls* (ca. 1700–1783), and Mary Ennalls, who married *Henry Hooper* (ca. 1687–1767). Her brother was *Robert Goldsborough* (1733–1788). Her first cousins were Elizabeth Goldsborough (ca. 1735–ca. 1786), who married second, *Benson Stainton* (?–ca. 1781); Mary Goldsborough (1755–1796), who married first, *Benedict Brice* (1749–1786); *Robert Goldsborough IV* (1740–1798); *Howes Goldsborough* (1747–1797); *William Goldsborough* (1750/51–1801); Mary Ennalls, who married *Ennalls Hooper* (?–ca. 1763); Ann Ennalls (ca. 1729–by 1790), who married *Henry Hooper, Jr.* (ca. 1727–1790); *Joseph Ennalls* (ca. 1745–1779); *John Ennalls* (by 1746–ca. 1778); *Henry Hooper, Jr.* (ca. 1727–1790); and Elinor Ennalls (ca. 1738–1793), who married *Joseph Daffin* (?–1796). Her nieces were Rebecca Goldsborough (ca. 1757–?), who married *Howes Goldsborough* (1747–1797); Sarah Goldsborough (ca. 1758–by 1832), who married *Henry Ennalls* (?–ca. 1803). CHILDREN. Probably died without progeny. PRIVATE CAREER. EDUCATION: literate. RELIGIOUS AFFILIATION: Protestant. SOCIAL STATUS AND

ACTIVITIES: Gent., by 1773; Esq., by 1783. OCCU-
PATIONAL PROFILE: merchant, by 1749; probably
also a planter. PUBLIC CAREER. LEGISLATIVE SER-
VICE: Lower House, Dorchester County, 1771
(Claims; Public Offices), 1773–1774; Conventions,
Dorchester County, 1st, 1774, 4th, 1775, 6th–8th,
1775–1776 (did not attend the 7th Convention);
Lower House, Dorchester County, 1777. LOCAL
OFFICES: justice, Dorchester County, 1760–1785
(quorum, 1770–1785); justice, Orphans' Court,
Dorchester County, 1777–1785; judge, court of
appeals, appointed under the Act to Procure
Troops for the American Army, Dorchester
County, appointed 1778; subscription officer, Con-
tinental Loan Office, Dorchester County, ap-
pointed 1779; commissioner of tax, Dorchester
County, 1779–1782. WEALTH DURING LIFETIME.
LAND AT FIRST ELECTION: at least 5,967 acres in
Dorchester County (2,288 acres inherited from his
father; 777 acres as heir-at-law of his sister; at
least 2,902 acres through marriage). SIGNIFICANT
CHANGES IN LAND BETWEEN FIRST ELECTION
AND DEATH: By 1783 Ennalls controlled 2,463
acres in Dorchester and Caroline counties as the
guardian for the son of his wife's half brother. He
also controlled 4,130 acres in Dorchester County
as heir-at-law of his brother, *John Ennalls* (by
1746–ca. 1778), all of which John had devised to
his sisters by his will. The will was witnessed by
only two people, and was, therefore, not legally
binding. William, as heir-at-law, chose to abide by
the will and by 1783 confirmed at least part of the
bequests his brother made. By 1783 William's
mother apparently had died and he inherited 698
acres in Dorchester County that his father had
entailed to him upon her death. WEALTH AT
DEATH. DIED: will probated on March 12, 1785, in
Dorchester County; buried on Col. George Aus-
tin's farm, near the Transquakin River, Bucktown
District, Dorchester County. PERSONAL PROP-
ERTY: assessed value £4,678.6.8, including 113
slaves in Dorchester and Caroline counties, 1783.
LAND: 6,879 acres in Dorchester and Caroline
counties, all of which was left to his wife for her
life. Ennalls probably still controlled 2,463 acres
in Dorchester and Caroline counties as guardian
of the son of his wife's half brother. He reaffirmed
in his own will probated in 1785 the bequests of
his brother *John Ennalls* (by 1746–ca. 1778) of
4,130 acres to his sisters.

EVANS, JAMES (ca. 1716–1788). BORN: ca.
1716, probably in Pennsylvania. IMMIGRATED:
possibly by 1760, from Pennsylvania. RESIDED: in
Lancaster County, Pennsylvania, 1739–ca. 1752;

West Nottingham, Chester County, Pennsylvania,
1751–1760; West Nottingham Hundred, Cecil
County, 1767. FAMILY BACKGROUND. FATHER:
John Evans (ca. 1680–?). BROTHERS: John, Jr.;
Robert (?–1775), of Milford Hundred, Cecil
County, a tanner, who married his sister-in-law
Margaret Kilpatrick. MARRIED first, Eleanor, possibly the widow of James Wright. MARRIED second, Isabella, daughter of John Kilpatrick. Her
sister was Margaret, who married her sister's
brother-in-law Robert Evans. CHILDREN. SON: Robert, who resided near Port Deposit, Cecil County.
DAUGHTERS: Jean, who married (first name un-
known) Thompson; Eleanor, who married James
Gordon Heron. PRIVATE CAREER. EDUCATION:
literate. SOCIAL STATUS AND ACTIVITIES: Gent.,
1750; Esq., 1788. OCCUPATIONAL PROFILE:
farmer. PUBLIC CAREER. LEGISLATIVE SERVICE:
Lower House, Cecil County, 1778–1779 (Laws to
Expire 3). LOCAL OFFICES: justice, Cecil County,
commissioned 1777; commissioner of tax, Cecil
County, 1783–1785. WEALTH DURING LIFETIME.
LAND AT FIRST ELECTION: probably 983 acres in
Cecil County. WEALTH AT DEATH. DIED: between
July 14 and August 19, 1788, in West Nottingham
Hundred, Cecil County. PERSONAL PROPERTY:
TEV, at least £1,160.0.9 current money (including
slaves). LAND: 983 acres in Cecil County.

EVANS, JOHN (?–1768). BORN: probably in
Somerset County, but possibly in Virginia; proba-
bly eldest son. NATIVE: at least second generation.
RESIDED: in Somerset County, 1720 (later became
part of Worcester County). FAMILY BACKGROUND.
FATHER: John Evans, Gent. (?–1720), of Somerset
County. BROTHERS: Edward, probably died young;
Ebenezer; and Samuel. SISTERS: Mary; Elizabeth.
MARRIED on February 22, ca. 1727, Sarah Campbell. CHILDREN. SONS: Elisha (1730–?); John
(1732–?); Ebenezer (1737–?); Edward (1747–1754);
probably Isaac (1750–?); and David (1753–?).
DAUGHTERS: Elizabeth, who married (first name
unknown) Tunel; Sophia (1745–?), who married
(first name unknown) Hopkins. PRIVATE CAREER.
EDUCATION: literate. RELIGIOUS AFFILIATION: An-
glican. OCCUPATIONAL PROFILE: probably a
planter. PUBLIC CAREER. LEGISLATIVE SERVICE:
Lower House, Worcester County, 1751–1754,
1754–1757. LOCAL OFFICES: justice, Worcester
County, 1754–1768 (quorum, 1761–1768); justice,
Court of Oyer and Terminer and Gaol Delivery,
Worcester County, commissioned 1766. MILITARY
SERVICE: captain, by 1753; major, by 1756.
WEALTH DURING LIFETIME. LAND AT FIRST
ELECTION: 972 acres in Somerset and Worcester

counties (inherited 325 acres from his father and brother). SIGNIFICANT CHANGES IN LAND BETWEEN FIRST ELECTION AND DEATH: purchased 603 acres in Worcester County, 1752–1764; sold 306 acres in Worcester County, 1752–1768. WEALTH AT DEATH. DIED: between April 25 and May 19, 1768; will probated in Worcester County. PERSONAL PROPERTY: TEV, at least £1,125.13.6 current money (including 14 slaves and 17 books). LAND: 1,269 acres in Worcester County.

EVANS, WILLIAM (?–1668/69). BORN: probably in England. IMMIGRATED: in 1646 as a free adult. RESIDED: in Newtown Hundred, St. Mary's County. MARRIED first, in 1651/52 Ann, widow of William Thompson. MARRIED second, Elizabeth, who subsequently married both John Jordaine and Cuthbert Scott. CHILDREN. Died without progeny. PRIVATE CAREER. EDUCATION: literate. RELIGIOUS AFFILIATION: Catholic. SOCIAL STATUS AND ACTIVITIES: low status on arrival; rose through years of faithful service. OCCUPATIONAL PROFILE: planter. PUBLIC CAREER. LEGISLATIVE SERVICE: Lower House, St. Mary's County, 1658, 1659/60 (election voided, but was reelected), 1661, 1662; Upper House, 1664, 1666. OTHER PROVINCIAL OFFICES: mustermaster general, 1661–1668/69; Council, 1664–1668/69; justice, Provincial Court, 1664–1668/69. LOCAL OFFICES: justice, St. Mary's County, 1658–1663 (quorum, 1661–1663); sheriff, St. Mary's County, 1663–1664. MILITARY SERVICE: lieutenant, 1646–1658; captain, 1658–1660; colonel, 1660–1668/69. STANDS ON PUBLIC/PRIVATE ISSUES: strong supporter of the proprietary interests against Ingle's Rebellion and the Parliamentary Commissioners. WEALTH DURING LIFETIME. LAND AT FIRST ELECTION: probably ca. 200 acres; over 650 acres by 1665. WEALTH AT DEATH. DIED: in March 1668/69. LAND: 900 acres.

EVELYN (EVELIN), GEORGE (1592/93–?). BORN: on January 31, 1592/93, in London, England; first son. IMMIGRATED: in 1636 as a free adult with his family. RESIDED: on Kent Island; St. Mary's County, by 1638; returned to England, ca. 1639. FAMILY BACKGROUND. FATHER: Robert Evelyn, Sr. (ca. 1570–1639), son of George Evelyn, of Wotton, Surrey, England; a member of the Virginia Company, 1609. MOTHER: Susannah, daughter of Gregory Young, Esq., of York, England. BROTHER: *Robert Evelyn* (?–ca. 1649). MARRIED in 1623 Jane, daughter of Richard Crane, of Dorset, England. CHILDREN. SONS: George (1623–?); Mountjoy (?–by 1662), who married Dorothea, daughter of Obedience Robins. DAUGHTER: Rebecca (ca. 1635–1701), who married first, Bar-

tholomew Knipe, and second, Daniel Parke. PRIVATE CAREER. EDUCATION: literate; entered the Middle Temple, London, England, 1620. SOCIAL STATUS AND ACTIVITIES: his family was prominent in colonial activities; probably returned to England after his father's death to assume ownership of the family estate there. OCCUPATIONAL PROFILE: agent, Cloberry & Company, 1636 (held one-sixth interest in the joint-stock venture); planter. PUBLIC CAREER. LEGISLATIVE SERVICE: Assembly, special writ, 1637/38 (Laws). LOCAL OFFICE: commander, Kent Isle, 1637–1638. STANDS ON PUBLIC/PRIVATE ISSUES: assisted the proprietary forces in subduing the forces of *William Claiborne* (1600–ca. 1677) on Kent Island for Lord Baltimore, for which he was rewarded with patronage. WEALTH DURING LIFETIME. LAND AT FIRST ELECTION: 400 acres, which he signed over to brother *Robert Evelyn* (?–ca. 1649) in 1638. WEALTH AT DEATH. DIED: after 1649; size of estate unknown.

EVELYN (EVELIN), ROBERT (?–ca. 1649). BORN: in London, England; probably second son. IMMIGRATED: ca. 1635 as a free adult, probably from Virginia. RESIDED: in St. Mary's County; left Maryland in 1642 or later. FAMILY BACKGROUND. FATHER: Robert Evelyn, Sr. (ca. 1570–1639), son of George Evelyn, of Wotton, Surrey, England; a member of the Virginia Company in 1609. MOTHER: Susannah, daughter of Gregory Young, Esq., of York, England. BROTHER: *George Evelyn* (1592/93–?). PRIVATE CAREER. EDUCATION: literate; probably well educated. SOCIAL STATUS AND ACTIVITIES: immigrated to Virginia in July 1634 with his uncle Thomas Young as agents of the crown; called "Lt. Evelin"; he returned to England in December 1634, but was back in Virginia by the following May on a "special and very important service"; Gent. on first appearance in Maryland records. OCCUPATIONAL PROFILE: agent of the crown, 1634–1635; planter. PUBLIC CAREER. LEGISLATIVE SERVICE: Assembly, present 1637/38, special writ 1642A (Laws). MILITARY SERVICE: captain, 1637–still serving in 1642. OUT OF COLONY SERVICE: surveyor and councilor, Virginia, 1636/37. WEALTH DURING LIFETIME. LAND AT FIRST ELECTION: received 400 acres from his brother *George Evelyn* (1592/93–?) in 1638. WEALTH AT DEATH. DIED: ca. 1649, probably in Virginia or the West Indies; size of estate unknown.

EVERDEN (EVERNDEN), THOMAS (?–1710). BORN: probably in Kent, England. IMMIGRATED: in 1681 as a free adult from Rhode Island. RE-

SIDED: in Somerset County; Dorchester County at the time of his death. MARRIED Katherine, widow of George Johnson (1627–1681). CHILDREN. SON: Nathaniel. DAUGHTER: Martha, who married Joshua Kennerly. STEPDAUGHTER: Katherine, who married *John Goddin* (?–1712/13). PRIVATE CAREER. EDUCATION: literate. RELIGIOUS AFFILIATION: Quaker; as a "traveling Friend," he did extensive missionary work in several English colonies. SOCIAL STATUS AND ACTIVITIES: first appeared in the Chesapeake area in the 1670s. OCCUPATIONAL PROFILE: planter; merchant. PUBLIC CAREER. LEGISLATIVE SERVICE: Lower House, Somerset County, 1692 (disqualified, because as a Quaker would not subscribe to the required oaths). LOCAL OFFICE: justice, Somerset County, 1685. WEALTH DURING LIFETIME. LAND AT FIRST ELECTION: 500 acres. WEALTH AT DEATH. DIED: between May 4 and June 15, 1710, at the home of his son-in-law, Joshua Kennerly. PERSONAL PROPERTY: TEV, £439.7.5 sterling (including 6 slaves and a part interest in a sloop); FB, £255.7.10. LAND: 1,350 acres, plus land in St. Dunstan's Parish, Kent, England and a house in Philadelphia. ADDITIONAL COMMENTS: left bequests of land and money to Quakers in Maryland and England.

EWEN (EWENS, OWENS, OWINGS), RICHARD (?–1660). BORN: probably in England. IMMIGRATED: in 1649 as a free adult with his wife and four children, probably from Virginia. RESIDED: in Calvert County; Anne Arundel County by 1659. ADDITIONAL COMMENTS: probably the same Richard Ewen who had 150 acres in Upper Norfolk County, Virginia in 1638. MARRIED Sophia, who subsequently married *William Burgess* (ca. 1622–1686/87). CHILDREN. SONS: Richard, a justice of Anne Arundel County from 1663/64 to 1676, the sheriff of Anne Arundel County from 1665 to 1666, and a lieutenant colonel in 1664; John (?–1669), a justice of Anne Arundel County from 1668 to 1669, and a lieutenant colonel in 1664, who married Sarah. DAUGHTERS: Ann; Sophia (?–1671), who married Richard Wells, son of *Richard Wells* (?–1667); Elizabeth, who married first, Richard Talbot, and second, ca. 1663 *William Richardson* (?–1698); Susanna (?–1664/65), who married James Billingsley (?–by 1664/65), son of *Francis Billingsley* (?–1695). PRIVATE CAREER. EDUCATION: literate. RELIGIOUS AFFILIATION: Protestant; came to Maryland during the Puritan migration from Virginia; his family had close Quaker ties. SOCIAL STATUS AND ACTIVITIES: brought four others, besides his family, on his ar-

rival in Maryland; no title at the time of his first appearance in records; Mr., by 1654. OCCUPATIONAL PROFILE: planter. PUBLIC CAREER. LEGISLATIVE SERVICE: Parliamentary Commission, 1654–1657/58; Assembly, Patuxent (Calvert County) 1654, 1657 (speaker); Lower House, Anne Arundel County, 1659/60 (speaker). OTHER PROVINCIAL OFFICE: justice, Provincial Court, 1654–1657/58. LOCAL OFFICE: justice, Anne Arundel County, 1658 (refused to sit because of military duties). MILITARY SERVICE: captain, 1654–1657/58; major, 1658. STANDS ON PUBLIC/PRIVATE ISSUES: a primary leader in Maryland under the Bennett-Claiborne commission, 1654–1657/58; refused to subscribe to an oath because he viewed it as unlawful, 1657. WEALTH DURING LIFETIME. LAND AT FIRST ELECTION: rights to 1,000 acres. WEALTH AT DEATH. DIED: in 1660. LAND: at least 350 acres.

EWEN (EWENS), WILLIAM (ca. 1609–ca. 1675/76). BORN: ca. 1609, probably in England. IMMIGRATED: in 1651 as a free adult with his wife, probably from Virginia. RESIDED: in Calvert County; Anne Arundel County, by 1658. ADDITIONAL COMMENTS: probably the William Ewen, merchant of James City County, Virginia, who received 1,400 acres in July 1648 for transporting himself and twenty-eight others to that colony. MARRIED Ann. CHILDREN. Probably died without progeny. PRIVATE CAREER. EDUCATION: literate. RELIGIOUS AFFILIATION: Protestant, with strong Quaker ties. SOCIAL STATUS AND ACTIVITIES: brought four servants with him on his arrival in Maryland; no title on first appearance in Maryland records; Mr., by 1654; no relationship proven between William and *Richard Ewen* (?–1660); public offices limited to jury service after 1658. OCCUPATIONAL PROFILE: planter. PUBLIC CAREER. LEGISLATIVE SERVICE: Assembly, Patuxent (Calvert County), 1654; Parliamentary Commission, 1656/57–1657/58; Assembly, Anne Arundel County, 1658. OTHER PROVINCIAL OFFICES: justice, Provincial Court, 1656/57–1657/58. MILITARY SERVICE: captain, by 1658. STANDS ON PUBLIC/PRIVATE ISSUES: his active role under the Bennett-Claiborne commission may account for his failure to hold office after the restoration of the proprietary government. WEALTH DURING LIFETIME. LAND AT FIRST ELECTION: at least 363 acres. WEALTH AT DEATH. DIED: will probated on February 16, 1675/76. LAND: 212 acres, plus 2 tracts of unspecified acreage.

EWING, PATRICK (?–1819). BORN: of age by 1765; eldest son. NATIVE: at least second generation. RESIDED: in Octarara Hundred, Cecil County. FAMILY BACKGROUND. FATHER: Joshua Ewing (?–1753), a yeoman. MOTHER: Jane. BROTHERS: Robert; Samuel; and Nathaniel. SISTER: Catherine, who married William Ewing. MARRIED first, by 1765 Jane. MARRIED second, on July 16, 1789, Elizabeth, daughter of James Porter. CHILDREN. SONS: Patrick; Putnam; and James. DAUGHTERS: Jane Elinor, who married by 1811 Nathaniel Ewing; Catherine Elizabeth, who married by 1811 Andrew Porter; and Elizabeth. PRIVATE CAREER. EDUCATION: literate. SOCIAL STATUS AND ACTIVITIES: Esq., 1790. OCCUPATIONAL PROFILE: yeoman. PUBLIC CAREER. LEGISLATIVE SERVICE: Conventions, Cecil County, 5th, 1775 (elected, but did not attend), 6th–8th, 1775–1776 (Manufactories 8th), 9th, 1776 (Manufactories); Lower House, Cecil County, 1777 (Manufactories 1), 1792, 1793. LOCAL OFFICES: justice, Cecil County, 1782–at least 1795; judge, Court of Appeals for Tax Assessment, Cecil County, appointed 1786. ADDITIONAL COMMENTS: In December 1788 Ewing's commission as justice was discouraged by all four Cecil County delegates, who charged that Ewing had become "extremely obnoxious. . ., inasmuch as he is generally esteemed a promoter of violence & outrage against the Laws. . ." Nevertheless, his commission was confirmed. WEALTH DURING LIFETIME. PERSONAL PROPERTY: assessed value £199.0.0, including 5 slaves and 8 oz. plate, 1783; 3 slaves, 1790. LAND AT FIRST ELECTION: at least 219 acres in Cecil County (inherited from his father). SIGNIFICANT CHANGES IN LAND BETWEEN FIRST ELECTION AND DEATH: acquired at least 41 acres in Cecil County; owned at least 249 acres in Cecil County, 1783. WEALTH AT DEATH. DIED: will probated on May 25, 1819, in Cecil County. PERSONAL PROPERTY: TEV, $3,166.70; FB, $2,544.64. LAND: possibly ca. 260 acres in Cecil County.

FALCONAR, ABRAHAM (?–1754). BORN: in Kent County. NATIVE: at least second generation. RESIDED: in Kent County. FAMILY BACKGROUND. FATHER: Gilbert Falconar (?–by 1736). MOTHER: Hannah (?–by 1766), daughter of William Barnes, of Kent County, Delaware. BROTHER: John (ca. 1720–?). SISTERS: Margaret (?–1738); Christian. MARRIED Elizabeth (?–1766), possibly his first cousin, daughter of William Barnes (?–1753), of Kent County, Delaware, and wife Ann (?–1759). Her brothers were William; John; and Stephen. Her sisters were Sarah; Jane; Catherine; Prisiler

(Priscilla), who married (first name unknown) Green; and Rebecca, who married (first name unknown) Massey. CHILDREN. SONS: Gilbert (1741–?); Abraham (1749–?), possibly a Queen Anne's County justice in 1788; he probably married by 1794 Sarah Hall, of Queen Anne's County. DAUGHTERS: Sarah (1743–?); Hannah (1744/45–?); Ann (1746–?); Priscilla (1747–?); and Elizabeth (1752–?). PRIVATE CAREER. EDUCATION: literate. RELIGIOUS AFFILIATION: Protestant. SOCIAL STATUS AND ACTIVITIES: Gent., 1754. OCCUPATIONAL PROFILE: planter. PUBLIC CAREER. LEGISLATIVE SERVICE: Lower House, Kent County, 1751–1754 (discharged on December 11, 1751, for being an ordinary keeper at the time of first election; reelected and seated during the 2nd session; died before the 6th session). WEALTH DURING LIFETIME. LAND AT FIRST ELECTION: 560 acres in Kent and Queen Anne's counties (410 acres inherited from his father, 150 acres by patent). ADDITIONAL COMMENTS: in 1738 Falconar inherited 2,135 acres in Kent County from his father; in 1742 he conveyed 1,725 acres of this property to his father-in-law. SIGNIFICANT CHANGES IN LAND BETWEEN FIRST ELECTION AND DEATH: he acquired 100 acres in Kent County, and was charged quitrents on 858 acres, composed of 2 tracts which he had previously deeded to his father-in-law. WEALTH AT DEATH. DIED: ca. July 1754 in Kent County. PERSONAL PROPERTY: TEV, £385.3.4 current money (including 1 slave and books); FB, £1.5.1. LAND: ca. 1,685 acres in Kent and Queen Anne's counties.

FAW, ABRAHAM (?–1828). BORN: of age by 1770. RESIDED: in Frederick County, 1770–1791; Montgomery County, 1793; Alexandria, Fairfax County, Virginia, 1794; Alexandria, Virginia, 1817. MARRIED first, by 1779 Juliana Boyer. Her brothers were Michael; Jonathan; and Abraham. Her sisters were Catherine, who married (first name unknown) Leatherman; Barbara, who married (first name unknown) Young; Christiana, who married (first name unknown) Koinitz; Mary, who married (first name unknown) Hay; and Susana, who married (first name unknown) Funk. MARRIED second, on March 28, 1790, Mary Ann Steiner. CHILDREN. SONS: William H. S. (?–by 1824); possibly Walter Reed. DAUGHTERS: Juliana M. Lowe; Sophia Elizabeth, who married Jacob Leonard. PRIVATE CAREER. EDUCATION: literate. RELIGIOUS AFFILIATION: Evangelical Reformed. SOCIAL STATUS AND ACTIVITIES: Esq., 1788. OCCUPATIONAL PROFILE: merchant. PUBLIC CAREER. LEGISLATIVE SERVICE: Lower House, Frederick County, 1785 (Claims), 1786–1787 (Claims 1, 2), 1787–1788 (Claims 1, 2; Grievances 1; Elections 2), 1788 (Claims; Elections; Grievances), 1789 (Claims; Laws to Expire). OTHER STATE OFFICE: Constitution Ratification Convention, Frederick County, 1788. LOCAL OFFICE: sheriff, Frederick County, elected 1777 (resigned same year). OUT OF STATE SERVICE: justice, Alexandria County, District of Columbia, in office 1806 and 1821; commissioner, Alexandria County, District of Columbia, in office 1812 and 1818. ADDITIONAL COMMENTS: unsuccessful candidate for a seat in the U.S. Congress, 1788. WEALTH DURING LIFETIME. PERSONAL PROPERTY: 2 slaves, 1790. LAND AT FIRST ELECTION: 841 acres in Frederick County, plus 2 lots in Frederick Town and 2 lots in Middletown, Frederick County (by purchase and patent). SIGNIFICANT CHANGES IN LAND BETWEEN FIRST ELECTION AND DEATH: acquired by purchase and patent 983 acres in Frederick and Montgomery counties, plus 5 lots in Frederick Town, Frederick County, 1785–1801; sold 929 acres in Frederick and Montgomery counties, 1787–1794; owned 900 acres in Allegany County, plus 4 lots in Cumberland, Allegany County, 1793. WEALTH AT DEATH. DIED: will probated on July 8, 1828, in Alexandria, Virginia. LAND: owned property in Kentucky, acreage unknown.

FELL, WILLIAM (1759–1786). BORN: on August 29, 1759, in St. John's Parish, Baltimore County; only child. NATIVE: third generation. RESIDED: on Fell's Point, Baltimore Town. FAMILY BACKGROUND. FATHER: Edward Fell (1736–1763), of Baltimore County, a merchant; son of William Fell (?–1746), who immigrated from Lancashire, England, in 1730. STEPFATHER: *James Giles* (1749/50–?). MOTHER: Ann (?–1785), daughter of John Bond and wife Alice Anna Webster. AUNT: Catherine Fell, who married *Thomas Bond, of Thomas* (?–1800). HALF BROTHER: Jacob Washington (Worthington) Giles (ca. 1776–1851). HALF SISTERS: Johanna Giles (ca. 1771–?), who married Dr. Thomas Johnson, of Baltimore County; Susanna Giles (ca. 1775–1797), who married Philip Moore. MARRIED never. PRIVATE CAREER. EDUCATION: literate; his father's will directed that he be "educated to understand law." RELIGIOUS AFFILIATION: gave 6 lots on Fell's Point in Baltimore Town for the erection of a Presbyterian church, 1782. SOCIAL STATUS AND ACTIVITIES: Gent., by 1782; Esq., by 1783; traveled in Europe from 1783 until at least 1784. OCCUPATIONAL PROFILE: merchant, who probably had a store on Fell's Point; landlord; continued the development of Fell's Point in Baltimore Town begun by his father. PUBLIC CAREER. LEGISLATIVE SERVICE: Lower House, Baltimore Town, 1782–1783 (Grievances 1, 2). WEALTH DURING LIFETIME. LAND AT FIRST ELECTION: possibly 1,470 acres in Baltimore, Harford, and Frederick counties, including two-thirds of Fell's Point in Baltimore Town (all inherited from his father, 1766). SIGNIFICANT CHANGES IN LAND BETWEEN FIRST ELECTION AND DEATH: secured the title to 1,014 acres of Fell's Point in Baltimore Town and his father's other land in Baltimore, Harford, and Frederick counties in 1783. In division of his father's Fell's Point land with his mother and his stepfather *James Giles* (1749/50–?), Fell acquired 100 lots on Fell's Point in Baltimore Town with their rents from 1782. WEALTH AT DEATH. DIED: a few days before October 10, 1786, in Baltimore Town. PERSONAL PROPERTY: TEV, £2,093.12.1 current money (including 7 books); FB, estate overpaid £105.15.4. LAND: ca. 349 lots on Fell's Point in Baltimore Town leased out; probably ca. 1,000 acres in Baltimore, Harford, and Frederick counties. ADDITIONAL COMMENTS: income at death was ca. £1,800 current money per year in rents from Fell's Point lots. Fell named his half brother Jacob and his two half sisters Johanna and Susanna as his principal heirs. Depositions by several of Ann Bond Fell Giles's cousins, the possible legal heirs of Fell, described him as a man in a "weak state of mind" for some time before his death. This testimony was challenged by Fell's contemporaries, however, and the terms of his will were honored.

FENDALL, JOHN (1674–1734). BORN: in 1674 in Charles County; probably second son. NATIVE: second generation. RESIDED: in Charles County, moved to Carolina with his parents in the 1680s, but returned to Charles County permanently in 1702. FAMILY BACKGROUND. FATHER: *Josias Fendall* (?–by 1688). MOTHER: Mary, daughter of *John Hatch* (ca. 1614–1681). BROTHERS: Robert (1672–1711/12); Josias (?–1723); and Henry (?–1736). SISTERS: Jane; Mary (1673–1751), who married first, John Theobald (1666–1713), and second, Matthew Barnes (1670–1745). MARRIED by 1702 Elizabeth (?–1736), widow of William Marshall (?–1697); daughter of Randolph Hinson. Her sisters were Mary; Barbara, who married John Spiring. CHILDREN. SON: Benjamin (?–1764), who married first, Eleanor (1710–1759), daughter of *Philip Lee* (ca. 1681–1744), and second, Priscilla (ca. 1714–1763). STEPSON: William Marshall (?–1697). DAUGHTERS: Elizabeth, who married John Beall

(?–1757), son of James Beall (?–1725); Mary (?–ca. 1759), who married Samuel Hanson, son of *Robert Hanson* (ca. 1680–1748). PRIVATE CAREER. EDUCATION: literate. RELIGIOUS AFFILIATION: Anglican. SOCIAL STATUS AND ACTIVITIES: Mr., 1702; Gent., by 1715. PUBLIC CAREER. LEGISLATIVE SERVICE: Lower House, Charles County, 1712–1714, 1715, 1716–1718, 1719–1721/22, 1728–1731 (Aggrievances 1–5). LOCAL OFFICES: William and Mary Parish Vestry, Charles County, 1705, 1718; justice, Charles County, 1712–1729 (quorum, by 1722–1729). MILITARY SERVICE: captain, by 1715; colonel, by 1721. WEALTH DURING LIFETIME. LAND AT FIRST ELECTION: over 115 acres in his own right and 450 acres belonging to minor stepchildren. SIGNIFICANT CHANGES IN LAND BETWEEN FIRST ELECTION AND DEATH: by 1718 he had acquired an additional 800 acres; between 1729 and 1732 he disposed of 1,474 acres (much of it to his son); acquired 225 acres in 1731. ADDITIONAL COMMENTS: established his family's claims to 650 acres in North Carolina in 1694. WEALTH AT DEATH. DIED: will probated on October 28, 1734. PERSONAL PROPERTY: TEV, £1,579.11.9 current money (including 22 slaves); FB, £1,435.0.5. LAND: over 225 acres.

FENDALL, JOSIAS (?–by 1688). BORN: in England. IMMIGRATED: by 1654/55 as a free adult with his wife. RESIDED: in Charles County; immigrated to North Carolina, ca. 1683. FAMILY BACKGROUND. BROTHER: Samuel (?–1694), who immigrated in 1664. COUSINS: John Fendall, a mariner of Devonshire, England; James Fendall (?–1689), of Baltimore County. OTHER KINSHIP: probably a relative of Henry Fendall, a citizen and cutler of London, England. MARRIED first, Mary, daughter of *John Hatch* (ca. 1614–1681). MARRIED second, Mary (?–1691). CHILDREN. SONS: Josias (?–by 1723); Robert (1672–1711/12); *John Fendall* (1674–1734), who married Elizabeth (?–1736), widow of William Marshall (?–1697) and daughter of Randolph Hinson; and Henry. DAUGHTERS: Jane; Mary (1673–1751), who married first, John Theobald (1666–1713), and second, Matthew Barnes (1670–1745). PRIVATE CAREER. EDUCATION: literate. RELIGIOUS AFFILIATION: Protestant. SOCIAL STATUS AND ACTIVITIES: Gent. on first appearance; arrived with eighteen servants. OCCUPATIONAL PROFILE: planter; attorney in 1662. PUBLIC CAREER. LEGISLATIVE SERVICE: Lower House, Charles County, 1678 (elected to the 3rd session, but was not allowed to sit). OTHER PROVINCIAL OFFICE: governor, 1656–1660. MILITARY SERVICE: captain, by 1654/55–1660 (for the pro-

prietary government). STANDS ON PUBLIC/PRIVATE ISSUES: in 1654/55 he was an officer in Gov. William Stone's forces, for which he was placed in custody by the government of Parliamentary Commissioners; in 1657/58 he led the proprietary soldiers in recapturing Maryland's government from the commissioners; in 1659/60 he joined with a majority of the Lower House members in a rebellion that resulted in the colony's becoming a commonwealth; he was permanently barred from holding office in 1661; in 1678/79 he was accused of making scandalous speeches against the government; and in 1681 he was arrested for an alleged conspiracy against the government. He left the colony soon thereafter. WEALTH DURING LIFETIME. LAND AT FIRST ELECTION: over 4,050 acres. SIGNIFICANT CHANGES IN LAND BETWEEN FIRST ELECTION AND DEATH: sold most of his land by 1683. WEALTH AT DEATH. DIED: by May 14, 1688; size of estate unknown.

FENDALL, PHILIP RICHARD (?–?). BORN: of age by 1756. NATIVE: fourth generation. RESIDED: in William and Mary Parish, Charles County; left Maryland during the Revolution; Fairfax County, Virginia, 1786; Alexandria, Virginia, 1790. FAMILY BACKGROUND. FATHER: Benjamin Fendall (?–1764), clerk of Charles County from 1752 to 1756, son of *John Fendall* (1674–1734). MOTHER: Eleanor (1710–1759), daughter of *Philip Lee* (ca. 1681–1744). STEPMOTHER: Priscilla (ca. 1714–1763). UNCLES: *Richard Lee* (ca. 1707–1787); *Arthur Lee* (?–1760); *Francis Lee* (?–1749). HALF UNCLES: *Corbin Lee* (?–1774); *George Lee* (ca. 1736–?). STEPAUNT: Hannah Lee Bowie, who married second, *Joseph Sprigg* (1736–1800). BROTHERS: John (?–by 1777); Benjamin; Rev. Henry, rector of Durham Parish, Charles County from 1767 to 1775; and Samuel. SISTER: Sarah (ca. 1732–1793), who married *Thomas Contee* (ca. 1729–1811). FIRST COUSINS: *Thomas Sim Lee* (1745–1819); *Philip Thomas Lee* (1738–1778); *Richard Potts* (1753–1808); Rebecca Potts, who married *Benjamin Mackall IV* (1745–by 1810); Sarah Potts, who married *Thomas Gantt, Jr.* (?–1808); and Hannah Lee, who married *George Plater* (1735–1792). MARRIED first, on September 30, 1759, his first cousin Sarah Lettice (?–1761), eldest daughter of *Richard Lee* (ca. 1707–1787); niece of *Francis Lee* (?–1749), *Arthur Lee* (?–1760), and Hannah Lee Bowie, who married second, *Joseph Sprigg* (1736–1800); half niece of both *Corbin Lee* (?–1774) and *George Lee* (ca. 1736–?). Her brothers were Richard, Jr. (?–1834); *Philip Thomas Lee* (1738–1778). Her sisters were Hannah (?–1763), who married *George Plater* (1735–1792); Alice (?–1789), who married, in 1788, *John Weems* (1737–1813); and Eleanor Ann (?–1806). Her first cousins were *Thomas Sim Lee* (1745–1819); Sarah Fendall (ca. 1732–1793), who married *Thomas Contee* (ca. 1729–1811); *Richard Potts* (1753–1808); Rebecca Potts, who married *Benjamin Mackall IV* (1745–by 1810); and Sarah Potts, who married *Thomas Gantt, Jr.* (?–1808). MARRIED second, by 1786, Elizabeth. PRIVATE CAREER. EDUCATION: literate. SOCIAL STATUS AND ACTIVITIES: Gent., 1758. OCCUPATIONAL PROFILE: officeholder, 1756–1778; merchant. Before the Revolution Fendall was the principal agent on the Potomac River for James Russell, merchant, of London, England. PUBLIC CAREER. LEGISLATIVE SERVICE: Conventions, Charles County, 4th, 1775 (elected, but did not attend), 5th, 1775. LOCAL OFFICES: clerk, Charles County, 1756–1778, succeeded his father; receiver of alienation fines, Charles County, 1768; clerk and cryer, Court of Oyer and Terminer and Gaol Delivery, Charles County, 1772; clerk, Court of Oyer and Terminer and Gaol Delivery, Charles County, appointed 1773 and 1776; Committee of Observation, Charles County, elected 1775. WEALTH DURING LIFETIME. LAND AT FIRST ELECTION: probably 690 acres in Charles County (495 acres by gift and inheritance from his father, 195 acres by purchase and patent); also owned land in Virginia. SIGNIFICANT CHANGES IN LAND BETWEEN FIRST ELECTION AND DEATH: sold 690 acres in William and Mary Parish, Charles County, 1786. WEALTH AT DEATH. DIED: after 1798, probably in Virginia; size of estate unknown.

FENWICK, CUTHBERT (1614–1655). BORN: in 1614 in England. IMMIGRATED: in 1633/34 as an indentured servant from Virginia. RESIDED: in St. Mary's County. MARRIED first, probably (first name unknown) Cornwaleys. MARRIED second, in 1649 Jane Eltonhead (?–by 1661), widow of Robert Moryson, of Kecoughtan, Virginia. Her brothers were *William Eltonhead* (ca. 1616–1655); Richard. CHILDREN. SONS: Cuthbert (1640–1676), a justice of Calvert County from 1674 to 1676; Ignatius; Thomas (?–by 1655); Robert (ca. 1651–1676); Richard (ca. 1653–1714), a justice of Calvert County from 1685 to 1689; and John (ca. 1655–1720). DAUGHTER: Theresa. PRIVATE CAREER. EDUCATION: literate; probably well educated. RELIGIOUS AFFILIATION: Catholic. SOCIAL STATUS AND ACTIVITIES: arrived as a servant; probably served *Thomas Cornwaleys* (ca. 1605–1675/76) in a responsible administrative capacity; free by 1637/38 and called Gent. almost immedi-

ately thereafter. OCCUPATIONAL PROFILE: servant, 1633/34; overseer, steward, and attorney for *Thomas Cornwaleys* (ca. 1605–1675/76); probably an independent planter from the early 1650s until his death. PUBLIC CAREER. LEGISLATIVE SERVICE: Assembly, present 1637/38, present 1638/39, special writ 1640 (did not attend), Mattapanient Hundred, St. Mary's County, 1641 (elected to the 2nd session), special writ 1642A, present 1647/48, St. Mary's County, 1649 (Accounts); Lower House, St. Inigoe's Hundred, St. Mary's County, 1650–1650/51 (elected to fill vacancy in the 1st session; Laws, chairman 1). OTHER PROVINCIAL OFFICE: proprietary agent to New England, 1643. LOCAL OFFICE: justice, St. Mary's County, 1644. MILITARY SERVICE: commission to seize illegal traders, 1638–1639. STANDS ON PUBLIC/PRIVATE ISSUES: supporter of the Jesuits and upholder of Cornwaleys's position against proprietary policies in the struggles of the first decade with Lord Baltimore. WEALTH DURING LIFETIME. PERSONAL PROPERTY: at least 6 Negro servants in 1649 (from his marriage settlement). LAND AT FIRST ELECTION: 2,000 acres in 1651. WEALTH AT DEATH. DIED: prior to December 1655. LAND: at least 2,000 acres.

FENWICK, IGNATIUS (?–1784). BORN: probably in St. Mary's County, of age by 1763; probably eldest son. NATIVE: fifth generation. RESIDED: in Charles County from at least 1763 until about 1774; "Wallington," St. Mary's County, until death. FAMILY BACKGROUND. FATHER: Ignatius Fenwick (?–1776), of St. Mary's County, served on the Committee of Correspondence for St. Mary's County in 1775; owned 922 acres in St. Mary's County at the time of his death. MOTHER: Mary, daughter of Edward Cole (?–1761), of St. Mary's County, and wife Ann Neale (?–1768). BROTHERS: Edward; James, a mariner and ship's captain in partnership with his brother Joseph in a merchant firm in Georgetown, Montgomery County, who married Catherine Ford in 1778; Henry; Joseph (by 1773–?), who married ca. 1792 Elenoire Menoir, of Bordeaux, France, and who served as U.S. consul in Bordeaux, France from 1790 to 1801; Richard; and Rev. John Ceslas, O.P. (?–1815). SISTERS: Helena; Elizabeth; Ann, who married (first name unknown) Clarke; and Mary, who married (first name unknown) Jenkins. MARRIED by 1761 Sarah (ca. 1744–by 1784), daughter of Michael Taney (ca. 1695–1743/44), of Calvert County, and second wife Sarah; stepdaughter of George Cole III; granddaughter of John Brooke. Her half nephew was *Michael Taney* (1750–ca.

1820). **CHILDREN. SONS:** James (?–1823), who married first, Mary Lancaster, and second, Teresa; Edward, who was educated in France and became a Dominican priest and the first Catholic bishop of Cincinnati; Michael, who was educated in France and who married Ann Anita Manning; Thomas, who married Eleanor Young; Nicholas; and Charles, who drowned at sea in childhood. **DAUGHTERS:** Mary (?–died young); Sarah, who married Nicholas Young. **PRIVATE CAREER. EDUCATION:** literate. **RELIGIOUS AFFILIATION:** Catholic. **OCCUPATIONAL PROFILE:** planter. **PUBLIC CAREER. LEGISLATIVE SERVICE:** Convention, St. Mary's County, 9th, 1776. **LOCAL OFFICES:** justice, St. Mary's County, 1777–1784; commissioner of tax, St. Mary's County, 1779–1784; justice, Orphans' Court, St. Mary's County, 1782–1784. **MILITARY SERVICE:** colonel, Lower Battalion, St. Mary's County, by 1777. **WEALTH DURING LIFETIME. LAND AT FIRST ELECTION:** probably at least 2,092 acres in St. Mary's, Prince George's, and Charles counties (inherited ca. 1,000 acres in St. Mary's County from his maternal grandfather; at least 710 acres of the land in Prince George's and Charles counties were held in trust for four of his children under the terms of the will of their uncle, James Cole). **SIGNIFICANT CHANGES IN LAND BETWEEN FIRST ELECTION AND DEATH:** sold 86 acres in Charles County in 1780; purchased ca. 10 acres in Prince George's County in 1778 and 417 acres in Charles County in 1783. He also purchased additional land in St. Mary's County in the 1780s. **WEALTH AT DEATH. DIED:** between March 16 and April 6, 1784, in St. Mary's County. **PERSONAL PROPERTY:** TEV, at least £2,533.11.1 current money; FB, £2,140.7.10. **LAND:** probably at least 2,500 acres in St. Mary's, Charles, and Prince George's counties.

FERY (FERRY), JOHN (?–1698/99). **IMMIGRATED:** by 1691, probably much earlier, possibly as a servant. **RESIDED:** Patapsco Hundred, Baltimore County. **MARRIED** probably Ann, widow of John Boring (?–1690), a justice of Baltimore County in 1679. **CHILDREN.** Probably died without progeny. **PRIVATE CAREER. EDUCATION:** literate. **RELIGIOUS AFFILIATION:** Anglican. **OCCUPATIONAL PROFILE:** possibly a servant; planter; merchant in partnership with Capt. Thomas Todd, of Virginia. **PUBLIC CAREER. LEGISLATIVE SERVICE:** Lower House, Baltimore County, 1694–1697, 1697/98–1698 (died before the 3rd session). **LOCAL OFFICES:** justice, Baltimore County, 1691–1698/99 (quorum, 1692–1698/99); St. Paul's Parish Vestry, Baltimore

County 1693–1697. **MILITARY SERVICE:** captain, by 1696. **STANDS ON PUBLIC/PRIVATE ISSUES:** an opponent of slavery. **WEALTH DURING LIFETIME. PERSONAL PROPERTY:** headed a household of 10 taxables in 1692 and 1694. **LAND AT FIRST ELECTION:** at least 257 acres, plus 530 acres in trust for his Boring stepchildren. **WEALTH AT DEATH. DIED:** will probated on March 11, 1698/99. **PERSONAL PROPERTY:** TEV, £367.8.9 sterling, plus 9,666 pounds of tobacco (including 5 servants). **LAND:** 596 acres. **IDENTIFICATION PROBLEMS.** No definite determination of origins. There were two men with the name John Fery. One was a servant who entered in 1674; another with the same name immigrated in 1680.

FINNEY, WILLIAM (ca. 1637–1696). **BORN:** ca. 1637. **IMMIGRATED:** in 1670 as a free adult with his wife and three daughters. **RESIDED:** in Talbot County. **MARRIED** first, Mary. **MARRIED** second, Katherine. **CHILDREN. SON:** William (?–ca. 1723), who married Rachel, daughter of William Clayton (ca. 1655–1721). **DAUGHTERS:** Elizabeth; Mary, who married Joseph Semphill; and Susanna. **PRIVATE CAREER. EDUCATION:** literate. **RELIGOUS AFFILIATION:** Anglican. **SOCIAL STATUS AND ACTIVITIES:** transported three people to Maryland in addition to family; Gent. on arrival. **OCCUPATIONAL PROFILE:** attorney, admitted to the Talbot County Court in 1678/79 (disbarred in 1678 for fighting); planter; tanner and shoemaker. **PUBLIC CAREER. LEGISLATIVE SERVICE:** Lower House, Talbot County, 1692–1693. **LOCAL OFFICES:** justice, Talbot County, 1687–1695/96 (quorum, 1692–1695/96); deputy commissary, Talbot County, 1692–1694; St. Paul's Parish Vestry, Talbot County, 1693–1695/96. **MILITARY SERVICE:** major, 1692–1694; lieutenant colonel, 1694–1695/96. **WEALTH DURING LIFETIME. LAND AT FIRST ELECTION:** ca. 725 acres. **WEALTH AT DEATH. DIED:** administration bond dated April 23, 1696. **PERSONAL PROPERTY:** TEV, £221.13.6 sterling (including 1 slave, 4 servants, and a parcel of books). **LAND:** ca. 725 acres.

FISCHER (FISHER), ADAM (ca. 1736–1787). **BORN:** ca. 1736. **RESIDED:** in Frederick Town, Frederick County. **MARRIED** Margaret (ca. 1739–1799). **CHILDREN. SONS:** John; Adam (1773–1835), who married Elizabeth (1777–1860). **DAUGHTERS:** Elizabeth; Amelia; Catherine; Christiana; and Barbara. **PRIVATE CAREER. EDUCATION:** trained as a surgeon. **SOCIAL STATUS AND ACTIVITIES:** Esq., 1782. **OCCUPATIONAL PROFILE:** surgeon, 1767; probably a planter. **PUBLIC CAREER. LEGISLATIVE**

SERVICE: Convention, Frederick County, 9th, 1776; Lower House, Frederick County, 1778–1779 (Laws to Expire 2; Claims 3). LOCAL OFFICES: Committee of Observation, Frederick County, in office 1776; deputy of the committee to recommend officers for the two German companies and lieutenants for the rifle company, Frederick County, 1776; sheriff, Frederick County, 1782–at least 1785; collector of tax, Frederick County, in office 1785. MILITARY SERVICE: supplied a substitute to serve in the militia, 1778. WEALTH DURING LIFETIME. PERSONAL PROPERTY: assessed value £250.0.0, including 3 slaves and 3 oz. plate, 1782. LAND AT FIRST ELECTION: at least 172 acres in Frederick County and 2 lots in Frederick Town, Frederick County. SIGNIFICANT CHANGES IN LAND BETWEEN FIRST ELECTION AND DEATH: sold one and three-fourths lots in Frederick Town, by 1782. WEALTH AT DEATH. DIED: on August 16, 1787, in Frederick Town, Frederick County. PERSONAL PROPERTY: TEV, at least £315.14.3 current money (including 4 slaves). LAND: ca. 172 acres, plus one-fourth of a lot in Frederick Town, Frederick County. His property was seized after his death to pay £7,690.3.0, tax monies he allegedly owed the state as Frederick County tax collector; at least 13.25 acres of land seized by the state was later recovered by his wife and Fischer's name was cleared.

FISHER, THOMAS (?–1721/22). BORN: of age by 1699. NATIVE: probably, if so, probably second generation. RESIDED: in Talbot County (later became, part of Queen Anne's County). FAMILY BACKGROUND. FATHER: Thomas Fisher, Gent. (?–ca. 1698), of Kent Island, Talbot County; a merchant. MOTHER: Anne. MARRIED by 1699 Sarah. CHILDREN. SONS: Thomas; John; Joseph; Richard; William; and Flower. DAUGHTERS: Susanna; Jane; Elizabeth; Sarah; and Mary. PRIVATE CAREER. EDUCATION: literate. OCCUPATIONAL PROFILE: planter. PUBLIC CAREER. LEGISLATIVE SERVICE: Lower House, Queen Anne's County, 1719–1721/22 (Aggrievances 1–4). LOCAL OFFICES: commissioner to lay out fifty acres for a town at the mouth of Tuckahoe Creek, Queen Anne's County, appointed 1708; justice, Queen Anne's County, 1710–1721/22 (quorum, 1716–1721/22). MILITARY SERVICE: captain. WEALTH DURING LIFETIME. LAND AT FIRST ELECTION: 2,827 acres in Queen Anne's and Dorchester counties (2,147 acres, the remainder of 2,747 acres inherited from his father; 680 acres by purchase). SIGNIFICANT CHANGES IN LAND BETWEEN FIRST ELECTION AND DEATH: surveyed 166 acres in Queen Anne's and Dorchester counties. WEALTH AT DEATH. DIED: will probated on March 1, 1721/22, in Queen Anne's County. PERSONAL PROPERTY: TEV, £764.19.2 (including 6 slaves, 1 servant, and books); FB, £747.4.4. LAND: 2,993 acres in Queen Anne's and Dorchester counties.

FITZHERBERT, EDWARD (?–?). IMMIGRATED: in 1670 as a free adult. RESIDED: in St. Mary's County; probably returned to England, 1673. FAMILY BACKGROUND. BROTHER: John, who married Mary, daughter of *Giles Brent* (1600–ca. 1671/72) and wife Kittamaquund. PRIVATE CAREER. EDUCATION: almost certainly literate and probably well educated. RELIGIOUS AFFILIATION: Catholic. SOCIAL STATUS AND ACTIVITIES: very high status on arrival; Esq., by 1670/71; appointed to the Council within a few months of his arrival in the colony; no record of his presence in colony after November 1673. OCCUPATIONAL PROFILE: probably a planter. PUBLIC CAREER. LEGISLATIVE SERVICE: Upper House, 1671 (no attendance recorded after the 2nd session). OTHER PROVINCIAL OFFICES: Council, 1670/71–1673; justice, Provincial Court, 1670/71–1673. LOCAL OFFICES: alderman, St. Mary's City, 1671. MILITARY SERVICE: major, 1671–1673.

FITZHUGH, WILLIAM (ca. 1722–1798). BORN: ca. 1722 in Virginia. IMMIGRATED: ca. 1752 from Virginia. RESIDED: in Calvert County until ca. 1793; Washington County, ca. 1793–1798. FAMILY BACKGROUND. FATHER: George Fitzhugh (ca. 1690–1722), of Virginia. MOTHER: Mary (ca. 1697–1728), daughter of Col. George Mason, of Virginia. MARRIED first, (first name unknown), widow of George Turberville; daughter of Richard Lee, of London, England. MARRIED second, in January 1752 Ann (1727–1793), widow of John Rousby (1728–1750/51); daughter of *Peregrine Frisby* (1688–1739); granddaughter of both *Nicholas Sewall* (ca. 1655–1737) and *James Frisby* (ca. 1651–1704); niece of *Thomas Frisby* (1681–ca. 1715/16) and *James Frisby* (1684–1719). Her brothers were Peregrine Frisby (1713/14–?); Nicholas (?–died in infancy); James (?–died in infancy); and James (1722–1755). Her sisters were Susannah (1718–?); Sarah (1727–?); and Elizabeth (1729/30–?). Her first cousin was Ariana Margaret Frisby (1717–?), who married *William Harris* (1704–1748). Her nephews were *Peregrine Tilghman* (ca. 1741–1807); *James Tilghman* (1743–1809). Her niece was Henrietta Maria Lloyd (?–1822), who married *William Hayward, Jr.* (ca. 1758–1834). CHILDREN. SONS: George, who was an intimate friend of Gov. Robert Eden and served as clerk of Caroline County from 1774 to 1777; John, who married Elizabeth, daughter of *Richard Parran* (?–by 1783); *William Fitzhugh, Jr.* (1761–1839); and Capt. Peregrine (ca. 1760–?), who resided in Queen Anne's County in 1792, Washington County in 1797, and Soder's Bay, Lake Ontario from 1799 until death. Peregrine was an aide to Gen. George Washington during the Revolution and he married Elizabeth Crowley, daughter of *Samuel Chew* (by 1734–1786). STEPDAUGHTER: Elizabeth Rousby, who married *George Plater* (1735–1792). PRIVATE CAREER. EDUCATION: literate. RELIGIOUS AFFILIATION: Anglican, Christ Church Parish, Calvert County. SOCIAL STATUS AND ACTIVITIES: Esq., 1752; frequently entered his horses in the Annapolis races. ADDITIONAL COMMENTS: Fitzhugh was a close friend of George Washington and of *Thomas Sim Lee* (1745–1819), who wrote letters of recommendation for Fitzhugh's sons when they were applying for military offices. He became blind in later life. OCCUPATIONAL PROFILE: planter; owned a gristmill, fulling mills, and a distillery in Calvert County, by 1783. PUBLIC CAREER. LEGISLATIVE SERVICE: Lower House, Calvert County, 1754–1757 (Grievances 1–6; Arms and Ammunition 5, 6), 1758–1761 (Elections 2; Arms and Ammunition 2); Upper House, 1769–1770 (appointed before the 2nd session), 1771, 1773–1774; Convention, Calvert County, 9th, 1776 (Elections); Lower House, Calvert County, 1777, 1777–1778 (Manufactories 1; speaker 2, 3), 1778–1779 (speaker 1–3), 1779–1780 (Grievances 1; Elections 3), 1780–1781 (elected to the 1st session to fill vacancy), 1781–1782, 1782–1783. OTHER PROVINCIAL OFFICES: Council, 1769–at least 1774 (appointed and qualified on November 12, 1769); treasurer, Western Shore, appointed 1772 and 1773; commissary general, appointed 1773; chairman, Patuxent Association, in office 1781. LOCAL OFFICES: justice, Calvert County, 1752–at least 1769 (quorum, 1758–at least 1769); recruiting officer, Calvert County, appointed 1780. MILITARY SERVICE: colonel, by 1752; fought in the French and Indian War and participated in the West Indian expedition. STANDS ON PUBLIC/PRIVATE ISSUES: At the outbreak of the Revolution Fitzhugh declined to continue receiving his half pay from the British government for former military service, which would have required him to remain neutral. WEALTH DURING LIFETIME. PERSONAL PROPERTY: In July 1780 Fitzhugh's home was raided by the British and by August 1781 he claimed 30 slaves had gone off with the enemy. Assessed value

£957.15.0, including 13 slaves, 1783; listed as one of the largest creditors against the estate of *Robert Eden* (1741–1784), which owed him £1,642.5.2 in 1787. LAND AT FIRST ELECTION: 4,651 acres in Talbot, Queen Anne's, and Calvert counties (all acquired through his marriage to his second wife). SIGNIFICANT CHANGES IN LAND BETWEEN FIRST ELECTION AND DEATH: owned 2,300 acres, 3 lots, and mills in Calvert County, 1783; owned 2,500 acres in Washington County in 1785, of which at least 1,500 acres were deeded to his sons prior to his death. WEALTH AT DEATH. DIED: on February 10, 1798, in Washington County. PERSONAL PROPERTY: TEV, $17,405.68 current money (including 34 slaves); FB, estate overpaid $385.06. LAND: 43,000 acres in Kentucky, 2 lots in Washington, D.C., and an unspecified number of lots in Richmond, Virginia, mentioned in his will. ADDITIONAL COMMENTS: In his will Fitzhugh instructed his executors to petition for compensation of losses caused by British raids on, and threats to, his dwelling plantation during the Revolution.

FITZHUGH, WILLIAM, JR. (1761–1839). BORN: in 1761 in Calvert County. NATIVE: second generation. RESIDED: in Calvert County; "The Hive," near Hagerstown, Washington County, probably by the 1790s; Genesee, Livingston County, New York, ca. 1800 until death. FAMILY BACKGROUND. FATHER: *William Fitzhugh* (ca. 1722–1798). MOTHER: Ann (1727–1793), daughter of *Peregrine Frisby* (1688–1739). BROTHERS: George; Capt. Peregrine (ca. 1760–?); and John. STEPSISTER: Elizabeth Rousby, who married *George Plater* (1735–1792). STEPNIECE: Ann, who married *Uriah Forrest* (1746–1805). OTHER KINSHIP: his great-grandfathers were *Nicholas Sewall* (ca. 1655–1737) and *James Frisby* (ca. 1651–1704); his great-uncles were *Thomas Frisby* (1681–ca. 1715/16) and *James Frisby* (1684–1719). MARRIED Ann (Nancy) (1771–?), daughter of Col. Daniel Hughes (?–1818), of Hagerstown, Washington County, and wife Rebeccca Lux; stepdaughter of both Susannah Schlatter, of Germantown, Pennsylvania, and Ann Elliott, of Carlisle, Pennsylvania; granddaughter of *Darby Lux* (ca. 1698–1750); niece of *Samuel Hughes* (ca. 1741–?), *William Lux* (ca. 1730–1778), *Darby Lux* (?–1795), and Elizabeth Hughes (?–1793), who married *Richard Potts* (1753–1808). Her brothers were Robert (1767–?), who married Susannah Purviance; William (1769–?); Samuel (1773–?), who married (first name unknown) Holker; and James (1775–?), who never married. Her sister was Rebecca (ca. 1777–1800). Her first cousin was Richard Potts (1786–

1865), a member of the Maryland Senate from 1838 to 1844, who married Ahn, daughter of *George Murdock* (ca. 1742–1805). CHILDREN. SONS: William H. (1786–1829), a presidential elector (for Andrew Jackson), who married Mary, daughter of Samuel Hughes; Dr. Daniel, one of the wealthier men of western New York, who married Ann Dana; Samuel, a judge in New York, who married Ann Addison; James, of Kentucky; Henry, of New York, who married (first name unknown), daughter of Charles Carroll, of "Bellevue," Washington County, who was a cousin of *Charles Carroll of Carrollton* (1737–1832); Richard, who married Mary Jones, of Livingston County, New York, and who died in a railroad accident; Robert, who married Maria, daughter of Daniel Carroll, of Duddington (?–1849). DAUGHTERS: (first name unknown), who married Rev. (first name unknown) Backus; (first name unknown), who married in 1841 James Birney (1792–1857), an anti-slavery leader and Abolition candidate for the presidency; (first name unknown), who married (first name unknown) Tallman, of Rochester, New York; Ann Carroll, who married Gerritt Smith (1797–1874), a philanthropist and abolitionist, of Petersboro, New York; and (first name unknown), who married Comdr. (first name unknown) Swift, of Geneva, New York. One of these daughters was named Rebecca Ann. PRIVATE CAREER. EDUCATION: literate. RELIGIOUS AFFILIATION: his great-grandmother was a Catholic; his grandfather was Protestant. OCCUPATIONAL PROFILE: probably a planter. PUBLIC CAREER. LEGISLATIVE SERVICE: Lower House, Calvert County, 1786–1787, 1787–1788, 1788. MILITARY SERVICE: captain, by 1783; colonel, period of service unknown. WEALTH DURING LIFETIME. PERSONAL PROPERTY: 16 slaves inherited from his father, 1798. LAND AT FIRST ELECTION: although he appeared to own no land in his own right, he probably had control of at least part of his aging father's vast holdings. SIGNIFICANT CHANGES IN LAND BETWEEN FIRST ELECTION AND DEATH: acquired a total of 2,646 acres in Washington County between 1787 and 1807, of which 500 acres were a deed of gift from his father, 1787; 2,000 acres were inherited from his father, 1798; and 146 acres were purchased and patented in 1792 and 1807. WEALTH AT DEATH. DIED: in 1839 in New York; size of estate unknown.

FORBES, JAMES (ca. 1731–1780). BORN: ca. 1731, near Benedict, Charles County. NATIVE: probably second generation. RESIDED: in St. Mary's County, 1766; Charles County, 1770. FAM-ILY BACKGROUND. FATHER: John Forbes, Gent. (?–by 1732); probably emigrated from Scotland; he resided in St. Mary's County and was in debt at the time of his death. MOTHER: Dryden (1687–1760), widow of *Henry Peregrine Jowles* (1681–1720); daughter of *Kenelm Cheseldyne* (1640–1708). UNCLES: *Kenelm Cheseldyne* (1683–1719); *Thomas Trueman Greenfield* (1682–1733). STEP-BROTHERS: Henry Greenfield Jowles; Kenelm Jowles. STEPSISTERS: Mary Jowles; Sybill Jowles; and Rebecca Jowles. CHILDREN. SON: John (1757–1804), who married Elizabeth and in his will summarized his "wordly transactions" as "both intricate and numerous." PRIVATE CAREER. EDUCATION: literate. RELIGIOUS AFFILIATION: Anglican. SOCIAL STATUS AND ACTIVITIES: Gent., 1759; Hon., 1780. OCCUPATIONAL PROFILE: merchant, in partnership with George Maxwell, 1757–1762. PUBLIC CAREER. LEGISLATIVE SERVICE: Lower House, Charles County, 1777–1778 (Grievances 1, 3; Claims 1, 3). LOCAL OFFICES: justice, Charles County, commissioned 1770 and 1777; commissioner of tax, Charles County, appointed 1777. OUT OF STATE SERVICE: delegate, Continental Congress, 1777–1780 (elected on December 22, 1777, to fill vacancy, but did not attend until January 1778; reelected in November 1778 and December 1779; died while in office). WEALTH DURING LIFETIME. LAND AT FIRST ELECTION: at least 2 lots in Charles County; possibly ca. 1,000 acres in St. Mary's County. WEALTH AT DEATH. DIED: on March 25, 1780, in Philadelphia, Pennsylvania; buried at Christ Protestant Episcopal Church; size of estate unknown.

FORD, ATHANASIUS (ca. 1728–?). BORN: ca. 1728 in St. Mary's County. NATIVE: fourth generation. RESIDED: on Beaverdam Manor, St. Mary's County. FAMILY BACKGROUND. FATHER: possibly John Ford, son of Robert Ford. BROTHER: possibly John, Jr. PRIVATE CAREER. EDUCATION: literate. RELIGIOUS AFFILIATION: Catholic. SOCIAL STATUS AND ACTIVITIES: Gent., 1782. OCCUPATIONAL PROFILE: planter; retail merchant, trading with Christopher Court, a London merchant, 1772. PUBLIC CAREER. LEGISLATIVE SERVICE: Conventions, St. Mary's County, 7th–8th, 1776; Lower House, St. Mary's County, 1777, 1777–1778 (Loan Office 1), 1778–1779 (Elections 2), 1782–1783, 1784 (elected, but did not attend). WEALTH DURING LIFETIME. LAND AT FIRST ELECTION: 1,447 acres in St. Mary's County (63 acres that his father was leasing for the lifetime of his two sons, but which Athanasius possessed; 191 acres by purchase; 1,193 acres by patent). He was also leasing 18 acres, 1762. SIGNIFICANT CHANGES IN LAND BETWEEN FIRST ELECTION AND DEATH: purchased 365 acres in Charles County in 1782, and immediately traded it for an unspecified amount of acreage in St. Mary's County; patented 14.5 acres in St. Mary's County, 1783. WEALTH AT DEATH. DIED: possibly between 1785 and 1790; size of estate unknown. According to his London creditor Christopher Court, Ford sold his property between 1785 and 1786, moved from Maryland, and died insolvent.

FORD, WILLIAM (?–1678/79). BORN: in England. IMMIGRATED: in 1670 as a free adult from Bristol. RESIDED: in Dorchester County. MARRIED in 1670/71 Sarah, daughter of *Richard Preston* (?–ca. 1669/70). Her brothers were Richard (?–by 1669); James (?–by 1673/74); and Samuel. Her sisters were Naomi (?–1663), who married *William Berry* (ca. 1636–1691); Margaret; and Rebecca. CHILDREN. SONS: Samuel (1673–?); Josias. DAUGHTER: Rebecca. PRIVATE CAREER. EDUCATION: literate. RELIGIOUS AFFILIATION: Quaker. SOCIAL STATUS AND ACTIVITIES: Gent. on arrival. OCCUPATIONAL PROFILE: planter. PUBLIC CAREER. LEGISLATIVE SERVICE: Lower House, Dorchester County, 1674/75 (elected to the 4th session; Laws 4), 1676–1678 (Elections and Privileges 2; died before the 3rd session). LOCAL OFFICE: justice, Dorchester County, 1674 (refused to take the required oath). WEALTH DURING LIFETIME. LAND AT FIRST ELECTION: at least 900 acres; patented and sold an additional 1,400 acres ca. 1675. WEALTH AT DEATH. DIED: will probated on March 4, 1678/79. PERSONAL PROPERTY: TEV, 57,581 pounds of tobacco (including 5 servants); FB, estate overpaid 20,175 pounds of tobacco. LAND: over 900 acres.

FORMAN, EZEKIEL (?–?). NATIVE: second generation. RESIDED: in Kent County; Princeton, New Jersey. FAMILY BACKGROUND. FATHER: Joseph Forman, banished from Scotland; settled in Monmouth, New Jersey in 1765. MOTHER: (first name unknown), daughter of William Hemsley. BROTHER: Gen. David, who married Ann, daughter of Thomas Marsh, and died in Natchez, Mississippi. MARRIED by 1768 Augustina, daughter of Thomas Marsh. Her sister was Ann, who married by 1768 David Forman. CHILDREN. SON: William Gordon, who married his first cousin Sarah Marsh. DAUGHTERS: Elizabeth (1768–?); Sarah (1768–?). PRIVATE CAREER. EDUCATION: literate. OCCUPATIONAL PROFILE: officeholder; probably a planter. PUBLIC CAREER. LEGISLATIVE SERVICE:

Lower House, Kent County, 1777 (Claims 1; discharged on November 4, 1777, for serving as a county clerk at the time of election). LOCAL OFFICES: sheriff, Kent County, 1774–1776; Committee of Correspondence, Kent County, in office 1774; clerk, Kent County, 1777–1800; judge, court of appeals, appointed under the Act to Procure Troops for the American Army, Kent County, appointed 1778. MILITARY SERVICE: paymaster, marching militia, Eastern Shore. WEALTH DURING LIFETIME. PERSONAL AND REAL PROPERTY: his wife received the use and profits of £750.0.0 from her aunt Sarah Marsh Emory, ca. 1774; assessed value £1,215.15.0, including 34 slaves, 1783; assessed value $186.00 (combined real and personal property), 1804; assessed value $267.00 (combined real and personal property), 1808; assessed value $534.00 (combined real and personal property), 1812. LAND AT FIRST ELECTION: 768 acres in Cecil and Queen Anne's counties. WEALTH AT DEATH. DIED: possibly in Princeton, New Jersey; size of estate unknown.

FORREST, URIAH (1746–1805). BORN: in 1746 in St. Mary's County. NATIVE: the Forrest family immigrated to Jamestown, Virginia in 1607; descendants appear in St. Mary's County by the mid-seventeenth century. RESIDED: in St. Mary's County until ca. 1783; London, England, until ca. 1786; Georgetown, Montgomery County, ca. 1786 until death. FAMILY BACKGROUND. FATHER: probably Thomas Forrest, of St. Mary's County. BROTHER: *Zachariah Forrest* (ca. 1743–ca. 1817). MARRIED Rebecca, daughter of *George Plater* (1735–1792); stepdaughter or daughter of either Hannah Lee (?–1763) or Elizabeth Rousby (?–1750); granddaughter or stepgranddaughter of *Richard Lee* (ca. 1707–1787); stepgranddaughter of *William Fitzhugh* (ca. 1722–1798). Her brothers or half brothers were George; John Rousby; Thomas; and William. Her sister was Ann, who married Philip Barton Key. CHILDREN. SONS: probably Joseph; Henry; and Uriah. DAUGHTERS: Ann, who married (first name unknown) Green; Maria, who married (first name unknown) Bohrer. PRIVATE CAREER. EDUCATION: literate. RELIGIOUS AFFILIATION: Anglican, St. Andrew's Parish, St. Mary's County. SOCIAL STATUS AND ACTIVITIES: Gent., 1776; Esq., 1797. OCCUPATIONAL PROFILE: at the close of the Revolutionary War, Forrest went to London, England, as the resident partner of Forrest, Stoddert & Murdock. With *Benjamin C. Stoddert* (ca. 1751–1813), Forrest and Murdock engaged in trade on the Potomac River. Forrest was also instrumental in the incorporation of the

Georgetown Bridge Company, the Bank of Columbia, and the Georgetown Mutual Insurance Company. **PUBLIC CAREER.** LEGISLATIVE SERVICE: Lower House, St. Mary's County, 1781–1782 (Claims 1, 2), 1782–1783 (Manufactories 2), 1786–1787 (Grievances 1; Claims 1; discharged on January 15, 1787 for failure to meet the residency requirement), 1787–1788 (Claims 2), 1788 (Elections), Montgomery County, 1789 (Elections; Laws to Expire), 1790; Senate, Western Shore, Term of 1796–1801: 1796 (did not serve), 1797, 1798, 1799, 1800. OTHER STATE OFFICES: commissioner, confiscated British property, qualified February 1781, resigned July 1781; Executive Council, elected 1791 and 1792. LOCAL OFFICES: churchwarden, St. Andrew's Parish, St. Mary's County, in office 1782–1783; mayor, Georgetown, Montgomery County, elected 1792; justice, Montgomery County, 1799–at least 1800. MILITARY SERVICE: 1st lieutenant, Gunby's Independent Maryland Company, 1776; captain, Third Maryland Battalion, Flying Camp, 1776; major, Third Maryland Regiment, 1776; wounded and lost a leg at the Battle of Germantown, 1776; lieutenant colonel, First Maryland Regiment, 1777; transferred to Seventh Maryland Regiment, 1779; resigned 1781; brigadier general, Fourth Brigade (Prince George's County and the lower part of Montgomery County), Maryland Militia, 1794–1795; major general, First Division, Maryland Militia, commissioned 1795–served until 1801 (out of state). OUT OF STATE SERVICE: delegate, Continental Congress, 1786–1787 (elected in December 1786, but did not attend until February 1787; resigned on May 11, 1787); representative, U.S. Congress, 1793–1794 (resigned on November 8, 1794); clerk, Circuit Court, District of Columbia, 1801–1805. STANDS ON PUBLIC/PRIVATE ISSUES: elected as a Federalist to the U.S. Congress. **WEALTH DURING LIFETIME.** PERSONAL PROPERTY: 5 slaves, 1790; assessed value £480.0.0, including 5 slaves and 50 oz. plate, 1793; assessed value £700.0.0, including 14 slaves and 150 oz. plate, 1798; assessed value £398.10.0, including 9 slaves, 1801; owned one-third interest in a sailing vessel, 1800. SIGNIFICANT CHANGES IN LAND BETWEEN FIRST ELECTION AND DEATH: owned a lot in Alexandria, Virginia, by 1790; purchased 202 acres in Montgomery County in 1791, which he sold in 1797; patented 1,257 acres (1,013.5 in Allegany County and 243.5 in St. Mary's County), 1795–1798; owned 150 lots in Washington, D.C., plus 1,229.5 acres in Montgomery County and the District of Columbia, 1798; sold the lot in Alexandria, Virginia, in 1790, and 806.5 acres in Montgomery County, Maryland, 1802. WEALTH AT DEATH. DIED: on July 6, 1805, at his home "Rosedale," Georgetown, D.C. He was buried at Oak Hill Cemetery, Washington, D.C. LAND: ca. 1,680 acres in Allegany, St. Mary's, and Montgomery counties, and the District of Columbia, plus ca. 150 lots in the District of Columbia. ADDITIONAL COMMENTS: Assignees handled the administration of his estate, which was deeply in debt. The Bank of Columbia requested a quick administration because of suits pending in the General Court and on the Court of Appeals docket.

FORREST, ZACHARIAH (ca. 1743–ca. 1817). BORN: ca. 1743 in St. Mary's County. NATIVE: the Forrest family immigrated to Jamestown, Virginia in 1607; descendants had settled in St. Mary's County by the mid-seventeenth century. RESIDED: in Lower Resurrection Hundred, St. Mary's County. **FAMILY BACKGROUND.** FATHER: probably Thomas Forrest, of St. Mary's County. BROTHER: *Uriah Forrest* (1746–1805). MARRIED first, Anne (Nancy), daughter of Stourton Edwards and wife Barbara, of St. Mary's County. MARRIED second, in 1800 Ann, daughter of Henrietta Ford, of St. Mary's County. CHILDREN. SONS: Richard (1767–?); James; and Uriah. DAUGHTERS: Catherine; Sarah, who married (first name unknown) Abell; Ann, who married (first name unknown) Good; Elizabeth, who married (first name unknown) Cooke; and (first name unknown), who married (first name unknown) Johnson. **PRIVATE CAREER.** RELIGIOUS AFFILIATION: Anglican, All Faiths Parish and St. Andrew's Parish, St. Mary's County. OCCUPATIONAL PROFILE: probably a planter. **PUBLIC CAREER.** LEGISLATIVE SERVICE: Lower House, St. Mary's County, 1787 (elected to the 2nd session of the 1786–1787 Assembly to fill vacancy; Grievances 2), 1789. OTHER STATE OFFICE: associate justice, First District, 1791–1792 (resigned). LOCAL OFFICES: tobacco inspector, Cole's warehouse, St. Mary's County, appointed 1770 and 1773; militia recruiting officer, St. Mary's County, appointed ca. 1777; sheriff, St. Mary's County, 1778–1782; All Faiths Parish Vestry, St. Mary's County, in office 1782 and 1792; justice, St. Mary's County, in office 1785–1789, 1794, 1801–at least 1805; justice, Orphans' Court, St. Mary's County, in office 1785–1789, and 1793; commissioner of tax, St. Mary's County, 1786–1798. MILITARY SERVICE: 2nd lieutenant, Upper Battalion, St. Mary's County Militia, commissioned 1777; captain, Lower Battalion, St. Mary's County Militia, commissioned 1780. **WEALTH DURING LIFETIME.** PERSONAL PROPERTY: 15

slaves, 1790; assessed value £413.0.0, including 18 slaves and plate, 1793; assessed value £432.12.6, including 18 slaves and 13 oz. plate, 1809; assessed value $1,453.00, including 21 slaves and 18 oz. plate, 1813. LAND AT FIRST ELECTION: possibly ca. 400 acres in St. Mary's County. SIGNIFICANT CHANGES IN LAND BETWEEN FIRST ELECTION AND DEATH: patented 1,504 acres in St. Mary's County between 1787 and 1798; owned 2,761 acres in St. Mary's County from 1809 until death. WEALTH AT DEATH. DIED: will probated in February 1817 in St. Mary's County. LAND: 2,761 acres in St. Mary's County.

FOWKE (FOULKE), GERARD (1625–1669). BORN: in 1625, probably in Staffordshire, England; younger son. IMMIGRATED: by 1664 as a free adult from Westmoreland County, Virginia. RESIDED: in Charles County. ADDITIONAL COMMENTS: in Virginia by 1651. FAMILY BACKGROUND. FATHER: Roger Fowke. MOTHER: Mary Bayley. BROTHER: John Fowke, of Gunston, Staffordshire, England, who married Joyce March. MARRIED first, Hope. MARRIED second, in 1661/62 Anne, widow of *Job Chandler* (?–1659); daughter of Adam Thorowgood (1602–1641) and wife Sarah Offley (1609–?), of Lower Norfolk County, Virginia; stepdaughter of *Francis Yardley* (ca. 1624–by 1655). CHILDREN. SONS: *Gerard Fowke* (1662/63–ca. 1734/35), who married first, Mary Lomax, and second, in 1686 Sarah, daughter of Thomas Burdett and wife Verlinda Cotton; Adam. DAUGHTERS: Jean, who married (first name unknown) Mercer; Elizabeth (?–1698/99), who married *William Dent* (ca. 1660–1704); and Mary, who married in 1680 George Mason (1660–1716). PRIVATE CAREER. EDUCATION: literate. RELIGIOUS AFFILIATION: Protestant. SOCIAL STATUS AND ACTIVITIES: Gent., of Westmoreland County, Virginia, 1661/62. PUBLIC CAREER. LEGISLATIVE SERVICE: Lower House, Charles County, 1666. LOCAL OFFICE: justice, Charles County, 1667 (did not qualify). MILITARY SERVICE: colonel, by 1667. OUT OF COLONY SERVICE: justice, 1655, 1662; burgess, James City, Virginia, 1658–1659, Westmoreland County, Virginia, 1663. MILITARY SERVICE: captain, 1658; colonel, by 1662. STANDS ON PUBLIC/PRIVATE ISSUES: he was disciplined by the Virginia House of Burgesses for "injuries and affronts done to Wahangonche, King of the Potomac Indians," and was disfranchised and disqualified from holding office in that colony in 1661/62. WEALTH DURING LIFETIME. LAND AT FIRST ELECTION: owned extensive acreage in Virginia, perhaps only the 2,550 acres owned by his wife and stepchildren in Maryland.

SIGNIFICANT CHANGES IN LAND BETWEEN FIRST ELECTION AND DEATH: claimed he had no freehold in Charles County in 1668. WEALTH AT DEATH. DIED: by October 12, 1669. PERSONAL PROPERTY: TEV, 47,813 pounds of tobacco (including 3 slaves and 3 servants). LAND: 1,200 acres in Virginia.

FOWKE (FOULKE), GERARD (1662/63–ca. 1734/35). BORN: in 1662/63 in either Charles County or Westmoreland County, Virginia; oldest son. NATIVE: second generation. RESIDED: in Charles County. FAMILY BACKGROUND. FATHER: *Gerard Fowke* (1625–1669). MOTHER: Anne, widow of *Job Chandler* (?–1659); daughter of Adam Thorowgood (1602–1641), of Lower Norfolk County, Virginia. BROTHER: Adam. SISTERS: Elizabeth (?–1698/99), who married *William Dent* (ca. 1660–1704); and Mary, who married George Mason (1660–1716). HALF SISTER: Jean, who married (first name unknown) Mercer. MARRIED first, Mary Lomax. MARRIED second, in 1686 Sarah (?–1747), daughter of Thomas Burdett and wife Verlinda Cotton. CHILDREN. SONS: Gerard (1687–?); Chandler (1692–1745), who married Mary Fossaker; and Roger (1696–?), who married Anne, daughter of *Thomas Stone* (1677–1727). DAUGHTERS: Ann (1689/90–1739), who married Robert Alexander; Frances (1691/92–1744), who married in 1711 Gustavus Brown; Catherine (1694–?), who married Ellsworth Bayne, son of *John Bayne* (ca. 1662–1701); and Elizabeth. PRIVATE CAREER. EDUCATION: literate. RELIGIOUS AFFILIATION: Anglican. SOCIAL STATUS AND ACTIVITIES: second generation burgess. OCCUPATIONAL PROFILE: planter. PUBLIC CAREER. LEGISLATIVE SERVICE: Lower House, Charles County, 1704–1707. LOCAL OFFICES: Nanjemoy Parish Vestry, Charles County, 1696–1697, 1703; sheriff, Charles County, 1699–1701; justice, Charles County, 1704–1720 (quorum, 1714–1720). WEALTH DURING LIFETIME. LAND AT FIRST ELECTION: 1,279 acres. WEALTH AT DEATH. DIED: will probated on January 24, 1734/35. PERSONAL PROPERTY: TEV, £521.4.4 current money (including 16 slaves); FB, £485.9.5. LAND: over 1,279 acres in Maryland, plus land in Virginia.

FRANCIS, RICHARD (?–?). BORN: in Ireland, of age by 1729; younger son. IMMIGRATED: ca. 1729 from Ireland. RESIDED: in Annapolis, Anne Arundel County; moved to Virginia in 1739; probably moved to Philadelphia, Pennsylvania, after 1739. FAMILY BACKGROUND. FATHER: Rev. John Francis, dean of Lismore and rector of St. Mary's,

Dublin, Ireland. MOTHER: (first name unknown) Tench. BROTHERS: *Tench Francis* (1701–1758); Philip (ca. 1708–1773), immigrated to New York in 1755, after receiving a chaplaincy of a regiment and later became an English clergyman and writer, who married in 1739 Elizabeth Rowe (?–ca. 1744/45). NIECE: Ann (Anna) Francis (1727–?), who married *James Tilghman* (1716–1793). PRIVATE CAREER. EDUCATION: literate. RELIGIOUS AFFILIATION: Protestant. ADDITIONAL COMMENTS: wrote *Maxims in Equity.* OCCUPATIONAL PROFILE: lawyer, admitted to the following courts: Provincial Court in May 1729; Prerogative Court in May 1729; Court of Chancery in December 1729; Prince George's County in August 1730; Anne Arundel County by June 1734; and Baltimore County by March 1736/37. PUBLIC CAREER. LEGISLATIVE SERVICE: Lower House, Annapolis, 1734/35–1737 (Laws 1; discharged on April 3, 1735, after several Annapolis voters were declared ineligible by the Assembly; reseated on April 12, 1735, after reelection; Laws Cv, 2–4). OTHER PROVINICAL OFFICES: examiner general, 1732–1738; commissioner of the Paper Currency Office, 1734–1738. WEALTH DURING LIFETIME. LAND AT FIRST ELECTION: no evidence of landownership while in Maryland. WEALTH AT DEATH. DIED: after 1739, out of Maryland; size of estate unknown.

FRANCIS, TENCH (1701–1758). BORN: in 1701 in Ireland; eldest son. IMMIGRATED: by 1724 from Ireland. RESIDED: in Kent County, by 1724; Talbot County, by December 1724; Philadelphia, Pennsylvania, 1737. FAMILY BACKGROUND. FATHER: Rev. John Francis, dean of Lismore, rector of St. Mary's, Dublin, Ireland. MOTHER: (first name unknown) Tench. BROTHERS: *Richard Francis* (?–?); Philip (ca. 1708–1773), who immigrated to New York in 1755, having received a chaplaincy of a British regiment, and who returned to England where he served as a clergyman and miscellaneous writer, and who married in 1739 Elizabeth Rowe (?–ca. 1744/45). MARRIED on December 29, 1724, Elizabeth (ca. 1708–?), daughter of *Foster Turbutt* (1679–1720/21); niece of *William Turbutt* (1683/84–1739). Her brother was Henry (ca. 1703–?). Her sisters were Sarah (1706–1773), who married *Nicholas Goldsborough* (ca. 1689–1766); Mary Anne (1711–1794); Mary (1713–?); Anne (1715–1766), who married *John Goldsborough* (1711–1778); and Rachel (1718–?). Her first cousins were Elizabeth Turbutt, who married *Thomas Harris* (?–1760); Anna Maria Turbutt, who married *Edward Tilghman* (1713–

1786); Mary Anne Wright (?–1747), who married *William Hopper* (1707–1772); and Anne Wright (?–by 1754), who married *Edward Oldham* (1709–1773). Her nephews were *Thomas Goldsborough* (ca. 1728–1793); *Howes Goldsborough* (1747–1797); and *William Goldsborough* (1750/51–1801). Her nieces were Elizabeth Goldsborough (1735–ca. 1786), who married second, *Benson Stainton* (?–ca. 1781); Mary Goldsborough (1755–1796), who married *Benedict Brice* (1749–1786); and Ann Goldsborough (1732–?), who married *Edward Oldham* (1709–1773). CHILDREN. SONS: John (ca. 1725–?); Tench (1731–1800), who married in 1762 Anne, eldest daughter of Charles Willing and wife Anne; Turbutt (1740–1797), a colonel in the British army, who married Rebecca, only daughter of Samuel Mifflin; and Philip (1748–?), who married his first cousin Henrietta Maria (ca. 1753–1839), daughter of *John Goldsborough* (1711–1778). DAUGHTERS: Ann (1727–?), who married *James Tilghman* (1716–1793); Mary (1729–?), who married William Coxe, of New Jersey; Elizabeth (1733–1800), who married John Lawrence; Margaret (1735–1794), who married in 1753 Edward Shippen (1728/29–1806), a lawyer, member of the provincial council of Pennsylvania from 1770 to 1775, associate justice of the Pennsylvania Supreme Court from 1791 to 1799, and justice of the Pennsylvania Supreme Court from 1799 to 1805; Rachel (1737–?), who married first, John Retfe, and second, Matthew Pearce. ADDITIONAL COMMENTS: his granddaughter was Margaret Shippen, who married in 1779 Benedict Arnold (ca. 1741–1801), revolutionary war general and traitor. PRIVATE CAREER. EDUCATION: received a legal education in England. RELIGIOUS AFFILIATION: Anglican, St. Peter's Parish, Talbot County. SOCIAL STATUS AND ACTIVITIES: Esq. ADDITIONAL COMMENTS: one of the founders of the Philadelphia Academy, 1743; trustee for the College of Philadelphia when it opened in 1757. OCCUPATIONAL PROFILE: a lawyer, admitted to the following courts: Talbot County in June 1724; Kent County by 1725; Queen Anne's County by August 1728; Provincial Court in October 1728; Dorchester County by June 1734. Officeholder. PUBLIC CAREER. LEGISLATIVE SERVICE: Lower House, Talbot County, 1734/35–1737 (Laws 1, Cv, 2–4). LOCAL OFFICES: clerk of Indictments, Kent County, by 1725, Talbot County, by 1734; clerk, Talbot County, 1727–1738; deputy commissary, Talbot County, 1734–1738. ADDITIONAL COMMENTS: Francis hired and trained Thomas Bullen to perform his duties as clerk of Talbot County from June 1734 to 1738. In 1738 Francis sold the clerkship to John Leeds for a sum in excess of £130 sterling. OUT OF PROVINCE SERVICE: attorney general, Pennsylvania, 1744–1752; Pennsylvania commissioner, in office 1750; recorder, Philadelphia, Pennsylvania, 1750–1754. WEALTH DURING LIFETIME. LAND AT FIRST ELECTION: 2,022 acres in Talbot and Dorchester counties (713 acres through his marriage; 1,309 acres by purchase). SIGNIFICANT CHANGES IN LAND BETWEEN FIRST ELECTION AND DEATH: he had sold almost all of his Maryland land by 1743, including 800 acres in Talbot County, which he sold to his daughter Ann and her husband *James Tilghman* (1716–1793). WEALTH AT DEATH. DIED: in 1758, probably in Philadelphia, Pennsylvania; size of estate unknown.

FRANKLIN (FRANKLYN), ROBERT (?–1682). BORN: probably in England. IMMIGRATED: in 1664 as a free adult. RESIDED: in Anne Arundel County. MARRIED first, (name unknown). MARRIED second, by 1674 Sarah, daughter of *George Puddington* (?–1674). CHILDREN. SON: Robert, Jr. (1659–?). DAUGHTER: Sarah, who married William Herne (?–1698). PRIVATE CAREER. EDUCATION: literate. SOCIAL STATUS AND ACTIVITIES: no title on arrival in the colony; proved rights in 1667 to 200 acres for transporting himself and three others (not members of his family); his son apparently migrated later. OCCUPATIONAL PROFILE: planter; merchant. PUBLIC CAREER. LEGISLATIVE SERVICE: Lower House, Anne Arundel County, 1671–1674/75 (Accounts 2). LOCAL OFFICES: justice, Anne Arundel County, 1668–1678/79 (quorum, 1676–1678/79); sheriff, Anne Arundel County, 1678/79–1682. WEALTH DURING LIFETIME. LAND AT FIRST ELECTION: at least 1,040 acres. WEALTH AT DEATH. DIED: by October 1682. PERSONAL PROPERTY: TEV, £139.15.7 sterling (including 1 servant); FB, estate overpaid 50,000 pounds of tobacco. LAND: 814 acres.

FRANKLIN, THOMAS (ca. 1706–1787). BORN: ca. 1706. IMMIGRATED: by 1728. RESIDED: at "Blenheim," Baltimore County. MARRIED first, by 1730 Ruth. MARRIED second, by 1744 Ruth, widow of Peasley Ingram, of Baltimore County; daughter of *Charles Hammond* (ca. 1670–1713); stepdaughter of *Edmond Benson* (1687–1734); niece of *Thomas Hammond* (?–ca. 1724/25) and *John Hammond* (ca. 1665–1742/43). Her brothers were *Charles Hammond* (1692/93–1772); *Philip Hammond* (1697–1760); Nathan (1708–1762); Rezin (?–1739); and John (?–1753). Her sister was Hamutel. Her first cousin was *Thomas Hammond*

(1693–?). Her nephews were *Nathan Hammond* (1731–1811); *Rezin Hammond* (?–1783); *John Hammond* (1735–1784); *Rezin Hammond* (1745–1809); and *Matthias Hammond* (1740–1786). Her niece was Anne Hammond (1716–?), who married second, *William Govane* (1716/17–1768). CHILDREN. SONS: Thomas Heath (?–1794); Benjamin (?–1794); and James (?–1792). ADDITIONAL COMMENTS: Thomas and Benjamin died within a few days of each other; both were alcoholics with impaired mental and physical health. DAUGHTERS: Sarah, who married (first name unknown) Smith, of Baltimore County; Elizabeth (1745–1771), who married *Aquila Paca* (1738–1788). STEPDAUGHTER: Ruth Ingram (?–by 1794). PRIVATE CAREER. EDUCATION: literate. RELIGIOUS AFFILIATION: Anglican, St. John's Parish, Baltimore County. SOCIAL STATUS AND ACTIVITIES: Esq.; Gent.; married into a very prominent Anne Arundel County family. OCCUPATIONAL PROFILE: planter. PUBLIC CAREER. LEGISLATIVE SERVICE: Lower House, Baltimore County, 1751 (elected to the 3rd session to fill vacancy), 1751–1752 (election of entire county delegation voided on December 12, 1751, because of illegal actions of the sheriff; reelected to the 2nd session; resigned before the 3rd session to become sheriff). LOCAL OFFICES: St. John's Parish Vestry, Baltimore County, in office 1738–1741, 1759–1762, 1768, and 1772; St. Paul's Parish Vestry, Baltimore County, in office 1747 and 1748; justice, Baltimore County, 1747–at least 1775 (quorum, 1748–at least 1775); justice, Court of Oyer and Terminer and Gaol Delivery, Baltimore County, commissioned 1750, 1751, 1753, 1758, 1759, 1760, 1761, and 1763; sheriff, Baltimore County, commissioned 1752; churchwarden, St. John's Parish, Baltimore County, in office 1771 and 1772. JURY SERVICE: foreman, grand jury, Baltimore County, appointed 1732. MILITARY SERVICE: captain, by 1747; major, by 1754; colonel, by 1771. WEALTH DURING LIFETIME. PERSONAL PROPERTY: assessed value £1,412.0.0, including 32 slaves and 42 oz. plate, 1783. LAND AT FIRST ELECTION: at least 1,040 acres in Baltimore and Anne Arundel counties (at least 570 acres in Baltimore and Anne Arundel counties through his marriage, 470 acres in Baltimore County by patent and purchase). SIGNIFICANT CHANGES IN LAND BETWEEN FIRST ELECTION AND DEATH: purchased an additional 1,564 acres in Baltimore County, plus 2 lots in Baltimore Town, in the 1760s; transferred some of his wife's land in Baltimore County and 300 acres of his own to his stepdaughter, 1765; sold 244 acres of his wife's land in Anne Arundel County in 1782. WEALTH

AT DEATH. DIED: administration bond granted on April 27, 1787, in Baltimore County. PERSONAL PROPERTY: TEV, £1,759.9.2 current money (including 42 slaves and plate); FB, estate overpaid £355.16.6. His debts included over £1,800 current money owed to *Daniel Dulany, Jr.* (1722–1797) as executor of the estate of Ann Tasker, widow of *Benjamin Tasker* (ca. 1690–1768). LAND: ca. 2,064 acres in Baltimore County, plus 2 lots in Baltimore Town.

FRANKLYN, JOHN (?–1727). IMMIGRATED: by 1687. RESIDED: in All Hallow's Parish, Somerset County. CHILDREN. SON: Ebenezer (?–1728). DAUGHTERS: Elizabeth, who married (first name unknown) Wallon; Mary, who married William Collins; and (first name unknown), who married William Fassitt. PRIVATE CAREER. EDUCATION: literate. RELIGIOUS AFFILIATION: Protestant, possibly a Presbyterian. SOCIAL STATUS AND ACTIVITIES: Gent., 1726/27. OCCUPATIONAL PROFILE: planter. PUBLIC CAREER. LEGISLATIVE SERVICE: Lower House, Somerset County, 1701–1704, 1708A, 1708B–1711. LOCAL OFFICES: Snow Hill Parish Vestry, Somerset County, 1696/97; justice, Somerset County, 1697–1715 (quorum, 1705–1715). MILITARY SERVICE: captain, 1701–1711; major, 1711–1715; lieutenant colonel, 1715–1727. WEALTH DURING LIFETIME. LAND AT FIRST ELECTION: 1,225 acres in 1709. WEALTH AT DEATH. DIED: will probated on November 24, 1727. PERSONAL PROPERTY: TEV, £70.7.6. LAND: 1,425 acres.

FRASER (FRAZER, FRAZIER), GEORGE (?–1764). BORN: probably after 1709. NATIVE: second generation. RESIDED: at "Bowplains" on the Potomac River, Prince George's County, opposite Alexandria, Virginia. FAMILY BACKGROUND. FATHER: Rev. John Fraser (?–1742), who immigrated from Virginia in 1701; rector of Durham Parish in Charles County from 1705 to 1710, and King George's Parish in Prince George's County by 1733 to 1742. MOTHER: Ann (?–after 1764), daughter of Giles Blyzard and wife Mary. BROTHER: John (?–1742). SISTERS: Mary (by 1709–?), who married William Magruder (?–1765), son of *Samuel Magruder* (1654–1711) and brother of *John Magruder* (1694–1750); Susannah (?–by 1746), who married *John Hawkins, Jr.* (1713–1757); Anne (1718–1779), who married in 1748 Allen Bowie; and Verlinda. NEPHEW: *George Fraser Hawkins* (ca. 1741–1785). NIECE: Susanna Fraser Hawkins, who married *William Bayly* (ca. 1742–1824). OTHER KINSHIP: his stepgrandfather

was *James Smallwood* (ca. 1639–ca. 1714/15). PRIVATE CAREER. EDUCATION: literate. RELIGIOUS AFFILIATION: Anglican, King George's Parish, Prince George's County. SOCIAL STATUS AND ACTIVITIES: Mr., 1739; Gent., 1742; Esq., 1764. OCCUPATIONAL PROFILE: probably a planter. PUBLIC CAREER. LEGISLATIVE SERVICE: Lower House, Prince George's County, 1752–1754 (elected to the 2nd session to fill vacancy), 1754–1757 (Arms and Ammunition 1–6; Bills of Credit 5), 1757–1758 (Arms and Ammunition 1, Cv, 2), 1758–1761 (Arms and Ammunition 2, 3, Cv 3). LOCAL OFFICES: King George's Parish Vestry, Prince George's County, in office 1741–1743, 1747–1750, 1752–1755, 1760–1763; justice, Prince George's County, 1741–at least 1757 (quorum, 1752–at least 1757). WEALTH DURING LIFETIME. LAND AT FIRST ELECTION: 2,190 acres in Prince George's and Frederick counties (1,170 acres in Prince George's County, part of which was deeded as a gift by his father the remainder inherited from his father and brother; 355 acres in Prince George's County by purchase; and 665 acres in Frederick County by patent). SIGNIFICANT CHANGES IN LAND BETWEEN FIRST ELECTION AND DEATH: acquired an additional 300 acres in Prince George's County to add to his 500-acre dwelling plantation between 1753 and 1761; acquired a house and lot in Georgetown, Frederick County, by 1764. WEALTH AT DEATH. DIED: in December 1764 at his seat in Prince George's County. LAND: 2,490 acres in Prince George's and Frederick counties, plus a house and a lot in Georgetown, Frederick County. ADDITIONAL COMMENTS: His principal heirs were his mother, his sister Verlinda, and his nephew *George Fraser Hawkins* (ca. 1741–1785).

FRAZIER (FRAIZER, FRASER, FRAZER), ALEXANDER (?–1790). BORN: between 1756 and 1763, probably in Calvert County. NATIVE: at least second generation. RESIDED: at "Sterlings Nest," Calvert County. FAMILY BACKGROUND. FATHER: Alexander Frazier (?–1779), of Calvert County. BROTHER: John, a minor in 1790. MARRIED never. CHILDREN. Died without progeny. PRIVATE CAREER. EDUCATION: literate. OCCUPATIONAL PROFILE: planter; ran a blacksmith shop on his property with James Patison as his partner. PUBLIC CAREER. LEGISLATIVE SERVICE: Lower House, Calvert County, 1784 (Elections), 1785, 1788, 1789. WEALTH DURING LIFETIME. PERSONAL PROPERTY: assessed value £711.10.0, including 18 slaves, 1783. LAND AT FIRST ELECTION: charged with at least 740 acres in Calvert County in 1783, one-half of which belonged to his brother. **WEALTH AT DEATH. DIED**: on June 9, 1790, at "Sterlings Nest," Calvert County. **PERSONAL PROPERTY**: his inventory was appraised at £850.13.4 current money, but was then sold by order of the Calvert County Orphans' Court for £625.9.7 current money. **LAND**: a moiety of 888 acres in Calvert County. **ADDITIONAL COMMENTS**: on November 30, 1795, because of the heavy indebtedness of Frazier's estate, the chancellor decreed that all of Frazier's land, which he and his brother had inherited from their father, be sold. One-half of the profits went to Frazier's creditors and one-half to his brother John. The 888 acres sold for £2,930.8.0.

FREELAND, FRISBY (by 1747–?). **BORN**: in Calvert County, between 1742 and 1747; younger son. **NATIVE**: third generation. **RESIDED**: in the Second District, Calvert County, 1783; All Saints' Parish, Calvert County, 1800. **FAMILY BACKGROUND. FATHER**: Robert Freeland (?–ca. 1757), a planter, of Upper Cliffs, Calvert County, son of Robert Freeland (?–ca. 1695), who immigrated ca. 1659 and resided in Calvert County. **MOTHER**: Sarah, widow of Thomas Holland (1700–1742). **BROTHERS**: Robert, Jr.; Francis; Jacob; *Peregrine Freeland* (?–?); and Benjamin (?–by 1757). **SISTERS**: Mary, who married William Harrison, Jr.; Sarah; and Rebecca. **MARRIED** Sarah (1770–1843), widow of Allen Bowie (ca. 1768–1795); daughter of William Chew (1746–1801) and wife Elizabeth Reynolds (?–1801); granddaughter of Thomas Reynolds. Sarah was married either prior to, or subsequently to, Beverly R. Grayson. Her brothers were Francis Holland (1774–1834), who married (first name unknown) Calvit, of Mississippi; William Lock (1778–1858), who married in 1805 Rebecca Freeland (1785–1840). Her sisters were Elizabeth (1772–1828), who married both (first name unknown) Mosely, of Kentucky, and (first name unknown) Smith; Mary (1776–1821), who married Thomas Reynolds, of Mississippi; and Ann Reynolds (1780–?), who married (first name unknown) Craig, of Kentucky. **CHILDREN. SON**: possibly Frisby Freeland, Jr. (ca. 1774–?). **STEPSON**: Fielder Bowie, Jr. (1792–1866); possibly Thomas Grayson. **ADDITIONAL COMMENTS**: his household contained 2 boys and 3 girls, all minors in 1800. **PRIVATE CAREER. EDUCATION**: literate. **SOCIAL STATUS AND ACTIVITIES**: listed as one of the fifteen wealthiest people living in Calvert County, 1782. **OCCUPATIONAL PROFILE**: probably a planter. **PUBLIC CAREER. LEGISLATIVE SERVICE**: Lower House, Calvert County, 1779–1780, 1780–

1781. **LOCAL OFFICES**: coroner, Calvert County, appointed 1774, 1790, and 1795; Committee of Observation, Calvert County, elected 1774; tobacco inspector, Lower Marlboro warehouse, Calvert County, appointed 1786, 1787, 1788, 1790 (recommended, but not commissioned); justice, Calvert County, 1787–at least 1793; commissioner of tax, Calvert County, appointed 1798. **MILITARY SERVICE**: captain, Calvert County Militia, commissioned 1776. **WEALTH DURING LIFETIME. PERSONAL PROPERTY**: assessed value £1,032.17.6, including 30 slaves and 30 oz. plate, 1783; 56 slaves, 1800. **LAND AT FIRST ELECTION**: at least 931 acres, plus 1 lot in Huntington, Calvert County (323 acres inherited from his father). **SIGNIFICANT CHANGES IN LAND BETWEEN FIRST ELECTION AND DEATH**: purchased more than 391 acres and sold 99 acres in Calvert County, 1780–1796. **WEALTH AT DEATH. DIED**: after 1807. **LAND**: possibly 1,223 acres, plus 1 lot in Huntington, Calvert County.

FREELAND, PEREGRINE (?–?). **BORN**: in Calvert County, a minor in 1757; younger son. **NATIVE**: third generation. **RESIDED**: in "Upper Hundreds of the Cliffs," Second Tax District, Calvert County. **FAMILY BACKGROUND. FATHER**: Robert Freeland (?–ca. 1757), a planter, of Upper Cliffs, Calvert County, son of Robert Freeland (?–ca. 1695), who immigrated ca. 1695 and resided in Calvert County. **MOTHER**: Sarah, widow of Thomas Holland (1700–1742), of Anne Arundel County. **BROTHERS**: Robert, Jr.; Francis; Jacob; *Frisby Freeland* (by 1747–?); and Benjamin (?–by 1757). **SISTERS**: Mary, who married William Harrison, Jr.; Sarah; and Rebecca. **CHILDREN**. His household contained 2 boys and 2 girls, all between 10 and 16 years of age, 1800. **PRIVATE CAREER. EDUCATION**: literate. **PUBLIC CAREER. LEGISLATIVE SERVICE**: Lower House, Calvert County, 1789, 1790, 1792, 1793, 1794. **LOCAL OFFICE**: coroner, Calvert County, 1783–1789. **WEALTH DURING LIFETIME. PERSONAL PROPERTY**: assessed value £604.19.2, including 17 slaves and 3.5 oz. plate, 1783; 22 slaves, 1800; 28 slaves, 1810. **LAND AT FIRST ELECTION**: at least 323 acres in Calvert County (inherited from his father). **WEALTH AT DEATH. DIED**: possibly between 1810 and 1820, probably in Calvert County; size of estate unknown.

FREEMAN, WILLIAM (ca. 1668–ca. 1737/38). **BORN**: ca. 1668. **RESIDED**: in Cecil County. **MARRIED** Anne, a Quaker, who subsequently married William Hutchinson. **CHILDREN. SONS**: Isaac; Jacob (?–by 1735/36); William, Jr.; Thomas; and Richard. DAUGHTER: Mary, who married in 1731 William Abott. PRIVATE CAREER. EDUCATION: literate. RELIGIOUS AFFILIATION: his wife was a Quaker; son Jacob probably Anglican. SOCIAL STATUS AND ACTIVITIES: Gent. at death. OCCUPATIONAL PROFILE: planter. PUBLIC CAREER. LEGISLATIVE SERVICE: Lower House, Cecil County, 1722–1724. WEALTH DURING LIFETIME. LAND AT FIRST ELECTION: at least 1,324 acres and possibly 1,424 acres in Cecil and Kent counties and Sussex County, Delaware. SIGNIFICANT CHANGES IN LAND BETWEEN FIRST ELECTION AND DEATH: sold 400 acres in Cecil County, 1733; acquired 180 acres in Cecil County and possibly patented 94 acres in Sussex County, Delaware, 1734. WEALTH AT DEATH. DIED: will probated on February 13, 1737/38, in Cecil County. PERSONAL PROPERTY: TEV, £188.19.9 (including 2 slaves); FB, estate overpaid £4.6.5. LAND: over 1,400 acres in Cecil and Kent counties, and possibly Sussex County, Delaware.

FRISBY, JAMES (ca. 1651–1704). BORN: ca. 1651 in England. IMMIGRATED: by 1665 as a minor with his parents from Virginia. RESIDED: in Baltimore County; Cecil County after 1676. FAMILY BACKGROUND. FATHER: James Frisby (?–1674), who immigrated to Virginia with his family in 1654, owned 600 acres in Lower Norfolk County, Virginia, and eventually owned 1,950 acres in Maryland. He was a planter, merchant, and served as a justice of Baltimore County from 1665 to 1674. MOTHER: Mary. BROTHERS: *William Frisby* (by 1664–1713); Thomas. MARRIED ca. 1675 Sarah Read. Her brother was Peregrine Browne, of London, England, a shipmaster and merchant involved in trade with Maryland. CHILDREN. SONS: James (1676–died young); *Thomas Frisby* (1681–ca. 1715/16), who married first in 1702/3 Frances (?–1713), daughter of *George Wells* (?–1696), and second, Augustina, daughter of *Casparus Augustus Herman* (1656–1697); *James Frisby* (1684–1719), who married in 1713/14 Ariana, daughter of *Matthias Vanderheyden* (?–1729); *Peregrine Frisby* (1688–1739), who married Elizabeth, daughter of *Nicholas Sewall* (ca. 1655–1737); Jacob (1693–by 1704); Francis (1697–?); and William (1699–1724), who married Mary, daughter of *Nicholas Sewall* (ca. 1655–1737). DAUGHTERS: Mary (1678/79–?); Sarah (1680–1731), who married first, Thomas Robinson, and second, Stephen Knight; Mary (1690–1704); and Frances (1696–by 1704). PRIVATE CAREER. EDUCATION: literate, probably attended school in En-

gland; he sent his sons to England for their education. RELIGIOUS AFFILIATION: Protestant. SOCIAL STATUS AND ACTIVITIES: his father established a prominent family in Maryland; his business frequently carried him to England. OCCUPATIONAL PROFILE: planter; merchant. PUBLIC CAREER. LEGISLATIVE SERVICE: Lower House, Cecil County, 1676–1682, 1682–1684 (Accounts 2, 3; Laws 3), Associators' Convention, Cecil County, 1689 (no evidence of attendance after the 1st session); Upper House, 1692 (did not attend the 1st session; dismissed before the 2nd session), 1694–1697 (Accounts 1), 1697/98–1700, 1701–1704 (attended only the 1st session). OTHER PROVINCIAL OFFICES: Council, 1691–1692 (dismissed), 1694–1704. LOCAL OFFICE: justice, Cecil County, 1676–1685 (quorum, 1681–1685). MILITARY SERVICE: captain, by 1683/84. STANDS ON PUBLIC/PRIVATE ISSUES: defended Lord Baltimore's government against the Protestant Associators in 1689; recommended by Lord Baltimore to be on first royal Council; removed by Gov. Lionel Copley in 1692, but restored by Gov. Francis Nicholson in 1694; refused out of "Scruple of Conscience" to take the required oaths in October 1695 and was removed from the Court of Delegates. WEALTH DURING LIFETIME. LAND AT FIRST ELECTION: over 700 acres; 2,770 acres by 1691 when appointed to the Council. WEALTH AT DEATH. DIED: will probated on June 19, 1704. PERSONAL PROPERTY: TEV, £4,874.4.11 sterling (including 28 slaves); balance in England of £3,012.15.11. LAND: over 4,033 acres.

FRISBY, JAMES (1684–1719). BORN: in 1684 in Cecil County; second surviving son. NATIVE: third generation. RESIDED: in Cecil County. FAMILY BACKGROUND. FATHER: *James Frisby* (ca. 1651–1704). MOTHER: Sarah Read. UNCLE: *William Frisby* (by 1664–1713). BROTHERS: James (1676–died young); *Thomas Frisby* (1681–ca. 1715/16), who married first, in 1702/3 Frances (?–1713), daughter of *George Wells* (?–1696), and second, Augustina, daughter of *Casparus Augustus Herman* (1656–1697); *Peregrine Frisby* (1688–1739), married Elizabeth, daughter of *Nicholas Sewall* (ca. 1655–1737); Jacob (1693–by 1704); Francis (1697–?); and William (1699–1724), who married Margaret, daughter of *Nicholas Sewall* (ca. 1655–1737). SISTERS: Mary (1678/79–?); Sarah (1680–1731); Mary (1690–1704); and Frances (1696–by 1704). MARRIED in 1713/14 Ariana (1690–1741), who died in England following a smallpox inoculation, daughter of *Matthias Vanderheyden* (?–1729) and wife Anna Margareta Herman, widow of *Henry Ward* (?–1683/84); niece of both *Casparus Augustus Herman* (1656–1697) and Judith Herman, who subsequently married *John Thompson* (?–1701). Ariana subsequently married by 1723 *Thomas Bordley* (ca. 1683–1726), and finally *Edmund Jennings* (?–1756). Her half brother was *Henry Ward* (?–1734). Her sisters were Jane; Augustina, who married *James Harris* (1682–1743); and Francina, who married second, *Charles Hynson* (1692–1748). Her nephew was *Matthias Harris* (1718–1773). Her first cousins were *Ephraim Augustus Herman* (1683–1734/35); *Richard Thompson* (ca. 1680–by 1775); *Augustine Thompson* (1691–ca. 1738/39); and *Joseph Wood* (?–1738). CHILDREN. DAUGHTERS: Sarah (1714–1782), who married in 1730 John Brice (1706–1766); Ariana Margaret (1717–?), who married *William Harris* (1704–1748); and Francina Augustina (1719–1766), who married first, Dr. William Stevenson (?–1739), and second, Daniel Cheston. PRIVATE CAREER. EDUCATION: literate, probably attended school in England. RELIGIOUS AFFILIATION: Anglican. SOCIAL STATUS AND ACTIVITIES: second generation burgess; third generation county officeholder. OCCUPATIONAL PROFILE: merchant; planter. PUBLIC CAREER. LEGISLATIVE SERVICE: Lower House, Cecil County, 1712–1714, 1716–1718, 1719 (died before the 2nd session). LOCAL OFFICE: North Sassafras Parish Vestry, Cecil County, 1718–1719. MILITARY SERVICE: captain by 1718. WEALTH DURING LIFETIME. LAND AT FIRST ELECTION: over 1,720 acres inherited from his father in 1704. WEALTH AT DEATH. DIED: will probated on December 30, 1719. PERSONAL PROPERTY: TEV, £896.16.0 sterling (including 11 slaves and 1 servant). LAND: over 1,720 acres.

FRISBY, PEREGRINE (1688–1739). BORN: in 1688 in Cecil County; third surviving son. NATIVE: third generation. RESIDED: in Cecil County. FAMILY BACKGROUND. FATHER: *James Frisby* (ca. 1651–1704). MOTHER: Sarah Read. UNCLE: *William Frisby* (by 1664–1713). BROTHERS: James (1676–died young); *Thomas Frisby* (1681–ca. 1715/16), who married first, Frances (?–1713), daughter of *George Wells* (?–1696), and second, Augustina, daughter of *Casparus Augustus Herman* (1656–1697); *James Frisby* (1684–1719), who married Ariana, daughter of *Matthias Vanderheyden* (?–1729); Jacob (1693–by 1704); Francis (1697–?); and William (1699–1724), who married Mary, daughter of *Nicholas Sewall* (ca. 1655–1737). SISTERS: Mary (1678/79–?); Sarah (1680–1731); Mary (1690–1704); and Frances (1696–by

1704). MARRIED Elizabeth, daughter of *Nicholas Sewall* (ca. 1655–1737); granddaughter of both *Henry Sewall* (?–1665) and *William Burgess* (ca. 1622–1686/87); stepgranddaughter of *Charles Calvert, 3rd Lord Baltimore* (1637–1714/15); niece of *Cecilius Calvert* (1667–1681), *Benedict Leonard Calvert, 4th Lord Baltimore* (1679–1715), *Philip Calvert* (1626–1682), *Jesse Wharton* (?–1676), *William Digges* (ca. 1650–1697), *Benjamin Rozer* (?–1681), and *Edward Pye* (?–1696). CHILDREN. SONS: Peregrine (1713/14–?); Nicholas (?–died in infancy); and James (1722–1725). DAUGHTERS: Susanna (1718–?), who married in 1738 Richard Tilghman (1705–1766), son of *Richard Tilghman* (1672/73–1738/39); Sarah (1727–?), who married Philemon Charles Blake (?–1761); Ann (1727–1793), who married first, John Rousby (1728–1750/51), son of *John Rousby* (1685–1744), and second, *William Fitzhugh* (ca. 1722–1798); and Elizabeth (1729/30–?), who married James Lloyd (1716/17–1768), son of *James Lloyd* (1679/80–1723). PRIVATE CAREER. EDUCATION: literate, probably attended school in England. RELIGIOUS AFFILIATION: Protestant. SOCIAL STATUS AND ACTIVITIES: second generation burgess. OCCUPATIONAL PROFILE: planter. PUBLIC CAREER. LEGISLATIVE SERVICE: Lower House, Cecil County, 1712–1714. WEALTH DURING LIFETIME. LAND AT FIRST ELECTION: ca. 2,100 acres. WEALTH AT DEATH. DIED: will probated on September 5, 1739. PERSONAL PROPERTY: TEV, £11.10.9 gold, £619.6.1 sterling, £31.19.9 current money, £1,679.12.4 paper currency (including 28 slaves). LAND: ca. 2,100 acres.

FRISBY, THOMAS (1681–ca. 1715/16). BORN: in 1681 in Cecil County; oldest surviving son. NATIVE: third generation. RESIDED: in Cecil County. FAMILY BACKGROUND. FATHER: *James Frisby* (ca. 1651–1704). MOTHER: Sarah Read. UNCLE: *William Frisby* (by 1664–1713). BROTHERS: James (1676–died young); *James Frisby* (1684–1719), who married in 1713/14 Ariana, daughter of *Matthias Vanderheyden* (?–1729); *Peregrine Frisby* (1688–1739), who married Elizabeth, daughter of *Nicholas Sewall* (ca. 1655–1737); Jacob (1693–by 1704); Francis (1697–?); and William (1699–1724), who married Mary, daughter of *Nicholas Sewall* (ca. 1655–1737). SISTERS: Mary (1678/79–?); Sarah (1680–1731); Mary (1690–1704); and Frances (1696–by 1704). MARRIED first, in 1702/3 Frances (?–1713), daughter of *George Wells* (?–1696) and wife Blanche Goldsmith. MARRIED second, Augustina, daughter of *Casparus Augustus Herman* (1656–1697); niece of *Henry Ward* (?–1683/84),

Matthias Vanderheyden (?–1729), and *John Thompson* (?–1701). She subsequently married *Roger Larramore* (?–1721), and finally, Henry Rippin. Her brother was *Ephraim Augustus Herman* (1683–1734/35). Her cousins were *Henry Ward* (?–1734); *Richard Thompson* (ca. 1680–by 1775); and *Augustine Thompson* (1691–ca. 1738/39). CHILDREN. SONS: Thomas (1703/4–1734); James (1711–1734); Peregrine (1711–1747), who married Mary, daughter of Francis Holland and wife Susanna Utie. DAUGHTERS: Mary (1705–?); Mary (1709–?), who married in 1729 Thomas Henderson; and Sarah (1713–1757), who married first, Thomas Holland, son of *William Holland* (?–1732), and second, Robert Freeland. PRIVATE CAREER. EDUCATION: literate, almost certainly attended school in England. RELIGIOUS AFFILIATION: Anglican. SOCIAL STATUS AND ACTIVITIES: second generation burgess and third generation local officeholder. OCCUPATIONAL PROFILE: planter; merchant. PUBLIC CAREER. LEGISLATIVE SERVICE: Lower House, Cecil County, 1702 (elected to the 3rd session, but disqualified for not being of age), 1703–1704 (probably elected to the 4th session, certainly elected by the 5th session), 1704–1707 (Elections and Privileges 3), 1708A, 1708B–1711. LOCAL OFFICES: surveyor, Cecil County, 1698–1700; North Sassafras Parish Vestry, Cecil County, 1703–1704, 1713; justice, Cecil County, by 1708/9–1715. WEALTH DURING LIFETIME. LAND AT FIRST ELECTION: controlled ca. 2,700 acres of his father's estate. WEALTH AT DEATH. DIED: inventory dated February 8, 1715/16. PERSONAL PROPERTY: TEV, £884.12.4 sterling; FB, £855.13.9. LAND: ca. 2,100 acres.

FRISBY, WILLIAM (by 1664–1713). BORN: by 1664 in Virginia; younger son. IMMIGRATED: by 1665 as a minor with his father from Virginia. RESIDED: in Baltimore County; Kent County. FAMILY BACKGROUND. FATHER: James Frisby (?–1674), who immigrated to Virginia with his family in 1654. He owned 600 acres in Lower Norfolk County, Virginia, and eventually acquired 1,950 acres in Maryland. He was a planter, merchant, and justice of Baltimore County from 1665 to 1674. MOTHER: Mary. BROTHERS: *James Frisby* (ca. 1651–1704); Thomas. MARRIED first, in 1684 Mary (?–1699), daughter of Symon Carpenter. MARRIED second, Rachel (?–1703). MARRIED third, Ann (?–1721). CHILDREN. SONS: William Frisby (1684–1738), who married Jane, daughter of *John Thompson* (?–1701); James (1685–1721); Richard (?–1703); Thomas (?–1711); and Stephen (?–1712). DAUGHTER: Anne (1713/14–after 1775),

who married Peregrine Frisby. PRIVATE CAREER. EDUCATION: literate. RELIGIOUS AFFILIATION: Anglican. SOCIAL STATUS AND ACTIVITIES: went to England in 1693 and 1695, and possibly in 1697–1698, when he was again out of the province. OCCUPATIONAL PROFILE: planter; merchant. PUBLIC CAREER. LEGISLATIVE SERVICE: Lower House, Kent County, 1694–1697 (Aggrievances 5), 1704–1707 (Elections and Privileges 1), 1708A. OTHER PROVINCIAL OFFICE: agent to England, 1695. LOCAL OFFICES: justice, Kent County, 1685–1689 (quorum, 1688–1689), 1693 (refused to take the required oath), 1694–1697 (president), 1701/2 (refused to take the required oath), 1702 (refused to take the required oath); St. Paul's Parish Vestry, Kent County, 1693–1706, 1711–1713. STANDS ON PUBLIC/PRIVATE ISSUES: opposed the revolution of Protestant Associators in 1689. WEALTH DURING LIFETIME. LAND AT FIRST ELECTION: probably 1,250 acres. WEALTH AT DEATH. DIED: buried on December 17, 1713. PERSONAL PROPERTY: TEV, £1,318.17.1 sterling (including 14 slaves). LAND: 1,250 acres.

FULLER, WILLIAM (?–by 1695) IMMIGRATED: in 1651 as a free adult with his family, probably from Virginia. RESIDED: in Broad Neck Hundred, Anne Arundel County; left Maryland probably by 1664; in Barbados by 1671; settled in South Carolina in 1678. MARRIED Sarah, daughter of Nicholas Martiau (1592–1657), a French Protestant, naturalized in England, who immigrated to Virginia in 1620 as an agent for the earl of Huntington, and served as a Virginia burgess in 1632, and as a justice of York County, Virginia, from 1633 to 1657. CHILDREN. SON: William (1673–1732), a burgess in South Carolina in 1712. DAUGHTERS: Elizabeth (ca. 1655–?), who married (first name unknown) Cattell; probably Maryann; and probably Belinda. PRIVATE CAREER. EDUCATION: literate. RELIGIOUS AFFILIATION: Protestant; Quaker by 1657. SOCIAL STATUS AND ACTIVITIES: probably left Virginia because of religious persecution; called a captain at his first appearance in Maryland records; quickly assumed leadership of the Protestant forces in the colony. OCCUPATIONAL PROFILE: planter. PUBLIC CAREER. LEGISLATIVE SERVICE: Assembly, Providence (Anne Arundel County), 1654; Parliamentary Commission, 1654–1657/58; Lower House, Anne Arundel County, 1658, 1659/60. OTHER PROVINCIAL OFFICES: justice, Provincial Court, 1654–1657/58. governor, 1655; MILITARY OFFICES: captain, 1652–1657/58; commander of an expedition against the Eastern Shore Indians, 1652. OUT OF

COLONY SERVICE: Council, South Carolina, 1679–1682. STANDS ON PUBLIC/PRIVATE ISSUES: executive leader in the Puritan government, 1654–1657/58; supporter of Fendall's Rebellion, 1659/60–1660; a warrant issued for his arrest in 1660/61 after the restoration of the proprietary government probably motivated him to leave the colony. WEALTH DURING LIFETIME. LAND AT FIRST ELECTION: 300 acres; patented an additional 500 acres in 1658–1659; received a warrant for 1,020 acres in South Carolina, 1683. WEALTH AT DEATH. DIED: by 1695 in South Carolina; size of estate unknown.

FUNK, JACOB (ca. 1725–1794). BORN: ca. 1725; probably eldest son. IMMIGRATED: probably from Virginia. RESIDED: in Frederick County (later became part of Washington County); migrated to Jefferson County, Kentucky, 1791. FAMILY BACKGROUND. FATHER: Jacob Funk (?–1746), died in Frederick County, Virginia. MOTHER: Frances. BROTHERS: Henry; John. SISTERS: Frances; Elizabeth; Mary; and Barbara. MARRIED ca. 1749 Ann (ca. 1727–?). CHILDREN. SONS: John (ca. 1750–ca. 1818); Jacob (?–by 1793). DAUGHTERS: Ann, who married Frederick Geiger; Mary, who married Philip Ashert; Elizabeth, who married Abraham Bains; and Rosina, who married Robert Martin. PRIVATE CAREER. EDUCATION: literate. RELIGIOUS AFFILIATION: Protestant. SOCIAL STATUS AND ACTIVITIES: Gent., 1778. ADDITIONAL COMMENTS: Funk founded the town of Jerusalem (later called Funkstown), located two and one-half miles south of Elizabeth Town (later called Hagerstown) in Washington County. Jerusalem and Elizabeth Town were in competition to be named the county seat. Because of the personal influence of Gen. Daniel Heister and others, Elizabeth Town was selected. Thereafter, Jerusalem, or Funkstown, remained a village. In 1772 Funk deeded land to both the Presbyterian and Lutheran congregations in Jerusalem for the purpose of building churches. Funk was part of a group of about fifty persons who migrated from Funkstown to Kentucky in 1791. OCCUPATIONAL PROFILE: farmer, by 1755–1763; merchant, 1768; yeoman, 1772; farmer, 1773–1777; land speculator. PUBLIC CAREER. LEGISLATIVE SERVICE: Lower House, Frederick County, 1773–1774 (elected to the 2nd session to fill vacancy); Conventions, Frederick County, 2nd–3rd, 1774, 4th, 1775, 5th, 1775; Lower House, Washington County, 1785, 1786–1787, 1787–1788. LOCAL OFFICE: Committee of Observation, Frederick County, elected 1775. **WEALTH DURING LIFETIME.** PERSONAL PROP-

ERTY: assessed value £237.12.6, including 1 mill, Upper Antietam Hundred, Washington County, 1783; 1 slave, Jefferson County, Kentucky, 1793. LAND AT FIRST ELECTION: ca. 1,700 acres in Frederick County and ca. 420 acres in Prince George's County (including a section called Hamburgh, later part of Washington, D.C., which was divided into 287 lots). SIGNIFICANT CHANGES IN LAND BETWEEN FIRST ELECTION AND DEATH: purchased 750 acres in Washington County between 1777 and 1779, of which 130 acres were later sold; sold 25 lots in Hamburgh between 1780 and 1788; time of disposal of remaining Maryland land unknown; owned 983 acres in Jefferson County, Kentucky, plus land in other Kentucky counties, 1793. WEALTH AT DEATH. DIED: will probated on May 6, 1794, in Jefferson County, Kentucky. LAND: over 7,400 acres in Kentucky.

GALE, GEORGE (1671–1712). BORN: in 1671 in Whitehaven, Cumberland, England; younger son. IMMIGRATED: by 1707 as a free adult from Virginia. RESIDED: in Monie Hundred, Somerset County. ADDITIONAL COMMENTS: immigrated to Virginia, ca. 1690. FAMILY BACKGROUND. FATHER: John Gale. BROTHERS: Mathias Gale, a merchant of London, England; John Gale. MARRIED first, in 1700 Mildred (?–1701), widow of Lawrence Washington (1650–1698); daughter of Col. Augustine Warner, of Gloucester County, Virginia. MARRIED second, Elizabeth (1674–1736), daughter of Levin Denwood (ca. 1648–1726). Her brothers were Levin (1670–1703); Arthur (1671/72–1720). Her sister was Mary (1676–1735), who married Henry Hill, son of *Richard Hill* (ca. 1640–1700). CHILDREN. SONS: *Levin Gale* (ca. 1704–1744), who married Leah Littleton; *George Gale* (?–ca. 1772), who married Elizabeth; *John Gale* (?–ca. 1744), who married Milcah Hill; Mathias (?–1748), who married Margaret Gordon, of Virginia. STEPSONS: Augustine Washington (1695–1743); John Washington (1691–?). DAUGHTER: Mildred (January 25, 1701–March 26, 1701). STEPDAUGHTER: Mildred Washington (ca. 1698–?). PRIVATE CAREER. EDUCATION: literate, probably well educated. RELIGIOUS AFFILIATION: Anglican; his second wife was a devout Quaker, but his children were raised as Anglicans. SOCIAL STATUS AND ACTIVITIES: owned part of the ship *Cumberland* in the late 1600s; in 1700 he returned to Whitehaven, England, with his wife and her children, where she died in early 1701; a dispute over the Washington estate brought him back to Virginia by 1704, and he moved to Maryland soon thereafter; Gent. on arrival in Maryland; his education and status brought him immediate appointment to high offices and a recommendation for a seat on the Council. OCCUPATIONAL PROFILE: merchant. PUBLIC CAREER. LEGISLATIVE SERVICE: Lower House, Somerset County, 1708A, 1708B–1711 (Laws 1–4). LOCAL OFFICE: chief justice, Somerset County, 1708/9–1712. MILITARY SERVICE: major, 1707; lieutenant colonel, 1711/12–1712. WEALTH DURING LIFETIME. PERSONAL PROPERTY: £1,000 bequeathed from his first wife. LAND AT FIRST ELECTION: at least 400 acres, probably more. WEALTH AT DEATH. DIED: in August 1712. PERSONAL PROPERTY: TEV, £3,348.12.5 sterling (including 10 slaves, silver plate worth £28, one-half interest in the sloop *Dolphin*, one-half interest in the *Bonetta*, one-half interest in the *Mulberry*, part interest in the *Cumberland*, surveying instruments, a microscope, and books).

GALE, GEORGE (?–ca. 1772). BORN: of age in 1727; probably second son. NATIVE: second generation. RESIDED: in Somerset County. FAMILY BACKGROUND. FATHER: *George Gale* (1671–1712). MOTHER: Betty (1674–1736), daughter of Levin Denwood and wife Priscilla. BROTHERS: *Levin Gale* (ca. 1704–1744); *John Gale* (?–ca. 1744); and Matthias (?–1748). NEPHEW: *Levin Gale* (ca. 1730–1791). NIECE: Mary Gale (ca. 1734–?), who married *Samuel Wilson* (1735–1790). OTHER KINSHIP: his great-nephew was *George Gale* (1756–1815). ADDITIONAL COMMENTS: his father's first wife was probably Mildred (?–1701), widow of Lawrence Washington (1650–1698), and the daughter of Col. Augustine Warner, of Gloucester County, Virginia. She was the grandmother of George Washington (1731/32–1799). MARRIED by 1736 Elizabeth. CHILDREN. No surviving children. PRIVATE CAREER. EDUCATION: literate. RELIGIOUS AFFILIATION: Anglican. His father was an Anglican; his mother was a Quaker. SOCIAL STATUS AND ACTIVITIES: Gent., 1736; Esq., 1760. OCCUPATIONAL PROFILE: merchant; probably a planter. PUBLIC CAREER. LEGISLATIVE SERVICE: Lower House, Somerset County, 1742–1744 (Laws 1; Accounts 2). LOCAL OFFICES: commissioner to establish a town at the head of the Manokin River, Somerset County, appointed 1733; justice, Court of Oyer and Terminer and Gaol Delivery, Somerset County, commissioned 1742; justice, Somerset County, 1757–at least 1762. MILITARY SERVICE: colonel, ca. 1744. WEALTH DURING LIFETIME. LAND AT FIRST ELECTION: possibly ca. 2,900 acres in Somerset, Dorchester, Queen Anne's, Calvert, and Baltimore counties. WEALTH AT DEATH.

DIED: will probated on January 11, 1772, in Somerset County. PERSONAL PROPERTY: TEV, at least £1,982.5.5 current money (including 34 slaves and more than 74 books). LAND: possibly 2,588 acres in Somerset, Dorchester, and Cecil counties.

GALE, GEORGE (1756–1815). BORN: on June 3, 1756, in Somerset County. NATIVE: fourth generation. RESIDED: in Somerset County until ca. 1794; Baltimore County, 1794; on the Susquehanna River, Cecil County, 1795–1815. FAMILY BACKGROUND. FATHER: *Levin Gale* (ca. 1730–1791). MOTHER: Leah Littleton, his father's first cousin, daughter of *Levin Gale* (ca. 1704–1744). BROTHERS: Levin; Lyttleton (?–1815); and Robert. SISTER: Leah. OTHER KINSHIP: his great-uncles were *George Gale* (?–ca.1772) and *John Gale* (?–ca. 1744); his second cousin was Mary Gale (ca. 1734–by 1790), who married *Samuel Wilson* (1735–1790). MARRIED Anna Maria (1756–1817), daughter of *Henry Hollyday* (ca. 1725–1789); granddaughter of *George Robins* (1697–1742); niece of *James Hollyday* (1722–1786), Margaret Robins (1734–1808), who married *William Hayward* (?–1791), and Henrietta Maria Robins (1736–1791), who married *James Lloyd Chamberlaine* (1732–1783); half niece of both *Richard Lloyd* (1717–1786) and *Edward Lloyd* (1711–1770). Her brothers were Henry (?–died young); Thomas; *James Hollyday* (1758–1807); and Henry (1771–?). Her sisters were Henrietta Maria (1750–1832), who married *Samuel Chamberlaine* (1742–1811); Sarah (1753–?); Rebecca (1762–?), who married *Nicholas Hammond* (1758–1830); Elizabeth (1768–?); and Margaret (1774–?). Her first cousin was Henrietta Maria Chamberlaine (?–1804), who married *William Hayward, Jr.* (ca. 1758–1834). Other relatives included great-aunt Elizabeth Robins (1710–1746), who married *William Goldsborough* (1709–1760). CHILDREN. SONS: Levin (1784–1834), a representative to the U.S. Congress from 1827 to 1829, who married in 1813 his first cousin Harriet Rebecca (1783–?), daughter of *Samuel Chamberlaine* (1742–1811); George (1794–1863), who married Anna Maria Dove (Done); and Henry Hollyday (1797–1800). DAUGHTERS: Anna Maria (1782–1847); Leah (ca. 1785–1857), who never married and died in Baltimore County; Henrietta Maria Elizabeth, who married in 1811 her first cousin Henry Chamberlaine, son of *Samuel Chamberlaine* (1742–1811); Sarah (Sally) Hollyday, never married; Harriet (1796–1830), died without progeny; Margaret (1797–1798); and Georgianna (1803–1856), who married Cornelius McLean (1807–1861), of

Baltimore County. PRIVATE CAREER. EDUCATION: literate; may have entered the College of New Jersey (later Princeton University) in 1774, but was a nongraduate. RELIGIOUS AFFILIATION: Anglican. OCCUPATIONAL PROFILE: owned 5 mill seats and races and probably a sawmill; his inventory included "2,600 ft. of pine plank for decking vessels" ; first president of the Baltimore branch of the Bank of the United States, established in February 1792; stockholder in the Havre de Grace Company, established ca. 1795. PUBLIC CAREER. LEGISLATIVE SERVICE: Lower House, Somerset County, 1784 (resigned on December 6, 1784); Senate, Eastern Shore, Term of 1781–1786: 1784 (elected on December 4, 1784, to fill vacancy; qualified on December 6, 1784), 1785, Term of 1786–1791: 1786–1787, 1787–1788, 1788, 1789, 1790. OTHER STATE OFFICE: Constitution Ratification Convention, Somerset County, 1788. LOCAL OFFICES: justice, Somerset County, commissioned 1785 and 1786; justice, Orphans' Court, Somerset County, commissioned 1785 and 1786, Cecil County, commissioned 1799. OUT OF STATE SERVICE: representative, U. S. Congress, 1789–1791; appointed supervisor of distilled liquors for the district of Maryland by President Washington, 1791. WEALTH DURING LIFETIME. PERSONAL PROPERTY: 15 slaves, 1783; assessed value £615.0.0, including 25 slaves, 1793–1795. LAND AT FIRST ELECTION: at least 799 acres in Somerset County, 1783. SIGNIFICANT CHANGES IN LAND BETWEEN FIRST ELECTION AND DEATH: sold all of his land in Somerset County, at least 842 acres, by ca. 1796; purchased 2,831 acres in Cecil County, of which 1,050 acres were mortgaged, plus ca. 55 acres of lots in Havre de Grace, Cecil County, 1795–1800; sold 1,088 acres and mortgaged an additional 625 acres in Cecil County, and sold his lots in Harve de Grace, Cecil County, 1800–1815. WEALTH AT DEATH. DIED: on January 2, 1815, in Cecil County; buried in St. Mark's (Episcopal) churchyard, Aiken, Cecil County. PERSONAL PROPERTY: TEV, $8,806.35 (including more than 20 slaves); FB, $479.78. LAND: possibly 1,743 acres in Cecil County, of which 625 acres were mortgaged. ADDITIONAL COMMENTS: Gale's estate was not settled until 1840. Some real and personal property was sold to settle debts, and some debts were assumed by his son Levin prior to 1835. A large tract of land that remained as part of the estate was sold in 1838 to settle the combined estates of Gale and his son Levin.

GALE, JOHN (?–ca. 1744). BORN: by 1712 in Somerset County; probably third son. NATIVE: second generation. RESIDED: in Somerset County (probably in that section that later became part of Wicomico County). FAMILY BACKGROUND. FATHER: *George Gale* (1671–1712). MOTHER: Betty (1674–1736). BROTHERS: *Levin Gale* (ca. 1704–1744); *George Gale* (?–ca. 1772); and Matthias (?–1748). NEPHEW: *Levin Gale* (ca. 1730–1791). OTHER KINSHIP: his great-nephew was *George Gale* (1756–1815). ADDITIONAL COMMENTS: his father's first wife was probably Mildred (?–1701), widow of Lawrence Washington (1650–1698), and the daughter of Col. Augustine Warner, of Gloucester County, Virginia. She was the grandmother of George Washington (1731/32–1799). MARRIED his first cousin Milcah (Mileah, Miliah), daughter of Henry Hill, a mariner of Anne Arundel and Dorchester counties, and wife Mary Denwood; stepdaughter of Sarah; granddaughter of both *Richard Hill* (ca. 1640–1700) and Levin Denwood; niece of *Joseph Hill* (ca. 1670–1724). Milcah subsequently married Rev. Thomas Airey, rector of Christ Church, Cambridge, Dorchester County. Her brothers were Joseph; Richard, who married Deborah; and Levin, who married Elizabeth. Her sisters were Mary Gillespie, who married Ezekiel Gilliss; Priscilla, who married Caleb Dorsey. CHILDREN. SONS: George (ca. 1731–1765), who married on January 30, 1750, his stepsister Elizabeth (?–1799), daughter of Rev. Thomas Airey and wife Elizabeth Pitt; Henry (ca. 1740–?); and Levin (ca. 1743–?). DAUGHTERS: Mary (ca. 1734–by 1790), who married *Samuel Wilson* (1735–1790); Betty (ca. 1737–?). PRIVATE CAREER. EDUCATION: literate. RELIGIOUS AFFILIATION: Protestant. His father was an Anglican; his mother and wife were Quakers. He specified in his will that his sons were to be raised as Anglicans. SOCIAL STATUS AND ACTIVITIES: Gent., 1733. OCCUPATIONAL PROFILE: merchant; probably a planter. PUBLIC CAREER. LEGISLATIVE SERVICE: Lower House, Somerset County, 1739–1741 (Bills of Credit 3). LOCAL OFFICE: justice, Somerset County, commissioned 1738. MILITARY SERVICE: captain, by 1741. WEALTH DURING LIFETIME. PERSONAL PROPERTY: his wife's dower was £48.0.0. LAND AT FIRST ELECTION: ca. 1,872 acres in Somerset, Queen Anne's, Calvert, and Baltimore counties (ca. 988 acres inherited; ca. 884 acres purchased at public auction). SIGNIFICANT CHANGES IN LAND BETWEEN FIRST ELECTION AND DEATH: sold 287 acres in Queen Anne's County in 1740; purchased and patented ca. 566 acres in Somerset County, 1741–1742. WEALTH AT DEATH. DIED: in Somerset County; administration

bond given in January ca. 1744. PERSONAL PROP-
ERTY: TEV, £2,343.17.3 current money (including
37 slaves and books); FB, £1,013.18.5. LAND:
probably ca. 2,300 acres in Somerset, Queen Anne's, and probably Calvert and Baltimore
counties.

GALE, JOHN (1753–1813). BORN: on September
25, 1753; eldest son. NATIVE: fourth generation.
RESIDED: in Great Annamessex Hundred, Somer-
set County. FAMILY BACKGROUND. FATHER:
George Gale (1731–1765), son of *John Gale* (?–ca.
1744). MOTHER: Elizabeth (?–1799), daughter of
Rev. Thomas Airey and wife Elizabeth Pitt.
BROTHER: George Gale (1756–?). SISTERS: Mileah
(1751–1780), who married *Robert Harrison* (1740–
1802); Mary (1759–1760); Elizabeth (1762–?); and
Leah. OTHER KINSHIP: his great-grandfather was
George Gale (1671–1712); his great-uncles were
George Gale (?–ca. 1772) and *Levin Gale* (ca.
1704–1744); his second cousin was *Levin Gale* (ca.
1730–1791). MARRIED Amelia, daughter of
Thomas Williams; granddaughter of David Wil-
liams. CHILDREN. SON: John Planner. DAUGHTERS:
Mary; Milcah; and Amelia Caroline. All the chil-
dren were minors in 1811. PRIVATE CAREER. EDU-
CATION: literate. RELIGIOUS AFFILIATION: Angli-
can, Coventry Parish, Somerset County.
OCCUPATIONAL PROFILE: probably a planter. PUB-
LIC CAREER. LEGISLATIVE SERVICE: Lower House,
Somerset County, 1785, 1786–1787, 1787–1788,
1788 (elected, but did not attend), 1789, 1806,
1807, 1808–1809, 1809. OTHER STATE OFFICES:
Constitution Ratification Convention, Somerset
County, 1788; associate justice, Fourth District,
appointed 1794. LOCAL OFFICES: Coventry Parish
Vestry, Somerset and Worcester counties, elected
1788 (did not serve) and 1792; justice, Somerset
County, appointed 1793. MILITARY SERVICE: 2nd
lieutenant, Second Maryland Regiment, 1776; 1st
lieutenant, January 1777; taken prisoner at Staten
Island in August 1777 and exchanged in October
1778; captain, December 1777; transferred to Fifth
Maryland Regiment, January 1781; aide-de-camp
to Gen. Mordecai Gist, December 1782 until the
end of the Revolutionary War; brevet major, September 1783; colonel, Maryland Militia, by 1794;
brigadier general, Tenth Brigade (Somerset and
Worcester counties), Maryland Militia, commissioned 1801. WEALTH DURING LIFETIME. PER-
SONAL PROPERTY: assessed value £1,090.0.0, including 28 slaves, 1793. LAND AT FIRST
ELECTION: at least 1,450 acres in Somerset County
(through marriage); possibly owned as much as
1,729 acres in Somerset and Dorchester counties

combined. SIGNIFICANT CHANGES IN LAND BE-
TWEEN FIRST ELECTION AND DEATH: charged
with 3,399 acres in Somerset County in 1793.
WEALTH AT DEATH. DIED: will probated on March
3, 1813, in Somerset County; buried at "Cedar
Grove" on the Annamessex River in Somerset
County. PERSONAL PROPERTY: assessed value
£7,220.0.0, including 80 slaves, 1813. LAND: 3,340
acres in Somerset County, plus 200 acres that he
referred to in his will as military lands.

GALE, LEVIN (ca. 1704–1744). BORN: ca. 1704,
probably in Somerset County. NATIVE: second
generation. RESIDED: in Somerset County. FAMILY
BACKGROUND. FATHER: *George Gale* (1671–1712).
MOTHER: Betty (1674–1736), daughter of Levin
Denwood (ca. 1648–1726) and wife Priscilla.
BROTHERS: *George Gale* (?–ca. 1772); *John Gale*
(?–ca. 1744); and Matthias (?–1748). NEPHEW: *Levin Gale* (ca. 1730–1791). NIECE: Mary Gale (ca.
1734–by 1790), who married *Samuel Wilson*
(1735–1790). MARRIED by 1726 Leah, daughter of
Southy Littleton, of Accomack County, Virginia,
and wife Mary Browne; stepdaughter of Hancock
Custis; granddaughter of both Col. Southy Littleton and wife Sarah Bowman, and of Thomas
Browne and wife Susanna. Her brother was
Southy (?–died young). CHILDREN. DAUGHTER:
Leah, who married her first cousin *Levin Gale* (ca.
1730–1791). PRIVATE CAREER. EDUCATION: literate. RELIGIOUS AFFILIATION: Anglican; made a
gift of one acre of land to the Presbyterians to
erect a house of worship, 1742. SOCIAL STATUS
AND ACTIVITIES: Hon., 1742. OCCUPATIONAL
PROFILE: attorney, admitted to the Somerset
County Court in November 1722; planter; officeholder; merchant, engaged in mercantile activities
with his brothers Matthias, *George Gale* (?–ca.
1772), and *John Gale* (?–ca. 1744); as Col. Levin
Gale & Company, Gale, and his partners, *John
Caldwell* (?–1747), *Robert King* (1689–1755), Archibald Smith, and Alexander Draper owned an
ironworks and a schooner, 1728. PUBLIC CAREER.
LEGISLATIVE SERVICE: Lower House, Somerset
County, 1725–1727 (Laws 1–4), 1728–1731 (Laws
3), 1732–1734 (Laws 1–Cv; discharged during the
convention for accepting a government position of
"trust and profit" after the election), 1734/35–
1737 (Laws 1, Cv, 2–4; Bills of Credit 1, Cv, 2–4),
1738 (Laws; Bills of Credit; appointed to the
Council during the convention); Upper House,
1738 (appointed during the convention), 1739–
1741 (Bills of Credit–Paper Currency Cv, 1, 3),
1742 (Bills of Credit–Paper Currency 1; died before the 2nd session). OTHER PROVINCIAL OF-

FICES: justice, Provincial Court, 1726–1744 (quorum, 1732–1744); judge, Assize Court, Eastern Shore, 1731–at least 1739; naval officer, Pocomoke, 1733–1740 (resigned); Council, 1738–1744 (qualified on May 15, 1738); judge, Land Office, 1738–1744; major general, Eastern Shore, commissioned 1742. LOCAL OFFICES: clerk of Indictments, Somerset County, appointed 1723/24; ranger, Somerset County, appointed 1724/25; justice, Court of Oyer and Terminer and Gaol Delivery, Somerset County, commissioned 1736, 1742, and 1743; churchwarden, St. Anne's Parish, Anne Arundel County, elected 1740. MILITARY SERVICE: lieutenant colonel, militia, by 1727; colonel, by 1729. WEALTH DURING LIFETIME. LAND AT FIRST ELECTION: 709 acres in Somerset County (all inherited from his father). SIGNIFICANT CHANGES IN LAND BETWEEN FIRST ELECTION AND DEATH: acquired 2,270 acres in Accomack County, Virginia, through his marriage, by 1726–1731; purchased or patented at least 3,715 acres in Somerset County between 1726 and 1742; owned one-eighth of 823 acres as a partner in the firm of Col. Levin Gale & Company, 1728; inherited 280 acres in Somerset County from his mother, 1736; sold 1,223 acres in Somerset County by 1743. WEALTH AT DEATH. DIED: will probated on April 24, 1744, in Somerset County. PERSONAL PROPERTY: TEV, £9,078.18.5 current money (including 43 slaves, 416 oz. 15 dwt. 17 gr. silver plate, 5 gold rings weighing 12 dwt. 5 gr., books; and the ironworks property, which included 1 servant and 1 schooner); FB, estate overpaid £527.15.0. LAND: at least 3,481 acres in Somerset County, plus one-eighth of 823 acres in Somerset County, which belonged to the partnership of Col. Levin Gale & Company, plus 2,270 acres in Accomack County, Virginia.

GALE, LEVIN (ca. 1730–1791). BORN: ca. 1730, probably in Somerset County; only son. NATIVE: third generation. RESIDED: in Somerset County. FAMILY BACKGROUND. FATHER: Capt. Matthias Gale (?–1748), a merchant of Somerset County, son of *George Gale* (1671–1712). MOTHER: Margaret Gordon, of Virginia. UNCLES: *Levin Gale* (ca. 1704–1744); *George Gale* (?–ca. 1772); and *John Gale* (?–ca. 1744). MARRIED on February 20, 1755, his first cousin Leah Littleton, daughter of *Levin Gale* (ca. 1704–1744). CHILDREN. SONS: Robert, who married Jane; Littleton (?–1815), who married Margaret (1774–1848), daughter of *Henry Hollyday* (ca. 1725–1789); *George Gale* (1756–1815); and Levin (?–by 1806). DAUGHTER: Leah Littleton, who married Samuel Wilson. PRIVATE

CAREER. EDUCATION: literate. RELIGIOUS AFFILIATION: Anglican. OCCUPATIONAL PROFILE: attorney, admitted to Somerset County Court in August 1754; merchant, by 1766, in partnership with *John Stewart* (?–?) and *Henry Jackson* (?–1795) between at least 1774 and 1787; officeholder. PUBLIC CAREER. LEGISLATIVE SERVICE: Lower House, Somerset County, 1756–1757 (elected to the 5th session to fill vacancy), 1757–1758 (Bills of Credit 1), 1758–1761 (Bills of Credit 1), 1768–1770 (Grievances 3), 1771, 1773–1774 (elected, but did not attend). OTHER PROVINCIAL OFFICE: riding surveyor, Pocomoke, 1763–1776. LOCAL OFFICES: justice, Somerset County, 1766–at least 1777 (quorum, 1766–at least 1777); trustee for the Nanticoke Indians, in office 1768; Somerset Parish Vestry, Somerset County, in office 1769, elected 1779 (fined £20 for refusing to serve), in office 1783 and 1787; justice, Court of Oyer and Terminer and Gaol Delivery, Somerset County, commissioned 1770, 1771, and 1772; commissioner of tax, Somerset County, 1777–1779; justice, Orphans' Court, Somerset County, commissioned 1777; judge, Court of Appeals for Tax Assessment, Somerset County, appointed 1786. WEALTH DURING LIFETIME. PERSONAL PROPERTY: assessed value £5,583.0.0 current money, including 51 slaves and 708 oz. plate, 1783. LAND AT FIRST ELECTION: at least 2,462 acres in Somerset County and Virginia, plus 1 lot in Princess Anne, Somerset County (inherited at least 170 acres in Somerset County from his father; acquired at least 2,270 acres in Virginia through his marriage in 1755). SIGNIFICANT CHANGES IN LAND BETWEEN FIRST ELECTION AND DEATH: sold 2,270 acres in Virginia, 1759; purchased 1,731 acres in Somerset County and inherited an unspecified number of acres in Somerset County from his uncle *George Gale* (?–ca. 1772) between 1766 and 1772; deeded or sold 480 acres in Somerset County between 1778 and 1786; charged with 2,412 acres in Somerset County, plus 1.5 lots in Princess Anne, 1783; purchased 1,000 acres in Somerset County, 1785. WEALTH AT DEATH. DIED: on October 9, 1791, probably in Somerset County. LAND: at least 3,412 acres in Somerset County, plus 1.5 lots in Princess Anne, Somerset County.

GALLOWAY, BENJAMIN (1752–1831). BORN: in 1752 at his family's home on the West River, Anne Arundel County; third son. NATIVE: fifth generation. RESIDED: in Rhode River Hundred, Anne Arundel County, until ca. 1796 when he moved to Washington County, settling in Elizabeth Town (later called Hagerstown). FAMILY

BACKGROUND. FATHER: Samuel Galloway (1720–1785), of "Tulip Hill," West River, Anne Arundel County. MOTHER: Anne (1725–1756), daughter of Dr. Samuel Chew and wife Mary Galloway. BROTHERS: John (1748–1810), who married in 1786 Sarah Chew; Samuel, Jr. (1751–?). SISTERS: Mary (1746–?), who married *Thomas Ringgold* (1744–1776); Anne (1755–?), who married in 1775 James Cheston. MARRIED on October 5, 1775, Henrietta Maria (1759–1847), daughter of *Samuel Chew* (by 1734–1786); niece of Henrietta Maria Chew (1731–1762), who married *Edward Dorsey* (1718–1760); Margaret Chew (?–1773), who married *John Beale Bordley* (1726/27–1804); and Ann Mary Chew (?–1774), who married *William Paca* (1740–1799). Her brothers were Samuel Lloyd (1756–1796); John Croley (by 1767–by 1786). Her sisters were Elizabeth (1765–?); Ann (after 1770–?). CHILDREN. Died without progeny. PRIVATE CAREER. EDUCATION: sent to school in England. RELIGIOUS AFFILIATION: his family was traditionally Quaker, but Galloway was married in St. James' Parish, Anne Arundel County, and his wife owned a pew in St. John's Protestant Episcopal Church in Hagerstown at her death. SOCIAL STATUS AND ACTIVITIES: Gent., by 1783; Esq., at death; member of a prominent southern Anne Arundel County family. OCCUPATIONAL PROFILE: lawyer, 1779; planter, 1795. PUBLIC CAREER. LEGISLATIVE SERVICE: Lower House, Anne Arundel County, 1777. OTHER STATE OFFICE: attorney general, appointed 1778. LOCAL OFFICES: justice, Orphans' Court, Anne Arundel County, 1782–at least 1785; justice, Anne Arundel County, 1783–at least 1785. STANDS ON PUBLIC/PRIVATE ISSUES: his obituary called him a "Republican from his youth" and a "sterling Jeffersonian Republican." WEALTH DURING LIFETIME. PERSONAL PROPERTY: assessed value £1,820.10.0, including 36 slaves, 1783; assessed value £702.0.0 including 16 slaves and 192 oz. plate, 1803–1804. LAND AT FIRST ELECTION: none in his own name, but he was probably living on and managing ca. 1,500 acres of his father's land in Anne Arundel County. SIGNIFICANT CHANGES IN LAND BETWEEN FIRST ELECTION AND DEATH: purchased 750 acres in Montgomery County in 1779, but sold it in 1795. In 1782 his wife received 800 acres of a large tract in Washington County from her father *Samuel Chew* (by 1734–1786). Inherited ca. 1,500 acres in Anne Arundel County from his father in 1785. His wife was bequeathed an additional 1,351 acres by her uncle Bennett Chew (?–1793) in 1793. Shortly afterwards, the Galloways moved to Washington County, probably to live in Hagerstown where

they purchased several lots and occasionally sold off pieces of the large tract. He had apparently sold about 450 acres of his land in Anne Arundel County by 1798. WEALTH AT DEATH. DIED: on August 18, 1831, in Hagerstown, Washington County. LAND: ca. 1,000 acres in Anne Arundel County, plus 7 lots in Hagerstown and his wife's remaining ca. 1,300 acres in Washington County.

GANTT, EDWARD (?–by 1783). BORN: by 1725 in Prince George's County; younger son. NATIVE: third generation. RESIDED: in the First District, Calvert County. FAMILY BACKGROUND. FATHER: *Thomas Gantt* (?–1765). MOTHER: Priscilla, daughter of *Thomas Brooke* (ca. 1659–1730/31). STEPMOTHER: Margery (?–1764), widow of Levin Covington (?–1725), daughter of *Thomas Hollyday* (ca. 1661–1702/3). UNCLE: *Thomas Brooke* (1683–1744). STEPUNCLE: *James Hollyday* (1696–1747). AUNT: Sarah Brooke (?–1724), who married first, *William Dent* (ca. 1660–1704), and second, *Philip Lee* (ca. 1681–1744). HALF AUNTS: Jane Brooke, who married *Alexander Contee* (ca. 1691–1740); Margery Wight, who married second, *Joseph Belt* (ca. 1680–1761). BROTHERS: *Thomas Gantt* (ca. 1710–1785); George (?–1779); and *Fielder Gantt* (?–1807). STEPBROTHER: Leonard Covington. SISTERS: Priscilla; Elizabeth; and probably Ann, who married *John Brome* (1703–1748). STEPSISTER: Elizabeth Covington. FIRST COUSINS: *Richard Brooke* (1716–1783); Eleanor Brooke, who married *Samuel Beall* (ca. 1713–ca. 1778); *Richard Lee* (ca. 1707–1787); *Arthur Lee* (?–1760); *Francis Lee* (?–1749); and Hannah Lee, who married *Joseph Sprigg* (1736–1800). HALF FIRST COUSINS: *John Contee* (1722–ca. 1796); *Thomas Contee* (ca. 1729–1811); Jane Contee (1728–1812), who married *John Hanson, Jr.* (1721–1783); *Edward Sprigg* (?–?); *Thomas Sprigg* (1715–1781); and *Thomas Beall, of George* (1735–1819). NEPHEWS: *Thomas Gantt, Jr.* (?–1808); *Erasmus Gantt* (?–?). NIECES: Ann Gantt, who married *Thomas Harwood III* (by 1757–by 1805); Rachel Gantt (?–1793), who married *Richard Brooke* (1716–1783); and Sarah Gantt, who married *Osborn Sprigg* (ca. 1741–1815). MARRIED by 1749 Elizabeth, daughter of Robert Wheeler, of Charles County, and wife Mary. CHILDREN. SONS: *Thomas Gantt* (?–ca. 1802); Edward (?–ca. 1811), an Anglican priest who was ordained in 1770 in London, England, and who married Mary Crompton. DAUGHTER: Mary, who married Bishop Thomas John Claggett (1742–1816), the first Protestant Episcopal bishop of Maryland, 1792–1816. PRIVATE CAREER. EDUCATION: literate. RELIGIOUS AFFILIATION: Anglican, All Saints' Parish, Calvert County. SOCIAL STATUS AND ACTIVITIES: Gent. OCCUPATIONAL PROFILE: planter. **PUBLIC CAREER.** LEGISLATIVE SERVICE: Lower House, Calvert County, 1751–1754 (Arms and Ammunition 3), 1757–1758, 1758–1761, 1762–1763, 1765–1766 (Grievances 2–4), 1768–1770 (Grievances 3, Public Offices 2, 3); Conventions, Calvert County, 5th 1775, 6th–8th, 1775–1776. LOCAL OFFICES: All Saints' Parish Vestry, Calvert County, appointed 1747 and 1751. MILITARY SERVICE: captain, by 1751. **WEALTH DURING LIFETIME.** LAND AT FIRST ELECTION: probably ca. 800 acres in Calvert County. SIGNIFICANT CHANGES IN LAND BETWEEN FIRST ELECTION AND DEATH: paid quitrents on 907 acres in Calvert County, 1755; patented 12 acres in Calvert County in 1760 and obtained a certificate of patent for 156 acres in Calvert County, 1763; paid quitrents on 910 acres in Calvert County in 1761; inherited one-quarter lot in Nottingham, Prince George's County, from his father in 1765. Paid quitrents on 826 acres in Calvert County, 1774. ADDITIONAL COMMENTS: Gantt acted as security for *Fielder Gantt* (?–1807) on bonds totaling over £650 sterling given in 1768 and 1771 to cover the debts of the Fielderia Furnace in Frederick County. He accepted mortgages on land and personal property in Prince George's and Frederick counties from *Fielder Gantt* (?–1807). The property was then sold to pay off himself and Fielder's other creditors. **WEALTH AT DEATH.** DIED: between mid-1775 and 1783 in Calvert County. LAND: probably 826 acres in Calvert County.

GANTT, ERASMUS (?–?). BORN: in Prince George's County, of age by 1780; fifth son. NATIVE: fourth generation. RESIDED: in Prince George's County; moved to Washington County before May 1794; lived in Berkley County, Virginia, by May 1797. **FAMILY BACKGROUND.** FATHER: *Thomas Gantt* (ca. 1710–1785), son of *Thomas Gantt* (?–1765). MOTHER: Eleanor Hillary (?–1787). UNCLES: *Fielder Gantt* (?–1807); *Edward Gantt* (?–by 1783). AUNT: Ann Gantt, who married *John Brome* (1703–1748). BROTHERS: Levi; Fielder (ca. 1764–1824). HALF BROTHERS: *Thomas Gantt, Jr.* (?–1808); John (1740–?); and Edward (ca. 1741–1837). SISTERS: Ann; Elizabeth; Priscilla (?–ca. 1784); and Sarah, who married *Osborn Sprigg* (ca. 1741–1815). HALF SISTERS: Rachel (?–1793), who married *Richard Brooke* (1716–1783). FIRST COUSINS: *Thomas Gantt* (?–ca. 1802); Ann Gantt, who married *Thomas Harwood III* (by 1757–by 1805). **PRIVATE CAREER.** EDUCATION: literate. SOCIAL STATUS AND ACTIVITIES: Esq., by

1791. OCCUPATIONAL PROFILE: lawyer, admitted to the Prince George's County Court in 1783; practiced in Prince George's County in at least 1783, 1784, and 1789. **PUBLIC CAREER.** LEGISLATIVE SERVICE: Lower House, Prince George's County, 1784 (Grievances). LOCAL OFFICES: justice, Prince George's County, in office 1787–at least 1788, 1790–at least 1792. **WEALTH DURING LIFETIME.** PERSONAL PROPERTY: 12 slaves, 1790. LAND AT FIRST ELECTION: possibly 106 acres in Prince George's County. SIGNIFICANT CHANGES IN LAND BETWEEN FIRST ELECTION AND DEATH: inherited ca. 350 acres in Prince George's County from his father, 1785; sold all of his land in Prince George's County in 1794; purchased 250 acres in Washington County in 1797. **WEALTH AT DEATH.** DIED: out of state. LAND: probably none in Maryland.

GANTT (GAUNT, GAUNTT), FIELDER (?–1807). BORN: of age by 1753, in Prince George's County. NATIVE: at least third generation. RESIDED: Prince George's County until 1764; Frederick County, 1764 until death. **FAMILY BACKGROUND.** FATHER: *Thomas Gantt* (?–1765). MOTHER: Priscilla, daughter of *Thomas Brooke* (ca. 1659–1730/31). STEPMOTHER: Margery Holliday (1688–1764), widow of Levin Covington. UNCLE: *Thomas Brooke* (1683–1744). STEPUNCLE: *James Hollyday* (1696–1747). AUNT: Sarah Brooke (?–1724), who married first, *William Dent* (ca. 1660–1704), and second, *Philip Lee* (ca. 1681–1744). HALF AUNT: Jane Brooke, who married *Alexander Contee* (ca. 1691–1740). BROTHERS: *Thomas Gantt* (ca. 1710–1785); *Edward Gantt* (?–by 1783); and George (?–1779). STEPBROTHER: Leonard Covington. SISTERS: Priscilla; Elizabeth; and probably Ann. FIRST COUSINS: *Richard Brooke* (1716–1783); Eleanor Brooke, who married *Samuel Beall* (ca. 1713–ca. 1778); *Richard Lee* (ca. 1707–1787); *Arthur Lee* (?–1760); *Francis Lee* (?–1749); and Hannah Lee, who married *Joseph Sprigg* (1736–1800). HALF FIRST COUSINS: *John Contee* (1722–ca. 1796); *Thomas Contee* (ca. 1729–1811); Jane Contee (1728–1812), who married *John Hanson, Jr.* (1721–1783); *Thomas Beall, of George* (1735–1819); *Thomas Sprigg* (1715–1781); and *Edward Sprigg* (?–?). NEPHEWS: *Thomas Gantt* (?–ca. 1802); *Thomas Gantt, Jr.* (?–1808); and *Erasmus Gantt* (?–?). NIECES: Ann Gantt, who married *Thomas Harwood III* (by 1757–by 1805); Rachel Gantt (?–1793), who married *Richard Brooke* (1716–1783); and Sarah Gantt, who married *Osborn Sprigg* (ca. 1741–1815). MARRIED Susannah. **CHILDREN.** SON: John (1775–1803), a lawyer. DAUGHTER: Margaretta, who married Nicholas King, of Washington County. **PRIVATE CAREER**. EDUCATION: literate. RELIGIOUS AFFILIATION: Anglican. SOCIAL STATUS AND ACTIVITIES: Gent., 1765; Esq., 1766. OCCUPATIONAL PROFILE: ironmaster, Fielderia Furnace, Frederick County. Gantt testified in the Chancery Court in 1804 concerning alleged illegal and unethical practices by his business partner, James Hunter, of Virginia, in the Fielderia Furnace between ca. 1767 and ca. 1791. He stated that his life had been ruined by Hunter, and that his credit and reputation had never recovered. **PUBLIC CAREER**. LEGISLATIVE SERVICE: Lower House, Frederick County, 1765–1766, 1779–1780 (Grievances 1, 2; Tax Commissioners 1; Manufactories 2), 1780–1781 (Grievances 1, 2). LOCAL OFFICES: justice, Frederick County, 1779–1785, 1786 (did not qualify); overseer of roads, Frederick County, in office in 1788. **WEALTH DURING LIFETIME**. PERSONAL PROPERTY: assessed value £2,038.11.8, including 16 slaves and plate, 1778; 6 slaves, 1790. LAND AT FIRST ELECTION: 13,081 acres in Prince George's and Frederick counties (inherited 400 acres from his father, 1765; purchased and patented 12,681 acres). SIGNIFICANT CHANGES IN LAND BETWEEN FIRST ELECTION AND DEATH: mortgaged at least 9,179 acres in 1766 and 1767 to help pay business debts of the Fielderia Furnace, incurred in part by his business partner, James Hunter. By 1779 he contemplated selling off his land in divided sections, but waited until the 1780s for the price he wanted. **WEALTH AT DEATH**. DIED: on November 14, 1807, on his farm near Frederick Town, Frederick County. PERSONAL PROPERTY: TEV, $1,223.00 current money (including 3 slaves and 30 books); FB, estate overpaid $5.72. LAND: at least 600 acres in Frederick County.

GANTT, THOMAS (?–1765). BORN: by 1691 in Prince George's County; elder son. NATIVE: second generation. RESIDED: in Prince George's County. **FAMILY BACKGROUND**. FATHER: Thomas Gantt (Gaunt) (?–ca. 1691), of Calvert County, immigrated as an indentured servant in 1654. STEPFATHER: *John Wight* (?–1705). MOTHER: Ann (?–1726). BROTHER: Edward. STEPBROTHER: John Wight, who married Ann, daughter of *Thomas Greenfield* (ca. 1649–1715). SISTERS: Ann; Elizabeth (?–1718). HALF SISTERS: Margery Wight, who married first, Thomas Sprigg, son of *Thomas Sprigg* (ca. 1670–by 1739), and second, *Joseph Belt* (ca. 1680–1761); Mary Wight, who married Jeremiah Belt; and Feilder Wight, who married John Powell. HALF NEPHEWS: *Edward*

Sprigg (?–?); *Thomas Sprigg* (1715–1781). MARRIED first, by 1726 Priscilla, daughter of *Thomas Brooke* (ca. 1659–1730/31). Her brother was *Thomas Brooke* (1683–1744). Her sisters were Sarah (?–1724), who married first, *William Dent* (ca. 1660–1704), and second, *Philip Lee* (ca. 1681–1744); Eleanor. Her half sister was Jane, who married *Alexander Contee* (ca. 1691–1740). Her nephews were *Richard Brooke* (1716–1783); *Richard Lee* (ca. 1707–1787); *Arthur Lee* (?–1760); and *Francis Lee* (?–1749). Her half nephews were *Thomas Beall, of George* (1735–1819); *John Contee* (1722–ca. 1796); and *Thomas Contee* (ca. 1729–1811). Her nieces were Hannah Lee, who married *Joseph Sprigg* (1736–1800); Eleanor Brooke, who married *Samuel Beall* (ca. 1713–ca. 1778). Her half niece was Jane Contee (1728–1812), who married *John Hanson, Jr.* (1721–1783). MARRIED second, in 1737 Margery (?–1764), widow of Levin Covington (?–1725); daughter of *Thomas Hollyday* (ca. 1661–1702/3); niece of both Martha Trueman, who married *Thomas Greenfield* (ca. 1649–1715), and Ann Trueman, who married *John Bigger* (ca. 1654–1714); half niece of *Adderton Skinner* (ca. 1677–1756); stepniece of *Robert Skinner* (?–1713). Her brothers were Leonard (1692–1741); *James Hollyday* (1696–1747). Her first cousins were *Thomas Trueman Greenfield* (1682–1733); Jane Greenfield, who married *Henry Holland Hawkins* (1683–1751). Her nephews were *James Hollyday* (1722–1786); *Henry Hollyday* (ca. 1725–1789). Her nieces were Elizabeth Hollyday, who married *Francis Lee* (?–1749); Mary Hollyday, who married *Francis Waring* (1715–1769). **CHILDREN**. SONS: *Thomas Gantt* (ca. 1710–1785); George (?–1779), who married Hannah; *Fielder Gantt* (?–1807); and *Edward Gantt* (?–by 1783). STEPSON: Leonard Covington. DAUGHTERS: Elizabeth, who married Rev. Samuel Clagget; Priscilla; and probably Ann, who married *John Brome* (1703–1748). STEPDAUGHTER: Elizabeth Covington. **PRIVATE CAREER**. EDUCATION: literate. RELIGIOUS AFFILIATION: Anglican, St. Paul's Parish, Prince George's County. SOCIAL STATUS AND ACTIVITIES: Gent., by 1726. OCCUPATIONAL PROFILE: planter; owned a storehouse in Nottingham, Prince George's County. **PUBLIC CAREER**. LEGISLATIVE SERVICE: Lower House, Prince George's County, 1722–1724 (Accounts 1–3), 1725–1727. LOCAL OFFICES: justice, Prince George's County, 1719–at least 1732 (chief justice, by 1729); St. Paul's Parish Vestry, Prince George's County, 1732–1733, 1735–1738, 1744–1746. **WEALTH DURING LIFETIME**. LAND AT FIRST ELECTION: at least 784 acres in Prince George's and Charles counties (at least 370 acres inherited from his father; 254 by patent). SIGNIFICANT CHANGES IN LAND BETWEEN FIRST ELECTION AND DEATH: patented an additional 729 acres in Charles and Prince George's counties in the 1720s; acquired an interest in 290 acres in Prince George's County, plus 1 lot in Nottingham, Prince George's County, as a gift from his father-in-law, *Thomas Brooke* (ca. 1659–1730/31), in 1726. He continued to purchase and patent land in Prince George's County throughout the 1730s and 1750s, and combined several tracts into a 1,294-acre patent in 1753. Gantt secured an interest in 584 acres in Prince George's County upon his marriage to Margery, but released 500 acres to her daughter in 1754. He probably gave 300 acres in Prince George's County to his son *Thomas Gantt* (ca. 1710–1785) by 1760. WEALTH AT DEATH. DIED: between February 19 and August 29, 1765, in Prince George's County. LAND: 2,764 acres in Prince George's and Charles counties, plus 1 lot in Nottingham, Prince George's County.

GANTT (GAUNT), THOMAS (ca. 1710–1785).

BORN: ca. 1710 in Prince George's County; eldest son. NATIVE: third generation. RESIDED: in Prince George's County. FAMILY BACKGROUND. FATHER: *Thomas Gantt* (?–1765). MOTHER: Priscilla, daughter of *Thomas Brooke* (ca. 1659–1730/31). STEPMOTHER: Margery (?–1764), widow of Levin Covington (?–1725); daughter of *Thomas Hollyday* (ca. 1661–1702/3). UNCLE: *Thomas Brooke* (1683–1744). STEPUNCLE: *James Hollyday* (1696–1747). AUNT: Sarah Brooke (?–1724), who married first, *William Dent* (ca. 1660–1704), and second, *Philip Lee* (ca. 1681–1744). HALF AUNT: Jane Brooke, who married *Alexander Contee* (ca. 1691–1740). BROTHERS: George (?–1779); *Fielder Gantt* (?–1807); *Edward Gantt* (?–by 1783). STEPBROTHER: Leonard Covington. SISTERS: Priscilla; Elizabeth; and probably Ann, who married *John Brome* (1703–1748). STEPSISTER: Elizabeth Covington. FIRST COUSINS: *Richard Brooke* (1716–1783); Eleanor Brooke, who married *Samuel Beall* (ca. 1713–ca. 1778); *Richard Lee* (ca. 1707–1787); *Arthur Lee* (?–1760); *Francis Lee* (?–1749); and Hannah Lee, who married *Joseph Sprigg* (1736–1800). HALF FIRST COUSINS: *John Contee* (1722–ca. 1796); *Thomas Contee* (ca. 1729–1811); Jane Contee (1728–1812), who married *John Hanson, Jr.* (1721–1783); *Thomas Beall, of George* (1735–1819); *Thomas Sprigg* (1715–1781); and *Edward Sprigg* (?–?). NEPHEW: *Thomas Gantt* (?–ca. 1802). NIECE: Ann Gantt, who married *Thomas Harwood III* (by 1757–by 1805). MARRIED first, by 1734

Rachel, daughter of *John Smith* (?–1738). Her sisters were Jane; Sarah, who married *Joseph Hall* (ca. 1701–?); and Tabitha (ca. 1690–1769), who married *Thomas Sheredine* (1699–1752). Her nephew was *Upton Sheredine* (1740–1800). MARRIED second, by 1754 Eleanor (?–1787), daughter of Thomas Hillary (?–ca. 1728/29), of Prince George's County. Her brothers were Thomas; John; William; and Henry. Her sisters were Sarah; Elizabeth. CHILDREN. SONS: *Thomas Gantt, Jr.* (?–1808); Edward (ca. 1741–1837), A.B., College of New Jersey (later became Princeton University) in 1762, M.D., University of Leiden, Netherlands, in 1767, a physician, who married in 1768 Ann Houghton (Stoughton) Sloss, of Somerset County, and later moved to Kentucky; John (1740–?), who moved to Berkley County, Virginia by 1778; Levi, who married Harriet Lowndes; *Erasmus Gantt* (?–?); and Fielder (ca. 1764–1824). DAUGHTERS: Rachel (?–1793), who married *Richard Brooke* (1716–1783); Elizabeth; Priscilla (?–ca. 1784); Ann, who married Basil Waring; and Sarah, who married *Osborn Sprigg* (ca. 1741–1815). ADDITIONAL COMMENTS: Sarah may have been Eleanor's child by a previous marriage. PRIVATE CAREER. EDUCATION: literate. RELIGIOUS AFFILIATION: Anglican. SOCIAL STATUS AND ACTIVITIES: Gent., by 1773. OCCUPATIONAL PROFILE: planter. PUBLIC CAREER. LEGISLATIVE SERVICE: Lower House, Prince George's County, 1757 (elected to the 6th session of the 1754–1757 Assembly to fill vacancy), 1757–1758. LOCAL OFFICES: Queen Anne Parish Vestry, Prince George's County, 1735–1738, 1742–1744, 1751–1754, 1761; justice, Prince George's County, 1738–1740, 1748–at least 1751 (quorum, 1748–at least 1751); commissioner to purchase land to lay out Bladensburg, Prince George's County, 1742. MILITARY SERVICE: captain, by 1743. WEALTH DURING LIFETIME. LAND AT FIRST ELECTION: 985 acres in Prince George's County (287 acres received from John Smith as a dower upon his marriage to Rachel; at least 600 acres by purchase). SIGNIFICANT CHANGES IN LAND BETWEEN FIRST ELECTION AND DEATH: obtained about 400 acres in Prince George's County as a gift from his father by 1760, and inherited ca. 1,014 acres in Prince George's County from his father, 1765. Gantt purchased 1,550 acres in Frederick County in 1766, but exchanged it with his son *Thomas Gantt, Jr.* (?–1808) for 452 acres in Prince George's County in 1773. He purchased or patented a few small tracts in Prince George's County during the early 1770s, but sold 4 of these, plus the 452-acre tract, in 1776 and 1777. He gave at least 200 acres to his son John in 1775. WEALTH

AT DEATH. DIED: will probated on March 28, 1785, in Prince George's County. PERSONAL PROPERTY: TEV, at least £1,907.9.8 current money (including 26 slaves and old books). LAND: 2,296 acres in Prince George's County.

GANTT, THOMAS (?–ca. 1802). BORN: in Calvert County; probably elder son. NATIVE: fourth generation. RESIDED: in the First District, Calvert County. **FAMILY BACKGROUND. FATHER:** *Edward Gantt* (?–by 1783), son of *Thomas Gantt* (?–1765). MOTHER: Elizabeth Wheeler. UNCLES: *Fielder Gantt* (?–1807); *Thomas Gantt* (ca. 1710–1785). AUNT: probably Ann Gantt, who married *John Brome* (1703–1748). BROTHER: Edward (?–ca. 1811). SISTER: Mary, who married Bishop Thomas John Claggett (1742–1816). FIRST COUSINS: *Thomas Gantt, Jr.* (?–1808); *Erasmus Gantt* (?–?); Rachel Gantt (?–1793), who married *Richard Brooke* (1716–1783); Sarah Gantt, who married *Osborn Sprigg* (ca. 1741–1815); and Ann Gantt, who married *Thomas Harwood III* (by 1757–by 1805). MARRIED Barbara, who subsequently married George F. Janny, a Quaker. **CHILDREN.** SONS: Edward (?–ca. 1812); Thomas; and John (?–1818). **PRIVATE CAREER.** EDUCATION: literate. OCCUPATIONAL PROFILE: physician. **PUBLIC CAREER.** LEGISLATIVE SERVICE: Lower House, Calvert County, 1780–1781, 1785, 1786–1787, 1787–1788, 1788, 1789, 1790, 1791–1792. LOCAL OFFICE: Maryland Senate elector, Calvert County, elected 1791, 1801. **WEALTH DURING LIFETIME.** PERSONAL PROPERTY: assessed value £797.3.4, including 20 slaves and 22 oz. plate, 1783. LAND AT FIRST ELECTION: possibly 67 acres in Calvert County. SIGNIFICANT CHANGES IN LAND BETWEEN FIRST ELECTION AND DEATH: inherited 826 acres in Calvert County from his father by 1783. In return for acting as security for *Fielder Gantt* (?–1807), he accepted a mortgage on Fielder's land and personal property in Frederick County, which was later sold to pay himself and Fielder's other creditors. He purchased 259 acres in Calvert County in 1795 and sold 40 acres in Calvert County in 1801. Gantt acquired 178 acres in Prince George's County by 1796 and 45 acres in Anne Arundel County prior to his death. **WEALTH AT DEATH.** DIED: ca. 1802 in Calvert County. LAND: at least 3,070 acres in Calvert, Anne Arundel, and Prince George's counties. **IDENTIFICATION PROBLEMS.** Dr. Thomas Gantt, son of *Edward Gantt* (?–by 1783), has been assigned the legislative service from Calvert County in the name of Thomas Gantt, Jr., because he was consistently described as being "of Calvert County" in the Frederick

County land records during the 1780s and he termed himself "Dr. Thomas Gantt" or "Dr. Thomas Gantt, Jr." in deeds recorded in those land records. There was no other Thomas Gantt of the appropriate age in Calvert County during his period of service in the legislature.

GANTT, THOMAS, JR. (?–1808). BORN: in Prince George's County, of age by 1758; probably eldest son. NATIVE: fourth generation. RESIDED: in Prince George's County until at least March, 1781; probably moved to Frederick County before October 1781 where be remained until shortly after his father's death in 1785; moved back to Prince George's County by July 1786 and lived there until his death. **FAMILY BACKGROUND. FATHER:** *Thomas Gantt* (ca. 1710–1785), son of *Thomas Gantt* (?–1765). MOTHER: Rachel Smith. STEPMOTHER: Eleanor Hillary (?–1787). UNCLES: *Fielder Gantt* (?–1807); *Edward Gantt* (?–by 1783). AUNTS: probably Ann Gantt, who married *John Brome* (1703–1748); Sarah Smith, who married *Joseph Hall* (ca. 1701–?); Tabitha Smith (ca. 1690–1769), who married *Thomas Sheredine* (1699–1752). BROTHERS: Edward (ca. 1741–1837); John (1740–?). HALF BROTHERS: Levi; *Erasmus Gantt* (?–?); and Fielder (ca. 1764–1824). SISTER: Rachel (?–1793), who married *Richard Brooke* (1716–1783). HALF SISTERS: Elizabeth; Ann; Priscilla (?–ca. 1784); and Sarah, who married *Osborn Sprigg* (ca. 1741–1815). FIRST COUSINS: *Thomas Gantt* (?–ca. 1802); Ann Gantt, who married *Thomas Harwood III* (by 1757–by 1805); and *Upton Sheredine* (1740–1800). MARRIED first, Susanna (1737–by 1782), daughter of *James John Mackall* (1717–1772); niece of *Samuel Hance* (by 1732–?). Her brothers were *John Mackall* (1740–1799); *Benjamin Mackall IV* (1745–by 1810); James (1747–1837); Richard (1749–?); and *Thomas Mackall* (1751–1799). Her sisters were Priscilla, who married *Robert Bowie* (ca. 1750–1818); Mary, who married *Edward Reynolds* (?–?); Elizabeth; Sarah; Barbara; Ann; and Margaret. MARRIED second, on November 7, 1782, Sarah Eleanor, daughter of William Potts (1718–1761), of Barbados, and wife Sarah; granddaughter of *Philip Lee* (ca. 1681–1744); niece of *Richard Lee* (ca. 1707–1787), *Arthur Lee* (?–1760), *Francis Lee* (?–1749), and Hannah Lee, who married *Joseph Sprigg* (1736–1800). Her brothers were *Richard Potts* (1753–1808); William (?–by 1817), a merchant. Her sister was Rebecca (?–by 1810), who married *Benjamin Mackall IV* (1745–?). Her first cousins were *Philip Thomas Lee* (1738–1778); *Thomas Sim Lee* (1745–1819); Sarah Lee, who married *Philip Richard*

Fendall (?–?); Alice Lee (?–1789), who married *John Weems* (1737–1813); Hannah Lee, who married *George Plater* (1735–1792); and *Philip Richard Fendall* (?–?). CHILDREN. SONS: Thomas (1760–1780); John Mackall (1762–1811), who married in 1798 Mary Sprigg, widow of (first name unknown) Hermance; Benjamin (1764–1808), who moved to Georgia; Richard (1767–?), who married Sarah Allen and later moved to South Carolina; Daniel (1770–?), who moved to Virginia; Charles (1773–?), who married (first name unknown) Parran; and Thomas (1783–?). DAUGHTERS: Betty Heighe (1756–?); Mary (1765–?), who married in 1791 James Newbern; Ann (1771–?), who married Peter Wood; and Sarah Eleanor (1787–?), who married (first name unknown) Beall. PRIVATE CAREER. EDUCATION: literate. RELIGIOUS AFFILIATION: Anglican. SOCIAL STATUS AND ACTIVITIES: Gent., by 1778, Esq., 1784. OCCUPATIONAL PROFILE: planter, 1778; farmer, 1783. PUBLIC CAREER. LEGISLATIVE SERVICE: Conventions, Prince George's County, 2nd, 1774, 4th, 1775, 5th, 1775; Lower House, Prince George's County, 1778–1779 (Laws to Expire 3), Frederick County, 1784. LOCAL OFFICES: King George's Parish Vestry, Prince George's County, 1764; constable, New Scotland Hundred, Prince George's County, 1767; justice, Prince George's County, 1773–1782 (out of county), 1787–at least 1800, Frederick County, commissioned 1784 (moved); Committee of Observation, Prince George's County, elected 1775. STANDS ON PUBLIC/PRIVATE ISSUES: attended meeting in Prince George's County that appointed committees to support the association against the Townsend Acts, 1770. WEALTH DURING LIFETIME. PERSONAL PROPERTY: mortgaged his personal property and crops in Frederick County for £70.0.0, 1783; assessed value $785.00, including 30 slaves and 48 oz. plate, 1793; assessed value $825.00, including 29 slaves and 40 oz. plate, 1807. LAND AT FIRST ELECTION: ca. 1,660 acres in Frederick and Prince George's counties (1,550 acres in Frederick County received from his father in exchange for 452 acres in Prince George's County). SIGNIFICANT CHANGES IN LAND BETWEEN FIRST ELECTION AND DEATH: purchased 400 acres in Prince George's County, but sold it in 1778. Gantt probably inherited 682 acres in Prince George's County from his father, 1785. He purchased 605 acres in Prince George's County in 1787 and sold a 1,550-acre tract in Frederick County in 1787 and 1788. He gave 320 acres in Prince George's County to his son John and sold 605 acres in Prince George's County by 1796. WEALTH AT DEATH. DIED: will

probated on May 30, 1808, in Prince George's County. PERSONAL PROPERTY: inventories totaled $1,754.03 (including 8 slaves and 4 books). LAND: 621 acres in Prince George's County. IDENTIFICATION PROBLEMS. There was a problem identifying the Thomas Gantt who served in Frederick County in 1784. The Frederick County service has been assigned to this Thomas Gantt on the basis of a careful study of land records and family history. This Thomas Gantt had land in Frederick County from 1773 on, but he, according to the land records, was living in Prince George's County until at least March 1781. There was no Thomas Gantt in the 1776 or 1778 Census or Oaths of Fidelity lists from Frederick County, nor was there any Thomas Gantt living in Frederick County mentioned in that county's deeds until October 1781. From October 1781 to October 1784, there are four entries in the Frederick County and Provincial Court deeds for a "Thomas Gantt, Jr.," a "Thomas Gantt, farmer," and a "Thomas Gantt, Jr., Esq.," all of Frederick County. There are no Prince George's County land transactions for a Thomas Gantt, Jr., during these three years. The records for justice of the peace appointments show Thomas as "out of county" in Prince George's County after 1782 and "removed" from Frederick County after 1784. Unfortunately no definite link can be made using land transactions between the Thomas Gantt of Frederick County and the Thomas Gantt of Prince George's County. However, after 1784 there are no further entries in the Frederick County deed books for a Thomas Gantt, of Frederick. The Thomas Gantt described in this biography must be the man who married Sarah Eleanor Potts in Frederick County in 1782. He names children Thomas and Sarah Eleanor in his will and there are no other known Thomas Gantts of age in Prince George's or Frederick counties at this time. *Thomas Gantt* (?–ca. 1802) is always referred to as "Dr. Thomas Gantt of Calvert County" in the Frederick County land records.

GARDINER, LUKE (1622–1674). BORN: in 1622, probably in England; second son. IMMIGRATED: in 1637 as a minor with parents from Virginia. RESIDED: in St. Mary's County; returned briefly to Virginia during Ingle's Rebellion. FAMILY BACKGROUND. FATHER: Richard Gardiner (?–ca. 1651), served in three unelected assemblies, but not a man of great wealth. MOTHER: Elizabeth. BROTHERS: Richard (1616–?); John (1633–?). SISTER: Elizabeth (1618–?), who married *Richard Lusthead* (?–1642). MARRIED Elizabeth, daughter of

Richard Hatton; niece of *Thomas Hatton* (?–1654/55). She subsequently married *Clement Hill* (?–1708). Her brothers were *William Hatton* (?–1712); Richard. Her sisters were Mary, who married *Zachary Wade* (ca. 1627–1678); Elinor (1642–1725), who married first, *Thomas Brooke* (1632–1676), and second, *Henry Darnall* (ca. 1645–1711); and Barbara, who married *James Johnson* (?–?). CHILDREN. SONS: *Richard Gardiner* (?–1687), who married Elizabeth, daughter of Maj. John Ware, of Rappahannock, Virginia; John, who married Mary, daughter of *William Boreman* (ca. 1630–1709); Luke, who married Monica; and Thomas. PRIVATE CAREER. EDUCATION: literate. RELIGIOUS AFFILIATION: Catholic. SOCIAL STATUS AND ACTIVITIES: servant or apprentice to Thomas Copley in 1637; designated Gent. or by a military title after 1660. OCCUPATIONAL PROFILE: servant or apprentice, 1637; planter. PUBLIC CAREER. LEGISLATIVE SERVICE: Lower House, St. Mary's County, 1659/60 (elected to fill vacancy), 1661, 1662, 1671 (resigned after the 2nd session to become sheriff). LOCAL OFFICES: justice, St. Mary's County, 1661–1666, 1668–1672 (quorum, 1664–1666, 1668–1672); sheriff, St. Mary's County, 1672–1674. MILITARY SERVICE: lieutenant by 1660/61; captain, by 1664, still serving in 1670. WEALTH DURING LIFETIME. LAND AT FIRST ELECTION: operated 4 separate plantations. WEALTH AT DEATH. DIED: by August 1674. PERSONAL PROPERTY: TEV, £632.18.0 sterling (including 3 slaves and 10 servants). LAND: over 5,000 acres.

GARDINER, RICHARD (?–1687). BORN: in St. Mary's County; oldest son. NATIVE: third generation. RESIDED: in St. Mary's County. FAMILY BACKGROUND. FATHER: *Luke Gardiner* (1622–1674). STEPFATHER: *Clement Hill* (?–1708). MOTHER: Elizabeth Hatton. UNCLES: *Richard Lusthead* (?–1642); *William Hatton* (?–1712); *Zachary Wade* (ca. 1627–1678); *Thomas Brooke* (1632–1676); *Henry Darnall* (ca. 1645–1711); and *James Johnson* (?–?). BROTHERS: John, who married Mary, daughter of *William Boreman* (ca. 1630–1709); Luke; and Thomas. FIRST COUSIN: *Thomas Brooke* (ca. 1659–1730/31). MARRIED Elizabeth, daughter of Maj. John Ware, of Rappannock, Virginia. CHILDREN. SONS: John; Luke. PRIVATE CAREER. EDUCATION: literate. RELIGIOUS AFFILIATION: Catholic. SOCIAL STATUS AND ACTIVITIES: third generation burgess; sons held no known office. OCCUPATIONAL PROFILE: planter; merchant; owned a gristmill. PUBLIC CAREER. LEGISLATIVE SERVICE: Lower House, St. Mary's

County, 1681–1682 (elected to the 3rd session), 1686 (died before the 2nd session). LOCAL OFFICES: coroner, St. Mary's County, 1676; justice, St. Mary's County, 1677–1687 (quorum, 1686–1687). WEALTH DURING LIFETIME. LAND AT FIRST ELECTION: at least 1,200 acres inherited from his father. WEALTH AT DEATH. DIED: will probated on December 3, 1687. PERSONAL PROPERTY: TEV, £1,338.17.8 sterling (including 17 slaves and 3 servants); FB, £26.3.8. LAND: over 1,200 acres.

GARRETT, AMOS (1671–1727/28). BORN: in 1671 in England. IMMIGRATED: by 1701 as a free adult. RESIDED: in Annapolis, Anne Arundel County. FAMILY BACKGROUND. FATHER: James Garrett. MOTHER: Sarah, by 1727/28, "late of St. Olives St., Southwark," England. SISTERS: Mary, who married Henry Woodward; Elizabeth Ginn. NEPHEW: Amos Woodward. MARRIED never. CHILDREN. Died without progeny. PRIVATE CAREER. EDUCATION: literate. RELIGIOUS AFFILIATION: Anglican. SOCIAL STATUS AND ACTIVITIES: served as agent for Sir *Thomas Lawrence* (ca. 1645–1714); one of the richest men in Maryland; important in development of Annapolis. OCCUPATIONAL PROFILE: merchant; planter. PUBLIC CAREER. LEGISLATIVE SERVICE: Lower House, Annapolis, 1712–1714 (Laws 2–4; Aggrievances 1), 1715, 1720–1721/22 (elected to the 2nd session to fill vacancy). LOCAL OFFICES: justice, Anne Arundel County, by 1702–1706 (quorum, 1704–1706); St. Anne's Parish Vestry, Anne Arundel County, 1704–1706; mayor, Annapolis, 1708; alderman, Annapolis, by 1720–1726. WEALTH DURING LIFETIME. LAND AT FIRST ELECTION: 8,000 acres in 1714. WEALTH AT DEATH. DIED: on March 8, 1727/28; excessive drinking may have caused his death; the total cost for his funeral exceeded £442.19.2, with over 1,000 Bibles and other holy books distributed to mourners. PERSONAL PROPERTY: TEV, £1,047.11.10 sterling, £11,508.5.3 current money (including 68 slaves and 10 servants). LAND: over 8,000 acres.

GARRETT, AMOS (1723–ca. 1789). BORN: on June 10, 1723, in St. George's Parish, Baltimore County; elder son. NATIVE: probably third generation. RESIDED: in Baltimore County (later became Harford County); Spesutia Lower Hundred, Harford County, by 1783. FAMILY BACKGROUND. FATHER: Bennett Garrett (?–1740), of St. George's Parish, Baltimore County, who was probably the son of Richard Garrett (?–1709). MOTHER: Arabella (?–1737). STEPMOTHER: Martha Presbury.

HALF BROTHER: Edward Beedle Garrett (1738–1739). SISTER: Ruth (1729–?). MARRIED on August 23, 1744, Frances (1727–by 1786), daughter of George Drew (?–1735) and wife Hannah Lisbury (?–1733); stepdaughter of Johannah Phillips (1720–?), who subsequently married Jacob Giles. Her brother was Anthony (1726–?). Her sisters were Mary Ann (1723–?); Druscilla (1733–?). Her half sister was Susannah (1736–?). ADDITIONAL COMMENTS: Her stepmother's son was *James Giles* (1749/50–?). CHILDREN. SON: Bennett (1745/46–by 1786). DAUGHTERS: Cassandra (1750–?), who married Isaac Penrose (ca. 1747–?), of Harford County; Milcah (1756–?), who married *Benedict Edward Hall* (ca. 1744–1822); and Frances (ca. 1763–?). PRIVATE CAREER. EDUCATION: literate. RELIGIOUS AFFILIATION: Anglican, St. George's Parish, Baltimore County (later became Harford County). SOCIAL STATUS AND ACTIVITIES: Mr., 1744; Gent., by 1786. OCCUPATIONAL PROFILE: planter. PUBLIC CAREER. LEGISLATIVE SERVICE: Convention, Harford County, 3rd, 1774. LOCAL OFFICES: St. George's Parish Vestry, Baltimore County, in office 1757–1760, 1770–1773, 1779–1781; coroner, Baltimore County, appointed 1765 and 1773; justice, Baltimore County, 1769–1773 (quorum, 1772–1773), Harford County, 1773–at least 1774 (quorum, 1773–at least 1774). WEALTH DURING LIFETIME. PERSONAL PROPERTY: 36 slaves, 1776; assessed value £319.0.0, including 6 slaves, 1783. LAND AT FIRST ELECTION: 786.5 acres in Harford County. SIGNIFCANT CHANGES IN LAND BETWEEN FIRST ELECTION AND DEATH: sold 29 acres in 1776 and probably 122 acres by 1783; assessed with 659 acres, 1783; gave all his land and personal property to his daughter Milcah and son-in-law *Benedict Edward Hall* (ca. 1744–1822) in 1786. In exchange Hall was to pay Garrett's debts and honor his bequests to his granddaughters. Garrett retained a life estate in the property. WEALTH AT DEATH. DIED: will probated on February 2, 1789, in Harford County. PERSONAL PROPERTY: TEV, at least £329.3.6 (including 9 slaves).

GARRETT, NATHANIEL (?–1688). IMMIGRATED: by 1671. RESIDED: in Cecil County. MARRIED never. CHILDREN. Died without progeny. PRIVATE CAREER. EDUCATION: literate. SOCIAL STATUS AND ACTIVITIES: no title on arrival; will mentioned his "good friend" *John Thompson* (?–1701). OCCUPATIONAL PROFILE: planter. PUBLIC CAREER. LEGISLATIVE SERVICE: Lower House, Cecil County, 1676–1682. LOCAL OFFICE: justice, Cecil County, 1676–1688 (quorum, 1685–1688).

WEALTH DURING LIFETIME. LAND AT FIRST ELECTION: 650 acres. WEALTH AT DEATH. DIED: will probated on April 27, 1688. PERSONAL PROPERTY: TEV, £95.15.0 sterling (including 2 servants), plus 9,692 pounds of tobacco in debts owed to his estate. LAND: 650 acres.

GASSAWAY, JOHN (1707–1762). BORN: on September 16, 1707, in All Hallow's Parish, Anne Arundel County; eldest son. NATIVE: third generation. RESIDED: on his plantation on the South River, Anne Arundel County. FAMILY BACKGROUND. FATHER: *Thomas Gassaway* (1683/84–1739), son of *Nicholas Gassaway* (1634–1691/92). MOTHER: Susanna Hanslap (1682/83–?). BROTHERS: Thomas (ca. 1710–1745); Nicholas (?–1775); Hanslap (?–1717); and Henry (1723–1776). SISTERS: Anne (1705–1717); Elizabeth (?–1707); and Elizabeth (ca. 1712–?), who married Capt. John Howard, of Baltimore County. NEPHEW: *John Beale Howard* (by 1739–1799). MARRIED on December 5, 1727, his first cousin Sarah (1701/2–?), daughter of William Cotter (?–1702) and wife Jane Gassaway; granddaughter of *Nicholas Gassaway* (1634–1691/92); niece of *Thomas Gassaway* (1683/84–1739). Her brothers were John (?–by 1736); William. Her sister was Ann (?–by 1736). CHILDREN. SONS: Thomas (1730/31–ca. 1774), who married Mary Cowman; John (1732–1752), of Frederick County, who married Rachel; William (1734–ca. 1735); William (1736–?); Nicholas (1738–?); Henry (1740–1756); and Isaac (1742–?). DAUGHTER: Anne (1728/29–1755), who married first, Isaac Johns, second, William Chapman, and third, Gassaway Rawlings. PRIVATE CAREER. EDUCATION: literate. RELIGIOUS AFFILIATION: Anglican. SOCIAL STATUS AND ACTIVITIES: Gent., 1742. OCCUPATIONAL PROFILE: planter. PUBLIC CAREER. LEGISLATIVE SERVICE: Lower House, Anne Arundel County, 1753–1754 (elected to the 3rd session to fill vacancy), 1754–1757 (Bills of Credit 5), 1757–1758 (Accounts 1, Cv, 2), 1758–1761 (Accounts Cv 1, 1, Cv 2, 2, 3, Cv 3; Grievances Cv 1, 1, Cv 2, 2, 3, Cv 3). LOCAL OFFICES: justice, Anne Arundel County, in office 1742–1747, 1752–1762 (quorum, 1746–1747, 1752–1762); sheriff, Anne Arundel County, 1748–1751. MILITARY SERVICE: captain, by 1754. WEALTH DURING LIFETIME. LAND AT FIRST ELECTION: 1,128 acres in Anne Arundel County (552 acres probably inherited from his father, 1739). SIGNIFICANT CHANGES IN LAND BETWEEN FIRST ELECTION AND DEATH: acquired an additional 232 acres in Anne Arundel County by 1761. WEALTH AT DEATH. DIED: on June 15, 1762, at his plantation in Anne Arundel County after a long illness. PERSONAL PROPERTY: TEV, £3,006.7.1 current money (including 54 slaves); FB, estate overpaid £5.1.10. LAND: 1,360 acres in Anne Arundel County. ADDITIONAL COMMENTS: his obituary characterized him as "an honest upright man."

GASSAWAY, NICHOLAS (1634–1691/92). BORN: in 1634 in London, England. IMMIGRATED: in 1649 or 1650 as an indentured servant or apprentice to *Richard Ewen* (?–1660). RESIDED: in Anne Arundel County. FAMILY BACKGROUND. FATHER: Thomas Gassaway. MOTHER: Ann Collingwood. UNCLE: John Collingwood, of London, England, a merchant. MARRIED first, (name unknown). MARRIED second, by 1672 Anne, daughter of *Thomas Besson* (ca. 1617–1679). CHILDREN. SONS: Nicholas, Jr. (ca. 1668–1699), a justice of Anne Arundel County from 1691 to 1699, who married Ann, daughter of *James Saunders* (?–1707); John, who married Elizabeth Lawrence; and *Thomas Gassaway* (1683/84–1739), the sheriff of Anne Arundel County from 1711 to 1714, who married Susannah, daughter of Henry Hanslop. DAUGHTERS: Hester, who married first, Nicholas Gross, and second, Stephen Warman; Anne, who married first, John Watkins, second, William Burgess, son of *William Burgess* (ca. 1622–1686/87), and third, *Richard Jones* (ca. 1671–1714); Jane (?–1736), who married first, William Cotter (?–1702), second, James Saunders, son of *James Saunders* (?–1707); and Margaret, who married first, Thomas Larkin, second, William Galloway, and third, James Durham. PRIVATE CAREER. EDUCATION: literate. RELIGIOUS AFFILIATION: Protestant. SOCIAL STATUS AND ACTIVITIES: achieved rapid upward mobility. OCCUPATIONAL PROFILE: servant or apprentice; planter; merchant. PUBLIC CAREER. LEGISLATIVE SERVICE: Associators' Convention, Anne Arundel County, 1690–1691/92 (elected to the 2nd or 3rd session); Grand Committee of Twenty, 1690–1691/92. OTHER PROVINCIAL OFFICE: justice, Provincial Court, 1691–1691/92. LOCAL OFFICE: justice, Anne Arundel County, by 1679–1691/92 (quorum, 1685–1691/92). MILITARY SERVICE: captain, by 1679–1685; major, 1685–1690; colonel, 1690–1691/92. STANDS ON PUBLIC/PRIVATE ISSUES: his initial response to the revolution of 1689 is unknown, but he extended his support to the Associators by the summer of 1690. WEALTH DURING LIFETIME. LAND AT FIRST ELECTION: over 1,320 acres. WEALTH AT DEATH. DIED: between January 10 and January 27, 1691/92. PERSONAL PROPERTY: TEV, £1,144.14.7 sterling, plus 109,898 pounds of tobacco (including 20 slaves and 1 servant). LAND: over 1,320 acres.

GASSAWAY, THOMAS (1683/84–1739). BORN: on February 20, 1683/84, in All Hallow's Parish, Anne Arundel County; third son. NATIVE: second generation. RESIDED: in Anne Arundel County. FAMILY BACKGROUND. FATHER: *Nicholas Gassaway* (1634–1691/92). MOTHER: Anne, daughter of *Thomas Besson* (ca. 1617–1679). GUARDIAN: his brother-in-law John Watkins. BROTHERS: Nicholas, Jr. (ca. 1668–1699), who married Anne, daughter of *James Saunders* (?–1707); John. SISTERS: Hester; Anne, who married John Watkins; Jane (?–1736); and Margaret. MARRIED by January 7, 1702, Susanna (1682/83–?), daughter of Henry Hanslap (?–1698), of Anne Arundel County, and wife Elizabeth (?–after 1702). Her brother was Joseph (?–by 1702). Her sisters were Elizabeth, who married first, (first name unknown) Battee, and second, Joseph Chew (?–1716), a Quaker; Frances (?–by 1697), who married Benjamin Wells. CHILDREN. SONS: *John Gassaway* (1707–1762); Thomas (ca. 1710–1745), who married first, Sarah Geist (?–1735), and second, Sarah Watkins; Nicholas (?–1775), who married Catherine (1720–1788), daughter of *Thomas Worthington* (ca. 1691–1753); Hanslap (?–1717); Henry (1723–1776), who married first, Rebecca Chapman, and second, Dinah Battee. DAUGHTERS: Anne (1705–1717); Elizabeth (?–1707); and Elizabeth (ca. 1712–?), who married Capt. John Howard, of Baltimore County. PRIVATE CAREER. EDUCATION: literate. RELIGIOUS AFFILIATION: Anglican. SOCIAL STATUS AND ACTIVITIES: Gent., 1720. OCCUPATIONAL PROFILE: planter; merchant. PUBLIC CAREER. LEGISLATIVE SERVICE: Lower House, Anne Arundel County, 1739 (Elections Cv; Aggrievances Cv; died before the 1st session). LOCAL OFFICES: sheriff, Anne Arundel County, by 1715–1716; justice, Court of Oyer and Terminer and Gaol Delivery, Anne Arundel County, commissioned 1715, 1716, 1717, 1718, and 1720; justice, Anne Arundel County, 1716–at least 1723 (quorum, 1720–at least 1723). MILITARY SERVICE: captain, by 1721. WEALTH DURING LIFETIME. LAND AT FIRST ELECTION: 1,671 acres in Anne Arundel and Baltimore counties, plus 1 lot in Annapolis (1,030 acres in Baltimore County inherited from his father in 1691/92; 400 acres in Anne Arundel County through his marriage). WEALTH AT DEATH. DIED: on September 12, 1739; buried in All Hallow's Church Cemetery, Anne Arundel County. PERSONAL PROPERTY: TEV, £1,654.16.6 current money (including 19 slaves and 4 servants); FB, £181.9.9. LAND: 1,671 acres in Anne Arundel and Baltimore counties, plus 1 lot in Annapolis.

GEORGE, JOSHUA (ca. 1695–1748). BORN: ca. 1695. IMMIGRATED: arrived in the colony by October 1720. RESIDED: in Annapolis, Anne Arundel County; Cecil County, by 1728. MARRIED in May 1722 Allice Docwray. CHILDREN. SONS: Maj. Joshua; *Sidney George* (?–1774). DAUGHTERS: Mary, who married by 1766 James Louttet; Alice, who married by 1749 Charles Gordon. PRIVATE CAREER. EDUCATION: literate. RELIGIOUS AFFILIATION: Protestant. SOCIAL STATUS AND ACTIVITIES: Gent., 1730; Esq. at death. OCCUPATIONAL PROFILE: lawyer, admitted to the following courts: Annapolis Mayor's Court in April 1721; Anne Arundel County in August 1721; Baltimore County in March 1721/22; Provincial Court in April 1722; Prince George's County in June 1722; Court of Chancery by July 1722; Cecil County by June 1723; Kent County by November 1731; Queen Anne's County in November 1739. Planter. PUBLIC CAREER. LEGISLATIVE SERVICE: Lower House, Cecil County, 1728–1731 (Laws 1–5), 1732–1734 (Laws 1–Cv), 1734/35–1737 (Laws 1, Cv, 2–4; Elections 1, Cv, 2–4), 1738 (Laws; Elections), 1739–1741 (Laws Cv–3), 1742–1744 (Laws 1, 2), 1745 (Laws), 1745/46–1748 (Laws 1–3, 4). OTHER PROVINCIAL OFFICE: surveyor general, Western Shore, 1746–1748. LOCAL OFFICES: clerk of Indictments, Baltimore County, commissioned 1722, 1723, and 1733, Cecil County, commissioned 1724. WEALTH DURING LIFETIME. LAND AT FIRST ELECTION: he was leasing a house and part of a lot in Annapolis by April 1723; 521 acres in Baltimore County, which he sold to *Charles Carroll* (1691–1755) the year of his first election, 1728. SIGNIFICANT CHANGES IN LAND BETWEEN FIRST ELECTION AND DEATH: purchased 2,803 acres in Cecil County and sold 550 acres in Cecil County, 1730–1744. WEALTH AT DEATH. DIED: between November 1 and December 16, 1748, in Cecil County. PERSONAL PROPERTY: TEV, £3,460.17.0 current money (including 46 slaves, law books, books on other topics, 19 oz. plate, and carpenter's tools); FB, £550.18.0. LAND: at least 1,258 acres, possibly as much as 2,803 acres in Cecil County.

GEORGE, SIDNEY (?–1774). BORN: in Cecil County, of age by 1748; eldest son. NATIVE: second generation. RESIDED: in Cecil County. FAMILY BACKGROUND. FATHER: *Joshua George* (ca. 1695–1748). MOTHER: Allice Docwray. BROTHER: Maj.

Joshua. SISTERS: Mary; Alice. CHILDREN. SONS: Sidney, a justice of the Orphans' Court of Cecil County from 1802 to 1805, who married Mary; Joshua, who was underage in 1774. DAUGHTERS: Rebecca, who was underage in 1774; Sarah, who was underage in 1774. PRIVATE CAREER. EDUCATION: literate. RELIGIOUS AFFILIATION: Protestant. SOCIAL STATUS AND ACTIVITIES: Gent., 1749. OCCUPATIONAL PROFILE: attorney, admitted to the following courts: Baltimore County by March 1754; Cecil County by March 1759. PUBLIC CAREER. LEGISLATIVE SERVICE: Lower House, Cecil County, 1751–1754. LOCAL OFFICE: justice, Cecil County, 1762–at least 1769 (quorum, 1768–at least 1769). WEALTH DURING LIFETIME. LAND AT FIRST ELECTION: 1,000 acres in Cecil County (inherited from his father); also controlled 776 acres in Cecil County during the minority of his brother Joshua. SIGNIFICANT CHANGES IN LAND BETWEEN FIRST ELECTION AND DEATH: owned 1,513 acres in Cecil County, 1767; purchased and quickly sold a 2,900-acre tract in Kent County for a profit of £250.0.0, 1765–1767; relinquished control of his brother's land when Joshua reached his majority. WEALTH AT DEATH. DIED: between March 2 and April 21, 1774, in Cecil County. LAND: 1,513 acres in Cecil County.

GERARD, THOMAS (1608–1673). BORN: in 1608 at New Hall, Lancashire, England; oldest son. IMMIGRATED: in 1638 as a free adult; returned to England in 1640, but resettled in the colony with his family soon thereafter. RESIDED: on St. Clement's Manor, St. Mary's County; moved to Virginia, 1664. FAMILY BACKGROUND. FATHER: John Gerard, of New Hall, England, son of Thomas Gerard and wife Jane, of Garswood, England. MOTHER: Isabell. BROTHERS: Marmaduke; William; Francis; and Richard. MARRIED first, Susannah, daughter of John Snowe, of Brookehouse, Chedulton, England. Her brothers were Abel; Justinian; and Marmaduke. MARRIED second, Rose Tucker. CHILDREN. SONS: Thomas (?–1686), a justice of St. Mary's County from 1676 to 1679, who married Ann (?–1702/3), daughter of Richard Hawkins or William Smallwood; Justinian (?–1688), a justice of St. Mary's County from 1676 to 1677, who married Sarah; and John, who married Elizabeth. DAUGHTERS: Susannah, who married first, *Robert Slye* (ca. 1628–1670/71), and second, *John Coode* (ca. 1648–1708/9); Frances, who married first, Thomas Speke, second, Valentine Peyton, third, John Appleton, fourth, John Washington, and fifth, William Hardwick; Temperance, who married first, Daniel Hutt, second, John Crabbe, and third, Benjamin Blanchflower; Elizabeth (?–1716), who married first, *Nehemiah Blakiston* (?–1693), second, Ralph Rymer, and third, *Joshua Guibert* (?–1713); and Mary, who married *Kenelm Cheseldyne* (1640–1708). PRIVATE CAREER. EDUCATION: literate; probably well educated. RELIGIOUS AFFILIATION: Catholic, but his wife and children were Protestants. SOCIAL STATUS AND ACTIVITIES: Gent. with high status on arrival in the colony; brought five servants with him, and by 1648 he had imported over forty servants; became manor lord of St. Clement's in 1639; sold his English holdings and brought his family to Maryland in 1650; involved in a celebrated legal action against his brothers-in-law over control of extensive lands in Maryland. OCCUPATIONAL PROFILE: physician; planter. PUBLIC CAREER. LEGISLATIVE SERVICE: Assembly, St. Mary's County, 1638/39, special writ 1641, special writ 1641/42, special writ 1642A; Upper House, 1658, 1659/60. OTHER PROVINCIAL OFFICES: Council, 1643–1649, 1651–1660 (suspended from October 1658 to October 1659 for maligning other councilors); justice, Provincial Court, 1643–1649, 1650/51–1660. LOCAL OFFICE: conservator of the peace, St. Clement's Hundred, St. Mary's County, 1639/40. STANDS ON PUBLIC/PRIVATE ISSUES: a very controversial figure in provincial politics and frequently at odds with the proprietor's spokesmen, Gerard supported Fendall's Rebellion in 1659/60, for which he was permanently barred from voting or holding office in the colony. WEALTH DURING LIFETIME. PERSONAL PROPERTY: valued at £299.11.3 in 1664. LAND AT FIRST ELECTION: 1,030 acres in 1639; 11,000 acres by 1642; 14,000 acres by 1651, plus 3,500 acres in Virginia. WEALTH AT DEATH. DIED: by October 19, 1673. LAND: ca. 16,000 acres.

GIBBONS, EDWARD (?–1654). BORN: probably in England. IMMIGRATED: no definite record that he ever lived in Maryland. Gibbons lived in New England at Mount Wollaston prior to 1630, when he moved to Charleston, South Carolina, and became a freeman. He lived in Virginia at least briefly in 1646, and he was well acquainted with Barbados through his mercantile activities. MARRIED Margaret. CHILDREN. Jothan (1633–1658); Edward (1638–?); and John (1655–?). DAUGHTER: Jerusha (?–died in infancy). PRIVATE CAREER. EDUCATION: literate. RELIGIOUS AFFILIATION: converted to Puritanism in 1630. OCCUPATIONAL PROFILE: merchant of Boston; a pioneer in the development of New England's export trade. PUBLIC CAREER. PROVINCIAL OFFICE: Council, 1650/51

(no record of actual service). MILITARY SERVICE: commissioned an admiral and lieutenant, 1650/51, but no record of service. OUT OF COLONY SERVICE: Massachusetts General Court, 1635; assistant, Massachusetts General Court, 1650; major general of United Colonies of New England, 1649. STANDS ON PUBLIC/PRIVATE ISSUES: sought by Lord Baltimore in an effort to attract New Englanders to Maryland and to appoint influential Protestants to his government; no evidence that Gibbons ever accepted his commission. WEALTH DURING LIFETIME. PERSONAL PROPERTY: owner of the ship *Artillery*, in partnership with Edmund Scarburgh of Virginia; owned a windmill in St. Mary's County. WEALTH AT DEATH. DIED: on December 9, 1654; size of estate unknown.

GIBSON, JOHN (?–1790). BORN: in Talbot County, of age by 1754; probably third son. NATIVE: at least third generation. RESIDED: in Talbot County. FAMILY BACKGROUND. FATHER: Woolman (Wollman) Gibson, Gent. (ca. 1695–1742), of Talbot County. STEPFATHER: William Trippe. MOTHER: Elizabeth, daughter of John Dawson, granddaughter of Bryant Omealy. BROTHERS: *Woolman Gibson* (?–1786); Jonathan; Jacob (?–ca. 1789), who married Rachel; and Bartholomew. SISTERS: Margaret; Mary; and Alice. MARRIED by 1766 Elizabeth (?–1797). CHILDREN. SONS: *Woolman Gibson, Jr.* (?–ca. 1798); *John Gibson III* (?–1819). DAUGHTERS: Elizabeth, who married first, John Thomas, and second, by 1807 (first name unknown) Stewart; Mary (1766–1790), who married *Richard Tilghman* (1740–1809); and Anna, who married first, Dr. John Elbert, and second, Dr. William E. Seth. PRIVATE CAREER. EDUCATION: literate. RELIGIOUS AFFILIATION: Anglican. SOCIAL STATUS AND ACTIVITIES: Gent., 1777; Esq. at death. OCCUPATIONAL PROFILE: planter. PUBLIC CAREER. LEGISLATIVE SERVICE: Conventions, Talbot County, 9th, 1776; Lower House, Talbot County, 1777, 1777–1778 (Manufactories 2), 1778–1779 (elected to the 1st session to fill vacancy), 1779–1780 (Manufactories 2), 1781–1782 (Elections 1). LOCAL OFFICES: churchwarden, St. Paul's Parish, Queen Anne's County, in office 1757; St. Paul's Parish Vestry, Queen Anne's County, in office 1763, 1769, 1779–1780, 1782–1784; justice, Talbot County, commissioned 1774, 1777, and 1778; Committee of Observation, Talbot County, elected 1775; justice, Orphans' Court, Talbot County, commissioned 1777 and 1778; commissary for horses, Talbot County, appointed 1781; judge, Court of Appeals for Tax Assessment, Talbot County, commissioned 1786.

WEALTH DURING LIFETIME. PERSONAL PROPERTY: 30 slaves, 1776; assessed value £966.15.0, including 23 slaves and 45 oz. plate, 1783. LAND AT FIRST ELECTION: 386 acres in Talbot County (all by purchase). ADDITIONAL COMMENTS: Gibson had inherited 150 acres from his father and had purchased 536 acres, all prior to his first election. In 1774 he gave 300 acres of this land by deed of gift to his son *Woolman Gibson, Jr.* (?–ca. 1798). SIGNIFICANT CHANGES IN LAND BETWEEN FIRST ELECTION AND DEATH: purchased 30 acres in Queen Anne's County, 1779. In 1789 Gibson bound himself to convey 165 acres in Talbot County, which were in the possession of his son *John Gibson III* (?–1819), and this tract was conveyed by his executors after his death. Without recording a deed, Gibson conveyed a mill and mill seat to his son *Woolman Gibson, Jr.* (?–ca. 1798). Three months before his death in 1790, he purchased 350 acres in Talbot and Queen Anne's counties, but paid only a small down payment on it. In his will Gibson directed that the 350 acres should be sold if necessary to discharge his contract with the seller, and his executors did dispose of it at public auction, with the purchaser being the previous owner of the tract. WEALTH AT DEATH. DIED: in May 1790 in Talbot County. PERSONAL PROPERTY: TEV, £2,456.1.11 current money (including 53 slaves, 61 oz. plate, and books); FB, £2,230.12.7. LAND: 859 acres in Talbot and Queen Anne's counties.

GIBSON, JOHN, III (?–1819). BORN: in Talbot County, of age by 1783; younger son. NATIVE: at least fourth generation. RESIDED: in Talbot County; Anne Arundel County, 1795; Annapolis, Anne Arundel County, 1801; Baltimore City, 1811; Annapolis, 1813; on the Magothy River, Anne Arundel County, at death. FAMILY BACKGROUND. FATHER: *John Gibson* (?–1790). MOTHER: Elizabeth (?–1797). UNCLE: *Woolman Gibson* (?–1786). BROTHER: *Woolman Gibson, Jr.* (?–ca. 1798). SISTERS: Elizabeth; Mary (1766–1790), who married *Richard Tilghman* (1740–1809); and Anna. MARRIED in 1785 Ann Ogle (ca. 1766–1821), daughter of *John Ridout* (1732–1797); granddaughter of *Samuel Ogle* (1694–1752); niece of *Benjamin Ogle* (1748/49–1809). Her brothers were Samuel (ca. 1765–1840); Horatio. Her sister was Meliora Ogle (1780–1781). CHILDREN. SONS: John James; Horatio Samuel. DAUGHTERS: Maria E., who married in 1807 John Tilghman, of Talbot County; Ann Ogle. PRIVATE CAREER. EDUCATION: literate. SOCIAL STATUS AND ACTIVITIES: Gent., 1793; Esq., 1795. OCCUPATIONAL PROFILE: probably a planter; partner with Richard Caton and others in the Cape Sable Company in Anne Arundel County in 1812, which was formed to search for coal and other mineral ores on the company's land. The company was incorporated in 1818 to produce copperas and alum. *Charles Carroll of Carrollton* (1737–1832) held the land in trust for the owners. After Gibson's death, a court case arose involving the disposition of his one-third interest in the company, or 20 shares valued at $20,000. Gibson entailed the shares to his heirs in 1815, then allegedly sold them to Alexander Mitchell in 1817. Richard Caton stated that he had been the sole purchaser of the company lands, that Gibson was merely his agent, and that he was included in the company only out of Caton's kindness and goodwill. Caton said he knew Gibson "to be poor, but a man whose integrity and worth" had led him to grant Gibson shares in the company. One of the company's creditors deposed that Gibson's "credit and reputation" was "at too low an ebb" to be of any help to the company in terms of loans or other means of raising capital. According to Caton, however, Gibson proved deceitful and dishonest by applying to his own use "several and large sums of money which Caton had confidently placed in his hands" for the use of the company. In reply, the chancellor in the court case said that Gibson appeared to have discovered some coal or other valuable minerals on a tract of land on the Magothy River in Anne Arundel County. Gibson informed Caton of his discovery and together they bought the land. Therefore, the titles of neither were due to the generosity of the other, but to the good management of a fortunate find. Whether the shares belonged to Gibson's heirs or to the man he supposedly sold them to was not resolved, however, because the company's property had to be sold to pay its creditors. PUBLIC CAREER. LEGISLATIVE SERVICE: Lower House, Talbot County, 1784, 1786–1787 (Claims 1). LOCAL OFFICES: militia recruiting officer, Talbot County, appointed 1778; register of wills, Talbot County, 1787–1792; justice, Anne Arundel County, 1794–at least 1800. WEALTH DURING LIFETIME. PERSONAL PROPERTY: assessed value £218.0.0, including 6 slaves, 1783; £1,000.0.0 current money devised to his wife from her father, 1797; assessed value £1,390.0.0, including 50 slaves and 13.10 oz. plate, Talbot County, 1798; 35 slaves, Anne Arundel County, 1798; one-third interest in the Cape Sable Company valued at $20,000, including land and other company property, 1813. LAND AT FIRST ELECTION: controlled 137 acres in Talbot County (actual ownership of this land belonged to his father); also held 201 acres in Talbot County for Miller's heirs. SIGNIFICANT CHANGES IN LAND BETWEEN FIRST ELECTION AND DEATH: purchased 173 acres in Talbot County, 1786; inherited at least 331 acres from his father in Talbot County, 1790; mortgaged lands inherited from his father in Talbot County, 1793; inherited 250 acres from his brother *Woolman Gibson, Jr.* (?–ca. 1798) in Talbot County, by 1805; had sold all of his Talbot County land by 1806; acquired 1,637 acres in Baltimore County through his marriage, 1791; sold ca. 1,450 acres of his wife's land in Baltimore County, between 1794 and 1818; owned 2,058 acres in Anne Arundel County, by 1798; purchased 216 acres in Anne Arundel County, 1807; sold 288 acres in Anne Arundel County to son Horatio, 1808; mortgaged 1,986 acres in Anne Arundel County, 1809; sold 365 acres in Anne Arundel County, part of the land mortgaged in 1810; owned one-third of ca. 782 acres in Anne Arundel County, which formed the Cape Sable Company, 1812–1813; deeded all of his property, real, personal, and mixed, except his lands in Pennsylvania, to two men to hold in trust for himself and his wife for life, and then to transfer it to his children and their issue, 1815. WEALTH AT DEATH. DIED: on December 6, 1819, at his seat near the Magothy River, Anne Arundel County. PERSONAL PROPERTY: TEV, $5,210.13 (including 14 slaves, 1 sloop, and 3 books); FB, $2,114.48, however all of this was recovered in a judgment against him by Elizabeth Thomas for the use of William Baker and his sons. LAND: at least 1,577 acres in Anne Arundel and Baltimore counties, plus one-third of ca. 782 acres in Anne Arundel County, which was in dispute at the time of his death; plus unspecified acreage in Pennsylvania.

GIBSON, MILES (ca. 1646–1692). BORN: ca. 1646, probably in England. IMMIGRATED: before 1668 as an indentured servant to John Bradford. RESIDED: in Baltimore County. MARRIED first, Ann, daughter of *Thomas Thurston* (ca. 1622–1693). MARRIED second, in 1692 Elizabeth, widow of both Henry Hazelwood (?–1680) and Richard Edmonds (?–by 1692). CHILDREN. SON: Robert (?–1704). DAUGHTER: Sarah. PRIVATE CAREER. EDUCATION: literate. RELIGIOUS AFFILIATION: Protestant. OCCUPATIONAL PROFILE: indentured servant, free by 1668 when he purchased 240 acres; planter. PUBLIC CAREER. LEGISLATIVE SERVICE: Lower House, Baltimore County, 1682 (resigned after the 1st session to become sheriff). LOCAL OFFICES: justice, Baltimore County, 1679–1683;

sheriff, Baltimore County, 1683–1686. STANDS ON PUBLIC/PRIVATE ISSUES: supported Lord Baltimore's government against Protestant Associators in the revolution of 1689. WEALTH DURING LIFETIME. PERSONAL PROPERTY: 6 slaves in 1692. LAND AT FIRST ELECTION: ca. 340 acres by 1682; ca. 2,549 acres by 1684. WEALTH AT DEATH. DIED: by May 26, 1692. PERSONAL PROPERTY: TEV, £516.2.1 sterling, plus 28,458 pounds of tobacco (including 9 slaves). LAND: probably ca. 2,540 acres.

GIBSON, WOOLMAN (?–1786). BORN: in Talbot County, of age by 1747; eldest son. NATIVE: at least third generation. RESIDED: on the St. Michael's River, Talbot County. FAMILY BACKGROUND. FATHER: Woolman (Wollman) Gibson, Gent. (ca. 1695–1742), of Talbot County. STEPFATHER: William Trippe. MOTHER: Elizabeth, daughter of John Dawson; granddaughter of Bryant Omealy. BROTHERS: Jonathan; *John Gibson* (?– 1790); Jacob (?–ca. 1789), who married Rachel; and Bartholomew. SISTERS: Margaret; Mary; and Alice. NEPHEWS: *Woolman Gibson, Jr.* (?–ca. 1798); *John Gibson III* (?–1819). NIECE: Mary Gibson (1766–1790), who married in 1784 *Richard Tilghman* (1740–1809). MARRIED Rachel. CHILDREN. SONS: John; Jonathan (?–1783); Capt. Woolman (?–1781), who married Rebecca; and Jacob. DAUGHTER: Mary, who married in 1786 Samuel Seney, of Queen Anne's County. PRIVATE CAREER. EDUCATION: literate. RELIGIOUS AFFILIATION: Anglican. OCCUPATIONAL PROFILE: probably a planter. PUBLIC CAREER. LEGISLATIVE SERVICE: Lower House, Talbot County, 1758–1761, 1765–1766. LOCAL OFFICES: churchwarden, St. Michael's Parish, Talbot County, in office 1745/46, 1749–1750; St. Michael's Parish Vestry, Talbot County, elected 1759 and 1764; sheriff, Talbot County, 1761–1764. MILITARY SERVICE: lieutenant, Talbot County Militia, 1748; captain, by 1759. WEALTH DURING LIFETIME. PERSONAL PROPERTY: mortgaged 16 slaves, 1773; assessed value £599.10.0, including 13 slaves, 1783; 9 slaves given by deeds of gift to his children, 1786. LAND AT FIRST ELECTION: 386 acres in Talbot County (all inherited from his father). SIGNIFICANT CHANGES IN LAND BETWEEN FIRST ELECTION AND DEATH: mortgaged all his lands in 1773 (no record of the mortgage being released, but all of the tracts are listed under his name on the 1783 tax assessment although the total is only 310 acres); conveyed 200 acres in Talbot County by a deed of gift to his son in 1782, but he retained a life estate in the property; patented 25 acres in

Talbot County, 1785–1786. WEALTH AT DEATH. DIED: between April 22 and May 12, 1786, in Talbot County. PERSONAL PROPERTY: TEV, £556.9.1 current money (including 3 slaves and 1 book); FB, estate overpaid £25.3.5. LAND: 335 acres in Talbot County (including 200 acres given to his son, but in which he retained a life estate).

GIBSON, WOOLMAN, JR. (?–ca. 1798). BORN: in Talbot County, of age by 1776; elder son. NATIVE: at least fourth generation. RESIDED: near head of Wye River, Talbot County. FAMILY BACKGROUND. FATHER: *John Gibson* (?–1790). MOTHER: Elizabeth (?–1797). UNCLE: *Woolman Gibson* (?–1786). BROTHER: *John Gibson III* (?–1819). SISTERS: Elizabeth; Mary (1766–1790), who married *Richard Tilghman* (1740–1809); and Anna. MARRIED by 1778 Frances (?–1805), daughter of *Thomas Reynolds* (?–1778). Her brothers were William; *Edward Reynolds* (?–?). Her sisters were Elizabeth (?–1801); Margaret; Ann; Sarah; Rebecca; and Mary, who married *John Mackall* (1740–1799). PRIVATE CAREER. EDUCATION: literate. OCCUPATIONAL PROFILE: probably a planter. PUBLIC CAREER. LEGISLATIVE SERVICE: Lower House, Talbot County, 1782–1783, 1783 (elected, but did not attend), 1791–1792, 1792. LOCAL OFFICES: justice, Talbot County, 1779–at least 1794 (heads list in 1794); justice, Orphans' Court, Talbot County, 1785–at least 1788. WEALTH DURING LIFETIME. PERSONAL PROPERTY: 10 slaves, 1776; his wife's share of her father's personal estate was approximately £1,400 current money and 500 pounds of tobacco, ca. 1778; assessed value £950.0.0, including 19 slaves and 30 oz. plate, 1783; 18 slaves, 1790. LAND AT FIRST ELECTION: 200 acres in Talbot County (the remainder of 300 acres received by deed of gift from his father). SIGNIFICANT CHANGES IN LAND BETWEEN FIRST ELECTION AND DEATH: received a mill and mill seat and a tract of land in Talbot County from his father, but the date of the conveyance is unknown. WEALTH AT DEATH. DIED: will probated on February 2, 1798, in Talbot County. PERSONAL PROPERTY: TEV, £1,685.4.11 current money (including 20 slaves and books); FB, £169.13.11. LAND: 250 acres in Talbot County, plus a mill and mill seat in Talbot County.

GILES, JAMES (1749/50–?). BORN: on February 2, 1749/50, in St. George's Parish, Baltimore County (later became part of Harford County); fourth son. NATIVE: at least third generation. RESIDED: in Harford County until ca. 1788; Baltimore County; Harford County again by 1794.

FAMILY BACKGROUND. FATHER: Jacob Giles (1705–1784), of Baltimore County (later became part of Harford County), a Quaker, and a partner in the Bush River Ironworks and Cumberland Forge. MOTHER: Johanna (1720–?), widow of George Drew (?–1735/36); daughter of *James Phillips* (?–1720) and wife Johanna Kemp. HALF UNCLE: *Aquila Hall* (1727–1779). BROTHERS: Jacob (1753–by 1784); Thomas (1754–1798); Aquila (1757–?); and Edward (1759–1783). HALF BROTHERS: John (1729–by 1784); Jacob (1733–?); and *Nathaniel Giles* (1735–1775). SISTERS: Elizabeth (1747–by 1784), who married William Smith; Johanna (1751–?). HALF SISTERS: Susanna Drew (1736–?), who married (first name unknown) Scott; Sarah Giles (?–by 1784), who married Nathaniel Rigbie, Jr. ADDITIONAL COMMENTS: his father's first wife was Hannah. MARRIED Ann (?–1785), widow of Edward Fell (1736–1766); daughter of John Bond and wife Alice Anna Webster; niece of *Jacob Bond* (ca. 1725–1780). Her first cousins were *Thomas Bond, of Thomas* (?–1800); *William Bond, of Joshua* (ca. 1747–1788); *James Bond* (ca. 1757–1803); and Catherine Fell (by 1746–by 1795), who married *Thomas Bond, of Thomas* (?–1800). CHILDREN. SON: Jacob Washington (1776–1851). STEPSON: *William Fell* (1759–1786). DAUGHTERS: Johannah (1771–?), who married Dr. Thomas Johnson, of Baltimore County; Susanna (1775–1797), who married Philip Moore. PRIVATE CAREER. EDUCATION: literate. RELIGIOUS AFFILIATION: strong Quaker background; his children's births were registered in the Deer Creek Meeting records, Baltimore County; Giles was not a practicing Quaker in 1778 when he took the oath of fidelity. SOCIAL STATUS AND ACTIVITIES: Gent., by 1787. OCCUPATIONAL PROFILE: landlord; planter. PUBLIC CAREER. LEGISLATIVE SERVICE: Lower House, Harford County, 1780–1781 (elected to the 1st session to fill vacancy). LOCAL OFFICES: justice, Harford County, appointed 1778, 1779 ("left out at request of court"), 1780, and 1794. JURY SERVICE: first petit jury, Harford County, period of service unknown. MILITARY SERVICE: 2nd lieutenant and adjutant, Fifth Company, Harford County Militia, by 1775. WEALTH DURING LIFETIME. PERSONAL PROPERTY: 15 slaves, 1776; assessed value £719.6.8, including 11 slaves and 20 oz. plate, 1783. Filed for relief as an insolvent debtor in February 1788. At that time he owned 13 slaves and was receiving an annual income of £662 sterling from rental property on Fells Point, Baltimore Town, in which he held a life interest because of his marriage to Ann Fell. LAND AT FIRST ELECTION: probably ca. 620 acres in Harford County (500 acres by deed of gift from his parents in 1766 that were entailed to his male heirs), plus a life estate in one-third of both Fells Point and 400 acres in Baltimore County (through his marriage). SIGNIFICANT CHANGES IN LAND BETWEEN FIRST ELECTION AND DEATH: assessed with 619 acres in Harford County, 1783; his 500-acre home plantation in Harford County was deeded as security for his debts in 1787. His insolvency petition in 1788 listed the 620 acres in Harford County (500 of which were already mortgaged), his life estate in the one-third of both Fells Point and the 400 acres in Baltimore County, and 2 lots on Fells Point held in his own right. WEALTH AT DEATH. DIED: sometime after 1794; size of estate unknown.

GILES, NATHANIEL (1735–1775). BORN: on October 2, 1735, in St. George's Parish, Baltimore County (later became part of Harford County); third son. NATIVE: at least third generation. RESIDED: at Lapidam Mill, Baltimore County (later became part of Harford County). FAMILY BACKGROUND. FATHER: Jacob Giles (1705–1784), of Baltimore County (later became part of Harford County), a Quaker, and a partner in the Bush River Ironworks and Cumberland Forge. MOTHER: Hannah. STEPMOTHER: Johanna (1720–?), widow of George Drew (?–1735/6); daughter of *James Phillips* (?–1720) and wife Johanna Kemp. BROTHERS: John (1729–by 1784); Jacob (1733–?). HALF BROTHERS: *James Giles* (1749/50–?); Jacob (1753–by 1784); Thomas (1754–1798); Aquila (1757–?); and Edward (1759–1783). SISTERS: Sarah (?–by 1784), who married Nathaniel Rigbie, Jr. HALF SISTERS: Elizabeth (1747–by 1784), who married William Smith; Johanna (1751–?). STEPSISTER: Susanna Drew (1736–?), who married (first name unknown) Scott. MARRIED on March 7, 1762, Sarah (1742–1775), daughter of Col. William Hammond (1702–1752) and wife Sarah Sheredine (1721–?); granddaughter of both *Thomas Sheredine* (1699–1752) and *Thomas Hammond* (?–ca. 1724/25); niece of *Upton Sheredine* (1740–1800). Her brothers were William (1743–1810), who married Mary; Thomas (1744–?); Larkin (1746–?); and James (1749–?). Her sisters were Rebecca (1741–?), who married Caleb Dorsey; Elizabeth (1747–?). CHILDREN. DAUGHTERS: Hannah (1762–?), who married (first name unknown) Gover; Sarah (1767–?), who married (first name unknown) Gover; Elizabeth (1770–?); Caroline (1772–?), who married Edward Shoemaker; and Charlotte (?–died young). PRIVATE CAREER. RELIGIOUS AFFILIATION: strong Quaker background;

family records are found in the Deer Creek Meeting registers, Baltimore County. SOCIAL STATUS AND ACTIVITIES: Gent., by 1770. OCCUPATIONAL PROFILE: planter; owned a small gristmill and store and one-third interest in a sloop. PUBLIC CAREER. LEGISLATIVE SERVICE: Convention, Harford County, 1st, 1774 (appointed, but did not attend). STANDS ON PUBLIC/PRIVATE ISSUES: his will provided for the manumission of his slaves and the disinheritance of any of his children who tried to claim them. WEALTH DURING LIFETIME. PERSONAL PROPERTY: 9 slaves, 1775. LAND AT FIRST ELECTION: 1,118 acres in Harford County (at least 712 acres from his father by deed of gift, 1766). WEALTH AT DEATH. DIED: on May 23, 1775, in Harford County. PERSONAL PROPERTY: TEV, at least £1,766.17.0 current money (including 9 slaves, plate, 28 books, and one-third interest in a sloop). LAND: probably 1,118 acres in Harford County.

GILLIS (GILLISS), JOSEPH (ca. 1706–?). BORN: ca. 1706, probably in Somerset County; probably fourth son. NATIVE: third generation. RESIDED: in Somerset County. FAMILY BACKGROUND. FATHER: John Gillis (ca. 1662–1720). MOTHER: Mary. BROTHERS: John; Thomas, who married Anne Lackey; and Ezekial. SISTERS: Rebecca; Sarah; Betty; and Bridget. MARRIED by 1735/36 Eleanor, daughter of William Bozman, Sr. (?–1749), of Somerset County, and wife Sarah. Her brother was Ballard. CHILDREN. SONS: George, of age by 1761; William. PRIVATE CAREER. EDUCATION: literate. RELIGIOUS AFFILIATION: Anglican. SOCIAL STATUS AND ACTIVITIES: Gent., 1749. OCCUPATIONAL PROFILE: probably a planter. PUBLIC CAREER. LEGISLATIVE SERVICE: Lower House, Somerset County, 1751–1754. LOCAL OFFICES: justice, Somerset County, 1754–at least 1774 (quorum, 1758–at least 1774); Somerset Parish Vestry, Somerset County, in office 1767–1770; justice, Court of Oyer and Terminer and Gaol Delivery, Somerset County, commissioned 1771. MILITARY SERVICE: captain, by 1755. WEALTH DURING LIFETIME. PERSONAL PROPERTY: assessed value £992.0.0, including 29 slaves and 48 oz. plate, 1783. LAND AT FIRST ELECTION: 708 acres in Somerset County (550 acres inherited from his father; 158 acres by purchase). SIGNIFICANT CHANGES IN LAND BETWEEN FIRST ELECTION AND DEATH: deeded as gifts to his sons 550 acres in 1761 and 158 acres in 1777, all of which were in Somerset County. WEALTH AT DEATH. DIED: probably in Somerset County; lived until at least 1783; not listed in the 1790 census.

GILPIN, JOSEPH (ca. 1727–1790). BORN: ca. 1727; eldest son. NATIVE: third generation. RESIDED: in North Milford Hundred, Cecil County. FAMILY BACKGROUND. FATHER: Samuel Gilpin (1694–1767), who immigrated in 1733 from Delaware County, Pennsylvania; son of Joseph Gilpin, a Quaker, who immigrated in 1695 from England to Pennsylvania. MOTHER: Jane Parker, of Pennsylvania. BROTHERS: Thomas (?–1778), a Quaker, of Philadelphia, Pennsylvania, who was exiled from his home during the Revolutionary War for declining to serve in the military, and who died in Winchester, Virginia; Samuel; and George, a close friend of George Washington. SISTERS: Hannah; Mary; and Rachel. MARRIED by 1765 Elizabeth Reed. CHILDREN. SONS: John (1765–1808), who married on September 20, 1797, Mary, daughter of *Henry Hollingsworth* (1737–1803); Joseph. DAUGHTERS: Elizabeth, who married on April 12, 1798, Mark Alexander; Hannah, who married on November 17, 1789, Francis Partridge; Mary, who married on May 1, 1800, James Partridge; and Rachel. PRIVATE CAREER. EDUCATION: literate. RELIGIOUS AFFILIATION: Anglican, St. Mary Anne's Parish, Cecil County. SOCIAL STATUS AND ACTIVITIES: Mr., 1756; Gent., 1767; Esq., 1769. OCCUPATIONAL PROFILE: miller; owned a sawmill; purchased a lot in Elkton, Cecil County, in 1783 with *Henry Hollingsworth* (1737–1803) and others where they planed to build a market. PUBLIC CAREER. LEGISLATIVE SERVICE: Lower House, Cecil County, 1770 (elected to the 3rd session to fill vacancy; Accounts 3), 1773–1774 (Bills of Credit 2, 3); Conventions, Cecil County, 3rd, 1774, 5th, 1775, 6th–8th, 1775–1776 (Manufactories 8th), 9th, 1776 (Manufactories; Elections); Lower House, Cecil County, 1777 (Manufactories 1, 2; Grievances 2). OTHER STATE OFFICE: Constitution Ratification Convention, Cecil County, 1788. LOCAL OFFICES: justice, Cecil County, 1764–1790 (quorum, 1774–1790); justice, Orphans' Court, Cecil County, 1777–1790; collector of clothing, Cecil County, appointed 1777; subscription officer, Continental Loan Office, Cecil County, appointed 1779. WEALTH DURING LIFETIME. PERSONAL PROPERTY: assessed value £216.0.0, including 70 oz. plate, 1783. LAND AT FIRST ELECTION: 993 acres in Cecil County (143 acres from his father as a gift, 850 acres by purchase and patent). SIGNIFICANT CHANGES IN LAND BETWEEN FIRST ELECTION AND DEATH: purchased and patented 394 acres in Cecil County, 1771–1786; sold 54 acres in 1772 and 1783. He was charged with 1,017 acres in Cecil County in 1783. By 1786 he owned 1,622 acres in Pennsylvania, which was probably family land. WEALTH AT DEATH. DIED: will probated on April 13, 1790, in Cecil County. PERSONAL PROPERTY: TEV, £1,997.3.10 current money (including 1 black servant, 125 oz. plate, and at least 22 books); FB, £1,495.0.8. LAND: 1,302 acres in Cecil County and 1,622 acres in Pennsylvania.

GIST, CHRISTOPHER (?–1690/91). IMMIGRATED: by 1677 as a free adult with his wife. RESIDED: in Baltimore County. MARRIED Edith (?–1694), sister of Richard Cromwell. She subsequently married in 1691 Joseph Williams, and finally in 1692 John Beecher. CHILDREN. SON: *Richard Gist* (1683–1741), who married Zipporah Murray. PRIVATE CAREER. EDUCATION: literate. RELIGIOUS AFFILIATION: Protestant. OCCUPATIONAL PROFILE: planter. PUBLIC CAREER. LEGISLATIVE SERVICE: Associators' Convention, Baltimore County, 1689–1690/91. LOCAL OFFICES: overseer of highways, Baltimore County, 1685; justice, Baltimore County, 1689–1690/91. WEALTH DURING LIFETIME. LAND AT FIRST ELECTION: 581 acres. WEALTH AT DEATH. DIED: will probated on March 10, 1690/91. LAND: 581 acres.

GIST (GUEST, GEIST), RICHARD (1683–1741). BORN: in 1683 in Baltimore County; only child. NATIVE: second generation. RESIDED: in Garrison Forest, Baltimore County. FAMILY BACKGROUND. FATHER: *Christopher Gist* (?–1690/91). STEPFATHERS: Joseph Williams (?–1692); John Beecher. GUARDIANS: his uncle, Richard Cromwell (?–ca. 1717), with whom Gist lived after his mother's death; Thomas Staley (?–1700). MOTHER: Edith (?–1694), daughter of (first name unknown) Cromwell. MARRIED on December 7, 1704, Zipporah, daughter of James Murray (?–1704) and wife Jemima Morgan. Her brothers were Josephus (ca. 1688–1772), who married Ruth Hawkins; Morgan (?–by 1741), who married Sarah Hawkins; Melchizedek (?–by 1748), who married Sophia Giles; and Jabez (?–by 1761), who married Mary Wheeler. Her sisters were Jemima (?–1725), who married first, John Eager, and second, Philip Jones; Keziah, who married Johathan Hanson. CHILDREN. SONS: Christopher (ca. 1705–?), who married Sarah Howard; Nathaniel (ca. 1707–?), who married Mary Howard; William (ca. 1711–?), who married Violetta Howard; Thomas (1712–?), who married Susannah Cockey; and John (ca. 1722–?), who married Mary. DAUGHTERS: Edith (ca. 1709–?), who married Abraham Vaughan; Jemima (ca. 1714–?), who married William Seabrook; Ruth (ca. 1716–?), who married William Lewis; and Sarah (ca. 1724–?), who married John Kennedy. PRIVATE CAREER. EDUCATION: literate; his mother specified in her will that he be taught writing and accounts to fit him for the "merchant business." RELIGIOUS AFFILIATION: Anglican; his wife was a Quaker. SOCIAL STATUS AND ACTIVITIES: Gent., 1733; Mr., 1740. ADDITIONAL COMMENTS: after his mother's death, Gist lived with his uncle Richard Cromwell. OCCUPATIONAL PROFILE: merchant. PUBLIC CAREER. LEGISLATIVE SERVICE: Lower House, Baltimore County, 1740–1741 (elected to the 1st session to fill vacancy). OTHER PROVINCIAL OFFICE: surveyor, Western Shore, period of service unknown. LOCAL OFFICES: justice, Baltimore County, 1727–1741 (quorum, 1737–1741); commissioner, Baltimore County, appointed to purchase land upon which Baltimore Town was to be built, 1729. JURY SERVICE: foreman, Baltimore County, appointed 1722. WEALTH DURING LIFETIME. LAND AT FIRST ELECTION: 1,804 acres in Baltimore County, plus 1 lot in Baltimore Town (including at least 100 acres obtained through marriage). SIGNIFICANT CHANGES IN LAND BETWEEN FIRST ELECTION AND DEATH: gave 216 acres in Baltimore County to his son Thomas, 1738/39. WEALTH AT DEATH. DIED: on August 22, 1741, in Baltimore County. PERSONAL PROPERTY: TEV, £86.1.3 sterling, £1,189.17.11 current money, plus 8,420 pounds of tobacco; FB, estate overpaid £274.6.5 sterling, £1,105.2.4 current money, plus 5,315 pounds of tobacco. LAND: ca. 1,538 acres in Baltimore County.

GITTINGS, JAMES (1735–ca. 1823). BORN: on April 23, 1735; second son. NATIVE: at least second generation. RESIDED: at "Long Green," Gunpowder River Upper Hundred, Baltimore County. FAMILY BACKGROUND. FATHER: Thomas Gittings (?–1760). STEPFATHER: Thomas Treadway. MOTHER: Mary (?–1779), widow of James Lynch; daughter of James Lee, of Bush River, Baltimore County. BROTHER: Asael (1739–1776), of Kent County, who married Mary. HALF BROTHER: Thomas Gittings (?–1784), who married Hannah Clark. HALF SISTERS: Margaret Gittings, who married John Chamberlaine; Elizabeth Gittings, who married (first name unknown) Gover; Mary Gittings, who married Richard Wilmot; Susannah Gittings, who married John Wilson; and possibly Mary Lynch. ADDITIONAL COMMENTS: his father's first wife was Elizabeth Redgrave, of Kent County. MARRIED Elizabeth, daughter of Dr. *George Buchanan* (ca. 1697–1750) and wife Eleanor Rogers. Her brothers were *Lloyd Buchanan*

(1729–ca. 1762); *Andrew Buchanan* (ca. 1733–1786); Archibald (1736–1785); George (1739–?); James (1744–1783); and William (1748–?). Her sister was Eleanor (1732–?). CHILDREN. SONS: Thomas (ca. 1762–ca. 1804), who married Mary Wilmot; Richard (1763–1830), who married Mary (Polly), daughter of *John Sterett* (1750/51–1787); James, Jr. (1769–1820), who married Harriett, daughter of *John Sterett* (1750/51–1787); Archibald (1776–by 1832), who married first, Elizabeth Bosley, and second, Martha Rumsey. DAUGHTERS: Elizabeth (1774–?), who married Lambert Smith; Ann, who married William Patterson, Jr., Esq.; Mary, who married Thomas Ringgold (1768–1818), son of *Thomas Ringgold* (1744–1776); and Eleanor, who married James Croxall. PRIVATE CAREER. EDUCATION: literate. RELIGIOUS AFFILIATION: Anglican, St. John's Parish, Baltimore County. His wife and a least one son were Presbyterians. SOCIAL STATUS AND ACTIVITIES: Mr., 1772; Gent., 1774; Esq., 1783. OCCUPATIONAL PROFILE: planter; active in the development of Baltimore Town. PUBLIC CAREER. LEGISLATIVE SERVICE: Convention, Baltimore County, 5th, 1775; Lower House, Baltimore County, 1789. LOCAL OFFICES: churchwarden, St. John's Parish, Baltimore County, in office 1759–1760; St. John's Parish Vestry, Baltimore County, in office 1762–1765, 1767–1770, and 1780; justice, Baltimore County, 1768–at least 1775 (quorum, 1772–at least 1775); commissioner of tax, Baltimore County, 1777–at least 1783; judge, Court of Appeals for Tax Assessment, Baltimore County, appointed 1786 and 1787. MILITARY SERVICE: captain, Gunpowder Hundred Company, Baltimore County Militia, elected May 6, 1776; 1st major, Gunpowder Battalion, Baltimore County Militia, commissioned May 25, 1776; lieutenant colonel, Gunpowder Battalion, Baltimore County Militia, commissioned August 30, 1777; called colonel, 1782. STANDS ON PUBLIC/PRIVATE ISSUES: specified in his will that one slave be manumitted for faithful service. WEALTH DURING LIFETIME. PERSONAL PROPERTY: inherited 3 slaves from his father, 1760; assessed value £2,705.0.0, including 31 slaves and 84 oz. plate, 1783. LAND AT FIRST ELECTION: 1,231 acres in Baltimore County (845 acres inherited from his father in 1760; remainder resurveyed and patented, 1770), plus 1 lot in Baltimore Town and a lease on 207 acres in Baltimore Town. SIGNIFICANT CHANGES IN LAND BETWEEN FIRST ELECTION AND DEATH: patented 984 acres in Baltimore County in 1788, and purchased an additional 1,210 acres in Baltimore County in the early 1790s. After 1798

Gittings bought a few tracts in Baltimore County and divested himself of ca. 1,754 acres, with all but 400 acres of it being given to his sons. From the mid-1780s until his death Gittings was involved in land transactions in Baltimore Town, particularly in the Fell's Point and Franklin Street areas. WEALTH AT DEATH. DIED: will probated on February 26, 1823, in Baltimore County. PERSONAL PROPERTY: requested no appraisal of his estate. LAND: ca. 2,010 acres in Baltimore County, plus a number of lots in Baltimore City.

GODDIN, JOHN (?–1712/13). IMMIGRATED: in 1677 as a free adult. RESIDED: in Somerset County. MARRIED by 1681 Katherine, daughter of George Johnson (1627–1681), sheriff of Somerset County from 1668 to 1669; stepdaughter of *Thomas Everden* (?–1710). CHILDREN. SON: John (1681–?). DAUGHTER: Katherine (?–1753), who married *Thomas Purnell* (?–1723). PRIVATE CAREER. EDUCATION: literate. RELIGIOUS AFFILIATION: Quaker. SOCIAL STATUS AND ACTIVITIES: no title on arrival in the colony. OCCUPATIONAL PROFILE: planter. PUBLIC CAREER. LEGISLATIVE SERVICE: Lower House, Somerset County, 1681–1682 (elected to the 3rd session), 1692 (disqualified, because as a Quaker he would not subscribe to the required oaths). LOCAL OFFICE: justice, Somerset County, 1680/81 (probably never served). WEALTH DURING LIFETIME. LAND AT FIRST ELECTION: 1,200 acres; 5,273 acres by 1690. WEALTH AT DEATH. DIED: on February 20, 1712/13. PERSONAL PROPERTY: TEV, £322.3.7 sterling (including 4 slaves). LAND: 5,273 acres.

GOLDSBOROUGH, CHARLES (1707–1767). BORN: on June 26, 1707, in Talbot County; third son. NATIVE: second generation. RESIDED: in Dorchester County, by 1727; Cambridge, Dorchester County. FAMILY BACKGROUND. FATHER: *Robert Goldsborough* (1660–1746). MOTHER: Elizabeth (1678–1719/20), daughter of *Nicholas Greenberry* (1627–1697). UNCLE: *Charles Greenberry* (1672–1713). HALF UNCLE: *Thomas Robins* (1672–1721). AUNT: Ann Greenberry, who married *John Hammond* (ca. 1665–1742/43). BROTHERS: Robert (ca. 1704–1777); Nicholas (ca. 1704–1756); *William Goldsborough* (1709–1760); *John Goldsborough* (1711–1778); Greenberry (1713–ca. 1716); Howes (1715–1746); Greenberry (1717–1717); and (first name unknown) (1718–1718). SISTERS: Ann (1698–ca. 1708); Elizabeth (ca. 1700–ca. 1708); and Mary (1702–ca. 1742). FIRST COUSINS: *Nicholas Goldsborough* (ca. 1689–1766); Elizabeth Ridgely (?–1734), who married *Thomas Worthing-*

ton (ca. 1691–1753); and Elizabeth Standley, who married second, *Thomas Robins* (1672–1721). NEPHEWS: *Robert Goldsborough IV* (1740–1798); *Howes Goldsborough* (1747–1797); and *William Goldsborough* (1750/51–1801). NIECES: Elizabeth Goldsborough (ca. 1735–ca. 1786), who married second, *Benson Stainton* (?–ca. 1781); and Mary Goldsborough (1755–1796), who married first, *Benedict Brice* (1749–1786). MARRIED first, on July 18, 1730, Elizabeth (?–by 1739), daughter of *Joseph Ennalls* (?–1709) and wife Mary Brooke; granddaughter of both *Bartholomew Ennalls* (1643–1688) and *John Brooke* (by 1646–1692/93); niece of *Thomas Ennalls* (?–1718), *Henry Ennalls* (1675–1734), Elizabeth Ennalls, who married *Roger Woolford* (1670–1730), and Ann Brooke, who married first, *Thomas Cooke* (?–1692/93). Her brothers were *William Ennalls* (?–1731); *Bartholomew Ennalls* (ca. 1700–1783); Thomas (?–1753); Henry (?–1734); and Joseph (1702–1759). Her sister was Mary, who married *Henry Hooper* (ca. 1687–1767). Her first cousin was *Thomas Woolford* (ca. 1699–ca. 1750/51). Her nephews were *Joseph Ennalls* (ca. 1745–1779); *William Ennalls* (?–1785); *John Ennalls* (by 1746–ca. 1778); and *Henry Hooper, Jr.* (ca. 1727–1790). Her nieces were Mary Ennalls, who married *Ennalls Hooper* (?–ca. 1763); Ann Ennalls (ca. 1729–by 1790), who married *Henry Hooper, Jr.* (ca. 1727–1790); Elinor Ennalls (ca. 1738–1793), who married *Joseph Daffin* (?–1796). MARRIED second, on August 2, 1739, Elizabeth (1723–?), daughter of Samuel Dickinson, Gent. (ca. 1689–1760), of Kent County on Delaware, Pennsylvania, presiding judge of the Court of Common Pleas of Kent County, Delaware, in 1740, associate judge of the Supreme Court of Delaware, in 1754, and wife Judith Troth; stepdaughter of Mary Cadwalader; granddaughter of William Troth; stepgranddaughter of John Cadwalader, of Pennsylvania. Her brothers were William (1711–?), Walter (ca. 1712–?), and Samuel, all of whom died young; and Henry (1718–?). Her half brother was John Dickinson (1732–1808), of Pennsylvania, statesman, author of *Letters from a Farmer in Pennsylvania to the Inhabitants of the British Colonies* (1768), president of the Supreme Executive Council of Delaware in 1781, and later elected to the same office in Pennsylvania, who married Mary, daughter of Isaac Norris. Her sisters were Elizabeth, Rebecca, Rachel, and Rachel, all of whom died young. CHILDREN. SONS: *Robert Goldsborough* (1733–1788); Charles (1740–1769), who married Anna Maria Lloyd (1737–1768), daughter of *William Tilghman* (1711–1782). Charles entered the University of Pennsylvania in May 1758, but never graduated. DAUGHTER: Elizabeth Greenberry (ca. 1731–1820), who married *William Ennalls* (?–1785). PRIVATE CAREER. EDUCATION: literate; in a petition to the Provincial Court he claimed that he had studied to be a lawyer. RELIGIOUS AFFILIATION: Anglican, St. Peter's Parish, Talbot County. SOCIAL STATUS AND ACTIVITIES: Gent., 1741; Esq., 1756. OCCUPATIONAL PROFILE: lawyer, admitted to the following courts: Talbot County in August 1728; Somerset County in November 1736; Provincial Court in October 1738; Talbot County by March 1738/39; Queen Anne's County in March 1740/41; and Dorchester County by August 1762. ADDITIONAL COMMENTS: In an effort to resolve the problem the Worcester County sheriff was having in demanding quitrents on those lands lying north of a boundary line that had been run in 1751 from Fenwick's Island between Maryland and Delaware, Gov. Horatio Sharpe asked Goldsborough's legal opinion. Goldsborough replied that he believed those people living north of the line were no longer subject to Maryland laws, nor were they liable to pay Maryland taxes. PUBLIC CAREER. LEGISLATIVE SERVICE: Lower House, Dorchester County, 1751–1754 (Laws 1–6), 1754–1757 (Laws 1–4; Grievances 3), 1758–1761 (Grievances 3, Cv 3), 1762 (appointed to Council before the 2nd session); Upper House, 1763 (appointed before the 2nd session), 1765–1766. OTHER PROVINCIAL OFFICES: Council, 1762–1767 (appointed and qualified in July 1762); commissary general, 1764–1767. LOCAL OFFICE: clerk, Dorchester County, 1728–1738 (resigned). ADDITIONAL COMMENTS: A report from the Lower House Committee of Aggrievances and Courts of Justice in May 1739 stated that Charles Goldsborough, while he was clerk of Dorchester County, had demanded recognizances in large sums from people before he would conduct their business in the county courts. The condition of these recognizances required a person to pay the officer's fees immediately. If they did not, Goldsborough, who in the meantime had become a lawyer, obtained judgments against them that resulted in prison terms for some. The Committee determined, and the Lower House concurred, that Goldsborough's methods were illegal. He was reprimanded by the Lower House for his "vexatious, litigious and crewell" [*sic*] practices and ordered to pay the fees arising from the inquiry or be committed to the sergeant's custody until he complied with the order. In 1753 Goldsborough intended to apply for a seat in the Council, but Gov. Sharpe opposed his appointment. In a letter to Frederick

Calvert, 6th Lord Baltimore, Sharpe stated that the Goldsborough family had always presented itself in opposition to the government and that there was no reason to assume that Charles would be any different. Sharpe, however, did recommend him for a seat in the Lower House. He felt Goldsborough had the "Cunning & Capacity to lead or impose on some of the Burgesses. . . ." By 1760, though, Gov. Sharpe had changed his opinion of Goldsborough, stating that the family had been misrepresented to him at first and that he now believed them to be moderate and respectful towards the government. Sharpe felt Goldsborough had proven himself a man of ability and recommended that he be appointed to fill the Council seat vacated by the death of *Benjamin Tasker, Jr.* (1720/21–1760). WEALTH DURING LIFETIME. PERSONAL PROPERTY: his father bequeathed Goldsborough and his brother *William Goldsborough* (1709–1760) £146.4.6 sterling, money he had in the hands of Mr. John Hanbury, merchant, to be divided equally between them. LAND AT FIRST ELECTION: at least 5,908 acres in Dorchester County, plus 3 lots in Cambridge, Dorchester County (263 acres through second marriage; at least 5,645 acres by purchase and patent). ADDITIONAL COMMENTS: Charles's father did not leave him any land because, as he stated in his will, Charles had already been blessed with a handsome estate. SIGNIFICANT CHANGES IN LAND BETWEEN FIRST ELECTION AND DEATH: Goldsborough patented 2 tracts totalling 4,353 acres in Dorchester County in 1759 and 1760. These tracts were apparently on the Maryland-Delaware border, and when the Mason-Dixon line was drawn in ca. 1764 the land probably became part of Delaware. Goldsborough purchased or patented at least 6,875 additional acres in Dorchester County and 356 acres in Kent County, Delaware, and at least 4 lots in Cambridge, Dorchester County, between 1752 and 1765. He sold 256 acres in Dorchester County between 1756 and 1764. He received by deed of gift 1 lot in Cambridge, Dorchester County, from his second wife's father, 1760. Goldsborough stated in his will that he had already conveyed 600 acres in Dorchester County to his daughter, but no date was given. WEALTH AT DEATH. DIED: on July 14, 1767, about 7:00 in the morning, in Dorchester County, of a "Dropsy." PERSONAL PROPERTY: requested no appraisal of his estate. LAND: at least 11,927 acres in Dorchester County, plus at least 7 lots in Cambridge, Dorchester County, and lodgings in Annapolis; he also owned at least 356 acres in Kent County, Delaware, and he may have owned 4,353 acres more in Delaware, which had originally been patented in Dorchester County. ADDITIONAL COMMENTS: There is a discrepancy of at least 3,026 acres between what the Dorchester County debt books list Goldsborough as owning and the total figure obtained from deeds. The figure in the debt books may be too low because some of the land may have been included in Delaware when the Mason-Dixon line was drawn.

GOLDSBOROUGH, HOWES (1747–1797). BORN: on Friday afternoon, September 4, 1747, in Talbot County; second son. NATIVE: third generation. RESIDED: in Mill Hundred, Talbot County. FAMILY BACKGROUND. FATHER: Robert Goldsborough (ca. 1704–1777), of "Myrtle Grove," Talbot County; a justice of Talbot County from 1734 to 1741 and from 1749 to 1766; son of *Robert Goldsborough* (1660–1746). MOTHER: Mary Anne (1711–1794), widow of John Robins (?–1739), a lawyer; daughter of *Foster Turbutt* (1679–1720/21). UNCLES: *Charles Goldsborough* (1707–1767); *William Goldsborough* (1709–1760); and *John Goldsborough* (1711–1778). AUNTS: Sarah Turbutt (1706–1773), who married *Nicholas Goldsborough* (ca. 1689–1766); Elizabeth Turbutt (1708–?), who married *Tench Francis* (1701–1758); and Anne Turbutt (1715–1766), who married *John Goldsborough* (1711–1778). BROTHER: *William Goldsborough* (1750/51–1801). HALF BROTHER: *Robert Goldsborough IV* (1740–1798). SISTERS: Elizabeth (1745–1748); Mary Anne Turbutt (1752–1811), never married. FIRST COUSINS: *Thomas Goldsborough* (ca. 1728–1793); *Robert Goldsborough* (1733–1788); Ann Francis (1727–?), who married *James Tilghman* (1716–1793); Elizabeth Greenberry Goldsborough (ca. 1731–1820), who married *William Ennalls* (?–1785); Ann Goldsborough (1732–?), who married *Edward Oldham* (1709–1773); Elizabeth Goldsborough (ca. 1735–ca. 1786), who married second, *Benson Stainton* (?–ca. 1781); and Mary Goldsborough (1755–1796), who married *Benedict Brice* (1749–1786). ADDITIONAL COMMENTS: his father's first wife was Sarah (?–1740), daughter of Rev. Henry Nicols (1687–ca. 1749), rector of St. Michael's Parish, Talbot County. MARRIED on November 16, 1773, his second cousin Rebecca (ca. 1757–?), daughter of *Robert Goldsborough* (1733–1788); granddaughter of *Charles Goldsborough* (1707–1767); niece of Elizabeth Greenberry Goldsborough (ca. 1731–1820), who married *William Ennalls* (?–1785). Her brothers were Charles (ca. 1756–ca. 1759); Charles (1761–1801); Robert (ca. 1766–1790); John (by 1766–?); William; Richard;

and Howes. Her sisters were Sarah (ca. 1758–by 1832), who married *Henry Ennalls* (?–ca. 1803); Elizabeth; and Rachel (?–1811). CHILDREN. SONS: Robert (1776–1777); Charles (1779–1824), who married in 1802 Sarah (1789–1819), daughter of Vachel Keene; Robert Yerbury (1782–by 1805); Henry Turbutt (1783–1785); William Henry (1785–1842); Howes (1789–?), a physician by 1812, who married in 1814 Henrietta Maria Ward; and Henry (1792–1832), who married first, in 1817 Eliza Ann Thomas (?–1817), second, Susannah Shippley (?–by 1823), third, in 1823 Anne Keene (?–1824), and fourth, in 1825 Margaret, daughter of *James Tilghman, Jr.* (ca. 1748–1796). DAUGHTERS: Sarah (1774–?), who married in 1802 Dr. Samuel Y. Keene; Mary Ann (1778–by 1812), who married in 1804 Dr. Tristram Thomas; Ann (1787–1855), who married in 1810 Charles Louis Pascault, of Baltimore; Rebecca (1790–1792); and Elizabeth (1791–1791). PRIVATE CAREER. EDUCATION: literate. RELIGIOUS AFFILIATION: Anglican, St. Michael's Parish, Talbot County. OCCUPATIONAL PROFILE: probably a planter. PUBLIC CAREER. LEGISLATIVE SERVICE: Lower House, Talbot County, 1777–1778, 1778–1779 (Claims 3), 1781 (elected, but did not attend the 1781–1782 Assembly; resigned on November 16, 1781), 1785 (Claims). LOCAL OFFICES: justice, Talbot County, 1777–at least 1782; justice, Orphans' Court, Talbot County, 1777–at least 1783; commissioner of Tax, Talbot County, 1777–at least 1792; St. Michael's Parish Vestry, Talbot County, in office 1780–1784, 1796; trustee of the Alms- and Workhouse, Talbot County, in office 1787 and 1789; commission to build a courthouse at Easton, Talbot County, in office 1789; associate justice, Second District, Talbot County, appointed 1795. WEALTH DURING LIFETIME. PERSONAL PROPERTY: 23 slaves, 1776; assessed value £1,180.6.8, including 28 slaves and 71 oz. plate, 1783; 37 slaves, 1790. LAND AT FIRST ELECTION: 642 acres in Talbot County (all inherited from his father). SIGNIFICANT CHANGES IN LAND BETWEEN FIRST ELECTION AND DEATH: purchased 332 acres in Talbot County, 1788; inherited one-third of 2 tracts in Queen Anne's County from his mother with his portion totaling 369 acres, ca. 1794; purchased 76 acres in Talbot County, 1795. ADDITIONAL COMMENTS: Howes was an heir of his mother's estate with his brother *William Goldsborough* (1750/51–1801) and his sister Mary Anne Turbutt Goldsborough. WEALTH AT DEATH. DIED: between January 1 and February 16, 1797, in Talbot County. PERSONAL PROPERTY: TEV, £6,936.11.0 current money (including 41 slaves,

180 oz. plate, a library of books, maps, and pamphlets); FB, £6,165.1.2. LAND: 1,419 acres in Talbot and Queen Anne's counties.

GOLDSBOROUGH, JOHN (1711–1778). BORN: on Friday, October 12, 1711, in Talbot County; fifth son. NATIVE: second generation. RESIDED: at "Four Square," Talbot County. FAMILY BACKGROUND. FATHER: *Robert Goldsborough* (1660–1746). MOTHER: Elizabeth (1678–1719/20), daughter of *Nicholas Greenberry* (1627–1697). UNCLE: *Charles Greenberry* (1672–1713). HALF UNCLE: *Thomas Robins* (1672–1721). AUNT: Ann Greenberry, who married *John Hammond* (ca. 1665–1742/43). BROTHERS: Robert (ca. 1704–1777); Nicholas (ca. 1704–1756); *Charles Goldsborough* (1707–1767); *William Goldsborough* (1709–1760); Greenberry (1713–ca. 1716); Howes (1715–1746); Greenberry (1717–1717); and (first name unknown) (1718–1718). SISTERS: Ann (1698–ca. 1708); Elizabeth (ca. 1700–ca. 1708); and Mary (1702–ca. 1742). FIRST COUSINS: *Nicholas Goldsborough* (ca. 1689–1766); Elizabeth Ridgely (?–1734), who married *Thomas Worthington* (ca. 1691–1753); Elizabeth Standley, who married second, *Thomas Robins* (1672–1721). NEPHEWS: *Robert Goldsborough IV* (1740–1798); *Howes Goldsborough* (1747–1797); *William Goldsborough* (1750/51–1801); and *Robert Goldsborough* (1733–1788). NIECE: Elizabeth Greenberry Goldsborough (ca. 1731–1820), who married *William Ennalls* (?–1785). MARRIED first, on October 31, 1733, Anne (1715–1766), daughter of *Foster Turbutt* (1679–1720/21); niece of *William Turbutt* (1683/84–1739). Her brother was Henry (ca. 1703–?). Her sisters were Sarah (1706–1773), who married *Nicholas Goldsborough* (ca. 1689–1766); Elizabeth (ca. 1708–?), who married *Tench Francis* (1701–1758); Mary Anne (1711–1794); Mary (1713–?); and Rachel (1718–?). Her first cousins were Anna Maria Turbutt, who married *Edward Tilghman* (1713–1786); Elizabeth Turbutt (?–ca. 1760), who married *Thomas Harris* (?–1760); Mary Anne Wright (?–1747), who married *William Hopper* (1707–1772); and Anne Wright (?–by 1754), who married *Edward Oldham* (1709–1773). Her nephews were *Thomas Goldsborough* (ca. 1728–1793); *Howes Goldsborough* (1747–1797); and *William Goldsborough* (1750/51–1801). Her nieces were Ann Francis (1727–?), who married *James Tilghman* (1716–1793); Ann Goldsborough (1732–?), who married *Edward Oldham* (1709–1773). MARRIED second, by 1774 Mary, widow of John Lookerman (?–1766), of Queen Anne's County; daughter of Richard Skinner and wife Katherine Sherwood.

CHILDREN. SONS: Robert (ca. 1736–1770); John (1740–1803), deputy commissary of Dorchester County from 1765 to 1777, coroner of Dorchester County in 1766, justice of Dorchester County from 1766 to 1773, register of wills of Dorchester County from 1777 to 1803, and commissioner of tax of Dorchester County from 1783 to 1792, who married in 1762 Caroline, daughter of Howes Goldsborough (1715–1746) and wife Roseanna Piper; Capt. Greenbury (1742–1829); Charles (1744–1774), who married Ann, daughter of *Edward Tilghman* (1713–1786), and who was accidentally killed in a shooting incident; William (1759–1794), a first lieutenant in the Fourth Independent Company of Talbot County Militia in 1776, who was nicknamed "Hessian Billy," because he killed three Hessian soldiers who simultaneously attacked him, he was also appointed a major in the Talbot County Militia in 1794, joined the Society of Cincinnati, and never married; and Robert, a physician, who married Henrietta, widow of Dr. John Bracco (ca. 1763–1794), daughter of Joseph Nicholson, of Kent County, and wife Mary. STEPSONS: Richard Lookerman (?–1792), who married first, in 1775 Mary Darden, and second, in 1779 Ann Wood; Jacob Lookerman (1759–1839), who married first, in 1784 Eleanor Clarke, and second, in 1802 Mary, daughter of *Robert Harrison* (1740–1802). DAUGHTERS: Elizabeth (ca. 1735–ca. 1786), who married first, John Campbell (?–ca. 1766), second, *Benson Stainton* (?–ca. 1781), and third, Richard Kennard (?–1796); Anne (1751–1781), who married Vincent Loockerman, of Dover, Delaware; Henrietta Maria (ca. 1753–1839), who married Philip Francis (1748–?), son of *Tench Francis* (1701–1758); Mary (1755–1796), who married first, *Benedict Brice* (1749–1786), and second, Dr. James Cooke (?–1794); and Anna Maria, who married Arthur Emory, of Queen Anne's County. STEPDAUGHTER: Elizabeth Loockerman. PRIVATE CAREER. EDUCATION: literate. RELIGIOUS AFFILIATION: Anglican, St. Peter's Parish, Talbot County. OCCUPATIONAL PROFILE: probably a planter. PUBLIC CAREER. LEGISLATIVE SERVICE: Lower House, Talbot County, 1742–1744, 1745 (Elections), 1745/46–1748 (Elections Cv 1, 1–3, 4; Aggrievances Cv 1, 1–3, 4), 1749–1751 (Elections Cv–3; Aggrievances Cv–3; Bills of Credit 1), 1751–1754 (Elections 1–6; Grievances 1–6; Accounts 3–6), 1754–1757 (Elections 1–6; Grievances 1–6; Accounts 1–6), 1757–1758 (Elections 1, Cv, 2; Grievances 1, Cv, 2; Accounts 1, Cv, 2), 1758–1761 (Elections Cv 1, 1, Cv 2, 3, Cv 3; Grievances Cv 1, 1, Cv 2; Accounts Cv 1, 1, Cv 2, 3, Cv 3), 1762–1763 (Elections 1, 2;

Accounts 1, 2), 1765–1766 (Accounts 2, 3; Laws to Expire 2, 3; Grievances 2), 1768–1770 (Elections 1–3; Accounts 1–3; Public Offices 1; Laws to Expire 1–3). LOCAL OFFICES: sheriff, Talbot County, 1736–1739; justice, Talbot County, 1741–at least 1777 (quorum, 1751–at least 1777), he was a member of the "Stamp Act Court" that adjourned in 1765 rather than enforce the act; St. Peter's Parish Vestry, Talbot County, in office 1742–1745, 1747–1750, and 1761–1764; trustee of the charity work school, St. Peter's Parish, Talbot County, in office ca. 1750; justice, Court of Oyer and Terminer and Gaol Delivery, Talbot County, commissioned 1768 and 1771; justice, Orphans' Court, Talbot County, commissioned 1777; commissioner of tax, Talbot County, 1777–1779. WEALTH DURING LIFETIME. PERSONAL PROPERTY: inherited slaves, chattels, and one-third of a cargo from his father in 1746. LAND AT FIRST ELECTION: 450 acres in Talbot County (all acquired through his first marriage). SIGNIFICANT CHANGES IN LAND BETWEEN FIRST ELECTION AND DEATH: inherited at least 795 acres in Talbot County from his father, 1746; patented 56 acres in Talbot County, 1754; acquired 690 acres in Talbot County between 1744 and 1761; gave 586 acres in Talbot County by deed of gift to his son Charles, 1774. WEALTH AT DEATH. DIED: on January 18, 1778, in Talbot County, probably at his dwelling plantation, "Four Square." PERSONAL PROPERTY: TEV, £7,805.14.0 current money (including 36 slaves, 144.25 oz. plate, and books); FB, £6,315.1.8. LAND: 1,557 acres in Talbot County.

GOLDSBOROUGH, NICHOLAS (ca. 1689–1766). BORN: ca. 1689 at "Boston," Talbot County; elder son. NATIVE: second generation. RESIDED: in Talbot County. FAMILY BACKGROUND. FATHER: Nicholas Goldsborough (1662–1705); immigrated from England in 1679; resided in Talbot County; deputy sheriff of Talbot County in 1689; justice of Talbot County in 1705. MOTHER: Ann (?–by 1702), daughter of Thomas Powell. STEPMOTHER: Elizabeth (?–1708), daughter of John Sargeant and wife Mary. UNCLE: *Robert Goldsborough* (1660–1746). HALF UNCLE: *Thomas Robins* (1672–1721). BROTHER: Robert (1696–1696). SISTER: Rachel (1692–?), who married in 1712 Samuel Turbutt. HALF SISTERS: Mary (1702–?), who married in 1720 Henry Bowdle; Elizabeth (1704–1765), who married in 1734 Thomas Martin. FIRST COUSINS: Elizabeth Standley, who married second, *Thomas Robins* (1672–1721); *Charles Goldsborough* (1707–1767); *William Goldsborough* (1709–1760); and *John Goldsborough* (1711–1778).

MARRIED on January 25, 1721/22, Sarah (1706–1773), daughter of *Foster Turbutt* (1679–1720/21); niece of *William Turbutt* (1683/84–1739). Her brother was Henry (ca. 1703–?). Her sisters were Elizabeth (ca. 1708–?), who married *Tench Francis* (1701–1758); Mary Anne (1711–1794); Mary (1713–?); Anne (1715–1766), who married *John Goldsborough* (1711–1778); and Rachel (1718–?). Her first cousins were Anna Maria Turbutt, who married *Edward Tilghman* (1713–1786); Elizabeth Turbutt (?–ca. 1760), who married *Thomas Harris* (?–1760); Mary Anne Wright (?–1747), who married *William Hopper* (1707–1772); and Anne Wright (?–by 1754), who married *Edward Oldham* (1709–1773). Her nephews were *Howes Goldsborough* (1747–1797); *William Goldsborough* (1750/51–1801). Her nieces were Ann Francis (1727–?), who married *James Tilghman* (1716–1793); Elizabeth Goldsborough (1735–ca. 1786), who married second, *Benson Stainton* (?–ca. 1781); and Mary Goldsborough (1755–1796), who married *Benedict Brice* (1749–1786). CHILDREN. SONS: Nicholas (1726/27–1777), who married first, in 1759 Mary (ca. 1741–1768), daughter of *William Thomas* (1705–1767), and second, ca. 1769 Rebecca Dickinson; *Thomas Goldsborough* (ca. 1728–1793); Robert (1730–1736); Robert (1736/37–1740); and Foster (ca. 1738–1777), who married Rachel Bruff. DAUGHTERS: Ann (1722/23–ca. 1726), who died of "dropsy"; Sarah (1724–?), who married first, in 1742 Standley Robins (1715–1742), son of *Thomas Robins* (1672–1721), and second, Richard Turbot; Ann (1732–?), who married *Edward Oldham* (1709–1773); Rachel (1734–1796), who married in 1768 Rev. John Barclay (?–1772), rector of St. Peter's Parish, Talbot County from 1762 to 1772; Mary (1740–1812), who was buried at White Marsh Church, St. Peter's Parish, Talbot County; Elizabeth (1742–1776); and Bridget (1744–1774), who married in 1774 John Singleton (1750–1819), nephew and heir of *James Dickinson* (ca. 1726–1787). PRIVATE CAREER. EDUCATION: literate. RELIGIOUS AFFILIATION: Anglican, St. Peter's Parish, Talbot County. SOCIAL STATUS AND ACTIVITIES: Gent., 1723. OCCUPATIONAL PROFILE: planter. PUBLIC CAREER. LEGISLATIVE SERVICE: Lower House, Talbot County, 1725–1727, 1732–1734 (Laws 2), 1734/35–1737 (Aggrievances 1, Cv, 2–4), 1738 (Aggrievances), 1739–1741 (Aggrievances Cv–3), 1742–1744 (Aggrievances 1, 2; Laws 1, 2), 1745 (Aggrievances; Laws), 1745/46–1748 (Aggrievances 1; Laws 1–3, 4), 1749–1751 (Aggrievances Cv–3; Laws Cv–3). LOCAL OFFICES: St. Peter's Parish Vestry, Talbot County, elected 1717, 1718 (refused to serve), 1719, 1720, 1733, and 1741; justice, Talbot County, by 1720–at least 1745 (quorum, 1727–at least 1745); justice, Court of Oyer and Terminer and Gaol Delivery, Talbot County, commissioned 1720; tobacco inspector, Fourth Precinct, Talbot County, appointed 1729 (refused to serve). STANDS ON PUBLIC/PRIVATE ISSUES: In 1744 *Joshua George* (ca. 1695–1748) reported to the Council a conversation he had had with Goldsborough. George had told Goldsborough that he thought it "a very hard Affair" that sheriffs and others were not being compensated for the trouble and money they expended on Indians who were committed to their custody. Goldsborough responded that he thought it "a very cruel Affair on the Indians" who had been given passes by Governor Ogle to meet, but were then molested by the sheriffs of the various counties. His defense of the Indians was taken by George to be an offense against the governor. The Council ordered the attorney general to prosecute Goldsborough in the Provincial Court, although apparently no action was taken. WEALTH DURING LIFETIME. LAND AT FIRST ELECTION: 1,934 acres in Talbot, Queen Anne's, and Dorchester counties (1,234 acres inherited from his father; 700 acres acquired through his marriage). SIGNIFICANT CHANGES IN LAND BETWEEN FIRST ELECTION AND DEATH: resurveyed 300 acres of the land he had inherited from his father, resulting in a new total of 821 acres in Dorchester County, 1728; his wife inherited her father's dwelling plantation containing 730 acres in Talbot County after the death of her brother, by 1738; purchased 630 acres in Queen Anne's, Talbot, and Dorchester counties between 1738 and 1749; purchased at least 74 acres in Talbot County in 1751, but he gave all of it to his son *Thomas Goldsborough* (ca. 1728–1793) by deed of gift, 1753. WEALTH AT DEATH. DIED: in September 1766 in Talbot County. PERSONAL PROPERTY: TEV, £3,638.3.8 as calculated (including 40 slaves, 5 servants, 67 oz. 8 dwts. plate, and books); FB, £3,592.15.9. LAND: 3,848 acres in Talbot, Dorchester, and Queen Anne's counties.

GOLDSBOROUGH (GOULDESBOROUGH), ROBERT (1660–1746).

BORN: in 1660 in Dorset, England; oldest son. IMMIGRATED: in 1677 as a free adult with his brother, probably from England. RESIDED: in Dorchester County; Talbot County, by 1690. FAMILY BACKGROUND. FATHER: Nicholas Goldsborough (ca. 1640–1670), a merchant of Blandford, Dorset, England in 1659, who went to Barbados in 1669, then to New England, and finally to Maryland in 1670. MOTHER: Margaret, daughter of Abraham Howes. She subsequently married in 1671 George Robins (1635–1674). BROTHER: Nicholas (1662–1705), who married first, Ann, daughter of Thomas Powell, and second, Elizabeth, daughter of John Sargent. HALF BROTHER: *Thomas Robins* (1672–1721). SISTER: Judith, who married first, John Standley, and second, Robert Grundy. MARRIED in 1697 Elizabeth (1678–1719/20), daughter of *Nicholas Greenberry* (1627–1697). Her brother was *Charles Greenberry* (1672–1713). Her sisters were Katherine, who married Henry Ridgely (1669–1699/1700), son of *Henry Ridgeley* (?–1710); Ann, who married *John Hammond* (ca. 1665–1742/43). Her niece was Elizabeth Ridgely (?–1734), who married *Thomas Worthington* (ca. 1691–1753). CHILDREN. SONS: Robert (ca. 1704–1777), who married first, Sarah (?–1740), daughter of Henry Nichols, and second, Mary Anne (1711–1794), widow of John Robins and daughter of *Foster Turbutt* (1679–1720/21); Nicholas (ca. 1704–1756), who married Jane, widow of James Banning; *Charles Goldsborough* (1707–1767), who married first, Elizabeth, daughter of *Joseph Ennalls* (?–1709), and second, Elizabeth, daughter of Samuel Dickinson; *William Goldsborough* (1709–1760), who married first in 1734/35 Elizabeth, daughter of *Thomas Robins* (1672–1721), and second, in 1747 Henrietta Maria (1707–1771), widow of George Robins (1697–1742) and daughter of *Richard Tilghman* (1672/73–1738/39); *John Goldsborough* (1711–1778), who married Ann (1715–1766), daughter of *Foster Turbutt* (1679–1720/21); Greenberry (1713–ca. 1716); and Howes (1715–1746), who married Rosanna, daughter of Michael Piper. DAUGHTERS: Ann (1698–ca. 1708); Elizabeth (ca. 1700–ca. 1708); and Mary (1702–ca. 1742), who married (first name unknown) Mooney. PRIVATE CAREER. EDUCATION: literate, probably had considerable schooling. RELIGIOUS AFFILIATION: Anglican. OCCUPATIONAL PROFILE: lawyer, admitted to the following courts: Talbot County in 1687; Provincial Court in 1693. Planter; merchant. PUBLIC CAREER. LEGISLATIVE SERVICE: Lower House, Talbot County, 1704–1707 (Elections and Privileges 1; Laws 1). OTHER PROVINCIAL OFFICES: clerk, Committee of Aggrievances, 1695; clerk, Committee of Laws, 1696. LOCAL OFFICES: clerk of Indictments, Talbot County, 1692, 1716–1717/18; justice, Talbot County, 1695/96–1697 (quorum); chief justice, Talbot County, 1699–1705, 1719–1738. STANDS ON PUBLIC/PRIVATE ISSUES: opposed the government of Protestant Associators in 1689. WEALTH DURING LIFETIME. LAND AT

FIRST ELECTION: over 900 acres; patented or bought over 2,000 acres, 1688–1735. WEALTH AT DEATH. DIED: on December 25, 1746; size of estate unknown.

GOLDSBOROUGH, ROBERT (1733–1788).

BORN: on December 3, 1733, in Cambridge, Dorchester County; elder son. NATIVE: third generation. RESIDED: in Dorchester County, 1733–1752; England, 1752–1759; Dorchester County, 1759; "The Point," Dorchester County, 1767. FAMILY BACKGROUND. FATHER: *Charles Goldsborough* (1707–1767), son of *Robert Goldsborough* (1660–1746). MOTHER: Elizabeth (?–by 1739), daughter of *Joseph Ennalls* (?–1709) and wife Mary Brooke. STEPMOTHER: Elizabeth (1723–?), daughter of Samuel Dickinson (ca. 1689–1760) and wife Judith Troth. UNCLES: *William Goldsborough* (1709–1760); *John Goldsborough* (1711–1778); *William Ennalls* (?–1731); and *Bartholomew Ennalls* (ca. 1700–1783). AUNT: Mary Ennalls, who married *Henry Hooper* (ca. 1687–1767). HALF BROTHER: Charles Goldsborough (1740–1769). SISTER: Elizabeth Greenberry (ca. 1731–1820), who married *William Ennalls* (?–1785). FIRST COUSINS: *Henry Hooper, Jr.* (ca. 1727–1790); *Robert Goldsborough IV* (1740–1798); *Howes Goldsborough* (1747–1797); *William Goldsborough* (1750/51–1801); *Joseph Ennalls* (ca. 1745–1779); *William Ennalls* (?–1785); *John Ennalls* (by 1746–ca. 1778); Mary Ennalls, who married *Ennalls Hooper* (?–ca. 1763); Ann Ennalls (ca. 1729–by 1790), who married *Henry Hooper, Jr.* (ca. 1727–1790); Elizabeth Goldsborough (ca. 1735–ca. 1786), who married second, *Benson Stainton* (?–ca. 1781); Mary Goldsborough (1755–1796), who married first, *Benedict Brice* (1749–1786); and Elinor Ennalls (ca. 1738–1793), who married *Joseph Daffin* (?–1796). MARRIED on March 27, 1755, in England, Sarah, daughter of Richard Yerbury (?–1754), of London, England. Her brother was Richard, who married, but died without progeny. Her sister was Rachel, who married Thomas Watson. CHILDREN. SONS: Charles (ca. 1756–ca. 1759), born and died in England; Charles (1761–1801), who married Williamina Elizabeth, daughter of Rev. William Smith, of Philadelphia, Pennsylvania; John (by 1766–?), probably died young; Robert (ca. 1766–1790), drowned, never married; William, who married Sarah (1770–?), daughter of *Nicholas Worthington* (1734–1793); Richard, who married Achash (1768–?), daughter of *Nicholas Worthington* (1734–1793); and Howes, died without progeny. DAUGHTERS: Rebecca (ca. 1757–?), who married *Howes Goldsborough* (1747–1797);

Sarah (ca. 1758–by 1832), who married *Henry Ennalls* (?–ca. 1803); Elizabeth, who married James Sykes; Rachel (?–1811), who married in 1791 Horatio Ridout, son of *John Ridout* (1732–1797). PRIVATE CAREER. EDUCATION: entered the Middle Temple, London, England, in December 1752; graduated from the College of Philadelphia, 1760. RELIGIOUS AFFILIATION: Anglican. SOCIAL STATUS AND ACTIVITIES: Esq., 1755. OCCUPATIONAL PROFILE: lawyer, called to the bar in February 1757, London, England; returned to Maryland to practice law in 1759, admitted to the following courts: Queen Anne's County in March 1760; Provincial Court in April 1760; Dorchester County by November 1772. PUBLIC CAREER. LEGISLATIVE SERVICE: Lower House, Dorchester County, 1765–1766 (Accounts 2, 3; Public Offices 2); Conventions, Dorchester County, 1st, 1774, 4th, 1775, 5th, 1775, 6th–8th, 1775–1776 (did not attend the 6th Convention), 9th, 1776; Senate, Eastern Shore, Term of 1776–1781: 1777, 1777–1778, 1778–1779, 1779–1780, 1780–1781 (did not serve), Term of 1781–1786: 1781–1782, 1782–1783 (resigned on May 29, 1783), 1783 (elected on November 24, 1783, to fill vacancy after giving his assurance that he would attend "whenever his health would permit" ; did not serve), 1784 (declined to serve on November 25, 1784). OTHER PROVINCIAL/STATE OFFICES: attorney general, 1766–1768 (resigned); 1st Council of Safety, Eastern Shore, 1775 (elected, but did not serve); Consititution Ratification Convention, Dorchester County, 1788. LOCAL OFFICES: sheriff, Dorchester County, 1761–1764; judge, Court of Appeals for Tax Assessment, Dorchester County, appointed 1786; Great Choptank Parish Vestry, Dorchester County, in office 1788. OUT OF STATE SERVICE: delegate, Continental Congress, 1774–1776 (elected in June 1774, December 1774, April 1775, August 1775, and May 1776). WEALTH DURING LIFETIME. PERSONAL PROPERTY: 15 slaves, 1775; assessed value £6,103.13.4, including 123 slaves and 376 oz. plate, 1783. LAND AT FIRST ELECTION: 185 acres in Dorchester County (all by patent), plus a large estate in Wiltshire and London, England (acquired through marriage). SIGNIFICANT CHANGES IN LAND BETWEEN FIRST ELECTION AND DEATH: inherited at least 4,608 acres in Dorchester County from his father, 1767; owned a total of 8,631 acres in Dorchester County, 1783; in an exchange of land with his son Charles, Robert gave him 1,050 acres in Dorchester County, 1783; resurveyed several tracts and added 380 acres of vacant land in Dorchester County to his total acreage, between 1784 and 1788. WEALTH AT DEATH. DIED: on

Monday, December 22, 1788, between 8:00 and 9:00 in the evening in Dorchester County; interred in Cambridge Churchyard, Dorchester County. LAND: 7,961 acres in Dorchester County; possibly still owned the estate in Wiltshire and London, England.

GOLDSBOROUGH, ROBERT, IV (1740–1798).

BORN: on Saturday, November 8, 1740, at "Myrtle Grove," Talbot County; first son. NATIVE: third generation. RESIDED: in Talbot County. FAMILY BACKGROUND. FATHER: Robert Goldsborough (ca. 1704–1777), of "Myrtle Grove," Talbot County; a justice of Talbot County from 1734 to 1741 and from 1749 to 1766; son of *Robert Goldsborough* (1660–1746). MOTHER: Sarah (?–1740), daughter of Rev. Henry Nicols (1687–ca. 1749), rector of St. Michael's Parish, Talbot County, and wife Elizabeth Gatchell. STEPMOTHER: Mary Anne (1711–1794), widow of John Robins (?–1739), a lawyer; daughter of *Foster Turbutt* (1679–1720/21). UNCLES: *Charles Goldsborough* (1707–1767); *William Goldsborough* (1709–1760); and *John Goldsborough* (1711–1778). STEPAUNTS: Sarah Turbutt (1706–1773), who married *Nicholas Goldsborough* (ca. 1689–1766); Elizabeth Turbutt (1708–?), who married *Tench Francis* (1701–1758); and Anne Turbutt (1715–1766), who married *John Goldsborough* (1711–1778). HALF BROTHERS: *Howes Goldsborough* (1747–1797); *William Goldsborough* (1750/51–1801). HALF SISTERS: Elizabeth (1745–1748); Mary Anne Turbutt (1752–1811), who never married. FIRST COUSINS: *Robert Goldsborough* (1733–1788); Elizabeth Greenberry Goldsborough (ca. 1731–1820), who married *William Ennalls* (?–1785); Elizabeth Goldsborough (ca. 1735–ca. 1786), who married second, *Benson Stainton* (?–ca. 1781); Mary Goldsborough (1755–1796), who married *Benedict Brice* (1749–1786); and *Jeremiah Nichols* (1748–ca. 1806). MARRIED on Thursday, September 22, 1768, Mary Emerson (ca. 1739–1811), youngest daughter of *Henry Trippe* (?–1744); granddaughter of *Henry Trippe* (?–ca. 1723/24); niece of both Elizabeth Trippe, who married second, *Bartholomew Ennalls* (ca. 1700–1783) and Mary Trippe (?–1782), who married *Jacob Hindman* (by 1713–1766). Her brother was Henry (?–ca. 1770). Her sisters were Sarah; Ann, who married *John Dickinson* (ca. 1726–1789); and Elizabeth. Her first cousins were *James Hindman* (1741–1830); *William Hindman* (1743–1822); and Elizabeth Hindman (?–by 1788), who married *William Perry* (1746–1799). CHILDREN. SONS: Robert (1771–1771); Robert Henry (1774–1777); Robert Henry (1779–1836), a member of

the House of Delegates from Talbot County in 1804 and 1825, a U.S. senator from 1813 to 1819 and from 1835 to 1836, and a presidential elector (for Jackson) in 1833, he married in 1800 Henrietta Maria, second daughter of Col. Robert Lloyd Nicols, of "Mt. Pleasant," Talbot County. DAUGHTERS: (first name unknown) (1769–?); Elizabeth (1776–1798), who married in 1793 Charles Goldsborough, Esq. (1765–1834), of Dorchester County, governor of Maryland in 1819, grandson of *Charles Goldsborough* (1707–1767). PRIVATE CAREER. EDUCATION: entered the University of Pennsylvania on August 12, 1757, as a member of the class of 1760. RELIGIOUS AFFILIATION: Anglican; appointed by the St. Michael's Parish Vestry, Talbot County, to be the deputy at a meeting of the representatives from several parishes in Chestertown, Kent County, to frame a petition to the General Assembly for the better support of ministers, 1781. SOCIAL STATUS AND ACTIVITIES: Esq., 1779; Hon., 1784; a member of the American Philosophical Society, 1791. OCCUPATIONAL PROFILE: lawyer, admitted to the following courts: Talbot County in November 1759; Provincial Court in April 1765; Queen Anne's County in June 1765; Dorchester County by November 1772. Officeholder; probably also a planter. PUBLIC CAREER. LEGISLATIVE SERVICE: Convention, Talbot County, 1st, 1774; Lower House, Talbot County, 1778 (elected to the 2nd session of the 1777–1778 Assembly to fill vacancy), 1778–1779 (Claims 2). OTHER STATE OFFICES: judge, General Court, 1784–1798; Constitution Ratification Convention, Talbot County, 1788. LOCAL OFFICES: clerk of Indictments, Talbot County, sworn 1759; St. Michael's Parish Vestry, Talbot County, elected 1779 and 1784; visitor, Talbot County School, in office 1783. STANDS ON PUBLIC/PRIVATE ISSUES: signed a nonimportation resolution at a meeting in Annapolis in June 1769. WEALTH DURING LIFETIME. PERSONAL PROPERTY: 24 slaves, 1776; assessed value £1,769.11.3, including 46 slaves and 134.25 oz. plate, 1783; 41 slaves, 1790; assessed value £2,258.12.6, including 78 slaves and 193.5 oz. plate, Talbot County, 1798; 7 slaves, Queen Anne's County, 1798. LAND AT FIRST ELECTION: 1,129 acres in Talbot and Queen Anne's counties (250 acres inherited from his grandfather; 679 acres acquired through his marriage; 200 acres by purchase). SIGNIFICANT CHANGES IN LAND BETWEEN FIRST ELECTION AND DEATH: inherited 965 acres in Talbot County from his father; purchased 111 acres of confiscated British property in Baltimore County, 1783; sold 320 acres in Talbot County, 1784. WEALTH AT

DEATH. DIED: on Saturday morning, November 24, 1798, in Talbot County. PERSONAL PROPERTY: TEV, £8,197.0.0 current money (including 79 slaves, 227.5 oz. plate, a library of law books and other books); FB, £6,235.19.3. LAND: at least 1,828 acres in Talbot, Queen Anne's, and Baltimore counties.

GOLDSBOROUGH, THOMAS (ca. 1728–1793).

BORN: on February 24, ca. 1728, probably at "Otwell," Talbot County; second son. NATIVE: probably third generation. RESIDED: in Talbot County; Upper Choptank District, Caroline County, 1773; Talbot County, by 1792 until death. FAMILY BACKGROUND. FATHER: *Nicholas Goldsborough* (ca. 1689–1766). MOTHER: Sarah (1706–ca. 1772), daughter of *Foster Turbutt* (1679–1720/21). AUNTS: Elizabeth Turbutt (ca. 1708–?), who married in 1724 *Tench Francis* (1701–1758); Anne Turbutt (1715–1766), who married *John Goldsborough* (1711–1778). BROTHERS: Nicholas (1726/27–1777); Robert (1730–1736); Robert (1736/37–1740); and Foster (ca. 1738–1777). SISTERS: Ann (1722/23–ca. 1726); Sarah (1724–?); Ann (1732–?), who married *Edward Oldham* (1709–1773); Rachel (1734–1796); Mary (1740–1812); Elizabeth (1742–1776); and Bridget (1744–1774). FIRST COUSINS: *Howes Goldsborough* (1747–1797); *William Goldsborough* (1750/51–1801); Ann Francis (1727–?), who married *James Tilghman* (1716–1793); Elizabeth Goldsborough (1735–ca. 1786), who married second, *Benson Stainton* (?–ca. 1781); and Mary Goldsborough (1755–1796), who married *Benedict Brice* (1749–1786). MARRIED after 1775 Catherine (ca. 1755–1825), daughter of Griffin Fauntleroy (?–by 1774), of Northumberland County, Virginia, and wife Judith Swan (?–1774). Catherine was a niece of George Washington (1731/32–1799). Her brothers were Griffin, who married Sarah; Capt. John (?–1785), who married (first name unknown) Keene, daughter of William Keene, of Virginia, and died in Kentucky; and Swan. Her sisters were Sarah; Ann, who married first, (first name unknown) Colson, and second, William Keene, of Virginia. CHILDREN. SONS: Thomas, who married on October 2, 1801, Maria, daughter of the Hon. James Thomas, of Annapolis; Griffin (?–by 1791). DAUGHTERS: Sarah Fauntleroy, who married in 1808 Dr. John Barnett; Catherine, who married on June 3, 1798, Dr. Nathaniel Potter (1770–1843), son of *Zabdiel Potter* (?–1793). PRIVATE CAREER. EDUCATION: literate. RELIGIOUS AFFILIATION: Anglican; baptized by Rev. Daniel Maynadier, of St. Peter's Parish, Talbot County. SOCIAL STATUS

AND ACTIVITIES: Esq., 1762. OCCUPATIONAL PROFILE: lawyer, admitted to the following courts: Talbot County in 1752; Queen Anne's County in 1755; Provincial Court in 1765. Probably also a planter. PUBLIC CAREER. LEGISLATIVE SERVICE: Conventions, Caroline County, 1st, 1774, 4th, 1775; Lower House, Caroline County, 1786–1787 (elected, but did not attend). LOCAL OFFICES: St. Peter's Parish Vestry, Talbot County, by 1756–at least 1759, by 1763–at least 1766; commissioner to purchase land for a courthouse and prison, Caroline County, appointed 1773; commissioner of tax, Caroline County, 1777–at least 1782; justice, Orphans' Court, Caroline County, commissioned 1781; judge, Court of Appeals for Tax Assessment, Caroline County, 1786. WEALTH DURING LIFETIME. PERSONAL PROPERTY: assessed value £1,681.0.0, including 32 slaves and 49 oz. plate, 1783; 13 slaves, 1790. LAND AT FIRST ELECTION: 1,042 acres in Queen Anne's and Talbot counties (974 acres from his father, 68 acres by purchase). WEALTH AT DEATH. DIED: on March 9, 1793, in Talbot County. PERSONAL PROPERTY: TEV, £5,059.7.7 current money (including 30 slaves, 60 oz. plate, 11 law books, plus other books); FB, £2,238.9.3. LAND: 1,315 acres in Caroline and Talbot counties. ADDITIONAL COMMENTS: In his will he instructed that his son, Thomas, be educated in mathematics and English grammar and then be apprenticed to a worthy attorney for a minimum of five years.

GOLDSBOROUGH, WILLIAM (1709–1760).

BORN: on Wednesday, July 6, 1709, at "Ashby," Talbot County; fourth son. NATIVE: second generation. RESIDED: on Island Creek, Talbot County; at "Peach Blossom," Talbot County, after 1747. FAMILY BACKGROUND. FATHER: *Robert Goldsborough* (1660–1746). MOTHER: Elizabeth (1678–1719/20), daughter of *Nicholas Greenberry* (1627–1697). UNCLE: *Charles Greenberry* (1672–1713). HALF UNCLE: *Thomas Robins* (1672–1721). AUNT: Ann Greenberry, who married *John Hammond* (ca. 1665–1742/43). BROTHERS: Robert (ca. 1704–1777); Nicholas (ca. 1704–1756); *Charles Goldsborough* (1707–1767); *John Goldsborough* (1711–1778); Greenberry (1713–ca. 1716); Howes (1715–1746); Greenberry (1717–1717); and (first name unknown) (1718–1718). SISTERS: Ann (1698–ca. 1708); Elizabeth (ca. 1700–ca. 1708); and Mary (1702–ca. 1742). FIRST COUSINS: *Nicholas Goldsborough* (ca. 1689–1766); Elizabeth Ridgely (?–1734), who married *Thomas Worthington* (ca. 1691–1753); and Elizabeth Standley, who married second, *Thomas Robins* (1672–1721). NEPHEWS:

Robert Goldsborough IV (1740–1798); *Howes Goldsborough* (1747–1797); *William Goldsborough* (1750/51–1801); and *Robert Goldsborough* (1733–1788). NIECES: Elizabeth Greenberry Goldsborough (ca. 1731–1820), who married *William Ennalls* (?–1785); Elizabeth Goldsborough (ca. 1735–ca. 1786), who married second, *Benson Stainton* (?–ca. 1781); and Mary Goldsborough (1755–1796), who married *Benedict Brice* (1749–1786). MARRIED first, on January 23, 1734/35, Elizabeth (1710–1746), daughter of *Thomas Robins* (1672–1721); half niece of *Robert Goldsborough* (1660–1746). Her brothers were Thomas (1705–1718); William (1707–?); John (1707–?); Lambert (1712–1718); and Standley (1715–1742). Her half brother was *George Robins* (1697–1742). MARRIED second, on September 2, 1747, Henrietta Maria (1707–1771), widow of *George Robins* (1697–1742); daughter of *Richard Tilghman* (1672/73–1738/39); granddaughter of *Philemon Lloyd* (1646–1685); niece of *Edward Lloyd* (1670–1718/19), *Philemon Lloyd* (ca. 1674–1732/33), *James Lloyd* (1679/80–1723), Rebecca Tilghman (?–1725), who married *Simon Wilmer* (ca. 1656–1699), and Margaret Lloyd (1683–1747), who married *Matthew Tilghman Ward* (ca. 1676–1741); half niece of Susanna Bennett (1666–1714), who married first, *John Darnall* (?–1684), and second, *Henry Lowe* (?–1717). Her brothers were Philemon (1704–1724); Richard (1705–1768); *William Tilghman* (1711–1782); *Edward Tilghman* (1713–1786); *James Tilghman* (1716–1793); and *Matthew Tilghman* (1717/18–1790). Her sisters were Mary (1702–1736), who married *James Earle, Jr.* (ca. 1694–1739); Anna Maria (1709–1763), who married first, *William Hemsley* (1703–1736), and second, *Robert Lloyd* (ca. 1712–1770). Her first cousins were *Matthew Tilghman Ward* (ca. 1676–1741); *Lambert Wilmer* (1682–1732); *Simon Wilmer* (1686–1737); *Edward Lloyd* (1711–1770); *Robert Lloyd* (ca. 1712–1770); *Richard Lloyd* (1717–1786); Henrietta Maria Lloyd Chew (?–1765), who married second, *Daniel Dulany* (1685–1753); Henrietta Maria Lloyd (ca. 1711–1748), who married *Samuel Chamberlaine* (1698–1773); Margaret Lloyd (1714–ca. 1785), who married *William Tilghman* (1711–1782); and Anne Lloyd (ca. 1723–1794), who married *Matthew Tilghman* (1717/18–1790). Her nephews were *Michael Earle* (1722–1787); *Richard Tilghman Earle* (1728/29–1788); *William Hemsley* (1736/37–1812); *Richard Tilghman* (1740–1809); *Matthew Tilghman* (1760–ca. 1801); *James Tilghman* (1743–1809); *Peregrine Tilghman* (ca. 1741–1807); *James Tilghman, Jr.* (ca. 1748–1796); and *William Tilghman* (1756–

1827). Her nieces were Anna Maria Earle (1725–1795), who married *Thomas Ringgold* (1715–1772); Henrietta Maria Earle (1730–1767), who married *William Hemsley* (1736/37–1812); Deborah Lloyd, who married *Peregrine Tilghman* (ca. 1741–1807); Margaret Tilghman (1742–1817), who married *Charles Carroll, Barrister* (1723–1783); Anna Maria Tilghman, who married *William Hemsley* (1736/37–1812); and Elizabeth Tilghman, who married *James Lloyd* (1745–1820). CHILDREN. SONS: Greenbury (?–died young); William (?–died young). STEPSON: Thomas Robins (1740–1762). DAUGHTERS: Henrietta Maria (?–died young); Elizabeth H. (1743–died young). STEPDAUGHTERS: Anna Maria Robins (1732–1806), who married *Henry Hollyday* (ca. 1725–1789); Margaret Robins (1734–1808), who married *William Hayward* (?–1791); Henrietta Maria Robins (1736–1791), who married *James Lloyd Chamberlaine* (1732–1783); Susannah Robins (1738–?), who married first, Thomas Chamberlaine (1731–1764), and second, Robert Lloyd Nicols; and Elizabeth Robins (1742–by 1764). PRIVATE CAREER. EDUCATION: literate. RELIGIOUS AFFILIATION: Anglican, St. Peter's Parish, Talbot County. SOCIAL STATUS AND ACTIVITIES: Gent., 1740; Esq. and Hon. at death. OCCUPATIONAL PROFILE: attorney, but actively practiced law only briefly; admitted to the bar to practice law in November 1733; admitted to the following courts: Dorchester County by November 1733; Queen Anne's County in November 1733; Somerset County in November 1733; Talbot County in November 1733; Provincial Court in October 1734. Planter. PUBLIC CAREER. LEGISLATIVE SERVICE: Upper House, 1755–1757 (appointed during the 2nd session), 1757–1758, 1758–1760 (died before the 3rd session). OTHER PROVINCIAL OFFICES: justice, Provincial Court, 1754–at least 1757; judge, Assize Court, Eastern Shore, appointed 1754; Council, 1755–1760 (appointed and qualified on March 11, 1755); judge, Court of Vice-Admiralty, appointed 1756. LOCAL OFFICES: clerk of Indictments, Somerset County, sworn 1733; St. Peter's Parish Vestry, Talbot County, elected 1743 and 1747; trustee, charity work school, St. Peter's Parish, Talbot County, elected 1750. MILITARY SERVICE: colonel, militia, 1755. WEALTH DURING LIFETIME. PERSONAL PROPERTY: his father left William and his brother *Charles Goldsborough* (1707–1767) £146.4.6 sterling, then in the hands of John Hanbury, a London merchant, to be equally divided according to the terms of his will, 1746. LAND AT FIRST ELECTION: 2,013 acres in Talbot, Queen Anne's, and Dorchester counties

(1,000 acres through his second marriage; 1,013 acres by purchase); also controlled 5,303 acres in Talbot, Queen Anne's, and Dorchester counties for the heirs of *George Robins* (1697–1742). ADDITIONAL COMMENTS: William's father did not leave his son any land, because, as he stated in his will, William had already been blessed with a handsome estate. SIGNIFICANT CHANGES IN LAND BETWEEN FIRST ELECTION AND DEATH: sold 1,000 acres in Queen Anne's County, 1757. WEALTH AT DEATH. DIED: on Sunday morning, September 21, 1760, at "Peach Blossom," his seat near Talbot County Courthouse; buried at "Peach Blossom," Talbot County; his health had begun to fail ca. 1756. PERSONAL PROPERTY: requested no appraisal of his estate; at least 6 slaves mentioned in his will. LAND: 1,013 acres in Talbot and Dorchester counties; still controlled 5,303 acres in Talbot, Queen Anne's, and Dorchester counties for the heirs of *George Robins* (1697–1742). ADDITIONAL COMMENTS: William was held in high esteem by Gov. Horatio Sharpe, who wrote of him, "No person in the Country had a better character than this Gent'n. . . ."

GOLDSBOROUGH, WILLIAM (1750/51–1801). BORN: on Sunday evening, March 17, 1750/51, in Talbot County; third son. NATIVE: third generation. RESIDED: on the St. Michael's River, Talbot County. FAMILY BACKGROUND. FATHER: Robert Goldsborough (ca. 1704–1777), of "Myrtle Grove," Talbot County; a justice of Talbot County from 1734 to 1741 and from 1749 to 1766; son of *Robert Goldsborough* (1660–1746). MOTHER: Mary Anne (1711–1794), widow of John Robins (?–1739), a lawyer; daughter of *Foster Turbutt* (1679–1720/21). UNCLES: *Charles Goldsborough* (1707–1767); *William Goldsborough* (1709–1760); and *John Goldsborough* (1711–1778). AUNTS: Sarah Turbutt (1706–1773), who married *Nicholas Goldsborough* (ca. 1689–1766); Elizabeth Turbutt (1708–?), who married *Tench Francis* (1701–1758); Anne Turbutt (1715–1766), who married *John Goldsborough* (1711–1778). BROTHER: *Howes Goldsborough* (1747–1797). HALF BROTHER: *Robert Goldsborough IV* (1740–1798). SISTERS: Elizabeth (1745–1748); Mary Anne Turbutt (1752–1811), who never married. FIRST COUSINS: *Thomas Goldsborough* (ca. 1728–1793); *Robert Goldsborough* (1733–1788); Ann Francis (1727–?), who married *James Tilghman* (1716–1793); Elizabeth Greenberry Goldsborough (ca. 1731–1820), who married *William Ennalls* (?–1785); Ann Goldsborough (1732–?), who married *Edward Oldham* (1709–1773); Elizabeth Golds-

borough (ca. 1735–ca. 1786), who married second, *Benson Stainton* (?–ca. 1781); and Mary Goldsborough (1755–1796), who married *Benedict Brice* (1749–1786). ADDITIONAL COMMENTS: his father's first wife was Sarah (?–1740), daughter of Rev. Henry Nicols (1687–ca. 1749), rector of St. Michael's Parish, Talbot County. PRIVATE CAREER. EDUCATION: literate. RELIGIOUS AFFILIATION: Anglican, St. Michael's Parish, Talbot County. SOCIAL STATUS AND ACTIVITIES: Gent., 1781; Esq., 1783. OCCUPATIONAL PROFILE: probably a planter. PUBLIC CAREER. LEGISLATIVE SERVICE: Lower House, Talbot County, 1778 (elected to the 3rd session of the 1777–1778 Assembly to fill vacancy), 1779 (elected to the 2nd session of the 1778–1779 Assembly to fill vacancy; Claims 2; Tax Commissioners 3). LOCAL OFFICES: trustee for the poor, Talbot County, in office 1774; justice, Talbot County, 1779–at least 1785; justice, Orphans' Court, Talbot County, 1779–at least 1784; commissioner of tax, Talbot County, appointed 1786; trustee of the Alms- and Workhouse, Talbot County, in office 1789; St. Michael's Parish Vestry, Talbot County, in office 1791–1796. WEALTH DURING LIFETIME. PERSONAL PROPERTY: his father left him £300 toward cost of building a house, 1777; assessed value £712.11.8, including 14 slaves and 68 oz. plate, 1783; 22 slaves, 1790; assessed value £900.6.8, including 26 slaves and 71 oz. plate, 1798. LAND AT FIRST ELECTION: 736 acres in Talbot County (all inherited from his father). SIGNIFICANT CHANGES IN LAND BETWEEN FIRST ELECTION AND DEATH: inherited one-third of a tract in Queen Anne's County from his mother and received another one-third of the same tract from his sister Mary Anne, for a total increase of 279 acres between 1794 and 1801. ADDITIONAL COMMENTS: William was heir to his mother's estate with his brother *Howes Goldsborough* (1747–1797) and his sister Mary Anne Turbutt Goldsborough. WEALTH AT DEATH. DIED: on January 23, 1801, in Talbot County; buried at "Ashby," Talbot County. LAND: at least 1,100 acres in Talbot and Queen Anne's counties.

GOLDSMITH, GEORGE (?–1666). IMMIGRATED: in 1656 as a free adult with his wife and son. RESIDED: in Baltimore County. ADDITIONAL COMMENTS: may be either the George Goldsmith who transported his wife, three children, and eight others to Virginia in 1650 and settled on the north side of the Rappahannock River, or his son. FAMILY BACKGROUND. UNCLE: *Samuel Goldsmith* (?–1671). BROTHERS: Matthew; Thomas, from Isle of Wight County, Virginia. MARRIED Mary Collet, who subsequently married Capt. Samuel Boston. CHILDREN. SON: George (?–1692), a justice of Baltimore County from 1686 to 1688, who married Martha, daughter of Edward Beadle. Martha Goldsmith subsequently married *John Hall* (ca. 1658–1737). DAUGHTERS: Elizabeth (?–by 1677); Mary, who probably married Edward Beadle. PRIVATE CAREER. EDUCATION: literate. RELIGIOUS AFFILIATION: probably a Protestant. OCCUPATIONAL PROFILE: planter. PUBLIC CAREER. LEGISLATIVE SERVICE: Lower House, Baltimore County, 1659/60. LOCAL OFFICES: justice, Baltimore County, 1664, 1665–1666; sheriff, Baltimore County, 1664–1665; deputy surveyor, Baltimore County, 1664–1666. MILITARY SERVICE: captain, 1664–1666. STANDS ON PUBLIC/PRIVATE ISSUES: supported Fendall's Rebellion, 1659/60–1660, but was pardoned in 1661. WEALTH DURING LIFETIME. LAND AT FIRST ELECTION: over 500 acres (patented 500 acres in 1658/59). WEALTH AT DEATH. DIED: will probated on July 20, 1666. PERSONAL PROPERTY: TEV, 92,555 pounds of tobacco (including 4 slaves and 5 servants). LAND: over 2,150 acres.

GOLDSMITH, SAMUEL (?–1671). BORN: probably in England. IMMIGRATED: in 1658 as a free adult with his wife and two daughters. RESIDED: in Baltimore County. FAMILY BACKGROUND. NEPHEW: *George Goldsmith* (?–1666). MARRIED Johanna. CHILDREN. DAUGHTERS: Elizabeth; Blanche, who married *George Wells* (?–1696); and Susannah, who married *George Utie* (?–1678). PRIVATE CAREER. EDUCATION: literate. RELIGIOUS AFFILIATION: probably a Protestant. SOCIAL STATUS AND ACTIVITIES: brought four servants with him to the colony. OCCUPATIONAL PROFILE: planter. PUBLIC CAREER. LEGISLATIVE SERVICE: Lower House, Baltimore County, 1659/60, 1663–1664. MILITARY SERVICE: major, 1658/59–1660, 1661–?. STANDS ON PUBLIC/PRIVATE ISSUES: supported Fendall's Rebellion, 1659/60–1660, but was pardoned in 1661. WEALTH DURING LIFETIME. LAND AT FIRST ELECTION: ca. 800 acres. WEALTH AT DEATH. DIED: will probated on October 6, 1671. PERSONAL PROPERTY: TEV, 86,076 pounds of tobacco. LAND: ca. 800 acres.

GORDON, ROBERT (ca. 1676–1753). BORN: ca. 1676. IMMIGRATED: ca. 1719 probably from Scotland. RESIDED: in Annapolis, Anne Arundel County. FAMILY BACKGROUND. COUSIN: James Gordon, of Cecil County, merchant. CHILDREN. DAUGHTER: Agnes (?–1759). PRIVATE CAREER. EDUCATION: literate. RELIGIOUS AFFILIATION: Anglican, St. Anne's Parish, Anne Arundel County. SOCIAL STATUS AND ACTIVITIES: Esq., 1724; a founder of the Tuesday Club, 1745; member of the Red House Club. ADDITIONAL COMMENTS: apparently a member of the Gordon clan in Maryland, Scotland, and Barbados; described by *Alexander Hamilton* (1712–1756) in the Tuesday Club minutes as a quiet man with an "excellent muscial voice." OCCUPATIONAL PROFILE: merchant; officeholder. PUBLIC CAREER. LEGISLATIVE SERVICE: Lower House, Annapolis, 1725–1727 (Accounts 4), 1728–1731, 1732–1734 (election voided; re-elected to the 1st session; Accounts 1–Cv; discharged during the convention for accepting an office "of trust and profit" from the government), 1734/35–1737 (Accounts 1, Cv, 2–4), 1738 (elected to fill vacancy), 1739–1741, 1742–1744, 1745, 1745/46–1748, 1749–1751, 1751–1752 (died before the 3rd session). OTHER PROVINCIAL OFFICES: justice, Provincial Court, 1732–at least 1751 (quorum, 1734–at least 1751); commissioner of the Paper Currency Office, 1733–1753; judge, Assize Court, Western Shore, in office 1739–1740. LOCAL OFFICES: St. Anne's Parish Vestry, Anne Arundel County, in office 1723–1727; alderman, Annapolis, 1726–1728; justice, Anne Arundel County, 1727–at least 1731; judge, Court of Oyer and Terminer and Gaol Delivery, Anne Arundel County, commissioned 1731, 1734, 1736, 1738/39, and 1751. MILITARY SERVICE: captain, by 1723. WEALTH DURING LIFETIME. LAND AT FIRST ELECTION: 5.5 acres adjoining Annapolis, a strip of valuable land along the Market Space in Annapolis, and a 76-year lease on a lot in Annapolis (on which he built a house). SIGNIFICANT CHANGES IN LAND BETWEEN FIRST ELECTION AND DEATH: acquired additional land in Annapolis and 1 lot in Baltimore Town, plus ca. 150 acres in Anne Arundel County in the late 1720s and 1730s; sold or mortgaged the lot in Baltimore Town and all of his Annapolis land, except the lot where his house stood, between 1739 and 1751. WEALTH AT DEATH. DIED: on September 9, 1753, in Anne Arundel County, of "gout in his lungs." PERSONAL PROPERTY: TEV, at least £993.12.3, current money (including 19 slaves and books). LAND: ca. 150 acres in Anne Arundel County, plus a lease on 1 lot in Annapolis.

GOUGH (GOFF), HARRY DORSEY (ca. 1745–1808). BORN: on January 28, ca. 1745, in Anne Arundel County. NATIVE: second generation. RESIDED: at "Perry Hall," Baltimore County. FAMILY BACKGROUND. FATHER: Thomas Gough, Gent. (?–by 1760), immigrated from England by

1733; resided in Anne Arundel County. By 1746 he was in debt to several creditors, including Onorio Razolini and Philpott & Lee, to whom he was bound for over £92 sterling, plus interest. He was forced to sell his personal property (including household items, livestock, and crops) to pay his accounts; he apparently held no land in his own name. MOTHER: Sophia (1707–?), daughter of Caleb Dorsey (1685–1742) and wife Eleanor Warfield (?–1752); Sophia inherited the plantation on which she and her husband lived from her brother, *Edward Dorsey* (1718–1760). UNCLE: *Edward Dorsey* (1718–1760). AUNT: Mary Dorsey (1725–ca. 1787), who married *John Ridgely* (?–1771). FIRST COUSINS: *Charles Ridgely, of John* (?–ca. 1787); *Thomas Dorsey* (?–1790); Achsah Dorsey (1746–1799), who married *Ephraim Howard* (1745–1788); Rebecca Dorsey (1739–1812), who married *Charles Ridgely* (1733–1790); Eleanor Dorsey (ca. 1739–1825), who married *John Hall* (1729–1797); Eleanor Dorsey, who married *Upton Sheredine* (1740–1800); Mary Dorsey (?–1816), who married *John Weems* (1727–1794); Deborah Ridgely (1749–1817), who married *John Sterett* (1750/51–1787); and Mary Ridgely (?–1804), who married *Benjamin Nicholson* (?–1792). MARRIED on May 2, 1771, Prudence (1755–1822), daughter of John Carnan and wife Achsah Ridgely Holliday; stepdaughter of Daniel Chamier; granddaughter of *Charles Ridgely* (?–1772); niece of *Charles Ridgely* (1733–1790), *John Ridgely* (?–1771), and Rachel Ridgely, who married *Darby Lux* (?–1795). Her brother was Charles Ridgely of Hampton (1760–1829), governor of Maryland from 1816 to 1819. Her half brother was John Robert Holliday. Her sister was Elizabeth, who married Thomas Bond Onion. Her first cousins were Deborah Ridgely (1749–1817), who married *John Sterett* (1750/51–1787); Mary Ridgely (?–1804), who married *Benjamin Nicholson* (?–1792); *Charles Ridgely, of John* (?–ca. 1787); and Rachel Goodwin, who married *Jesse Hollingsworth* (1732/33–1810). CHILDREN. DAUGHTER: Sophia (1772–1816), who married in 1787 *James (Maccubbin) Carroll* (1761–1832). PRIVATE CAREER. EDUCATION: literate. RELIGIOUS AFFILIATION: Anglican, until he converted to Methodism in 1775. In his journal Francis Asbury mentioned that he was "treated with great kindness" at Gough's home where he often visited, and commended the religious fervor of the Gough family. Gough and his wife were members of the first Methodist class in Baltimore and Gough occasionally preached. SOCIAL STATUS AND ACTIVITIES: Esq.; president of the Maryland Society for Promoting Agriculture, 1786. OCCUPA-TIONAL PROFILE: land developer and speculator, primarily in Baltimore City; merchant. PUBLIC CAREER. LEGISLATIVE SERVICE: Lower House, Baltimore County, 1787–1788, 1790, 1791–1792, 1792. LOCAL OFFICES: justice, Baltimore County, commissioned 1768 and 1769; St. Paul's Parish Vestry, Baltimore County, in office 1772–1774; Committee of Observation, Middle River Lower Hundred, Baltimore County, elected 1774. WEALTH DURING LIFETIME. PERSONAL PROPERTY: assessed value £871.5.0, not including his Baltimore Town property, 1783. LAND AT FIRST ELECTION: ca. 4,300 acres in Baltimore and Harford counties, plus 5 lots in Baltimore Town (all through personal acquisition). With his wife and her family, Gough was a leasor of some 40 lots in Baltimore Town, part of his father-in-law's estate. SIGNIFICANT CHANGES IN LAND BETWEEN FIRST ELECTION AND DEATH: In addition to his dealings as part of the Carnan-Onion family, Gough was involved in more than 150 land transactions in Baltimore City and Baltimore County between 1768 and 1807, two-thirds of which occurred after 1787. He held mortgages and assignments of leases, but his major activity was the development of land in Baltimore City, principally on Charles, St. Paul, Light, and Baltimore streets. He usually sold lots, or parts of lots, outright, but in some cases he leased lots, retaining the title and ground rents. An example of his business transactions was the development of a 475-acre tract adjoining Baltimore Town, named "Huntington," patented by John and Achsah Carnan in 1761. In the early 1780s the land was divided into lots and leased out by Gough and his wife and her sister and brother-in-law, Elizabeth and Thomas Bond Onion. Gough purchased the property in 1790 and sold it off in small parcels over the next 15 years. His Harford County land was sold before his death, but he continued to deal in Baltimore County land throughout the period. WEALTH AT DEATH. DIED: on May 5, 1808, in Baltimore County. PERSONAL PROPERTY: TEV, $107,289.75; FB, $39,180.62. LAND: ca. 2,500 acres in Baltimore County and lots in Baltimore City, primarily on Light Street.

GOVANE, WILLIAM (1716/17–1768). BORN: on February 4, 1716/17, in Anne Arundel County; only child. NATIVE: probably second generation. RESIDED: in Anne Arundel County; Baltimore County, 1750. FAMILY BACKGROUND. FATHER: James Govane (?–1739), who married first, Mary, widow of Thomas Homewood (?–1709). MOTHER: Elizabeth, widow of William Hammond (?–

1710/11); daughter of William Cockey and wife Sarah. HALF BROTHERS: *Thomas Hammond* (1693–?); Mordecai Hammond (1695–1734), who married Frances Lillingston; Benjamin Hammond (1706/7–?), who married first, Sarah Eagle, and second, Margaret Talbot; Lawrence Hammond (1709–1784), who married first, Ruth Greniffe, and second, Margaret Hughes; and William Hammond (1710/11–?), who married Mary Merriken. HALF SISTERS: Sarah Hammond (1691/2–?); Susannah Hammond (1697–?), who married Carpenter Lillingston; and Jane Hammond (1700–1703). MARRIED between July 1740 and August 1741, Anne (1716–1785), widow of Thomas Homewood (1704–1739); daughter of *Charles Hammond* (1692/93–1772); niece of *Philip Hammond* (1697–1760), Ruth Hammond, who married second, *Thomas Franklin* (ca. 1706–1787), and Comfort Stimpson, who married *John Dorsey* (ca. 1682–?). Her first cousins were *John Hammond* (1735–1784); *Rezin Hammond* (1745–1809); *Matthias Hammond* (1740–1786); *Nathan Hammond* (1731–1811); *Rezin Hammond* (?–1783); and *John Hammond Dorsey* (1718–1774). ADDITIONAL COMMENTS: In 1750 Govane was accused of ill-treating his wife Anne and mismanaging Thomas Homewood's estate worth approximately £3,000 current money. By a Chancery Court decree in 1750 Anne was granted a separation and Govane was denied any control over the Homewood estate. Govane then moved to Baltimore County where he lived with Mary Salisbury (?–ca. 1768), by whom he had two children. CHILDREN. NATURAL SON: James Govane. STEPSON: Charles Homewood (1734–?), who married Elizabeth Wright. NATURAL DAUGHTER: Mary Govane. STEPDAUGHTERS: Ann Homewood (1736–?), who married Joseph Marriott; Rebecca Homewood (1738–?), who married (first name unknown) Bishop. PRIVATE CAREER. EDUCATION: literate. RELIGIOUS AFFILIATION: Anglican. SOCIAL STATUS AND ACTIVITIES: Gent., 1752. OCCUPATIONAL PROFILE: merchant, by 1739. Active in trade in the West Indies where he often traveled on business. PUBLIC CAREER. LEGISLATIVE SERVICE: Lower House, Baltimore County, 1751–1754 (election of entire county delegation voided on December 12, 1751, because of illegal actions of the sheriff; reelected to the 2nd session), 1754–1757 (Arms and Ammunition 5, 6; Bills of Credit 5; Accounts 6), 1757–1758 (Accounts 1, Cv, 2), 1758–1761 (Accounts Cv 1, 1, Cv 2, 2, 3, Cv 3; Public Offices Cv 1, 1, Cv 2, 2, 3, Cv 3). LOCAL OFFICES: constable, Broad Neck Hundred, Anne Arundel County, appointed 1749; St. Margaret's Parish Vestry, Anne

Arundel County, in office 1750. JURY SERVICE: grand jury, Anne Arundel County, in office 1743; jury, Anne Arundel County, in office 1748. MILITARY SERVICE: captain, by 1754. WEALTH DURING LIFETIME. PERSONAL PROPERTY: used the profits of his wife's dower of £1,700 current money as widow of Thomas Homewood, and controlled the Homewood children's portion of their father's estate until 1750 when he was denied that right by the Chancery Court. LAND AT FIRST ELECTION: 540 acres in Baltimore County (all by personal acquisition). Lost any legal claim to his portion of the Homewood estate of ca. 2,000 acres in Anne Arundel County in 1752. SIGNIFICANT CHANGES IN LAND BETWEEN FIRST ELECTION AND DEATH: consolidated his 540-acre holdings with adjoining vacant lands to obtain an 810-acre patent in Baltimore County in 1755; purchased an additional 400 acres in Baltimore County in 1757. WEALTH AT DEATH. DIED: in September 1768 in Baltimore County. PERSONAL PROPERTY: TEV, £1,405.8.0 current money (including 39 slaves, plate, and books); FB, estate overpaid £127.18.0. LAND: 1,210 acres in Baltimore County, all of which were devised to his son James.

GRAHAME (GRAHAM), CHARLES (ca. 1721–1779). BORN: ca. 1721 in Scotland. IMMIGRATED: by 1751 with his brother. RESIDED: in Lower Marlboro, Calvert County. FAMILY BACKGROUND. FATHER: John Grahame. MOTHER: Ann Campbell. BROTHER: David (?–ca. 1754), of Queen Anne's County, who married Charlotte Hyde, a cousin of Lord Baltimore. MARRIED ca. 1753 Aesneath Hutton. CHILDREN. SON: *John Grahame* (1760–1833). DAUGHTER: Aesneath (Asenath, Azenath) (by 1758–?); Ann (?–by 1790), who married *Thomas Mackall* (1751–1799). PRIVATE CAREER. EDUCATION: literate. RELIGIOUS AFFILIATION: Protestant. SOCIAL STATUS AND ACTIVITIES: Mr., 1753; Gent., 1769. OCCUPATIONAL PROFILE: merchant, in partnership with John Wardrop, 1753; member of the merchant firm of William Lux & Company, 1767. Other partners in the firm were *William Lux* (ca. 1730–1778), James Dick, and William Lyon. Before the Revolution, Grahame was the principal agent for James Russell, an important London merchant. He supervised both Russell's extensive mercantile interests in Maryland and his share of the Nottingham Ironworks in Baltimore County. PUBLIC CAREER. LEGISLATIVE SERVICE: Lower House, Calvert County, 1762–1763 (Bills of Credit 1, 2), 1765–1766 (Bills of Credit 2, 4; Public Offices 3; Laws to Expire 4), 1768–1770 (Claims 1–4), 1771 (Claims); Convention, Calvert County,

9th, 1776 (Elections, Claims, Loan Office); Senate, Western Shore, Term of 1776–1781: 1777 (elected on March 18, 1777, to fill vacancy in the 1777 Assembly; qualified on March 25, 1777; appointed to the Loan Office Committee on April 14, 1777 to replace Turbutt Wright), 1777–1778, 1778–1779 (did not serve; died before the 3rd session). OTHER PROVINCIAL OFFICES: naval officer, Pocomoke, in office 1754–1755; surveyor general, Eastern Shore, in office 1754–1755; 5th Council of Safety, Western Shore, 1776–1777 (declined). LOCAL OFFICES: sheriff, Calvert County, 1755–1756; justice, Calvert County, 1756–1779 (quorum, 1766–1779); trustee for building All Saints' Church, Calvert County, in office 1774; justice, Orphans' Court, Calvert County, 1777–1779. STANDS ON PUBLIC/PRIVATE ISSUES: served on a committee of the General Assembly to protest the Stamp Act, 1765; protested the Fee Bill promulgated by Gov. Robert Eden in 1772. WEALTH DURING LIFETIME. LAND AT FIRST ELECTION: 1,044 acres in Calvert and Frederick counties (195 acres in Frederick County held jointly with John Cooke); jointly held a mortgage with David Arnold on a lot in Lower Marlboro, Calvert County. SIGNIFICANT CHANGES IN LAND BETWEEN FIRST ELECTION AND DEATH: obtained 103 acres in Anne Arundel County through a defaulted mortgage, 1763; ca. 2,906 acres in Baltimore County by purchase and patent of resurveys in 1776 (this was his share of the land held originally in partnership with William Lux and James Dick). WEALTH AT DEATH. DIED: in 1779, probably in Calvert County. PERSONAL PROPERTY: size of estate unknown. LAND: at least 952 acres in Calvert and Anne Arundel counties, and possibly 2,906 acres in Baltimore County.

GRAHAME (GRAHAM), JOHN (1760–1833). BORN: on August 8, 1760, in Lower Marlboro, Calvert County; only surviving son. NATIVE: second generation. RESIDED: in Lower Marlboro, Calvert County, until 1788; "Rose Hill Farm," Frederick County, 1788–1833. FAMILY BACKGROUND. FATHER: *Charles Grahame* (ca. 1721–1779). MOTHER: Aesneath Hutton. SISTERS: Aesneath (Asenath, Azenath) (by 1758–?); Ann (?–by 1790), who married *Thomas Mackall* (1751–1799). MARRIED in January 1788 Anne Jennings (1759–1835), daughter of *Thomas Johnson* (1732–1819); granddaughter of both Thomas Johnson (1702–1777), of Calvert County, and Thomas Jennings (?–1759), of Annapolis; niece of *Baker Johnson* (1747–1811). Her brothers were Thomas Jennings; James; and Joshua. Her sisters were Elizabeth; Rebecca; and

Dorcas. CHILDREN. SON: Thomas J. (1794–1827), who married his first cousin Caroline Worthington Goldsborough (1803–1831), daughter of *Baker Johnson* (1747–1811). DAUGHTER: Ann Rebecca (1798–1816). PRIVATE CAREER. EDUCATION: attended, but did not graduate from, the College of New Jersey (later Princeton University), 1777. RELIGIOUS AFFILIATION: Anglican, All Saints' Parish, Frederick County. SOCIAL STATUS AND ACTIVITIES: Esq., 1795. OCCUPATIONAL PROFILE: merchant in the firm of John Graham & Company, Calvert County, 1785; president of the Frederick County Bank, 1818–1833; planter. PUBLIC CAREER. LEGISLATIVE SERVICE: Lower House, Calvert County, 1783, 1784 (Claims), 1785 (Claims), 1786–1787, 1787–1788 (Claims 1); Senate, Western Shore, Term of 1796–1801: 1796, 1797, 1798, 1799, 1800. OTHER STATE OFFICE: associate justice, Fifth District Court, appointed 1793. LOCAL OFFICES: justice, Calvert County, 1782–1787 ("desires to be left out"); justice, Orphans' Court, Calvert County, commissioned 1786 and 1787; All Saints' Parish Vestry, Frederick County, in office 1812; Maryland Senate elector, Frederick County, elected 1816. MILITARY SERVICE: 2nd lieutenant, Calvert County Militia, commissioned 1778. WEALTH DURING LIFETIME. PERSONAL PROPERTY: assessed value £117.0.0, including 3 slaves, 1783; 11 slaves, 1790; 19 slaves, 1800; 29 slaves, 1810; 16 slaves, 1825; 6 slaves, 1833. LAND AT FIRST ELECTION: at least 263 acres in Calvert County (inherited from his father). SIGNIFICANT CHANGES IN LAND BETWEEN FIRST ELECTION AND DEATH: obtained 225 acres through his wife's dower, "Rose Hill Farm," Frederick County, 1788; owned 1 lot in Cumberland, Allegany County, 1793; obtained 2,419 acres in Frederick County, 1793–1829 (136 acres as a gift from his father-in-law; 849 acres probably inherited from his sister). He sold 1,298 acres in Calvert and Frederick counties, 1816–1829. All of his remaining land was mortgaged in 1829 and remained so until his death. He sold 687 acres of the mortgaged land in Frederick County in 1830. ADDITIONAL COMMENTS: Grahame suffered severe financial reverses later in his life. In the mid-1820s he was forced to start selling slaves and land. In 1829 he took out a $20,000 mortgage on "Rose Hill," continued his land sales, and mortgaged his remaining slaves and stock. WEALTH AT DEATH. DIED: on March 20, 1833, at "Rose Hill Farm," Frederick County. PERSONAL PROPERTY: TEV, $1,524.72 (including 6 slaves, all of whom were mortgaged for the sum of $5,800.00); FB, $1,145.68 as recorded in the final accounting of the estate. LAND: probably ca. 444 acres in Frederick County, all of which appeared to be still mortgaged. ADDITIONAL COMMENTS: after the final accounting of the estate, his wife sold his entire assets to pay his outstanding debts. Although $25,000 was received from the sales, only $3,662 was left after settlement with his creditors.

GRAVES, RICHARD (1739–1792). BORN: on December 18, 1739, in Kent County; younger son. NATIVE: at least second generation. RESIDED: at "Buck Neck," District 3, Kent County. FAMILY BACKGROUND. FATHER: William Graves (?–1751). MOTHER: Sarah Hynson (?–1773). BROTHER: William Hynson (1737–?). SISTERS: Mary (1742–?), who married Dr. Thomas Van Dyke; Elizabeth (1746–?). MARRIED Mary, daughter of *John Gresham* (ca. 1703–ca. 1752). Her brothers were *Richard Gresham* (?–1780); John (ca. 1742–ca. 1772); and Thomas (probably born after 1750–?). Her sister was Sarah (1730–?). CHILDREN. SONS: William; Richard. DAUGHTERS: Mary, who married (first name unknown) Crockett; Sarah, who married (first name unknown) Clarkson. PRIVATE CAREER. EDUCATION: literate. RELIGIOUS AFFILIATION: Anglican, Emmanuel Church, Chester Parish, Kent County. SOCIAL STATUS AND ACTIVITIES: Gent., 1775; Esq., 1778. OCCUPATIONAL PROFILE: farmer. PUBLIC CAREER. LEGISLATIVE SERVICE: Lower House, Kent County, 1784 (discharged on November 24, 1784, for serving as a field officer at the time of first election; reelected and seated), 1785. LOCAL OFFICE: justice, Kent County, 1782–1792. MILITARY SERVICE: field officer, 1784; colonel, 1792. WEALTH DURING LIFETIME. PERSONAL PROPERTY: assessed value £3,600.0.0, including 45 slaves and 100 oz. plate, 1783. LAND AT FIRST ELECTION: 2,295 acres in Kent and Harford counties (340 acres from father, 393 acres from mother). WEALTH AT DEATH. DIED: between September 24 and October 15, 1792, in Kent County. PERSONAL PROPERTY: TEV, £2,833.6.4 current money (including 36 slaves and 8 books); FB, £1,591.11.1. LAND: 1,006 acres in Kent, Queen Anne's, and Harford counties, plus 4 houses and lots in Chestertown, Kent County; owned land and fisheries in North Carolina.

GRAY, FRANCIS (?–1667). BORN: probably in England. IMMIGRATED: by 1637. RESIDED: in St. Mary's County; moved to Virginia, 1647. MARRIED in 1638 Alice Moreman. PRIVATE CAREER. RELIGIOUS AFFILIATION: Protestant. SOCIAL STATUS AND ACTIVITIES: no title on arrival; probably a tenant on land owned by Leonard Calvert, 1643.

OCCUPATIONAL PROFILE: carpenter. PUBLIC CAREER. LEGISLATIVE SERVICE: Assembly, present 1637/38, St. Mary's County, 1638/39, St. George's Hundred, St. Mary's County, 1640. STANDS ON PUBLIC/PRIVATE ISSUES: assisted the rebels during Ingle's Rebellion, which probably accounts for his subsequent removal to Virginia. WEALTH DURING LIFETIME. LAND AT FIRST ELECTION: sold rights to 500 acres, 1650/51. WEALTH AT DEATH. DIED: in 1667. LAND: probably 1,000 acres patented in Virginia, 1654.

GRAY, JOSEPH (?–1724). BORN: probably elder son. IMMIGRATED: by 1678, probably as a minor with his mother and siblings. RESIDED: in Coventry Parish, Somerset County. FAMILY BACKGROUND. STEPFATHER: probably Thomas Jones, who served as sheriff, justice, and militia captain in Somerset County. MOTHER: probably Jane Gray Jones. ADDITIONAL COMMENTS: probably the same Joseph Gray for whom Jane Gray Jones claimed rights in 1679/80, as well as for her other three children. BROTHER: probably James. SISTERS: probably Mary; Elizabeth. MARRIED first, by 1687 Elizabeth. MARRIED second, by 1692 Mary. MARRIED third, Elizabeth. CHILDREN. SONS: Thomas (1687–?); Wescott (1692–?). DAUGHTERS: Jane Pittman (1689–?), who married *Peter Dent* (ca. 1665–1710/11); Jemima (1692–?). PRIVATE CAREER. EDUCATION: literate. RELIGIOUS AFFILIATION: Protestant. OCCUPATIONAL PROFILE: planter; contractor; commissioned to build new pillory, 1708/9. PUBLIC CAREER. LEGISLATIVE SERVICE: Lower House, Somerset County, 1704–1707. LOCAL OFFICE: justice, Somerset County, 1707–1724 (quorum, by 1715–1724). STANDS ON PUBLIC/PRIVATE ISSUES: called before the Somerset County Court for speaking against the justices, 1698/99. WEALTH DURING LIFETIME. LAND AT FIRST ELECTION: patented 600 acres with James Gray, 1678; ca. 450 acres, 1704. WEALTH AT DEATH. DIED: ca. November 1724. PERSONAL PROPERTY: TEV, £434.15.3 (including 13 slaves); FB, £255.3.3. LAND: probably 550 acres.

GRAY, JOSEPH COX (?–1764). BORN: of age by 1742. NATIVE: possibly. RESIDED: in Dorchester County. FAMILY BACKGROUND. MOTHER: possibly Elizabeth Lemee (?–ca. 1736), of Dorchester County. MARRIED first, by 1741 Sarah (?–by 1745), daughter of *Govert Lookerman* (ca. 1681–1728); granddaughter of both *Jacob Lookerman* (1652–1730) and *Roger Woolford* (?–ca. 1701/2); niece of *Roger Woolford* (1670–1730), Mary Woolford (1663–1740), who married *Henry Hooper* (ca. 1643–1720), Elizabeth Woolford (1664–1738), who married first, *Thomas Ennalls* (?–1718), and second, *William Holland* (?–1732), and Mary Lookerman, who married third, *Francis Allen* (?–1745). Her brothers were Jacob (?–ca. 1741); Govert (?–1753). Her sisters were Elizabeth; Mary (?–ca. 1772). Her first cousins were *Thomas Woolford* (ca. 1699–ca. 1750/51); *Henry Hooper* (ca. 1687–1767); *Jacob Hindman* (by 1713–1766); *William Allen* (?–1792); Rosannah Woolford; Mary Hooper (?–ca. 1757), who married second, *John Rider* (1686–1739/40); Anne Hooper (?–1761), who married *John Broome* (1676–ca. 1738/39); and *James Woolford* (ca. 1736–ca. 1783). Her nephews were *Thomas Ennalls* (?–by 1783); *Henry Ennalls* (ca. 1741–by 1788). Her niece was Margaret Ennalls (?–by 1795), who married *William Maynadier* (1747–1795). MARRIED second, by 1745 his first wife's first cousin Rosannah Woolford, widow of Jacob Lookerman (?–ca. 1741); daughter of James Woolford (ca. 1680–1758), of Dorchester County, a planter; granddaughter of *Roger Woolford* (?–ca. 1701/2); niece of *Roger Woolford* (1670–1730), Mary Woolford (1663–1740), who married *Henry Hooper* (ca. 1643–1720), Elizabeth Woolford (1664–1738), who married first, *Thomas Ennalls* (?–1718), and second, *William Holland* (?–1732), and Sarah Woolford (ca. 1672–?), who married *Govert Lookerman* (ca. 1681–1728). Her brothers or half brothers were John (ca. 1701–?); Roger (ca. 1715–?); Levin (?–ca. 1773), who married Jane, daughter of John Stewart; Thomas; David; William; and *James Woolford* (ca. 1736–ca. 1783). Her sisters or half sisters were Elizabeth; Ann; and Sarah. Her natural sister was Mary, who married by 1729 Thomas Stewart. Her first cousins were Sarah Lookerman (?–by 1745); Mary Hooper (?–ca. 1757), who married second, *John Rider* (1686–1739/40); Anne Hooper (?–1761), who married *John Broome* (1676–ca. 1738/39); *Thomas Woolford* (ca. 1699–ca. 1750/51); and *Henry Hooper* (ca. 1687–1767). Her nephews were *Thomas Ennalls* (?–by 1783); *Henry Ennalls* (ca. 1741–by 1788). Her niece was Margaret Ennalls (?–by 1795), who married *William Maynadier* (1747–1795). CHILDREN. SONS: James; Joseph; and John. STEPSON: Jacob Lookerman (?–by 1767). DAUGHTER: Sarah Lookerman, who married (first name unknown) Coleburn; Rosalinda. STEPDAUGHTER: Elizabeth Lookerman, who married (first name unknown) Wing. PRIVATE CAREER. EDUCATION: literate. RELIGIOUS AFFILIATION: Protestant. SOCIAL STATUS AND ACTIVITIES: Gent., by 1747. OCCUPATIONAL PROFILE: planter. PUBLIC CAREER. LEGISLATIVE SERVICE: Lower House, Dorchester County, 1753–1754 (elected to

the 3rd session to fill vacancy), 1754–1757, 1757–1758, 1762–1763. LOCAL OFFICE: justice, Dorchester County, 1754–1764. WEALTH DURING LIFETIME. LAND AT FIRST ELECTION: 100 acres in Dorchester County (had acquired 300 acres through first marriage, but had sold 200 acres of it before his first election); controlled 1,391 acres in Dorchester County for his second wife and her children by her first marriage. SIGNIFICANT CHANGES IN LAND BETWEEN FIRST ELECTION AND DEATH: patented 281 acres in Dorchester County, 1764. WEALTH AT DEATH. DIED: in Dorchester County; obituary appeared on May 24, 1764. PERSONAL PROPERTY: TEV, £932.2.3 current money (including 15 slaves, 43 oz. 6 dwt. 12 gr. plate, and books); FB, £541.17.9 as calculated. LAND: 381 acres in Dorchester County; controlled 1,391 acres in Dorchester County for his second wife and her children by her first marriage.

GREENBERRY (GREENBURY), CHARLES (1672–1713). BORN: in 1672, probably in England. IMMIGRATED: in 1674 as a minor with his parents. RESIDED: in Anne Arundel County. FAMILY BACKGROUND. FATHER: *Nicholas Greenberry* (1627–1697). MOTHER: Ann (1648–1698). SISTERS: Katherine, who married first, Henry Ridgeley (1669–1699/1700), son of *Henry Ridgeley* (?–1710), and second, John Howard; Ann, who married *John Hammond* (ca. 1665–1742/43); and Elizabeth (1678–1719/20), who married in 1697 *Robert Goldsborough* (1660–1746). NEPHEWS: *Charles Goldsborough* (1707–1767); *William Goldsborough* (1709–1760); and *John Goldsborough* (1711–1778). NIECE: Elizabeth Ridgely (?–1734), who married *Thomas Worthington* (ca. 1691–1753). MARRIED by March 1700/1 Rachel (?–1748/49), daughter of John Stimpson, Gent. (?–by 1692), of Anne Arundel County, and wife Rachel (?–after 1724), widow of Neale Clarke (?–1676); stepdaughter of Robert Proctor (?–by 1695), Richard Kilburne (?–by 1698), and Thomas Freeborne (?–1713); granddaughter of *Richard Beard* (?–1681). Rachel Stimpson Greenberry subsequently married in 1715 *Charles Hammond* (1692/93–1772). Her brother was John (?–by 1718). Her half brothers were Neale Clarke; Richard Clarke. Her stepbrothers were William Kilburne; Richard Freeborne. Her sister was Comfort (ca. 1684–ca. 1747), who married *John Dorsey* (ca. 1682–?). Her half sisters were Ruth (surname unknown), who married (first name unknown) Williams; Rachel Robinson, who married (first name unknown) Edney. Her stepsisters were Elizabeth Kilburne; Sarah Freeborne, who married (first name unknown)

Sampson; Jane Freeborne, who married (first name unknown) Thomas; Priscilla Freeborne; and Ann Freeborne. Her nephew was *John Hammond Dorsey* (1718–1774). CHILDREN. Three, sex and names unknown, all died young. PRIVATE CAREER. EDUCATION: literate. RELIGIOUS AFFILIATION: Anglican. SOCIAL STATUS AND ACTIVITIES: second generation burgess and councilor; closely related to several important Maryland families. OCCUPATIONAL PROFILE: planter; merchant. PUBLIC CAREER. LEGISLATIVE SERVICE: Lower House, Anne Arundel County, 1701/2–1704 (elected to the 2nd session; Aggrievances 5), 1704–1707 (Laws 1–5, chairman 4), 1708A (Laws, probably chairman), 1708B (Laws, chairman 1; appointed to Council after the 1st session of 1708B–1711 Assembly); Upper House, 1709–1711 (appointed before the 2nd session), 1712–1713 (died before the 3rd session). OTHER PROVINCIAL OFFICES: Council, 1708–1713; associate justice, Court of Chancery, 1709–1713. LOCAL OFFICES: justice, Anne Arundel County 1702–1709 (quorum); St. Margaret's Parish Vestry, Anne Arundel County, 1707. MILITARY SERVICE: major, 1701/2–1707; colonel, 1707. WEALTH DURING LIFETIME. LAND AT FIRST ELECTION: at least 615 acres. WEALTH AT DEATH. DIED: on November 19, 1713. PERSONAL PROPERTY: TEV, £1,474.14.11 sterling (including 16 slaves). LAND: probably ca. 615 acres.

GREENBERRY (GREENBURY), NICHOLAS (1627–1697). BORN: in 1627 in England. IMMIGRATED: in 1674 as a free adult with his wife and two children. RESIDED: in Anne Arundel County. MARRIED Ann (1648–1698). CHILDREN. SON: *Charles Greenberry* (1672–1713), who married Rachel (?–1748/49), daughter of John Stimpson. DAUGHTERS: Katherine, who married first, Henry Ridgeley (1669–1699/1700), son of *Henry Ridgeley* (?–1710), and second, John Howard; Ann, who married *John Hammond* (ca. 1665–1742/43); and Elizabeth (1678–1719/20), who married in 1697 *Robert Goldsborough* (1660–1746). PRIVATE CAREER. EDUCATION: literate. RELIGIOUS AFFILIATION: Protestant. SOCIAL STATUS AND ACTIVITES: immigrated with three servants; Gent. on arrival. OCCUPATIONAL PROFILE: planter; merchant. PUBLIC CAREER. LEGISLATIVE SERVICE: Associators' Convention, Anne Arundel County, 1690–1692 (elected to the 2nd or 3rd session); Grand Committee of Twenty, 1690–1692; Upper House, 1692–1693 (Laws 1), 1694–1697. OTHER PROVINCIAL OFFICES: Council, 1691–1697 (president, 1693–1694); justice, Provincial Court, 1691–1694 (quorum); chancellor, 1693/94–1694. LOCAL OFFICE: justice, Anne Arundel County, 1686–1692 (quorum, 1689–1692). MILITARY SERVICE: captain, 1686–1687, 1689–1691; major, 1691–1692; colonel, 1692–1697. STANDS ON PUBLIC/PRIVATE ISSUES: his initial attitude toward the revolution of 1689 is uncertain, but he supported the new government by the late spring of 1690 and he rose rapidly in colonial politics after the revolution; his appointment as president of the Council, and thus acting chief executive, by Edmund Andros in 1693, was strongly opposed by Sir Thomas Lawrence. WEALTH DURING LIFETIME. LAND AT FIRST ELECTION: over 700 acres. WEALTH AT DEATH. DIED: on December 17, 1697. PERSONAL PROPERTY: TEV, £1,045.15.3 sterling (including 6 slaves and 1 servant); FB, £903.5.8, cash balance in England of £363.12.4. LAND: ca. 700 acres.

GREENE, LEONARD (?–1688). BORN: in St. Mary's County; probably second son. NATIVE: second generation. RESIDED: in St. Mary's County. FAMILY BACKGROUND. FATHER: *Thomas Greene* (?–ca. 1651/52). MOTHER: probably Winifred, widow of Nicholas Harvey. She subsequently married *Robert Clarke* (ca. 1611–1664). BROTHERS: Thomas; Robert, who married Mary, daughter of *William Boreman* (ca. 1630–1709); and Francis. MARRIED Anne. CHILDREN. SON: Thomas. DAUGHTERS: Winifred, who married Francis Wheeler; Mary, who married Francis Marbury; and Margaret, who married Joseph Alvey. PRIVATE CAREER. EDUCATION: literate. RELIGIOUS AFFILIATION: Catholic. SOCIAL STATUS AND ACTIVITIES: second generation burgess; godson of Gov. Leonard Calvert. OCCUPATIONAL PROFILE: planter; possibly also mercantile activity. PUBLIC CAREER. LEGISLATIVE SERVICE: Lower House, St. Mary's City, 1682–1684. LOCAL OFFICES: constable, St. George's Hundred, St. Mary's County, 1676; deputy sheriff, St. Mary's County, 1679. WEALTH AT DEATH. DIED: will probated on July 4, 1688. PERSONAL PROPERTY: TEV, £238.12.7 sterling (including 1 slave and 3 servants). LAND: 1,300 acres.

GREENE, THOMAS (?–ca. 1651/52). BORN: in England. IMMIGRATED: in 1633/34 as a free adult. RESIDED: in St. Mary's County. FAMILY BACKGROUND. BROTHER: Robert, Esq. MARRIED first, Ann Cox. MARRIED second, in 1643 Millicent Browne. MARRIED third, by 1647 Winifred Seyborn, widow of Nicholas Harvey. She subsequently married *Robert Clarke* (ca. 1611–1664). CHILDREN. SONS: Thomas; *Leonard Greene* (?–1688), who married Ann; Robert, who married Mary, daughter of *William Boreman* (ca. 1630–

1709); and Francis. **PRIVATE CAREER.** EDUCATION: literate. RELIGIOUS AFFILIATION: Catholic. SOCIAL STATUS AND ACTIVITIES: an original adventurer in founding of the colony; brought two servants with him on his arrival in Maryland; his wife immigrated in 1638, and two of his children followed in 1644; he was a close friend of Leonard Calvert and Father Thomas Copley, a Jesuit priest; Gent., by 1637/38. OCCUPATIONAL: PROFILE: planter. **PUBLIC CAREER.** LEGISLATIVE SERVICE: Assembly, present 1637/38, special writ 1638/39, St. Mary's Hundred, St. Mary's County, 1640–1641, special writ 1641/42 (Aggrievances), St. Mary's Hundred, St. Mary's County, 1642A (Accounts; probably Laws), present 1642B (Laws); Upper House, 1646/47, 1649, 1650 (Laws 1; dismissed by the 2nd session). OTHER PROVINCIAL OFFICES: Council, 1644–1647, 1648–1650; justice, Provincial Court, 1644–1647, 1648–1650; appointed governor by Leonard Calvert on June 9, 1647, but he was never commissioned and was superseded by William Stone on August 6, 1648; acting governor, 1649. LOCAL OFFICE: justice, St. Mary's County, 1644–1650. STANDS ON PUBLIC/PRIVATE ISSUES: a strong supporter of the Jesuits against Lord Baltimore in first decade of settlement of the colony; he was accused of partiality as acting governor, 1648; as acting governor in October 1649, he proclaimed Charles Stuart the "undoubted rightfull heire" to the English throne; discharged from all offices on August 6, 1650, for usurping authority. **WEALTH DURING LIFETIME.** LAND AT FIRST ELECTION: ca. 2,000 acres. **WEALTH AT DEATH.** DIED: will probated on January 23, 1651/52. LAND: ca. 2,500 acres.

GREENFIELD, THOMAS (ca. 1649–1715). BORN: ca. 1649 in Gedling, England. IMMIGRATED: ca. 1674/75 as a free adult. RESIDED: in Calvert County; Prince George's County after 1695. MARRIED by 1677 Martha, daughter of Dr. James Trueman and wife Ann Stoner; stepdaughter of Robert Skinner (?–1686); niece of *Thomas Trueman* (ca. 1625–1685). Her stepbrother was *Robert Skinner* (?–1713). Her half brothers were Clark Skinner; William Skinner; and *Adderton Skinner* (ca. 1677–1756). Her sisters were Mary, who married *Thomas Hollyday* (ca. 1661–1702/3); Ann, who married *John Bigger* (ca. 1654–1714); and Elizabeth. Her stepsister or half sister was Mary Skinner, who married Joseph Letchworth (?–1713), son of *Thomas Letchworth* (?–1667). CHILDREN. SONS: *Thomas Trueman Greenfield* (1682–1733), who married first, by 1708 Susannah (1680–1730), daughter of *Kenelm Cheseldyne*

(1640–1708), and second, Anne (1694–1759), widow of Francis Wilkinson and daughter of *Walter Smith* (?–1711); Trueman; James; and Micajah. DAUGHTERS: Jane, who married *Henry Holland Hawkins* (1683–1751); Martha, who married Basil Waring (1683–1733); Elizabeth, who married Gabriel Parker; and Ann, who married John Wight, son of *John Wight* (?–1705). **PRIVATE CAREER.** EDUCATION: literate, attended Cambridge University. RELIGIOUS AFFILIATION: Anglican. SOCIAL STATUS AND ACTIVITIES: Gent., by 1691; Esq. from 1697; attorney in fact by 1677 for *Thomas Trueman* (ca. 1625–1685), whose estate he managed for almost two decades; a founder and leading figure of Prince George's County. OCCUPATIONAL PROFILE: planter. **PUBLIC CAREER.** LEGISLATIVE SERVICE: Lower House, Calvert County, 1692–1693 (Laws 1; Aggrievances 2), 1694–1695 (Accounts 3, 4; resigned after the 4th session to become sheriff), Prince George's County, 1699–1700 (elected to the 3rd session; Elections and Privileges 4), 1701–1704 (Elections and Privileges, chairman 1), 1704–1707 (Aggrievances 1, 4, 5; chairman 1, 4; Elections and Privileges, chairman 3); Upper House, 1708A, 1708B–1711, 1712–1714, 1715. OTHER PROVINCIAL OFFICES: justice, Provincial Court, 1699–1707 (quorum, 1704–1707); Council, 1708–1715; assistant judge, Court of Chancery, 1714/15. LOCAL OFFICES: justice, Calvert County, 1689–1696 (quorum, 1692–1696); St. Paul's Parish Vestry, Calvert County, 1693–1696; coroner, Calvert County, 1694; sheriff, Prince George's County, 1695/96–1699; MILITARY SERVICE: major, 1694; colonel, 1707–1715. STANDS ON PUBLIC/PRIVATE ISSUES: recommended by Lord Baltimore for appointment to the first royal Council, but he was not actually appointed until Gov. John Seymour sought an alternative to the Addison-Brooke clique in Prince George's County in 1708; he was criticized for his highhanded behavior while sheriff of Prince George's County. **WEALTH DURING LIFETIME.** LAND AT FIRST ELECTION: 1,299 acres in 1692, with stewardship of an additional 4,800 acres; 1,586 acres in 1706, with stewardship of an additional 2,500 acres. **WEALTH AT DEATH.** DIED: will probated on November 7, 1715. PERSONAL PROPERTY: TEV, £459.8.4 sterling. LAND: 2,309 acres.

GREENFIELD, THOMAS (ca. 1715–1774). BORN: ca. 1715 in St. Mary's County. NATIVE: third generation. RESIDED: in St. Mary's County. FAMILY BACKGROUND. FATHER: Maj. Trueman Greenfield, Gent. (?–ca. 1726), son of *Thomas Greenfield* (ca. 1649–1715). STEPFATHER: John

Chesley (?–1767). MOTHER: Elizabeth. UNCLE: *Thomas Trueman Greenfield* (1682–1733). AUNT: Jane Greenfield, who married *Henry Holland Hawkins* (1683–1751). BROTHERS: George (?–ca. 1751); Henry (?–1748). HALF BROTHER: Benjamin Chesley (ca. 1737–?). SISTERS: Elizabeth, who married (first name unknown) Cartwright; Rebecca. HALF SISTER: Elizabeth, who married (first name unknown) Pile (Peles). FIRST COUSINS: *Francis Waring* (1715–1769); *Josias Hawkins* (ca. 1735–1789); Eleanor Hawkins, who married *George Dent* (?–1785); and Marianne Greenfield, who married *John Stoddert* (?–1767). MARRIED Dorothy Barber, of St. Mary's County. CHILDREN. SONS: Trueman (?–1775), who married Susannah; Thomas. DAUGHTERS: Rebecca, who married (first name unknown) Broome; Dorothy, who married (first name unknown) Tubman. PRIVATE CAREER. EDUCATION: literate. RELIGIOUS AFFILIATION: Anglican. SOCIAL STATUS AND ACTIVITIES: Mr., 1741. OCCUPATIONAL PROFILE: probably a planter; owned a water mill. PUBLIC CAREER. LEGISLATIVE SERVICE: Lower House, St. Mary's County, 1758–1761. LOCAL OFFICES: churchwarden, All Faith's Parish, St. Mary's County, in office 1741 and 1749; inspector, Benedict warehouse, Charles County, appointed 1750; justice, St. Mary's County, in office 1755–at least 1773 (quorum, 1768–at least 1773); vestry, All Faith's Parish, 1764–at least 1768. MILITARY SERVICE: captain, by 1749. WEALTH DURING LIFETIME. PERSONAL PROPERTY: 10 slaves, 1773. LAND AT FIRST ELECTION: 1,018 acres in St. Mary's County (probably all inherited). SIGNIFICANT CHANGES IN LAND BETWEEN FIRST ELECTION AND DEATH: sold or gave away most of his land before his death. WEALTH AT DEATH. DIED: will probated on April 15, 1774, in St. Mary's County. PERSONAL PROPERTY: TEV, at least £542.4.2 current money (including 8 slaves, 57 oz. old silver, 1 book, and 1 pair of millstones). LAND: 300 acres in St. Mary's County.

GREENFIELD, THOMAS TRUEMAN (1682–1733).

BORN: in 1682 in Calvert County; oldest son. NATIVE: second generation. RESIDED: in Calvert County; Prince George's County, after 1695; Resurrection Hundred, St. Mary's County, by 1708. FAMILY BACKGROUND. FATHER: *Thomas Greenfield* (ca. 1649–1715). MOTHER: Martha Trueman. UNCLES: *Thomas Hollyday* (ca. 1661–1702/3); *John Bigger* (ca. 1654–1714); *Robert Skinner* (?–1713); and *Adderton Skinner* (ca. 1677–1756). BROTHERS: Trueman; James; and Micajah. SISTERS: Jane, who married *Henry Hol-*

land Hawkins (1683–1751); Martha; Ann; and Elizabeth. MARRIED first, by 1708 Susannah (1680–1730), daughter of *Kenelm Cheseldyne* (1640–1708); granddaughter of *Thomas Gerard* (1608–1673); niece of *John Coode* (ca. 1648–1708/9), *Nehemiah Blakiston* (?–1693), and *Joshua Guibert* (?–1713). Her brother was *Kenelm Cheseldyne* (1683–1719). Her sisters were Mary (1678–?), who married first, *James Hay* (?–by 1717/18), and second, George Fobes; Dryden (1687–1760), who married first, *Henry Peregrine Jowles* (1681–1720), and second, John Fobes. MARRIED second, Anne (1694–1759), widow of Francis Wilkinson; daughter of *Walter Smith* (?–1711). Her brothers were Richard (?–1732); Walter Smith (ca. 1692–1734). Her sisters were Lucy (1688–1770), who married *Thomas Brooke* (1683–1744); Eleanor (1690–1761), who married *Thomas Addison* (1679–1727); Rebecca (1696–1737), who married *Daniel Dulany* (1685–1753); Elizabeth; and Mary. Her nephews were *Daniel Dulany, Jr.* (1722–1797); *Walter Dulany* (?–1773); *Richard Brooke* (1716–1783); and *John Addison* (1713–1764). Her nieces were Margaret Dulany, who married first, *Alexander Hamilton* (1712–1756), and second, *William Murdock* (?–1769); Eleanor Brooke, who married *Samuel Beall* (ca. 1713–ca. 1778); and Ann Addison (1711/12–?), who married *William Murdock* (?–1769). CHILDREN. SONS: Thomas Trueman; Kenelm Trueman; Gerard Trueman; Nathaniel; Walter (?–by 1745); and James. DAUGHTERS: Marianne, who married by 1728 *John Stoddert* (?–1767); Sabrina, who married Thomas Marshall. PRIVATE CAREER. EDUCATION: literate. RELIGIOUS AFFILIATION: Anglican. SOCIAL STATUS AND ACTIVITIES: second generation burgess. OCCUPATIONAL PROFILE: planter. PUBLIC CAREER. LEGISLATIVE SERVICE: Lower House, St. Mary's County, 1708A (election voided), 1708B–1711, 1712–1714 (Accounts 3, 4), 1715 (Accounts), 1716–1718 (Accounts 1–3), 1719–1721/22 (appointed sheriff before the 3rd session; reelected to the 4th session), 1725–1727 (Laws 1–4; Elections 1–3), 1728–1731 (Laws 3). LOCAL OFFICES: justice, St. Mary's County, 1708–probably continuously to 1733, except for the year he served as sheriff (quorum, 1727–1733); sheriff, St. Mary's County, 1721. MILITARY SERVICE: captain, 1708; colonel, by 1723. WEALTH DURING LIFETIME. LAND AT FIRST ELECTION: over 2,300 acres; heir to the extensive landholdings of his great-uncle *Thomas Trueman* (ca. 1625–1685) and his grandfather James Trueman. WEALTH AT DEATH. DIED: on December 10, 1733. PERSONAL PROPERTY: TEV, £194.14.0 sterling, £1,896.14.2

current money (including 24 slaves); FB, £58.18.0 sterling, £476.5.7 current money. LAND: 6,194 acres, plus 5 tracts of unspecified acreage.

GRESHAM (GRASHAM), JOHN (ca. 1703–ca. 1752). BORN: ca. 1703, probably in Anne Arundel County; eldest son. NATIVE: probably, if so, third generation. RESIDED: at "Greshams Calledge," Kent County, by 1728. FAMILY BACKGROUND. FATHER: John Gresham, Esq. (?–1723), of Annapolis; planter; sheriff of Anne Arundel County from ca. 1722 until death; examiner general from 1722 until death; owned ca. 5,000 acres at death; son of John Gresham (?–1713), of Anne Arundel County. MOTHER: Sarah (?–1756), owned real estate in England at time of death. BROTHERS: Thomas (?–ca. 1731/32), died without progeny; *Richard Gresham* (?–ca. 1773). SISTERS: Priscilla; Sarah, who married Solomon Wooden; and Elizabeth, who married Jacob Jones. NIECE: Sarah Gresham, who married *Thomas Smyth* (1730–1819). OTHER KINSHIP: his great-nephew was *Thomas Smyth, Jr.* (1757–1807). MARRIED first, Hannah (1705–?), daughter of *Nathaniel Hynson* (?–ca. 1721/22). MARRIED second, (name unknown), a widow. Her sister was Mary (1711–?). CHILDREN. SONS: John (ca. 1742–ca. 1772); *Richard Gresham* (?–1780); and Thomas (probably after 1750–?). STEPSON: William. DAUGHTERS: Sarah (1730–?), who married by 1750 James Frisby; Mary, who married *Richard Graves* (1739–1792). PRIVATE CAREER. EDUCATION: literate. RELIGIOUS AFFILIATION: Anglican. SOCIAL STATUS AND ACTIVITIES: Gent., 1728. OCCUPATIONAL PROFILE: probably a planter. PUBLIC CAREER. LEGISLATIVE SERVICE: Lower House, Kent County, 1742–1744 (Arms and Ammunition 1, 2; Elections 2), 1745 (Arms and Ammunition; Elections), 1745/46–1748 (Elections Cv 1, 1–3, 4; Laws 3), 1751 (elected to the 1751–1754 Assembly, but did not attend; died before the 2nd session). LOCAL OFFICES: deputy commissary, Kent County, 1727–1742; sheriff, Kent County, 1727–1729, 1732–1735; justice, Kent County, 1729–at least 1731. WEALTH DURING LIFETIME. LAND AT FIRST ELECTION: 3,185 acres in Kent, Anne Arundel, and Queen Anne's counties, plus 1 lot in Chestertown, Kent County (1,336 acres inherited from father; 550 acres through marriage to first wife; 1,299 acres by personal acquisition). SIGNIFICANT CHANGES IN LAND BETWEEN FIRST ELECTION AND DEATH: acquired 1,222 acres in Anne Arundel and Kent counties, 1743–1754; gave 400 acres in Anne Arundel County to his sister Sarah and her husband Solomon Wooden, 1744. WEALTH AT DEATH. DIED: will probated in January 1752 in Kent County. PERSONAL PROPERTY: TEV, £1,655.18.4 current money (including 34 slaves and numerous silver and gold items); FB, £1,099.16.2. LAND: 3,399 acres (2,163 acres in Kent County; 236 acres in Anne Arundel County; 1,000 acres in Queen Anne's County; plus 2 lots in Chestertown, Kent County).

GRESHAM, RICHARD (?–ca. 1773). BORN: probably in Anne Arundel County, of age by 1729; younger son. NATIVE: third generation. RESIDED: in Kent County. FAMILY BACKGROUND. FATHER: John Gresham, Esq. (?–1723), of Annapolis; planter; sheriff of Anne Arundel County from ca. 1722 until death; examiner general from 1722 until death; owned ca. 5,000 acres at death; son of John Gresham (?–1713), of Anne Arundel County. MOTHER: Sarah (?–1756), owned real estate in England at time of death. BROTHERS: *John Gresham* (ca. 1703–ca. 1752); Thomas (?–ca. 1731/32), died without progeny. SISTERS: Priscilla; Sarah, who married Solomon Wooden; and Elizabeth, who married Jacob Jones. NEPHEW: *Richard Gresham* (?–1780). MARRIED Martha (1712–?), daughter of *Thomas Smith* (1656–1719). Her brother was *Thomas Smith* (1710–ca. 1742). CHILDREN. Possible natural SON: Thomas Gresham, son of Sophia Whalen and grandson of Edward Whalen, to whom Gresham devised a large part of his estate. DAUGHTER: Sarah, who married *Thomas Smyth* (1730–1819), of Chestertown, Kent County, merchant. PRIVATE CAREER. EDUCATION: literate. RELIGIOUS AFFILIATION: Anglican, Chester Parish, Kent County. SOCIAL STATUS AND ACTIVITIES: Gent., 1743; Esq., 1748. OCCUPATIONAL PROFILE: merchant. PUBLIC CAREER. LEGISLATIVE SERVICE: Lower House, Kent County, 1742–1744, 1745 (Aggrievances), 1745/46–1748 (Aggrievances Cv 1, 1–3, 4), 1752–1754 (elected to the 2nd session to fill vacancy), 1754–1757, 1758–1761, 1768–1770, 1771. LOCAL OFFICE: justice, Kent County, 1760–at least 1769 (quorum, 1762–at least 1769). WEALTH DURING LIFETIME. LAND AT FIRST ELECTION: 960 acres in Kent and Baltimore counties (150 acres in Baltimore County remaining from his inheritance from his father in 1723). SIGNIFICANT CHANGES IN LAND BETWEEN FIRST ELECTION AND DEATH: patented 564 acres and purchased 965 acres, plus parts of 2 lots in Chestertown, all in Kent County, 1743–1773. Sold at least 351 acres in Kent and Baltimore counties, 1743–1773. Inherited land in England from his mother in 1756. WEALTH AT DEATH. DIED: between December 4, 1772, and January 6, 1773, in Kent County. PERSONAL PROPERTY: TEV, at least

£3,790.2.3 current money (including 45 slaves and 7 servants). LAND: ca. 2,193 acres in Kent County, plus lots in Chestertown, Kent County.

GRESHAM, RICHARD (?–1780). BORN: in Kent County, less than 20 years of age in 1750; younger son. NATIVE: probably fourth generation. RESIDED: in Kent County. FAMILY BACKGROUND. FATHER: *John Gresham* (ca. 1703–ca. 1752). UNCLE: *Richard Gresham* (?–ca. 1773). BROTHERS: John (ca. 1742–probably 1772); Thomas (probably after 1750–?). STEPBROTHER: William. SISTERS: Sarah (1730–?); Mary, who married *Richard Graves* (1739–1792). MARRIED Ann. CHILDREN. SONS: Richard Montgomery; John. DAUGHTERS: Maria; Ann. PRIVATE CAREER. EDUCATION: literate. RELIGIOUS AFFILIATION: Anglican, Shrewsbury Parish, Kent County. SOCIAL STATUS AND ACTIVITIES: Gent., 1771; Esq., 1778. OCCUPATIONAL PROFILE: probably a planter. PUBLIC CAREER. LEGISLATIVE SERVICE: Lower House, Kent County, 1777–1778 (elected to the 1st session to fill vacancy); 1778–1779 (Elections 2; Grievances 3), 1779 (Manufactories 1; Tax Commissioners 1; died before the 2nd session of the 1779–1780 Assembly). LOCAL OFFICE: justice, Kent County, 1774, 1777. WEALTH DURING LIFETIME. LAND AT FIRST ELECTION: ca. 1,156 acres in Kent and Queen Anne's counties. WEALTH AT DEATH. DIED: between February 4 and February 19, 1780, in Kent County. PERSONAL PROPERTY: TEV, at least $7,158.78 current money (including 32 slaves, 1 servant, and 10 books). LAND: probably 1,156 acres in Kent and Queen Anne's counties.

GRIFFITH, (GRIFFETH), CHARLES GREENBURY (1744–1792). BORN: on May 17, 1744, in Queen Caroline Parish, Anne Arundel County; youngest son. NATIVE: third generation. RESIDED: in Frederick County (later became part of Montgomery County), by 1770. FAMILY BACKGROUND. FATHER: Orlando Griffith (1688–1757), son of William Griffith. MOTHER: Katherine Howard. BROTHERS: *Henry Griffith* (ca. 1720–1794); Nicholas (?–died young); Greenbury (1727–?), who married Ruth Biggs; Joshua (1730–?), who married Ann Hall; Benjamin (1732–?), who married Mary Biggs; and Orlando (1741–1774). SISTERS: Lucretia (1739–?), who married first, Caleb Davis, and second, Azel Waters; Sarah (1718–?), who married Nicholas Dorsey. MARRIED Sarah (1745–?), daughter of Henry Ridgely (?–1750) and wife Elizabeth Warfield; niece of Elizabeth Ridgely, who married *Thomas Worthington* (ca. 1691–1753). Her brothers were Greenbury (1726–?);

Henry Ridgely (1728–1791); Nicholas (1729/30–1732); Benjamin (1731/32–?); Joshua (1733/34–?); Charles Greenbury (1735–?); Thomas (1740–?); and Nicholas Greenbury (1742–?). Her sisters were Katherine (1723–ca. 1753), who married Capt. Phileman Dorsey (1714–1772); Anne (1725–?), who married *Brice T. B. Worthington* (1727–1794); and Elizabeth (1737–by 1761), who married Col. *Thomas Dorsey* (?–1790). CHILDREN. DAUGHTER: Elizabeth (1764–1824), who married *Jeremiah Crabb* (1760–1800). PRIVATE CAREER. EDUCATION: literate. RELIGIOUS AFFILIATION: Anglican. OCCUPATIONAL PROFILE: planter. PUBLIC CAREER. LEGISLATIVE SERVICE: Lower House, Montgomery County, 1781–1782 (Public Taxes 1), 1782–1783, 1787–1788. LOCAL OFFICES: Committee of Observation, Frederick County, in office 1777; county lieutenant, Frederick County, appointed 1777; justice, Montgomery County, commissioned 1777; subscription officer, Continental Loan Office, Montgomery County, appointed 1779. MILITARY SERVICE: colonel, First Battalion of the Flying Camp, 1776. WEALTH DURING LIFETIME. PERSONAL PROPERTY: assessed value £1,278.0.0, including 22 slaves and 16 oz. plate, 1783. LAND AT FIRST ELECTION: 640 acres in Frederick and Anne Arundel counties (250 acres inherited from his father, 390 acres by personal acquisition). SIGNIFICANT CHANGES IN LAND BETWEEN FIRST ELECTION AND DEATH: acquired by purchase and patent 1,119 acres in Montgomery County, 1783–1789; sold 537 acres in Montgomery County in 1791. WEALTH AT DEATH. DIED: on August 12, 1792, probably in Montgomery County. LAND: probably ca. 1,222 acres in Frederick, Montgomery, and Anne Arundel counties, 1792; ca. 561 acres in Montgomery County were sold by Griffith's heirs to *Richard Ridgely* (1755–1824) in 1798.

GRIFFITH, HENRY (ca. 1720–1794). BORN: on February 14, ca. 1720, in Queen Caroline Parish, Anne Arundel County; second son. NATIVE: third generation. RESIDED: in Anne Arundel County; Frederick County (later became part of Montgomery County), by 1772. FAMILY BACKGROUND. FATHER: Orlando Griffith. MOTHER: Katherine Howard. BROTHERS: Nicholas (?–died young); Greenbury (1727–?), who married in 1752 Ruth Biggs; Joshua (1730–?), who married Ann Hall; Benjamin (1732–?), who married Mary Biggs; Orlando (1741–1774); and *Charles Greenbury Griffith* (1744–1792). SISTERS: Sarah (1718–?), who married Nicholas Dorsey; Lucretia (1739–?), who married Caleb Davis. MARRIED first, on April 9,

1741, Elizabeth (?–1749), daughter of Edward Dorsey and wife Sarah Todd. MARRIED second, on June 3, 1751, Ruth, daughter of John Hammond (?–1753) and wife Anne Dorsey. Her brothers were John (1739–?); Charles (?–1796). Her sisters were Hannah (1723–?), who married John Welsh; Ann, who married Francis Davis; Hamutel, who married Benjamin Welch, of John; and Rachel, who married John Mackelfresh. CHILDREN. SONS: Henry (1744/45–1809), who married first, Sarah Warfield, and second, Sarah Davis; Samuel (1752–?), who married first, Rachel Warfield, and second, Ruth Berry; John Hammond (1754–?), who married Elizabeth Ridgely; Philemon (1756–?), who married Eleanor Jacob; Charles (1758–?); and Joshua (1764–?), who married Elizabeth Ridgely. DAUGHTERS: Sarah (1741/42–?), who married Rezin Todd; Ruth (1747–?), who married Amon Riggs; Rachel (1749–?), who married Samuel Welsh; Ann (1762–?), who married in 1779 Nicholas Hall; Eleanor (1766–?), who married John Burgess; Elizabeth (1768–?); and Ruth, who married Joab Waters. PRIVATE CAREER. RELIGIOUS AFFILIATION: Protestant. SOCIAL STATUS AND ACTIVITIES: Gent., 1757. OCCUPATIONAL PROFILE: planter; merchant; land speculator. PUBLIC CAREER. LEGISLATIVE SERVICE: Lower House, Anne Arundel County, 1768–1770 (Arms and Ammunition 1–3; Public Offices 2, 3), Frederick County, 1773–1774 (Arms and Ammunition 2,3; Public Offices 1, Cv, 2, 3; Accounts Cv, 2, 3); Conventions, Frederick County, 1st, 1774, 2nd–3rd, 1774, 4th, 1775, 5th, 1775, 6th–8th, 1775–1776. LOCAL OFFICES: tobacco inspector, Queen Caroline Parish, Anne Arundel County, appointed 1749, 1750, 1753, and 1755; justice, Anne Arundel County, 1755–at least 1760, Montgomery County, 1777; Queen Caroline Parish Vestry, Anne Arundel County, in office 1757–1761; constable, Huntington Hundred, Anne Arundel County, appointed 1758; commissioner to examine evidence to prove boundaries of land, Anne Arundel County, appointed 1761; commissioner for the formation of Montgomery County, in office 1776; commissioner of tax, Montgomery County, 1777–at least 1792. MILITARY SERVICE: captain, by 1768. STANDS ON PUBLIC/PRIVATE ISSUES: supported *Charles Carroll of Carrollton* (1737–1832) in his newspaper debate with *Daniel Dulany, Jr.* (1722–1797) concerning Governor Eden's Fee Bill, 1773. WEALTH DURING LIFETIME. PERSONAL PROPERTY: assessed value £823.0.0 current money, including 18 slaves and 4.5 oz. plate, 1783. LAND AT FIRST ELECTION: 6,957 acres in Anne Arundel and Frederick counties (6,549 acres by patent).

SIGNIFICANT CHANGES IN LAND BETWEEN FIRST ELECTION AND DEATH: most of Griffith's land transactions were speculative in nature. He patented or purchased large tracts of land and then subdivided them and sold the smaller parcels. However, in at least one case in which a tract of ca. 1,900 acres in Frederick County was sold in at least 20 parcels betwen ca. 1784 and 1794 he made very little profit. By 1789 he had sold or agreed to sell most of his speculative land. WEALTH AT DEATH. DIED: will probated October 10, 1794, in Montgomery County. PERSONAL PROPERTY: TEV, £4,329.5.2 (including 19 slaves, 3 oz. plate, and an "electrical machine"); FB, estate overpaid £194.18.2. LAND: ca. 1,325 acres in Anne Arundel, Montgomery, Frederick, and Allegany counties.

GRIFFITH (GRIFFEN, GRIFFIN, GRIFFETH), JOHN (?–?). RESIDED: in St. Mary's County. MARRIED by 1735 Elizabeth, widow of both Darby Morris (?–by 1727), of St. Mary's County, and John Downe (Downie, Downey) (?–by 1735). CHILDREN. STEPSONS: John Morris; Darby Morris; David Downey (?–1764), who married Elizabeth; and John Downey (?–1774). STEPDAUGHTERS: Elizabeth Morris; Rachel Morris. PUBLIC CAREER. LEGISLATIVE SERVICE: Lower House, St. Mary's County, 1742–1744. WEALTH DURING LIFETIME. LAND AT FIRST ELECTION: 110 acres in St. Mary's County (all by patent); surveyed but never patented an additional 188 acres in St. Mary's County. SIGNIFICANT CHANGES IN LAND BETWEEN FIRST ELECTION AND DEATH: sold 110 acres in St. Mary's County, 1743.

GUIBERT, JOSHUA (?–1713). BORN: in Rheims, France. IMMIGRATED: by 1667 as a free adult from France. RESIDED: at "Lukeland," Chaptico Hundred, St. Mary's County. MARRIED first, by 1673 Elizabeth, daughter of *Luke Barber* (?–1668). MARRIED second, Elizabeth (?–1716), widow of both *Nehemiah Blakiston* (?–1693) and Ralph Rymer; daughter of *Thomas Gerard* (1608–1673). CHILDREN. SONS: Thomas; Matthew; and Joshua. DAUGHTERS: Elizabeth; Ann, who married John Blakiston, son of *Nehemiah Blakiston* (?–1693). PRIVATE CAREER. EDUCATION: literate. RELIGIOUS AFFILIATION: Protestant, probably a Huguenot. SOCIAL STATUS AND ACTIVITIES: naturalized by an Act of Assembly, 1678. OCCUPATIONAL PROFILE: planter, by 1669; attorney, 1677; merchant, 1682. PUBLIC CAREER. LEGISLATIVE SERVICE: Lower House, St. Mary's County, 1708A (election voided), 1708B–1711. LOCAL OFFICE: justice, St.

Mary's County, 1694–still sitting in 1708. STANDS ON PUBLIC/PRIVATE ISSUES: charged with involvement in the conspiracy of *John Coode* (ca. 1648–1708/9) and *Philip Clarke* (?–1699) against Gov. Francis Nicholson, 1698. WEALTH DURING LIFETIME. LAND AT FIRST ELECTION: over 160 acres, plus substantial acreage in his wife's name. WEALTH AT DEATH. DIED: will probated on May 16, 1713. PERSONAL PROPERTY: TEV, £445.19.1 sterling (including 11 slaves). LAND: over 160 acres.

GWINN (GWYNN), JOHN (ca. 1756–1807). BORN: ca. 1756. NATIVE: at least second generation. RESIDED: in Frederick County, 1786–1802; Annapolis, Anne Arundel County, 1803–1807. FAMILY BACKGROUND. FATHER: John Gwinn (?–1785). MARRIED Mary, daughter of Jacob Good (?–1783). CHILDREN. Six, but sex and names unknown. PRIVATE CAREER. EDUCATION: literate. SOCIAL STATUS AND ACTIVITIES: Esq., 1790. ADDITIONAL COMMENTS: prior to his marriage he owned only 10.5 acres in his own right. Shortly after his marriage and the acquisition of his wife's landed estate, he was elected to the legislature and assumed the title of Esq. OCCUPATIONAL PROFILE: merchant, by 1795. PUBLIC CAREER. LEGISLATIVE SERVICE: Lower House, Frederick County, 1788, 1798. LOCAL OFFICES: justice, Frederick County, 1785–at least 1800; commissioner of tax, Frederick County, 1798–1800. WEALTH DURING LIFETIME. PERSONAL PROPERTY: 1 slave, 1790. LAND AT FIRST ELECTION: 311 acres in Frederick County, plus 21 lots in Taney Town, Frederick County (his wife had inherited 300 acres and the 21 lots from her father prior to their marriage). SIGNIFICANT CHANGES IN LAND BETWEEN FIRST ELECTION AND DEATH: sold all of the town lots, plus 34 acres in Frederick County, and purchased 2 lots in Westminster, Frederick County, by 1800. WEALTH AT DEATH. DIED: on February 11, 1807, at Fells Point, Baltimore City; size of estate unknown.

GWITHER (GWYTHER, GUITHER), NICHOLAS (ca. 1626–ca. 1665/66). BORN: in ca. 1626. IMMIGRATED: in 1639 as a indentured servant to *Thomas Cornwaleys* (ca. 1605–1675/76); free by 1647/48. RESIDED: in St. Inigoe's Hundred, St. Mary's County. MARRIED by 1650 Mary, a servant in 1649 to *Cuthbert Fenwick* (1614–1655). CHILDREN. SONS: John; Owen; William; and Nicholas (1651–1680). PRIVATE CAREER. EDUCATION: literate. OCCUPATIONAL PROFILE: servant; planter. PUBLIC CAREER. LEGISLATIVE SERVICE: Lower House, St. Mary's County, 1663. LOCAL OFFICES:

sheriff, St. Mary's County, 1650–1653, 1657/58–1662, Charles County, 1658–1661. MILITARY SERVICE: lieutenant, 1650; captain, by 1657/58. STANDS ON PUBLIC/PRIVATE ISSUES: supported Lord Baltimore against the Puritans in 1655. WEALTH DURING LIFETIME. LAND AT FIRST ELECTION: at least 100 acres; obtained a 21-year lease on 700 acres in partnership with Thomas Jackson in 1647/48, which he sold to Jackson in 1652; patented 900 acres in 1658, which he sold in 1662. WEALTH AT DEATH. DIED: by March 24, 1665/66. PERSONAL PROPERTY: TEV, 31,888 pounds of tobacco (including 1 slave and 2 servants).

HAGAR, JONATHAN (ca. 1719–1775). BORN: ca. 1719, probably in Germany. IMMIGRATED: ca. 1730 from Germany as a freeman. RESIDED: at "Hagar's Choice," Salisbury Hundred, Frederick County. MARRIED in 1740 Elizabeth (?–1765), daughter of Martin Kirshner (?–1769) and wife Margaretha. Her brothers were Martin; David; and George. Her sisters were Modalena; Morgeth. CHILDREN. SON: Jonathan, Jr. (1756–1798), wounded and taken prisoner by the British at the Battle of Long Island in 1776, confined at Halifax, Nova Scotia. DAUGHTER: Rosina (Rosannah) (1752–1810), who married Gen. Daniel Heister (?–1804), of Philadelphia County, Pennsylvania and died childless . PRIVATE CAREER. EDUCATION: literate. RELIGIOUS AFFILIATION: German Reformed. SOCIAL STATUS AND ACTIVITIES: Mr., 1753. ADDITIONAL COMMENTS: founded Hagerstown (originally Elizabeth Town, named for his wife). OCCUPATIONAL PROFILE: farmer. PUBLIC CAREER. LEGISLATIVE SERVICE: Lower House, Frederick County, 1771 (discharged on October 8, 1771; even though Hagar had been naturalized earlier in 1771, the law disallowed any but natural-born subjects or descendants of natural-born subjects from serving as delegates. On October 16, 1771 the Assembly passed a bill granting full rights to naturalized Protestants. Hagar was re-elected and seated on November 16, 1771), 1773 (discharged on October 15, 1773; the Lower House ruled that the law it had approved during the previous Assembly concerning the rights of naturalized Protestants was automatically void since the lord proprietor had died in September 1771 and the Assembly should then have been dissolved). MILITARY SERVICE: captain. WEALTH DURING LIFETIME. LAND AT FIRST ELECTION: 9,871 acres in Frederick County. SIGNIFICANT CHANGES IN LAND BETWEEN FIRST ELECTION AND DEATH: patented 1,077 acres in Frederick

County, 1773. WEALTH AT DEATH. DIED: on November 6, 1775, in Frederick County; killed in an accident at his sawmill; buried in a vault near his house, but later interred in the graveyard of Zion Church in Hagerstown. LAND: at least 5,000 acres in Frederick County, plus 5 lots in Hagerstown.

HALL, AQUILA (ACQUILA) (1727–1779). BORN: in 1727 in Baltimore County; younger surviving son. NATIVE: fourth generation. RESIDED: in Baltimore County (later became part of Harford County). FAMILY BACKGROUND. FATHER: Aquila Hall (1699–1728), of "Cranberry Hall," Baltimore County; son of *John Hall* (ca. 1658–1737). GUARDIAN AND UNCLE: *John Hall* (1701–1774). MOTHER: Johanna Kemp (?–1735), widow of *James Phillips* (?–1720). BROTHERS: John (1722–1768), of Swantown, Baltimore County, who married Cordelia Holland; Aquila (1724–1724); and Aquila (1725–1725). SISTER: Martha (1725–1725). FIRST COUSINS: *John Hall, Jr.* (1737–1770); *Josias Carvil Hall* (1746–1814); *Benedict Edward Hall* (ca. 1744–1822); Martha Hall, who married *Walter Tolley* (?–1783); Martha Hall, who married *John Rumsey* (ca. 1742–1828); Mary Hall, who married *Benjamin Rumsey* (1734–1808); and Blanche Hall, who married *John Beale Howard* (by 1739–1799). NIECE: Susannah Hall, who married *James Heath* (?–1766). MARRIED in 1750 his cousin Sophia (?–1780), daughter of Col. Thomas White (1705–1774), of Philadelphia, and wife Sophia Hall (1709/10–?); stepdaughter of Esther Hewlings Newman; granddaughter of *John Hall* (ca. 1658–1737); niece of *John Hall* (1701–1774). Her half brother was William White (1748–1836), first Protestant Episcopal bishop of the diocese of Pennsylvania. Her sisters were Mary (?–1827), who married Robert Morris (1734–1806), a merchant of Philadelphia, financier of the American Revolution, member of the Continental Congress from 1776 to 1778, signer of the Declaration of Independence, member of the Pennsylvania assembly from 1778 to 1780 and from 1785 to 1787, member of the U.S. Senate from 1789 to 1795, founder of the Bank of North America; Sarah Charlotte. Her first cousins were Martha Hall, who married *Walter Tolley* (?–1783); *Aquila Hall* (1727–1779); *John Hall, Jr.* (1737–1770); *Benedict Edward Hall* (ca. 1744–1822); *Josias Carvil Hall* (1746–1814); Martha Hall, who married *John Rumsey* (ca. 1742–1828); Mary Hall, who married *Benjamin Rumsey* (1734–1808); and Blanche Hall, who married *John Beale Howard* (by 1739–1799). CHILDREN. SONS: Thomas (1750–1804), a lawyer, who married Isabella Presbury; James White

(1754–1808); Aquila (1754–1754); William (1756–1818); John (1762–1804), who never married; Edward (1763–?); and Benedict (1771–?). DAUGHTERS: Charlotte (1758–1838), who married *Nathaniel Ramsay* (1741–1817); Mary (1760–?), who married Richard K. Heath; Sophia (1765–?), who married *Philip Key* (1750–1820); Martha (1768–?), who married John McHenry, of Allegany County; and Elizabeth (1770–?). PRIVATE CAREER. EDUCATION: literate. RELIGIOUS AFFILIATION: Anglican, St. George's Parish, Harford County. SOCIAL STATUS AND ACTIVITIES: Mr., 1773; Esq., 1779. OCCUPATIONAL PROFILE: merchant, in partnership with Michael Gilbert in Bushtown, Harford County, 1771–1776; planter; mill owner. PUBLIC CAREER. LEGISLATIVE SERVICE: Lower House, Baltimore County, 1770 (elected to the 3rd session to fill vacancy; Accounts 3), 1773, (resigned during or after the 2nd session to become a representative from Harford County); Lower House, Harford County, 1774 (elected to the 3rd session to represent the newly formed county); Conventions, Harford County, 1st, 1774 (appointed, but did not attend), 2nd–3rd, 1774, 6th–8th, 1775–1776; Lower House, Harford County, 1777–1778 (Manufactories 2). LOCAL OFFICES: justice, Baltimore County, 1757–1762, 1769–1773 (quorum, 1769–1773), Harford County, 1774–1779 (quorum, 1774–1779); sheriff, Baltimore County, 1762–1763 (resigned); Committee of Observation, Harford County, elected 1774; county lieutenant, Harford County, appointed 1777. MILITARY SERVICE: organized a militia company and was elected captain, 1775; colonel, 1776. STANDS ON PUBLIC/PRIVATE ISSUES: signed the Bush Declaration on March 22, 1775. WEALTH DURING LIFETIME. PERSONAL PROPERTY: The firm of Hall & Gilbert was indebted to Christopher Court, a London merchant, for £480.3.10 by 1776. Hall was personally indebted to Court for £1,282.5.9 by 1776, but the amount was contested by Hall's heirs and remained unpaid until at least 1807. LAND AT FIRST ELECTION: 882 acres in Baltimore County. SIGNIFICANT CHANGES IN LAND BETWEEN FIRST ELECTION AND DEATH: purchased 356.5 acres in Baltimore County by 1770; his wife inherited a life estate to more than 3,200 acres in Harford County from her father in 1774, but the land was entailed to her children. WEALTH AT DEATH. DIED: will probated on April 10, 1779, in Harford County. PERSONAL PROPERTY: mentioned 32 slaves in his will. LAND: 1,233.75 acres in Baltimore and Harford counties, plus land in Frederick County.

HALL, BENEDICT EDWARD (ca. 1744–1822).
BORN: ca. 1744 in St. George's Parish, Baltimore
County; second surviving son. NATIVE: fourth gen-
eration. RESIDED: at "Shandy Hall," Spesutia
Lower Hundred, Harford County. FAMILY BACK-
GROUND. FATHER: *John Hall* (1701–1774).
MOTHER: Hannah (1711–1782). BROTHERS: *John
Hall, Jr.* (1737–1770); Josiah (1739–1739); Aquila
(1742–1743); and *Josias Carvil Hall* (1746–1814).
SISTERS: Martha (1735–?), who married second,
John Rumsey (ca. 1742–1828); Mary (1740–?),
who married *Benjamin Rumsey* (1734–1808).
FIRST COUSINS: *Aquila Hall* (1727–1779); Martha
Hall, who married *Walter Tolley* (?–1783); Blanche
Hall, who married *John Beale Howard* (by 1739–
1799); and Sophia White (?–1780), who married
Aquila Hall (1727–1779). MARRIED in 1781 Mil-
cah (1756–?), daughter of *Amos Garrett* (1723–ca.
1789) and wife Frances Drew (1727–by 1786). Her
brother was Bennett (1745/46–by 1786). Her sis-
ters were Cassandra (1750–?); Frances (ca. 1763–
?). CHILDREN. SONS: Henry (by 1786–?); Benedict
Charles; and Edward Carvil. DAUGHTERS: Anne
Maria Caroline; Hannah Elizabeth; Charlotte; and
Harriet. PRIVATE CAREER. EDUCATION: literate.
RELIGIOUS AFFILIATION: Anglican, St. George's
Parish, Harford County; elected lay delegate to
the Protestant Episcopal Church Convention,
1788. SOCIAL STATUS AND ACTIVITIES: Gent.;
third generation legislator. OCCUPATIONAL PRO-
FILE: planter; associated with the mercantile firm
of Walter T. Hall & Co., Havre de Grace, Harford
County. PUBLIC CAREER. LEGISLATIVE SERVICE:
Conventions, Harford County, 1st, 1774, 4th,
1775, 5th, 1775; Senate, Western Shore, Term of
1776–1781: 1781 (elected on June 12, 1781, to fill
vacancy in the 1780–1781 Assembly; qualified on
June 17, 1781), Term of 1781–1786: 1781–1782,
1782–1783, 1783, 1784, 1785. LOCAL OFFICES: St.
George's Parish Vestry, Harford County, in office
1771–1774, 1784, 1787, 1792–1793, 1798–1800;
justice, Baltimore County, 1772–1773, Harford
County, 1774–1788; commissioner, Harford
County, appointed 1773; Committee of Correspondence, Harford County, elected 1774; justice,
Orphans' Court, Harford County, appointed 1777,
in office 1784–1789; commissioner of tax, Harford
County, 1777–1779; commissioner, Havre de
Grace, Harford County, appointed 1785; associate
justice, Third District Circuit Court, Harford
County, 1789–at least 1800. MILITARY SERVICE:
enrolled in Company No. 1, Harford County Mili-
tia, 1775; enrolled in Company No. 2, Harford
Rifles, Flying Camp, 1776. WEALTH DURING
LIFETIME. PERSONAL PROPERTY: 13 slaves, 1776;

assessed value £1,349.0.0 current money, including 26 slaves, 1783; inherited the personal estate of
Amos Garrett (1723–ca. 1789) in 1789, with a
value of at least £329.0.0 current money before
payment of debts. LAND AT FIRST ELECTION:
1,971 acres in Harford County (inherited from his
father in 1774). SIGNIFICANT CHANGES IN LAND
BETWEEN FIRST ELECTION AND DEATH: purchased ca. 400 acres in Harford County in the
1780s; assessed for 2,133 acres in Harford County,
1783; inherited a life estate in ca. 659 acres from
Amos Garrett (1723–ca. 1789) in 1789; mortgaged
his home plantation in 1801 (released in 1811) and
sold over 425 acres by 1810 to pay debts, some of
which had been incurred by Walter T. Hall & Co.;
purchased 5 lots in Havre de Grace, Harford
County, and gave his eldest son at least 1,300
acres of his home plantation shortly before his
death. WEALTH AT DEATH. DIED: will probated on
April 24, 1822, in Harford County. PERSONAL
PROPERTY: TEV, $1,794.44 current money; FB,
$653.46. LAND: at least 236 acres in Harford
County were mentioned in his will, all of which
were probably already in the possession of his
sons; 5 lots in Havre de Grace, Harford County.

HALL, BENJAMIN (1667–1721). BORN: in 1667
in Calvert County; third son. NATIVE: second generation. RESIDED: in Calvert County; St. Mary's
County briefly in the 1690s; Charles County,
1696. FAMILY BACKGROUND. FATHER: *Richard
Hall* (?–1688). MOTHER: Elizabeth. BROTHERS: *Elisha Hall* (1663–ca. 1716/17); Joseph (1665–1705);
and Aaron (1669–1704). SISTERS: Rachel (1671–
1730), who married *Walter Smith* (?–1711);
Elizabeth (1673–1743); Lucia (1675–?), who married *John Smith* (?–1738); and Sarah (1677–?),
who married *Robert Bradley* (?–1724). MARRIED
by 1696/97 Mary (1678–1742), widow of James
Bowling (?–1693); daughter of *Thomas Brooke*
(1632–1676) and wife Elinor Hatton; stepdaughter
of *Henry Darnall* (ca. 1645–1711); granddaughter
of *Robert Brooke* (1602–1655); niece of *Baker
Brooke* (1628–1678/79), *Charles Brooke* (1636–
1671), *William Hatton* (?–1712); *Zachary Wade*
(ca. 1627–1678), *Luke Gardiner* (1622–1674),
Clement Hill (?–1708), and *James Johnson* (?–?).
Mary Brooke Hall subsequently married Henry
Witham. Her brothers were *Thomas Brooke* (ca.
1659–1730/31); Robert (1663–1714); Ignatius
(1670–1751); Matthew (1672–1703); and Clement
(1676–1737). Her sister was Elinor. CHILDREN.
SON: Francis (1696–1785), who married Dorothy,
daughter of *Henry Lowe* (?–1717). PRIVATE CA-
REER. EDUCATION: literate. RELIGIOUS AFFILIA-

TION: raised as a Quaker; presumably a lapsed Quaker and a nominal Anglican during the period of his officeholding, 1694–1704; converted to Catholicism sometime after his marriage. SOCIAL STATUS AND ACTIVITIES: second generation burgess; son held no known office. OCCUPATIONAL PROFILE: possibly an agent in 1688 for the London merchant firm of Lane, Perry, & Paggan; merchant; planter. PUBLIC CAREER. LEGISLATIVE SERVICE: Lower House, Charles County, 1697/98–1700, 1701–1704. LOCAL OFFICES: justice, St. Mary's County, 1694–1694/95, Charles County, 1696–1698, 1700–1704; coroner, Charles County, 1697, 1699, 1702. MILITARY SERVICE: captain, 1700–1702. STANDS ON PUBLIC/PRIVATE ISSUES: Jacobite activity brought his dismissal from his justiceship in 1698. WEALTH DURING LIFETIME. LAND AT FIRST ELECTION: over 773 acres, of which 500 acres was inherited from his father in 1688. WEALTH AT DEATH. DIED: will probated on March 29, 1721. PERSONAL PROPERTY: TEV, £1,419.8.2 (including 31 slaves and 2 servants); FB, £1,301.1.6. LAND: 2,099 acres.

HALL, BENJAMIN, OF FRANCIS (?–1803). BORN: probably between 1730 and 1735 in Prince George's County; youngest son. NATIVE: fourth generation. RESIDED: at "Pleasant Hill," Prince George's County. FAMILY BACKGROUND. FATHER: Francis Hall, Gent. (ca. 1696–1785), son of *Benjamin Hall* (1667–1721). MOTHER: Dorothy (1704–?), daughter of *Henry Lowe* (?–1717) and wife Susanna Maria Bennett Darnall (1666–1714). UNCLES: *Henry Lowe* (?–1721); *Nicholas Lowe* (?–1728). AUNT: Jane Lowe, who married *James Bowles* (?–ca. 1727/28). BROTHERS: Francis; Richard Bennett (?–1805), who married Margaret. SISTERS: Eleanor, who married William Digges, Jr.; Susannah, who married Henry Darnall; and Henrietta, who married John Waring, Sr. OTHER KINSHIP: his great-grandfather was *Richard Hall* (?–1688); his great-uncle was *Elisha Hall* (1663–ca. 1716/17); his great-aunts were Rachel Hall, who married Col. *Walter Smith* (?–1711) and Lucia Hall, who married *John Smith* (?–1738). MARRIED in 1757 Elinor (?–1796), daughter of *William Murdock* (?–1769); stepdaughter of Margaret Dulany; granddaughter of *Thomas Addison* (1679–1727); stepgranddaughter of *Daniel Dulany* (1685–1753); niece of *John Addison* (1713–1764); half niece of both Rebecca Addison (1703–?), who married first, *James Bowles* (?–ca. 1727/28), and second, *George Plater* (1695–1755), and Elinor Addison, who married fourth, *Corbin Lee* (?–1774). Her brothers were John (1729–?); *Addison Murdock*

(1731–1793); and John (1733–1791). Her sisters were Catherine (?–1771); Ann; and Mary (?–1792). Elinor Hall's stepmother Margaret Dulany was the widow of Dr. *Alexander Hamilton* (1712–1756). CHILDREN. SONS: William Murdock (1759–ca. 1792), who married Ann Duckett; Henry Lowe (1761–1817), who died without progeny. DAUGHTERS: Anne (1762–?), who married *Thomas Clark* (ca. 1760–1796); Eleanor (1768–?), who married first, Dr. David Clarke, and second, (first name unknown) Magruder; and Catherine (1778–?), who married John Burgess Bowie. PRIVATE CAREER. RELIGIOUS AFFILIATION: his grandfather *Benjamin Hall* (1667–1721) was a Catholic convert by his death and his father received his education at a Jesuit College. SOCIAL STATUS AND ACTIVITIES: Gent., 1787. OCCUPATIONAL PROFILE: probably a planter; he was given one-half of the merchandise in his father's store in 1772, but did not take ownership until his father's death in 1785; he owned a tanyard at the time of his death. PUBLIC CAREER. LEGISLATIVE SERVICE: Conventions, Prince George's County, 1st, 1774, 4th, 1775, 5th, 1775, 9th, 1776 (elected to the Convention after election of first delegation was voided); Lower House, Prince George's County, 1779–1780 (Claims 2). OTHER STATE OFFICE: Constitution Ratification Convention, Prince George's County, 1788. LOCAL OFFICE: justice, Prince George's County, commissioned 1750, 1751, 1777, 1778, and 1779. WEALTH DURING LIFETIME. PERSONAL PROPERTY: his wife's inheritance amounted to £500 sterling, 1769; 35 slaves, plus one-half of the goods in his father's store inherited from his father, 1785; 49 slaves, 1798. LAND AT FIRST ELECTION: he owned no land in his own name; but he was probably living on the land that was later devised to him by his father. SIGNIFICANT CHANGES IN LAND BETWEEN FIRST ELECTION AND DEATH: inherited 1,844 acres in Prince George's and Frederick counties, 1785; purchased 80 acres in Prince George's County, 1787; taxed for 5 tenant and overseer houses, his own house, and the houses and outbuildings of his two sons, 1798. WEALTH AT DEATH. DIED: between February and April 1803 in Prince George's County, at an advanced age. PERSONAL PROPERTY: TEV, £3,319.15.6 current money (including 64 slaves, 184 oz. plate, and 2 stills); FB, £2,101.8.6. LAND: at least 1,924 acres in Prince George's and Frederick counties.

HALL, CHRISTOPHER (?–1746). BORN: in Kent County, of age by 1722; eldest son. NATIVE: at least second generation. RESIDED: in Shrewsbury Parish, Kent County. FAMILY BACKGROUND.

FATHER: John Hall (?–1736), of Kent County. MOTHER: Ann (?–after 1736). BROTHERS: George; John. MARRIED Mary (?–by 1746). CHILDREN. SON: *William Hall* (1723–1780). DAUGHTERS: Elizabeth, who married by 1745 James Gray; Sarah, who married by 1745 James Woodland; Mary; Rachel, who married Andrew Hynson; and Margaret, who married by 1745 George Wilson. PRIVATE CAREER. EDUCATION: literate. RELIGIOUS AFFILIATION: Anglican, Shrewsbury Parish, Kent County. SOCIAL STATUS AND ACTIVITIES: Gent., 1745/46. OCCUPATIONAL PROFILE: planter. PUBLIC CAREER. LEGISLATIVE SERVICE: Lower House, Kent County, 1732–1734, 1734/35–1737. LOCAL OFFICES: churchwarden, Shrewsbury Parish, Kent County, in office 1724, 1729; Shrewsbury Parish Vestry, Kent County, in office 1725, 1726–1729, and 1745–1746. WEALTH DURING LIFETIME. LAND AT FIRST ELECTION: 115 acres in Kent County. SIGNIFICANT CHANGES IN LAND BETWEEN FIRST ELECTION AND DEATH: acquired an additional 435 acres in Kent County by 1737. WEALTH AT DEATH. DIED: between March 13, 1745/46, and April 7, 1746, in Kent County. PERSONAL PROPERTY: TEV, £1,234.13.4 current money (including 16 slaves and 1 servant); FB, £141.12.0. LAND: possibly 550 acres in Kent County.

HALL, ELIHU (1724–ca. 1791). BORN: in 1724 in Cecil County; second son. NATIVE: fourth generation. RESIDED: in North Susquehanna and Octarara hundreds, Cecil County. FAMILY BACKGROUND. FATHER: Elihu Hall (1692–1753), of Calvert, Anne Arundel, and Cecil counties; son of *Elisha Hall* (1663–ca. 1716/17). MOTHER: Elizabeth, daughter of Richard Harrison (?–1716/17), of Calvert County. BROTHER: Elisha Hall (1723–1757), who married in 1746 Ruth, daughter of Jacob Hall. SISTERS: Elizabeth; Sarah, who married Andrew Bay, of South Carolina. OTHER KINSHIP: his father married first, in 1730 Elizabeth, daughter of Philip Coale. His great-grandfather was *Richard Hall* (?–1688); his great-uncle was *Benjamin Hall* (1667–1721); his great-aunts were Rachel Hall (1671–1730), who married *Walter Smith* (?–1711); Lucia Hall (1675–?), who married *John Smith* (?–1738); and Sarah Hall (1677–?), who married *Robert Bradley* (?–1724). MARRIED on June 16, 1757, Catharine (1736–?), daughter of John Orrick (?–1749) and wife Susannah. Her brothers were John; Nicholas; and Charles. Her sisters were Rachel; Rebecca; Sarah; and Susanna. CHILDREN. SONS: Elihu (1758–ca. 1793), who married Charity; John (1760–1826);

James (1762–1793); Elisha John (1764–1835); Charles (1767–1821); Samuel Chew (1769–?), who never married; George Whitefield (1770–?), who never married; Henry (1773–1808), a physician, who married Hester, daughter of the Hon. William Maclay, the first U.S. senator from Pennsylvania; and Washington (1776–?). DAUGHTERS: Susan (1766–1852), who married Robert Lyon (1754–1842), of Baltimore County; Elizabeth Harrison (1772–?), who married first, (first name unknown) Ogle, and second, (first name unknown) Gordon; Catharine Orrick (1775–?), who married (first name unknown) Churchman; and Julia Reed (1778–?), who never married. PRIVATE CAREER. EDUCATION: literate. RELIGIOUS AFFILIATION: he came from a Quaker family; his son Elihu was an elder of the Presbyterian Church, West Nottingham, Cecil County, 1792. SOCIAL STATUS AND ACTIVITIES: Mr., 1779; Esq., 1790. OCCUPATIONAL PROFILE: probably a planter. PUBLIC CAREER. LEGISLATIVE SERVICE: Lower House, Cecil County, 1779–1780 (resigned on April 29, 1780). LOCAL OFFICES: justice, Cecil County, 1756–1771 (quorum, 1758–1771), probably 1772–1776 (probably quorum; records missing), 1777 (quorum); justice, Court of Oyer and Terminer and Gaol Delivery, Cecil County, commissioned 1762; justice, Orphans' Court, Cecil County, commissioned 1777. MILITARY SERVICE: 2nd major, Susquehanna Battalion, Maryland Militia, appointed 1766. ADDITIONAL COMMENTS: His son, Elihu, served in the First Maryland Regiment and was taken prisoner at Staten Island in August 1777, where he remained until exchanged in October 1780. He resigned in May 1781, but later served in the Maryland Militia. WEALTH DURING LIFETIME. PERSONAL PROPERTY: assessed value £627.0.0, including 12 slaves and 8 oz. plate, 1783. LAND AT FIRST ELECTION: 1,353 acres in Cecil County (inherited 1,746 acres from his father in 1754, but sold 393 acres of it by 1764). SIGNIFICANT CHANGES IN LAND BETWEEN FIRST ELECTION AND DEATH: he was charged with 610 acres in Cecil County, 1783. WEALTH AT DEATH. DIED: between December 17, 1790, and February 16, 1791. LAND: 270 acres in Cecil County mentioned in his will, plus several other tracts with unspecified acreage; may have had as much as 600 acres.

HALL, ELISHA (1663–ca. 1716/17). BORN: in 1663 in Calvert County; first son. NATIVE: second generation. RESIDED: in Calvert County. FAMILY BACKGROUND. FATHER: *Richard Hall* (?–1688). MOTHER: Elizabeth. BROTHERS: Joseph (1665–1705), who married Ann; *Benjamin Hall* (1667–

1721), who married Mary (1678–1742), widow of James Bowling (?–1693) and daughter of *Thomas Brooke* (1632–1676); and Aaron (1669–1704). SIS-TERS: Rachel (1671–1730), who married *Walter Smith* (?–1711); Elizabeth (1673–1743); Lucia (1675–?), who married *John Smith* (?–1738); and Sarah (1677–?), who married *Robert Bradley* (?–1724). MARRIED in 1688 Sarah, widow of Jonas Wingfield; daughter of Richard Hooper. CHIL-DREN. SONS: Richard (1690–1739); Elisha (1692–1753), who married first, Elizabeth (?–1721), daughter of Philip Coale, and second, ca. 1722 Elizabeth, widow of John Chew (1687–1718) and daughter of Richard Harrison. DAUGHTERS: Elizabeth (1691–?), who married in 1708 Richard Harrison, Jr.; Sarah (1694–1741), who married in 1711 Samuel Harrison; and Mary. PRIVATE CA-REER. EDUCATION: literate. RELIGIOUS AFFILIA-TION: raised as a Quaker; a nominal Anglican (at least during his period of officeholding, 1696–1704) who had pew in All Saints' Church, Calvert County, 1703/4; a practicing Quaker by the spring of 1704. SOCIAL STATUS AND ACTIVITIES: second generation burgess. OCCUPATIONAL PROFILE: planter. PUBLIC CAREER. LEGISLATIVE SERVICE: Lower House, Calvert County, 1697/98–1700 (Aggrievances 2, 3; Elections and Privileges 3, 4, probably chairman 4), 1701–1704 (Elections and Privileges 1, 3; dismissed from the 5th session for failure to subscribe to the required oaths). LOCAL OFFICE: justice, Calvert County, 1696–1698, by 1700–?. STANDS ON PUBLIC/PRIVATE ISSUES: op-posed the revolution of 1689; Jacobite activity brought his dismissal from his justiceship, 1698. WEALTH DURING LIFETIME. LAND AT FIRST ELECTION: ca. 1,500 acres (inherited from his fa-ther in 1688). WEALTH AT DEATH. DIED: will pro-bated on February 8, 1716/17. PERSONAL PROP-ERTY: TEV, £1,465.0.11 (including 31 slaves); FB, £1,415.7.3. LAND: ca. 1,500 acres.

HALL, HENRY (1702/3–1756). BORN: on March 2, 1702/3, in St. James' Parish, Anne Arundel County; eldest son. NATIVE: second generation. RESIDED: at "Morley's Lott," South River, Anne Arundel County. FAMILY BACKGROUND. FATHER: Rev. Henry Hall (1676–1722), A.B., Cambridge University, 1697; immigrated in 1698 from Hor-sham, England, to become the first rector of St. James' Parish, Anne Arundel County. MOTHER: Mary (ca. 1682–?), daughter of Mareen Duvall (?–1694). BROTHERS: Benjamin (1706–1709); Benja-min (1710–1760), who married in 1731 Sophia Welsh; Edward (1714–1744), who married Mary Belt; John (1716–1790), who married in 1745

Anne Wells; and William (1719–1770), who mar-ried Rachel. SISTERS: Mary (1704–?), who married first, Gundar Erickson, and second, John Smith; Magdalene, who married Jonathan Davies; and Martha (1708–1752), who married in 1726 Stephen West (1682–1752). NEPHEW: *Stephen West* (1727–1790). MARRIED first, on September 25, 1723, Martha (?–1734), daughter of Ishmeal Bate-man and wife Mary. MARRIED second, on Novem-ber 12, 1734, Elizabeth Lansdale. CHILDREN. SONS: *Henry Hall* (1727–1770); *John Hall* (1729–1797); Benjamin (1732–?); Edward (1735–?), who mar-ried in 1756 Martha Duckett; Isaac (1737–?), who married in 1760 Ruth, daughter of *Mordecai Jacob* (1714–1771); Thomas Henry (1744–1788), who married Barbara Bowie, who subsequently mar-ried *Ignatius Taylor* (?–1807); and William (1748–?), who married Margaret Harwood. DAUGHTERS: Mary (1724/25–?); Elizabeth (1739–?), who mar-ried in 1768 John Dorsey; Martha (1741–1747); Margaret (1746–?), who married Col. *Richard Harwood* (1738–1826); Mary (1752–1771); and Martha (1755–?), who married in 1769 (first name unknown) Lawrence. PRIVATE CAREER. EDUCA-TION: literate. RELIGIOUS AFFILIATION: Anglican, All Hallow's Parish, Anne Arundel County. SO-CIAL STATUS AND ACTIVITIES: Gent., by 1742. OCCUPATIONAL PROFILE: planter; merchant, deal-ing with John Buchanan and Silvanus Grove, mer-chants of London, England, to whom he owed £767.1.5 sterling at the time of his death. PUBLIC CAREER. LEGISLATIVE SERVICE: Lower House, Anne Arundel County, 1740–1741 (elected to the 1st session to fill vacancy; Arms and Ammunition 3), 1742–1744 (Arms and Ammunition 1, 2; Laws 2; Elections 2), 1745 (Arms and Ammunition; Laws), 1745/46–1748 (Arms and Ammunition Cv 1, 1–3, 4; Laws Cv, 1–3, 4; Bills of Credit 1, 2), 1751–1754 (Laws 1–6), 1754–1756 (Laws 1–4; died during the 4th session). LOCAL OFFICES: jus-tice, Anne Arundel County, 1739–at least 1743 (quorum, 1742–at least 1743). WEALTH DURING LIFETIME. LAND AT FIRST ELECTION: ca. 1,713 acres in Anne Arundel, Prince George's, and Baltimore counties, plus 2 lots in Queen Anne, Prince George's County (ca. 1,115 acres inherited from his father, 1722; 350 acres by deed of gift from his mother, 1724). SIGNIFICANT CHANGES IN LAND BETWEEN FIRST ELECTION AND DEATH: purchased over 800 acres in Anne Arundel County between 1742 and 1744 to enlarge his holdings along the Patuxent River. Sold 275 acres in Baltimore County in 1746 and 110 acres in Prince George's County in 1756. WEALTH AT DEATH. DIED: on May 18, 1756, at "Morley's Lott" near the head of the South River, Anne Arundel County. PERSONAL PROPERTY: TEV, £553.5.4 sterling, £4,239.17.10 current money, 2,161 pounds of tobacco (including 41 slaves, 1 servant, and new goods in his store valued at £295.11.5 current money); FB, estate overpaid £308.1.6 sterling, but with positive balances of £4,202.8.8 current money and 2,161 pounds of tobacco. LAND: 2,218 acres in Anne Arundel and Prince George's counties, plus 2 lots in Queen Anne, Prince George's County.

HALL, HENRY (1727–1770). BORN: on May 27, 1727, in All Hallow's Parish, Anne Arundel County; eldest son. NATIVE: third generation. RESIDED: in Anne Arundel County. FAMILY BACKGROUND. FATHER: *Henry Hall* (1702/3–1756). MOTHER: Martha Bateman (?–1734). STEPMOTHER: Elizabeth Lansdale. BROTHERS: *John Hall* (1729–1797); Benjamin (1732–?). HALF BROTHERS: Edward (1735–?); Isaac (1737–?), who married in 1760 Ruth, daughter of *Mordecai Jacob* (1714–1771); Thomas Henry (1744–1788), who married Barbara Bowie, who subsequently married *Ignatius Taylor* (?–1807); and William (1748–?). SISTER: Mary (1724/25–?). HALF SISTERS: Elizabeth (1739–?); Martha (1741–1747); Margaret (1746–?), who married Col. *Richard Harwood* (1738–1826); Mary (1752–1771); and Martha (1755–?). COUSIN: *Stephen West* (1727–1790). MARRIED in 1748 Elizabeth (?–1789), daughter of Nicholas Watkins (?–1770), of Anne Arundel County, planter, and wife Margaret. Her brothers were John; Gassaway; Joseph; Thomas; and Jeremiah. Her sister was Ann. CHILDREN. SONS: Maj. Henry (1751–?), who married first, Margery Howard, and second, Rachel Harwood; Nicholas, who married first, Martha Hall Howard, and second, Ann Griffith; William, who married in 1782 Martha Duckett; and John Stephen, who married in 1788 Elizabeth Boyd. DAUGHTERS: Martha (1755–?), who married in 1770 Joseph Howard; Mary, who married in 1778 David Steuart; Margaret (?–1805); Anne, who married first, Thomas Rutland, and second, John Watkins; and Elizabeth, who married John Watkins. PRIVATE CAREER. EDUCATION: literate. RELIGIOUS AFFILIATION: Anglican, All Hallow's Parish, Anne Arundel County. SOCIAL STATUS AND ACTIVITIES: Gent., by 1764. OCCUPATIONAL PROFILE: merchant; land speculator. PUBLIC CAREER. LEGISLATIVE SERVICE: Lower House, Anne Arundel County, 1762–1763 (Grievances 1, 2; Bills of Credit 1, 2), 1765–1766 (Bills of Credit 2, 4; Elections 4; Public Offices 3, 4). LOCAL OFFICES: justice, Anne Arundel County, 1752–1770

(quorum, 1761–1770); justice, Court of Oyer and Terminer and Gaol Delivery, Anne Arundel County, commissioned 1764. MILITARY SERVICE: major, period of service unknown. WEALTH DURING LIFETIME. LAND AT FIRST ELECTION: 2,157 acres in Anne Arundel, Prince George's, and Frederick counties (ca. 980 acres inherited from his father, 1756), plus control of his younger brother's 452-acre inheritance until 1764. SIGNIFICANT CHANGES IN LAND BETWEEN FIRST ELECTION AND DEATH: during the 1760s Hall patented ca. 7,815 acres in Frederick County and ca. 163 acres in Anne Arundel County. He sold off the land in Frederick County piecemeal, with several sales still pending at the time of his death, and mortgaged over 3,000 acres in Prince George's, Frederick and Anne Arundel counties to his brother *John Hall* (1729–1797) in 1764 and 1767. WEALTH AT DEATH. DIED: on January 11, 1770, in Anne Arundel County. PERSONAL PROPERTY: TEV, £1,358.4.5 current money (including 6 slaves, 49.5 oz. plate, books, dry goods, and hardware); FB, £105.10.1 current money. LAND: 7,605 acres in Anne Arundel, Prince George's, and Frederick counties. He had already made contracts to sell at least 1,000 acres in Prince George's and Frederick counties, however, and directed in his will that ca. 5,700 acres in Frederick County should be sold to pay his debts and mortgages.

HALL, JOHN (ca. 1658–1737). BORN: ca. 1658 in Anne Arundel County; only son. NATIVE: second generation. RESIDED: in Anne Arundel County; Baltimore County after 1682. FAMILY BACKGROUND. FATHER: John Hall (?–by 1660), who immigrated in 1640. MOTHER: Mary (1632–1699), daughter of *William Parker* (?–1673/74). She subsequently married by 1661 Robert Paca (?–1681). HALF BROTHER: *Aquila Paca* (early 1670s–1721). MARRIED first, Sarah (?–1693), widow of both George Hooper and John Collier. Her brother was Abraham Homan. MARRIED second, in 1693 Martha, widow of George Goldsmith (?–1692); daughter of Edward Beadle and wife Susannah. CHILDREN. SONS: John (1694/95–1701); Edward (1697–1738), a justice of Baltimore County from 1721 to 1732, who married in 1717 Avarilla, daughter of *John Carvile* (ca. 1670–1709); Acquila (1699–1728), who married Johanna, widow of *James Phillips* (?–1720); *John Hall* (1701–1774), who married in 1734 Hannah Johns; and Parker (1707–1756), a justice of Baltimore County from 1736/37 to 1751, who married Blanche, daughter of *John Carvile* (ca. 1670–1709). DAUGHTER: Sophia (1709/10–?), who married Col. Thomas White.

STEPDAUGHTERS: Isabella Hooper; Ann Collier. PRIVATE CAREER. EDUCATION: literate. RELIGIOUS AFFILIATION: Anglican. SOCIAL STATUS AND ACTIVITIES: became a leading figure in Baltimore County and one of the largest landowners in that county in the 1690s. OCCUPATIONAL PROFILE: planter, by 1683. PUBLIC CAREER. LEGISLATIVE SERVICE: Lower House, Baltimore County, 1696–1697 (elected to the 6th session), 1697/98–1700 (Accounts 1, 2; Aggrievances 4), 1701–1704 (Accounts 1–3), 1707 (elected to the 5th session); Upper House, 1709–1711 (appointed before the 2nd session), 1712–1714, 1715, 1716–1718, 1719–1721/22, 1722–1724, 1725–1727, 1728–1731, 1732–1734, 1734/35–1737 (president, 1, Cv, 2; did not attend the 3rd session; died during the 4th session). OTHER PROVINCIAL OFFICES: justice, Provincial Court, 1700–1707 (quorum, 1704–1707); Council, 1709–1737 (president, 1733/34–1737). LOCAL OFFICES: sheriff, Baltimore County, 1691–1693/94; justice, Baltimore County, 1694–1701; deputy commissary, Baltimore County, 1698/99. MILITARY SERVICE: captain, 1695. WEALTH DURING LIFETIME. PERSONAL PROPERTY: headed a household of 5 taxables with 1 slave, 1692; 6 taxables including 1 slave, 1695. LAND AT FIRST ELECTION: over 2,000 acres. WEALTH AT DEATH. DIED: will probated on August 27, 1737. PERSONAL PROPERTY: TEV, £1,547.11.6 (including 26 slaves and books); FB, £41.5.6. LAND: over 6,738 acres.

HALL, JOHN (1701–1774). BORN: in 1701 in St. George's Parish, Baltimore County; third surviving son. NATIVE: third generation. RESIDED: in St. George's Parish, Baltimore County (later became Harford County). FAMILY BACKGROUND. FATHER: *John Hall* (ca. 1658–1737). MOTHER: Martha. BROTHERS: John (1694/95–1701); Edward (1697–1738); Aquila (1699–1728/29); and Parker (1707–ca. 1756). SISTER: Sophia (1709/10–?). NEPHEW: *Aquila Hall* (1727–1779). NIECES: Martha Hall, who married *Walter Tolley* (?–1783); Blanche Hall, who married *John Beale Howard* (by 1739–1799); and Sophia White, who married *Aquila Hall* (1727–1779). MARRIED in 1734 Hannah (1711–1782), widow of Abraham Johns (?–1731), chirurgeon, of Baltimore County; daughter of *Roger Matthews* (ca. 1686–1741) and wife Mary Carvil (?–1718); stepdaughter of Elizabeth Garrett; niece of *John Carvile* (ca. 1670–1709). Her brothers were John (1714–?), who married Ann Maxwell; Roger (1718–?). Her half brothers were James (1727–?); Aquila (1733–?); Leven (1736–?); and Bennett (1739–?). Her half sister was Emolia

(1729–by 1740). CHILDREN. SONS: *John Hall, Jr.* (1737–1770); Josiah (1739–1739); Aquila (1742–1743); *Benedict Edward Hall* (ca. 1744–1822); and *Josias Carvil Hall* (1746–1814). DAUGHTERS: Martha (1735–?), who married first, (first name unknown) Giles, and second, *John Rumsey* (ca. 1742–1828); Mary (1740–?), who married *Benjamin Rumsey* (1734–1808). WARDS: the sons of his brother Aquila, John (1722–1768), who married Cordelia Holland, and *Aquila Hall* (1727–1779). PRIVATE CAREER. EDUCATION: literate. RELIGIOUS AFFILIATION: Anglican, St. George's Parish, Baltimore County. SOCIAL STATUS AND ACTIVITIES: Gent. OCCUPATIONAL PROFILE: planter. PUBLIC CAREER. LEGISLATIVE SERVICE: Lower House, Baltimore County, 1745, 1745/46–1748. LOCAL OFFICES: justice, Baltimore County, in office 1728–1730; 1734–1735; 1746 (quorum) and 1747; sheriff, Baltimore County, 1730–1733, January–November 1735; St. George's Parish Vestry, Baltimore County, in office 1730–1733, 1741–1744, 1749–1752, 1754–1757; justice, Court of Oyer and Terminer and Gaol Delivery, Baltimore County, commissioned 1759, 1760, 1761, and 1763. MILITARY SERVICE: major, by 1737; colonel, by 1743. WEALTH DURING LIFETIME. LAND AT FIRST ELECTION: 5,265 acres in Baltimore County (1,740 acres inherited from his father, 1737; 260 acres by marriage). SIGNIFICANT CHANGES IN LAND BETWEEN FIRST ELECTION AND DEATH: purchased several small pieces of land in Baltimore County in the 1750s and 1760s and leased out lots in Joppa, Baltimore County, owned by his wife before their marriage; assessed for 5,516 acres in Baltimore County in 1768; inherited 142 acres in Baltimore County from his son *John Hall, Jr.* (1737–1770) in 1770; gave at least 923 acres in Baltimore County to his two daughters and their husbands in 1770 and 1771. WEALTH AT DEATH. DIED: will probated on May 11, 1774, in Harford County. LAND: at least 4,462 acres in Baltimore County (some of which had become part of Harford County).

HALL, JOHN (1729–1797). BORN: on November 23, 1729, in All Hallow's Parish, Anne Arundel County; second son. NATIVE: third generation. RESIDED: in St. Mary's County until ca. 1764; Annapolis, Anne Arundel County, 1765; "Vineyard," Anne Arundel County, ca. 1788. FAMILY BACKGROUND. FATHER: *Henry Hall* (1702/3–1756). MOTHER: Martha Bateman (?–1734). STEPMOTHER: Elizabeth Lansdale. BROTHERS: *Henry Hall* (1727–1770); Benjamin (1732–?). STEPBROTHERS: Edward (1735–?); Isaac (1737–?), who married in 1760

Ruth, daughter of *Mordecai Jacob* (1714–1771); Thomas Henry (1744–1788), who married Barbara Bowie, who subsequently married *Ignatius Taylor* (?–1807); and William (1748–?). SISTER: Mary (1724/25–?). STEPSISTERS: Elizabeth (1739–?); Martha (1741–1747); Margaret (1746–?), who married *Richard Harwood* (1738–1826); Mary (1752–1771); and Martha (1755–?). FIRST COUSIN: *Stephen West* (1727–1790). MARRIED on August 23, 1767, Eleanor (ca. 1739–1805), daughter of Richard Dorsey (1714–1760), of Anne Arundel County, and wife Elizabeth (1711–ca. 1776); granddaughter of *John Beale* (?–1734); niece of both *Edward Dorsey* (1718–1760) and Mary Dorsey (1725–ca. 1787), who married *John Ridgely* (?–1771). Her brothers were Caleb, who married Mary Rutland; Richard; and Edward. Her sisters were Mary (?–1816), who married *John Weems* (1727–1794); Anne, who married Benjamin Beall; Elizabeth, who married first, (first name unknown) MacGoway, and second, Elijah Harrison. Her first cousins were *Thomas Dorsey* (?–1790); *Harry Dorsey Gough* (ca. 1745–1808); *Charles Ridgely, of John* (?–ca. 1787); Eleanor Dorsey (ca. 1739–1805), who married *Upton Sheredine* (1740–1800); Achsah Dorsey (1746–1799), who married *Ephraim Howard* (1745–1788); Rebecca Dorsey (1739–1812), who married *Charles Ridgely* (1733–1790); Deborah Ridgely (1749–1817), who married *John Sterett* (1750/51–1787); and Mary Ridgely (?–1804), who married *Benjamin Nicholson* (?–1792). CHILDREN. Died without progeny. PRIVATE CAREER. EDUCATION: received legal training. RELIGIOUS AFFILIATION: Anglican, St. Anne's Parish, Anne Arundel County. SOCIAL STATUS AND ACTIVITIES: Esq., by 1754. OCCUPATIONAL PROFILE: lawyer, admitted to the following courts: Prince George's County in June 1752; Charles County in March 1753; Provincial Court in April 1753; Anne Arundel County in November 1754; Chancery Court by February 1761; Frederick County Court in August 1763. He appeared as an attorney in the Anne Arundel County Court over 300 times between 1754 and 1768. PUBLIC CAREER. LEGISLATIVE SERVICE: Lower House, St. Mary's County, 1762–1763 (Elections 1, 2; Grievances 1, 2; Public Offices 1), Annapolis, 1765–1766 (elected to the 2nd session to fill vacancy; Public Offices 2–4; Grievances 4; Laws to Expire 4), 1768–1770 (Public Offices 2, 3; Elections 3), 1771 (Elections), Anne Arundel County, 1773–1774 (Elections 1, Cv, 2, 3; Public Offices 1, Cv, 2, 3); Conventions, Anne Arundel County, 1st, 1774, 2nd–3rd, 1774 (chairman 3rd), 4th, 1775, 5th, 1775, 9th, 1776 (Elected to fill va-

cancy); Lower House, Anne Arundel County, 1777 (Elections 1; Grievances 1, 2; Laws to Expire 1), 1777–1778 (Elections 1, 2; Grievances 1; Manufactories 1; resigned on June 9, 1778), 1778–1779 (Elections 1; Grievances 1, 3), 1779–1780 (Elections 1; Grievances 1), 1780–1781, 1781–1782 (Grievances 1, 2), 1782–1783 (Grievances 1, 2), 1783 (Grievances), 1784 (Grievances), 1785; Senate, Western Shore, Term of 1786–1791: 1786–1787, 1787–1788, 1788, 1789, 1790, Term of 1791–1796: 1791–1792, 1792, 1793, 1794, 1795. OTHER STATE OFFICE: Council of Safety, Western Shore, 2nd, 1776, 3rd 1776, 4th, 1776, 5th, 1776–1777. LOCAL OFFICES: recorder, Annapolis, in office 1766; St. Anne's Parish Vestry, Anne Arundel County, in office 1769–1772. OUT OF STATE SERVICE: delegate, Continental Congress, 1774 (elected in December 1774, but no meetings of Congress were held), 1775 (elected in April 1775 and August 1775; resigned on December 9, 1775), 1779 (elected in December 1779, but did not attend), 1783 (elected on December 9, 1783, to fill vacancy, but did not attend; resigned by March 8, 1784, because of poor health). STANDS ON PUBLIC/PRIVATE ISSUES: he was allied with *Matthias Hammond* (1740–1786) and *Rezin Hammond* (1745–1809) in a radical coalition of the Popular Party, 1774–1776. He voted to exempt military personnel from the General Assembly in 1777 because of his belief in the complete separation of the legislative and executive branches of government. Because the executive controlled the military, Hall believed that there was the potential for conflict of interest. WEALTH DURING LIFETIME. PERSONAL PROPERTY: assessed value £1,270.0.0, including 27 slaves and 60 oz. plate, 1783. Throughout his career Hall held a number of mortgages on land and personal property. LAND AT FIRST ELECTION: 317 acres in St. Mary's and Anne Arundel counties, plus 3.5 lots in Annapolis (probably all by purchase). SIGNIFICANT CHANGES IN LAND BETWEEN FIRST ELECTION AND DEATH: owned and leased out at least 2 additional lots in Annapolis; increased his home plantation on the south side of the Severn River to over 880 acres (ca. 660 acres of which he acquired through his marriage); bought a 5,400-acre tract in Frederick County from the estate of his brother *Henry Hall* (1727–1770) in 1772, and sold off at least 3,800 acres of it during the next 25 years; acquired 670 acres in Anne Arundel County from a default on a mortgage he held. WEALTH AT DEATH. DIED: on March 8, 1797, at "Vineyard," Anne Arundel County. PERSONAL PROPERTY: TEV, £5,811.19.5 current money (including 31 slaves and law books); FB, £1,363.11.9. LAND: 1,570 acres in Frederick County and 1,554 acres in Anne Arundel County, plus 2.5 lots in Annapolis. ADDITIONAL COMMENTS: his principal heirs were the children of his brother *Henry Hall* (1727–1770), although his wife received a life estate in his Annapolis and Anne Arundel County land. His will provided for the manumission of his slaves.

HALL, JOHN, JR. (1737–1770). BORN: in 1737 in St. George's Parish, Baltimore County; eldest son. NATIVE: fourth generation. RESIDED: probably with his father in St. George's Parish, Baltimore County. FAMILY BACKGROUND. FATHER: *John Hall* (1701–1774). MOTHER: Hannah (1711–1782). BROTHERS: Josiah (1739–1739); Aquila (1742–1743); *Benedict Edward Hall* (ca. 1744–1822); and *Josias Carvil Hall* (1746–1814). SISTERS: Martha (1735–?), who married second, *John Rumsey* (ca. 1742–1828); Mary (1740–?), who married *Benjamin Rumsey* (1734–1808). FIRST COUSINS: *Aquila Hall* (1727–1779); Martha Hall, who married *Walter Tolley* (?–1783); Blanche Hall, who married *John Beale Howard* (by 1739–1799); and Sophia White (?–1780), who married *Aquila Hall* (1727–1779). MARRIED never. CHILDREN. Died without progeny. PRIVATE CAREER. EDUCATION: literate. RELIGIOUS AFFILIATION: Anglican, St. George's Parish, Baltimore County. SOCIAL STATUS AND ACTIVITIES: Gent.; third generation legislator. OCCUPATIONAL PROFILE: planter. PUBLIC CAREER. LEGISLATIVE SERVICE: Lower House, Baltimore County, 1765–1766 (Grievances 2; Public Offices 3). WEALTH DURING LIFETIME. LAND AT FIRST ELECTION: 142 acres in Baltimore County. WEALTH AT DEATH. DIED: will probated on July 16, 1770, in Baltimore County. LAND: 142 acres in Baltimore County.

HALL, JOSEPH (ca. 1701–?). BORN: ca. 1701 in Calvert County; only surviving son. NATIVE: third generation. RESIDED: in Calvert County. FAMILY BACKGROUND. FATHER: Joseph Hall (?–1705), son of *Richard Hall* (?–1688). STEPFATHER: Rev. Thomas Cockshutt (?–1722), of All Saints' Parish, Calvert County. MOTHER: Ann (?–1742). UNCLES: *Elisha Hall* (1663–ca. 1716/17); *Benjamin Hall* (1667–1721). AUNTS: Rachel Hall (1671–1730), who married *Walter Smith* (?–1711); Lucia Hall (1675–?), who married *John Smith* (?–1738); and Sarah Hall (1677–?), who married *Robert Bradley* (?–1724). STEPBROTHER: Thomas Cockshutt (ca. 1708–1734), who married Rebecca. STEPSISTER: Martha Cockshutt, who married ca. 1714 Thomas Lingan. STEPSISTERS OR HALF SISTERS: Elizabeth

Cockshutt; Ann Cockshutt. MARRIED in 1722 Sarah, widow of William Richardson; daughter of *John Smith* (?–1738), of Hall's Creek, Calvert County, a merchant, and wife Sarah. Her brother was John Smith. Her sisters were Rachel, who married *Thomas Gantt* (ca. 1710–1785); Jane (?–by 1738); and Tabitha (ca. 1690–1769), who married *Thomas Sheredine* (1699–1752). Her nephews were *Upton Sheredine* (1740–1800); *Thomas Gantt, Jr.* (?–1808). Her niece was Rachel Gantt (?–1793), who married *Richard Brooke* (1716–1783). CHILDREN. SON: John (by 1738–?). DAUGHTERS: Rachel; Ann. PRIVATE CAREER. RELIGIOUS AFFILIATION: Anglican. SOCIAL STATUS AND ACTIVITIES: Gent., 1728. OCCUPATIONAL PROFILE: probably a planter. PUBLIC CAREER. LEGISLATIVE SERVICE: Lower House, Calvert County, 1739–1741 (Aggrievances 3), 1742–1744 (Aggrievances 1, 2), 1745, 1745/46–1748. LOCAL OFFICES: Christ Church Parish Vestry, Calvert County, 1725–1730, 1736–1739; deputy commissary, Calvert County, by 1730–1734; justice, Calvert County, in office by 1731–at least 1733 (quorum); churchwarden, Christ Church Parish, Calvert County, 1735–1736. WEALTH DURING LIFETIME. LAND AT FIRST ELECTION: 934 acres in Calvert and Prince George's counties (287 acres through his marriage). SIGNIFICANT CHANGES IN LAND BETWEEN FIRST ELECTION AND DEATH: mortgaged 647 acres in Calvert County, 1747; may have patented 128 acres in Anne Arundel County and 45 acres in Sussex County, Delaware, 1749–1753. WEALTH AT DEATH. LAND: probably 934 acres in Calvert and Prince George's counties.

HALL, JOSIAS CARVIL (1746–1814). BORN: on July 7, 1746, in St. George's Parish, Baltimore County; youngest son. NATIVE: fourth generation. RESIDED: in Baltimore County, (later became Harford County); Baltimore County, 1811 until death. FAMILY BACKGROUND. FATHER: *John Hall* (1701–1774). MOTHER: Hannah (1711–1782). BROTHERS: *John Hall, Jr.* (1737–1770); Josiah (1739–1739); Aquila (1742–1743); and *Benedict Edward Hall* (ca. 1744–1822). SISTERS: Martha (1735–?), who married second, *John Rumsey* (ca. 1742–1828); Mary (1740–?), who married *Benjamin Rumsey* (1734–1808). FIRST COUSINS: *Aquila Hall* (1727–1779); Martha Hall, who married *Walter Tolley* (?–1783); Blanche Hall, who married *John Beale Howard* (by 1739–1799); and Sophia Hall (?–1780), who married *Aquila Hall* (1727–1779). MARRIED by 1775 Janet (Jane) (1752–1812), daughter of William Smith (1728–1814), a merchant of Baltimore Town, who immigrated from

Lancaster County, Pennsylvania in 1761, and his wife Elizabeth Buchanan (1733–1784); niece of both *William Buchanan* (1732–1804) and Mary Buchanan (1729–1782), who married *John Smith* (1718–1794). Her brother was William Buchanan. Her sisters were Mary (?–by 1812), who married Otho Holland Williams (1749–1794); Margaret, who married Robert Smith. CHILDREN. SON: Benedict William (1790–?). DAUGHTER: Hannah Elizabeth (1785–by 1814). PRIVATE CAREER. EDUCATION: M.B., College of Medicine, Philadelphia, Pennsylvania, 1769. RELIGIOUS AFFILLIATION: Presbyterian, by 1786. SOCIAL STATUS AND ACTIVITIES: Gent.; third generation legislator; member of the Maryland Society of Cincinnati. OCCUPATIONAL PROFILE: physician; planter. PUBLIC CAREER. LEGISLATIVE SERVICE: Convention, Harford County, 3rd, 1774. OTHER STATE OFFICE: Executive Council, 1788–1789. LOCAL OFFICES: Committee of Observation, Harford County, in office 1775; justice, Harford County, appointed 1795. MILITARY SERVICE: captain, First Company, Harford County Militia, 1775; colonel, Second Battalion, Flying Camp, 1776; colonel, Fourth Battalion of Regulars, 1777; supernumerary colonel, Maryland Line, 1781; brigadier general, First Brigade (Harford and Cecil counties), Maryland Militia, 1794–1795 (resigned); lieutenant colonel, Ninth U.S. Infantry, 1799–1800. STANDS ON PUBLIC/PRIVATE ISSUES: signed the Bush Declaration, Harford County, 1775; his will included details on the manumission and care of his slaves. WEALTH DURING LIFETIME. PERSONAL PROPERTY: 14 slaves, 2 servants, 1776; assessed value $882.80 current money, including 23 slaves and 16 oz. plate, 1783. LAND AT FIRST ELECTION: 1,461 acres in Harford County (inherited from his father in 1774). SIGNIFICANT CHANGES IN LAND BETWEEN FIRST ELECTION AND DEATH: he was entitled to 400 acres in Allegany County for his service in the Revolution; acquired the lease on at least 1 lot in Baltimore Town in 1792; bought an additional 600 acres in Harford County, 1786–1800, and sold ca. 900 acres in Harford County, 1800–1811. WEALTH AT DEATH. DIED: between June 18 and November 12, 1814, in Baltimore County. PERSONAL PROPERTY: his will mentioned 15 slaves. LAND: at least 1,124 acres in Harford County and probably a lease on 1 lot in Baltimore City.

HALL, RICHARD (?–1688). IMMIGRATED: ca. 1658 as a free adult with his wife, perhaps from Virginia. RESIDED: in Calvert County. MARRIED Elizabeth. CHILDREN. SONS: *Elisha Hall* (1663–ca.

1716/17), who married in 1688 Sarah, widow of Jonas Wingfield and daughter of Richard Hooper; Joseph (1665–1705), who married Ann; *Benjamin Hall* (1667–1721), who married Mary (1678–1742), widow of James Bowling (?–1693) and daughter of *Thomas Brooke* (1632–1676); and Aaron (1669–1704). DAUGHTERS: Rachel (1671–1730), who married *Walter Smith* (?–1711); Elizabeth (1673–1743), who married first, Richard Evans, and second, Dr. James Kingsbury; Lucia (1675–?), who married *John Smith* (?–1738); and Sarah (1677–?), who married *Robert Bradley* (?–1724). PRIVATE CAREER. EDUCATION: literate. RELIGIOUS AFFILIATION: Quaker. SOCIAL STATUS AND ACTIVITIES: claimed rights in 1663 for transporting thirteen people (himself, his wife, and eleven others); he served five terms in the Assembly, one of the longest legislative records in seventeenth-century Maryland; his two sons and three sons-in-law also served in the Assembly. OCCUPATIONAL PROFILE: carpenter; planter. PUBLIC CAREER. LEGISLATIVE SERVICE: Lower House, Calvert County, 1666, 1669, 1674–1674/75 (elected to the 3rd session; Laws 4), 1676–1682 (Accounts 1, 3), 1682–1684 (Accounts 2; Laws 2). WEALTH DURING LIFETIME. LAND AT FIRST ELECTION: ca. 2,500 acres in 1666; over 3,700 acres by 1676. WEALTH AT DEATH. DIED: will probated on August 28, 1688. LAND: ca. 5,100 acres.

HALL, WALTER (?–1678). IMMIGRATED: in 1652 as a free adult. RESIDED: in Newtown, St. Mary's County. MARRIED first, by 1658 (name unknown), widow of Henry Fox. MARRIED second, by 1663 Margaret, widow of John Lloyd. She subsequently married James Pattison. CHILDREN. Probably died without progeny. PRIVATE CAREER. EDUCATION: literate. RELIGIOUS AFFILIATION: Catholic. SOCIAL STATUS AND ACTIVITIES: Mr. on arrival, but not alway referred to as such thereafter; not Gent. until the mid-1670s. OCCUPATIONAL PROFILE: planter. PUBLIC CAREER. LEGISLATIVE SERVICE: Lower House, St. Mary's County, 1676–1678 (died before the 3rd session). LOCAL OFFICES: clerk, St. Mary's County, 1661–1673/74; coroner, St. Mary's County, 1676; justice, St. Mary's County, 1677–1678. WEALTH DURING LIFETIME. LAND AT FIRST ELECTION: over 1,250 acres. WEALTH AT DEATH. DIED: in November 1678. PERSONAL PROPERTY: TEV, 74,461 pounds of tobacco (including 2 slaves and 2 servants). LAND: 1,200 acres.

HALL, WILLIAM (1723–1780). BORN: on December 22, 1723, in Shrewsbury Parish, Kent

County. NATIVE: at least third generation. RE-SIDED: in Chestertown, Kent County. FAMILY BACKGROUND. FATHER: *Christopher Hall* (?–1746). MOTHER: Mary. SISTERS: Elizabeth; Sarah; Mary; Rachel; and Margaret. PRIVATE CAREER. EDUCATION: probably literate. RELIGIOUS AFFILIATION: Anglican, Shrewsbury Parish, Kent County. PUBLIC CAREER. LEGISLATIVE SERVICE: Convention, Kent County, 1st, 1774 (appointed, but did not attend). LOCAL OFFICE: sheriff, Kent County, elected 1779. WEALTH DURING LIFETIME. SIGNIFICANT CHANGES IN LAND BETWEEN FIRST ELECTION AND DEATH: purchased 1 lot in Chestertown, Kent County, 1779. WEALTH AT DEATH. DIED: ca. April 1780 in Kent County. PERSONAL PROPERTY: TEV, £3,358.5.0 current money (including 1 slave); FB, £174.11.1. LAND: 1 lot in Chestertown, Kent County.

HAMBLETON (HAMILTON), WILLIAM (ca. 1636–1677). BORN: ca. 1636. IMMIGRATED: in 1657 as a free adult. RESIDED: in Kent County; St. Michael's River, Talbot County, by 1663. MARRIED Sarah, who subsequently married Richard Collins. CHILDREN. SONS: John; Edward; Samuel; Philemon; and William. DAUGHTERS: Mary; Frances. PRIVATE CAREER. EDUCATION: literate. SOCIAL STATUS AND ACTIVITIES: no title on arrival in the colony. OCCUPATIONAL PROFILE: planter. PUBLIC CAREER. LEGISLATIVE SERVICE: Lower House, Talbot County, 1666, 1669, 1671–1674/75 (Accounts 3). LOCAL OFFICES: sheriff, Talbot County, 1663; justice, Talbot County, 1663/64, first evidence of service 1668/69–1675/76. WEALTH DURING LIFETIME. LAND AT FIRST ELECTION: ca. 1,000 acres. WEALTH AT DEATH. DIED: will probated on October 10, 1677. PERSONAL PROPERTY: TEV, 64,271 pounds of tobacco (including 6 servants and 6 books); FB, 57,719 pounds of tobacco. LAND: 1,724 acres.

HAMILTON, ALEXANDER (1712–1756). BORN: on September 26, 1712, in Edinburgh, Scotland; sixth son. IMMIGRATED: to Annapolis, Anne Arundel County, in 1739. RESIDED: in Annapolis. FAMILY BACKGROUND. FATHER: Rev. William Hamilton, professor of divinity and principal of the University of Edinburgh. BROTHERS: included John, a physician, who married in 1722 Mary Scott, of Calvert County; Gavin. MARRIED on May 29, 1747, Margaret, daughter of *Daniel Dulany* (1685–1753); stepdaughter of Henrietta Maria Lloyd Chew Dulany (?–1766); granddaughter of *Walter Smith* (?–1711); niece of Lucy Smith (1688–1770), who married *Thomas Brooke* (1683–

1744), Eleanor Smith (1690–1761), who married *Thomas Addison* (1679–1727), and Ann Smith (1694–1759), who married second, *Thomas Trueman Greenfield* (1682–1733). Margaret Dulany Hamilton subsequently married in 1757 *William Murdock* (?–1769). Her brothers were *Daniel Dulany, Jr.* (1722–1797); *Walter Dulany* (?–1773); and Dennis (1730–1779). Her stepbrother was *Samuel Chew* (by 1734–1786). Her sisters were Rachel; Rebecca; and Mary. Her stepsisters were Henrietta Maria Chew (1731–1762), who married *Edward Dorsey* (1718–1760); Margaret Chew (?–1773), who married *John Beale Bordley* (1726/27–1804); and Ann Mary Chew (1736–1774), who married *William Paca* (1740–1799). Her first cousins were *Richard Brooke* (1716–1783); Eleanor Brooke, who married *Samuel Beall* (ca. 1713–ca. 1778); *John Addison* (1713–1764); Ann Addison (1711/12–1753), who married *William Murdock* (?–1769); and Marianne Greenfield, who married *John Stoddert* (?–1767). Her nephews were *Benjamin Tasker Dulany* (1752–1816); *James Heath* (?–1766). CHILDREN. Probably none who survived infancy, although Hamilton mentioned in his will written in October 1747 that his wife was pregnant. PRIVATE CAREER. EDUCATION: received a medical degree from the University of Edinburgh, 1737. RELIGIOUS AFFILIATION: Anglican, St. Anne's Parish, Anne Arundel County; converted from Presbyterianism. SOCIAL STATUS AND ACTIVITIES: known by his contemporaries as a man of "wit, humor and drollery in which acquirement he had no equal," and as a person with a "friendly benevolent disposition" and "strict honor and integrity." He wrote the *Itinerarium* , a journal describing his travels through the northern colonies during the summer of 1744, in which he commented on the opportunities for genteel conversation and "public gay diversions." In 1745 Hamilton founded the Tuesday Club, which was devoted to literary farce, satire, and elegant humor. A colleague noted that Hamilton was so much the "life and soul of the Tuesday Club as it expired with him." Hamilton also frequently contributed amusing anecdotes to the *Maryland Gazette* . OCCUPATIONAL PROFILE: physician, with "a respectable practice among the wealthier colonials" ; also trained young men for medical careers. Wrote *A Defence of Dr. Thomson's Discourse* (1752) supporting the practice of inoculation. PUBLIC CAREER. LEGISLATIVE SERVICE: Lower House, Annapolis, 1753–1754 (elected to the 3rd session to fill vacancy). LOCAL OFFICES: common councilman, Annapolis, 1743–1756; St. Anne's Parish Vestry, Anne Arundel County, in office 1749–

1753. **WEALTH DURING LIFETIME**. LAND AT FIRST ELECTION: 130 acres in Anne Arundel County; 2 lots in Annapolis (acquired through his marriage). **WEALTH AT DEATH**. DIED: on May 11, 1756, at his home in Annapolis. LAND: 130 acres in Anne Arundel County and 2 lots in Annapolis.

HAMILTON, ANDREW (1676–1741). BORN: in 1676, probably in Scotland. IMMIGRATED: in 1709/10 as a free adult with his wife and children from Virginia. RESIDED: in Kent County; moved to Philadelphia in late 1715. ADDITIONAL COMMENTS: he was in Virginia by 1700, where he practiced law; he bought a large plantation in Maryland in 1707, but did not migrate there until two years later. MARRIED ca. 1707 Ann (?–1736), widow of Joseph Preeson; daughter of Thomas Browne (?–1705), a Quaker of Northampton County, Virginia, and his wife Susannah Denwood. Her sisters were Elizabeth, who married Thomas Preeson, and Mary, who married first, Southy Littleton, and second, Hancock Custis. CHILDREN. SONS: Andrew (1708–1747); James (1710–1783), who became governor of Pennsylvania. DAUGHTER: Margaret (1709–1760), who married William Allen, a mayor of Philadelphia. PRIVATE CAREER. EDUCATION: literate; possibly attended St. Andrew's University in 1690, and Glasgow University in 1694; attended Gray's Inn, London, England, 1713/14. RELIGIOUS AFFILIATION: Protestant; his wife was a Quaker. SOCIAL STATUS AND ACTIVITIES: Gent. by 1713; went to England in 1713 and again in 1725–1726 when he represented the Penns in litigation against Sir William Keith; achieved fame for his design of the Pennsylvania Statehouse in Philadelphia, now known as Independence Hall. OCCUPATIONAL PROFILE: attorney, admitted to the following courts: Somerset County in 1703; Provincial Court in 1712. Practiced in Accomack County and Northampton County courts in Virginia from 1703 to 1712; practiced in Pennsylvania from 1715. PUBLIC CAREER. LEGISLATIVE SERVICE: Lower House, Kent County, 1715 (Laws). OUT OF COLONY SERVICE: attorney general of Pennsylvania, 1717–1723/24; Pennsylvania Council, 1721–1723/24; Pennsylvania Assembly, Bucks County, 1727–1733 (speaker 1729–1733), 1734–1739 (speaker); Delaware Assembly, Kent County, 1727–1733; (speaker 1728–1733). 1734–1739 (speaker); judge of the Vice-Admiralty Court, Pennsylvania, 1737–1741. STANDS ON PUBLIC/PRIVATE ISSUES: defender of John Peter Zenger in the celebrated trial concerning freedom of the press, 1735. **WEALTH DURING LIFETIME**. LAND AT FIRST ELECTION: at least 885 acres (sold in 1717), plus land in Virginia. **WEALTH AT DEATH**. DIED: on August 4, 1741, in Bush Hill, Pennsylvania. LAND: 653 acres, plus 2 tracts of unspecified acreage.

HAMILTON, WILLIAM (ca. 1682–1759). BORN: ca. 1682. IMMIGRATED: probably by 1710. RESIDED: in St. Thomas Parish, Baltimore County. MARRIED by 1716 Sarah. CHILDREN. SONS: John (1716–?); William (?–1770). DAUGHTERS: Sarah, who married (first name unknown) Gardner; Katherine (1718–?), who married (first name unknown) Gardner; Helen, who married George Ogg; Rachel, who married George Sayter; Ruth (1720–?), who married Masack Baker or William Beasman; (first name unknown), who married either Masack Baker or William Beasman. PRIVATE CAREER. EDUCATION: literate. RELIGIOUS AFFILIATION: Anglican; one of the first trustees of St. Thomas Parish, Baltimore County. SOCIAL STATUS AND ACTIVITIES: Gent., 1729. OCCUPATIONAL PROFILE: planter. PUBLIC CAREER. LEGISLATIVE SERVICE: Lower House, Baltimore County, 1722–1724, 1725–1727, 1728–1731 (Aggrievances 1–5), 1732–1734 (Aggrievances 1–Cv), 1734/35–1737 (Aggrievances 1, Cv, 2–4). LOCAL OFFICES: justice, Baltimore County, by 1728–at least 1735 (quorum, 1729–at least 1735); commissioner, Baltimore County, appointed to purchase land upon which Baltimore Town was to be built, 1729. MILITARY SERVICE: colonel, 1734. **WEALTH DURING LIFETIME**. LAND AT FIRST ELECTION: first appeared in Baltimore County in 1710 when he purchased with *Peter Bond* (?–1718) a 243-acre tract in that county; at least 150 acres in Baltimore County. SIGNIFICANT CHANGES IN LAND BETWEEN FIRST ELECTION AND DEATH: began to patent land in Baltimore County in 1724 and consolidated his holdings by 1752 into a 966-acre patent located along the falls of the Patapsco River, part of which was in Anne Arundel County; also patented 213 acres in Baltimore County in 1745. **WEALTH AT DEATH**. DIED: between October 15 and November 7, 1759, in Baltimore County. PERSONAL PROPERTY: TEV, £786.6.10 current money (including 14 slaves and plate); FB, £31.6.4. LAND: 1,221.5 acres in Baltimore and Anne Arundel counties.

HAMMOND, CHARLES (ca. 1670–1713). BORN: ca. 1670 in Anne Arundel County; probably fourth son. NATIVE: third generation. RESIDED: in Anne Arundel County. FAMILY BACKGROUND. FATHER: *John Hammond* (1643–1707). MOTHER:

Mary (?–by 1678), daughter of Matthew Howard and wife Ann. UNCLE: *Cornelius Howard* (?–1680). AUNT: Elizabeth Howard, who married *Henry Ridgeley* (?–1710). BROTHERS: *Thomas Hammond* (?–ca. 1724/25); *John Hammond* (ca. 1665–1742/43); and William (?–1711/12), who married Elizabeth Cockey. SISTERS: Mary, who married Cornelius Howard (ca. 1670–1717), son of *Cornelius Howard* (?–1680); and Elizabeth, who married first, Richard Moss, and second, Thomas Cockey. FIRST COUSINS: *Matthew Howard* (ca. 1675–1750); Sarah Howard, who married first, *John Worthington* (1650–1701), and second, *John Brice* (?–1713). MARRIED his first cousin Hannah (1678–1752), daughter of Philip Howard and wife Ruth Baldwin; niece of both *Cornelius Howard* (?–1680) and Mary Howard, who married *John Hammond* (1643–1707). Hannah subsequently married *Edmond Benson* (1687–1734). Her first cousins were *Matthew Howard* (ca. 1675–1750); Sarah Howard, who married first, *John Worthington* (1650–1701), and second, *John Brice* (?–1713). CHILDREN. SONS: *Charles Hammond* (1692/93–1772), who married in 1715 Rachel (?–1748/49), widow of *Charles Greenberry* (1672–1713) and daughter of John Stimpson; *Philip Hammond* (1697–1760), who married first, Comfort, and second, Rachel (1711–1781), daughter of *John Brice* (?–1713); John (?–1755), who married Ann, daughter of *Edward Dorsey* (?–1705); Rezin (?–1739); and Nathaniel (1708–1762), who married Ann Welsh. DAUGHTERS: Mehitabel (Hamutel) (baptized 1713–?), who married Charles Worthington (1701–?), son of *John Worthington* (1650–1701); and Ruth (baptized 1713–?), who married first, in 1730 Peasley Ingram, and second, *Thomas Franklin* (ca. 1706–1788). PRIVATE CAREER. EDUCATION: literate. RELIGIOUS AFFILIATION: Anglican. SOCIAL STATUS AND ACTIVITIES: second generation burgess. OCCUPATIONAL PROFILE: planter; merchant. PUBLIC CAREER. LEGISLATIVE SERVICE: Lower House, Anne Arundel County, 1710–1711 (elected to the 3rd session), 1712–1713 (died before the 3rd session). LOCAL OFFICE: justice, Anne Arundel County, by 1702–1713 (quorum, 1708–1713). MILITARY SERVICE: officer, by 1696; major, 1708–1713. WEALTH DURING LIFETIME. LAND AT FIRST ELECTION: over 1,039 acres (796 acres inherited from his father). WEALTH AT DEATH. DIED: on November 23, 1713. PERSONAL PROPERTY: TEV, £1,090.14.0 sterling (including 14 slaves); FB, £1,056.10.2. LAND: ca. 1,500 acres.

HAMMOND, CHARLES (1692/93–1772).

BORN: in 1692/93 in St. Anne's Parish, Anne Arundel County; eldest son. NATIVE: fourth generation. RESIDED: on the north side of the Severn River, Anne Arundel County. FAMILY BACKGROUND. FATHER: *Charles Hammond* (ca. 1670–1713), son of *John Hammond* (1643–1707). STEPFATHER: *Edmond Benson* (1687–1734). MOTHER: Hannah, daughter of Philip Howard and wife Ruth Baldwin. UNCLES: *Thomas Hammond* (?–ca. 1724/25); *John Hammond* (1665–1742/43). BROTHERS: John (?–1755); *Philip Hammond* (1697–1760); Rezin (?–1739); and Nathaniel (1708–1762). SISTERS: Hamutel; Ruth, who married second, *Thomas Franklin* (ca. 1706–1787). FIRST COUSIN: *Thomas Hammond* (1693–?). NEPHEWS: *John Hammond* (1735–1784); *Rezin Hammond* (1745–1809); *Matthias Hammond* (1740–1786); *Nathan Hammond* (1731–1811); and *Rezin Hammond* (?–1783). MARRIED on October 24, 1715, Rachel (?–1748/49), widow of *Charles Greenberry* (1672–1713); daughter of John Stimpson, Gent. (?–by 1692), of Anne Arundel County, and wife Rachel (?–after 1724), widow of Neale Clarke (?–1676); stepdaughter of Robert Proctor (?–by 1695), Richard Kilburne (?–by 1698), and Thomas Freeborne (?–1713); granddaughter of *Richard Beard* (?–1681). Her brother was John (?–by 1718). Her sister was Comfort (ca. 1684–ca. 1747), who married *John Dorsey* (ca. 1682–?). Her nephew was *John Hammond Dorsey* (1718–1774). CHILDREN. DAUGHTER: Ann (1716–1785); who married first, Thomas Homewood, and second, *William Govane* (1716/17–1768). Hammond supported his daughter in her suit against *William Govane* (1716/17–1768) for cruelty and for the mismanagement of the estate of Thomas Homewood. Hammond assisted in the maintenance of his grandchildren, and after 1750 administered the Homewood estate. PRIVATE CAREER. EDUCATION: literate. RELIGIOUS AFFILIATION: Anglican, St. Margaret's Parish, Anne Arundel County. SOCIAL STATUS AND ACTIVITIES: Gent., 1718; Esq., by 1736; Hon., by 1748. OCCUPATIONAL PROFILE: planter; officeholder. PUBLIC CAREER. LEGISLATIVE SERVICE: Upper House, 1735/36–1737 (appointed before convention), 1738, 1739–1741, 1742–1744, 1745, 1745/46–1748, 1749–1751, 1751–1754, 1754–1757, 1757–1758, 1758–1761, 1762–1763, 1765–1766, 1768–1770, 1771. OTHER PROVINCIAL OFFICES: justice, Provincial Court, 1732–at least 1735 (quorum, 1734, 1735); commissioner of the Paper Currency Office, 1733/34–1766; Council, 1735–1772 (qualified on July 15, 1735; president 1768–1772); treasurer, Western Shore, 1736–1772. LOCAL OFFICES: justice, Court of Oyer and Terminer and Gaol Delivery, Anne

Arundel County, commissioned 1715, 1716, 1717, 1718, 1720, 1731, and 1734; justice, Anne Arundel County, 1716–at least 1731 (quorum, 1727–at least 1731). MILITARY SERVICE: colonel, by 1767. WEALTH DURING LIFETIME. LAND AT FIRST ELECTION: 1,732 acres in Anne Arundel County (ca. 845 acres through his marriage, ca. 282 acres inherited from his parents). SIGNIFICANT CHANGES IN LAND BETWEEN FIRST ELECTION AND DEATH: purchased or patented an additional 1,237 acres in Anne Arundel County, but sold or assigned 1,073 acres; gave 1,150 acres to his daughter and grandchildren by deed of gift in 1744, retaining a life interest in the estate. WEALTH AT DEATH. DIED: on September 13, 1772, at his home in St. Margaret's Parish, Anne Arundel County. PERSONAL PROPERTY: his will mentioned more than 38 slaves. LAND: title to 746 acres and a life estate in 1,150 acres in Anne Arundel County.

HAMMOND, JOHN (1643–1707). BORN: in 1643, probably on Isle of Wight, England; probably second son. IMMIGRATED: ca. 1655 as a minor with his father and brother. RESIDED: in Anne Arundel County. FAMILY BACKGROUND. FATHER: Thomas Hammond, a colonel in the Parliamentary army. BROTHER: Thomas Hammond. MARRIED first, Mary (?–by 1678), daughter of Matthew Howard and wife Ann. Her brothers were *Cornelius Howard* (?–1680), Matthew (ca. 1640–1692/93), who married Sarah Dorsey; Samuel; John; and Philip, who married Ruth Baldwin. Her sisters were Elizabeth, who married *Henry Ridgeley* (?–1710); Anne. Her nephew was *Matthew Howard* (ca. 1675–1750). Her nieces were Sarah Howard, who married first, *John Worthington* (1650–1701), and second, *John Brice* (?–1713); Hannah Howard, who married first, *Charles Hammond* (ca. 1670–1713), and second, *Edmond Benson* (1687–1734). MARRIED second, by November 1678 Mary, widow of (first name unknown) Roper. CHILDREN. SONS: *Thomas Hammond* (?–ca. 1724/25), who married first, Rebecca Larkin Lightfoot, and second, Mary Heath; *John Hammond* (ca. 1665–1742/43), who married Ann, daughter of *Nicholas Greenberry* (1627–1697); William (?–1711/12), who married Elizabeth Cockey; and *Charles Hammond* (ca. 1670–1713). DAUGHTERS: Mary, who married Cornelius Howard (ca. 1670–1717), son of *Cornelius Howard* (?–1680); Elizabeth, who married first, Richard Moss, and second, Thomas Cockey. PRIVATE CAREER. EDUCATION: literate. RELIGIOUS AFFILIATION: a Quaker as a young man; converted to Anglicanism by the late 1680s. SOCIAL STATUS AND

ACTIVITIES: established one of the most prominent families on the Western Shore; his business often carried him to England; he was a critical figure in the selection of the first royal Council in 1691. OCCUPATIONAL PROFILE: a merchant active in the transatlantic trade; planter. PUBLIC CAREER. LEGISLATIVE SERVICE: Lower House, Anne Arundel County, 1692–1693 (Elections and Privileges, probably chairman 1; Accounts 1; Aggrievances 2), 1694–1697 (Laws 7; Elections and Privileges, chairman 7), 1697/98–1698 (Elections and Privileges, chairman 1; appointed to Council after the 2nd session); Upper House, 1699–1700 (appointed before the 3rd session), 1701–1704, 1704–1707. OTHER PROVINCIAL OFFICES: justice, Provincial Court, 1694–1698 (quorum, 1696–1698); Council, 1698–1707; associate justice, Court of Chancery, 1699; justice, Vice-Admiralty Court, 1702. LOCAL OFFICES: justice, Anne Arundel County, 1685–1694 (quorum, 1689–1694); St. Anne's Parish Vestry, Anne Arundel County, 1704–1705. MILITARY SERVICE: captain, 1691 or 1692–1694; major, 1694–1698; lieutenant colonel, 1698–1707; major general of the Western Shore, 1707. STANDS ON PUBLIC/PRIVATE ISSUES: supported the revolution of 1689. WEALTH DURING LIFETIME. LAND AT FIRST ELECTION: over 614 acres. WEALTH AT DEATH. DIED: on November 24, 1707. PERSONAL PROPERTY: TEV, £1,8710.1.6 (including 22 slaves); FB, £1,631.3.8. LAND: ca. 2,609 acres.

HAMMOND, JOHN (1665–1742/43). BORN: in 1665 in Anne Arundel County, second son. NATIVE: third generation. RESIDED: in Anne Arundel County. FAMILY BACKGROUND. FATHER: *John Hammond* (1643–1707). MOTHER: Mary (?–by 1678), daughter of Matthew Howard and wife Ann. UNCLE: *Cornelius Howard* (?–1680). AUNT: Elizabeth Howard, who married *Henry Ridgeley* (?–1710). BROTHERS: *Thomas Hammond* (?–ca. 1724/25); William (?–1711/12); and *Charles Hammond* (ca. 1670–1713). SISTERS: Mary, who married Cornelius Howard (ca. 1670–1717), son of *Cornelius Howard* (?–1680); Elizabeth, who married first, Richard Moss, and second, Thomas Cockey. FIRST COUSINS: *Matthew Howard* (ca. 1675–1750); Sarah Howard, who married first, *John Worthington* (1650–1701), and second, *John Brice* (?–1713); and Hannah Howard, who married first, *Charles Hammond* (ca. 1670–1713), and second, *Edmond Benson* (1687–1734). MARRIED in 1696 Ann, daughter of *Nicholas Greenberry* (1627–1697). Her brother was *Charles Greenberry* (1672–1713). Her sisters were Katherine, who married Henry Ridgely; Elizabeth (1678–

1719/20), who married *Robert Goldsborough* (1660–1746). Her nephews were *Charles Goldsborough* (1707–1767); *William Goldsborough* (1709–1760); and *John Goldsborough* (1711–1778). Her niece was Elizabeth Ridgely, who married *Thomas Worthington* (ca. 1691–1753). CHILDREN. SONS: Thomas John (1697–1767), who married in 1721 Anne Cockey; Nicholas (1703/4–1743), who married Mary. DAUGHTERS: Elizabeth, who married in 1711 John Burley; Anne (1697–1708); Comfort, (1701–probably 1741/42), who probably married John Worthington, son of *John Worthington* (1650–1701); and Rachel (1708–?), who married in 1727 John Moale. PRIVATE CAREER. EDUCATION: literate. RELIGIOUS AFFILIATION: baptized as an Anglican along with his children in 1713 but he probably had previous Quaker leanings. SOCIAL STATUS AND ACTIVITIES: second generation burgess; inactive in public life after 1715. OCCUPATIONAL PROFILE: planter; merchant. PUBLIC CAREER. LEGISLATIVE SERVICE: Lower House, Anne Arundel County, 1704 (dismissed from the 1st session for refusal to subscribe to the required oaths), 1714 (elected to the 4th session). LOCAL OFFICE: justice, Anne Arundel County, 1711–1715 (quorum, 1714–1715). STANDS ON PUBLIC/PRIVATE ISSUES: his Quaker beliefs or leanings probably kept him out of public life before 1711. WEALTH DURING LIFETIME. LAND AT FIRST ELECTION: 500–1,000 acres. WEALTH AT DEATH. DIED: on February 9, 1742/43. PERSONAL PROPERTY: TEV, £24.13.9 sterling, £1,221.11.10 current money (including 18 slaves); FB, £177.11.8 sterling, £445.7.7 current money. LAND: 958 acres.

HAMMOND, JOHN (1735–1784). BORN: in 1735 in Anne Arundel County; younger son. NATIVE: fifth generation. RESIDED: in Anne Arundel County. FAMILY BACKGROUND. FATHER: *Philip Hammond* (1697–1760), son of *Charles Hammond* (ca. 1670–1713). MOTHER: Rachel (1711–1786), daughter of *John Brice* (?–1713). UNCLE: *Charles Hammond* (1692/93–1772). AUNTS: Ruth Hammond, who married second, *Thomas Franklin* (ca. 1706–1787); Anne Brice (1708–1765), who married *Vachel Denton* (ca. 1696–1752). BROTHERS: Charles (1729–by 1786); Philip (?–1783); Denton (?–1782); *Matthias Hammond* (1740–1786); and *Rezin Hammond* (1745–1809). HALF BROTHER: Joshua (1719–died a minor). SISTER: Anne. FIRST COUSINS: *Nathan Hammond* (1731–1811); *Rezin Hammond* (?–1783); Anne Hammond (1716–?), who married second, *William Govane* (1716/17–1768); *John Brice* (1738–1820); *James Brice* (1746–

1801); and *Benedict Brice* (1749–1786). MARRIED by March 24, 1772, Ann. CHILDREN. SONS: William, never married; Thomas. DAUGHTERS: Sarah, who married on May 31, 1788, Richard Marriott; Mary, who married on April 4, 1789, John Marriott; Elizabeth, who married on August 4, 1784, William King, a Baltimore County merchant; and Henrietta, who married Basil Brown. PRIVATE CAREER. EDUCATION: admitted to the Middle Temple, London, England, in February 1753; entered Oriel College, Oxford University in January 1758. RELIGIOUS AFFILIATION: Anglican. SOCIAL STATUS AND ACTIVITIES: fourth generation legislator. OCCUPATIONAL PROFILE: lawyer, called to the bar in England in February 1760; admitted to the following courts: Frederick County in August 1760; Provincial Court in September 1760; Anne Arundel County in November 1760; Court of Chancery by February 1761. PUBLIC CAREER. LEGISLATIVE SERVICE: Lower House, Anne Arundel County, 1760–1761 (elected to the 3rd session to fill vacancy; Grievances 3, Cv 3), 1762–1763 (Grievances 2; Public Offices 1, 2), 1765–1766 (Grievances 2–4; Public Offices 2–4; Laws to Expire 2, 4), 1771 (Elections). LOCAL OFFICE: churchwarden, St. Anne's Parish, Anne Arundel County, 1762–1763. WEALTH DURING LIFETIME. PERSONAL PROPERTY: assessed value £2,258.15.0, including 58 slaves and 162 oz. plate, 1783. LAND AT FIRST ELECTION: undivided one-sixth interest in his father's ca. 23,000 acres in Anne Arundel and Baltimore counties. SIGNIFICANT CHANGES IN LAND BETWEEN FIRST ELECTION AND DEATH: Hammond began patenting small tracts of land in Anne Arundel County in 1761, and over the next eleven years he patented 29 tracts totaling 3,244 acres. During this twelve year period he also acquired 3,432 acres in Anne Arundel County by purchase or mortgage and sold 375 acres. After their father's death, John and his five brothers began dividing his land amongst themselves. John's share, confirmed to him by all his brothers by 1772, equaled 2,663 acres in Anne Arundel County, including the family estate, "Acton," adjacent to Annapolis, plus 1 lot in Annapolis and 2 lots in Elk Ridge, Anne Arundel County. After 1772 Hammond sold 994 acres, lost 207 acres in a resurvey of 2 tracts, and by 1783 had given 1,300 acres to his son William. He acquired over 626 acres in Anne Arundel County, 1772–1784. WEALTH AT DEATH. DIED: between January 14 and February 21, 1784, in Anne Arundel County. PERSONAL PROPERTY: TEV, £3,655.14.11 current money (including more than 23 slaves); FB, £3,327.10.0. LAND: ca. 7,100 acres in Anne Arundel County, plus 2 lots in Elkridge, Anne Arundel County, and 1 lot in Annapolis and his share of any of his father's land still undivided.

HAMMOND, MATTHIAS (1740–1786). BORN: on May 24, 1740, in Anne Arundel County; younger son. NATIVE: fifth generation. RESIDED: in Anne Arundel County. FAMILY BACKGROUND. FATHER: *Philip Hammond* (1697–1760), son of *Charles Hammond* (ca. 1670–1713). MOTHER: Rachel (1711–1786), daughter of *John Brice* (?–1713). UNCLE: *Charles Hammond* (1692/93–1772). AUNTS: Ruth Hammond, who married second, *Thomas Franklin* (ca. 1706–1787); Anne Brice (1708–1765), who married *Vachel Denton* (ca. 1696–1752). BROTHERS: Charles (1729–by 1786); *John Hammond* (1735–1784); Philip (?–1783); Denton (?–1782); and *Rezin Hammond* (1745–1809). HALF BROTHER: Joshua (1719–died a minor). SISTER: Anne. FIRST COUSINS: *Nathan Hammond* (1731–1811); *Rezin Hammond* (?–1783); Anne Hammond (1716–?), who married second, *William Govane* (1716/17–1768); *John Brice* (1738–1820); *James Brice* (1746–1801); and *Benedict Brice* (1749–1786). MARRIED never. CHILDREN. Died without progeny. PRIVATE CAREER. EDUCATION: literate. RELIGIOUS AFFILIATION: Anglican. SOCIAL STATUS AND ACTIVITIES: Gent.; fourth generation legislator. ADDITIONAL COMMENTS: built the "Hammond-Harwood" mansion in Annapolis, which was designed by William Buckland, ca. 1772. OCCUPATIONAL PROFILE: planter. PUBLIC CAREER. LEGISLATIVE SERVICE: Lower House, Annapolis, 1773–1774 (Elections 1, Cv, 2, 3); Conventions, Anne Arundel County, 1st, 1774, 2nd–3rd, 1774, 4th, 1775, 5th, 1775. LOCAL OFFICES: St. Anne's Parish Vestry, Anne Arundel County, in office 1773–1776; Committee of Correspondence, Annapolis and Anne Arundel County, elected 1774. MILITARY SERVICE: quartermaster, Severn Battalion, Anne Arundel County Militia, appointed 1776. STANDS ON PUBLIC/PRIVATE ISSUES: supported *Charles Carroll of Carrollton* (1737–1832) in the fee controversy debate with *Daniel Dulany, Jr.* (1722–1797), 1773; leader of the anti-Stewart group that forced Anthony Stewart to set fire to his ship, the *Peggy Stewart*, in the Annapolis harbor in October 1774, because Stewart had paid the required tax on the tea imported in his vessel. WEALTH DURING LIFETIME. PERSONAL PROPERTY: assessed value £2,928.0.0 current money, including 62 slaves and 168 oz. plate, 1783. LAND AT FIRST ELECTION: at least 6,900 acres in Anne Arundel County, plus 2 lots in Annapolis (3,677 acres received as his share of

his father's land confirmed to Matthias by his brothers in 1772; part interest in 785 acres of his father's land conveyed to Matthias by his brother John Hammond in 1772; 1,144 acres by patent; remaining acreage and lots acquired by purchase). SIGNIFICANT CHANGES IN LAND BETWEEN FIRST ELECTION AND DEATH: purchased 2 additional lots in Annapolis in 1774 and ca. 1,400 acres in Anne Arundel County, 1774–1786. Patented 243 acres in Anne Arundel County into 10 small tracts as additions to property already owned, 1784. Sold 773 acres, 1775–1786. WEALTH AT DEATH. DIED: on November 11, 1786, in Anne Arundel County; buried in the family cemetery near Gambrills, Anne Arundel County. LAND: probably ca. 7,800 acres in Anne Arundel County. ADDITIONAL COMMENTS: he was described in his obituary as a respected and esteemed gentleman of a "most amicable and benevolent disposition." Named as his principal heirs Philip and John Hammond, sons of his deceased brother Charles.

HAMMOND, NATHAN (1731–1811). BORN: in 1731 in Anne Arundel County; eldest son. NATIVE: fifth generation. RESIDED: in Anne Arundel County until 1777; Frederick County; in both counties alternately during the 1790s and early 1800s. FAMILY BACKGROUND. FATHER: Maj. Nathan Hammond (1708–1762), of Elkridge, Anne Arundel County; sheriff of Anne Arundel County in 1751; son of *Charles Hammond* (ca. 1670–1713). MOTHER: Ann (?–1780), daughter of John Welsh and wife Rachel. UNCLES: *Charles Hammond* (1692/93–1772); *Philip Hammond* (1697–1760). AUNT: Ruth Hammond, who married second, *Thomas Franklin* (ca. 1706–1787). BROTHERS: *Rezin Hammond* (?–1783); Philip (1744–1799), of Anne Arundel County, who married Barbara Riatt; Charles; Capt. John, who married Martha Hawkins; Ormand (ca. 1754–?), of Frederick County, who married Elizabeth Duckett; Aquilla (1744–1797); and Thomas (?–1786), of Frederick County. SISTERS: Ann (?–1790); Hannah, who married John Riatt, Jr.; Ruth; Caroline (?–ca. 1772); Mary, who married Vachel Hammond; and Hamutal (?–ca. 1772). FIRST COUSINS: *Matthias Hammond* (1740–1786); *John Hammond* (1735–1784); *Rezin Hammond* (1745–1809); and Anne Hammond, who married second, *William Govane* (1716/17–1768). MARRIED between March 27 and April 4, 1759, Ann (?–by 1802), widow of John Riatt, Gent., of Annapolis, merchant. Agreed in marriage contract to give each Riatt child £1,000 current money if he had no issue of his own by Ann; released from this obligation by his stepchildren in 1802 after paying them a total of £1,000 current money. **CHILDREN.** STEPSONS: John Riatt, Jr., who married Hannah, sister of *Nathan Hammond* (1731–1811); George Riatt. STEPDAUGHTERS: Ann Riatt, who married by 1767 John Duckett; Barbara Riatt (1743–?), who married Philip Hammond (1744–1799), brother of *Nathan Hammond* (1731–1811); and Harriott Riatt (?–by 1802), who married by 1767 Marmaduke Winell. **PRIVATE CAREER.** EDUCATION: literate. RELIGIOUS AFFILIATION: Anglican, St. Anne's Parish, Anne Arundel County, until 1777 when he moved to Frederick County. SOCIAL STATUS AND ACTIVITIES: Gent., 1759. OCCUPATIONAL PROFILE: merchant; farmer; land speculator. Maintained a store in Annapolis in 1761 until at least 1773; in partnership with *Stephen West* (1727–1790) 1761. After 1782 Hammond called himself a farmer. **PUBLIC CAREER.** LEGISLATIVE SERVICE: Lower House, Frederick County, 1783 (Claims). OTHER STATE OFFICE: commissioner and endorser of bills of credit, 1776–1783. LOCAL OFFICES: sheriff, Annapolis, 1753–1754; churchwarden, St. Anne's Parish, Anne Arundel County, 1769–1770, 1774–1775; St. Anne's Parish Vestry, Anne Arundel County, 1770–1773, 1775–1777; trustee of the poor, Anne Arundel County, in office in 1772. **WEALTH DURING LIFETIME. PERSONAL PROPERTY:** settled the estate of John Riatt with his wife Ann; final distribution was made in 1769. Her portion was £171.17.4 sterling, £1,404.11.2 current money, and 3,036 pounds of tobacco. Riatt also had held a lease to part of a lot in Annapolis and Hammond leased the remainder of the lot in 1762. Assessed value £391.0.0, including 12 slaves, Anne Arundel County 1783. ADDITIONAL COMMENTS: Subleased land and a store near the dock in Annapolis after 1777. By 1798 Hammond had two tenants on his Anne Arundel County land. LAND AT FIRST ELECTION: 1,512 acres in Anne Arundel and Frederick counties, plus 2 lots in Annapolis and a 97-year lease on 1 lot near the dock in Annapolis. (480 acres in Frederick County inherited from his father, 152 acres in Frederick County inherited upon the death of sister his Caroline, ca. 1772). SIGNIFICANT CHANGES IN LAND BETWEEN FIRST ELECTION AND DEATH: patented 40 acres in Frederick County in 1790 and 1798; probably sold his 2 lots in Annapolis before 1798; purchased ca. 200 acres in Anne Arundel County in 1801 and sold 687 acres in that county in 1802 and 1803; purchased 2,265 acres in Kentucky prior to 1802. **WEALTH AT DEATH. DIED:** on November 4, 1811, in Frederick County; buried in Mt. Olivet Cemetery, Frederick County. LAND:

1,065 acres in Frederick and Anne Arundel counties, plus a lease on 1 lot in Annapolis, and 2,265 acres in Kentucky.

HAMMOND, NICHOLAS (1758–1830). BORN: on May 26, 1758, on the Isle of Jersey, England. IMMIGRATED: by 1780 from Philadelphia, Pennsylvania. RESIDED: in Cambridge, Dorchester County, 1780; Easton, Talbot County, 1798; built "St. Aubins," Talbot County, 1808. **FAMILY BACKGROUND. FATHER:** Nicholas Hammond, immigrated in 1730 from the Isle of Jersey, England, to Philadelphia, Pennsylvania. He had returned to the Isle of Jersey by 1758. MOTHER: Margaret Lampriere. MARRIED first, in 1780 his cousin Sarah George (?–1787), of Philadelphia, Pennsylvania. MARRIED second, in 1792 Rebecca (1762–1801), daughter of *Henry Hollyday* (ca. 1725–1789); granddaughter of both *James Hollyday* (1696–1747) and *George Robins* (1697–1742); stepgranddaugher of *William Goldsborough* (1709–1760); niece of *James Hollyday* (1722–1786), Margaret Robins (1734–1808), who married *William Hayward* (?–1791), Henrietta Maria Robins (1736–1791), who married *James Lloyd Chamberlaine* (1732–1783); half niece of both *Edward Lloyd* (1711–1770) and *Richard Lloyd* (1717–1786). Her brothers were Henry (?–died young); *James Hollyday* (1758–1807); Thomas (1760–1823); and Henry (1771–1850). Her sisters were Henrietta Maria (1750–1832), who married *Samuel Chamberlaine* (1742–1811); Sarah (1753–1829); Anna Maria (1756–1817), who married *George Gale* (1756–1815); Elizabeth (1768–1810); and Margaret (1774–?). Her first cousin was Henrietta Maria Chamberlaine (?–1804), who married *William Hayward, Jr.* (ca. 1758–1834). **CHILDREN.** SON: Nicholas (1795–1831), a physician, who married in 1823 Anne Caroline, daughter of Howes Goldsborough and wife Mary. DAUGHTERS: Anna Maria, who married in 1818 her first cousin James Lloyd Chamberlaine (1785–1844), son of *Samuel Chamberlaine* (1742–1811); Rebecca Hollyday (1801–?), who married in 1833 Rev. Robert William Goldsborough. **PRIVATE CAREER.** EDUCATION: sent from England to Philadelphia, Pennsylvania, to study law, ca. 1772. RELIGIOUS AFFILIATION: Anglican, St. Peter's Parish, Talbot County. SOCIAL STATUS AND ACTIVITIES: Gent., 1785; Esq., 1789; Freemason, participated in the establishment of the first lodge formed in Dorchester County, No. 29, delegate from Lodge No. 29 to the convention which organized the Grand Lodge; Hammond was elected junior grand warden in 1789, and senior grand warden in 1790, and deputy grand master from 1791 to 1794; one of the original corporators of Easton Academy in 1798, and first secretary of its' board of trustees; president of the Society for the Promotion of Agriculture and Rural Economy for the Eastern Shore of Maryland, 1805; president of the Board of Trustees of the Agricultural Society for the Eastern Shore in 1823, and reelected in 1825. ADDITIONAL COMMENTS: Hammond had a hearing defect. OCCUPATIONAL PROFILE: lawyer; president of the Farmers Bank, Easton, Talbot County, 1805–1808, 1813–1830. PUBLIC CAREER. LEGISLATIVE SERVICE: Senate, Eastern Shore, Term of 1786–1791: 1788 (elected on November 28, 1788 to fill vacancy; qualified on December 8, 1788), 1789, 1790, Term of 1791–1796: 1793 (elected on November 16, 1793 to fill vacancy; declined to serve on November 22, 1793), Term of 1796–1801: 1796 (did not serve), 1797, 1798 (did not serve), 1799, 1800 (resigned on November 26, 1800). OTHER STATE OFFICE: Constitution Ratification Convention, Dorchester County, 1788. LOCAL OFFICES: clerk, Dorchester County, 1777–1788; Maryland Senate elector, Dorchester County, elected 1786; Great Choptank Parish Vestry, Dorchester County, in office 1788–1791; justice, Orphans' Court, Dorchester County, commissioned and resigned 1791. STANDS ON PUBLIC/PRIVATE ISSUES: Hammond introduced a bill entitled "An Act to promote the gradual abolition of Slavery and to prevent the rigorous Exportation of Negros [*sic*] and Mulattos from this State" into the Maryland Senate at the November Session, 1789; the bill occassioned much conversation amongst the members and the populace, and many members of the House of Delegates professed a strong aversion to it; to "avoid the temper and Irritation" that discussion of such a bill would have caused, it was tabled. WEALTH DURING LIFETIME. PERSONAL PROPERTY: assessed value £473.10.0, including 12 slaves and 60 oz. plate, Talbot County, 1798; obtained £895.8.4 current money through second marriage, ca. 1801; assessed value $2,328.00, including 17 slaves and 60 oz. plate, Talbot County, 1817. LAND AT FIRST ELECTION: lots in Cambridge, Dorchester County. SIGNIFICANT CHANGES IN LAND BETWEEN FIRST ELECTION AND DEATH: owned 15 acres in Talbot County, 1798; obtained lots in Easton, Talbot County, plus other real estate in Talbot County, through second marriage, 1804; owned a total of 959 acres in Talbot County, 1817; resurveyed several tracts in Talbot County between 1820 and 1827 for a net gain of 54 acres. WEALTH AT DEATH. DIED: on November 11, 1830, in Talbot County; buried at "Rat-

cliffe," Talbot County. PERSONAL PROPERTY: requested no appraisal of his estate; assessed value $1,508.00, including 16 slaves and 70 oz. plate, Talbot County, 1832. LAND: 785 acres in Talbot County, plus lots in Dorchester County.

HAMMOND, PHILIP (1697–1760). BORN: in 1697 in St. Anne's Parish, Anne Arundel County; probably second son. NATIVE: fourth generation. RESIDED: at "Howard's Adventure," Anne Arundel County, and "Acton," adjacent to Annapolis, Anne Arundel County. FAMILY BACKGROUND. FATHER: *Charles Hammond* (ca. 1670–1713), son of *John Hammond* (1643–1707). STEPFATHER: *Edmond Benson* (1687–1734). MOTHER: Hannah, daughter of Philip Howard and wife Ruth Baldwin. UNCLES: *Thomas Hammond* (?–ca. 1724/25); *John Hammond* (ca. 1665–1742/43). BROTHERS: *Charles Hammond* (1692/93–1772); John (?–1755); Nathan (1708–1762); and Rezin (?–1739). SISTERS: Hamutel; Ruth, who married second, *Thomas Franklin* (ca. 1706–1787). FIRST COUSIN: *Thomas Hammond* (1693–?). NEPHEWS: *Nathan Hammond* (1731–1811); *Rezin Hammond* (?–1783). NIECE: Anne Hammond (1716–?), who married second, *William Govane* (1716/17–1768). MARRIED first, Comfort Duval. MARRIED second, Rachel (1711–1786), daughter of *John Brice* (?–1713); niece of *Matthew Howard* (ca. 1675–1750). Her brother was John (1705–1766). Her half brother was *Thomas Worthington* (ca. 1691–1753). Her sister was Anne (1708–1765), who married *Vachel Denton* (ca. 1696–1752). Her nephews were *John Brice* (1738–1820); *James Brice* (1746–1801); and *Benedict Brice* (1749–1786). Her half nephews were *Samuel Worthington* (1734–1815); *Brice T. B. Worthington* (1727–1794); and *Nicholas Worthington* (1734–1793). CHILDREN. SONS: Joshua (1719–died a minor); Charles (1729–by 1786); *John Hammond* (1735–1784); Philip (?–1783); Denton (?–1782); *Matthias Hammond* (1740–1786); and *Rezin Hammond* (1745–1809). DAUGHTER: Anne, who married (first name unknown) Hopkins. PRIVATE CAREER. EDUCATION: literate. RELIGIOUS AFFILIATION: Anglican, St. Anne's Parish, Anne Arundel County; undertook to have a chapel of ease completed for the parishioners in the northern part of the county, 1729. SOCIAL STATUS AND ACTIVITIES: Gent. and Esq., by death. OCCUPATIONAL PROFILE: planter; established Philip Hammond & Co. in 1729 and remained active as a merchant until his death. PUBLIC CAREER. LEGISLATIVE SERVICE: Lower House, Anne Arundel County, 1732–1734 (Laws 1–Cv), 1734/35–1737 (Laws 1, Cv, 2–4; Elections 1, Cv, 2–4), 1738

(Laws; Elections), 1739–1741 (Laws Cv; elected speaker of the 1st session; resigned as speaker during the 3rd session because of the severe illness of his son), 1742–1744 (Laws 1, 2; Bills of Credit 2), 1745 (Laws), 1745/46–1748 (Laws Cv 1, 1–3, 4), 1749–1751 (speaker), 1751–1754 (speaker), 1754–1757 (Laws 1–4; Grievances 3), 1757–1758 (Grievances 1, Cv, 2; Public Offices 1, Cv, 2), 1758–1760 (died before the 3rd session). OTHER PROVINCIAL OFFICE: clerk, Prerogative Office, 1718–1721. LOCAL OFFICES: deputy commissary, Anne Arundel County, in office 1718–1720; St. Anne's Parish Vestry, Anne Arundel County, in office 1727–1730, 1740–1743. WEALTH DURING LIFETIME. LAND AT FIRST ELECTION: 3,683 acres in Anne Arundel and Baltimore counties (ca. 400 acres inherited from his father, 1713; 250 acres inherited from his grandfather Philip Howard, with title to the property assured by his brothers, 1730; ca. 200 acres by his second marriage); Philip Hammond & Co. owned at least 900 additional acres in Anne Arundel County by 1732. SIGNIFICANT CHANGES IN LAND BETWEEN FIRST ELECTION AND DEATH: patented 2,171 acres in Anne Arundel County, 1732–1758. Purchased at least 9,189 acres in Anne Arundel County, 1732–1758. Charged with quit-rents on an additional 5,200 acres in Anne Arundel County by 1760. Sold only a few small tracts during this period. WEALTH AT DEATH. DIED: on May 3, 1760; buried in the family cemetery near Gambrills, Anne Arundel County. PERSONAL PROPERTY: 107 slaves and 528 oz. plate valued at £3,828.13.0 current money. LAND: ca. 20,000 acres in Anne Arundel and Baltimore counties according to patents and assessments. Heirs divided 23,000 acres by 1772, all of it supposedly Philip's land. ADDITIONAL COMMENTS: he was described in his obituary as a gentleman of "great natural abilities" with a large fortune.

HAMMOND, REZIN (?–1783). BORN: in Anne Arundel County, of age by 1760; probably second son. NATIVE: fifth generation. RESIDED: in Anne Arundel County, 1760; Baltimore County, by 1770. FAMILY BACKGROUND. FATHER: Maj. Nathan Hammond (1708–1762), of Elkridge, Anne Arundel County; sheriff of Anne Arundel County in 1751; son of *Charles Hammond* (ca. 1670–1713). MOTHER: Ann (?–1780), daughter of John Welsh and wife Rachel. UNCLES: *Charles Hammond* (1692/93–1772); *Philip Hammond* (1697–1760). AUNT: Ruth Hammond, who married second, *Thomas Franklin* (ca. 1706–1787). BROTHERS: *Nathan Hammond* (1731–1811); Philip (1744–1799), of Anne Arundel County, who mar-

ried Barbara Riatt; Charles; Capt. John, who married Martha Hawkins; Ormand (ca. 1754–?), of Frederick County, who married Elizabeth Duckett; Aquilla (1744–1797); and Thomas (?–1786), of Frederick County. SISTERS: Ann (?–1790); Hannah, who married John Riatt, Jr.; Ruth; Caroline (?–ca. 1772); Mary, who married Vachel Hammond; and Hamutal (?–ca. 1772). FIRST COUSINS: *Matthias Hammond* (1740–1786); *John Hammond* (1735–1784); *Rezin Hammond* (1745–1809); and Anne Hammond, who married second, *William Govane* (1716/17–1768). MARRIED on September 2, 1760, Rebecca (?–1805), daughter of Matthew Hawkins and wife Rachel Burley. CHILDREN. SONS: Rezin (?–1796); Matthias (?–1798); and Nathan (?–1818), who married Martha. DAUGHTER: Rebecca, who married David Gist. PRIVATE CAREER. EDUCATION: literate. SOCIAL STATUS AND ACTIVITIES: Gent., by 1781. OCCUPATIONAL PROFILE: planter. PUBLIC CAREER. LEGISLATIVE SERVICE: Lower House, Baltimore County, 1778–1779, 1779–1780, 1780–1781 (resigned on May 25, 1781). LOCAL OFFICES: Committee of Observation, Delaware Hundred, Baltimore County, elected 1774; justice, Baltimore County, commissioned 1774 and 1775. WEALTH DURING LIFETIME. LAND AT FIRST ELECTION: 876 acres in Baltimore and Anne Arundel counties (195 acres inherited from his father in 1762; 261 acres through his marriage; remainder by purchase). WEALTH AT DEATH. DIED: between February 14 and April 10, 1783, in Baltimore County. PERSONAL PROPERTY: TEV, £2,385.7.0 current money (including 30 slaves); FB, £2,250.14.4. LAND: 876 acres in Baltimore and Anne Arundel counties.

HAMMOND, REZIN (1745–1809). BORN: in 1745 in Anne Arundel County; youngest son. NATIVE: fifth generation. RESIDED: in Severn Hundred, Anne Arundel County. FAMILY BACKGROUND. FATHER: *Philip Hammond* (1697–1760), son of *Charles Hammond* (ca. 1670–1713). MOTHER: Rachel (1711–1786), daughter of *John Brice* (?–1713). UNCLE: *Charles Hammond* (1692/93–1772). AUNTS: Ruth Hammond, who married second, *Thomas Franklin* (ca. 1706–1787); Anne Brice (1708–1765), who married *Vachel Denton* (ca. 1696–1752). BROTHERS: Charles (1729–by 1786); *John Hammond* (1735–1784); Philip (?–1783); Denton (?–1782); and *Matthias Hammond* (1740–1786). HALF BROTHERS: Joshua (1719–died a minor). SISTER: Anne. FIRST COUSINS: *Nathan Hammond* (1731–1811); *Rezin Hammond* (?–1783); Anne Hammond, who married second, *William Govane* (1716/17–1768);

John Brice (1738–1820); *James Brice* (1746–1801); and *Benedict Brice* (1749–1786). MARRIED never. CHILDREN. Died without progeny. PRIVATE CAREER. EDUCATION: literate. SOCIAL STATUS AND ACTIVITIES: Esq., 1773; Gent., 1774; fourth generation legislator. OCCUPATIONAL PROFILE: planter. PUBLIC CAREER. LEGISLATIVE SERVICE: Conventions, Anne Arundel County, 1st, 1774, 2nd–3rd, 1774 (elected to the 3rd Convention, but did not attend), 4th, 1775, 5th, 1775, 9th, 1776; Lower House, Anne Arundel County, 1777, 1777–1778 (resigned during the 3rd session). LOCAL OFFICES: Committee of Observation, Annapolis and Anne Arundel County, elected 1774 and 1775; commissioner of tax, Anne Arundel County, 1783–1785. MILITARY SERVICE: lieutenant colonel, Severn Battalion, Anne Arundel County Militia, appointed 1776; colonel, by 1795. STANDS ON PUBLIC/PRIVATE ISSUES: active in radical patriotic politics during 1774 and 1775 with his brother *Matthias Hammond* (1740–1786). His obituary described him as having been a leader of a "little warrior band," with a "sincere and ardent attachment" to the American cause. At his death, Hammond provided for the manumission and support of his slaves. WEALTH DURING LIFETIME. PERSONAL PROPERTY: assessed value £10,057.0.0 current money, including 72 slaves, 1783; 102 slaves, 1798. ADDITIONAL COMMENTS: Hammond, with his brother Denton and his sister Anne, were the heirs of *Vachel Denton* (ca. 1696–1752). LAND AT FIRST ELECTION: at least 5,500 acres in Anne Arundel County (more than 4,000 acres inherited from his father in 1760 and confirmed to him by his brothers by 1772). SIGNIFICANT CHANGES IN LAND BETWEEN FIRST ELECTION AND DEATH: charged with 6,311 acres in Anne Arundel County, 1783; charged with 10,484 acres in Anne Arundel County, 1798; during the 1780s and 1790s he consolidated his land into three large tracts; leased out ca. 10,000 acres to 31 tenants, 1798; he continued to acquire and patent large holdings until his death, selling very little. WEALTH AT DEATH. DIED: on September 1, 1809, at his farm in Anne Arundel County, after a long and painful illness; buried in the family cemetery near Gambrills, Anne Arundel County. PERSONAL PROPERTY: included 166 slaves, and a law library. LAND: 12,671 acres in Anne Arundel County, plus one-fourth interest in 2,286 acres in Frederick County, a part of his father's estate not patented until 1796. ADDITIONAL COMMENTS: his obituary lauded him as an "inflexible friend," a "charitable Christian," and an "upright citizen." Named as his principal heirs the sons of his nephew Philip

Hammond, probably the son of his brother Charles.

HAMMOND, THOMAS (?–ca. 1724/25). BORN: in Anne Arundel County; first son. NATIVE: third generation. RESIDED: in Anne Arundel County; Baltimore County by 1694. FAMILY BACKGROUND. FATHER: *John Hammond* (1643–1707). MOTHER: Mary (?–by 1678), daughter of Matthew Howard and wife Ann. UNCLE: *Cornelius Howard* (?–1680). AUNT: Elizabeth Howard, who married *Henry Ridgeley* (?–1710). BROTHERS: *John Hammond* (ca. 1665–1742/43), who married Ann, daughter of *Nicholas Greenberry* (1627–1697); William (?–1711/12); and *Charles Hammond* (ca. 1670–1713). SISTERS: Mary, who married Cornelius Howard, son of *Cornelius Howard* (?–1680); Elizabeth. FIRST COUSINS: *Matthew Howard* (ca. 1675–1750); Sarah Howard, who married first, *John Worthington* (1650–1701), and second, *John Brice* (?–1713); and Hannah Howard, who married first, her first cousin *Charles Hammond* (ca. 1670–1713), and second, *Edmond Benson* (1687–1734). MARRIED first, ca. 1687/88 Rebecca, widow of Thomas Lightfoot; probably daughter of John Larkin. MARRIED second, by 1718 Mary Heath. CHILDREN. SONS: John (1694–1739); Thomas; William (1702–1752), the sheriff of Baltimore County in 1737, who married first, Elizabeth Hughes Raven, and second, Sarah Sheredine; Lawrence, who married Aborila Simpkins; Henry; Haman; and Charles. DAUGHTERS: Helen, who married John Worthington, son of *John Worthington* (1650–1701); Susannah, who married in 1719 John Orick; and Katherine. PRIVATE CAREER. EDUCATION: literate. RELIGIOUS AFFILIATION: Protestant. SOCIAL STATUS AND ACTIVITIES: second generation burgess; his sons held no elective offices. OCCUPATIONAL PROFILE: planter. PUBLIC CAREER. LEGISLATIVE SERVICE: Lower House, Baltimore County, 1701–1704, 1712–1714 (election voided at the 1st session; reelected to the 2nd session), 1722–1724. LOCAL OFFICES: justice, Baltimore County, 1694 (no evidence that he ever sat, and he was not reappointed in 1696), sitting in 1701. MILITARY SERVICE: captain, 1694; major, by 1701; colonel at death. WEALTH DURING LIFETIME. PERSONAL PROPERTY: had household of 6 taxables, including 3 slaves, 1692–1695. LAND AT FIRST ELECTION: heir-at-law; at least 300 acres by 1707, probably much more; at least 500 acres by 1712. WEALTH AT DEATH. DIED: between December 2, 1724, and February 2, 1724/25. PERSONAL PROPERTY: TEV, £535.13.2 (including 12 slaves); FB, estate overpaid £24.0.0. LAND: at least 500 acres, probably much more.

HAMMOND, THOMAS (1693–?). BORN: on December 19, 1693, in St. Margaret's Parish, Anne Arundel County; eldest son. NATIVE: fourth generation. RESIDED: on Kent Island, Queen Anne's County, by 1722; Kent County, 1723; Queen Anne's County, 1724–at least 1751. FAMILY BACKGROUND. FATHER: William Hammond (?–1710/11), of Anne Arundel County, son of *John Hammond* (1643–1707). STEPFATHER: James Govane, Gent. (?–1739), of Anne Arundel County. MOTHER: Elizabeth (?–ca. 1731), daughter of William Cockey and wife Sarah. UNCLES: *Thomas Hammond* (?–ca. 1724/25); *John Hammond* (ca. 1665–1742/43); and *Charles Hammond* (ca. 1670–1713). BROTHERS: Mordecai (1695–1746), of Anne Arundel County, who married in 1719 Frances, daughter of Rev. John Lillingston (?–1709); Benjamin (1706/7–?), who married first, Sarah Eagle, and second, Margaret Talbot; Lawrence (1709–1784), who married first, Ruth Greniffe, and second, Margaret Hughes; William (1710/11–?), who married Mary Merriken. HALF BROTHER: *William Govane* (1716/17–1768). SISTERS: Sarah (1691/92–?); Susannah (1697–?), who married Carpenter Lillingston (?–ca. 1724), of Queen Anne's County, son of Rev. John Lillingston (?–1709), but by the time her husband made his will he stated that she had left his home and was therefore disbarred from any part of his estate; and Jane (1700–1703). FIRST COUSINS: *Charles Hammond* (1692/93–1772); *Philip Hammond* (1697–1760); and Ruth Hammond, who married second, *Thomas Franklin* (ca. 1706–1787). MARRIED first, on January 6, 1714, Jane (?–by 1738), widow of *John Wells* (?–1714); daughter of Rev. John Lillingston (?–1709), rector of St. Paul's Parish in Queen Anne's County from 1691 to 1709, and wife Mary Carpenter; granddaughter of Symon Carpenter (?–1670) and wife Elizabeth (?–1702); stepgranddaugher of *Henry Coursey* (ca. 1629–1695). Her brothers were Carpenter (?–ca. 1724), who married Susannah (1697–?), daughter of William Hammond (?–1710/11); George. Her sisters were Mary; Frances, who married Mordecai Hammond (1695–1746), son of William Hammond (?–1710/11). Her first cousins were *James Earle, Jr.* (ca. 1694–1739); Elizabeth Earle (ca. 1694–?), who married *William Turbutt* (1683/84–1739). MARRIED second, by 1738 Elizabeth. CHILDREN. SONS: Lillingston (1719–?); Thomas (1720–?), who married Sarah. STEPSON: John Wells (ca. 1704–?). STEPDAUGHTER: Mary Ann Wells (1714–?). PRI-

VATE CAREER. EDUCATION: literate. RELIGIOUS AFFILIATION: Anglican. OCCUPATIONAL PROFILE: planter. PUBLIC CAREER. LEGISLATIVE SERVICE: Lower House, Queen Anne's County, 1741 (elected to the 3rd session to fill vacancy), 1742–1744, 1745, 1745/46–1748. LOCAL OFFICES: counter of tobacco plants, Queen Anne's County, appointed 1729 (declined); St. Paul's Parish Vestry, Queen Anne's County, 1735–1738; justice, Queen Anne's County, 1749–1751. WEALTH DURING LIFETIME. LAND AT FIRST ELECTION: 380 acres in Queen Anne's County (had inherited 510 acres in Anne Arundel County from his father, but sold all of it before his first election; life estate to 305 acres in Queen Anne's County through his first marriage; 75 acres in Queen Anne's County by purchase). SIGNIFICANT CHANGES IN LAND BETWEEN FIRST ELECTION AND DEATH: purchased 60 acres in Queen Anne's County in 1749; sold his rights to the 305 acres owned by his first wife and the 75 acres that he had purchased before his first election in June 1751. In October 1751 he sold the 60-acre tract purchased in 1749. ADDITIONAL COMMENTS: A few days after Hammond sold his last tract of land he executed a deed stating that he was indebted to Mr. Charles Brown & Co., merchants, for at least 9,000 pounds of tobacco; and, "not having wherewith to pay them," he requested that all the tobacco due to him for his services as an assemblyman and justice of the peace for Queen Anne's County be assigned to Brown to pay his debts. In addition he assigned all the tobacco on his dwelling plantation to Brown. WEALTH AT DEATH. DIED: after 1751, probably heavily in debt. LAND: none.

HANCE, SAMUEL (?–?). BORN: probably in Calvert County, of age by 1753. NATIVE: third generation. RESIDED: in Calvert County; Talbot County, 1785. FAMILY BACKGROUND. FATHER: Benjamin Hance (1684–1738), of "Overton," Calvert County, son of John Hance (?–1709) and wife Sarah. MOTHER: Mary, daughter of Col. Francis Hutchins and wife Elizabeth. SISTER: Mary, who married ca. 1736 *James John Mackall* (1717–1772). NEPHEWS: *John Mackall* (1740–1799); *Benjamin Mackall IV* (1745–by 1810). CHILDREN. SON: Benjamin. PRIVATE CAREER. EDUCATION: literate. RELIGIOUS AFFILIATION: Anglican; his grandfather was a Quaker. SOCIAL STATUS AND ACTIVITIES: Mr., 1781. OCCUPATIONAL PROFILE: probably a planter. PUBLIC CAREER. LEGISLATIVE SERVICE: Lower House, Calvert County, 1777–1778 (elected, but did not attend). LOCAL OFFICES: justice, Calvert County, commissioned 1777 (did not qualify); committee of observation to watch for British warships, Calvert County, 1780; Christ Church Parish Vestry, 1781–1782. WEALTH DURING LIFETIME. PERSONAL PROPERTY: assessed value £1,445.3.4, including 35 slaves and 100 oz. plate, 1783. LAND AT FIRST ELECTION: 394 acres in Calvert County. SIGNIFICANT CHANGES IN LAND BETWEEN FIRST ELECTION AND DEATH: acquired more than 653 acres in Calvert and Talbot counties by 1785. WEALTH AT DEATH. DIED: after 1785, possibly in Talbot County; size of estate unknown.

HANDS, THOMAS BEDINGFIELD (?–1811). BORN: in Kent County, of age by 1767; only son. NATIVE: at least second generation. RESIDED: in Chestertown, Kent County. FAMILY BACKGROUND. FATHER: Thomas Bedingfield Hands (?–1769), of Kent County, who was treasurer of the Eastern Shore and justice of the Provincial Court. MOTHER: Sarah (1721–1754), daughter of Alexander McGahon. SISTERS: Margaret (1745–1794), who married *Thomas Smyth* (1730–1819); Elizabeth, who married on February 16, 1796, (name unknown). MARRIED first, by July 1780 Mary. MARRIED second, in 1801 Mary Jackson, of Chestertown, Kent County. CHILDREN. SONS: Bedingfield (?–1821), who married Catherine (1782–1849). Catherine subsequently married Richard Ringgold; Alexander. DAUGHTER: Sarah, who married William Barroll. PRIVATE CAREER. EDUCATION: studied law. RELIGIOUS AFFILIATION: Anglican, Chestertown Church, Kent County. SOCIAL STATUS AND ACTIVITIES: Gent., 1767. OCCUPATIONAL PROFILE: lawyer, admitted to the following courts: Annapolis Mayor's Court in April 1765; Queen Anne's County in June 1765; Baltimore County in August 1765; Kent County by March 1766; Provincial Court in May 1767; Cecil County by March 1771. PUBLIC CAREER. LEGISLATIVE SERVICE: Conventions, Kent County, 4th, 1775, 5th, 1775; Senate, Eastern Shore, Term of 1776–1781: 1777 (elected on February 15, 1777, to fill vacancy; probably declined to serve, but date unknown). OTHER STATE OFFICE: Councils of Safety, Eastern Shore, 2nd, 1776, 3rd, 1776, 4th, 1776 (declined). LOCAL OFFICES: Chester Parish Vestry, Kent County, in office 1800–1811; visitor, Kent County Free School, in office 1801. WEALTH DURING LIFETIME. PERSONAL PROPERTY: assessed value £1,337.10.0, including 27 slaves and 378 oz. plate, 1783; assessed value $9,099.00 (combined real and personal property), 1804–1811. LAND AT FIRST ELECTION: 400 acres in Kent County (inherited from his father), plus 2 water lots and 1 land lot in Chestertown, Kent County. SIGNIFICANT CHANGES IN LAND BETWEEN FIRST ELECTION AND DEATH: purchased 520 acres in Kent County, plus 4 lots in Chestertown, Kent County, 1777–1798. WEALTH AT DEATH. DIED: ca. June 1811. PERSONAL PROPERTY: requested no appraisal of his estate. LAND: probably 1,000 acres in Kent County, plus 2 lots in Chestertown, Kent County.

HANDY, BENJAMIN (?–ca. 1763). BORN: probably in Somerset County, a minor in 1735; possibly eldest son. NATIVE: third generation. RESIDED: in Somerset County; Worcester County, by 1748/49. FAMILY BACKGROUND. FATHER: Ebenezer Handy (?–ca. 1735/36), son of Samuel Handy (?–1721) and wife Mary Sewell. MOTHER OR STEPMOTHER: Betty. UNCLE AND GUARDIAN: *Isaac Handy* (?–1762). BROTHERS: John; Robert. SISTERS: Mary Elizabeth; Mary. OTHER KINSHIP: his first cousin was *John Handy* (ca. 1724–1756). MARRIED first, his first cousin Priscilla (?–by 1748/49), daughter of John Handy, Gent. (1695–1745) and wife Jane Dashiell (1698–?); stepdaughter of Thomas Gillis; granddaughter of *Thomas Dashiell* (1666–ca. 1756). Her brothers were *John Handy* (ca. 1724–1756); Charles, of Newport, Rhode Island, 1755; Samuel (?–by 1760), who married Sarah; and Levin. Her sisters were Easter (ca. 1720–1748), who married first, Robert Dashiell (?–1744/45), son of George Dashiell (?–1733/34), and second, Day Scott (1746–by 1773); Ann (?–by 1761); and Mary (1740–1766), who married William Geddes, Esq. Her first cousins were *Thomas Dashiell* (1733–1771); *Joseph Dashiell* (1736–ca. 1787); and *George Dashiell* (1743–?); and *John Dashiell* (ca. 1740–1817), a possible legislator. Her other relatives included her great-grandfather *James Dashiell* (ca. 1634–1697). MARRIED second, by 1756 Elizabeth. CHILDREN. SON: John. PRIVATE CAREER. EDUCATION: literate. RELIGIOUS AFFILIATION: Protestant. SOCIAL STATUS AND ACTIVITIES: Gent., 1748/49. OCCUPATIONAL PROFILE: planter, 1751; owned a sawmill in partnership with Thomas and George Martin, 1763. PUBLIC CAREER. LEGISLATIVE SERVICE: Lower House, Worcester County, 1756–1757 (elected to the 4th session to fill vacancy), 1757–1758 (Arms and Ammunition 2), 1758 (appointed sheriff before the 1st session). LOCAL OFFICES: justice, Worcester County, ca. 1747–1763 (quorum, 1754–1763); sheriff, Worcester County, 1758–1761; collector of the excise tax, Worcester County, in office 1758; collector of the land tax, Worcester County, in office 1759. MILITARY SERVICE: captain, by 1756; major, by 1758. WEALTH DURING

LIFETIME. PERSONAL PROPERTY: 3 slaves and a stallion inherited from his father, 1735/36; his wife inherited more than £500 from her father, ca. 1745. LAND AT FIRST ELECTION: 615 acres in Somerset and Worcester counties (inherited all except 5 acres from his father). SIGNIFICANT CHANGES IN LAND BETWEEN FIRST ELECTION AND DEATH: patented 1,165 acres in Worcester and Somerset counties in 1763 in partnership with George and Thomas Martin, with whom he owned a sawmill; purchased and patented 270 acres in Worcester and Somerset counties, 1760–1763. WEALTH AT DEATH. DIED: "soon after April 25, 1763;" administration bond granted on June 4, 1764, in Worcester County. PERSONAL PROPERTY: TEV, £958.3.6 current money (including 16 slaves and 7 books); FB, £519.3.10. LAND: 885 acres in Worcester County, plus 1,165 acres in Somerset and Worcester counties held with his two business partners.

HANDY, ISAAC (?–1762). BORN: in Somerset County, of age by 1726; younger son. NATIVE: second generation. RESIDED: in Somerset County. FAMILY BACKGROUND. FATHER: Samuel Handy (?–1721). MOTHER: Mary Sewell. BROTHERS: Samuel (?–1734/35); Thomas (?–between 1722 and 1727), a mariner, who married Martha; Stephen (?–1724), who died without progeny; Benjamin; William (1686–1734); Ebenezer (?–ca. 1735/36); and John (1695–1745), who married Jane (Jean) (1698–?), daughter of *Thomas Dashiell* (1666–ca. 1756), subsequently the wife of Thomas Gillis. SISTERS: Rachel, who married (first name unknown) Colbourn; Jane, who married (first name unknown) Colbourn; Priscilla; Sarah, who married (first name unknown) Tull; and Mary. NEPHEWS: *John Handy* (ca. 1724–1756); *Benjamin Handy* (?– ca. 1763). MARRIED on April 27, 1726, Anne (1707–?), daughter of *Thomas Dashiell* (1666–ca. 1756). Her brothers were *George Dashiell* (1690/91–1748); Thomas (1700–by 1765); Henry (1702/3–1756); Charles (1705–1765); Levin (1711/12–1795); and John (1711/12–1736), who was probably a twin to Levin. Her sisters were Priscilla (1688/89–?); Elizabeth (Betty) (1693/94–1762); Isabel (1695–?); Jean (Jane) (1698–?); and Sarah (1709–?). Her nephews were *Thomas Dashiell* (1733–1771); *Joseph Dashiell* (1736–ca. 1787); *George Dashiell* (1743–?), and *John Dashiell* (ca. 1740–1817), a possible legislator. CHILDREN. SONS: Capt. George (1727–1782), builder of "Handy Hall," Somerset County, captain and master of the sloop *George*, which was insured and probably owned by his father, married on Febru-

ary 9, 1755, Nellie, daughter of Thomas Gillis and wife Priscilla Denwood; Thomas (1737–?), who died at sea; William (1739–1791); *Isaac Handy* (1743–ca. 1774); and Capt. Henry (1747–?), who married Jane, daughter of *William Winder* (1714/15–1792). DAUGHTERS: Sarah (1731–?), who married by 1755 Rev. Hugh Henry; Mary (1733–died young); Elizabeth (1741–1796), who married John Harris; and Ann, who married Thomas Gillis. PRIVATE CAREER. EDUCATION: literate. RELIGIOUS AFFILIATION: Protestant. SOCIAL STATUS AND ACTIVITIES: Gent., 1734. OCCUPATIONAL PROFILE: a mariner, 1726; his father left him and his brother Stephen one-half interest in the sloop *Samuel & Mary* with the provision that they would receive the other half if their brother Thomas died without issue; a merchant in 1741, involved in the shipping business with the sloop *George* . PUBLIC CAREER. LEGISLATIVE SERVICE: Lower House, Somerset County, 1747–1748 (elected to the 3rd session to fill vacancy), 1749–1751. LOCAL OFFICES: justice, Somerset County, 1734–1762 (quorum, 1746–1762); justice, Court of Oyer and Terminer and Gaol Delivery, Somerset County, commissioned 1750 and 1753. MILITARY SERVICE: captain, by 1744; colonel, by 1755. WEALTH DURING LIFETIME. LAND AT FIRST ELECTION: at least 1,392 acres in Somerset County (all through purchase). SIGNIFICANT CHANGES IN LAND BETWEEN FIRST ELECTION AND DEATH: gave 350 acres to his son George in 1751; obtained 311 acres between 1752 and 1759; sold 303 acres by 1759, all acreage was in Somerset County. WEALTH AT DEATH. DIED: on November 12, 1762, in Somerset County. PERSONAL PROPERTY: TEV, £962.19.2 current money (including 17 slaves and books); FB, £302.15.1. LAND: 1,018 acres in Somerset County.

HANDY, ISAAC (1743–ca. 1774). BORN: on December 19, 1743, in Somerset County; younger son. NATIVE: third generation. RESIDED: in Somerset County; Princess Anne, Somerset County, by October 1769. FAMILY BACKGROUND. FATHER: *Isaac Handy* (?–1762). MOTHER: Anne (1707–?), daughter of *Thomas Dashiell* (1666–ca. 1756). UNCLE: *George Dashiell* (1690/91–1748). BROTHERS: George (1727–1782); Thomas (1737–?); William (1739–1791); and Henry. SISTERS: Sarah (1731–?); Mary (1733–died young); Elizabeth (1741–1796); and Ann. FIRST COUSINS: *John Handy* (ca. 1724– 1756); *Thomas Dashiell* (1733–1771); *Joseph Dashiell* (1736–ca. 1787); *George Dashiell* (1743–?); and *John Dashiell* (ca. 1740–1817), a possible legislator. MARRIED Esther, daughter of *William*

Winder (1714/15–1792) and wife Esther Gillis. Esther Handy subsequently married *William Polk* (1752–1812). CHILDREN. SON: Richard Henry. DAUGHTER: Margaret Winder. PRIVATE CAREER. EDUCATION: A.B., graduated from the College of New Jersey (later Princeton University) in 1761. RELIGIOUS AFFILIATION: Protestant; came from a Presbyterian family. OCCUPATIONAL PROFILE: attorney, admitted to the following courts: Somerset County in June 1763; Worcester County by June 1769; Provincial Court in October 1769. PUBLIC CAREER. LEGISLATIVE SERVICE: Lower House, Somerset County, 1771 (Laws to Expire; Public Offices). WEALTH DURING LIFETIME. LAND AT FIRST ELECTION: 290 acres, plus 2 lots in Somerset County (all purchased except for 15 acres that he probably inherited from his father). SIGNIFICANT CHANGES IN LAND BETWEEN FIRST ELECTION AND DEATH: acquired an additional 122.5 acres in Somerset County. WEALTH AT DEATH. DIED: inventory made on June 17, 1774, in Somerset County. PERSONAL PROPERTY: TEV, £1,136.15.2 current money (including 13 slaves and 79 books); FB, £220.11.9. LAND: 412.5 acres, plus 2 lots in Somerset County.

HANDY, JOHN (ca. 1724–1756). BORN: ca. 1724 in Somerset County; eldest son. NATIVE: third generation. RESIDED: in Somerset County. FAMILY BACKGROUND. FATHER: John Handy, Gent. (1695–1745), sheriff of Somerset County in 1743; son of Samuel Handy (?–1721) and wife Mary Sewell. STEPFATHER: Thomas Gillis. MOTHER: Jane (Jean) (1698–?), daughter of *Thomas Dashiell* (1666–ca. 1756). UNCLES: *George Dashiell* (1690/91–1748); *Isaac Handy* (?–1762). AUNT: Anne Dashiell (1707–?), who married *Isaac Handy* (?–1762). BROTHERS: Charles, who resided in Newport, Rhode Island, 1755; Samuel (a minor in 1744–by 1760), who married Sarah; and Levin (a minor in 1744–by 1761). SISTERS: Easter (ca. 1720–1748), who married first, Robert Dashiell (?–1744/45), son of George Dashiell (?–1733/34), and second, Day Scott (1746–by 1773); Priscilla (?–by 1748/49), who married *Benjamin Handy* (?–ca. 1763); Ann (?–by 1761); and Mary (1740–1766), who married William Geddes, Esq. FIRST COUSINS: *John Dashiell* (ca. 1740–1817), a possible legislator; *Thomas Dashiell* (1733–1771); *Joseph Dashiell* (1736–ca. 1787); *George Dashiell* (1743–?); and *Isaac Handy* (1743–ca. 1774). OTHER KINSHIP: his great-grandfather was *James Dashiell* (ca. 1634–1697). MARRIED on December 25, 1748, Ann (?–by 1760), daughter of Christopher Nutter (?–ca. 1741) and wife Sarah; stepdaughter of George Hardy; granddaughter of Christopher Nutter (?–1729), of Stepney Parish, Somerset County, and wife Margaret. Ann Handy subsequently married Ephraim King. Her brother was Christopher Nutter (?–ca. 1744), who died a minor. CHILDREN. SONS: Thomas (1749–1776), who married Sarah; Levin. DAUGHTERS: Amelia; Priscilla (1757–?). PRIVATE CAREER. EDUCATION: literate. RELIGIOUS AFFILIATION: Protestant. SOCIAL STATUS AND ACTIVITIES: Gent., 1755. OCCUPATIONAL PROFILE: merchant. PUBLIC CAREER. LEGISLATIVE SERVICE: Lower House, Somerset County, 1751–1754, 1754–1756 (Bills of Credit 1–3, 5; died before the 6th session). LOCAL OFFICE: justice, Somerset County, 1751–1756. MILITARY SERVICE: captain, by 1752. WEALTH DURING LIFETIME. PERSONAL PROPERTY: £156.19.10, by 1761 (a legacy from his father's estate). LAND AT FIRST ELECTION: 1,541 acres in Somerset County (342 acres inherited from his father; 1,099 acres of his wife's land purchased from her stepfather for £50). SIGNIFICANT CHANGES IN LAND BETWEEN FIRST ELECTION AND DEATH: purchased at least 200 acres in Somerset County, 1755. WEALTH AT DEATH. DIED: on November 6, 1756, in Somerset County of a "nervous fever." PERSONAL PROPERTY: TEV, £1,751.10.0 current money (including 18 slaves and more than 18 books); FB, £897.7.4. LAND: ca. 1,898 acres in Somerset County.

HANDY, SAMUEL (1751/52–1828). BORN: on March 5, 1751/52, in Somerset County; probably second son. NATIVE: at least second generation. RESIDED: in Somerset County; Worcester County, 1768. FAMILY BACKGROUND. FATHER: Samuel Handy (?–1755). STEPFATHER: John Pollett. GUARDIAN: *Littleton Dennis* (ca. 1728–1774). MOTHER: Mary, daughter of *John Dennis* (1704–1767). UNCLES: *Littleton Dennis* (ca. 1728–1774); *John Dennis, Jr.* (ca. 1724–1782). BROTHERS: John (1749–?); William, Esq. (?–1790), who married Mary King. SISTERS: Mary (1743–?); Elizabeth (1747–by 1827), who married (first name unknown) Davis. FIRST COUSIN: *Henry Dennis* (?–1785). MARRIED by 1768 Mary. CHILDREN. SON: John C. DAUGHTERS: Harriet G., who married (first name unknown) Stevenson; Mary D., who married (first name unknown) Henry; and (first name unknown), who married Ephraim K. Wilson. PRIVATE CAREER. EDUCATION: literate. RELIGIOUS AFFILIATION: Anglican; held pews in both Rehobeth Church and Dividing Creek Chapel, Coventry Parish, Somerset County. SOCIAL STATUS AND ACTIVITIES: Esq., 1791. OCCUPATIONAL PROFILE: merchant. PUBLIC CAREER. LEGISLATIVE

SERVICE: Conventions, Worcester County, 3rd, 1774, 5th, 1775, 6th–8th, 1775–1776, 9th, 1776 (election voided on August 15, 1776, because voter qualifications had not been ascertained as prescribed by the 8th Convention resolves; reelected and seated); Lower House, Worcester County, 1781–1782 (Public Taxes 2). LOCAL OFFICES: All Hallow's Parish Vestry, Worcester County, in office 1773; justice, Worcester County, commissioned 1775, 1777, and 1784 (did not qualify); commissioner of tax, Worcester County, 1777–at least 1798. MILITARY SERVICE: colonel, Synnapuxent Battalion, Worcester County Militia, commissioned 1777. WEALTH DURING LIFETIME. PERSONAL PROPERTY: assessed value £727.0.0, including 24 slaves and 22 oz. plate, 1783; 35 slaves, 1790. LAND AT FIRST ELECTION: 815 acres in Somerset and Worcester counties (all by personal acquisition). SIGNIFICANT CHANGES IN LAND BETWEEN FIRST ELECTION AND DEATH: purchased 3,596 acres and sold 940 acres in Worcester County, 1783–1828. WEALTH AT DEATH. DIED: will probated on June 10, 1828, in Worcester County. PERSONAL PROPERTY: TEV, $5,819.97 (including 14 slaves and more than 16 books); FB, $4,811.10. LAND: at least 3,476 acres in Worcester County.

HANSON, ALEXANDER CONTEE (1749–1806). BORN: on October 22, 1749, in Charles County; eldest son. NATIVE: probably fourth generation. RESIDED: in Frederick County; Church Street, Annapolis, Anne Arundel County, ca. 1778 until death. FAMILY BACKGROUND. FATHER: *John Hanson, Jr.* (1721–1783). MOTHER: Jane (1728–1812), daughter of *Alexander Contee* (ca. 1691–1740). BROTHERS: John (1753–1760); Samuel (1756–1781); and Peter Contee (1758–1776). SISTERS: Catherine Contee (1744–?); Jane Contee (1747–1781), who married Dr. *Philip Thomas* (1747–1815); Elizabeth (1751–1753); and Grace (1762–1763). MARRIED on June 4, 1778, Rebecca Howard (1758–1806). CHILDREN. SONS: Charles Wallace, associate judge, Sixth Judicial District; Alexander Contee, Jr. (1786–1819), of Rockville, Montgomery County, a lawyer who established and edited the ·*Federal Republican,* was an unsuccessful candidate for the Lower House in 1816, elected as a Federalist to the Thirteenth and Fourteenth Congress, 1813–1816, elected to U.S. Senate, 1816–1819, and who married on June 25, 1805, Priscilla Dorsey. DAUGHTER: (first name unknown), who married Thomas Peabody Grosvenor, of New York. PRIVATE CAREER. EDUCATION: educated at the College of Philadelphia; later stud-

ied law. RELIGIOUS AFFILIATION: Protestant. SOCIAL STATUS AND ACTIVITIES: Esq., 1801. OCCUPATIONAL PROFILE: lawyer, admitted to the following courts: Frederick County in March 1773; Provincial Court in April 1773; Charles County by November 1773; Prince George's County in March 1774. Assistant private secretary to Gen. George Washington, 1776; officeholder. He compiled the *Laws of Maryland* (Annapolis, 1787), which included acts passed from November 1763 to 1784; authored numerous political pamphlets, as well as a compilation of the state's testamentary laws, published in Annapolis in 1798. PUBLIC CAREER. LEGISLATIVE SERVICE: Convention, Frederick County, 1st, 1774. OTHER STATE OFFICES: clerk of the Senate, elected 1777, resigned 1778; judge, General Court, 1778–1789; Constitution Ratification Convention, Annapolis, 1788; chancellor and judge, Land Office, 1789–1806; presidential elector, 1789, 1792. LOCAL OFFICES: Committee of Observation, Frederick County, elected 1774 and 1775. STANDS ON PUBLIC/PRIVATE ISSUES: writing under the pseudonym "Aristides," he was an articulate supporter for the ratification of the U.S. Constitution. WEALTH DURING LIFETIME. PERSONAL PROPERTY: assessed value £246.13.4, including 2 slaves and 40 oz. plate, Anne Arundel County, 1783. LAND AT FIRST ELECTION: 364 acres in Frederick County, plus 2 lots in Annapolis. SIGNIFICANT CHANGES IN LAND BETWEEN FIRST ELECTION AND DEATH: patented 64 acres and sold at least 109 acres in Frederick County, and rented 2 lots in Annapolis, 1775–1807. WEALTH AT DEATH. DIED: on January 16, 1806, in Annapolis, of apoplexy. PERSONAL PROPERTY: TEV, at least $4,838.72 (including 11 slaves, 55 volumes, plus a 97-volume law library); FB, $3,476.26. LAND: probably 428 acres in Frederick County, plus part of lots 48 and 49 on Church Street, Annapolis, where he lived.

HANSON, HANS (ca. 1647–1704). BORN: ca. 1647 in Delaware Bay, New Sweden. IMMIGRATED: in 1653 as a minor with his parents. RESIDED: in Kent County; Cecil County, by 1697/98. FAMILY BACKGROUND. FATHER: Andrew Hanson (?–1655). MOTHER: Annicak. MARRIED in 1679 Martha, widow of John Wells. She subsequently married William Pott. CHILDREN. SONS: George, who married first, (name unknown), second, Sarah, daughter of *Daniel Pearce* (1677–1727), and third, Jane Hynson; Frederick; William; and Hans. DAUGHTERS: Ann; Mary, who married *St. Leger Codd* (?–1730). PRIVATE CAREER. EDUCATION: literate. RELIGIOUS AFFILIATION: Anglican.

SOCIAL STATUS AND ACTIVITIES: apprenticed to *Joseph Wickes* (ca. 1620–1692) in 1655 after his father's death; acquired the first land in his own name in 1667; he was naturalized in 1671. OCCUPATIONAL PROFILE: apprentice, 1655; planter; owned a gristmill. **PUBLIC CAREER.** LEGISLATIVE SERVICE: Associators' Convention, Kent County, 1689–1692; Lower House, Kent County, 1692–1693, 1694–1697 (Aggrievances 3, 4, 8), Cecil County, 1697/98–1700. LOCAL OFFICES: justice, Kent County, 1685–1697 (quorum, 1689–1697), Cecil County by 1702; St. Paul's Parish Vestry, Kent County, 1693–1703. MILITARY SERVICE: captain, by 1693; lieutenant colonel, 1694; colonel at the time of his death. STANDS ON PUBLIC/PRIVATE ISSUES: supported the revolution of 1689. **WEALTH DURING LIFETIME. LAND AT FIRST ELECTION:** probably over 1,000 acres. **WEALTH AT DEATH. DIED:** will probated on April 27, 1704. PERSONAL PROPERTY: TEV, £1,066.4.1 sterling. LAND: 1,175 acres.

HANSON, JOHN, JR. (1721–1783). BORN: on April 3, 1721, in Port Tobacco Parish, Charles County; third surviving son. NATIVE: at least third generation. RESIDED: in Charles County; Frederick County, 1769. **FAMILY BACKGROUND. FATHER:** *Samuel Hanson* (ca. 1685–1740). MOTHER: Elizabeth (ca. 1688–1764), daughter of *Walter Storey* (ca. 1666–1726). UNCLE: *Robert Hanson* (ca. 1680–1748). BROTHERS: *Walter Hanson* (1711/12–1794); *Samuel Hanson* (1716–1794); William (1718/19–1721); and William (1726–?). SISTERS: Elizabeth (1707–?); Mary (1709/10–?); Sarah (1714–?); Jane (1721/22–?); Charity (1724–?), who married second, *Arthur Lee* (?–1760); and Chloe. FIRST COUSINS: Dorothy Hanson (1721–1752), who married *Richard Harrison* (?–1780); Mary Hanson, who married *Daniel Jenifer* (?–1795). NEPHEW: *Samuel Hanson, of Samuel* (ca. 1752–1830). MARRIED in 1747 Jane (1728–1812), daughter of *Alexander Contee* (ca. 1691–1740); granddaughter of *Thomas Brooke* (ca. 1659–1730/31); half niece of *Thomas Brooke* (1683–1744), Sarah Brooke (?–1724), who married first, *William Dent* (ca. 1660–1704) and second, *Philip Lee* (ca. 1681–1744), and Priscilla Brooke, who married *Thomas Gantt* (?–1765). Her brothers were *John Contee* (1722–ca. 1796); Alexander, Jr. (1724–1734); Peter (1726–ca. 1779); *Thomas Contee* (ca. 1729–1811); Alexander (1734–1744); and Theodore (1736–ca. 1764). Her sisters were Catherine (1732–1831); Grace (1738–?); and Barbara (1741–1796). Her first cousin was *Thomas Beall, of George* (1735–1819). **CHILDREN. SONS:** *Alexander Contee Hanson*

(1749–1806); John (1753–1760); Samuel (1756–1781), a physician; and Peter Contee (1758–1776), who died at Fort Washington during the Revolutionary War. DAUGHTERS: Catherine Contee (1744–?), who married Philip Alexander; Jane Contee (1747–1781), who married in 1773 Dr. *Philip Thomas* (1747–1815); Elizabeth (1751–1753); and Grace (1762–1763). **PRIVATE CAREER.** EDUCATION: literate. RELIGIOUS AFFILIATION: Protestant. SOCIAL STATUS AND ACTIVITIES: Gent., 1744; Esq., by 1778. OCCUPATIONAL PROFILE: merchant, 1769; by 1772 he and his brother-in-law *Thomas Contee* (ca. 1729–1811) owned a store and warehouse in Frederick Town. **PUBLIC CAREER.** LEGISLATIVE SERVICE: Lower House, Charles County, 1757–1758 (Bills of Credit 1, Cv, 2), 1758–1761 (Bills of Credit Cv 1, 1, Cv 2, 2, 3, Cv 3), 1762–1763 (Bills of Credit 1, 2), 1765–1766 (Bills of Credit 2, 4; Accounts 3, 4; Laws to Expire 4), 1768–1769 (Claims 1; discharged from the Assembly at the beginning of the 2nd session after he had accepted the office of deputy surveyor of Frederick County); Conventions, Frederick County, 1st, 1774 (appointed, but did not attend), 4th, 1775 (elected, but did not attend), 5th, 1775; Lower House, Frederick County, 1777 (elected, but did not attend; resigned early in the 1st session), 1778–1779 (Claims 1, 2), 1779–1780 (Elections and Privileges 1; Claims 1; Manufactories 1), 1780–1781 (elected, but did not attend), 1781–1782 (elected, but did not attend; resigned early in the 1st session). LOCAL OFFICES: sheriff, Charles County, 1750–1753, Frederick County, commissioned 1771; deputy surveyor, Frederick County, commissioned 1769, 1771, 1773, and 1777 (resigned 1777); chairman, Committee of Observation, Frederick County, 1775; treasurer, Frederick County, elected 1775; commissioner to establish gunlock manufactory in Frederick Town, 1776; loan officer (to receive subscriptions for loan of money to the Continental Congress and to the State of Maryland), appointed 1777; judge, court of appeals, appointed under the Act to Procure Troops for the American Army, Frederick County, appointed 1778. OUT OF STATE SERVICE: delegate, Continental Congress, 1779–1782 (elected in December 1779, but did not attend until June 1780; reelected in November 1780 and November 1781). ADDITIONAL COMMENTS: Hanson was elected president of Congress on November 5, 1781. One week later he considered resigning from this position because of poor health, family responsibilities, and the "irksome" qualities of the "form and ceremonies" required as president. He was urged to continue by fellow members who cited the great difficulty Congress would have selecting a replacement, since only seven states were then represented. Hanson decided to remain as president contingent upon his reelection as a delegate by the Maryland Assembly. On November 28, 1781, Maryland returned him as one of her four delegates, and he continued as president of Congress until November 4, 1782. STANDS ON PUBLIC/PRIVATE ISSUES: as part of the Maryland congressional delegation he signed the Articles of Confederation in 1781, causing their adoption and closing a prolonged debate over the dispositon of western lands that had at last been resolved to Maryland's satisfaction. WEALTH DURING LIFETIME. LAND AT FIRST ELECTION: 1,312 acres in Charles County. SIGNIFICANT CHANGES IN LAND BETWEEN FIRST ELECTION AND DEATH: by 1769 Hanson had sold all of his land in Charles County and moved to Frederick County. During the next ten years he purchased 223 acres in Frederick County, took two 14-year leases on another 255 acres there, purchased 1 lot in Georgetown, Frederick County (later Montgomery County), and at least 2 lots in Frederick Town. In 1779 he purchased part of a tract adjoining Frederick Town for £4,000 current money, and divided it into lots, possibly totaling 10 lots. Hanson sold 6 of these lots for £4,008 current money between 1780 and 1781. WEALTH AT DEATH. DIED: on November 15, 1783, at the home of his nephew, Thomas Hanson, at Oxon Hill, Prince George's County; buried at Oxon Hill, Prince George's County. PERSONAL PROPERTY: requested no appraisal of his estate; 11 slaves were mentioned in his will. LAND: probably owned 223 acres and leased 255 acres, all in Frederick County, plus at least 6 lots in Frederick Town, Frederick County, and 1 lot in Georgetown, Montgomery County.

HANSON, ROBERT (ca. 1680–1748). BORN: ca. 1680 in Port Tobacco Hundred, Charles County; eldest son. NATIVE: at least second generation. RESIDED: in Charles County. FAMILY BACKGROUND. FATHER: John Hanson (?–1714), of Charles County; possibly an immigrant; planter. MOTHER: Mary, daughter of Thomas Hussey, of Charles County. BROTHERS: John (ca. 1681–1754), who married Elizabeth Hussey, a widow; Benjamin (?–1719); and *Samuel Hanson* (ca. 1685–1740). SISTERS: Mary, who married first, Rev. William Maconchie (1710–1742), and second, Theophilus Swift; Anne (1692–?); and Sarah. MARRIED first, by 1705 Benedicta. MARRIED second, ca. 1714 Mary (1692–1718), daughter of *Philip Hoskins* (ca. 1650–1718). Her brothers were William

(1690–1727); Philip, Jr. (1696–?); Oswald (1699–1720); Bennett (1701–?); and Ballard (1703–?). Her sisters were Benedicta (1679–1685); Jane (1681–?); Benedicta (1685–?); Elizabeth (1687–?); Margaret (1696–?); Mary Ann; and Martha (ca. 1705–?), who married *Thomas Stone* (1677–1727). MARRIED third, ca. 1720/21 Dorothy, widow of *John Parry* (?–1719); daughter of Cornelius White. MARRIED fourth, ca. 1727 Violetta, widow of William Hoskins (1690–1727); daughter of Francis Harrison. MARRIED fifth, on April 14, 1747, Anne, widow of John Maconchie. CHILDREN. SONS: Robert (?–1734); William (ca. 1717–1766), who married Mary, daughter of *Thomas Stone* (1677–1727); Samuel (1705–1749), who married Mary, daughter of *John Fendall* (1674–1734); Benjamin; and Robert (?–1770). STEPSONS: Thomas Parry (Perry); William Maconchie; and Alexander Maconchie. DAUGHTERS: Dorothy (1721–1752), who married *Richard Harrison* (?–1780); Mary, who married *Daniel Jenifer* (?–1795); Sarah, who married Gerard Fowke; and Violetta (?–1786). STEPDAUGHTERS: Elizabeth Hoskins (1721–1773), who married *Walter Hanson* (1711/12–1794); Mary Hoskins, who married first, John Cunningham, and second, Mungo Muschett. PRIVATE CAREER. EDUCATION: literate. RELIGIOUS AFFILIATION: Protestant. OCCUPATIONAL PROFILE: probably a planter. PUBLIC CAREER. LEGISLATIVE SERVICE: Lower House, Charles County, 1719–1721/22 (Aggrievances 1), 1728–1731 (Elections 1–5), 1732–1734 (Elections 1–Cv), 1734/35–1737 (Elections 1, Cv, 2–4), 1738 (Elections; Arms and Ammunition), 1739–1741 (Elections Cv–3; Arms and Ammunition Cv–3). OTHER PROVINCIAL OFFICE: justice, Provincial Court, commissioned 1741 (quorum, 1741). LOCAL OFFICES: sheriff, Charles County, commissioned 1715; justice, Charles County, at least by 1718–1748 (quorum, at least by 1718–1748); justice, Court of Oyer and Terminer and Gaol Delivery, Charles County, commissioned 1718, 1720, 1731, 1733, 1743, and 1744; clerk, Port Tobacco Parish Vestry, Charles County, in office 1722. JURY SERVICE: jury member, Charles County Court, served in 1712. MILITARY SERVICE: major, 1730; called "colonel," 1738. WEALTH DURING LIFETIME. LAND AT FIRST ELECTION: at least 1,649 acres in Charles County (including at least 100 acres inherited from his father and 609 acres obtained through his second marriage). SIGNIFICANT CHANGES IN LAND BETWEEN FIRST ELECTION AND DEATH: purchased an additional 1,254 acres in Charles County, plus 1 lot in Chandlertown, Charles County, 1720–1746; sold 809 acres, 1720–1746;

deeded 434 acres as a gift to his son and daughter. **WEALTH AT DEATH.** DIED: will probated on September 27, 1748, in Charles County. PERSONAL PROPERTY: TEV, £1,024.6.11 current money (including 18 slaves and 2 servants); FB, £429.14.1. LAND: over 986 acres, plus 6 lots in Charles County.

HANSON, SAMUEL (ca. 1685–1740). BORN: ca. 1685 in Charles County; youngest son. NATIVE: at least second generation. RESIDED: at "The Hills," Charles County. **FAMILY BACKGROUND. FATHER:** John Hanson (?–1714), a planter; possibly an immigrant. MOTHER: Mary, daughter of Thomas Hussey, of Charles County. BROTHERS: *Robert Hanson* (ca. 1680–1748); Benjamin (?–1719); and John (ca. 1681–1754). SISTERS: Mary, who married first, Rev. William Maconchie (1710–1742), and second, Theophilus Swift; Ann (1692–?); and Sarah. NIECES: Dorothy Hanson (1721–1752), who married *Richard Harrison* (?–1780); Mary Hanson, who married *Daniel Jenifer* (?–1795). MARRIED by 1707 Elizabeth (ca. 1688–1764), widow of Benjamin Warren (?–1706); daughter of *Walter Storey* (ca. 1666–1726). Her sisters were Sarah; Charity; and Jane. **CHILDREN. SONS:** *Walter Hanson* (1711/12–1794); *Samuel Hanson* (1716–1794); William (1718/19–1721); *John Hanson, Jr.* (1721–1783); and William (1726–?). DAUGHTERS: Elizabeth (1707–?), who married Benjamin Douglas; Mary (1709/10–?); Sarah (1714–?); Jane (1721/22–?); Charity (1724–?), who married first, John Howard (?–1749), and second, *Arthur Lee* (?–1760); and Chloe, who married Philip Briscoe. **PRIVATE CAREER. EDUCATION:** literate. RELIGIOUS AFFILIATION: Anglican. SOCIAL STATUS AND ACTIVITIES: Gent., by 1717. OCCUPATIONAL PROFILE: planter; officeholder. **PUBLIC CAREER. LEGISLATIVE SERVICE:** Lower House, Charles County, 1716–1717 (Laws 1; resigned between the 2nd and 3rd sessions to become sheriff), 1728–1731 (Laws 1–5). LOCAL OFFICES: sheriff, Charles County 1717–at least 1720; clerk, Charles County, 1720–1740; deputy commissary, Charles County, 1724–1733/34. MILITARY SERVICE: captain, period of service unknown. **WEALTH DURING LIFETIME.** LAND AT FIRST ELECTION: 190 acres in Charles County (acquired through his marriage). SIGNIFICANT CHANGES IN LAND BETWEEN FIRST ELECTION AND DEATH: acquired nearly 1,400 acres in Charles County by purchase and patent between 1717 and 1736; sold 300 acres in Charles County in 1722/23, and gave 340 acres in Charles County (including his dwelling house) to his son *Walter Hanson* (1711/12–1794) in 1738. **WEALTH AT**

DEATH. DIED: on October 26, 1740, in Charles County; buried at "Equality," Charles County. PERSONAL PROPERTY: TEV, £1,361.0.0 current money (including 22 slaves and books); FB, £1,258.2.11. LAND: ca. 750 acres in Charles County.

HANSON, SAMUEL (1716–1794). BORN: on December 20, 1716, in Port Tobacco Parish, Charles County; second son. NATIVE: third generation. RESIDED: at "Green Hill," Port Tobacco Upper Hundred, Charles County. **FAMILY BACKGROUND. FATHER:** *Samuel Hanson* (ca. 1685–1740). MOTHER: Elizabeth (ca. 1688–1764), widow of Benjamin Warren (?–1706); daughter of *Walter Storey* (ca. 1666–1726). UNCLE: *Robert Hanson* (ca. 1680–1748). BROTHERS: *Walter Hanson* (1711/12–1794); William (1718/19–1721); *John Hanson, Jr.* (1721–1783); and William (1726–?). SISTERS: Elizabeth (1707–?); Mary (1709/10–?); Sarah (1714–?); Jane (1721/22–?); Charity (1724–?), who married second, *Arthur Lee* (?–1760); and Chloe. FIRST COUSINS: Dorothy Hanson (1721–1752), who married *Richard Harrison* (?–1780); Mary Hanson, who married *Daniel Jenifer* (?–1795). NEPHEW: *Alexander Contee Hanson* (1749–1806). NIECE: Jane (1747–1781), who married *Philip Thomas* (1747–1815). MARRIED first, Anne, daughter of Thomas Hawkins and wife Sarah. MARRIED second, ca. 1774 Anne Brown (?–ca. 1800), widow of both Samuel Clagett and Robert Horner. Her brother was Dr. Gustavus Brown. **CHILDREN. SONS:** Thomas Hawkins (1750–1810), who married Rebecca, daughter of *Walter Dulany* (?–1773); *Samuel Hanson, of Samuel* (ca. 1752–1830). DAUGHTERS: Chloe (ca. 1743–?), who married *George Lee* (ca. 1736–?); Mildred (ca. 1746–by 1796), who married *William Baker* (ca. 1749–1812); Sarah Hawkins (1750–1822), who married Dr. William Beans (1748/49–1828); Nancy, who married John Addison, son of *John Addison* (1713–1764); Eleanor (?–1796), who married *Henry Henley Chapman* (?–1821); Anne, who married Nicholas Lingan; and Elizabeth, who married John Anderson. STEPSONS: Samuel Clagett; Gustavus Brown Horner; William Horner (ca. 1765–?); and John Horner. **PRIVATE CAREER. EDUCATION:** literate. SOCIAL STATUS AND ACTIVITIES: Mr., by 1744; Gent., by 1746; Esq., by 1783. OCCUPATIONAL PROFILE: merchant, by 1764; planter. **PUBLIC CAREER. LEGISLATIVE SERVICE:** Conventions, Charles County, 2nd, 1774, 4th 1775 (elected, but did not attend), 5th, 1775 (elected, but did not attend); Lower House, Charles County, 1778–1779 (Elections 2; Laws to Expire 3), 1779–1780

(Manufactories 1); 1780–1781 (elected to the 1st session to fill vacancy; Grievances 1; resigned on May 25, 1781). LOCAL OFFICES: sheriff, Charles County, 1744–47, 1749–1750; justice, Charles County, 1755–at least 1778 (quorum, 1769–at least 1778); justice, Court of Oyer and Terminer and Gaol Delivery, Charles County, commissioned 1772; justice, Orphans' court, Charles County, commissioned 1777 and 1778; judge, court of appeals, appointed under the Act to Procure Troops for the American Army, Charles County, appointed 1778; subscription officer, Continental Loan Office, Charles County, appointed 1779. STANDS ON PUBLIC/PRIVATE ISSUES: provided for the care, schooling, and manumission of his slaves in his will. WEALTH DURING LIFETIME. PERSONAL PROPERTY: assessed value £1,321.0.0, including 25 slaves and 69 oz. plate, 1783. LAND AT FIRST ELECTION: 5,225 acres in Charles and Frederick counties (ca. 370 acres inherited from his father). SIGNIFICANT CHANGES IN LAND BETWEEN FIRST ELECTION AND DEATH: gave at least 283 acres in Charles County to his son Thomas in 1776, and 1,770 acres in Charles County to his son *Samuel Hanson, of Samuel* (ca. 1752–1830) between 1776 and 1779. Hanson purchased approximately 227 acres in Charles County and sold 423 acres in Charles County. He apparently also divested himself of his land in Frederick and Montgomery counties prior to his death. WEALTH AT DEATH. DIED: will probated on November 25, 1794, in Charles County. PERSONAL PROPERTY: TEV, £3,498.8.5 current money (including 26 slaves); FB, £439.1.8. LAND: 2,005 acres in Charles County. IDENTIFICATION PROBLEMS. The legislative service and officeholding attributed to *Samuel Hanson* (1716–1794) was the result of an analysis of records pertaining to the six men of that name living in Charles County during the period 1774–1784. However, these conclusions cannot be positively verified. See also the profiles of *Samuel Hanson, Jr.* (?–1817) and *Samuel Hanson, of Samuel* (ca. 1752–1830).

HANSON, SAMUEL, JR. (?–1817). BORN: in Charles County, of age by 1759; second son. NATIVE: fourth generation. RESIDED: in Port Tobacco Parish, Charles County. FAMILY BACKGROUND. FATHER: Maj. Samuel Hanson (1705–1749), son of *Robert Hanson* (ca. 1680–1748) and wife Benedicta; a justice of Charles County from 1736 to at least 1747/48 (quorum, 1741–at least 1747/48). MOTHER: Mary (?–ca. 1759), daughter of *John Fendall* (1674–1734) and wife Elizabeth. HALF AUNTS: Dorothy Hanson (1721–1752), who mar-

ried *Richard Harrison* (?–1780); Mary Hanson, who married *Daniel Jenifer* (?–1795). BROTHERS: Robert; Josias (?–1764). SISTERS: Elizabeth; Benedicta (?–1790); Mary; Dorothy; and Martha (?–1765). FIRST COUSINS: *Philip Richard Fendall* (?–?); Sarah Fendall (ca. 1732–1793), who married *Thomas Contee* (ca. 1729–1811); and *Josias Beall* (ca. 1725–1803). MARRIED first, by 1759 Margaret (?–by 1793). MARRIED second, ca. 1793 Sarah, widow of Basil Beall (?–1792). CHILDREN. SONS: Samuel (?–ca. 1823), a physician and justice of Charles County from 1799 to 1801 and in 1803, who married Elizabeth Fendall, daughter of Thomas Marshall (?–1801); John Beall, who married Elizabeth Marshall. DAUGHTERS: Margaret Beall, who married John Fendall Beall; Charity Fendall Noble; Mary Fendall, who married (first name unknown) Cawood; Elizabeth Beall, who married (first name unknown) McPherson. STEPSONS: William Beall; Benjamin Beall. STEPDAUGHTERS: Elizabeth Duvall; Elinor MacGill; and Mary Beall. PRIVATE CAREER. EDUCATION: literate. SOCIAL STATUS AND ACTIVITIES: Gent., 1759. OCCUPATIONAL PROFILE: planter. PUBLIC CAREER. LEGISLATIVE SERVICE: Lower House, Charles County, 1778 (elected to the 3rd session of the 1777–1778 Assembly to fill vacancy; discharged on June 17, 1778, for serving as a field officer at the time of his election). MILITARY SERVICE: second major, Upper Battalion, Charles County Militia, appointed 1776; called major, 1783. WEALTH DURING LIFETIME. PERSONAL PROPERTY: assessed value £324.10.0, including 5 slaves, 1783; 34 slaves, 1798. LAND AT FIRST ELECTION: probably 1,192 acres in Charles County (82 acres by purchase; ca. 1,100 acres inherited from his father). SIGNIFICANT CHANGES IN LAND BETWEEN FIRST ELECTION AND DEATH: assessed for 860 acres in Charles County in 1783; deeded 800 acres in Charles County to his son Samuel in 1797; assessed for 513 acres in 1798. WEALTH AT DEATH. DIED: between September 21 and October 15, 1817, in Charles County. PERSONAL PROPERTY: inventory totaled $10,262.00 (including 29 slaves, plate, and books). LAND: about 250 acres in Charles County. IDENTIFICATION PROBLEMS. There were at least six Samuel Hansons of age in Charles County between 1774 and 1784. At least three of these men were known as "junior." The Samuel Hanson dismissed from the 1777–1778 General Assembly was referred to in the proceedings of that Assembly as both "junior" and "major." After an analysis of the records pertaining to all of the Samuel Hansons, this service was assigned to Samuel Hanson (?–1817), but it can not be positively verified. See also the profiles of *Samuel Hanson* (1716–1794) and *Samuel Hanson, of Samuel* (ca. 1752–1830).

HANSON, SAMUEL, OF SAMUEL (ca. 1752–1830). BORN: ca. 1752 in Port Tobacco Parish, Charles County; probably younger son. NATIVE: fourth generation. RESIDED: in Port Tobacco Upper Hundred, Fourth District, Charles County; Alexandria, Virginia, by 1787. FAMILY BACKGROUND. FATHER: *Samuel Hanson* (1716–1794). MOTHER: Anne, daughter of Thomas Hawkins. STEPMOTHER: Anne Brown (?–ca. 1800), widow of both Samuel Clagett and Robert Horner. UNCLES: *John Hanson, Jr.* (1721–1783); *Walter Hanson* (1711/12–1794). BROTHER: Thomas Hawkins (1750–1810). SISTERS: Chloe (ca. 1743–?), who married *George Lee* (ca. 1736–?); Mildred (ca. 1746–by 1796), who married *William Baker* (ca. 1749–1812); Sarah Hawkins (1750–1822); Nancy; Eleanor (?–1796), who married *Henry Henley Chapman* (?–1821); Anne; and Elizabeth. STEPBROTHERS: Samuel Clagett; Gustavus Brown Horner; William Horner (ca. 1765–?); and John Horner. FIRST COUSIN: *Alexander Contee Hanson* (1749–1806). MARRIED ca. 1777 Mary Key (Kay), of Philadelphia, Pennsylvania. CHILDREN. SONS: Samuel (1786–?), who married Matilda Calloway Hickman and by 1807 had moved to Bourbon County, Kentucky; Isaac Kay (1790–?), who married Maria H. Jones; Thomas (1792–?); and John (1795–1796). DAUGHTERS: Maria (1781–?); Ann (1793–1872); and Lousia Serena (1799–1840), who married Roger Chew Weightman. PRIVATE CAREER. EDUCATION: literate. OCCUPATIONAL PROFILE: planter; cashier, Bank of Columbia, Washington, D.C. PUBLIC CAREER. LEGISLATIVE SERVICE: Convention, Charles County, 5th, 1775; Lower House, Charles County, 1782 (elected to the 2nd session of the 1781–1782 Assembly to fill vacancy), 1783, 1784. LOCAL OFFICE: justice, Charles County, 1779–at least 1786. MILITARY SERVICE: lieutenant colonel, Charles County Militia, appointed 1776, served at least until 1778. WEALTH DURING LIFETIME. PERSONAL PROPERTY: assessed value £583.0.0, including 4 slaves and 50 oz. plate, 1783. LAND AT FIRST ELECTION: 1,549 acres in Charles County (the remainder of a total of 1,770 acres given to him by his father between 1776 and 1779). SIGNIFICANT CHANGES IN LAND BETWEEN FIRST ELECTION AND DEATH: sold all of his Charles County land except 355 acres, and had moved to Alexandria, Virginia, by 1787. Apparently sold his remaining Charles County land by 1798. WEALTH AT DEATH. DIED: in 1830 in Washington, D.C. IDENTIFICATION PROBLEMS. The legislative service and officeholding included in this profile have been attributed to Samuel Hanson, of Samuel on the basis of an analysis of the careers, titles, and other information found for the several Samuel Hansons living in Charles County during the period. The service and offices cannot, however, be positively verified. See also the profiles of *Samuel Hanson, Jr.* (?–1817) and *Samuel Hanson* (1716–1794).

HANSON, WALTER (1711/12–1794). BORN: on March 11, 1711/12, in Port Tobacco Parish, Charles County; eldest son. NATIVE: at least third generation. RESIDED: in Port Tobacco, West Hundred, District 5, Charles County. FAMILY BACKGROUND. FATHER: *Samuel Hanson* (ca. 1685–1740). MOTHER: Elizabeth (ca. 1688–1764), daughter of *Walter Storey* (ca. 1666–1726). UNCLE: *Robert Hanson* (ca. 1680–1748). BROTHERS: *Samuel Hanson* (1716–1794); William (1718/19–1721); *John Hanson, Jr.* (1721–1783); and William (1726–?). SISTERS: Elizabeth (1707–?); Mary (1709/10–?); Sarah (1714–?); Jane (1721/22–?); and Charity (1724–?), who married second, *Arthur Lee* (?–1760); and Chloe. FIRST COUSINS: Dorothy Hanson (1721–1752), who married *Richard Harrison* (?–1780); Mary Hanson (?–?), who married *Daniel Jenifer* (?–1795). NEPHEW: *Samuel Hanson, of Samuel* (ca. 1752–1830). MARRIED first, by 1740 Elizabeth (1721–1773), daughter of William Hoskins (1690–1727); stepdaughter of *Robert Hanson* (ca. 1680–1748); granddaughter of *Philip Hoskins* (ca. 1650–1718). Her sister was Mary, who married first, John Cunningham, and second, Mungo Muschett. MARRIED second, on April 20, 1783, Elizabeth Hanson. CHILDREN. SONS: Hoskins (?–1796), who married Catherine Queen Thompson; Samuel (?–1810); William (?–1796), who married Sarah Sinnett; and Walter. DAUGHTERS: Elizabeth Hoskins, who married William Barton Smoot; Violetta, who married Henry Barnes; Anne, who married first, Hugh Mitchell, and second, Samuel Stone; Heloise (?–1763); and Margaret, who married John Muschett. PRIVATE CAREER. EDUCATION: literate. SOCIAL STATUS AND ACTIVITIES: Gent., 1744; Esq., 1773. OCCUPATIONAL PROFILE: planter, 1738; merchant, 1756; planter, 1775; officeholder. PUBLIC CAREER. LEGISLATIVE SERVICE: Convention, Charles County, 1st, 1774 (appointed, but did not attend). LOCAL OFFICES: sheriff, Charles County, 1738–1741; deputy commissary, Charles County, in office 1740–1751, 1767–1773, 1776–1777; justice, Charles County, 1741–1794 (quorum, 1749–1794); deputy controller, Charles County, 1768; justice, Court of Oyer and Terminer and Gaol Delivery, Charles County, commissioned 1772 and 1773; Committee of Observation, Charles County, elected 1774; judge, court of appeals, appointed under the Act to Procure Troops for the American Army, Charles County, appointed 1778; subscription officer, Continental Loan Office, Charles County, appointed 1779; justice, Orphans' Court, Charles County, 1779–at least 1789. WEALTH DURING LIFETIME. PERSONAL PROPERTY: assessed value £1,121.0.0, including 24 slaves and 6 oz. plate, 1783. LAND AT FIRST ELECTION: 2,840 acres in Charles County (including 340 acres received as a gift from his parents, 1738; ca. 1,432 acres obtained through his marriage; at least 948 acres by purchase). SIGNIFICANT CHANGES IN LAND BETWEEN FIRST ELECTION AND DEATH: sold at least 169 acres in 1775. Gave 392 acres to his son Hoskins in 1782, but retained a life estate in the property. By 1783 Hanson was assessed for only 1,466 acres; his sons paid taxes on 710 acres of their father's property and 200 acres had apparently been given to his daughter Margaret and her husband. In 1792 Hanson resurveyed and patented a large tract of his land gaining 82 acres, but he immediately sold 158 acres of it. All of his land was in Charles County. WEALTH AT DEATH. DIED: between May 21 and December 1, 1794, in Charles County. PERSONAL PROPERTY: TEV, at least £817.12.2 current money (including 14 slaves). LAND: probably 2,276 acres in Charles County, of which at least 760 acres were already in the hands of his sons, Walter, Jr., and Hoskins.

HARBERT (HERBERT), WILLIAM (?–1718). BORN: perhaps in Maryland, of age by 1690. NATIVE: perhaps second generation. RESIDED: in Charles County. FAMILY BACKGROUND. FATHER: perhaps William Harbert, who died in Calvert County, ca. 1679. MARRIED first, by 1690 Mary Sentel. MARRIED second, possibly Elinor, widow of John Angell; daughter of James Pattison, of St. Mary's County. MARRIED third, Sarah (?–1718), probably widow of both John Douglas (?–1705/6) and Ralph Smith. CHILDREN. DAUGHTERS: Ann, who married *George Dent* (1690–1754); Catherine (1692–?). PRIVATE CAREER. EDUCATION: literate. RELIGIOUS AFFILIATION: Anglican. OCCUPATIONAL PROFILE: planter. PUBLIC CAREER. LEGISLATIVE SERVICE: Lower House, Charles County, 1708A. LOCAL OFFICES: William and Mary Parish Vestry, Charles County, 1696–1697; justice, Charles County, 1700–1714 (quorum, 1708–1714). MILITARY SERVICE: captain, 1705. WEALTH DURING LIFETIME. LAND AT FIRST ELECTION: ca. 1,574 acres. WEALTH AT DEATH. DIED: will probated on July 26, 1718. PERSONAL PROPERTY: TEV, £1,083.14.8 (including 9 slaves, 1 servant, and 18 books); FB, £1,001.0.0. LAND: over 500 acres. IDENTIFICATION PROBLEMS. Career and origins uncertain; two other William Harberts lived in neighboring counties.

HARDCASTLE, THOMAS (ca. 1737–1808). BORN: in either 1736 or 1737, probably in Queen Anne's County; eldest son. NATIVE: second generation. RESIDED: in Queen Anne's County (later became part of Caroline County); Tuckahoe Hundred, Caroline County, 1778; built "Castle Hall," Caroline County, in 1781. FAMILY BACKGROUND. FATHER: Robert Hardcastle (?–1760), immigrated ca. 1730 from Yorkshire, England; resided in Queen Anne's County; saddler; planter. MOTHER: possibly Elinor (?–by 1736), widow of James London, of Queen Anne's County, carpenter; or possibly (name unknown). STEPMOTHER: Jamson (?–by 1769), widow of both Richard Eubanks (?–1746) and Ralph Ellston (?–by 1756). BROTHERS OR HALF BROTHERS: John; Robert (1740–1831), of Queen Anne's County and Wheeling, West Virginia, who married Jane Pratt; Solomon; Peter; James; and William. HALF BROTHERS OR STEPBROTHERS: Richard London; James London. STEPBROTHERS: Henry Eubanks; William Elston. SISTERS OR HALF SISTERS: Ann, who married William Bell; Elizabeth. HALF SISTER OR STEPSISTER: Rebecka London. STEPSISTERS: Rachel Elston (?–by 1769, died an infant); Elizabeth Elston. MARRIED on November 8, 1756, Henrietta (1739–1812), daughter of John Downes, Sr. (?–1758), of Queen Anne's County. Her brothers were Hynson; James (?–by 1758); John, Jr.; Henry; Charles; and Hawkins. Her sisters were Margaret, who married (first name unknown) Kenton; and Ann, who married Lodman Elbert. Her first cousins were *Philemon Downes* (ca. 1741–ca. 1796); *Henry Downes* (ca. 1748–1816). CHILDREN. SONS: John (1757–1810), who married first, Jane (1759–1786), widow of *Nathaniel Potter* (?–1780), and second, in 1790 Polly Costen (1774–1854); Aaron (1759–1795), who married in 1788 Arabella Stokely; Thomas (1763–1824); Robert (1768–1852), who married in 1796 Sarah Baynard; Philip (1776–1815); William Molleson (1779–1874), who was elected eleven times to the Maryland Assembly, and who married Anne, daughter of Henry Colston, of Talbot County; Matthew (1786–1835); and Peter, who married in 1797 Mary Baynard. DAUGHTER: Henrietta (1765–1805), who married

James Pearce. **PRIVATE CAREER. EDUCATION:** literate. **SOCIAL STATUS AND ACTIVITIES:** Mr., 1774; Gent., 1778; Esq., 1788. **OCCUPATIONAL PROFILE:** planter, 1760, 1779; farmer, 1772. **PUBLIC CAREER. LEGISLATIVE SERVICE:** Lower House, Caroline County, 1783 (elected, but did not attend), 1784, 1786–1787. **LOCAL OFFICES:** tobacco inspector, Queen Anne's County, in office 1762, 1766; churchwarden, St. John's Parish, Queen Anne's County, in office 1762–1763; St. John's Parish Vestry, Queen Anne's County, in office 1763–1766; justice, Caroline County, 1777–at least 1787; commissioner of tax, Caroline County, appointed 1777 and 1779; justice, Orphans' Court, Caroline County, commissioned 1779, 1780, 1786, and 1787. **WEALTH DURING LIFETIME. PERSONAL PROPERTY:** assessed value £1,251.0.0, including 18 slaves, 1783; 20 slaves, 1790; 25 slaves, 1798. **LAND AT FIRST ELECTION:** 1,575 acres in Caroline County (all by purchase or patent). **ADDITIONAL COMMENTS:** Hardcastle had inherited at least 257 acres from his father, but had given it to his son John, Jr., before his first election. **SIGNIFICANT CHANGES IN LAND BETWEEN FIRST ELECTION AND DEATH:** by ca. 1805 he owned 1,890 acres in Caroline County, but his will indicated that most of it had been given or sold to his children before the will was written. **WEALTH AT DEATH. DIED:** on September 29, 1808, in Dorchester County. **PERSONAL PROPERTY:** TEV, £1,147.10.0 (including 16 slaves and books); FB, estate overpaid £51.13.2. **LAND:** he gave or sold most of his land to his children prior to his death.

HARFORD, HENRY (ca. 1759–1834). **BORN:** ca. 1759 in London, England; eldest child, natural son. **RESIDED:** in England, at his house in London or his country estate, "Down Place," near Windsor, Berkshire, England; in Maryland, at the Annapolis home of Dr. Upton Scott, 1783–1786. **FAMILY BACKGROUND. FATHER:** *Frederick Calvert, 6th Lord Baltimore* (1731/32–1771). **STEPFATHER:** Peter Prevost, Esq. **GUARDIANS:** Dr. John Moore (1730–1805), archbishop of Canterbury; Hugh Hammersley, Esq., principal secretary of Maryland from 1765 to at least 1771 (date of last commission); and his stepfather Peter Prevost, Esq. **MOTHER:** Hester Whalen (?–1812), of Ireland. **HALF UNCLE:** *Benedict Calvert* (ca. 1724–1788). **AUNT:** Caroline Calvert, who married *Robert Eden* (1741–1784). **SISTER:** Frances Mary (ca. 1760–1822). **HALF SISTERS:** Sophia Hales (1765–?); Elizabeth Hales (1765–?); and Charlotte Hope (1770–?). **MARRIED** first, in June 1792 Louisa (?–ca. 1802), daughter of Peter Pigou, Esq. **MARRIED**

second, in June 1806 Esther Ryecroft (ca. 1775–1853). **CHILDREN. SONS:** Henry (1793–died in infancy); Frederick Paul (ca. 1802–1860), who married Elizabeth Louisa Halifax (ca. 1810–1876); George (1807–?); and Charles (1811–?). **DAUGHTERS:** Louisa Ann (1794–?); Frances (1796–?); Fredericka Louisa Elizabeth (1797–?), who married Robert T. J. Glyn; Charlotte Penelope (1808–died young); Esther (1810–?); and Emily (1814–?), who married Rev. William H. W. Bowyer. **PRIVATE CAREER. EDUCATION:** Richmond School near Epsom, Eton, England, 1772–1775; Exeter College, Oxford University, 1776–1779. **RELIGIOUS AFFILIATION:** Anglican. **SOCIAL STATUS AND ACTIVITIES:** Esq.; did not inherit the title of Lord Baltimore because of his illegitimacy. **PUBLIC CAREER. PROVINCIAL OFFICE:** proprietor of Maryland, 1771–1776. **OUT OF STATE SERVICE:** tied for a seat in Parliament from Lyme Regis, Dorsetshire, in 1780, but lost when the election was decided by the House of Commons. **WEALTH DURING LIFETIME. PERSONAL PROPERTY:** inherited ca. £96,000 in deposits and investments from his father's estate. Received a £60,000 settlement from proprietorship litigation, 1781. Submitted a claim of £327,441 to the Maryland government for the loss of land and revenues, which was denied by the General Assembly in 1786. A similar claim for £447,000 presented to the British government was partially allowed and Harford received probably £70,000 in compensation. He also received £10,000, which was deducted from Maryland's bank stock in England in 1805. After further petitions to the British government for compensation for debts owed him by Maryland residents but not paid because of the war, Harford's claim was allowed in 1813 and he may have received a part of the £43,000 requested. **LAND AT FIRST ELECTION:** during Harford's minority his father left Maryland in the control of his executors *Robert Eden* (1741–1784), Hugh Hammersley, Esq., Peter Prevost, Esq., and Robert Morris (who was removed by 1776). The provisions in the will of *Frederick Calvert, 6th Lord Baltimore* (1731/32–1771), leaving the proprietorship to his illegitimate Harford children was contested by John Browning and the Edens and remained in litigation until 1781. Although Harford inherited the proprietor's rights to lands in Maryland under the will of his father in 1771, the resulting litigation and war made his ownership of little value. **SIGNIFICANT CHANGES IN LAND BETWEEN FIRST ELECTION AND DEATH:** Harford estimated that his inheritance included 71,000 acres of manor lands and 125,000 acres of undeveloped land west of Fort Cumberland, 1786.

The proprietary lands confiscated by the Maryland government totaled about 245,000 acres. WEALTH AT DEATH. DIED: on December 8, 1835, at "Down Place"; buried in St. Michael's Churchyard, Bray, England. LAND: probably a house in London and a country estate near Windsor.

HARRIS, BENTON (ca. 1716–1777). BORN: ca. 1716. RESIDED: in Worcester County, 1743 (probably lived in that part of Somerset County that later became part of Worcester County). FAMILY BACKGROUND. FATHER: probably John Harris, of Somerset County. SISTERS: Rebecca, who married (first name unknown) Costin (Caster); (first name unknown), who married (first name unknown) Perkins; (first name unknown), who married (first name unknown) Hayman; (first name unknown), who married (first name unknown) Boughton; (first name unknown), who married (first name unknown) Riggin. MARRIED ca. 1753 Betty, widow of both William Whittington, a possible legislator, and Hampton Hopkins (?–1746); daughter of Robert Martin (?–1725), who immigrated from Scotland in the early-eighteenth century, and wife Mary Downes (?–1774); stepdaughter of *James Martin* (?–ca. 1748). Her brother was Capt. John. Her sister was Mary, who married (first name unknown) Schoolfield. CHILDREN. STEPSONS: William Whittington (?–1769), who married Mary King; Samuel Hopkins. PRIVATE CAREER. EDUCATION: literate. RELIGIOUS AFFILIATION: Protestant. SOCIAL STATUS AND ACTIVITIES: Gent., 1746. OCCUPATIONAL PROFILE: planter; officeholder. PUBLIC CAREER. LEGISLATIVE SERVICE: Lower House, Worcester County, 1757–1758 (Accounts 1), 1758–1761 (Public Offices Cv 3), 1762–1763 (Elections 1, 2; Public Offices 1, 2; Accounts 2), 1765–1766 (Public Offices 2; Grievances 3). LOCAL OFFICES: deputy commissary, Worcester County, 1743–1777; sheriff, Worcester County, 1745–1746; justice, Worcester County, 1762–1777 (quorum, 1769–1777); justice, Court of Oyer and Terminer and Gaol Delivery, Worcester County, commissioned 1770 and 1771; chairman, Committee of Observation, Worcester County, in office 1776; register of wills, Worcester County, appointed 1777. MILITARY SERVICE: captain, by 1745. WEALTH DURING LIFETIME. LAND AT FIRST ELECTION: 706 acres in Somerset and Worcester counties (probably inherited 151 acres from his father), plus control of 396 additional acres in Worcester County, which he was holding for his stepson, 1756. SIGNIFICANT CHANGES IN LAND BETWEEN FIRST ELECTION AND DEATH: by 1774 he no longer controlled the 396 acres belong-

ing to his stepson; he was charged with more than 300 additional acres, 1757–1774; he acquired 307 acres through a patent resurvey in 1776. WEALTH AT DEATH. DIED: between April and September 1777; will probated in Worcester County. PERSONAL PROPERTY: TEV, at least £5,956.12.10 current money (including 17 slaves). LAND: more than 1,369 acres in Somerset and Worcester counties.

HARRIS, EDWARD (ca. 1757–ca. 1837). BORN: ca. 1757 in Queen Anne's County; probably youngest son. NATIVE: at least third generation. RESIDED: in Queen Anne's County; Talbot County, 1783; Queen Anne's County, 1790; Baltimore City, 1804; Queen Anne's County, 1822. FAMILY BACKGROUND. FATHER: *Thomas Harris* (?–1760). MOTHER: Elizabeth (?–ca. 1760), daughter of *William Turbutt* (1683/84–1739). STEPFATHER: Richard Keene, of Queen Anne's County. GUARDIAN: *Edward Lloyd* (1711–1770), responsible for the care of Edward until he was twenty-one years old. AUNT: Anna Maria Turbutt, who married *Edward Tilghman* (1713–1786). BROTHERS: William (?–by 1795); Thomas. SISTERS: Elizabeth; Sarah; Margaret; and Mary (ca. 1755–?). MARRIED by 1784 Sarah, daughter of *Pollard Edmondson* (ca. 1718–1794); granddaughter of *John Edmondson* (1692–1743). Her mother was either Mary Dickinson or Rachel Birckhead McManus (by 1740–1818). CHILDREN. SONS: Turbutt, who married in 1807 Maria, daughter of *Samuel Earle* (1756–1790), and who was declared incompetent by his father in 1822 because of several blows he had received to his head in 1819; Pollard; and Edward. DAUGHTERS: Maria, who married by 1820 James Sterett; Eliza; Mary; and Sarah. PRIVATE CAREER. EDUCATION: literate; his father's will specified that Edward and his brothers be kept in school until they were of a suitable age and had attained sufficient education to be apprenticed to a practitioner of some art or science to which their natural genius inclined them. RELIGIOUS AFFILIATION: Anglican, Chester Church, St. Paul's Parish, Queen Anne's County. SOCIAL STATUS AND ACTIVITIES: Gent., 1791. OCCUPATIONAL PROFILE: physician in 1792, but did not practice before 1797; farmer. PUBLIC CAREER. LEGISLATIVE SERVICE: Lower House, Talbot County, 1783, 1784, Queen Anne's County, 1790. LOCAL OFFICES: justice of the peace, Queen Anne's County, in office 1791; associate justice, Second District, Queen Anne's County, appointed 1791. WEALTH DURING LIFETIME. PERSONAL PROPERTY: £221.18.4 received as part of his share of his father's estate, ca. 1773; assessed value £402.0.0, including 7 slaves, 1783;

20 slaves, 1790; 2 slaves received from his father's estate, 1792; a moiety of approximately £745.17.10 being the remainder of his share of his father's estate, ca. 1796; 26 slaves, 1798; assessed value $3,795.00, including 36 slaves and 300 oz. plate, 1824; gave 41 slaves to his daughters by deeds of gift, 1835. LAND AT FIRST ELECTION: 1,019 acres in Queen Anne's County (at least 919 acres from his father). No land was found listed in his name in Talbot County in 1783, but he married the daughter of a Talbot County legislator, and it was probably through her dower that he was elected a delegate from Talbot County. SIGNIFICANT CHANGES IN LAND BETWEEN FIRST ELECTION AND DEATH: sold 422 acres and purchased 345 acres in Queen Anne's County, 1791; owned 2 lots in Easton, Talbot County, plus a moiety of 494 acres in Talbot County possessed in right of his son, 1798; no Talbot County land appeared under his name after 1798; purchased 166 acres in Queen Anne's County, 1804; purchased 236 acres in Queen Anne's County, 1821; bought, sold, mortgaged, leased, and resurveyed some 1,193 acres and 18 lots in Baltimore County between 1800 and 1835, but all or most of it was sold before his death, including at least 165 acres given in a deed of trust to his daughter. WEALTH AT DEATH. DIED: will probated on February 9, 1837, in Queen Anne's County. PERSONAL PROPERTY: TEV, $39,098.30 (including 40 slaves probably the same ones given to his daughters in 1835, servants, 1,116 oz. plate, and books); FB, $35,063.72. LAND: at least 1,316 acres in Queen Anne's County, possibly also 191 acres and some lots in Baltimore County.

HARRIS, JAMES (1682–1743). BORN: in 1682 in Kent County; only son. NATIVE: second generation. RESIDED: in Kent County; Cecil County by 1693; Kent County by 1707. FAMILY BACKGROUND. FATHER: *William Harris* (ca. 1644–1712). MOTHER: Joan. SISTERS: Tabitha, who married *Marmaduke Tilden* (?–1726); (first name unknown), who married Thomas Brown, stepson of *William Hopkins* (?–1702); Mary, who married Robert Dunn, son of *Robert Dunn* (ca. 1630–1676); and Margaret, who married *Charles Hynson* (1663–1711). MARRIED first, in 1701 Elizabeth (?–1716), daughter of *Edward Jones* (?–1697). MARRIED second, Augustina (?–1775), daughter of *Matthias Vanderheyden* (?–1729). Her half brother was *Henry Ward* (?–1734). Her sisters were Jane; Francina; and Ariana (1690–?), who married first *James Frisby* (1684–1719), second, *Thomas Bordley* (ca. 1683–1726), and third, *Edmund Jennings*

(?–1756). CHILDREN. SONS: *William Harris* (1704–1748), who married Ariana Margaretta, daughter of *James Frisby* (1684–1719); *Matthias Harris* (1718–1773), who married first, Mary, daughter of Rev. James Wilkinson, and second, Hester Bailey, of Delaware. DAUGHTERS: Elizabeth, who married John Conner; Jane, who married John Carvill; Mary, who married Hercules Coutts; and Sarah, who married Stephen Bordley. PRIVATE CAREER. EDUCATION: literate. RELIGIOUS AFFILIATION: Anglican. SOCIAL STATUS AND ACTIVITIES: second generation burgess; Mr., by 1707; Esq., by 1717. OCCUPATIONAL PROFILE: planter; surveyor; owned a mill at the time of his death. PUBLIC CAREER. LEGISLATIVE SERVICE: Lower House, Kent County, 1710 (elected to the 3rd session; resigned to become sheriff before the 4th session), 1715 (Elections and Privileges; Laws), 1716–1718 (Laws 1–3), 1725–1727 (Laws 1–4), 1728–1731 (Laws 1–5), 1734/35–1737 (speaker 1–5,); Upper House, 1739–1741, 1742 (died before the 2nd session). OTHER PROVINCIAL OFFICES: justice, Provincial Court, 1716–1726 (quorum, 1718–1726); surveyor general, Eastern Shore, 1737–1743; Council, 1739–1742. LOCAL OFFICES: coroner, Cecil County, 1703; justice, Cecil County, 1706, Kent County, 1707–1708, 1714–1716, 1733–1738/39 (quorum, 1708, 1714–1716, 1733–1738/39); St. Paul's Parish Vestry, Kent County, 1709–1711, 1715–1716, 1725; sheriff, Kent County, 1711–1713; surveyor, Talbot County, 1730. MILITARY SERVICE: captain, by 1709–1716; major, 1716–?; colonel, by 1742. WEALTH DURING LIFETIME. LAND AT FIRST ELECTION: heir-at-law to over 1,600 acres by 1713. WEALTH AT DEATH. DIED: will probated on December 10, 1743. PERSONAL PROPERTY: TEV, £350.14.5 sterling, £3,125.10.4 current money (including 50 slaves and books); FB, £199.17.4 sterling, £91.10.11 current money. LAND: ca. 4,450 acres.

HARRIS, MATTHIAS (1718–1773). BORN: in 1718 in Kent County; probably second son. NATIVE: third generation. RESIDED: in Kent County, 1718–1752; London, England, ca. 1752; Accomack Parish, Virginia, and All Hallow's Parish, Worcester County, ca. 1753–1759; Lewes (Lewistown), Delaware, ca. 1760; Chester Parish, Kent County, 1767–1769; Christ Church Parish, Kent Island, Queen Anne's County, 1769–1773. FAMILY BACKGROUND. FATHER: *James Harris* (1682–1743), son of *William Harris* (ca. 1644–1712), who married first, Elizabeth (?–1716), daughter of *Edward Jones* (?–1697). MOTHER: Augustina, daughter of *Matthias Vanderheyden* (?–1729). AUNTS: Ariana

Vanderheyden (1690–1741), who married first, *James Frisby* (1684–1719), second; *Thomas Bordley* (ca. 1683–1726), and third, *Edmund Jennings* (?–1756); Francina Vanderheyden, who married second, *Charles Hynson* (1692–1748). HALF BROTHER: *William Harris* (1704–1748). HALF SISTERS: Jane; Mary; Elizabeth; and Sarah. FIRST COUSINS: Ariana Margaret Frisby (1717–?), who married *William Harris* (1704–1748); *John Beale Bordley* (1726/27–1804). MARRIED first, by 1745 Mary, daughter of Rev. James Williamson, originally from Shrewsbury Parish, Kent County, later moved to Calvert County. Her brother was Alexander, a minister of Prince George's Parish, Frederick County. MARRIED second, Hester, daughter of Judge (first name unknown) Bailey, of Delaware. CHILDREN. SONS: Joseph (?–died young); William, who moved to Delaware; and James, who married (first name unknown), daughter of James Burke. DAUGHTERS: Elizabeth, who married (first name unknown) Anderson; Margaret, who married (first name unknown) Anderson; Augusta, who married Thomas Carter; and Hester, who married D. Ridgely, of Delaware. PRIVATE CAREER. EDUCATION: studied to become a clergyman. RELIGIOUS AFFILIATION: Anglican. SOCIAL STATUS AND ACTIVITIES: Gent., 1743. OCCUPATIONAL PROFILE: officeholder; Anglican minister, ordained 1753. Made chaplain of Maryland by Lord Baltimore, 1753. A scandal concerning alleged forgery by Harris caused Governor Sharpe to refuse him a permanent appointment to a parish. Governor Eden finally gave Harris a permanent parish in 1769. PUBLIC CAREER. LEGISLATIVE SERVICE: Lower House, Kent County, 1745 (Laws), 1745/46–1748 (Laws Cv 1, 1–3, 4), 1749–1751 (Laws Cv-3). LOCAL OFFICES: clerk, Court of Oyer and Terminer and Gaol Delivery, Kent County, commissioned 1742; rector *locus tenens* , All Hallow's Parish, Worcester County, before 1760; probationer, Chester Parish, Kent County, 1767–1769; rector, Christ Church Parish, Kent County, 1769–1773; rector, Chester Parish, Kent County, 1773. OUT OF COLONY SERVICE: minister, Accomac Parish, Eastern Shore, Virginia, before 1760; minister, Lewes, Delaware, ca. 1760. WEALTH DURING LIFETIME. LAND AT FIRST ELECTION: 1,235 acres, plus 7 lots in Kent County (legacy from his father). SIGNIFICANT CHANGES IN LAND BETWEEN FIRST ELECTION AND DEATH: purchased 987 acres in Cecil County, which he mortgaged to *Edward Lloyd* (1711–1770) and later forfeited; received ca. 1,164 acres in Kent County in 1748 from the estate of his brother William, which he mortgaged and then sold. WEALTH AT

DEATH. DIED: between March 18 and May 3, 1773; buried at Christ Church, Kent Island, Queen Anne's County. LAND: 322 acres, plus 6.5 lots in Kent County; possibly an insolvent debtor at death.

HARRIS, THOMAS (?–1760). BORN: of age by 1737; probably younger son. NATIVE: at least second generation. RESIDED: in St. Paul's Parish, Queen Anne's County. FAMILY BACKGROUND. FATHER: Edward Harris (?–1717), of Queen Anne's County; a planter. MOTHER: Elizabeth. BROTHER: Edward (?–1740), died without progeny, killed by Peter, one of his slaves. SISTERS: Anne, who married (first name unknown) Vicars, of Talbot County; Elizabeth, who married (first name unknown) Millington; and (first name unknown), who married George Bessicks. OTHER KINSHIP: his godfather was Dr. Thomas Godman, who according to the terms of Edward Harris's will was to supervise Thomas's education. MARRIED by 1742 Elizabeth (?–ca. 1760), daughter of *William Turbutt* (1683/84–1739); niece of both *Foster Turbutt* (1679–1720/21) and *James Earle, Jr.* (ca. 1694–1739). Elizabeth Turbutt Harris subsequently married Richard Keene, of Queen Anne's County. Her brother was Michael. Her sisters were Anna Maria, who married *Edward Tilghman* (1713–1786); Mary. Her first cousins were Sarah Turbutt (1706–1773), who married *Nicholas Goldsborough* (ca. 1689–1766); Anne Turbutt (1715–1766), who married *John Goldsborough* (1711–1778); Elizabeth Turbutt (ca. 1708–?), who married *Tench Francis* (1701–1758); Mary Anne Wright (?–1747), who married *William Hopper* (1707–1772); Anne Wright (?–by 1754), who married *Edward Oldham* (1709–1773); *Michael Earle* (1722–1787); *Richard Tilghman Earle* (1728/29–1788); *Joseph Earle* (1739–1777); Anna Maria Earle (1725–1795), who married *Thomas Ringgold* (1715–1772); and Henrietta Maria Earle (1730–1767), who married *William Hemsley* (1736/37–1812). CHILDREN. SONS: William (?–by 1795); Thomas; and *Edward Harris* (ca. 1757–ca. 1837). DAUGHTERS: Elizabeth, who married Dr. George Garnett, Jr.; Sarah, who married Rev. Samuel Keene; Margaret, who married Vachel Keene; and Mary (ca. 1755–?), who married Thomas Hill Airey, of Dorchester County. PRIVATE CAREER. EDUCATION: literate. RELIGIOUS AFFILIATION: Anglican. SOCIAL STATUS AND ACTIVITIES: Gent., by 1742. OCCUPATIONAL PROFILE: planter, 1746; mariner, 1748. PUBLIC CAREER. LEGISLATIVE SERVICE: Lower House, Queen Anne's County, 1758–1759 (died before the 2nd session). LOCAL OF-

FICES: visitor, Queen Anne's County Free School, elected 1746 and 1759; Old Chester Church Vestry, St. Paul's Parish, Queen Anne's County, 1748–1750; sheriff, Queen Anne's County, 1751–1754. MILITARY SERVICE: captain, by 1741. **WEALTH DURING LIFETIME.** LAND AT FIRST ELECTION: at least 2,863 acres in Queen Anne's, Cecil, and Kent counties (272 acres inherited from his father after his brother died childless; 279 acres through his marriage; at least 2,140 acres by purchase or patent). SIGNIFICANT CHANGES IN LAND BETWEEN FIRST ELECTION AND DEATH: 2,345 acres in Queen Anne's County by patent, 1759; 281 acres in Queen Anne's County by purchase, 1759. WEALTH AT DEATH. DIED: on a Tuesday in March 1760 in Queen Anne's County, of smallpox. PERSONAL PROPERTY: TEV, £3,216.9.5 current money (including 29 slaves, 1 servant, 90 books, and 36.5 oz. silver); FB, £2,723.4.7. LAND: at least 6,045 acres in Queen Anne's, Kent, and Cecil counties. A portion of 2,345 acres in Queen Anne's County owned by Harris at his death was escheated land that he had patented in 1759. Someone apparently disputed his claim to the land and in his will he ordered his son-in-law, George Garnett, Jr., to commence a lawsuit to recover possession. Garnett never did this, but Harris's heirs nevertheless appear to have retained title to the land.

HARRIS, WILLIAM (ca. 1644–1712). BORN: ca. 1644, probably in England. IMMIGRATED: by 1674, perhaps as early as 1668 as a free adult. RESIDED: in Kent County; Cecil County, by 1693. MARRIED by 1680 Joan. CHILDREN. SON: *James Harris* (1682–1743), who married first, Elizabeth, daughter of *Edward Jones* (?–1697), and second, Augustina, daughter of *Matthias Vanderheyden* (?–1729). DAUGHTERS: (first name unknown), who married Thomas Brown, stepson of *William Hopkins* (?–1702); Mary, who married Robert Dunn, son of *Robert Dunn* (ca. 1630–1676); Tabitha, who married *Marmaduke Tilden* (?–1726); and Margaret, who married *Charles Hynson* (1663–1711). PRIVATE CAREER. EDUCATION: literate. RELIGIOUS AFFILIATION: Protestant. SOCIAL STATUS AND ACTIVITIES: perhaps the "Mr. William Harris" involved in a lawsuit in Kent County in 1668; he began actively patenting land in the 1680s; he made a trip to England in 1687. OCCUPATIONAL PROFILE: attorney; factor; planter; owned a water mill in partnership with *Hans Hanson* (ca. 1647–1704). PUBLIC CAREER. LEGISLATIVE SERVICE: Lower House, Kent County, 1686–1688 (elected to the 1st session to fill vacancy); Associators'

Convention, Kent County, 1689–1692; Grand Committee of Twenty, 1690–1692; Lower House, Kent County, 1692–1693 (Accounts 1; Elections and Privileges 1), Cecil County, 1697/98–1700 (Elections and Privileges 1, 3, chairman 3; Aggrievances 1–3, chairman 2, 3), 1701–1704 (Elections and Privileges, chairman 2, 3; Aggrievances 1, 5, chairman 5; Laws 1). LOCAL OFFICES: justice, Kent County, 1686–1692, Cecil County, 1692–1704 (quorum); St. Paul's Parish Vestry, Kent County 1699–1702, 1707–1708, 1711. MILITARY SERVICE: major, by 1701; colonel at the time of his death. STANDS ON PUBLIC/PRIVATE ISSUES: supported the revolution of 1689; recommended for appointment to Council in 1691, 1702, and 1707, but he was never actually commissioned. WEALTH DURING LIFETIME. LAND AT FIRST ELECTION: 1,900 acres by 1689. WEALTH AT DEATH. DIED: will probated on November 21, 1712. PERSONAL PROPERTY: TEV, £960.19.9 sterling (including 17 slaves); FB, £93.4.2. LAND: probably over 1,900 acres.

HARRIS, WILLIAM (1704–1748). BORN: in 1704 in St. Paul's Parish, Kent County; eldest son. NATIVE: third generation. RESIDED: on Fairly (Fairlee) Creek, Kent County. FAMILY BACKGROUND. FATHER: *James Harris* (1682–1743), son of *William Harris* (ca. 1644–1712). MOTHER: Elizabeth (?–1716), daughter of *Edward Jones* (?–1697). STEPMOTHER: Augustina, daughter of *Matthias Vanderheyden* (?–1729). STEPAUNTS: Ariana Vanderheyden (1690–1741), who married first, *James Frisby* (1684–1719), second *Thomas Bordley* (ca. 1683–1726), and third, *Edmund Jennings* (?–1756); Francina Vanderheyden, who married second, *Charles Hynson* (1692–1748). HALF BROTHER: *Matthias Harris* (1718–1773). SISTERS: Jane; Mary; Elizabeth; and Sarah. MARRIED Ariana Margaretta (1717–?), daughter of *James Frisby* (1684–1719); stepdaughter of both *Thomas Bordley* (ca. 1683–1726) and *Edmund Jennings* (?–1756); niece of *Henry Ward* (?–1734), Augustina Vanderheyden, who married *James Harris* (1682–1743), and Francina Vanderheyden, who married second, *Charles Hynson* (1692–1748). Her half brother was *John Beale Bordley* (1726/27–1804). Her sisters were Sarah (1714–1730); Francina Augustina (1719–1766). Her nephews were *William Stevenson* (1739–1785); *John Brice* (1738–1820); *James Brice* (1746–1801); and *Benedict Brice* (1749–1786). CHILDREN. SON: James, who never married. DAUGHTER: Ariana. PRIVATE CAREER. EDUCATION: literate. RELIGIOUS AFFILIATION: Anglican, St. Paul's Parish, Kent County.

SOCIAL STATUS AND ACTIVITIES: Esq., 1744. OC-CUPATIONAL PROFILE: probably a planter. PUBLIC CAREER. LEGISLATIVE SERVICE: Lower House, Kent County, 1739–1741. LOCAL OFFICES: sheriff, Kent County, 1735–1737, 1741–1743; justice, Kent County, 1738–1748 (quorum, 1740–1748). WEALTH DURING LIFETIME. LAND AT FIRST ELECTION: 145 acres in Kent County (a gift from his father), plus 1.5 lots in Chestertown, Kent County. SIGNIFICANT CHANGES IN LAND BE-TWEEN FIRST ELECTION AND DEATH: patented 483 acres in Cecil County in partnership with Daniel Cheston and John Brice. Harris received 890 acres in Cecil County as the eldest son and heir-in-law of his mother, only daughter of *Edward Jones* (?–1697), to whom the land had been entailed. Certificates for this land had been issued to Jones, but no patents were recorded until Harris demanded his rights in 1744. Harris sold at least 765 acres of this land shortly after recovering it, 1744. He inherited 300 acres in Cecil County from his father's estate, which he also sold in 1744. Harris received at least additional 991 acres in Kent County from his father's estate, by 1747. He resurveyed the 145-acre tract he owned at first election into a 554-acre tract in Kent County, 1746. Harris, Brice, and Cheston sold 350 acres of the land they held in partnership in Cecil County, 1747. Harris purchased 474 acres in Kent County, 1747. WEALTH AT DEATH. DIED: on June 22, 1748, at his plantation on Fairly Creek, Kent County. PERSONAL PROPERTY: TEV, £113.2.11 sterling, £1,537.15.4 current money, plus 52,344 pounds of tobacco (including books and plate); FB, £1,944.14.11 current money. LAND: at least 1,844 acres in Cecil and Kent counties; plus 133 acres in Cecil County in partnership with John Brice and Daniel Cheston.

HARRISON, BENJAMIN (ca. 1754–1825). BORN: ca. 1754, mentioned as unborn in father's will written in August 1754; second son, youngest child. NATIVE: fourth generation. RESIDED: in Herring Creek Hundred, West River, Anne Arundel County. FAMILY BACKGROUND. FATHER: Richard Harrison (?–1761), of Anne Arundel County, son of Samuel Harrison (1679–1733) and wife Sarah Hall (?–ca. 1741/42). MOTHER: Rachel. BROTHER: Samuel. SISTERS: Sarah; Susannah; Araminta; Rachel; and Margaret. MARRIED on February 23, 1775, Sarah (?–by 1803), daughter of Stephen Steward (?–ca. 1790), of Anne Arundel County, a shipbuilder and merchant. Her brother was Stephen, Jr. Her sister was Elizabeth, who married Frederick Skinner, of Calvert County. CHILDREN.

SON: John, who married Holland and moved to Washington County by 1805. DAUGHTERS: Eleanor, who married in 1803 John Stevenson; Anne, who married in 1809 Thomas Tongue, Jr. PRIVATE CAREER. EDUCATION: literate. RELIGIOUS AFFILIA-TION: his father, of Quaker background, specified in his will that his sons should not be educated in the Roman Catholic faith of his wife. SOCIAL STA-TUS AND ACTIVITIES: Esq., 1787. OCCUPATIONAL PROFILE: mariner, 1774, possibly master of the ship *Gedder* that imported goods for an Annapolis merchant. Known as "captain" from at least 1776 until at least 1808, although he called himself a planter in 1803. PUBLIC CAREER. STATE OFFICES: Executive Council, 1787–1788; Constitution Rati-fication Convention, Anne Arundel County, 1788. WEALTH DURING LIFETIME. PERSONAL PROP-ERTY: assessed value £1,169.0.0, including 16 slaves and 90 oz. plate, 1783; 31 slaves, 1790; 34 slaves, 1798. In 1792 Harrison was appointed ad-ministrator of the estate of his father-in-law to replace his brother-in-law, Stephen Steward, Jr., who had petitioned for relief as an insolvent debtor. The estate of Stephen Steward, Sr., was responsible for the debts of Col. John Steward, as well as his own, and his personal property was insufficient to satisfy all their creditors. Harrison applied for relief as an insolvent debtor in April 1795, appointing a trustee for his real and per-sonal estate. He eventually sold the real property of Stephen Steward, Sr., but he was forced to pay many of the debts himself until the transactions were confirmed. LAND AT FIRST ELECTION: prob-ably 501 acres in Anne Arundel County (400 acres were a gift from his uncle, Benjamin Harrison, 1774). SIGNIFICANT CHANGES IN LAND BETWEEN FIRST ELECTION AND DEATH: obtained warrants and surveyed ca. 150 acres in Anne Arundel County in 1796, but sold the land before patenting it. Assessed for 538 acres in Anne Arundel County, 1798. Probably purchased 100 acres in Anne Arundel County during the 1790s, but sold 50 acres of that tract in addition to 15 acres of his uncle's gift in the early 1800s. Purchased 124 acres in Anne Arundel County, 1806. Sold the remain-der of his uncle's gift in 1812 and 1815. WEALTH AT DEATH. DIED: between September 1 and No-vember 10, 1825, in Anne Arundel County. LAND: probably 271 acres in Anne Arundel County.

HARRISON, JOSEPH (ca. 1623–1673). BORN: ca. 1623, probably in England. IMMIGRATED: in 1653 as a free adult. RESIDED: in Charles County. MARRIED Elizabeth. CHILDREN. SONS: Joseph (1659–1710), who married Jane; Francis; Richard

(1659–1710), who married Jane, daughter of *Zachary Wade* (ca. 1627–1678); and Benjamin. DAUGHTERS: Elizabeth (1663/64–?); Katherine (1666/67–?). PRIVATE CAREER. EDUCATION: literate. RELIGIOUS AFFILIATION: probably a Protestant. SOCIAL STATUS AND ACTIVITIES: no title on arrival. OCCUPATIONAL PROFILE: planter. PUBLIC CAREER. LEGISLATIVE SERVICE: Lower House, Charles County, 1661, 1663–1664. LOCAL OFFICE: justice, Charles County, 1660–1673. WEALTH DURING LIFETIME. LAND AT FIRST ELECTION: 300 acres. WEALTH AT DEATH. DIED: will probated on December 26, 1673. PERSONAL PROPERTY: TEV, 23,631 pounds of tobacco (including 1 servant). LAND: 500 acres.

HARRISON, JOSEPH (1687–1727). BORN: on October 27, 1687, in Charles County; probably a younger son. NATIVE: third generation. RESIDED: in Charles County. FAMILY BACKGROUND. FATHER: Richard Harrison (1659–1710), a justice of Charles County from 1694 to 1708/9; son of *Joseph Harrison* (ca. 1623–1673). MOTHER: Jane, daughter of *Zachary Wade* (ca. 1627–1678). She subsequently married Stephen Evans. BROTHERS: Thomas; Benjamin; and Richard. SISTERS: Elizabeth (1685–1718); Tabitha. MARRIED Verlinda, daughter of *William Stone* (1666–1731). CHILDREN. SONS: *Richard Harrison* (?–1780), who married first, Dorothy (1721–1752), daughter of *Robert Hanson* (ca. 1680–1748), and second, Elizabeth, daughter of *George Dent* (1690–1754); *Joseph Hanson Harrison* (?–1785), who married Mary; and William. DAUGHTERS: Tabitha; Elizabeth. PRIVATE CAREER. EDUCATION: literate. RELIGIOUS AFFILIATION: Protestant. SOCIAL STATUS AND ACTIVITIES: third generation local officeholder. OCCUPATIONAL PROFILE: planter. PUBLIC CAREER. LEGISLATIVE SERVICE: Lower House, Charles County, 1715, 1722–1724 (Aggrievances 1–3), 1725–1726 (Aggrievances 1–3; died before the 4th session). LOCAL OFFICE: justice, Charles County, 1712–1727. MILITARY SERVICE: captain, by 1722–1727. WEALTH DURING LIFETIME. LAND AT FIRST ELECTION: at least 500 acres inherited from his father. WEALTH AT DEATH. DIED: will probated on May 5, 1727. PERSONAL PROPERTY: TEV, £697.12.8 (including 11 slaves); FB, £215.17.7. LAND: over 2,600 acres.

HARRISON, JOSEPH HANSON (?–1785). BORN: of age by 1746. NATIVE: fourth generation. RESIDED: in Lower Hundred, Durham Parish, Charles County. FAMILY BACKGROUND. FATHER: *Joseph Harrison* (1687–1727). MOTHER: Verlinda,

daughter of *William Stone* (1666–1731). BROTHERS: *Richard Harrison* (?–1780); William. SISTERS: Tabitha, who married (first name unknown) Hooe; Elizabeth. NEPHEWS: *William Harrison* (?–1789); *Robert Townshend Hooe* (ca. 1743–1809). MARRIED by 1763 Mary. CHILDREN. SONS: Joseph White and Richard, were merchants in Alexandria, Virginia, by 1782. DAUGHTERS: Dorothy; Mary, who married George Hutchinson. PRIVATE CAREER. EDUCATION: literate. RELIGIOUS AFFILIATION: Protestant. SOCIAL STATUS AND ACTIVITIES: Gent., 1746. OCCUPATIONAL PROFILE: probably a planter. PUBLIC CAREER. LEGISLATIVE SERVICE: Lower House, Charles County, 1768–1770 (Public Offices 2, 3; Grievances 2, 4), 1771 (Public Offices; Grievances); Conventions, Charles County, 1st, 1774, 2nd, 1774, 4th, 1775 (elected, but did not attend), 5th, 1775 (elected, but did not attend), 7th–8th, 1776; Lower House, Charles County, 1777, 1778–1779 (Laws to Expire 3), 1779–1780 (Claims 2). LOCAL OFFICES: justice, Charles County, 1759–at least 1773; Durham Parish Vestry, Charles County, in office 1774–1776, 1779–1780, 1784–1787; Committee of Observation, Charles County, elected 1774. MILITARY SERVICE: captain by 1774. WEALTH DURING LIFETIME. PERSONAL PROPERTY: assessed value £320.17.6, including 6 slaves and 18.5 oz. plate, 1783. LAND AT FIRST ELECTION: 1,233 acres in Charles County, 831 of which were mortgaged. SIGNIFICANT CHANGES IN LAND BETWEEN FIRST ELECTION AND DEATH: lost possession of 831 mortgaged acres and sold or otherwise disposed of the 402 acres remaining from his original holdings; acquired 620 acres in Charles County through patent and possibly purchase by 1783. WEALTH AT DEATH. DIED: will probated on May 28, 1785, in Charles County. PERSONAL PROPERTY: at least 2 slaves. LAND: 620 acres in Charles County.

HARRISON, RICHARD (?–1780). BORN: in Charles County; eldest son. NATIVE: fourth generation. RESIDED: in Lower Hundred, Durham Parish, Charles County. FAMILY BACKGROUND. FATHER: *Joseph Harrison* (1687–1727). MOTHER: Verlinda, daughter of *William Stone* (1666–1731). BROTHERS: *Joseph Hanson Harrison* (?–1785); William. SISTERS: Tabitha; Elizabeth. OTHER KINSHIP: his great-grandfather was *Joseph Harrison* (ca. 1623–1673). MARRIED first, by 1746 Dorothy (1721–1752), daughter of *Robert Hanson* (ca. 1680–1748); niece of *Samuel Hanson* (ca. 1685–1740). Her brother was Benjamin. Her sister was Mary, who married *Daniel Jenifer* (?–1795). Her stepsister was Elizabeth Hoskins, who married

Walter Hanson (1711/12–1794). Her first cousins were *Samuel Hanson* (1716–1794); *John Hanson, Jr.* (1721–1783); Charity Hanson (1724–?), who married second, *Arthur Lee* (?–1760); and *Walter Hanson* (1711/12–1794). MARRIED second, Elizabeth (?–1781), widow of William Penn; daughter of *George Dent* (1690–1754); granddaughter of both *William Dent* (ca. 1660–1704) and *William Harbert* (?–1718); niece of *Thomas Dent* (1685–1725). Her brothers were *George Dent* (?–1785); *John Dent, of George* (ca. 1733–1809). Her sisters were Ann; Sarah; Rebecca (1714–died young); Letty; Mary; Eleanor; Margaret; and Rebecca (1735–1770), who married *Thomas Hanson Marshall* (1731–1801). Her nephew was *George Dent* (ca. 1758–1813). CHILDREN. SONS: Robert Hanson, who married Grace, daughter of William Dent (?–1756/57); *William Harrison* (?–1789); and Walter Hanson, rector of Durham Parish, Charles County. STEPSONS: Jezreal Penn; William Penn. PRIVATE CAREER. EDUCATION: literate. RELIGIOUS AFFILIATION: Protestant. SOCIAL STATUS AND ACTIVITIES: Gent., 1744; Esq., 1754. OCCUPATIONAL PROFILE: probably a planter. PUBLIC CAREER. LEGISLATIVE SERVICE: Lower House, Charles County, 1742–1744, 1745, 1745/46–1748, 1751–1754 (Bills of Credit 1–6). LOCAL OFFICES: justice, Charles County, 1741–at least 1769 (quorum, 1755–at least 1769). MILITARY SERVICE: captain, 1747; colonel, 1754. WEALTH DURING LIFETIME. LAND AT FIRST ELECTION: 1,127 acres in Charles County (700 acres inherited from his father in 1727, 150 acres by personal acquisition, 277 acres from his first wife's dower). SIGNIFICANT CHANGES IN LAND BETWEEN FIRST ELECTION AND DEATH: acquired 1,534 acres in Charles County, 1747–1773. WEALTH AT DEATH. DIED: will probated on September 16, 1780, in Charles County. LAND: at least 2,661 acres in Charles County.

HARRISON, ROBERT (1740–1802). BORN: on November 5, 1740, in Appleby, Westmoreland County, England; eldest son. IMMIGRATED: in March 1755 from England. RESIDED: at "Appleby," near Cambridge, Dorchester County. FAMILY BACKGROUND. FATHER: Christopher (1717–1799), of Appleby, Westmoreland County, England, a grocer. MOTHER: Mary (1716–1782), daughter of John Caile (?–1747), of England, and wife Margaret. BROTHERS: John Caile (1747–1780), who married in 1773 his first cousin Mary Caile, daughter of Hall Caile and wife Elizabeth Haskins; Christopher (1749–1752); Thomas (1751–1830), who married Margaret Birbeck (ca.

1754–1833); and William (1753–1835). SISTERS: Sarah (1743–1745); Margaret (1745–1785), who married Gilpin Gorst (1726–1803), son of William Gorst, steward of Appleby Castle; Jane (1755–1755); and Mary (1758–1759). MARRIED on October 10, 1770, Milcah (1751–1780), daughter of George Gale (ca. 1731–1765) and wife Elizabeth Airey (?–1799); granddaughter of both *John Gale* (?–ca. 1744) and Rev. Thomas Airey and wife Elizabeth Pitt; niece of Mary Gale (ca. 1734–by 1790), who married *Samuel Wilson* (1735–1790); half niece of Milcah Airey, who married *Thomas Firmin Eccleston* (ca. 1738–1785). Her brothers were *John Gale* (1753–1813); George (1756–?). Her sisters were Mary (1759–1760); Elizabeth (ca. 1762–?); and Leah. CHILDREN. SONS: Christopher (1775–1862), first lieutenant governor of Indiana from 1816 to 1818, helped layout the city of Indianapolis, Indiana, never married; John Gale (1779–1802), never married. DAUGHTERS: Mary (1774–1840), who married in 1802 Jacob Loockerman (1759–1839), son of John Loockerman, Jr., and stepson of *John Goldsborough* (1711–1778); Elizabeth (1777–1857), who married in 1803 Andrew Skinner. PRIVATE CAREER. EDUCATION: literate. RELIGIOUS AFFILIATION: Anglican, Great Choptank Church, Cambridge, Dorchester County. SOCIAL STATUS AND ACTIVITIES: one of the trustees for building a ballroom in Cambridge, Dorchester County, for the use of those people who had subscribed money toward its construction, 1770. OCCUPATIONAL PROFILE: merchant, Cambridge, Dorchester County, by 1764; owned a brick storehouse on High Street, Cambridge, Dorchester County, 1785; planter, by 1793. PUBLIC CAREER. LEGISLATIVE SERVICE: Conventions, Dorchester County, 1st, 1774, 5th, 1775. OTHER STATE OFFICE: associate justice, Fourth Judicial District, 1791–1794 (resigned). LOCAL OFFICES: sheriff, Dorchester County, 1767–1770; justice, Dorchester County, 1777–at least 1785; justice, Orphans' Court, Dorchester County, commissioned 1777 and 1778 (did not qualify); subscription officer, Continental Loan Office, Dorchester County, appointed 1777 and 1779; commissioner of tax, Dorchester County, 1779–at least 1792; Maryland Senate elector, Dorchester County, elected 1791. ADDITIONAL COMMENTS: Harrison arrived in Maryland in 1755 with letters of introduction to Governor Sharpe recommending that he be appointed to an office "on account of his alliance." No office was found for him until he was appointed sheriff of Dorchester County in 1767. MILITARY SERVICE: 1st major, Lower Battalion, Dorchester County, appointed 1776; colonel, Lower Battalion, Dorchester County, commissioned 1778. WEALTH DURING LIFETIME. PERSONAL PROPERTY: Harrison inherited from his uncle, John Caile, a one-sixth share of Caile's original capital stock in trade and the increase and profits on it, 1767. By the time he inherited the property he was already managing it for his uncle. Assessed value £1,149.15.0, including 18 slaves and 132 oz. plate, 1783. LAND AT FIRST ELECTION: 528 acres in Dorchester County (all by purchase). WEALTH AT DEATH. DIED: on May 16, 1802, probably in Dorchester County. PERSONAL PROPERTY: size of estate unknown. LAND: 572 acres in Dorchester County.

HARRISON, THOMAS (?–1782). BORN: in Great Britain, of age by 1742. IMMIGRATED: in 1742 as a free adult. RESIDED: in Baltimore Town. CHILDREN. Died without progeny. PRIVATE CAREER. EDUCATION: literate. SOCIAL STATUS AND ACTIVITIES: Gent., 1782. OCCUPATIONAL PROFILE: a merchant; owned the firm named Thomas Harrison & Co., Baltimore Town. PUBLIC CAREER. LEGISLATIVE SERVICE: Conventions, Baltimore County, 4th, 1775, 5th, 1775. LOCAL OFFICES: commissioner, Baltimore Town, 1745–1782; Committee of Observation, Baltimore Town, elected 1774. WEALTH DURING LIFETIME. LAND AT FIRST ELECTION: at least 13,587 acres in Baltimore, Anne Arundel, and Harford counties, plus 6 lots in Baltimore Town under development and leased out (all through personal acquisition). SIGNIFICANT CHANGES IN LAND BETWEEN FIRST ELECTION AND DEATH: sold much of his Baltimore County land, but continued to concentrate on the development of lots in Baltimore Town. WEALTH AT DEATH. DIED: on October 14, 1782, in Baltimore Town after an illness lasting about three weeks. PERSONAL PROPERTY: TEV, £5,216.1.3 current money (including 31 slaves); FB, estate overpaid £8,910.19.10. LAND: 7,926 acres in Baltimore, Harford, and Anne Arundel counties, plus 18 acres and 35 lots in Baltimore Town. His real and personal property was estimated to be worth more than £150,000 current money. ADDITIONAL COMMENTS: his income at death from ground rents in Baltimore Town amounted to £385.0.0 current money per annum. His principal heirs were his nephew John Harrison, of Lincolnshire, England, his niece Elizabeth Irvine, of County Sligo, Ireland, and his executors, *William West* (1739–1791), *Daniel Bowley* (1745–1807), and *Richard Ridgely* (1755–1824). A dispute arose after Harrison's death over whether or not his estate left to his British heirs

should be confiscated. *Luther Martin* (1744–1826), attorney general, argued for the commissioners of confiscated British property that Harrison had intended to devise the bulk of his property to his executors in trust for his British relatives and therefore the property should be confiscated. West, Bowley, and Ridgely denied any such trust arrangement and claimed the property as their own. Although the chancellor's decree was in favor of the commissioners, an Act of Assembly passed in 1790 removed the matter from the Chancery Court and negated the state's claim to Harrison's estate.

HARRISON, WILLIAM (?–1789). BORN: prior to 1752, in Charles County; probably second son. NATIVE: fifth generation. RESIDED: in Charles County; at times in Alexandria, Virginia, where his brother Robert practiced law. FAMILY BACKGROUND. FATHER: *Richard Harrison* (?–1780), son of *Joseph Harrison* (1687–1727). MOTHER: Dorothy (1721–1752), daughter of *Robert Hanson* (ca. 1680–1748). STEPMOTHER: Elizabeth (?–1781), widow of William Penn; daughter of *George Dent* (1690–1754). UNCLE: *Joseph Hanson Harrison* (?–1785). STEPUNCLES: *George Dent* (?–1785); *John Dent, of George* (ca. 1733–1809). AUNT: Mary Hanson, who married *Daniel Jenifer* (?–1795). STEPAUNTS: Elizabeth Hoskins, who married *Walter Hanson* (1711/12–1794); Rebecca Dent (1735–1770), who married *Thomas Hanson Marshall* (1731–1801). BROTHERS: Robert Hanson, military secretary to George Washington and chief judge of the General Court; Walter Hanson, rector of Durham Parish, Charles County. STEPBROTHERS: Jezereal Penn; William Penn. MARRIED first, Rebecca, daughter of William Dent (1706–1757) and wife Anne Warren; granddaughter of *Thomas Dent* (1685–1725) and wife Ann Bayne. Her brothers were George, who married first, Rose Townshend Knox (?–1794), and second, Elizabeth Harrison Knox; *Warren Dent* (?–1794). Her sisters were Eleanor, who married *John Jordan* (?–1763); Judith, who married *Jeremiah Chase* (?–1755); Mary, who married Rev. William Dowie; Ann, who married Samuel Briscoe; and Grace, who married Robert Harrison. Her niece was Mary Hanson Briscoe, who married *Michael Jenifer Stone* (1747–1812). MARRIED second, Ann. CHILDREN. SONS: William Dent; probably also Robert Hanson. DAUGHTERS: Ann Warren; Rebecca; and Grace. PRIVATE CAREER. EDUCATION: literate. RELIGIOUS AFFILIATION: Protestant. SOCIAL STATUS AND ACTIVITIES: Esq.; Hon. OCCUPATIONAL PROFILE: probably a planter. PUBLIC CAREER.

LEGISLATIVE SERVICE: Conventions, Charles County, 5th, 1775, 7th–8th, 1776; Senate, Western Shore, Term of 1786–1791: 1786–1787 (elected on December 22, 1786 to fill vacancy; qualified on April 14, 1787), 1787–1788 (elected, but did not serve), 1788 (elected, but did not serve), 1789 (died before the beginning of the Assembly). LOCAL OFFICES: Committee of Observation, Charles County, elected 1775; justice, Charles County, 1778–at least 1788. MILITARY SERVICE: colonel, 1781. OUT OF STATE SERVICE: delegate, Continental Congress, 1785–1786 (elected in November 1785, but did not attend until March 1786), 1786 (elected in December 1786, but did not attend), 1787 (elected in December 1787, but did not attend). WEALTH DURING LIFETIME. PERSONAL PROPERTY: assessed value £1,661.5.0, including 36 slaves and 99 oz. plate, 1783. SIGNIFICANT CHANGES IN LAND BETWEEN FIRST ELECTION AND DEATH: owned 1,679 acres in Charles County, 1783 (inherited at least 1,141 acres from his father). WEALTH AT DEATH. DIED: on July 21, 1789; will probated in Charles County. PERSONAL PROPERTY: TEV, £2,727.11.3 current money; FB, £2,450.3.0. LAND: probably 1,679 acres in Charles County.

HART, JOHN (?–?). BORN: in Ireland. IMMIGRATED: in 1714 as a free adult with his wife. RESIDED: in Annapolis, Anne Arundel County; returned to England in May 1720. FAMILY BACKGROUND. FATHER: Merrick Hart, of Crobert, County Craven, Ireland. MOTHER: Lettice Vesey, daughter of Thomas Vesey. UNCLE: John Vesey, archbishop of Tuam. MARRIED Anne. CHILDREN. SON: Henry (1717–1718). DAUGHTER: Marylandia (1716–?). PRIVATE CAREER. EDUCATION: literate. RELIGIOUS AFFILIATION: Anglican. SOCIAL STATUS AND ACTIVITIES: arrived as governor; he received his commission through the support of Benedict Leonard Calvert and on promising to give Calvert £500 annually from the profits of the office. OCCUPATIONAL PROFILE: military officer who had served as a captain in Spain and Portugal before coming to Maryland; colonial bureaucrat. PUBLIC CAREER. PROVINCIAL OFFICES: governor, 1713/14–1720; chancellor, 1715–1719/20; surveyor general of the Eastern Shore, 1716/17–1720; surveyor general of the Western Shore, 1716/17–1720. OUT OF COLONY SERVICE: governor of the Leeward Islands, 1721–1727. WEALTH DURING LIFETIME. LAND AT FIRST ELECTION: took a 31-year lease on 200 acres in 1715.

HART, THOMAS (?–1808). BORN: in Hanover County, Virginia; eldest child; he moved to Orange County, North Carolina, ca. 1760. IMMIGRATED: ca. 1780 from North Carolina. RESIDED: in Hagerstown, Washington County; moved to Kentucky in the spring of 1794. FAMILY BACKGROUND. FATHER: Thomas Hart, of Hanover County, Virginia. BROTHERS: John; Benjamin; David; and Nathaniel. SISTER: Susannah. MARRIED Susannah (?–1832), possibly of Orange County, North Carolina. CHILDREN. SONS: Thomas, Jr. (?–1809), who married Eleanor, daughter of Peter Grosh. Thomas was a partner with his father in the firm of Hart, Barton, & Hart in Lexington, Kentucky. He was also a partner in the firm of Hart, Bartlett, & Cox in New Orleans, Louisiana; Nathaniel Gray (?–1813), captain, died at the Battle of Raisins in the War of 1812; and John. DAUGHTERS: Susannah, who married (first name unknown) Price; Elizabeth (?–by 1807), who married (first name unknown) Pindell; Anne, who married James Brown (1766–1835), of Kentucky, a U.S. senator and diplomat; Lucretia, who married Henry Clay (1777–1852), of Kentucky, a U.S. congressman, senator, and secretary of state. PRIVATE CAREER. EDUCATION: literate. RELIGIOUS AFFILIATION: In a letter written in 1805 to his son-in-law the Hon. James Brown he described his attempt to establish "a new religion, similar to the Dunkars and Quakers" in Lexington, Kentucky; however, no other record has been found regarding this endeavor. SOCIAL STATUS AND ACTIVITIES: one of the founders of a library in Lexington, Kentucky, 1795; first president of the Lexington Immigration Society, 1797. OCCUPATIONAL PROFILE: yeoman, 1784; merchant, by 1786; with partner Col. Nathaniel Rochester he manufactured nails, brads, and sprigs in Hagerstown, Washington County; after moving to Kentucky he and his son established the firm of Hart, Barton, & Hart in Lexington; built a nail factory, 1794; opened a general merchandise store, 1795; owned a brick-making machine, 1798; involved in the formation of an insurance company, 1802. PUBLIC CAREER. LEGISLATIVE SERVICE: Lower House, Washington County, 1784 (elected, but did not attend). LOCAL OFFICES: commissioner of tax, Washington County, appointed 1783; justice, Orphans' Court, Washington County, appointed 1792 (refused to serve). MILITARY SERVICE: colonel, 1787. WEALTH DURING LIFETIME. PERSONAL PROPERTY: assessed value £3,006.6.8, including 25 slaves and 44 oz. plate, 1783; owned 18 slaves, 1790. LAND AT FIRST ELECTION: 700 acres in Elizabeth Hundred, Washington County. SIGNIFICANT CHANGES IN

LAND BETWEEN FIRST ELECTION AND DEATH: apparently sold all of his Washington County land, 1783–1804. WEALTH AT DEATH. DIED: on June 23, 1808, in Lexington, Kentucky. PERSONAL PROPERTY: TEV, at least $13,751.08 (including approximately 70 volumes in his library). LAND: 2 houses and lots in Lexington, Kentucky, plus an unspecified number of acres in Kentucky and Tennessee.

HARWOOD, RICHARD (1738–1826). BORN: on December 1, 1738, in All Hallow's Parish, Anne Arundel County; eldest son. NATIVE: third generation. RESIDED: in Rhode River Hundred, Anne Arundel County. FAMILY BACKGROUND. FATHER: Capt. Richard Harwood (?–1754), of West River, Anne Arundel County. MOTHER: Ann (1719–1804), daughter of Gassaway Watkins and wife Ann. BROTHERS: Joseph (1739/40–died young); Gassaway (1741–died young); Thomas, Esq. (1743–1804), of Annapolis, treasurer of the Western Shore from 1775 to 1804; John (1744–?); Samuel (1746–?); Nicholas (1748–?); William (1749–?); and Benjamin (1751–1826), treasurer of the Western Shore from 1804 to 1826. SISTERS: Mary (1753–?); Elizabeth (1753–died young). MARRIED first, on February 3, 1767, Margaret (1746–?), daughter of *Henry Hall* (1702/3–1756). Her brothers were Edward (1735–?); Isaac (1737–?); Thomas Henry (1744–1788); and William (1748–?). Her half brothers were *Henry Hall* (1727–1770); *John Hall* (1729–1797). Her sisters were Elizabeth (1739–?); Mary (1752–1771); and Martha (1755–?). Her first cousin was *Stephen West* (1727–1790). MARRIED second, in 1806 Lucinda, widow of John Battee (?–1803); probably the daughter of Capt. Thomas Harwood. CHILDREN. SONS: Richard Hall (?–1819), member of the Maryland House of Delegates in 1798. STEPSONS: Richard Battee; Thomas Battee; and John Osborn Battee. DAUGHTERS: Priscilla, who married in 1806 John Beale Weems (?–1814), son of *John Weems* (1727–1794); Rachel Sprigg. STEPDAUGHTERS: Henrietta Battee; Caroline Battee. PRIVATE CAREER. EDUCATION: literate. RELIGIOUS AFFILIATION: Anglican, All Hallow's Parish, Anne Arundel County. SOCIAL STATUS AND ACTIVITIES: Gent., 1767. OCCUPATIONAL PROFILE: planter. PUBLIC CAREER. LEGISLATIVE SERVICE: Lower House, Anne Arundel County, 1786–1787 (Grievances 1, 2), 1787–1788 (Elections 1), 1788, 1789, 1790, 1791–1792, 1792, 1793; Senate, Western Shore, Term of 1801–1806: 1801 (president), 1802 (president), 1803 (president), 1804 (president), 1805 (president). LOCAL OFFICES: justice, Anne Arundel County, 1771–1782 (resigned); justice, Court of Oyer and Terminer and Gaol Delivery, Anne Arundel County, commissioned 1775; justice, Orphans' Court, Anne Arundel County, 1777–1782; commissioner of tax, Anne Arundel County, 1777–at least 1786; subscription officer, Continental Loan Office, Anne Arundel County, appointed 1779; sheriff, Anne Arundel County, in office 1782–1785, 1794–1797; All Hallow's Parish Vestry, Anne Arundel County, in office 1810. JURY SERVICE: juror, Anne Arundel County, served 1762, 1763, and 1765; grand juror, Anne Arundel County, served 1761, 1763, and 1764 (foreman). MILITARY SERVICE: lieutenent colonel, by May 1776; colonel, by 1783. WEALTH DURING LIFETIME. PERSONAL PROPERTY: assessed value £1,095.15.0, including 23 slaves and 21 oz. plate, 1783; 40 slaves, 1798. In the late 1790s Harwood was involved in litigation to collect debts owed to him and to have that money assigned to his creditors. In 1800 he mortgaged all of his property to his brother Benjamin to cover a debt of £2,993.0.0 and to insure future credit. The mortgage included 17 adult slaves, livestock, a plantation, and household equipment. When Harwood married Lucy Battee their marriage agreement specified that neither was responsible for the other's debts. LAND AT FIRST ELECTION: 877 acres in Anne Arundel County. SIGNIFICANT CHANGES IN LAND BETWEEN FIRST ELECTION AND DEATH: by 1798 Harwood owned 955 acres in Anne Arundel County, but the mortgage in 1800 assigned all of this land to his brother Benjamin. WEALTH AT DEATH. DIED: on February 21, 1826, in Anne Arundel County. PERSONAL PROPERTY: inventory totaled $705.75, composed of cash and stock in both the Planter's Bank of Prince George's County and the South River Bridge Company. LAND: probably none.

HARWOOD, THOMAS, III (by 1757–by 1805). BORN: probably in Prince George's County, of age by 1778. NATIVE: fourth generation. RESIDED: alternately in Calvert and Prince George's counties. FAMILY BACKGROUND. FATHER: either Capt. Thomas Harwood (1698–1770) or Benjamin Harwood, son of Maj. Thomas Harwood, of Prince George's County, and wife Sarah Belt. OTHER KINSHIP: his great-uncle was possibly *Joseph Belt* (ca. 1680–1761). MARRIED by May 20, 1779, Ann, daughter of George Gantt (?–1779) and wife Hannah; granddaughter of *Thomas Gantt* (?–1765); niece of *Thomas Gantt* (ca. 1710–1785), *Edward Gantt* (?–by 1783), *Fielder Gantt* (?–1807), and probably Ann Gantt, who married *John Brome*

(1703–1748). Her brothers were James; George; William Pitt; Joseph; and Edward. Her sisters were Priscilla, who married (possibly Jeremiah) Belt; Eleanor. Her first cousins were *Thomas Gantt, Jr.* (?–1808); *Erasmus Gantt* (?–?); *Thomas Gantt* (?–ca. 1802); Rachel Gantt (?–1793), who married Dr. *Richard Brooke* (1716–1783); and Sarah Gantt, who married *Osborn Sprigg* (ca. 1741–1815). CHILDREN. SON: Thomas. DAUGHTER: Caroline, who married R. H. Smith. PRIVATE CAREER. EDUCATION: literate. SOCIAL STATUS AND ACTIVITIES: Gent., 1781. OCCUPATIONAL PROFILE: probably a planter. PUBLIC CAREER. LEGISLATIVE SERVICE: Lower House, Calvert County, 1783. LOCAL OFFICES: justice, Calvert County, 1789–1791 (resigned); justice, Orphans' Court, Calvert County, appointed 1789; associate justice, First District Court, Calvert County, appointed 1793 (did not qualify). MILITARY SERVICE: called major at death. WEALTH DURING LIFETIME. PERSONAL PROPERTY: assessed value £204.10.0, including 5 slaves and 12 oz. plate, 1783. LAND AT FIRST ELECTION: at least 400 acres in Prince George's County (by purchase), plus 2 lots in Lower Marlboro, Calvert County. SIGNIFICANT CHANGES IN LAND BETWEEN FIRST ELECTION AND DEATH: mortgaged 400 acres in Prince George's County, 1789; mortgaged an additional 61.75 acres in Calvert County, 1797. ADDITIONAL COMMENTS: He deeded his personal property (including 17 slaves, livestock, and household items) and 62 acres of land in trust to Joseph Wilkinson to be sold at a public sale for the benefit of his son and daughter and his creditors. He valued the property at £1,590.10.8, but it sold for £1,441.14.1 WEALTH AT DEATH. DIED: between 1797 and 1805, probably in Calvert County. IDENTIFICATION PROBLEMS. The distinguishing characteristic that helped to identify the legislator was his signature, "the 3rd." However in 1792 while serving as a justice of the peace he signed his name "jr."

HATCH, JOHN (ca. 1614–1681). BORN: ca. 1614, probably in England. IMMIGRATED: in 1637 as an indentured servant to Cloberry & Company. RESIDED: in Kent County; St. Mary's County, by 1641; Charles County, by 1658. MARRIED Alice. CHILDREN. DAUGHTERS: Mary, who married *Josias Fendall* (?–by 1688); Mary, who married John Dent (?–1712), probably a nephew of *Thomas Dent* (ca. 1630–1676). PRIVATE CAREER. EDUCATION: literate. RELIGIOUS AFFILIATION: Protestant. OCCUPATIONAL PROFILE: servant to Cloberry & Company, 1637; farm laborer, 1642; often an attorney in the Provincial Court, 1644/45–?; planter.

PUBLIC CAREER. LEGISLATIVE SERVICE: Assembly, present, 1647/48 (Defense); Lower House, St. George's Hundred, St. Mary's County, 1650–1650/51 (Laws 1; Accounts 1); Parliamentary Commission, 1654–1657/58; Assembly, Potomac (St. Mary's County), 1654; Lower House, Charles County, 1658, 1659/60. OTHER PROVINCIAL OFFICES: justice, Provincial Court, 1654–1657/58; Council, 1660. LOCAL OFFICES: sheriff, St. Mary's County, 1646–1648; justice, Charles County, 1658–1660. STANDS ON PUBLIC/PRIVATE ISSUES: supported the rebellion led by his son-in-law *Josias Fendall* (?–by 1688) in 1659/60; in 1660/61 he was fined, bonded, and ordered to leave the province within one year for his role in rebellion, but the sentence of banishment was remitted in November 1661; held no offices thereafter. WEALTH DURING LIFETIME. LAND AT FIRST ELECTION: ca. 450 acres. WEALTH AT DEATH. DIED: in 1681. LAND: ca. 450 acres.

HATTON, THOMAS (?–1654/55). BORN: England. IMMIGRATED: in 1648 as a free adult with his wife and two sons. RESIDED: at "Pope's Freehold," St. Mary's County. FAMILY BACKGROUND. FATHER: John Hatton. BROTHERS: Richard (?–by 1649); John (?–1654), of London, England; Henry; and Samuel. SISTERS: Sarah; Susan; and Hanna. MARRIED Margaret (?–1657). CHILDREN. SONS: Robert; Thomas (ca. 1642/43–1675), who married first, (first name unknown), daughter of Randolph Hanson, and second, Elizabeth, daughter of John Waughop. PRIVATE CAREER. EDUCATION: literate, with considerable clerical skills. RELIGIOUS AFFILIATION: Protestant. SOCIAL STATUS AND ACTIVITIES: brought two servants with him on his arrival in the colony, and the next year assisted his sister-in-law and her children, including his nephew *William Hatton* (?–1712), in settling in Maryland; had a commission as a Councilor and secretary on his arrival in the colony; probably met Cecil Calvert through his friend Thomas Motham, Gent., a clerk in Chancery Lane. OCCUPATIONAL PROFILE: placeman; planter. PUBLIC CAREER. LEGISLATIVE SERVICE: Assembly, special writ 1649; Upper House, 1650–1650/51 (Laws 1); Parliamentary Commission, 1652–1653; Assembly, Potomac (St. Mary's County), 1654 (declined to sit because of his oath to Lord Baltimore). OTHER PROVINCIAL OFFICES: Council, 1648–1654; justice, Provincial Court, 1648–1654; secretary, 1648–1654; judge of Probate, 1648–1654; receiver general, 1648–1651; attorney general, 1650–1654. STANDS ON PUBLIC/PRIVATE ISSUES: staunch supporter of Lord Baltimore's rights against the assumption of government by the Parliamentary Commissioners, 1654. WEALTH DURING LIFETIME. LAND AT FIRST ELECTION: 500 acres in 1650; acquired an additional 600 acres in 1652. WEALTH AT DEATH. DIED: on March 5, 1654/55; killed at the Battle of the Severn. PERSONAL PROPERTY: no inventory, but owned much livestock. LAND: 1,600 acres.

HATTON, WILLIAM (?–1712). BORN: in England; probably oldest son. IMMIGRATED: in 1649 as a minor with his mother and siblings. RESIDED: in St. Mary's County; Charles County, by 1689; Prince George's County after 1695. FAMILY BACKGROUND. FATHER: Richard Hatton. STEPFATHER: *Richard Banks* (ca. 1612–ca. 1667). MOTHER: Margaret. UNCLE: *Thomas Hatton* (?–1654/55). BROTHER: Richard, who married by 1674 Ann (1659–?), daughter of *John Price* (ca. 1607–1660/61). SISTERS: Elinor (1642–1725), who married first, *Thomas Brooke* (1632–1676), and second, *Henry Darnall* (ca. 1645–1711); Mary, who married *Zachary Wade* (ca. 1627–1678); Elizabeth, who married first, *Luke Gardiner* (1622–1674), and second, *Clement Hill* (?–1708); and Barbara, who married *James Johnson* (?–?). MARRIED first, Elizabeth, daughter of Rev. William Wilkinson. Her sister was Rebecca, who married first, *Thomas Dent* (ca. 1630–1676), and second, *John Addison* (?–ca. 1705/6). MARRIED second, Mary. CHILDREN. SON: Joseph, a member of the Piscattaway Parish Vestry in Charles County from 1713 to 1715, who married in 1710 Lucy, daughter of Francis Marbury. DAUGHTER: Penelope, who married Thomas Middleston, son of Robert Middleston. PRIVATE CAREER. EDUCATION: literate. RELIGIOUS AFFILIATION: Presbyterian. SOCIAL STATUS AND ACTIVITIES: Gent. before his appointment as a justice. OCCUPATIONAL PROFILE: planter. PUBLIC CAREER. LEGISLATIVE SERVICE: Lower House, St. Mary's County, 1671–1674/75 (Laws 3), 1676–1682, 1682–1684 (Accounts 1), Prince George's County, 1696–1697 (elected to the 5th session). OTHER PROVINCIAL OFFICE: justice, Provincial Court, 1694–1699. LOCAL OFFICES: justice, St. Mary's County, 1675/76–1689, Charles County, 1689–1694; coroner, St. Mary's County, 1676; Piscattaway Vestry, Charles County, 1693–1704. STANDS ON PUBLIC/PRIVATE ISSUES: often consulted on Indian affairs; refused to take the oath as a justice in 1690, and probably was a reluctant supporter of Protestant Associators' government; recommended for a position on the Council in 1697, but was not appointed. WEALTH DURING LIFETIME. LAND AT FIRST ELECTION: ca. 1,868 acres; at least 1,738 acres in 1696. WEALTH AT

DEATH. DIED: on August 2, 1712. PERSONAL PROPERTY: TEV, £422.8.5 sterling (including 5 slaves, 1 servant, and 2 parcels of books); FB, £315.13.7. LAND: 1,620 acres.

HAWKINS, GEORGE FRASER (FRAZIER) (ca. 1741–1785). BORN: ca. 1741 in Prince George's County; probably third son. NATIVE: fourth generation. RESIDED: at "Bowplains" on the Potomac River, Prince George's County, opposite Alexandria, Virginia. FAMILY BACKGROUND. FATHER: *John Hawkins, Jr.* (1713–1757). MOTHER: Susannah Fraser (?–by 1746). STEPMOTHER: Priscilla Magruder Covington. UNCLE: *George Fraser* (?–1764). BROTHERS: Giles Blizzard (1732–?); John Stone (1734–1764); and Alexander Thomas, who was a minor in 1757. STEPBROTHER: Levin Covington. SISTERS: Ann Fraser (1736–1738); Elizabeth Lawrance; and Susanna Fraser, who married *William Bayly* (ca. 1742–1824). STEPSISTER: Rebecca Covington, who married *Benjamin Mackall, Jr.* (ca. 1723–1795). MARRIED by 1769 Susannah Trueman Somerville (ca. 1750–by 1792), daughter of Margaret Somerville (?–1785), of St. Mary's County (?–1785). Her sister was Margaret Trueman (?–by 1796), who married *John DeButts* (?–1796). CHILDREN. SONS: John Trueman (by 1771–by 1799); George Fraser Hawkins (1777–?). DAUGHTERS: Peggy, who married Nathaniel Hawkins; Susannah Greenfield. PRIVATE CAREER. EDUCATION: literate. RELIGIOUS AFFILIATION: Anglican. SOCIAL STATUS AND ACTIVITIES: Mr., 1784; Gent., 1784. OCCUPATIONAL PROFILE: partner in land transactions ca. 1770 with *Charles Beatty* (ca. 1736–1804); a merchant in partnership with Bernard O'Niell (O'Neal), of St. Mary's County, 1771; owned a ferry house; probably also a planter. PUBLIC CAREER. LEGISLATIVE SERVICE: Lower House, Prince George's County, 1781–1782 (Public Taxes 1, 2), 1782–1783. LOCAL OFFICES: King George's Parish Vestry, Prince George's County, in office 1769–1772; justice, Prince George's County, in office 1769–at least 1773; coroner, Prince George's County, appointed 1785. WEALTH DURING LIFETIME. PERSONAL PROPERTY: 22 slaves, 1776. LAND AT FIRST ELECTION: 6,029 acres in Prince George's and Frederick counties (2,425 acres inherited from his uncle George Fraser; 3,603 acres by purchase and patent). SIGNIFICANT CHANGES IN LAND BETWEEN FIRST ELECTION AND DEATH: purchased an unspecified amount of land near Redstone, Pennsylvania; sold all of his Frederick County land, totaling probably 5,482 acres, by 1785. ADDITIONAL COMMENTS: he was deeply in debt by the 1770s and 1780s; accounts show that he ran up high tavern bills. **WEALTH AT DEATH. DIED:** will probated on September 13, 1785, in Prince George's County. **PERSONAL PROPERTY:** TEV, £2,210.2.5 (including 29 slaves and books); FB, estate overpaid £349.5.3. **LAND:** 547 acres in Prince George's County, plus unspecified acreage in Pennsylvania. **ADDITIONAL COMMENTS:** After his death claims against his estate totaled £4,500. His land was sold to pay his creditors.

HAWKINS, HENRY (?–1699). **IMMIGRATED:** in 1665 as a free adult with his wife and son. **RESIDED:** in Talbot County; Port Tobacco Hundred, Charles County, by 1671. **MARRIED** first, Eleanor (?–by 1681). **MARRIED** second, Elizabeth, widow of Francis Wynn. Her niece was Elizabeth Teares, who married *William Middleton* (1686–1769). **CHILDREN. SONS:** John; Henry (ca. 1667–1702), who married Susan, daughter of Alexander Smith; *Henry Holland Hawkins* (1683–1751), who married Jane, daughter of *Thomas Greenfield* (ca. 1649–1715). **DAUGHTERS:** Ruth, who married James Rooch; Mary; and Eleanor, who married first, Rev. George Tubman, and second, William Smallwood, son of *James Smallwood* (ca. 1639–ca. 1714/15). **PRIVATE CAREER. EDUCATION:** literate. **RELIGIOUS AFFILIATION:** Anglican. **SOCIAL STATUS AND ACTIVITIES:** Mr., by 1669. **OCCUPATIONAL PROFILE:** tanner; planter. **PUBLIC CAREER. LEGISLATIVE SERVICE:** Lower House, Charles County, 1688 (elected to the 2nd session); Associators' Convention, Charles County, 1689–1692; Lower House, Charles County, 1692–1693, 1694–1697, 1697/98–1698 (Elections and Privileges 1; died before the 3rd session). **LOCAL OFFICES:** constable, Charles County, 1670/71–1672; justice, Charles County, 1680–1699 (quorum, 1690–1699); Port Tobacco Parish Vestry, Charles County, 1693–1697. **MILITARY SERVICE:** captain, 1694. **STANDS ON PUBLIC/PRIVATE ISSUES:** initially hesitant to support the revolution of 1689. **WEALTH DURING LIFETIME. LAND AT FIRST ELECTION:** ca. 2,000 acres; his wife Elizabeth held 2,264 acres from her previous husband's estate. **WEALTH AT DEATH. DIED:** will probated on May 12, 1699. **PERSONAL PROPERTY:** TEV, £327.18.8 sterling (including 3 slaves and 11 servants). **LAND:** 2,775 acres.

HAWKINS, HENRY HOLLAND (1683–1751). **BORN:** in 1683 in Charles County; youngest son. **NATIVE:** second generation. **RESIDED:** at "Hawkins Purchase," Charles County. **FAMILY BACKGROUND. FATHER:** *Henry Hawkins* (?–1699).

MOTHER: Elizabeth. **BROTHERS:** John; Henry (ca. 1667–1702). **SISTERS:** Ruth; Mary; and Eleanor. **MARRIED** Jane, daughter of *Thomas Greenfield* (ca. 1649–1715); niece of Mary Truman, who married *Thomas Hollyday* (ca. 1661–1702/3); half niece of *Adderton Skinner* (ca. 1677–1756); stepniece of *Robert Skinner* (?–1713). Her brothers were *Thomas Trueman Greenfield* (1682–1733); Micajah; Truman; and James. Her sisters were Martha; Elizabeth; and Ann. Her first cousin was *James Hollyday* (1696–1747). Her nephew was *Francis Waring* (1715–1769). Her niece was Marianne Truman Greenfield, who married *John Stoddert* (?–1767). **CHILDREN. SONS:** Samuel; *Josias Hawkins* (ca. 1735–1789); and Henry. **DAUGHTERS:** Elizabeth, who married Richard Marsham Waring, Sr.; Martha, who married (first name unknown) Portase (Porteus); Eleanor, who married *George Dent* (?–1785); Jane; Susannah; and Ruth. **PRIVATE CAREER. EDUCATION:** literate. **RELIGIOUS AFFILIATION:** Protestant; his son-in-law, Richard Marsham Waring, Sr., specified in his will that his children remain with their mother, Elizabeth Hawkins, and "be educated in the Catholic church." **SOCIAL STATUS AND ACTIVITIES:** Gent., 1727; Mr., 1751. **OCCUPATIONAL PROFILE:** planter. **PUBLIC CAREER. LEGISLATIVE SERVICE:** Lower House, Charles County, 1722–1724, 1725–1727, 1732–1734, 1734/35–1737. **LOCAL OFFICE:** justice, Charles County, 1728–at least 1740 (quorum, 1735–at least 1740). **WEALTH DURING LIFETIME. LAND AT FIRST ELECTION:** at least 300 acres in Charles County (devised to him by his father, 1699). **SIGNIFICANT CHANGES IN LAND BETWEEN FIRST ELECTION AND DEATH:** purchased 1,459 acres in Charles County, 1735–1751; obtained at least 173 acres in Charles County, through his marriage. **WEALTH AT DEATH. DIED:** will probated on April 22, 1751, in Charles County. **PERSONAL PROPERTY:** TEV, £2,203.8.3 current money (including 36 slaves, books, and 55 oz. plate); FB, £2,115.4.0. **LAND:** at least 2,757 acres in Charles County.

HAWKINS, JOHN (ca. 1657–1717). **BORN:** ca. 1657 in Talbot County; second son. **NATIVE:** second generation. **RESIDED:** in Talbot County; Kent County, by 1696; Queen Anne's County, after 1707. **FAMILY BACKGROUND. FATHER:** almost certainly Thomas Hawkins (?–1656), who immigrated by 1656 from Westmoreland County, Virginia. **STEPFATHER:** by 1658, Seth Foster (?–1675). **MOTHER:** Elizabeth. **BROTHER:** Thomas (1645–1677). **HALF SISTERS:** Elizabeth (1658/59–1726), who married first, *Vincent Lowe* (?–1692), and second, *William Coursey* (?–ca. 1717/18); Sarah, who married first, Michael Turbutt, and second, Jacob Covington (?–1726). ADDITIONAL COMMENTS: Thomas Hawkins did not mention a son named John in his will, but his son Thomas's will, written in 1677, stated that the John Hawkins who became a burgess was his brother; John was probably born after his father's death, which would coincide with his first appearance in records; Foster was definitely his stepfather. MARRIED first, by 1680 Frances. Her brother was John Grosse, of Anne Arundel County. MARRIED second, by 1691 Judith. CHILDREN. SONS: John; Ernault, who married Elizabeth. DAUGHTER: Elizabeth, who married Thomas Marsh. PRIVATE CAREER. EDUCATION: literate. RELIGIOUS AFFILIATION: Anglican. SOCIAL STATUS AND ACTIVITIES: Gent., 1680; Esq., by 1701. OCCUPATIONAL PROFILE: planter. PUBLIC CAREER. LEGISLATIVE SERVICE: Lower House, Queen Anne's County, 1714 (elected to the 4th session), 1716–1717 (died before the 3rd session). OTHER PROVINCIAL OFFICES: justice, Provincial Court, 1697 (refused oath), sitting by August 1698–1707 (quorum, 1702–1707). LOCAL OFFICES: justice, Talbot County, 1694–1695/96, Kent County, 1696–1697; St. Paul's Parish Vestry, Queen Anne's County 1711–1712. MILITARY SERVICE: captain, 1692; major, by 1708. STANDS ON PUBLIC/PRIVATE ISSUES: opposed the revolution of 1689; he was recommended for appointment to Council in 1707, but was never commissioned. WEALTH DURING LIFETIME. LAND AT FIRST ELECTION: ca. 1,000 acres (gave his son John 2 plantations in 1701). WEALTH AT DEATH. DIED: will probated in September 1717. PERSONAL PROPERTY: TEV, £1,206.5.10 (including 26 slaves and 2 servants). LAND: 1,000 acres, plus 3 plantations of unspecified acreage.

HAWKINS, JOHN, JR. (1713–1757). BORN: on August 15, 1713, in Piscataway Parish, Prince George's County. NATIVE: third generation. RESIDED: at "Hawkins Lot," King George's Parish, Prince George's County until 1751; on his plantation in St. Paul's Parish, Prince George's County, 1752 until death. FAMILY BACKGROUND. FATHER: John Hawkins (ca. 1690–1772), of Prince George's County, a tobacco inspector in Prince George's County in 1751. MOTHER: Elizabeth (?–1772). MARRIED first, on February 17, 1731, Susannah (?–by 1746), daughter of Rev. John Fraser (?–1742), rector of Durham Parish in Charles County from 1705 to 1710 and King George's Parish in Prince George's County by 1733 to 1742, and wife Ann Blyzard (?–after 1764); stepgranddaughter of

James Smallwood (ca. 1639–ca. 1714/15). Her brothers were John (?–by 1742); *George Fraser* (?–1764). Her sisters were Mary (by 1709–?), who married William Magruder; Anne (1718–1779), who married in 1748 Allen Bowie; and Verlinda. MARRIED second, between 1742 and 1746 Priscilla (probably Magruder), widow of Leonard Covington (?–ca. 1742). Priscilla subsequently married by 1762 Benjamin Fendall, Esq. CHILDREN. SONS: Giles Blizzard (1732–?); John Stone (1734–1764); *George Fraser Hawkins* (ca. 1741–1785); and Alexander Thomas, who was a minor in 1757. STEPSON: Levin Covington. DAUGHTERS: Ann Fraser (1736–1738); Elizabeth Lawrance; Susanna Fraser, who married *William Bayly* (ca. 1742–1824). STEPDAUGHTER: Rebeckah Covington, who married *Benjamin Mackall, Jr.* (ca. 1723–1795). PRIVATE CAREER. RELIGIOUS AFFILIATION: Anglican, King George's Parish, Prince George's County until 1751, St. Paul's Parish, Prince George's County, 1752 until death. OCCUPATIONAL PROFILE: a merchant; in 1750 he was appointed attorney, agent, and factor for a group of merchants of Liverpool, England. PUBLIC CAREER. LEGISLATIVE SERVICE: Lower House, Prince George's County, 1753–1754 (elected to the 3rd session to fill vacancy), 1754–1756 (Accounts 1–5; Bills of Credit 5; died before the 6th session). LOCAL OFFICES: justice, Prince George's County, 1740–1757 (quorum, 1741–1757); churchwarden, King George's Parish, Prince George's County, in office 1746 and 1747; King George's Parish Vestry, Prince George's County, in office 1748–1751; St. Paul's Parish Vestry, Prince George's County, in office 1752 and 1753. WEALTH DURING LIFETIME. LAND AT FIRST ELECTION: 6,565 acres in Prince George's, Frederick, and Charles counties (ca. 334 acres by deed of gift from his parents and inheritance from his father; 886 acres through his marriage; 5,333 acres by purchase and patent). SIGNIFICANT CHANGES IN LAND BETWEEN FIRST ELECTION AND DEATH: purchased 200 acres in Frederick County, 1757. WEALTH AT DEATH. DIED: in February 1757 in Prince George's County, "after a few hours illness." PERSONAL PROPERTY: TEV, £1,923.19.0 current money (including 35 slaves, 43 oz. plate, and 3 books); FB, £1,122.12.9. LAND: 6,765 acres in Prince George's, Frederick, and Charles counties.

HAWKINS, JOSIAS (ca. 1735–1789). BORN: ca. 1735, probably at "Hawkins Purchase," Port Tobacco, East Hundred, Charles County. NATIVE: third generation. RESIDED: probably at "Hawkins Purchase," East Hundred, Port Tobacco, Charles

County. FAMILY BACKGROUND. FATHER: *Henry Holland Hawkins* (1683–1751), son of *Henry Hawkins* (?–1699). MOTHER: Jane, daughter of *Thomas Greenfield* (ca. 1649–1715). UNCLE: *Thomas Trueman Greenfield* (1682–1733). BROTHERS: Samuel; Henry. SISTERS: Elizabeth; Martha; Eleanor, who married *George Dent* (?–1785); Jane; Susannah; and Ruth. FIRST COUSINS: *Francis Waring* (1715–1769); *Thomas Greenfield* (ca. 1715–1774); Marianne Greenfield, who married *John Stoddert* (?–1767). NIECE: Anne Dent, who married *John Parnham* (ca. 1748–1813). MARRIED by 1777 Ann. CHILDREN. SONS: Thomas; Francis Waring; Henry Holland; Caleb; and Samuel. DAUGHTERS: Martha Porteus; Eleanor; and Mary Holliday, who married (first name unknown) Hanson. PRIVATE CAREER. EDUCATION: literate. RELIGIOUS AFFILIATION: Protestant. SOCIAL STATUS AND ACTIVITIES: Gent., by 1770. OCCUPATIONAL PROFILE: planter. PUBLIC CAREER. LEGISLATIVE SERVICE: Lower House, Charles County, 1771 (discharged on October 14, 1771 for "treating" at the election; re-elected to session), 1773–1774 (Public Offices 1, 2, 3; Claims 2, 3); Conventions, Charles County, 1st, 1774, 2nd, 1774, 4th, 1775, 5th, 1775 (elected, but did not attend), 6th–8th, 1775–1776; Lower House, Charles County, 1783 (Claims), 1784 (elected, but did not attend). LOCAL OFFICES: justice, Charles County, 1762–at least 1777 (quorum, 1770–at least 1777); Committee of Observation, Charles County, elected 1774; justice, Orphans' Court, Charles County, commissioned 1777, 1779, 1782, and 1783; commissioner of tax, Charles County, 1777–at least 1783; trustee, Charlotte Hall School, 1778; judge, Court of Appeals for Tax Assessment, Charles County, appointed 1786. MILITARY SERVICE: colonel, 1778. WEALTH DURING LIFETIME. PERSONAL PROPERTY: assessed value £2,018.8.4, including 40 slaves and 1 oz. plate, 1783. LAND AT FIRST ELECTION: 3,161 acres in Charles and Prince George's counties (inherited 629 acres from his father in 1751, and 1,628 acres, which were his brothers' shares of their father's estate, by 1770). WEALTH AT DEATH. DIED: on October 30, 1789, in Charles County. PERSONAL PROPERTY: TEV, £2,104.12.8 current money (including 33 slaves and books); FB, £1,985.6.4. LAND: at least 2,415 acres in Charles and Prince George's counties.

HAWKINS, RALPH (?–ca. 1669/70). IMMIGRATED: in 1652 as a free adult from England. RESIDED: in Broad Neck Hundred, Anne Arundel County. MARRIED first, (name unknown). MARRIED second, Margaret. CHILDREN. SONS: William; Ralph. PRIVATE CAREER. EDUCATION: literate. RELIGIOUS AFFILIATION: Quaker. SOCIAL STATUS AND ACTIVITIES: no title on arrival; no record of any office besides burgess. OCCUPATIONAL PROFILE: planter; merchant. PUBLIC CAREER. LEGISLATIVE SERVICE: Lower House, Anne Arundel County, 1662. WEALTH AT DEATH. DIED: after September 19, 1669; will probated on January 4, 1669/70. PERSONAL PROPERTY: TEV, 26,780 pounds of tobacco (including 1 servant). LAND: probably 350 acres.

HAWLEY, JEROME (1590–1638). BORN: in 1590 in Middlesex, England; younger son. IMMIGRATED: in 1633 as a free adult with his wife and family. RESIDED: in St. Mary's County; moved to Virginia, 1637/38. FAMILY BACKGROUND. FATHER: James Hawley (1558–1622), of Brentford, Middlesex, England. MOTHER: Susann, daughter of Robert Tuthill, of Amersham, England. BROTHERS: William Hawley, Esq., of Grossment, Monmouth, England; James Hawley, Esq. (?–by 1667), of New Brandford, Middlesex, England; Henry (?–1679), governor of Barbados; and Gabriel (1609–by 1636/37). MARRIED first, (first name unknown) Hawkins. MARRIED second, Eleanor, widow of Thomas Courtney. CHILDREN. STEPSON: Sir William Courtney, of Newhouse, Wiltshire, England. PRIVATE CAREER. EDUCATION: literate. RELIGIOUS AFFILIATION: Catholic. SOCIAL STATUS AND ACTIVITIES: his family was very active in colonizing both Virginia and Barbados; he was a one-eighth partner in the *Ark*, 1633; returned to England in 1635–1637, where he successfully lobbied for high appointments in Virginia; coauthored with *John Lewger* (1602–1665), *A Relation of Maryland*, 1635; "gentleman server" to Queen Henrietta Maria, 1637. OCCUPATIONAL PROFILE: colonial investor; merchant; placeman. PUBLIC CAREER. LEGISLATIVE SERVICE: Assembly, 1637/38. OTHER PROVINCIAL OFFICES: commissioner, 1633–1637; Council, 1637–1638. OUT OF COLONY SERVICE: councilor and treasurer of Virginia, 1636/37–1638. STANDS ON PUBLIC/PRIVATE ISSUES: accused of weakly defending Lord Baltimore's claims to Kent Island and of being excessively avaricious, 1638. WEALTH AT DEATH. DIED: prior to August 2, 1638. PERSONAL PROPERTY: TEV, £944.13.0 sterling; most of his estate went to satisfy his creditors. LAND: rights to 6,000 acres.

HAY (KEY, HEY), JAMES (?–by 1717/18). BORN: of age by 1699. NATIVE: origins uncertain, but definitely in Maryland by 1699; possibly second generation. RESIDED: in St. Mary's County.

FAMILY BACKGROUND. FATHER: possibly James Hay, who was in Maryland in 1670. MARRIED by 1707, probably by 1702, Mary (1678–?), daughter of *Kenelm Cheseldyne* (1640–1708). She subsequently married by 1717/18 George Fobes. Her brother was *Kenelm Cheseldyne* (1683–1719). Her sisters were Susannah (1680–1730), who married *Thomas Trueman Greenfield* (1682–1733); Dryden (1687–1760), who married first, *Henry Peregrine Jowles* (1681–1720), and second, John Fobes. CHILDREN. SON: probably James. DAUGHTER: Mary (by 1708–?). PRIVATE CAREER. EDUCATION: literate. RELIGIOUS AFFILIATION: Protestant. SOCIAL STATUS AND ACTIVITIES: Gent., by 1705; probably had married the daughter of *Kenelm Cheseldyne* (1640–1708) by 1702 when he was appointed sheriff. PUBLIC CAREER. LEGISLATIVE SERVICE: Lower House, St. Mary's City, 1704–1707 (Elections and Privileges 4). LOCAL OFFICE: sheriff, St. Mary's County, 1702–1704. WEALTH AT DEATH. DIED: by 1717/18. LAND: ca. 400 acres.

HAYWARD, WILLIAM (?–1791).

BORN: of age by 1756. NATIVE: at least second generation. RESIDED: in Somerset County; "Locust Grove," Bayley's Neck, Talbot County, 1767; "Marshy Point," Talbot County, 1789. FAMILY BACKGROUND. BROTHER: George Hayward (?–1773). NEPHEW: *William Hayward, Jr.* (ca. 1758–1834). MARRIED in November 1760 Margaret (1734–1808), daughter of *George Robins* (1697–1742); stepdaughter of *William Goldsborough* (1709–1760); granddaughter of both *Thomas Robins* (1672–1721) and *Richard Tilghman* (1672/73–1738/39); niece of *William Tilghman* (1711–1782), *Edward Tilghman* (1713–1786), *James Tilghman* (1716–1793), *Matthew Tilghman* (1717/18–1790), Mary Tilghman (1702–ca. 1736), who married *James Earle, Jr.* (ca. 1694–1739), and Anna Maria Tilghman (1709–1763), who married first, *William Hemsley* (1703–1736), and second, *Robert Lloyd* (ca. 1712–1770); stepniece of Elizabeth Robins (1710–1746), who married *William Goldsborough* (1709–1760). Her brother was Thomas (1740–1762). Her sisters were Anna Maria (1732–1806), who married *Henry Hollyday* (ca. 1725–1789); Henrietta Maria (1736–1791), who married *James Lloyd Chamberlaine* (1732–1783); Susannah (1738–?); and Elizabeth (1742–by 1764). Her first cousins were *Michael Earle* (1722–1787); *Richard Tilghman Earle* (1728/29–1788); *William Hemsley* (1736/37–1812); *Richard Tilghman* (1740–1809); *Matthew Tilghman* (1760–ca. 1801); *James Tilghman* (1743–1809); *Peregrine Tilghman* (ca. 1741–1807); *James Tilghman, Jr.* (ca. 1748–1796); *William Tilghman* (1756–1827); Anna Maria Earle (1725–1795), who married *Thomas Ringgold* (1715–1772); Henrietta Maria Earle (1730–1767), who married *William Hemsley* (1736/37–1812); Deborah Lloyd, who married *Peregrine Tilghman* (ca. 1741–1807); Margaret Tilghman (1742–1817), who married *Charles Carroll, Barrister* (1723–1783); Anna Maria Tilghman (?–1817), who married *William Hemsley* (1736/37–1812); and Elizabeth Tilghman, who married *James Lloyd* (1745–1820). Her nephew was *James Hollyday* (1758–1807). Her nieces were Henrietta Maria Hollyday (1750–1832), who married *Samuel Chamberlaine* (1742–1811); Anna Maria Hollyday (1756–1817), who married *George Gale* (1756–1815); Rebecca (1762–1801), who married *Nicholas Hammond* (1758–1830); and Henrietta Maria Chamberlaine (?–1804), who married *William Hayward, Jr.* (ca. 1758–1834). Her other relatives included her great-grandfather *Philemon Lloyd* (1646–1685). CHILDREN. SONS: George Robins (1767–1811), who married Margaret Smyth, of Kent County; Thomas (1771–?), who married first, in 1795 Mary, daughter of Thomas Smyth and wife Margaret, and second, Mary, widow of William S. Bond. DAUGHTERS: Henrietta Maria (1761–1761); Sarah (1763–1764). PRIVATE CAREER. EDUCATION: literate. RELIGIOUS AFFILIATION: Anglican. SOCIAL STATUS AND ACTIVITIES: Gent., 1758. OCCUPATIONAL PROFILE: planter; officeholder; attorney, admitted to the following courts; Somerset County in November 1750; Talbot County in November 1762; Provincial Court in April 1764. PUBLIC CAREER. LEGISLATIVE SERVICE: Lower House, Somerset County, 1762–1763 (Accounts 1, 2), 1768–1769 (Elections 1, 2; Grievances 1, 2; Public Offices 1; appointed to the Council before the 3rd session); Upper House, 1770 (appointed before the 3rd session), 1771, 1773–1774. OTHER PROVINCIAL/STATE OFFICES: Council, 1770–1776 (appointed and qualified on September 24, 1770); justice, Provincial Court, 1771–1776; rent roll keeper, Western Shore, appointed 1772 and 1773; judge, Admiralty Court, appointed 1776; 3rd Council of Safety, Eastern Shore, 1776; chief judge, General Court, appointed 1777 (declined). LOCAL OFFICES: acting clerk of Indictments, Somerset County, appointed 1750 and 1752; justice, Somerset County, commissioned 1763 (quorum). WEALTH DURING LIFETIME. PERSONAL PROPERTY: assessed value £1,200.0.0, including 35 slaves, 1783. LAND AT FIRST ELECTION: 2,284 acres in Somerset and Talbot counties. SIGNIFICANT CHANGES IN LAND BETWEEN FIRST ELECTION AND DEATH: acquired an additional 2,120 acres in Somerset and Talbot counties (at least 1,706 acres inherited from his wife's brother, ca. 1764) 1763–1789; transferred by deeds of gift at least 1,915 acres in Talbot County to his sons and nephew, 1782–1789; sold at least 838 acres in Talbot and Somerset counties, 1763–1789. WEALTH AT DEATH. DIED: will probated on March 21, 1791, in Talbot County. PERSONAL PROPERTY: TEV, at least £3,781.11.10 current money (including 59 slaves, 139 law books, and ca. 49 other books). LAND: ca. 1,500 acres in Somerset and Talbot counties, plus he mentioned in his will unspecified acreage in Worcester County and on the Western Shore, 1789.

HAYWARD, WILLIAM, JR. (ca. 1758–1834). BORN: ca. 1758. RESIDED: near the Miles River Ferry and Easton, Talbot County. FAMILY BACKGROUND. UNCLE: *William Hayward* (?–1791). BROTHER: Thomas (?–ca. 1811), of Baltimore City, a mariner, who married Anne and was lost at sea. SISTERS: Elizabeth, of Somerset County; Augusta, of Somerset County. MARRIED first, between 1783 and 1787 Henrietta Maria (?–1804), daughter of *James Lloyd Chamberlaine* (1732–1783); granddaughter of both *George Robins* (1697–1742) and *Samuel Chamberlaine* (1698–1773); stepgranddaughter of *William Goldsborough* (1709–1760); niece of *Samuel Chamberlaine* (1742–1811), Anne Chamberlaine (1734–1786), who married *Richard Tilghman Earle* (1728/29–1788), Anna Maria Robins (1732–1806), who married *Henry Hollyday* (ca. 1725–1789), and Margaret Robins (1734–1808), who married *William Hayward* (?–1791). Her brothers were Samuel (?–1784); Robins (?–by 1773); and Robins (1773–1808). Her sister was Margaret. Her first cousins were *James Hollyday* (1758–1807); *Samuel Earle* (1756–1790); Henrietta Maria Hollyday (1750–1832), who married *Samuel Chamberlaine* (1742–1811); Anna Maria Hollyday (1756–1817), who married *George Gale* (1756–1815); and Rebecca Hollyday (1762–by 1830), who married *Nicholas Hammond* (1758–1830). MARRIED second, by 1810 Henrietta Maria (?–1822), daughter of James Lloyd (1716/17–1768), of Parson's Landing, Talbot County, a mariner, and wife Elizabeth Frisby (1729–?); stepdaughter of Elizabeth Ward; granddaughter of both *James Lloyd* (1679/80–1723) and *Peregrine Frisby* (1688–1739); niece of *Robert Lloyd* (ca. 1712–1770), Henrietta Maria Lloyd (ca. 1711–1748), who married *Samuel Chamberlaine* (1698–1773), Margaret Lloyd (1714–ca. 1785), who married *William Tilghman* (1711–1782), Ann Lloyd (ca. 1723–1794), who married *Matthew Tilghman*

(1717/18–1790), and Ann Frisby (1727–1793), who married second, *William Fitzhugh* (ca. 1722–1798). Her brothers were James (?–1815), a captain in the Fourth Battalion of Maryland Militia during the Revolution, who married Sarah, daughter of Thomas Martin; Peregrine; Robert, Gent. (?–1784), of Talbot County, a physician; Philemon, Gent. (?–1827), of Queen Anne's County by 1796 and of Cecil County at death; Frisby, Gent., of Cecil County by 1796; and Nicholas. Her sisters were Ann; Elizabeth (?–1813), of Talbot County; and Deborah. Her first cousins were Deborah Lloyd, who married *Peregrine Tilghman* (ca. 1741–1807); *James Lloyd Chamberlaine* (1732–1783); *Samuel Chamberlaine* (1742–1811); Anne Chamberlaine (1734–1786), who married *Richard Tilghman Earle* (1728/29–1788); *Richard Tilghman* (1740–1809); Margaret Tilghman (1742–1817), who married *Charles Carroll, Barrister* (1723–1783); *William Fitzhugh, Jr.* (1761–1839); Elizabeth Rousby, who married *George Plater* (1735–1792); *Peregrine Tilghman* (ca. 1741–1807); and *James Tilghman* (1743–1809). CHILDREN. SONS: William (1787–1836), of Easton, Talbot County, a lawyer, who was a member of the Maryland House of Delegates from 1818 to 1820 and was elected to the U.S. Congress as a Democratic representative for the 1825 session, who married in 1809 Elizabeth Haskins Bullitt, of Easton, Talbot County; and James Chamberlaine (?–ca. 1832), who never married. DAUGHTERS: Henrietta Maria, who never married; Sarah (?–1821), who never married and died of consumption. PRIVATE CAREER. EDUCATION: literate. RELIGIOUS AFFILIATION: Anglican, St. Michael's Parish, Talbot County. ADDITIONAL COMMENTS: in 1805 he was elected vice president of the newly formed Agricultural Society that met at Easton, Talbot County, to promote new methods of crop rotation and fertilization. OCCUPATIONAL PROFILE: attorney at law; planter. PUBLIC CAREER. LEGISLATIVE SERVICE: Lower House, Talbot County, 1787–1788; Senate, Eastern Shore, Term of 1801–1806: 1801, 1802, 1803 (did not serve), 1804, 1805. LOCAL OFFICES: St. Michael's Parish Vestry, Talbot County, elected 1790, 1797, 1822, 1827, 1830, 1831, 1833, 1834, and 1835; associate justice, Talbot County, in office 1798; Commission to divide Talbot County into election districts, appointed 1800; trustee, Easton Academy, Talbot County, in office 1800; judge of elections, First District, Talbot County, in office 1800; Maryland Senate elector, Talbot County, 1821. MILITARY SERVICE: colonel, by 1804. WEALTH DURING LIFETIME. PERSONAL PROPERTY: 28 slaves, 1790; assessed value £1,296.19.8, including 35 slaves and 221 oz. plate, 1798; assessed value £1,560.9.2, including 49 slaves and 221 oz. plate, 1804; gave 3 slaves to his son William, 1809; assessed value $4,445.00, including 46 slaves and 220 oz. plate, 1817; assigned all slaves, livestock, and other effects in trust to his son William to be sold to pay his debts, 1819; 11 slaves sold at public auction to pay a debt, but they were purchased by his son William, 1820; several articles sold at public sale to pay a debt, but again they were purchased by his son William, ca. 1828; assessed value $345.00, including 220 oz. plate, 1832. LAND AT FIRST ELECTION: at least 709 acres in Talbot County (200 acres acquired as a gift from his uncle; at least 509 acres obtained through his first marriage). SIGNIFICANT CHANGES IN LAND BETWEEN FIRST ELECTION AND DEATH: Hayward and his wife received life estates in 393 acres in Talbot County, plus a moiety of 2 lots in Easton, Talbot County, from his mother-in-law, 1791. He purchased at least 1,371 acres in Talbot County between 1796 and 1811, but sold 26 acres of it in 1806. He owned a total of 2,816 acres in Talbot County, 1817. Hayward mortgaged 1,013 acres in Talbot County to the president and directors of the Farmers Bank of Maryland at Easton in 1817. Apparently in financial difficulty, Hayward assigned all of his land, including that mortgaged to the bank, to his son William in trust to be sold to pay his debts, 1819. After William discharged this trust, he was to transfer any remaining land back to Hayward or his heirs. In ca. 1825 the sheriff of Talbot County put 550 acres of Hayward's Talbot County land up for public sale. It was purchased by Hayward's son William. By 1832 Hayward was assessed for 1,298 acres in Talbot County, all of which were probably still held in trust by his son. The Farmers Bank continued to hold the 1,013 acres in Talbot County and to pay the taxes on it until 1834 when Hayward, having defaulted on his mortgage payments, relinquished all of his rights to the land. WEALTH AT DEATH. DIED: on November 11, 1834, in Talbot County; size of estate unknown, although he probably had little of significance.

HEATH, JAMES (?–1766). BORN: in Cecil County, of age by 1758; younger son. NATIVE: at least third generation. RESIDED: in Cecil County; moved to Baltimore County between December 1759 and May 1761. FAMILY BACKGROUND. FATHER: James Paul Heath (?–1746), of Cecil County. STEPFATHER: William Hedges. MOTHER: Rebecca, daughter of *Daniel Dulany* (1685–1753), and wife Rebecca Smith (ca. 1695–1737). UNCLES:

Daniel Dulany, Jr. (1722–1797); *Walter Dulany* (?–1773). STEPUNCLE: *Samuel Chew* (by 1734–1786). AUNT: Margaret Dulany, who married first, Dr. *Alexander Hamilton* (1712–1756), and second, *William Murdock* (?–1769). STEPAUNTS: Margaret Chew (?–1773), who married *John Beale Bordley* (1726/27–1804); Ann Mary Chew (1736–1777), who married *William Paca* (1740–1799); and Henrietta Maria Chew (1731–1762), who married *Edward Dorsey* (1718–1760). BROTHER: Daniel. FIRST COUSIN: *Benjamin Tasker Dulany* (1752–1816). MARRIED on October 25, 1759, Susannah, daughter of John Hall (1722–1768), of Swantown, Baltimore County, and wife Cordelia Holland; niece of *Aquila Hall* (1727–1779). Her brothers were William (1749–?); Parker (1765–?); and Aquila. Her half brother was *Francis Holland* (ca. 1745–1795). Her sisters were Cordelia (1758–?); Sarah (1760–?). Her half sister was Frances Holland (ca. 1747–?). Her first cousins were Charlotte Hall (1758–1838), who married *Nathaniel Ramsay* (1741–1817); Sophia Hall (1765–?), who married *Philip Key* (1750–1820). CHILDREN. Died without progeny. PRIVATE CAREER. EDUCATION: literate; served in the counting house of William Allen, of Philadelphia, Pennsylvania, ca. 1754. His father's will directed that Heath be sent to the Jesuit College of St. Omer in France, but his training in the Philadelphia mercantile firm was arranged by his uncle *Daniel Dulany, Jr.* (1722–1797). RELIGIOUS AFFILIATION: his father's will directed that James be brought up as a Catholic. SOCIAL STATUS AND ACTIVITIES: Gent., 1785; Esq. at death; his father and paternal grandfather owned extensive landholdings in Cecil and Kent counties; the executors of his father's estate included Richard Bennett (1667–1749), *Daniel Dulany, Jr.* (1722–1797), and probably *Charles Carroll, Sr.* (1702–1782). OCCUPATIONAL PROFILE: merchant; planter. PUBLIC CAREER. LEGISLATIVE SERVICE: Lower House, Baltimore County, 1765–1766 (died during the 4th session). WEALTH DURING LIFETIME. LAND AT FIRST ELECTION: 5,202 acres in Cecil, Kent, Baltimore, and Anne Arundel counties, plus 3 lots in Chestertown, Kent County, and other lots in Warwick, Cecil County (at least 5,100 acres inherited from his father). WEALTH AT DEATH. DIED: on November 27, 1766, in Baltimore County. PERSONAL PROPERTY: TEV, £4,430.16.2 gold (including 42 slaves); FB, £462.9.5. LAND: 5,185 acres in Cecil, Kent, and Baltimore counties, plus lots in Chestertown, Kent County, and Warwick, Cecil County. ADDITIONAL COMMENTS: he named as his principal heirs the children of his uncles *Daniel*

Dulany, Jr. (1722–1797) and *Walter Dulany* (?–1773).

HEIGHE, JAMES (?–1757). BORN: probably in Calvert County, under 18 years of age in 1725; only surviving son. NATIVE: at least second generation. RESIDED: on the bay side near Plum Point, Calvert County. FAMILY BACKGROUND. FATHER: James Heighe (?–1725). MOTHER: Ann. SISTERS: Elizabeth, who married (first name unknown) Sollers; Mary, who married (first name unknown) Sollers; and Althea, underage in 1725. MARRIED Betty (1715–?), daughter of *Thomas Holdsworth* (ca. 1692–1718); stepdaughter of *Benjamin Mackall* (1675–1761); niece of *Walter Smith* (ca. 1693–1748); half niece of *John Rousby* (1685–1744); stepniece of both *John Mackall* (1669–1739) and *James Mackall* (1671–1717). Her half brother was *Benjamin Mackall, Jr.* (ca. 1723–1795). Her sisters were Mary (1713–?), who married *Benson Bond* (1710–1750); Rebecca (1716–?); and Ann (1719–?). Her half sister was Barbara Mackall, who married *William Wilkinson* (?–1755). Her half first cousins were Anne Rousby (1721–1769), who married *Edward Lloyd* (1711–1770); Elizabeth Rousby, who married *Abraham Barnes* (?–ca. 1778); and Gertrude Rousby (?–ca. 1770), who married *Robert Jenkins Henry* (ca. 1712–1766). Her half nephew was *William Mackall Wilkinson* (1752–1799). CHILDREN. SONS: James, who married Elizabeth (1743–?), daughter of *James John Mackall* (1717–1772); Thomas Holdsworth. DAUGHTERS: Ann, who married George Gantt; Betty; Barbara; and Mary. PRIVATE CAREER. EDUCATION: literate. RELIGIOUS AFFILIATION: Anglican. SOCIAL STATUS AND ACTIVITIES: Mr., 1734. OCCUPATIONAL PROFILE: probably a planter. PUBLIC CAREER. LEGISLATIVE SERVICE: Lower House, Calvert County, 1749–1751. LOCAL OFFICES: churchwarden, All Saints' Parish, Calvert County, elected 1734 and 1736; justice, Calvert County, commissioned 1734, 1754, and 1756; All Saints' Parish Vestry, Calvert County, in office 1739–1742, elected 1746 and 1751. MILITARY SERVICE: captain, troop of horse, Prince Frederick, Calvert County, by 1748. WEALTH DURING LIFETIME. LAND AT FIRST ELECTION: more than 531 acres in Calvert County. SIGNIFICANT CHANGES IN LAND BETWEEN FIRST ELECTION AND DEATH: owned 900 acres in 1753. WEALTH AT DEATH. DIED: between November 23, 1756, and September 12, 1757, in Calvert County. PERSONAL PROPERTY: TEV, £1,489.0.9 current money (including 32 slaves, books, 28 oz. old silver, and one-third in-terest in a boat); FB, £18.0.6. LAND: 900 acres in Calvert County.

HEMSLEY, PHILEMON (1670–1719). BORN: in 1670 in Kent County; third son. NATIVE: second generation. RESIDED: in Kent County; Talbot County, by 1671; Queen Anne's County, after 1707; Charles County, by 1713. FAMILY BACKGROUND. FATHER: William Hemsley (ca. 1634–1685), immigrated in 1658 from Yorkshire, England, with his wife and daughter. A Catholic, he was a merchant, doctor, and planter as well as sheriff of Kent County in 1663, clerk of Talbot County from 1668 to 1674, and justice of Talbot County from 1681 to 1685. During his lifetime he patented ca. 5,000 acres. MOTHER: Judith (ca. 1633–?). BROTHERS: *William Hemsley* (1661/62–1699); Charles (1665–1698/99); and Vincent (1672–1729). SISTERS: Penelope (1657–?); Judith. MARRIED first, Frances, daughter of Robert Noble (?–1684). MARRIED second, Mary Townley, widow of *John Contee* (?–1708). Her first cousin was Gov. *John Seymour* (1649–1709). CHILDREN. SON: *William Hemsley* (1703–1736), who married in 1725 Anna Maria (1709–1763), daughter of Col. *Richard Tilghman* (1672/73–1738/39). DAUGHTER: Ann. PRIVATE CAREER. EDUCATION: literate. RELIGIOUS AFFILIATION: Protestant, converted from Roman Catholicism by 1689. SOCIAL STATUS AND ACTIVITIES: Gent., by 1709; Esq. by death. OCCUPATIONAL PROFILE: a merchant, who traded with Barbados; in partnership with Jonathan Forward, a merchant of London, England; contractor; planter. PUBLIC CAREER. LEGISLATIVE SERVICE: Lower House, Queen Anne's County, 1708A, 1708B–1710 (resigned before the 4th session to become sheriff). LOCAL OFFICES: justice, Talbot County, 1701–1707, Queen Anne's County, 1707–1710; sheriff, Queen Anne's County, 1711–ca. 1713. STANDS ON PUBLIC/PRIVATE ISSUES: opposed the revolution of Protestant Associators in 1689. WEALTH DURING LIFETIME. LAND AT FIRST ELECTION: at least 356 acres and an unspecified amount of land inherited from his father. WEALTH AT DEATH. DIED: will probated on November 10, 1719. PERSONAL PROPERTY: TEV, £3,034.1.9 current money (including 44 slaves, 7 servants, and books); FB, estate overpaid £189.19.7. LAND: over 1,000 acres, plus a house in Annapolis.

HEMSLEY, WILLIAM (1661/62–1699). BORN: in 1661/62 in Kent County; first son. NATIVE: second generation. RESIDED: in Kent County; Talbot County, by 1671. FAMILY BACKGROUND. FATHER:

William Hemsley (ca. 1634–1685), who immigrated in 1658 from Yorkshire, England, with his wife and daughter. He was a Catholic, whose occupations included those of merchant, doctor, and planter. He served as sheriff of Kent County in 1663, clerk of Talbot County from 1668 to 1674, and justice of Talbot County from 1681 to 1685. During his lifetime he patented ca. 5,000 acres in Maryland. MOTHER: Judith (ca. 1633–?). BROTHERS: Charles (1665–1698/99); *Philemon Hemsley* (1670–1719); and Vincent (1672–1729), the sheriff of Talbot County in 1702. SISTERS: Penelope (1657–?); Judith. MARRIED first, by 1685/86 Cornelia, widow of Robert Noble (?–1684). MARRIED second, Jane. CHILDREN. SON: William (?–1699). STEPSON: Robert Noble. DAUGHTER: Elizabeth. STEPDAUGHTER: Frances Noble, who married *Philemon Hemsley* (1670–1719). PRIVATE CAREER. EDUCATION: literate; possibly educated in England. RELIGIOUS AFFILIATION: Protestant; converted from Roman Catholicism by 1693. SOCIAL STATUS AND ACTIVITIES: Gent., by 1685/86. OCCUPATIONAL PROFILE: lawyer, admitted to the following courts: Provincial Court in 1695/96; Kent County in 1696. Planter. PUBLIC CAREER. LEGISLATIVE SERVICE: Lower House, Talbot County, 1696–1697 (elected to the 5th session; Laws 5), 1697/98–1698 (Laws 1; died before the 3rd session). LOCAL OFFICES: deputy commissary, Talbot County, 1685; justice, Talbot County, 1695/96–1699 (quorum, 1697–1699). STANDS ON PUBLIC/PRIVATE ISSUES: opposed the revolution of Protestant Associators in 1689; a political opponent of Thomas Lawrence, secretary of the Province, who blocked Hemsley's appointment as clerk of Talbot County in 1693. WEALTH DURING LIFETIME. LAND AT FIRST ELECTION: over 3,500 acres. WEALTH AT DEATH. DIED: will probated on May 6, 1699. PERSONAL PROPERTY: TEV, £783.17.11 sterling (including 12 servants and 21 books); FB, £413.6.1. LAND: over 2,116 acres.

HEMSLEY (HAMSLEY, HANSLEY, HEMESLEY, HEMSELY, HENESLEY, HENSLEY), WILLIAM (1703–1736). BORN: in 1703; only son. NATIVE: third generation. RESIDED: at "Cloverfields," near Queenstown, Queen Anne's County. FAMILY BACKGROUND. FATHER: *Philemon Hemsley* (1670–1719). MOTHER: Frances Noble. STEPMOTHER: Mary Townley, widow of *John Contee* (?–1708). UNCLE: *William Hemsley* (1661/62–1699). SISTER: Anne. MARRIED on December 9, 1725, Anna Maria (1709–1763), daughter of *Richard Tilghman* (1672/73–1738/39); granddaughter of *Philemon Lloyd* (1646–1685); niece of *Edward*

Lloyd (1670–1718/19), *Philemon Lloyd* (ca. 1674–1732/33), *James Lloyd* (1679/80–1723), Rebecca Tilghman (?–1725), who married *Simon Wilmer* (ca. 1656–1699), and Margaret Lloyd (1683–1747), who married *Matthew Tilghman Ward* (ca. 1676–1741); half niece of Susanna Bennett (1666–1714), who married first, *John Darnall* (?–1684), and second, *Henry Lowe* (?–1717). Anna Maria Hemsley subsequently married *Robert Lloyd* (ca. 1712–1770). Her brothers were Philemon (1704–ca. 1724); Richard (1705–1768); *William Tilghman* (1711–1782); *Edward Tilghman* (1713–1786); *James Tilghman* (1716–1793); and *Matthew Tilghman* (1717/18–1790). Her sisters were Mary (1702–ca. 1736), who married *James Earle, Jr.* (ca. 1694–1739); Henrietta Maria (1707–1771), who married first, *George Robins* (1697–1742), and second, *William Goldsborough* (1709–1760). Her first cousins were *Matthew Tilghman Ward* (ca. 1676–1741); *Lambert Wilmer* (1682–1732); *Simon Wilmer* (1686–1737); *Edward Lloyd* (1711–1770); *Richard Lloyd* (1717–1786); *Robert Lloyd* (ca. 1712–1770); Henrietta Maria Lloyd Chew (?–1765), who married second, *Daniel Dulany* (1685–1753); Henrietta Maria Lloyd (ca. 1711–1748), who married *Samuel Chamberlaine* (1698–1773); Margaret Lloyd (1714–ca. 1785), who married *William Tilghman* (1711–1782); and Anne Lloyd (ca. 1723–1794), who married *Matthew Tilghman* (1717/18–1790). Her nephews were *Michael Earle* (1722–1787); *Richard Tilghman Earle* (1728/29–1788); *Richard Tilghman* (1740–1809); *Matthew Tilghman* (1760–ca. 1801); *James Tilghman* (1743–1809); *Peregrine Tilghman* (ca. 1741–1807); *James Tilghman, Jr.* (ca. 1748–1796); and *William Tilghman* (1756–1827). Her nieces were Anna Maria Earle (1725–1795), who married *Thomas Ringgold* (1715–1772); Henrietta Maria Earle (1730–1767), who married *William Hemsley* (1736/37–1812); Margaret Tilghman (1742–1817), who married *Charles Carroll, Barrister* (1723–1783); Anna Maria Tilghman, who married *William Hemsley* (1736/37–1812); Elizabeth Tilghman, who married *James Lloyd* (1745–1820); Anna Maria Robins (1732–1806), who married *Henry Hollyday* (ca. 1725–1789); Margaret Robins (1734–1808), who married *William Hayward* (?–1791); and Henrietta Maria Robins (1736–1791), who married *James Lloyd Chamberlaine* (1732–1783). CHILDREN. SONS: Philemon (1728–1752), who died of smallpox in London, England, where he was studying law at the Middle Temple, never married; Richard (?–died young); and *William Hemsley* (1736/37–1812). DAUGHTERS: Anna Maria (1726–1790), who never married; Henrietta

Maria (1730–?); and Mary (1733–ca. 1750). PRI-VATE CAREER. EDUCATION: literate. RELIGIOUS AFFILIATION: Anglican, Wye Chapel, St. Paul's Parish, Queen Anne's County. SOCIAL STATUS AND ACTIVITIES: Gent., by 1722. OCCUPATIONAL PROFILE: probably a planter; merchant. PUBLIC CAREER. LEGISLATIVE SERVICE: Lower House, Queen Anne's County, 1728–1731, 1732–1734 (Elections 1–Cv; Accounts Cv), 1734/35–1736 (Elections 1, Cv, 2; Bills of Credit 1, Cv, 2; died before the 3rd session). LOCAL OFFICES: sheriff, Queen Anne's County, 1724–1727; deputy com-missary, Queen Anne's County, 1724–1733; St. Paul's Church Vestry, St. Paul's Parish, Queen Anne's County, in office 1728, 1732–1735; justice, Queen Anne's County, 1729–at least 1733. WEALTH DURING LIFETIME. LAND AT FIRST ELECTION: at least 2,403 acres in Queen Anne's and Talbot counties (255 acres from his father; 2,148 acres by purchase or resurvey). SIGNIFICANT CHANGES IN LAND BETWEEN FIRST ELECTION AND DEATH: acquired 2,390 additional acres in Queen Anne's and Talbot counties through pur-chase or patent. WEALTH AT DEATH. DIED: on Oc-tober 2, 1736, in Queen Anne's County. PERSONAL PROPERTY: TEV, £3,518.8.7 current money (in-cluding 33 slaves, 8 servants, books, 79.25 oz. sil-ver, large quantities of molasses and rum, and a schooner); FB, could not be calculated, because Hemsley's administratrix requested time to submit another account due to foreign accounts requiring settlement, but no additional account was found. LAND: 4,793 acres in Queen Anne's and Talbot counties.

HEMSLEY (HAMSLEY, HANSLEY, HEMES-LEY, HEMSELY, HENESLEY, HENSLEY), WILLIAM (1736/37–1812). BORN: on January 23, 1736/37, at "Cloverfields," near Queenstown, Queen Anne's County, nearly four months after the death of his father. NATIVE: fourth generation. RESIDED: at "Cloverfields," Queen Anne's County. FAMILY BACKGROUND. FATHER: *William Hemsley* (1703–1736), son of *Philemon Hemsley* (1670–1719). STEPFATHER: *Robert Lloyd* (ca. 1712–1770). MOTHER: Anna Maria (1709–1763), daughter of *Richard Tilghman* (1672/73–1738/39). UNCLES: *William Tilghman* (1711–1782); *Edward Tilgh-man* (1713–1786); *James Tilghman* (1716–1793); and *Matthew Tilghman* (1717/18–1790). AUNTS: Mary Tilghman (1702–ca. 1736), who married *James Earle, Jr.* (ca. 1694–1739); Henrietta Maria Tilghman (1707–1771), who married first, *George Robins* (1697–1742), and second, *William Golds-borough* (1709–1760). BROTHERS: Philemon (1728–

1752); Richard (?–died young). HALF BROTHER: Richard Lloyd. SISTERS: Anna Maria (1726–1790); Henrietta Maria (1730–?); and Mary (1733–ca. 1750). HALF SISTERS: Deborah Lloyd, who mar-ried *Peregrine Tilghman* (ca. 1741–1807); Anna Maria Lloyd. FIRST COUSINS: *Michael Earle* (1722–1787); *Richard Tilghman Earle* (1728/29–1788); *Richard Tilghman* (1740–1809); *Matthew Tilghman* (1760–ca. 1801); *James Tilghman* (1743–1809); *Peregrine Tilghman* (ca. 1741–1807); *James Tilghman, Jr.* (ca. 1748–1796); *William Tilghman* (1756–1827); Anna Maria Earle (1725–1795), who married *Thomas Ringgold* (1715–1772); Margaret Tilghman (1742–1817), who mar-ried *Charles Carroll, Barrister* (1723–1783); Elizabeth Tilghman, who married *James Lloyd* (1745–1820); Anna Maria Robins (1732–1806), who married *Henry Hollyday* (ca. 1725–1789); Margaret Robins (1734–1808), who married *Wil-liam Hayward* (?–1791); and Henrietta Maria Ro-bins (1736–1791), who married *James Lloyd Chamberlaine* (1732–1783). MARRIED first, on April 3, 1758, his first cousin Henrietta Maria (1730–1767), daughter of *James Earle, Jr.* (ca. 1694–1739); stepdaughter of Sarah Crapp Che-tham; granddaughter of *Richard Tilghman* (1672/73–1738/39); niece of *William Tilghman* (1711–1782), *Edward Tilghman* (1713–1786), *James Tilghman* (1716–1793), *Matthew Tilghman* (1717/18–1790), Elizabeth Earle (ca. 1694–?), who married *William Turbutt* (1683/84–1739), Hen-rietta Maria Tilghman (1707–1771), who married first, *George Robins* (1697–1742), and second, *Wil-liam Goldsborough* (1709–1760), and Anna Maria Tilghman (1709–1763), who married first, *William Hemsley* (1703–1736), and second, *Robert Lloyd* (ca. 1712–1770). Her brothers were *Michael Earle* (1722–1787); Richard (1727–1728); *Richard Tilghman Earle* (1728/29–1788); Joseph (1732–1732); and James (1734–1810). Her half brother was *Joseph Earle* (1739–1777). Her sister was Anna Maria (1725–1795), who married *Thomas Ringgold* (1715–1772). Her first cousins were *Richard Tilghman* (1740–1809); *Matthew Tilgh-man* (1760–ca. 1801); *James Tilghman* (1743–1809); *Peregrine Tilghman* (ca. 1741–1807); *James Tilghman, Jr.* (ca. 1748–1796); *William Tilghman* (1756–1827); Anna Maria Turbutt, who married *Edward Tilghman* (1713–1786); Elizabeth Turbutt (?–ca. 1760), who married *Thomas Harris* (?–1760); Deborah Lloyd, who married *Peregrine Tilghman* (ca. 1741–1807); Margaret Tilghman (1742–1817), who married *Charles Carroll, Barris-ter* (1723–1783); Anna Maria Tilghman (?–1817), who married *William Hemsley* (1736/37–1812);

Elizabeth Tilghman, who married *James Lloyd* (1745–1820); Anna Maria Robins (1732–1806), who married *Henry Hollyday* (ca. 1725–1789); Margaret Robins (1734–1808), who married *William Hayward* (?–1791); and Henrietta Maria Robins (1736–1791), who married *James Lloyd Chamberlaine* (1732–1783). Her nephew was *Thomas Ringgold* (1744–1776). MARRIED second, Sarah (1749–1794), daughter of *Alexander Williamson* (ca. 1712–1760); niece of *Thomas Ringgold* (1715–1772). Her brothers were Alexander (?–1760); James. Her sisters were Ann; Henrietta; and Rebecca. Her first cousin was *Thomas Ringgold* (1744–1776). MARRIED third, his first cousin Anna Maria (?–1817), who moved to Philadelphia after William's death and died there without progeny, daughter of *James Tilghman* (1716–1793); granddaughter of both *Richard Tilghman* (1672/73–1738/39) and *Tench Francis* (1701–1758); niece of *William Tilghman* (1711–1782), *Edward Tilghman* (1713–1786), *Matthew Tilghman* (1717/18–1790), Mary Tilghman (1702–ca. 1736), who married *James Earle, Jr.* (ca. 1694–1739), Henrietta Maria Tilghman (1707–1771), who married first, *George Robins* (1697–1742), and second, *William Goldsborough* (1709–1760), Anna Maria Tilghman (1709–1763), who marrried first, *William Hemsley* (1703–1736), and second, *Robert Lloyd* (ca. 1712–1770). Her brothers were Tench (1744–1786); Richard (1746–1796); *James Tilghman, Jr.* (ca. 1748–1796); *William Tilghman* (1756–1827); Philemon (1760–1797); and Thomas Ringgold (1765–1789). Her sisters were Elizabeth, who married *James Lloyd* (1745–1820); Mary; and Henrietta Maria (1763–1796). Her first cousins were *Michael Earle* (1722–1787); *Richard Tilghman Earle* (1728/29–1788); *Richard Tilghman* (1740–1809); *Matthew Tilghman* (1760–ca. 1801); *James Tilghman* (1743–1809); *Peregrine Tilghman* (ca. 1741–1807); Anna Maria Earle (1725–1795), who married *Thomas Ringgold* (1715–1772); Henrietta Maria Earle (1730–1767), who married *William Hemsley* (1736/37–1812); Deborah Lloyd, who married *Peregrine Tilghman* (ca. 1741–1807); Margaret Tilghman (1742–1817), who married *Charles Carroll, Barrister* (1723–1783); Anna Maria Robins (1732–1806), who married *Henry Hollyday* (ca. 1725–1789); Margaret Robins (1734–1808), who married *William Hayward* (?–1791); and Henrietta Maria Robins (1736–1791), who married *James Lloyd Chamberlaine* (1732–1783). CHILDREN. SONS: William (1766–1825), died without progeny, who married Maria (1784–1805), daughter of *James Lloyd* (1745–1820); Philemon (?–by 1822), who married first, Elizabeth (1784–

1808), daughter of *James Lloyd* (1745–1820), and second, in 1813 Ann, daughter of Daniel Fiddeman; Thomas, who married in 1808 Elizabeth (1783–1839), daughter of *James Tilghman, Jr.* (ca. 1748–1796); Alexander, who married first, in 1808 Henrietta Maria (?–1817), daughter of Lloyd Tilghman, and second, Elizabeth Ann, daughter of Francis West, of Philadelphia, Pennsylvania, and wife Mary Nixon; and James, who never married. DAUGHTERS: Mary (1760–1798), buried at "Cloverfields," Queen Anne's County, who married ca. 1782 Joseph Forman, of Chestertown, Kent County; Charlotte (1762–1822), who never married; Anna Maria (?–died young); Sarah, who married Dr. John Irvine Troup; Henrietta Maria (1779–1821), died without progeny, who married Thomas Chamberlaine Earle (1771–?), son of *Richard Tilghman Earle* (1728/29–1788); Anna Maria, who married in 1805 Thomas Emory, of "Poplar Grove," Queen Anne's County; and Juliana, who never married. PRIVATE CAREER. EDUCATION: literate. RELIGIOUS AFFILIATION: Anglican, St. Paul's Parish, Queen Anne's County. SOCIAL STATUS AND ACTIVITIES: Gent., 1759; Esq. at death; one of the five largest subscribers to the endowment of Washington College, Chestertown, Kent County, 1782. OCCUPATIONAL PROFILE: planter; owned two mills, one of which was Wye Mills in Talbot County valued at £450 in 1804; owned a privateer during the Revolution. PUBLIC CAREER. LEGISLATIVE SERVICE: Lower House, Queen Anne's County, 1778 (elected to the 2nd session of the 1777–1778 Assembly, but did not attend); Senate, Eastern Shore, Term of 1776–1781: 1779–1780 (elected on November 9, 1779, to fill vacancy; qualified on November 13, 1779), 1780–1781, Term of 1781–1786: 1784 (elected on December 4, 1784, to fill vacancy; declined to serve on December 9, 1784), Term of 1786–1791: 1786–1787, 1787–1788, 1788 (did not serve), 1789 (did not serve), 1790. OTHER PROVINCIAL/STATE OFFICES: treasurer, Eastern Shore, commissioned 1769 and 1773; 5th Council of Safety, Eastern Shore, 1776–1777 (appointed on December 13, 1776, but declined to serve); Executive Council, 1777 (elected on November 25, 1777, to fill vacancy, but declined to serve); Constitution Ratification Convention, Queen Anne's County, 1788. LOCAL OFFICES: St. Paul's Church Vestry, St. Paul's Parish, Queen Anne's County, in office 1760–1763, 1766–1768, 1772–1779, 1789–1792; churchwarden, St. Paul's Church, St. Paul's Parish, Queen Anne's County, in office 1771; appointed by the Council of Safety to purchase gold and silver coin in Queen Anne's County "to enable Congress to conduct the operations in Canada," 1776; county lieutenant, Queen Anne's County, in office 1777; loan officer, Continental Loan Office, Queen Anne's County, appointed 1777 and 1779; justice, Queen Anne's County, commissioned 1777 and 1778 (did not qualify); justice, Orphans' Court, Queen Anne's County, commissioned 1778 (did not qualify); purchasing agent, Queen Anne's County, appointed 1779; judge, Court of Appeals for Tax Assessment, Queen Anne's County, appointed 1786. MILITARY SERVICE: major, by 1760; colonel, Twentieth Battalion, Queen Anne's County Militia, commissioned 1777. OUT OF STATE SERVICE: delegate, Continental Congress, 1782–1783 (elected on June 15, 1782, to fill vacancy; reelected in November 1782; resigned on May 7, 1783). WEALTH DURING LIFETIME. PERSONAL PROPERTY: 44 slaves, 1776; assessed value £8,182.10.0, including 49 slaves and 142 oz. plate, 1783; 49 slaves, 1798. LAND AT FIRST ELECTION: 3,395 acres in Queen Anne's County and 750 acres in Delaware (formerly Queen Anne's County) (3,331 acres from his brother; 650 acres from his maternal grandfather; 31 acres by patent; 133 acres by purchase). SIGNIFICANT CHANGES IN LAND BETWEEN FIRST ELECTION AND DEATH: sold 650 acres in Caroline County (formerly Queen Anne's County), 1777; owned 2,465 acres in Queen Anne's County, 1783; owned 2,959 acres in Talbot and Queen Anne's counties, 1798 (including 1,309 acres from his sister); by 1804 his son Philemon was assessed as owning 570 acres of his father's land in Talbot County; purchased at least 143 acres in Queen Anne's and Caroline counties between 1803 and 1812; owned 5,451 acres in Green County, Pennsylvania, his part of over 40,000 acres of land that had formerly belonged to Edward Tilghman, and that was held in trust by William Cooke for Hemsley and others, by 1807; sold 754 acres in Delaware (formerly Queen Anne's County), 1808. WEALTH AT DEATH. DIED: on June 5, 1812, at "Cloverfields," Queen Anne's County; buried in the "Cloverfields" cemetery. PERSONAL PROPERTY: TEV, $101,212.79 current money (including 138 slaves, 270 oz. plate, books, 78 shares of stock in the Farmers Bank at Easton, and 10 shares in the Chesapeake and Delaware Canal Company); FB, $90,258.17. LAND: at least 2,289 acres in Queen Anne's, Talbot, and Caroline counties, plus town lots in Washington, D.C., and 5,451 acres in Green County, Pennsylvania.

HENLEY (HENLY), ROBERT (ca. 1617–1684). BORN: ca. 1617, probably in England. IMMI-GRATED: in 1648 as a free adult. RESIDED: in Charles County. MARRIED in 1664 Sarah, widow of Francis Batchelor. CHILDREN. DAUGHTER: Charity, who married first, *John Courts* (1655/56–1702), and second, *John Contee* (?–1708). PRIVATE CAREER. EDUCATION: illiterate. RELIGIOUS AFFILIATION: probably a Protestant. OCCUPATIONAL PROFILE: planter; perhaps some mercantile activity. PUBLIC CAREER. LEGISLATIVE SERVICE: Lower House, Charles County, 1659/60, 1676–1682 (Accounts 1). LOCAL OFFICES: justice, Charles County, 1658–1660, 1672–1684 (quorum, 1676–1684). STANDS ON PUBLIC/PRIVATE ISSUES: probably supported Fendall's Rebellion in 1659/60, which cost him his justiceship and kept him out of public office for a decade. WEALTH DURING LIFETIME. LAND AT FIRST ELECTION: 275 acres in 1660; 875 acres in 1676. WEALTH AT DEATH. DIED: will probated on March 31, 1684. PERSONAL PROPERTY: TEV, £558.2.2 sterling (including 9 slaves and 6 servants). LAND: 875 acres.

HENRY, FRANCIS JENKINS (?–1796). BORN: prior to 1750, probably in Worcester County; second son. NATIVE: third generation. RESIDED: in Buckingham Hundred, Worcester County. FAMILY BACKGROUND. FATHER: *John Henry* (ca. 1714–1781). MOTHER: Dorothy (1725–by 1781), daughter of *John Rider* (1686–1739/40). UNCLE: *Robert Jenkins Henry* (ca. 1712–1766). STEPAUNT: Ann Hicks, who married *Henry Travers* (?–1765). BROTHERS: Charles Rider; Rider; *John Henry, Jr.* (ca. 1750–1798); and Robert. ADDITIONAL COMMENTS: Brothers Charles Rider and Rider may possibly be the same person. SISTERS: Charlotte, who married *William Winder, Jr.* (?–1808); Niturah; Dorothy (Dolly), who married *Isaac Henry* (?–ca. 1802); Nancy; and Sarah. FIRST COUSIN: Ann Billings, who married *Henry Steele* (ca. 1718–1782). OTHER KINSHIP: his great-uncle was *Robert King* (1689–1755); his great-aunt was Eleanor King, daughter of *Robert King* (?–1697), who married *Charles Ballard* (ca. 1670–ca. 1724/25); his second cousin was Mary Elizabeth King (1715–1739), who married *Abraham Barnes* (?–ca. 1778). PRIVATE CAREER. EDUCATION: literate. SOCIAL STATUS AND ACTIVITIES: Gent., 1786. OCCUPATIONAL PROFILE: probably a planter. PUBLIC CAREER. LEGISLATIVE SERVICE: Lower House, Worcester County, 1786–1787, 1787–1788. ADDITIONAL COMMENTS: It is presumed that Francis Jenkins Henry was the full name of the delegate serving in the 1786–1787 Assembly, although the proceedings refer only to "Jenkins Henry." No individual by the name of Jenkins Henry could be identified in Worcester County. LOCAL OFFICE: justice, Worcester County, commissioned 1794 and 1795. WEALTH DURING LIFETIME. PERSONAL PROPERTY: assessed value £1,204.5.0, including 32 slaves, 1783; 50 slaves, 1790. LAND AT FIRST ELECTION: ca. 2,244 acres in Worcester and Dorchester counties (2,008 acres inherited from his father; 236 acres purchased as confiscated British property). WEALTH AT DEATH. DIED: will probated on June 8, 1796, in Worcester County. PERSONAL PROPERTY: TEV, $6,011.14 current money (including 40 slaves and books); FB, $4,453.76. LAND: ca. 2,100 acres in Worcester and Dorchester counties.

HENRY, ISAAC (?–ca. 1802). BORN: of age by 1775; probably eldest son. NATIVE: at least second generation. RESIDED: in Rewastico Hundred, Somerset County. FAMILY BACKGROUND. FATHER: Rev. Hugh Henry (?–1762/63), A.B. in 1748 from the College of New Jersey (later became Princeton University); ordained a Presbyterian minister at Pocomoke Church, Rehobeth, Somerset County, 1751, and resided at Rehobeth from 1751 to 1763; was minister to the following churches, Wicomico Church, Salisbury, Dorchester County; Manokin Church, Princess Anne, Somerset County; and Laurel, Delaware. He died in Rehobeth. STEPFATHER: John Darby, of Dorchester County. MOTHER: Sarah, daughter of *Isaac Handy* (?–1762). UNCLE: *John Handy* (ca. 1724–1756). BROTHERS: James; William Blair; and Hugh. SISTER: Nancy. OTHER KINSHIP: his great-grandfather was *Thomas Dashiell* (1666–ca. 1756); his great-uncle was *George Dashiell* (1690/91–1748). MARRIED by 1781 Dorothy (Dolly), daughter of *John Henry* (ca. 1714–1781); granddaughter of *John Rider* (1686–1739/40); niece of *Robert Jenkins Henry* (ca. 1712–1766). Her brothers were *Francis Jenkins Henry* (?–1796); *John Henry, Jr.* (ca. 1750–1798); Charles Rider; Rider; and Robert. ADDITIONAL COMMENTS: brothers Charles Rider and Rider may possibly be the same person. Her sisters were Charlotte, who married *William Winder, Jr.* (?–1808); Niturah; Nancy; and Sarah. PRIVATE CAREER. EDUCATION: literate. RELIGIOUS AFFILIATION: Presbyterian. SOCIAL STATUS AND ACTIVITIES: Esq., 1793. OCCUPATIONAL PROFILE: planter. PUBLIC CAREER. LEGISLATIVE SERVICE: Lower House, Somerset County, 1779–1780 (Manufactories 2). LOCAL OFFICE: trustee, Washington Academy, Somerset County, 1779–1801. WEALTH DURING LIFETIME. PERSONAL PROPERTY: assessed value £679.5.0, including 22 slaves and 15 oz. plate, 1783; assessed value £575.0.0,

including 21 slaves and 7 oz. plate, 1793. LAND AT FIRST ELECTION: 253 acres in Somerset County (all inherited from his father). SIGNIFICANT CHANGES IN LAND BETWEEN FIRST ELECTION AND DEATH: resurveyed inherited lands and some purchased lands into 1 tract of 464 acres in Somerset County, 1786. WEALTH AT DEATH. DIED: between October 1801 and November 17, 1802. PERSONAL PROPERTY: TEV, $3,314.92 current money (including 15 slaves, 20 oz. plate, law books, and "English books"); FB, $1,151.55. LAND: at least 420 acres in Somerset County.

HENRY, JOHN (ca. 1714–1781). BORN: between 1713 and 1715 in Somerset County; second son. NATIVE: second generation. RESIDED: in Worcester County; Dorchester County, by 1765; Somerset County. FAMILY BACKGROUND. FATHER: Rev. John Henry (?–1717), who immigrated from Ireland in 1710; resided in Pocomoke, Somerset County; a Presbyterian minister of Pocomoke Church, Somerset County from 1710 to 1717. GUARDIAN: *Robert King* (1689–1755). STEPFATHER AND GUARDIAN: Rev. John Hampton (?–1721/22), Presbyterian minister of Snow Hill Church, Somerset County from 1707 to 1718, Pitts Creek Church, Somerset County from 1709 to 1717, Pocomoke Church, Somerset County from 1717 to 1722. Rev. Hampton left his wife, Mary, his entire estate in America and one-third of his estate in Europe. MOTHER: Mary (1674–1744), widow of *Francis Jenkins* (ca. 1650–1710); daughter of *Robert King* (?–1697). UNCLE: *Robert King* (1689–1755). AUNT: Eleanor King, who married *Charles Ballard* (ca. 1670–ca. 1724/25). BROTHER: *Robert Jenkins Henry* (ca. 1712–1766). SISTER: (first name unknown) (?–1722). FIRST COUSIN: Mary Elizabeth King (1715–1739), who married *Abraham Barnes* (?–ca. 1778). MARRIED Dorothy (1725–by 1781), daughter of *John Rider* (1686–1739/40); stepdaughter of Mary Hooper Hicks; granddaughter of Capt. *Thomas Hicks* (1659–1722); stepgranddaughter of *Henry Hooper* (ca. 1643–1720); niece of both *Henry Hooper* (ca. 1687–1767) and Ann Hooper, who married *John Broome* (1676–ca. 1738/39); half niece of both Mary Hooper (1674–1745), who married *Henry Ennalls* (1675–1734) and Elizabeth Hooper, who married *Matthew Travers* (ca. 1672–1742). Her brothers were John (1708–1733); Charles (1716–1741); and Hutchins (1718–1732). Her sisters were Ann; Sarah. Her stepsister was Ann Hicks, who married *Henry Travers* (?–1765). Her niece was Ann Billings, who married *Henry Steele* (ca. 1718–1782). Her other relatives included great-grandfather *Charles Hutchins* (?–1700); half first cousin *Henry Travers* (?–1765); and step-first cousin *Henry Hooper, Jr.* (ca. 1727–1790). CHILDREN. SONS: Charles Rider; Rider; *Francis Jenkins Henry* (?–1796); *John Henry, Jr.* (ca. 1750–1798); and Robert. ADDITIONAL COMMENTS: brothers Charles Rider and Rider may possibly be the same person. DAUGHTERS: Charlotte, who married *William Winder, Jr.* (?–1808); Niturah; Dorothy (Dolly), who married *Isaac Henry* (?–ca. 1802); Nancy; and Sarah. PRIVATE CAREER. EDUCATION: literate; his father's will requested that his guardian provide him with a "genteel education." RELIGIOUS AFFILIATION: his father and stepfather were both Presbyterian ministers; his wife's family and his son are buried at Christ Church graveyard (Anglican), Cambridge, Dorchester County. OCCUPATIONAL PROFILE: merchant, in partnership with *Henry Steele* (ca. 1718–1782). PUBLIC CAREER. LEGISLAIVE SERVICE: Lower House, Worcester County, 1744, 1745 (Bills of Credit), 1745/46–1748 (Bills of Credit Cv 1, 1–3, 4), 1749–1751 (Bills of Credit Cv–3), 1754 (elected to the 6th session of the 1751–1754 Assembly to fill vacancy), 1754–1757 (Bills of Credit 1–6; Accounts 6), 1757–1758 (Bills of Credit 1, Cv, 2), Dorchester County, 1766 (elected to the 3rd session to fill vacancy; Laws to Expire 3). LOCAL OFFICE: justice, Worcester County, in office 1742. MILITARY SERVICE: colonel, by 1749. WEALTH DURING LIFETIME. PERSONAL PROPERTY: inherited one-third of his father's personal estate, including one-half of his historical books, 1717; his wife inherited £700.5.3 current money and 6,091 pounds of tobacco, 1750. LAND AT FIRST ELECTION: at least 1,893 acres in Worcester County, plus a moiety of a storehouse and a lot in Snow Hill, Worcester County (997 acres, plus the storehouse and lot, inherited from his father; 897 acres purchased from his brother). His mother retained the use and occupation of the inherited lands and paid the quitrents on them until her death in 1744. SIGNIFICANT CHANGES IN LAND BETWEEN FIRST ELECTION AND DEATH: obtained an additional 2,670 acres in Dorchester County through his wife's inheritance, by 1750. WEALTH AT DEATH. DIED: will probated on September 13, 1781, in Somerset County. PERSONAL PROPERTY: requested no appraisal of his estate. LAND: ca. 5,700 acres in Dorchester, Somerset, and Worcester counties, and Delaware, plus a moiety of 2 lots in Vienna, Dorchester County.

HENRY, JOHN, JR. (ca. 1750–1798). BORN: ca. 1750 in Dorchester County, probably at his fa-

ther's estate, "Weston" ; third son. NATIVE: third generation. RESIDED: at "Weston," near Vienna, Dorchester County. FAMILY BACKGROUND. FATHER: *John Henry* (ca. 1714–1781). MOTHER: Dorothy (1725–?), daughter of *John Rider* (1686–1739/40) and wife Ann Hicks (ca. 1684–ca. 1733); stepdaughter of Mary Hooper Hicks Rider (?–ca. 1757). UNCLE: *Robert Jenkins Henry* (ca. 1712–1766). BROTHERS: Charles Rider; *Francis Jenkins Henry* (?–1796); Robert; and possibly also Rider (?–by 1787), but he and Charles Rider are probably the same person. SISTERS: Charlotte, who married *William Winder, Jr.* (?–1808); Niturah; Dolly, who married *Isaac Henry* (?–ca. 1802); Nancy; and Sarah. FIRST COUSIN: Ann Billings, who married *Henry Steele* (ca. 1718–1782). OTHER KINSHIP: his stepaunt was Ann Hicks, who married *Henry Travers* (?–1765); his great-grandfather was *Thomas Hicks* (1659–1722); and his great-stepgrandfather was *Henry Hooper* (ca. 1643–1720). MARRIED on March 6, 1787, Margaret (ca. 1766–1789), daughter of John Campbell (?–ca. 1766), of Dorchester County, a merchant, and wife Elizabeth Goldsborough (ca. 1735–ca. 1786); stepdaughter of both *Benson Stainton* (?–ca. 1781) and Richard Kinnard (?–1796); granddaughter of *John Goldsborough* (1711–1778); niece of Mary Goldsborough (1755–1796), who married *Benedict Brice* (1749–1786). Her sister was Ann (?–died young). CHILDREN. SONS: John Campbell (1787–1857), of Hambrooks, Dorchester County, who married in 1808 Mary Nevett (1789–1873), daughter of *James Steele* (ca. 1760–1816); Francis Jenkins (1789–?), who never married. After John Henry died in 1798, the boys' guardian, Levin H. Campbell, sent them to the College of New Jersey (later became Princeton University) to be educated. PRIVATE CAREER. EDUCATION: sent to West Nottingham Academy, Cecil County, under the tutelage of Rev. Samuel Finley, D.D.; graduated from the College of New Jersey (later became Princeton University) ca. 1769; studied law at Middle Temple, London, England, ca. 1769–ca. 1775. RELIGIOUS AFFILIATION: Anglican; his father's family was Presbyterian. SOCIAL STATUS AND ACTIVITIES: Gent., by 1776; Esq. and Hon., by 1789; member of the Robin Hood Club, London, England, which debated the issues of the separation of America and Great Britain, ca. 1769–1775. ADDITIONAL COMMENTS: The Henry estate in Dorchester County, "Weston," was burned by the British in 1780, but it was probably still in the possession of his father, *John Henry* (ca. 1714–1781) at that time. OCCUPATIONAL PROFILE: lawyer, practiced law in Dorchester County and was admitted to the Caroline County Court in September 1775. PUBLIC CAREER. LEGISLATIVE SERVICE: Lower House, Dorchester County, 1777 (Elections 1; Grievances 1, 2), 1777–1778 (Grievances 3), 1778–1779 (elected, but did not attend), 1779–1780 (Grievances 1, 2; Tax Commissioners 1, 2; Elections 2), 1780 (elected to the 1780–1781 Assembly, but did not attend; resigned on December 11, 1780, following his election to the Senate); Senate, Eastern Shore, Term of 1776–1781: 1780 (elected on May 16, 1780 to fill vacancy in the 1779–1780 Assembly; did not serve), 1780–1781 (qualified on December 11, 1780), Term of 1781–1786: 1781–1782, 1782–1783, 1783, 1784, 1785, Term of 1786–1791: 1786–1787, 1787–1788, 1788, 1789 (did not serve), 1790. OTHER STATE OFFICE: governor, 1797–1798 (resigned due to ill health). LOCAL OFFICES: judge, court of appeals, appointed under the Act to Procure Troops for the American Army, Dorchester County, appointed 1778. OUT OF STATE SERVICE: delegate, Continental Congress, 1777–1779 (elected on December 22, 1777, to fill vacancy, but did not attend until January 1778; reelected in November 1778), 1780 (elected on March 31, 1780, to fill vacancy), 1784–1786 (elected on December 17, 1784, to fill vacancy, but did not attend until March 1785; reelected in November 1785); senator, U.S. Congress, 1789–1791, 1791–1793, 1793–1795, 1795–1797, 1797 (resigned on December 10, 1797 to become governor). WEALTH DURING LIFETIME. LAND AT FIRST ELECTION: no acreage found, but father had been a member of the legislature and was land wealthy. SIGNIFICANT CHANGES IN LAND BETWEEN FIRST ELECTION AND DEATH: at least 694 acres in Somerset County inherited from his father, 1781; approximately 1,960 acres in Dorchester and Caroline counties through marriage, 1787; after the deaths of his elder brothers, John inherited at least 1,546 acres in Dorchester County that his father had entailed to his sons. WEALTH AT DEATH. DIED: on December 16, 1798, at "Weston," Dorchester County; retired from governorship one month earlier "due to ill health"; his body was moved to Christ Church Graveyard, Cambridge, Dorchester County, 1908. PERSONAL PROPERTY: size of estate unknown. LAND: at least 4,226 acres in Somerset, Dorchester, and Caroline counties.

HENRY, ROBERT JENKINS (JENCKINS) (ca. 1712–1766).

BORN: ca. 1712 in Somerset County; elder son. NATIVE: second generation. RESIDED: in Somerset County. FAMILY BACKGROUND. FATHER: Rev. John Henry (?–1717), a graduate of the University of Edinburgh, who was ordained by the Presbytery of Dublin, Ireland. He immigrated to the American colonies in 1710 and was a Presbyterian minister of Pocomoke Church in Somerset County from 1710 to 1717. MOTHER: Mary (1674–1744), widow of *Francis Jenkins* (ca. 1650–1710); daughter of *Robert King* (?–1697). She subsequently married ca. 1718 Rev. John Hampton (?–1721/22), a Presbyterian minister of Snow Hill Church from 1707 to 1718, Pitts Creek Church from 1709 to 1717, and Pocomoke Church from 1717 to 1722, all in Somerset County. UNCLE: *Robert King* (1689–1755). AUNT: Eleanor King, who married *Charles Ballard* (ca. 1670–ca. 1724/25). BROTHER: *John Henry* (ca. 1714–1781). SISTER: (first name unknown) (?–1722). FIRST COUSIN: Mary Elizabeth King (1715–1739), who married *Abraham Barnes* (?–ca. 1778). NEPHEWS: *Francis Jenkins Henry* (?–1796); *John Henry, Jr.* (ca. 1750–1798). NIECES: Charlotte Henry, who married *William Winder, Jr.* (?–1808); Dorothy (Dolly) Henry, who married *Isaac Henry* (?–ca. 1802). MARRIED in May 1746 Gertrude (?–ca. 1770), daughter of *John Rousby* (1685–1744); granddaughter of both *Thomas Burford* (?–1686/87) and *John Rousby* (?–1685/86); half niece of both *Walter Smith* (ca. 1693–1748) and Barbara Smith (1693–1764), who married first, *Thomas Holdsworth* (ca. 1692–1718), and second, *Benjamin Mackall* (1675–1761). At the time of their marriage, Gertrude was described as "an agreeable young Lady with a handsome Fortune." Her brother was John (1728–1750/51), who married Ann (1727–1791), daughter of *Peregrine Frisby* (1688–1739). Her stepbrother was *George Plater* (1695–1755). Her sisters were Anne (1721–1769), who married *Edward Lloyd* (1711–1770); Elizabeth, who married *Abraham Barnes* (?–ca. 1778). Her half first cousins were Mary Holdsworth (1713–?), who married *Benson Bond* (1710–1750); Betty Holdsworth 1715–?) who married *James Heighe* (?–1757); *Benjamin Mackall* (ca. 1723–1795); and Barbara Mackall, who married *William Wilkinson* (?–1755). Her nephews were *Edward Lloyd* (1744–1796); *John Barnes* (ca. 1743–1800); and *Richard Barnes* (?–1804). Her nieces were Elizabeth Lloyd (1741/42–?), who married *John Cadwalader* (1741/42–1786); Elizabeth Rousby, who married *George Plater* (1735–1792). CHILDREN. SONS: Robert Jenkins (ca. 1755–?); Edward. DAUGHTERS: Mary King; Ann; Elizabeth; and Gertrude. PRIVATE CAREER. EDUCATION: literate. RELIGIOUS AFFILIATION: Presbyterian. He donated during his lifetime and in his will, the land which the Presbyterian Meeting House and Retiring House occupied in the town of Rehobeth, and also a small quantity of ground around them, so that "they may be forever quietly and peaceably used and without interruptions, as they heretofore have done." OCCUPATIONAL PROFILE: attorney, admitted to the following courts: Somerset County in March 1731/32; Provincial Court in October 1739. Planter; merchant, owner and part owner in several sloops, all of which were captured by the French and taken to Martinique in 1746 while on a voyage from Maryland to the British West Indies. PUBLIC CAREER. LEGISLATIVE SERVICE: Lower House, Somerset County, 1738, 1739–1741 (Laws Cv–3), 1747–1748 (elected to the 3rd session to fill vacancy; Laws 4), 1749–1751 (Laws Cv–3), 1751–1754 (Laws 1–6), 1754–1756 (Laws 1–4; appointed to the Council before the 5th session); Upper House, 1756–1757 (appointed before the 5th session), 1757–1758, 1758–1761, 1762–1763, 1765–1766 (died before the 4th session). OTHER PROVINCIAL OFFICES: justice, Provincial Court, 1746–at least 1756 (quorum, 1754–at least 1756); judge, Assize Court, Eastern Shore, 1747–1766; Council, 1756–1766 (appointed and qualified on May 22, 1756); naval officer, Pocomoke, 1762–1766. LOCAL OFFICES: clerk of Indictments, Somerset County, in office 1732, 1737/38, and 1747; justice, Somerset County, in office 1747; justice, Court of Oyer and Terminer and Gaol Delivery, Somerset County, commissioned 1750, 1753, and 1754. MILITARY SERVICE: captain, by 1735; major, by 1745; colonel, by 1752. STANDS ON PUBLIC/PRIVATE ISSUES: in his will he requested that "my Negros may be treated with Humanity into whosesoever Hands they may Come." WEALTH DURING LIFETIME. LAND AT FIRST ELECTION: 500 acres in Somerset County (all through personal acquisition). He also held title to 1,696 acres in Somerset County and 1,570 acres in North Carolina, all of which he had inherited from his father, but his mother had control of it during her lifetime. SIGNIFICANT CHANGES IN LAND BETWEEN FIRST ELECTION AND DEATH: acquired more than 6,100 acres in Somerset, Worcester, and Calvert counties, and Sussex County, Delaware, and North Carolina, plus lots in Rehobeth, Somerset County (after the death of his mother, he attained possession of the land he had inherited from his father. He also inherited from his mother an additional 909 acres in Somerset County and Sussex County, Delaware, plus lots in Rehobeth, Somerset County. He acquired 976 acres in Calvert County as a result of his marriage in 1746. He also purchased over 1,000 acres in Somerset and Worcester counties between 1740 and 1765). He sold 930 acres in North Carolina by 1764, and

gave 896 acres in Worcester County to his brother *John Henry* (ca. 1714–1781) in 1754. WEALTH AT DEATH. DIED: in October 1766 of the gout in Dorchester County at the house of his brother *John Henry* (ca. 1714–1781) while on his return home from a meeting of the Assize Court. PERSONAL PROPERTY: TEV, £6,797.15.8 current money (including 86 slaves, 1 servant, law books, and other books); FB, £6,247.4.10. LAND: over 3,964 acres in Somerset, Worcester, and Calvert counties, and Sussex County, Delaware, plus lots in Rehobeth, Somerset County.

HERMAN (HERRMAN), CASPARUS AUGUSTUS (1656–1697). BORN: in 1656 in New Amsterdam; second son. IMMIGRATED: in 1661 as a minor with his parents. RESIDED: near New Castle, Pennsylvania, by 1676; resettled in Maryland, ca. 1687; Cecil County. FAMILY BACKGROUND. FATHER: Augustine Herman (1621–1686), born in Prague; moved to Holland, and by 1644 was a factor in New Amsterdam; began preparation of map of Maryland in 1660 for which he received 5,000 acres; immigrated in 1661 with his family and servants, settling on Bohemia Manor, which eventually included 25,000 acres; served as a justice of both Baltimore and Cecil counties. MOTHER: Jane. BROTHER: Ephraim (?–by 1689). SISTERS: Anna Margarita, who married first, *Henry Ward* (?–1683/84), and second, *Matthias Vanderheyden* (?–1729); Judith, who married *John Thompson* (?–1701); and Francina, who married Joseph Wood. MARRIED first, Susanna Huyberts. MARRIED second, in 1682 Anna Reyniers. MARRIED third, Catherine Williams, who subsequently married John Jawort. CHILDREN. SON: *Ephraim Augustus Herman* (1683–1734/35), who married first, Isabella, daughter of Maurice Trent, of Pennsylvania, and second, Araminta. DAUGHTERS: Augustina, who married first, *Thomas Frisby* (1681–ca. 1715/16), second, *Roger Larramore* (?–1721), and third, Henry Rippin; Catherine (1697–?). PRIVATE CAREER. EDUCATION: literate. RELIGIOUS AFFILIATION: Protestant. SOCIAL STATUS AND ACTIVITIES: established a residence on the Delaware River in the vicinity of New Castle, Pennsylvania; carried on commercial activities in New York; on the death of his brother he inherited Bohemia Manor and moved to Maryland by late 1687 or early 1688. OCCUPATIONAL PROFILE: planter; merchant; contractor (built the first State House in Annapolis). PUBLIC CAREER. LEGISLATIVE SERVICE: Lower House, Cecil County, 1694–1696 (died before the 7th session). LOCAL OFFICES: justice, Cecil County, 1687–1697 (quorum, 1688–

1697; president, 1694–1697); North Sassafras Parish Vestry, Cecil County, 1693–1697. MILITARY SERVICE: colonel, 1692–1697. OUT OF COLONY SERVICE: Pennsylvania Assembly, 1683–1685. STANDS ON PUBLIC/PRIVATE ISSUES: opposed the revolution of 1689; accused of treason and popery; did not subscribe to the required oaths as a justice under the new government until August 1691. WEALTH DURING LIFETIME. LAND AT FIRST ELECTION: over 5,000 acres. WEALTH AT DEATH. DIED: by June 1697. PERSONAL PROPERTY: TEV, £1,587.8.1 sterling (including 11 slaves, 1 servant, 2 sloops, and 1 shallop); FB, £412.5.10. LAND: over 9,000 acres.

HERMAN (HERRMAN), EPHRAIM AUGUS-TUS (1683–1734/35). BORN: in 1683 near New Castle, Pennsylvania; only son. IMMIGRATED: in 1687 or early 1688 as a minor with his father from Pennsylvania. RESIDED: on Bohemia Manor, Cecil County. FAMILY BACKGROUND. FATHER: *Casparus Augustus Herman* (1656–1697). STEPFATHER: John Jawort. MOTHER: Anna Reyniers. STEPMOTHER: Catherine Williams. UNCLES: *Henry Ward* (?–1683/84); *Matthias Vanderheyden* (?–1729); and *John Thompson* (?–1701). SISTERS: Augustina, who married first, *Thomas Frisby* (1681–ca. 1715/16), second, *Roger Larramore* (?–1721), and third, Henry Rippin; and Catherine (1697–?). FIRST COUSINS: *Henry Ward* (?–1734); *Richard Thompson* (ca. 1680–by 1775); and *Augustine Thompson* (1691–ca. 1738/39). MARRIED first, by 1714 Isabella (?–1732), daughter of Maurice Trent, of Pennsylvania; stepdaughter of Robert French, of New Castle, Pennsylvania. MARRIED second, Araminta, who subsequently married by 1737 (first name unknown) Young, and finally, by 1742 William Alexander. CHILDREN. SONS: Casparus (?–1732); Ephraim Augustus (1734–1751). DAUGHTERS: Catherine, who married Peter Bouchell; Mary, who married John Lawson (?–1755). PRIVATE CAREER. EDUCATION: literate. RELIGIOUS AFFILIATION: Anglican. SOCIAL STATUS AND ACTIVITIES: second generation burgess and third generation county officeholder; Gent., by 1713. OCCUPATIONAL PROFILE: planter. PUBLIC CAREER. LEGISLATIVE SERVICE: Lower House, Cecil County, 1715, 1716–1718, 1719–1721/22, 1725–1727 (Elections 4), 1728–1731 (Elections 1–5), 1732–1734 (Elections 1–Cv), 1734/35 (elected, but did not serve; died before the 1st session). LOCAL OFFICES: justice, Cecil County, 1714–1721; North Sassafras Parish Vestry, Cecil County, 1716–1722, 1724–1725, 1734–1734/35. MILITARY SERVICE: colonel, 1714. WEALTH DURING LIFETIME. LAND

AT FIRST ELECTION: over 9,000 acres inherited from his father. WEALTH AT DEATH. DIED: by March 20, 1734/35. PERSONAL PROPERTY: TEV, £1,038.15.6 sterling (including 18 slaves); FB, £629.11.1. LAND: over 13,000 acres.

HEUGH (HEUGHES, HEWS, HOUGHES, HUES, HUGH, HUGHE, HUGHES, HUGHS), ANDREW (ca. 1727–ca. 1789). BORN: ca. 1727, probably in Scotland. IMMIGRATED: probably from Scotland. RESIDED: in Lower Potomac Hundred, Frederick County (later became part of Montgomery County). FAMILY BACKGROUND. BROTHER: Charles Heugh, died in Scotland by 1788. MARRIED by 1752 Sarah (1731–1800). CHILDREN. SONS: John (1765–?); Andrew, Jr. (1770–1796). DAUGHTERS: Elizabeth (1755–?); Sarah (1757–?); Ann (1759–?); Margaret (1761–?); Jeane (1764–?); Mary (1768–?); Harriot (1774–?); Christina, who married in 1796 Walter C. Williams; and Martha. PRIVATE CAREER. EDUCATION: literate. RELIGIOUS AFFILIATION: Protestant. SOCIAL STATUS AND ACTIVITIES: Gent., 1773. OCCUPATIONAL PROFILE: merchant. PUBLIC CAREER. LEGISLATIVE SERVICE: Lower House, Frederick County, 1769–1770 (elected to the 2nd session to fill vacancy). LOCAL OFFICES: justice, Frederick County, 1754–at least 1775 (quorum, 1763–at least 1775), Montgomery County, 1787–at least 1788; justice, Court of Oyer and Terminer and Gaol Delivery, Frederick County, commissioned 1765; coroner, Frederick County, commissioned 1773. WEALTH DURING LIFETIME. LAND AT FIRST ELECTION: 489 acres in Frederick County. SIGNIFICANT CHANGES IN LAND BETWEEN FIRST ELECTION AND DEATH: purchased 390 acres in Frederick and Montgomery counties and sold 246 acres in Frederick County, 1769–1773. WEALTH AT DEATH. DIED: between December 22, 1788, and February 10, 1789, in Montgomery County. PERSONAL PROPERTY: requested no appraisal of his estate; his will mentioned 12 slaves. LAND: at least 500 acres in Montgomery County, plus property in Falkirk, Scotland, inherited from his brother and an estate in Scotland inherited from his father.

HICKS, THOMAS (1659–1722). BORN: in 1659, probably in England. IMMIGRATED: by 1678, probably as a free adult. RESIDED: in Dorchester County. MARRIED Sarah, daughter of Levin Denwood (ca. 1602–after 1663). Her brothers were Thomas; Luke, and Levin. Her sisters were Elizabeth, who married *Henry Hooper* (ca. 1643–1720); Mary, who married *Roger Woolford* (?–ca. 1701/2); Susanna; and Rebecca. CHILDREN. SONS:

Levin (?–1732), a justice of Dorchester County by 1709, who married Mary (?–1757), daughter of *Henry Hooper* (ca. 1643–1720); Thomas, who married Elizabeth, daughter of *Roger Woolford* (1670–1730). DAUGHTER: Ann (1684–1733), who married *John Rider* (1686–1739/40). PRIVATE CAREER. EDUCATION: literate. RELIGIOUS AFFILIATION: Protestant. SOCIAL STATUS AND ACTIVITIES: no title on earliest appearance in records; Mr., by 1690; his sons held no known provincial office. OCCUPATIONAL PROFILE: planter. PUBLIC CAREER. LEGISLATIVE SERVICE: Lower House, Dorchester County, 1694–1697, 1697/98–1700, 1710–1711 (elected to the 3rd session). OTHER PROVINCIAL OFFICE: justice, Provincial Court, 1704–1707. LOCAL OFFICES: justice, Dorchester County, 1690–1697, 1706–1707 (quorum, 1694–1697, 1706–1707). MILITARY SERVICE: major, by 1698–1722. WEALTH DURING LIFETIME. LAND AT FIRST ELECTION: ca. 944 acres. WEALTH AT DEATH. DIED: will probated on August 6, 1722. PERSONAL PROPERTY: TEV, £722.18.11 (including 11 slaves). LAND: over 1,680 acres.

HICKS, WILLIAM (ca. 1732–?). BORN: ca. 1732 in St. Mary's County. NATIVE: second generation. RESIDED: in St. Mary's County; Whitehaven, Cumberland County, England, by 1749; St. Mary's County, by 1753; Whitehaven, Cumberland County, England, 1759. FAMILY BACKGROUND. FATHER: Capt. John Hicks (?–1753), who immigrated from Whitehaven, Cumberland County, England. He was a sea captain, tobacco planter, and justice of the peace for St. Mary's County by 1730, sheriff for St. Mary's County in 1732, and a judge of the Provincial Court from 1738 to 1742. MOTHER: Ann. BROTHER: George. SISTERS: Mary, who married William Hennor (Kenner?), of Cherry Point, Northumberland County, Virginia; Elizabeth, of England, who married (first name unknown) Hall. MARRIED between 1753 and 1757 Priscilla, daughter of William Hebb (?–1758), of St. Mary's County, and wife Hopewell (?–ca. 1769). Her brother was Vernon. Her sisters were Elizabeth, who married (first name unknown) Wilson; Grace, who married (first name unknown) Gwyther; and Ann, who married Edward Fenwick. CHILDREN. SON: (first name unknown). Possibly other children. PRIVATE CAREER. EDUCATION: educated in Whitehaven, Cumberland County, England. RELIGIOUS AFFILIATION: Anglican; his mother was a Catholic. SOCIAL STATUS AND ACTIVITIES: Esq., by 1759. OCCUPATIONAL PROFILE: a merchant and factor; continued the factorial business of his uncle

in Whitehaven, Cumberland County, England; sent large cargoes of goods to Maryland in return for shipments of tobacco. PUBLIC CAREER. LEGISLATIVE SERVICE: Lower House, St. Mary's County, 1754–1757. OUT OF COLONY SERVICE: high sheriff, Cumberland County, England, 1772; magistrate, Cumberland County, England, period of service unknown. STANDS ON PUBLIC/PRIVATE ISSUES: Hicks left Maryland with his wife and family in 1759 to settle in Whitehaven, Cumberland County, England. He never returned to Maryland. During the Revolution his property in Maryland and Virginia was confiscated and sold. William sent his son to Maryland in 1784 in an unsuccessful attempt to recover what he had lost. WEALTH DURING LIFETIME. PERSONAL PROPERTY: £425.11.6 sterling, plus outstanding debts of approximately £300 sterling as of September 12, 1775, according to his petition concerning his confiscated property. LAND AT FIRST ELECTION: at least 232 acres in St. Mary's County, and 1 lot in Alexandria, Virginia (all inherited from his father and an uncle). SIGNIFICANT CHANGES IN LAND BETWEEN FIRST ELECTION AND DEATH: He acquired 750 acres by deed in St. Mary's County and resurveyed it into a 1,003-acre tract, 1757. Hicks's lands (consisting of 1 lot in Alexandria, Virginia, and 1,055 acres in St. Mary's County) were confiscated and sold during the Revolution. WEALTH AT DEATH. DIED: after 1784, probably in Whitehaven, Cumberland County, England. PERSONAL PROPERTY: size of estate unknown. LAND: probably owned land in England; all land in Maryland and Virginia was confiscated and sold.

HILL, CLEMENT (?–1708). IMMIGRATED: by 1665/66 as a free adult. RESIDED: in St. Mary's County. MARRIED Elizabeth, widow of *Luke Gardiner* (1622–1674); daughter of Richard Hatton; stepdaughter of *Richard Banks* (ca. 1612–ca. 1667); niece of *Thomas Hatton* (?–1654/55). Her brothers were *William Hatton* (?–1712), who married Elizabeth Wilkinson; and Richard, who married by 1674 Ann (1659–?), daughter of *John Price* (ca. 1607–1660/61). Her sisters were Elinor (1642–1725), who married first, *Thomas Brooke* (1632–1676), and second, *Henry Darnall* (ca. 1645–1711); Mary, who married *Zachary Wade* (ca. 1627–1678); and Barbara, who married *James Johnson* (?–?). CHILDREN. STEPSONS: *Richard Gardiner* (?–1687); John Gardiner; Luke Gardiner; and Thomas Gardiner. PRIVATE CAREER. EDUCATION: literate. RELIGIOUS AFFILIATION: Catholic. SOCIAL STATUS AND ACTIVITIES: his marriage brought rapid upward mobility. OCCUPATIONAL

PROFILE: planter. **PUBLIC CAREER.** LEGISLATIVE SERVICE: Lower House, St. Mary's County, 1678–1682 (elected to the 2nd session), 1682–1684 (Accounts 1–3; Laws 3), 1686 (appointed to Council before the 1st session met); Upper House, 1686–1688 (Accounts 2). OTHER PROVINCIAL OFFICES: Board of Deputy Governors, 1685–1689; Council, 1685–1689; justice, Provincial Court, 1685–1689; joint commissary general, 1685–1689; deputy surveyor general, 1685. LOCAL OFFICES: sheriff, St. Mary's County, 1674–1677; justice, St. Mary's County, 1677–1685. STANDS ON PUBLIC/PRIVATE ISSUES: displaced by the revolution of 1689 because as a Catholic he was ineligible to hold public office under the royal government. **WEALTH DURING LIFETIME.** LAND AT FIRST ELECTION: 1,400 acres. **WEALTH AT DEATH.** DIED: will probated in April 1708; named nephew Clement Hill as his heir. PERSONAL PROPERTY: TEV, £568.6.6 sterling (including 7 slaves and 2 servants); FB, £524.8.11. LAND: 2,400 acres.

HILL, EDWARD (?–1663). IMMIGRATED: in 1646 as a free adult from Virginia. RESIDED: briefly in St. Mary's County. ADDITIONAL COMMENTS: in Virginia by 1622; no evidence that he ever established a permanent residence in Maryland, but he was present to preside over a session of the Assembly in 1646. **FAMILY BACKGROUND.** BROTHER: John Hill, a mercer of Lombard Street, London, England. MARRIED (first name unknown), daughter of Richard Boyle, of London, England. CHILDREN. SON: Edward Hill, who served as a burgess and councilor in Virginia. **PUBLIC CAREER.** PROVINCIAL OFFICE: governor, 1646 (appointed by Leonard Calvert on July 30, 1646, but his commission was illegal since Hill was not a councilor). OUT OF COLONY SERVICE: speaker, House of Burgesses, Virginia, 1644, 1645, 1654, 1659; Council, Virginia, 1655, 1660–1663; colonel, by 1654. STANDS ON PUBLIC/PRIVATE ISSUES: much controversy arose over the legality of the Assembly that met during his interim governorship; he was suspended from all of his offices by the Virginia Assembly in 1656 for "crimes and misdemeanors," resulting from the overwhelming defeat of his expedition against the Indians earlier that year. **WEALTH DURING LIFETIME.** LAND AT FIRST ELECTION: patented at least 6,926 acres in Virginia. **WEALTH AT DEATH.** DIED: in 1663; size of estate unknown.

HILL, JOSEPH (ca. 1670–1724). BORN: ca. 1670 in Anne Arundel County; probably first son. NATIVE: second generation. RESIDED: in Anne Arun-

del County. **FAMILY BACKGROUND.** FATHER: *Richard Hill* (ca. 1640–1700). MOTHER: Milcah, widow of *Robert Clarkson* (?–1666). BROTHERS: Richard (1673–1729); Henry. HALF BROTHER: Robert Clarkson. HALF SISTERS: Mary Clarkson, who married first, Thomas Francis, and second, *Samuel Young* (1662–1736); Elizabeth Clarkson. MARRIED never. CHILDREN. Died without progeny. **PRIVATE CAREER.** EDUCATION: literate. RELIGIOUS AFFILIATION: Protestant, probably a nominal Anglican, but his brothers were devout Quakers and he never served on the bench or in the militia. SOCIAL STATUS AND ACTIVITIES: second generation burgess. OCCUPATIONAL PROFILE: planter; merchant. **PUBLIC CAREER.** LEGISLATIVE SERVICE: Lower House, Anne Arundel County, 1704–1707 (Accounts 1–5, probably chairman 5; Elections and Privileges, chairman 4, 5; temporarily dismissed from the 5th session for alleged involvement with a traitor, Richard Clarke, but was exonerated and reseated), 1708A (Accounts, chairman), 1708B–1711 (Accounts 1–4), 1712–1714 (Accounts 1–4, probably chairman 3, 4), 1715 (Accounts, probably chairman), 1716–1718 (Accounts 1–3), 1719–1721/22 (Accounts 1–5, probably chairman), 1722–1723 (Accounts 1, 2; died before the 3rd session). LOCAL OFFICE: St. Anne's Parish Vestry, Anne Arundel County, 1713–1715. STANDS ON PUBLIC/PRIVATE ISSUES: he was often in strong opposition to the executive during his eight terms in the Assembly; called a leader of the "native" party. **WEALTH DURING LIFETIME.** LAND AT FIRST ELECTION: at least 759 acres inherited from his father in 1700; acquired 1,400 acres from his brother, Richard, in 1712. **WEALTH AT DEATH.** DIED: on May 24, 1724. PERSONAL PROPERTY: TEV, £2,653.19.9 (including 22 slaves); FB, £2,161.15.3. LAND: 2,000 acres.

HILL, RICHARD (ca. 1640–1700). BORN: ca. 1640, probably in England. IMMIGRATED: by 1659, possibly as an indentured servant. RESIDED: in Anne Arundel County. **FAMILY BACKGROUND.** SISTER: Abigail Parr, of Worcestershire, England. MARRIED in 1666 Milcah, widow of *Robert Clarkson* (?–1666). CHILDREN. SONS: *Joseph Hill* (ca. 1670–1724); Richard (1673–1729), mayor of Philadelphia, speaker of the Assembly and president of the Council of Pennsylvania, who married in 1700 Hannah, widow of John Delaval and daughter of Thomas Lloyd (both men were councilors in Pennsylvania); Henry, who married Mary (1676–1735), daughter of Levin Denwood (ca. 1648–1726). STEPSON: Robert Clarkson. STEPDAUGHTERS: Mary Clarkson, who married first, Thomas

Francis, and second, *Samuel Young* (1662–1736); Elizabeth Clarkson. PRIVATE CAREER. EDUCATION: literate. RELIGIOUS AFFILIATION: Protestant with Quaker leanings; two of his sons were Quakers. SOCIAL STATUS AND ACTIVITIES: transported by John Cisson, possibly as his servant; became a leading figure in Anne Arundel County, and had one of the most active legislative careers in seventeenth-century Maryland; Gent., by 1675/76. OCCUPATIONAL PROFILE: planter, 1676; ordinary keeper; merchant engaged in trade with England and Guinea. PUBLIC CAREER. LEGISLATIVE SERVICE: Lower House, Anne Arundel County, 1681–1682 (elected to the 3rd session), 1682–1684 (Accounts 2; Laws 3), 1686–1688, 1694–1697 (Laws 3, 5, 8, chairman 5), 1697/98–1700 (Laws 1, 4). OTHER PROVINCIAL OFFICES: special agent to New York to negotiate regarding Indian affairs, 1681; justice, Provincial Court, 1694–1696, 1696–1700 (quorum, 1697–1700; chief justice, 1699–1700); naval officer, Annapolis, 1694–1696; Council, special writ, 1698 (never officially commissioned). LOCAL OFFICE: justice, Anne Arundel County, 1674–1689 (quorum, 1676–1689; president, 1685–1689). MILITARY SERVICE: captain, 1675–1689, 1694–1698; colonel, 1698–1700. STANDS ON PUBLIC/PRIVATE ISSUES: an adamant opponent of the revolution of 1689, he was forced to flee to Virginia; from Virginia he went to England where he testified against rebel government; he was brought back into public office by Gov. Francis Nicholson, who bestowed considerable patronage on him. WEALTH DURING LIFETIME. LAND AT FIRST ELECTION: over 1,700 acres by 1681. WEALTH AT DEATH. DIED: will probated on November 5, 1700. PERSONAL PROPERTY: TEV, £1,103.8.9 sterling (including 9 slaves and 4 servants). LAND: over 1,721 acres.

HINDMAN, JACOB (by 1713–1766). BORN: between 1705 and 1713, probably in Queen Anne's County; only son. NATIVE: second generation. RESIDED: in Dorchester County; Talbot County, ca. 1744. FAMILY BACKGROUND. FATHER: Rev. James Hindman (?–1713), who immigrated from England ca. 1710 and was rector of St. Paul's Parish in Queen Anne's County from May 1710 until death. STEPFATHERS: Hugh Eccleston, Jr. (?–by 1717), son of *Hugh Eccleston* (?–1710/11); *Francis Allen* (?–1745). MOTHER: Mary, daughter of *Jacob Lookerman* (1652–1730) and wife Elinor Ketin; stepdaughter of Dorothy Lookerman. UNCLE: *Govert Lookerman* (ca. 1681–1728). HALF BROTHERS: Moses Allen; *William Allen* (?–1792); and Joseph Allen. STEPBROTHERS: John Allen (?–ca. 1738);

Francis Allen (ca. 1715–?), of Worcester County, a planter who married Mary, the widow of William Brady. SISTER: (first name unknown) (ca. 1713–?). HALF SISTERS: Mary Allen, who married in 1759 Rev. John Rosse, of Snow Hill, Worcester County; Eleanor Allen; and Elizabeth Allen. FIRST COUSIN: Sarah Lookerman (?–by 1745), who married *Joseph Cox Gray* (?–1764). MARRIED on January 29, 1739, Mary (?–1782), daughter of *Henry Trippe* (?–ca. 1723/24); stepdaughter of John Eccleston; granddaughter of *Henry Trippe* (1632–1697/98); stepniece of *John Brooke* (by 1646–1692/93). Her brothers were Edward (?–1772); *Henry Trippe* (?–1744); and John. Her sisters were Sarah (?–1755); Elizabeth, who married second, *Bartholomew Ennalls* (ca. 1700–1783). Her nieces were Mary Emerson Trippe (ca. 1739–1811), who married *Robert Goldsborough IV* (1740–1798); Ann Trippe, who married *John Dickinson* (ca. 1726–1789). CHILDREN. SONS: *James Hindman* (1741–1830); *William Hindman* (1743–1822); Jacob Henderson (?–1781), ordained in 1769, rector of St. Peter's Parish in Talbot County from 1772 to 1780 and Great Choptank Parish in Dorchester County from 1773 to 1783; Edward (?–1781), who married in 1775 Ann, widow of Andrew Mein, of Talbot County, daughter of Rev. Philip Walker (?–1776), of Caroline County; and Col. John (?–by 1794), a physician, who married Esther, daughter of Elizabeth Nicholson. DAUGHTERS: Mary, who drowned at the age of 12; Elizabeth (?–by 1788), who married *William Perry* (1746–1799); and Sarah (?–ca. 1782), who never married. PRIVATE CAREER. EDUCATION: literate. RELIGIOUS AFFILIATION: Anglican, St. Peter's Parish Church, Talbot County; St. Michael's Parish Church, Talbot County. SOCIAL STATUS AND ACTIVITIES: Gent., by 1741; Esq., by 1758. OCCUPATIONAL PROFILE: farmer; planter. PUBLIC CAREER. LEGISLATIVE SERVICE: Lower House, Dorchester County, 1741 (elected to the 3rd session to fill vacancy), 1742–1744. LOCAL OFFICES: sheriff, Dorchester County, 1737–1740, Talbot County, 1745–1748, 1755–1758; St. Michael's Parish Vestry, Talbot County, in office 1745, 1749, 1759, and 1764; justice, Talbot County, 1749–1766. MILITARY SERVICE: captain, by 1741. STANDS ON PUBLIC/PRIVATE ISSUES: as a justice of the peace of Talbot County, Hindman joined the other Talbot County justices in refusing to meet in court to carry out the provisions of the Stamp Act, 1765. WEALTH DURING LIFETIME. LAND AT FIRST ELECTION: 484 acres in Dorchester, Queen Anne's, and Talbot counties (184 acres inherited from his father; 200 acres by purchase). SIGNIFICANT CHANGES IN LAND BE-

TWEEN FIRST ELECTION AND DEATH: acquired 924 acres in Talbot County, between 1742 and 1758; sold 184 acres in Queen Anne's County, 1746. WEALTH AT DEATH. DIED: on September 9, 1766, in Talbot County. PERSONAL PROPERTY: TEV, £2,088.12.8 current money (including 32 slaves, 24 books, and 94 oz. 5 dwt. 21 gr. plate); FB, £807.6.8. LAND: 1,120 acres in Talbot and Dorchester counties.

HINDMAN, JAMES (1741–1830). BORN: on June 20, 1741, in Dorchester County; probably eldest son. NATIVE: third generation. RESIDED: in Talbot County, by 1744; Queen Anne's County, by 1788; Baltimore City, by 1809. FAMILY BACKGROUND. FATHER: *Jacob Hindman* (by 1713–1766), stepson of *Francis Allen* (?–1745). MOTHER: Mary (?–1782), daughter of *Henry Trippe* (?–ca. 1723/24). UNCLE: *Henry Trippe* (?–1744). HALF UNCLE: *William Allen* (?–1792). AUNT: Elizabeth Trippe, who married second, *Bartholomew Ennalls* (ca. 1700–1783). BROTHERS: *William Hindman* (1743–1822); Jacob Henderson (?–1781); Edward (?–1781); and John (?–by 1794). SISTERS: Elizabeth (?–by 1788), who married *William Perry* (1746–1799); Sarah (?–ca. 1782); and Mary (?–died young). FIRST COUSINS: Mary Emerson Trippe (ca. 1739–1811), who married *Robert Goldsborough IV* (1740–1798); Ann Trippe, who married *John Dickinson* (ca. 1726–1789). MARRIED first, ca. 1774 Marian (?–by 1788), of Anne Arundel County, daughter of William Anderson (?–by 1774), of Great Tower Hill, London, England, a merchant, and wife Rebecca Covington Lloyd (1713–ca. 1776); granddaughter of *Edward Lloyd* (1670–1718/19); stepgranddaughter of *James Hollyday* (1696–1747); niece of both *Edward Lloyd* (1711–1770) and *Richard Lloyd* (1717–1786); half niece of *James Hollyday* (1722–1786) and *Henry Hollyday* (ca. 1725–1789). Her brothers were Samuel (?–by 1774), of Great Tower Hill, London, England, a merchant; James (?–ca. 1785), of Queen Anne's County; William (?–by 1788), of Talbot County; and Edward (?–by 1788), of Anne Arundel County. Her sister was Harriet Rebecca, of Talbot County. Her first cousins were *Edward Lloyd* (1744–1796); *James Lloyd* (1745–1820); and Elizabeth Lloyd (1741/42–?), who married *John Cadwalader* (1741/42–1786). MARRIED second, in March 1797 Elizabeth Hamilton. CHILDREN. Probably died without progeny. PRIVATE CAREER. EDUCATION: literate; a subscriber to Washington College, Chestertown, Kent County. SOCIAL STATUS AND ACTIVITIES: Gent., 1774; Esq., 1790. ADDITIONAL COMMENTS: Hindman was said to be "be-

yond sea," ca. 1766, according to a note in his father's will. OCCUPATIONAL PROFILE: planter; merchant; owned a brewery. PUBLIC CAREER. LEGISLATIVE SERVICE: Lower House, Talbot County, 1780–1781 (Claims 1, 2; suspended from the Assembly November 16–29, 1780, for making slanderous statements in public), 1781–1782 (Claims 1, 2), 1782–1783 (Claims 1, 2), 1783 (Elections; Claims; Grievances), 1784 (Claims). ADDITIONAL COMMENTS: On November 16, 1780 the Lower House voted to reprimand and censure Hindman for some remarks he made in public against certain members of the legislature. He said that those who had voted against calling in the state and convention money then in circulation were scoundrels, rascals, and fools, and that the speaker gave his vote from a nod or wink from another member. Hindman apologized to the Lower House and the speaker, but not to the specific members, and he was therefore ordered committed to the custody of the sergeant-at-arms. On November 29, 1780 Hindman was released from custody and permitted to take his seat. OTHER STATE OFFICES: Executive Council, 1777–1778, 1778–1779 (resigned on June 26, 1779), 1786–1787, 1788–1789; treasurer, Eastern Shore, 1777–1778 (resigned). LOCAL OFFICES: Committee of Observation, Talbot County, elected 1775; deputy assistant commissary of purchases for the army, Talbot County, in office by 1779, resigned 1780; justice, Queen Anne's County, 1788–at least 1800, Baltimore County, 1814–at least 1817. JURY SERVICE: jury, Baltimore County, 1811. MILITARY SERVICE: captain, Fourth Independent Company, Talbot County Militia, January 1776; lieutenant colonel, Fifth Maryland Regiment, December 1776; called colonel, by 1778. ADDITIONAL COMMENTS: While Hindman was in command of the Fourth Independent Company of Militia at Oxford, Talbot County, he was ordered by the Talbot County Committee of Observation to arrest some Talbot County legislators who, against the orders of the committee, had boarded Gov. Robert Eden's ship to bid him farewell after he had been ordered to leave the country. STANDS ON PUBLIC/PRIVATE ISSUES: manumitted ten slaves between 1799 and 1801; manumitted one slave in his will. WEALTH DURING LIFETIME. PERSONAL PROPERTY: his first wife's inheritance from her mother was £1,500, ca. 1776; assessed value £263.0.0, including 4 slaves, 1783; 35 slaves, 1790; 31 slaves, 1798; owned a brewery on Philpotts Point, Baltimore City, 1802–1818. LAND AT FIRST ELECTION: 630 acres in Talbot and Dorchester counties (inherited 720 acres from his father, but gave 620 acres of it by deed of gift to his brother William Hindman before his first election; received at least 300 acres by deed of gift from Edward Lloyd, which he then resurveyed). SIGNIFICANT CHANGES IN LAND BETWEEN FIRST ELECTION AND DEATH: purchased 355 acres in Queen Anne's County and sold 530 acres in Talbot County, 1793; sold at least 452 acres in Queen Anne's and Dorchester counties, 1801; bought and sold tracts and lots in Baltimore City and Baltimore County, 1793–1827. WEALTH AT DEATH. DIED: on February 18, 1830, in Baltimore City. PERSONAL PROPERTY: TEV, $75,094.42 (including extensive stockholdings, with at least 881 shares in several banks and road companies, over $10,000 in U.S. government stock issued in 1814 and 1815 bearing 6 percent interest, and $3,700 in city corporate stock bearing 5 percent interest; and at least 4 slaves, 1 of whom he manumitted in his will); FB, $82.13. LAND: 1 dwelling house and a lot on North Calvert Street, Baltimore City. ADDITIONAL COMMENTS: his principal heirs were his nephews Archibald Hindman Campbell, William Hindman Campbell, William Hindman, and Henry Hindman, and his nieces Maria Winchester, Elizabeth Augusta Goodwin, Sophia Campbell, and Elizabeth Barney.

HINDMAN, WILLIAM (1743–1822). BORN: on April 1, 1743, in Dorchester County; second son. NATIVE: third generation. RESIDED: in Talbot County, by 1744. FAMILY BACKGROUND. FATHER: *Jacob Hindman* (by 1713–1766), stepson of *Francis Allen* (?–1745). MOTHER: Mary (?–1782), daughter of *Henry Trippe* (?–ca. 1723/24). UNCLE: *Henry Trippe* (?–1744). HALF UNCLE: *William Allen* (?–1792). AUNT: Elizabeth Trippe, who married second, *Bartholomew Ennalls* (ca. 1700–1783). BROTHERS: *James Hindman* (1741–1830); Jacob Henderson (?–1781); Edward (?–1781); and John (?–by 1794). SISTERS: Elizabeth (?–by 1788), who married *William Perry* (1746–1799); Sarah (?–ca. 1782); and Mary (?–died young). FIRST COUSINS: Mary Emerson Trippe (ca. 1739–1811), who married *Robert Goldsborough IV* (1740–1798); Ann Trippe, who married *John Dickinson* (ca. 1726–1789). MARRIED never. PRIVATE CAREER. EDUCATION: attended the University of Pennsylvania from May 1758 to 1761, but was a nongraduate; entered the Inns of Court, London, England, and graduated in 1765; subscribed to Washington College, Chestertown, Kent County. RELIGIOUS AFFILIATION: Anglican, St. Michael's Parish, Talbot County; Methodist, by 1795; gave land to the trustees for the meetinghouse of the Methodist Episcopal Church, Wye Chapel, to

erect a place of public worship, 1795. SOCIAL STATUS AND ACTIVITIES: Gent., 1771; Esq., 1783; Hon., 1795. OCCUPATIONAL PROFILE: lawyer, admitted to the following courts: Queen Anne's County in June 1765; Somerset County in June 1765; Talbot County in June 1765; Dorchester County by November 1772. Land speculator; planter after he retired from politics, ca. 1801. PUBLIC CAREER. LEGISLATIVE SERVICE: Conventions, Talbot County, 4th, 1775, 5th, 1775; Senate, Eastern Shore, Term of 1776–1781: 1777 (elected on April 12, 1777, to fill vacancy in the 1777 Assembly; qualified on June 17, 1777), 1777–1778, 1778–1779, 1779–1780, 1780–1781, Term of 1781–1786: 1781–1782, 1782–1783, 1783, 1784, 1785 (did not serve), Term of 1791–1796: 1791–1792, 1792, 1793 (resigned on November 15, 1793, after his election to the U.S. Congress), Term of 1796–1801: 1798 (elected on January 12, 1799, to serve during the last week of the 1798 Assembly), 1799, 1800. OTHER STATE OFFICES: treasurer, Eastern Shore, 1775–1777 (resigned); clerk, Eastern Shore branch of the Council of Safety of Maryland, in office 1775; Executive Council, 1789–1790, 1790–1791. LOCAL OFFICES: St. Michael's Parish Vestry, Talbot County, in office 1771–1772, 1773, 1779–1780, 1784–1785; secretary, Committee of Observation, Talbot County, elected 1775; justice, Talbot County, appointed 1778 (did not qualify), 1779; justice, Orphans' Court, Talbot County, appointed 1778 (did not qualify), 1779; board of visitors, Washington College, Chestertown, Kent County, in office 1782; board of visitors, Talbot County School, in office 1783. OUT OF STATE SERVICE: delegate, Continental Congress, 1784–1786 (elected on December 17, 1784, to fill vacancy, but did not attend until February 1785; reelected in November 1785 and December 1786; no record of attendance after November 1786); representative, U.S. Congress, 1793 (elected to fill vacancy; seated on January 30, 1793), 1793–1795, 1795–1797, 1797–1799; senator, U.S. Congress, 1800–1801 (elected to fill vacancy; seated on December 15, 1800), 1801 (reappointed to fill vacancy caused by the failure of the legislature to elect his successor; seated on March 5, 1801). ADDITIONAL COMMENTS: During a heated campaign for a U.S. Senate seat in 1798, Hindman's opponent, *Joshua Seney* (1756–1798), accused him of falling asleep in Congress. STANDS ON PUBLIC/PRIVATE ISSUES: opposed confiscating British property, 1779, 1781; supported Jay's Treaty and the Alien and Sedition Acts; represented the Federalist party in his unsuccessful campaign for the U.S. Senate, 1798. In his will Hindman manumitted all of his slaves giving them the rooms they occupied and the gardens they cultivated. WEALTH DURING LIFETIME. PERSONAL PROPERTY: 39 slaves, 1776; assessed value £1,686.15.0, including 35 slaves and 75 oz. plate, 1783; 61 slaves, 1790; 86 slaves, 1798. LAND AT FIRST ELECTION: 620 acres in Talbot County (inherited 400 acres from his father, but sold it before his first election; received 620 acres as a deed of gift from his brother). SIGNIFICANT CHANGES IN LAND BETWEEN FIRST ELECTION AND DEATH: purchased 2,335 acres of confiscated British property along with *William Perry* (1746–1799) and *Gabriel Duvall* (1752–1844) in 1782 and sold it in 1784; purchased 2,547 acres in Talbot County between 1790 and 1794; sold at least 1,437 acres in Talbot County between 1790 and 1794; sold at least 1,437 acres in Talbot County between 1790 and 1799; resurveyed all of his remaining Talbot County land into one 1,872-acre tract, 1803; sold 714 acres in Talbot County between 1803 and 1813. WEALTH AT DEATH. DIED: on January 19, 1822, at the residence of his brother *James Hindman* (1741–1830) in Baltimore City; interred at St. Paul's Cemetery, Baltimore City. PERSONAL PROPERTY: requested no appraisal of his estate; manumitted all of his slaves; 1 servant was also mentioned in his will. LAND: 1,160 acres in Talbot County. ADDITIONAL COMMENTS: his principal heir was his nephew Henry Hindman.

HOLDSWORTH, THOMAS (ca. 1692–1718). BORN: ca. 1692 in Calvert County; first son. NATIVE: second generation. RESIDED: in Calvert County. FAMILY BACKGROUND. FATHER: Samuel Holdsworth (?–1710/11), who immigrated by 1676, served as a justice of Calvert County from 1696 to 1706, and was a parish vestryman. MOTHER: Rozamond, widow of both Joseph Horsey and *Richard Ladd* (?–ca.1691/92). MARRIED in 1712/13 Barbara (1693–1764), daughter of Richard Smith (?–1714) and wife Barbara Morgan, widow of *John Rousby* (?–1685/86); stepdaughter of Maria Johanna Somerset, widow of Col. Lowther; granddaughter of both *Richard Smith* (?–ca. 1690) and *Henry Morgan* (ca. 1616–1663); niece of *Walter Smith* (?–1711). She subsequently married *Benjamin Mackall* (1675–1761). Her brother was *Walter Smith* (ca. 1693–1748). Her half brothers were Richard Smith; Charles Somerset Smith (1698–1738); and *John Rousby* (1685–1744). Her sisters were Frances (by 1698–by 1714); Susanna (by 1698–by 1714). Her half sisters were Anne, who married William Dankins; Elizabeth, who married William Tom; Gertrude Rousby; and Elizabeth Rousby (1682–1740), who

married Richard Bennett (1667–1749). Her first cousin was Rebecca Smith (1696–1737), who married *Daniel Dulany* (1685–1753); Lucy Smith, who married *Thomas Brooke* (1683–1744); Eleanor Smith, who married *Thomas Addison* (1679–1727); and Ann Smith (1694–1759), who married second, *Thomas Trueman Greenfield* (1682–1733). Her half nieces were Anne Rousby, who married *Edward Lloyd* (1711–1770); Elizabeth Rousby, who married *Abraham Barnes* (?–ca. 1778); and Gertrude Rousby, who married *Robert Jenkins Henry* (ca. 1712–1766). CHILDREN. DAUGHTERS: Mary (1713–?), who married *Benson Bond* (1710–1750); Betty (1715–?), who married *James Heighe* (?–1757); Rebecca, who married Richard Young, son of *Samuel Young* (1662–1736); and Ann, who married John Bond. PRIVATE CAREER. EDUCATION: literate. RELIGIOUS AFFILIATION: Anglican. OCCUPATIONAL PROFILE: planter; merchant. PUBLIC CAREER. LEGISLATIVE SERVICE: Lower House, Calvert County, 1715. LOCAL OFFICE: justice, Calvert County, 1714/15–still sitting in 1715. WEALTH DURING LIFETIME. LAND AT FIRST ELECTION: ca. 750 acres. WEALTH AT DEATH. DIED: administration bond dated December 15, 1718. PERSONAL PROPERTY: TEV, £2,467.10.10 (including 50 slaves); FB, £2,167.11.10. LAND: 2,065 acres.

HOLLAND, FRANCIS (ca. 1745–1795). BORN: ca. 1745 in Baltimore County; elder child, only son. NATIVE: at least fourth generation. RESIDED: in Spesutia Hundred, Harford County. FAMILY BACKGROUND. FATHER: Francis Holland, Gent. (1719–1746/47), of Baltimore County; son of Francis Holland and wife Susannah. STEPFATHER: John Hall (1722–1768), of Swantown, Baltimore County. MOTHER: Cordelia. STEPUNCLE: *Aquila Hall* (1727–1779). SISTER: Frances (ca. 1747–?), who married Thomas Gassaway Howard, brother of *John Beale Howard* (by 1739–1799). HALF SISTER: Susannah Hall, who married *James Heath* (?–1766). OTHER KINSHIP: his great-grandfather was *William Holland* (?–1732). MARRIED by 1776 Hannah (ca. 1751–?). CHILDREN. SONS: Francis Utie (ca. 1771–?), who married Syball, daughter of *William West* (1739–1791); John (ca. 1773–by 1795); Thomas; and Robert. PRIVATE CAREER. EDUCATION: literate. RELIGIOUS AFFILIATION: Anglican, St. George's Parish and St. John's Parish, Harford County. SOCIAL STATUS AND ACTIVITIES: Gent., by 1769. OCCUPATIONAL PROFILE: planter; merchant in the firm of Holland & Cowan with a warehouse and shipyard in the 1780s. The property of Holland & Cowan was valued at £386 current money in 1783. **PUBLIC CAREER. LEGISLATIVE SERVICE:** Conventions, Harford County, 3rd, 1774, 4th, 1775, 5th, 1775. **LOCAL OFFICES:** St. George's Parish Vestry, Harford County, in office 1769, 1770, 1772; Committee of Observation, Harford County, elected 1775; justice, Harford County, appointed 1777, 1778 (did not qualify). **MILITARY SERVICE:** enrolled in Josias Carvil Hall's First Company, Harford County Militia, 1775; captain, Harford County Company, Flying Camp, 1776; colonel, 1779. **STANDS ON PUBLIC/PRIVATE ISSUES:** signed the Bush Declaration on March 22, 1775. Holland manumitted four slaves in 1794 and sold two more to his son in 1795, with the stipulations that they not be sold unwillingly out of the state and that they be freed in seven years. His will provided that the remainder of his slaves twenty-five years of age or above be manumitted one year after his death. **WEALTH DURING LIFETIME. PERSONAL PROPERTY:** 8 slaves and 2 servants, 1776; assessed value £1,026.5.0, including 15 slaves and 80 oz. plate, 1783. **LAND AT FIRST ELECTION:** 2,367 acres in Harford County (at least 2,300 acres inherited from his father, 1746/47). **SIGNIFICANT CHANGES IN LAND BETWEEN FIRST ELECTION AND DEATH:** purchased 321 acres in Harford County in 1775. Sold the 2,300-acre tract in Harford County in 1779 and the 321-acre plantation before 1787. Acquired 500 acres in Harford County before 1793, possibly through his marriage. **WEALTH AT DEATH. DIED:** buried on August 14, 1795, in St. John's Parish, Harford County. **PERSONAL PROPERTY:** TEV, at least £931.7.11 current money (including 18 slaves, 12 oz. plate, and more than 3 books). **LAND:** probably 500 acres in Harford County.

HOLLAND, NEHEMIAH (?–1788). **BORN:** in Somerset County, of age by 1751; eldest son. **NATIVE:** fourth generation. **RESIDED:** in Worcester County. **FAMILY BACKGROUND. FATHER:** Nehemiah Holland (?–by 1760), of Worcester County; a planter; son of Nehemiah Holland (?–1721) and wife (first name unknown) Idolet. **STEPMOTHER:** Ann. **BROTHERS:** Thomas; William. **HALF BROTHER:** Benjamin. **SISTERS:** Sarah, who married (first name unknown) Tarr; Tabitha, who married (first name unknown) Price; Bridget, who married (first name unknown) Johnson; Betty, who married (first name unknown) Moore. **ADDITIONAL COMMENTS:** Nehemiah was either the nephew, father, brother, or first cousin of *William Holland* (identity questionable). **MARRIED** by 1771 Scarborough (?–1814), who subsequently married *Peter Chaille* (?–1802). **CHILDREN. SONS:** John; William;

Nehemiah; Thomas; and Peter. **DAUGHTER:** Anne. **PRIVATE CAREER. EDUCATION:** literate. **RELIGIOUS AFFILIATION:** Protestant. **SOCIAL STATUS AND ACTIVITIES:** Esq., 1774. **OCCUPATIONAL PROFILE:** planter. **PUBLIC CAREER. LEGISLATIVE SERVICE:** Lower House, Worcester County, 1771, 1773–1774; Convention, Worcester County, 3rd, 1774; Lower House, Worcester County, 1777–1778 (resigned on March 14, 1778, because of pains in his limbs which were "at times violent"), 1779–1780 (resigned on June 17, 1780), 1782–1783, 1783. **LOCAL OFFICES:** justice, Worcester County, 1768–at least 1785 (quorum, 1773–at least 1785); justice, Orphans' Court, Worcester County, 1777–at least 1785; subscription officer, Continental Loan Office, Worcester County, commissioned 1779. **WEALTH DURING LIFETIME. PERSONAL PROPERTY:** inherited 4 slaves, personalty, and £30 current money from his uncle William Holland, Gent., 1752. **LAND AT FIRST ELECTION:** 518 acres in Worcester County (186 acres inherited from his father; 332 acres by purchase and patent). **SIGNIFICANT CHANGES IN LAND BETWEEN FIRST ELECTION AND DEATH:** purchased and patented more than 629 acres in Worcester County, 1771–1788. **WEALTH AT DEATH. DIED:** will probated on June 20, 1788, in Worcester County. **PERSONAL PROPERTY:** requested no appraisal of his estate. **LAND:** more than 1,147 acres in Worcester County.

HOLLAND, WILLIAM (identity questionable). **PUBLIC CAREER. LEGISLATIVE SERVICE:** Lower House, Worcester County, 1778 (elected to the 2nd session to fill vacancy; election voided on April 6, 1778; reelected to the 3rd session, but did not attend). **IDENTIFICATION PROBLEMS.** There are at least five William Hollands in Worcester County of age in 1777: William Holland (ca. 1707–1786), son of Nehemiah Holland (?–1721) and uncle of *Nehemiah Holland* (?–1788); William Holland (probably ca. 1735–?), son of Nehemiah Holland (?–1760) and brother of *Nehemiah Holland* (?–1788); William Holland (probably ca. 1735–after 1786), son of William Holland (ca. 1707–1786) and first cousin of *Nehemiah Holland* (?–1788); William Holland (probably ca. 1740–?), son of Israel Holland and first cousin of *Nehemiah Holland* (?–1788); and William Holland (probably ca. 1755–after 1788), son of *Nehemiah Holland* (?–1788). There is no information in the legislative proceedings that indicates which of these five men was elected to the Lower House in 1778. The *Maryland Archives* and *Inventory of Maryland State Papers* contain references to a Maj. William Holland who was commissioned a captain in 1777 and a major in 1779 in the Snow Hill Battalion of the Worcester County Militia. Maj. William Holland is listed with his title in the 1790 census for Worcester County and may be the William Holland who died in 1805 (only the administrative bond in the name of Rebecca Holland exists for his estate). Because of his military service, Maj. William Holland would have been ineligible to serve in the legislature. Because of his age, family connections, and wealth, it seems probable that William Holland (probably ca. 1755–after 1788), son of *Nehemiah Holland* (?–1788) was the Maj. Holland and hence not the legislator. William Holland (ca. 1707–1786) probably could be eliminated from consideration for this legislative service because of his age. Even if these two men are assumed not to have served, there are, however, still the three others who could have.

HOLLAND, WILLIAM (?–1732). BORN: of age by 1684. NATIVE: possibly second generation. RESIDED: in Anne Arundel County. FAMILY BACKGROUND. FATHER: possibly William Holland, who was in Maryland in 1669/70. MARRIED first, Margaret, daughter of Francis Holland and wife Margaret. Her brother was Francis Holland, Jr. MARRIED second, by 1724 Elizabeth (1664/65–1739), widow of Col. *Thomas Ennalls* (?–1718); daughter of *Roger Woolford* (?–ca. 1701/2) and wife Mary Denwood. Her brother was *Roger Woolford* (1670–1730). Her sisters were Sarah (1672–by 1730), who married *Govert Lookerman* (ca. 1681–1728); Mary, who married *Henry Hooper* (ca. 1643–1720). CHILDREN. SONS: Francis (1691–?); William (1695–?); and Thomas (?–1742), who married Sarah (1713–1757), daughter of *Thomas Frisby* (1681–ca. 1715/16). DAUGHTERS: Margaret (1701–?); Frances (?–by 1724), who married *Philip Thomas* (1693/94–1762). PRIVATE CAREER. EDUCATION: literate. RELIGIOUS AFFILIATION: Anglican, but he had close ties to Quakers (perhaps a Quaker himself in 1684). SOCIAL STATUS AND ACTIVITIES: Gent., by 1686; called William Holland, Jr., in 1696; a good friend and business associate of Quakers *Richard Harrison* (?–1780) and Samuel Chew. OCCUPATIONAL PROFILE: planter; merchant. PUBLIC CAREER. LEGISLATIVE SERVICE: Lower House, Anne Arundel County, 1701 (Laws 1; appointed to the Council after the 1st session); Upper House, 1701/2–1704 (appointed before the 2nd session), 1704–1707, 1708A, 1708B–1711, 1712–1714, 1715, 1716–1718, 1719–1721/22, 1722–1724, 1725–1727, 1728–1731, 1732 (appointed, but did not serve; died before the 2nd session). OTHER PROVINCIAL OFFICES: Council,

1701–1732 (president, 1722–1728/29); assistant justice, Court of Chancery, 1705–1720; justice, Provincial Court, 1707–1719 (chief justice, 1708–1719); chancellor, 1719/20–1721; naval officer, Patuxent, 1720–1722; commissary general, 1721–1727. LOCAL OFFICES: justice, Anne Arundel County, 1692–1694, 1695–1700 (quorum, 1694–1700); St. James' Parish Vestry, Anne Arundel County, 1695–1703. MILITARY SERVICE: captain, by 1691; lieutenant colonel, by 1701; colonel, by 1716. WEALTH DURING LIFETIME. LAND AT FIRST ELECTION: 1,438 acres. WEALTH AT DEATH. DIED: will probated on October 25, 1732. PERSONAL PROPERTY: TEV, £3,220.12.11 (including 67 slaves and 1 servant). LAND: ca. 3,000 acres.

HOLLINGSWORTH, HENRY (1737–1803). BORN: on September 17, 1737, at Head of Elk, Cecil County; fourth son. NATIVE: third generation. RESIDED: at Elkton, Cecil County. FAMILY BACKGROUND. FATHER: Zebulon Hollingsworth (ca. 1696–1763), of Cecil County, an innholder, a presiding justice of the Cecil County Court, and a vestryman of St. Mary Anne's Parish, Cecil County, in 1743; the son of Henry Hollingsworth (1658–1721) and wife Lydia Atkinson; immigrated in 1712 from Pennsylvania. MOTHER: Ann (?–1740), daughter of *Francis Mauldin* (?–1734/35). STEPMOTHER: Mary (?–1807), daughter of Thomas Jacobs and wife Mary Robinson. UNCLE: *Francis Mauldin* (ca. 1719–1762). AUNT: Fransinah Mauldin, who married Samuel Bayard (1705–1776). BROTHERS: Steven (1730–1740); *Jesse Hollingsworth* (1732/33–1810); Zebulon (1735–?); and Levi (1739–?). HALF BROTHERS: Jacob (1742–1803); Thomas; Stephen (1749–1822), who never married; John; David (1754–1775), who never married; Samuel (1757–?); and William (?–died young). SISTER: Elizabeth (1727/28–?), who married (first name unknown) Veazey. HALF SISTER: Lydia, who married Samuel Wallis. MARRIED first, on November 4, 1769, Sarah Husbands (1748–1775). MARRIED second, by 1786 Jane. CHILDREN. SONS: William (1773–1817), who married first, Ann Black, and second, Margaret Evans; Henry (1790–?), who never married. DAUGHTERS: Mary (1772–1850), who married first, John Gilpin (1765–1808), son of *Joseph Gilpin* (ca. 1727–1790), and second, Frisby Henderson (1767–1845); Hannah (1782–1844), who married James R. Partridge; Betsy (1785–?); and Nancy (1787–?), who married Rev. John Tally. PRIVATE CAREER. EDUCATION: literate. RELIGIOUS AFFILIATION: Anglican. SOCIAL STATUS AND ACTIVITIES: Gent., 1786; Esq., 1793. OCCUPATIONAL PROFILE: a mill owner; a manufacturer of gun barrels and bayonets, he was said to be the first manufacturer of munitions in Maryland. Part owner of a market house, 1783; merchant in Elkton, Cecil County, and partner in a store, 1786; sold land mills, water mills, merchant's mills, and sawmills, 1786; farmer, 1786; owned a saltpeter works in Cecil County. He organized the Cecil Manufacturing Company in Little Elk Creek, Cecil County in 1794, and with nine other partners he built a stone mill in 1796 and purchased 500 acres adjoining the mill site for sheep pasturage to keep the mill supplied with wool. He sold his interest in the company in 1800. PUBLIC CAREER. LEGISLATIVE SERVICE: Lower House, Cecil County, 1789 (elected to session to fill vacancy), 1790, 1791–1792, 1792, 1793, 1794; Senate, Eastern Shore, Term of 1801–1806: 1801, 1802, 1803 (died before the beginning of the Assembly). OTHER STATE OFFICES: commissary, Eastern Shore, in office by 1776; commissioner to auction confiscated British property, in office ca. 1785; Constitution Ratification Convention, Cecil County, 1788. LOCAL OFFICES: churchwarden, North Elk Parish, Cecil County, in office 1764; North Elk Parish Vestry, Cecil County, in office 1779–1783, 1784–1786; appointed to carry out the "act to prohibit for a limited time the exportation of Indian corn etc. by land" 1780; justice, Cecil County, 1789–1803. MILITARY SERVICE: lieutenant colonel, Elk Battalion, Cecil County Militia, by 1776; colonel, Elk Battalion, Cecil County Militia, by 1779–1781. WEALTH DURING LIFETIME. PERSONAL PROPERTY: assessed value £485.0.0, including 8 slaves, 1783. LAND AT FIRST ELECTION: 817 acres in Cecil County, including 389 acres purchased as confiscated British property belonging to *Robert Alexander* (1740–1805) and *Henry Harford* (ca. 1759–1834). Alexander's wife protested the confiscation and sale of her husband's property ca. 1786 and Hollingsworth promised to restore the land should Alexander return to Maryland to claim it. SIGNIFICANT CHANGES IN LAND BETWEEN FIRST ELECTION AND DEATH: acquired 669 additional acres in Cecil County, and sold 4 lots in Elkton, Cecil County, 1794–1797. WEALTH AT DEATH. DIED: on September 29, 1803, in Cecil County. PERSONAL PROPERTY: TEV, $21,380.71 (including 14 slaves and books); FB, estate overpaid $66.42. LAND: over 1,138 acres in Cecil County.

HOLLINGSWORTH, JESSE (1732/33–1810).

BORN: on March 12, 1732/33, in St. Mary Anne's Parish, Cecil County; eldest surviving son. NATIVE: third generation. RESIDED: in Cecil County; Baltimore Town, by 1772. FAMILY BACKGROUND. FATHER: Zebulon Hollingsworth (ca. 1696–1763), of Cecil County, an innholder, a presiding justice of Cecil County Court, and a vestryman of St. Mary Anne's Parish, Cecil County, in 1743; son of Henry Hollingsworth (1658–1721) and wife Lydia Atkinson; immigrated in 1712 from Pennsylvania. MOTHER: Ann (?–1740), daughter of *Francis Mauldin* (?–1734/35). STEPMOTHER: Mary (?–1807), daughter of Thomas Jacobs and wife Mary Robinson. UNCLE: *Francis Mauldin* (ca. 1719–1762). AUNT: Fransinah Mauldin, who married Samuel Bayard (1705–1776). BROTHERS: Steven (1730–1740); Zebulon (1735–?); *Henry Hollingsworth* (1737–1803); and Levi (1739–?). HALF BROTHERS: Jacob (1742–1803); Thomas; Stephen (1749–1822), who never married; John; David (1754–1775), who never married; Samuel (1757–?); and William (?–died young). SISTER: Elizabeth (1727/28–?), who married (first name unknown) Veazey. HALF SISTER: Lydia, who married Samuel Wallis. MARRIED first, ca. 1758 Sinai Ricketts (1737–1786). MARRIED second, in 1790 Rachel Lyde (?–1819), widow of (first name unknown) Parkins; daughter of Lyde Goodwin (1725–1801), a physician, and wife Pleasance Ridgely; granddaughter of *Charles Ridgely* (?–1772); niece of Capt. *Charles Ridgely* (1733–1790), *John Ridgely* (?–1771), and Rachel Ridgely, who married *Darby Lux* (?–1795). Her brothers were William; Lyde. Her sisters were Susannah; Pleasance, who married John Coleman. Her first cousins were *Charles Ridgely, of John* (?–ca. 1787); Deborah Ridgely (?–1817), who married *John Sterett* (1750/51–1787); Mary (?–1804), who married *Benjamin Nicholson* (?–1792); and Prudence Carnan (1755–1822), who married *Harry Dorsey Gough* (ca. 1745–1808). CHILDREN. SONS: Zebulon, associate judge, Sixth District Court, 1806–by 1817, who married in 1790 Elizabeth Ireland; Francis (1773–1826), a merchant and partner in the firm of Hollingsworth & Worthington, who married Mary; John (1771–?), who married Rachel Wilkins. STEPSON: Thomas Parkins (?–1797). DAUGHTERS: Ann, who married in 1792 Rev. Henry Willis; Mary (1760–?), who married in 1781 Capt. Jeremiah Yellott. PRIVATE CAREER. EDUCATION: literate. RELIGIOUS AFFILIATION: Methodist; active in organizing the Methodist Society in Baltimore Town, which built the first Methodist Church in that town in 1775. SOCIAL STATUS AND ACTIVITIES: Esq. at death. OCCUPATIONAL PROFILE: merchant; owned a privateer during the Revolution. PUBLIC CAREER. LEGISLATIVE SERVICE: Lower House, Baltimore Town, 1786–1787 (Claims 1, 2). OTHER STATE OFFICES:

served as agent for the state during the Revolution: procured supplies and vessels, superintended the construction and outfitting of vessels for the Maryland navy, arranged for the transport of troops and supplies, was involved in exporting goods from Baltimore Town for the state. LOCAL OFFICES: commissioner to make roads leading to Baltimore Town, appointed 1774; agent to purchase provisions, Baltimore County, appointed 1778; Board of Commissioners, Baltimore County, in office ca. 1781; councilman (first branch), Baltimore City, elected 1797. WEALTH DURING LIFETIME. PERSONAL PROPERTY: store or warehouse on "Hollingsworth's Wharf," Baltimore Town, which burned in 1794. Built a large brick warehouse at the head of his dock before his death. His marriage contract with Rachel Parkins provided that each partner would hold his or her property individually and choose his or her heirs. LAND AT FIRST ELECTION: at least 456 acres in Washington and Anne Arundel counties, plus 16 lots in Baltimore Town (8 owned outright, 5 held by lease, 3 leased out for ground rent). SIGNIFICANT CHANGES IN LAND BETWEEN FIRST ELECTION AND DEATH: sold his land in Anne Arundel and Washington counties and bought a house and lot in Alexandria, Virginia. During the 1790s he sold or leased out almost all of his lots in Baltimore City, reserving ground rents on at least 4 lots (as well as the leases he already held on 3 others). By the early 1800s he mortgaged or sold additional lots and leases to pay the creditors of his son Zebulon. WEALTH AT DEATH. DIED: will probated on October 6, 1810, in Baltimore City. PERSONAL PROPERTY: included stock in the Bank of Maryland, Bank of Baltimore, Frederick Turnpike Road, Reisterstown and York roads, 2 houses on Calvert Street and 2 houses on East Street, Baltimore City. Requested no appraisal of his estate. LAND: 2 lots in Baltimore City, plus ground rents on 3 more lots in Baltimore City and 1 lot in Baltimore City leased to him; also a house and lot in Alexandria, Virginia.

HOLLYDAY (HOLLIDAY), HENRY (ca. 1725–1789). BORN: on March 9, ca. 1725, at "Wye House," Talbot County; younger son. NATIVE: third generation. RESIDED: in Philadelphia, Pennsylvania, ca. 1739; Queen Anne's County, after 1747; "Ratcliffe Manor," Talbot County, by 1768. FAMILY BACKGROUND. FATHER: *James Hollyday* (1696–1747), son of *Thomas Hollyday* (ca. 1661–1702/3). MOTHER: Sarah (1683–1755), widow of *Edward Lloyd* (1670–1718/19); daughter of Nehemiah Covington (?–ca. 1713), of Somerset County,

and wife Rebecca Denwood. AUNTS: Margery Hollyday Covington (?–1764), who married second, *Thomas Gantt* (?–1765); Elizabeth Covington, who married *Benjamin Wailes* (?–ca. 1729); and Priscilla Covington, who married *Robert King* (1689–1755). BROTHER: *James Hollyday* (1722–1786). HALF BROTHERS: Philemon Lloyd (1709–1729); *Edward Lloyd* (1711–1770); James Lloyd (1715–1738); and *Richard Lloyd* (1717–1786). SISTER: Sarah (1727–1729). HALF SISTER: Rebecca Lloyd (1713–ca. 1776). FIRST COUSINS: Mary King (1715–1739), who married *Abraham Barnes* (?–ca. 1778); Elizabeth Hollyday, who married *Francis Lee* (?–1749); and Mary Hollyday, who married *Francis Waring* (1715–1769). MARRIED on December 9, 1748, Anna Maria (ca. 1732–1804), daughter of *George Robins* (1697–1742); stepdaughter of *William Goldsborough* (1709–1760); granddaugher of both *Thomas Robins* (1672–1721) and *Richard Tilghman* (1672/73–1738/39); niece of *William Tilghman* (1711–1782), *Edward Tilghman* (1713–1786), *James Tilghman* (1716–1793), *Matthew Tilghman* (1717/18–1790), Mary Tilghman (1702–1736), who married *James Earle, Jr.* (ca. 1694–1739), and Anna Maria Tilghman (1709–1763), who married first, *William Hemsley* (1703–1736), and second, *Robert Lloyd* (ca. 1712–1770); half niece of Elizabeth Robins (1710–1746), who married *William Goldsborough* (1709–1760). Her brother was Thomas (1740–1762). Her sisters were Margaret (1734–1808), who married *William Hayward* (?–1791); Henrietta Maria (1736–1791), who married *James Lloyd Chamberlaine* (1732–1783); Susanna (1738–?); and Elizabeth (1742–by 1764). Her first cousins were *Richard Tilghman* (1740–1809); *Michael Earle* (1722–1787); *Richard Tilghman Earle* (1728/29–1788); *Peregrine Tilghman* (ca. 1741–1807); *James Tilghman* (1743–1809); *William Tilghman* (1756–1827); *Matthew Tilghman* (1760–ca. 1801); *James Tilghman, Jr.* (ca. 1748–1796); *William Hemsley* (1736/37–1812); Margaret Tilghman (1742–1817), who married *Charles Carroll, Barrister* (1723–1783); Anna Maria Earle (1725–1795), who married *Thomas Ringgold* (1715–1772); Henrietta Maria Earle (1730–1767), who married *William Hemsley* (1736/37–1812); Deborah Lloyd, who married *Peregrine Tilghman* (ca. 1741–1807); Anna Maria Tilghman (?–1817), who married *William Hemsley* (1736/37–1812); and Elizabeth Tilghman, who married *James Lloyd* (1745–1820). Her niece was Henrietta Maria Chamberlaine (?–1804), who married *William Hayward, Jr.* (ca. 1758–1834). CHILDREN. SONS: Henry, who died at age two; *James Hollyday* (1758–1807); Thomas (1760–1823), who never married and suffered from mental illness; and Henry (1771–1850), a lawyer in Easton, Talbot County, lieutenant in the Talbot County Militia in 1799, paymaster of the Eastern Shore Militia in 1812, and Federalist Maryland state senator from the Eastern Shore in 1818, who married in 1798 Ann, daughter of *Richard Bennett Carmichael* (1753–1824). DAUGHTERS: Henrietta Maria (1750–1832), who married *Samuel Chamberlaine* (1742–1811); Sarah (1753–1829), who married in 1812 Henry Nicols, of Baltimore County; Anna Maria (1756–1817), who married *George Gale* (1756–1815); Rebecca (1762–1801), who married *Nicholas Hammond* (1758–1830); Elizabeth (1768–1810), who never married; and Margaret (1774–?), who married Littleton Gale. PRIVATE CAREER. EDUCATION: literate. RELIGIOUS AFFILIATION: Anglican, St. Peter's Parish, Talbot County; probably also a member of St. Michael's Parish, Talbot County. SOCIAL STATUS AND ACTIVITIES: Mr., 1756; Gent., 1784; Esq. at death. OCCUPATIONAL PROFILE: apprenticed to a merchant in Philadelphia, Pennsylvania, at the age of fourteen; farmer; planter; after the ban on importation of salt from British manufacturers prior to the Revolutionary War, Hollyday operated a salt factory on his plantation. PUBLIC CAREER. LEGISLATIVE SERVICE: Lower House, Talbot County, 1765–1766 (Elections 2, 4; Public Offices 2). OTHER PROVINCIAL OFFICE: deputy naval officer, deputy collector, and deputy receiver of sixpence per month of seaman's wages, Oxford, 1746–1747 (resigned). LOCAL OFFICES: sheriff, Queen Anne's County, 1748–1751; deputy commissary, Talbot County, in office 1753–1755; St. Michael's Parish Vestry, Talbot County, elected 1753, 1768, and 1774; farmer of the quitrents, Talbot County, appointed 1755; visitor, Talbot County Free School, in office ca. 1764. MILITARY SERVICE: sergeant, 1746. STANDS ON PUBLIC/PRIVATE ISSUES: during the Revolution Hollyday refused to sign the Association of Freemen or take the Oath of Fidelity to the new government. As a result, he was barred from holding public office and was treble-taxed. WEALTH DURING LIFETIME. PERSONAL PROPERTY: 55 slaves, 1776; assessed value £2,961.0.0, including 77 slaves and 315 oz. plate, Queen Anne's and Talbot counties, 1783. The heavy taxes imposed on Hollyday during the Revolution proved extremely burdensome. In a letter to his brother he wrote that he had "not a single shilling with which to buy supplies for my family. . .they are barefooted; except for the help of my daughter and her husband, many a morning I would have no butter or milk for my family." LAND AT FIRST ELEC-

TION: 2,008 acres in Queen Anne's and Talbot counties (inherited 714 acres from his father and 150 acres from his mother; 1,024 acres acquired through his marriage). SIGNIFICANT CHANGES IN LAND BETWEEN FIRST ELECTION AND DEATH: his wife inherited 800 acres in Talbot County after her mother's death, 1771; owned a total of 2,831 acres in Caroline, Queen Anne's, and Talbot counties, plus lots in Chestertown, Kent County in 1783; inherited 1,088 acres in Queen Anne's County from his brother *James Hollyday* (1722–1786) in 1786. WEALTH AT DEATH. DIED: on November 11, 1789, in Talbot County. PERSONAL PROPERTY: TEV, £18,431.1.3 current money (including 131 slaves, 204 oz. 15 dwt. 5 gr. plate, 269 dwt. 16 gr. gold, and books); FB, £12,505.6.11. LAND: 3,119 acres in Talbot, Queen Anne's, and Caroline counties, plus 1 lot in Chestertown, Kent County, and 1 lot at Talbot County Courthouse (now Easton).

HOLLYDAY (HOLLIDAY), JAMES (1696–1747). BORN: on June 18, 1696, probably in Prince George's County; younger son. NATIVE: second generation. RESIDED: at "Wye House," Talbot County, ca. 1721–1732; London, England, 1733–1736; "Readbourne," Queen Anne's County, 1736 until death. FAMILY BACKGROUND. FATHER: *Thomas Hollyday* (ca. 1661–1702/3). MOTHER: Mary (?–by 1702/3), daughter of Dr. James Trueman and wife Ann Storer. HALF UNCLE: *Adderton Skinner* (ca. 1677–1756). STEPUNCLE: *Robert Skinner* (?–1713). AUNTS: Martha Trueman, who married *Thomas Greenfield* (ca. 1649–1715); Ann Trueman, who married *John Bigger* (ca. 1654–1714). BROTHER: Leonard (1692–1741). SISTER: Margery (?–1764), who married first, Levin Covington (?–1725), and second, *Thomas Gantt* (?–1765). FIRST COUSINS: *Thomas Trueman Greenfield* (1682–1733); Jane Greenfield, who married *Henry Holland Hawkins* (1683–1751). NIECES: Elizabeth Hollyday, who married *Francis Lee* (?–1749); Mary Hollyday, who married *Francis Waring* (1715–1769). MARRIED on May 3, 1721, Sarah (1683–1755), who was born in Somerset County and died in London, England; widow of *Edward Lloyd* (1670–1718/19); daughter of Nehemiah Covington (?–ca. 1713), of Somerset County, and wife Rebecca Denwood. Her brother was Levin, of Prince George's County, who married Margery (?–1764), daughter of *Thomas Hollyday* (ca. 1661–1702/3). Her sisters were Elizabeth, who married *Benjamin Wailes* (?–ca. 1729); Priscilla, who married *Robert King* (1689–1755). Her niece was Mary King (1715–1739), who married *Abraham*

Barnes (?–ca. 1778). CHILDREN. SONS: *James Hollyday* (1722–1786); *Henry Hollyday* (ca. 1725–1789). STEPSONS: Philemon Lloyd (1709–1729); *Edward Lloyd* (1711–1770); James Lloyd (1715–1738); and *Richard Lloyd* (1717–1786). DAUGHTER: Sarah (1727–1729), who died by accidental drowning. STEPDAUGHTER: Rebecca Lloyd (1713–ca. 1776), who married William Anderson, of London, England, a merchant. PRIVATE CAREER. EDUCATION: literate. RELIGIOUS AFFILIATION: Anglican, St. Luke's Parish, Queen Anne's County; his wife was a Quaker. SOCIAL STATUS AND ACTIVITIES: Esq., 1738. OCCUPATIONAL PROFILE: probably a planter; officeholder. PUBLIC CAREER. LEGISLATIVE SERVICE: Lower House, Talbot County, 1725–1727 (Accounts 1–3; Laws 3, 4), 1728–1731 (Accounts 1–5; Elections 1–5); Upper House, 1735/36–1737 (appointed before the convention; did not attend until the 3rd session), 1738, 1739–1741, 1742–1744, 1745, 1745/46–1747 (died before the 2nd convention). ADDITIONAL COMMENTS: in 1726 *Charles Carroll, Sr.* (1702–1782) challenged Hollyday to a duel, which he accepted. Their dispute was over legislation concerning control of the planting, quantity, and quality of tobacco. The Lower House intervened, prevented the duel, and censured them both. OTHER PROVINCIAL OFFICES: treasurer, Eastern Shore, 1727–1747; justice, Provincial Court, 1732–at least 1735 (quorum, 1732–at least 1735); justice, Court of Assize, Eastern Shore, 1732–at least 1734; Council, 1735–1747 (appointed on July 15, 1735, but did not qualify until February 17, 1736/37, having been in Europe since his nomination); naval officer, Oxford, 1737–1747. LOCAL OFFICES: visitor, Talbot County School, in office 1727; justice, Talbot County, 1727–at least 1732 (quorum, 1732); justice, Court of Oyer and Terminer and Gaol Delivery, Talbot County,/appointed 1728; St. Luke's Parish Vestry, Queen Anne's County, elected 1734. MILITARY SERVICE: called "colonel," but no evidence of military service found. WEALTH DURING LIFETIME. LAND AT FIRST ELECTION: 800 acres in Prince George's and Talbot counties (700 acres inherited from his father; 100 acres acquired through his marriage), also controlled 6,163 acres in Talbot and Queen Anne's counties for the heirs of *Edward Lloyd* (1670–1718/19). SIGNIFICANT CHANGES IN LAND BETWEEN FIRST ELECTION AND DEATH: resurveyed the 700 acres he owned at first election in Prince George's County into a 1,069-acre tract, 1729; patented 1,440 acres in Queen Anne's County, 1733; purchased 200 acres in Queen Anne's County between 1734 and 1737. WEALTH AT DEATH. DIED: on October 8, 1747, in Queen Anne's County. PERSONAL PROPERTY: requested no appraisal of his estate. LAND: 2,809 acres in Prince George's, Talbot, and Queen Anne's counties.

HOLLYDAY (HOLLIDAY), JAMES (1722–1786). BORN: on October 30, 1722, at "Wye House," Talbot County; elder son. NATIVE: third generation. RESIDED: in Queen Anne's County; London, England, 1754–1758; "Readbourne," Queen Anne's County, 1758 to death. FAMILY BACKGROUND. FATHER: *James Hollyday* (1696–1747), son of *Thomas Hollyday* (ca. 1661–1702/3). MOTHER: Sarah Covington (1683–1765), widow of *Edward Lloyd* (1670–1718/19); daughter of Nehemiah Covington (?–ca. 1713), of Somerset County, and wife Rebecca Denwood. AUNTS: Margery Hollyday Covington (?–1764), who married second, *Thomas Gantt* (?–1765); Elizabeth Covington, who married *Benjamin Wailes* (?–ca. 1729); and Priscilla Covington, who married *Robert King* (1689–1755). BROTHER: *Henry Hollyday* (ca. 1725–1789). HALF BROTHERS: Philemon Lloyd (1709–1729); *Edward Lloyd* (1711–1770); James Lloyd (1715–1738); and *Richard Lloyd* (1717–1786). SISTER: Sarah (1727–1729). HALF SISTER: Rebecca Lloyd (1713–ca. 1776). FIRST COUSINS: Mary King (1715–1739), who married *Abraham Barnes* (?–ca. 1778); Elizabeth Hollyday, who married *Francis Lee* (?–1749); and Mary Hollyday, who married *Francis Waring* (1715–1769). NEPHEW: *James Hollyday* (1758–1807). NIECES: Henrietta Maria Hollyday (1750–1832), who married *Samuel Chamberlaine* (1742–1811); Anna Maria Hollyday (1756–1817), who married *George Gale* (1756–1815); and Rebecca Hollyday (1762–1801), who married *Nicholas Hammond* (1758–1830). MARRIED never. CHILDREN. Died without progeny. PRIVATE CAREER. EDUCATION: almost certainly trained under *Joshua George* (ca. 1695–1748) as a lawyer; admitted to the Middle Temple in December 1754 and returned to Maryland in 1758. RELIGIOUS AFFILIATION: Anglican. OCCUPATIONAL PROFILE: lawyer, admitted to the following courts: Baltimore County in June 1744; Queen Anne's County in November 1748; Kent County by March 1749/50; Provincial Court in September 1758; Cecil County by November 1759. PUBLIC CAREER. LEGISLATIVE SERVICE: Lower House, Queen Anne's County, 1751–1754 (Laws 1–6), 1762–1763, 1765–1766, 1768–1770 (Grievances 1–3); Conventions, Queen Anne's County, 3rd, 1774, 4th, 1775, 5th, 1775, 6th–8th, 1775–1776. OTHER PROVINCIAL/STATE OFFICES: treasurer, Eastern Shore, appointed 1758 (declined); attorney general, appointed 1763 (declined); 1st Council of Safety, Eastern Shore, 1775; chancellor, appointed 1777 (declined). LOCAL OFFICES: sheriff, Queen Anne's County, 1745–1748. WEALTH DURING LIFETIME. PERSONAL PROPERTY: assessed value £2,690.0.0, including 56 slaves and 365 oz. plate, 1783. LAND AT FIRST ELECTION: 114 acres in Queen Anne's County (96 acres as a gift from his father; 18 acres by purchase). SIGNIFICANT CHANGES IN LAND BETWEEN FIRST ELECTION AND DEATH: purchased 134 acres in Queen Anne's County, 1753; according to the terms of his father's will, James's mother held a life estate in 1,440 acres in Queen Anne's County. When she died in 1755, James and his brother *Henry Hollyday* (ca. 1725–1789) inherited the land, with James's portion being 840 acres. WEALTH AT DEATH. DIED: will probated on November 16, 1786, in Queen Anne's County. Hollyday died from malaria, a disease he had suffered from for years; buried at his home "Readbourne Rectified." PERSONAL PROPERTY: requested no appraisal of his estate; left legacies of over £2,000 current money. LAND: 1,088 acres in Queen Anne's County, plus 1 lot in Chestertown, Kent County, and 1 lot in Havre de Grace, Harford County. ADDITIONAL COMMENTS: his principal heir was his brother *Henry Hollyday* (ca. 1725–1789).

HOLLYDAY (HOLLADAY, HOLLIDAY), JAMES (1758–1807). BORN: on November 1, 1758, probably in Talbot County; eldest surviving son. NATIVE: fourth generation. RESIDED: spent much of his early life with his uncle *James Hollyday* (1722–1786); at "Readbourne," Queen Anne's County, 1779 until death. FAMILY BACKGROUND. FATHER: *Henry Hollyday* (ca. 1725–1789), son of *James Hollyday* (1696–1747). MOTHER: Anna Maria (ca. 1732–1804), daughter of *George Robins* (1697–1742). UNCLE: *James Hollyday* (1722–1786). HALF UNCLES: *Richard Lloyd* (1717–1786); *Edward Lloyd* (1711–1770). AUNTS: Margaret Robins (1734–1808), who married *William Hayward* (?–1791); Henrietta Maria Robins (1736–1791), who married *James Lloyd Chamberlaine* (1732–1783). BROTHERS: Henry, who died at age two; Thomas (1760–1823); and Henry (1771–1850). SISTERS: Henrietta Maria (1750–1832), who married *Samuel Chamberlaine* (1742–1811); Sarah (1753–1829); Anna Maria (1756–1817), who married *George Gale* (1756–1815); Rebecca (1762–1801), who married *Nicholas Hammond* (1758–1830); Elizabeth (1768–1810); and Margaret (1774–?). FIRST COUSIN: Henrietta Maria Chamberlaine (?–1804), who married *William Hayward, Jr.* (ca.

1758–1834). MARRIED in 1790 Susanna (Susan) (1774–1849), daughter of *James Tilghman* (1743–1809); granddaughter of *George Steuart* (1700–ca. 1784); niece of *Peregrine Tilghman* (ca. 1741–1807). Her brothers were George (1771–1792); Frisby (1773–1847). CHILDREN. SONS: James (1792–1832), who went to Louisiana and lost his entire fortune; Henry (1798–1865), who married in 1826 his first cousin Anna Maria Hollyday; George Steuart (1799–1870), who served in the Maryland legislature ca. 1842, and who married in 1825 Caroline Matilda Carvill; Frisby (1801–1821), who went to sea and died of yellow fever; William (1804–1868), who married first, in 1830 Ann Cheston Tilghman (?–1834), and second, in 1837 Louisa Lamar Tilghman, his first wife's half sister; and Richard Tilghman (1806–?), who married Susan Regan. DAUGHTER: Anna Maria Chew (1796–1823), who married Arthur Tilghman Jones. PRIVATE CAREER. EDUCATION: received his early education at the Talbot County Free School. He later entered the Kent County Free School and completed his academic courses when that school became Washington College in 1782; studied law first with his uncle *James Hollyday* (1722–1786), and later under *Thomas Bedingfield Hands* (?–1811). SOCIAL STATUS AND ACTIVITIES: Esq., 1798; fourth generation legislator. OCCUPATIONAL PROFILE: lawyer. PUBLIC CAREER. LEGISLATIVE SERVICE: Lower House, Queen Anne's County, 1788; Senate, Eastern Shore, Term of 1791–1796: 1791–1792, 1792, 1793, 1794 (did not serve), 1795 (did not serve), Term of 1796–1801: 1796, 1797 (did not serve), 1798, 1799 (did not serve), 1800. OTHER STATE OFFICE: Constitution Ratification Convention, Queen Anne's County, 1788. LOCAL OFFICE: associate justice, Second District, Queen Anne's County, appointed January 1791, resigned by October 1791. MILITARY SERVICE: assigned to a company of horse, 1777; lieutenant, Queen Anne's County Militia, by 1794; captain, by 1799. WEALTH DURING LIFETIME. PERSONAL PROPERTY: inherited 18 slaves from his father and all of the law books of his uncle *James Hollyday* (1722–1786), 1789; from ca. 1791 until his death, James controlled the estate of his brother Thomas, who suffered from mental illness and lived with him; 42 slaves, 1798; held stock in the Havre de Grace Company, 1804. LAND AT FIRST ELECTION: 1,088 acres in Queen Anne's County, 1789. This land belonged to his uncle *James Hollyday* (1722–1786), with whom he lived from 1779, but he did not receive actual title to the property until his own father's death in 1789. Managed the 598 acres in Queen Anne's County that belonged to his brother

Thomas's estate. WEALTH AT DEATH. DIED: on January 8, 1807, in Queen Anne's County. PERSONAL PROPERTY: TEV, $17,689.67, as calculated (including 49 slaves, 395 oz. 18 dwt. of silver, and books); FB, $2,516.43, as calculated. LAND: 1,089 acres in Queen Anne's County, plus he had control of 598 acres in Queen Anne's County for his brother Thomas.

HOLLYDAY, THOMAS (ca. 1661–1702/3). BORN: ca. 1661 in Nottinghamshire, England; probably first son. IMMIGRATED: ca. 1678 as a free adult. RESIDED: in Calvert County; "Billingsley," Patuxent Hundred, Prince George's County. FAMILY BACKGROUND. FATHER: probably Thomas Hollyday, a militia captain in Virginia. MARRIED ca. 1690 Mary, daughter of Dr. James Trueman and wife Ann Storer; stepdaughter of Robert Skinner; niece of *Thomas Trueman* (ca. 1625–1685). Her stepbrother was *Robert Skinner* (?–1713). Her half brothers were Clark Skinner: William Skinner; and *Adderton Skinner* (ca. 1677–1756). Her sisters were Martha, who married *Thomas Greenfield* (ca. 1649–1715); Ann, who married *John Bigger* (ca. 1654–1714); and Elizabeth, who married Charles Greene, of Norfolk, England. Her half sister or stepsister was Mary Skinner, who married Joseph Letchworth, son of *Thomas Letchworth* (?–1667). CHILDREN. SONS: *James Hollyday* (1696–1747), who married Sarah, widow of *Edward Lloyd* (1670–1718/19); Col. Leonard (1692–1741), a justice of Prince George's County from 1721 to 1733, who married first, (first name unknown) Smith, and second, Eleanor (ca. 1700–1750), widow of Marsham Waring (?–1732) and daughter of Clement Hill (?–1743) and wife Eleanor Darnall. DAUGHTER: Margery (?–1764), who married first, Levin Covington (?–1725), son of Nehemiah Covington, and second, *Thomas Gantt* (?–1765). PRIVATE CAREER. EDUCATION: literate. RELIGIOUS AFFILIATION: Anglican. SOCIAL STATUS AND ACTIVITIES: descendant of Sir Leonard Hollyday, lord mayor of London, England, in 1605/6; he held no office before his marriage into the prominent Trueman family. OCCUPATIONAL PROFILE: apprentice and factor for the merchant Timothy Keyser upon arrival; planter; a merchant, who was prosecuted in 1696 for violating the Navigation Acts, but he obtained a *nolle prosequi* . PUBLIC CAREER. LEGISLATIVE SERVICE: Lower House, Prince George's County, 1696 (election to the 7th session voided). LOCAL OFFICES: justice, Calvert County, 1690–1696 (quorum, 1692–1696); St. Paul's Parish Vestry, Calvert County, 1693–1702/3; chief justice, Prince George's County,

1696–1702/3. MILITARY SERVICE: captain, 1694–1695/96; lieutenant colonel, 1695/96–1702/3. STANDS ON PUBLIC/PRIVATE ISSUES: probably opposed the Protestant Associators' Revolution in 1689, but accepted an office under the new government in 1690. WEALTH DURING LIFETIME. LAND AT FIRST ELECTION: at least 3,487 acres; his wife's dower was ca. 1,900 acres. WEALTH AT DEATH. DIED: shortly before February 20, 1702/3. PERSONAL PROPERTY: TEV, £1,059.18.5 sterling (including 18 slaves and 2 servants); FB, £743.2.0. LAND: 3,488 acres.

HOLMES, WILLIAM (ca. 1746–1825). BORN: ca. 1746, probably in Frederick County (later became part of Montgomery County); probably eldest son. NATIVE: at least second generation. RESIDED: in Anne Arundel County, probably from at least 1769 until 1778; Montgomery County from at least 1780 until death. FAMILY BACKGROUND. FATHER: John Holmes (?–1778), of Montgomery County. MOTHER: Isabella. BROTHERS: John (?–1797), who married Mary Benson; Basil; Josiah; Ely; and Richard. SISTERS: Nancy; Betsey, who married by 1777 (first name unknown) Estep. MARRIED Eleanor. CHILDREN. SONS: Richard, who married Rebecca, daughter of George Warfield; possibly a second son, William. PRIVATE CAREER. EDUCATION: literate. RELIGIOUS AFFILIATION: Anglican. SOCIAL STATUS AND ACTIVITIES: Gent., 1778; Esq., 1801. OCCUPATIONAL PROFILE: probably a scrivener, by 1769; planter. Occasional moneylender, accepting either land or livestock, crops, and plantation utensils as security. PUBLIC CAREER. LEGISLATIVE SERVICE: Lower House, Montgomery County, 1786–1787, 1787–1788 (Claims 2). OTHER STATE OFFICE: defeated as a candidate for the Constitution Ratification Convention of 1788. LOCAL OFFICES: commissioner of tax, Montgomery County, 1782–at least 1800; justice, Orphans' Court, Montgomery County, appointed 1803. WEALTH DURING LIFETIME. PERSONAL PROPERTY: assessed value £450.0.0, including 8 slaves, 1783; 30 slaves, 1790; assessed value £826.0.0, including 32 slaves and 2.5 oz. plate, 1795; assessed value £983.10.0, including 47 slaves and 2.5 oz. plate, 1796; assessed value £1,314.2.6, including 48 slaves and 1.5 oz. plate, 1801; assessed value £1,181.11.8, including 55 slaves and 77 oz. plate, 1812; assessed value £5,362.3.3, including 89 slaves and 77 oz. plate, 1824. LAND AT FIRST ELECTION: 629 acres in Montgomery County (all by personal acquisition). SIGNIFICANT CHANGES IN LAND BETWEEN FIRST ELECTION AND DEATH: over the next 30 years, Holmes acquired almost 3,600 additional acres in Montgomery County. Most of this land adjoined his previously held 400 acres in Lower Newfoundland Hundred (later became the 5th District) and on it he built a large dwelling house. Although some of the 3,600 acres were acquired through small patents and purchases, Holmes made two major purchases, ca. 900 acres in 1794 and 1,678 acres in 1816. He sold 295 acres in 1816. WEALTH AT DEATH. DIED: buried on August 29, 1825, in Prince George's Parish, Prince George's County; size of estate unknown. LAND: probably ca. 4,000 acres in Montgomery County.

HOMEWOOD, JOHN (?–1682). IMMIGRATED: ca. 1649 as a minor with his father or brother. RESIDED: in Anne Arundel County. FAMILY BACKGROUND. FATHER: possibly James Homewood, a justice of Anne Arundel County in 1650 (or this may have been his brother). BROTHER: Thomas. MARRIED by 1664 Sarah, daughter of *Thomas Meeres* (ca. 1602–ca. 1674). She subsequently married John Bennett. PRIVATE CAREER. EDUCATION: literate. RELIGIOUS AFFILIATION: Quaker. OCCUPATIONAL PROFILE: planter. PUBLIC CAREER. LEGISLATIVE SERVICE: Lower House, Anne Arundel County, 1663–1664, 1676–1682 (Elections and Privileges 2). LOCAL OFFICE: justice, Anne Arundel County, 1674–1679. STANDS ON PUBLIC/PRIVATE ISSUES: active in the 1670s with his fellow Quakers in seeking relief from taking legally required oaths. WEALTH DURING LIFETIME. LAND AT FIRST ELECTION: 470–1,000 acres. WEALTH AT DEATH. DIED: will probated on September 28, 1682. PERSONAL PROPERTY: at least 1 servant. LAND: 1,970 acres.

HOOD, JOHN, JR. (?–ca. 1795). BORN: of age by 1765. NATIVE: fourth generation. RESIDED: in Upper Fork Hundred or Bearground Hundred, Anne Arundel County. FAMILY BACKGROUND. FATHER: John Hood (1712–1786), of Elk Ridge, Anne Arundel County. MOTHER: Elizabeth Shipley (?–1795). MARRIED first, Hannah Poole. MARRIED second, after 1772 Rachel, daughter of Cornelius Howard (1717–1772), of Queen Caroline Parish, Anne Arundel County, and wife Rachel Worthington. Her brothers were Joseph; Thomas Cornelius; and Brice. Her sisters were Elizabeth, who married (first name unknown) Davis; Sarah. MARRIED third, in 1785 Elizabeth (1746–1807), daughter of Henry Gaither (1724–1783), of Montgomery County, and wife Martha Ridgely (?–1797). Her brothers were Beale (?–1839); William; Henry; Ephraim; Gerrard; Benjamin; Daniel; and Freder-

ick. Her sisters were Ann; Deborah; Mary; and Amelia. CHILDREN. SONS: James; Joshua (?–by 1795); John; Benjamin, who married in 1797 Sally Wayman; Thomas; and Henry Gaither. DAUGHTERS: Hannah, who married Jesse Owings; Sarah (1772–1833), who married Walter Tolley Worthington, son of *Samuel Worthington* (1734–1815); and Elizabeth, who married in 1797 Nicholas Merriweather. PRIVATE CAREER. EDUCATION: literate. OCCUPATIONAL PROFILE: planter; farmer, by 1782. Maintained extensive apple orchards. Hood had approximately 1,300 fruit-bearing trees on his and his sons' land at the time of his death. His leases to tenants stipulated that they plant apple trees. PUBLIC CAREER. LEGISLATIVE SERVICE: Conventions, Anne Arundel County, 1st, 1774 (appointed, but did not attend), 2nd, 1774. WEALTH DURING LIFETIME. PERSONAL PROPERTY: assessed value £880.0.0, including 24 slaves and 1.5 oz. plate, 1783. LAND AT FIRST ELECTION: ca. 1,524 acres in Anne Arundel and Baltimore counties (ca. 1,300 acres obtained as gifts from his father). SIGNIFICANT CHANGES IN LAND BETWEEN FIRST ELECTION AND DEATH: as his father's only heir, Hood's lands were closely tied with those of his father. When John Hood, Sr., died in 1786 he devised ca. 3,500 acres to his grandchildren, but since most were minors his son controlled the land. Hood acquired ca. 1,300 acres in Anne Arundel and Baltimore counties by purchase and patent and an additional 221 acres in Hampshire County, Virginia, through his marriage to Elizabeth Gaither. In 1782 he leased some of his land in Baltimore County for £12 per year, and prior to his death he gave ca. 1,100 acres in Baltimore County to two of his sons. WEALTH AT DEATH. DIED: will probated on February 10, 1795, in Anne Arundel County. PERSONAL PROPERTY: TEV, £5,333.11.8 current money (including 12 slaves); FB, £2,316.6.6. LAND: 2,708 acres in Anne Arundel and Baltimore counties.

HOOE, ROBERT TOWNSHEND (ca. 1743–1809). BORN: ca. 1743; second son. NATIVE: at least second generation. RESIDED: in Charles County; Alexandria, Virginia, by 1781. FAMILY BACKGROUND. MOTHER: Tabitha (?–1758), daughter of *Joseph Harrison* (1687–1727) and wife Verlinda. UNCLES: *Richard Harrison* (?–1780); *Joseph Hanson Harrison* (?–1785). BROTHER: Joseph (?–1760). SISTERS: Verlinda Harrison; Mary Townsend; and Sarah (?–1769). PRIVATE CAREER. EDUCATION: literate. OCCUPATIONAL PROFILE: surveyor, 1766; merchant; his firm of Hooe & Harrison, of Alexandria, Virginia, owned privateers during the American Revolution. **PUBLIC CAREER.** LEGISLATIVE SERVICE: Conventions, Charles County, 1st, 1774 (appointed, but did not attend), 2nd, 1774, 4th, 1775, 5th, 1775, 6th–8th, 1775–1776 (Claims 6th; Claims 7th; Claims 8th), 9th, 1776 (Claims). LOCAL OFFICE: deputy surveyor, Charles County, appointed 1766; Committee of Observation, Charles County, elected 1774. MILITARY SERVICE: lieutenant colonel, Twelfth Battalion, 1776; colonel, by 1781. **WEALTH DURING LIFETIME.** LAND AT FIRST ELECTION: ca. 556 acres in Charles County. **WEALTH AT DEATH.** DIED: on March 16, 1809, in Alexandria, Virginia; size of estate unknown.

HOOPER, ENNALLS (?–ca. 1763). BORN: probably of age by 1735. RESIDED: in Dorchester County; Virginia, 1753; apparently returned to Dorchester County sometime in the 1750s. MARRIED by 1739 Mary, daughter of *William Ennalls* (?–1731); ward and niece of Maj. Joseph Ennalls (1702–1759); granddaughter of *Joseph Ennalls* (?–1709); niece of *Bartholomew Ennalls* (ca. 1700–1783), Elizabeth Ennalls (?–by 1739), who married *Charles Goldsborough* (1707–1767), and Mary Ennalls, who married *Henry Hooper* (ca. 1687–1767). Her sisters were Anne (ca. 1729–by 1790), who married *Henry Hooper, Jr.* (ca. 1727–1790); Betty. Her first cousins were *Joseph Ennalls* (ca. 1745–1779); *William Ennalls* (?–1785); *John Ennalls* (by 1746–ca. 1778); *Henry Hooper, Jr.* (ca. 1727–1790); *Robert Goldsborough* (1733–1788); Elinor Ennalls (ca. 1738–1793), who married *Joseph Daffin* (?–1796); and Elizabeth Greenbery Goldsborough (ca. 1731–1820), who married *William Ennalls* (?–1785). Her nephew was *William Ennalls Hooper* (?–1795). **CHILDREN.** SONS: Henry (?–1771); James. DAUGHTERS: Ann; Mary. **PRIVATE CAREER.** EDUCATION: literate. RELIGIOUS AFFILIATION: Anglican, Cambridge Church, Dorchester County. SOCIAL STATUS AND ACTIVITIES: Gent., by 1744. OCCUPATIONAL PROFILE: probably a planter. **PUBLIC CAREER.** LEGISLATIVE SERVICE: Lower House, Dorchester County, 1751–1752 (resigned and left the province before the 3rd session). LOCAL OFFICES: deputy commissary, Dorchester County, in office 1744–1748, 1750–1751; sheriff, Dorchester County, 1746–1749; justice, Dorchester County, 1749–at least 1751. MILITARY SERVICE: major, by 1746; colonel, by 1751. **WEALTH DURING LIFETIME.** PERSONAL PROPERTY: sold 28 slaves, livestock, and all of his implements of household and husbandry, and other personalty to *Henry Hooper, Jr.* (ca. 1727–1790) and Joseph Ennalls in 1752. They were to dispose

of this property to pay the debts Ennalls Hooper owed to various people amounting to £1,062.16.3 current money, plus 70,800 pounds of tobacco. He sold 3 additional slaves and his interest in a church pew, between 1755 and 1757. LAND AT FIRST ELECTION: at least 2,576 acres in Dorchester County (3,660 acres through his marriage, of which 1,184 acres were sold before his first election; 100 acres by patent). SIGNIFICANT CHANGES IN LAND BETWEEN FIRST ELECTION AND DEATH: sold 2,129 acres in Dorchester County between 1753 and 1758; his wife sold 245 acres in Dorchester County, 1762. By 1752, when he gave power of attorney to *Henry Hooper, Jr.* (ca. 1727–1790) and Joseph Ennalls to schedule payment of his debts, he was in financial difficulties. **WEALTH AT DEATH.** DIED: by June 1763, possibly in Dorchester County, probably insolvent. PERSONAL PROPERTY: administration bond was in the amount of £500.0.0 sterling. LAND: 202 acres in Dorchester County, all of which he had leased out for his lifetime.

HOOPER, HENRY (ca. 1643–1720). BORN: ca. 1643, probably in England; probably oldest son. IMMIGRATED: in 1651 as a minor with his parents and three siblings. RESIDED: in Calvert County; Dorchester County, by 1667. **FAMILY BACKGROUND.** FATHER: Henry Hooper (?–ca. 1676), who was illiterate, accorded the title Mr. on arrival and who served as a justice of Calvert County from 1658 to 1661, and was a captain in 1658. MOTHER: Sarah. BROTHERS: Richard (?–1673); Robert. SISTERS: Elizabeth; Sarah. MARRIED first, in 1669 Elizabeth, daughter of Levin Denwood (ca. 1602–after 1663). Her brothers were Thomas; Luke; and Levin. Her sisters were Sarah, who married *Thomas Hicks* (1659–1722); Mary, who married *Roger Woolford* (?–ca. 1701/2); Susanna; and Rebecca. MARRIED second, Mary, daughter of *Roger Woolford* (?–ca. 1701/2). Her brother was *Roger Woolford* (1670–1730). Her sisters were Sarah (1672–by 1730), who married *Govert Lookerman* (ca. 1681–1728); Elizabeth (1664/65–1739), who married first, *Thomas Ennalls* (?–1718), and second, *William Holland* (?–1732). **CHILDREN.** SONS: Richard, who married Anne, daughter of William Dorrington; John (?–1754); Roger, who married (first name unknown) Hicks; *Henry Hooper* (ca. 1687–1767), who married Mary, daughter of *Joseph Ennalls* (?–1709); Thomas; and James (1703–1789). DAUGHTERS: Mary (1674–1745), who married *Henry Ennalls* (1675–1734); Priscilla, who married John Stevens; Elizabeth, who married *Matthew Travers* (ca.

1672–1742); Rebecca, who married John Hudson; Anne (?–1761), who married *John Broome* (1676– ca. 1738/39); Mary (?–ca. 1757), who married first, Levin Hicks (?–ca. 1731), son of *Thomas Hicks* (1659–1722), and second, *John Rider* (1686– 1739/40); Rosannah, who married John Hudson, Quartus (?–1751), son of of *John Hudson* (1653– 1730); and Sarah, who married John Heyward, stepson of *Bartholomew Ennalls* (1643–1688). PRIVATE CAREER. EDUCATION: literate. RELIGIOUS AFFILIATION: Protestant. OCCUPATIONAL PROFILE: planter. PUBLIC CAREER. LEGISLATIVE SERVICE: Lower House, Dorchester County, 1694– 1697. LOCAL OFFICE: justice, Dorchester County, 1669–1697 (quorum, 1690–1697). WEALTH DURING LIFETIME. LAND AT FIRST ELECTION: over 1,600 acres. WEALTH AT DEATH. DIED: will probated on August 30, 1720. PERSONAL PROPERTY: TEV, £598.8.11 current money (including 12 slaves and 1 servant). LAND: 2,481 acres, plus 2 tracts of unspecified acreage.

HOOPER, HENRY (ca. 1687–1767). BORN: ca. 1687 in Dorchester County. NATIVE: third generation. RESIDED: in Dorchester County. FAMILY BACKGROUND. FATHER: *Henry Hooper* (ca. 1643– 1720), who married first, Elizabeth, daughter of Levin Denwood. MOTHER: Mary (1663–1740), daughter of *Roger Woolford* (?–ca. 1701/2). UNCLE: *Roger Woolford* (1670–1730). AUNTS: Elizabeth Woolford (1664–1738), who married first, *Thomas Ennalls* (?–1718), and second, *William Holland* (?–1732); Sarah Woolford (ca. 1672– ?), who married *Govert Lookerman* (ca. 1681– 1728). BROTHERS: Thomas; John (?–1754); Roger; and James (1703–1789). HALF BROTHER: Richard. SISTERS: Anne (?–1761), who married *John Broome* (1676–ca. 1738/39); Mary (?–ca. 1757), who married second, *John Rider* (1686–1739/40); Rosannah; Sarah; Rebecca; and Priscilla. HALF SISTERS: Mary (1674–1745), who married *Henry Ennalls* (1675–1734); Elizabeth, who married *Matthew Travers* (ca. 1672–1742). FIRST COUSINS: *Thomas Woolford* (ca. 1699–ca. 1750/51); Sarah Lookerman (?–by 1745), who married *Joseph Cox Gray* (?–1764); Rosannah Woolford, who married second, *Joseph Cox Gray* (?–1764); and *James Woolford* (ca. 1736–ca. 1783). NEPHEW: *John Brome* (1703–1748). NIECE: Ann Hicks (?–1773), who married *Henry Travers* (?–1765). MARRIED by 1712 Mary, daughter of *Joseph Ennalls* (?–1709) granddaughter of both *Bartholomew Ennalls* (1643– 1688) and *John Brooke* (by 1646–1692/93); niece of *Thomas Ennalls* (?–1718), *Henry Ennalls* (1675–1734), Elizabeth Ennalls, who married *Ro-*

ger Woolford (1670–1730), and Ann Brooke, who married first, *Thomas Cooke* (?–1692/93). Her brothers were *William Ennalls* (?–1731); *Bartholomew Ennalls* (ca. 1700–1783); Thomas (?–1753); Joseph (1702–1759); and Henry (?–1734). Her sister was Elizabeth (?–by 1739), who married *Charles Goldsborough* (1707–1767). Her first cousin was *Thomas Woolford* (ca. 1699–ca. 1750/51). Her nephews were *Joseph Ennalls* (ca. 1745–1779); *William Ennalls* (?–1785); *John Ennalls* (by 1746–ca. 1778); and *Robert Goldsborough* (1733–1788). Her nieces were Elinor Ennalls (ca. 1738–1793), who married *Joseph Daffin* (?–1796); Elizabeth Greenbery Goldsborough (ca. 1731–1820), who married *William Ennalls* (?– 1785); Mary Ennalls, who married *Ennalls Hooper* (?–ca. 1763); and Ann Ennalls (ca. 1729–by 1790), who married *Henry Hooper, Jr.* (ca. 1727–1790). CHILDREN. SON: *Henry Hooper, Jr.* (ca. 1727– 1790). DAUGHTERS: Ann, who married Denwood Hicks; Mary, who married first, Bartholomew Ennalls, and second, Levin Hicks (?–1753). PRIVATE CAREER. EDUCATION: literate. RELIGIOUS AFFILIATION: Anglican, Cambridge Church and Vienna Chapel, Great Choptank Parish, Dorchester County. SOCIAL STATUS AND ACTIVITIES: Gent., by 1733; Esq., by 1738; Hon. at death. ADDITIONAL COMMENTS: In his will Hooper left £10 to the public freeschool in Annapolis. OCCUPATIONAL PROFILE: a mariner, by 1712; planter; attorney, admitted to the following courts: Dorchester County by August 1742; Talbot County in August 1744. PUBLIC CAREER. LEGISLATIVE SERVICE: Lower House, Dorchester County, 1722– 1724 (Elections 1–3), 1725–1727 (Elections 1–3; Laws 3), 1732–1734 (Laws 1–Cv; Accounts Cv), 1734/35–1737 (Laws 1, Cv, 2–4), 1738 (Laws; Arms and Ammunition), 1739–1741 (Laws Cv–3; Arms and Ammunition Cv–3), 1745 (Laws; Arms and Ammunition; Aggrievances), 1745/46–1748 (Laws Cv 1, 1–3, 4; Arms and Ammunition Cv 1, 1–3, 4; Aggrievances Cv 1, 1–3, 4), 1749–1751 (Laws Cv–3; Aggrievances Cv–3; Arms and Ammuntion Cv–3), 1751–1754 (Laws 1–6; Grievances 1–6), 1754–1757 (speaker 1–5; resigned as speaker on September 30, 1756, because of illness; reelected speaker for the 6th session), 1757–1758 (speaker 1, Cv, 2), 1758–1761 (speaker Cv 1, 1, Cv 2, 2, 3, Cv 3), 1762–1763 (speaker 1, 2); Upper House, 1765–1766 (appointed during the 1st session). OTHER PROVINCIAL OFFICES: judge, Assize Court, Eastern Shore, commissioned 1734–1739, 1743, and 1747; justice, Provincial Court, commissioned 1735, 1738, 1741, 1743, 1744, 1747, 1749, and 1766 (chief justice, by 1766); Council, 1765–

1767 (appointed and qualified on September 23, 1765). LOCAL OFFICES: school board, Dorchester County, in office 1723; justice, Dorchester County, in office 1732–1734 (quorum, 1734), 1751–at least 1764 (quorum, 1751–at least 1764); justice, Court of Oyer and Terminer and Gaol Delivery, Dorchester County, commissioned 1738, 1742, 1748, and 1754; clerk of Indictments, Dorchester County, appointed 1744. MILITARY SERVICE: captain, by 1723; colonel, in the militia, by 1744. WEALTH DURING LIFETIME. LAND AT FIRST ELECTION: 2,684 acres in Dorchester and Calvert counties (1,281 acres from his father; 1,403 acres by purchase). SIGNIFICANT CHANGES IN LAND BETWEEN FIRST ELECTION AND DEATH: purchased 600 acres in Dorchester County, 1728; resurveyed several tracts for a net gain of 1,147 acres in Dorchester County, 1739; sold 981 acres in Dorchester County between 1739 and 1748; patented and sold approximately 500 acres in Dorchester County between 1722 and 1767. WEALTH AT DEATH. DIED: on Monday, April 20, 1767, in Dorchester County; on the same day his brick dwelling house burned to the ground and his "Corps sic being then in the house was with much difficulty saved from flames." PERSONAL PROPERTY: TEV, £1,551.16.9 current money, 9,981 pounds of tobacco (including 24 slaves, books, new silver plate from England no weight given, and 64 oz. country plate); FB, £1,440.6.3 current money, 9,085 pounds of tobacco. LAND: at least 2,900 acres in Dorchester County, plus 1 lot in Georgetown, Kent County; plus he possibly still owned 500 acres in Calvert County, which he had inherited from his father.

HOOPER, HENRY, JR. (ca. 1727–1790). BORN: ca. 1727 in Dorchester County; only son. NATIVE: fourth generation. RESIDED: in Transquakin Hundred, Dorchester County. FAMILY BACKGROUND. FATHER: *Henry Hooper* (ca. 1687–1767), son of *Henry Hooper* (ca. 1643–1720). MOTHER: Mary, daughter of *Joseph Ennalls* (?–1709). UNCLES: *William Ennalls* (?–1731); *Bartholomew Ennalls* (ca. 1700–1783). AUNTS: Mary Hooper (?–ca. 1757), who married second, *John Rider* (1686–1739/40); Anne Hooper (?–1761), who married *John Broome* (1676–ca. 1738/39); and Elizabeth Ennalls (?–by 1739), who married *Charles Goldsborough* (1707–1767). HALF AUNTS: Mary Hooper (1674–1745), who married *Henry Ennalls* (1675–1734); Elizabeth Hooper, who married *Matthew Travers* (ca. 1672–1742). SISTERS: Ann; Mary. FIRST COUSINS: *John Brome* (1703–1748); *Robert Goldsborough* (1733–1788); *Joseph Ennalls* (ca. 1745–

1779); *William Ennalls* (?–1785); *John Ennalls* (by 1746–ca. 1778); Ann Hicks (?–1773), who married *Henry Travers* (?–1765); Elizabeth Greenbery Goldsborough (ca. 1731–1820), who married *William Ennalls* (?–1785); Elinor Ennalls (ca. 1738–1793), who married *Joseph Daffin* (?–1796); and Mary Ennalls, who married *Ennalls Hooper* (?–ca. 1763). NIECE: Mary Hicks (ca. 1745–1779), who married *Zachariah Campbell* (?–1777). MARRIED by 1746 his first cousin Ann (ca. 1729–by 1790), daughter of *William Ennalls* (?–1731); ward and niece of Maj. Joseph Ennalls (1702–1759); granddaughter of *Joseph Ennalls* (?–1709); niece of *Bartholomew Ennalls* (ca. 1700–1783), Elizabeth Ennalls (?–by 1739), who married *Charles Goldsborough* (1707–1767), and Mary Ennalls, who married *Henry Hooper* (ca. 1687–1767). Her sisters were Mary, who married *Ennalls Hooper* (?–ca. 1763); Betty. Her first cousins were *Joseph Ennalls* (ca. 1745–1779); *William Ennalls* (?–1785); *John Ennalls* (by 1746–ca. 1778); *Robert Goldsborough* (1733–1788); Elinor Ennalls (ca. 1738–1793), who married *Joseph Daffin* (?–1796); and Elizabeth Greenbery Goldsborough (ca. 1731–1820), who married *William Ennalls* (?–1785). CHILDREN. SONS: *William Ennalls Hooper* (?–1795); Henry, Jr., who married first, Mary Price, and second, in 1783 Mary Ennalls; and Maj. John (?–ca. 1798), who married in 1781 Elizabeth Scott. DAUGHTERS: Mary, who married Denwood Hicks; Sarah (Sally), who married Bartholomew Ennalls; and Anne Elizabeth, who married William Barrow. PRIVATE CAREER. EDUCATION: literate. RELIGIOUS AFFILIATION: Anglican, Cambridge Church and Vienna Chapel, Great Choptank Parish, Dorchester County. SOCIAL STATUS AND ACTIVITIES: Gent., by 1750; Esq., by 1786. OCCUPATIONAL PROFILE: probably a planter. PUBLIC CAREER. LEGISLATIVE SERVICE: Lower House, Dorchester County, 1768–1770 (Grievances 1–3; Public Offices 2, 3; Accounts 3); Conventions, Dorchester County, 1st, 1774, 4th, 1775, 5th, 1775, 6th–8th, 1775–1776; Senate, Eastern Shore, Term of 1776–1781: 1777 (date of election to the 1777 Assembly is unknown, but a "Mr. Hooper" declined to serve on April 12, 1777; identification is assumed); Lower House, Dorchester County, 1780 (elected to the 3rd session of the 1779–1780 Assembly, but did not attend; resigned on June 21, 1780). OTHER STATE OFFICES: 1st Council of Safety, Eastern Shore, 1775; judge, General Court, in office, 1778. LOCAL OFFICES: deputy commissary, Dorchester County, in office 1748–1750; justice, Dorchester County, 1754–at least 1769; county lieutenant, Dorchester County, appointed 1777; militia recruiter, Dorchester County, appointed 1781; trustee for the poor, Dorchester County, in office 1785. MILITARY SERVICE: captain, by 1751; colonel, by 1772; brigadier general, militia, lower Eastern Shore district, 1776–1783. WEALTH DURING LIFETIME. PERSONAL PROPERTY: £720.3.2 current money, and 4,542 pounds of tobacco, a legacy from his father's estate, 1771; 59 slaves, 1776; assessed value £2,510.5.0, including 48 slaves and 189 oz. plate, 1783. LAND AT FIRST ELECTION: approximately 5,990 acres in Dorchester County (at least 1,946 acres from his father; approximately 2,532 acres through his marriage, of which 600 acres were sold before his first election; at least 1,611 acres by purchase and/or patent). SIGNIFICANT CHANGES IN LAND BETWEEN FIRST ELECTION AND DEATH: gave 898 acres in Dorchester County by deed of gift to his son John, 1786. WEALTH AT DEATH. DIED: between September and December 1790 in Dorchester County. PERSONAL PROPERTY: size of estate unknown. LAND: at least 4,491 acres in Dorchester County.

HOOPER, WILLIAM ENNALLS (?–1795). BORN: in Dorchester County, of age by 1781; eldest son. NATIVE: fifth generation. RESIDED: in Dorchester County. FAMILY BACKGROUND. FATHER: *Henry Hooper, Jr.* (ca. 1727–1790), son of *Henry Hooper* (ca. 1687–1767). MOTHER: Ann (ca. 1729–by 1790), daughter of *William Ennalls* (?–1731). AUNT: Mary Ennalls, who married *Ennalls Hooper* (?–ca. 1763). BROTHERS: Henry, Jr.; Maj. John (?–ca. 1798). SISTERS: Mary; Sarah (Sally); and Anne Elizabeth. FIRST COUSIN: Mary Hicks (ca. 1745–1779), who married *Zachariah Campbell* (?–1777). MARRIED by 1783 Sarah (?–1798), daughter of (first name unknown) Ridgway, of Talbot County, and wife Mabel Sherwood (?–1796); stepdaughter of both Risdon Bozman (?–1774) and *Charles Daffin* (?–1794); granddaughter of Phillip Sherwood (?–ca. 1789), of Talbot County. Her brother was William. CHILDREN. SON: Henry. DAUGHTERS: Anne, who married Joseph Sullivane; Sally Ennalls, "Maid of the Oaks," who married in 1811 John W. Henry. Hooper was also the guardian for the children of *Zachariah Campbell* (?–1777), ca. 1783. PRIVATE CAREER. EDUCATION: literate. RELIGIOUS AFFILIATION: Anglican, Great Choptank Parish, Dorchester County. SOCIAL STATUS AND ACTIVITIES: Gent., by 1788; fourth generation legislator. OCCUPATIONAL PROFILE: physician, by 1781. PUBLIC CAREER. LEGISLATIVE SERVICE: Lower House, Dorchester County, 1785, 1786–1787. LOCAL OFFICES: com-

missary for horses, Dorchester County, appointed 1781; justice, Dorchester County, appointed 1791. MILITARY SERVICE: captain, Light Dragoons, Maryland Militia, by 1794. WEALTH DURING LIFETIME. PERSONAL PROPERTY: assessed value £672.16.8, including 14 slaves and 20 oz. plate, 1783; controlled 18 slaves for the heirs of *Zachariah Campbell* (?–1777), 1783. LAND AT FIRST ELECTION: 157 acres in Talbot County (all through his marriage), plus control of 585 acres in Dorchester County for the heirs of *Zachariah Campbell* (?–1777). SIGNIFICANT CHANGES IN LAND BETWEEN FIRST ELECTION AND DEATH: probably inherited approximately 1,200 acres in Dorchester County from his father in 1790, although some of this may have been bequeathed to his sisters; sold 157 acres in Talbot County, 1790; purchased and resurveyed 334 acres in Dorchester County, 1791. WEALTH AT DEATH. DIED: buried on July 24, 1795, in Great Choptank Parish, Dorchester County. PERSONAL PROPERTY: size of estate unknown. LAND: possibly as much as 1,500 acres in Dorchester County.

HOPEWELL, JAMES (?–1817). BORN: after 1756 in St. Mary's County. NATIVE: at least fourth generation. RESIDED: in Harvey Hundred, St. Mary's County. FAMILY BACKGROUND. FATHER: Hugh Hopewell (?–1777). MOTHER: Elizabeth (?–1787). BROTHERS: Hugh (?–1785), eldest son; Thomas (?–1781); and Pollard (?–1796), who married in 1785 Catherine Gaither. SISTERS: Elizabeth, who married (first name unknown) Emery; Ann, who married by 1779 (first name unknown) Hebb. OTHER KINSHIP: his great-grandfather was *Richard Hopewell* (?–ca. 1745); his great-aunt was Ann Hopewell, who married *Thomas Aisquith* (?–1761). MARRIED in 1798 probably Angelina (Ann), daughter of Robert Chesley and wife Maréia, of St. Mary's County. CHILDREN. SON: James Robert. DAUGHTERS: Ann Maréia, who married in 1815 George W. Biscoe; Olivia Caroline; and Henrietta Rebecca. PRIVATE CAREER. RELIGIOUS AFFILIATION: Anglican, St. Andrew's Parish, St. Mary's County. OCCUPATIONAL PROFILE: probably a planter. PUBLIC CAREER. LEGISLATIVE SERVICE: Lower House, St. Mary's County, 1786–1787, 1789, 1791–1792, 1794, 1795, and 1796. LOCAL OFFICES: St. Andrew's Parish Vestry, St. Mary's County, in office 1786–1791, 1793–1796, 1797–1807, 1809–1810, and 1812–1816; churchwarden, St. Andrew's Parish, St. Mary's County, in office 1791–1792; justice, St. Mary's County, 1793–at least 1805; coroner, St. Mary's County, appointed 1798. WEALTH DURING LIFETIME. PERSONAL

PROPERTY: 25 slaves, 1790; assessed value £563.0.0, including 20 slaves and plate, 1793; assessed value £725.0.0., including 24 slaves and 34 oz. plate, 1800; assessed value $822.45, including 27 slaves and 34 oz. plate, 1813. LAND AT FIRST ELECTION: ca. 319 acres in St. Mary's County (inherited from his father and probably his brother). SIGNIFICANT CHANGES IN LAND BETWEEN FIRST ELECTION AND DEATH: patented 358 acres in St. Mary's County, 1796; owned 935 acres in St. Mary's County from 1808 until death. WEALTH AT DEATH. DIED: will probated in December 1817 in St. Mary's County. PERSONAL PROPERTY: requested no appraisal of his estate. LAND: 935 acres in St. Mary's County.

HOPEWELL, RICHARD (?–ca. 1745). BORN: by 1681. NATIVE: second generation. RESIDED: in either Harvey Hundred or Resurrection Hundred, St. Mary's County. FAMILY BACKGROUND. FATHER: Hugh Hopewell (?–1690), an immigrant. MOTHER OR STEPMOTHER: Ann, who subsequently married by 1695 John Duckworth. BROTHERS: Francis; Hugh; and Joseph. SISTER: Ann, who married first, by 1724 Adam Bell (?–1718), and second, *Thomas Aisquith* (?–1761). MARRIED Elizabeth. CHILDREN. SONS: Richard (?–1732); Joseph; Hugh; John; Thomas Francis (?–1747); and William. DAUGHTERS: Ann; Mary; Susannah; and Elizabeth. PRIVATE CAREER. EDUCATION: literate. RELIGIOUS AFFILIATION: Anglican, All Faiths Parish, St. Mary's County. SOCIAL STATUS AND ACTIVITIES: Gent., 1734. OCCUPATIONAL PROFILE: probably a planter. PUBLIC CAREER. LEGISLATIVE SERVICE: Lower House, St. Mary's County, 1732–1734. LOCAL OFFICES: All Faiths Parish Vestry, St. Mary's County, in office 1708; justice, St. Mary's County, 1720–1722 (records not complete), 1730–at least 1733 (quorum, by 1730–at least 1733); sheriff, St. Mary's County, in office 1724–1726 and 1735–1738. MILITARY SERVICE: captain, by 1723. WEALTH DURING LIFETIME. LAND AT FIRST ELECTION: 2,122 acres in Kent, Talbot, and St. Mary's counties (150 acres by purchase; 1,672 acres inherited from his father). SIGNIFICANT CHANGES IN LAND BETWEEN FIRST ELECTION AND DEATH: acquired 222 acres in St. Mary's County, ca. 1733; sold 800 acres in Kent County, 1734. WEALTH AT DEATH. DIED: will probated on January 6, ca. 1745, in St. Mary's County. PERSONAL PROPERTY: TEV, at least £655.3.5 current money (including 16 slaves). LAND: 1,544 acres in Talbot and St. Mary's counties.

HOPKINS, NATHANIEL (?–1739/40). BORN: by 1680; second son. NATIVE: second generation, immigrated in 1680 as a minor with his parents. RESIDED: near Snow Hill, Somerset County (later became part of Worcester County). FAMILY BACKGROUND. FATHER: *Samuel Hopkins* (ca. 1636–1711). MOTHER: Hannah. BROTHER: *Samuel Hopkins* (1668–1744). SISTERS: Hannah, who married *William Whittington* (ca. 1650–1720); Temperance, who married Andrew Durrickson. MARRIED by 1699 Dennis, daughter of *Matthew Scarborough* (ca. 1649–1724). CHILDREN. SONS: Matthew; Samuel; and Hampton. DAUGHTERS: Mary; Hannah, who married by 1739 (first name unknown) Murray; and Dennis, who married by 1739 (first name unknown) Johnson. PRIVATE CAREER. EDUCATION: literate. RELIGIOUS AFFILIATION: Presbyterian, Snow Hill Congregation, Worcester County. SOCIAL STATUS AND ACTIVITIES: Mr., 1720. OCCUPATIONAL PROFILE: planter. PUBLIC CAREER. LEGISLATIVE SERVICE: Lower House, Somerset County, 1722–1724. MILITARY SERVICE: captain, by 1724. WEALTH DURING LIFETIME. LAND AT FIRST ELECTION: 450 acres in Somerset County (300 acres inherited from his father; 150 acres through his marriage). WEALTH AT DEATH. DIED: will probated on March 20, 1739/40, in Somerset County. PERSONAL PROPERTY: his will mentioned 1 slave. LAND: probably 450 acres in Somerset County.

HOPKINS, SAMUEL (ca. 1636–1711). BORN: ca. 1636. IMMIGRATED: in 1680 as a free adult with his wife and four children from Virginia. RESIDED: in Somerset County. ADDITIONAL COMMENTS: moved from Connecticut to Accomack County, Virginia, by 1678. FAMILY BACKGROUND. FATHER: probably Samuel Hopkins, who was in New Haven Colony by 1639. MARRIED in December 1667 Hannah, probably the daughter of Capt. Nathaniel Turner (?–1646), of New Haven, Connecticut, a merchant who traded in the Delaware Bay area. CHILDREN. SONS: *Samuel Hopkins* (1668–1744), who married Jennet; *Nathaniel Hopkins* (?–1739/40). DAUGHTERS: Hannah (1670–?), who married *William Whittington* (ca. 1650–1720); Temperance, who married Andreas Durrickson. PRIVATE CAREER. EDUCATION: literate. RELIGIOUS AFFILIATION: Presbyterian. SOCIAL STATUS AND ACTIVITIES: no title on arrival in Maryland. OCCUPATIONAL PROFILE: attorney for Richard Daughan, a mariner of London, England, 1690; planter. PUBLIC CAREER. LEGISLATIVE SERVICE: Associators' Convention, Somerset County, 1689–1692. LOCAL OFFICES: justice, Somerset County, 1687–

1699 (quorum, 1699); deputy commissary, Somerset County, 1692–1699. ADDITIONAL COMMENTS: he was indicted for extortion and malfeasance in 1700, but the indictment was dismissed on a technicality in 1701. STANDS ON PUBLIC/PRIVATE ISSUES: supported the Protestant Associators' revolution in 1689. WEALTH DURING LIFETIME. LAND AT FIRST ELECTION: 350 acres. WEALTH AT DEATH. DIED: by October 3, 1711. PERSONAL PROPERTY: TEV, £77.10.7 sterling (including 1 slave and 1 servant). LAND: 1,450 acres.

HOPKINS, SAMUEL (1668–1744). BORN: in 1668 in New Haven, Connecticut; first son. IMMIGRATED: in 1680 as a minor with his parents from Virginia. RESIDED: in Somerset County; Worcester County at death. FAMILY BACKGROUND. FATHER: *Samuel Hopkins* (ca. 1636–1711). MOTHER: Hannah. BROTHER: *Nathaniel Hopkins* (?–1739/40). SISTERS: Hannah, who married *William Whittington* (ca. 1650–1720); Temperance. MARRIED Jennet. CHILDREN. SONS: Samuel, a justice of Somerset County in 1738; Josiah; and John. PRIVATE CAREER. EDUCATION: literate. RELIGIOUS AFFILIATION: Presbyterian; commissioner to presbytery meetings in Philadelphia, 1714. SOCIAL STATUS AND ACTIVITIES: second generation burgess; Mr., 1712; Gent., 1721. OCCUPATIONAL PROFILE: planter. PUBLIC CAREER. LEGISLATIVE SERVICE: Lower House, Somerset County, 1715, 1716–1718. LOCAL OFFICES: justice, Somerset County, 1705/6–1731/32 (quorum, 1715–1731/32; chief justice, 1724–1731/32); deputy commissary, Somerset County, 1709–1715, 1718–1721; coroner, Somerset County, 1713. WEALTH DURING LIFETIME. LAND AT FIRST ELECTION: 850 acres. WEALTH AT DEATH. DIED: will probated on November 28, 1744. LAND: over 411 acres, but he had previously given much land to his sons.

HOPKINS, WILLIAM (?–1702). BORN: probably in England. IMMIGRATED: ca. 1653 as an indentured servant. RESIDED: in Annapolis, Anne Arundel County. MARRIED after 1673 (name unknown), widow of Thomas Browne. CHILDREN. STEPSON: Thomas Browne, who married (first name unknown), daughter of *William Harris* (ca. 1644–1712). DAUGHTER: probably Ann, who married John Jobson. PRIVATE CAREER. EDUCATION: literate. RELIGIOUS AFFILIATION: Anglican. SOCIAL STATUS AND ACTIVITIES: arrived as an indentured servant, but was free by 1659 when he patented his first land; eventually patented over 1,800 acres in a series of small parcels. OCCUPATIONAL PROFILE: servant; planter; storekeeper. PUBLIC CA-

REER. LEGISLATIVE SERVICE: Associators' Convention, Anne Arundel County, 1690–1692 (elected to the 2nd or 3rd session). LOCAL OFFICES: justice, Anne Arundel County, 1690–1692; Broad Neck Parish Vestry, Anne Arundel County, 1693–1696. STANDS ON PUBLIC/PRIVATE ISSUES: evidently became a strong supporter of the revolution of 1689, which brought political offices he would not ordinarily have held; no record of any officeholding other than vestry service after 1692. WEALTH DURING LIFETIME. LAND AT FIRST ELECTION: over 1,000 acres. WEALTH AT DEATH. DIED: will probated on August 6, 1702. PERSONAL PROPERTY: TEV, £405.3.5 sterling (including 1 slave and 2 servants). LAND: over 1,000 acres.

HOPPER, WILLIAM (1707–1772). BORN: on July 11, 1707, probably in Queen Anne's County; only son. NATIVE: second generation. RESIDED: on the Chester River, St. Paul's Parish, Queen Anne's County. FAMILY BACKGROUND. FATHER: William Hopper (?–1711), who immigrated from the bishopric of Durham, England, and resided in Queen Anne's County; a husbandman. GUARDIANS: Joseph Earle, 1726; Thomas Murphey, 1727. MOTHER: possibly Dorothy, of the bishopric of Durham, England, his father's first wife; or possibly Mary, his father's second wife. SISTERS: Jane (of Dorothy); Jane (of Mary), one of whom was his half sister. MARRIED first, by 1739 Esther (?–1740), daughter of William Sweatnam (?–1720) and wife Sarah. Her sister was Sarah. MARRIED second, on May 21, 1741, Mary Anne (?–1747), daughter of Thomas Hynson Wright (1688–1747) and wife Mary Turbutt Coursey; granddaughter of both *Solomon Wright* (ca. 1655–1717) and Michael Turbutt (?–1696) and wife Sarah Foster; niece of *Charles Wright* (?–1720), *Foster Turbutt* (1679–1720/21), and *William Turbutt* (1683/84–1739). Her brothers were *Thomas Wright* (?–ca. 1784); Nathan Samuel Turbutt Wright (?–1792). Her sisters were Anne, who married *Edward Oldham* (1709–1773); Sarah. Her half sisters were Mary Coursey, who married *Solomon Wright* (?–ca. 1729); Elizabeth Coursey, who married *Thomas Wilkinson* (1700/1–ca. 1758). Her first cousins were *Robert Norrest Wright* (?–ca. 1746/47); Sarah Turbutt (1706–1773), who married *Nicholas Goldsborough* (ca. 1689–1766); Elizabeth Turbutt (ca. 1708–?), who married *Tench Francis* (1701–1758); Anne Turbutt (1715–1766), who married *John Goldsborough* (1711–1778); Anna Maria Turbutt, who married *Edward Tilghman* (1713–1786); and Elizabeth Turbutt (?–ca. 1760), who married *Thomas Harris* (?–1760).

Her nephew was *Samuel Turbutt Wright* (1749–1810). Her nieces were Ann Oldham (?–by 1794), who married *Joshua Clarke* (?–1781); Elizabeth Oldham (?–by 1776), who married *William Hopper* (by 1747–1806); and Hannah Oldham (?–1828), who married *Nicholas Martin* (1743–ca. 1808). MARRIED third, in 1763 Sarah (?–ca. 1775), widow of Matthew Dockery (?–1763). CHILDREN. SON: *William Hopper* (by 1747–1806). DAUGHTERS: Mary, who married by 1772 Joseph Nicholson, Gent., of Kent County; Elizabeth (1739–1806), who married *Joseph Nicholson, Jr.* (?–1786); Henrietta (?–by 1772), who married by 1765 Hugh Neil, a clergyman of Philadelphia, Pennsylvania; Mary Ann (1742–?), who married first, Philemon Charles Blake (?–1765), and second, *James Bordley* (?–ca. 1793); Sally (?–1761); and Dorothy, who married (first name unknown) Hutchings. PRIVATE CAREER. EDUCATION: literate. RELIGIOUS AFFILIATION: Anglican, Chester Church, St. Paul's Parish, Queen Anne's County. SOCIAL STATUS AND ACTIVITIES: Mr., 1734; Gent., 1736; Esq., 1756. ADDITIONAL COMMENTS: Hopper was called before the vestry of St. Paul's Parish in 1762 to answer for his cohabitation with Jane Brown. They refused to separate, with Hopper stating that "she was his tenant, and a useful woman to him as being his Taylor, his barber, his laundress, and one who taught his young Negroes to sew." OCCUPATIONAL PROFILE: carpenter, 1729; merchant, by 1737; built a school with Christopher Cox, by 1747. PUBLIC CAREER. LEGISLATIVE SERVICE: Lower House, Queen Anne's County, 1745, 1745/46–1748, 1749–1751 (Bills of Credit 1), 1751–1754 (Arms and Ammunition 1–6), 1758–1761, 1770 (elected to the 3rd session to fill vacancy). LOCAL OFFICES: counter of tobacco plants, Queen Anne's County, appointed 1730; St. Paul's Parish Vestry, Queen Anne's County, in office 1733–1737, 1740–1746, 1748–1751, 1754–1756; justice, Queen Anne's County, 1743–1772 (quorum, 1749–1772); sheriff, Queen Anne's County, 1754–1757; receiver or collector of land tax, Queen Anne's County, in office by 1756; deputy commissary, Queen Anne's County, 1758–1759. MILITARY SERVICE: captain, by 1746; major, by 1756; colonel, by 1758. WEALTH DURING LIFETIME. LAND AT FIRST ELECTION: at least 3,287 acres in Queen Anne's County (at least 2,887 acquired through his first two marriages). SIGNIFICANT CHANGES IN LAND BETWEEN FIRST ELECTION AND DEATH: acquired 1,024 additional acres in Queen Anne's County between 1747 and 1768 by purchase or patent; acquired 113 acres in Queen Anne's County apparently through his third marriage, ca.

1763; gave 2,187 acres in Queen Anne's County to his children by deeds of gift, between 1765 and 1772. WEALTH AT DEATH. DIED: between February 5 and April 16, 1772, in Queen Anne's County. PERSONAL PROPERTY: TEV, £4,258.6.4 specie (including 31 slaves, 3 servants, 185.75 oz. plate, and books); FB, £1,263.4.7. LAND: at least 2,124 acres in Queen Anne's County.

HOPPER, WILLIAM (by 1747–1806). BORN: between 1741 and 1747 in Queen Anne's County; only son. NATIVE: third generation. RESIDED: in Queen Anne's County (later became part of Caroline County) until 1785; Queen Anne's County, 1785 until death. FAMILY BACKGROUND. FATHER: *William Hopper* (1707–1772). MOTHER: Mary Anne (?–1747), daughter of Thomas Hynson Wright (1688–1747) and wife Mary Turbutt; granddaughter of *Solomon Wright* (ca. 1655–1717). STEPMOTHER: Sarah Dockery (?–ca. 1775). UNCLE: *Thomas Wright* (?–ca. 1784). AUNT: Ann Wright (?–by 1754), who married *Edward Oldham* (1709–1773). SISTER: Mary Anne (1742–by 1792), who married second, *James Bordley* (?–ca. 1793). HALF SISTERS: Mary; Elizabeth (1739–1806), who married *Joseph Nicholson, Jr.* (?–1786); Henrietta; Sally (?–1761); and Dorothy. FIRST COUSINS: *Samuel Turbutt Wright* (1749–1810); Ann Oldham (?–by 1794), who married *Joshua Clarke* (?–1781); Hannah Oldham (?–1828), who married *Nicholas Martin* (1743–ca. 1808). MARRIED first, by 1769 his first cousin Elizabeth (?–by 1776), daughter of *Edward Oldham* (1709–1773) and wife Ann Wright (?–by 1754); stepdaughter of Ann Goldsborough (1732–?); granddaughter of *John Oldham* (?–1729); stepgranddaughter of *Nicholas Goldsborough* (ca. 1689–1766); niece of Hannah Oldham (1702–1759), who married *James Edge* (ca. 1710–1757), Mary Anne Wright (?–1747), who married *William Hopper* (1707–1772), and *Thomas Wright* (?–ca. 1784); stepniece of *Thomas Goldsborough* (ca. 1728–1793). Her sisters were Anne (?–by 1794), who married *Joshua Clarke* (?–1781); Hannah (?–1828), who married *Nicholas Martin* (1743–ca. 1808); and Mary (?–by 1772). Her first cousins were *Samuel Turbutt Wright* (1749–1810); Mary Ann Hopper (1742–by 1792), who married second, *James Bordley* (?–ca. 1793). ADDITIONAL COMMENTS: by 1759 Elizabeth and her sister Anne were living with their aunt Hannah Oldham Edge from whom they inherited the lands of their uncle *James Edge* (ca. 1710–1757). MARRIED second, on April 17, 1776, Ann, daughter of Daniel Cox. CHILDREN. SONS: William (?–1793); Daniel Cox (1777–?), a lawyer by 1807; Thomas Wright

(1783–?), a surgeon's mate in the Thirty-eighth Regiment, Maryland Militia in 1808, who married on August 9, 1808, Ann Emory (ca. 1789–1821); Philemon Blake (1791–?), a lawyer, who married first, Rebecca (ca. 1794–1822), and second, on September 2, 1822, Margaret Anne Thomas; and William (a minor in 1807). DAUGHTERS: Sarah (1779–?); Mary (1787–?); and Anna Maria. PRIVATE CAREER. EDUCATION: entered the University of Pennsylvania on May 3, 1762, attended until 1765, but did not graduate. RELIGIOUS AFFILIATION: Anglican; Methodist by 1794. SOCIAL STATUS AND ACTIVITIES: Gent., 1767; subscriber to Washington College, Chestertown, Kent County. OCCUPATIONAL PROFILE: merchant, 1774, in partnership with *James Kent* (ca. 1738–1805); farmer, 1795. PUBLIC CAREER. LEGISLATIVE SERVICE: Convention, Caroline County, 5th, 1775; Lower House, Caroline County, 1780 (elected, but did not attend; resigned on November 1, 1780), 1781–1782, 1782–1783, 1783. LOCAL OFFICES: St. Paul's Parish Vestry, Queen Anne's County, in office 1771–1774; justice, Queen Anne's County, commissioned 1773 and 1794; Committee of Correspondence, Caroline County, elected 1774; sheriff, Caroline County, commissioned 1774, 1775, 1777, and 1778; trustee for the poor, Queen Anne's County, 1801–1805. MILITARY SERVICE: captain, Caroline County Militia, by 1777; colonel, by 1806. Criticized by Col. Mordecai Gist in a letter to Gov. Thomas Johnson after the Battle of Germantown in 1777 in which Hopper was said to have been attacked "with qualms of sickness" that forced him to leave his regiment when under attack. WEALTH DURING LIFETIME. PERSONAL PROPERTY: assessed value £1,015.0.0 current money, including 20 slaves, 1783; at least 21 slaves, 1803. Declared insolvent in 1788, at which time his personal property included 59 slaves and 86 oz. plate; he was able to repurchase 21 of these slaves in 1803. LAND AT FIRST ELECTION: at least 3,167 acres in Queen Anne's, Talbot, and Caroline counties (at least 1,028 acres inherited from his father; 1,877 acres through his first marriage, at least 1,297 acres of which was given to his wife in 1759 by her aunt Hannah Edge, widow of James Edge; and one-third share of 786 acres held in partnership with John Markland and John Brown). SIGNIFICANT CHANGES IN LAND BETWEEN FIRST ELECTION AND DEATH: obtained 1,713 acres through his second marriage, 1776; charged with 4,246 acres in Queen Anne's, Talbot, and Caroline counties, 1783; turned at least 4,753 acres over to trustees when he declared insolvency, 1788; repurchased ca. 3,400 acres, 1803. WEALTH

AT DEATH. DIED: in late November 1806 in Queen Anne's County; size of estate unknown.

HORSEY, STEPHEN (ca. 1620–1671). BORN: ca. 1620, probably in England. IMMIGRATED: in 1661 as a free adult with his wife and five children from Northampton County, Virginia. RESIDED: in Annemesex Hundred, Somerset County. ADDITIONAL COMMENTS: transported to Virginia by 1643, probably as an indentured servant, by Obedience Robins; owned land in Northampton County, Virginia, by 1647. MARRIED by December 1650 Sarah, widow of Michael Williams, of Northampton County, Virginia. CHILDREN. SONS: Stephen (ca. 1651–1722), a shipwright and justice of Somerset County from 1691 to 1699, who married in 1681 Hannah, daughter of *Randall Revell* (ca. 1611–1686/87); John (ca. 1653–1678); Samuel (ca. 1655–1736), who married Ann; Nathaniel (1664/65–1721), who married in 1687 Sarah, daughter of *Randall Revell* (ca. 1611–1686/87); and Isaac (1665–1752), who married Sarah. DAUGHTERS: Mary (ca. 1657–1678); Abigail (ca. 1659–?), who married first, in 1672/73 John Kibble, and second, Richard Stevens. PRIVATE CAREER. EDUCATION: literate. RELIGIOUS AFFILIATION: a dissenting Protestant; closely associated with the Quakers, but probably not a member. SOCIAL STATUS AND ACTIVITIES: in the 1650s he was called an "ignorant yet insolvent officer. . .a fractious pretentious person. . .his children at great ages yet uncristened." OCCUPATIONAL PROFILE: probably an indentured servant, free by 1647; cooper; planter. PUBLIC CAREER. LEGISLATIVE SERVICE: Lower House, Somerset County, 1669 (did not attend). LOCAL OFFICES: justice, Somerset County, 1662/63–1666, 1666–1671 (quorum, 1666–1671); sheriff, Somerset County, 1666–1668; deputy surveyor, Somerset County, 1666. OUT OF PROVINCE SERVICE: burgess, Northampton County, Virginia, 1652, 1653. WEALTH DURING LIFETIME. LAND AT FIRST ELECTION: 800 acres. WEALTH AT DEATH. DIED: on August 8, 1671. LAND: 800 acres.

HORSEY, WILLIAM (ca. 1745–1786). BORN: in January ca. 1745; second son. NATIVE: at least second generation. RESIDED: in the Second District, Rewastico, Somerset County. FAMILY BACKGROUND. FATHER: Outerbridge Horsey (?–1788). MOTHER: Mary Dixon (?–by 1772). STEPMOTHER: Sarah Milbourn. BROTHERS: Nathaniel (1740–?); Isaac (1748–1790), who married Mary; Outerbridge (1751–?); and Stephen. HALF BROTHER: Lazarus (of age in 1785–?). SISTERS: Elizabeth

(1742–?); Martha (1747–?); Mary (1753–?); and Nancy, who married (first name unknown) Moore. HALF SISTERS: Sally (of age in 1785–?); Martha Outerbridge (of age in 1785–?). MARRIED first, (first name unknown), daughter of Rev. Alexander Adams, Jr. (ca. 1725–1767), of St. James Parish at Herring Creek, Anne Arundel County from 1748 to 1767, and wife Sarah Jones (?–ca. 1782); niece of both *William Adams* (?–1795) and *John Adams* (?–?). Her brothers were Alexander; Josiah (?–1789), who married Louisa. Her sisters were Amelia, who married Ebenezer Handy; Sarah, who married (first name unknown) Hamilton (Hambleton); Betty; and Louisa, who married Charles Nutter. MARRIED second, by 1775 Nelly (Eleanor) Wailes (?–1787). Her brother was Levin, who married Mary. Her sister was Sarah Hast. CHILDREN. SONS: Outerbridge (1775–?); Isaac; George Wailes; and William (1780–?). PRIVATE CAREER. EDUCATION: literate. RELIGIOUS AFFILIATION: Anglican. SOCIAL STATUS AND ACTIVITIES: Esq., 1774. OCCUPATIONAL PROFILE: planter; a merchant by 1772 in partnership with his brother Isaac; owner of a sawmill in partnership with Isaac Handy; owned a sloop. PUBLIC CAREER. LEGISLATIVE SERVICE: Convention, Somerset County, 9th, 1776; Lower House, Somerset County, 1777 (election voided on March 5, 1777, because at the time of the election thirty men "armed with firearms affixed with sticks and spears" had intimidated the voters). LOCAL OFFICE: justice, Somerset County, 1768–at least 1777 (quorum, 1775–at least 1777). WEALTH DURING LIFETIME. PERSONAL PROPERTY: assessed value £1,530.0.0, including 16 slaves and 12 oz. plate, 1783. LAND AT FIRST ELECTION: 1,278 acres in Somerset and Worcester counties (William owned 1,277 acres of this land jointly with his brother Isaac. They had acquired this acreage by purchasing bonds of conveyance between 1771 and 1776). SIGNIFICANT CHANGES IN LAND BETWEEN FIRST ELECTION AND DEATH: William and Isaac partitioned their jointly owned lands in 1782 and William's share totaled at least 600 acres in Worcester County. By 1783 he was charged with 99 acres in Somerset County and had patented an additional 189 acres in Worcester County. WEALTH AT DEATH. DIED: between June 16 and November 11, 1786, in Somerset County. PERSONAL PROPERTY: TEV, £1,772.5.4 (including 16 slaves, books, and a sloop); FB, £1,611.18.2. LAND: more than 900 acres in Somerset and Worcester counties, plus an unspecified amount of land in Somerset County that is mentioned in his will as having been devised to him by his great-grandfather.

HOSIER, HENRY (?–1686). BORN: in England. IMMIGRATED: probably in 1668, definitely by 1671, as a free adult from Bristol, England. RESIDED: in Calvert County; Kent County, by 1671. MARRIED Johanna. CHILDREN. SON: Henry (?–1710), who married Rebecca. DAUGHTERS: Johanna, who married first, Morgan Jones, and second, Thomas Pyner; Elizabeth; and Mary (1656–?), who married Lewis Stephens. PRIVATE CAREER. EDUCATION: literate. RELIGIOUS AFFILIATION: Protestant, perhaps a Quaker. SOCIAL STATUS AND ACTIVITIES: Gent. on arrival; transported his wife and four children to the colony by 1673. OCCUPATIONAL PROFILE: merchant of Bristol, England, and in Maryland, 1668; merchant; planter. PUBLIC CAREER. LEGISLATIVE SERVICE: Lower House, Kent County, 1676–1682, 1682–1684 (Trade 1), 1686 (died before the 1st session). LOCAL OFFICES: justice, Kent County, 1671–1683; coroner, Kent County, 1673. ADDITIONAL COMMENTS: He was dismissed from his justiceship for misbehavior in 1683. WEALTH DURING LIFETIME. LAND AT FIRST ELECTION: patented 700 acres by 1672; actively selling land in 1673. WEALTH AT DEATH. DIED: will probated on May 23, 1686. PERSONAL PROPERTY: TEV, £168.15.3 sterling (including 4 servants and books); FB, £59.19.11.

HOSKINS, PHILIP (ca. 1650–1718). BORN: ca. 1650, probably in England. IMMIGRATED: by 1671 as a free adult. RESIDED: in Charles County. FAMILY BACKGROUND. OTHER KINSHIP: Oswald Hoskins, a draper of London, England; probably related to Richard Hoskins, Gent., who was in Maryland by 1651/52, or Bennett Hoskins, who took out a warrant for a 1,000-acre manor in 1654. MARRIED first, by 1680 Elizabeth, daughter of Archibald Wahob. MARRIED second, by 1698 Anne, widow of Thomas Mudd; daughter of *Thomas Mathews* (ca. 1622–1675/76). CHILDREN. SONS: William (1690–1727), who married Violetta, daughter of Francis Harrison; Philip, Jr. (1696–?); Oswald (1699–1720); Bennett (1701–?); and Ballard (1703–?). DAUGHTERS: Benedicta (1679–1685); Jane (1681–?); Benedicta (1685–?); Elizabeth (1687–?); Mary (1692–1718), who married *Robert Hanson* (ca. 1680–1748); Mary Ann; and Martha (ca. 1705–?), who married *Thomas Stone* (1677–1727). PRIVATE CAREER. EDUCATION: literate. RELIGIOUS AFFILIATION: Anglican. OCCUPATIONAL PROFILE: arrived in 1671 as Bennett Hoskins's agent to secure the patent for a 2,000-acre tract called "Friendship Manor"; planter; merchant. PUBLIC CAREER. LEGISLATIVE SERVICE: Lower House, Charles County, 1692–1693 (Aggrievances 1, 2), 1696–1697 (elected to the 7th session), 1697/98–1700 (Accounts 1–4; Elections and Privileges 1), 1712–1714, 1716–1717 (died before the 3rd session). OTHER PROVINCIAL OFFICE: justice, Provincial Court, 1696–1707 (quorum, 1699–1707). LOCAL OFFICES: justice, Charles County, 1690–1696, 1710–1718 (quorum, 1694–1696, 1710–1718; president, 1710–1718); Port Tobacco Parish Vestry, Charles County, 1693–1696. MILITARY SERVICE: captain, 1690–1702; colonel, by 1705. STANDS ON PUBLIC/PRIVATE ISSUES: his support of the revolution of 1689 brought the first appointments to local offices; he was recommended for appointment to the Council in 1701/2, but he was never commissioned. WEALTH DURING LIFETIME. LAND AT FIRST ELECTION: over 1,256 acres; by 1698 he had acquired an additional 2,189 acres from the Mudd estate. WEALTH AT DEATH. DIED: will probated on April 30, 1718. PERSONAL PROPERTY: TEV, £1,347.5.3 (including 21 slaves). LAND: 1,314 acres.

HOUSTON, ISAAC (?–1797). BORN: in Worcester County, of age by 1775. NATIVE: at least third generation. RESIDED: in Acquango Hundred, Worcester County. FAMILY BACKGROUND. FATHER: James Houston (?–1761), of Worcester County; son of Joseph Houston. STEPFATHER: William Lane, a Quaker. MOTHER: Mary (?–by 1773), widow of Levi Purnell (Purnall) (?–1751), of Worcester County. BROTHERS: *James Houston* (?–1809); John. STEPBROTHERS: Thomas Purnell; Levi Purnell. SISTER: Mary. STEPSISTER: Sarah Purnell. MARRIED by 1776 Mary, widow of Capt. Joshua Sturgis (?–1774). CHILDREN. SON: James, Jr. (?–1814), a lunatic. DAUGHTERS: Mary Dixon (?–1800), who died without progeny; Sarah, who married by 1799 William Quinton; and Amelia (ca. 1784–?). STEPDAUGHTER: Martha Purnell Sturgis. PRIVATE CAREER. EDUCATION: literate. RELIGIOUS AFFILIATION: Anglican. SOCIAL STATUS AND ACTIVITIES: Esq., 1777; Gent., 1778. OCCUPATIONAL PROFILE: probably a planter; owned a mill; owned one-half interest in a sloop. PUBLIC CAREER. LEGISLATIVE SERVICE: Lower House, Worcester County, 1780–1781, 1789, 1793. LOCAL OFFICES: justice, Worcester County, commissioned 1777, 1778, and 1779 (did not qualify); justice, Orphans' Court, Worcester County, commissioned 1778 (did not qualify). MILITARY SERVICE: captain of a militia company in the Wicomico Battalion, Worcester County, commissioned 1777, resigned 1778; called colonel, by 1797. WEALTH DURING LIFETIME. PERSONAL PROPERTY: his wife's inheritance from her first

marriage was £636.5.4, 1776; assessed value £973.18.4, including ca. 23 slaves and 43 oz. plate, 1783. LAND AT FIRST ELECTION: owned ca. 556 acres in Worcester County (more than 294 acres inherited from his father; 262 acres by purchase); he had control of 782 acres in Worcester County for the heirs of his wife's first husband. SIGNIFICANT CHANGES IN LAND BETWEEN FIRST ELECTION AND DEATH: owned 819 acres in Worcester County, including a mill lot and a water mill, 1783; purchased 222 acres, plus 1 tract of unspecified acreage in Worcester County between 1789 and 1793; controlled 782 acres in Worcester County until 1786. WEALTH AT DEATH. DIED: administration bond taken on July 15, 1797, in Worcester County. PERSONAL PROPERTY: TEV, $4,730.64 current money (including 16 slaves and more than 9 books); FB, $4,253.64. LAND: ca. 1,040 acres in Worcester County.

HOUSTON, JAMES (?–1809). BORN: in Worcester County, of age by 1782. NATIVE: at least third generation. RESIDED: in Acquango Hundred, Worcester County. FAMILY BACKGROUND. FATHER: James Houston (?–1761), of Worcester County, son of Joseph Houston. STEPFATHER: William Lane, a Quaker. MOTHER: Mary (?–by 1773), widow of Levi Purnell (Purnall) (?–1751), of Worcester County. BROTHERS: *Isaac Houston* (?–1797); John. STEPBROTHERS: Thomas Purnell; Levi Purnell. SISTER: Mary. STEPSISTER: Sarah Purnell. MARRIED first, by 1791 Martha Purnell. MARRIED second, in 1806 Gertrude Parker. CHILDREN. SONS: Isaac; James. PRIVATE CAREER. EDUCATION: literate. RELIGIOUS AFFILIATION: Anglican, All Hallow's Parish, Worcester County. OCCUPATIONAL PROFILE: probably a planter. PUBLIC CAREER. LEGISLATIVE SERVICE: Lower House, Worcester County, 1788. LOCAL OFFICES: All Hallow's Parish Vestry, Worcester County, in office 1798; justice, Worcester County, 1799–at least 1800. MILITARY SERVICE: captain, Thirty-seventh Regiment, Worcester County Militia, commissioned 1794; major, Thirty-seventh Regiment, Worcester County Militia, commissioned 1796; lieutenant colonel, Thirty-seventh Regiment, Worcester County Militia, commissioned 1800; called colonel at death. WEALTH DURING LIFETIME. PERSONAL PROPERTY: 19 slaves, 1790. LAND AT FIRST ELECTION: 241 acres in Worcester County (121 acres inherited from his father's estate after his brother John died; 120 acres by purchase). SIGNIFICANT CHANGES IN LAND BETWEEN FIRST ELECTION AND DEATH: sold 120 acres in Worcester County, 1791; purchased 9 acres in Worcester County, 1792. **WEALTH AT DEATH. DIED:** between January 31 and February 14, 1809, in Worcester County. **PERSONAL PROPERTY:** TEV, $4,186.44 (including 11 slaves, 4 oz. old silver, and books); FB, $2,820.69. **LAND:** 129 acres in Worcester County.

HOWARD, CORNELIUS (?–1680). **BORN:** ca. 1630s, probably in Virginia; probably third son. **IMMIGRATED:** in 1659 as a free adult from Virginia. **RESIDED:** in Anne Arundel County. **FAMILY BACKGROUND. FATHER:** probably Matthew Howard, of Lower Norfolk County, Virginia. **MOTHER:** probably Ann. **BROTHERS:** Samuel; John; Matthew (ca. 1640–1692/93), who married Sarah Dorsey; and Philip, who married Ruth Baldwin. **SISTERS:** Elizabeth, who married *Henry Ridgeley* (?–1710); Ann; and Mary, who married *John Hammond* (1643–1707). **NEPHEWS:** *Charles Hammond* (ca. 1670–1713); *Thomas Hammond* (?–ca. 1724/25); *John Hammond* (ca. 1665–1742/43); and *Matthew Howard* (ca. 1675–1750). **NIECES:** Sarah Howard, who married first, *John Worthington* (1650–1701), and second, *John Brice* (?–1713); Hannah Howard, who married first, *Charles Hammond* (ca. 1670–1713), and second, *Edmond Benson* (1687–1734). **ADDITIONAL COMMENTS:** a relationship to Matthew Howard and wife Anne, who were in Virginia in the early 1630s is almost certain; when the family was living in Virginia they had close ties to *Edward Lloyd* (ca. 1620–1696) of Maryland. **MARRIED** Elizabeth. **CHILDREN. SONS:** Cornelius (ca. 1670–1717), a member of the Middleneck Parish Vestry, Anne Arundel County, from 1693 to 1697, who married Mary, daughter of *John Hammond* (1643–1707); Joseph (1676–1736), a member of the St. Anne's Parish Vestry, Anne Arundel County, in 1713, who married first, Hannah, daughter of *Edward Dorsey* (?–1705), second, Anne, and third, Margery. **DAUGHTERS:** Sarah; Mary; and Elizabeth, who married first, Andrew Norwood, second, Andrew Wellsley, and third, Charles Kilbourne. **PRIVATE CAREER. EDUCATION:** literate. **RELIGIOUS AFFILIATION:** Protestant. **SOCIAL STATUS AND ACTIVITIES:** transported two others on his arrival in Maryland in 1659, two more in 1661, and another in 1662; no title on arrival in the colony. **OCCUPATIONAL PROFILE:** planter. **PUBLIC CAREER. LEGISLATIVE SERVICE:** Lower House, Anne Arundel County, 1671–1674/75. **LOCAL OFFICE:** justice, Anne Arundel County, 1679. **MILITARY SERVICE:** ensign, 1661. **WEALTH DURING LIFETIME. LAND AT FIRST ELECTION:** ca. 1,300 acres. **WEALTH AT DEATH. DIED:** will probated on October 15, 1680. **PERSONAL PROPERTY:** TEV, 53,515 pounds of tobacco (including 2 servants). **LAND:** over 1,370 acres.

HOWARD, EPHRAIM (1745–1788). **BORN:** on December 3, 1745, in Queen Caroline Parish, Anne Arundel County; fifth child, second son. **NATIVE:** fifth generation. **RESIDED:** at "Talbott's Resolution Manor," Elk Ridge Hundred, Anne Arundel County. **FAMILY BACKGROUND. FATHER:** Henry Howard (1707–1773), son of Joseph Howard (?–1736). **MOTHER:** Sarah (?–1791), daughter of John Dorsey. **BROTHERS:** James (1744–?); John Beale (1748–1788), who married Rebecca Boone; Vachel Denton (1751–1778), captain of a cavalry unit in the Continental Army of Virginia; and Joshua (1752–?). **SISTERS:** Rachel (1732–?), who married in 1751 Dr. Joshua Warfield (?–1759); Sarah (1733/34–?), who married first, (first name unknown) Green, and second, (first name unknown) Nelson; Onner (1740–?), who married first, (first name unknown) Warfield, second, (first name unknown) Davidge, and third, (first name unknown) Wilkins. **MARRIED** Achsah (1746–1799), daughter of John Dorsey (1708–1765) and wife Elizabeth Dorsey (?–1803); granddaughter (paternal) of Caleb Dorsey (1685–1742); niece of both *Edward Dorsey* (1718–1760) and Mary Dorsey (1725–ca. 1787), who married *John Ridgely* (?–1771). Her brothers were Caleb (1740–1795), who married first, Sophia Dorsey, and second, Rebecca Hammond; John (1751–1796), who married Margaret Boone; and Richard (1756–1826), who married Ann Wayman. Her sisters were Elinor (1743–?), who married Richard Stringer; Ann (1748–?), who married Philemon Dorsey; and Elizabeth (1753–?), who married (first name unknown) Burgess. Her first cousins were *Thomas Dorsey* (?–1790); *Harry Dorsey Gough* (ca. 1745–1808); Eleanor Dorsey (ca. 1739–1805), who married *John Hall* (1729–1797); Rebecca Dorsey (1739–1812), who married *Charles Ridgely* (1733–1790); Mary Dorsey (?–1816), who married *John Weems* (1727–1794); *Charles Ridgely, of John* (?–ca. 1787); Deborah Ridgely (1749–1817), who married *John Sterett* (1750/51–1787); Mary Ridgely (?–1804), who married *Benjamin Nicholson* (?–1792); and Eleanor Dorsey, who married *Upton Sheredine* (1740–1800). **CHILDREN. SONS:** Henry (?–1817), a physician, who married in 1803 Rebecca Bond; Brutus (?–1816); Cincinnatus (?–by 1799); and Ephraim (after 1783–1811), who died without progeny. **DAUGHTERS:** Sarah, who married Charles Elder; Achsah (?–1788); and Elizabeth (?–1826), who was described by her sister in 1820 as having been in a "deranged state for many years past." **PRIVATE**

CAREER. EDUCATION: literate. OCCUPATIONAL PROFILE: a physician, who practiced near Elk Ridge, Anne Arundel County; planter; also owned an artillery forge and mill. Involved in the manufacture of saltpeter and munitions, 1775. PUBLIC CAREER. LEGISLATIVE SERVICE: Convention, Anne Arundel County, 5th, 1775. LOCAL OFFICES: justice, Anne Arundel County, 1755–at least 1764. MILITARY SERVICE: surgeon to a battalion of marching militia under Col. Thomas Dorsey, appointed 1777. STANDS ON PUBLIC/PRIVATE ISSUES: a leader of those citizens who forced Anthony Stewart to set fire to his ship, the *Peggy Stewart*, in the Annapolis harbor in October 1774, because Stewart had paid the required tax on tea imported in his vessel. WEALTH DURING LIFETIME. PERSONAL PROPERTY: assessed value £1,823.0.0, including 33 slaves and 20 oz. plate, 1783. Borrowed £5,191.0.0 sterling from *Charles Carroll of Carrollton* (1737–1832), 1785. LAND AT FIRST ELECTION: 768 acres in Anne Arundel County (156 acres from his mother by deed of gift, 1760; 250 acres inherited from his father, 1773). SIGNIFICANT CHANGES IN LAND BETWEEN FIRST ELECTION AND DEATH: purchased 200 acres in Anne Arundel County, 1780; assessed for 1,153 acres, 1783. Mortgaged 406 acres to *Charles Carroll of Carrollton* (1737–1832) as security for debts owed to him, 1787. Purchased over 2,000 acres in Kentucky. WEALTH AT DEATH. DIED: will probated on December 6, 1788, in Anne Arundel County. PERSONAL PROPERTY: TEV, £2,500.0.3 current money (including 25 slaves, one-third interest in 1 other slave, 1 servant, medical and other books, and a microscope); FB, £68.2.4, not including proceeds from sale of land. His executor stated that Howard's personal estate was insufficient to pay the debts owed. At least 431.5 acres of Howard's land was sold after his death to pay his debts. LAND: ca. 1,000 acres in Anne Arundel County (including 406 acres still mortgaged at the time of his death), plus land in Kentucky.

HOWARD, JOHN BEALE (by 1739–1799). BORN: by September 7, 1739, probably in Baltimore County; elder son. NATIVE: fourth generation. RESIDED: probably in Baltimore County (later became part of Harford County); Gunpowder Hundred, Baltimore County, by 1781; Baltimore Town, by 1792. FAMILY BACKGROUND. FATHER: Capt. John Howard (ca. 1709–1805), son of Cornelius Howard (1670–1717) and wife Mary Hammond; ward of *John Beale* (?–1734). MOTHER: Elizabeth, daughter of *Thomas Gassaway* (1683/84–1739). UNCLE: *John Gassaway* (1707–

1762). BROTHER: Thomas Gassaway (ca. 1745–1803), who married Frances (ca. 1747–?), sister of *Francis Holland* (ca. 1745–1795). FIRST COUSIN: *John Eager Howard* (1752–1827). MARRIED on April 18, 1765, Blanche (ca. 1742–1800), daughter of Parker Hall (?–ca. 1756) and wife Blanche Carvile; granddaughter of both *John Hall* (ca. 1658–1737) and *John Carvile* (ca. 1670–1709); niece of *John Hall* (1701–1774). Her brother was Edward. Her sister was Mary. Her first cousins were Martha Hall, who married *Walter Tolley* (?–1783); *Aquila Hall* (1727–1779); *John Hall, Jr.* (1737–1770); *Benedict Edward Hall* (ca. 1744–1822); *Josias Carvil Hall* (1746–1814); Martha Hall, who married *John Rumsey* (ca. 1742–1828); and Mary Hall, who married *Benjamin Rumsey* (1734–1808). CHILDREN. SONS: Parker (?–died in infancy); John Beal (1770–?), who married Margaret, daughter of Rev. *William West* (1739–1791); Edward Aquilla (1775–1854), who married first, in 1798 Charlotte Rumsey, and second, in 1809 Agnes; and Mathias (1777–1781). DAUGHTER: Elizabeth (1767–1848), who married Benjamin Richardson. PRIVATE CAREER. EDUCATION: literate. RELIGIOUS AFFILIATION: Anglican, St. John's Parish, Baltimore County (later became part of Harford County). SOCIAL STATUS AND ACTIVITIES: Esq., by 1777. OCCUPATIONAL PROFILE: planter; merchant, in partnership with James Osborne (?–1793) with connections in London. PUBLIC CAREER. LEGISLATIVE SERVICE: Convention, Harford County, 5th, 1775; Lower House, Baltimore County, 1781–1782. LOCAL OFFICES: St. John's Parish Vestry, Baltimore County (later became part of Harford County), in office 1764–at least 1781; justice, Baltimore County, 1768–1773 (quorum, 1772–1773), Harford County, appointed 1774 (quorum, 1774), Baltimore County, 1777–at least 1782; deputy commissary, Harford County, 1774–1777; justice, Orphans' Court, Baltimore County, appointed 1777; subscription officer, Continental Loan Office, Baltimore County, appointed 1779. MILITARY SERVICE: 1st lieutenant, Harford County Militia, 1776. WEALTH DURING LIFETIME. PERSONAL PROPERTY: assessed value £663.7.0, including 13 slaves and 50 oz. plate, 1783; 3 slaves, 1792. Filed a petition of insolvency in April 1792 listing the debts owed by the firm of Howard & Osborne. LAND AT FIRST ELECTION: 939 acres in Baltimore and Harford counties (125 acres in Baltimore County inherited from his mother's family; ca. 370 acres in Harford County by marriage). SIGNIFICANT CHANGES IN LAND BETWEEN FIRST ELECTION AND DEATH: owned at least 845 acres in Baltimore and Harford counties, plus 2 lots in Joppa, Baltimore County, 1783. His insolvency petition in 1792 listed 1 house and lot in Joppa, plus 1,196 acres in Baltimore and Harford counties, but 369 acres of this were already mortgaged, 200 acres had been given to his son, and 250 acres were still technically owned by his father. Howard and his wife deeded the ca. 370 acres in Harford County she had brought with her at their marriage to his trustee in 1794 to satisfy his creditors. WEALTH AT DEATH. DIED: buried on July 17, 1799, in St. John's Parish, Harford County; size of estate unknown.

HOWARD, JOHN EAGER (1752–1827). BORN: on June 4, 1752, in Baltimore County; third son. NATIVE: fourth generation. RESIDED: at "Belvedere," Baltimore City. FAMILY BACKGROUND. FATHER: Cornelius Howard (ca. 1706–1777). MOTHER: Ruth (ca. 1721–1796), daughter of John Eager. BROTHERS: George (1740–1766); Joshua (1745–1767); Cornelius (1754–?), a member of the Maryland House of Delegates in 1793; James (1757–1806); and Philip (1762–1764). SISTERS: Rachel (1743–1747); Ruth (1747–?), who married Charles Elder; Rachel (1749–1750); Violetta (1759–?), who married Joseph West; and Anne (1765–1770). FIRST COUSIN: *John Beale Howard* (by 1739–1799). MARRIED on May 18, 1787, Margaret (Peggy) Oswald, daughter of Benjamin Chew (1722–1810), an attorney of Philadelphia, chief justice of the Pennsylvania Supreme Court from 1774 to 1776, a Loyalist, judge, and president of the Pennsylvania High Court of Errors and Appeals from 1791 to 1808. CHILDREN. SONS: George (1789–1846), the governor of Maryland from 1831 to 1833, who married Prudence Gough, daughter of Charles Ridgely, of "Hampton" (1760–1829), the governor of Maryland from 1816 to 1819; John Eager, Jr. (?–by 1822), who married Cornelia Reed; Benjamin Chew (1791–1872), a member of the Maryland House of Delegates in 1824 and a representative to the U.S. Congress from 1829 to 1833 and from 1835 to 1839; Charles (1802–?); William; and James, who married Sophia J. Ridgley. DAUGHTERS: Juliana Elizabeth (1796–1821), who married John McHenry, son of *James McHenry* (1753–1816); Sophia, who married William George Reed, of South Carolina. PRIVATE CAREER. EDUCATION: received his early education from private tutors. RELIGIOUS AFFILIATION: Anglican, St. Thomas Parish and St. Paul's Parish, Baltimore County. SOCIAL STATUS AND ACTIVITIES: a member of the Jockey Club, Annapolis; a founding member of the Society of Cincinnati. OCCUPATIONAL PROFILE: major developer of Baltimore City; planter; officeholder. PUBLIC CAREER. LEGISLATIVE SERVICE: Senate, Western Shore, Term of 1791–1796: 1791–1792, 1792, 1793, 1794 (president), 1795, Term of 1796–1801: 1796 (resigned on December 1, 1796, after his election to the U.S. Senate), Term of 1816–1821: 1816 (declined to serve because of his "delicate state of. . .health"). OTHER STATE OFFICES: governor, 1788–1791; associate justice, Third District, appointed by May 1792, resigned by July 1792; commissioner, Maryland Penitentiary, in office 1804. LOCAL OFFICES: Committee of Observation, Baltimore County, elected 1774; committee to license suits of law, in office 1775; justice, Baltimore County, 1785–1787; justice, Orphans' Court, Baltimore County, 1786–1787; Maryland Senate elector, Baltimore County and Baltimore Town, elected 1786; commissioner, Baltimore Town, in office 1792; Committee of Supply, Baltimore City, War of 1812, in office 1812. MILITARY SERVICE: captain, Second Maryland Battalion, Flying Camp, July 1776; commander of a company at the Battle of White Plains, October 1776; major, Fourth Maryland Regiment, February 1777; lieutenant colonel, Fifth Maryland Regiment, March 1778, transferred to the Second Maryland Regiment, October 1779; fought in the Battle of Cowpens in January 1781 for which he received a medal for heroism from Congress, March 1781; fought in the battles of Guilford Courthouse, Hobkirk's Hill, and Eutaw Springs, 1781; wounded at the Battle of Eutaw Springs, September 1781; colonel, 1781; retired 1783; major general, Third Division, Maryland Militia, commissioned in May 1794, resigned by April 1795. OUT OF STATE SERVICE: delegate, Continental Congress, 1787–1788 (elected in December 1787, but did not attend until January 1788); declined the position as U.S. secretary of war, 1795; senator, U.S. Congress, 1796–1797 (elected to fill vacancy; seated on December 27, 1796), 1797–1799, 1799–1801, 1801–1803; defeated as a Federalist party candidate for vice president of the U.S., 1816. STANDS ON PUBLIC/PRIVATE ISSUES: His philanthropic endeavors in Baltimore City included a gift of land for the construction of the Washington Monument, as well as land for various churches, a cemetery for the interment of strangers, and a market house. Howard offered land to the State of Maryland if the state would move the captial from Annapolis to Baltimore City. WEALTH DURING LIFETIME. PERSONAL PROPERTY: 3 slaves inherited from his father, 1777; 2 slaves inherited from his mother, 1796; 13 slaves on his Anne Arundel County farm, 1798. LAND AT FIRST ELECTION: he held title to at least 200 lots in Baltimore Town, plus additional acreage within the city or adjacent to it under development. SIGNIFICANT CHANGES IN LAND BETWEEN FIRST ELECTION AND DEATH: Howard continued to develop lots in and near Baltimore City, most of which he leased out, retaining the fee simple title. He acquired 2 large tracts totaling 570 acres in Baltimore County and by 1798 owned 450 acres in Anne Arundel County, which he incorporated into a 771-acre patent in 1805. As a result of his service in the Revolution he received 750 acres in Allegany County. WEALTH AT DEATH. DIED: on October 12, 1827, as a result of a severe cold, at "Belvedere," Baltimore City; buried in old St. Paul's Cemetery, Baltimore City. PERSONAL PROPERTY: requested no appraisal of his estate, however the value of his ground rents on 289 lots in Baltimore City totaled $119,758.00 and "Belvedere House," with its 3 lots on Calvert and St. Paul streets in Baltimore City, was appraised at $18,513.00. LAND: ca. 400 lots in Baltimore City; 2,092 acres in Baltimore, Anne Arundel, and Allegany counties, plus 1 lot in Bath, Berkeley County, Virginia. Total value of real estate was $1,084,745.00

HOWARD, MATTHEW (ca. 1675–1750). BORN: ca. 1675; probably second son. NATIVE: at least second generation. RESIDED: in Kent County. FAMILY BACKGROUND. FATHER: Matthew Howard (ca. 1640–1692/93), of Anne Arundel County. MOTHER: Sarah, daughter of Edward Dorsey. UNCLE: *Cornelius Howard* (?–1680). AUNTS: Elizabeth Howard, who married *Henry Ridgeley* (?–1710); Mary Howard, who married *John Hammond* (1643–1707). BROTHERS: John; Samuel (?–by 1691). SISTER: Sarah, who married first, *John Worthington* (1650–1701), and second, *John Brice* (?–1713). FIRST COUSINS: Hannah Howard, who married first, *Charles Hammond* (ca. 1670–1713), and second, *Edmond Benson* (1687–1734); *Charles Hammond* (ca. 1670–1713); *Thomas Hammond* (?–ca. 1724/25); and *John Hammond* (ca. 1665–1742/43). NEPHEW: *Thomas Worthington* (ca. 1691–1753). NIECES: Ann Brice (1708–1765), who married *Vachel Denton* (ca. 1696–1752); Rachel Brice (1711–1786), who married *Philip Hammond* (1697–1760). MARRIED first, on October 26, 1714, Mary (?–1736), widow of both (first name unknown) Kennard and George Browning (?–by 1714). MARRIED second, Elizabeth, a Quaker, who subsequently married both William Redgrave and William Delehunte. CHILDREN. SONS: James; John. STEPSONS: Richard Kennard; Nathaniel Kennard; and George Browning (?–1735). DAUGHTERS: Su-

san; Hannah; Martha; and Ann. STEPDAUGHTER: Elizabeth (surname unknown), who married (first name unknown) Williams. PRIVATE CAREER. EDUCATION: literate. RELIGIOUS AFFILIATION: Protestant. SOCIAL STATUS AND ACTIVITIES: Mr., 1727. OCCUPATIONAL PROFILE: carpenter, 1730; planter. PUBLIC CAREER. LEGISLATIVE SERVICE: Lower House, Kent County, 1732–1734. LOCAL OFFICE: Shrewsbury Parish Vestry, Kent County, in office 1727–1729. WEALTH DURING LIFETIME. LAND AT FIRST ELECTION: 343 acres in Kent County (100 acres belonged to his first wife). SIGNIFICANT CHANGES IN LAND BETWEEN FIRST ELECTION AND DEATH: resurveyed several pieces of land into one 570-acre tract in Kent County, 1744. WEALTH AT DEATH. DIED: between October 24 and November 19, 1750, in Kent County. PERSONAL PROPERTY: TEV, £446.16.4 current money (including 8 slaves, 1 servant, and books); FB, £416.16.10. LAND: 666 acres in Kent County.

HOWARD, MICHAEL (?–1737). BORN: probably in Ireland, of age by 1717. IMMIGRATED: by 1717, probably from Ireland. RESIDED: in Annapolis, Anne Arundel County, 1717; Talbot County, March 1720/21. FAMILY BACKGROUND. BROTHERS: Adam, of County Westmeath, Ireland; Francis, of County Westmeath, Ireland; Rochford; and Matthew (?–by 1734/35), of Dublin, Ireland, who married Sarah. SISTERS: Ann, who married (first name unknown) Plunkett; Rose, who married (first name unknown) Wilson. MARRIED never. PRIVATE CAREER. EDUCATION: attended Gray's Inn, London, England. RELIGIOUS AFFILIATION: Protestant. ADDITIONAL COMMENTS: in August 1735 Edward Fotterell alleged that Howard owed him money "won at gameing"; Fotterell challenged him to a fight, but Howard refused. OCCUPATIONAL PROFILE: lawyer, admitted to the following courts: Kent County in March 1717/18; Anne Arundel County in June 1717; Prince George's County in June 1717; Provincial Court in September 1717; Talbot County in June 1718; Court of Chancery by June 1718; Queen Anne's County by November 1718; Cecil County by June 1719; Dorchester County by August 1728. He was also engaged in mercantile activities. Officeholder. PUBLIC CAREER. LEGISLATIVE SERVICE: Upper House, 1732–1734, 1734/35–1737. OTHER PROVINCIAL OFFICES: attorney general, 1725–1734 (resigned); surveyor general, Eastern Shore, 1726–1737; naval officer, Oxford, 1727–1737; Council, 1732–1737 (qualified on April 18, 1732). LOCAL OFFICES: deputy commissary, Talbot County, 1722–1724; clerk of Indictments, Talbot County, in office 1722; commissioner, Talbot County School, in office 1727. **WEALTH DURING LIFETIME.** LAND AT FIRST ELECTION: none; lived in lodgings in Talbot County. **WEALTH AT DEATH.** DIED: between August 3 and 27, 1737, possibly in Annapolis; will probated in Talbot County. PERSONAL PROPERTY: TEV, £522.8.10 current money, plus £129.12.6 gold (including a law library and other books); FB, £323.8.2 current money, plus £22.10.3 gold. LAND: none. ADDITIONAL COMMENTS: his principal heirs were his nephew Michael William Howard, his niece Elizabeth Howard, his brother Adam and Adam's two eldest sons, his brother Francis, his sister Ann Plunkett and her two eldest sons, his sister Rose Wilson and her eldest son, and his brother Rochford.

HOWE, THOMAS (?–1720/21). BORN: probably in Maryland, of age by 1683. NATIVE: probably second generation. RESIDED: in Calvert County. **FAMILY BACKGROUND.** FATHER: probably Thomas Howe (ca. 1634–1676), who immigrated by 1656. MOTHER: probably Phyllis, who subsequently married Gustavus White. MARRIED Rebecca (?–by 1720). **CHILDREN.** SON: Thomas (1689–?). DAUGHTERS: Sarah (1693–?), who married James Somervell; Maulden (1697–?), who married Charles Claggett, son of Thomas Claggett; Rebecca (1699–?); Elizabeth (1705–?); and Mary (1709–?). **PRIVATE CAREER.** EDUCATION: literate. RELIGIOUS AFFILIATION: Protestant. SOCIAL STATUS AND ACTIVITIES: Mr. at death. OCCUPATIONAL PROFILE: planter. **PUBLIC CAREER.** LEGISLATIVE SERVICE: Lower House, Calvert County, 1704–1707. **WEALTH DURING LIFETIME.** LAND AT FIRST ELECTION: at least 200 acres. **WEALTH AT DEATH.** DIED: between January 23 and March 16, 1720/21. PERSONAL PROPERTY: TEV, £982.12.8 (including 16 slaves and 1 servant). LAND: at least 680 acres.

HOWELL, THOMAS (?–1675). IMMIGRATED: by 1658 as a free adult. RESIDED: Anne Arundel County; Baltimore County, by 1661; Cecil County, by 1674. MARRIED Elizabeth. **CHILDREN.** SONS: John; Nathaniel. DAUGHTER: Sarah, who married *John Vanhack* (?–ca. 1675/76). **PRIVATE CAREER.** EDUCATION: literate. RELIGIOUS AFFILIATION: Protestant. SOCIAL STATUS AND ACTIVITIES: a justice with his first appearance in the records of the colony. OCCUPATIONAL PROFILE: planter. **PUBLIC CAREER.** LEGISLATIVE SERVICE: Lower House, Anne Arundel County, 1659/60, Baltimore County, 1666, 1671–1674/75 (Laws 3; Accounts 3). LOCAL OFFICES: justice, Anne Arundel County, by 1658–61, Baltimore County, 1661–1674 (quorum), Cecil County, 1674–1675 (presi-

dent). MILITARY SERVICE: captain, by 1658–1675. **WEALTH DURING LIFETIME.** LAND AT FIRST ELECTION: ca. 1,250 acres. **WEALTH AT DEATH.** DIED: will probated on November 28, 1675. PERSONAL PROPERTY: TEV, 197,752 pounds of tobacco (including 6 servants); FB, 49,322 pounds of tobacco. LAND: over 1,000 acres.

HUDSON (HODSON), JOHN (?–1677). IMMIGRATED: by 1659 as a free adult with his family from Virginia. RESIDED: in Dorchester County. MARRIED first, name unknown. MARRIED second, Hester. **CHILDREN.** SONS: *John Hudson* (1653–1730); *John Hudson, Secundus* (?–1745), who married Anne, daughter of John Worth (?–1703/4); Joseph; and Thomas. **PRIVATE CAREER.** EDUCATION: literate. RELIGIOUS AFFILIATION: Quaker. SOCIAL STATUS AND ACTIVITIES: no title on arrival. OCCUPATIONAL PROFILE: planter. **PUBLIC CAREER.** LEGISLATIVE SERVICE: Lower House, Dorchester County, 1676 (died before the 2nd session). LOCAL OFFICE: justice, Dorchester County, 1674 (quorum; refused to take the required oath). **WEALTH AT DEATH.** DIED: will probated on July 14, 1677. PERSONAL PROPERTY: TEV, 25,640 pounds of tobacco (including 4 servants); FB, 7,416 pounds of tobacco. LAND: ca. 484 acres.

HUDSON (HODSON), JOHN (1653–1730). BORN: in 1653, probably in Virginia; oldest son. IMMIGRATED: by 1659 as a minor with his father from Virginia. RESIDED: in Dorchester County. **FAMILY BACKGROUND.** FATHER: *John Hudson* (?–1677). STEPMOTHER: Hester. BROTHERS OR HALF BROTHERS: *John Hudson, Secundus* (?–1745); Joseph; and Thomas. MARRIED (name unknown). **CHILDREN.** SONS: John, Jr. (?–ca. 1749), who married Elizabeth; John Quartus (?–1751), who married Rosannah, daughter of *Henry Hooper* (ca. 1643–1720); and James. **PRIVATE CAREER.** EDUCATION: literate. RELIGIOUS AFFILIATION: Protestant, converted from Quakerism to Anglicanism by the mid-1690s. SOCIAL STATUS AND ACTIVITIES: second generation burgess; Mr., by 1704. OCCUPATIONAL PROFILE: planter. **PUBLIC CAREER.** LEGISLATIVE SERVICE: Lower House, Dorchester County, 1704–1707, 1708A, 1710–1711 (elected to the 3rd session), 1715. LOCAL OFFICE: justice, Dorchester County, 1685–1692. MILITARY SERVICE: captain, by 1696. **WEALTH DURING LIFETIME.** LAND AT FIRST ELECTION: ca. 1,300 acres. **WEALTH AT DEATH.** DIED: will probated on April 21, 1730. PERSONAL PROPERTY: TEV, £609.6.7 (including 10 slaves). LAND: ca. 1,300 acres, plus several tracts of unspecified acreage that probably amounted to an additional 1,000 acres.

HUDSON (HODSON), JOHN, SECUNDUS (?–1745). BORN: after 1665, possibly in Virginia. NATIVE: second generation. RESIDED: in Dorchester County. FAMILY BACKGROUND. FATHER: *John Hudson* (?–1677). MOTHER: Hester. BROTHERS OR HALF BROTHERS: Thomas; Joseph. HALF BROTHER: *John Hudson* (1653–1730). MARRIED by 1703/4 Anne, daughter of John Worth (?–1703/4), of Kent County, and wife Sarah (Shara). Her brothers were John; William. CHILDREN. SON: John. DAUGHTERS: Hester Anne (?–1763), who never married; Sophia; and Vienna, who married Thomas Lookerman. PRIVATE CAREER. EDUCATION: literate. RELIGIOUS AFFILIATION: Protestant; his father was a Quaker. SOCIAL STATUS AND ACTIVITIES: Gent., by 1712. OCCUPATIONAL PROFILE: yeoman. PUBLIC CAREER. LEGISLATIVE SERVICE: Lower House, Dorchester County, 1722–1724. LOCAL OFFICES: land commissioner, Dorchester County, in office 1728; justice, Dorchester County, 1729–at least 1733. MILITARY SERVICE: captain, by 1730. WEALTH DURING LIFETIME. LAND AT FIRST ELECTION: 676 acres in Dorchester County (100 acres from his father, 576 acres by purchase and patent). SIGNIFICANT CHANGES IN LAND BETWEEN FIRST ELECTION AND DEATH: sold 248 acres in Dorchester County, 1724; mortgaged his 422-acre dwelling plantation in Dorchester County, 1730; patented 100 acres in Dorchester County, 1731; sold the 422-acre tract, 1739. WEALTH AT DEATH. DIED: administration bond dated December 13, 1745, in Dorchester County. PERSONAL PROPERTY: TEV, £323.11.1 current money (including 4 slaves and books); FB, £307.9.8. LAND: at least 106 acres in Dorchester County.

HUETT (HEWITT), JOHN (ca. 1640–1698). BORN: ca. 1640 in England; first son. IMMIGRATED: ca. 1677 as a free adult from England. RESIDED: in Somerset County. FAMILY BACKGROUND. FATHER: Rev. John Huett, Pembrooke College, Cambridge University, and D.D., Oxford University; minister of St. Gregory's by St. Paul's, London, England; executed in 1658 for his support of the unsuccessful pro-Stuart uprising. MARRIED ca. 1686, Rachel (Battian?) (?–1726), who subsequently married Col. Nicholas Evans. CHILDREN. DAUGHTERS: Anne, who married first, Matthew Nutter (?–1720), and second, Alexander Leckie; Susanna, who married Joseph Johnson. PRIVATE CAREER. EDUCATION: literate, schooled through deacon's orders (a stage of education for clerics short of full ordination). RELIGIOUS AFFILI-ATION: Anglican. SOCIAL STATUS AND ACTIVITIES: after the Stuart restoration, he received an annuity of £100 from the crown in appreciation for his father's loyalty; he may have come to Virginia in 1663 and returned later to England; ordained in 1682 by the bishop of London; one of only three or four practicing Anglican ministers in the colony during his early career. OCCUPATIONAL PROFILE: minister, Stepney Parish, Somerset County, 1682–1695, Somerset Parish, Somerset County, 1691–1695, Dorchester Parish, Dorchester County, 1671–1695. PUBLIC CAREER. LEGISLATIVE SERVICE: Lower House, Somerset County, 1692 (discharged from the 1st session; as an ordained minister he was ineligible to serve in the Assembly.) OTHER PROVINCIAL OFFICE: chaplain of the Assembly, 1692–1694. WEALTH AT DEATH. DIED: by June 24, 1698; size of estate unknown.

HUGHES, SAMUEL (ca. 1741–?). BORN: ca. 1741. NATIVE: second generation. RESIDED: in Frederick County (later became part of Washington County); "Mount Pleasant," Harford County, by 1779. FAMILY BACKGROUND. FATHER: Barnabas Hughes (?–1765), born in Donegal, Ireland; immigrated to Lancaster, Pennsylvania; resided in Baltimore, Frederick, and Washington counties; owner of the Mount Etna Ironworks. MOTHER: Elizabeth Waters (?–1793). BROTHERS: Col. Daniel (?–1818), who married first, Rebecca Lux (1731–?), second, Susannah Schlatter, and third, Ann Elliott; John, a captain in the Revolutionary army; and Barnabas, who married (first name unknown) Beltzhower. SISTERS: Elizabeth (?–1793), who married *Richard Potts* (1753–1808); Margaret. NIECE: Ann Hughes, who married *William Fitzhugh, Jr.* (1761–1839). MARRIED by 1781 Sarah (?–after 1818). CHILDREN. Probably died without progeny. PRIVATE CAREER. EDUCATION: literate. RELIGIOUS AFFILIATION: Anglican, Spesutia Church, St. George's Parish, Harford County. SOCIAL STATUS AND ACTIVITIES: Gent., 1779; Esq., 1779. OCCUPATIONAL PROFILE: ironmaster. His brothers Samuel and Daniel gained control of the Antietam and other ironworks in the Antietam Valley, Washington County, just prior to the outbreak of the Revolution. Samuel directly supervised the Antietam furnace, which produced cannon for the Baltimore Town Committee of Correspondence, the Continental Marine Committee, and the Continental Army. After the war, Samuel terminated his Washington County iron-making operations, and between 1786 and 1789 sold or leased his property there. He continued as ironmaster in Harford County near "Mount Pleasant." The main thrust of his business operations, however, was directed to the Susquehanna River area, where he entered into the iron-smelting and cannon-casting business on the old Principio Ironworks property. He named his business the Cecil Furnace, one of several iron-making ventures he had in Cecil County. Another was a partnership with John Churchman in a forge on Octorara Creek (later known as Frey's Forge). Cecil Furnace was his chief interest, however; in 1796 Samuel secured a contract with the government to produce cannon for new frigates. His iron operations in Cecil County were generally successful until the War of 1812, when the Cecil Furnace was attacked by Admiral Cockburn. The buildings and facilities were burned and the cannon on hand were destroyed. Samuel rebuilt, but it was a financial strain and the business suffered. He mortgaged and then sold the Cecil Furnace to two Baltimore merchants, Robert Gilmore and Robert Smith in 1820 to discharge debts totaling $39,081.50. Hughes was also involved in land speculation, specifically as a partner in the Havre de Grace Company, which was formed in 1797 to acquire land adjacent to Havre de Grace. PUBLIC CAREER. LEGISLATIVE SERVICE: Convention, Frederick County, 9th, 1776; Lower House, Washington County, 1777 (Manufactories 2), 1777–1778 (Manufactories 3), 1778–1779 (Tax Commissioners 1; Claims 3); Senate, Western Shore, Term of 1776–1781: 1781 (elected on January 2, 1781 to fill vacancy in the 1780–1781 Assembly; qualified on January 12, 1781), Term of 1781–1786: 1783 (elected on May 9, 1783 to fill vacancy in the 1782–1783 Assembly; qualified on May 23, 1783), 1783, 1784, 1785, Term of 1786–1791: 1786–1787 (elected on December 2, 1786 to fill vacancy; qualified on December 12, 1786), 1787–1788, 1788, 1789, 1790. LOCAL OFFICES: Committee of Observation, Frederick County, elected 1774 and 1775; justice, Washington County, 1777–at least 1778 (moved to Baltimore County), Harford County, 1782–at least 1797; justice, Orphans' Court, Washington County, 1777–at least 1778 (moved to Baltimore County), Harford County, commissioned 1784; town commissioner, Havre de Grace, Harford County, 1785; judge, Court of Appeals for Tax Assessment, Harford County, appointed 1786; associate justice, Circuit Court, Harford County, appointed 1789. ADDITIONAL COMMENTS: The Washington County clerk's reference to Hughes having moved to Baltimore County was not substantiated by landownership. JURY SERVICE: petit jury, Harford County, term began in 1801. MILITARY SERVICE: colonel. WEALTH DURING LIFETIME. PERSONAL PROPERTY: assessed value £864.0.0, including 15 slaves and 30 oz. plate, Harford County, 1783; 13 slaves, 1790. LAND AT FIRST ELECTION: 1,138 acres in Frederick, Baltimore (later became Harford County), and Washington counties. SIGNIFICANT CHANGES IN LAND BETWEEN FIRST ELECTION AND DEATH: purchased 6,038 acres in Washington and Harford counties and sold 4,351 acres in Washington and Harford counties, 1779–1813; acquired 200 lots near Havre de Grace, Harford County, upon the dissolution of the Havre de Grace Company, of which he was entitled to seven thirty-seconds share of the capital stock, 1806. Patented and acquired by purchase or mortgage at least 4,717 acres in Cecil County, by 1799–1816. Sold this land and the ironworks located on it in 1820. WEALTH AT DEATH. Size of estate unknown.

HUGHLETT, THOMAS (ca. 1739–ca. 1803). BORN: ca. 1739, probably in Virginia; only son. NATIVE: second generation. ADDITIONAL COMMENTS: immigrated ca. 1749 as a minor with his father from St. Stephen's Parish, Northumberland County, Virginia. RESIDED: in Queen Anne's County (later became part of Caroline County); Choptank Hundred, Caroline County, 1778. FAMILY BACKGROUND. FATHER: William Hughlett (?–1771), immigrated ca. 1749 from Virginia; resided in Queen Anne's County; merchant; planter. MOTHER: Mary. SISTERS: Anne, who married in 1758 William Harrington (1737–?); Mary, who married (first name unknown) Harrington; and Winefred, who married Cooper Kendardine. MARRIED by 1767 Sarah (ca. 1748–1772), daughter of Obediah Dixon (ca. 1709–1780), of Dorchester and Caroline counties, planter, and wife Sarah. Her brothers were Robert; Benjamin; and Joseph. Her sisters were Martha; Rebecca; and China, who married (first name unknown) Dill. MARRIED second, in January 1778 Rebeckah, daughter of *Richard Mason* (?–ca. 1782). Her brother was Thomas. Her sisters were Sarah; Margaret. CHILDREN. SONS: William (1769–?), who was elected to the Maryland Senate in 1816 and married Elizabeth S. (ca. 1774–1810); Richard (ca. 1782–1827), who married Anna. DAUGHTERS: Mary (ca. 1767–?), who married Charles Adams; Ann (?–1806), who married Dr. Timothy Caldwell. PRIVATE CAREER. EDUCATION: literate. RELIGIOUS AFFILIATION: Anglican, St. John's Parish, Caroline County. SOCIAL STATUS AND ACTIVITIES: Gent., 1793; Esq., 1797. OCCUPATIONAL PROFILE: farmer, 1778; in partnership with his son Richard in a tannery, Caroline County; probably also a merchant in partnership with his son Richard;

owned a schooner. **PUBLIC CAREER. LEGISLATIVE SERVICE:** Lower House, Caroline County, 1783, 1784, 1785, 1787–1788, 1792, 1793, 1798. **LOCAL OFFICES:** coroner, Caroline County, 1778 (resigned), commissioned 1791, resigned 1792; appointed to execute the "act to prohibit for a limited time the exportation of Indian corn etc. by land," Caroline County, 1780; justice, Caroline County, 1782–at least 1800; Maryland Senate elector, Caroline County, in office 1786; tobacco inspector, Choptank Bridge, Caroline County, commissioned 1786; sheriff, Caroline County, commissioned 1787, serving in 1791; commissioner of tax, Caroline County, appointed 1798. **MILITARY SERVICE:** captain, Caroline County Militia, 1786. **WEALTH DURING LIFETIME. PERSONAL PROPERTY:** assessed value £322.0.0, including 7 slaves, 1783; 11 slaves, 1790; 15 slaves, 1798. **LAND AT FIRST ELECTION:** 406 acres in Caroline County (at least 125 acres from his father, probably 125 additional acres from his father; 156 acres by patent); may also have had lands in Kent County, Delaware, left to him by his father in 1771. **WEALTH AT DEATH. DIED:** ca. 1803 in Caroline County. **PERSONAL PROPERTY:** TEV, £2,555.0.4 (including 3 slaves, books, a schooner, large quantities of cloth, leather hides, and other merchandise); FB, £1,741.15.3. **LAND:** 588 acres in Caroline County; may also have possessed land in Kent County, Delaware.

HUMPHRYS (HUMPHREYS), THOMAS (?–ca. 1726). **BORN:** of age by December 1718. **IMMIGRATED:** ca. 1718. **RESIDED:** in Annapolis, Anne Arundel County, at least 1720–1723. **MARRIED** by October 30, 1723, Mary. **PRIVATE CAREER. EDUCATION:** literate. **SOCIAL STATUS AND ACTIVITIES:** Gent., 1722; Esq., 1723; probably well-connected, because in December 1718 he was recommended to Gov. John Hart in a letter written by Lord Guilford, the guardian of *Charles Calvert, 5th Lord Baltimore* (1699–1751). **OCCUPATIONAL PROFILE:** attorney, admitted to the following courts: Anne Arundel County in June 1720; Provincial Court in September 1720. Officeholder. **PUBLIC CAREER. LEGISLATIVE SERVICE:** Lower House, Annapolis, 1722–1724 (Elections 1–3). **OTHER PROVINCIAL OFFICE:** naval officer, Patuxent, 1722–1726. **WEALTH DURING LIFETIME. LAND AT FIRST ELECTION:** at least a house and lot in Annapolis (by purchase). **SIGNIFICANT CHANGES IN LAND BETWEEN FIRST ELECTION AND DEATH:** sold his house and lot in Annapolis, 1723. **WEALTH AT DEATH. DIED:** by November 15, 1726, "near New York" ; size of estate unknown.

HUNGERFORD, CHARLES (?–ca. 1805). **BORN:** probably in Charles County, of age by 1769. **NATIVE:** probably fifth generation. **RESIDED:** in Charles County; Frederick County (later became part of Montgomery County), by 1769; Virginia, after 1800. **FAMILY BACKGROUND. FATHER:** (first name unknown) Hungerford, son of Barton Hungerford (1687–1758). **MARRIED** Mary, who survived her husband. **CHILDREN. SON:** William, of Montgomery County. **DAUGHTERS:** probably six, but names unknown. **PRIVATE CAREER. EDUCATION:** literate. **OCCUPATIONAL PROFILE:** tavernkeeper, Frederick County, 1770; planter, 1800. **PUBLIC CAREER. LEGISLATIVE SERVICE:** Lower House, Montgomery County, 1780–1781. **LOCAL OFFICE:** justice, Montgomery County, 1780–at least 1785. **STANDS ON PUBLIC/PRIVATE ISSUES:** His tavern was a meeting place of Montgomery County patriots, who on June 11, 1774, passed what became known as the Hungerford Tavern "Resolves." The "Resolves" called for every "lawful means" to be used to secure relief from the oppressive acts of the British Parliament, including ceasing all commerce between Britain and her colonies. **WEALTH DURING LIFETIME. PERSONAL PROPERTY:** assessed value £908.0.0, including 20 slaves and 3 oz. plate, 1783; 29 slaves, 1790; assessed value £632.0.0, including 27 slaves and 3 oz. plate, 1793; assessed value £485.0.0, including 18 slaves and 2 oz. plate, 1798. **LAND AT FIRST ELECTION:** 350 acres of leasehold land in Montgomery County. **SIGNIFICANT CHANGES IN LAND BETWEEN FIRST ELECTION AND DEATH:** acquired 298 acres in Montgomery County, 1787–1800; sold 89 acres in Montgomery County, 1800. **WEALTH AT DEATH. DIED:** between December 1805 and January 1806, probably in Virginia; size of estate unknown.

HUNT, WORNELL (?–by 1728/29). **BORN:** probably in Yonghall, Ireland. **IMMIGRATED:** by November 1706 from Nevis. **RESIDED:** in Annapolis, Anne Arundel County; moved to West Indies in late 1716 or early 1717. **FAMILY BACKGROUND. FATHER:** John Hunt, of Ireland. **MARRIED** by 1707 Caroline. **CHILDREN. DAUGHTER:** Judith (1707–?). **PRIVATE CAREER. EDUCATION:** literate; admitted to Lincoln's Inn in 1704. **RELIGIOUS AFFILIATION:** Anglican. **SOCIAL STATUS AND ACTIVITIES:** called "of Middlesex, Gent." in 1704; an officeholder in Nevis, 1705/6; Esq. on arrival; imported twenty Negroes in 1709. **OCCUPATIONAL PROFILE:** lawyer, admitted to the following courts: Prince George's County in 1706; Anne Arundel County in 1706; Provincial Court in 1707. **PUBLIC CAREER. LEGIS-**

LATIVE SERVICE: Lower House, Annapolis, 1708A (election voided), 1708B–1711 (dismissed from the 2nd session for failure to meet the residency requirement of three years in the colony; reelected late in the 2nd session; Laws 2). LOCAL OFFICES: alderman, Annapolis, 1708; St. Anne's Parish Vestry, Anne Arundel County, 1716–1717. WEALTH DURING LIFETIME. LAND AT FIRST ELECTION: 480 acres by 1712, which he sold in 1716. WEALTH AT DEATH. DIED: by March 1728/29; size of estate unknown.

HUTCHINS, CHARLES (?–1700). BORN: in England. IMMIGRATED: in 1672 as a free adult. RESIDED: in Dorchester County. MARRIED first, Dorothy. MARRIED second, Anne. CHILDREN. SON: (first name unknown), left in England. DAUGHTER: Anne, who married John Rider, of England. PRIVATE CAREER. EDUCATION: literate. RELIGIOUS AFFILIATION: Anglican. SOCIAL STATUS AND ACTIVITIES: estranged from first wife and son who did not accompany him to Maryland, he remarried without obtaining a divorce. His first wife later sued him for one-third of his estate, most of which went to his grandson *John Rider* (1686–1739/40). Hutchins was probably related to *Francis Hutchins* (?–1698), to whom he assigned his headright claim. He was appointed to the county bench within two years of arrival, but he was called "broken London carpenter" by Edward Randolph in 1692. OCCUPATIONAL PROFILE: planter; merchant. PUBLIC CAREER. LEGISLATIVE SERVICE: Associators' Convention, Dorchester County, 1689–1692; Upper House, 1692–1693 (Laws 2), 1694–1697, 1697/98–1700. OTHER PROVINCIAL OFFICES: Council, 1691–1700; justice, Provincial Court, 1693–1694 (quorum). LOCAL OFFICE: justice, Dorchester County, 1674–1692 (quorum, 1689–1692). MILITARY SERVICE: colonel, by 1690–1700. STANDS ON PUBLIC/PRIVATE ISSUES: he supported the revolution of Protestant Associators in 1689 and rose rapidly in office thereafter. WEALTH DURING LIFETIME. LAND AT FIRST ELECTION: ca. 5,000 acres. WEALTH AT DEATH. DIED: will probated on October 23, 1700. PERSONAL PROPERTY: TEV, £1,058.8.7 sterling (including 18 slaves and 6 servants). LAND: over 3,918 acres.

HUTCHINS, FRANCIS (?–1698). IMMIGRATED: in 1652 as a indentured servant to *Richard Preston* (?–ca. 1669/70). RESIDED: in Calvert County. MARRIED Elizabeth. Her sister was Margaret Burrage, who married first, Nathan Smith, and second, *Thomas Tench* (?–1708). CHILDREN. SON:

John. DAUGHTERS: Margaret, who married Abraham Johns (1677–1707), son of *Richard Johns* (1649–1717); Elizabeth, who married first, Roger Brooke, son of Roger Brooke (1637–1700), and second, Richard Smith; Sarah; Frances; Priscilla, who married Richard Johns, Jr. (1687–1719); and Mary, who married Samuel Thomas, son of *Philip Thomas* (?–1675). PRIVATE CAREER. EDUCATION: illiterate. RELIGIOUS AFFILIATION: Protestant; his wife and at least some of his children were Quakers. OCCUPATIONAL PROFILE: servant, 1652; planter; merchant. PUBLIC CAREER. LEGISLATIVE SERVICE: Lower House, Calvert County, 1682–1684, 1694–1697 (Aggrievances 3). LOCAL OFFICE: justice, Calvert County, 1679–1698 (quorum, 1697–1698). STANDS ON PUBLIC/PRIVATE ISSUES: he opposed the Protestant Associators' revolution of 1689; he was nominated by Lord Baltimore to the first royal Council in 1690, but he was not appointed. WEALTH AT DEATH. DIED: will probated on July 14, 1698. PERSONAL PROPERTY: TEV, £813.17.3 sterling (including 8 slaves, 2 servants, and merchandise worth £209.5.9). LAND: 1,000 acres.

HUTCHINSON (HUTCHISON), WILLIAM (?–1711). BORN: in Scotland. IMMIGRATED: by 1685 as a free adult. RESIDED: in Charles County; Piscattaway Hundred, Prince George's County, after 1695. FAMILY BACKGROUND. FATHER: John Hutchinson, a landowner of Ayrshire, Scotland. BROTHER: George. MARRIED Sarah. CHILDREN. SONS: John; William. DAUGHTERS: Ann, who married Gabriel Parker; Mary, who married John Abington; and Elizabeth, who married William Pile. PRIVATE CAREER. EDUCATION: literate. RELIGIOUS AFFILIATION: Presbyterian. SOCIAL STATUS AND ACTIVITIES: a close associate of *John Addison* (?–ca. 1705/6); "out of the country" in 1704, which probably accounts for the termination of his assembly and judicial service; his sons held no major offices. OCCUPATIONAL PROFILE: surveyor; acquired great wealth through Indian trade and land speculation; planter; merchant. PUBLIC CAREER. LEGISLATIVE SERVICE: Lower House, Charles County, 1694–1696 (resigned during or after the 5th session as a Charles County burgess upon election from the newly established county of Prince George's), Prince George's County, 1696–1697 (Laws 8), 1697/98–1700 (Laws 3, 4; Aggrievances 1, 2). LOCAL OFFICES: justice, Charles County, 1689–1696, Prince George's County, 1696–1697, 1699–1704 (quorum, 1696–1697, 1699–1704; president, 1702–1704); coroner, Charles County, 1690; surveyor, Charles and St. Mary's counties, 1692;

Piscattaway Parish Vestry, Charles County, 1693–1704. MILITARY SERVICE: captain, 1696–1701. STANDS ON PUBLIC/PRIVATE ISSUES: he supported the revolution of 1689. WEALTH DURING LIFETIME. LAND AT FIRST ELECTION: 3,811 acres in 1692; 7,684 acres in 1704. WEALTH AT DEATH. DIED: by April 23, 1711. PERSONAL PROPERTY: TEV, £1,428.2.6 sterling (including 29 slaves and 2 servants); FB, £93.2.0. LAND: 6,002 acres in Maryland, plus land in Scotland.

HYLAND, NICHOLAS (?–1774). BORN: in Cecil County, of age by 1739; probably second son. NATIVE: second generation. RESIDED: in Cecil County. FAMILY BACKGROUND. FATHER: Nicholas Hyland (?–1719), possibly immigrated from Labadun, England. MOTHER: Millicent. BROTHER: Capt. John (1716–1756), who married on April 29, 1739, Martha (?–1766), daughter of *Marmaduke Tilden* (?–1726). NEPHEW: *Stephen Hyland* (1744–1806). MARRIED Elizabeth. CHILDREN. SONS: John (?–by 1765), who married Mary Tilden; Nicholas (1733–1785), who married Margery, daughter of John Kankey and wife Ann; twins Isaac (1735/36–?) and Jacob (1735/36–?); Samson (1742–?); and Michael (1744–?). DAUGHTER: Millicent (1740–?), who married Alexander Williamson. PRIVATE CAREER. EDUCATION: literate. RELIGIOUS AFFILIATION: Anglican, St. Mary Anne's Church, North Elk Parish, Cecil County; favored legislation against "Popish Priests and Jesuits." SOCIAL STATUS AND ACTIVITIES: Gent., 1769. OCCUPATIONAL PROFILE: yeoman. PUBLIC CAREER. LEGISLATIVE SERVICE: Lower House, Cecil County, 1742–1744, 1745, 1745/46–1748, 1750–1751 (elected to the 2nd session to fill vacancy; Arms and Ammunition 2), 1751–1754 (Elections 1–6), 1754–1757 (Elections 1–6; Arms and Ammunition 5, 6), 1757–1758 (Elections 1, Cv, 2; Arms and Ammunition 1, Cv, 2), 1765–1766 (Grievances 2). LOCAL OFFICES: justice, Cecil County, 1740–1774 (quorum, 1749–1774); North Elk Parish Vestry, Cecil County, in office 1743–1748, 1751–1754; justice, Court of Oyer and Terminer and Gaol Delivery, Cecil County, commissioned 1752, 1759, 1761, and 1762. MILITARY SERVICE: captain, by 1742; colonel, by 1761. WEALTH DURING LIFETIME. LAND AT FIRST ELECTION: 1,500 acres in Cecil County (inherited from his father). SIGNIFICANT CHANGES IN LAND BETWEEN FIRST ELECTION AND DEATH: purchased several small tracts in Cecil County, and deeded 100 acres in Cecil County to his son Nicholas. WEALTH AT DEATH. DIED: between October 3, 1773, and April 27, 1774, in Cecil County. PER-

SONAL PROPERTY: TEV, £2,507.15.5 current money (including 19 slaves and plate); FB, £2,462.15.4. LAND: ca. 1,600 acres in Cecil County.

HYLAND, STEPHEN (1744–1806). BORN: on December 26, 1744, at "Harmony Hall," North Elk Parish, Cecil County; second son. NATIVE: second or third generation. RESIDED: in North Elk Parish, Cecil County. FAMILY BACKGROUND. FATHER: Capt. John Hyland (1716–1756), of "Harmony Hall," Cecil County. MOTHER: Martha (?–1766), daughter of *Marmaduke Tilden* (?–1726). UNCLE: Col. *Nicholas Hyland* (?–1774). AUNT: Wealthy Ann Tilden, who married Thomas Hynson, son of *Charles Hynson* (1663–1711). BROTHERS: Nicholas Hyland (1742–?); John (1746–?); Charles (1749–?); and Lambert (1751–?). SISTERS: Rebecca (1739/40–?), who married Josiah Kankey; Millicent (1754–?), who married Capt. John Lord. MARRIED first, in 1774 Rebecca Tilden (?–1775). MARRIED second, in 1777 Araminta, daughter of Dr. Thomas Hamm and wife Ann. CHILDREN. SONS: John (1775–?); Nicholas (1779–?); Jacob; Stephen; and Lambert. DAUGHTERS: Mary; Martha. PRIVATE CAREER. EDUCATION: literate. RELIGIOUS AFFILIATION: Anglican, St. Mary Anne's Church, North Elk Parish, Cecil County. SOCIAL STATUS AND ACTIVITIES: Gent., 1773; Esq., 1774. OCCUPATIONAL PROFILE: probably a planter. PUBLIC CAREER. LEGISLATIVE SERVICE: Lower House, Cecil County, 1773–1774; Conventions, Cecil County, 1st, 1774, 5th, 1775 (elected, but did not attend); Lower House, Cecil County, 1777–1778. OTHER STATE OFFICE: associate justice, Second District, 1789–at least 1791. LOCAL OFFICES: North Elk Parish Vestry, Cecil County, in office 1771–1774, 1779–1791; justice, Cecil County, 1772–1788; justice, Orphans' Court, Cecil County, 1777–at least 1789; sheriff, Cecil County, elected 1779 (not commissioned), 1782 (not commissioned); commissioner of tax, Cecil County, 1783–at least 1786. MILITARY SERVICE: colonel, Thirtieth or Susquehanna Battalion, Cecil County Militia, commissioned September 1778. WEALTH DURING LIFETIME. PERSONAL PROPERTY: assessed value £595.0.0, including 11 slaves and 12 oz. plate, 1783. LAND AT FIRST ELECTION: 1,138 acres in Cecil County. SIGNIFICANT CHANGES IN LAND BETWEEN FIRST ELECTION AND DEATH: owned 1,261 acres in Cecil County, 1783; purchased 136 acres in Cecil County and 3 lots in Elkton, Cecil County, between 1796 and 1799, but sold this 136 acres and 3 lots between 1799 and 1800. WEALTH AT DEATH. DIED: administration bond filed on December 13, 1806, in Cecil County. PERSONAL PROPERTY: TEV, $5,325.87 (including 7 slaves and silver valued at $46.50); FB, $3,650.73. LAND: 1,261 acres in Cecil County.

HYNSON (HINSON), CHARLES (1663–1711).

BORN: in 1663 in Kent County; third son. NATIVE: second generation. RESIDED: in Kent County. FAMILY BACKGROUND. FATHER: *Thomas Hynson* (1620–ca. 1667/68). MOTHER: Grace. BROTHERS: *John Hynson* (?–1705); Thomas (?–1679). SISTERS: Grace; Ann, who married first, Benjamin Randall, second, *Joseph Wickes* (ca. 1620–1692), and third, *St. Leger Codd* (ca. 1634–ca. 1707/8). MARRIED in 1686/87 Margaret, daughter of *William Harris* (ca. 1644–1712). Her brother was *James Harris* (1682–1743). Her sisters were Tabitha, who married *Marmaduke Tilden* (?–1726); Mary. CHILDREN. SONS: Thomas (1688–?); *Charles Hynson* (1692–1748); and *William Hynson* (1708–1767). DAUGHTERS: Dorcas (1690–?); Judith (1694–1703); Margaret (1697–?); Jane (1700–1702); and Jane (Joan) (1702–?). PRIVATE CAREER. EDUCATION: literate. RELIGIOUS AFFILIATION: Anglican. SOCIAL STATUS AND ACTIVITIES: second generation burgess. OCCUPATIONAL PROFILE: planter. PUBLIC CAREER. LEGISLATIVE SERVICE: Lower House, Kent County, 1700 (elected to the 4th session). ADDITIONAL COMMENTS: he stood three times as an unsuccessful candidate for burgess, 1701–1708. LOCAL OFFICES: clerk, Kent County, 1692–1694; justice, Kent County, 1694–1696, 1697–1704 (quorum, 1701/2–1704); St. Paul's Parish Vestry, Kent County, 1699–1703, 1708–1710. WEALTH DURING LIFETIME. PERSONAL PROPERTY: inherited 11,000 pounds of tobacco from his father's estate. LAND AT FIRST ELECTION: at least 250 acres; 150 acres from his wife's dower. WEALTH AT DEATH. DIED: buried on May 24, 1711. PERSONAL PROPERTY: TEV, £432.12.7 sterling (including 6 slaves); FB, £358.5.0. LAND: at least 250 acres.

HYNSON (HINSON), CHARLES (1692–1748).

BORN: on August 27, 1692, in Kent County; second son. NATIVE: third generation. RESIDED: in Chestertown, Kent County. FAMILY BACKGROUND. FATHER: *Charles Hynson* (1663–1711). MOTHER: Margaret, daughter of *William Harris* (ca. 1644–1712). UNCLES: *James Harris* (1682–1743); *John Hynson* (?–1705). AUNT: Ann Hynson, who married second, *Joseph Wickes* (ca. 1620–1692), and third, *St. Leger Codd* (ca. 1634–ca. 1707/8). BROTHERS: Thomas (1688–?); *William Hynson* (1708–1767). SISTERS: Dorcas (1690–?);

Judith (1694–1703); Margaret (1697–?); Jane (1700–1702); and Jane (Joan) (1702–?). FIRST COUSINS: *John Hynson* (ca. 1670–1708); *Nathaniel Hynson* (?–ca. 1721/22). NEPHEW: *Matthias Harris* (1718–1773). MARRIED Francina, widow of (first name unknown) Shippen; daughter of *Matthias Vanderheyden* (?–1729) and wife Anna Margaretta Herman, widow of *Henry Ward* (?–1683/84). Her half brother was *Henry Ward* (?–1734). Her sisters were Jane; Augustina, who married *James Harris* (1682–1743); and Ariana, who married first, *James Frisby* (1684–1719), second, *Thomas Bordley* (ca. 1683–1726), and third, *Edmund Jennings* (?–1756). Her nephews were *Matthias Harris* (1718–1773); *John Beale Bordley* (1726/27–1804). Her niece was Ariana Margaretta Frisby (1717–?), who married *William Harris* (1704–1748). CHILDREN. In his will he mentioned "my dear child Margaret," daughter of Mrs. Margaret (surname unknown), of Philadelphia, Pennsylvania. PRIVATE CAREER. EDUCATION: literate. RELIGIOUS AFFILIATION: Anglican. SOCIAL STATUS AND ACTIVITIES: Gent., 1723. OCCUPATIONAL PROFILE: a merchant. PUBLIC CAREER. LEGISLATIVE SERVICE: Lower House, Kent County, 1738, 1739–1741 (Elections Cv–3; Bills of Credit 1–3). LOCAL OFFICES: deputy commissary, Kent County, 1722–1727, 1742–1748; justice, Kent County, 1730–at least 1747 (quorum, 1733–at least 1747); justice, Court of Oyer and Terminer and Gaol Delivery, Kent County, commissioned 1737, 1740, 1742, 1744, and 1746. MILITARY SERVICE: colonel, 1748. WEALTH DURING LIFETIME. LAND AT FIRST ELECTION: 1,873 acres in Kent County, plus 2 lots in Chestertown, Kent County (all by personal acquisition). SIGNIFICANT CHANGES IN LAND BETWEEN FIRST ELECTION AND DEATH: purchased at least 246 acres in Kent County, 1742–1747; sold 859 acres in Kent County, 1741–1747. By 1747 he held his two Chestertown lots as a tenant in common with William Murray and Bedingfield Hands. WEALTH AT DEATH. DIED: will probated on April 11, 1748, in Kent County. PERSONAL PROPERTY: TEV, at least £1,431.10.5 current money (including 32 slaves). LAND: 1,260 acres in Kent County; also houses and lots in Chestertown, Kent County.

HYNSON (HINSON), JOHN (?–1705).

BORN: probably in the late 1640s, probably in Virginia, of age by 1667; first or second son. IMMIGRATED: in 1651 as a minor with his father from Virginia. RESIDED: in Kent County; Talbot County, by 1670; Kent County again by 1674. FAMILY BACKGROUND. FATHER: *Thomas Hynson* (1620–ca.

1667/68). MOTHER: Grace. BROTHERS: Thomas (?–1679); *Charles Hynson* (1663–1711), who married Margaret, daughter of *William Harris* (ca. 1644–1712). SISTERS: Ann, who married first, Benjamin Randall, second, *Joseph Wickes* (ca. 1620–1692), and third, *St. Leger Codd* (ca. 1634–ca. 1707/8); Grace. MARRIED first, by 1670 Rachel. MARRIED second, ca. 1693 Ann, widow of Jonathan Grafton. CHILDREN. SONS: *John Hynson* (ca. 1670–1708), who married Mary, daughter of John Stoops; *Nathaniel Hynson* (?–ca. 1721/22), who married first, Hannah, and second, Mary Kelley. DAUGHTERS: Elizabeth, who married (first name unknown) Rogers; Jane, who married Philip Holeager; Mary, who married William Glanville; Ann, who married Rev. Stephen Bordley (ca. 1675–1709); and Sarah, who married *James Smith* (ca. 1683–1760). PRIVATE CAREER. EDUCATION: literate. RELIGIOUS AFFILIATION: Anglican. SOCIAL STATUS AND ACTIVITIES: second generation burgess. OCCUPATIONAL PROFILE: planter. PUBLIC CAREER. LEGISLATIVE SERVICE: Lower House, Kent County, 1681–1682 (elected to the 3rd session), 1694–1697, 1701–1704. LOCAL OFFICES: justice, Kent County, 1674–1683, 1684–1692, 1694–1701 (quorum, 1688–1692, 1694–1701); sheriff, Kent County, 1683; St. Paul's Parish Vestry, Kent County, 1697–1702. MILITARY SERVICE: lieutenant, by 1681/82; captain, 1689; colonel, 1694–1705. STANDS ON PUBLIC/PRIVATE ISSUES: opposed the revolution of Protestant Associators in 1689; testified personally in London for Lord Baltimore against the rebels in 1690; called a "grand leader of Jacobite party," 1692; reappointed to his civil and military offices by Gov. Francis Nicholson in 1694. WEALTH DURING LIFETIME. LAND AT FIRST ELECTION: at least 850 acres inherited from his father. PERSONAL PROPERTY: 10,400 pounds of tobacco from his father's estate. WEALTH AT DEATH. DIED: buried on May 10, 1705. LAND: over 1,000 acres.

HYNSON (HINSON), JOHN (ca. 1670–1708). BORN: ca. 1670 in Kent County; oldest son. NATIVE: third generation. RESIDED: in Cecil County. FAMILY BACKGROUND. FATHER: *John Hynson* (?–1705), son of *Thomas Hynson* (1620–ca. 1667/68). MOTHER: Rachel. UNCLE: *Charles Hynson* (1663–1711). BROTHER: *Nathaniel Hynson* (?–ca. 1721/22). SISTERS: Mary; Elizabeth; Jane; and Sarah, who married *James Smith* (ca. 1683–1760). MARRIED in 1693 Mary, daughter of John Stoops. She subsequently married in 1710 Benjamin Pearce (1683–1734), son of *William Pearce* (ca. 1641–1720/21). CHILDREN. SONS: John, Thomas

(1700–?); and Nathaniel. DAUGHTERS: Hannah (1708–?); Rachel; and Jane. PRIVATE CAREER. EDUCATION: literate. RELIGIOUS AFFILIATION: Anglican. SOCIAL STATUS AND ACTIVITIES: third generation burgess. OCCUPATIONAL PROFILE: planter. PUBLIC CAREER. LEGISLATIVE SERVICE: Lower House, Cecil County, 1708A (died before the Assembly met). LOCAL OFFICES: justice, Cecil County, probably 1697/98–1708; North Sassafras Parish Vestry, Cecil County, 1701–1708. WEALTH DURING LIFETIME. LAND AT FIRST ELECTION: over 1,300 acres (at least 876 acres inherited from his father). WEALTH AT DEATH. DIED: buried on September 30, 1708. PERSONAL PROPERTY: TEV, £434.14.4 sterling (including 5 slaves and 3 servants). LAND: over 1,300 acres.

HYNSON (HINSON), NATHANIEL (?–ca. 1721/22). BORN: in Kent County, of age by 1698; probably second son. NATIVE: third generation. RESIDED: at "Sutton," Kent County. FAMILY BACKGROUND. FATHER: *John Hynson* (?–1705). MOTHER: Rachel (?–by 1693). STEPMOTHER: Anne, widow of Jonathan Grafton. UNCLE: *Charles Hynson* (1663–1711). BROTHER: *John Hynson* (ca. 1670–1708). SISTERS: Mary; Elizabeth; Anne; Jane; and Sarah, who married *James Smith* (ca. 1683–1760). FIRST COUSINS: *William Hynson* (1708–1767); *Charles Hynson* (1692–1748). MARRIED first, Hannah (?–1713). MARRIED second, on August 16, 1714, Mary Kelley, who subsequently married Joseph Young. CHILDREN. SONS: Nathaniel (1709–1712); Nathaniel (1714–?), who married on October 29, 1735, Mary Smith. DAUGHTERS: Hannah (1705–?), who married *John Gresham* (ca. 1703–ca. 1752); Mary (?–1710); Mary (1711–?); Martha; and Rebecca. OTHER CHILDREN: an unborn child was mentioned in his will. PRIVATE CAREER. EDUCATION: literate. RELIGIOUS AFFILIATION: Anglican, St. Paul's Parish, Kent County. SOCIAL STATUS AND ACTIVITIES: Gent., 1709; Esq., 1721. OCCUPATIONAL PROFILE: merchant; probably a planter. PUBLIC CAREER. LEGISLATIVE SERVICE: Lower House, Kent County, 1716–1718 (Aggrievances 1–3), 1719–1721 (Aggrievances 1–4; died during the 4th session). OTHER PROVINCIAL OFFICE: justice, Provincial Court, 1720–1721 (quorum, 1720). LOCAL OFFICES: St. Paul's Parish Vestry, Kent County, in office 1715–1717; justice, Kent County, before 1716–at least 1720 (quorum, 1716–at least 1720). MILITARY SERVICE: colonel, 1709. WEALTH DURING LIFETIME. LAND AT FIRST ELECTION: 2,760 acres in Kent County (1,050 acres from his father, 300 of which he managed for his nephew). SIGNIFICANT CHANGES IN

LAND BETWEEN FIRST ELECTION AND DEATH: purchased 1,362 acres in Kent County, 1717–1718; he released the 300 acres under his control to his nephew in 1721. **WEALTH AT DEATH. DIED:** between May 14, 1721, and January 26, 1721/22, in Kent County. PERSONAL PROPERTY: TEV, £3,183.12.5 current money (including 30 slaves, 6 servants, 24 books, and 1 sloop); FB, £2,269.0.5. LAND: at least 3,052 acres in Kent County.

HYNSON (HINSON), THOMAS (1620–ca. 1667/68). BORN: in 1620, probably in England. IMMIGRATED: in 1651 as a free adult with his wife and children from Isle of Wight County, Virginia. ADDITIONAL COMMENTS: in Virginia by 1646. RESIDED: in Kent County. **MARRIED** Grace. **CHILDREN. SONS:** *John Hynson* (?–1705), who married first, by 1670 Rachel, and second, ca. 1693 Ann, widow of Jonathan Grafton; Thomas (?–1679), a sheriff of Talbot County in 1666, who married Ann Gaines; and *Charles Hynson* (1663–1711), who married in 1686/87 Margaret, daughter of *William Harris* (ca. 1644–1712). DAUGHTERS: Ann, who married first, Benjamin Randall, second, *Joseph Wickes* (ca. 1620–1692), and third, *St. Leger Codd* (ca. 1634–ca. 1707/8); Grace, who married by 1663 Thomas South, of Talbot County. **PRIVATE CAREER.** EDUCATION: literate. RELIGIOUS AFFILIATION: Protestant. SOCIAL STATUS AND ACTIVITIES: he was a pioneer settler of Kent County. OCCUPATIONAL PROFILE: planter. **PUBLIC CAREER.** LEGISLATIVE SERVICE: Assembly, Kent County, 1654; Lower House, Kent County, 1659/60. LOCAL OFFICES: justice, Kent County, 1652–1655, 1656–1658; sheriff, Kent County, 1655–1656. STANDS ON PUBLIC/PRIVATE ISSUES: supported Fendall's Rebellion in 1659/60–1660, for which he was fined 2,000 pounds of tobacco and barred from office for seven years in 1661. **WEALTH DURING LIFETIME. LAND AT FIRST ELECTION:** rights to 800 acres; patented over 4,000 acres. **WEALTH AT DEATH.** DIED: administration bond dated January 25, 1667/68. PERSONAL PROPERTY: TEV, 80,679 pounds of tobacco (in-

cluding 1 slave and 4 servants). LAND: over 4,000 acres.

HYNSON (HINSON), WILLIAM (1708–1767). BORN: on December 23, 1708, in St. Paul's Parish, Kent County; youngest son. NATIVE: third generation. RESIDED: in Kent County. **FAMILY BACKGROUND. FATHER:** *Charles Hynson* (1663–1711). MOTHER: Margaret, daughter of *William Harris* (ca. 1644–1712). UNCLES: *John Hynson* (?–1705); *James Harris* (1682–1743). AUNT: Ann Hynson, who married second, *Joseph Wickes* (ca. 1620–1692), and third, *St. Leger Codd* (ca. 1634–ca. 1707/8). BROTHERS: Thomas (1688–?); *Charles Hynson* (1692–1748). SISTERS: Dorcas (1690–?); Judith (1694–1703); Margaret (1697–?); Jane (1700–1702); and Jane (Joan) (1702–?). FIRST COUSINS: *John Hynson* (ca. 1670–1708); *Nathaniel Hynson* (?–ca. 1721/22). NEPHEW: *Matthias Harris* (1718–1773). **MARRIED** Martha Wickes. Her brother was Joseph Wickes. **CHILDREN.** Probably died without progeny. **PRIVATE CAREER.** EDUCATION: literate. RELIGIOUS AFFILIATION: Anglican. SOCIAL STATUS AND ACTIVITIES: Gent., 1763. OCCUPATIONAL PROFILE: planter. **PUBLIC CAREER.** LEGISLATIVE SERVICE: Lower House, Kent County, 1754–1757 (Bills of Credit 5), 1757–1758 (Accounts 1, Cv, 2), 1758–1761 (Accounts Cv 1, 1, Cv 2, 2, 3, Cv 3), 1762–1763 (Accounts 1, 2), 1765–1766 (Accounts 2; Grievances 2). LOCAL OFFICE: justice, Kent County, 1748–at least 1759 (quorum, 1756–at least 1759). MILITARY SERVICE: called major. **WEALTH DURING LIFETIME. LAND AT FIRST ELECTION:** 200 acres in Kent County, received from his grandfather *William Harris* (ca. 1644–1712). SIGNIFICANT CHANGES IN LAND BETWEEN FIRST ELECTION AND DEATH: acquired 75 acres in Kent County, 1762–1763. **WEALTH AT DEATH.** DIED: administration bond dated October 17, 1767, in Kent County. PERSONAL PROPERTY: TEV, at least £1,085.2.4 (including 25 slaves and books). LAND: 278 acres in Kent County.